Tuesday 1:30 — 2:30 pm

Software: Multiframe

Collabrate & VoiceThread.   DELTA Testing Center

Architectural
Structures

Architectural Structures

Wayne Place

BICENTENNIAL
1807
WILEY
2007
BICENTENNIAL

JOHN WILEY & SONS, INC.

Published by John Wiley & Sons, Inc., Hoboken, New Jersey

Published simultaneously in Canada

Designations used by companies to distinguish their products are often claimed as trademarks. In all instances where John Wiley & Sons, Inc. is aware of a claim, the product names appear in initial capital or all capital letters. Readers, however, should contact the appropriate companies for more complete information regarding trademarks and registration.

Limit of Liability/Disclaimer of Warranty: While the publisher and the author have used their best efforts in preparing this book, they make no representations or warranties with respect to the accuracy or completeness of the contents of this book and specifically disclaim any implied warranties of merchantability or fitness for a particular purpose. No warranty may be created or extended by sales representatives or written sales materials. The advice and strategies contained herein may not be suitable for your situation. You should consult with a professional where appropriate. Neither the publisher nor the author shall be liable for any loss of profit or any other commercial damages, including but not limited to special, incidental, consequential, or other damages.

For general information about our other products and services, please contact our Customer Care Department within the United States at (800) 762-2974, outside the United States at (317) 572-3993 or fax (317) 572-4002.

Wiley also publishes its books in a variety of electronic formats. Some content that appears in print may not be available in electronic books. For more information about Wiley products, visit our web site at www.wiley.com.

Wiley Bicentennial Logo: Richard J. Pacifico

Library of Congress Cataloging-in-Publication Data:

Place, Wayne.
   Architectural structures / Wayne Place.
      p. cm.
   Includes bibliographical references and index.
   ISBN: 978-0-471-72551-0 (cloth)
   1. Structural design. 2. Structural design—Case studies.
   I. Title.
   TA658.P625 2006
   624.1'7—dc22
                                           2005034525

Printed in the United States of America

10 9 8 7 6 5 4 3 2 1

To Leslie
whose courage, wisdom, beauty, and passion inspire me.
She never lets me forget my dreams, of which this book is one.
Without her love and encouragement, it would never have been finished.

Acknowledgments

My thanks go to:

Wendy Fuller, who proofed text, generated drawings, manipulated images, solved computer problems, typeset equations, created data bases, and helped to keep several graduate students working productively on this book.

Jonathan Priest, who used his skills for negotiation and foreign languages to persuade a host of busy and gifted people to share their designs, data, and photographs for use in this book. He wrote hundreds of e-mails, made hundreds of phone calls, and scanned hundreds of images.

Sydney Ohare, who stepped in for Wendy Fuller, when Wendy departed for Prague.

Tom Place, who built and photographed many of the models in this book and who managed to salvage and refine numerous computer drawings that were wasting away on an obsolete computer.

James Sweeney, who took my Multiframe renderings and made them more beautiful and communicative. He also generated original renderings, which are noted where they occur.

T.C. Howard, who taught me more about architecture and engineering than anyone else. Without his tutelage, this book would never have come to be.

Charles Lysaght, who has served as one of my great role models in life. He is the person I have turned to when the burdens have gotten too heavy and I needed someone who would shoulder some of the load. He is also a superb engineer.

To the many wonderful people in design firms who have shared their creative masterpieces:

T.C. Howard of Synergetics, Inc., Raleigh, North Carolina
Curt Fentress of Fentress-Bradburn, Denver, Colorado
William Baker, Robert Sinn, John Zils, Lawrence Novak, Shane McCormick, Stan Korista, Christopher Brown, Dane Rankin, Christopher Rockey, and David Horos of Skidmore Owings and Merrill, LLP, Chicago, Illinois
Hal Iyengar of Structural Design International

Mark Williard and Ola Ferm of WilliardFerm Architects
Charles Lysaght and Pat Kyzer of Lysaght and Associates
Dorothy Candela, wife and partner of Felix Candela
Gunnar Birkert of Gunnar Birkert Associates, Boston, Massachsetts
Leslie Robertson of Leslie Robertson Associates, New York, New York
Ed DePaola of Severud Associates, New York, New York
Jeffrey Feingold of Skidmore Owings and Merrill, LLP, New York, New York

The host of good people in various professional organizations who have labored long and honorably to advance human knowledge and make our built environments safer and better for human habitation. The number of people is simply too great to list all of them here, including every person who has ever served on a committee or generated technical data for one of the following great organizations that have contributed to the knowledge base in this book. It is impossible to quantify the magnitude of their contributions. Everything we do is built on the foundation of knowledge that they have provided for us.

American Institute of Steel Construction (AISC)
American Society of Civil Engineers (ASCE)
Precast/Prestressed Concrete Institute (PCI)
Steel Joist Institute (SJI)
National Forest and Paper Association (NFPA)

Specific manufacturers of structural products:

Vulcraft, Inc.
Boise Caskade, Inc.
Copperweld Corporation

My parents Mary and Jeff Place, who let their bending in the archer's hand be for gladness. My mother gave me unconditional love, and my father lit the candle to show me the way. Their love for each other and zest for life made me believe in dreams.

Contents

1

Structural Design Process

1.1 Nature of the Process

This book is primarily intended as a textbook for students enrolled in professionally accredited architecture programs. A secondary audience includes interns preparing for the architectural registration exams. There may also be limited markets for professional architects, structural engineers desiring to better understand the architect's approach to structures in the context of the larger design problem, and persons interested in pursuing a career in either architecture or structural engineering.

Architects have a huge array of issues to address in architectural practice. Among these are the following: keeping rain out of a building, getting water off a site, thermal comfort, visual comfort, space planning, fire egress, fire resistance, corrosion and rot resistance, vermin resistance, marketing, client relations, the law, contracts, construction administration, the functional purposes of architecture, the role of the building in the larger cultural context, security, economy, resource management, codes and standards, and how to make a building withstand all the forces to which it will likely be subjected during its lifetime. This last subject area is referred to as *architectural structures.*

Because of the extraordinary range of demands on an architect's time and skills and the extraordinary number of subjects that architecture students must master, architectural structures are typically addressed in only two or three lecture courses in an accredited architectural curriculum in the United States. These two or three lecture courses must be contrasted with the ten or twelve courses that will normally be taken by a graduate of an accredited structural engineering curriculum. This contrast in level of focus makes it clear why a good structural engineering consultant is a very valuable asset to an architect. However, having a good structural consultant does not relieve the architect of serious responsibility in the structural domain. All architects must be well versed in matters related to structures. The architect has the primary responsibility for establishing the structural concept for a building, as part of the overall design concept, and must be able to speak the language of the structural consultant with sufficient skill and understanding to take full advantage of the consultant's capabilities.

Most books on structures are written by structural engineers for an audience of structural engineers. This focus is not appropriate in nature to the needs of the architect, who must understand how structure fits into the larger design context. Furthermore, it is not appropriate in scale, inasmuch as the texts required by an engineering student over the course of that student's education will fill an entire cabinet. Given the wide range of other learning responsibilities of an architecture student, there is not enough money to acquire, or time to use, an entire cabinet full of books on structures. To support the learning needs of architecture students, a text is needed that is different in both scope and approach from the reference material provided for engineers.

It is the goal of this text to supply the architecture student with a comprehensive set of learning and reference materials to help prepare that student to enter the workforce as a serious professional, competent to deal with structural issues at the level, and in the manner, appropriate to architects. This book can also serve as a valuable reference for architectural interns preparing for the architectural registration examinations.

1.2 General Comments Regarding Architectural Education

Structural design is one of the more rigorous aspects of architectural design. Much knowledge has been generated and codified over the centuries that human beings have been practicing in and developing this field. This book gives primary attention to those things that are known, quantified, and codified.

However, very few things in the realm of architecture yield a single solution. To any given design problem, there are many possible solutions, and picking the best solution is often the subject of intense debate. Therefore, no one should come to this subject matter assuming that this text, or any text, is going to serve up a single, optimized solution to any design problem, unless that design problem has been so narrowly defined as to be artificial.

In design, there is always a great deal of latitude for personal expression. Design is purposeful action. The designer must have an attitude to act. Architecture students develop an attitude through a chaotic learning process involving a lot of trial and error. In going through this process, an architecture student must remain aware of a fundamental premise: the process is more important than the product; that is, the student's learning and development are more important than the output. The student has a license to make mistakes. It is actually more efficient to plow forward and make mistakes than to spend too much time trying to figure out how to do it perfectly the first time. To paraphrase the immortal words of Thomas Edison: To have good ideas, you should have many ideas and then throw out the bad ones. Of course, throwing out the bad ones requires a lot of rigorous and critical thinking. No one should ever fall in love with any idea that has not been subjected to intense and prolonged critical evaluation and withstood the test with flying colors. Furthermore, important ideas should be subjected to periodic reevaluation. Times and conditions change. Ideas that once seemed unassailable may outlive their usefulness or, at the very least, need updating in the light of new knowledge and insights.

This text focuses primarily on exploring the known, quantified, and codified, but it also honors the chaotic learning process described here. On some projects, students will be given fairly wide latitude to generate concepts and to explore. Optimally, the educational experience will be stronger if the student explores this subject matter in the context of a design process, such as would occur in a studio environment, where feedback is provided by enlightened people with a wide range of experience and philosophical points of view.

In pursuing this subject matter, it is valuable to have a frame of reference regarding the roles of the architect, as the leader of the design team, and the structural engineer, as a crucial contributor of expertise and hard work needed to execute the project safely and effectively. The diagram in Figure 1.1 will help provide that frame of reference.

In contemplating the diagram in Figure 1.1, keep in mind that design and analysis are two sides of the same coin and that the skills and points of view of architects and engineers, although distinctive, also overlap and sometimes blur together. The most effective design teams consist of individuals with strong foci who can play their respective roles while having enough overlap in understanding and purpose that they can see each other's point of view and cooperate in working toward mutually understood and shared goals. The most harmful poison to a design team is to have such a separation in points of view and understanding that a rift develops between the members of the team. Cooperation is the watchword in this process, as in all other team efforts.

1.3 Background of the Reader

The prerequisites of a student for optimum utilization of this text include the following:

- A working knowledge of plane and solid geometry (This is absolutely fundamental to the design of architecture and should be a part of any architect's basic repertoire.)
- A working knowledge of arithmetic (This is part of the basic repertoire of any educated, thinking person. No architect can make good judgments without the arithmetic that reinforces a sense of scale, proportions, and economy.)
- An introduction to trigonometry and vectors
- Basic skills in sketching
- Basic skills in fashioning scale models out of cardboard, wood, plastic, and/or metals
- A basic knowledge of computers, including word processing, spreadsheet analysis, and computer-aided design (CAD)

An understanding of calculus is helpful, but this book is crafted in such a manner that calculus is not crucial to grasping the concepts.

A computer with appropriate software is such a powerful tool for learning and exploration that any course of study that does not take advantage of that tool is far from ideal in preparing an architecture student for the future workplace. Therefore, students intending to use this text to maximum advantage in a full assault on the subject

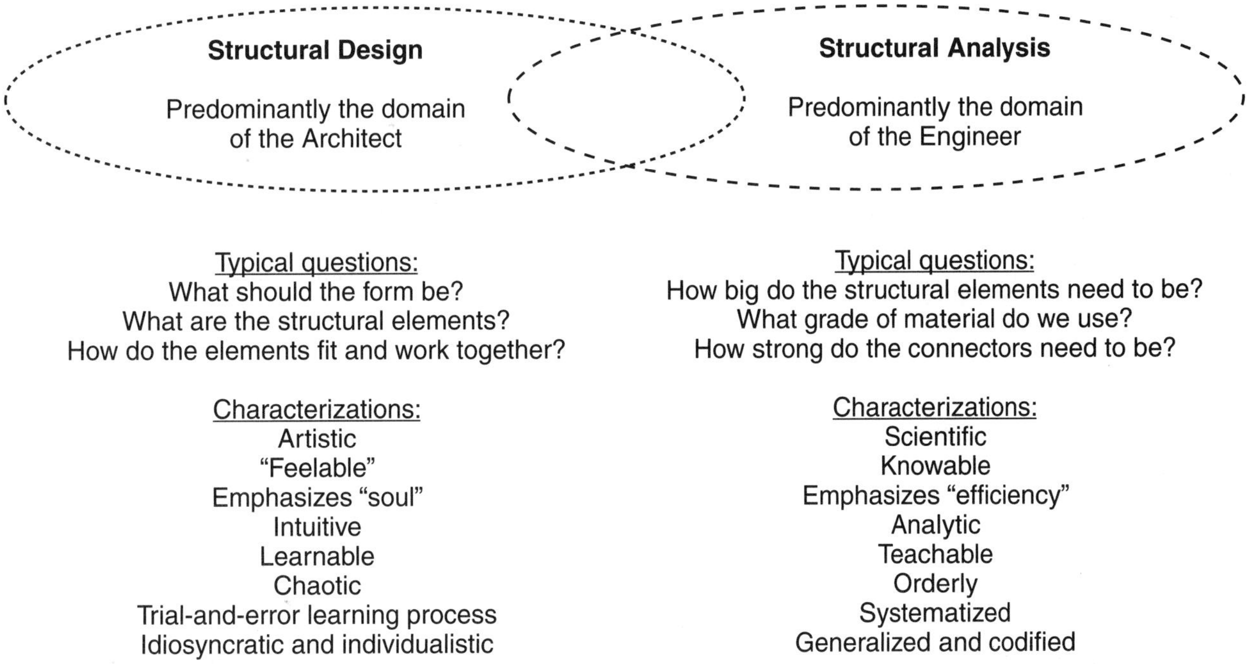

Structural Design

Predominantly the domain of the Architect

Structural Analysis

Predominantly the domain of the Engineer

Typical questions:
What should the form be?
What are the structural elements?
How do the elements fit and work together?

Typical questions:
How big do the structural elements need to be?
What grade of material do we use?
How strong do the connectors need to be?

Characterizations:
Artistic
"Feelable"
Emphasizes "soul"
Intuitive
Learnable
Chaotic
Trial-and-error learning process
Idiosyncratic and individualistic

Characterizations:
Scientific
Knowable
Emphasizes "efficiency"
Analytic
Teachable
Orderly
Systematized
Generalized and codified

Figure 1.1 Nature of the design process and roles of the design participants.

should have access to a computer with word processing, a spreadsheet program, and a structural analysis program. Examples of the latter are Multiframe, Strudl, SAP, RISA, STAAD.Pro, Tekla Xsteel, S-Frame, ETABS, MIDAS, ProSteel 3D, and RamSteel. This book will provide examples of the principles of analysis on which these programs are based. It will also take the student through many of these examples in the form of assignments designed to reinforce the concepts.

The computer analysis programs are important for several reasons:

1. They eliminate much of the tedious math, allowing the student to focus on concepts and to explore the behavior and attributes of many more structural forms than would be possible if the student were straddled with the responsibility of carrying out all of the math longhand.
2. The computer facilitates the analysis of very complex three-dimensional structures that simply could not be done reliably by longhand analysis.
3. The programs provide visualization tools that are invaluable for exploring both geometry and structural behavior.

1.4 Vehicles for Delivering the Concepts

1. Freebody diagrams. These are at the absolute heart of structural design. Understanding how freebodies are constructed and interpreted is vital to the most basic concepts in structures.
2. Math (primarily geometry and arithmetic). These give scale and rigor to everything the architect does in structural design.
3. Spreadsheet programs for computers. These programs are powerful aids in organizing and carrying out computations. They provide:
   - Sophisticated and rapid computational tools
   - Ease of use
   - A record of the inputs that can be used in checking and troubleshooting
   - A record of the equations that can be used in checking and troubleshooting
   - Graphic output for visualization and presentations

   These programs are already commonplace tools for architects to use in generating budgets and doing value analysis. Applying them in a structures course to generate computational templates is an obvious match.
4. Computer simulations showing axial forces, axial stresses, moments, bending stresses, shear forces, shear stresses, and deformation under various loading conditions. These programs are a requirement in any serious course in structures. The ease they pro-

vide in visualizing and exploring structural behavior is simply unprecedented. The use of these programs is featured heavily in the examples and assignments in this book.

5. Physical testing and physical models demonstrating the structural behavior of elements and/or systems of elements. The tactile feedback provided by physical experiments and models is a powerful aid to a student's comprehension. They are not easy to make in a manner that truly simulates the behavior of a full-sized structure, but they are worth the effort. Some phenomena, such as buckling, are better understood in physical models than in any other learning media. Moreover, models teach students about statistical variations in performance that are not apparent in purely computational processes. There is nothing like testing a series of models that were intended to be identical to help students understand why safety factors are important.
6. Design solutions embodied in actual building structures. There are vast insights to be gathered from the successful designs born of great minds that have grappled with this subject over the centuries. These should be revisited often, each time with a fresh eye to see things that may have been overlooked before. They should include examples where the integration of structure with the other building systems has been addressed in at least a competent, if not inspired, manner.
7. Practical examples in value engineering—that is, demonstrating efficient ways to determine the structural costs of providing greater architectural amenities—such as the following:
   - The structural cost of increasing span to reduce the number of columns interfering with efficient space planning
   - The structural cost of using rigid frames, as opposed to shear walls or triangulating struts, as a way to promote freer movement of people and equipment through a structure
   - The structural cost of introducing openings for admitting natural light to illuminate the interior of a building
8. Data on properties of materials.
9. Data on dimensions and section properties for common structural elements, such as standard rolled and formed steel sections.
10. Load tables for columns, beams, and trusses. These are particularly helpful for quick sizing and for doing cost-benefit analysis for common building types. Introducing students to the great compendia that are the source of this information is also an important goal of this text.
11. The written word. Words alone are a poor means of understanding and communicating structural

behavior. However, words provide a indispensable tool in organizing our ideas about the subject.

12. Assignments and projects. Exercise is the primary road to learning.

1.5 Expectations Regarding the Outcome of the Learning Process

Learning goals for a student working with this book are expressed in terms of three levels of achievement in design activity.

The first level of structural design activity is primarily qualitative, including the following:

- Concept generation—that is, understanding what kinds of elements need to be included in the structural system to deal with the entire array of vertical and lateral loads on a structure; understanding how to make the structural system mesh with the spatial and functional requirements of the architectural design.
- Applying simple rules of thumb to establish the proportions of structural elements—for example, the depth of a parallel-chord truss will typically be in the range of 0.042 to 0.062 times the span of the parallel-chord truss; the final depth will depend on a variety of structural, economic, and architectural factors to be worked out in later stages of the design process.

Architects should be able to perform these design activities competently and should do them routinely in practice.

The second level of structural design activity is semi-quantitative, including the following:

- Geometric definition of a structure (This can be fairly straightforward, such as in the case of a system of beams and columns laid out on a regular grid, to quite challenging, such as in the case of a hyperbolic paraboloid network, a geodesic dome, or a free-form structure like architect Frank Gehry's art museum in Bilbão.)
- Quick, approximate sizing of elements, such as beams and open-web joists, using tables of standard elements
- Cost estimating

Architects should be able to perform these activities competently enough to have a sense of what an engineer might be doing in support of the architect on a given project. A significant goal of this text is to provide students with a sufficient understanding of the structural issues and engineering design processes to confidently engage an engineer in the overall design process. Some architects will choose to perform these functions in practice; others may choose to have their engineering consultants perform such functions.

The third level of structural design activity is highly quantitative, including the following:

- Final sizing of elements using precise computational processes
- Calculations involving complex interactions between structural members constituting structural systems

Architecture students completing a rigorous course of study using this text will:

- Be able to apply a standard software analysis program to simple structural systems
- Understand the principles and issues involved
- Understand the complexity of the process
- Understand the power and limitations of analytic methods
- Understand the issues, state of the art, and vocabulary necessary for interacting effectively with a structural engineer

Most architects will choose to have their engineering consultants perform these highly quantitative design functions. However, the computer analysis tools used in this course are examples of what will be prevalent in practice within the next decade. The architect and engineer can use these tools in a collaborative process of generating architectural form.

The education that an architecture student can receive in completing a rigorous course of study using this text will provide a very good commonsense understanding of architectural structures. As indicated earlier, this educational experience is not the equivalent of a full education in structural engineering. Structural engineers take many more courses in this focus area and are responsible for a great many kinds of information that the architect will typically be unprepared to address. Sometimes, the commonsense understanding that architects acquire from this text, and as a byproduct of experience as an architect, will provide the architect with some insights that some engineers do not have. However, the architect should not allow that fact to delude him or her into believing that he or she has all the skills to produce a major architectural work without the assistance of a competent and motivated structural engineer. One of the architect's major tasks as a designer is to acquire and properly utilize good engineering consulting services to assist in generating economical and safe designs.

1.6 Types of Structural Action

There are three primary kinds of structural action that architects and engineers use in creating structures for human habitation and use:

1. Axial tension, involving a tension force along the axis of a member.

2. Axial compression, involving a compression force along the axis of a member. Such members are usually referred to as *columns* or *compression struts*.

3. *Bending*, also referred to as *flexure*, involving forces lateral to the axis of a member. Such members are usually referred to as *beams.*

In Figure 1.2(a), a ⅛ in.-diameter × 6 in.-long PVC rod is subjected to axial tension. More than 9 kg of weight has been hung off the rod. It would have supported substantially more weight, but the testing was limited by concern about dents in the floor. In Figure 1.2(b), the same rod is subjected to axial compression in a small testing device. Buckling failure occurred at 0.8 kg of axial compression force, which is less than a tenth of what it easily held in tension. In Figure 1.2(c), the same element is being used in bending, where massive deformations are observed at a lateral force of 0.4 kg. This demonstration illustrates the hierarchy of structural efficiency: tension members tend to be more efficient than compression members, which tend to be more efficient than bending members.

Tensile members are limited by the yield stress of the material. They can also be severely limited by means of making connections at the ends of the members. In Figure 1.2, the PVC rod was glued deep into the two sturdy wooden blocks, which ensured that the end connections would develop most or all of the potential tension capacity of the rod.

Compression members are limited by the yield stress of the material and by buckling, wherein the element begins to radically change shape, moving laterally out from under the load, before the yield stress of the material is reached. (*Laterally* means to the side, i.e., perpendicular to the axis of the element.) The tendency to buckle can be diminished by redistributing the material in the member cross section. For example, a ¹⁄₁₆ in.-thick × 3 in.-wide × 36 in.-long piece of styrene plastic will not support its own weight without buckling laterally. If that same sheet of material is cut lengthwise into seven equal-width strips and those strips are glued together, they form a solid bar that is almost exactly square. This solid, square bar not only supports its own weight, it can support about 15 lbs of compression force, as shown in Figure 1.3(a). If that same sheet is cut into four ¾ in.-wide strips and reassembled into a square, hollow section 36 in. long—see Figure 1.3(b)—that section can hold over 100 lbs in compressive force. The process of reconfiguring the material has given the column extra breadth, which has stiffened it against buckling. This idea of configuring material to achieve structural efficiency is at the heart of the design process.

In regard to spanning methods, suspension structures rely primarily on elements working in pure tension, arches rely primarily on elements acting in pure compression, and trusses are composed of an assembly of elements that are each working in either pure tension or pure compression. As such, these methods of spanning tend to be more structurally efficient than the use of beams. However, beams are simple to design and fabricate and in many situations are the most economical means of spanning. It would be difficult to imagine replacing a standard 2 × 6 wood rafter in the roof of a house with a tiny truss. The minor material savings achieved by the truss would never offset the cost of detailing the truss. At the other extreme, we would have difficulty imagining replacing the lacy cable structure of the Golden Gate Bridge with a huge, solid beam. Structural efficiency tends to be more important for long spans or heavy loads. For short spans and light loads, the simplest

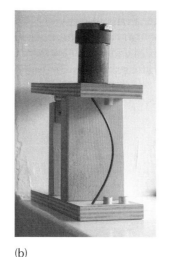

(a)   (b)   (c)

Figure 1.2 (a) Axial tension, (b) axial compression, and (c) bending.

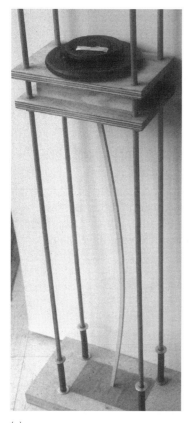

(a)   (b)

Figure 1.3 (a) A solid rod and (b) a hollow tube.

and most expedient structure is generally the most economical and appropriate. How to achieve structural efficiency is a major theme of this book.

Bending elements are limited by leverage effects. Beams, particularly shallow beams, have a major mechanical disadvantage relative to the applied forces. This point is addressed in more detailed and more precise terms in later chapters. In the meantime, simple experience and intuition can be used to develop the idea of leverage. It can be clear from experience that the shape of a structural element is important and that "structural depth" is crucial to structural performance. For example, if we want a strong beam, we will set a wood 2 × 10 on edge to resist gravity forces. Yet if we wanted to break the same board, we would lay it on its side. Laying the board on its side reduces both the strength and the stiffness of the element in responding to gravity forces. A wide, flat beam is not only weaker, that is, easier to break, but also less stiff. Typically in our culture, we associate stiffness with strength. When we pound on a wall or jump up and down on a floor and perceive very little movement, we assume that these elements are very strong. Although there is a correlation between stiffness and strength, the correlation between those properties is far from perfect.

For example, we can create a broad, flat cantilever beam that is both flexible enough and strong enough to be used as a diving board. This apparently contradictory set of traits is also useful in the leaf springs of a motor vehicle. However, in structural applications, stiffness and strength will be highly correlated, and we will be seeking to create structures that are both strong and very stiff. Most of the time the primary motive for seeking stiffness is either to reduce distracting vibrations or to improve the perception of quality on the part of the building occupants. Sometimes, however, the desirability of stiffness goes beyond perception and becomes a life safety issue. For example, an overflexible flat roof may begin to deflect under the weight of a deluge of rain. The deflection creates a bowl shape that causes more water to accumulate. The added water causes a deeper bowl to form, resulting in an even greater accumulation. This process is referred to as *ponding*. Ponding has more to do with the stiffness of the roof than with the initial strength of the roof. Two roofs may both be rated to carry the prescribed snow or live load, but one may be flexible enough to accumulate water and the other stiff enough to resist that accumulation. Ponding takes the importance of stiffness beyond perception and comfort into the realm of life safety.

In Figure 1.4(a), the $1/16$ in.-thick × 3 in.-wide styrene sheet is being used as a beam oriented with the broad faces horizontal. Just as it failed to hold its own weight as a column, it fails to hold its own weight as a beam. In Figure 1.4(b), the beam is oriented with the broad faces vertical; that is, it is set up on edge. In this case, it supports its own weight plus a small additional weight. The top edge of the beam is in compression and is starting to buckle to the side, accounting for the curved top edge of the beam.

Adding more weight causes the beam to buckle quickly to the side, as shown in Figure 1.5(a). Although this beam has the attribute of being quite deep, which is the direction we want to take it, it has the disadvantage of not being laterally very stiff. To help address this deficiency, we can cut the sheet of styrene into three strips of about equal width and glue them back together to form an I-section, as shown in Figure 1.5(b). The I-beam tends to exhibit slightly greater vertical deflection than the simple sheet set on edge, which means that the I-beam is slightly less stiff relative to vertical deformation. However, the I-beam is much stronger, by virtue of the fact that it is laterally much more stable than the simple sheet in Figure 1.4(b). The greater strength is apparent in the fact that it carries more than ten times as much weight.

There is a consistent theme in both columns and beams. The columns need breadth in both directions to avoid buckling in either direction. Beams need depth to provide leverage in resisting the load and lateral breadth to avoid lateral buckling. In the preceding examples, breadth and depth have been achieved by connecting

(a)

(b)

Figure 1.4 (a) A very shallow beam and (b) a deep beam.

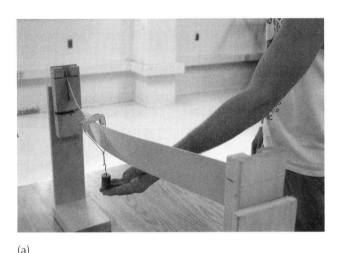

(a)

(b)

Figure 1.5 A sheet of material (a) set on edge and (b) configured as an I-beam.

perpendicular sheets of material to form a shape that is substantially more stable than either sheet would be on its own. Each sheet has a weak direction, which is shored up by the perpendicular sheet material connected edge-on to it. This notion of mutually stabilizing sheets of material is one to which we will return many times in conceptualizing structures.

I-beams are a classic example of combining perpendicular sheets of material to form a stronger composite shape. In the United States, most I-beams are not fashioned by joining sheets of material, but are made by a rolling process in which a big lump of steel, called a *billet,* is gradually squeezed and deformed until it takes on the final I-shaped section. In this manner, the perpendicular sheets of material are made as integral parts of the whole and there is no process required to connect the parts. For very large I-beams, the rolling process is not economical and the beams are made by welding steel plates together. The quality of the welds is crucial to ensuring the composite action of the plates.

The importance of ensuring composite action is illustrated by the following experiment. A shallow beam is made of acrylic plastic ⅛ in. deep and 1.5 in. wide. Under a 0.1 kg force, it deflects noticeably, as shown in Figure 1.6(a). Stacking ten of these beams and imposing ten times as much load produces almost exactly the same deflection, as shown in Figure 1.6(b).

Effectively, each beam in the stack of ten beams is acting to resist one tenth of the load. In other words, the stacked beams look like a very deep beam, but the stack is actually acting like ten independent beams. In essence, stacking the ten beams with 1.0 kg on top is equivalent to placing the ten beams side by side and putting 0.1 kg on each beam. In contrast, when the ten beams are not

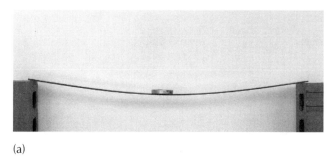
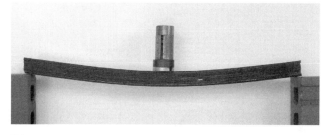

(a)   (b)

Figure 1.6 (a) A shallow beam and (b) ten shallow beams stacked.

simply stacked, but are properly glued together, they deflect much less and can carry much more load, as shown in Figure 1.7.

The message of this demonstration is that achieving structural depth by combining elements requires that the elements are sufficiently well connected that they can resist the shear forces occurring between them during bending. The classic example of this effect is making a concrete deck work in composite action with the steel beam supporting the deck. Achieving this composite action can significantly increase the effective overall depth of the spanning system. For example, a 6 in.-deep concrete slab working in composite action with a 12 in.-deep steel I-beam increases the structural depth from 12 in. to 18 in. To achieve this composite action, steel shear studs are welded to the top of the beam. These shear studs are embedded in the concrete, which is poured around them.

The concept of perpendicular sheets of material, which accounts for the outstanding structural performance of building components, such as I-beams and square tubes, can also be applied at the scale of the building itself. For example, a thin wall is the structural equivalent of a thin sheet of material. The base of that wall can be broadened by attaching it to a footing, as shown in the model in Figure 1.8(a). This base is typically very narrow because the gravity force transmitted down through the wall is distributed along a long footing, which distributes the force

very evenly into the soil. In a house, the wall footing is usually a 1 ft.-wide strip of concrete. In some situations, where the soil quality is particularly poor, the footing might be slightly wider than 1 ft. This footing does little to help stabilize the wall, which can be blown over in a slight breeze; see Figure 1.8(b).

This is true even of walls that we think of as heavy and stable, such as walls made of concrete masonry units. One of the most common causes of death on construction

(a)

(b)

Figure 1.7 Ten shallow beams glued to form one deep beam.

Figure 1.8 (a) A thin wall (b) subjected to lateral force.

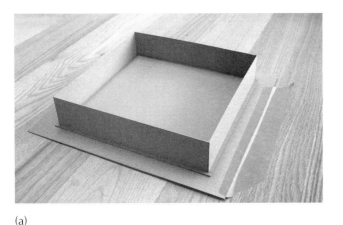

(a)

(b)

Figure 1.9 (a, b) Walls stabilizing each other at the ends.

sites is the overturning of masonry walls that have not been properly shored up during the construction process. Clearly, an individual wall of this sort is of no structural value by itself. This wall makes sense only as part of a larger system, with other parts that compensate for the weaknesses of this wall. One way to help this wall is to connect it to other walls perpendicular to it. This is what is normally done anyway, inasmuch as achieving an enclosed space requires more than one wall. Figure 1.9 illustrates the idea. Each of the four walls is stabilized at its ends by other walls set perpendicular to it. Now the weakness of each wall is near the center of the wall, where it is far removed from the stabilizing benefits of any perpendicular sheets of material.

The walls perpendicular to the wall being exposed to wind overpressure are put in a state of shear as the wall being loaded leans against them. These perpendicular walls are sometimes referred to as *shear walls*. They must be properly constituted to resist a shearing force. Many of the walls used in standard construction are capable of resisting substantial shear force. However, this is not al-

ways true. For example, classic post-and-beam construction is very poor in resisting lateral forces, as illustrated in Figure 1.10.

Standard wood stud construction eliminates this deformation of the wood frame by adding sheets of material in the plane of the wall, such as plywood or oriented strand board (OSB), which provide the diagonal forces to keep the wall from racking. See Figures 1.11, 1.12, and 1.13.

The composite construction of sheet material, such as plywood or OSB, with studs is another example of mutually bracing, perpendicular sheets of material, in that the studs are set with their long cross-sectional dimension perpendicular to the OSB sheet. The OSB sheet is very thin and very vulnerable to lateral buckling, similar to that observed in the thin sheet of plastic that we tried to use as a beam in Figure 1.5. By itself, the OSB is not a very effective structural element, but when braced frequently by studs, its structural effectiveness is greatly enhanced. OSB and plywood are typically considered as providing the shear resistance for walls in one- or two-story buildings, using only nails to connect the OSB or plywood to

(a)

(b)

Figure 1.10 (a, b) Post-and-beam construction deforming (racking) under shearing load.

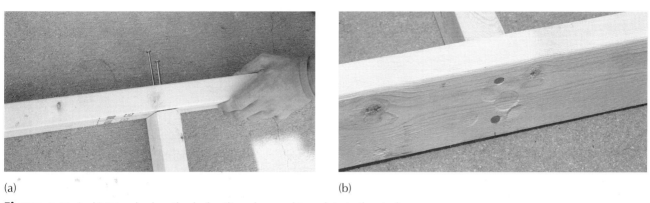

Figure 1.11 (a, b) Sstandard method of nailing shoe and top plate to the studs.

Figure 1.12 (a, b) Racking of studs under shearing force of a single finger.

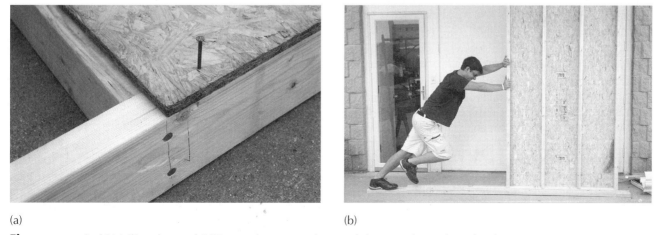

Figure 1.13 (a, b) Nailing sheets of OSB to studs, a top a plate, and shoe to enhance lateral resistance.

(a)

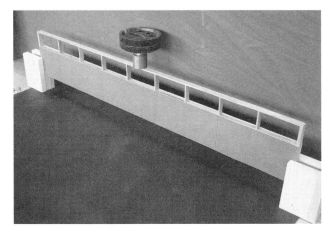

(b)

Figure 1.14 (a) 2×6 wood beams nailed together and (b) creating a box beam using plywood and 2×6 wood beams.

the studs. However, with the use of screws and glue, plywood box beams can be used for roofs spanning up to a hundred feet. Figure 1.14 illustrates the point. The model in (a) shows an assembly of wood sticks scaled to be the equivalent of a 2×6 wood beam, which is deflecting dramatically under a 0.5 kg weight. The model in (b) has chipboard glued to each side to create a box beam, similar to what could be done using plywood in a real structure. The model in Figure 1.14(b) barely deflects under five times as much load.

These kinds of box beams can be put together to form a folded-plate roof like the one in the model in the Figure 1.15.

Openings, such as doors and windows, undermine the shear capacity of a stud-and-plywood wall. Windows and doors are architecturally essential elements. Therefore, understanding the amount of opening that can be made in a shear wall without undermining its structural effectiveness is crucial. The building codes give pre-

Figure 1.15 Model of folded-plate roof.

scriptive rules for the percentages of walls in various situations that can be given over to openings. When the designer wants to exceed those limits, a more detailed analysis has to be done and special measures beyond the standard stud construction methods may be required.

Good shear walls perpendicular to the ends of the wall being loaded still do not solve the problem of the weakness of the wall being loaded near the center of that wall (Figure 1.9(b)). This weakness near the center of the wall can be addressed by using another perpendicular sheet of material, which may be either a floor or roof diaphragm, as shown in Figure 1.16.

A floor or roof acting in this mode is called a *diaphragm floor* or *diaphragm roof*. A diaphragm is a planar element that:

• Serves a primary purpose, such as roof decking spanning from roof joist to roof joist, to support forces perpendicular to the planar element, such as snow or maintenance workers on the roof

Figure 1.16 Floor or roof diaphragm stabilizing the top edge of a loaded wall.

- Serves a secondary role as a deep beam resisting forces parallel to the plane of the element

In Figure 1.16, the force parallel to the plane of the roof decking is created by the wall pressing against the edge of the roof. The diagram in Figure 1.17 suggests the nature of the interaction, wherein:

- The upper edge of the loaded wall presses against the edge of the roof.

- The diaphragm roof acts as a very deep, horizontal beam carrying the horizontal force on its edge to the tops of the side walls (i.e., the walls parallel to the direction of the force).
- The side walls serve as shear walls, carrying the force down to the footings.
- The horizontal force of the roof diaphragm along the top edge of one of the side shear walls, combined with the horizontal force in the other direction of the footing

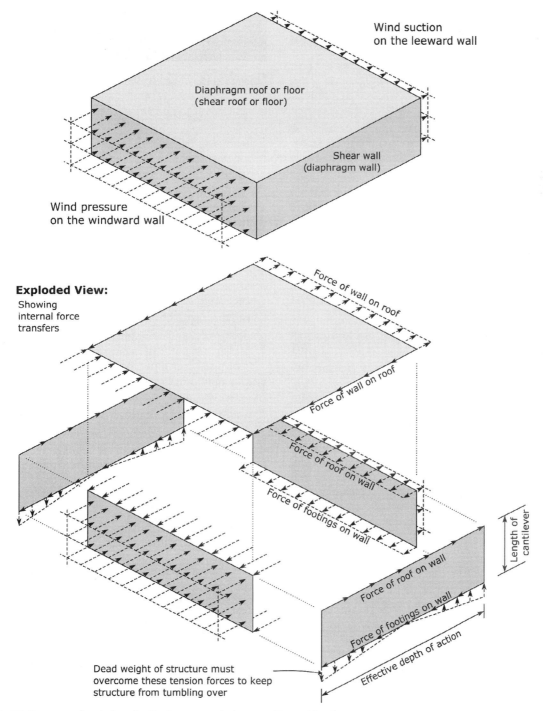

Figure 1.17 Forces on loaded wall, diaphragm roof, shear walls, and footings.

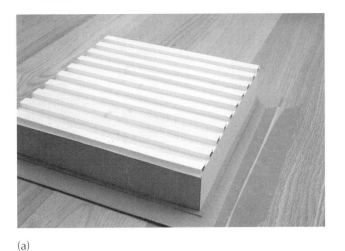

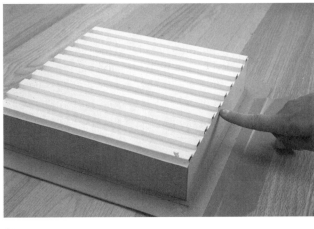

(a) (b)

Figure 1.18 (a, b) Diaphragm action of corrugated roof for force parallel to corrugations.

on the bottom of the side shear wall, tends to make the shear wall rotate. To avoid this, the footing must also create hold-down forces on the shear wall on the windward end of the shear wall and upward forces on the leeward end of the shear wall. These forces have to do with the overturning effect, which can be equilibrated only by the self-weight of the wall and of the footing.

The properties that allow a roof to work as a horizontal beam, that is, as a diaphragm, are the same properties that allow a wall to work as a cantilevered beam relative to forces parallel to the wall; that is, to work as a shear wall. Shear walls could be referred to as *diaphragm walls,* or diaphragm roofs as *shear roofs.* This text, however, sticks to the custom of associating the word *shear* with walls and the word *diaphragm* with roofs and floors.

In steel construction, the roof diaphragm is normally made of corrugated steel decking. A very thin steel sheet is run through a rolling system to form it into corrugated deck. It resists buckling really well for forces parallel to the corrugations, as shown in Figure 1.18.

In this model, the corrugations are represented as very coarse; that is, they are out of scale with the rest of the model. This was done to make the effects more apparent and to simplify the model building process. The decking is vulnerable to forces perpendicular to the corrugations, where the decking acts somewhat like an accordion. In a sense, the corrugations represent a kind of "prebuckling" of the steel sheet. The effect is demonstrated in Figure 1.19.

Corrugated decking, like the OSB in the shear wall example shown in Figure 1.13, is greatly benefited by the other structural elements in the system. For example, the

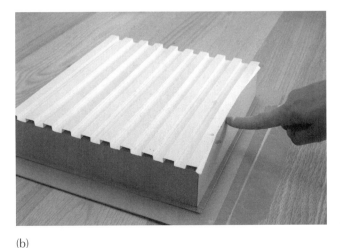

(a) (b)

Figure 1.19 (a, b) Corrugations crumpling at the point of application of the force.

(a)

(b)

Figure 1.20 Drag strut (a) improves decks' resistance to crumpling (b).

corrugated decking will be supported every few feet by spanning members, such as trusses or beams. These spanning members connect all the flutes of the corrugated decking by a continuous strut. Any force delivered to that spanning member is then delivered to every flute of the deck, which helps to distribute the forces over the decking and allow the decking to function more effectively as a diaphragm. This suggests that the connection at the top of the wall should be detailed in such a way that the forces of the wall go directly to the spanning members, rather than directly to the decking. This normally happens if the wall is working in bearing to support the spanning members. Sometimes a stiff wall engages the

roof decking at a location where there is not a spanning member. To get a force transfer between the wall and the diaphragm, a special element called a *drag strut* can be welded to the bottom of the decking, similar to what is shown on the left in Figure 1.20.

In addition to wind forces, we sometimes want walls to resist the pressure of soil, which is normally much higher than wind pressure. Thin walls on narrow footings are totally inappropriate for resisting such large lateral forces, as shown in Figure 1.21.

With relatively minor additional thickness and reinforcing, such walls can be made to work well in situations where the soil pressure is exerted from all sides of the

(a)

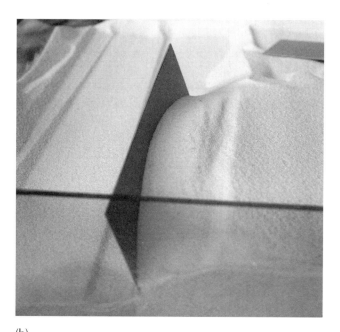

(b)

Figure 1.21 Thin wall on narrow footing, (a) standing alone and (b) under soil pressure.

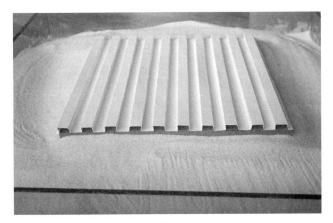

Figure 1.22 Soil on all sides of a basement wall.

building and the floor or roofing system at the top of the loaded wall is capable of taking the inward force of the soil in compression. This is the geometric and structural situation normally encountered in full basements in buildings. In this situation, the wall is spanning from the footing up to the roof or floor diaphragm, which works in compression to keep the tops of the walls from falling inward (see Figure 1.22).

Sometimes the terrain makes it desirable to have a walkout basement, which means that there is soil pressure on one side of the building, but not the other. This situation is depicted in Figure 1.23, in which (a) shows the model with no soil pressure and (b) shows the model with soil pressure on the right side. The image in (b) shows that the model has skidded to the left under the influence of the soil pressure. This behavior can be observed in a lightweight building with shallow footings. Usually, the side walls start to skid, but the walls perpendicular to the force cannot skid because the soil resistance at the footing is too great. This causes the building to break up as it moves laterally.

This loading condition creates forces in the structure that are difficult to analyze and design for. It also transmits a substantial amount of force through many building components that do not need to be loaded. Therefore, it is customary to account for unbalanced soil loads by designing the loaded wall as a cantilevered retaining wall. In this mode of operation, the wall has no restraint at the top and it must be connected to the foundation with a strong enough joint that the wall functions as a vertical cantilever beam. To make this work, the footing must be very strong and must be designed to avoid turning over under the influence of the wall. The standard design for a cantilevered retaining wall works similarly to a classic sheet metal bookend, where the weight of the books rests on the foot of the bookend, thereby stabilizing the bookend against overturning. In the case of the cantilevered retaining wall, soil rests on the top of the broad foundation, stabilizing it against overturning. This arrangement is shown in Figure 1.24, in which (a) shows the wide footing and (b) shows the soil against the right face of the wall, which is called the *stem*.

The footers for cantilevered retaining walls require much more excavation than wall footings that are designed to carry only gravity forces. This can be a serious issue where site limitations make it difficult to perform the excavations without encroaching on adjacent property or structures. Cantilevered walls are self-sustaining, or without the benefit of other, perpendicular walls to brace them, which requires that they be very thick walls. The benefit of cantilevered retaining walls is that they take the burden of the load at the point of application of the load, protecting the rest of the structure from that burden.

In the case of a wide building, such as the one shown in Figure 1.23, lateral forces tend to make the building skid across the land. For narrow buildings, the major concern becomes overturning of the entire structure, as shown in Figure 1.25. Such structures need to be held

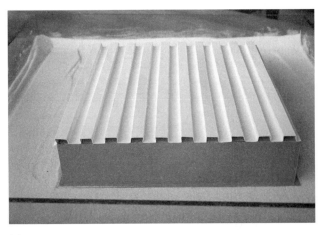

(a)

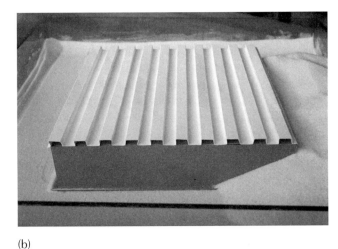

(b)

Figure 1.23 (a, b) Building skidding under influence of soil on one side.

(a)

(b)

Figure 1.24 Cantilevered retaining wall (a) before and (b) after loading.

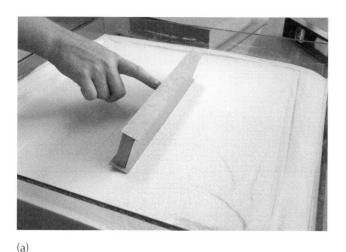
(a)

(b)

Figure 1.25 Buildings with tall, narrow proportions tending to turn over under lateral forces.

down by large, heavy footings or by piles or ground augers reaching deep into the soil.

Thus far, the focus has been on the structural benefits of mutually bracing, perpendicular sheets of material. These sheets can have openings in them to serve a variety of purposes. For example, in walls, door and window openings are normally desired. Typically, doors are rectangular because that shape is simple to frame and fits the human body. Windows are usually rectangular simply because of the simplicity of framing. From a structural point of view, other shapes may be preferable to rectangles. For example, circular or triangular holes can be cut in the solid web of a beam, as shown in Figure 1.26(a), or, for maximum lightness and transparency, slender struts can be used in a triangular pattern, like the truss in Figure 1.26(b). In (a), the beams are triangular in cross-section, consisting of three sheets of mutually bracing material. No additional bracing material is required. In

(b), the truss supports the roof diaphragm, which in turn provides lateral stabilization for the top edge, or top chord, of the truss. The bottom edge, or bottom chord, of the truss needs lateral bracing struts because there is no sheet of material available at the bottom of the truss to stabilize the bottom of the truss.

These spanning elements can have large rectangular openings, although this configuration is far from optimal from a structural point of view. In this case, the portions of the structure that remain must be very strong beamlike elements that are joined with rigid connections to produce something called a *rigid frame*. A *rigid joint* is defined as a joint that maintains the angle between the elements being joined, even under full loading on the structure. A rigid frame that is used to span is sometimes called a *Verendeel truss*. Rigid frames tend to be much heavier and more difficult to fabricate than triangulated trusses. As a consequence, they are rarely used for resisting gravity forces.

(a)

(b)

Figure 1.26 Beams with (a) holes and (b) a truss.

The term *truss* has come to be associated with fully tri-angulated spanning elements, and the terminology *Verendeel truss* is at odds with the common usage of the term. For example, it would be rare that the mention of the word *truss* would bring the image of a rigid frame to mind.

Verendeel trusses can be quite elegant, as illustrated in Figure 1.27, showing a pedestrian bridge in the Oakbrook shopping mall in Oakbrook, Illinois.

The bridge in Figure 1.28 represents the ultimate in lightness and transparency in structural sheets. Uniform

Figure 1.27 Rigid-frame spanning elements (Verendeel trusses) supporting a pedestrian bridge.

Figure 1.28 The Golden Gate Bridge.

gravity loads are being carried by two suspension cables. These cables would change shape drastically under a concentrated gravity force, such as the weight of a very heavily loaded vehicle or a closely spaced convoy of trucks. To "smooth out" the nonuniformity of the gravity loads, trusses are provided in the same vertical plane with the suspension cables. The trusses are supported by suspenders hanging from the suspension cables. Each cable, with its associated truss, forms a very strong and rigid "sheet" of material that is minimal and very transparent. Material has been put only where it needs to be. It may initially be difficult for the student to think of these slender cables as part of a sheet of material, but getting that concept established in his or her mind is crucial to understanding this subject matter.

In the same bridge, lateral forces of wind are resisted by horizontal trusses, one at the bottom of the side trusses and one at the top of the side trusses (just below the roadbed). These horizontal trusses are the perpendicular "sheets" of material that reinforce the vertical "sheets" consisting of the cables and the side trusses.

The principles and structural systems applied to resisting gravity loads can also be applied to resisting lateral forces on buildings. Figure 1.29 shows a building with no appreciable resistance being racked by a lateral force (a). That same structure can be stabilized by shear walls (b). These shear walls are the structural analog of the solid-web beam in gravity systems.

The same structure can also be stabilized by triangulation, such as cross-bracing, which would be the analog

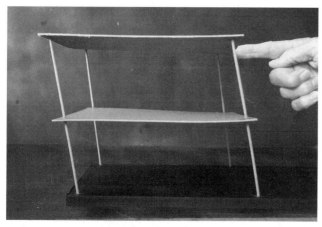

(a)

(b)

Figure 1.29 (a, b) Structural frame stabilized by adding shear panels.

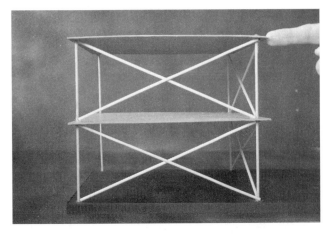

(a)

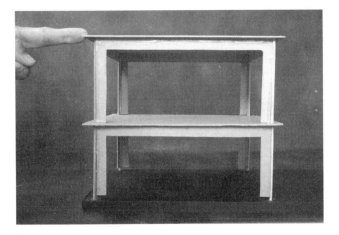

(b)

Figure 1.30 Bracing with (a) triangulation and (b) a rigid frame.

of a truss used to span against the forces of gravity; see Figure 1.30(a). It can also be braced using beamlike elements forming a rigid frame; see Figure 1.30(b).

The use of rigid frames is much more common in dealing with lateral bracing than in gravity spanning for buildings because they provide the kind of openings that allow human traffic to easily pass through at a variety of locations. Moreover, for some very tall buildings, the inherently large dimensions of the columns make rigid-frame action very effective and practical. One of the most beautiful and practical examples of this mode of construction is the Sears Tower, designed by Skidmore, Owings & Merrill of Chicago (see Chapters 7 and 10). In the Sears Tower, as is the case in most rigid-frame steel structures, the rigid joints were achieved through welding, which makes the material essentially continuous in all directions. Achieving rigid joints with wood is much more problematical than with steel. The unidirectional nature of wood fibers creates a challenge in making the material continuous in more than one direction through a joint. The only effective way to achieve this result is to split the

material in one direction and let material running in another direction pass between the two split pieces. To get a rigid connection between the intersecting members, the material that has been split apart must effectively encase the material passing through. This arrangement is illustrated in Figure 1.31, wherein 2 × 6 wood beams, with blocking elements in between, have been sandwiched around a 2 × 4 wood beam running perpendicular to the two 2 × 6 wood beams. In a really good rigid joint, the blocking members should be pressed down against the 2 × 4 and glue should be used to fill any fine voids and to ensure that the blocking elements do not slip where they are connected to the 2 × 6s. In this demonstration model, there was no glue. In spite of that fact, this single joint is now more than capable of taking the maximum force from the person who was able to rack the standard stud wall frame with a single finger (as was shown in Figure 1.12(b)). The use of moment joints is clearly a more complicated method of achieving lateral stability in a wood structure than by the use of plywood or OSB sheathing to create a shear wall.

(a)

(b)

Figure 1.31 (a, b) Rigid joint in wood.

The mutually bracing sheets of material do not have to be perpendicular to each other. They simply have to meet at an angle that puts each sheet substantially out of the plane of the other sheet. For example, a tube with a triangular cross section can function extremely well structurally, even though the sheets of each face are meeting each other at 60°, instead of 90°. In fact, such a tube can even work well with a cross section that is a 45°-45°-90° right triangle.

Sometimes, the sheets of material may not even be planar elements. In Figure 1.32(a), a thin-shelled barrel vault is extremely vulnerable to lateral forces, which cause roll-through deformation. The curved sheets of material in the thin-shelled cross vault in Figure 1.32(b) are very effective at bracing each other everywhere except at the top, where the sheets merge into a locally flat area where the sheets become essentially coplanar.

Domes, which have no flat parts, are even subtler examples of this phenomenon. No matter in which direction you push on a dome, there is part of the dome that is essentially "edge on" to the force. That material is crucial in keeping the dome surface from deforming; see Figure 1.33.

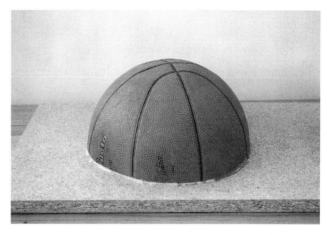

(a)

(b)

Figure 1.33 (a, b) A dome subjected to lateral load.

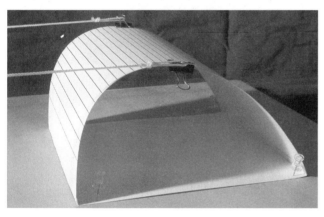

(a)

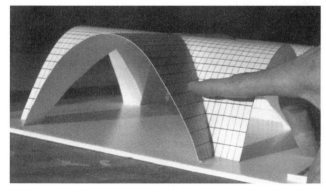

(b)

Figure 1.32 (a) A thin-shelled barrel vault and (b) a thin-shelled cross vault.

In Figure 1.34(a), the sides of the dome are cut away. The remaining portion of the dome is extremely vulnerable to lateral force on its surface (b).

There is a fourth, somewhat less common form of structural action called *torsion*. Torsion involves an element's being subjected to a torque that causes it to twist about its axis. The most common form of torsion is seen in the drive shaft of a motor vehicle. Elements that work well in other kinds of structural action, such as bending, do not necessarily work well in torsion. For example, I-beams work very well in bending and are about the worst structural form for addressing torsion. Closed tubes are the best structural form for working in torsion. Figure 1.35 illustrates this point. There are three plastic elements, each constructed from the same amount and type of styrene plastic. The elements are a square tube (top), a thick, solid bar (middle), and an I-section (bottom). The I-section has the smallest torque and largest amount of twist. The hollow tube has the largest torque and the least amount of twist.

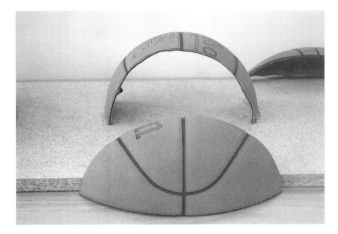

(a)

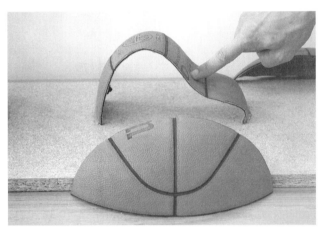

(b)

Figure 1.35 Torsion in a tube, a slab, and an I-section.

Figure 1.34 (a, b) Dome with sides sliced away, showing roll-through deformation.

The Sunshine Skyway Bridge in Tampa, Florida, is an example of a structure that relies on torsion for stability. The roadway is supported along its centerline by a plane of tension stays that are in turn supported by the towers. If these stays were the only means of support for the roadway, any asymmetric loading, such as might occur with heavy traffic on one side of the bridge, would cause the bridge to twist over, dumping the traffic into the bay. The cross section of the roadway is a closed tube that is connected at the towers so that it will not rotate. Asymmetric loading on the roadway is carried through this torsional action. It is crucial that this tube closes on itself. The following figures illustrate this point. In Figure 1.36, stays support the centerline of the roadway, which is tubular in cross section and is restrained against rotation at the towers by wooden pins above and below the roadway. Asymmetric loading is simulated by a heavy chain resting on the right side of the roadway. Removing the pins at the towers causes the roadway to tilt dramati-

cally, dumping the load. The tubular roadway is working very well in torsion to resist this asymmetric loading.

Figure 1.37 shows what happens when the tube is split along two lines on the bottom of the roadway. Neither the total amount of material in the cross section nor the depth of the cross section has been changed by making these slices. However, the torsional capacity of the roadway has been drastically diminished, as indicated by the amount of twist. The twist has induced such a severe tilt in the roadway that the chain has to be tied to the bridge to keep it from slipping off.

The most common situation in which torsion is encountered in buildings is in curved beams, which tend to twist under loading. For such structures, the ideal beam cross section is a closed tube. However, thin-walled tubes have serious problems with wall buckling when an attempt is made to roll them into a curved form. Wide-flange elements are usually much easier to roll into a curved shape. Sometimes it is more economical to simply use a heavy wide-flange beam, even though that may not be the most structurally efficient shape.

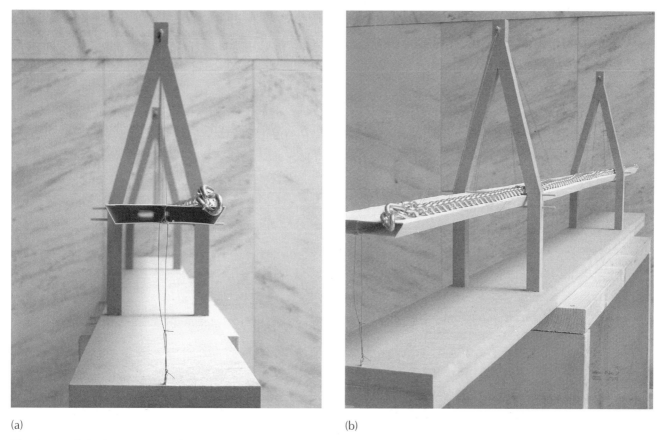

(a) (b)

Figure 1.36 (a, b) Two views of a model bridge with stays down the centerline.

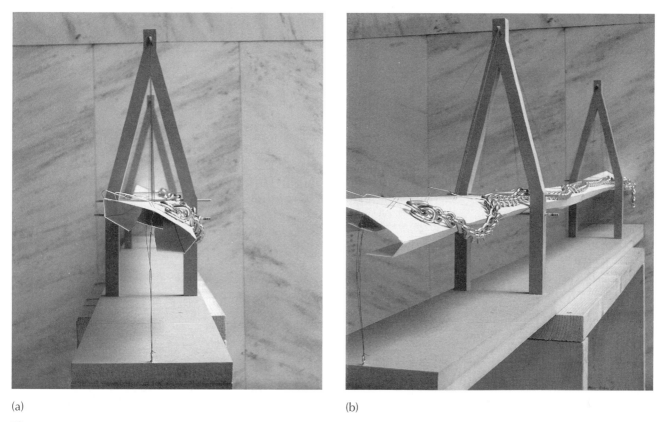

(a) (b)

Figure 1.37 (a, b) Effect of slicing a roadway so that it is no longer a closed tube.

1.7 Design Guidelines for Spans and Proportions of Common Members and Systems

As demonstrated with the plastic beams (Figure 1.4 and Figure 1.5), depth is crucial to their being able to span effectively. The required depth of a beam is not an ab-

solute matter, but a relative matter. It has to do with proportions: the longer the beam, the deeper the beam needs to be. The same general argument applies to all kinds of spanning elements. The tables in Figures 1.38 through 1.44 show typical spans and proportions for some of the common spanning systems that are discussed in more detail in other parts of this book. The spanning members are drawn to scale, with the scale being indicated at the top

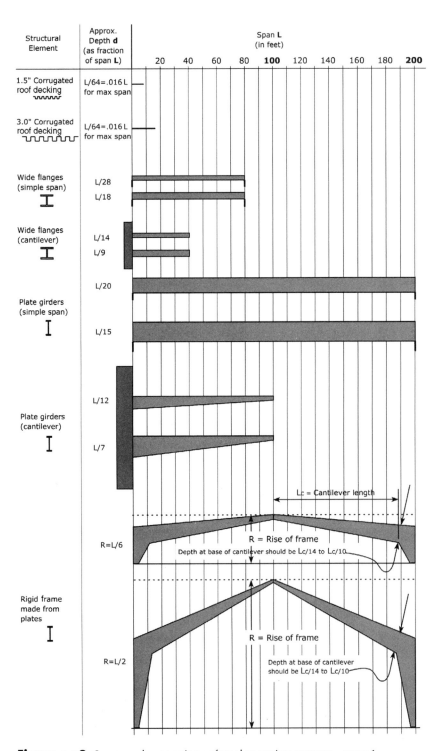

Figure 1.38 Spans and proportions of steel spanning systems—page 1.

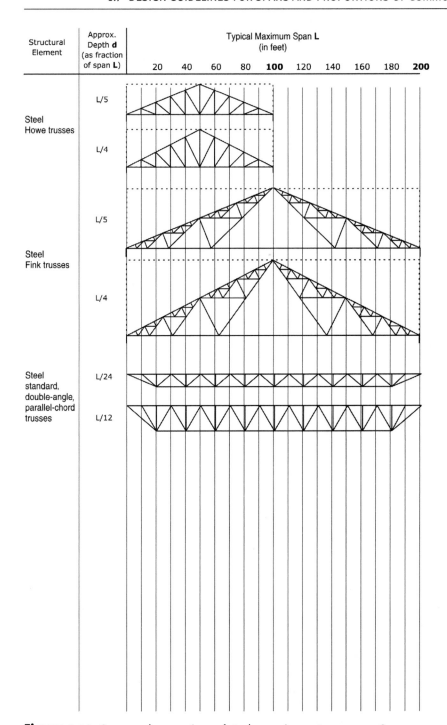

Structural Element	Approx. Depth d (as fraction of span L)	Typical Maximum Span L (in feet)								
		20 40 60 80 **100** 120 140 160 180 **200**								

Figure 1.39 Spans and proportions of steel spanning systems—page 2.

of each page. Most of the pages put the top of the scale at a span of 200 ft and one page goes to 1,000 ft. In interpreting the data, the first thing the reader should look at is the scale at the top of the page.

For each spanning system, there are two diagrams drawn, one indicating the shallowest proportions that would be commonly used and the other indicating the deepest proportions that would commonly be used. Both

the diagrams shown for a particular spanning element are drawn at a length indicative of the maximum length that is commonly expected to be seen for that element. All these spans and proportions are indicative of common practice at the time of the writing of this book. Every one of these spanning systems could be driven to greater spans by a highly motivated designer. Therefore, these upper limits should not be interpreted as absolute, but

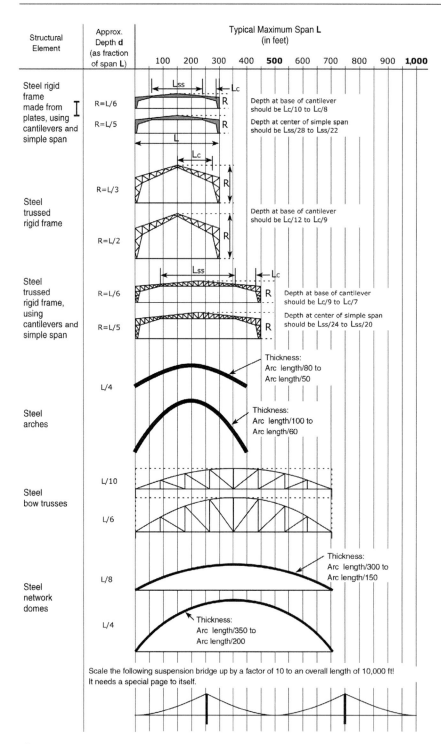

Figure 1.40 Spans and proportions of steel spanning systems—page 3.

simply as indicators of the practical limits to the span of the system. Similarly, the limits of the proportions, as indicated by the two diagrams, should also be understood as indicators of common practice, and not as any kind of absolute limits. These pages can be consulted in the early stages of design to get an idea of what is economically practical with these systems.

Assignment 1.1: Problem on Spans and Proportions of Steel Spanning Elements

1. A steel parallel-chord truss is to span 80 ft. With proportions near the shallower end of the range indicated in the guidelines, its depth would be what?

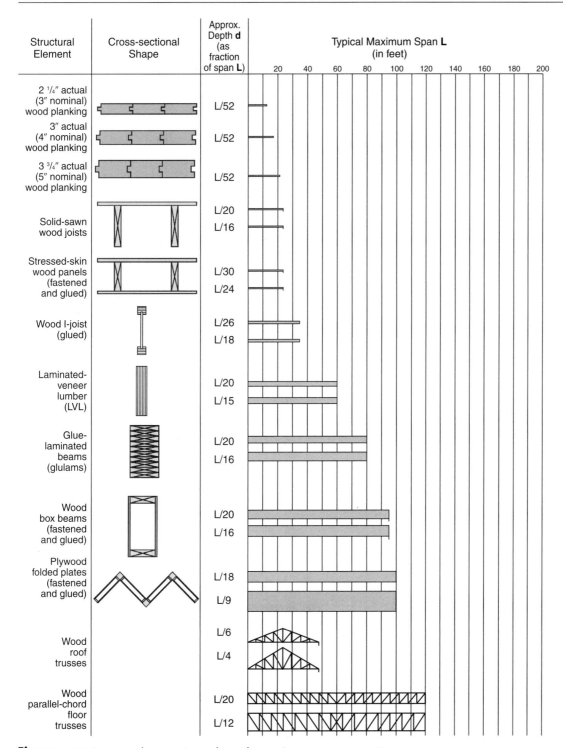

Figure 1.41 Spans and proportions of wood spanning systems—page 1.

With proportions near the deeper end of the range indicated in the guidelines, its depth would be what?

_____

2. For a steel bow truss of relatively deep proportions spanning 60 ft, what would the depth at the center of the truss be? _____

3. A wide-flange cantilevered beam projecting out 20 ft, having fairly shallow proportions, would be how deep? _____

4. A solid-sawn wood joist is spanning 16 ft. With proportions near the shallower end of the range indicated in the guidelines, its depth would be what?

_____

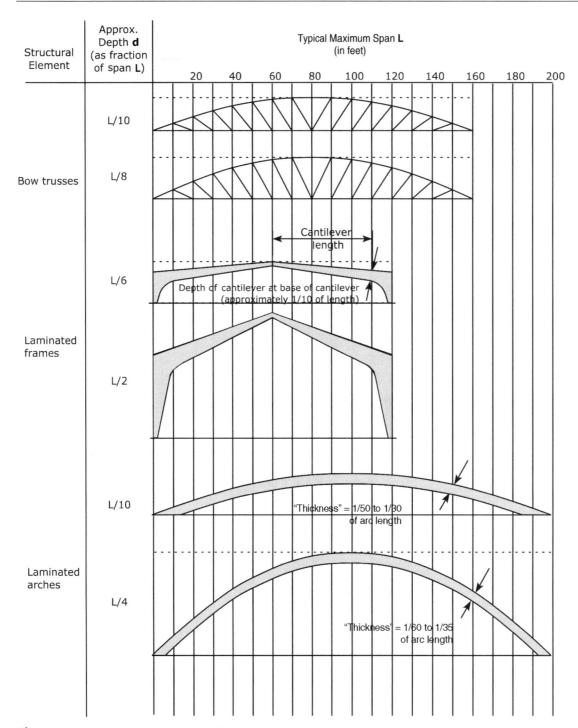

Structural Element	Approx. Depth **d** (as fraction of span **L**)	Typical Maximum Span **L** (in feet)
Bow trusses	L/10	
	L/8	
Laminated frames	L/6	
	L/2	
Laminated arches	L/10	
	L/4	

Figure 1.42 Spans and proportions of wood spanning systems—page 2.

With proportions near the deeper end of the range indicated in the guidelines, its depth would be what? _____

5. A steel rigid frame is spanning 140 ft. What would be the shallowest rise within the range indicated in the guidelines? _____ What would be the highest rise within the range indicated in the guidelines? _____

6. For a simple concrete slab spanning 25 ft in two directions and supported continuously around the boundary by beams or bearing walls, what is the shallowest depth within the guidelines? _____

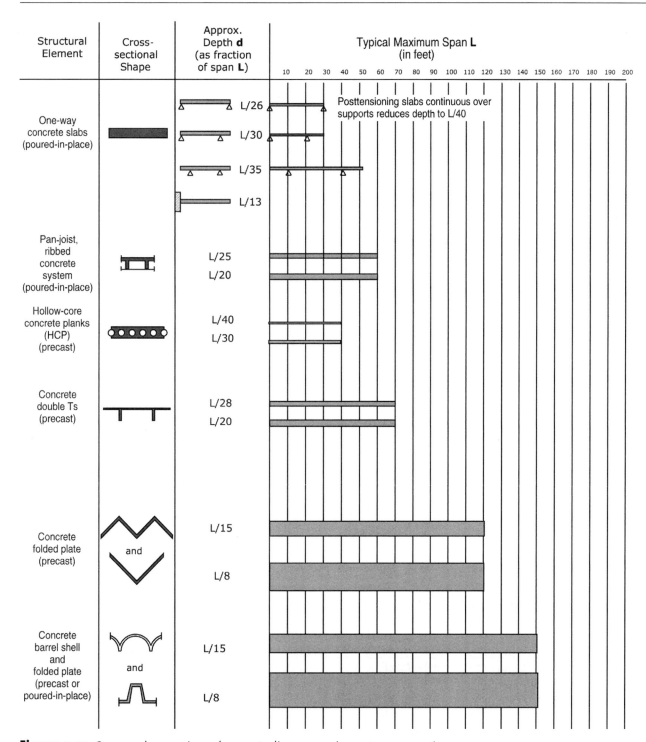

Figure 1.43 Spans and proportions of concrete, linear spanning systems—page 1.

What is the maximum depth within the guidelines?

_____

Assignment 1.2: Structural Design/Model Project

Providing interior illumination using natural light is commonly referred to as *daylighting.* Daylighting involves an interesting challenge in structural design, inasmuch as it requires extensive openings, or apertures, to admit the light. In this project, students will design a steel structure that admits daylight for illumination. The building will have an identified purpose and will address the following requirements:

1. Most of the roof surface will be opaque and well insulated.

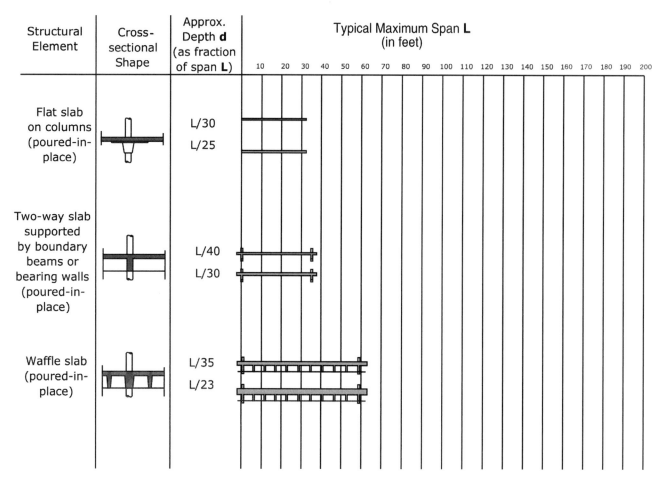

Structural Element	Cross-sectional Shape	Approx. Depth **d** (as fraction of span **L**)	Typical Maximum Span **L** (in feet)
Flat slab on columns (poured-in-place)		L/30 L/25	
Two-way slab supported by boundary beams or bearing walls (poured-in-place)		L/40 L/30	
Waffle slab (poured-in-place)		L/35 L/23	

Figure 1.44 Spans and proportions of concrete, two-way spanning systems—page 1.

2. Within the roof will be openings to admit daylight.

3. These openings will represent approximately 20 percent of the floor area being illuminated.

4. The openings will be vertical and facing north and south.

5. The openings will be distributed/located in such a manner as to produce fairly uniform light throughout the interior of the structure.

6. A means will be identified by which glare from beam sunlight can be avoided at all times of year. This may involve the use of baffles, banners, or some other elements that intercept the beam sunlight admitted through the south-facing glazing.

7. The spans involved should be large enough to be challenging—at least 50 ft.

8. The design must provide adequate rigidity so that the glass in the openings will not shatter.

9. The spanning members will have appropriate proportions.

For the physical model:

• Materials and connections used in the model should behave in a manner that is reasonably representative of the materials from which the actual structure would be created. In your model, as in the real structure, connections that work are more important than pretty connections. Realistic simulation of structural behavior suggests that you do *not* build your model on a thick, rigid slab of material. One of the most tenuous parts of a structure is the connection to the ground. The ground generally has significant compressive capacity, minimal shear capacity, and no tensile or bending capacity. The model should attempt to reflect these facts. This is a tough part of the assignment. Start collecting

Model Creator(s):	If there are multiple creators, evaluators should keep in mind the level of effort and quality of work appropriate to the number of creators.	
Model Evaluators:		

1. Evaluate the elements for resisting each of the following forces: Vertical forces: Dead load: Snow/live load on roof: Live load on floors: Wind suction on roof: Horizontal forces: Wind, earthquake, live, or impact forces in N–S direction: Wind, earthquake, live, or impact forces in E–W direction:	Total value: 50 pts	Points deducted
	With regard to each of these forces: A. Are the proportions of the bending elements **(d/L)** consistent with the guidelines? B. Do the compressive elements have adequate **breadth** and/or **bracing** to resist buckling? C. Are there elements that looke like some common structural element, but are really acting like something else?	
2. Is the model-building technique effective in simulating the structural behavior that would be expected from the structure?	Total value: 10 pts	Points deducted
3. Are the daylighting apertures appropriately - oriented? - sized? - located? - protected with overhangs? - provided with beam sunlight blockers/diffusers?	Total value: 20 pts	Points deducted
4. Does the design show innovation, creativity, or a willingness to take risks?	Total value: 5 pts	Points deducted
5. Artistic/aesthetic evaluation: Is the structure inspiring? Is it dramatic? Does it stimulate curiosity? Does it have pleasing proportions?	Total value: 5 pts	Points deducted
6. Would the structure serve the intended function well? Does it shed rain well? Are there heat trains? Does the space have sufficient size and the right proportions for the function? Are entry and egress properly provided? Are there safety issues?	Total value: 10 pts	Points deducted
	Total points deducted	
	Final evaluation of DL model: /100	

Figure 1.45 Evaluation of Structural Design/Model Project.

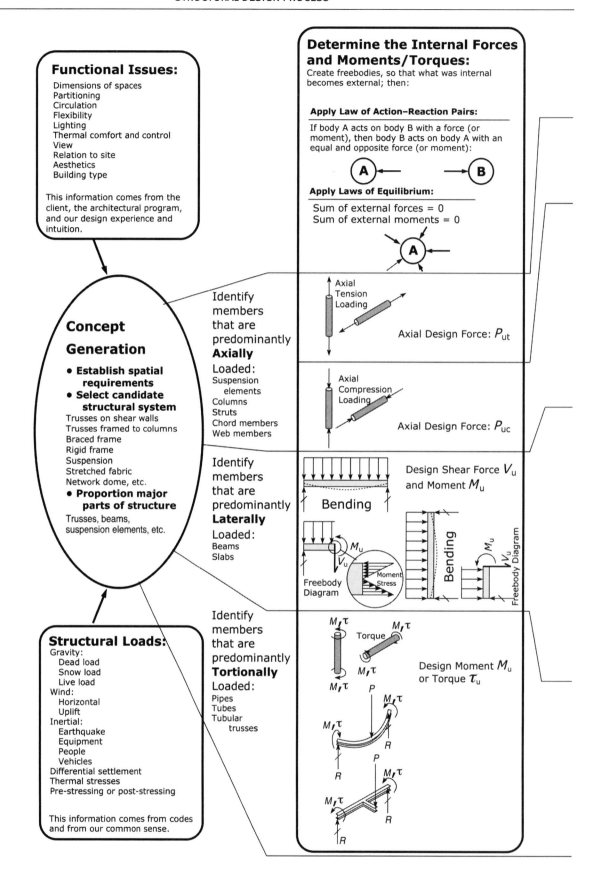

(a)

Figure 1.46 Flowchart for structural design process—page 1.

Design Members

Choose material: note yield stress
and material stiffness E

Choose shape of X-section
Choose connector concept
Size X-section
Work out details of connections

Tension element

(Fails by material tearing (yielding))

$$A_t \geq \frac{P_{ut}}{\Phi_t F_y}$$ P_{ut} from factored loads

"Slender" Compression Element

(Fails by crushing of material or buckling of the element)
Chose radius of gyration large enough that slenderness ratio (L/r) allows a reasonably high allowed compressive stress F_{CR}.

$$A_c \geq \frac{P_{uc}}{\Phi_C F_{CR}}$$

P_{uc} from factored loads

Other issues:

Buckling of parts of X-section (e.g., wall buckling)

Shear (use reasonable area in vertical rectangle)

A = area of rectangle
= cross-sectional strength for shear

$$A \geq \frac{3}{2} \frac{V_u}{\Phi_v F_{yv}}$$ V from factored loads

3/2 factor accounts for nonuniform stress distribution

Moment (use I-section with wide flange for stability)

S = section modulus
= cross-sectional strength in resisting moment.

$$S \geq \frac{M_u}{\Phi_b F_y}$$ M_u from factored loads

(**b** is for bending. It should be **m**, for moment stresses, but history has made it otherwise.)

Deflection (use deep I-section)

I = moment of inertia - cross-sectional stiffness

$$I \geq \frac{f(w,L)}{E} \times \frac{L}{\Delta}$$

where f(w,L) is a function of the unfactored load and span

Other Issues:

Lateral stability, flange buckling
bearing surface, bolt sizing, etc.

To achieve tortional strength and stiffness:
Use a section with a large

Angular Moment of Inertia J.

Tubular elements (e.g., round pipe, round tube, square tube, tubular truss) are ideal.

Some of the above are hard to produce in curved forms (e.g., the walls of square tube buckles during rolling). In such applications, the I section may prove to be satisfactory if a version is used with thick flanges and web:

Design Members with Combined Stresses

Some members are in multiple states of stress. For example, the vertical members in the following structure have axial forces from the weight of the roof and lateral forces from the wind. The top chord members are in compression under the influence of the overall truss action and they are bending under the influence of the deck resting on them.

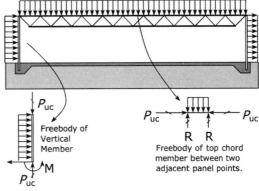

P_{uc}
Freebody of Vertical Member
M
P_{uc}

P_{uc} — R R — P_{uc}
Freebody of top chord member between two adjacent panel points.

For a member to be satisfactory under the combined axial load and bending load, it must satisfy the following condition:

The fraction of the member's capacity consumed for axial compression + the fraction of the member's capacity consumed for bending
must be less than or equal to 1.

$$\left(\frac{f_c}{\Phi_c F_{CR}} \right) =$$ the fraction of the element's compressive capacity that is consumed under axial load

f_c = actual compressive stress under the axial load

$\Phi_c F_{CR}$ = allowed compressive stress under the axial load

$$\left(\frac{f_b}{\Phi_b F_y} \right) =$$ the fraction of the element's moment capacity that is consumed in the lateral loading, where

f_b = actual moment stress under the lateral load

$\Phi_b F_y$ = allowed moment stress under the lateral load

Procedure: Add together the two fractions from above.

$$\left(\frac{f_c}{\Phi_c F_{CR}} \right) + \left(\frac{f_b}{\Phi_b F_y} \right) \leq 1$$

This equation states that the fraction of the element's capacity that is consumed for all the loads on it, i.e., for the combination of axial and lateral loads, must not exceed ONE, i.e., it will not exceed the safe capacity of the member.

This design process is highly itertive, involving trial and error. In such a situation, we:
1. Make an educated guess regarding which loading condition is the most demanding on the member
2. Oversize the member for that loading condition
3. Test the member to see if it is adequate to resist the combined stresses from the two loading conditions
This is called a UNITY check.

The details of the equation above vary from material to material and over time, as refinements are made in the methodology, but for purposes of this text the equation above captures the gist of the sizing process for combined stresses. The more detailed calculations for combined stress should be performed by a qualified structural engineer.

(b)

Figure 1.46 Flowchart for structural design process—page 2 *(Continued).*

materials early and do experiments to see how best to connect those materials. Explore how best to express the structural behavior of your design.

- A sequence of models in partially completed states would be useful if you are exploring a new structural concept. In this manner, the structural function of each part can be demonstrated as it is added to the structure. If you want to build several good models, group projects will be considered. Discuss your team plan with the instructor before proceeding. The additional level of effort needed to justify additional team members should be apparent in the project.
- Write a succinct one-page description of the rationales underlying your design. This should include a description of which elements bear primary responsibility for each of the common loads that would have to be addressed, especially gravity and wind in all directions, including wind suction on the roof. See the loads checklist at the beginning of Chapter 2. Discuss materials, methods of connection, and fabrication and construction issues.
- Put a scale figure in the model to indicate its size.

Make your design something that excites you. It should represent structural beauty, as you define it at this stage in your development as a designer.

Assignment 1.3: Structural Model Analysis/Evaluation

To stimulate active student participation in the discussion and analysis of the structural models, the class will be divided into groups. (Three students per group seems to be a manageable size that offers diversity of ideas without being so large that voices get lost. The instructor will make the final decision on the size of the groups.) Each group will prepare a detailed (but concise) written analysis of four models other than their own.

The student groups will be formed by students signing up together. The sign-up sheet will indicate the method by which three models will be assigned to each group. In addition to the three assigned models, each group will select one other model for review. Each group is encouraged to select a model that is as different as possible from the models that are assigned. If a group has been assigned a model that is substantially incomplete, the group is encouraged to choose another model to replace it.

Each group is to choose a location in which to work and to mark that location with a sheet of paper with the letter representing the group (A, B, C, etc.). Then, each person in the class is responsible for taking his or her model to the location of the group that will be reviewing it.

To bring some structure and discipline to this process, an evaluation sheet has been provided (see Figure 1.45). On the evaluation sheet, various design issues are listed

and point values are assigned. This evaluation sheet will be the point of departure for all discussions of the models. As you proceed in your discussions, you may want to make suggestions regarding additional issues that should be included on the sheet or for changes in the assignment of points. It is recommended that you use a pencil so that you can edit your work.

When the instructors do the final grading of the models, they will simultaneously grade these reviews. Serious, thoughtful reviews will get high marks.

In each group, all three individuals will participate in all four reviews. A review should reflect the sentiments of all the members of the group. Moreover, the grade for all group members will be the same, so it is truly a collective effort. To ensure that the work is fairly distributed, each group member should assume responsibility for the actual write-up of at least one of the model projects.

Each group member should review all write-ups and provide editorial comments to the person primarily responsible for the write-up.

One week later, lab time will be allocated for students to present their evaluations to the class and to lead class discussion of the projects. As you write up the evaluations, think about what you consider important to present to the class. Prioritize the issues for each model. These presentations should not ramble. They must get to key issues and should focus on a few key points, such as: "This aspect of the design/model is particularly deficient" or "one of the really strong points of this design/model was . . ." Think of your task as being to enlighten your fellow students—not to fill time.

1.8 Flowchart of the Structural Design Process

The flowchart in Figure 1.46 describes the structural design process that is followed in practice. Some of the concepts outlined here will be fully understood only as the reader goes through each of the chapters of this book. However, the gist of the process should be apparent in what is shown. This flowchart will be a kind of road map for the process. As you learn new things, you will periodically return to this road map to help you know where you stand in learning about the process. At this first encounter with the road map, you are encouraged to study it and try to understand its salient features. Even though its details will in some ways exceed your understanding at first encounter, it is still worth beginning the process of getting the map in your head. Otherwise, there will be a tendency to see each chapter of this book as isolated and episodic, rather than as part of a coherent process.

2

Loads

2.1 Units of Measure

Localized force *(sometimes referred to as a point load or point force)*

Symbols:

P (uppercase *P* for point force) or

W (uppercase *W* for weight)

There is no such thing as a true point force, since a finite force on a point (which has zero area) would result in an infinite pressure. There are no materials that can withstand infinite pressure, so a point force is a meaningless concept. However, some forces are very localized and can, from the point of view of equilibrium, be treated as point forces. Even highly distributed forces can be replaced with a point force at the center of action of the distributed force, for certain computational purposes (see Figure 2.1).

Units:

Force, for example:

(pounds) or

K (kips—1 kip equals 1,000 pounds, i.e., a kilopound)

Force distributed along a line *(sometimes referred to as a line load); see Figure 2.2*

Symbols:

w (lowercase *w*)

Units:

Force per unit length, for example: $\frac{\#}{\text{ft}}$ or $\frac{\text{K}}{\text{ft}}$

Force distributed over an area *(usually referred to as a pressure or a stress); see Figure 2.3*

Symbols:

p (lowercase *p* for pressure)

f (lowercase *f* for stress in a material)

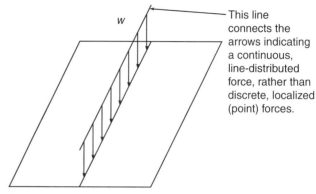

Figure 2.2 Line-distributed load.

F (uppercase *F* for a limit on stress in a material, e.g., yield stress)

S (uppercase *S* for stress in a material, typically used in Multiframe)

Note: In this text, *f* or *F* is generally used for stress, rather than *S*, since the symbol *S* is used for the section modulus, which occurs along with stress in some of the equations. Clearly, using the same symbol for two different quantities in one equation would be unacceptably confusing. However, Multiframe uses *S* for stress, so, when dealing with Multiframe, *S* is used for stress. In other words, the symbolism will not be completely consistent. The situation regarding symbols is further aggravated by the fact that different symbols are sometimes used in presenting design data for different materials, as set forth by the professional and industry organizations responsible for those materials.

Units:

Force per unit area, for example: $\frac{\#}{\text{ft}^2}$ or $\frac{\text{K}}{\text{ft}^2}$ or $\frac{\#}{\text{in.}^2}$ or $\frac{\text{K}}{\text{in.}^2}$

Force distributed over a volume *(usually referred to as a density); see Figure 2.4*

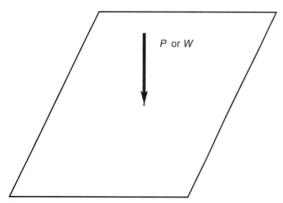

Figure 2.1 Point force.

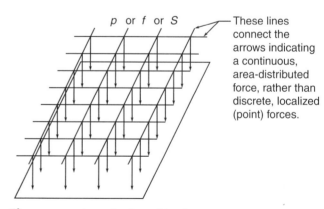

Figure 2.3 Area-distributed load.

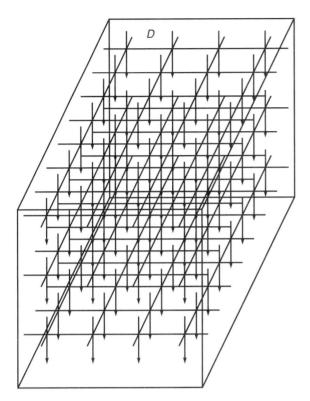

Figure 2.4 Volume-distributed force.

Symbols:

D (uppercase D for density)

Units:

Force per unit volume, for example: $\dfrac{\#}{\text{in.}^3}$ or $\dfrac{\#}{\text{ft}^3}$ or $\dfrac{K}{\text{in.}^3}$

These definitions can be understood in terms of the following example, dealing with the main floor of a residence constructed with plywood floors on solid-sawn lumber joists.

For floors and roofs, the decking must be thick enough to resist punch-through of localized forces (see Figure 2.5).

Once resistance to punch-through has been properly addressed, the remaining effect of the live load can be

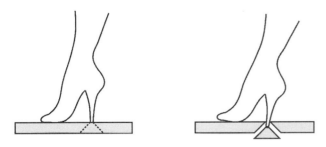

Figure 2.5 Localized force causing punch-through.

treated by assuming a uniform pressure over the entire floor. For the main floor of residences, a distributed load of $\dfrac{40\#}{\text{ft}^2}$ is prescribed. You can imagine that the weight of the human occupants has been reduced to an "equivalent" layer of water distributed over the entire floor (see Figure 2.6).

The force of gravity on the water is a force that is distributed throughout the volume of the water. However, from the point of view of designing the structure, the main effect of the water that needs to be considered is the effect of the water's weight on the plywood. The weight of the water is distributed over the area of the plywood, creating a pressure p on the top surface of the plywood:

$$p = \frac{W}{A} = \frac{D \cdot V}{A} = \frac{D \cdot A \cdot h}{A} = D \cdot h \qquad \textbf{[2.1]}$$

Where

W = weight of the water

A = area over which the water is distributed

D = density of water

h = height of the layer of water

The height of the "equivalent" layer of water can be determined by solving for h:

$$h = \frac{p}{D} = \frac{\dfrac{40\#}{\text{ft}^2}}{\dfrac{62.4\#}{\text{ft}^3}} \qquad \textbf{[2.2]}$$

This is a tangle of units that needs to be simplified. In this text, units are reorganized and simplified by multiplying by ratios of units that represent 1. Any mathematical expression can be multiplied by 1 without changing its value. Creative ways are sought to express 1 that will simplify the mathematical expression.

Examples of expressions for 1 are:

$$\left[\frac{12\ \text{in.}}{\text{ft}}\right] = 1$$

$$\left[\frac{1000\#}{K}\right] = 1 \qquad \textbf{[2.3]}$$

$$\left[\frac{\text{ft}^3}{\text{ft}^3}\right] = 1$$

Notice that in each case, the numerator and denominator of the ratio are encased in square brackets. This will be the convention to express the fact that the ratio of these quantities is 1 and that this ratio was introduced for the specific purpose of manipulating units.

Armed with this tool, the expression for h in Equation 2.2 can be tackled. To begin with, the denominator can

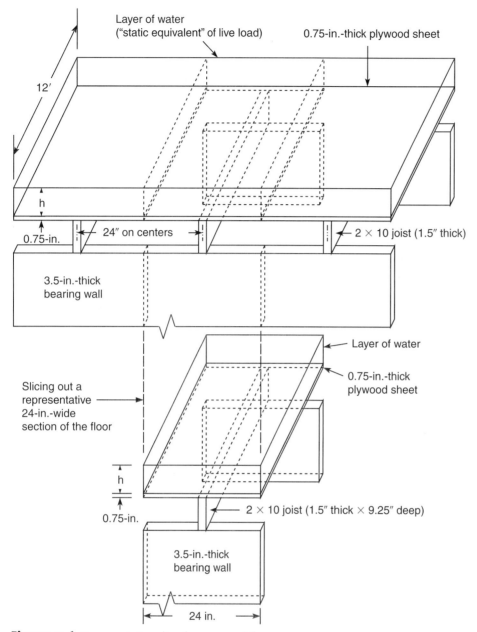

Figure 2.6 Representative slice from a wood floor.

be simplified by multiplying it by [ft³], which will eliminate the units in the denominator of the denominator. However, one cannot multiply the denominator of the expression for *h* by [ft³] without also multiplying the numerator of the expression for *h* by the same quantity. In other words, one can multiply the expression for *h* by

$$\left[\frac{ft^3}{ft^3} \right]$$ **[2.4]**

and not change its value.

$$h = \frac{p}{D} = \frac{\dfrac{40\#}{ft^2}}{\dfrac{62.4\#}{ft^3}} \times \left[\frac{ft^3}{ft^3} \right] = \frac{40\#\,ft}{62.4\#} = 0.641\,ft$$ **[2.5]**

To express *h* in terms of inches rather than feet, one needs to get rid of the ft unit and replace it with an in. unit. If the preceding expression is multiplied by $\left[\dfrac{12\,in.}{ft} \right] = 1$, then it will cancel out the ft and replace it with 12 in.:

$$h = \frac{p}{D} = 0.641 \text{ ft} \cdot \left[\frac{12 \text{ in.}}{\text{ft}}\right] = 7.69 \text{ in.} \qquad \textbf{[2.6]}$$

In other words, the floor should safely support a layer of water almost 8 in. deep over the entire floor. (Think of it as wall-to-wall water beds! Of course, long-term creep might make the floor sag somewhat, which would be visually disturbing to many people.)

In Figure 2.7, the pressure is shown in the customary symbolic manner, with numerous arrows connected by lines to indicate the continuous nature of the distributed force. In the original diagram, the length of the pressure arrows were 0.25 in. In other words, the scale was:

$$\frac{0.25 \text{ in.}}{\frac{40\#}{\text{ft}^2}} = \frac{0.00625 \text{ in.}}{\frac{\#}{\text{ft}^2}}.$$

Once a pressure was calculated in units of $\frac{\#}{\text{ft}^2}$, then that quantity was multiplied by the scaling factor $\dfrac{0.00625 \text{ in.}}{\frac{\#}{\text{ft}^2}}$ to get the appropriate length in inches of the arrows to represent that pressure. The original scale of the arrows was lost when the size of the drawings was adjusted to fit the drawings into a column of text. However, the relative lengths of all the pressures in Figure 2.7 through 2.12 are accurate.

The weight of the plywood can also be expressed as an area-distributed load. (This has less "reality" than using an area-distributed load for the water, since there is no surface over which this "pressure" is manifest. However,

for purposes of accounting for the loads on the structure, it is a completely valid and highly useful way to approach the problem.)

Area-distributed force associated with the weight of the 0.75 in.-thick plywood:

$$\begin{aligned}
p &= \frac{\text{Weight of plywood}}{\text{ft}^2} \\[2mm]
&= \frac{\text{Density of plywood} \cdot \text{Volume of plywood}}{\text{Area of plywood}} \qquad \textbf{[2.7]} \\[2mm]
&= \frac{\frac{35\#}{\text{ft}^3} \cdot 1 \text{ ft} \cdot 1 \text{ ft} \cdot 0.75 \text{ in.} \cdot \left[\frac{\text{ft}}{12 \text{ in.}}\right]}{\text{ft}^2} = \frac{2.2\#}{\text{ft}^2}
\end{aligned}$$

The total area-distributed load associated with the water and the plywood would be:

$$p = \frac{40\#}{\text{ft}^2} + \frac{2.2\#}{\text{ft}^2} = \frac{42.2\#}{\text{ft}^2} \qquad \textbf{[2.8]}$$

The total downward force of gravity on the water and plywood in the representative 24 in.-wide section of the structure would be:

$$W = \frac{42.2\#}{\text{ft}^2} \cdot 24 \text{ in.} \cdot 12 \text{ ft} \cdot \left[\frac{\text{ft}}{12 \text{ in.}}\right] = 1{,}013\# \qquad \textbf{[2.9]}$$

To keep the plywood in equilibrium, that is, to keep the plywood from falling, the downward force of gravity must be counteracted by an equal upward force. This equilibrating upward force is provided by the joist, which exerts an upward force of 1,013# on the underside of the plywood. This force is an area-distributed force with an associated pressure p of the joist on the plywood:

$$\begin{aligned}
p &= \frac{\text{Force}}{\text{Area of the top of the joist}} \\[2mm]
&= \frac{1{,}013\#}{1.5 \text{ in.} \cdot 12 \text{ ft}} \cdot \left[\frac{12 \text{ in}}{\text{ft}}\right] = \frac{675\#}{\text{ft}^2}
\end{aligned} \qquad \textbf{[2.10]}$$

Another way of thinking about this issue is that the area over which the 1,013# force is being distributed is changing from 12 ft × 24 in. for the area on the top of the plywood to 12 ft × 1.5 in. for the area on the bottom of the plywood. The area is, thus, reduced by a factor of 1.5/24, and, therefore, the total pressure must increase by a factor of 24/1.5 to keep the product of the pressure times the area equal to the constant value of 1,013#. Hence, the pressure on the bottom of the plywood must be:

$$p = \frac{42.2\#}{\text{ft}^2} \cdot \frac{24}{1.5} = \frac{675\#}{\text{ft}^2} \qquad \textbf{[2.11]}$$

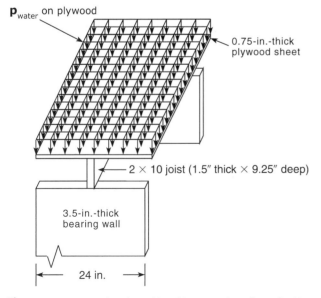

p~water~ on plywood

0.75-in.-thick plywood sheet

2 × 10 joist (1.5″ thick × 9.25″ deep)

3.5-in.-thick bearing wall

24 in.

Figure 2.7 Area-distributed load (pressure) on floor decking.

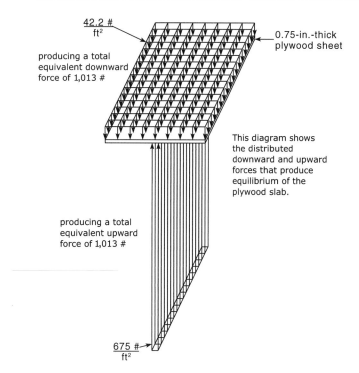

Figure 2.8 Pressure on top and bottom of the decking.

The differences in the pressure on the top and bottom of the plywood can be expressed graphically by scaling the length of the pressure arrows (see Figure 2.8).

Using the scaling factor established earlier, the upward arrows on the bottom of the plywood should be drawn at the following length:

$$\text{Length} = \frac{0.00625 \text{ in.}}{\frac{\#}{\text{ft}^2}} \cdot \frac{675\#}{\text{ft}^2} = 4.22 \text{ in.} \qquad \textbf{[2.12]}$$

According to the principles of action–reaction pairs,* the upward pressure (or stress) exerted on the bottom of the plywood by the top surface of the joist must, at all points of contact, be equal to the downward pressure (or stress) of the plywood on the top of the joist (see Figure 2.9).

The next interesting pressure (or stress) to determine is at the interface between the joist and the bearing wall. To find this pressure, one must first find the weight of the joist itself since the weight of the joist also bears on the wall:

W = density of the wood × volume of the joist

$$W = \frac{30\#}{\text{ft}^3} \cdot 1.5 \text{ in.} \cdot 9.25 \text{ in.} \cdot 12 \text{ ft} \cdot \left[\frac{\text{ft}}{12 \text{ in.}}\right] \cdot \left[\frac{\text{ft}}{12 \text{ in.}}\right]$$

$$= 34.7\# \qquad \textbf{[2.13]}$$

_____

*The principle of action/reaction pairs derives from Isaac Newton's laws of motion. The principles of equilibrium and action/reaction pairs will be discussed in more detail in Chapter 3.

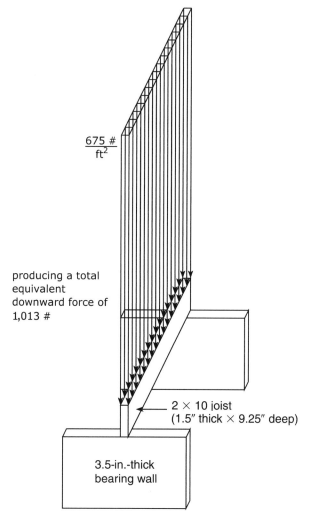

Figure 2.9 Pressure on top of joist.

The total downward force of gravity causing the beam to move downward is then:

= 1,013# + 34.7# = 1,048#

This can be converted to an equivalent pressure from the combined effect of the joist and the load on top of the joist:

$$p = \frac{\text{Force}}{\text{Area of the top of the joist}}$$

$$= \frac{1,048\#}{1.5 \text{ in.} \cdot 12 \text{ ft}} \cdot \left[\frac{12 \text{ in.}}{\text{ft}}\right] = \frac{699\#}{\text{ft}^2} \qquad \textbf{[2.14]}$$

$$\text{Length} = \frac{0.00625 \text{ in}}{\frac{\#}{\text{ft}^2}} \cdot \frac{699\#}{\text{ft}^2} = 4.37 \text{ in.}$$

Notice that the dead weight of the joist is only a small fraction of the load it supports (34.7#/1,013# = 0.034 or about 3 percent of the weight it supports). Therefore, when the pressure diagram is redrawn, the change is barely noticeable (see Figure 2.10).

It is customary on long, slender elements, such as a joist, to express the gravity load on the element as a line load, that is, as force per unit length along a line. Of course, a true line load cannot exist, since a line has no area and the pressure of a finite force on zero area would be infinite and there are no materials that can resist an infinite pressure. However, from the points of view of equilibrium and action–reaction pairs, the concept of a line force is completely legitimate and is computationally convenient (see Figure 2.11):

$$w = \frac{1,048\#}{12 \text{ ft}} = \frac{87.33\#}{\text{ft}} \qquad \textbf{[2.15]}$$

If the joist is to be kept in equilibrium and not start to fall downward under the influence of the gravity forces, the two bearing walls must be exerting a total upward force of 1,048#. By the symmetry of the situation, it is clear that the two bearing walls will share the load equally, so they will each be pushing up on the bottom of the joist with a force that is half of 1,048#, or 524#.

This force is distributed over a relatively small area of bearing surface equal to 1.5 in. × 3.5 in. The pressure will be the force divided by the area of interface:

$$p = \frac{524\#}{1.5 \text{ in.} \cdot 3.5 \text{ in.}} \cdot \left[\frac{12 \text{ in.}}{\text{ft}} \right] \cdot \left[\frac{12 \text{ in.}}{\text{ft}} \right] = \frac{14,373\#}{\text{ft}^2} \qquad \textbf{[2.16]}$$

which is 20.6 times greater than the total area-distributed downward force (14,373#/699# = 20.6).

It is also possible to arrive at a figure for the upward pressure of the wall on the joist by multiplying the area-distributed downward pressure on the top of the joist times a scaling factor equal to the ratio of the length of joist over which the gravity load occurs, divided by the length of joist involved in the bearing surface on the underside of the joist. That is,

$$p = \frac{699\#}{\text{ft}^2} \cdot \frac{\begin{array}{c}\text{Length of joist over which}\\ \text{gravity load is distributed}\end{array}}{\begin{array}{c}\text{Length of joist involved}\\ \text{in bearing surface}\end{array}}$$

$$\qquad \textbf{[2.17]}$$

$$= \frac{699\#}{\text{ft}^2} \cdot \frac{12 \text{ ft}}{7 \text{ in.}} \cdot \left[\frac{12 \text{ in.}}{\text{ft}} \right] = \frac{14,379\#}{\text{ft}^2}$$

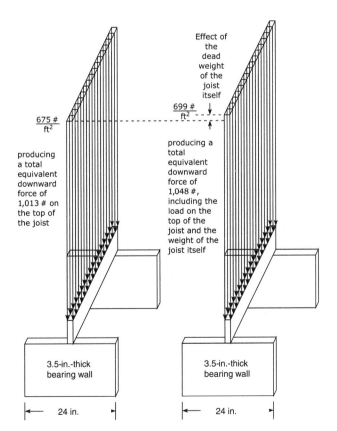

Figure 2.10 Adjusted pressure on top of joist, accounting for self-weight of the joist.

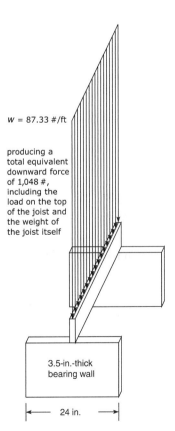

Figure 2.11 Equivalent line-distributed force.

which is consistent with the previous result to the number of significant figures being retained in the calculation.

$$\text{Length} = \frac{0.00625 \text{ in.}}{\frac{\#}{\text{ft}^2}} \cdot \frac{14{,}379\#}{\text{ft}^2} = 89.8 \text{ in.} \qquad \textbf{[2.18]}$$

Adding the upward pressure of the wall on the joist completes the equilibrium picture for the joist, as shown in the diagram in Figure 2.12.

Thus far, all of the stresses have been kept in the consistent units with which this process was begun, that is, $\#/\text{ft}^2$. In this manner, the amplification of stress, as loads are accumulated down through the structure, has been made graphically apparent. However, when pressures or stresses become large enough, it is customary to switch from pounds per square foot, which is a relatively small unit, to larger units that allow us to manipulate smaller numbers. For example, in wood, stresses are typically expressed in $\#/\text{in.}^2$, and for a very high strength material like steel, stresses are typically expressed in $K/\text{in.}^2$. Since the current problem involves wood, the bearing pressure is converted to $\#/\text{in.}^2$, in order to assess whether the wood is in jeopardy:

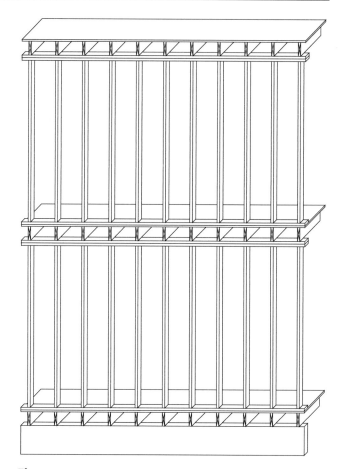

Figure 2.13 Wood framing without openings.

$$\frac{14{,}373\#}{\text{ft}^2} \cdot \left[\frac{\text{ft}}{12 \text{ in.}}\right] \cdot \left[\frac{\text{ft}}{12 \text{ in.}}\right] = \frac{100\#}{\text{in.}^2} \qquad \textbf{[2.19]}$$

Typically, wood can withstand compression stress perpendicular to the wood grain of several hundred $\#/\text{in.}^2$. Therefore, the joist and the top plate of the wall are not in jeopardy from a single floor. However, if extra floors are added, as shown in the framing plan in Figure 2.13, the stresses start to mount up.

The stresses become amplified even further when large openings concentrate forces in an even smaller number of members, as shown in the diagram in Figure 2.14.

Assignment 2.1: Units of Measure

Rework the floor example in Section 2.1, "Loads: Units of Measure," assuming the following parameters:

- The floor live load is 30#/ft².
- The decking consists of ⅝ in.-thick particle board (with a density of 45# per cubic foot) on top of ½ in.-thick plywood (with a density of 35# per cubic foot).
- The density of the solid lumber in the joists is 30# per cubic foot.

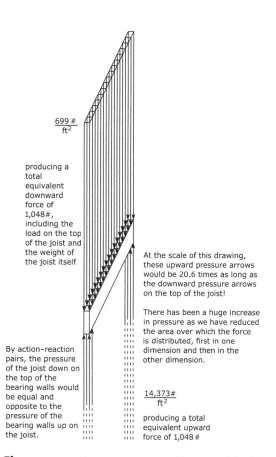

$\frac{699\#}{\text{ft}^2}$

producing a total equivalent downward force of 1,048#, including the load on the top of the joist and the weight of the joist itself

At the scale of this drawing, these upward pressure arrows would be 20.6 times as long as the downward pressure arrows on the top of the joist!

There has been a huge increase in pressure as we have reduced the area over which the force is distributed, first in one dimension and then in the other dimension.

By action–reaction pairs, the pressure of the joist down on the top of the bearing walls would be equal and opposite to the pressure of the bearing walls up on the joist.

$\frac{14{,}373\#}{\text{ft}^2}$

producing a total equivalent upward force of 1,048#

Figure 2.12 Pressure on top and bottom of the joist.

- The joists are nominal 2 × 8 (S4S) with finished dimensions of 1.5 in. × 7.25 in.
- The centerline-to-centerline spacing of the joists is 16 in.
- The length of the joists is 12 ft.
- The bearing walls are each 3.5 in. thick.

In presenting your solution, include *all* the steps, equations, and diagrams included in the example. Draw all elements and stresses to a consistent scale in a tidy and orderly way. To simplify the drawing, you can draw stresses with kfour scaled arrows at the corners of the distribution, with straight lines connecting their ends to indicate a continuous distribution of pressure. Present the work as if you were teaching it to someone else who has never encountered it before. Your assignment will be graded on the basis of its clarity. The grader will read it and evaluate it as if he or she were seeing the material for the first time. It needs to be crystal clear and effortless for the grader to read. As you work the problem, think about terminology, units, manipulation of units, scaling factors, basic concepts of equilibrium, and basic concepts of action–reaction pairs. The concepts embodied in this problem will carry over to everything you do in this course in structures.

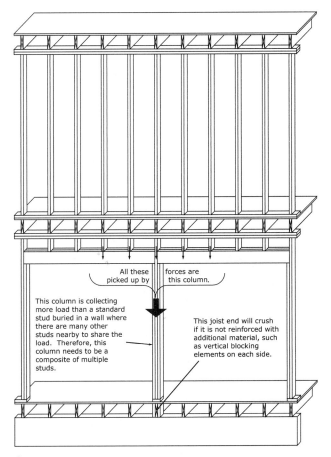

This column is collecting more load than a standard stud buried in a wall where there are many other studs nearby to share the load. Therefore, this column needs to be a composite of multiple studs.

All these forces are picked up by this column.

This joist end will crush if it is not reinforced with additional material, such as vertical blocking elements on each side.

Figure 2.14 Wood framing with openings.

2.2 Classification of Loads

2.2.1 GENERAL DEFINITIONS AND LOAD COMBINATIONS

In the design and construction of buildings, very little is known with great precision. This is particularly true of loads, some of which are highly unpredictable. An excellent example of this is wind. Instrumentation and qualified researchers have been considering the issue of wind speeds for only a century or two. The numbers of instruments and researchers have been limited by practical considerations, and they are often not in the right locations to properly record the most extreme wind conditions that may exist at any given moment on the planet. For practical reasons, the available instruments tend to be deployed near population centers. In spite of such limitations, there is beginning to emerge a fairly good picture of the most likely wind speeds that will occur in various locations. Yet it is also understood that a storm can occur at any time that would be so extreme that it would be necessary to redraw this picture. The researchers who prepare wind-speed data always speak in terms of statistical distributions and probabilities. From such data, someone has to make a decision about what will be chosen as a design wind speed. This information is codified and is then available to designers, to help in making decisions and moving forward. Designers are, thus, spared from doing their own wind research before they can start the design of a building.

In addition to uncertainty in loads, there is also uncertainty in how various structural members will perform. A precise determination of the structural performance of an element will depend on precise knowledge of the material composition and the geometry of the structural member. In standard practice, neither the material composition nor the geometry of any structural element is ever precisely known. Therefore, in standard practice, designers must accept an inherent uncertainty in the performance of any structural member.

For the purposes of this text, the focus is on a design method called *load and resistance factor design* (LRFD). In this method, uncertainty in the knowledge of loads is addressed by multiplying the design load by a load factor, which varies from one load type to another. Load factors are always greater than 1, with larger load factors for forces with greater uncertainty. The load factor provides a margin of safety relative to the maximum load that would be likely to occur over the life of a building. The load that results from multiplying the load factor times the design load is called the *factored load*. In the LRFD method, structural members are sized for the factored load, rather than the design load.

The uncertainty in our knowledge of the likely performance of a structural member will be addressed by

Table 2.1 Load Combinations

1. $1.2D + 1.6L + 1.6L_r$
2. $1.2D + 1.6W + 1.0L + 1.0L_r$
3. $0.9D + 1.6W$

Where:

D = dead load
L = live load
L_r = live/snow load on the roof
W = wind load

multiplying the theoretical structural performance of the member by a resistance factor, which varies from one member type to another. Resistance factors are always less than 1, with smaller resistance factors for structural members with less predictable structural performance. Resistance factors provide a margin of safety relative to the uncertainty in our knowledge of the performance of the structural member.

This book will focus on the LRFD method. The only exceptions to the LRFD procedure outlined earlier will be a limited set of design tables for specific manufactured products; their tables are expressed in terms of safe, imposable loads, and the load for comparison is the design load, rather than the factored load.

In the LRFD method, the building codes require that we design a building to withstand several factored load combinations, which can be found in *Minimum Design Loads for Buildings and Other Structures*, SEI/ASCE 7-02, published by the American Society of Civil Engineers and the Structural Engineering Institute. The list of load combinations in SEI/ASCE 7-02 is very long and complex. Table 2.1 is the simplified list of load combinations addressed in this book.

Load combination 3 involves a load factor of less than 1 for dead load, in combination with the maximum factored wind force. This load case is specifically targeted at the issue of whether a building has enough mass to keep from lifting up and toppling over under the lateral force of wind. The 0.9 factor on the dead load is intended to ensure that we do not overestimate the benefit of the dead load in anchoring the building on the land.

There are many loads that may affect a building during its useful life. Among the ways that these forces can be characterized is in terms of the probability of various intensities occurring within a given time frame and the likely duration of the forces when they do occur.

For buildings, the forces range from permanent, static loads to highly dynamic forces (see Figure 2.15). This spectrum can be broken down as follows:

- Static loads (sometimes called *dead loads*) such as might result from the weight of the structure itself
- Shifting and variable loads (sometimes called *live loads*) such as might be caused by occupants or moving equipment

- Oscillatory forces, such as might be caused by earthquakes, wind-induced oscillations, or vibrating equipment
- Impact forces, such as might result from having a large object dropped on the floor or a piece of moving equipment rammed into a support element

Dynamic forces tend to be more difficult to calculate than static forces, and the results of the calculations for dynamic forces tend to be less accurate than those for static forces. The importance of dynamic forces, such as wind gusts or earthquakes, vary from one geographic location to another and from one building type to another. In some locations earthquakes are quite common, and designers must account for them using a full dynamic analysis. In other locations they are relatively rare, and the codes allow seismic forces to be addressed using static approximations. The type of construction and the estimated natural frequency of the building also influence the decision regarding whether to do a static or dynamic analysis. The importance of some kinds of dynamic loading, such as wind-induced building oscillations, will depend on the type of structure, so judgment is required in determining the amount of dynamic analysis required in a given situation (see Figure 2.15).

Dynamic forces can sometimes be much larger than the weight of the objects causing such forces. In Figure 2.16(a), a 200# person is standing on a single nail, which does not penetrate any deeper into the wood under the influence of the force. This indicates that the force required to drive the nail into the wood is something greater than 200#. A 16 ounce hammer, which weighs 1#, can be used to drive the nail into the wood, which indicates that the 1# hammer is exerting a force greater than 200#; see Figure 2.16(b). This force is exerted for an extremely brief time, but it is very intense. Issues of this sort become extremely important in situations like a parking deck under a building, where a high-speed vehicle can cause forces drastically in excess of the weight of the car. A fast-moving car colliding with a column can collapse the building. As in the case of oscillatory forces induced by wind or earth movement, impact loads can be very difficult to estimate. However, they have to be accounted for, since they are sometimes the most severe loads exerted on a structure.

2.2.2 DEAD LOADS (FIXED ELEMENTS)

The dead loads (fixed elements) in a building will include:

- The structure itself
- Internal partitions
- Hung ceilings
- All internal and external surfaces and finishes

Fixed elements (dead loads. permanently).

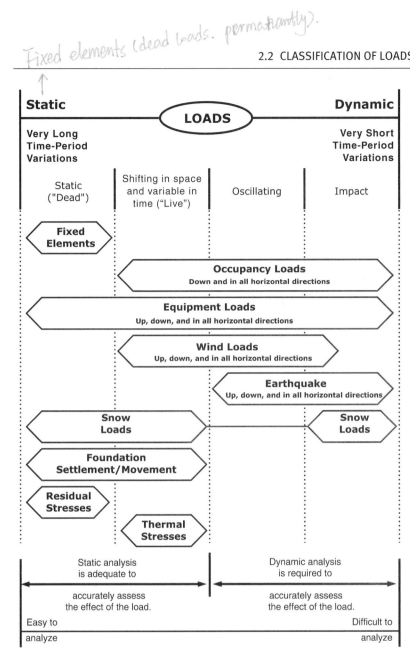

Figure 2.15 Time variations in loads of various types.

(a)

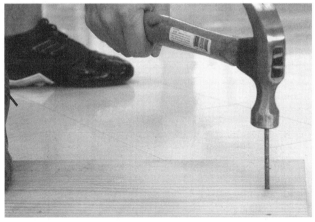

(b)

Figure 2.16 (a) Static 200# force and (b) impact force exceeding 200#.

speeding viechles might have large impact to building if it run into a column.

- Heating, ventilating, and air conditioning (HVAC) duct-work and equipment
- Permanently mounted equipment

An example of the latter would be large machines for manufacturing. For highly localized, fixed equipment, it is possible to reinforce the structure at the location of that equipment while leaving the rest of the structure with a more normal load-resisting capability. However, caution should be exercised in doing this because the occupants may decide to relocate the equipment after occupying the building. Moreover, the equipment will have to be moved to the designated location when the building is first occupied, and that may require moving the equipment across sections of the structure that are not adequate to hold it. This is an example of a construction load that may be more severe than the long-term load that will occur after the assembly of the structural system is complete.

Fixed loads are the most easily and accurately estimated of all the loads that impact buildings. Knowing the size of all the elements and the densities of the materials allows the accurate assessment of the size of the fixed loads. Table 2.2 gives examples of the densities of some common building materials.

Densities are fundamental information from which the weights of all fixed elements can be calculated. However, calculating the weights of some elements can be quite complicated. For example, to calculate the weight of a concrete masonry unit with voids requires detailed information about all the dimensions of the unit. To make

life easier for designers, the manufacturers of such products provide a listing of the weights of their products. This information is typically given in terms of a weight per square foot. For example, in Table 2.3, the weight per square foot of 8 in.-thick hollow concrete blocks made using lightweight aggregate is 38#/ft². Such a wall, built to a height of 10 ft, is shown in Figure 2.17.

The figures in Table 2.3 are fairly typical of the materials being characterized, although some of the figures tend to be slightly on the high (conservative) side to ensure safety in the design process. In many instances, you may want to be even more conservative. For example, suppose you estimate the weight of asphalt shingles on a roof to be 3#/ft². This is heavier than almost any shingle you can buy on the market today. However, suppose you construct the building and cover the roof with shingles weighing 2.5#/ft², which is an example of a good, heavy-duty shingle that is commonly available. Then suppose that 15 years from now the owners decide to put another layer of shingles over the first layer, and 15 years later they do it again. At that point, they will have a long-term load of 7.5#/ft², which is substantially more than the estimate of 3#/ft² on which the load calculations were based.

For analysis purposes, the dead load of the beam (i.e., self-weight) is usually assumed to be on top of the beam, thereby simplifying the analysis by treating the self-weight of the beam in exactly the same manner as the decking load and the applied load (live load or snow load), all of which are delivered to the top of the beam. Of course, the self-weight of the beam is actually distributed through the beam and is not on the top of the beam. However, typically the self-weight of the beam is only a small fraction of the imposed load on the beam, and, therefore, the self-weight of the beam can be presumed to be on top of the beam without significantly altering the distribution of stresses predicted by the analysis (see Figure 2.18).

As in the case of a beam, the dead load of a truss (i.e., self-weight) is usually assumed to be on top of the truss, thereby simplifying the analysis by treating the self-weight of the truss in exactly the same manner as the decking load and the applied load (live load or snow load), all of

Table 2.2 Average Densities of Materials

Material	lb/ft³
Metals	
Aluminum, cast	165
Copper, cast	556
Lead	710
Steel, rolled	490
Masonry	
Concrete, plain	
Stone aggregate	144
Light aggregate	75–110
Concrete, stone aggregate, reinforced	150
Brick	100–130
Earth	
Clay, dry	63
Clay, damp	110
Earth, dry	75–95
Earth, damp	80–100
Other	
Glass, common	156
Glass, plate	161
Pitch	69
Tar	75

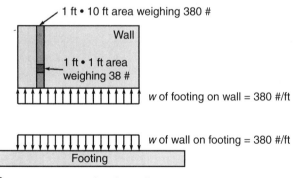

Figure 2.17 Weight of a wall.

Table 2.3 Weights of Building Materials

Materials		Weight #/ft²	Materials		Weight #/ft²
Ceilings				4 in. thick	18
Channel suspended system		1		6 in. thick	28
Lathing and plastering		See partitions		8 in. thick	34
				10 in. thick	40
Acoustical fiber tile		1	Gypsum block		
Floors				2 in. thick	9.5
Steel deck		2–4		3 in. thick	10.5
Concrete—reinforced				4 in. thick	12.5
Stone	1 in. thick	12.5		5 in. thick	14
Slag	1 in. thick	11.5		6 in. thick	18.5
Lightweight	1 in. thick	6–10	Wood studs 2 × 4		
Concrete—plain			(12–16 in. OC)		2
Stone	1 in. thick	12	Steel partitions		4
Slag	1 in. thick	11	Plaster	1 in. thick	
Lightweight	1 in. thick	3–9	Gypsum		5
Fills			Cement		10
Gypsum	1 in. thick	6	Lathing		
Sand	1 in. thick	8	Gypsum board	½ in. thick	2
Cinders	1 in. thick	4	Metal		0.5
Finishes			**Walls**		
Terrazzo	1 in. thick	13	Brick		
Ceramic or quarry tile	¾ in. thick	10		4 in. thick	40
Linoleum	¼ in. thick	1		8 in. thick	80
Mastic	¾ in. thick	9		12 in. thick	120
Hardwood	¾ in. thick	4	Hollow concrete block		
Softwood	¾ in. thick	2.5	(heavy aggregate)		
Roofs				4 in. thick	30
Copper or tin		1		6 in. thick	43
Single-ply membrane		1		8 in. thick	55
Three-ply felt and gravel		5.5		12 in. thick	80
Five-ply felt and gravel		6	Hollow concrete block		
Shingles			(light aggregate)		
Wood		2		4 in. thick	21
Asphalt		3		6 in. thick	30
Clay tile		9–14		8 in. thick	38
Slate	¼ in. thick	10		12 in. thick	55
Sheathing			Clay tile (load bearing)		
Wood	½ in. thick	2		4 in. thick	25
Wood	¾ in. thick	3		6 in. thick	30
Gypsum	1 in. thick	4		8 in. thick	33
Insulation	1 in. thick			12 in. thick	45
Loose		0.5	Stone	4 in. thick	55
Rigid		1.5	Glass block	4 in. thick	18
Partitions			Windows, glass frame and sash		8
Clay tile			Curtain walls	See manufacturer	
			Structural glass	1 in. thick	15
	3 in. thick	17	Corrugated cement asbestos	¼ in. thick	3

which are delivered to the top of the truss. Of course, the self-weight of the truss is actually distributed through the truss and is not on the top of the truss. However, typically the self-weight of the truss is only a small fraction of the imposed load on the truss, and, therefore, the self-weight of the truss can be presumed to be on top of the truss

without significantly altering the distribution of stresses predicted by the analysis (see Figure 2.19).

Trusses that are heavily loaded will tend to be more massive, but even in such cases the self-weight of a truss is small compared with the imposed load and the effect of moving the self-weight of the truss up to the top of the

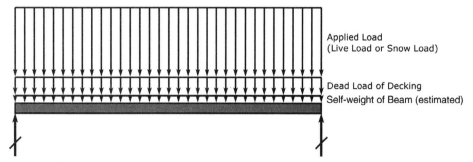

Figure 2.18 Putting the self-weight of a beam on top of the beam.

truss has a relatively small effect on the predictions of the analysis. This case is illustrated in Figure 2.20, in which all of the loads are simply scaled upward in proportion to each other.

For steel trusses of very long spans (several hundred feet) or for concrete trusses (which are intrinsically heavy because of the nature of the material), the self-weight may become large enough that it needs to be analyzed as distributed through the truss. This situation is shown in Figure 2.21, a diagram of the end of a very large truss, where the dead load is shown distributed on all the members.

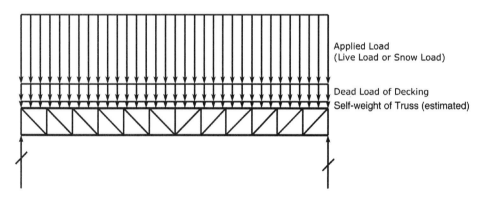

Figure 2.19 Putting the self-weight of a truss on top of the truss.

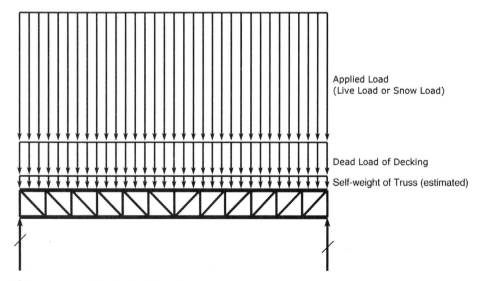

Figure 2.20 Heavier loads on the truss.

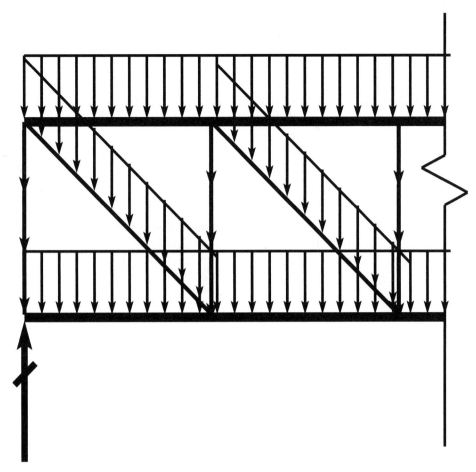

Figure 2.21 Self-weight of a truss distributed over the elements of the truss.

2.2.3 OCCUPANCY LOADS (LIVE LOADS)

The occupants of a building can produce loads that change in intensity and location, over time periods ranging from a few hours to fractions of a second.

Occupancy loads can be extremely localized and very intense. Probably the most severe situation commonly encountered is a woman standing on one high heel, so that the entire weight of the body is concentrated in one very small area of the floor. Almost as intense is a person rocking back in a chair, so that the entire load of the body and the chair is imposed on two very small areas. These loads tend to cause a localized failure of the floor decking, called *punch-through.* Material in the deck tends to shear along a surface, called the *cone of percussion,* shown in Figure 2.22.

Because these are shifting loads that can occur anywhere, the entire floor decking has to be made thick enough everywhere to resist a punch-through.

Once the deck is thick enough to resist punch-through, we are typically no longer obligated by code to account for localized effects resulting from occupancy. In other words, the structure supporting the decking can be ana-lyzed as if the occupancy load was uniformly distributed over the floor area, with no concern for exactly where people's feet are coming to rest on the floor. In a sense, the structure is being analyzed as if the occupants were replaced by a pool of water with the same equivalent weight as the occupants being simulated. This can be justified because the decking is fairly effective in distributing the load among the structural elements beneath it. Table 2.4 shows the usual loads prescribed by code for various occupancy types. These are typical, but check your local code for variations from these standards.

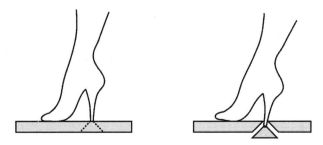

Figure 2.22 Punch-through.

So-called live loads account for occupants and the associated furniture and equipment they would typically be expected to use in the designated space. For example, in libraries, the prescribed occupancy load is 60#/ft² for

Table 2.4 Recommended Live Loads

Function of Space	Live Load (#/ft²)
Assembly Halls, Auditoriums, Churches, etc.	
Fixed seats	60
Movable seats	100
Restaurants, Gymnasiums, Grandstands, etc.	100
Theaters	
Aisles and lobbies	100
Balconies	60
Stage floors	150
Business Facilities	
Offices	80
Office corridors	100
Document storage systems	200
Educational Facilities	
Library reading rooms	60
Library stacks	150
Classrooms	40
Corridors	100
Manufacturing Facilities	
Light	125
Heavy	250
Labs	100
Hospitals	
Wards and private rooms	40
Operating rooms	60
Corridors	80
Private Dwellings	
First floor	40
Upper floors	30
Uninhabitable attics	20
Multifamily Dwellings	
Apartments	40
Corridors	60

reading rooms and 150#/ft² for stacks. The weight of the books and stacks are counted as part of the live load because they would typically be expected to be used in the designated spaces. Hence, the prescribed live load in the stack areas is very high. This is an example of an unusually high furnishing load, or special equipment load, that is peculiar to the function of the space. An even more extreme furnishing load is prescribed for document storage systems, which typically have to be designed for 200#/ft².

Design loads for similar functions may vary by situation. For example, because it is assumed that large parties will be typically be held on the first floor (or main floor) of a dwelling, the main floor has to be designed for 40#/ft², whereas the upper floors (secondary floors) have to be designed for only 30#/ft².

People do not actually distribute themselves uniformly over an entire floor area. Some portion of the floor area may be loaded up to the level prescribed by the code, whereas other portions of the floor area may have no occupancy load at all. This does not create a problem in most situations, but there are some situations in which it does. The designer has responsibility to account for all the possible distributions of occupancy load that may create special problems. For example, if occupancy load on some portion of a structure creates a more severe structural problem than occupancy load distributed uniformly over the entire floor area, then the designer has to decide what part of the floor needs to be loaded to create the worst structural problem and then design for that loading condition. The following illustrates some situations in which the design of part of the structure may be dictated by occupancy on only part of the floor area:

- *Load condition 1* (Figure 2.23): A uniform live load distributed over the entire truss produces no shearing force at the center panel. The lack of any shear force makes the presence of a diagonal web much less critical in that bay. Typically, the continuity of the chord members across that bay provides all the stability that is necessary. A reason for leaving out the diagonal web in that panel is to accommodate an air duct.
- *Load condition 2* (Figure 2.24): In contrast, a uniform load distributed over only half the truss generates a sig-

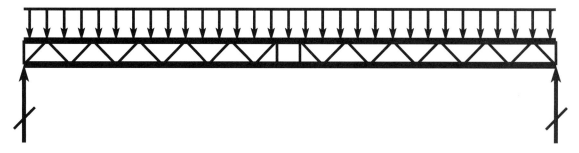

Figure 2.23 Symmetric load on truss (full live load).

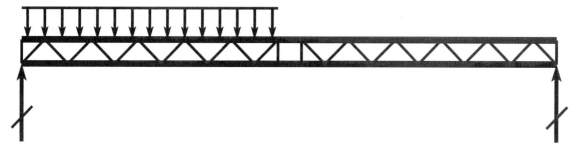

Figure 2.24 Asymmetric load on truss (shifting, nonuniform live load).

nificant shearing force in the center bay. The chord members at the center bay may snap owing to the lack of a diagonal web member to carry the shearing force. This shearing force may dictate the need for triangulation in this panel. Only an analysis or experimentation will determine whether the continuous chords alone (without a triangulating web member) will be adequate to withstand the shearing in this panel.

Load condition 1 will be critical in sizing the chord members for resisting the maximum axial force induced by the overall truss action.

Load condition 2 will be critical in determining the need (or lack of need) for a web member in the center bay. Load condition 2 may also become the controlling issue in sizing the chord members if a decision is made to leave out the web member in the center bay. Leaving out the web member in the center bay means that the chord members have to work in bending to keep the center bay stable. The chord members then have to be sized for both the axial forces, induced by the overall action of the truss, and the bending induced by the shearing force in the untriangulated center bay of the truss.

Factors other than shifting occupancy load can create shear problems in a nontriangulated panel of a truss. The following Figure 2.25 shows wood floor trusses spanning 26 ft over the basement of a house. The web members have been omitted from the center bays to accommodate a duct that has yet to be installed.

This was the builder's first experiment with using floor trusses. He chose trusses to span the full width of the house to provide a full basement with no columns or walls to interrupt the space. For reasons of economy, the builder decided to shift back to conventional framing on the second floor of the house. The savings were minimal, but they seemed worthwhile to the builder at the time. Figure 2.26 shows the framing on the second floor. Note that 14 ft-long floor joists frame into a flitch beam that delivers most of its loads to a single column, which is visible at the right side of the image.

The loads from that column are delivered to the top chord of a single floor truss below. This load on one side of the truss created a severe shearing force in the untriangulated center bay of the truss. This force is manifest in a racking of that bay, as shown in Figure 2.27. The column has also created another severe problem, in that it has delivered its load to the top chord midway between points that are supported by web members in the truss. This is putting the top chord in severe bending, in addition to the axial force that the chord member must withstand as part of its role in the overall action of the truss. Shortly after the picture in Figure 2.27 was taken, the top chord of the truss began to make snapping noises. In response, the builder attempted to relieve the top chord by jamming a 2 × 4 between the bottom joint and the underside of the top chord, just below the base of the column. Not long after that, the pressure plates on the bottom joint began to work loose from the wood. At that

Figure 2.25 Truss framing on main floor above the full basement.

Figure 2.26 Framing of the second floor (top of picture).

point, the builder constructed a stud wall under the truss and nailed up sheet rock on both sides in a vain attempt to secure the structure. The builder's solution never addressed the fact that the truss was still serving as mediator between the very large column element above and the distributed wall below. The truss was not suited to serve in that role. A better solution would have been to use two columns to support the truss at two bottom-chord joints to either side of the column above. Then the portion of the truss between the two support columns could be

sawn away and a third, more sturdy, column could be placed immediately below the large column above, giving the large force in that column a direct path to the foundation. This particular example illustrates the importance of carefully thinking through how to provide a continuous, properly sized path for transmitting all forces to the foundations. Do not "toss things into the stress path" and just assume, or hope, that they are going to work. Make sure those elements can actually carry the forces that they have to carry. More specifically, the fol-

Figure 2.27 Truss with a concentrated force in the wrong place.

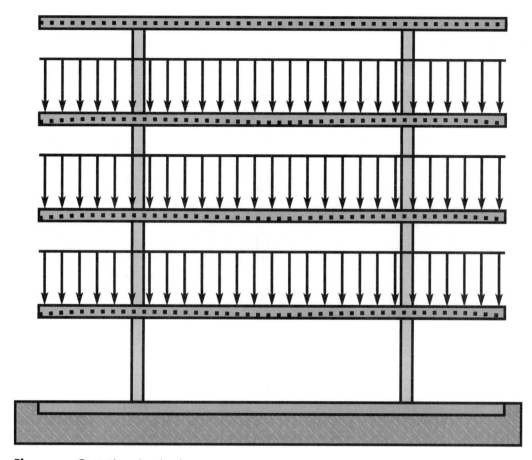

Figure 2.28 Uniform live load.

lowing advice should always be followed: (1) Deliver all concentrated forces on a truss to a panel point of the truss, and (2) make sure that all bays of a truss are triangulated if they are going to have significant shearing force on them.

The next two diagrams provide another example in which partial live load is a very serious concern:

- *Load condition 1* (Figure 2.28): The uniform live load is applied along the entire length of the beams, both between the columns and out on the cantilevered portions of the beams.
- *Load condition 2* (Figure 2.29): Occupants on some floors are having a Christmas party in the interior of the building, where their weight is concentrated. Other occupants are gathering at the windows to see an exceptional sunset.

The latter loading condition dictates using much deeper and stiffer beams than would the former loading condition.

Under some circumstances occupancy loads can be highly dynamic. For example, football fans moving in rhythmic unison in a stadium can cause severe oscillatory loads, particularly if the frequency of their movements matches one of the natural frequencies of the stadium structure. Moreover, if they stamp their feet in unison, the load becomes an impact force.

These dynamic problems can also occur in more mundane structures. For example, a large group of wild dancers moving in unison can cause severe loading on the floor of a dwelling. Many residential structures, such as outdoor decks, are not properly designed for these dynamic occupancy loads. Most codes assume that the static pressure loads are adequately conservative to solve the dynamic loading problem, and, fortunately, in most cases, they are. If there is any doubt about it, a dynamic analysis should be performed.

Finally, equipment and furnishings can cause severe impact loads. Sometimes these forces can come from unexpected sources. For example, an acquaintance of mine almost took a column out from under his house when he and some rowdy friends were moving a 1,500# pool table at very high speed from one part of his basement to another. I was called in for an engineering consultation to assess the significance of the dent that was left in the steel column.

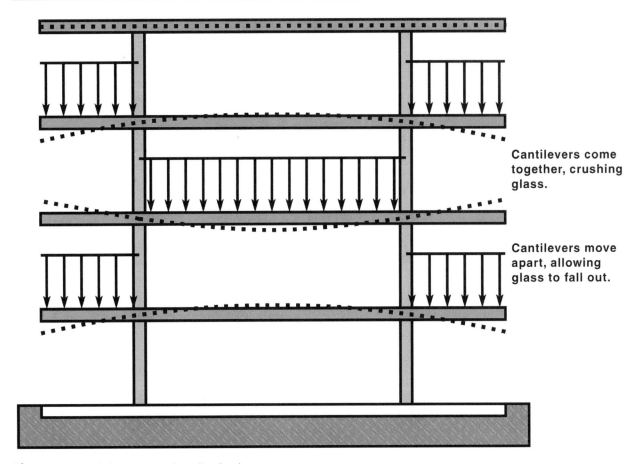

Figure 2.29 Shifting, nonuniform live load.

Example 1 of dead load and live load computation (Figure 2.30):

Consider a 5 in.-thick reinforced concrete slab floor made with heavy aggregate, spanning one way 16 ft between bearing walls in an apartment application. We would want to know what loads are delivered to the bearing

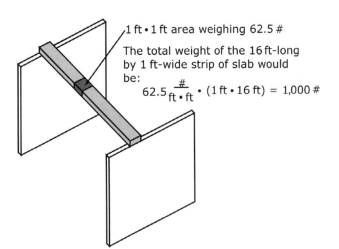

1 ft • 1 ft area weighing 62.5 #

The total weight of the 16 ft-long by 1 ft-wide strip of slab would be:

$$62.5 \frac{\#}{\text{ft} \cdot \text{ft}} \cdot (1 \text{ ft} \cdot 16 \text{ ft}) = 1{,}000 \text{ \#}$$

Figure 2.30 Calculating floor loads.

walls. In Table 2.3, the dead weight of reinforced concrete is given as $\dfrac{\frac{12.5\#}{\text{ft}^2}}{\text{in.}}$ of thickness. Therefore, the weight of the 5 in.-thick floor would be:

$$\frac{\frac{12.5\#}{\text{ft}^2}}{\text{in.}} \cdot 5 \text{ in.} = \frac{62.5\#}{\text{ft}^2} \qquad \text{[2.20]}$$

Table 2.4 shows that the design floor live load for apartments is 40#/ft^2.

Bearing walls at the end of the structure would have responsibility for supporting only half the span, that is, 8 ft, and the interior bearing walls would be supporting 8 ft on each side, for a total width of floor of 16 ft. (See Figure 2.31.)

For every linear foot along the top of the end wall, an area of 1 ft · 8 ft = 8 ft^2 of floor is supported.

For every linear foot along the top of an interior wall, an area of 1 ft · 16 ft = 16 ft^2 is supported.

For the end wall:

The dead load w_{dead} of the slab on the top of the end wall is:

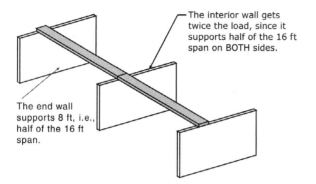

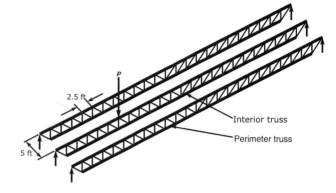

Figure 2.31 Calculating floor loads transferred to the support walls.

Figure 2.32 Calculating the force on the vertex of a truss.

$$W_{Dead} = \frac{\frac{62.5\#}{ft^2} \cdot 8 \ ft^2}{ft \ of \ wall} = \frac{500\#}{ft} \qquad [2.21]$$

The live load w_{live} on the top of the end wall is:

$$W_{Live} = \frac{\frac{40\#}{ft^2} \cdot 8 \ ft^2}{ft \ of \ wall} = \frac{320\#}{ft} \qquad [2.22]$$

The total load w_{total} on the top of the end wall is:

$$W_{Total} = \frac{500\#}{ft} + \frac{320\#}{ft} = \frac{820\#}{ft} \qquad [2.23]$$

For an interior wall:
The dead load w_{dead} of the slab on the top of the interior wall is:

$$W_{Dead} = \frac{\frac{62.5\#}{ft^2} \cdot 16 \ ft^2}{ft \ of \ wall} = \frac{1000\#}{ft} \qquad [2.24]$$

The live load w_{live} on the top of the interior wall is:

$$W_{Live} = \frac{\frac{40\#}{ft^2} \cdot 16 \ ft^2}{ft \ of \ wall} = \frac{640\#}{ft} \qquad [2.25]$$

The total load w_{total} on the top of the interior wall is:

$$W_{Total} = \frac{1000\#}{ft} + \frac{640\#}{ft} = \frac{1640\#}{ft} \qquad [2.26]$$

Example 2 of dead load and live load computation:

A series of truss joists span a distance, L, and are spaced 5 ft on center (OC). The spacing between panel points on a truss is 2.5 ft. Assume the dead weight of the floor system is approximately 36#/ft² and that the live load is 80#/ft². (See Figure 2.32.)

Find the line-distributed load *w* for dead, live, and total load for both an interior truss and a perimeter (end) truss.

Find the point force *P* for the dead, live, and total load on a representative panel point (vertex) on the interior truss.

In Figure 2.33, a blowup of one end of the spanning system indicates what areas of slab should be considered for calculating each of the quantities sought.

For a perimeter (end) truss:
The dead load w_{dead} of the slab on the top of the perimeter (end) truss is:

$$W_{Dead} = \frac{\frac{36\#}{ft^2} \cdot 2.5 \ ft^2}{ft \ of \ truss} = \frac{90\#}{ft} \qquad [2.27]$$

The live load w_{live} on the top of the perimeter (end) truss is:

$$W_{Live} = \frac{\frac{80\#}{ft^2} \cdot 2.5 \ ft^2}{ft \ of \ truss} = \frac{200\#}{ft} \qquad [2.28]$$

The total load w_{total} on the top of the perimeter (end) truss is:

$$W_{Total} = \frac{90\#}{ft} + \frac{200\#}{ft} = \frac{290\#}{ft} \qquad [2.29]$$

For an interior truss:
The dead load w_{dead} of the slab on the top of the interior truss is:

$$W_{Dead} = \frac{\frac{36\#}{ft^2} \cdot 5 \ ft^2}{ft \ of \ truss} = \frac{180\#}{ft} \qquad [2.30]$$

The live load w_{live} on the top of the interior truss is:

$$W_{Live} = \frac{\frac{80\#}{ft^2} \cdot 5 \ ft^2}{ft \ of \ truss} = \frac{400\#}{ft} \qquad [2.31]$$

The total load w_{total} on the top of the interior truss is:

$$W_{Total} = \frac{180\#}{ft} + \frac{400\#}{ft} = \frac{580\#}{ft} \qquad [2.32]$$

For an interior truss:
The dead load P_{dead} of the slab on the vertex of the interior truss is:

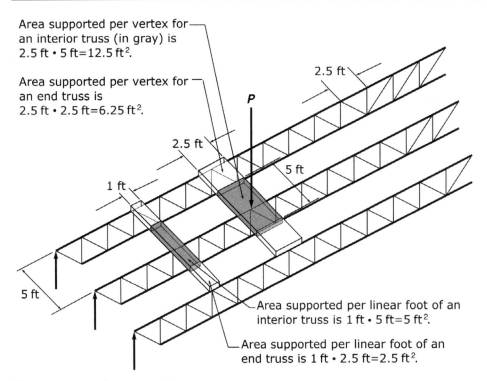

Area supported per vertex for an interior truss (in gray) is 2.5 ft · 5 ft=12.5 ft².

Area supported per vertex for an end truss is 2.5 ft · 2.5 ft=6.25 ft².

2.5 ft

1 ft

5 ft

P

2.5 ft

5 ft

Area supported per linear foot of an interior truss is 1 ft · 5 ft=5 ft².

Area supported per linear foot of an end truss is 1 ft · 2.5 ft=2.5 ft².

Figure 2.33 Influence area for a vertex on a truss.

$$P_{Dead} = \frac{36\#}{ft^2} \cdot 5\ ft \cdot 2.5\ ft = 450\# \qquad [2.33]$$

The live load P_{live} on the vertex of the interior truss is:

$$P_{Live} = \frac{80\#}{ft^2} \cdot 5\ ft \cdot 2.5\ ft = 1{,}000\# \qquad [2.34]$$

The total load P_{total} on the vertex of the interior truss is:

$$P_{Total} = 450\# + 1{,}000\# = 1{,}450\# \qquad [2.45]$$

2.2.4 SNOW LOADS

Snow loads on roofs vary widely, depending on such factors as the following:

- Latitude
- Elevation above sea level
- Solar exposure (roofs shaded by evergreen trees or situated on the north side of a hill are likely to retain snow much longer, allowing further accumulation to occur)
- Wind speed (high winds tend to blow snow off roofs)
- Local microclimate effects (e.g., the lake effect around the Great Lakes, special wind patterns in mountain environments, etc.)
- The slope of the roof

Design snow loads for typical urban areas in the United States range from 10#/ft² to 60#/ft². Snow loads in uninhabited areas have been recorded as high as 300#/ft². In addition to design codes, local experience should be checked because, in some areas, the snow loads may vary significantly from those indicated in the design figures in the code.

The code prescribes roof load requirements in terms of both snow load and roof live load, the latter accounting for persons on the roof for maintenance or inspection. For example, in Raleigh, North Carolina, the design roof live load is 20#/ft² and the snow load is 15#/ft². For a structure on which there is no possibility of human occupancy, such as a greenhouse covered with plastic film, the design roof load would be 15#/ft². However, for almost all buildings, there is a possibility that at some time in the life of the structure, human beings will be on the roof for inspection or maintenance. Therefore, designers typically refer to something called the *roof live load/snow load*. In Raleigh, North Carolina, this figure will be 20#/ft². Figure 2.34 depicts this load. In dealing with these roof loads, the assumption is made that the load is uniform as projected on the horizontal. In other words, the thickness of the layer of snow in the vertical direction is always the same, regardless of the angle of the roof surface.

Snow loads may endure anywhere from a few days to several months. Wood structures tend to do better under short-term loads than they do under long-term loads. In locations where the snow loads are normally fairly short-term, the stresses from snow are allowed to be as much as 15 percent higher than the stresses under the permanent loads on the structure.

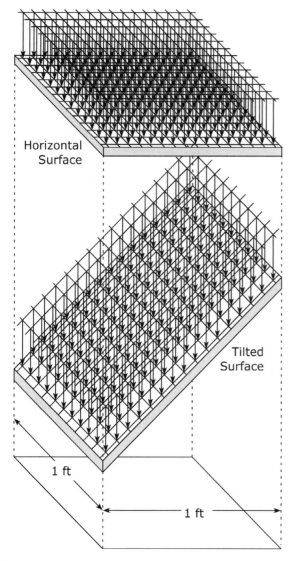

Figure 2.34 Snow load on horizontal and sloped surfaces.

Snow can also cause impact loads when it falls from a height. For example, snow can slide off a high roof onto a lower section of roof, as shown in Figure 2.35. Warm air stratifying under the high part of the roof can increase heat conduction through the roof, causing the bottom layer of snow to melt, creating a slick layer of snow that facilitates the sliding of the mass of snow off the high roof. In most situations, the code allows the calculation of these impact loads as some multiple of the static design

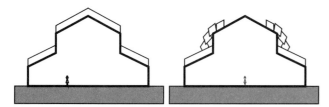

Figure 2.35 Impact snow loads.

snow load. However, for situations that may involve large amounts of snow falling substantial distances, some effort should be made to quantify the impact effect. In addition, structures should be designed to protect people from direct impact, which may occur when they are entering or exiting from a building.

Sometimes the effect of solid water can be quite shocking. For example, ice has been observed to build to substantial thicknesses on TV and radio towers. Sunlight passing through the ice can heat the steel on which the ice has accumulated, causing the ice to release from the tower. The resulting daggers of ice can be quite large and can reach speeds of several hundred miles per hour. Such pieces of ice have even been observed to shatter concrete roofs. The effects can be quite stunning when the ice falls from of a 2,000 ft-tall TV tower. Figure 2.36 shows a structure designed to protect a TV facility from ice falling from the tower (Architect: Thomas Crowder; Engineers: Lysaght and Associates). The roof trusses are covered with a steel grid that is capable of absorbing substantial amounts of energy as it deforms (see Figure 2.37). The grid also breaks up the ice so that none of the

Figure 2.36 Trusses supporting steel grid designed to stop ice missiles.

Figure 2.37 View of the steel grid from the rooftop.

pieces that get through are large enough to cause serious damage to the structure below. The large overhangs are intended to protect employees going to and from their cars, which are parked under the overhang.

2.2.5 WIND LOADS

2.2.5.1 Static Effects of Wind A structure in the path of a wind causes the wind to be deflected or, in some cases, stopped. As a consequence, the kinetic energy of the wind is transformed into the potential energy of pressure or suction. The magnitude of the pressure or suction caused by the wind at a point on a structure depends on the velocity of the wind; the mass density of the air; the geometrical shape, dimensions, and orientation of the structure; the location of the point affected on the structure; the nature of the surface that the wind acts on; and the overall stiffness of the structure.

As a fluid, such as air, flows around an immersed object, a complex flow pattern is generated around the object. The nature and complexity of the flow pattern depend on the shape of the object. Flows can be either smooth or turbulent. The forces acting on the object as a result of the impinging airflow can be either pressure forces or suction forces. The more an object is streamlined, the less the total reactive force exerted by the structure in opposing the motion of the air. Figure 2.38 illustrates airflows around objects.

The magnitude of the forces involved as air moves around a shape is dependent on the velocity of the wind, among other factors. Design wind velocities for different geographical locations are determined from empirical observations. Figure 2.39 shows overpressures and suctions on a typical residential form with a gently sloped roof. The only surface with an overpressure is the windward wall. It has a shape factor of +0.8. The plus sign signifies an overpressure; 0.8 is the highest shape factor, signifying that the overpressure on the windward wall is the highest pressure on the structure. All the other walls and the roof are subjected to wind suction or, more

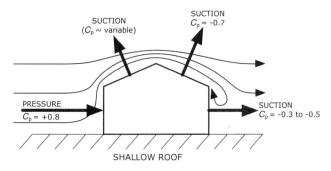

Figure 2.39 Shape coefficients, C_p, for a low-slope roof.

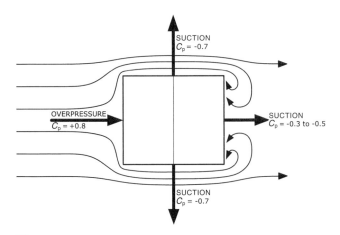

Figure 2.40 Plan view of structure, showing suction on side walls.

specifically, the air pressure on the outer surfaces of those elements is below ambient pressure. We refer to that condition as *suction*. The actual force on those elements is a result of the fact that the interior air pressure exceeds the exterior pressure on those elements. The shape coefficient for the leeward face of the roof is –0.7. The minus sign signifies a suction, or net outward force. The value 0.7 indicates that the magnitude of the suction pressure is $7/8$ as great as the magnitude of the overpressure on the

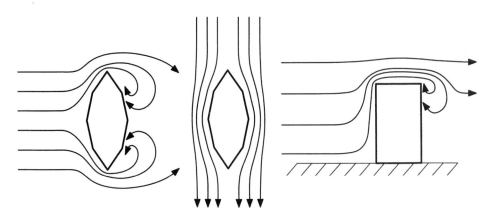

Figure 2.38 Wind patterns.

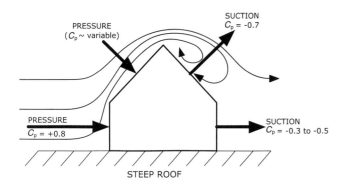

Figure 2.41 Shape coefficients, C_p, for a steep roof.

windward wall, which has a shape coefficient of +0.8. The shape coefficient of the side walls is also –0.7. (See Figure 2.40).

Figure 2.41 shows a steep roof, which has an overpressure on the windward side. When a roof gets steep enough, it begins to act like a wall to the wind and the force changes from suction to overpressure.

The wind design information in Figures 2.43, 2.44, 2.45, 2.48, 2.49, and 2.50 comes from SEI/ASCE 7-02, *Minimum Design Loads for Buildings and Other Structures*, produced by the American Society of Civil Engineers. The information in SEI/ASCE 7-02 has been adopted as the technical basis for the *2003 International Building Code.*

The interaction of wind with the vast array of building forms designers might contemplate is one of the most complex issues addressed in architecture and engineering. Addressing wind forces with a high degree of accuracy would drastically exceed the design budget for ordinary buildings. In the light of that fact, the codes used to address wind forces on most buildings are substantially simplified and fairly conservative to allow the practical design and analysis of buildings. Within the codes, there are three methods for accounting for wind forces.

Method 1, also referred to as the simplified method, is allowed only for rigid buildings less than 60 ft tall. This method makes some substantial simplifications, such as putting all the lateral force on the windward side of the structure. It also puts wind pressures in a series of tables that minimize the amount of computation that has to be done. Method 1 applies to a limited range of building geometries.

Method 2 applies to buildings of all heights. This method accounts for wind pressure or suction on all surfaces, including the suction on the leeward side of a building and suction on the side walls (i.e., the walls parallel to the wind direction). As compared with Method 1, Method 2 requires more computation. Method 2, like Method 1, is limited in the range of building geometries that it addresses, although not as limited as Method 1.

Method 3 uses wind-tunnel tests or dynamic computer analyses to estimate the effect of wind on a building. This method is the most expensive, most rigorous, and most widely applicable in terms of the range of building geometries to which it can be applied. It is usually used on large projects involving flexible structures that have a high probability of resonating in response to wind disturbance.

Both Methods 1 and 2 represent simplified summaries of the physics of wind forces (the so-called simplified method would more aptly be called the "more simplified method"). In spite of these simplifications, wind codes are still among the most complex and most difficult to understand and implement in the design process.

Further discussion of Methods 2 and 3 is beyond the scope of this text. However, they will not be missed because the important wind load concepts are very well illustrated by Method 1. As mentioned earlier, Method 1 is limited to rigid buildings less than 60 ft tall. There are a variety of factors or tests to determine if a building meets the standard of being "rigid." For the purposes of this book, it is simply assumed that the structures are rigid. However, in practice, the engineer will make an assessment regarding whether the simplified method applies or one of the more complicated methods is required.

This discussion starts with Method 1 and simplifies it further. The additional simplifications will allow students to make much more rapid (but still fairly accurate) comparative analyses between the effects of wind load and the effects of other forces on a building. These simplifications will also allow students to move forward in considering a host of other important issues that they would never get to if they became bogged down in the extremely fine details of the interaction of the wind with structures. Students should be aware of the nature of the simplifications and should understand that the full code should be adhered to in the design and analysis of any real building. Students should also understand that the full code is much more complicated than the simplified version used in this book and that the structural engineer of record does a substantial amount of work for a design team in addressing the more detailed analysis called for in the codes.

The wind pressure on a surface of a building depends on the following:

- The wind speed
- The shape of the building
- The direction of the wind relative to the building
- The location of the point on the building at which the wind pressure is being assessed
- The height and other dimensions of the structure

The map in Figure 2.42 shows the approximate wind speeds in the eastern United States. Maps of this sort are good indicators of what is likely to happen. However, they

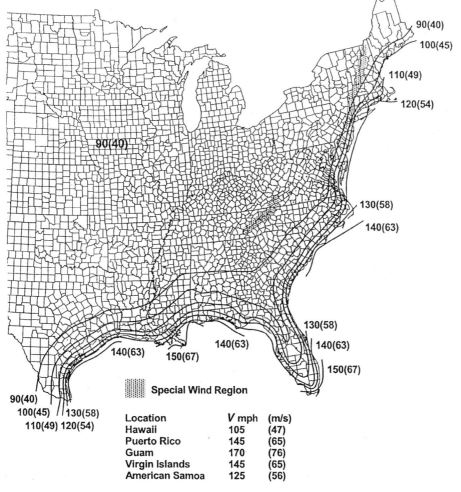

Special Wind Region

Location	V mph	(m/s)
Hawaii	105	(47)
Puerto Rico	145	(65)
Guam	170	(76)
Virgin Islands	145	(65)
American Samoa	125	(56)

Notes:
1. Values are nominal-design, 3-second-gust wind speeds in miles per hour (m/s) at 33 ft (10 m) above ground for Exposure C category.
2. Linear interpolation between wind contours is permitted.
3. Islands and coastal areas outside the last contour shall use the last wind-speed contour of the coastal area.
4. Mountainous terrain, gorges, ocean promontories, and special wind regions shall be examined for unusual wind conditions.

Figure 2.42 Wind-speed map for eastern United States. (Reprinted courtesy of the American Society of Civil Engineers.)

should not be the basis for the design of a real building. The governing codes in any particular locale should be consulted to determine the prescribed design wind speed. For the purposes of this text, this map will be quite adequate.

Wind pressure varies in proportion to the square of the wind speed:

$$pressure \propto V^2$$

The design wind speed in Wake County, North Carolina, is 95 mph. The design wind speed along the North Carolina coast is typically 135 mph. This means that the design wind pressure will be higher at the coast by a factor of $(135/95)^2 = 2.02$; that is, more than twice as great.

Wind speed is dependent on the driving force of weather conditions and can be altered by local condi-

tions—for example, it can be reduced by the roughness of the terrain and accelerated locally by escarpments, ridges, and hills. For the purposes of this text, this discussion does not address the special problems associated with escarpments, ridges, and hills, but the reader should be aware that substantial accelerations in air speed are possible in the vicinity of such landforms and, when confronted in practice with a site at or near the top of such a landform, should consult the detailed code to perform analyses at that site.

The wind-exposure categories noted below have to do with local conditions around a building. These categories are defined as follows.

Surface Roughness A was previously defined to refer to large city centers with at least 50 percent of the buildings

Table 2.5 Building Importance Factors

Building Importance Category	Importance Factor I (for wind)
I	.87
II	1.00
III	1.15
IV	1.15

having a height in excess of 70 ft. This surface roughness category has been subsumed into Surface Roughness B, and we no longer refer to Surface Roughness A.

Surface Roughness B is defined to refer to urban and suburban areas, wooded areas, or other terrain with numerous closely spaced obstructions having the size of a single-family dwelling or larger. Exposure B applies where the ground Surface Roughness B prevails in the upwind direction for a distance of at least 2,630 ft or 10 times the height of the building, whichever is greater.

Surface Roughness C is defined to refer to open terrain with scattered obstructions having heights generally less than 30 ft. This category includes flat, open country; grasslands; and all water surfaces in hurricane-prone regions. Exposure C applies for all cases where Exposures B and D do not apply.

Surface Roughness D is defined as referring to flat, unobstructed areas and water surfaces outside hurricane-prone regions. This category includes smooth mud flats, salt flats, and unbroken ice. Exposure D applies where the ground Surface Roughness D prevails in the upward direction for a distance of at least 5,000 ft or 10 times the height of the building, whichever is greater. Exposure D extends inland from the shoreline for a distance of 660 ft or 10 times the height of the building, whichever is greater.

For a site located in a transition zone between two exposure categories, the more severe exposure category should be used in accounting for wind effects. The roughness categories are used to define exposure factors used in adjusting wind-design pressures in a particular geographic location. Wind-pressure tables in the codes are expressed in terms of Exposure B, with adjustment factors for other exposures. Adjustment factors are also provided for building height and building importance. As examples of the latter, hospitals and other emergency facilities will be designed to a higher standard than a tobacco drying barn. Wind pressures will be adjusted by the building importance factors shown in Table 2.5, based on the building importance classification categories:

- Category I: Buildings and other structures that represent low hazard to human life in the event of failure
- Category II: All buildings not in the other three categories

- Category III: Buildings and other structures that represent a substantial hazard to human life in the event of failure, such as buildings where more than 300 people gather in one area, schools with capacity greater than 250 people, and daycare facilities with capacity greater than 150
- Category IV: Buildings and other structures designated as essential facilities, such as hospitals; emergency shelters; and fire, ambulance, rescue, and police stations

The concerns about the effect of wind loading are divided between the main wind force resisting system (MWFRS) and components and cladding of the building enclosure. The MWFRS reacts to average wind loading over various faces of the structure. Components and cladding are subjected to all the local variations in wind pressure, and in some locations, are subjected to much higher local pressures than the average pressure that impacts the MWFRS.

2.2.5.2 Design Pressures for Sizing the Main Wind Force Resisting System

Examine the wind pressures prescribed for the design of the MWFRS of a building. Figure 2.43 defines some zones on a building's surfaces and indicates the direction of various pressure components within those zones. Figures 2.44 and 2.45 list the design pressures associated with each of those zones, corresponding to various prevailing wind velocities.

First, consider Method 1. As mentioned earlier, there are a number of simplifications that can allow us to make much more rapid (but still reasonably accurate) comparative analyses between the effects of wind load and the effects of other forces on a building. These simplifications are the following:

- The pressure given in the tables (Figures 2.44 and 2.45) for Zone A will be assumed to be everywhere on the windward wall. Because the pressure for Zone A is larger than the pressure for Zone C, this is a conservative assumption.
- The pressure given in the tables for Zone B will be assumed to be the horizontal component everywhere on the windward slope of the roof. Because the pressure for Zone B is larger than the pressure for Zone D, this is a conservative assumption.
- The pressure given in the tables for Zone E will be assumed to be the vertical component everywhere on the windward half of the roof. Because the pressure for Zone E is larger than the pressure for Zone G, this is a conservative assumption.
- The pressure given in the tables for Zone F will be assumed to be the vertical component everywhere on the leeward half of the roof. Because the pressure for Zone F is larger than the pressure for Zone H, this is a conservative assumption.

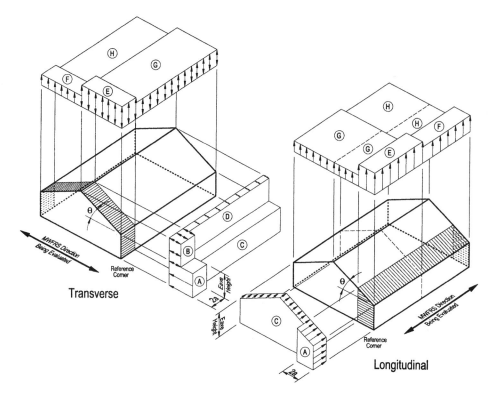

Figure 2.43 Effects of wind on a gabled building. (Reprinted courtesy of the American Society of Civil Engineers.)

• The pressure given in the tables for Zone EOH will be assumed to be everywhere under the overhang. Because the pressure for Zone EOH is larger than the pressure for Zone GOH, this is a conservative assumption.

These assumptions may seem at first unduly conservative and wasteful. However, in many cases, the impact of these assumptions on the cost of a structure will be small and the simplifications are appropriate to the task, particularly for the preliminary stages of design. As the project develops, a more detailed calculation can be made based on the full range of pressure variations given in the tables. The purpose of this more detailed calculation will be to save money on the structure. Before starting the more detailed calculations, it would be appropriate to assess the likely savings that might result from the more detailed calculations.

The pressure data distilling out of these simplifications have been surrounded with heavy lines in Figure 2.44. For the purposes of focusing this discussion, the wind-pressure data corresponding to a design wind speed of 100 mph has been highlighted.

The zones referred to in Figure 2.44 are defined in Figure 2.43.

Figure 2.46 shows the pressure distributions for a design wind speed of 100 mph, with wind movement from left to right, plotted to scale for a flat-roof building.

Figure 2.47 shows the pressure distributions for a design wind speed of 100 mph, with wind movement from left to right, plotted to scale, for a gable-roof building with the roof surfaces sloping at 45°.

Certain building shapes produce airflows that are unstable, i.e., they fluctuate. A gabled roof sloping at 45° tends to create such fluctuations. To properly account for the variations in pressure, two load cases are given in the tables in Figures 2.44 and 2.45. Those two load cases are plotted in Figure 2.47. To get factored wind loads, multiply all the numbers in Figures 2.46 and 2.47 by the load factor 1.6.

Assignments:

1. For a 100 mph wind speed on a flat-roof building of height 60 ft and width 80 ft, draw the pressure distributions to scale. Because the building is more than 30 ft high, the variation in pressure that occurs above 30 ft must be taken into account. This variation is accounted for through the height and exposure adjustment factor. For simplicity, use the height and exposure adjustment factor for 60 ft for all elevations between 30 ft and 60 ft.

2. Consider a 100 mph wind speed perpendicular to the ridge line on a gabled building that is 72 ft wide, has walls that are 50 ft high, and has roof facets with a slope of 3 in 12. Find the angle of the roof facets.

Main Wind Force Resisting System – Method 1		h ≤ 60 ft.
Design Wind Pressures		**Walls & Roofs**
Enclosed Buildings		

Simplified Design Wind Pressure, p_{S30} (psf) *(Exposure B at h = 30 ft. with I = 1.0)*

Basic Wind Speed (mph)	Roof Angle (degrees)	Load Case	Zones									
			Horizontal Pressures				Vertical Pressures				Overhangs	
			A	B	C	D	E	F	G	H	EOH	GOH
85	0 to 5°	1	11.5	-5.9	7.6	-3.5	-13.8	-7.8	-9.6	-6.1	-19.3	-15.1
	10°	1	12.9	-5.4	8.6	-3.1	-13.8	-8.4	-9.6	-6.5	-19.3	-15.1
	15°	1	14.4	-4.8	9.6	-2.7	-13.8	-9.0	-9.6	-6.9	-19.3	-15.1
	20°	1	15.9	-4.2	10.6	-2.3	-13.8	-9.6	-9.6	-7.3	-19.3	-15.1
	25°	1	14.4	2.3	10.4	2.4	-6.4	-8.7	-4.6	-7.0	-11.9	-10.1
		2	——	——	——	——	-2.4	-4.7	-0.7	-3.0	——	——
	30 to 45°	1	12.9	8.8	10.2	7.0	1.0	-7.8	0.3	-6.7	-4.5	-5.2
		2	12.9	8.8	10.2	7.0	5.0	-3.9	4.3	-2.8	-4.5	-5.2
90	0 to 5°	1	12.8	-6.7	8.5	-4.0	-15.4	-8.8	-10.7	-6.8	-21.6	-16.9
	10°	1	14.5	-6.0	9.6	-3.5	-15.4	-9.4	-10.7	-7.2	-21.6	-16.9
	15°	1	16.1	-5.4	10.7	-3.0	-15.4	-10.1	-10.7	-7.7	-21.6	-16.9
	20°	1	17.8	-4.7	11.9	-2.6	-15.4	-10.7	-10.7	-8.1	-21.6	-16.9
	25°	1	16.1	2.6	11.7	2.7	-7.2	-9.8	-5.2	-7.8	-13.3	-11.4
		2	——	——	——	——	-2.7	-5.3	-0.7	-3.4	——	——
	30 to 45°	1	14.4	9.9	11.5	7.9	1.1	-8.8	0.4	-7.5	-5.1	-5.8
		2	14.4	9.9	11.5	7.9	5.6	-4.3	4.8	-3.1	-5.1	-5.8
100	0 to 5°	1	15.9	-8.2	10.5	-4.9	-19.1	-10.8	-13.3	-8.4	-26.7	-20.9
	10°	1	17.9	-7.4	11.9	-4.3	-19.1	-11.6	-13.3	-8.9	-26.7	-20.9
	15°	1	19.9	-6.6	13.3	-3.8	-19.1	-12.4	-13.3	-9.5	-26.7	-20.9
	20°	1	22.0	-5.8	14.6	-3.2	-19.1	-13.3	-13.3	-10.1	-26.7	-20.9
	25°	1	19.9	3.2	14.4	3.3	-8.8	-12.0	-6.4	-9.7	-16.5	-14.0
		2	——	——	——	——	-3.4	-6.6	-0.9	-4.2	——	——
	30 to 45°	1	17.8	12.2	14.2	9.8	1.4	-10.8	0.5	-9.3	-6.3	-7.2
		2	17.8	12.2	14.2	9.8	6.9	-5.3	5.9	-3.8	-6.3	-7.2
110	0 to 5°	1	19.2	-10.0	12.7	-5.9	-23.1	-13.1	-16.0	-10.1	-32.3	-25.3
	10°	1	21.6	-9.0	14.4	-5.2	-23.1	-14.1	-16.0	-10.8	-32.3	-25.3
	15°	1	24.1	-8.0	16.0	-4.6	-23.1	-15.1	-16.0	-11.5	-32.3	-25.3
	20°	1	26.6	-7.0	17.7	-3.9	-23.1	-16.0	-16.0	-12.2	-32.3	-25.3
	25°	1	24.1	3.9	17.4	4.0	-10.7	-14.6	-7.7	-11.7	-19.9	-17.0
		2	——	——	——	——	-4.1	-7.9	-1.1	-5.1	——	——
	30 to 45°	1	21.6	14.8	17.2	11.8	1.7	-13.1	0.6	-11.3	-7.6	-8.7
		2	21.6	14.8	17.2	11.8	8.3	-6.5	7.2	-4.6	-7.6	-8.7
120	0 to 5°	1	22.8	-11.9	15.1	-7.0	-27.4	-15.6	-19.1	-12.1	-38.4	-30.1
	10°	1	25.8	-10.7	17.1	-6.2	-27.4	-16.8	-19.1	-12.9	-38.4	-30.1
	15°	1	28.7	-9.5	19.1	-5.4	-27.4	-17.9	-19.1	-13.7	-38.4	-30.1
	20°	1	31.6	-8.3	21.1	-4.6	-27.4	-19.1	-19.1	-14.5	-38.4	-30.1
	25°	1	28.6	4.6	20.7	4.7	-12.7	-17.3	-9.2	-13.9	-23.7	-20.2
		2	——	——	——	——	-4.8	-9.4	-1.3	-6.0	——	——
	30 to 45°	1	25.7	17.6	20.4	14.0	2.0	-15.6	0.7	-13.4	-9.0	-10.3
		2	25.7	17.6	20.4	14.0	9.9	-7.7	8.6	-5.5	-9.0	-10.3
130	0 to 5°	1	26.8	-13.9	17.8	-8.2	-32.2	-18.3	-22.4	-14.2	-45.1	-35.3
	10°	1	30.2	-12.5	20.1	-7.3	-32.2	-19.7	-22.4	-15.1	-45.1	-35.3
	15°	1	33.7	-11.2	22.4	-6.4	-32.2	-21.0	-22.4	-16.1	-45.1	-35.3
	20°	1	37.1	-9.8	24.7	-5.4	-32.2	-22.4	-22.4	-17.0	-45.1	-35.3
	25°	1	33.6	5.4	24.3	5.5	-14.9	-20.4	-10.8	-16.4	-27.8	-23.7
		2	——	——	——	——	-5.7	-11.1	-1.5	-7.1	——	——
	30 to 45°	1	30.1	20.6	24.0	16.5	2.3	-18.3	0.8	-15.7	-10.6	-12.1
		2	30.1	20.6	24.0	16.5	11.6	-9.0	10.0	-6.4	-10.6	-12.1

Unit Conversions – 1.0 ft = 0.3048 m; 1.0 psf = 0.0479 kN/m²

Figure 2.44 Wind pressures on Main Wind Force Resisting System for various design wind speeds. (Reprinted courtesy of the American Society of Civil Engineers.)

Main Wind Force Resisting System – Method 1		h ≤ 60 ft.
Design Wind Pressures		**Walls & Roofs**
Enclosed Buildings		

Simplified Design Wind Pressure, p_{S30} (psf) *(Exposure B at h = 30 ft. with I = 1.0)*

Basic Wind Speed (mph)	Roof Angle (degrees)	Load Case	Zones									
			Horizontal Pressures				Vertical Pressures				Overhangs	
			A	B	C	D	E	F	G	H	EOH	GOH
140	0 to 5°	1	31.1	-16.1	20.6	-9.6	-37.3	-21.2	-26.0	-16.4	-52.3	-40.9
	10°	1	35.1	-14.5	23.3	-8.5	-37.3	-22.8	-26.0	-17.5	-52.3	-40.9
	15°	1	39.0	-12.9	26.0	-7.4	-37.3	-24.4	-26.0	-18.6	-52.3	-40.9
	20°	1	43.0	-11.4	28.7	-6.3	-37.3	-26.0	-26.0	-19.7	-52.3	-40.9
	25°	1	39.0	6.3	28.2	6.4	-17.3	-23.6	-12.5	-19.0	-32.3	-27.5
		2	——	——	——	——	-6.6	-12.8	-1.8	-8.2	——	——
	30 to 45°	1	35.0	23.9	27.8	19.1	2.7	-21.2	0.9	-18.2	-12.3	-14.0
		2	35.0	23.9	27.8	19.1	13.4	-10.5	11.7	-7.5	-12.3	-14.0
150	0 to 5°	1	35.7	-18.5	23.7	-11.0	-42.9	-24.4	-29.8	-18.9	-60.0	-47.0
	10°	1	40.2	-16.7	26.8	-9.7	-42.9	-26.2	-29.8	-20.1	-60.0	-47.0
	15°	1	44.8	-14.9	29.8	-8.5	-42.9	-28.0	-29.8	-21.4	-60.0	-47.0
	20°	1	49.4	-13.0	32.9	-7.2	-42.9	-29.8	-29.8	-22.6	-60.0	-47.0
	25°	1	44.8	7.2	32.4	7.4	-19.9	-27.1	-14.4	-21.8	-37.0	-31.6
		2	——	——	——	——	-7.5	-14.7	-2.1	-9.4	——	——
	30 to 45°	1	40.1	27.4	31.9	22.0	3.1	-24.4	1.0	-20.9	-14.1	-16.1
		2	40.1	27.4	31.9	22.0	15.4	-12.0	13.4	-8.6	-14.1	-16.1
170	0 to 5°	1	45.8	-23.8	30.4	-14.1	-55.1	-31.3	-38.3	-24.2	-77.1	-60.4
	10°	1	51.7	-21.4	34.4	-12.5	-55.1	-33.6	-38.3	-25.8	-77.1	-60.4
	15°	1	57.6	-19.1	38.3	-10.9	-55.1	-36.0	-38.3	-27.5	-77.1	-60.4
	20°	1	63.4	-16.7	42.3	-9.3	-55.1	-38.3	-38.3	-29.1	-77.1	-60.4
	25°	1	57.5	9.3	41.6	9.5	-25.6	-34.8	-18.5	-28.0	-47.6	-40.5
		2	——	——	——	——	-9.7	-18.9	-2.6	-12.1	——	——
	30 to 45°	1	51.5	35.2	41.0	28.2	4.0	-31.3	1.3	-26.9	-18.1	-20.7
		2	51.5	35.2	41.0	28.2	19.8	-15.4	17.2	-11.0	-18.1	-20.7

Adjustment Factor
for Building Height and Exposure, λ

Mean roof height (ft)	Exposure		
	B	C	D
15	1.00	1.21	1.47
20	1.00	1.29	1.55
25	1.00	1.35	1.61
30	1.00	1.40	1.66
35	1.05	1.45	1.70
40	1.09	1.49	1.74
45	1.12	1.53	1.78
50	1.16	1.56	1.81
55	1.19	1.59	1.84
60	1.22	1.62	1.87

Unit Conversions – 1.0 ft = 0.3048 m; 1.0 psf = 0.0479 kN/m²

Figure 2.45 Wind pressures on Main Wind Force Resisting System for various design wind speeds (*Continued*). (Reprinted courtesy of the American Society of Civil Engineers.)

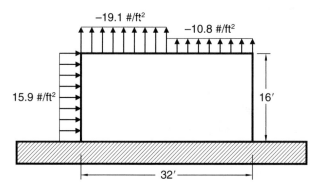

Figure 2.46 Pressure distributions on a flat-roof building of height ≤ 30 ft.

Choose the angle in the table in Figure 2.44 that is closest to the angle for 3 in 12 (i.e., do not bother interpolating in the tables). Draw the pressure distributions to scale. Because the building is more than 30 ft high, the variation in pressure that occurs above 30 ft must be taken into account. This variation is accounted for through the height- and exposure-adjustment factor. Find the mean roof height. Find the value in the table in Figure 2.45 for mean roof height that is closest to the value for this building. For simplicity, use the exposure factor for mean roof height for all elevations between 30 ft and the top of the roof.

3. Repeat problem 1 for a design wind speed of 130 mph.
4. Repeat problem 2 for a design wind speed of 130 mph.

2.2.5.3 Design Pressures for Sizing Components and Cladding
Figures 2.48 through 2.50 address wind pressures on components and cladding. This tends to be more the domain of the architect than the engineer, inasmuch as the engineer is typically focused on the MWFRS, and the architect needs to be careful to specify paneling and glazing systems that can withstand the local effects of

wind over the envelope of the building. However, a proper design process involves a close collaboration between architect and engineer in addressing both MWFRS and components and cladding.

In Figure 2.48, the building surface is divided into zones. The most intense wind pressures occur at corners of the building, where the Venturi/Bernoulli* effects are highest. The next most intense effects occur at end zones of the building surfaces. The least intense effects occur on interior portions of the building surfaces. The dimensions assigned to the various winds zones depend on the sizes of the surfaces and on other factors outlined in Figure 2.48. Complicating things further is the fact that various kinds of cladding on a building occur in their own patterns, which may have little correlation with the wind zones. One of the tasks of the architect and the engineer is to attempt to simplify this picture. For example, it would be suspect design practice to adjust the strength of components to tailor them precisely to every zone. This will tend to add more cost to the building than simply designing some of the components to a higher standard than required for the wind zone in which they occur. Furthermore, finely tailoring the strength of various components to where they occur on a building increases the

---

*The Venturi effect principle states that locally constricting the flow area for a moving fluid causes an increase in fluid speed at the constriction. One implication of the Venturi effect is that moving air has to speed up to "get around" the edges of a building. The Bernoulli effect principle states that increasing the speed of a fluid tangent to a surface reduces the pressure of the fluid on that surface. In the vernacular, this pressure reduction is called a *suction*. The concept of suction can be deceptive. The so-called suction force tending to tear a wall, or roof, away from the rest of the structure to which it is attached is actually a manifestation of the fact that the reduced outside pressure no longer fully counteracts the inside pressure. The dominance of the inside pressure produces a net outward force.

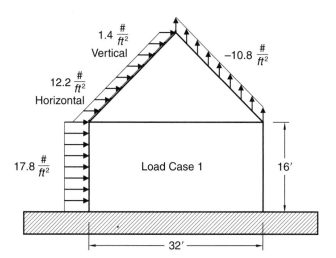

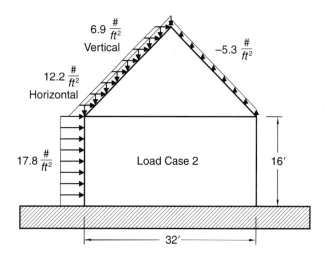

Figure 2.47 Pressure distributions on a building of height ≤ 30 ft, with roof facets at 45°.

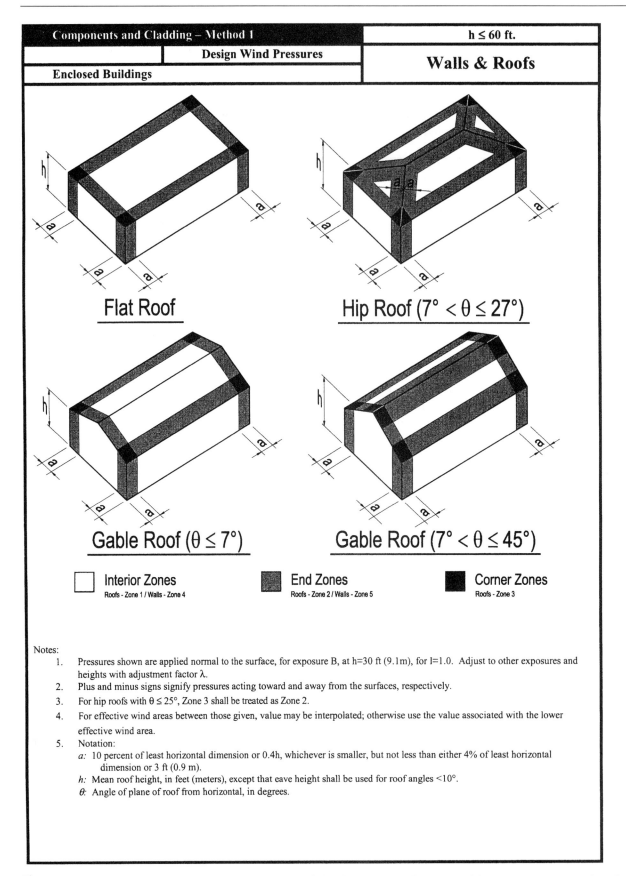

Components and Cladding – Method 1		h ≤ 60 ft.
	Design Wind Pressures	**Walls & Roofs**
Enclosed Buildings		

Flat Roof

Hip Roof (7° < θ ≤ 27°)

Gable Roof (θ ≤ 7°)

Gable Roof (7° < θ ≤ 45°)

☐ Interior Zones
Roofs - Zone 1 / Walls - Zone 4

▨ End Zones
Roofs - Zone 2 / Walls - Zone 5

■ Corner Zones
Roofs - Zone 3

Notes:
1. Pressures shown are applied normal to the surface, for exposure B, at h=30 ft (9.1m), for I=1.0. Adjust to other exposures and heights with adjustment factor λ.
2. Plus and minus signs signify pressures acting toward and away from the surfaces, respectively.
3. For hip roofs with θ ≤ 25°, Zone 3 shall be treated as Zone 2.
4. For effective wind areas between those given, value may be interpolated; otherwise use the value associated with the lower effective wind area.
5. Notation:
   a: 10 percent of least horizontal dimension or 0.4h, whichever is smaller, but not less than either 4% of least horizontal dimension or 3 ft (0.9 m).
   h: Mean roof height, in feet (meters), except that eave height shall be used for roof angles <10°.
   θ: Angle of plane of roof from horizontal, in degrees.

Figure 2.48 Effects of wind on building components and cladding. (Reprinted courtesy of the American Society of Civil Engineers.)

chance of components being installed in the wrong locations.

Another important variable is the area of a component. The variations in wind pressure occurring over a surface tend to be "smoothed out" for a component with a large area, whereby parts of the component may be subjected to very high pressure, but other parts will experience a lower pressure, thus producing a lower average pressure on the component. Components with a smaller area are more likely to be subjected to the full effects of large pressure fluctuations. In the tables in Figures 2.49 and 2.50, this effect is accounted for in the column labeled "Effective Wind Area."

To focus the discussion, bold boxes have been drawn around the wind-pressure data corresponding to a building with a flat roof subjected to a 100 mph wind. Notice the following trends:

- Pressures in Zone 3 are greater than pressures in Zone 2, which are greater than pressures in Zone 1.
- Pressures decrease with increased effective wind area.
- For each combination of zone, effective wind area, and wind speed, there are two pressure figures given: an overpressure and a suction. The component must be designed to meet both of these pressures. For most components, overpressure and suction will have to be accounted for separately because a component will have different structural mechanisms for addressing those two pressures. For example, overpressure on plywood sheathing presses the sheathing up against the studs in the wall, whereas suction tends to pull loose the nails securing the plywood to the studs.
- For components, the magnitude of the pressure produced by wind suction exceeds the magnitude of the wind overpressure, often by a substantial amount.

With regard to the last two points, the structural mechanisms for resisting overpressure are usually superior to the mechanism for resisting suction. Therefore, suction is normally the primary concern in component design.

Exercise 2.2: Wind Load Computation

A window that is 4 ft × 5 ft is located in Zone 5 of a wall in a building with a flat roof that is subjected to a wind speed of 100 mph.

- What is the average wind suction on the window component?
- What is the total suction force on the component?

The steel roof decking panel at the corner of a flat roof is 3 ft wide and spans 5 ft from the center of one roof truss to the center of the next roof truss. For a wind speed of 100 mph:

- What is the average suction pressure on the component?

- What is the total suction force on the component?
- What does this suction pressure translate to, in terms of the line-distributed force along the truss, $w_{suction}$ (in pounds per linear foot of truss)?
- What is the average overpressure on the component?
- What is the total overpressure force on the component?
- What does this overpressure translate to, in terms of the line-distributed force along the truss, $w_{Overpressure}$ (in pounds per linear foot of truss)?

For simplicity, do not bother interpolating between data points in the pressure tables. Take the most severe of the two pressures that bracket the effective wind area that you have calculated.

2.2.5.4 Wind Damping   When wind blows on a tall building constructed of structurally efficient, highly elastic material, oscillations can be induced via a process called *vortex shedding*.* When the frequency of the vortex shedding matches one of the normal modes of oscillation of the structure, energy can be stored in the structure over several oscillations, leading to large displacements and high stresses. The resulting movement can cause anxiety or physical discomfort for the building occupants and, in extreme cases, create stresses that threaten the integrity of the building structure.

There are four major mechanisms that can serve to damp oscillations:

1. Damping from the inherent "deadness" of the structural frame
2. Damping from partitions and exterior walls
3. Aerodynamic damping
4. Added damping

For a steel building, material damping intrinsic in the structure itself is usually very small, typically a fraction of 1 percent of critical damping. For concrete the damping is better, and for wood the inherent damping is very good.

Damping found in nonstructural elements results from the sliding of materials past each other as the building moves. Examples include the movement of a glass wall in its rubber edge, and the friction of partitions as they slide, the cracking of nonstructural parts, such as masonry shaft enclosures. These damping mechanisms can be very significant, but are very difficult to quantify and cannot, therefore, be relied upon in situations where the threat of oscillations is high.

Aerodynamic damping is associated with the shape of a building. Irregularly shaped buildings have greater aerodynamic damping than smooth, uniform shapes. For

---

*A vortex is a region of turbulent flow that reflects a break from smooth, laminar flow. Most buildings are not aerodynamic enough to maintain laminar flow and they therefore produce vortices.

Components and Cladding – Method 1 · **h ≤ 60 ft.**

Design Wind Pressures

Enclosed Buildings · **Walls & Roofs**

Net Design Wind Pressure, p_{net30} (psf) *(Exposure B at h = 30 ft. with I = 1.0)*

	Zone	Effective Wind Area (sf)	Basic Wind Speed V (mph)															
			85		90		100		110		120		130		140		150		170	
Roof 0 to 7 degrees	1	10	5.3	-13.0	5.9	-14.6	7.3	-18.0	8.9	-21.8	10.5	-25.9	12.4	-30.4	14.3	-35.3	16.5	-40.5	21.1	-52.0
	1	20	5.0	-12.7	5.6	-14.2	6.9	-17.5	8.3	-21.2	9.9	-25.2	11.6	-29.6	13.4	-34.4	15.4	-39.4	19.8	-50.7
	1	50	4.5	-12.2	5.1	-13.7	6.3	-16.9	7.6	-20.5	9.0	-24.4	10.6	-28.6	12.3	-33.2	14.1	-38.1	18.1	-48.9
	1	100	4.2	-11.9	4.7	-13.3	5.8	-16.5	7.0	-19.9	8.3	-23.7	9.8	-27.8	11.4	-32.3	13.0	-37.0	16.7	-47.6
	2	10	5.3	-21.8	5.9	-24.4	7.3	-30.2	8.9	-36.5	10.5	-43.5	12.4	-51.0	14.3	-59.2	16.5	-67.9	21.1	-87.2
	2	20	5.0	-19.5	5.6	-21.8	6.9	-27.0	8.3	-32.6	9.9	-38.8	11.6	-45.6	13.4	-52.9	15.4	-60.7	19.8	-78.0
	2	50	4.5	-16.4	5.1	-18.4	6.3	-22.7	7.6	-27.5	9.0	-32.7	10.6	-38.4	12.3	-44.5	14.1	-51.1	18.1	-65.7
	2	100	4.2	-14.1	4.7	-15.8	5.8	-19.5	7.0	-23.6	8.3	-28.1	9.8	-33.0	11.4	-38.2	13.0	-43.9	16.7	-56.4
	3	10	5.3	-32.8	5.9	-36.8	7.3	-45.4	8.9	-55.0	10.5	-65.4	12.4	-76.8	14.3	-89.0	16.5	-102.2	21.1	-131.3
	3	20	5.0	-27.2	5.6	-30.5	6.9	-37.6	8.3	-45.5	9.9	-54.2	11.6	-63.6	13.4	-73.8	15.4	-84.7	19.8	-108.7
	3	50	4.5	-19.7	5.1	-22.1	6.3	-27.3	7.6	-33.1	9.0	-39.3	10.6	-46.2	12.3	-53.5	14.1	-61.5	18.1	-78.9
	3	100	4.2	-14.1	4.7	-15.8	5.8	-19.5	7.0	-23.6	8.3	-28.1	9.8	-33.0	11.4	-38.2	13.0	-43.9	16.7	-56.4
Roof > 7 to 27 degrees	1	10	7.5	-11.9	8.4	-13.3	10.4	-16.5	12.5	-19.9	14.9	-23.7	17.5	-27.8	20.3	-32.3	23.3	-37.0	30.0	-47.6
	1	20	6.8	-11.6	7.7	-13.0	9.4	-16.0	11.4	-19.4	13.6	-23.0	16.0	-27.0	18.5	-31.4	21.3	-36.0	27.3	-46.3
	1	50	6.0	-11.1	6.7	-12.5	8.2	-15.4	10.0	-18.6	11.9	-22.2	13.9	-26.0	16.1	-30.2	18.5	-34.6	23.8	-44.5
	1	100	5.3	-10.8	5.9	-12.1	7.3	-14.9	8.9	-18.1	10.5	-21.5	12.4	-25.2	14.3	-29.3	16.5	-33.6	21.1	-43.2
	2	10	7.5	-20.7	8.4	-23.2	10.4	-28.7	12.5	-34.7	14.9	-41.3	17.5	-48.4	20.3	-56.2	23.3	-64.5	30.0	-82.8
	2	20	6.8	-19.0	7.7	-21.4	9.4	-26.4	11.4	-31.9	13.6	-38.0	16.0	-44.6	18.5	-51.7	21.3	-59.3	27.3	-76.2
	2	50	6.0	-16.9	6.7	-18.9	8.2	-23.3	10.0	-28.2	11.9	-33.6	13.9	-39.4	16.1	-45.7	18.5	-52.5	23.8	-67.4
	2	100	5.3	-15.2	5.9	-17.0	7.3	-21.0	8.9	-25.5	10.5	-30.3	12.4	-35.6	14.3	-41.2	16.5	-47.3	21.1	-60.8
	3	10	7.5	-30.6	8.4	-34.3	10.4	-42.4	12.5	-51.3	14.9	-61.0	17.5	-71.6	20.3	-83.1	23.3	-95.4	30.0	-122.5
	3	20	6.8	-28.6	7.7	-32.1	9.4	-39.6	11.4	-47.9	13.6	-57.1	16.0	-67.0	18.5	-77.7	21.3	-89.2	27.3	-114.5
	3	50	6.0	-26.0	6.7	-29.1	8.2	-36.0	10.0	-43.5	11.9	-51.8	13.9	-60.8	16.1	-70.5	18.5	-81.0	23.8	-104.0
	3	100	5.3	-24.0	5.9	-26.9	7.3	-33.2	8.9	-40.2	10.5	-47.9	12.4	-56.2	14.3	-65.1	16.5	-74.8	21.1	-96.0
Roof > 27 to 45 degrees	1	10	11.9	-13.0	13.3	-14.6	16.5	-18.0	19.9	-21.8	23.7	-25.9	27.8	-30.4	32.3	-35.3	37.0	-40.5	47.6	-52.0
	1	20	11.6	-12.3	13.0	-13.8	16.0	-17.1	19.4	-20.7	23.0	-24.6	27.0	-28.9	31.4	-33.5	36.0	-38.4	46.3	-49.3
	1	50	11.1	-11.5	12.5	-12.8	15.4	-15.9	18.6	-19.2	22.2	-22.8	26.0	-26.8	30.2	-31.1	34.6	-35.7	44.5	-45.8
	1	100	10.8	-10.8	12.1	-12.1	14.9	-14.9	18.1	-18.1	21.5	-21.5	25.2	-25.2	29.3	-29.3	33.6	-33.6	43.2	-43.2
	2	10	11.9	-15.2	13.3	-17.0	16.5	-21.0	19.9	-25.5	23.7	-30.3	27.8	-35.6	32.3	-41.2	37.0	-47.3	47.6	-60.8
	2	20	11.6	-14.5	13.0	-16.3	16.0	-20.1	19.4	-24.3	23.0	-29.0	27.0	-34.0	31.4	-39.4	36.0	-45.3	46.3	-58.1
	2	50	11.1	-13.7	12.5	-15.3	15.4	-18.9	18.6	-22.9	22.2	-27.2	26.0	-32.0	30.2	-37.1	34.6	-42.5	44.5	-54.6
	2	100	10.8	-13.0	12.1	-14.6	14.9	-18.0	18.1	-21.8	21.5	-25.9	25.2	-30.4	29.3	-35.3	33.6	-40.5	43.2	-52.0
	3	10	11.9	-15.2	13.3	-17.0	16.5	-21.0	19.9	-25.5	23.7	-30.3	27.8	-35.6	32.3	-41.2	37.0	-47.3	47.6	-60.8
	3	20	11.6	-14.5	13.0	-16.3	16.0	-20.1	19.4	-24.3	23.0	-29.0	27.0	-34.0	31.4	-39.4	36.0	-45.3	46.3	-58.1
	3	50	11.1	-13.7	12.5	-15.3	15.4	-18.9	18.6	-22.9	22.2	-27.2	26.0	-32.0	30.2	-37.1	34.6	-42.5	44.5	-54.6
	3	100	10.8	-13.0	12.1	-14.6	14.9	-18.0	18.1	-21.8	21.5	-25.9	25.2	-30.4	29.3	-35.3	33.6	-40.5	43.2	-52.0
Wall	4	10	13.0	-14.1	14.6	-15.8	18.0	-19.5	21.8	-23.6	25.9	-28.1	30.4	-33.0	35.3	-38.2	40.5	-43.9	52.0	-56.4
	4	20	12.4	-13.5	13.9	-15.1	17.2	-18.7	20.8	-22.6	24.7	-26.9	29.0	-31.6	33.7	-36.7	38.7	-42.1	49.6	-54.1
	4	50	11.6	-12.7	13.0	-14.3	16.1	-17.6	19.5	-21.3	23.2	-25.4	27.2	-29.8	31.6	-34.6	36.2	-39.7	46.6	-51.0
	4	100	11.1	-12.2	12.4	-13.6	15.3	-16.8	18.5	-20.4	22.0	-24.2	25.9	-28.4	30.0	-33.0	34.4	-37.8	44.2	-48.6
	4	500	9.7	-10.8	10.9	-12.1	13.4	-14.9	16.2	-18.1	19.3	-21.5	22.7	-25.2	26.3	-29.3	30.2	-33.6	38.8	-43.2
	5	10	13.0	-17.4	14.6	-19.5	18.0	-24.1	21.8	-29.1	25.9	-34.7	30.4	-40.7	35.3	-47.2	40.5	-54.2	52.0	-69.6
	5	20	12.4	-16.2	13.9	-18.2	17.2	-22.5	20.8	-27.2	24.7	-32.4	29.0	-38.0	33.7	-44.0	38.7	-50.5	49.6	-64.9
	5	50	11.6	-14.7	13.0	-16.5	16.1	-20.3	19.5	-24.6	23.2	-29.3	27.2	-34.3	31.6	-39.8	36.2	-45.7	46.6	-58.7
	5	100	11.1	-13.5	12.4	-15.1	15.3	-18.7	18.5	-22.6	22.0	-26.9	25.9	-31.6	30.0	-36.7	34.4	-42.1	44.2	-54.1
	5	500	9.7	-10.8	10.9	-12.1	13.4	-14.9	16.2	-18.1	19.3	-21.5	22.7	-25.2	26.3	-29.3	30.2	-33.6	38.8	-43.2

Unit Conversions – 1.0 ft = 0.3048 m; 1.0 sf = 0.0929 m^2; 1.0 psf = 0.0479 kN/m^2

Figure 2.49 Wind pressure on components and cladding. (Reprinted courtesy of the American Society of Civil Engineers.)

Components and Cladding – Method 1										h ≤ 60 ft.	
Design Wind Pressures										**Walls & Roofs**	
Enclosed Buildings											

Roof Overhang Net Design Wind Pressure, p_net30 (psf)
(Exposure B at h = 30 ft. with I = 1.0)

	Zone	Effective Wind Area (sf)	Basic Wind Speed V (mph)							
			90	100	110	120	130	140	150	170
Roof 0 to 7 degrees	2	10	-21.0	-25.9	-31.4	-37.3	-43.8	-50.8	-58.3	-74.9
	2	20	-20.6	-25.5	-30.8	-36.7	-43.0	-49.9	-57.3	-73.6
	2	50	-20.1	-24.9	-30.1	-35.8	-42.0	-48.7	-55.9	-71.8
	2	100	-19.8	-24.4	-29.5	-35.1	-41.2	-47.8	-54.9	-70.5
	3	10	-34.6	-42.7	-51.6	-61.5	-72.1	-83.7	-96.0	-123.4
	3	20	-27.1	-33.5	-40.5	-48.3	-56.6	-65.7	-75.4	-96.8
	3	50	-17.3	-21.4	-25.9	-30.8	-36.1	-41.9	-48.1	-61.8
	3	100	-10.0	-12.2	-14.8	-17.6	-20.6	-23.9	-27.4	-35.2
Roof > 7 to 27 degrees	2	10	-27.2	-33.5	-40.6	-48.3	-56.7	-65.7	-75.5	-96.9
	2	20	-27.2	-33.5	-40.6	-48.3	-56.7	-65.7	-75.5	-96.9
	2	50	-27.2	-33.5	-40.6	-48.3	-56.7	-65.7	-75.5	-96.9
	2	100	-27.2	-33.5	-40.6	-48.3	-56.7	-65.7	-75.5	-96.9
	3	10	-45.7	-56.4	-68.3	-81.2	-95.3	-110.6	-126.9	-163.0
	3	20	-41.2	-50.9	-61.6	-73.3	-86.0	-99.8	-114.5	-147.1
	3	50	-35.3	-43.6	-52.8	-62.8	-73.7	-85.5	-98.1	-126.1
	3	100	-30.9	-38.1	-46.1	-54.9	-64.4	-74.7	-85.8	-110.1
Roof > 27 to 45 degrees	2	10	-24.7	-30.5	-36.9	-43.9	-51.5	-59.8	-68.6	-88.1
	2	20	-24.0	-29.6	-35.8	-42.6	-50.0	-58.0	-66.5	-85.5
	2	50	-23.0	-28.4	-34.3	-40.8	-47.9	-55.6	-63.8	-82.0
	2	100	-22.2	-27.4	-33.2	-39.5	-46.4	-53.8	-61.7	-79.3
	3	10	-24.7	-30.5	-36.9	-43.9	-51.5	-59.8	-68.6	-88.1
	3	20	-24.0	-29.6	-35.8	-42.6	-50.0	-58.0	-66.5	-85.5
	3	50	-23.0	-28.4	-34.3	-40.8	-47.9	-55.6	-63.8	-82.0
	3	100	-22.2	-27.4	-33.2	-39.5	-46.4	-53.8	-61.7	-79.3

Adjustment Factor
for Building Height and Exposure, λ

Mean roof height (ft)	Exposure		
	B	C	D
15	1.00	1.21	1.47
20	1.00	1.29	1.55
25	1.00	1.35	1.61
30	1.00	1.40	1.66
35	1.05	1.45	1.70
40	1.09	1.49	1.74
45	1.12	1.53	1.78
50	1.16	1.56	1.81
55	1.19	1.59	1.84
60	1.22	1.62	1.87

Unit Conversions – 1.0 ft = 0.3048 m; 1.0 sf = 0.0929 m²; 1.0 psf = 0.0479 kN/m²

Figure 2.50 Wind pressure on components and cladding (*Continued*). (Reprinted courtesy of the American Society of Civil Engineers.)

example, the changing cross section of the Sears Tower, as a function of vertical position, causes it to produce different sizes of vortices at various levels. Varying the size of the vortices prevents them from reinforcing each other to produce large, coherent effects. Some buildings have negative aerodynamic damping; that is, they not only do not damp oscillations, they enhance the tendency to oscillate. Care must be taken in the design and analysis of a building to ensure that aerodynamic damping has been properly accounted for, particularly in tall, flexible buildings made from structural materials that have little inherent damping.

The fourth kind of damping is induced or added damping. It is used routinely for door closers and automobile shock absorbers. These are basically added damping systems.

One of the best examples of a wind-damping system was designed for the World Trade Center (see Figure 2.51). Nonstructural energy absorbers were installed at the ends of the bottom chords of the floor trusses. The use of hydraulic dampers, similar to the shock absorbers in automobiles, was considered, but these would have had to be very large and expensive. Dampers of this kind tend to be effective only for large displacements. Normally, we want to suppress wind oscillations before they become extreme. To address this issue, the design team for the World Trade Center chose to use viscoelastic damping. As the name implies, viscoelastic materials are both viscous and elastic; they are both liquidlike and springlike. A viscoelastic material is elastic to the extent that it will return to its original shape when deformed at moderate rates, but it absorbs substantial amounts of energy in the process of moving. Very thin layers of these materials are quite effective energy absorbers. After viscoelastic material has been strained in one direction, the

return is just slow enough to oppose the next cycle of oscillation. Most of the energy input in the viscoelastic material is not stored but is converted to heat. A "perfect" spring, in contrast, stores all the energy and returns all the energy when it returns to its undeformed shape.

The viscoelastic component of the damper was an acrylic copolymer produced by 3M. Approximately 10,000 dampers were installed in each 100-story tower. About 100 dampers were installed at each floor, from the 7th through the 107th. Each damper was composed of three steel elements: two 4 in. × 4 in. steel Ts and one $\frac{1}{2}$ in. × 4 in. bar. Between the steel Ts and the steel bar were sandwiched two 0.050 in. × 4 in. × 10 in. viscoelastic layers. These layers were epoxy bonded to the steel. One end of the bar extended beyond the bonded area for bolting between the double angles of the bottom chord of the truss, and the coped ends of the two Ts extended in the opposite direction for bolting to a seat on the column. In this system, even slight changes in the length of the damper produce large shear deformations in the viscoelastic sheet. In this manner, wind movement could be "nipped in the bud" before the magnitude of the displacements caused a serious structural or perceptual problem. When the building was "excited" by a gust of wind, the dampers ordinarily moved only a few thousandths of an inch, but they were designed for as much as 0.02 in. of movement. The dampers dissipated at least 300 in. • # of energy per cycle at maximum deflection.

Wind-induced oscillations are a particular concern in tall buildings, but they are not limited to that building type. An example of a long-span building with potential wind-flutter problems is the Dorton Arena, in Raleigh, North Carolina. Its cable roof is locally flat at the center, as shown in the Figure 2.52. Such an expanse of locally flat cables has a tendency to flutter under wind loading. To address this issue, wind-damping cables were connected to the underside of the cable network, as shown in Figure 2.53. These wind-damping cables were connected to dampers attached to the boundary columns, shown in Figure 2.54. Movement of the cable network

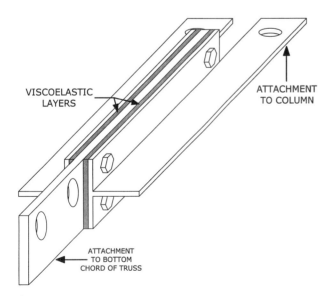

Figure 2.51 Wind damper in the World Trade Center.

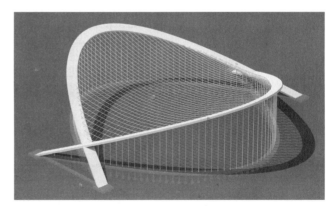

Figure 2.52 Cable network in the roof of Dorton Arena.

Figure 2.53 Wind-damping cables connecting cable network with dampers at side columns in the Dorton Arena.

Figure 2.54 Calibrated wind dampers in the Dorton Arena.

pulls on the damping cables, which subsequently activate the dampers.

2.2.6 EARTHQUAKE INERTIAL FORCES

2.2.6.1 General Inertia Issues   The sudden movement of the ground beneath a structure can induce large inertial forces in the structure.

The ground motion tends to be predominantly horizontal but may also involve extremely large vertical ac-

celerations. Accelerations on the order of 1 g have been measured for both horizontal and vertical movement of the ground (g = the acceleration of gravity near the surface of the earth). An acceleration of 1 g is not common, but it can occur near the epicenter of a large quake.

A sudden horizontal acceleration of 1 g would take the legs out from under even a very agile and gifted athlete. A person experiencing a vertical ground motion of 1 g would first feel twice as heavy and then be left "free floating" at the top of the ground motion. These large vertical accelerations tend to be most prevalent where loose or silty soil first liquefies and then develop a wave action that "crashes" against a rock formation. The liquefied soil then shoots upward, in a manner similar to an ocean wave focused in a crevice on a rocky coastline. The water speed increases as the crevice focuses the energy. When there is no place for the wave to move horizontally, the energy forces an explosive upward movement.

Large horizontal accelerations tend to be more common than large vertical accelerations. Moreover, most buildings that are properly designed for gravity loads will normally have enough excess capacity to withstand the vertical component of an earthquake. This excess capacity results from the margin of safety designed into the gravity system, combined with the fact that it is rare for a building to be subjected to its full gravity load inasmuch as most of the time the actual occupancy load is far below the design occupancy load. This leaves significant extra capacity for resisting the vertical ground acceleration.

Yet a building that is designed for wind load may not have anywhere near the capacity needed to resist the horizontal ground acceleration in a serious earthquake (see Figure 2.55). Of course, a proper design process will give ample attention to both forms of ground motion. In some buildings, in some situations, the vertical ground motion is far more deleterious than the horizontal ground motion, so it cannot be ignored.

If the building is anchored to the ground, it must either move with the earth or be sheared apart. The more massive the building, the more force it takes to make the building move with the earth, and the greater the internal stresses induced in the building. This fact is deduced from Newton's second law, which states that the force required to make a mass m accelerated with an acceleration a will be $F = ma$. The worst materials to use in resisting such forces are masonry, which have high mass and low stress capacity.

There are three common levels of analysis for dealing with earthquakes:

1. Ignore the issue altogether. This used to be the procedure in most of the United States.
2. Apply a lateral inertial force equal to some fraction of gravity (e.g., 0.1 g or 0.3 g) and do a simple static analysis of the structure under that load. This has been the approach in most of the United States for the last few years and will probably be the procedure for most buildings in most parts of the country for the foreseeable future.
3. Do a full dynamic analysis of the structure, using one of two methods, both of which require the use of computer computation methods:
   * Modal analysis
     1. Determine the structure's normal modes of oscillation.
     2. Determine the structure's tendency to dampen oscillatory motion.
     3. Compare the normal modes of the building to frequencies observed in documented earthquakes to see where there are matches that might strongly stimulate modes of oscillation in the building.
   * Time-history analysis
     1. Take ground-motion data from a representative earthquake.
     2. Apply the measured ground motion to the base of a computer model of the structure.
     3. Use the computer to calculate how these disturbances in the base of the structure propagate through the structure.

The *2003 International Building Code* (2003 IBC) requires some accounting of seismic forces everywhere in the country. In a significant departure from previous practice, the 2003 IBC also requires full dynamic analysis in parts of the country where it was never required before. Situations in which full dynamic analysis is particularly likely to be required include construction on sites with poor soil or buildings with large numbers of irregularities. Irregularities include such things as lateral bracing not in the plane of the frame being braced or places where there are breaks in the brace line, which can cause parts of the building to move independently of each other, creating serious stresses when they start moving rapidly toward each other.

When a building is drawn as a freebody, the effect of the earth on the base of the building can be represented

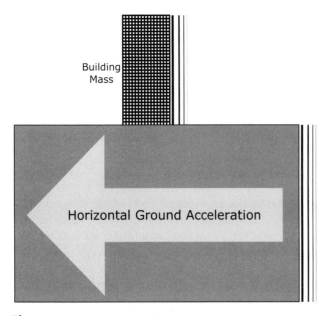

Figure 2.55 Ground acceleration.

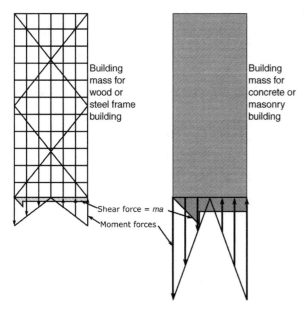

Figure 2.56 Inertial forces associated with ground acceleration.

Figure 2.57 Base isolation unit.

as a combination of a shearing force and an overturning moment on the base of the building, as shown in Figure 2.56.

The force can be reduced by decoupling the building from the earth. For example, the bases of columns can sit in broad, shallow dishes that allow the earth to accelerate without comparable accelerations in the base of the building. The sloped sides of the dish shape provide the restoring force to bring the building back to center when the earthquake disturbance has passed. Another method to achieve partial decoupling is to connect column bases to the footing through a flexible damping element. Figure 2.57 shows such an element being used as a retrofit in the San Francisco City Hall. The shiny cylindrical element at the base of the column is a rubber donut with a lead cylinder at its core. The rubber provides the restoring force, and the lead is the energy absorber. The cylinder is shiny because of a thin, aluminum covering. Visible outside the cylinder are two (of four) plates that are temporary connections between the column base and the footing. These rigid plates were rigid enough that they did not allow the rubber and lead to serve the decoupling function. When the construction was completed, these plates were removed to allow the rubber and lead to serve their intended roles. If the plates had not been kept in place during construction, some of the columns would be very free to move while others would still be connected rigidly to their footings. A seismic disturbance occurring during partial construction would have shifted all the shear force to the stiff (unretrofitted) columns, increasing the likelihood of collapse under even a minor quake.

For a low-mass structure, such as could be built from wood or steel, the shearing force at the base will be relatively modest. For a massive structure, however, such as concrete or masonry construction, the shearing force will be severe.

2.2.6.2 Oscillatory Movement Induced by Ground Motion
In addition to keeping the mass of a building low, it is desirable to create a "mechanically dead" structure.

In an earthquake, the earth moves back and forth, sometimes inducing oscillations in a building. If there is a frequency component in the ground motion that matches one of the natural frequencies of the building, then large amounts of oscillatory energy can build up in the structure over the duration of a quake. This phenomenon is demonstrated in Figure 2.58, where the columns of the structural frame are represented by steel piano wire. Movements of $1/8$ in. at the base are producing

Figure 2.58 Large-amplitude oscillations induced by small-amplitude base movements.

lateral movements of about 4 in. at the top of the structural frame. To get a gauge of the base movement, observe the two screws in the base at each end of the bottom beam of the frame. These screws were set to allow a maximum movement at the base of ⅛ in. The extremely large displacements at the top of the frame are produced by introducing small amounts of energy at the base and allowing that energy to build up over many cycles.

An analogy to this oscillatory phenomenon is the example of a child on a playground swing. Small impulses from the pusher, properly timed, gradually build up large amounts of energy in the motion. If the pusher continues to apply those impulses over several cycles of the motion, large amplitudes of motion can be built up. Another analogy is acoustic resonance. If two tuning forks that are precisely tuned to each other are placed side by side and one of them is rung, then the tiny stimulation transmitted through the air will start the other tuning fork ringing.

In both of these cases, the ability of modest stimulation to eventually generate a significant mechanical response depends on the ability of the mechanical system to retain the energy put into it over many cycles of the oscillatory stimulation. In the case of the swing, the very free movement of the hinge mechanism at the top of the swing and the relatively small effect of dissipation of energy in the air allows the swing to return to the pusher each time with almost all of the energy that the pusher put into the swing in previous cycles. In the case of the tuning fork, the steel dissipates almost no energy and the air is only a weak dissipater of the energy.

Most materials dissipate significant amounts of energy and work nothing like the steel in a tuning fork. For example, use a hammer to bang on a wood board or a concrete block and compare the response to banging on a piece of high-strength steel. The steel will ring, signifying that it is retaining the energy from the hammer over many cycles and that energy is, in fact, being dissipated into the air in the form of noise. In contrast, the wood or concrete block will give a dull thudding sound that dies almost immediately, as the mechanical energy induced by the hammer action becomes quickly absorbed in the form of internal heat in the material.

Of the common building materials, only steel requires special mechanisms to dampen earthquake oscillations. The viscoelastic devices incorporated into the World Trade Center constitute an example of such a mechanism. The devices were primarily installed to dampen wind-induced oscillations, but they would also help to dampen ground-induced oscillations. However, the energy absorbers in the World Trade Center were designed to work over a very narrow range of movement because the desire was to minimize perceivable motion for the building occupants. In contrast, good resistance to earthquakes requires a high degree of lateral flexibility to diminish the "shock" from abrupt ground movement. Large cylindrical

Figure 2.59 Shock absorber for seismic applications.

shock absorbers and joints in which highly ductile steel is used are both effective mechanisms for a structure to absorb large amounts of energy over proportionally large displacements (see Figure 2.59).

2.2.6.3 Ranking Structural Materials with Regard to Earthquake Resistance Wood, is in many ways, the ideal material because is has a very high strength-to-weight ratio and is a dead material that is self-damping, thereby rapidly suppressing any tendency to oscillate.

Steel has a very high strength-to-weight ratio, but requires added damping material.

Concrete has a lower strength-to-weight ratio than steel or wood and is brittle, which tends to make it vulnerable to earthquakes. However, with proper sizing of elements and incorporating a proper combination of prestressed reinforcing steel for strength and ductile reinforcing steel for damping, concrete structures can be very effective in resisting earthquakes.

Masonry has an extremely low strength-to-weight ratio and is a very bad choice for resisting earthquakes. In the Coalinga, California, earthquake, a survey of structures indicated that all of the wood-frame structures were safe for occupancy after the quake. In contrast, all of the unreinforced masonry structures collapsed except one, which was so badly damaged that it was condemned and ultimately torn down.

In designing for earthquake resistance, avoid weak stories and asymmetric resistance systems, such as shown in Figure 2.60. One of the challenges of structural design is the fact that the greatest forces occur at the base of a building, which is precisely where we desire the least obstruction to movement into, and through, the building.

Figure 2.61 is a generalized map of earthquake hazard in the United States. See also Table 2.6.

(a)

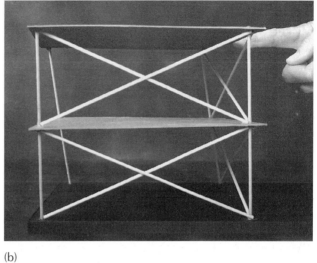

(b)

Figure 2.60 Weak story (a) and asymmetric lateral resistance (b). (Photograph reproduced courtesy of Richard K. Eisner.)

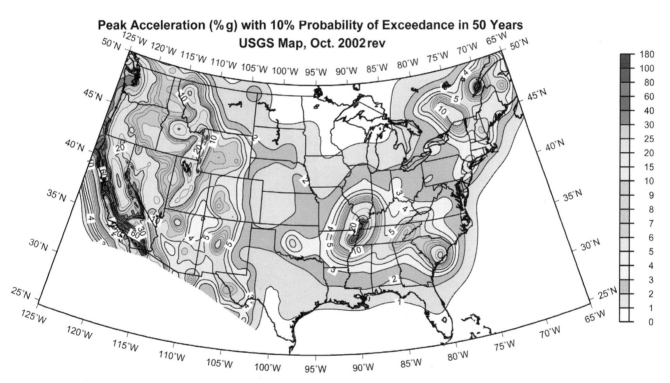

Figure 2.61 Generalized map of seismic hazard in the United States.

Table 2.6 Strongest Earthquakes in the Lower Forty-Eight States

	Year	Richter Scale Value		Year	Richter Scale Value
San Francisco, California	1906	8.25	New Madrid, Missouri	1812	7.8
New Madrid, Missouri	1812	8.2	Owens Valley, California	1972	7.8
New Madrid, Missouri	1811	8.0	Pleasant Valley, California	1915	7.8
Loma Prieta, California	1989	7.9	Kern County, California	1952	7.8
Fort Tejon, California	1857	7.9	Charleston, South Carolina	1886	7.7

2.2.7 RESIDUAL AND SETTLEMENT STRESSES

Residual stresses are stresses in a structure resulting from fabrication or erection processes. These stresses remain in the structure throughout its life, unless they are relieved by material creep or foundation settlement that serendipitously tends to equalize the stresses on various parts of the structure.

Residual stresses may result from:

- Cold bending or cold forging of ductile materials, such as steel or aluminum
- Rapid cooling of hot-formed elements (such as rolled or forged elements), which causes stress when some parts of the structure cool and contract more rapidly than other parts
- Welding, which causes stress when some parts of the material involved in the weld cool and contract more rapidly than other parts
- Inaccurate dimensioning of members in a redundant structure
- Inaccurate setting of foundations in a redundant structure

As an example of the latter phenomenon, consider the structure depicted in Figure 2.62. The top diagram represents the structure as designed. The bottom diagram represents the "as-built" structure, in which the foundations were not all set at the same level.

The space frame was constructed from left to right. Because of the intrinsic stiffness of the space frame, it cantilevered out over the last support. To complete the structure, the contractor bought some extra-long bolts, which his crew used to pull the space frame down to the last support. During this operation, some of the space-frame elements buckled. The structure did not collapse, but major repairs had to be made on the structure. This was actually quite fortunate. If evidence of the problem had not been immediately manifest in the buckling of those members, then large residual stresses would have been locked into the structure, waiting to combine with other stresses, perhaps induced by snow, to cause a catastrophic collapse. Similar stresses could also have been created by foundation settlement, assuming that the original foundation was set at the right height, but poor soils

and an inadequate footing under one support caused that support to settle over time.

Sometimes problematical movement of a support structure can occur immediately upon loading rather than by gradual settlement. For example, the spiral staircase in Figure 2.63 was initially analyzed assuming rigid supports at the landing side and simple column support on the other side.

Upon examination of the framing plan, it became apparent that the beams supporting the landing side of the stairs would not be perfectly rigid and their elastic movement had to be accounted for in the analysis of the stairs (see Figure 2.64).

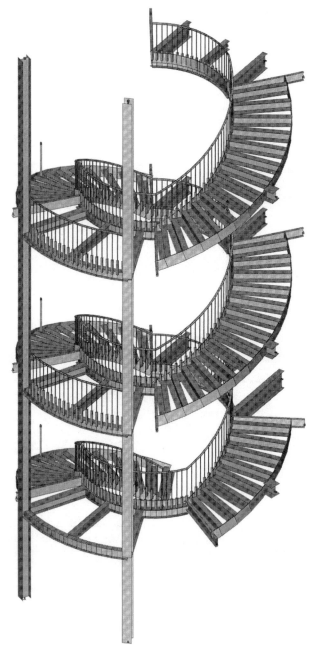

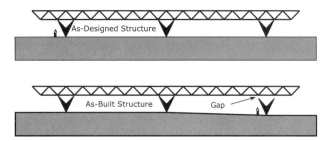

Figure 2.62 Residual stress induced by inaccurate foundations under a redundant structure.

Figure 2.63 Spiral stair supported on two rigid columns and two flexible beams.

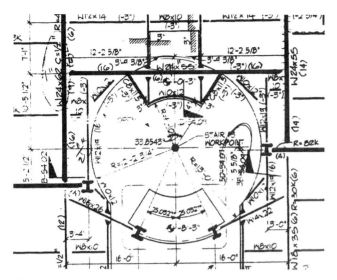

Figure 2.64 Framing plan showing support for stairs.

The beams supporting the landing side of the stairs are quite long, which means that they will deflect a substantial amount under the floor load and under loading from the stairs. Furthermore, they are supported at their ends by other long beams that will also deflect substantially, resulting in a very rubbery support system for the landing side of the spiral stairs. Because the stair looks a lot like a coil spring, one might imagine that it could accommodate the movement of the support beams without any serious problem. However, to avoid large torsional deformations, the stairs have to be framed in a manner that makes them torsionally very stiff. This is accomplished by welding the stair elements (treads and risers) into the side of the curved, helical stringers, thereby stabilizing the stringers against twisting under load. Introducing this torsional rigidity makes the stair act more like a rigid column than like a spring. When this happens, the movement of the support beams becomes a critical problem.

Figure 2.65 shows (a) the deformations in the stair, assuming rigid supports on the landing side; (b) the

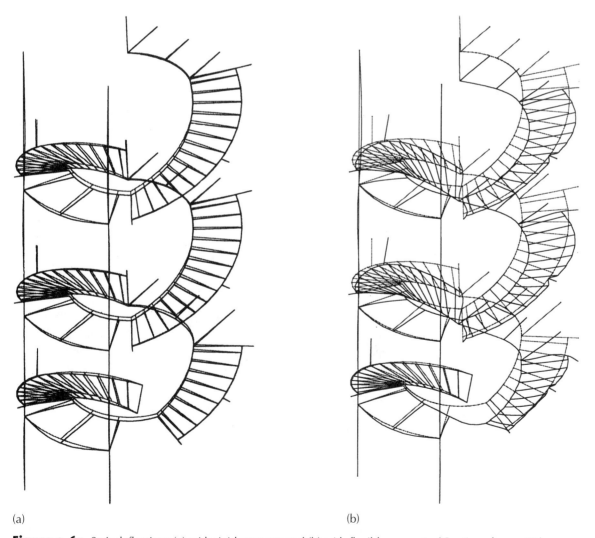

(a)   (b)

Figure 2.65 Stair deflections (a) with rigid supports and (b) with flexible supports. (*Continued on p. 78.*)

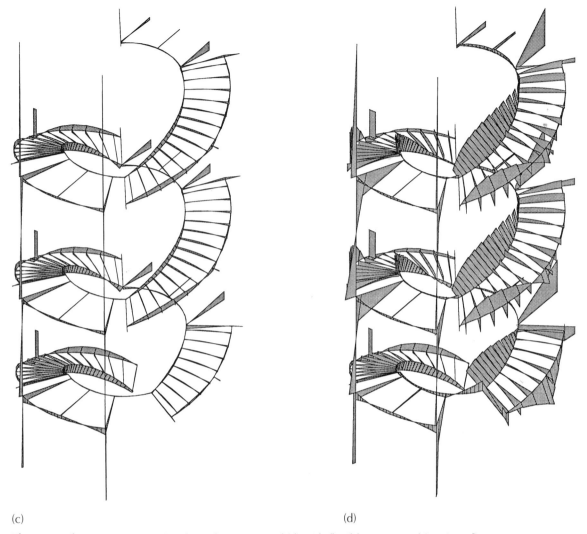

(c)   (d)

Figure 2.65 Stair stresses (c) with rigid supports and (d) with flexible supports. (*Continued*).

deformations in the stair, accounting for the deflection of the beams on the landing side of the stair; (c) the stresses in the stair, assuming rigid supports on the landing side; (d) the stresses in the stair, accounting for the deflection of the beams on the landing side of the stair.

Both the deformations and the stresses in the stair are radically larger when the deflections of the "support" beams are properly accounted for. In that case, the stair is actually acting as a column, supporting both the load on the stair and part of the load on the floors above. This is a serious role reversal, in which the stair, which is supposed to be supported by the beams, is actually supporting the beams instead.

This framing plan was seriously flawed in accounting for the relative stiffness of various stress paths. Here, as is always the case, the stiffest stress path picked up the greater share of the load. The ideal resolution to this design dilemma would be to add columns on the landing side of the stair, making both sides comparably stiff. However, an analysis of the stair was not initiated until after the design of the rest of the building was complete. The members of the design team were resistant to adding columns so late into the design process. The final resolution was to radically stiffen the beams on the landing side of the stair, using much heavier and deeper beam sections and taking maximum advantage of composite action between the beams and the concrete-slab-floor decking.

2.2.8 THERMAL STRESS

The figures in Table 2.7 can be used to determine the appropriate spacing of expansion joints. These figures can also be used to determine what materials are thermally incompatible. For example, steel has an expansion

Table 2.7 Coefficients of Thermal Expansion

Material Coefficient of Expansion	in./in./°F
Structural steel	.0000065
Aluminum	.0000128
Wrought iron	.0000067
Copper	.0000098
Brick	.0000035–.0000050
Cement mortar	.0000070
Concrete	.0000055–.0000070
Limestone	.0000040
Plaster	.0000090
Wood (fir), parallel to the grain	.0000023
Wood (fir), perpendicular to the grain (Moisture expansion perpendicular to the grain is also very large.)	.0000200–.0000300
Glass	.0000045
Acrylic plastic	.0000450–.0000500
Styrofoam	.0000400
Polyethylene	.0001000

coefficient in the range of the expansion coefficient of concrete. This allows steel to function as reinforcing for concrete. In contrast, aluminum has an expansion coefficient almost twice that of concrete. Introducing aluminum into concrete will cause it to crack severely when the temperature rises only a few degrees.

Sometimes thermal lag associated with differences in mass can also cause differential expansion problems. For example, a lightweight concrete grill surrounded by a very heavy, rigid concrete frame can cause problems. When the sun shines on the building, it will raise the temperature of the lightweight concrete grill faster than it raises the temperature of the heavy concrete frame. The grill will expand rapidly and can crush itself if expansion joints are not provided between the grill and the frame that contains the grill. In this situation, the materials have the same coefficient of expansion, but their temperatures do not track together.

3

Structural Analysis

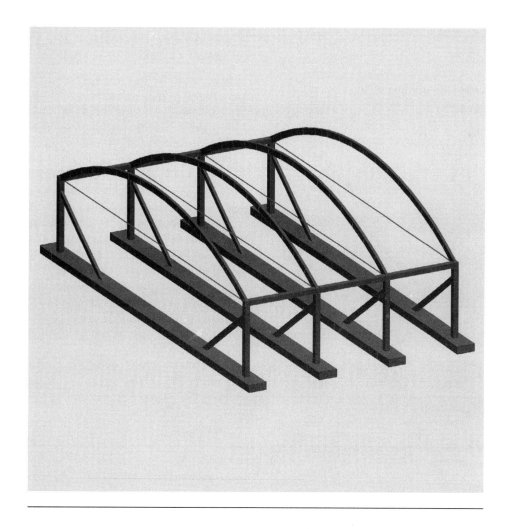

3.1 Forces and Moments

A vector is a quantity that has the following three properties:

1. Magnitude (a number plus units)
2. Direction (a line of action)
3. Sense (two possibilities, which we can label + or –)

Vector quantities are expressed in bold text. See Figure 3.1.

Vectors are best represented graphically, using arrows drawn to scale; for example, 1 in. = 10 mi, 1 in. = 50 #, and so forth. Table 3.1 lists examples of vector quantities.

Vectors can be manipulated mathematically, but the methods for doing that are somewhat more complicated than for simple numbers. The manipulation of vectors is best understood by beginning with the vector quantity *displacement* because of its conceptual simplicity. Displacement is a vector quantity indicating a distance in a direction.

Suppose you went for a walk along the following path:

D_1 = 5 mi east, D_2 = 3 mi south, D_3 = 9 mi west, D_4 = 7 mi north

The resultant displacement has a magnitude of

$$\sqrt{4^2 + 4^2} = 5.66 \text{ mi} \qquad [3.1]$$

and is directed toward the northwest (see Figure 3.2).

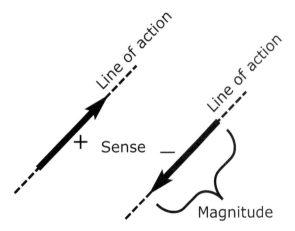

Figure 3.1 Vectors.

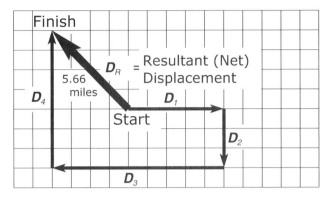

Figure 3.2 Sequence 1 of displacements.

$$D_R = 5.66 \text{ mi northwest} \qquad [3.2]$$

The magnitude of the resultant displacement is the straight-line distance from the initial point (start) to the terminal point (finish). (See Figure 3.2.)

In terms of displacement, the only relevant issue is where you finish, relative to where you started, not the total distance you walked. In this example, the total distance walked is:

$$D_1 + D_2 + D_3 + D_4$$
$$= 5 \text{ mi} + 3 \text{ mi} + 9 \text{ mi} + 7 \text{ mi} \qquad [3.3]$$
$$= 24 \text{ mi}$$

Experientially, the circuitous route and the direct route from the start to the finish are quite different. You, as the walker, are keenly interested in how far you walked. However, if you are a wilderness scout on a search and rescue mission, your helicopter pilot back at the start cares only about your resultant displacement and will not be interested in all the little details of how far you went or how bad your legs hurt. The pilot wants to know in what direction and how far to fly.

Suppose you execute the same displacements, but you walk them in a different order; that is, walk 3 mi south, then 5 mi east, then 7 mi north, then 9 mi west (see Figure 3.3):

The resultant (net) displacement is exactly the same. It makes no difference in what order you execute these displacements, the net effect is the same.

Consider a second example, involving displacements that are not in the cardinal directions. Again, changing

Table 3.1 Examples of Vector Quantities

Vector Name	Symbol	Magnitude Name	Symbol	Units
Displacement	D	Distance	D	Miles, feet, inches
Velocity	v	Speed	v	mi/hr, ft/sec
Acceleration	a	Acceleration	a	ft/sec/sec
Force	P	Force	P	lb (#), kip (1,000 lb)

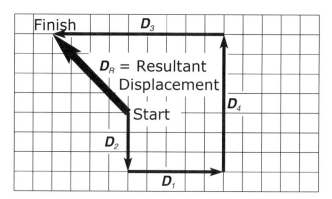

Figure 3.3 Sequence 2 of displacements.

the sequence for executing the displacements does not alter the resultant displacement. In the second case, the displacements are executed in the order D_4, D_3, D_1, and D_2. (See Figure 3.4.)

It can be said that the sequence of displacements is equivalent (in net effect) to the resultant displacement. The combined effect of the four displacements will be called the sum, and the sum is equal to the resultant:

$$D_{sum} = D_R = D_1 + D_2 + D_3 + D_4$$
$$= D_4 + D_3 + D_1 + D_2 \qquad [3.4]$$

In the terminology of mathematics, this formula demonstrates that addition of displacements is commutative, which means that the order in which the displacements are added does not affect the sum. (Note that the commutative property has only been demonstrated; it has not been proven.)

The preceding discussion provides a visual model for the addition of any sequence of vector quantities:

- Beginning with any vector in the sequence, the initial point of each new vector should be placed on the terminal point of the preceding vector.

- The resultant vector has its initial point at the initial point of the first vector and its terminal point at the terminal point of the last vector in the sequence.

As discussed shortly, this is not the only method of visualizing the addition of vectors, but it is the most intuitively obvious, particularly if displacements are kept in mind as the archetypical vector quantity.

Components:
Any vector (V) can be written in terms of two or more vectors that add together to give V:

$$V = A + B$$

A and B are referred to as the components of V. For any vector, there are an infinite number of components.

For the purpose of this book, the Cartesian components will almost always be chosen in a horizontal–vertical coordinate system, as shown in Figure 3.5.

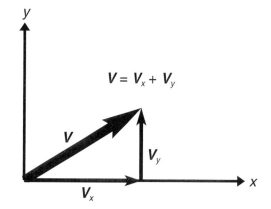

Figure 3.5 Vector components.

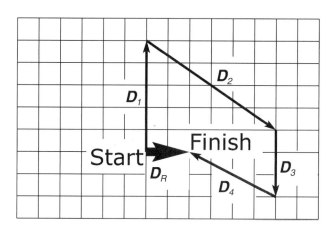
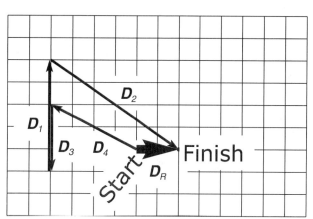

Figure 3.4 Two sequences of the same set of displacements.

Once the approach is limited to such a coordinate system, there are only two very precisely defined components for any vector. For all mathematical operations, the two components can substitute for the original vector.

At the moment, the focus is on the tip-to-tail method of visualizing vector addition. However, there is an alternate method of visualizing the addition of two components, which will become particularly useful later in this discussion in dealing with other issues or situations in which it is not useful to be picking up vectors and moving them around.

In this formulation, V_x and V_y have their initial points at the initial point of the resultant vector. V_x and V_y constitute two sides of a rectangle, of which the resultant vector V is a diagonal of the rectangle. This arrangement is shown in the Figure 3.6.

This formulation will be revisited when it becomes useful to do so.

Consider the following example. For the purposes of the immediate discussion, it continues to use the tip-to-tail formulation for visualizing the vectors and vector components (see Figure 3.7).

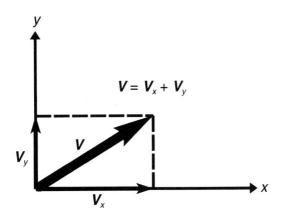

Figure 3.6 Alternate representation for vector components.

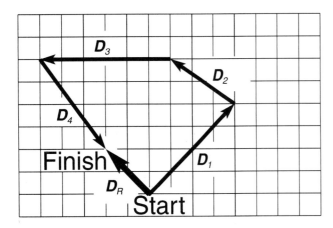

Figure 3.7 Sequence of displacements.

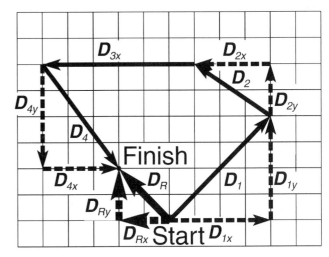

Figure 3.8 Representing displacements with their components.

Each of the vectors can be replaced by its components within the coordinate framework (see Figure 3.8):

  x-components produce movement only in the
    x-direction.
  y-components produce movement only in the
    y-direction.

Thus, only the *x*-components of the vectors can contribute to the *x*-component of the resultant vector, and only the *y*-components of the vectors can contribute to the *y*-component of the resultant vector. That is:

$$D_{Rx} = D_{1x} + D_{2x} + D_{3x} + D_{4x}$$
$$D_{Ry} = D_{1y} + D_{2y} + D_{3y} + D_{4y}$$

[3.5]

Adding vectors that all have the same direction is equivalent to adding real numbers. Therefore, we can write

$$D_{Rx} = D_{1x} + D_{2x} + D_{3x} + D_{4x}$$
$$D_{Ry} = D_{1y} + D_{2y} + D_{3y} + D_{4y}$$

[3.6]

where D_{1x}, D_{2x}, D_{3x}, D_{4x}, D_{1y}, D_{2y}, D_{3y}, and D_{4y} are scalars with an associated sign indicating direction along the appropriate line. The sign convention used in this book is as shown in Figure 3.9.

Thus, the diagram in Figure 3.10 is expressed mathematically as:

$$D_{Rx} = D_{1x} + D_{2x} + D_{3x} + D_{4x}$$
$$= 4 - 3 - 6 + 3 = -2$$
$$D_{Ry} = D_{1y} + D_{2y} + D_{3y} + D_{4y}$$
$$= 4 + 2 + 0 - 4 = 2$$

[3.7]

Through components, we see that the commutative nature of the addition of real numbers implies the commutative nature of the addition of vectors.

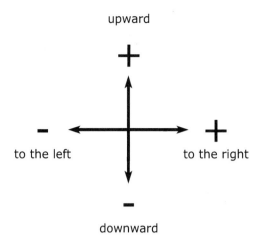

Figure 3.9 Sign convention.

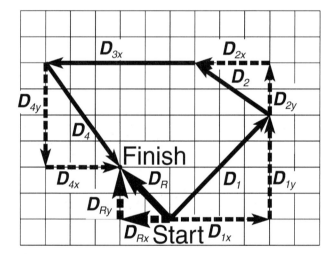

Figure 3.10 Vector representation of displacements.

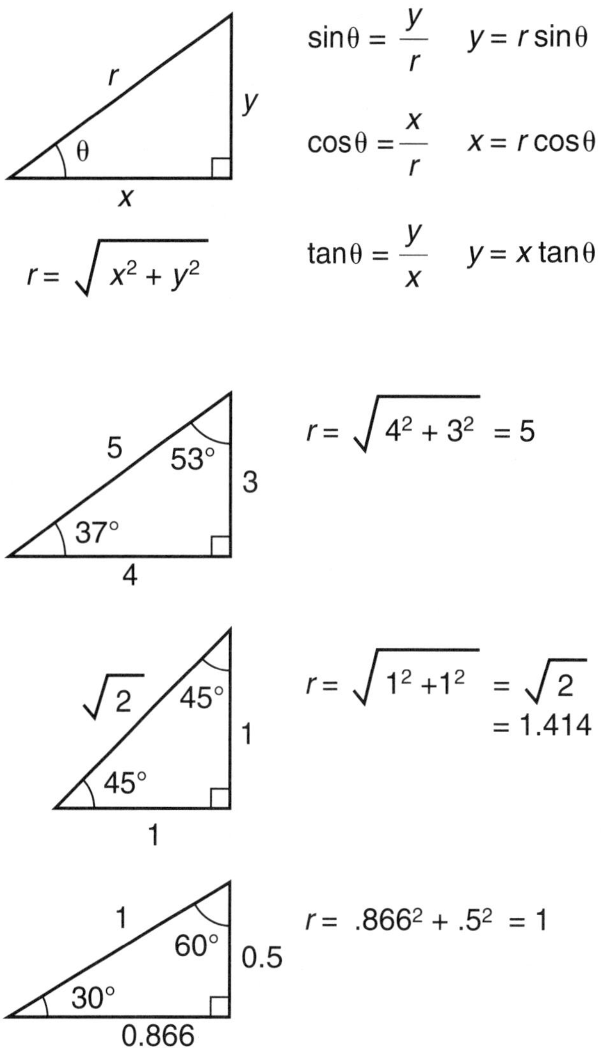

$$\sin\theta = \frac{y}{r} \qquad y = r\sin\theta$$

$$\cos\theta = \frac{x}{r} \qquad x = r\cos\theta$$

$$r = \sqrt{x^2 + y^2}$$

$$\tan\theta = \frac{y}{x} \qquad y = x\tan\theta$$

$$r = \sqrt{4^2 + 3^2} = 5$$

$$r = \sqrt{1^2 + 1^2} = \sqrt{2} = 1.414$$

$$r = \sqrt{.866^2 + .5^2} = 1$$

Figure 3.11 Trigonometry formulas and common triangles.

The use of components, plus a calculator, allows both greater precision and greater speed than the graphic solution method, which involves carefully drawing scaled arrows tip-to-tail. (It substitutes the more complex component formulation for the more difficult angle-magnitude formulation.)

In the course of resolving forces into components, some simple trigonometry formulas and special triangles will be used (see Figure 3.11).

A force is a push or a pull. Force is a vector quantity and is subject to the same rules of addition as all other vectors. Note that in the definition of addition of vectors, the only relevant factors are magnitude, direction, and sense. In terms of addition, the point of application of the force is irrelevant. Forces can be picked up and moved to serve the convenience of the process of addition. For example, they can be arranged in a tip-to-tail sequence to graphically generate the resultant force. At no time in

the process is information about the original location of the forces ever utilized.

Intuition and experience suggest that the point of application of the force can be very significant. For example, consider a flywheel constrained to rotate about an axle, as shown in Figure 3.12.

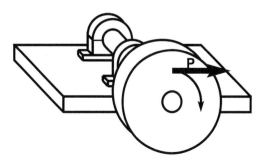

Figure 3.12 Flywheel with force applied.

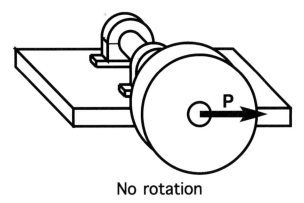

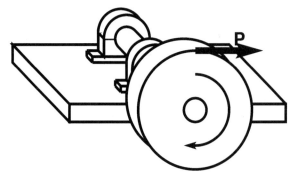

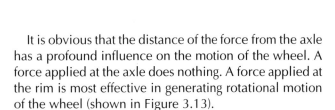

No rotation

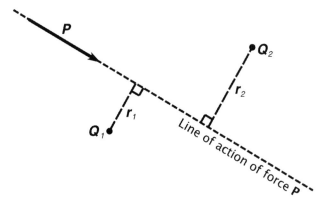

Maximum tendency to rotate

Figure 3.13 Different locations for the force.

It is obvious that the distance of the force from the axle has a profound influence on the motion of the wheel. A force applied at the axle does nothing. A force applied at the rim is most effective in generating rotational motion of the wheel (shown in Figure 3.13).

The question is, *How effective is the definition of addition used here, which ignores this position effect?* The answer is that addition, as defined here, is a valid and very useful tool, but it is not adequate by itself to describe all the phenomena to be dealt with.

Moment

The missing element in the current picture is called the *moment of the force.* A moment and a torque are conceptually similar and mathematically identical. It is customary to use the term *torque* when describing the behavior of objects constrained to move about a fixed axis of rotation, such as the flywheel in an engine, and to use the term *moment* to describe rotational influences involved in architectural structures, where the entire structure is fully constrained not to rotate about any axis.

Consider a force *P*, as shown in Figure 3.14.

P has a moment with respect to every point in the universe. In particular, two points, Q_1 and Q_2, have been identified for purposes of illustrating the process, as shown in Figure 3.15.

As the first step in the process, extend the line of action of *P* however far is necessary to allow the construction of two lines, both perpendicular to that line of action, one of which ends at Q_1 and the other of which ends at Q_2.

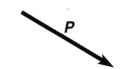

Figure 3.14 A force *P*.

Figure 3.15 Location of force relative to two points.

The moment of **P** about Q_1 is defined to be:

$$M_{P \text{ about } Q_1} = Pr_1 \qquad [3.8]$$

The moment of *P* about Q_2 is defined to be:

$$M_{P \text{ about } Q_2} = -Pr_2 \qquad [3.9]$$

To completely specify a moment requires the magnitude of the force, the location of the line of action of the force, and the location of the point about which the moment is to be calculated. Selecting the point about which moments are to be calculated depends on circumstances to be discussed later.

The preceding definition indicates the sign convention that will be used throughout this book, which is illustrated in Figure 3.16.

Clockwise (CW) and counterclockwise (CCW) moments tend to annihilate each other in the same manner as positive and negative numbers annihilate each other. In fact, the manipulation of moments (as dealt with here) boils down to the mathematics of real numbers. This is so because this discussion will deal only with planar sys-

A moment that tends to produce counterclockwise motion about the point shall be called *negative*.

A moment that tends to produce clockwise motion about the point shall be called *positive*.

CCW (neg)

CW (pos)

Figure 3.16 Sign convention for moments.

tems of forces that produce rotation only about one axial direction (that direction being perpendicular to the plane of the forces). Later, this simple treatment will be put in the context of a more general system.

Example:

Suppose you want to find the moment of *P* about Q (see Figure 3.17).

Extend the line of action of *P* and construct the perpendicular line that terminates on Q:

$$M_{P \text{ about} Q_1} = +Pr = +5\#r \qquad [3.10]$$

At this point, you do not know *r* or the point where the line of action and the perpendicular line intersect.

You need to find a right triangle relating Q to the line of action and about which you have sufficient information to define it completely. The various mathematical steps in this process are illustrated in Figure 3.18. The steps are as follows:

Draw a point B at coordinates (11,1).

Extend the line of action of the force out to point C, which has an *x*-coordinate of 11.

Determine that the vertical distance between B and C is 9 ft · tan37° = 9 ft (¾) = 6.75 ft.

Note that the vertical distance between Q and B is 1, so the vertical distance between Q and C is 6.75 ft – 1 ft = 5.75 ft.

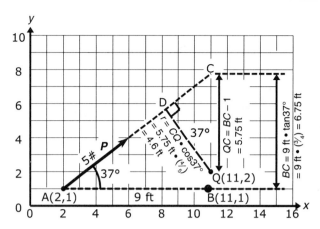

Figure 3.18 Resolving triangles and distances.

Note the similarity of triangle QDC to triangle ABC, which means that QDC is also a 3-4-5 right triangle.

The last point implies that r = CQ · cos37° = 5.75 (⅘) = 4.6 ft.

Calculate

$$M_{P \text{ about} Q} = (5\#)(4.6 \text{ ft}) = 23 \text{ ft\#} \qquad [3.11]$$

As in the case of the addition of vectors, using components can make the calculation of moments much less cumbersome and more orderly. To illustrate the point, the 5# force can be resolved into its components, leading to the diagram in Figure 3.19.

$$M_{P \text{ about} Q} = (3\#)(9 \text{ ft}) - (4\#)(1 \text{ ft}) = 23 \text{ ft\#} \qquad [3.12]$$

which demonstrates that the moment of a force about a point can be gotten by adding together the moments of the components of the force.

Note that, in this case, the component vectors (3# and 4#) have been located with their initial points at the initial point of the original vector (5#) rather than in the tip-to-tail configuration. Because the moment of a force is sensitive to the exact position of the line of action of the force, the initial point of the force has to be left where the

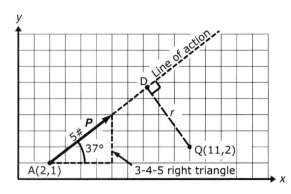

Figure 3.17 A 5 lb force producing a moment about point Q.

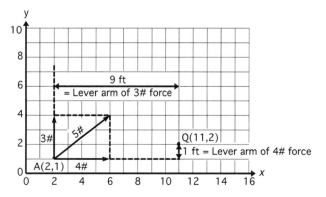

Figure 3.19 Calculating moments caused by the components of the force.

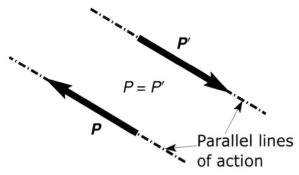

Figure 3.20 Force couple.

$$M_{C\ \text{about}\,Q} = M_{P\ \text{about}\,Q} + M_{P'\ \text{about}\,Q}$$

$$= P(r+L) - P'(r) = P(r+L) - P(r)$$

$$= Pr + PL - Pr$$

$$= +PL \qquad\qquad\qquad \textbf{[3.13]}$$

force is applied, rather than be moved around. The same rule applies to the components of the force if one intends to use the components to calculate the moment of the force. Forces can still be moved around for purposes of addition of forces, but not for purposes of calculating moments of forces. Forces can be slid along their lines of action without disturbing the moments, but they cannot be slid laterally—that is, off their lines of action.

Couples

A pair of equal but opposite forces is called a *force couple*, or simply a *couple* (see Figure 3.20).

The magnitude of **P** equals the magnitude of P', that is, P = P'.

A couple is a pure moment, in the sense that the two forces add to zero. In other words, there is no tendency for the object to which the couple is applied to translate, only a tendency to rotate under the influence of the couple.

To find the net moment of the force couple about a point Q, a line is constructed from the point Q to the lines of action, intersecting both lines of action at right angles (see Figure 3.21).

The plus sign indicates that the net effect of the couple is to cause clockwise rotation.

Notice that the term *r* has completely disappeared from the final formula. This means that *r* is irrelevant. However, *r* was the only quantity that provided a clue to where Q was located relative to the couple. Therefore, the location of the point Q is irrelevant to the value of the moment, or, putting it another way, the couple has the same moment about every point in the plane.

In summary, the magnitude of the moment of a couple is the product of the magnitude of one of the forces times the perpendicular distance between the lines of action of the two forces, for any and all points anywhere in the plane. This is a very powerful computational simplification that motivates one to group as many forces as possible into couples before commencing with calculating moments. In that sense, couples play a role in moments similar to the role of components in both vector addition and moment calculations.

3.2 Equilibrium

According to the laws of mechanics, any motion of any body can be described in terms of a combination of a translation (i.e., a movement in some direction) and a rotation about some axis.

Translational motion is described by Newton's second law, which states that a body subjected to a force **F** will accelerate in the direction of the force with an acceleration proportional to the force and inversely proportional to the mass of the object. In the shorthand of mathematics, this law is expressed by:

$$\textbf{F} = m\textbf{a}$$

This is a vector equation, with force and acceleration being vector quantities and mass being a scalar (i.e., it has magnitude but no direction). In this equation, vector quantities are expressed in bold type. The force in this equation is the resultant (sum) of all external forces on the object. Internal forces within the object will not cause it to accelerate. To make this all explicit, the equation might be rewritten as:

$$\Sigma \textbf{F}_{external} = m\textbf{a}$$

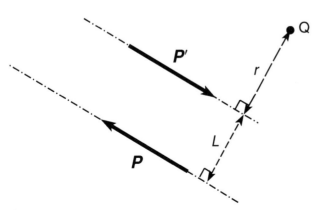

Figure 3.21 Location of force couple relative to point Q.

where the expression to the left of the equals sign is mathematical shorthand for "the sum of all the external forces on the object."

For historical reasons, architects and structural engineers have used the letter "F" to designate stress, rather than force, so the preceding equation must be rewritten using the letter "P" for force (as in Point force):

$$\Sigma P_{external} = m\mathbf{a}$$

The importance of the fact that these forces are external and not internal to the object cannot be overemphasized. Forces internal to the object in question are not part of the equation, and including them will always lead to an incorrect answer.

Rotational motion can be described by the rotational analog of Newton's first law. This rotational law states that a body subjected to an external torque τ will undergo a rotational (angular) acceleration α in the direction of the torque with a rotational acceleration proportional to the torque and inversely proportional to the rotational moment-of-inertia I of the object. In the shorthand of mathematics, this law is expressed by:

$$\Sigma\tau_{external} = I\alpha$$

Torque and acceleration are both vectors in this equation. The line of action of these vectors is the axis of rotation. By convention, the sense of these two vectors is defined to be the direction of the thumb on the right hand when the curled fingers of the right hand are pointing in the direction in which the torque is tending to produce rotational motion.

Civil engineers and architects use the word *moment,* rather than *torque,* so the preceding equation becomes:

$$\Sigma M_{external} = I\alpha$$

An object is said to be in equilibrium if it is not undergoing either translational or rotational acceleration:

$$\mathbf{a} = 0$$

$$\alpha = 0$$

Newton's first law implies that for an object to be in equilibrium, the sum of the external forces and the sum of the external torques must both be zero:

$$\Sigma P_{external} = 0$$

$$\Sigma M_{external} = 0$$

These are the generalized conditions of equilibrium.
$\Sigma P_{external}$ is equivalent to a single force, which is called the resultant P_R.

Hence, the equation

$$\Sigma P_{external} = 0$$

is equivalent to

$$P_R = 0$$

In order for a vector to be zero, all of its components must be zero. Hence:

$$P_{Rx} = 0$$

$$P_{Ry} = 0$$

$$P_{Rz} = 0$$

As demonstrated earlier, the x-component of the resultant is equal to the sum of the x-components of the vectors that sum together to produce the resultant:

$$P_{Rx} = P_{1x} + P_{2x} + P_{3x} + \dots + P_{nx}$$

$$P_{Ry} = P_{1y} + P_{2y} + P_{3y} + \dots + P_{ny}$$

$$P_{Rz} = P_{1z} + P_{2z} + P_{3z} + \dots + P_{nz}$$

Hence, if an object is in equilibrium:

$$0 = P_{1x} + P_{2x} + P_{3x} + \dots + P_{nx}$$

$$0 = P_{1y} + P_{2y} + P_{3y} + \dots + P_{ny}$$

$$0 = P_{1z} + P_{2z} + P_{3z} + \dots + P_{nz}$$

That is:

- The sum of the x-components of all the external forces must be zero.
- The sum of the y-components of all the external forces must be zero.
- The sum of the z-components of all the external forces must be zero.

Similarly, for rotational motion:

$$\Sigma M_{external} = 0$$

implies that

$$M_R = 0,$$

which implies that

$$M_{Rx} = 0$$

$$M_{Ry} = 0$$

$$M_{Rz} = 0,$$

which implies that

$$0 = M_{1x} + M_{2x} + M_{3x} + \dots + M_{nx}$$

$$0 = M_{1y} + M_{2y} + M_{3y} + \dots + M_{ny}$$

$$0 = M_{1z} + M_{2z} + M_{3z} + \dots + M_{nz}$$

That is:

- The sum of the x-components of all the external moments must be zero.
- The sum of the y-components of all the external moments must be zero.
- The sum of the z-components of all the external moments must be zero.

This text will deal predominantly with planar force systems, that is, with forces within the xy-plane. There are no z-forces within the xy-plane. Therefore, the equation

$$0 = P_{1z} + P_{2z} + P_{3z} + \ldots + P_{nz}$$

can be ignored because all the terms in this equation are zero.

Furthermore, forces within the xy-plane cannot produce moments about either the x-axis or the y-axis. Therefore, there will be no x-moments or y-moments, and the equations

$$0 = M_{1x} + M_{2x} + M_{3x} + \ldots + M_{nx}$$
$$0 = M_{1y} + M_{2y} + M_{3y} + \ldots + M_{ny}$$

can be ignored because all the terms in these equations are zero.

Hence, the meaningful equations of equilibrium are reduced to the following three equations:

$0 = P_{1x} + P_{2x} + P_{3x} + \ldots + P_{nx}$, which describes x-forces

$0 = P_{1y} + P_{2y} + P_{3y} + \ldots + P_{ny}$, which describes y-forces

$0 = M_{1z} + M_{2z} + M_{3z} + \ldots + M_{nz}$, which describes z-forces

For simplicity, this reduced set of equations of equilibrium is often written in the form:

$$\Sigma P_x = 0$$
$$\Sigma P_y = 0$$
$$\Sigma M_z = 0$$

The z is often left off the last equation because it is understood that the only moments generated by forces in the xy-plane are z-moments. This leads to the following reduced set of equations:

$\Sigma P_x = 0$ x-forces

$\Sigma P_y = 0$ y-forces

$\Sigma M = 0$ z-moments

Typically, a structure will be subjected to a set of forces called *applied forces* (such as wind and snow). To remain stable, the structure will be supported at one or more points by the ground or by some other stable structure. The forces exerted on the structure by its supports are called *reactive forces,* or *reactions* because they are activated in response to the applied forces.

Typically, either the applied forces are known or an intelligent estimate can be made of their magnitudes and directions. Once the applied forces are specified, the process of analyzing the structure can be initiated by using the equations of equilibrium to solve for the reactions.

The reduced set of three equations of equilibrium can be used to solve for up to three unknown reactions stabilizing an object.

The equation

$$\Sigma P_x = 0$$

can be used to solve only for x-forces because only x-forces would appear in this equation.

The equation

$$\Sigma P_y = 0$$

can be used to solve only for y-forces because only y-forces would appear in this equation.

The equation

$$\Sigma M = 0$$

can be used to solve for both x-forces and y-forces because both x-forces and y-forces can create moments about the z-axis, and, therefore, both x-forces and y-forces could appear in the z-moment equation. It may also be used to solve for any unknown moment.

Depending on the nature of the support system, these equations can be used to solve for any of the following combinations:

One x-force and two y-forces
Two x-forces and one y-force
One x-force, one y-force, and one moment

It is *not* possible to use this set of equations to solve for three y-forces because only two equations can be used to solve for y-forces, and three y-forces exceeds by one the number of unknowns that can be determined based on two equations. Additional information, in the form of another equation, must be generated to solve for the third y-force. By similar reasoning, it is not possible to use the preceding equations to solve for three x-forces.

Supports/Restraints

Supports are classified as one of three types, according to the number of degrees of constraint provided by the support on the structure being supported.

Support Type 1: Roller Joints

A support that provides a reactive force in a single specified direction is called a *roller joint* and is represented by the symbols shown in Figure 3.22.

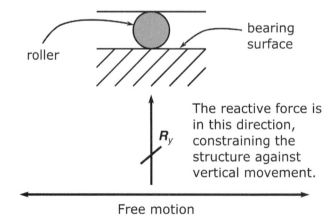

Figure 3.22 A roller joint capable of exerting a vertical force.

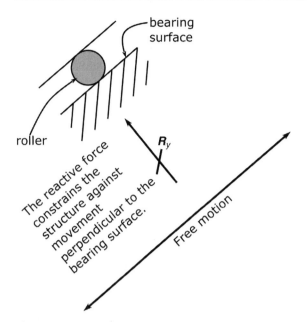

Figure 3.23 A roller joint capable of exerting a force perpendicular to a sloped bearing surface.

These symbols can be rotated to indicate a constraint in some other direction, as shown in Figure 3.23.

A roller joint may be either literal or figurative. For example, in a bridge structure in which the supports are an-chored to the ground, the supports move very little as compared with the thermal expansion exhibited by the spanning bridge that is thermally removed from the stabilizing thermal mass of the earth. (Remember the old rule of thumb that bridges always freeze first.) In such situations, the supports must be generous in accommodating movement caused by the thermal expansion and contraction of the bridge (see Figure 3.24).

The effect of a roller joint can be fairly closely simulated with a slotted bolt connection; see Figure 3.25. The hold-down nut at the slotted bolt hole is not tightened down against the flange of the I-beam, so that no more friction than necessary is acting to resist the movement of the beam. The locking out is used to keep the hold-down nut from moving.

The freedom of movement of a roller joint can sometimes be approximated by the inherent flexibility in the support structure, making either a roller joint or slotted connection unnecessary. For example, the design for an equestrian center, shown in Figure 3.26, involves glulam arches with steel-tie rods, supported at the ends by columns that are moment-connected to foundation-grade beams. The inherent flexibility of the columns will account for spreading of the arch structure due either to thermal expansion or to snow loads settling on the roof.

However, adding stringers to support stands may stiffen the columns to the point that they will not accommodate

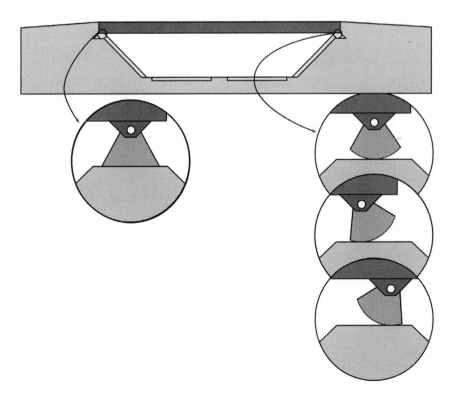

Figure 3.24 Classic rocker joint, which is a variant of a roller joint.

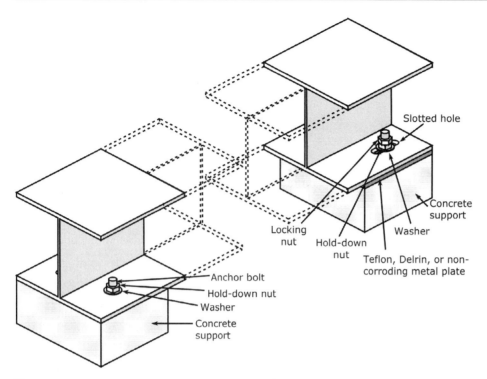

Figure 3.25 Approximations to pin joint (left) and to roller joint (right).

the required movement. The situation shown in Figure 3.27 is an example where the rigidity of the support structure will probably not accommodate changes in the length of the spanning system, and a slotted connection at one end of the arches would be appropriate. Stringers supporting the stands restrain the column at the connection point near the top of the column, preventing the outward movement of the column. Since the tie rod will stretch under the influence of the outward thrust of the arch, the rigidity of the support structure causes that structure to pick up a significant part of the force from the arch. Bending moment and shear force induced in the segment of column above the connection point could threaten the column.

Support Type 2: Pin Joints

A support that can provide a reactive force of any magnitude and direction required for stability of a structure is called a *pin joint* and is represented by the symbol shown in Figure 3.28.

The pin joint constrains the point of connection on the structure against translation in any direction by supplying a force of the required magnitude and direction (see Figure 3.29).

Like any other force, this reaction can be expressed in terms of its components, and, in setting up the problem, it is useful to depict this force in terms of its components immediately, thereby clearly indicating that there are two unknowns; those unknowns are the *x*-component of the

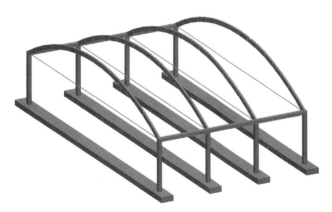

Figure 3.26 Tied arches on flexible columns.

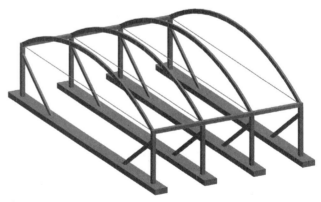

Figure 3.27 Tied arches on top of restrained columns.

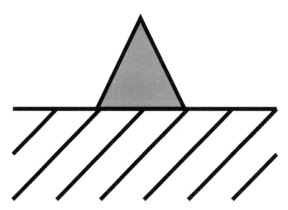

Figure 3.28 Symbol for a pin joint.

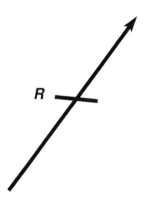

Figure 3.29 Reactive force from pin joint, which can be in any direction.

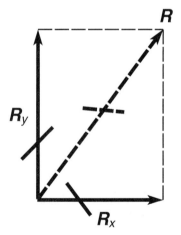

Figure 3.30 Horizontal reactive components can assume any value, independent of each other.

reaction and the *y*-component of the reaction (see Figure 3.30).

These two unknowns can vary independently of each other because the nature of the applied forces will determine the required size of the *x*-component and the re-

quired size of the *y*-component that will be necessary to keep the structure in equilibrium.

A pin joint may be either literal or figurative. An example of a literal pin joint is illustrated in Figure 3.31, which shows two beams meeting over the same support. The two beams are supporting portions of the same overpass. The end of the beam on the left is supported by a pivot rod that is supported by a rocker assembly, which allows both rotation and horizontal movement at the end of that beam. The end of the beam on the right is supported by a pivot rod that is supported by a tapered block that is bolted to the top of the column. The pivot rod allows rotation of the end of the beam, but the bolted block will not allow horizontal movement. The pin joint not only keeps the end of the bridge from falling under gravity forces, but also provides stabilization against horizontal forces, such as braking vehicles. (The horizontal force of a convoy of trucks slamming on the brakes can be very large.) The pin joint also pins down the structure and prevents it from "walking" off its supports as a result of many cycles of thermal expansion and contraction. Because the support of the beam on the left is a roller joint and the support of the beam on the right is a pin joint, the ends of the two beams can move back and forth relative to each other. To accommodate this motion, there is an expansion joint in the roadbed, between the ends of the two beams.

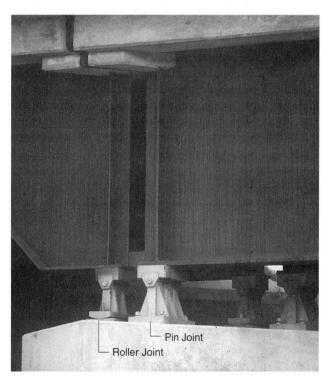

Figure 3.31 Roller joint and pin joint.

An example of a more figurative pin joint is a wide-flange beam, which can be bolted down to a support, as shown in the left connection in Figure 3.25. The hole in the flange is not made any larger than necessary to accommodate assembly of the structure. (To ensure that the structure can be assembled, the holes and anchor bolts must be precisely placed and must be slightly larger in diameter than the bolts.) The hold-down nut is tightened down against the flange of the I-beam to prevent any movement of the bolt in the hole and to utilize friction to reduce the shearing force on the bolt. This joint tends to inhibit rotational motion, and, therefore, its action goes somewhat beyond that of a true pin joint, which would allow completely free rotation at the point of support. However, the flange of the beam tends to be quite flexible under slight changes in the angle of the end of the beam, and, therefore, this connection approximates a pin joint very well for situations where only slight rotation would occur (e.g., for simply supported beams). Another example of a joint that approximates a pin joint is shown in Figure 3.32. The beam on the left is very deep and very stiff, so it will not tend to rotate very much at the end. The fin supporting the end of the beam utilizes four closely spaced bolts. The bolt holes are slightly oversized to facilitate assembly. The combination of the close spacing of the bolts and the oversized holes allows for enough play in the connection that no moment is generated by the bolts. There will be a slight moment resulting from friction between the beam web and the fin, induced by the snug tightening of the bolts. However, that moment will be negligible as compared with the moment-generating capacity of the beam itself.

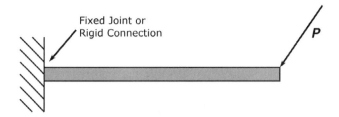

Figure 3.33 Cantilever beam.

Support Type 3: Fixed Joints (also called Rigid Connections)

A support that can provide:

- A reactive force in any direction required for stability of a structure, and
- A reactive pure moment of any magnitude and direction required for stability of the structure

is called a *fixed joint* (or *rigid connection*) and is represented by the symbol shown in Figure 3.33.

The fixed joint constrains the point of connection on the structure against translation in any direction, by supplying a force of the required magnitude and direction, and against rotation about the point of connection, by supplying a pure moment of the required magnitude and direction. The effect of the support structure can be represented by two force components and a curly arrow representing the direction of the constraining moment; see Figure 3.34.

These three unknowns can vary independently of each other because the nature of the applied forces will determine for each of the reactions the magnitude and direction that will be required to keep the structure in equilibrium. Examples of good moment connections are shown in Figure 3.35. In Figure 3.35(a), the beams have been attached to the column using bolted webs for shear capacity and welded flanges for moment capacity. In Figure 3.35(b), the thick joint at the top of the tapered column is an excellent moment connection. In comparison, the thin joint at the base of the column, with two small, closely spaced bolts, will generate negligible moment. In the context of this structure, the connection at the base would be regarded as a pin joint.

Figure 3.32 Effective pin joint in bolt connection.

Figure 3.34 Cantilever beam reactions.

(a)

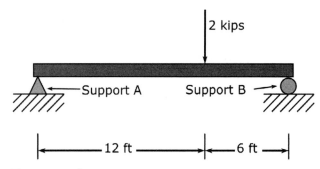

Figure 3.36 Simple-span beam with a point load.

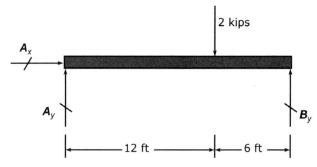

Figure 3.37 Reactive forces on simple-span beam.

Then the equations of equilibrium are applied:

$\Sigma P_x = 0$ As a convention, forces to the right are positive.

$\Sigma P_y = 0$ As a convention, upward forces are positive.

$\Sigma M = 0$ As a convention, clockwise moments are positive.

Applying the equation for the horizontal forces:

$$\sum P_x = 0 \pm_{\rightarrow} \quad \text{yields } A_x = 0$$

Applying the equation for the vertical forces:

$$\sum P_y = 0 \uparrow + \quad \text{yields } A_y + B_y - 2 \text{ kips} = 0$$

This does not allow one to immediately solve for one of the unknowns because it is a single equation with two unknowns. However, it does provide information regarding a relationship between the two remaining unknowns.

Applying the moment equation about the support point A

$$\sum M = 0 \;\widehat{+} \quad \text{yields } 2 \text{ kips} (12 \text{ ft}) - B_y (18 \text{ ft}) = 0,$$

which solves to give:

$$B_y = \frac{2 \text{ kips} (12 \text{ ft})}{(18 \text{ ft})} = 1.33 \text{ kips}$$

(b)

Figure 3.35 (a, b) Examples of good moment connections.

Example Problem 1

Find the reactions for the beam shown in Figure 3.36.

First, the supports are "interpreted" by replacing them with the forces or moments they can exert on the beam (Figure 3.37).

Now the value for B_y can be used in the equation for the sum of the vertical forces to get C

$A_y + B_y - 2$ kips $= 0$ becomes
$A_y + 1.33$ kips $- 2$ kips $= 0$,

which solves to $A_y = 0.67$ kips

To check the value for A_y, one can solve for A_y again using the moment equation, with moments taken about support point B

$$\sum M = 0 \curvearrowright \text{ yields } A_y (18 \text{ ft}) - 2 \text{ kips} (6 \text{ ft}) = 0$$

which solves to give $A_y = 0.67$ kips.

Example Problem 2

Find the reactions for the following beam in Figure 3.38.

$$w = \frac{1.5 \text{ kips}}{\text{ft}}$$

First, "interpret" the supports by replacing them with the forces or moments they can exert on the beam (see Figure 3.39).

Next, "interpret" the distributed force (with regard to its meaning in the context of concerns about equilibrium); see Figure 3.40. Knowledge of the precise distribution of pressure on the exterior surface of an object is required if the goal is to determine the precise distribution of stress within the object. However, from the point of view of

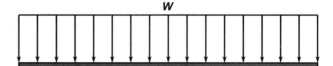

Figure 3.40 Uniformly distributed force.

equilibrium, it is *not* essential that all the details of the pressure distribution on the exterior surface of the object be addressed.

At this early stage of the analysis process, one can accurately deal with equilibrium by "distilling" the pressure distribution down to an equivalent force:

- The magnitude of the equivalent force is the net force associated with the pressure distribution, and
- The line of action of the equivalent force is the effective center of action of the pressure distribution.

The equivalent force can be understood in terms of its equilibrant. Consider a ruler (e.g., a meter stick). The force of gravity acts throughout the volume of the ruler. Because the ruler is quite small in two of its dimensions, the force of gravity will be depicted as a line force, rather than a volumetrically distributed force. For this distributed force, there exists only one "effective" center of action. One can understand immediately where that center is located by asking the question, *Where along the ruler would we place an upward force to equilibrate the ruler?* The answer, obviously, is in the center (see Figure 3.41).

From the point of view of equilibrium, the distributed line force w is equivalent to a single downward force at the center of the ruler, as shown in Figure 3.42.

Hence, from the point of view of applying the principles of equilibrium, any distributed force (i.e., real force) can be replaced by its equivalent point force. Once this substitution has been made, applying the principles of equilibrium to solve for the reactions is drastically simplified. (The equivalent force is easiest to find if the pres-

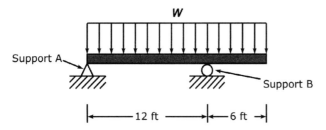

Figure 3.38 Continuous cantilever beam with two supports.

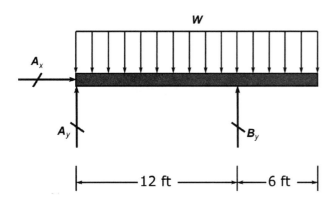

Figure 3.39 Reactive forces on cantilever beam.

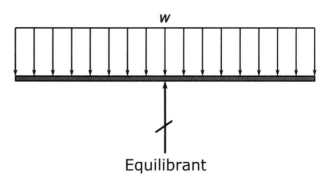

Figure 3.41 Equilibrant to a distributed force.

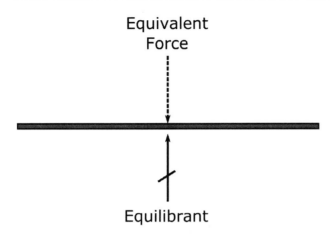

Figure 3.42 Localized equivalent to a distributed force.

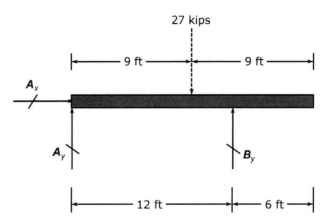

Figure 3.44 Replacing distributed force with localized equivalent force.

sure distribution is uniform, but it can be found for any pressure distribution.)

Returning to the problem to be solved, see Figure 3.43. The distributed force is replaced by its equivalent force (see Figure 3.44):

$$\text{Equivalent force} = wL = \frac{1.5 \text{ kips} \cdot 18 \text{ ft}}{\text{ft}} = \text{kips}$$

Then one begins applying the equations of equilibrium:

$$\sum P_x = 0 \pm_{\rightarrow}$$

$$\sum P_y = 0 \uparrow+$$

$$\sum M = 0 \; \stackrel{+}{\curvearrowright}$$

Previous conventions apply, as indicated by the symbols at the ends of the preceding equations.

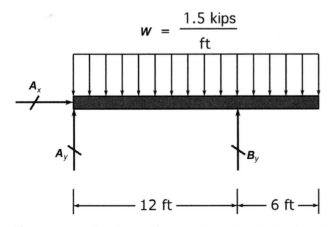

Figure 3.43 Cantilevered beam under uniformly distributed force.

Applying the equation for the horizontal forces:

$$\sum P_x = 0 \pm_{\rightarrow} \quad \text{yields } A_x = 0$$

There are two unknown y-forces. Previous experience indicates that writing out the equation for the y-forces will simply relate A_y to B_y. Rather than go through that relatively unsatisfying process, go directly to a moment equation that will eliminate one of the unknowns. Applying the moment equation about the support point A will eliminate A_y from the equation (since it will be multiplied by a zero lever arm) and allow solving for B_y directly

$$\sum M = 0 \; \stackrel{+}{\curvearrowright} \text{ yields } 27 \text{ kips (9 ft)} - B_y(12 \text{ ft}) = 0,$$

which solves to give $B_y = \dfrac{27 \text{ kips (9 ft)}}{(12 \text{ ft})} = 20.25 \text{ kips}$

Similarly, applying the moment equation about the support point B will eliminate B_y from the equation (since it will be multiplied by a zero lever arm) and allow solving for A_y directly

$$\sum M = 0 \; \stackrel{+}{\curvearrowright} \text{ yields } A_y(12 \text{ ft}) - 27 \text{ kips (3 ft)} = 0,$$

which solves to give $A_y = \dfrac{27 \text{ kips (3 ft)}}{(12 \text{ ft})} = 6.75 \text{ kips}$

Checking the values for A_y and B_y involves substituting them in the equation for the sum of the vertical forces:

$$\sum P_y = 0 \uparrow+ \text{ yields } A_y + B_y - 27 \text{ kips}$$

$$= 6.75 \text{ kips} + 20.25 \text{ kips} - 27 \text{ kips} = 0 \text{ kips}$$

Note that the equivalent force of 27 kips was generated for the entire distributed force over the full length of the beam and, therefore, applies only to dealing with the equilibrium equations for the full beam. Any freebody

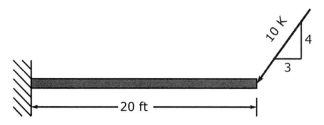

Figure 3.45 Cantilevered beam with point force at the end.

generated from some part of the beam would require that the equivalent force be recalculated.

Example Problem 3

Find the reactions for the beam in Figure 3.45.
As a first step:

- Resolve the 10 K applied force into its components.
- Replace the support by the forces and moment that it exerts on the beam (see Figure 3.46).

All of the reactions (i.e., the two reactive forces and the reactive moment) have been drawn in the directions conventionally designated as positive. This is an assumption that can be made without thinking. The machinery of the mathematics will tell whether or not these assumptions are correct. For example, simple inspection will reveal that M must be in the opposite direction shown to maintain equilibrium. However, there is no need to be concerned about that at this point in working the problem. The fact that one can make an arbitrary assumption and rely on the mathematics to tell whether it was correct is fortunate, inasmuch as there will be many complex structural situations in which determining the actual direction of a force a moment by simple inspection will be impossible. The way one is going about the problem to this point is exactly the way that any computer program would solve it.

Next, begin applying the equations of equilibrium:

$$\sum P_x = 0 \pm_{\rightarrow}$$

$$\sum P_y = 0 \uparrow +$$

$$\sum M = 0 \,\curvearrowright$$

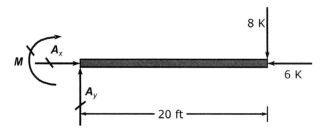

Figure 3.46 Resolving applied force into its components.

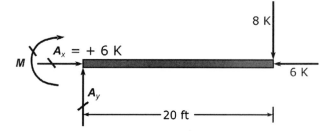

Figure 3.47 Resolved horizontal reaction.

Applying the equation for the horizontal forces,

$$\sum P_x = 0 \pm_{\rightarrow} \text{ yields } A_x - 6\,K = 0,$$

which solves to give $A_x = +6$ K.
The *plus* sign means, *Yes, the original direction assumed for* A_x *was correct; that is, the actual force is to the right.*
With this new piece of information, the diagram now looks like that in Figure 3.47.
Applying the equation for the vertical forces,

$$\sum P_y = 0 \uparrow +, \text{ yields } A_y - 8\,K = 0,$$

which solves to give $A_x = +8$ K
The plus sign means, Yes, the original direction assumed for A_y *was correct; that is, the actual force is upward.*
With this new piece of information, the diagram now looks like that in Figure 3.48.
Summing the moments about the point of support,

$$\sum M = 0 \,\curvearrowright \text{ yields } M + 8\,K(20\,\text{ft}) = 0,$$

which solves to give $M = -160$ K ft.
The *minus* sign means, *No, the original direction assumed for* M *was wrong; that is, the actual moment is counterclockwise, rather than the clockwise direction assumed in the original drawing.*

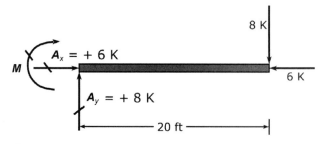

Figure 3.48 Resolved vertical reaction.

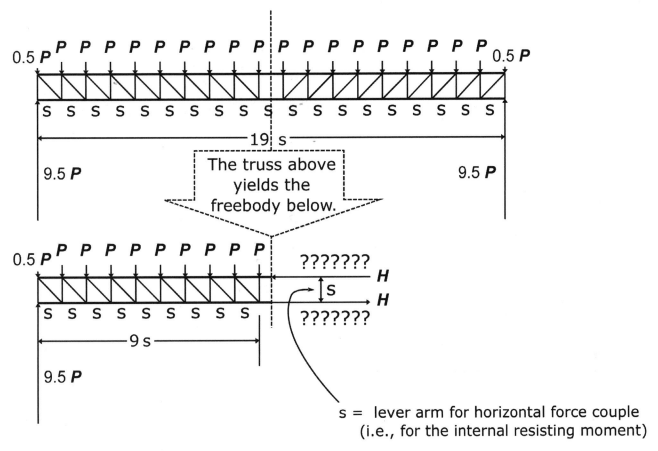

Figure 3.49 Creating a freebody by slicing through the center of the nineteen-bay truss.

3.3 Internal Resisting Moments of Spanning Members

Example 1

Using principles of equilibrium applied to a freebody to understand the forces of the internal resisting moment in a 19-bay parallel-chord truss.

Method: Clustering forces to produce two equal and opposite pure couples (see Figure 3.49).

Question: How big (i.e., how long) are the arrows representing the H forces if a single P force is drawn at $1/8$ in.?

Step 1: Replace the nine 1 P forces with a single 9 P force at the center of action of the original nine 1 P forces (see Figure 3.50).

Step 2: Add the 0.5 P downward force to the 9.5 P upward force, group the vertical forces into a pure couple (see Figure 3.51).

Step 3: Find H by setting the moment of the vertical forces equal to the moment of the horizontal forces.

The magnitude of the moment of the vertical 9 P forces is $9 P \times 5 s = 45 Ps$.

The moment of the horizontal H forces is Hs.

The moment of the horizontal H forces must be equal in magnitude to the moment of the vertical forces. Hence, $Hs = 45 Ps$. Hence, $H = 45 P$.

H is larger than the total downward force on the top of the truss by the factor $45 P/19 P = 2.37$, which indicates that spanning with such a shallow truss causes the verti-

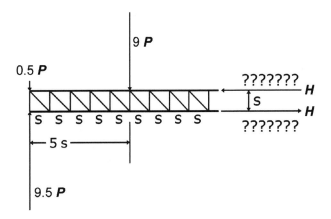

Figure 3.50 Clustering the nine 1 P applied forces into a 9 P force.

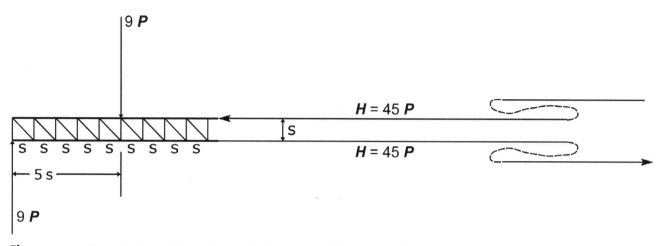

Figure 3.51 Clustering the end forces into a single, upward 9 *P* force, and solving for H.

cal load to be amplified in the form of horizontal forces in the resisting moment—and there are two members subjected to this large horizontal force (see Figure 3.51).

Example 2

Using principles of equilibrium applied to a freebody to understand the forces of the internal resisting moment in a twenty-bay parallel-chord truss (see Figure 3.52).

Method: Taking moments about selected points.

For a uniformly loaded, simple-span truss, the most severe chord forces occur at the center of the truss. The method of sections allows us to go directly to the center of the truss to determine the critical chord forces. To start the process with the truss shown in Figure 3.52, slice through bay 10 and use the left portion as a freebody (see Figure 3.53).

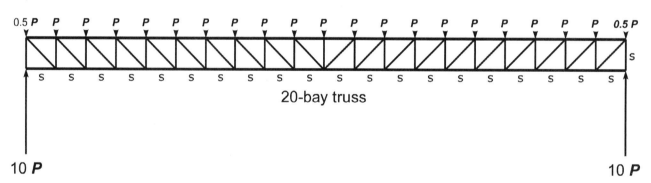

Figure 3.52 Twenty-bay, square-bay truss.

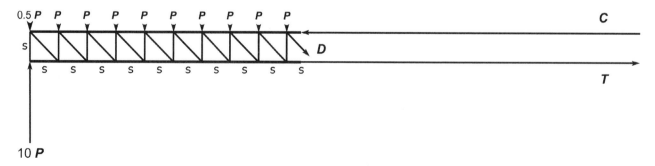

Figure 3.53 Creating freebody by slicing through the center of the twenty-bay truss.

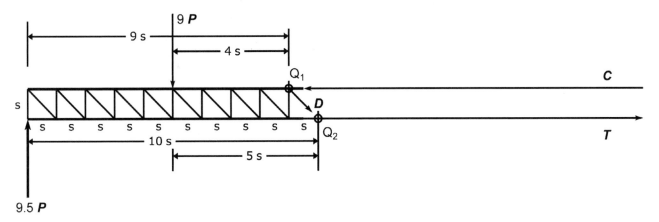

Figure 3.54 Clustering the nine 1 P applied forces into a single 9 P force and the end forces into a single 9.5 P force.

On the cut cross sections of the top and bottom chord, there will be compressive and tensile forces, respectively. In this case, a diagonal web member with a nonzero internal force has also been cut. Because D is not zero and it has a horizontal component, C and T are not equal in magnitude.

Next, the forces can be grouped together into larger equivalent forces to simplify the problem. For example:

The nine 1 P forces can be clustered into a single equivalent force of magnitude 9 P, and

The 10 P upward reaction and the 0.5 P downward force at the left end can be combined into a single upward force of magnitude 9.5 P at the left end (see Figure 3.54).

Taking a moment about point Q_1 eliminates the D and C forces from the moment equation because the lines of action of all of those forces go through point Q_1.

$$\sum M_{Q1} = 0 \; \curvearrowright$$

$$0 = -T(s) - 9P(4\,s) + 9.5(9\,s)$$

$$T = 49.5\ P$$

Taking moments about point Q_2 eliminates the D and T forces from the moment equation because the lines of action of all of those forces go through point Q_2.

$$\sum M_{Q2} = 0 \; \curvearrowright$$

$$0 = -C(s) - 9P(5\,s) + 9.5(10\,s)$$

$$C = 50\ P$$

$$\sum P_x = 0 \xrightarrow{+}$$

$$0 = -C - T + D_x$$

$$D = 0.5\ P$$

This x-component of D is to the right, which means it counteracts 0.5 P of the C force, leaving a net force of 49.5 P on point Q. Hence, the horizontal forces in the internal resisting moment are both 49.5 P.

Example 3

Using the principles of equilibrium applied to freebodies to explore the forces of the internal resisting moments in a variety of spanning systems.

The three structures in Figure 3.55 all have the same span and depth. A truss, suspension element, and arch are shown, with freebodies for each. In trusses, the horizontal forces of the internal resisting moment occur one above the other, and they are immediately apparent when we take the freebody by slicing through the center of the truss. In the case of a tension member or an arch, slicing through the center of the spanning element produced only one horizontal force. The other force in the force couple that constitutes the resisting moment is the buttressing force at the support. Other than this slight extra burden of forcing us to go looking for the second force in the force couple, the mathematics and physics of suspension members and arches are identical to the mathematics and physics of trusses.

In all three cases, the moment of the vertical forces (i.e, the applied forces) is:

$$M_v = \frac{wL}{2} \cdot \frac{L}{4} = \frac{wL^2}{8}$$

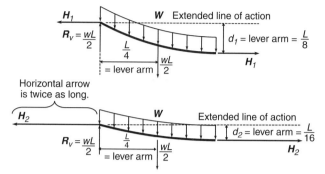

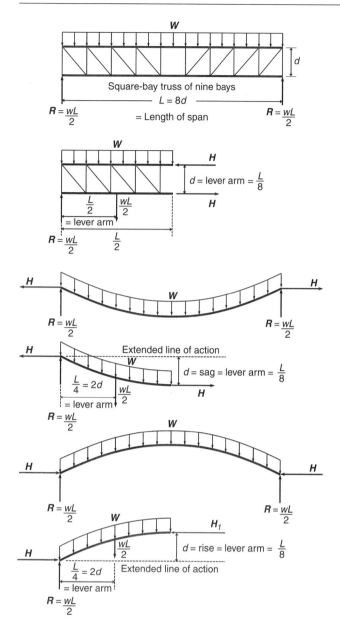

Figure 3.55 Creating a freebody by slicing through the center of a truss, suspension element, and arch.

In all cases, rotational equilibrium implies that the magnitude of the internal resisting moment = the magnitude of the moment of the vertical forces:

$$M_R = M_v$$

$$\left(H \cdot d_1\right) = \left(\frac{wL}{2} \cdot \frac{L}{4}\right)$$

$$\left(H \cdot \frac{L}{8}\right) = \left(\frac{wL}{2} \cdot \frac{L}{4}\right)$$

$$H = wL$$

Figure 3.56 Reducing the lever arm for the horizontal force couple.

The horizontal forces are the same for each spanning system.

Example 4

Using the principles of equilibrium applied to freebodies to explore the effect of depth of a spanning member on the magnitude of the forces in the internal resisting moment. In Figure 3.56, a suspension element has its depth reduced to half.

Taking moments about the left support of the deeper freebody implies:

$$0 = \left(\frac{wL}{2} \cdot \frac{L}{4}\right) - \left(H_1 \cdot d_1\right)$$

$$0 = \left(\frac{wL}{2} \cdot \frac{L}{4}\right) - \left(H_1 \cdot \frac{L}{8}\right)$$

$$H_1 = wL$$

Taking moments about the left support of the shallower freebody implies:

$$0 = \left(\frac{wL}{2} \cdot \frac{L}{4}\right) - \left(H_2 \cdot d_2\right)$$

$$0 = \left(\frac{wL}{2} \cdot \frac{L}{4}\right) - \left(H_2 \cdot \frac{L}{16}\right)$$

$$H_2 = 2wL$$

Changing the depth of the spanning element does not affect the moment of the vertical forces, which in every case is $\dfrac{M_R = wL^2}{8}$. This implies that the moment of the horizontal forces cannot change either. The lever arm for the horizontal forces is reduced to half its original value, requiring that the horizontal forces increase in magnitude by a factor of two. The same argument applies to *any* spanning system.

4

Materials

4.1 Materials: Basic Properties

A perfect crystal consists of approximately spherical atoms "nestled" together in a configuration, in which every atom in the interior of the crystal has the maximum number of nearest neighbor atoms that can be packed around it (see Figure 4.1).

This configuration is very stable, with each atom having bonds in many directions to help maintain its position within the crystal.

When a tensile stress is applied to the crystal, the atoms elongate in the direction of the stress, and, in response, the atoms contract in the directions perpendicular to the direction of the stress (see Figure 4.2).

When a compression stress is applied to the crystal, the atoms are "squashed" in the direction of the stress, and, in response, the atoms expand in the directions perpendicular to the direction of the stress (see Figure 4.3).

Atoms are perfectly elastic, so this process is completely reversible. That is, when the stress is removed, the crystal goes back to its original shape precisely.

Let:

P = force being applied to the material

A = area over which the force is being applied

Then the stress, f, applied to the material will be:

$$f = \frac{P}{A}$$

Let:

L = original length of the material

ΔL = change in length (elongation or shortening) of the material produced by the applied stress

Then the fractional change in length, ε, that is produced by the stress f will be:

$$\varepsilon = \frac{\Delta L}{L}$$

The technical name for ε is *strain*, but the best common-language descriptor is *the fractional change in length*.

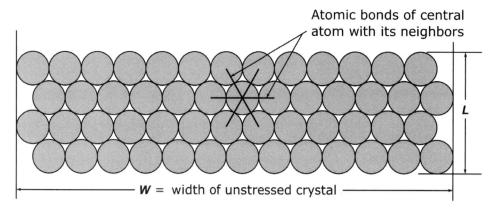

Figure 4.1 Perfectly ordered crystal of iron atoms.

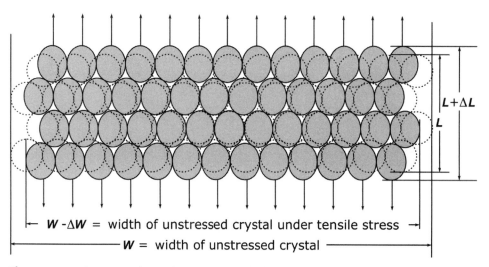

Figure 4.2 Elastic stretching of atoms in a perfectly ordered crystal of iron atoms.

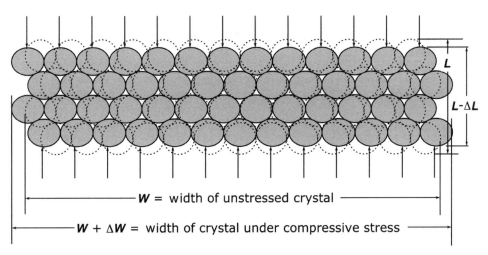

Figure 4.3 Elastic squashing of atoms in a perfectly ordered crystal of iron atoms.

A new quantity, E, can be defined, which is the ratio of the stress f to the strain ε that is produced by that stress:

$$E = \frac{f}{\varepsilon}$$

E is referred to by the technical names *Young's modulus* and the *elastic modulus*. However, the best common-language name for E is the *material stiffness*.

This common-language name can be deduced by a simple interpretation of the preceding equation. For example, compare two materials, called A and B. Suppose that material A must be subjected to twice the stress to reach a certain level of fractional deformation ε. It can be said that material A is twice is as stiff as material B. But E is twice as large for material A than it is for material B. So E is the indicator of the stiffness of the material. For simplicity, E can be called the *stiffness of the material*, or, even more briefly, the *material stiffness*.

The preceding equation can be rearranged to the following form:

$$f = E\varepsilon$$

At low stress, E is essentially a constant for all the common building materials. The range of stress and strain over which E is a constant is called the *linear region* of the material, inasmuch as the plot of f versus ε is a straight line over that region.

For all materials there is a limit to the linear region. For metals, such as steel and aluminum, the end of the linear region is marked by an abrupt yielding, during which the material deforms plastically into a new shape. Materials such as wood and concrete deviate from linear behavior in a more gradual way, with larger and larger deformation resulting from each incremental increase in stress. At its stress limit, concrete shatters without warning. Wood also shatters, but it usually provides warning in the form of creaking, groaning, and snapping sounds.

Materials that snap abruptly, such as concrete, are called *brittle*. Materials that exhibit plastic deformation, such as steel and aluminum, are called *ductile*.

Concrete and wood both exhibit creep at high stress levels. In other words, over a period of time with an unchanging stress level, the materials undergo a gradual and permanent change in shape. This trait is normally undesirable in building structures, but it can sometimes be an advantage, such as in the forming of curved wooden elements for furniture.

Yielding by plastic flow occurs when atoms in a metallic crystal slide by each other. This sliding process is enhanced by imperfections in the crystal structure. For example, if all the atoms in an iron crystal were perfectly arranged (such as in the preceding drawings), then the crystal would have very high strength. Perfect iron crystals, which have been produced in the laboratory in small samples called *iron whiskers*, have a stress capacity of over 2,000,000 lb/in.[2]. One of the most common grades of structural steel has a stress limit of 36,000 lb/in.[2], which means that the imperfections in the crystal structure of the steel have reduced its strength to about $1/60$ of the inherent strength of the iron in the perfect crystal.

By looking at the atoms along one of the planes on which there is a shearing stress, one can understand the plastic flow phenomenon. As the material cools from the molten state, it begins to solidify. Atoms stop migrating around in the molten liquid and begin to affix themselves to other atoms. In this process there is a lot of confusion. The number of atoms in any given layer is not always equal to the number of atoms in the adjacent layers. It is a bit like musical chairs, without enough sites for all the atoms in the layer that is in the process of deposition onto the surface of the existing crystal. Atoms that get deposited on the crystal and that are not bound to the maximum number of nearest neighbors will tend to be less stable, as shown in Figure 4.4.

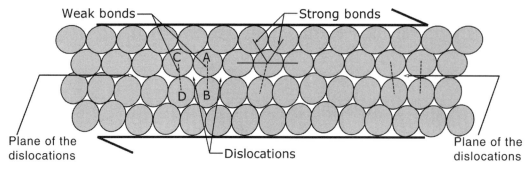

Figure 4.4 Iron atoms arrayed with dislocations interrupting the orderly array.

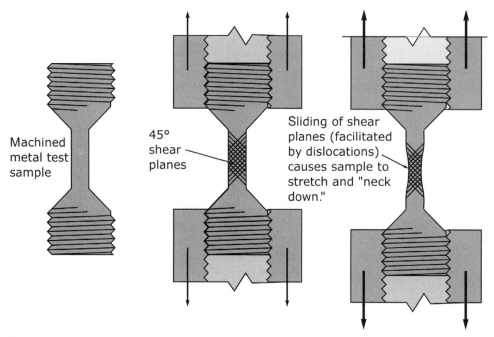

Figure 4.5 Shear planes in a sample under tension.

When a shear stress exists on the plane with the dislocations, the weak bonds facilitate sliding of atoms by each other. The weak bonds are the atomic equivalent of ball bearings. Atoms, such as A and B, poised straight across from each other on opposite sides of the plane of the dislocations, begin to move. As A and B move, A pulls atom C along with it, and B pushes atom D in front of it, until C and D are directly opposite each other. Then atoms C and D become the weakest links, and the facilitators of further movement.

The sliding of atoms by each other occurs under shear stress. Even in a sample of material subjected to "pure tension" or "pure compression," there are planes along which shear stress occurs. Therefore, this mode of material failure can be exhibited under all states of stress in a material (see Figure 4.5).

Figure 4.6 is a photograph of two steel samples, one in its original form and the other having been stretched to failure. The tendency of the material to neck down as the

plastic flow occurs is apparent in the shape of the end of the sample where the failure occurred.

This process of plastic flow can be inhibited by lodging small alloying atoms, such as carbon, in the dislocations.

Figure 4.6 Steel testing samples, in original shape (upper) and stretched to failure (lower).

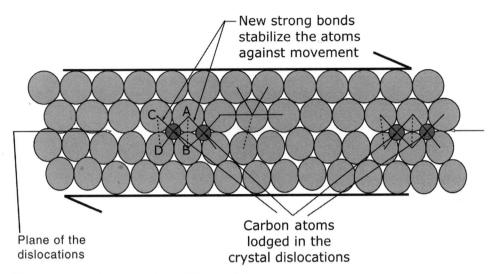

Figure 4.7 Carbon atoms lodged in crystal dislocations.

These alloy atoms become like the grit in gears. They bring the sliding process to a grinding halt. The key to the process is to get the carbon atoms to lodge in the dislocations, as shown in Figure 4.7.

Getting the carbon atoms into the dislocations is something of a random process and is never perfect. There are three ways to get the carbon atoms to preferentially lodge themselves in the dislocations. These three ways are the following:

1. Cool the material down quickly from a red-hot state by plunging it into a liquid, such as water or oil. This process is referred to as *case-hardening of the steel*. The flywheels of cars and steel tools are often case-hardened. Case-hardened material can have a yield stress as high as 250,000 lb/in.^{2}. The material tends to be brittle, giving no warning of failure.

2. Work-harden the material. As planes of iron atoms pass by each other during the process of plastic flow, the dislocations run back and forth along the dislocation planes. When the dislocations encounter carbon atoms, they tend to stop. If enough carbon atoms get lodged along the dislocation line, then the dislocation cannot move. After that, sliding ceases. If this process is done systematically enough, the material becomes very strong, with yield stresses as high as 250,000 lb/in.^{2}. The material tends to be brittle, giving no warning of failure. Drawn wire is an example of work-hardening. In this process, wire is repeatedly drawn through smaller and smaller openings. Material along the outer surface of the wire is "smeared," resulting in a work-hardened material. The resulting wire is sometimes called *piano wire*. When twisted into cable, it is called *high-strength steel cable*. This wire is used in steel suspension bridges.

3. Cool the material by blowing air over it. This will not produce material as strong as case-hardened steel or drawn wire. Steel used in conventional building structures is air-cooled. Yield stresses for these materials can range from 36,000 lb/in.^{2} to 100,000 lb/in.^{2}, but most structural elements are made from one of two grades, with yield stresses of 36,000 lb/in.^{2} and 50,000 lb/in.^{2}. All of these materials are ductile and exhibit plastic deformation after the yield stress has been reached. This plastic deformation is valuable for giving warning of failure and for absorbing energy during earthquakes. It can also be useful in shaping things by rolling or forging.

Figure 4.8 shows a plot of stress versus strain (fractional deformation) for low-grade structural steel. The portion of the region of plastic deformation shown in the diagram appears to be constant. The amount of plastic deformation that is possible with this "mild" grade of steel is very large (many times the width of that shown in the diagram). Over the plastic range, the yield stress of the material is actually increasing, as the plastic flow facilitates work-hardening. However, this upward trend is not apparent on the portion of the diagram shown because the upward slope is very slight and there is not enough of the diagram shown for any significant increase in yield stress to be apparent.

The same diagram shows the residual effect of plastic deformation. Removing the stress after plastic deformation has occurred produces an altered sample that, in the relaxed state, has a different shape from the sample before the plastic deformation occurred. In other words, there is a permanent deformation in the sample. If the plastic deformation was not too large, then the stiffness of the altered sample and the yield stress of the altered sample are not significantly changed by the occurrences of the plastic deformation. When stress is applied to the altered sample, it follows the same elastic deformation curve with the same yield stress as before the plastic deformation occurred. The

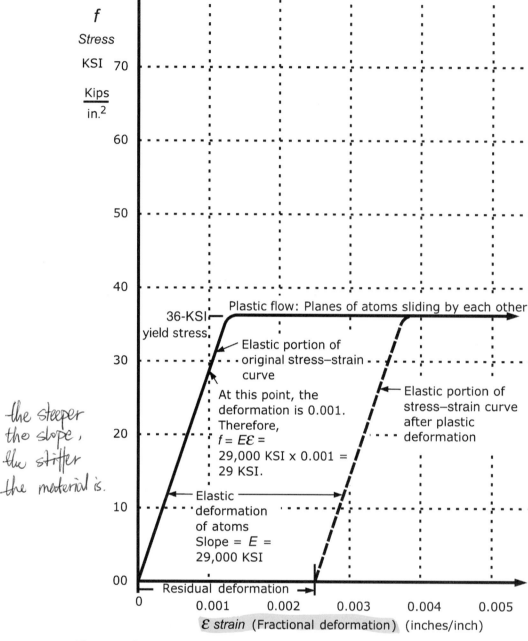

Figure 4.8 Stress–strain curves for 36-KSI steel.

only difference is that the starting length of the sample is different when the second stress–strain curve is run, as compared with the starting length of the sample when the first stress–strain curve was run.

Figure 4.9 shows the stress–strain curves for three common grades of steel: 36-KSI, 50-KSI, and 65-KSI. Each sample has the same material stiffness, inasmuch as this physical property is the result of the elastic deformation of the iron atoms. The only difference between the sam-

ples is the stress at which plastic deformation first occurs, that is, the yield stress of the material sample. Figure 4.9 also shows the stress–strain curves for 6061-T6 aluminum, three grades of concrete, and two grades of wood. Notice the nonlinear nature of concrete and wood.

Figure 4.9 gives the density and the specific gravity (SG) of the materials. Specific gravity is the ratio of the density of the material to the density of water. Because the specific gravity of steel is 7.85, steel is 7.85 times

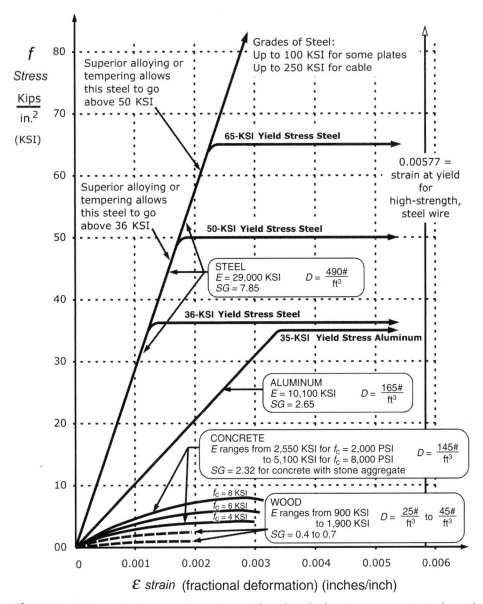

f **Stress**

$\dfrac{\text{Kips}}{\text{in.}^2}$

(KSI)

Grades of Steel:
Up to 100 KSI for some plates
Up to 250 KSI for cable

Superior alloying or tempering allows this steel to go above 50 KSI

65-KSI Yield Stress Steel

0.00577 = strain at yield for high-strength, steel wire

Superior alloying or tempering allows this steel to go above 36 KSI

50-KSI Yield Stress Steel

STEEL
$E = 29{,}000$ KSI $D = \dfrac{490\#}{\text{ft}^3}$
$SG = 7.85$

36-KSI Yield Stress Steel

35-KSI Yield Stress Aluminum

ALUMINUM
$E = 10{,}100$ KSI $D = \dfrac{165\#}{\text{ft}^3}$
$SG = 2.65$

CONCRETE
E ranges from 2,550 KSI for $f_c = 2{,}000$ PSI $D = \dfrac{145\#}{\text{ft}^3}$
to 5,100 KSI for $f_c = 8{,}000$ PSI
$SG = 2.32$ for concrete with stone aggregate

$f_c = 8$ KSI
$f_c = 6$ KSI
$f_c = 4$ KSI

WOOD
E ranges from 900 KSI $D = \dfrac{25\#}{\text{ft}^3}$ to $\dfrac{45\#}{\text{ft}^3}$
to 1,900 KSI
$SG = 0.4$ to 0.7

ε *strain* (fractional deformation) (inches/inch)

Figure 4.9 Stress–strain curves for various grades of steel, aluminum, concrete, and wood.

more dense than water. The density of water is 62.4 lb/ft³. Hence, the density of steel would be equal to the specific gravity for steel times the density of water, or 7.85 times 62.4 lb/ft³ = 490 lb/ft³.

Structural Efficiency of Materials

Consider a solid block of material of uniform cross-sectional area at all elevations (see Figure 4.10).

If the block is in equilibrium, the upward force P on the bottom of the block is equal to the weight W of the block:

$$P = W$$

P can be expressed as the product fA, where f is the stress on the base of the block and A is the area of the base of the block.

W can be expressed as the product DV, where D is the density of the material and V is the volume of the material. Furthermore, the volume of the block can be expressed as the product hA, where h is the height of the block and A is the area of the base of the block.

Then the equation of equilibrium becomes

$$fA = DV,$$

which in turn becomes

$$fA = DhA,$$

which simplifies to

$$f = Dh$$

In other words, the stress on the bottom of the block increases in proportion to the height of the block, with a

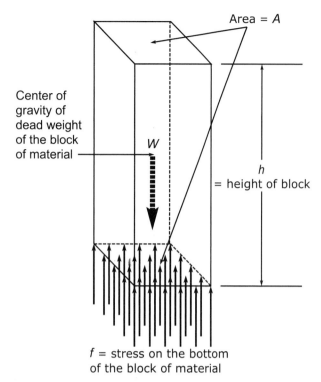

Center of gravity of dead weight of the block of material ⟶

W

h = height of block

Area = A

f = stress on the bottom of the block of material

Figure 4.10 Stress at the bottom of a prismatic block, under the self-weight of the block.

proportionality constant equal to the density of the material of which the block is made.

This equation can be reconfigured to express h in terms of f and D:

$$h = \frac{f}{D}$$

The highest value that f can have is F_y. This corresponds to the maximum height of the block. When the block is tall enough that the stress at the bottom reaches F_y, the bottom of the block will begin to crush under the weight of the block itself. The greatest height that a prismatic element can attain without crushing under its own weight is given by the following expression:

$$h_{max} = \frac{F_y}{D}$$

The quantity

$$\frac{F_y}{D}$$

is referred to as the "per-pound" strength of the material. The per-pound strength of a material is expressed in units of length (i.e., feet, meters, kilometers, etc.). The per-pound compression strength of a material is the height of a column (of constant cross section) at which the material at the bottom of the column begins to crush under the

self-weight of the column. The per-pound tensile strength of a material is the length of a vertical tension member (of constant cross section) at which the material at the top of the tension member begins to tear under the influence of the self-weight of the tension member.

An analogous per-pound measure of the stiffness of the material can be determined as follows. Divide both sides of the equation

$$f = E\varepsilon$$

by the density D of the material, to get the following equation:

$$\frac{f}{D} = \frac{E}{D} \cdot \varepsilon$$

Plots of f/D versus ε are given in Figure 4.11 for steel, aluminum, wood, and concrete. The slopes of the curves are the per-pound stiffness of the materials, and the highest f/D values achieved by the curves are the per-pound strengths of the materials. In Table 4.3, there is a numerical listing of the per-pound strengths and the per-pound stiffnesses of various materials, including some exotic materials that are not currently used in buildings, but which are used in aircraft, sporting equipment, and high-end yachts.

Notice that the elastic portions of the stress–strain diagrams for aluminum and the three grades of steel lie almost exactly on top of each other, signifying by their similar slopes that the per-pound stiffnesses for all four of these materials are essentially identical.

Figure 4.12 shows the stress–strain curves for both compression (upper right) and tension (lower left). The compression and tension stress–strain curves are the same for a grade of steel or a grade of aluminum. For concrete, the failure stresses in tension are drastically lower than the failure stresses in compression. For wood, the failures stresses in tension are slightly lower than the failure stresses in compression, primarily due to the effect of knots.

All of this information can be recast in terms of the concept of "per-pound strength" and "per-pound stiffness" by dividing the yield stress F_y and the stiffness E for each material by the density of the material. For example, for aluminum:

$$\frac{F_y}{D_{Al}} = \frac{35 \, \frac{K}{in.^2}}{0.165 \, \frac{K}{ft^3}} \cdot \left[\frac{12 \, in.}{ft} \right] \cdot \left[\frac{12 \, in.}{ft} \right] \cdot \left[\frac{12 \, in.}{ft} \right]$$

$$= 360,000 \, in.$$

This can be converted to feet:

$$360,000 \, in. \cdot \left[\frac{ft}{12 \, in.} \right] = 30,000 \, ft,$$

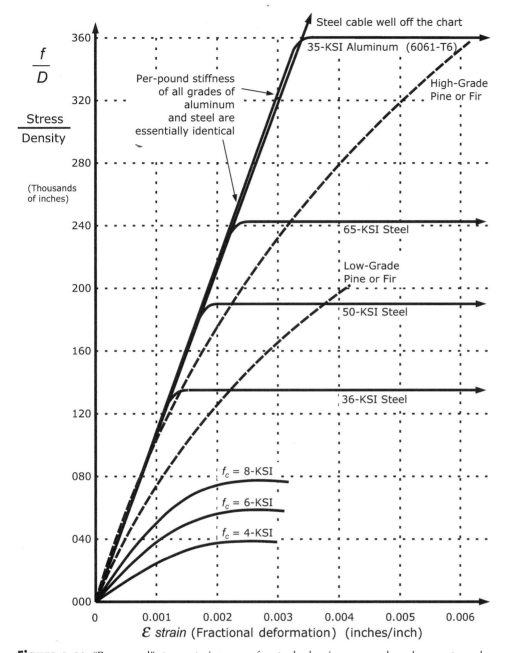

Figure 4.11 "Per-pound" stress–strain curves for steel, aluminum, wood, and concrete under compression.

which can also be converted to miles:

$$30{,}000 \text{ ft} \cdot \left[\frac{\text{mile}}{5{,}280 \text{ ft}} \right] = 5.7 \text{ miles}$$

Thus, 5.7 miles is the maximum length of 6061-T6 aluminum cable of uniform cross section that can support its own weight.

The per-pound stiffness of the material can be gotten in a similar manner by dividing the material stiffness by the material density:

$$\frac{E}{D_{\text{Al}}} = \frac{10{,}100 \; \frac{\text{K}}{\text{in.}^2}}{0.165 \; \frac{\text{K}}{\text{in.}^3}} \cdot \left[\frac{12 \text{ in.}}{\text{ft}} \right] \cdot \left[\frac{12 \text{ in.}}{\text{ft}} \right] \cdot \left[\frac{12 \text{ in.}}{\text{ft}} \right]$$

$$= 104{,}000{,}000 \text{ in.}$$

This can be converted to feet:

$$104{,}000{,}000 \text{ in.} \cdot \left[\frac{\text{ft}}{12 \text{ in.}} \right] = 8{,}630{,}000 \text{ ft,}$$

wood has higher strength to weight ratios than aluminum.

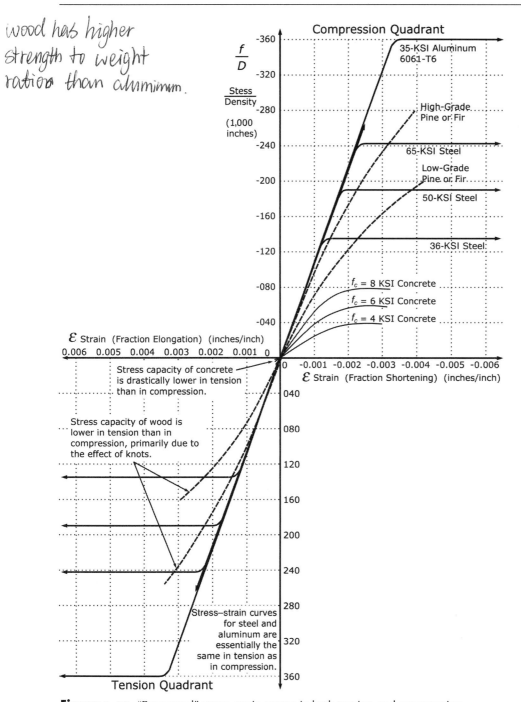

Figure 4.12 "Per-pound" stress–strain curves in both tension and compression.

which can also be converted to miles:

$$8{,}630{,}000 \text{ ft} \cdot \left[\frac{\text{mile}}{5{,}280 \text{ ft}} \right] = 1{,}630 \text{ miles}$$

The physical significance of this number is best understood in relative comparisons of various materials. The material with the higher per-pound stiffness will produce a lighter structure in situations where deflection or buckling is the limiting design factor (as opposed to tearing or crushing of the material). See Table 4.1.

The structural properties of earth/soil are listed separately, in Table 4.2, because they are given in different units.

To make a quick test at a construction site, take along wood blocks of areas 1 in.², 2 in.², 3 in.², and so on. Stand on the blocks and see how much area you need to avoid significant penetration into the soil. Divide your body

Table 4.1 Structural Properties of Common Building Materials

Material	F_y Material Strength (yield stress) $\dfrac{K}{in.^2}$	E Material Stiffness (elastic modulus) $\dfrac{K}{in.^2}$	D Density $\dfrac{K}{ft^3}$	$\dfrac{F_y}{D}$ Per-Pound Material Strength (miles)	$\dfrac{E}{D}$ Per-Pound Material Stiffness (miles)
Titanium (tempered β-alloys)	200	15,000	0.285	19.14	1,435
Titanium medium temper	110	15,000	0.285	10.53	1,435
Titanium (α-alloys)	25	15,000	0.285	2.39	1,435
High-strength steel wire/cable	250	26,000	0.490	13.91	1,447
Steel plate	100	29,000	0.490	5.57	1,614
	to	to	to	to	to
	32	29,000	0.490	1.78	1,614
Rolled steel sections	65	29,000	0.490	3.62	1,614
	50	29,000	0.490	2.78	1,614
	36	29,000	0.490	2.00	1,614
Aluminum (6061-T6)	35	10,100	0.165	5.79	1,669
Concrete	F_c				
	8	5,100	0.145	1.50	959
	7	4,770	0.145	1.32	897
	6	4,420	0.145	1.13	831
	5	4,030	0.145	0.94	758
	4	3,600	0.145	0.75	677
	3	3,120	0.145	0.56	587
	2	2,550	0.145	0.38	480
Pine, fir, hemlock	6	1,900	0.040	4.09	1,295
	to	to	to	to	to
	1.6	1,400	0.030	1.45	1,273

weight by the area of the smallest block that avoids significant penetration. Remember that the soil at the intended level of the foundation base will probably be denser and more compacted. To get a more accurate estimate of the soil capacity, excavate down to the intended base of the foundation before doing the block test. Before building a structure of significant size, hire a soils engineer. The soils engineer will have a better sense of substrata and variability of the soils on the site. For any really significant building, soil borings and soil analysis should be done, with a soils report being included as part of the design development documentation for the project.

These common building materials can be put in the context of more exotic materials, as shown in Table 4.3.

Example Problem

Distributing loads from materials of high-stress capacity to materials of low-stress capacity.

Suppose that the design forces on the top of a column are the following:

$$P_{dead} = 15 \text{ K}$$
$$P_{live} = 45 \text{ K}$$

The factored total load would be:

$$\text{Factored } P_{imposed} = 1.2 \, (P_{dead}) + 1.6 \, (P_{live})$$
$$= 1.2 \, (15 \text{ K}) + 1.6 \, (45 \text{ K}) = 90 \text{ K}$$

The column is made from 65-KSI steel (i.e, the yield stress of the steel is $F_{y \, steel} = 65$ kips/in.^{2}). The resistance factor for a steel column is $\Phi_{steel} = 0.85$. The design stress for the steel in the compression member, as limited by yielding of the material, is determined by multiplying the resistance factor times the yield stress: $\Phi_{steel} \cdot F_{y\_steel}$. For the moment, only the limit set by yielding of the material is addressed. Columns are also vulnerable to *buckling*,

Table 4.2 Structural Properties of Earth/Soil

Material	Design Stress ΦFy	
	$\dfrac{K}{ft^2}$	$\dfrac{lb}{in.^2}$
Massive igneous or metamorphic rock	300	2,100
Weathered rock	120	840
Dense sand	15	105
Stiff clay	9	63
Loose sand	3 to 6	21 to 42
Compacted controlled fill	4.5	30
Soft clay	3	21

Table 4.3 Comparison of Material Efficiencies

Material	$\dfrac{F_y}{D}$ (miles)	Normalized	$\dfrac{E}{D}$ (miles)	Normalized
Boron fibers	122	1	10,100	0.754
Graphite fibers	66.3	0.543	13,400	1
Glass fibers	66.3	0.543	1,800	0.134
Graphite fibers in epoxy	39.5	0.324	5,900	0.440
Boron fibers in aluminum	33.1	0.271	3,790	0.283
Titanium (tempered β-alloys)	19.14	0.157	1,435	0.107
High-strength steel wire/cable	13.91	0.114	1,447	0.108
50% glass fibers in polyester	13.1	0.107	521	0.039
Titanium (medium temper)	10.53	0.086	1,435	0.107
25% glass fibers in polyester	7.89	0.065	489	0.036
100-KSI steel plate	5.57	0.046	1,614	0.120
6061-T6 aluminum	5.79	0.047	1,669	0.125
High-grade pine or fir	4.09	0.034	1,300	0.097
65-KSI steel sections	3.62	0.030	1,614	0.120
50-KSI steel sections	2.78	0.023	1,614	0.120
Acrylic plastic	2.68	0.022		
Titanium (α-alloys)	2.39	0.020	1,435	0.107
36-KSI steel sections	2.00	0.016	1,614	0.120
Low-grade pine or fir	1.45	0.012	1,270	0.095
F_c = 8-KSI concrete	1.50	0.012	959	0.072
F_c = 2-KSI concrete	0.38	0.003	480	0.036

that is, to *elastic instability*, wherein a column begins to radically change shape at a stress level below the yield stress. Elastic instability is addressed in detail in Chapter 5. For the moment, we will simply note that the material in the cross-section of the column can be redistributed in a manner that will inhibit the tendency to buckle. However, no matter how well the material is distributed to resist buckling, the yield stress always sets a lower limit below which the cross-sectional area of the column cannot fall.

The height of the column is 10 ft. This would be useful information in dealing with buckling, if buckling were addressed in this example. However, for the purposes of this example, the length will be used only to calculate the self-weight of the column.

Welded to the base of the column is a 1.5 in.-thick base plate made of 65-KSI steel that is used to distribute the load from the column into a 12 in.-thick concrete spread footing. (Normally, one would size both the area and the thickness of this plate as part of the sizing procedure. However, to keep this particular example focused on issues most pertinent to this chapter, simply assume the thickness of the plate to be 1.5 in.) The crushing stress for the concrete in compression is $f_c = \dfrac{5,000\#}{\text{in.}^2}$. The resistance factor for the concrete spread footing is $\Phi_c = 0.65$. The design stress for the concrete is determined by multiply-

ing the resistance factor times the crushing stress of the concrete; that is, the design stress for the concrete is $\Phi_c \cdot f_c$.

The concrete spread footing rests on soil with a design compression stress of 2,300 lb/ft^2 = 2.3 K/ft^2. Neither the yield stress nor the resistance factor is specified for soil—only the design stress is specified. References to soil yielding are generally sidestepped for several reasons, among which are the following.

Soil failure is a complex process that occurs in several stages, which makes it difficult to describe (e.g., one stage often involves the squeezing out of moisture from between the solid particles, which may result in unacceptable foundation settlement, even though outright structural collapse does not occur), and there is an extreme lack of predictability regarding the stress levels at which the various stages of failure occur.

To avoid getting sidetracked in elaborate discussions of the nature and meaning of yielding in soils, the structural capacities of soils are expressed in terms of design stress, $\Phi_{soil} \cdot F_{y\_soil}$, rather than giving either Φ_{soil} or F_{y_soil} as separate quantities. This is similar to the treatment of wood, for which design stresses $\Phi_w \cdot F_{y\_w}$, are presented, but failure stress is not discussed in the design data.

(Note the different units in each preceding case. Do not get preoccupied with number manipulation and forget to look closely at the units. If you make a mistake with the unit conversions, then every number you generate will be utterly meaningless.)

Do the following:

1. Determine the design stress for the steel in the column, based on the resistance factor and the yield stress of the steel in the column, that is, $\Phi_{steel}F_{y\_steel}$.
2. Determine the column cross-sectional area required to support the factored load being delivered to the top of the column, based on the limit set by the design stress, $\Phi_{steel}F_{y\_steel}$.
3. Look up the density of steel and determine the column self-weight, W_{column}. What is the factored self-weight of the column?
4. Accounting for the factored self-weight of the column, determine the total factored force in the column, at the bottom of the column.
5. Determine the column cross-sectional area required to keep the stress at the bottom of the column within the design stress limit.
6. Repeat steps 3, 4, and 5 until you are totally bored. (Think about how you might shortcircuit some of this monotonous, repetitive number crunching. In the digital supplement on the CD-ROM that came with this text, digital computation is explored as a way to perform iterative calculations in a rapid and easy manner.)
7. What is the final value for the factored total force delivered to the steel base plate, that is, for factored $P_{imposed}$ + factored W_{column}?
8. Determine the design stress for the concrete in the spread footing, based on the resistance factor and the compression crushing stress of the concrete in the spread footing, that is, $\Phi_c F_c$.
9. Ignoring, for the moment, the self-weight of the steel base plate, what should the area of the steel base plate be to avoid exceeding the design stress in the concrete of the spread footing?
10. Using the density information you got for steel (in step 3), along with the area and thickness information for the steel base plate, what is the self-weight of the steel base plate? What is the factored self-weight of the plate?
11. Add the factored self-weight of the steel base plate to the load being delivered to the top of the steel base plate, to determine a new load being delivered to the top of the concrete spread footing.
12. What should the new area of the steel base plate be to avoid exceeding the design stress in the concrete of the spread footing?
13. Repeat steps 10 through 12 until you are totally bored. (Or shortcircuit the process through whatever technique you devised in step 6.)
14. Assuming for the moment that the self-weight of the concrete spread footing is negligible, what should the

area of the concrete spread footing be to avoid exceeding the design compressive stress for the soil?
15. Calculate the self-weight of the concrete spread footing. What is the factored self-weight?
16. What is the total factored force on the soil, including the factored weight of the concrete spread footing?
17. What should the new area of the concrete spread footing be to avoid exceeding the design compressive stress in the soil under the combined factored forces of imposed force, column weight, base plate weight, and concrete-spread-footing weight?
18. Repeat the last three steps until you are totally bored. (Or shortcircuit the process using whatever technique you devised in step 6.)

How much larger in area is the concrete spread footing than the cross-sectional area of the steel column? (Divide the area of the concrete spread footing by the cross-sectional area of the steel column.)

What does this last answer tell you about the relative stress capacity of high-grade steel and ordinary soil?

Draw squares showing the relative sizes of the areas determined earlier. (Suggestion: figure out a drawing scale that will allow the largest area [i.e., the concrete spread footing] to be depicted on a single sheet of 8.5 × 11 paper. Then draw the area of the steel plate and the cross-sectional area of the steel column at the same scale. The square for the concrete pad should fill most of the sheet of paper in order for the other two areas to be less than microscopic.)

This problem illustrates three important points:

- The principle of spreading the stresses from the materials of high structural efficiency to materials of low structural efficiency.
- The iterative nature of structural design. This is a classic chicken-and-egg problem: An element cannot be sized until its self-weight is known, and its self-weight cannot be known until it has been sized. To get out of the paralysis of this situation, make an assumption about the self-weight of the element and, through an iterative process, approach the final solution. Good structural designers develop simple estimation techniques, so that the number of iterations required to approach the final solution is small. Frequently, these estimation techniques yield a satisfactory answer on the first estimate and no iterations are required.
- The top-down nature of sizing structural elements. In other words, you have to size each element, starting with the elements at the top of the structure, to determine the loads on each element due to the dead weight of the elements resting on it. In this case, the sizing operations have been started at the column by simply specifying the total load delivered to the column from all the structure resting on the column. However, in a full design process, you would have had to size all the

elements above the column before you sized the column because all of the elements above the column impact the column. For the purposes of this illustrative problem, the aim was to focus on the column and the foundation and avoid getting involved in the more complicated mathematics necessary to deal with the structure resting on the column. So the process began with the load on the column.

Solution to Example Problem

Step 1:
For the 65-KSI steel column:

$$\Phi F_y = 0.85 \cdot \frac{65\ K}{\text{in.}^2} = \frac{55.25\ K}{\text{in.}^2}$$

Step 2:
The highest stress will occur at the base of the column, inasmuch as the cumulative effect of the self-weight of the column will be greatest at the base. However, it is not possible to know the self-weight of the column until the column has been sized. This is the classic "chicken-and-egg" problem: The column cannot be accurately sized without knowing its self-weight, and its self-weight cannot be known without sizing it. Coming to a satisfactory resolution is, therefore, an iterative process involving trial and error. First, the column cross section is sized to withstand the 90 kip imposed force on the top. Then the column is resized to account for the combined stress from the 90 kip imposed force and the self-weight of the column.

$$A_{column} = \frac{P_{imposed}}{\Phi F_y} = \frac{90\ K}{\dfrac{55.25\ K}{\text{in.}^2}} \cdot \left[\frac{\text{in.}^2}{\text{in.}^2}\right] = 1.629\ \text{in.}^2$$

Step 3:

$$
\begin{aligned}
\text{Weight of column} &= W_{column} \\
&= \text{density of steel} \cdot \\
&\quad \text{volume of steel column} \\
&= D \cdot V = D \cdot L \cdot A_{column} \\
&= \frac{490\#}{\text{ft}^3} \cdot 10\ \text{ft} \cdot 1.629\ \text{in.}^2 \cdot \\
&\quad \left[\frac{\text{ft}}{12\ \text{in.}}\right] \cdot \left[\frac{\text{ft}}{12\ \text{in.}}\right] \\
&= 55.4\# = 0.055\ K
\end{aligned}
$$

$$
\begin{aligned}
\text{Factored weight of column} &= 1.2(0.055\ K) \\
&= 0.0665\ K
\end{aligned}
$$

Step 4:
The factored axial force on the material at the base of the column is

$$P_{imposed} + W_{column} = 90\ K + 0.0665\ K = 90.067\ K$$

Step 5:

$$
\begin{aligned}
A_{column} &= \frac{P_{imposed} + 1.2\left(W_{column}\right)}{\Phi F_y} \\
&= \frac{90.067\ K}{\dfrac{55.25\ K}{\text{in.}^2}} \cdot \left[\frac{\text{in.}^2}{\text{in.}^2}\right] = 1.630\ \text{in.}^2
\end{aligned}
$$

This is, within three significant figures, the same size as determined in the preceding step.

Step 6:
The preceding step illustrates that for this column under this loading condition, to three-place accuracy, the self-weight of the column is negligible as compared with the imposed load. No further iterations are required.

Step 7:
The total load delivered to the steel baseplate is 90.07 K.

Step 8:

$$\Phi_c \cdot F_c = 0.65 \cdot \frac{5\ K}{\text{in.}^2} = \frac{3.25\ K}{\text{in.}^2}$$

Step 9:
When the principle of equilibrium is applied to the steel plate, the net force upward on the bottom of the steel plate must be 90.07 K plus the weight of the steel plate. Because the weight of the steel plate is unknown, the initial sizing will be based on 90.07 K.

The minimum area of the plate, required to keep the stress on the concrete below the design stress of 3.25 K/in.², is

$$
\begin{aligned}
A_{plate} &= \frac{P_{imposed} + 1.2\left(W_{column}\right)}{\Phi_c F_c} \\
&= \frac{90.07\ K}{\dfrac{3.25\ K}{\text{in.}^2}} \cdot \left[\frac{\text{in.}^2}{\text{in.}^2}\right] = 27.71\ \text{in.}^2
\end{aligned}
$$

Step 10:

$$
\begin{aligned}
\text{Weight of the steel base plate} &= D \cdot V = D \cdot t \cdot A_{plate} \\
&= \frac{490\#}{\text{ft}^3} \cdot 1.5\ \text{in.} \cdot 27.71\ \text{in.}^2 \cdot
\end{aligned}
$$

$$\left[\frac{ft}{12\ in.}\right]\cdot\left[\frac{ft}{12\ in.}\right]\cdot\left[\frac{ft}{12\ in.}\right]$$

$$= 11.8\# = 0.0118\ K$$

Factored weight of
the steel base plate $= 1.2(0.0118\ K) = 0.0141\ K$

Step 11:
The net force on the concrete is:

$P = 90.067\ K + .0141\ K = 90.081\ K$

Step 12:

$$A_{plate} = \frac{P_{imposed} + 1.2\left(W_{column} + W_{plate}\right)}{\Phi_c F_c}$$

$$= \frac{90.08\ K}{\dfrac{3.25\ K}{in.^2}}\cdot\left[\frac{in.^2}{in.^2}\right] = 27.72\ in.^2$$

To three significant figures, this is the same answer as derived in step 9.

Step 13:
No additional iterations are required.

Step 14:
Applying the principle of equilibrium to the concrete spread footing, the net upward force on the bottom of the spread footing is 90.08 K plus the self-weight of the spread footing. Because the self-weight of the spread footing is not known initially, a minimum area for the spread footing can be obtained by sizing the spread footing to distribute the 90.08 K over a sufficiently large area of soil that the design stress of the soil is not exceeded.

$$A_{concrete} = \frac{P_{imposed} + 1.2\left(W_{column} + W_{plate}\right)}{\Phi_{soil} F_{y\_soil}}$$

$$= \frac{90.08\ K}{\dfrac{2.3\ K}{ft^2}}\cdot\left[\frac{ft^2}{ft^2}\right] = 39.17\ ft^2$$

This is the required area of the concrete spread footing as limited by the design stress in the soil.

Step 15:

Weight of the
concrete pad $= D\cdot V = D\cdot t\cdot A_{concrete}$

$$= \frac{150\#}{ft^3}\cdot 12\ in.\cdot 39.17\ ft^2\cdot\left[\frac{ft}{12\ in.}\right]$$

$$= 5875\# = 5.875\ K$$

Factored weight of
the concrete pad $= 1.2(5.875\ K) = 7.050\ K$

Step 16:
The total force on the soil

$$= 90.08\ K + 7.05\ K = 97.13\ K$$

Step 17:

$$A_{concrete} = \frac{P_{imposed} + 1.2\left(W_{column} + W_{plate} + W_{concrete\ (previous)}\right)}{\Phi F_{y\_soil}}$$

$$= \frac{97.13\ K}{\dfrac{2.3\ K}{ft^2}}\cdot\left[\frac{ft^2}{ft^2}\right] = 42.23\ ft^2$$

This is the required area of the concrete pad as limited by the design stress in the soil.

Step 18:
Repeating step 15:

Weight of the
concrete pad $= D\cdot V = D\cdot t\cdot A_{concrete}$

$$= \frac{150\#}{ft^3}\cdot 12\ in.\cdot 42.23\ ft^2\cdot\left[\frac{ft}{12\ in.}\right]$$

$$= 6,335\# = 6.335\ K$$

Factored weight of
the concrete pad $= 1.2(6.335) = 7.602\ K$

Repeating step 16:
The total force on the soil

$$= 90.08\ K + 7.602\ K = 97.68\ K$$

Repeating step 17:

$$A_{concrete} = \frac{P_{imposed} + 1.2\left(W_{column} + W_{plate} + W_{concrete\ (previous)}\right)}{\Phi F_{y\_soil}}$$

$$= \frac{97.68\ K}{\dfrac{2.3\ K}{ft^2}}\cdot\left[\frac{ft^2}{ft^2}\right] = 42.47\ ft^2$$

Repeating step 15 again:

Weight of the
concrete spread footing $= D\cdot V = D\cdot t\cdot A_{concrete}$

$$= \frac{150\#}{ft^3}\cdot 12\ in.\cdot 42.47\ ft^2\cdot\left[\frac{ft}{12\ in.}\right]$$

$$= 6371\# = 6.371\ K$$

Factored weight of the
concrete spread footing $= 1.2(6.371\ K) = 7.645\ K$

Repeating step 16 again:
The total force on the soil

= 90.08 K + 7.645 K = 97.73 K

Repeating step 17 again:

$$A_{concrete} = \frac{P_{imposed} + 1.2\left(W_{column} + W_{plate} + W_{concrete\,(previous)}\right)}{\Phi F_{y\_soil}}$$

$$= \frac{97.73\text{ K}}{\dfrac{2.3\text{ K}}{\text{ft}^2}} \cdot \left[\frac{\text{ft}^2}{\text{ft}^2}\right] = 42.49\text{ ft}^2,$$

which is the same as the previous iteration. The solution has converged to the correct size for the concrete spread footing.

The fact that so many iterations were required for the concrete spread footing and that so few were required for the steel column and steel base plate reflects the high structural efficiency of steel as compared with concrete and soil.

Clearly, to avoid some of the work done in sizing the concrete spread footing, it would have been rational to make an estimate of the size of the footing; that is, it would have made sense to "kick the size up." Efficient estimating can drastically reduce computational effort. Iterative sizing procedures of this sort can also be done very efficiently using digital computational methods where the iterations are performed automatically.

Step 19:

$$\frac{\text{Area of concrete pad}}{\text{Area of steel column}} = \frac{42.49\text{ ft}^2}{1.63\text{ in.}^2} \cdot \left[\frac{12\text{ in.}^2}{\text{ft}}\right] \cdot \left[\frac{12\text{ in.}^2}{\text{ft}}\right]$$

$$= 3,756$$

Step 20:
The stress capacity of the steel is much higher than the stress capacity of the soil, which is why the interface elements, that is, the steel plate and the concrete pad, are required to distribute the force of the column over a drastically larger area of soil.

Step 21:
The areas shown in Figure 4.13 are drawn in proportion to each other:

The tiny black square in the middle represents the column area, the next larger square represents the steel base plate, and the largest square represents the concrete pad. This is a fairly extreme example because the stress capacity in the steel is about as high as can be attained and the stress capacity in the soil is near the bottom of the acceptable range. However, this example problem, which is more representative in terms of material stress capacities, illustrates that these areas are typically radically different.

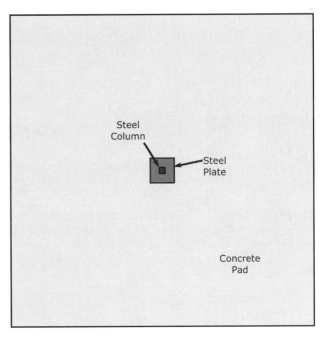

Figure 4.13 Relative areas of the column cross section, steel base plate, and concrete footing.

4.2 Wood Properties

In the early history of this country, there were vast expanses of old-growth wood from which large timbers could be cut. Furthermore, sawing and finishing wood was very energy-intensive, and mechanical equipment was not available for those tasks. Therefore, construction emphasized the use of large timbers, so that no more cutting than necessary would be required. Log cabins are the most extreme example of this approach, in which the only processing involved cutting to length, notching, and possibly using an adz to scrape a flat surface on the top and bottom of the log. Classic post-and-beam construction is a more refined example of this approach. Efficiency in reducing processing labor prevailed over efficiency in use of materials. For example, log cabins use the material with the grain oriented in the worst possible direction for resisting stresses. This weakness is compensated for by the use of extra material.

Today the economic factors have changed drastically in the following ways:

- Equipment for sawing, finishing, and processing lumber in a variety of ways is readily available.
- The energy to run that equipment is inexpensive.
- There is little old-growth wood from which large timbers can be cut.
- The curing time required for large timbers exceeds the patience of investors who want to see their money produce a financial return faster.

- The demand for the resource is so great that efficient structural utilization becomes crucial—a fact that is inconsistent with the structural diminishment associated with large shrinkage cracks and extensive knots prevalent in large structural timbers.

The effects of these economic factors have led to three trends that are ongoing:

1. Solid-sawn lumber is available only in smaller sizes.
2. Construction systems are emphasizing the use of these small elements—for example, balloon construction, involving the use of lots of thin, braced members (i.e., studs).
3. Methods of gluing small wood pieces together to produce larger structural elements are becoming more prevalent—for example, glue-laminate beams, wood I-beams with plywood or oriented strand board (OSB) webs, box beams, diaphragm roofs, and so on.

With regard to trend 1, there was a time in this country when it would be common to use a 6×12 timber as the main beam supporting a series of floor joists. Today such a large timber would be both rare and expensive. You would find it more economical to nail four 2×12s together to form such a large beam. In other words, enough money will be saved in reduced curing time to pay for the extra sawing, planing, gluing, and nailing required to make the equivalent beam as a composite of four 2×12s.

Furthermore, even 2×12s are becoming rare today. You will generally prefer to design for shorter spans, appropriate to 2×10s, or to choose a prefabricated element with greater structural depth, such as laminated veneer lumber (LVL), glulam beams, and I-joists.

Tables 4.4, 4.5, and 4.6 list properties of various species and grades of wood.

Table 4.6 contains reference design values for various types of stress and for material stiffness in a variety of species and grades of wood. These data were excerpted from (and are a tiny fraction of) the data available in the *National Design Specification (NDS) for Wood Construction*, 2005 edition, published by the American For-

Table 4.4 Density of Various Species of Wood

Species	lb/ft³
Ash, white	43
Basswood	26
Birch, sweet	47
Birch, yellow	43
Cedar, northern white	24
Cedar, western red	23
Douglas fir (coast)	34
Douglas fir (interior south)	31
Douglas fir (interior west)	32
Elm, rock	44
Elm, soft	36
Fir, balsam	27
Fir, white	27
Hemlock, eastern	29
Hemlock, western	30
Hickory	51
Maple, hard	44
Oak, white	47
Pine, eastern white	25
Pine, ponderosa	29
Pine, southern	36
Pine, southern longleaf	42
Poplar, yellow	30
Spruce, eastern	29

section modulus has to do with bending stress.

Table 4.5 Cross-Sectional Properties of Standard Dressed Solid-Sawn Lumber Surfaced Four Sides (S4S)

Nominal Size	Standard Dressed Size	Section Area A	Section Modulus S	Moment of Inertia I	# per Linear Foot When Density Equals			
					$\dfrac{25\#}{ft^3}$	$\dfrac{30\#}{ft^3}$	$\dfrac{35\#}{ft^3}$	$\dfrac{40\#}{ft^3}$
$b \times h$	$b \times h$	bh	$\dfrac{bh^2}{6}$	$\dfrac{bh^3}{12}$	$\dfrac{\#}{ft}$	$\dfrac{\#}{ft}$	$\dfrac{\#}{ft}$	$\dfrac{\#}{ft}$
in. × in.	in. × in.	in.²	in.³	in.⁴				
2×4	1.5 × 3.5	5.250	3.063	5.359	.911	1.094	1.276	1.458
2×6	1.5 × 5.5	8.250	7.563	20.797	1.432	1.719	2.005	2.292
2×8	1.5 × 7.25	10.875	13.141	47.635	1.888	2.266	2.643	3.021
2×10	1.5 × 9.25	13.875	21.391	98.932	2.409	2.891	3.372	3.854
2×12	1.5 × 11.25	16.875	31.641	177.979	2.930	3.516	4.102	4.688

b = base of section
h = height of section

moment of inertia: stiff

Table 4.6 Reference Design Values for Various Species and Grades of Lumber, to Be Used with Factored Loads

Species and Commercial Grade	Flexure (bending)		Tension Parallel to Grain	Horizontal Shear	Compression Perpendicular to Grain	Compression Parallel to Grain	Material Stiffness	
	Single Member Uses	Repetitive Member Uses						
	F_B (lb/in.²)	F_B (lb/in.²)	F_T (lb/in.²)	F_V (lb/in.²)	$F_C\perp$ (lb/in.²)	F_C (lb/in.²)	E (lb/in.²)	E_{min} (lb/in.²)
Douglas fir—larch								
# 1	1,836	2,111	1,166	292	1,055	2,916	1,700,000	790,500
# 2	1,652	1,900	994	292	1,055	2,624	1,600,000	739,500
Studs	1,285	1,478	778	292	1,055	1,652	1,400,000	650,250
Hemlock—fir								
# 1	1,790	2,059	1,080	243	683	2,624	1,500,000	701,250
# 2	1,561	1,795	907	243	683	2,527	1,300,000	599,250
Studs	1,239	1,425	691	243	683	1,555	1,200,000	561,000
Spruce—pine—fir (south)								
# 1	1,607	1,847	691	219	565	2,041	1,200,000	561,000
# 2	1,423	1,636	605	219	565	1,944	1,100,000	510,000
Studs	1,102	1,267	475	219	565	1,215	1,000,000	471,750
Southern pine								
# 1—6 in. wide	3,029	3,484	1,555	284	953	3,402	1,700,000	790,500
# 1—8 in. wide	2,754	3,167	1,512	284	953	3,208	1,700,000	790,500
# 1—10 in. wide	2,387	2,745	1,253	284	953	3,110	1,700,000	790,500
# 1—12 in. wide	2,295	2,639	1,166	284	953	3,110	1,700,000	790,500
# 2—6 in. wide	2,295	2,639	1,253	284	953	3,110	1,600,000	739,500
# 2—8 in. wide	2,203	2,534	1,123	284	953	3,013	1,600,000	739,500
# 2—10 in. wide	1,928	2,217	994	284	953	2,916	1,600,000	739,500
# 2—12 in. wide	1,790	2,059	950	284	953	2,819	1,600,000	739,500
Studs	1,561	1,795	821	284	953	1,895	1,400,000	650,250

[handwritten margin note: typically buy #2.]

est and Paper Association of the American Wood Council. The data in this table are in the format appropriate to load and resistance factor design (LRFD), so the stress values represent limits under the factored loads typical of the LRFD method. The reduction factors, Φ, for each type of stress/structural action, have already been incorporated into the stress values in the table. In other words, the design procedure simply requires that the stress in each case under factored loads must be less than or equal to the stress value listed in the table. This table is unlike any of the data tables listed in the NDS, in that all the tables in the NDS are based on the allowed stress design (ASD) method, which relates stress values to UN-factored loads. Because the structural-design field is moving away from ASD toward LRFD, this book has formatted the data in Table 4.5 to work with the factored loads appropriate to the LRFD method. Readers of this book who would like to access the more extensive data tables in the NDS can either learn the ASD method or use the information at the end of the NDS to convert the data tables to the LRFD format. All the values in Table 4.6 have to be adjusted further,

based on the time effect factor, λ, in Table 4.7. Columns 2 and 3 in Table 4.6 address stress-limits for flexure (bending). The stress limit for repetitive-member usage is 15 percent higher than for single-member usage. This higher value is applied to such things as floor joists that are spaced not more than 24 in. OC and to headers that are doubled-up, solid-sawn boards. The lower stress value for single-member usage is based on the statistical fact that a really bad single beam has no other beam with which to share its load. Sharing a load among multiple members smoothes out the statistical variations in the failure stress of the members, eliminating the most extreme low values.

The structural response of wood varies according to the duration of the load. The longer the load is applied, the greater the creep that will occur. Moreover, some force levels, when applied for a short period of time, will not damage the structure, but the same force levels applied for long periods of time will damage the structure. To account for this behavior, a time-effect factor is applied to the stresses in Table 4.6. Longer-term loads have lower time-effect factors, meaning that the adjusted ref-

Table 4.7 Time Effect Factor, λ, for Use with the LRFD Method

Load Combination	λ
$1.2D + 1.6L + 1.0L_r$	0.7 when L is from storage
	0.8 when L is from occupancy
	1.25 when L is from impact
$1.2D + 1.6W + 1.0L + 1.0L_r$	1.0

Where D = dead load, L = live load, L_r = live/snow load on roof, and W = wind load.

erence design value for stress will be lower for longer-term loads.

Table 4.7 gives the time effect factor, λ, for use with the LRFD method. Reference design values are multiplied by the time-effect factor indicated in the table, corresponding to the load combinations shown. Time-effect factors reduce the reference design values to account for the deleterious effect of long-duration loads.

4.3 Steel Properties

Steel Manufacturing Processes

Standard steel structural shapes of open cross section (such as channels, I-beams, wide flanges, angles, etc.) are rolled. In this process, a billet of steel is heated to about 1,600°F and then passed through a series of rollers that gradually form it into the desired shape. This process is very expensive—on the order of hundreds of thousands of dollars to tool up for a single shape.

Rolling improves the physical and mechanical properties of the steel. The steel is plastically deformed during the rolling process, which causes planes of atoms to slide past each other. This sliding is accommodated by dislocations in the crystal lattice. During the sliding process, carbon atoms get lodged in the dislocations, jamming the dislocations and inhibiting further movement. In this manner, the steel becomes stronger during the rolling process. For steel wide flanges, the rolling process occurs while the metal is orange hot. Some shapes, such as rod and plate, can be *cold-rolled*, producing a higher grade of steel and a superior finish on the product.

There are many steps in the rolling operation. These are required because of two factors: First, the steel shape cannot be reduced in cross section too rapidly, without danger of causing surface ruptures. Second, the rollers must pull the material through as it is being formed. In order to do this, the rollers must bite. Attempting a reduction too great on any single pass would cause the angle of bite to be too large, thereby preventing the bite from actually occurring.

Figure 4.14 illustrates the forces involved in rolling a steel section. Friction between the steel billet and the rollers pulls the billet through the rollers. The process of mashing the steel billet produces a force in the opposite direction to the friction force. This opposing force is tending to push the billet back out of the rollers. On the shallow slope of the interface between the roller and billet, the net force is tending to draw the billet through the rollers. On the steeply sloped part of the interface between the roller and the billet, the net force is tending to reject the billet. If a change in shape that is too great is attempted in any one pass, the force tending to reject the billet will exceed the friction force pulling the billet through the rollers.

Because of the expense of tooling for rolling steel sections, a designer usually tries to find a standard steel shape that will efficiently meet the structural requirements, rather than inventing a new shape. Where special shapes or very large sections are required, welded sections, called *plate girders*, can be made. (Wide-flange sections are available in depths up to 44 in.)

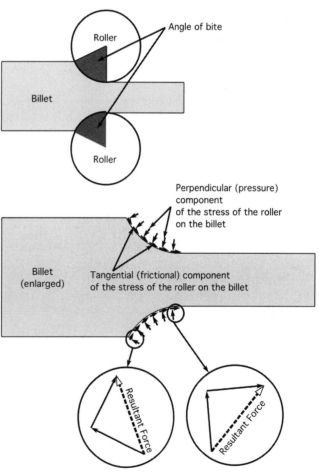

Figure 4.14 Force interaction between rollers and steel billet being rolled.

Figure 4.15 Coiled steel plate waiting to be used. (Image courtesy of Copperweld Corporation.)

Structural pipe or round tubing is made from flat coil stock that is formed into a closed shape by a series of rollers, then welded and trimmed smooth. Figure 4.15 shows coils of steel plate of various widths and thicknesses waiting to be formed into hollow steel sections. This is called *coil stock*.

Figure 4.16 shows steel coil stock being dragged into the coil holder before being fed into the rollers to be made into hollow steel sections. The coil holder twists and bends the coil stock to form it into a helix. This helix can grow larger or smaller, like a pulsating spring, to accommodate variations in the speed of the rolling system versus the speed at which coil stock is being fed into the system.

Figure 4.17 shows a convex roller pressing down on the coil stock from above and a concave roller pressing up on the coil stock from below. These concave rollers press against the outside surface of the steel coil stock. This pair of rollers is in the early stages of rolling the coil stock into a round tube.

Figure 4.18 shows a set of intermediate rollers. The upper, convex roller and the lower, concave roller are now joined by a series of concave rollers on the side. The side rollers press the coil stock together and start the process

Figure 4.16 Coiled steel plate stock being fed into holder. (Image courtesy of Copperweld Corporation.)

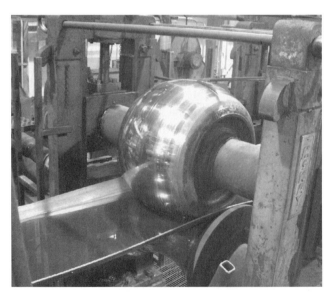

Figure 4.17 Convex roller above pressing coil stock down into concave roller below. (Image courtesy of Copperweld Corporation.)

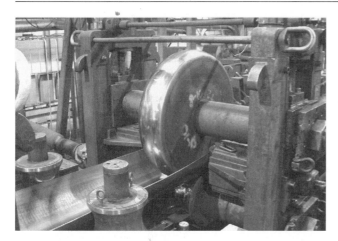

Figure 4.18 Concave rollers below and on the sides. (Image courtesy of Copperweld Corporation.)

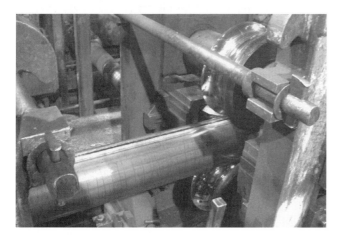

Figure 4.19 Final rollers are concave on all sides, including top. (Image courtesy of Copperweld Corporation.)

Figure 4.20 Induction welder. (Image courtesy of Copperweld Corporation.)

of curling it over the top, in the first step in bringing it to closure.

Figure 4.19 shows the final stages of the rolling process, in which concave rollers are on all sides. The concave roller on the top assists the side rollers in bringing the material together on the top.

Figure 4.20 shows a tube being welded with the use of an induction welder. Two side rollers press the curved coil stock inward to close the gap at the top. Power is delivered to the weld through the two large canted welding wheels straddling the seam where the weld is occurring. Getting the correct adjustment on each roller, the right speed of movement of the stock, and the appropriate power input to the welder are crucial to getting the correct outcome from the process. Once every variable is correctly set, it is crucial to keep the process going at a steady pace, to produce as much quality product as possible, before turning the machine off to change out the rollers to produce another size of tube. To provide high speeds of production, welders may operate at close to a megawatt of power. Production proceeds at about 10

ft/sec, and a long production space is required to stop the process when something in the process needs adjusting. The production line is also long because the circular saws that cut off the tube have to move with the tube. These saws are typically about 6 ft in diameter and about $1/2$ in. thick. They have to hack through the material very rapidly and then move back up the assembly line to make the next cut.

Square tube is made by mashing round tube, using rollers pressing in on four sides. Figure 4.21 shows two stages in that "mashing" operation.

Steel can also be formed into high-strength wire by repeatedly drawing it through drawing dies, each of which reduces the diameter of the material. The process of drawing the material through the die "smears" the material on the surface of the wire. This smearing work-hardens the wire, making the yield strength of the wire very high. The nib is made out of a very hard material, such as tungsten carbide sintered in a cobalt matrix (see Figure 4.22).

Steel Nomenclature

The terms and symbols defined here are occasionally referenced in this discussion and in other sections of this text. It would be useful for you to read each of the following definitions to see if you understand the concept that is described, and begin to familiarize yourself with them. Some will not be comprehensible at this point, but

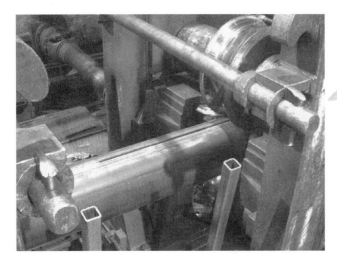

(a)

(b)

Figure 4.21 (a, b) Mashing round tube into square tube. (Image courtesy of Copperweld Corporation.)

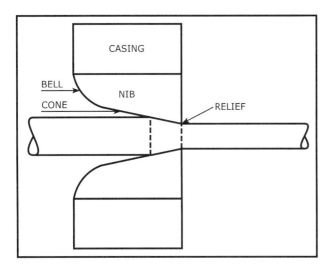

Figure 4.22 Diagram of die for drawing steel wire.

they will be revisited as your knowledge expands. In the meantime, remember where this section is, because you will occasionally have to refer to it to get the definition of terms and symbols that occur in your reading.

Glossary of Steel Symbols

A_g = gross cross-sectional area

A_n = net cross-sectional area

Actual stresses occurring under specified loading are designated using a lowercase f:

f_a = computed axial stress (K/in.^{2})

f_b = computed bending stress (K/in.^{2})

Limit stresses, as limited by the material or the building code, are designated using the capital letter F:

F_y = failure stress as limited by yielding of the steel, that is, as limited by plastic flow, in tension or compression, of the steel (ksi)

$F_{y'''}$ = failure stress as limited by web buckling (for any combinations of axial and bending loads) (ksi)

I_x = moment of inertia about the x–x (strong) axis (in.^{4})

I_y = moment of inertia about the y–y (weak) axis (in.^{4})

J = torsional constant (in.^{4})

K = effective length factor

L = length of spanning member or axially loaded member (ft)

L_c = maximum spacing between lateral bracing that will allow the compression flange of a bending member to achieve the full stress capacity of the material (F_y); that is, the spacing of lateral bracing that will prevent lateral buckling of the compression flange from limiting the strength of the beam (ft)

M = moment (kip · ft)

S = section modulus (in.^{3})

Z = plastic section modulus (in.^{3})

d = depth of column, beam, or girder (in.)

t_f = thickness of flange (in.)

t_w = thickness of web (in.)

Figure 4.23 shows dimensional data for some wide-flange sections from the *Manual of Steel Construction* from the American Institute of Steel Construction (AISC). In the designation of wide-flange sections, the *W* stands for wide flange, the first number is the nominal depth, and the second number is the weight in lb/ft. This particular figure illustrates dramatically that the nominal depth and the actual depth can be substantially different. In the system of rolling shapes, it is possible to get a whole series of different weights of beams using the same set of rollers by simply stopping the process at a different number of

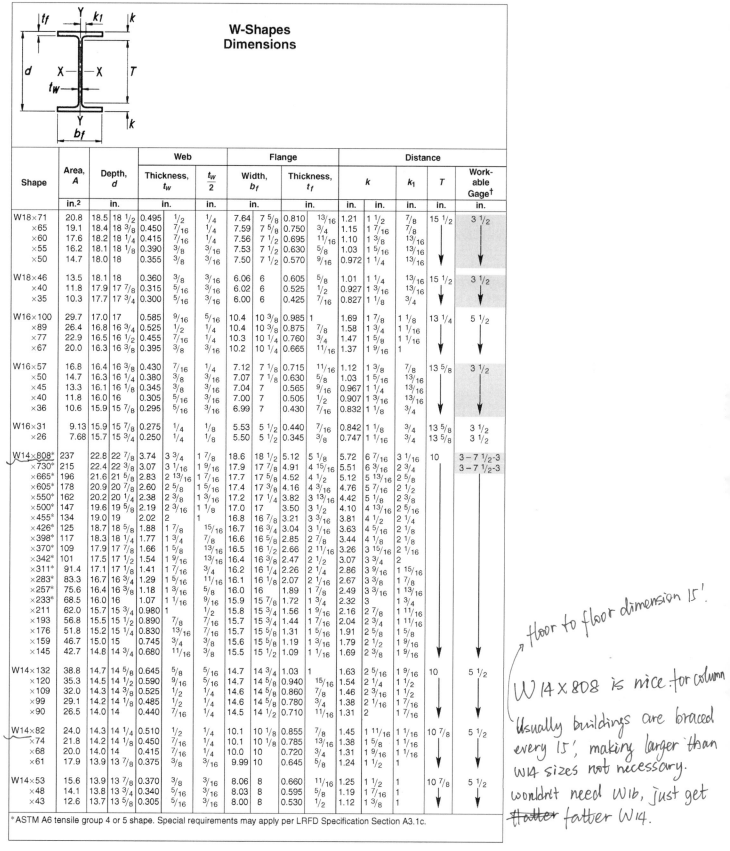

W-Shapes Dimensions

Shape	Area, A	Depth, d	Web Thickness, t_w	$\frac{t_w}{2}$	Flange Width, b_f	Flange Thickness, t_f	k	k_1	T	Workable Gage†
	in.²	in.	in.	in.	in.	in.	in.	in.	in.	in.
W18×71	20.8	18.5 18 1/2	0.495 1/2	1/4	7.64 7 5/8	0.810 13/16	1.21 1 1/2	7/8	15 1/2	3 1/2
×65	19.1	18.4 18 3/8	0.450 7/16	1/4	7.59 7 5/8	0.750 3/4	1.15 1 7/16	7/8		
×60	17.6	18.2 18 1/4	0.415 7/16	1/4	7.56 7 1/2	0.695 11/16	1.10 1 3/8	13/16		
×55	16.2	18.1 18 1/8	0.390 3/8	3/16	7.53 7 1/2	0.630 5/8	1.03 1 5/16	13/16		
×50	14.7	18.0 18	0.355 3/8	3/16	7.50 7 1/2	0.570 9/16	0.972 1 1/4	13/16		
W18×46	13.5	18.1 18	0.360 3/8	3/16	6.06 6	0.605 5/8	1.01 1 1/4	13/16	15 1/2	3 1/2
×40	11.8	17.9 17 7/8	0.315 5/16	3/16	6.02 6	0.525 1/2	0.927 1 3/16	13/16		
×35	10.3	17.7 17 3/4	0.300 5/16	3/16	6.00 6	0.425 7/16	0.827 1 1/8	3/4		
W16×100	29.7	17.0 17	0.585 9/16	5/16	10.4 10 3/8	0.985 1	1.69 1 7/8	1 1/8	13 1/4	5 1/2
×89	26.4	16.8 16 3/4	0.525 1/2	1/4	10.4 10 3/8	0.875 7/8	1.58 1 3/4	1 1/16		
×77	22.9	16.5 16 1/2	0.455 7/16	1/4	10.3 10 1/4	0.760 3/4	1.47 1 5/8	1 1/16		
×67	20.0	16.3 16 3/8	0.395 3/8	3/16	10.2 10 1/4	0.665 11/16	1.37 1 9/16	1		
W16×57	16.8	16.4 16 3/8	0.430 7/16	1/4	7.12 7 1/8	0.715 11/16	1.12 1 3/8	7/8	13 5/8	3 1/2
×50	14.7	16.3 16 1/4	0.380 3/8	3/16	7.07 7 1/8	0.630 5/8	1.03 1 5/16	13/16		
×45	13.3	16.1 16 1/8	0.345 3/8	3/16	7.04 7	0.565 9/16	0.967 1 1/4	13/16		
×40	11.8	16.0 16	0.305 5/16	3/16	7.00 7	0.505 1/2	0.907 1 3/16	13/16		
×36	10.6	15.9 15 7/8	0.295 5/16	3/16	6.99 7	0.430 7/16	0.832 1 1/8	3/4		
W16×31	9.13	15.9 15 7/8	0.275 1/4	1/8	5.53 5 1/2	0.440 7/16	0.842 1 1/8	3/4	13 5/8	3 1/2
×26	7.68	15.7 15 3/4	0.250 1/4	1/8	5.50 5 1/2	0.345 3/8	0.747 1 1/16	3/4	13 5/8	3 1/2
W14×808*	237	22.8 22 7/8	3.74 3 3/4	1 7/8	18.6 18 1/2	5.12 5 1/8	5.72 6 7/16	3 1/16	10	3 – 7 1/2 – 3
×730	215	22.4 22 3/8	3.07 3 1/16	1 9/16	17.9 17 7/8	4.91 4 15/16	5.51 6 3/16	2 3/4		3 – 7 1/2 – 3
×665*	196	21.6 21 5/8	2.83 2 13/16	1 7/16	17.7 17 5/8	4.52 4 1/2	5.12 5 13/16	2 5/8		
×605*	178	20.9 20 7/8	2.60 2 5/8	1 5/16	17.4 17 3/8	4.16 4 3/16	4.76 5 7/16	2 1/2		
×550*	162	20.2 20 1/4	2.38 2 3/8	1 3/16	17.2 17 1/4	3.82 3 13/16	4.42 5 1/8	2 3/8		
×500*	147	19.6 19 5/8	2.19 2 3/16	1 1/8	17.0 17	3.50 3 1/2	4.10 4 13/16	2 3/8		
×455*	134	19.0 19	2.02 2	1	16.8 16 7/8	3.21 3 3/16	3.81 4 1/2	2 1/4		
×426*	125	18.7 18 5/8	1.88 1 7/8	15/16	16.7 16 3/4	3.04 3 1/16	3.63 4 5/16	2 1/8		
×398*	117	18.3 18 1/4	1.77 1 3/4	7/8	16.6 16 5/8	2.85 2 7/8	3.44 4 1/8	2 1/8		
×370*	109	17.9 17 7/8	1.66 1 5/8	13/16	16.5 16 1/2	2.66 2 11/16	3.26 3 15/16	2 1/8		
×342*	101	17.5 17 1/2	1.54 1 9/16	13/16	16.4 16 3/8	2.47 2 1/2	3.07 3 3/4	2		
×311*	91.4	17.1 17 1/8	1.41 1 7/16	3/4	16.2 16 1/4	2.26 2 1/4	2.86 3 9/16	1 15/16		
×283*	83.3	16.7 16 3/4	1.29 1 5/16	11/16	16.1 16 1/8	2.07 2 1/16	2.67 3 3/8	1 7/8		
×257*	75.6	16.4 16 3/8	1.18 1 3/16	5/8	16.0 16	1.89 1 7/8	2.49 3 3/16	1 13/16		
×233*	68.5	16.0 16	1.07 1 1/16	9/16	15.9 15 7/8	1.72 1 3/4	2.32 3	1 3/4		
×211	62.0	15.7 15 3/4	0.980 1	1/2	15.8 15 3/4	1.56 1 9/16	2.16 2 7/8	1 11/16		
×193	56.8	15.5 15 1/2	0.890 7/8	7/16	15.7 15 3/4	1.44 1 7/16	2.04 2 3/4	1 11/16		
×176	51.8	15.2 15 1/4	0.830 13/16	7/16	15.7 15 5/8	1.31 1 5/16	1.91 2 5/8	1 5/8		
×159	46.7	15.0 15	0.745 3/4	3/8	15.6 15 5/8	1.19 1 3/16	1.79 2 1/2	1 9/16		
×145	42.7	14.8 14 3/4	0.680 11/16	3/8	15.5 15 1/2	1.09 1 1/16	1.69 2 3/8	1 9/16		
W14×132	38.8	14.7 14 5/8	0.645 5/8	5/16	14.7 14 3/4	1.03 1	1.63 2 5/16	1 9/16	10	5 1/2
×120	35.3	14.5 14 1/2	0.590 9/16	5/16	14.7 14 5/8	0.940 15/16	1.54 2 1/4	1 1/2		
×109	32.0	14.3 14 3/8	0.525 1/2	1/4	14.6 14 5/8	0.860 7/8	1.46 2 3/16	1 1/2		
×99	29.1	14.2 14 1/8	0.485 1/2	1/4	14.6 14 5/8	0.780 3/4	1.38 2 1/8	1 7/16		
×90	26.5	14.0 14	0.440 7/16	1/4	14.5 14 1/2	0.710 11/16	1.31 2	1 7/16		
W14×82	24.0	14.3 14 1/4	0.510 1/2	1/4	10.1 10 1/8	0.855 7/8	1.45 1 11/16	1 1/16	10 7/8	5 1/2
×74	21.8	14.2 14 1/8	0.450 7/16	1/4	10.1 10 1/8	0.785 13/16	1.38 1 5/8	1 1/16		
×68	20.0	14.0 14	0.415 7/16	1/4	10.0 10	0.720 3/4	1.31 1 9/16	1 1/16		
×61	17.9	13.9 13 7/8	0.375 3/8	3/16	9.99 10	0.645 5/8	1.24 1 1/2	1		
W14×53	15.6	13.9 13 7/8	0.370 3/8	3/16	8.06 8	0.660 11/16	1.25 1 1/2	1	10 7/8	5 1/2
×48	14.1	13.8 13 3/4	0.340 5/16	3/16	8.03 8	0.595 5/8	1.19 1 7/16	1		
×43	12.6	13.7 13 5/8	0.305 5/16	3/16	8.00 8	0.530 1/2	1.12 1 3/8	1		

* ASTM A6 tensile group 4 or 5 shape. Special requirements may apply per LRFD Specification Section A3.1c.

Figure 4.23 Dimensions for some steel wide-flange (W) sections. (Copyright American Institute of Steel Construction, Inc. Reprinted with permission. All rights reserved.)

[Handwritten margin notes:] floor to floor dimension 15'. W14×808 is nice for column. Usually buildings are braced every 15', making larger than W14 sizes not necessary. wouldn't need W16, just get ~~flatter~~ fatter W14.

passes through the rollers. A series of rollers that may have a 14 in.-deep beam as the end product of every rolling step can produce several beams much deeper than 14 in. deep by simply terminating the rolling process at an earlier step. In the Table 4.23, a W14 × 808 beam is nominally 14 in. deep because of the series that it is a part of, but its actual depth is 22.8 in. Its flanges are 18 in. wide. The beam weighs 808 lb/ft, which is extraordinarily heavy. There are many nominal 14 in. sections because 14 in. wide flanges make very good columns. They are large enough that buckling is not a problem, but compact enough that they do not take up much floor area. The pages on dimensional data are used by architects in practice more than any other part of the AISC manual because architects need to know how large things are in order to draw up details and to figure out how much volume the steel members are going to consume in the building. W-sections come in a range of stress grades, depending on the size of the member and the manufacturer.

Typically, they are available in grades $F_y = 36$ K/in.^{2} and 50 K/in.^{2}, and sometimes 65 K/in.^{2}. Before one proceeds with any design, it is appropriate to check on the availability of various grades of steel for various section sizes.

usually [handwritten annotation]

Some of the other data presented in these tables are addressed in Chapters 5 and 6.

Figure 4.24 contains dimensions and properties for round hollow steel sections (HSS). An HSS 3.000 × 0.250 has an outside diameter of 3 in. and a wall thickness of 0.25 in. The outer dimensions of the tubes are very regular, available in 1 in. or ½ in. increments, in contrast to the W-flange sections, which have all manner of odd dimensions. Round HSS sections are available in a stress grade of 42 K/in.^{2}. No tables are shown for square or rectangular HSS, but they also have very regular outside dimensions and regular wall thicknesses. Square tube and rectangular tube are available in 46 K/in.^{2} steel. *HSS* [handwritten]

Figure 4.25 contains dimensions and properties for steel pipe. Steel pipe was originally developed for

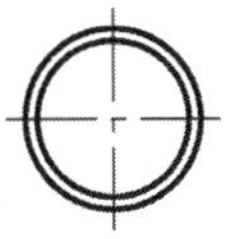

Shape	Wall Thickness, t		Nominal Wt.	Area, A	$\frac{D}{t}$	I	S	r	Z	Torsion		Surf. Area Per Ft
	nominal	design								J	C	
	in.	in.	lb/ft	in.^{2}		in.^{4}	in.^{3}	in.	in.^{3}	in.^{4}	in.^{3}	ft^2
HSS3.500	0.313	0.291	10.7	2.93	12.0	3.81	2.18	1.14	3.00	7.61	4.35	0.916
	0.300	0.280	10.3	2.83	12.5	3.70	2.11	1.14	2.91	7.40	4.23	0.916
	0.250	0.233	8.69	2.39	15.0	3.21	1.83	1.16	2.49	6.41	3.66	0.916
	0.216	0.201	7.58	2.08	17.4	2.84	1.63	1.17	2.19	5.69	3.25	0.916
	0.203	0.189	7.15	1.97	18.5	2.70	1.54	1.17	2.07	5.41	3.09	0.916
	0.188	0.174	6.66	1.82	20.1	2.52	1.44	1.18	1.93	5.04	2.88	0.916
	0.125	0.116	4.51	1.23	30.2	1.77	1.01	1.20	1.33	3.53	2.02	0.916
HSS3.000	0.300	0.280	8.66	2.39	10.7	2.24	1.49	0.967	2.08	4.47	2.98	0.785
	0.250	0.233	7.35	2.03	12.9	1.95	1.30	0.982	1.79	3.90	2.60	0.785
	0.216	0.201	6.43	1.77	14.9	1.74	1.16	0.992	1.58	3.48	2.32	0.785
	0.203	0.189	6.07	1.67	15.9	1.66	1.10	1.00	1.50	3.31	2.21	0.785
	0.188	0.174	5.65	1.54	17.2	1.55	1.03	1.00	1.39	3.10	2.06	0.785
	0.152	0.142	4.63	1.27	21.1	1.30	0.870	1.01	1.16	2.61	1.74	0.785
	0.134	0.125	4.11	1.13	24.0	1.17	0.779	1.02	1.03	2.34	1.56	0.785
	0.120	0.112	3.69	1.02	26.8	1.06	0.707	1.02	0.935	2.12	1.41	0.785
HSS2.875	0.250	0.233	7.02	1.93	12.3	1.70	1.18	0.938	1.63	3.40	2.37	0.753
	0.203	0.189	5.80	1.59	15.2	1.45	1.01	0.952	1.37	2.89	2.01	0.753
	0.188	0.174	5.40	1.48	16.5	1.35	0.941	0.957	1.27	2.70	1.88	0.753
	0.125	0.116	3.67	1.01	24.8	0.958	0.667	0.976	0.884	1.92	1.33	0.753
HSS2.500	0.250	0.233	6.01	1.66	10.7	1.08	0.862	0.806	1.20	2.15	1.72	0.654
	0.188	0.174	4.65	1.27	14.4	0.865	0.692	0.825	0.943	1.73	1.38	0.654
	0.125	0.116	3.17	0.869	21.6	0.619	0.495	0.844	0.660	1.24	0.990	0.654
HSS2.375	0.250	0.233	5.68	1.57	10.2	0.910	0.766	0.762	1.07	1.82	1.53	0.622
	0.218	0.204	5.03	1.39	11.6	0.827	0.696	0.771	0.964	1.65	1.39	0.622
	0.188	0.174	4.40	1.20	13.6	0.733	0.617	0.781	0.845	1.47	1.23	0.622
	0.154	0.143	3.66	1.00	16.6	0.627	0.528	0.791	0.713	1.25	1.06	0.622
	0.125	0.116	3.01	0.823	20.5	0.527	0.443	0.800	0.592	1.05	0.887	0.622
HSS1.900	0.145	0.135	2.72	0.749	14.1	0.293	0.309	0.626	0.421	0.586	0.617	0.497
HSS1.660	0.140	0.130	2.27	0.625	12.8	0.184	0.222	0.543	0.305	0.368	0.444	0.435

3.5 in outside dimension [handwritten annotation, left margin, pointing to HSS3.500]

Figure 4.24 Dimensions and properties for some round HSS sections. (Copyright American Institute of Steel Construction, Inc. Reprinted with permission.)

Diameter			Wall Thickness, t	Nominal Wt.	Area, A	$\frac{D}{t}$	I	S	r	Z	J
Nominal	Outside	Inside									
in.	in.	in.	in.	lb/ft	in.²		in.⁴	in.³	in.	in.³	in.⁴
Standard Weight (Std.)											
12	12.8	12.0	0.375	49.6	14.6	34.0	279	43.8	4.38	57.4	559
10	10.8	10.0	0.365	40.5	11.9	29.5	161	29.9	3.67	39.4	321
8	8.63	7.98	0.322	28.6	8.40	26.8	72.5	16.8	2.94	22.2	145
6	6.63	6.07	0.280	19.0	5.58	23.7	28.1	8.50	2.25	11.3	56.3
5	5.56	5.05	0.258	14.6	4.30	21.6	15.2	5.45	1.88	7.27	30.3
4	4.50	4.03	0.237	10.8	3.17	19.0	7.23	3.21	1.51	4.31	14.5
3 1/2	4.00	3.55	0.226	9.12	2.68	17.7	4.79	2.39	1.34	3.22	9.58
3	3.50	3.07	0.216	7.58	2.23	16.2	3.02	1.72	1.16	2.33	6.03
2 1/2	2.88	2.47	0.203	5.80	1.70	14.2	1.53	1.06	0.947	1.45	3.06
2	2.38	2.07	0.154	3.66	1.07	15.4	0.666	0.561	0.787	0.761	1.33
1 1/2	1.90	1.61	0.145	2.72	0.799	13.1	0.310	0.326	0.623	0.448	0.62
1 1/4	1.66	1.38	0.140	2.27	0.669	11.9	0.195	0.235	0.540	0.324	0.389
1	1.32	1.05	0.133	1.68	0.494	9.89	0.0873	0.133	0.421	0.187	0.175
3/4	1.05	0.824	0.113	1.13	0.333	9.29	0.0370	0.0705	0.334	0.0997	0.0741
1/2	0.840	0.622	0.109	0.852	0.250	7.71	0.0171	0.0407	0.261	0.0587	0.0342
Extra Strong (X-Strong)											
12	12.8	11.8	0.500	65.5	19.2	25.5	362	56.7	4.33	75.1	723
10	10.8	9.75	0.500	54.8	16.1	21.5	212	39.4	3.63	52.6	424
8	8.63	7.63	0.500	43.4	12.8	17.3	106	24.5	2.88	33.0	211
6	6.63	5.76	0.432	28.6	8.40	15.3	40.5	12.2	2.19	16.6	81.0
5	5.56	4.81	0.375	20.8	6.11	14.8	20.7	7.43	1.84	10.1	41.3
4	4.50	3.83	0.337	15.0	4.41	13.4	9.61	4.27	1.48	5.85	19.2
3 1/2	4.00	3.36	0.318	12.5	3.68	12.6	6.28	3.14	1.31	4.32	12.6
3	3.5	2.90	0.300	10.3	3.02	11.7	3.89	2.23	1.14	3.08	7.79
2 1/2	2.88	2.32	0.276	7.67	2.25	10.4	1.92	1.34	0.924	1.87	3.85
2	2.38	1.94	0.218	5.03	1.48	10.9	0.868	0.731	0.766	1.02	1.74
1 1/2	1.90	1.50	0.200	3.63	1.07	9.50	0.391	0.412	0.605	0.581	0.782
1 1/4	1.66	1.28	0.191	3.00	0.881	8.69	0.242	0.291	0.524	0.414	0.484
1	1.32	0.957	0.179	2.17	0.639	7.35	0.106	0.161	0.407	0.233	0.211
3/4	1.05	0.742	0.154	1.48	0.433	6.82	0.0448	0.0853	0.321	0.125	0.0896
1/2	0.840	0.546	0.147	1.09	0.320	5.71	0.0201	0.0478	0.250	0.0717	0.0402
Double-Extra Strong (XX-Strong)											
8	8.63	6.88	0.875	72.5	21.3	9.86	162	37.6	2.76	52.8	324
6	6.63	4.90	0.864	53.2	15.6	7.67	66.3	20.0	2.06	28.9	133
5	5.56	4.06	0.750	38.6	11.3	7.42	33.6	12.1	1.72	17.5	67.3
4	4.50	3.15	0.674	27.6	8.10	6.68	15.3	6.79	1.37	9.97	30.6
3	3.50	2.30	0.600	18.6	5.47	5.83	5.99	3.42	1.05	5.12	12.0
2 1/2	2.88	1.77	0.552	13.7	4.03	5.21	2.87	2.00	0.844	3.03	5.74
2	2.38	1.50	0.436	9.04	2.66	5.45	1.31	1.10	0.703	1.67	2.62

Steel Pipe Dimensions and Properties

Figure 4.25 Dimensions and properties for steel pipe. (Copyright American Institute of Steel Construction, Inc. Reprinted with permission.)

plumbing applications. The inside diameter of the pipe is about equal to the nominal diameter of the pipe, although even that dimension is not very regular. Typically, the inside diameter is slightly larger than the nominal diameter. The wall thickness increases with diameter, producing very odd outside diameters. These strange dimensions make steel pipe inappropriate for certain kinds of connection detailing. However, for most standard steel connection details, the odd dimensions of pipe cause no trouble. Extra-strong pipe has thicker walls, but the same inside diameter as standard pipe. Double-extra-strong pipe has even thicker walls. Steel pipe is available in a stress grade of 35 K/in.^{2}.

4.4 Concrete Properties

The primary ingredients of concrete are portland cement, water, sand, and stone aggregate. The water combines chemically with the portland cement in a chemical process called *hydration*, which causes the cement to harden and, in the process, to bind the sand and aggregate together into a monolithic material. Typically, the curing process achieves 90 percent of ultimate strength after about 28 days, but the concrete continues to grow stronger over the life of the material. Other chemicals, called *accelerants* and *retardants*, can be added to increase or slow the curing rate. Temperature also has a significant impact on the curing rate. Retardants tend to be needed to slow down the process during the hot months of summer, and accelerants are most appropriate during the cold months. Using accelerants during the warm months is problematical in that the heat of hydration during the curing process, combined with the high ambient temperatures, can cause severe cracking and damage to the concrete.

The main determinant of the strength of a concrete is the correct proportioning of the primary ingredients. Too little water can either cause incomplete hydration or cause the concrete to be sufficiently stiff and dry that it is difficult to place without having large voids that cause stress risers and reduced strength. Too much water will result in many tiny voids that cause local stress concentration and reduced strength. Too much aggregate and sand, and there will not be enough cement to bind it properly. Too little aggregate and sand will cause the concrete to overheat owing to the heat of hydration. Too little aggregate and sand will also adversely affect the economics, inasmuch as these ingredients are less expensive than the cement. Plasticizers can be added to make the concrete more fluid without adding excessive amounts of water.

Concrete is graded in terms of the compression stress that produces crushing of the material, designated by the symbol f_c'. Grades of concrete with f_c' in the range of

Table 4.8 Crushing Stress and Stiffness for Various Grades of Concrete

Grade	f_c' Crushing Stress (lb/in.^{2})	E Material Stiffness (lb/in.^{2})
2,000 psi	2,000	2,550,000
3,000 psi	3,000	3,120,000
4,000 psi	4,000	3,600,000
5,000 psi	5,000	4,030,000
6,000 psi	6,000	4,420,000
7,000 psi	7,000	4,770,000
8,000 psi	8,000	5,100,000

3,000 to 5,000 psi are commonly available everywhere in the United States. F_c' in the range of 5,000–6,000 psi is readily available in most precast plants. Much higher stress grades are available in some parts of the country where the technology is very advanced and the delivery infrastructure is in place.

Unlike steel, concrete has variable stiffness, which correlates with its crushing stress, as shown in Table 4.8.

Concrete is much weaker in tension than in compression. As a consequence, it must be reinforced anywhere that tension is going to occur. Reinforcement is most commonly a problem in beams, where the nature of the structural process produces tension in as many locations as it produces compression. This is typically accomplished using steel rebar or steel cable, similar to that shown in Figure 4.26. The image in (a) shows standard steel rebar, with ridges for enhancing the shear engagement with the concrete. The most common standard grade for steel rebar is F_y = 60-KSI (called *grade 60*), but F_y = 75-KSI (grade 75) is also available. Grades above 80 are not permitted except in precast concrete, where high-strength steel cable is used. The standard diameters for steel rebar are in increments of $\frac{1}{8}$ in. diameter. Rebar is designated by number. For example, a number 8 rebar has a diameter of $\frac{8}{8}$ in., or 1 in., and a number 13 rebar has a diameter of $\frac{13}{8}$ in., or $1\frac{5}{8}$ in. Figure 4.26 (b) shows steel cable that has been pretensioned in a casting bed being used to make a prestressed, precast wall. Because of its very high strength, steel cable is usually used in smaller diameters than steel rebar.

Sizing, spacing, and locating the steel reinforcing are beyond the scope of this book, except for some very basic examples that are given in Chapters 5 and 6. However, it is still possible for students using this text to tackle some fairly complicated concrete structures in a preliminary way, even including multistory, rigid frames, by using a computer and making some simplifying assumptions.

The concept behind the method is fairly straightforward. In general steel is being used to replace the con-

→ wire the steel to keep them from moving until concrete cures around it.

4.5 ALUMINUM PROPERTIES   **129**

(a)

(b)

Figure 4.26 (a) Steel reinforcing bar and (b) high-strength steel cable.

crete that does not work in tension. If adequate amounts of steel are supplied, then the steel essentially restores the capacity that is lost due to the weakness of the concrete in tension. Therefore, in regard to strength, computer analyses can be performed on members with rectangular cross sections by assuming that the entire section of concrete is active in both compression and tension. The primary flaw in this approach is that the steel deforms more than the concrete would, assuming that the concrete truly remained active in tension up to the appropriate stress levels. Therefore, the analysis will indicate a stiffer structure than will occur when the cracked concrete is accounted for. To compensate for this discrepancy, the computer simulation should be done for any members in bending using a stiffness that is half of the stiffness given in Table 4.8. A 4,000 psi concrete would be simulated with an $E = 0.5(3,600,000 \text{ lb/in.}^2) = 1,800,000 \text{ lb/in.}^2$ for all members in flexure. Columns that

are not in flexure can be simulated with the full E value of 3,600,000 lb/in.^{2}. In most rigid-frame concrete structures, all the vertical elements are in flexure under some loading condition, so the reduced E value will be used for those elements as well.

4.5 Aluminum Properties

Pure aluminum is a soft, extremely ductile metal. Although not classified as a noble metal, it is quite resistive to corrosion and is a much better choice than steel for direct exposure to the elements. There is a rich variety of alloying materials that can be used to modify the properties of aluminum. The designations for various alloys are given as a four-number sequence, each number indicating the amount of one of the common alloying materials that is mixed with the aluminum in the material. Understanding the complex array of properties possible with aluminum alloys is well beyond the capability of building designers. Therefore, the aluminum industry makes available, generally, a limited number of alloys of aluminum.

The common grade of aluminum for structural applications is 6061-T6, the first four numbers indicating the alloying composition and T6 meaning that the material has been heat tempered to a strength level of 6. The highest temper on the scale is 12. Some bicycle frames and some parts of airplanes may have a temper close to 12, but nothing in the building industry would have temper that high. Very high temper aluminum tends to loose some of its temper over time and also tends to be more susceptible to fatigue; that is, it tends to become brittle after millions of cycles of loading and unloading. This is more of a problem in airplanes and bicycle forks, where vibration can cause millions of cycles to occur, than it is in buildings.

For 6061-T6 aluminum, the yield stress is 35 KSI and the material stiffness is $E = 10,100$ KSI. This is the material depicted in the stress–strain diagrams in Section 4.1, "Materials: Basic Properties." In situations where finish and resistance to corrosion are more important than strength, the aluminum industry usually recommends a 3000 series alloy. These softer alloys are usually the materials of choice for framing around windows and doors. Special attention must be paid to the selection of an alloy when the local environment is fairly corrosive.

Among its other properties, aluminum:

- Can be extruded in complex and useful shapes while retaining structural strength.
- Can be extruded in closed shapes, such as tubes, without the need for rolling and welding, making these shapes much easier to achieve in aluminum than in steel.

(a)

(b)

Figure 4.27 (a, b) Hydraulic ram pushes billet into extrusion chamber and through the die.

- Can be forged into complex and useful shapes while retaining structural strength.
- Can be welded, but requires a more skillful welder and superior welding equipment than does steel.
- Can be machined more easily than steel.
- Tends to be weak and brittle when cast.

When reading the aluminum industry ratings on such properties as machinability and weldability, keep in mind that these ratings are relative to other aluminum alloys and not relative to steel. An A rating on weldability for an aluminum alloy does not mean that the material is as easy to weld as steel. It means that, as compared to other aluminum alloys, it welds fairly well.

Aluminum is extruded in a variety of standard shapes that duplicate many of the structural shapes in which steel is made, such as wide flanges, angles, pipe, round tube, and square tube. Because of limitations in the size of aluminum extruding equipment and a lack of demand, the standard structural shapes duplicate only the smaller sections made in the steel industry. The appeal of aluminum is not in the duplication of standard structural shapes, but in the huge variety of complex, intricate, and useful shapes that are possible in the extrusion process (such as in making slots for gaskets, thermal breaks, and other structural elements).

In Figure 4.27 (a) a hydraulic ram pushes a preheated billet of aluminum into the extrusion chamber and then (b) applies sufficient pressure to force the aluminum through the extrusion die. This particular machine is called a *10 in. press*, which accommodates a solid billet 10 in. in diameter. Presses ranging up to 12 in. are now common in the United States.

Figure 4.28 shows two plates of an extrusion die for making round tube. The image in (a) shows the first plate

in the die. The first plate is lying with its back side on the floor before assembly and use. In this case *back side* means the first face of the die against which the aluminum billet is pressed during the extrusion process. This particular die is being used on an extrusion press large enough that it allows the die to be configured to extrude four identical tubes at the same time. Aluminum is forced through twelve openings in the plate, three openings for each tube. The round elements at the center of three adjacent openings are the spreader elements that keep the aluminum from totally reconverging and forming a solid rod. The size of these spreader elements determine the inside diameter of a tube. The image in (b) shows the second plate of the two-plate extrusion die. Aluminum that comes through the first plate is forced up against the second plate. The spreader elements that are part of the first plate are long enough that they penetrate into the openings in the second plate. In this manner, the aluminum being extruded has die material both inside and outside simultaneously, which keeps the aluminum sufficiently contained so that the tubes can be formed. The pressure created by the constriction of the second plate causes the aluminum to re-fuse to itself, after having been separated into three "streams" of aluminum emerging from the three holes supplying a single tube.

Figure 4.29 shows an assembled two-plate die that is used to extrude one round tube at a time. The image in (a) shows the back side of the first plate, with four openings for allowing aluminum to be forced through the first plate. The image in (b) shows the other side of the assembled die. The small bolts that hold the two plates of the die together are for alignment purposes only. They could not possibly take the pressure of the aluminum being extruded. The entire die is placed internal to the extrusion chamber, so that the second plate is forced against

(a)

(b)

Figure 4.28 (a, b) Plates for a die to extrude four round tubes.

a very thick collar that defines the outlet from the chamber. This collar comes in very close to the extrusion opening, so that the effective span of the second plate in the extrusion die is fairly small. Furthermore, the net pressure of the aluminum tends to force the first plate of the extrusion die up against the second plate. Once the extrusion die is in place and the extrusion process is under way, the bolts are not necessary to hold the plates of the die together.

Aluminum emerging from the extruder is very hot and semimolten. It is cooled down either by water streams, air streams, or a combination of water and air. Aluminum is then stretched to produce a straighter, better tempered element with a better surface condition.

The benefits of aluminum are most apparent in situations where good structure, good appearance, corrosion resistance, and intricate linear details are required. For example, the extrusion shown in Figure 4.30, invented by TC Howard of Synergetics, Inc., is used in network domes. It has an I-section as the structural backbone. Integral with the I-section is a wide, flared flange that curls up to create a gutter for conducting water down the dome. Finally, it has integrated details that engage neoprene seals and the panels used to enclose the structure.

A widespread and excellent example of the use of aluminum mullions is illustrated in Figure 4.31, where the sequence of assembly is shown. The image in (a) shows

(a)

(b)

Figure 4.29 (a, b) Assembled die.

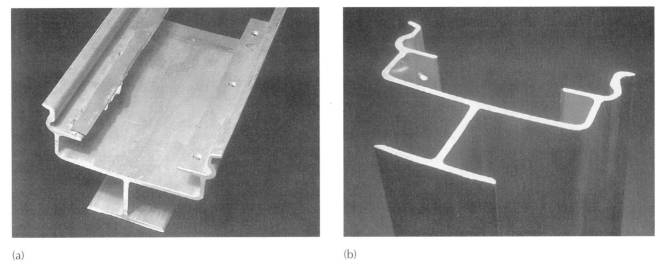

(a)   (b)

Figure 4.30 (a, b) Dome strut and gutter element by TC Howard.

(a)   (b)   (c)

Figure 4.31 (a–c) aluminum mullion assembly.

the main aluminum extrusion, consisting of a tube with slots for inserting neoprene gaskets and an integral, slotted fin for making connections to other parts of the assembly. The image in (b) shows a second aluminum extrusion being connected to the first using self-tapping screws that screw into the slot in the fin of the first extrusion.

The second extrusion also has neoprene gaskets for water-sealing the glass. The image in (c) shows a cap piece that snaps over the assembly, providing a visually finished product and obscuring the screws from any would-be burglar who may be tempted to unscrew the window framing.

5

Axial Members

5.1 Tension Members

Tension members fail by a yielding of the material. The design of a tension member requires two things:

- Sizing the cross-sectional area to safely resist yielding under the axial force
- Designing end connections that effectively transfer the force

Because there is no buckling involved in a tension member, the cross section can have any shape that is convenient, including being a solid rod.

With regard to sizing a cross section, the required area must be at least equal to the axial load under the factored load, divided by the resistance factor times the yield stress:

$$A_{required} \geq \frac{P_{factored}}{\Phi F_y} \qquad \textbf{[5.1]}$$

Some forms of end connections develop the full tension capacity of the member. For example, increasing the diameter of a tension rod at the ends of the rod can accommodate threading of the ends without diminishing the capacity of the ends. This geometry is shown in Figure 4.6. Threading the ends of the rod without increasing the diameter will drastically reduce the capacity of the end connection, because the threading operation reduces the effective cross-sectional area at the threads. The nature of the threads also causes stress concentration. Using flat plates with bolted connections for tension members has the same problem, in that the bolt holes remove useful tension material and cause stress concentration. Flat-plate tension members can also be increased in cross-sectional area at the end to avoid having the end connection govern the cross section. Such a tension member is called an *I-bar*, an example of which is shown in Figure 8.14. Well-designed and -executed welded connections can also develop the full capacity of a tension member. Stress distributions at connections are very complex, and the connections have to be sized for both yielding and fracture. Fracture occurs at the ultimate failure of the material. The details of connection design exceed the scope of this book. However, the basic issues involved in connections are an important part of conceptualizing structures.

The preceding equation for sizing the cross-sectional area of a tension member is one of the simplest used in designing structures. Sometimes, sizing a tension member is even easier than applying this equation. For example, in Section 5.3 of this chapter, tables are provided for the rapid selection of steel columns. These tables show a wide range of columns, even those of very short, fat proportions. Such a column fails by yielding; that is, it fails at the same stress at which it would if it were being used as a tension member. Using this table, a designer can select tension members by looking at the design axial force for columns of zero length. This topic is revisited in Section 5.3.

5.2 Columns: Generic Issues

Figure 5.1 shows the two classic modes of failure in columns.

In a column with fat proportions, failure occurs by crushing, that is, yielding of the material. For a fat column, the critical (or failure) force is given as follows:

$$F_{Cr\_Fat} = F_{yield} \qquad \textbf{[5.2]}$$

In columns of slender proportions, failure is initiated by elastic instability, which we usually refer to as *buckling*. The column moves out from under the load (buckles) before the stress reaches the yield stress of the material. The terminology *elastic instability* means that the structural element becomes unstable while the material is in a state of stress that is within the elastic range; that is, the stress has not exceeded the material's intrinsic stress limit, which is the yield stress. Instead the compression element fails at some lower stress level that is dictated by the geometry of the element in concert with inadequate stiffness of the material, which allows the compression member to "evade" the load by getting out from under it. This

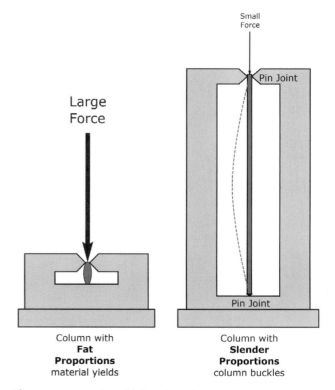

Figure 5.1 Modes of failure in columns.

process prevents the full utilization of the intrinsic stress capacity of the material.

In the buckling process, a deviation from straightness occurs. This deformation makes the column even less capable to withstand the load than it was in its original state. This causes further deviations, which results in even lower structural capacity. Once initiated, this process does not stop until the structural element fails catastrophically or until some other structural element picks up the load. In an actual building in which such a failure occurs, the material in the structural element will normally exceed its intrinsic stress capacity (the yield stress) before the building hits the ground. If this were not true, the building would "pop back up" after the load is removed. However, the fact remains that the failure was initiated by elastic instability and not by the stress reaching the yield stress of the material. Tracing the source of a building failure is often very difficult, inasmuch as almost all of the collapsed elements are severely damaged when the collapse is complete.

Buckling can occur even in a perfectly straight column. It is possible to prove this by describing a column that has an inherent lack of straightness and identifying a parameter that represents the deviation from straightness. Then a formula can be developed for the load that will fail the column. That formula contains the parameter that represents the deviation from straightness. When that parameter is allowed to approach zero, it produces a formula for the failure load for a perfectly straight column. The resulting formula is called *Euler's formula* for the failure load on a perfectly straight, slender column, which is the following:

$$F_{Cr\_slender} = \frac{\pi^2 E}{\left(\dfrac{L}{r}\right)^2},$$ **[5.3]**

where:

E = stiffness of material
L = length of column
r = radius of gyration
  = effective average distance of material in cross section from neutral axis of the cross section
  = indicator of "breadth" of column
L/r = slenderness ratio
π = pi = 3.14159

The critical material parameter is the material stiffness, E, rather than the yield stress, F_y.

The resistance factor, Φ, for a column will vary, depending on the material from which the column is made.

The radius of gyration, r, is an indicator of the effective structural breadth of the cross section. The radius of gyration is an area-weighted function that describes, on a kind of average basis, how far away the material in the cross section is from the neutral axis about which buckling is occurring. Typically, r is substantially smaller than the outer dimension of the cross section. Three examples are shown in Figure 5.2.

For the rectangle:
Radius of gyration with respect to buckling about the xx-axis (in this case, the strong axis).

$$r_{xx} = \frac{h}{\sqrt{12}} = 0.289\,h$$

Radius of gyration with respect to buckling about the yy-axis (in this case, the weak axis). Failure will occur about this axis, that is, with movement in the xx-direction, unless the column is braced against this mode of failure.

$$r_{yy} = \frac{b}{\sqrt{12}} = 0.289\,b$$

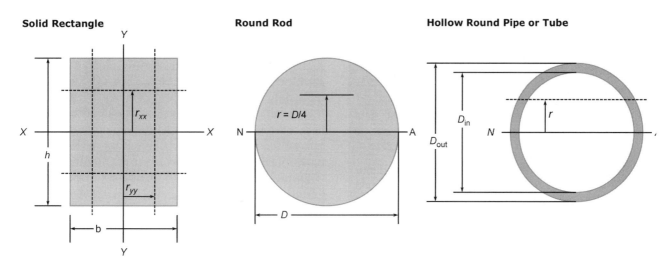

Figure 5.2 Radii of gyration for various cross sections.

For the rod:
Buckling about all axes:

$$r = \frac{D}{4} = 0.25\,D$$

For the pipe or round tube:

$$r = \frac{\sqrt{D_{in}^2 + D_{out}^2}}{4} = 0.25\,D$$

For very thin-walled round tube:

$$r = \frac{D_{out}^2}{2\sqrt{2}} = 0.354\,D$$

For slender columns, increasing the radius of gyration increases the stability of the compression member. A straightforward experiment serves to demonstrate the basic principles. The experiment began with a simple styrene sheet $\frac{1}{16}$ in. thick by 3 in. wide by 36 in. long. Attempting to use this sheet in its basic form as a column of length 36 in. with a cross section that measures $\frac{1}{16}$ in. by 3 in. proved to be fruitless because the "column" was so slender and unstable that it buckled under its own weight, that is, under zero applied axial load. This same size sheet can be cut up and reconfigured in a variety of ways to make stronger columns, such as the columns shown in Figure 5.3. From left to right are shown a simple angle, an angle with square block ends, an angle with beveled-edge block ends, an angle with a beveled-tip block end, the simple $\frac{1}{16}$ in. × 3 in. × 36 in. styrene sheet that is the basic unit of material from which all are made, a square tube, a triangular tube, and a solid square bar.

The simplest enhancement to the material configuration is to create a solid, square bar of cross-sectional area equal to that of the simple flat sheet. In this experiment, the basic sheet of material was cut into strips, which were glued together to form a solid bar 36 in. long with a square cross section, with each side of the square measuring 0.445 in. (approximately $\frac{7}{16}$ in.). This configuration proved to be significantly superior to the thin sheet, supporting about 15 lb of axial load before it buckled. See Figure 5.4.

Another $\frac{1}{16}$ in. × 3 in. × 36 in. sheet of material was cut into three strips, $\frac{1}{16}$ in. by 1 in., which were glued together to form a tube 36 in. long with a triangular cross section, with each side of the triangle measuring approximately $1\frac{1}{16}$ in. This column supported about 95 lb of axial load before it buckled, as shown in Figure 5.5.

Another $\frac{1}{16}$ in. × 3 in. × 36 in. sheet of material was cut into four strips, $\frac{1}{16}$ in. by $\frac{3}{4}$ in., which were glued together to form a tube 36 in. long with a square cross section, with each side of the square measuring approximately $\frac{13}{16}$ in. This column supported about 115 lb of axial load before it buckled, as shown in Figure 5.5.

A circular cross section would have supported an even greater axial load, but it was unknown how to fabricate a round tube out of styrene while still ensuring consistency with the material in the other columns. The increase in performance of the round column over the square column would have been very small, assuming that the two columns would have the same wall thickness and the same total amount of material.

The triangular and square columns tested in the preceding experiments are examples of closed sections. Closed sections are very effective columns because they place all the material a substantial distance away from the centroid of the section. The alternatives to closed sections, such as tubes, are open sections, such as wide-flanges or double angles. Open sections are not normally as efficient as closed tubes in resisting buckling under compressive loading, inasmuch as the open sections usually have a weak axis about which buckling occurs. They also have more material close to the centroid of the cross section, which means that the material is not doing much to contribute to the stiffness of the cross section (see Figure 5.7).

However, there are always two major reasons for using open sections rather than closed sections:

First, open sections are cheaper to fabricate. (Closed sections must be rolled to closure, welded along the seam, and trimmed smooth. In contrast, open sections require only rolling.)

Second, open sections are cheaper and easier to connect together. (Bolted connections are problematical for hollow sections. For bolts going all the way through a tube, it is difficult or impossible to pull the nut up tight without crushing the walls of the tube. For bolting through the wall of a tube, getting the nut down inside the tube can be a nuisance.)

There is a third reason that sometimes supports the decision to choose a closed shape over an open shape: In some instances the axial load is great enough that the amount of material needed in the cross section will result

Figure 5.3 Styrene columns: four angles of various end conditions: square, triangular, and solid.

(a)

(b)

Figure 5.4 (a, b) Column in shape of a solid, square bar.

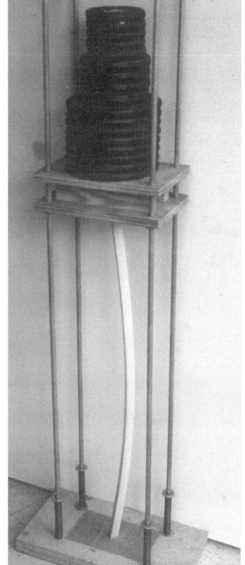

(a)

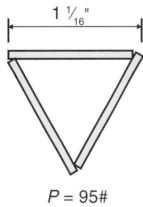

$P = 95\#$

(b)

Figure 5.5 (a, b) Column in shape of a triangular tube.

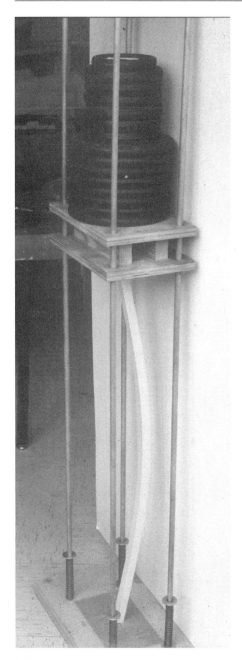

(a)

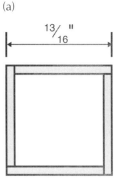

$$P = 115\#$$

(b)

Figure 5.6 (a, b) Column in shape of a square tube.

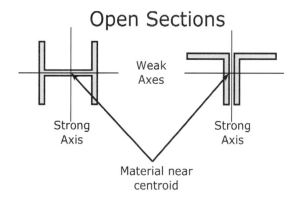

Open Sections

Closed Sections

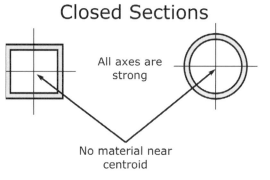

Figure 5.7 Cross sections suitable for compression struts and columns.

in sufficient cross-sectional breadth that the column is essentially fat, even for the open cross-sectional shape. If the column is already in the "fat" regime for the open shape, then crushing of the material, not buckling, is the determining issue and there is no benefit in further rearrangement of the cross-sectional material to add more "breadth" to the cross section. That is, there is no motivation to go to a tubular shape. Another way of thinking of this issue is the following: If the column is slender, so that it fails by buckling, then changing from an open section to a closed section may be motivated by a desire to make the column less slender. However, if the column is already fat (or close to fat) for the open section, there is little motivation to rearrange the cross-sectional material to increase the effective breadth of the cross section.

Returning to the column experiments, the same $1/16$ in. $\times 3$ in. $\times 36$ in. strip of styrene plastic can be cut into two strips, $1/16$ in. by $1\frac{1}{2}$ in., and glued together to form a column 36 in. long with an angle cross section (i.e., an L-shaped cross section) with each leg measuring approximately $1\frac{1}{2}$ in. Beveled wood blocks are glued to the ends of one of the angle columns (shown in Figure 5.3) to ensure that the ends will behave like ideal pin joints. (The length of the plastic is adjusted to ensure that the overall length of the column is still 36 in.) With pinned end conditions, this column supports about 40 lb of axial load before it buckles. This load is considerably less than the 115 lb required to fail the square column. The low failure load for the pinned-pinned angle column is due to its relatively low moment of inertia about its weak axis. The pinned-pinned column is shown in Figure 5.8. The curve assumed by the column during failure is half of a sine curve. The loading mechanism has been outfitted with clamps around the rods to stop the load before it totally destroys the column. When the load is removed, the column snaps back to its original shape, which is indicative of the fact that the buckling process occurred while the material was still within its elastic range. In an actual building, there would be no stops to limit the motion and the column would continue to collapse, eventually reaching plastic failure, from which the original column shape could never be recovered.

The pinned-pinned column constrained against lateral movement at the top is the reference column against which we compare everything else. (This is also called the *Euler column*, after the mathematician who first characterized the behavior of columns.) For the pinned-pinned column, the actual length of the column is half a sine curve, or $\lambda/2$. Thus, it can be said that $\lambda/2$ is the effective length for buckling. The critical force for buckling failure in an Euler column is given by the expression:

$$F_{Cr\_Slender} = \frac{\pi^2 E}{\left(\frac{L}{r}\right)^2}$$ [5.4]

This can be rewritten in terms of $\lambda/2$ to produce the following, more generalized, form:

$$F_{Cr\_Slender} = \frac{\pi^2 E}{\left(\frac{\left(\frac{\lambda}{2}\right)}{r}\right)^2}$$ [5.5]

The latter equation applies to buckling in all columns, regardless of the actual length of the column or how the column is restrained. If we can deduce the magnitude of $\lambda/2$ for the column, then the preceding equation tells us what the critical force is for buckling failure.

The effective length, $\lambda/2$, of a column can be altered by introducing moment connections at the ends. Figure 5.9 shows some of the common cases for columns with various degrees of end fixity.

For pinned-moment with sway and moment-pinned with sway:

Effective length = 2 · actual length

$$\frac{\lambda}{2} = 2L$$

$$P_{theoretical} = \frac{1}{4}P_{pin\text{-}pin} = 0.25\,P_{pin\text{-}pin}$$

(a)

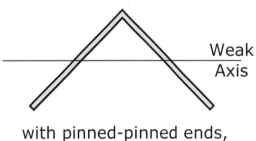

with pinned-pinned ends,
$$P = 40\#$$

(b)

Figure 5.8 (a, b) Angle column with beveled edge or tip.

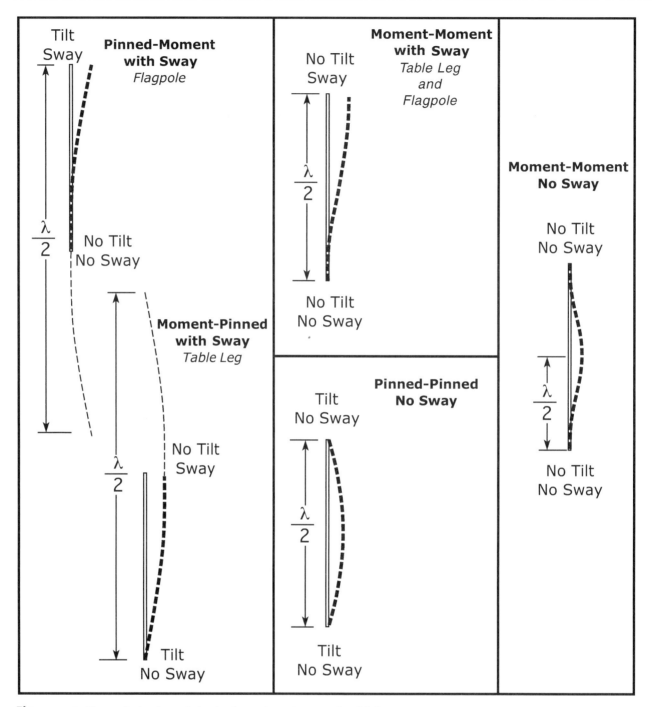

Figure 5.9 Theoretical column behavior for various degrees of end fixity.

For pinned-pinned, no sway, and moment-moment with sway:

Effective length $= 1 \cdot$ actual length

$$\frac{\lambda}{2} = L$$

$$P_{\text{theoretical}} = 1 P_{\text{pin-pin}}$$

For moment-moment, no sway:

Effective length $= \dfrac{\text{actual length}}{2}$

$$\frac{\lambda}{2} = 0.5 L$$

$$P_{\text{theoretical}} = 4 P_{\text{pin-pin}}$$

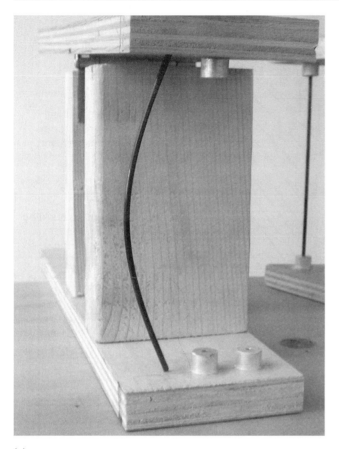

(a)

(b)

Figure 5.10 Pinned-pinned, no sway (a), and (b) moment-moment, no sway.

The angle column with the beveled ends corresponds to the case of pinned-pinned, no sway. (The nature of the testing apparatus inhibits lateral movement at the top; hence, no sway.) The effective length of this column is just equal to the actual length of the column, that is, 36 in. A second column was made with flat end blocks, which approximates the preceding case, called *moment-moment, no sway*. The buckled shapes of the two columns are compared in Figure 5.10: (a) the pinned-pinned, no sway column, and (b) the moment-moment, no sway column.

The effective length of the moment-moment, no sway column would be half of the actual length of the column, which means that the effective length would be 18 in. The effective length of the moment-moment, no sway column is half the effective length of the pinned-pinned, no sway column. Because the critical force for buckling failure varies as the inverse square of the effective length, as shown in the generalized buckling equation (5.5), the column with half the effective length of the other column should be four times as strong as the other column. Assuming the moment-moment, no sway column is still slender—that is, that reducing the effective length has not

taken the column from slender to fat proportions—it can be expected that the moment-moment, no sway column would have four times the axial load capacity of the pinned-pinned, no sway column; that is, the moment-moment, no sway column can be expected to buckle at an axial force of approximately 160 lb. However, the axial load capacity of the moment-moment, no sway column was measured to be only 60 lb; that is, instead of being 4 times as great it was only 1.5 times the axial load capacity of the pinned-pinned, no sway column.

The low failure load for the moment-moment, no sway column is attributable to a lack of compactness of the section. The unbraced outer extremes of the legs buckle before the overall section buckles. A member that exhibits this behavior is said to have a noncompact section or to exhibit local buckling or that part of the cross section gives up early. In most cases, when a part of the column cross section buckles, the rest of the column immediately fails when the load is transferred from the part that has buckled to the rest of the column. In such cases, tracing the source of the failure is very difficult, because the process occurs so rapidly that there is no chance to observe the development of the deformations that occur

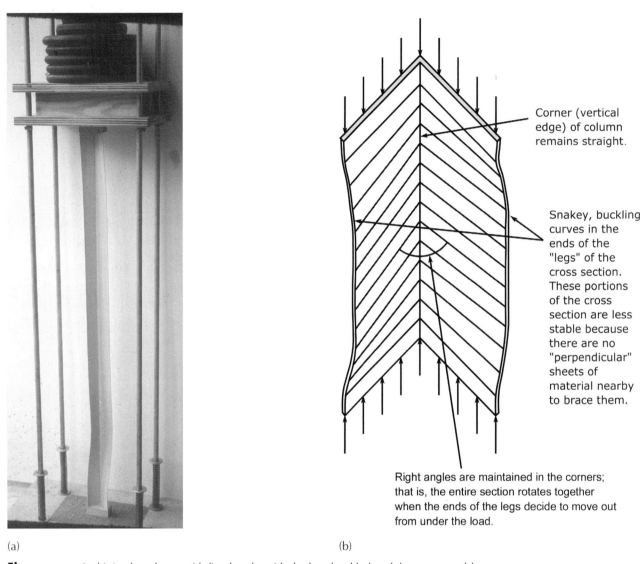

Corner (vertical edge) of column remains straight.

Snakey, buckling curves in the ends of the "legs" of the cross section. These portions of the cross section are less stable because there are no "perpendicular" sheets of material nearby to brace them.

Right angles are maintained in the corners; that is, the entire section rotates together when the ends of the legs decide to move out from under the load.

(a)   (b)

Figure 5.11 (a, b) Angle column with fixed ends, with the legs buckled and the corner stable.

during the process. In this particular experiment, the parts of the column cross section close to the corner, where mutually perpendicular materials are effectively bracing each other, remain adequately stable and continue supporting the load. In this manner, the failure process is frozen midway and it is possible to observe the stages of failure. By freezing the buckling process after the buckling deformation occurs in the legs, but before the overall column failure, one is afforded the luxury of standing back and studying the failure mechanism—like a frozen picture (see Figure 5.11).

This mode of failure can occur because of the lack of torsional stiffness of thin, open sections, such as angles. Closed, tubular sections do not exhibit this torsional mode of failure. For example, in the aforementioned column, you can easily visualize how a third rectangular

sheet of material glued along its edges to the edges of the legs of the angle would inhibit the lateral movement of the edges of the legs. This third sheet of material would complete a tube of triangular cross section, in which torsional deformation is so rigidly resisted that it would never be the mode of failure. Rather, the mode of failure would be overall buckling of the column or buckling of the walls of the tube out of the plane of the walls. Figure 5.12 shows two views of the column. The image in (a) shows a view down the column after the legs have buckled, but before the column has completely failed. The image in (b) shows the column after enough load has been added to totally fail the column. The twisted, distorted shape is typical of local, rather than overall, buckling. Even with this level of distortion, the column was able to return to its original shape. It was tested many

(a)

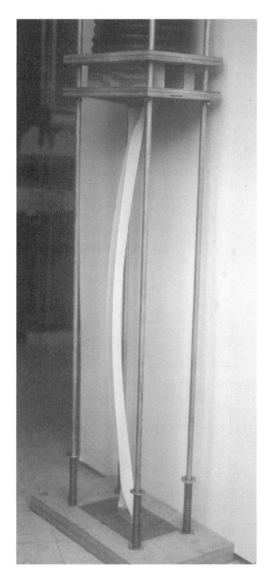

(b)

Figure 5.12 (a) Buckling of the legs and (b) after complete failure of the column.

times before the glue in the corner became too brittle and the column split at the joint.

To further illustrate the issue of end moments, the following examples of the various cases are presented. Figure 5.13 shows a case of pinned-moment with sway (flagpole). A flagpole column can be made more efficient by tapering the column, making it thicker at the base and narrower at the top. In the column in Figure 5.13(a), the baseplate is many times thicker than the column wall, as the column wall is in compression and the baseplate is in bending. The baseplate can be made somewhat thinner by adding stiffeners, as shown in Figure 5.13(b). In both cases, the anchor bolts penetrate deeply into the concrete pile. Two nuts are provided on each anchor bolt. The lower nut is for leveling, and the upper nut is for holding the baseplate down. The amount of material in the anchor bolts matches the amount of material in the wall of the tubular column, because the force in the column must ultimately be transferred to the foundation through the anchor bolts.

(a)

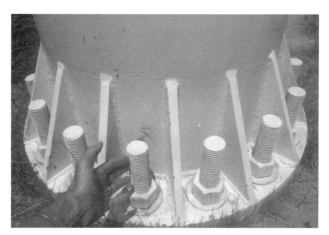

(b)

Figure 5.13 (a, b) Pinned-moment, with sway (flagpole).

Figure 5.14 shows one of the most famous examples of columns that are moment-pinned, with sway (table leg), the Johnson Wax Building, which Frank Lloyd Wright designed. The columns are moment-connected at the top to a grid of deep beams, which are visually obscured by the luminous ceiling. The columns are tapered from thick at the top to thin at the bottom, like the gracefully turned legs of a table. The wide, circular shapes at the tops of the columns were for visual and psychological effect, rather than for structure.

The column shown in Figure 5.15 is moment-pinned, with sway (table leg), relative to lateral movement parallel to the length of the large beam at the top. At 90° to the beam, the column is pinned-pinned, no sway. Sway in that direction is inhibited by the cross bracing rods.

The house in Figure 5.16 shows two kinds of fixed connection arrangements. The concrete columns at the bottom of the structure are rigidly connected into rigid grade beams, which hold the columns vertical at the foundation. The connections at the tops of these columns are not very substantial and would be regarded as pin joints. A column in this situation is referred to as a *flagpole* configuration. The columns in the next level up are embedded in box beams at both top and bottom, holding the columns vertical at both the ends. Such a column would be considered a combination of flagpole and table leg. There was no shear wall in this part of the house because the views were too important to allow them to be obscured by solid walls. Therefore, the burden of

(a)

(b)

Figure 5.14 (a) Johnson Wax Building designed by Frank Lloyd Wright (The image of the Johnson Wax Building is reprinted courtesy of HABS/HAER, the Historic American Buildings Survey/Historic American Engineering Record collection at the Library of Congress.) and (b) physical model expressing the structural action of the building.

Figure 5.15 Column with two modes: moment-pinned, with sway, and pinned-pinned, no sway.

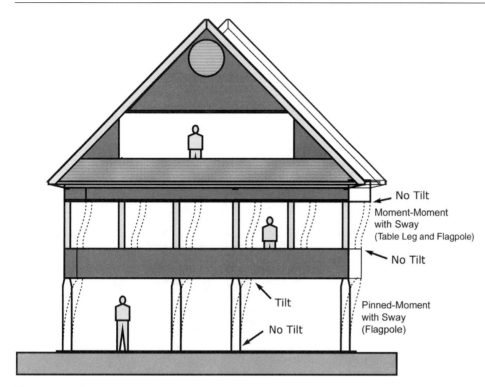

Figure 5.16 House with flagpole columns and combined table leg and flagpole.

both vertical and lateral forces ends up in these vertical elements.

Another example of the table-leg-and-flagpole combination is the structure shown in Figure 5.17, where the upper part of the column is moment-connected to the beam above and the lower part of the column is moment-connected to a grade beam that is hidden below the ground surface.

For plastic columns with an angle section, local buckling of the legs of the angle was observed. This kind of local buckling is not uncommon in open sections, particularly angles. However, buckling of parts of the cross section can also occur in closed sections, such as round tubes. In

the Firth of Forth Bridge, the trusses were made very deep to provide good leverage for the structure. The depth of the trusses resulted in very long compression members, which are vulnerable to buckling. To offset this tendency to buckle, large-diameter tubes were used, thereby producing favorable slenderness ratios for the overall columns (see Figure 5.18).

The loads in the tubes were not very great. Therefore, very little material was required in the cross sections of the tubes. In other words, the walls of the large-diameter tubes could be made very thin; so thin, in fact, that buckling of the walls of the tubes became a serious limitation. To resist wall buckling, ribs were riveted to the inside of

Figure 5.17 Combination table leg and flagpole.

Figure 5.18 Firth of Forth Bridge. (Photograph reproduced courtesy of Klaus Föhl.)

the tubular walls to stiffen the walls. These ribs were set parallel to the length of the tubes.

An alternative to using a single large-diameter, thin-walled tube is to lace several smaller tubes together in a trussed column (see Figure 5.19).

The material clustered together in the primary compression members and in the web members has a greater effective thickness than the material distributed over the thin, continuous sheet of material that constitutes the wall of the large-diameter tube. This means that the primary compression members and the web members are less vulnerable to buckling than the thin wall of the large-diameter tube. In a trussed column, the web members brace the primary compression members, thereby preventing lateral movement at the points of the connection. In this manner, a very long compression member is converted to many very short "members." The fabrication of the truss is usually less expensive than that of the large-diameter, thin-wall tube because the trussed column is made up of small, standard elements, whereas the large-

diameter tube requires special fabrication. Some very economical columns can be constructed by replacing the closed tubes with open sections like angles. Figure 5.20 illustrates a column that is made by shearing and punching steel angles (no cutting or drilling is required). The fabrication cost for such a column is minimal.

(a)

(b)

Figure 5.19 Small compression tubes laced together with web members.

Figure 5.20 (a, b) Trussed column constructed from steel angles bolted together.

The aforementioned column has a ragged exterior that detracts from its appearance and makes connecting panels and other architectural elements awkward. Using welded connections allows construction of angle columns with a smooth exterior, as shown in Figure 5.21(a). These trussed columns were covered with thin stone panels to make the columns visually more massive; see Figure 5.21(b).

A philosophical approach to designing compression members can be summarized in the following statement: Select a radius of gyration r that will keep the slenderness ratio in the range where buckling does not severely limit the effective utilization of the intrinsic stress capacity of the material, and then figure out how to configure the material in the cross section to produce that radius of gyration. In the process of configuring the cross section, remain cognizant of the potential hazards of creating a noncompact section, that is, a section in which some portion of the cross section is elastically unstable.

A trussed column with a large slenderness ratio will fail by overall column buckling, as shown in Figure 5.22(a). Increasing the cross section of the column makes the column more resistive to overall column buckling. However, the spacing between braced points on the compression elements increases, causing the effective slenderness ratio of the compression elements to increase. For trussed columns with large cross sections, the mode of failure is local buckling of segments of the individual compression elements as shown in Figure 5.22(b). The crossover between overall buckling and local buckling occurs at the point where the slenderness ratio of the overall column is just equal to the slenderness ratio of the segments of the individual compression members. Overall buckling and local buckling are illustrated in Figure 5.22. To inhibit local buckling, it is possible to truss the individual compression struts, as shown in Figure 5.22(c).

For the truss-column geometry shown in Figure 5.22(a, b), the optimum proportions are shown in the second image in Figure 5.23. These proportions cause overall column buckling to occur at the same load at which local buckling occurs. Making the cross section any smaller will cause the column to fail at a lower axial force, owing to overall column buckling (first image in Figure 5.23). Making the column cross section any larger will cause the column to fail at a lower axial load, due to local buckling of the segments of the compression struts (third image in Figure 5.23). Changing the geometry of the web members can reduce both the overall slenderness ratio of the column and the slenderness ratio of the segments of the individual compression struts, as shown in the fourth image in Figure 5.23. However, the web members in that column are very long, which means that they must be made larger in cross section to avoid being vulnerable to buckling failure. A geometry that addresses all these issues is shown in the final image of Figure 5.23. K-bracing

(a)

(b)

Figure 5.21 (a, b) Trussed column constructed of angles welded together.

(a)   (b)   (c)

Figure 5.22 (a) Overall buckling, (b) local buckling, and (c) trussing compression struts to inhibit local buckling.

allows for the web members to be shorter (or braced at mid-span) while the overall dimension of the column cross section is increased.

The George Washington Bridge in New York is evidence that trussed columns can be both structurally efficient and extraordinarily beautiful; see Figure 5.24.

The idea of trussing was introduced as a way of increasing the overall breadth of a column, to make the column less vulnerable to buckling. What emerged, in the course of discussion, was the notion that the web members in a trussed column can equally well be thought of as a way to reduce the effective length of the individual compression struts. The web members restrain points along the compression struts against lateral movement. Lateral movement associated with buckling can then occur only between the restrained points, but not at those points. The effective length for buckling of the compression struts then becomes the spacing between brace points. The lateral restraint depends on the continuous

webbing that ultimately traces the restraint back to the foundations.

It is possible to stabilize a compression strut without the diagonal elements that allow a stress path to be traced back to the foundations. The compression struts can be stiffened by moment-connecting them to thick cross members. The cross members restrain the compression struts against tilting at the points of connection. The compression struts are held close to vertical at the connections to the cross members, but are free to tilt away from vertical away from the points of connection to the cross members. To further strengthen the column, more rigid cross members can be used to pull parts of the column back to vertical. This process of stiffening compression members with moment joints is illustrated in Figure 5.25. For the models in parts (a), (b), and (c), there is no diagonal bracing anywhere. The compression struts are being braced exclusively by cross members that serve to hold the compression struts vertical at the points of connection.

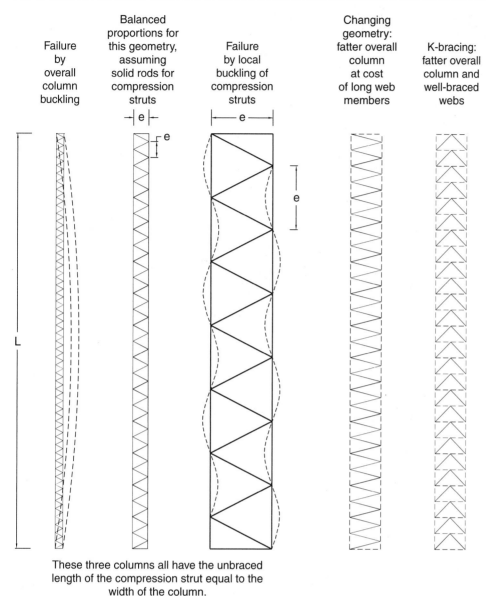

Failure by overall column buckling

Balanced proportions for this geometry, assuming solid rods for compression struts

Failure by local buckling of compression struts

Changing geometry: fatter overall column at cost of long web members

K-bracing: fatter overall column and well-braced webs

These three columns all have the unbraced length of the compression strut equal to the width of the column.

Figure 5.23 Proportions and web patterns for trussed columns.

These styrene models were warped substantially by the melting caused by the adhesive. In spite of the crudity of the models, the critical buckling loads that were observed were remarkably consistent with the underlying theory: Cutting the effective length in half increased the strength by a factor of four. This ratio began to break down for the last enhancement, involving adding diagonals, where the lack of straightness of the compression elements began to facilitate local buckling.

Verendeel columns are not typically as efficient as fully trussed columns. However, there are circumstances where a Verendeel column is extremely elegant, such as in the towers of the Golden Gate Bridge; see Figure 5.26.

Columns for which sway is allowed occur in structures where there are no other elements to inhibit sway. This implies that the columns themselves are the elements responsible for lateral stabilization of the structure. Under lateral forces on the structure, bending stresses will be induced in the columns at the moment-connections at the ends of the columns. Typically, these bending stresses resulting from lateral forces of wind or earthquake will be much larger than the axial stresses resulting from vertical forces of gravity or wind uplift. Therefore, these vertical elements must be analyzed in terms of combined bending and axial stresses, and referring to these vertical elements as *columns* is misleading.

Figure 5.24 George Washington Bridge, designed by Othmar Ammann. (Photograph reproduced courtesy of Leonhardt, Andrä, und Partner.)

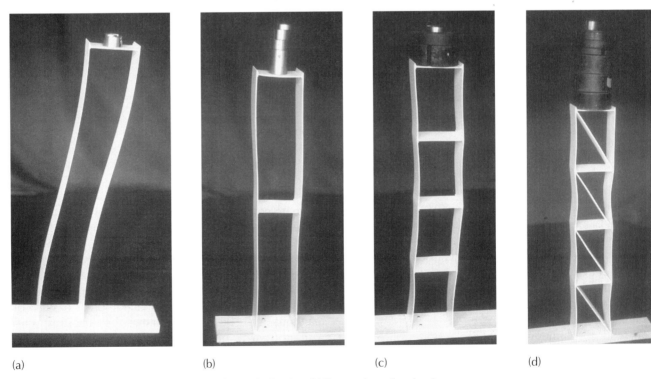

(a)   (b)   (c)   (d)

Figure 5.25 Rigid-frame (Verendeel) columns (a, b, c) and (d) one triangulated column.

Figure 5.26 Verendeel tower of the Golden Gate Bridge.

(a)

(b)

Figure 5.27 (a, b) Eccentric loading of columns.

They should technically be referred to as *beam-columns*. However, for reasons of verbal efficiency, it is typical to fall into the trap of simply calling them *columns*. This is a particularly easy trap into which to fall because, in this culture, the word *column* is traditionally applied to any vertical element in a structure. The issue of beam-columns and lateral bracing is discussed further in Chapter 10.

Bending stresses can also be introduced into vertical structural elements by applying a force that is off the centroid of the element's cross section. This situation, referred to as *eccentric loading*, occurs commonly in our methods of construction, as depicted in Figure 5.27.

Bending stress will also be introduced by any crookedness of a column because the forces applied to the centroids of the ends of the column will not align with the centroid of the cross sections near the center of the column. The nature of this process is outlined in the diagrams in Figures 5.28 through 5.31.

When a perfectly straight column is subjected to an axial force, the state of internal stress near the midpoint of the column is uniform compression; see Figure 5.28.

For a crooked column, the state of stress becomes more complicated than for a straight column. When a crooked column is subjected to an axial force, the state of internal stress near the midpoint of the column is not uniform; see Figure 5.29.

There must be an upward vertical force *P* on the cut face, to equilibrate the downward force *P* on the top of the column. The force on the cut face is not along the same line of action as the force on the top of the column. Therefore, those two forces constitute a couple, that is, a pure moment, that must be equilibrated by a moment *M* on the cut face (see Figure 5.30).

For modest deviations from straightness, the maximum bending stress associated with the moment *M* will be small as compared to the uniform stress associated with the axial force *P*. As the deviation from straightness increases, the maximum bending stress associated with the moment *M* will eventually equal the uniform stress

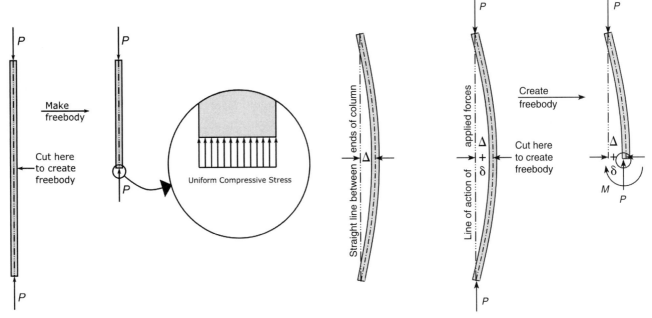

Figure 5.28 Stress pattern in a perfectly straight column.

Figure 5.29 Moment induced by crookedness of the column.

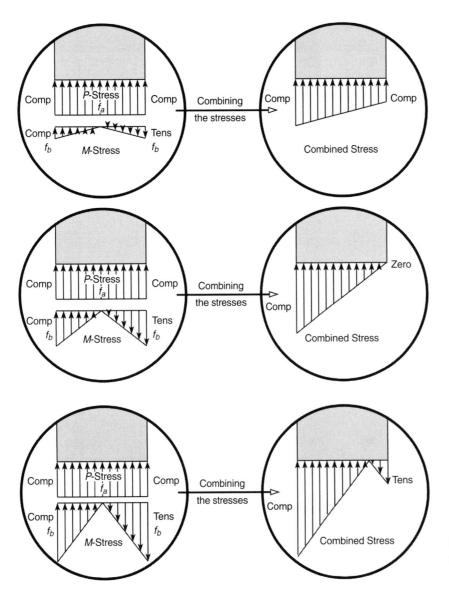

Figure 5.30 Combined bending and axial stresses in a crooked column.

associated with the axial force P. As the deviation from straightness continues to increase, the maximum bending stress associated with the moment M will surpass the uniform stress associated with the axial force P and a net tension stress will occur on the outer curve of the column.

To gain a sense of proportion regarding this problem, consider a 12 ft-high column made from a nominal 6 in. × 6 in. (5.5 in. × 5.5 in.) wood post, as shown in Figure 5.31.

This diagram shows a crooked column in which the maximum bending stress is just equal to the axial stress superimposed on a straight column of the same cross section and length. Notice how similar they are in shape. To detect this amount of deviation from straightness, one would have to use a straightedge or sight along the column. This issue of unexpected, amplified stress is one of the reasons that lower resistance factors, Φ, are used for columns, as compared to beams.

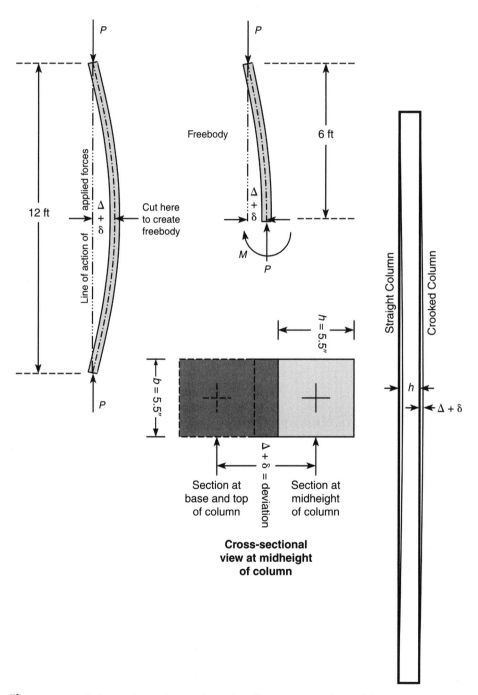

Figure 5.31 Column shape that produces bending stress equal to axial stress.

5.3 Steel Columns

As indicated in Figure 5.1, Section 5.2, very fat columns fail at the yield stress of the material and very slender columns fail by buckling.

Figure 5.32 demonstrates a plot of failure stress versus slenderness ratio, showing a horizontal line representing the limit set by yield stress and a curved, asymptotic line representing the limit set by the buckling stress. The column will always fail at whichever failure stress is reached first, either the yield stress or the buckling stress; this is determined by the slenderness ratio.

For a slender column, the critical (failure) stress is given by the buckling equation:

$$F_{cr} = \frac{\pi^2 E}{\left(\dfrac{L}{r}\right)^2} \qquad \text{[5.6]}$$

For a fat column, the critical (failure) stress is given by F_y.

For a grade of steel for which $F_y = 65$ KSI, the intersection of the curve described by the buckling equation

and the flat line represented by yielding will be given by the following equation:

$$\frac{65\ \text{K}}{\text{in.}^2} = \frac{\pi^2 E}{\left(\dfrac{L}{r}\right)^2} = \frac{3.14^2 \cdot \dfrac{29{,}000\ \text{K}}{\text{in.}^2}}{\left(\dfrac{L}{r}\right)^2} = \frac{\dfrac{286{,}200\ \text{K}}{\text{in.}^2}}{\left(\dfrac{L}{r}\right)^2}$$

$$\text{[5.7]}$$

$$\frac{L}{r} = \sqrt{\frac{286{,}200}{65}} = 66.3$$

Real columns do not exhibit a sharp transition from fat to slender behavior. Instead, there is a region between fat and slender where the tendency to crush and the tendency to buckle conspire to fail the column at stresses below either the yield stress or the stress predicted by Euler's buckling formula. This region is referred to as *intermediate between fat and slender behavior* (see Figure 5.33).

Table 5.1 gives the tabulated values for the critical compressive stress for four common grades of steel for slenderness ratios *KL* from zero to 200. *KL* is an alternate terminology for the effective length λ/2.

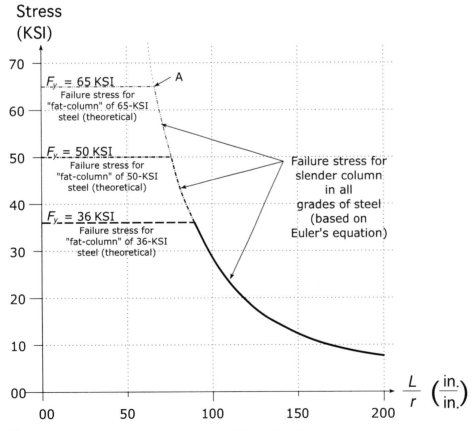

Figure 5.32 Theoretical transition from yielding to buckling.

Table 5.1 Critical Compressive Stress for Various Grades of Steel

KL/r	35-KSI Steel F_{cr}	42-KSI Steel F_{cr}	46-KSI Steel F_{cr}	50-KSI Steel F_{cr}	KL/r	35-KSI Steel F_{cr}	42-KSI Steel F_{cr}	46-KSI Steel F_{cr}	50-KSI Steel F_{cr}	KL/r	35-KSI Steel F_{cr}	42-KSI Steel F_{cr}	46-KSI Steel F_{cr}	50-KSI Steel F_{cr}
0	35.000	42.000	46.000	50.000	67	27.815	31.879	34.011	36.010	134	13.962	13.979	13.979	13.979
1	34.998	41.997	45.997	49.996	68	27.624	31.616	33.703	35.656	135	13.771	13.773	13.773	13.773
2	34.993	41.990	45.988	49.985	69	27.431	31.351	33.394	35.301	136	13.571	13.571	13.571	13.571
3	34.984	41.977	45.972	49.967	70	27.236	31.085	33.083	34.944	137	13.374	13.374	13.374	13.374
4	34.971	41.959	45.951	49.942	71	27.041	30.817	32.771	34.586	138	13.181	13.181	13.181	13.181
5	34.955	41.936	45.923	49.909	72	26.843	30.547	32.457	34.226	139	12.992	12.992	12.992	12.992
6	34.936	41.907	45.889	49.869	73	26.645	30.276	32.142	33.865	140	12.807	12.807	12.807	12.807
7	34.912	41.874	45.849	49.821	74	26.445	30.004	31.826	33.503	141	12.626	12.626	12.626	12.626
8	34.886	41.835	45.802	49.767	75	26.244	29.731	31.509	33.140	142	12.449	12.449	12.449	12.449
9	34.855	41.792	45.750	49.705	76	26.042	29.457	31.190	32.776	143	12.275	12.275	12.275	12.275
10	34.821	41.743	45.692	49.636	77	25.839	29.181	30.871	32.411	144	12.105	12.105	12.105	12.105
11	34.784	41.689	45.627	49.560	78	25.635	28.905	30.551	32.046	145	11.939	11.939	11.939	11.939
12	34.743	41.630	45.557	49.476	79	25.430	28.627	30.230	31.680	146	11.776	11.776	11.776	11.776
13	34.699	41.566	45.480	49.386	80	25.224	28.349	29.908	31.314	147	11.616	11.616	11.616	11.616
14	34.651	41.497	45.397	49.289	81	25.017	28.070	29.586	30.948	148	11.460	11.460	11.460	11.460
15	34.599	41.424	45.309	49.184	82	24.809	27.790	29.263	30.581	149	11.306	11.306	11.306	11.306
16	34.544	41.345	45.215	49.073	83	24.600	27.510	28.940	30.214	150	11.156	11.156	11.156	11.156
17	34.486	41.261	45.114	48.955	84	24.391	27.229	28.617	29.848	151	11.009	11.009	11.009	11.009
18	34.424	41.172	45.008	48.829	85	24.181	26.948	28.293	29.481	152	10.864	10.864	10.864	10.864
19	34.359	41.079	44.896	48.697	86	23.970	26.667	27.970	29.115	153	10.723	10.723	10.723	10.723
20	34.291	40.981	44.779	48.559	87	23.759	26.385	27.646	28.749	154	10.584	10.584	10.584	10.584
21	34.219	40.878	44.655	48.413	88	23.547	26.103	27.323	28.383	155	10.448	10.448	10.448	10.448
22	34.144	40.770	44.526	48.262	89	23.335	25.821	26.999	28.018	156	10.314	10.314	10.314	10.314
23	34.065	40.657	44.392	48.103	90	23.122	25.538	26.676	27.654	157	10.184	10.184	10.184	10.184
24	33.983	40.540	44.252	47.938	91	22.909	25.256	26.353	27.290	158	10.055	10.055	10.055	10.055
25	33.898	40.418	44.106	47.767	92	22.695	24.974	26.031	26.928	159	9.929	9.929	9.929	9.929
26	33.810	40.292	43.955	47.589	93	22.481	24.692	25.709	26.566	160	9.805	9.805	9.805	9.805
27	33.718	40.161	43.799	47.405	94	22.267	24.410	25.388	26.205	161	9.684	9.684	9.684	9.684
28	33.623	40.026	43.637	47.214	95	22.053	24.128	25.067	25.846	162	9.565	9.565	9.565	9.565
29	33.525	39.886	43.470	47.018	96	21.838	23.846	24.747	25.487	163	9.448	9.448	9.448	9.448
30	33.424	39.741	43.298	46.816	97	21.623	23.565	24.428	25.130	164	9.333	9.333	9.333	9.333
31	33.320	39.593	43.120	46.607	98	21.409	23.285	24.109	24.774	165	9.220	9.220	9.220	9.220
32	33.213	39.440	42.938	46.393	99	21.194	23.005	23.792	24.420	166	9.109	9.109	9.109	9.109
33	33.103	39.283	42.751	46.173	100	20.979	22.725	23.476	24.067	167	9.000	9.000	9.000	9.000
34	32.989	39.121	42.558	45.947	101	20.764	22.447	23.160	23.716	168	8.894	8.894	8.894	8.894
35	32.873	38.956	42.361	45.716	102	20.550	22.168	22.846	23.367	169	8.789	8.789	8.789	8.789
36	32.754	38.786	42.160	45.480	103	20.335	21.891	22.533	23.019	170	8.686	8.686	8.686	8.686
37	32.632	38.613	41.953	45.237	104	20.121	21.615	22.222	22.673	171	8.584	8.584	8.584	8.584
38	32.507	38.435	41.742	44.990	105	19.907	21.339	21.912	22.329	172	8.485	8.485	8.485	8.485
39	32.379	38.254	41.526	44.737	106	19.693	21.064	21.603	21.988	173	8.387	8.387	8.387	8.387
40	32.248	38.069	41.306	44.480	107	19.480	20.790	21.295	21.648	174	8.291	8.291	8.291	8.291
41	32.115	37.880	41.082	44.217	108	19.266	20.518	20.990	21.310	175	8.196	8.196	8.196	8.196
42	31.978	37.687	40.853	43.950	109	19.054	20.246	20.685	20.975	176	8.103	8.103	8.103	8.103
43	31.840	37.491	40.620	43.677	110	18.841	19.975	20.383	20.641	177	8.012	8.012	8.012	8.012
44	31.698	37.291	40.383	43.400	111	18.629	19.706	20.082	20.311	178	7.922	7.922	7.922	7.922
45	31.554	37.088	40.142	43.119	112	18.418	19.438	19.783	19.982	179	7.834	7.834	7.834	7.834
46	31.407	36.881	39.897	42.833	113	18.207	19.171	19.486	19.656	180	7.747	7.747	7.747	7.747
47	31.258	36.671	39.648	42.543	114	17.997	18.906	19.191	19.315	181	7.662	7.662	7.662	7.662
48	31.107	36.458	39.396	42.248	115	17.787	18.642	18.897	18.980	182	7.578	7.578	7.578	7.578
49	30.953	36.241	39.139	41.950	116	17.578	18.379	18.606	18.654	183	7.495	7.495	7.495	7.495
50	30.796	36.022	38.880	41.647	117	17.369	18.118	18.317	18.337	184	7.414	7.414	7.414	7.414
51	30.637	35.799	38.616	41.341	118	17.162	17.858	18.029	18.027	185	7.334	7.334	7.334	7.334
52	30.476	35.573	38.350	41.030	119	16.955	17.600	17.726	17.726	186	7.256	7.256	7.256	7.256
53	30.313	35.345	38.080	40.717	120	16.749	17.344	17.431	17.431	187	7.178	7.178	7.178	7.178
54	30.147	35.113	37.807	40.399	121	16.543	17.089	17.145	17.145	188	7.102	7.102	7.102	7.102
55	29.980	34.879	37.531	40.079	122	16.339	16.836	16.865	16.865	189	7.027	7.027	7.027	7.027
56	29.810	34.642	37.251	39.755	123	16.135	16.584	16.592	16.592	190	6.953	6.953	6.953	6.953
57	29.638	34.402	36.969	39.428	124	15.933	16.325	16.325	16.325	191	6.881	6.881	6.881	6.881
58	29.464	34.160	36.684	39.097	125	15.731	16.065	16.065	16.065	192	6.809	6.809	6.809	6.809
59	29.288	33.915	36.397	38.764	126	15.530	15.811	15.811	15.811	193	6.739	6.739	6.739	6.739
60	29.110	33.668	36.107	38.429	127	15.330	15.563	15.563	15.563	194	6.669	6.669	6.669	6.669
61	28.931	33.419	35.814	38.090	128	15.132	15.321	15.321	15.321	195	6.601	6.601	6.601	6.601
62	28.749	33.168	35.519	37.749	129	14.934	15.084	15.084	15.084	196	6.534	6.534	6.534	6.534
63	28.566	32.914	35.221	37.406	130	14.737	14.853	14.853	14.853	197	6.468	6.468	6.468	6.468
64	28.381	32.658	34.922	37.060	131	14.542	14.627	14.627	14.627	198	6.403	6.403	6.403	6.403
65	28.194	32.401	34.620	36.712	132	14.347	14.406	14.406	14.406	199	6.339	6.339	6.339	6.339
66	28.005	32.141	34.316	36.362	133	14.154	14.190	14.190	14.190	200	6.275	6.275	6.275	6.275

All the material behaves almost the same

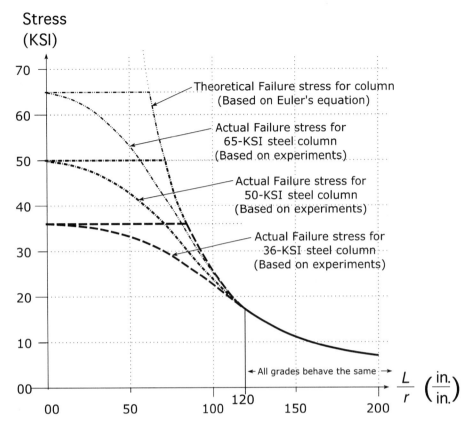

Figure 5.33 Failure stress intermediate between buckling and yielding.

As an example of how the allowed stress table can be used, consider a standard-weight, nominal, 4 in.-diameter pipe, used as a simple column 14 ft long.

As indicated in Section 4.3, "Steel Properties," for a 4 in. pipe:

$r = 1.51$ in.
$A = 3.17$ in.

For the 14 ft column:

$$\frac{KL}{r} = \frac{14\ \text{ft}}{1.51\ \text{in.}} \cdot \left[\frac{12\ \text{in.}}{\text{ft}}\right] = 111.3,$$

which, to be conservative, can be rounded up to 112. From Table 5.1, giving the critical compressive stress for various grades of steel and various slenderness ratios, for 35-KSI steel and $KL/r = 111.3$ (which requires interpolation), the critical concentric axial compression stress is:

$$F_{CR} = \frac{18.57\ \text{K}}{\text{in.}^2}$$

The critical axial compression force would be:

$$P_{CR} = F_{CR} \cdot A = \frac{18.57\ \text{K}}{\text{in.}^2} \cdot 3.17\ \text{in.}^2 = 58.85\ \text{K}$$

The design strength in axial compression would be:

$$\Phi P_{CR} = 0.85 \cdot 58.85\ \text{K} = 50.03\ \text{K}$$

which is approximately 50 K. This is consistent with the data in Figure 5.41, where, for a standard-weight, nominal 4 in.-diameter pipe column of effective length 14 ft, the design strength in axial compression is listed as 50 K. Figures 5.34 through 5.42 give design strength in axial compression for some of the standard steel shapes that are customarily used as compression members, thereby simplifying the sizing operations. Given a design force, the figures giving design axial strength in compression can be quickly scanned to find satisfactory columns that will be efficient and economical.

For nonstandard shapes, it becomes necessary to:

• Calculate r and A for the cross section
• Calculate KL/r
• Look up F_{cr}
• Multiply F_{cr} times A to get the critical axial compression force, P_n
• Multiply Φ_c times P_n to get the design strength in axial compression, $\Phi_c P_n$

For nonconcentric loading, the sizing operation is much more complicated. This topic is addressed in a later chapter.

		W12×									
Shape		336	305	279	252	230	210	190	170	152	136	120

W-Shapes
Design Strength in Axial
Compression, $\phi_c P_n$, kips

$F_y = 50$ ksi
$\phi_c P_n = 0.85 F_{cr} A_g$

Effective length KL (ft) with respect to least radius of gyration r_y	336	305	279	252	230	210	190	170	152	136	120
0	4200	3810	3480	3150	2880	2630	2370	2130	1900	1700	1500
6	4070	3690	3370	3040	2780	2540	2290	2050	1830	1630	1440
7	4020	3640	3330	3000	2740	2500	2260	2020	1810	1610	1420
8	3970	3590	3280	2960	2710	2470	2220	1990	1780	1590	1400
9	3910	3540	3230	2910	2660	2430	2190	1960	1750	1560	1380
10	3850	3480	3170	2860	2610	2380	2150	1920	1710	1530	1350
11	3780	3420	3110	2810	2560	2330	2100	1880	1680	1490	1320
12	3700	3350	3050	2750	2510	2280	2050	1840	1640	1460	1290
13	3620	3270	2980	2680	2450	2230	2000	1790	1590	1420	1250
14	3540	3190	2910	2610	2380	2170	1950	1740	1550	1380	1220
15	3450	3110	2830	2540	2320	2110	1900	1690	1510	1340	1180
16	3360	3020	2750	2470	2250	2040	1840	1640	1460	1290	1140
17	3260	2940	2670	2390	2180	1980	1780	1580	1410	1250	1100
18	3160	2840	2580	2320	2110	1910	1720	1530	1360	1210	1060
19	3060	2750	2500	2240	2030	1840	1650	1470	1310	1160	1020
20	2960	2660	2410	2160	1960	1780	1590	1420	1260	1110	976
22	2750	2460	2230	1990	1810	1640	1460	1300	1150	1020	892
24	2540	2270	2050	1830	1650	1490	1340	1180	1050	924	808
26	2330	2070	1870	1660	1500	1360	1210	1070	944	831	726
28	2120	1880	1690	1500	1350	1220	1090	959	844	742	646
30	1910	1690	1520	1340	1210	1090	967	852	749	656	569
32	1720	1510	1350	1190	1070	962	853	750	658	577	500
34	1520	1340	1200	1060	951	852	755	664	583	511	443
36	1360	1200	1070	944	848	760	674	593	520	456	395
38	1220	1080	960	847	761	682	605	532	467	409	355
40	1100	970	866	764	687	616	546	480	421	369	320

Properties											
P_{wo}, kips	1580	1340	1170	998	861	738	617	518	435	365	302
P_{wi}, kips/in.	89.0	81.5	76.5	70.0	64.5	59.0	53.0	48.0	43.5	39.5	35.5
P_{wb}, kips	15100	11600	9590	7320	5730	4400	3190	2370	1760	1320	957
P_{fb}, kips	2460	2070	1720	1420	1210	1020	852	684	551	439	347
L_p, ft	12.3	12.1	11.9	11.8	11.7	11.6	11.5	11.4	11.3	11.2	11.1
L_r, ft	131	119	110	99.7	91.9	84.2	76.6	68.9	62.1	55.7	50.0
A_g, in.^{2}	98.8	89.6	81.9	74.0	67.7	61.8	55.8	50.0	44.7	39.9	35.3
I_x, in.^{4}	4060	3550	3110	2720	2420	2140	1890	1650	1430	1240	1070
I_y, in.^{4}	1190	1050	937	828	742	664	589	517	454	398	345
r_y, in.	3.47	3.42	3.38	3.34	3.31	3.28	3.25	3.22	3.19	3.16	3.13
Ratio r_x/r_y	1.85	1.84	1.82	1.81	1.80	1.80	1.79	1.78	1.77	1.77	1.76
$P_{ex}(KL^2)/10^4$	116000	102000	89000	77900	69300	61300	54100	47200	40900	35500	30600
$P_{ey}(KL^2)/10^4$	34100	30100	26800	23700	21200	19000	16900	14800	13000	11400	9870

Figure 5.34 Design strength $\Phi_c P_N = 0.85 F_{CR} A_g$, in axial compression (K) for wide-flange sections. (Copyright American Institute of Steel Construction, Inc. Reprinted with permission. All rights reserved.)

$F_y = 50$ ksi
$\phi_c P_n = 0.85 F_{cr} A_g$

W-Shapes
Design Strength in Axial
Compression, $\phi_c P_n$, kips

Shape		W12×										
		106	96	87	79	72	65††	58	53	50	45	40
Effective length KL (ft) with respect to least radius of gyration r_y	0	1330	1200	1090	986	897	812	723	663	621	557	497
	6	1280	1150	1050	947	861	779	680	623	562	504	450
	7	1260	1140	1030	933	848	767	666	610	543	486	434
	8	1240	1120	1010	917	834	754	649	594	521	466	416
	9	1210	1100	994	900	818	739	631	577	497	445	396
	10	1190	1070	973	880	800	723	611	559	472	422	376
	11	1160	1050	950	860	781	706	590	539	445	398	354
	12	1130	1020	926	838	761	687	568	518	418	374	332
	13	1100	995	901	814	740	668	545	496	390	349	310
	14	1070	966	874	790	717	647	521	474	363	324	287
	15	1040	935	846	764	694	626	496	451	335	299	265
	16	1000	904	817	738	670	604	471	428	308	274	243
	17	968	871	788	711	645	581	446	404	281	250	222
	18	932	838	758	683	620	558	420	381	255	227	201
	19	895	805	727	655	594	535	395	357	230	204	181
	20	858	771	696	627	569	512	370	334	208	185	163
	22	783	703	634	570	517	464	322	290	172	152	135
	24	708	635	572	514	465	417	276	247	144	128	113
	26	635	569	511	459	415	372	235	210	123	109	96.5
	28	565	505	453	406	367	328	202	181	106	94.1	83.2
	30	497	443	397	355	321	287	176	158	92.3	82.0	72.5
	32	437	390	349	312	282	252	155	139	81.2	72.1	63.7
	34	387	345	309	277	250	223	137	123			
	36	345	308	276	247	223	199	122	110			
	38	310	276	248	221	200	179	110	98.4			
	40	279	249	223	200	181	161	99.2	88.9			
Properties												
P_{wo}, kips		242	206	182	156	137	117	112	101	105	90.5	75.2
P_{wi}, kips/in.		30.5	27.5	25.8	23.5	21.5	19.5	18.0	17.3	18.5	16.8	14.8
P_{wb}, kips		609	445	365	278	213	159	125	110	133	98.6	67.4
P_{fb}, kips		276	228	185	152	126	103	115	93.0	115	93.0	74.6
L_p, ft		11.0	10.9	10.8	10.8	10.7	11.9	8.87	8.76	6.92	6.89	6.85
L_r, ft		44.9	41.4	38.4	35.7	33.6	31.7	27.0	25.6	21.5	20.3	19.2
A_g, in.^{2}		31.2	28.2	25.6	23.2	21.1	19.1	17.0	15.6	14.6	13.1	11.7
I_x, in.^{4}		933	833	740	662	597	533	475	425	391	348	307
I_y, in.^{4}		301	270	241	216	195	174	107	95.8	56.3	50.0	44.1
r_y, in.		3.11	3.09	3.07	3.05	3.04	3.02	2.51	2.48	1.96	1.95	1.94
Ratio r_x/r_y		1.76	1.76	1.75	1.75	1.75	1.75	2.10	2.11	2.64	2.64	2.64
$P_{ex}(KL^2)/10^4$		26700	23800	21200	18900	17100	15300	13600	12200	11200	9960	8790
$P_{ey}(KL^2)/10^4$		8620	7730	6900	6180	5580	4980	3060	2740	1610	1430	1260

†† Flange is non-compact.
Note: Heavy line indicates Kl/r equal to or greater than 200.

Figure 5.35 Design strength $\Phi_c P_N = 0.85\, F_{CR} A_g$, in axial compression (K) for wide-flange sections (*Continued*). (Copyright American Institute of Steel Construction, Inc. Reprinted with permission. All rights reserved.)

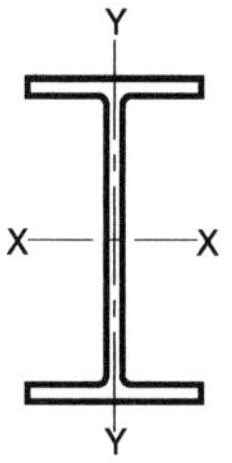

W-Shapes
Design Strength in Axial Compression, $\phi_c P_n$, kips

$F_y = 50$ ksi
$\phi_c P_n = 0.85 F_{cr} A_g$

Effective length *KL* (ft) with respect to least radius of gyration r_y	W10× 112	100	88	77	68	60	54	49	45	39	33
0	1400	1250	1100	961	850	748	672	612	565	489	413
6	1330	1180	1040	908	803	706	634	577	515	444	373
7	1300	1160	1020	890	787	692	621	565	497	428	360
8	1270	1140	999	869	769	675	606	551	478	412	345
9	1240	1110	973	847	749	657	590	536	458	393	329
10	1210	1080	945	822	727	638	572	520	436	374	312
11	1170	1040	916	796	703	617	553	502	412	353	294
12	1130	1010	884	768	678	595	533	484	388	332	276
13	1090	970	851	738	652	571	512	464	364	310	257
14	1050	931	817	708	625	547	490	444	339	289	238
15	1010	892	782	677	597	523	468	424	314	267	220
16	961	851	746	645	569	497	445	403	290	246	202
17	915	810	709	612	540	472	422	382	266	225	184
18	870	769	672	580	511	446	399	361	243	205	167
19	824	727	635	547	482	421	376	340	221	185	150
20	778	686	599	515	454	395	353	319	199	167	135
22	688	605	527	452	398	346	309	278	164	138	112
24	601	527	458	392	344	299	266	239	138	116	94.0
26	518	453	393	335	294	255	227	204	118	98.8	80.1
28	447	390	339	289	254	220	196	176	102	85.2	69.1
30	389	340	295	252	221	191	170	153	88.5	74.2	60.2
32	342	299	259	221	194	168	150	134	77.7	65.2	52.9
34	303	265	230	196	172	149	133	119			
36	270	236	205	175	153	133	118	106			
38	242	212	184	157	138	119	106	95.3			
40	219	191	166	141	124	108	95.9	86.0			

Properties

Shape	112	100	88	77	68	60	54	49	45	39	33
P_{wo}, kips	330	275	225	182	149	124	104	90.1	98	81.1	67.8
P_{wi}, kips/in.	37.8	34.0	30.3	26.5	23.5	21.0	18.5	17.0	17.5	15.8	14.5
P_{wb}, kips	1430	1040	732	494	344	245	168	130	142	103	80.7
P_{fb}, kips	439	353	276	213	167	130	106	88.2	108	79.0	53.2
L_p, ft	9.47	9.36	9.29	9.18	9.15	9.08	9.04	8.97	7.10	6.99	6.85
L_r, ft	56.5	50.8	45.1	39.9	36.0	32.6	30.2	28.3	24.1	21.9	19.8
A_g, in.^{2}	32.9	29.4	25.9	22.6	20.0	17.6	15.8	14.4	13.3	11.5	9.71
I_x, in.^{4}	716	623	534	455	394	341	303	272	248	209	171
I_y, in.^{4}	236	207	179	154	134	116	103	93.4	53.4	45.0	36.6
r_y, in.	2.68	2.65	2.63	2.60	2.59	2.57	2.56	2.54	2.01	1.98	1.94
Ratio r_x/r_y	1.74	1.74	1.73	1.73	1.71	1.71	1.71	1.71	2.15	2.16	2.16
$P_{ex}(KL^2)/10^4$	20500	17800	15300	13000	11300	9760	8670	7790	7100	5980	4890
$P_{ey}(KL^2)/10^4$	6750	5920	5120	4410	3840	3320	2950	2670	1530	1290	1050

Note: Heavy line indicates Kl/r equal to or greater than 200.

Figure 5.36 Design strength $\Phi_c P_N = 0.85\ F_{CR} A_g$, in axial compression (K) for wide-flange sections (*Continued*). (Copyright American Institute of Steel Construction, Inc. Reprinted with permission. All rights reserved.)

[handwritten note: square tube. yield stress: 46 kips/in².]

Shape	HSS12×12×				
	5/8	1/2	3/8††	5/16†	1/4†
t_{design}, in.	0.581	0.465	0.349	0.291	0.233
Wt/ft	93.1	75.9	58.0	48.8	39.4
Effective length KL (ft) with respect to least radius of gyration r_y					
0	1000	817	626	501	358
6	989	804	616	496	355
7	983	800	612	494	354
8	976	794	609	492	352
9	969	788	604	489	351
10	960	782	599	486	349
11	951	775	594	483	347
12	941	767	588	479	345
13	931	758	581	475	342
14	919	749	575	471	340
15	907	740	568	467	337
16	895	730	560	462	334
17	881	719	552	457	331
18	867	708	544	452	328
19	853	697	535	446	324
20	838	685	526	442	321
21	823	672	517	434	317
22	807	660	507	426	313
23	790	647	498	418	309
24	774	633	488	410	305
25	757	620	477	401	300
26	739	606	467	392	296
27	722	592	456	384	291
28	704	578	446	375	286
29	686	563	435	366	281
30	668	549	424	357	275
32	631	520	402	338	264
34	595	490	379	320	253
36	558	461	357	301	241
38	522	431	335	283	228
40	486	403	313	264	215
A_g, in.²	25.7	20.9	16.0	13.4	10.8
I_x, in.⁴	548	457	357	304	248
I_y, in.⁴	548	457	357	304	248
r_x/r_y	1.00	1.00	1.00	1.00	1.00
r_y, in.	4.62	4.68	4.73	4.76	4.79

†Section is a slender-element cross-section.
††Section is a non-compact cross-section.

Shape	HSS10×10×				
	5/8	1/2	3/8	5/16††	1/4†
t_{design}, in.	0.581	0.465	0.349	0.291	0.233
Wt/ft	76.1	62.3	47.8	40.3	32.6
Effective length KL (ft) with respect to least radius of gyration r_y					
0	821	673	516	434	328
6	802	657	505	424	323
7	795	651	500	421	321
8	787	645	496	417	319
9	778	638	490	413	317
10	768	630	485	408	314
11	757	622	478	402	311
12	745	612	471	397	308
13	733	603	464	391	304
14	720	592	456	384	301
15	706	581	448	377	297
16	692	569	439	370	292
17	676	557	430	362	288
18	661	545	421	355	283
19	645	532	411	346	278
20	628	519	401	338	273
21	611	505	391	330	267
22	593	491	380	321	260
23	576	477	370	312	253
24	558	462	359	303	246
25	540	448	348	294	239
26	522	433	337	285	231
27	504	419	326	275	224
28	485	404	315	266	216
29	467	389	304	257	209
30	449	375	293	248	201
32	413	346	271	229	187
34	378	317	249	211	172
36	344	290	228	193	158
38	311	263	208	176	144
40	281	237	188	160	131
Properties					
A_g, in.²	21.0	17.2	13.2	11.1	8.96
I_x, in.⁴	304	256	202	172	141
I_y, in.⁴	304	256	202	172	141
r_x/r_y	1.00	1.00	1.00	1.00	1.00
r_y, in.	3.80	3.86	3.92	3.94	3.97

†Section is a slender-element cross-section.
††Section is a non-compact cross-section.
Note: Heavy line indicates Kl/r equal to or greater than 200.

Figure 5.37 Design strength $P_n = 0.85\Phi F_{CR}A_g$, in axial compression (K) for square, hollow steel sections, F_y = 46-KSI (*Continued*). (Copyright American Institute of Steel Construction, Inc. Reprinted with permission. All rights reserved.)

Shape		HSS8×8×					Shape		HSS6×6×					
		$5/8$	$1/2$	$3/8$	$5/16$	$1/4$††			$5/8$	$1/2$	$3/8$	$5/16$	$1/4$	$3/16$††
t_{design}, in.		0.581	0.465	0.349	0.291	0.233	t_{design}, in.		0.581	0.465	0.349	0.291	0.233	0.174
Wt/ft		59.1	48.7	37.6	31.8	25.8	Wt/ft		42.1	35.1	27.4	23.3	19.0	14.5
Effective length KL (ft) with respect to least radius of gyration r_y	0	641	528	407	343	278	Effective length KL (ft) with respect to least radius of gyration r_y	0	457	381	296	251	205	156
	6	617	508	392	331	268		6	425	355	277	236	192	146
	7	608	501	387	326	265		7	414	346	271	230	188	143
	8	598	494	381	322	261		8	401	336	263	224	183	139
	9	587	485	375	316	257		9	387	325	255	217	178	135
	10	575	475	368	310	252		10	372	313	246	210	172	131
	11	562	465	360	304	247		11	357	301	237	202	165	126
	12	549	454	352	297	241		12	340	288	227	194	159	121
	13	534	442	343	290	235		13	323	274	216	185	152	116
	14	519	430	334	282	229		14	306	260	206	176	145	111
	15	503	417	324	274	223		15	288	246	195	167	138	106
	16	486	404	314	266	216		16	270	231	184	158	130	100
	17	469	390	304	257	209		17	252	217	173	149	123	94.5
	18	451	376	293	249	202		18	235	203	162	140	116	89.0
	19	434	362	283	240	195		19	218	189	151	131	108	83.5
	20	416	347	272	231	188		20	201	175	141	122	101	78.1
	21	398	332	261	221	180		21	185	161	130	113	93.9	72.7
	22	380	318	250	212	173		22	169	148	120	104	87.0	67.5
	23	361	303	239	203	166		23	154	136	110	96.1	80.4	62.5
	24	344	289	228	194	158		24	142	125	101	88.3	73.8	57.5
	25	326	274	217	185	151		25	131	115	93.4	81.3	68.0	53.0
	26	308	260	206	176	143		26	121	106	86.4	75.2	62.9	49.0
	27	291	246	195	167	136		27	112	98.4	80.1	69.7	58.3	45.4
	28	274	232	185	158	129		28	104	91.5	74.5	64.8	54.2	42.2
	29	258	219	174	149	122		29	97.1	85.3	69.4	60.4	50.5	39.4
	30	241	205	164	141	115		30	90.7	79.7	64.9	56.5	47.2	36.8
	32	212	181	145	124	102		32	79.7	70.1	57.0	49.6	41.5	32.3
	34	188	160	128	110	90.3		34	70.6	62.1	50.5	44.0	36.8	28.7
	36	168	143	114	98.1	80.5		36	63.0	55.4	45.0	39.2	32.8	25.6
	38	150	128	103	88.1	72.3		38			40.4	35.2	29.4	22.9
	40	136	116	92.6	79.5	65.2		40						
Properties														
A_g, in.^{2}		16.4	13.5	10.4	8.76	7.10	A_g, in.^{2}		11.7	9.74	7.58	6.43	5.24	3.98
I_x, in.^{4}		146	125	99.6	85.6	70.7	I_x, in.^{4}		55.2	48.3	39.5	34.3	28.6	22.3
I_y, in.^{4}		146	125	99.6	85.6	70.7	I_y, in.^{4}		55.2	48.3	39.5	34.3	28.6	22.3
r_x/r_y		1.00	1.00	1.00	1.00	1.00	r_x/r_y		1.00	1.00	1.00	1.00	1.00	1.00
r_y, in.		2.99	3.04	3.10	3.13	3.15	r_y, in.		2.17	2.23	2.28	2.31	2.34	2.37

† Section is a slender-element cross-section.
†† Section is a non-compact cross-section.
Note: Heavy line indicates Kl/r equal to or greater than 200.

† Section is a slender-element cross-section.
†† Section is a non-compact cross-section.
Note: Heavy line indicates Kl/r equal to or greater than 200.

Figure 5.38 Design strength $\Phi_c P_n = 0.85\, F_{CR} A_g$, in axial compression (K) for square, hollow steel sections, $F_y = 46$-KSI (*Continued*). (Copyright American Institute of Steel Construction, Inc. Reprinted with permission. All rights reserved.)

Shape	HSS5×5×					Shape	HSS4×4×					
	$1/2$	$3/8$	$5/16$	$1/4$	$3/16$		$1/2$	$3/8$	$5/16$	$1/4$	$3/16$	$1/8$[††]
t_{design}, in.	0.465	0.349	0.291	0.233	0.174	t_{design}, in.	0.465	0.349	0.291	0.233	0.174	0.116
Wt/ft	28.3	22.3	19.0	15.6	12.0	Wt/ft	21.5	17.2	14.8	12.2	9.40	6.45

Effective length KL (ft) with respect to least radius of gyration r_y						Effective length KL (ft) with respect to least radius of gyration r_y						
0	308	242	206	168	128	0	235	187	160	132	101	69.2
1	307	241	205	168	128	1	234	186	160	131	100	68.9
2	305	239	203	166	127	2	231	184	158	130	99.3	68.1
3	300	236	201	164	125	3	225	180	154	127	97.3	66.8
4	294	231	197	161	123	4	218	174	150	123	94.6	65.0
5	286	225	192	158	120	5	208	167	144	119	91.2	62.8
6	277	219	187	153	117	6	198	159	137	113	87.2	60.2
7	267	211	180	148	113	7	185	150	129	107	82.8	57.2
8	256	202	173	142	109	8	172	140	121	101	77.9	54.0
9	243	193	165	136	105	9	159	130	113	93.8	72.8	50.5
10	230	183	157	130	99.7	10	145	119	104	86.6	67.4	46.9
11	216	173	149	123	94.5	11	131	109	94.6	79.3	61.9	43.3
12	202	162	140	116	89.2	12	117	98.0	85.5	72.0	56.4	39.6
13	188	151	131	108	83.7	13	103	87.6	76.7	64.9	51.0	35.9
14	174	140	122	101	78.2	14	90.5	77.6	68.2	57.9	45.8	32.3
15	160	130	112	93.7	72.7	15	78.8	68.0	59.9	51.3	40.7	28.9
16	146	119	103	86.4	67.3	16	69.3	59.8	52.7	45.1	35.9	25.6
17	132	109	94.7	79.3	61.9	17	61.4	53.0	46.7	39.9	31.8	22.7
18	119	98.5	86.2	72.4	56.7	18	54.7	47.2	41.6	35.6	28.3	20.2
19	107	88.7	77.9	65.8	51.6	19	49.1	42.4	37.4	32.0	25.4	18.1
20	96.7	80.1	70.3	59.3	46.7	20	44.3	38.3	33.7	28.8	23.0	16.4
21	87.7	72.6	63.8	53.8	42.3	21	40.2	34.7	30.6	26.2	20.8	14.8
22	79.9	66.2	58.1	49.0	38.6	22	36.6	31.6	27.9	23.8	19.0	13.5
23	73.1	60.5	53.2	44.9	35.3	23	33.5	28.9	25.5	21.8	17.4	12.4
24	67.1	55.6	48.8	41.2	32.4	24		26.6	23.4	20.0	15.9	11.4
25	61.9	51.2	45.0	38.0	29.9	25				18.5	14.7	10.5
26	57.2	47.4	41.6	35.1	27.6	26						9.68
27	53.1	43.9	38.6	32.6	25.6	27						
28	49.3	40.8	35.9	30.3	23.8	28						
29	46.0	38.1	33.5	28.2	22.2	29						
30	43.0	35.6	31.3	26.4	20.7	30						

Properties

	HSS5×5×						HSS4×4×					
A_g, in.^{2}	7.88	6.18	5.26	4.30	3.28	A_g, in.^{2}	6.02	4.78	4.10	3.37	2.58	1.77
I_x, in.^{4}	26.0	21.7	19.0	16.0	12.6	I_x, in.^{4}	11.9	10.3	9.14	7.80	6.21	4.40
I_y, in.^{4}	26.0	21.7	19.0	16.0	12.6	I_y, in.^{4}	11.9	10.3	9.14	7.80	6.21	4.40
r_x/r_y	1.00	1.00	1.00	1.00	1.00	r_x/r_y	1.00	1.00	1.00	1.00	1.00	1.00
r_y, in.	1.82	1.87	1.90	1.93	1.96	r_y, in.	1.41	1.47	1.49	1.52	1.55	1.58

[†] Section is a slender-element cross-section.
Note: Heavy line indicates Kl/r equal to or greater than 200.

[†] Section is a slender-element cross-section.
[††] Section is a non-compact cross-section.
Note: Heavy line indicates Kl/r equal to or greater than 200.

Figure 5.39 Design strength $\Phi_c P_n = 0.85\ F_{CR}A_g$, in axial compression (K) for square, hollow steel sections, $F_y = 46$-KSI (*Continued*). (Copyright American Institute of Steel Construction, Inc. Reprinted with permission. All rights reserved.)

Shape	HSS3$\frac{1}{2}$×3$\frac{1}{2}$×					HSS3×3×					HSS2$\frac{1}{2}$×2$\frac{1}{2}$×			
	$^3/_8$	$^5/_{16}$	$^1/_4$	$^3/_{16}$	$^1/_8$	$^3/_8$	$^5/_{16}$	$^1/_4$	$^3/_{16}$	$^1/_8$	$^5/_{16}$	$^1/_4$	$^3/_{16}$	$^1/_8$
t_{design}, in.	0.349	0.291	0.233	0.174	0.116	0.349	0.291	0.233	0.174	0.116	0.291	0.233	0.174	0.116
Wt/ft	14.6	12.7	10.5	8.13	5.60	12.1	10.5	8.78	6.85	4.75	8.40	7.08	5.57	3.90

Effective length KL (ft) with respect to least radius of gyration r_y

	$^3/_8$	$^5/_{16}$	$^1/_4$	$^3/_{16}$	$^1/_8$	$^3/_8$	$^5/_{16}$	$^1/_4$	$^3/_{16}$	$^1/_8$	$^5/_{16}$	$^1/_4$	$^3/_{16}$	$^1/_8$
0	160	138	114	87.6	60.2	133	115	95.4	73.9	50.8	91.9	77.0	60.2	41.8
1	159	137	113	87.1	59.9	131	114	94.7	73.4	50.5	90.7	76.1	59.6	41.4
2	156	134	111	85.7	59.0	128	111	92.5	71.7	49.4	87.4	73.5	57.6	40.1
3	151	131	108	83.5	57.5	123	107	88.9	69.1	47.7	82.1	69.3	54.5	38.1
4	145	125	104	80.4	55.4	115	101	84.1	65.6	45.4	75.2	63.8	50.5	35.4
5	137	119	99	76.7	52.9	107	93.4	78.4	61.3	42.6	67.2	57.4	45.7	32.3
6	128	112	93.1	72.3	50.0	97.2	85.2	71.9	56.5	39.4	58.6	50.5	40.5	28.8
7	119	103	86.6	67.5	46.8	86.9	76.5	64.9	51.3	35.9	49.8	43.3	35.1	25.1
8	108	94.8	79.7	62.3	43.3	76.3	67.6	57.7	45.9	32.3	41.3	36.3	29.7	21.5
9	97.6	85.9	72.5	56.9	39.6	65.9	58.7	50.5	40.4	28.7	33.3	29.7	24.6	18.0
10	86.9	76.9	65.3	51.5	35.9	56.0	50.1	43.5	35.1	25.0	27.0	24.1	20.0	14.8
11	76.4	68.1	58.1	46.0	32.2	46.6	42.0	36.8	30.0	21.6	22.3	19.9	16.6	12.2
12	66.4	59.5	51.1	40.7	28.6	39.2	35.3	30.9	25.3	18.3	18.7	16.7	13.9	10.3
13	56.9	51.4	44.5	35.7	25.2	33.4	30.1	26.4	21.5	15.6	16.0	14.2	11.9	8.74
14	49.1	44.3	38.3	30.9	21.9	28.8	25.9	22.7	18.6	13.5	13.8	12.3	10.2	7.53
15	42.8	38.6	33.4	26.9	19.0	25.1	22.6	19.8	16.2	11.7		10.7	8.90	6.56
16	37.6	33.9	29.3	23.6	16.7	22.0	19.8	17.4	14.2	10.3				5.77
17	33.3	30.0	26.0	20.9	14.8	19.5	17.6	15.4	12.6	9.12				
18	29.7	26.8	23.2	18.7	13.2		15.7	13.7	11.2	8.14				
19	26.7	24.0	20.8	16.8	11.9				10.1	7.30				
20	24.1	21.7	18.8	15.1	10.7									
21	21.8	19.7	17.0	13.7	9.71									
22			15.5	12.5	8.85									
23														

Properties														
A_g, in.^{2}	4.09	3.52	2.91	2.24	1.54	3.39	2.94	2.44	1.89	1.30	2.35	1.97	1.54	1.07
I_x, in.^{4}	6.49	5.84	5.04	4.05	2.90	3.78	3.45	3.02	2.46	1.78	1.82	1.63	1.35	0.998
I_y, in.^{4}	6.49	5.84	5.04	4.05	2.90	3.78	3.45	3.02	2.46	1.78	1.82	1.63	1.35	0.998
r_x/r_y	1.00	1.00	1.00	1.00	1.00	1.00	1.00	1.00	1.00	1.00	1.00	1.00	1.00	1.00
r_y, in.	1.26	1.29	1.32	1.35	1.37	1.06	1.08	1.11	1.14	1.17	0.880	0.908	0.937	0.965

Note: Heavy line indicates Kl/r equal to or greater than 200.

Figure 5.40 Design strength $\Phi_c P_n = 0.85 F_{CR} A_g$, in axial compression (K) for square, hollow steel sections, $F_y = 46$-KSI (*Continued*). (Copyright American Institute of Steel Construction, Inc. Reprinted with permission. All rights reserved.)

<table>
<tr><th colspan="2" rowspan="3">Shape</th><th colspan="11" style="text-align:center">Steel Pipe
Design Strength in Axial
Compression, $\phi_c P_n$, kips</th></tr>
</table>

$F_y = 35$ ksi
$\phi_c P_n = 0.85 F_{cr} A_g$

Shape		Pipe 12		Pipe 10		Pipe 8			Pipe 6		
		XS	Std.	XS	Std.	XXS	XS	Std.	XXS	XS	Std.
Wall Thkns., in.		0.500	0.375	0.500	0.365	0.875	0.500	0.322	0.864	0.432	0.280
Wt/ft		65.5	49.6	54.8	40.5	72.5	43.4	28.6	53.2	28.6	19.0
Effective length KL (ft) with respect to radius of gyration r	0	571	434	479	354	634	381	250	464	250	166
	6	563	428	469	347	612	369	242	436	236	158
	7	560	426	466	345	604	365	240	426	232	155
	8	557	424	462	342	596	360	237	415	226	151
	9	553	421	458	339	586	354	233	403	221	148
	10	549	418	453	335	575	348	229	390	214	144
	11	545	415	448	331	564	342	225	376	207	139
	12	540	411	442	327	551	335	221	361	200	135
	13	534	407	436	323	538	328	216	346	193	130
	14	529	403	429	318	524	320	211	330	185	125
	15	523	398	422	313	510	312	206	314	177	120
	16	517	394	415	308	495	303	201	298	169	114
	17	510	389	407	302	479	295	195	281	160	109
	18	503	384	400	297	463	286	190	264	152	104
	19	496	378	391	291	447	276	184	248	143	98.1
	20	488	372	383	284	430	267	178	232	135	92.7
	22	472	361	365	272	397	248	165	200	119	82.1
	24	455	348	347	258	363	228	153	170	103	71.8
	25	447	342	338	251	346	219	147	157	95.5	66.8
	26	438	335	328	245	329	209	140	145	88.3	61.9
	28	420	321	309	231	297	190	128	125	76.1	53.4
	30	401	307	290	216	265	171	116	109	66.3	46.5
	31	391	300	280	209	250	162	110	102	62.1	43.6
	32	382	293	270	202	235	153	104	95.8	58.3	40.9
	34	363	279	251	188	208	136	93.1	84.9	51.6	36.2
	36	343	264	232	174	186	121	83.0		46.1	32.3
	37	333	257	223	167	176	115	78.6			30.6
	38	324	249	214	161	166	109	74.5			
	40	305	235	196	148	150	98.3	67.2			
Properties											
A_g, in.^{2}		19.2	14.6	16.1	11.9	21.3	12.8	8.40	15.6	8.40	5.58
I, in.^{4}		362	279	212	161	162	106	72.5	66.3	40.5	28.1
r, in.		4.33	4.38	3.63	3.67	2.76	2.88	2.94	2.06	2.19	2.25

XS = x-strong.
XXS = xx-strong.
Note: Heavy line indicates Kl/r equal to or greater than 200.

Figure 5.41 Design strength $\Phi_c P_n = 0.85 F_{CR} A_g$, in axial compression (K) for steel pipe. (Copyright American Institute of Steel Construction, Inc. Reprinted with permission. All rights reserved.)

→ self-weight of the column.

Extra Heavy.

standard.

$F_y = 35$ ksi

$\phi_c P_n = 0.85 F_{cr} A_g$

**Steel Pipe
Design Strength in Axial
Compression, $\phi_c P_n$, kips**

Shape	Pipe 5			Pipe 4			Pipe 3¹/₂		Pipe 3		
	XXS	XS	Std.	XXS	XS	Std.	XS	Std.	XXS	XS	Std.
Wall Thkns., in.	0.750	0.375	0.258	0.674	0.337	0.237	0.318	0.226	0.600	0.300	0.216
Wt/ft	38.6	20.8	14.6	27.6	15.0	10.8	12.5	9.12	18.6	10.3	7.58
0	336	182	128	241	131	94.3	109	79.7	163	89.8	66.3
6	307	168	119	209	116	83.9	93.8	68.8	128	73.3	54.5
7	298	163	115	199	111	80.5	88.7	65.2	117	68.0	50.7
8	287	158	112	187	106	76.7	83.2	61.3	106	62.5	46.7
9	275	152	108	175	99.9	72.6	77.3	57.2	94.7	56.8	42.6
10	262	146	104	163	93.7	68.3	71.3	52.9	83.4	51.0	38.4
11	249	140	99.4	150	87.3	63.8	65.1	48.5	72.5	45.2	34.2
12	235	133	94.7	137	80.8	59.2	59.0	44.1	62.1	39.7	30.1
13	221	126	89.9	124	74.3	54.6	53.0	39.8	52.9	34.4	26.3
14	206	119	85.0	112	67.8	50.0	47.2	35.7	45.6	29.7	22.7
15	192	111	80.0	99.6	61.5	45.6	41.6	31.7	39.7	25.8	19.8
16	178	104	75.0	88.0	55.4	41.2	36.6	27.9	34.9	22.7	17.4
17	164	96.9	70.0	77.9	49.5	37.1	32.4	24.7	30.9	20.1	15.4
18	150	89.8	65.1	69.5	44.2	33.1	28.9	22.0		17.9	13.7
19	137	82.8	60.3	62.4	39.6	29.7	25.9	19.8		16.1	12.3
20	124	76.1	55.6	56.3	35.8	26.8	23.4	17.8			
22	102	63.3	46.5	46.5	29.6	22.1		14.7			
24	86.0	53.2	39.1		24.8	18.6					
25	79.3	49.0	36.0			17.1					
26	73.3	45.3	33.3								
28	63.2	39.1	28.7								
30		34.1	25.0								
31			23.4								
32											
Properties											
A_g, in.²	11.3	6.11	4.30	8.10	4.41	3.17	3.68	2.68	5.47	3.02	2.23
I, in.⁴	33.6	20.7	15.2	15.3	9.61	7.23	6.28	4.79	5.99	3.89	3.02
r, in.	1.72	1.84	1.88	1.37	1.48	1.51	1.31	1.34	1.05	1.14	1.16

Effective length KL (ft) with respect to radius of gyration r

XS = x-strong.
XXS = xx-strong.
Note: Heavy line indicates Kl/r equal to or greater than 200.

Figure 5.42 Design strength $\Phi_c P_n = 0.85 F_{CR} A_g$, in axial compression (K) for steel pipe (*Continued*). (Copyright American Institute of Steel Construction, Inc. Reprinted with permission. All rights reserved.)

A designer can use the tables of design strength in axial compression, $\Phi_c P_n$, in Figures 5.34 through 5.42, to size tension members, by looking in the tables for columns of zero length, that is, columns that are not limited by buckling. For much more valuable information on steel columns, consult the *AISC Manual of Steel Construction*.

In the *Manual of Steel Construction*, the tables giving design strength in axial compression for wide-flange columns are limited to columns at least 10 in. deep. However, the manual includes tools to generate tables for any sections a designer may want to consider. For example, for fairly light-load situations, the designer may want to consider 6 in.-deep, wide-flange sections. Table 5.2 was generated by:

- Looking up A and r_y for the section
- Calculating KL/r
- Calculating the critical stress F_{cr} (which can be gotten from the table or from a curve-fit equation provided in the manual)
- Multiplying F_{cr} times the cross-sectional area A to get P_n
- Multiplying P_n by $\Phi_c = 0.85$ to get the design strength in axial compression

Table 5.2 Design Strength in Axial Compression of 6 in.-Deep, Wide-Flange Columns

Effective Length KL (ft) with respect to least radius of gyrations r_y	Design Strength in Axial Compression, $\Phi_c P_n$, Kips		
	W 6		
	25	20	15
0	312.0	249.5	188.3
1	310.5	248.3	187.3
2	306.3	244.8	184.5
3	299.4	239.2	180.0
4	290.0	231.5	173.8
5	278.4	221.9	166.1
6	264.7	210.8	157.2
7	249.5	198.4	147.3
8	233.0	184.9	136.6
9	215.7	170.8	125.5
10	197.8	156.2	114.1
11	179.7	141.6	102.7
12	161.8	127.2	91.5
13	144.4	113.1	80.8
14	127.7	99.7	70.6
15	111.7	87.0	61.3
16	98.2	76.4	53.9
17	86.9	67.7	47.8
18	77.6	60.4	42.6
19	69.6	54.2	38.2
20	62.8	48.9	34.5
21	57.0	44.4	31.3
22	51.9	40.4	28.5
23	47.5	37.0	26.1
24	43.6	34.0	24.0
25	40.2	31.3	22.1

This table is not complete, however, because some of the sections listed are not compact and they will be limited by local buckling for low slenderness ratios. This is particularly a concern for the W 6 × 15, which has thin flanges and web. The tables in the *AISC Manual of Steel Construction* account for the limitations of local buckling. Accounting for local buckling is beyond the scope of this book, so we will not adjust Table 5.2 to account for that effect. However, this table will be used as part of the following illustrative example, as local buckling will not be the limiting factor for any situation in which these sections will be used.

Steel-column Sizing Example—Statement of Problem

The problem is to size a 14 ft-tall column that is pinned at the bottom and the top and is restrained against sway (lateral movement) at the top (so the effective length is 14 ft). The axial force will vary to illustrate certain patterns of behavior. Observations will be made regarding how the self-weight and structural efficiency of the column varies with the applied load.

Part A: Sizing the column as limited only by yielding of the material

Loading Condition 1 (light load)

The column supports part of a lightweight metal roof that delivers the following compressive forces to the top of the column:

$P_{dead} = 6.00$ K
$P_{live} = 18.00$ K

1. Standard steel pipe is manufactured in 35-KSI steel. Find the required cross-sectional area A as limited by the yield stress of the material.
2. Calculate the weight of a column with that cross-sectional area by multiplying the cross-sectional area by the conversion factor: $\left(\dfrac{\dfrac{3.40\#}{\text{linear foot}}}{\text{in.}^2 \text{ of cross-sectional area}} \right)$.

This conversion factor is gotten from the following:

$$D_{steel} = \frac{490\#}{\text{ft}^3}$$

The aim is to determine the weight of a piece of steel 1 ft long, with a cross-sectional area of 1 in.^{2}. One cubic foot consists of 144 such columns of material. Therefore, the desired weight is 490 lb/144 = 3.40 lb, leading to the conversion factor:

$$\left(\frac{\dfrac{3.40\#}{\text{linear foot}}}{\text{in.}^2 \text{ of cross-sectional area}} \right).$$

3. Square steel tube is manufactured in 46-KSI steel. Find the required cross-sectional area A as limited by the yield stress.
4. Calculate the weight of a column with that cross-sectional area by multiplying the cross-sectional area by the conversion factor noted in step 2.
5. W-flange steel columns of the sizes appropriate to this problem are manufactured in 50-KSI steel. Find the required cross-sectional area A as limited by the yield stress.
6. Calculate the weight of a column with that cross-sectional area by multiplying the cross-sectional area by the conversion factor in step 3.

Loading Condition 2 (heavy load)

The column supports part of a multistory building that delivers the following compressive forces to the top of the column.

$P_{dead} = 100.00$ K
$P_{live} = 200.00$ K

1. Standard steel pipe is manufactured in 35-KSI steel. Find the required cross-sectional area A as limited by the yield stress of the material.
2. Calculate the weight of a column with that cross-sectional area by multiplying the cross-sectional area

by the conversion factor: $\left(\dfrac{\dfrac{3.40\#}{\text{linear foot}}}{\text{in.}^2 \text{ of cross-sectional area}} \right)$.

3. Square steel tube is manufactured in 46-KSI steel. Find the required cross-sectional area A as limited by the yield stress of the material.
4. Calculate the weight of a column with that cross-sectional area by multiplying the cross-sectional area by the conversion factor noted earlier.
5. W-flange steel columns of the sizes appropriate to this problem are manufactured in 50-KSI steel. Find the required cross-sectional area A as limited by the yield stress of the material.
6. Calculate the weight of a column with that cross-sectional area by multiplying the cross-sectional area by the conversion factor noted earlier.

Part B: Sizing the column to resist both crushing and buckling, using standard tables

Loading Condition 1 (light load)

The column supports part of a lightweight metal roof that delivers the following compressive forces to the top of the column:

$P_{dead} = 6.00$ K
$P_{live} = 18.00$ K

1. From Figures 5.41 and 5.42 specifying the design strength in axial compression, $\Phi_c P_n$, for steel pipe

columns of various cross sections and lengths, find the lightest-weight, standard pipe column in 35-KSI steel that will safely support the load. (These tables account for both buckling and crushing of the material and the resistance factor has already been provided for; that is, these tables give the design strength in axial compression, $\Phi_c P_n$, accounting for all modes of failure.)
2. How much does the pipe column weigh? (This number can be found at the top of Figure 5.41.)
3. By what factor is the weight of this column greater than the weight of the column you derived from consideration of material crushing alone (Part A, Loading Condition 1, Question 2)? This ratio tells you how important buckling is in the behavior of this column. If this number is much greater than 1, then buckling is a major limitation on the capacity of the column.
4. From Figures 5.37 through 5.40, specifying the design strength in axial compression, $\Phi_c P_n$, for square steel tube columns of various cross sections and lengths, find the lightest-weight square-tube column in 46-KSI steel that will safely support the load.
5. How much does the square-tube column weigh?
6. By what factor is the weight of this column greater than the weight of the column you derived from consideration of material crushing alone (Part A, Loading Condition 1, Question 4)?
7. From Figures 5.34, 5.35, and 5.36, specifying the design strength in axial compression, $\Phi_c P_n$, for W-flange steel columns of various cross sections and lengths, find the lightest-weight, wide-flange column in 50-KSI steel that will safely support the load.
8. How much does the wide-flange column weigh?
9. By what factor is the weight of this column greater than the weight of the column you derived from consideration of material crushing alone (Part A, Loading Condition 1, Question 6)?

Loading Condition 2 (heavy load)

The column supports part of a multistory building that delivers the following compressive forces to the top of the column:

$P_{dead} = 100.00$ K
$P_{live} = 200.00$ K

1. From Figures 5.41 and 5.42 specifying the design strength in axial compression, $\Phi_c P_n$, for steel pipe columns of various cross sections and lengths, find the lightest-weight, standard pipe column in 35-KSI steel that will safely support the load.
2. How much does the pipe column weigh?
3. By what factor is its weight greater than the weight of the column you derived from consideration of yielding alone (without consideration of buckling

limitations) (Part A, Loading Condition 2, Question 2)?

4. From the tables specifying the design strength in axial compression, $\Phi_c P_n$, for square-tube steel columns of various cross sections and lengths, find the lightest-weight, square-tube column in 46-KSI steel that will safely support the load.

5. How much does the square-tube column weigh?

6. By what factor is its weight greater than the weight of the column you derived from consideration of yielding alone (without consideration of buckling limitations) (Part A, Loading Condition 2, Question 4)?

7. From the tables specifying the design strength in axial compression, $\Phi_c P_n$, for W-flange steel columns of various cross sections and lengths (in the section on steel columns), find the lightest-weight, W-flange column in 50-KSI steel that will safely support the load. (These tables account for both buckling and crushing of the material, and a safety factor has been provided for.)

8. How much does the W-flange column weigh?

9. By what factor is the weight of this column greater than the weight of the column you derived from consideration of material crushing alone (Part A, Loading Condition 1, Question 6)? This ratio tells you how important buckling is in the behavior of this column. If this number is much greater than one, then buckling is a major limitation on the capacity of the column.

   Comparison of results for light load and heavy load:

10. What is the ratio of the axial force (accounting for both crushing and buckling) to the total self-weight of the column for:

    • The 36-KSI pipe column under light load?
    • The 36-KSI pipe column under heavy load?
    • The 46-KSI tube column under light load?
    • The 46-KSI tube column under heavy load?
    • The 50-KSI W-flange column under light load?
    • The 50-KSI W-flange column under heavy load?

The ratio of axial force to self-weight can be taken as an indicator of structural efficiency. Figures 5.43 through 5.46 provide the solution to this example problem.

Assignment 5.3.1

A 14 ft-long column is rigidly connected at the base to intersecting deep grade beams and is rigidly connected at the top to intersecting deep beams. Sway is not inhibited at the top of the column. Find the effective length. On the top of the column, the dead-load axial force is 8 kips, and

the live-load axial force is 16 kips. Find the factored total load on the top of the column. Find the lightest wide-flange section that will support the load. Find the lightest, hollow square steel section that will support the load. Find the lightest steel pipe that will support the load.

Assignment 5.3.2

A 14 ft-long column is rigidly connected at the base to intersecting deep grade beams and is rigidly connected at the top to intersecting deep beams. Sway is inhibited at the top of the column by bracing elements in other parts of the structure. Find the effective length. On the top of the column, the dead-load axial force is 130 kips, and the live-load axial force is 280 kips. Find the factored total load on the top of the column. Find the lightest wide-flange section that will support the load. Find the lightest, hollow square steel section that will support the load. Find the lightest steel pipe that will support the load.

Assignment 5.3.3

A 20 ft-long pinned-pinned column is restrained against lateral movement at the top by shear walls and a diaphragm roof. Find the effective length. On the top of the column, the dead-load axial force is 20 kips, and the live-load axial force is 40 kips. Find the factored total load on the top of the column. Find the lightest wide-flange section that will support the load. Find the lightest, hollow square steel section that will support the load. Find the lightest steel pipe that will support the load.

Assignment 5.3.4

Rework the preceding assignment, assuming

• A heavy load case of unfactored P_{dead} = 90 K; unfactored P_{live} = 160 K
• An 18 ft-long pinned-pinned column
• A light load case of unfactored P_{dead} = 10 K; unfactored P_{live} = 15 K
• A heavy load case of unfactored P_{dead} = 80 K; unfactored P_{live} = 180 K

If you set up this first problem in a spreadsheet, then solving the next problem is very easy. You can use the same spreadsheet template to do all the mathematical manipulations by just changing the inputs. The only work to be done is scanning the tables to find the right cross section. The solution to the example problem (see Figures 5.43 through 5.46) was performed in the spreadsheet, and images from the spreadsheet were used to present the solution.

Steel Column Sizing Example Problem Solution

Part A (sizing based on limit set by yielding of material): Loading Condition 1 (light load)

Factored force on column:

P_{dead} (K)	P_{live} (K)	$1.2P_{dead} + 1.6P_{live}$ (K)
6	18	36

Step

1

Yield stress = $F_y=$ 35 K/in.^{2}

Design stress = $\Phi c\ F_y = .85 \bullet 35$ K/in.$^2=$ 29.75 K/in.^{2}

$$A = \frac{36\ K}{29.75\ \frac{K}{in.^2}} = 1.210\ in.^2$$

2

$$Wt = A \bullet \frac{3.4\ \#}{\frac{ft}{in.^2}} = 1.210\ in.^2 \bullet \frac{3.4\ \#}{\frac{ft}{in.^2}} = 4.11\ \frac{\#}{ft}$$

3

Yield stress = $F_y=$ 46 K/in.^{2}

Design stress = $\Phi c\ F_y = .85 \bullet 46$ K/in.$^2=$ 39.1 K/in.^{2}

$$A = \frac{36\ K}{39.1\ \frac{K}{in.^2}} = 0.921\ in.^2$$

4

$$Wt = A \bullet \frac{3.4\ \#}{\frac{ft}{in.^2}} = 0.921\ in.^2 \bullet \frac{3.4\ \#}{\frac{ft}{in.^2}} = 3.13\ \frac{\#}{ft}$$

5

Yield stress = $F_y=$ 50 K/in.^{2}

Design stress = $\Phi c\ F_y = .85 \bullet 50$ K/in.$^2=$ 42.5 K/in.^{2}

$$A = \frac{36\ K}{42.5\ \frac{K}{in.^2}} = 0.847\ in.^2$$

6

$$Wt = A \bullet \frac{3.4\ \#}{\frac{ft}{in.^2}} = 0.847\ in.^2 \bullet \frac{3.4\ \#}{\frac{ft}{in.^2}} = 2.88\ \frac{\#}{ft}$$

Figure 5.43 Image 1 from spreadsheet template used to solve the example problem.

Steel Column Sizing Example Problem Solution (*Continued*)

Part A (sizing based on limit set by yielding of material): Loading Condition 2 (heavy load)

Factored force on column:

P_{dead}	P_{live}	$1.2P_{dead} + 1.6P_{live}$
(K)	(K)	(K)
100	200	440

Step

1 Yield stress = F_y = 35 K/in.^{2}

   Design stress = $\Phi c\ F_y$ = .85 • 35 K/in.^{2} = 29.75 K/in.^{2}

   $$A = \frac{440 \text{ K}}{29.75 \ \frac{\text{K}}{\text{in.}^2}} = 14.790 \text{ in.}^2$$

2 $$Wt = A \bullet \frac{3.4 \ \frac{\#}{ft}}{\text{in.}^2} = 14.790 \text{ in.}^2 \bullet \frac{3.4 \ \frac{\#}{ft}}{\text{in.}^2} = 50.28 \ \frac{\#}{ft}$$

3 Yield stress = F_y = 46 K/in.^{2}

   Design stress = $\Phi c\ F_y$ = .85 • 46 K/in.^{2} = 39.1 K/in.^{2}

   $$A = \frac{440 \text{ K}}{39.1 \ \frac{\text{K}}{\text{in.}^2}} = 11.253 \text{ in.}^2$$

4 $$Wt = A \bullet \frac{3.4 \ \frac{\#}{ft}}{\text{in.}^2} = 11.253 \text{ in.}^2 \bullet \frac{3.4 \ \frac{\#}{ft}}{\text{in.}^2} = 38.26 \ \frac{\#}{ft}$$

5 Yield stress = F_y = 50 K/in.^{2}

   Design stress = $\Phi c\ F_y$ = .85 • 50 K/in.^{2} = 42.5 K/in.^{2}

   $$A = \frac{440 \text{ K}}{42.5 \ \frac{\text{K}}{\text{in.}^2}} = 10.353 \text{ in.}^2$$

6 $$Wt = A \bullet \frac{3.4 \ \frac{\#}{ft}}{\text{in.}^2} = 10.353 \text{ in.}^2 \bullet \frac{3.4 \ \frac{\#}{ft}}{\text{in.}^2} = 35.20 \ \frac{\#}{ft}$$

Figure 5.44 Image 2 from spreadsheet template used to solve the example problem.

Steel Column Sizing Example Problem Solution (*Continued*)

Part B (sizing to resist yielding and buckling): Loading Condition 1 (light load)

Factored force on column:		
P_{dead}	P_{live}	$1.2P_{dead} + 1.6P_{live}$
(K)	(K)	(K)
6	18	36

Effective length =   14 ft

Step

1   4 in. standard pipe

2   10.8 #
                    ft

3   2.63 This says that buckling is causing us to use 2.63 times as much
                    material as we would if all we had to account for was material yielding.

4   4" x 4" x $\frac{3}{16}$"

5   7.3 #
                    ft

6   2.33 This says that buckling is causing us to use 2.33 times as much
                    material as we would if all we had to account for was material yielding.

7   W6 x 15

8   15 #
                    ft

9   5.21 This says that buckling is causing us to use 5.21 times as much
                    material as we would if all we had to account for was material yielding!

Part B (sizing to resist yielding and buckling): Loading Condition 2 (heavy load):

Factored force on column:		
P_{dead}	P_{live}	$1.2P_{dead} + 1.6P_{live}$
(K)	(K)	(K)
100	200	440

Effective length =   14 ft

Step

1   12 in. extra-strong pipe

2   65.5 #
                    ft

3   1.30 This says that buckling is causing us to use 1.30 times as much
                    material as we would if all we had to account for was material yielding.

4   HSS 10" x 10" x $\frac{3}{8}$" square tube

5   47.8 #
                    ft

6   1.25 This says that buckling is causing us to use 1.25 times as much
                    material as we would if all we had to account for was material yielding.

7   W10 x 49

8   49 #
                    ft

9   1.39 This says that buckling is causing us to use 1.39 times as much
                    material as we would if all we had to account for was material yielding.

Figure 5.45 Image 3 from spreadsheet template used to solve the example problem.

Steel Column Sizing Example Problem Solution (*Continued*)

Comparison of results for light load and heavy load

	Factored Axial Force K	Self-Weight K/ft	Factored Axial Force / Self-Weight
A	36	0.0108	238
B	**440**	**0.0655**	**480**
C	36	0.0073	352
D	**440**	**0.0478**	**658**
E	36	0.0150	171
F	**440**	**0.0490**	**641**

These results indicate that the columns under heavy loading are performing substantially more efficiently than columns under light loading. This can be explained in the following manner:
Columns for lighter loads tend to have smaller cross sections:
> which makes them more slender
> which makes them more vulnerable to buckling
> which means the allowed stress will be lower
> which makes them less efficient

Columns subjected to very high loads tend to have large cross sectional areas:
> which means they tend to be fat
> which means that their failure tends to be governed more by yielding than by buckling
> which means that columns made of higher-grade steel tend to perform more efficiently

We expect closed sections, such as pipes, to make more efficient columns than wide flanges because of the shape. However, the numbers above indicate that for heavily loaded columns, the wide-flange column is actually lighter than the pipe column. This can be explained in the following manner:
> Highly loaded columns tend to be governed more by material yielding than by buckling. For the columns chosen for this example, the wide-flange column had a higher yield stress than the pipe.
> Therefore, the wide-flange column was more efficient.

When we account for the added cost of, and complexity of making connections to, pipe columns, it is not surprising that we still use a lot of wide-flange columns.

Figure 5.46 Image 4 from spreadsheet template used to solve the example problem.

5.4 Precast Concrete Columns

Figures 5.47 and 5.48 show design curves for precast concrete columns.

In steel columns, increasing the moment reduces the amount of axial force that the column can withstand, and increasing the axial force reduces the amount of moment that the column can withstand. The curves for concrete columns, shown in Figures 5.47 and 5.48, show a different, and more complex, behavior. Up to a point, increasing the axial force increases the moment that a column can resist. This behavior is attributable to the fact that, under moment, both concrete and steel are acting in compression, but only steel is acting in tension. Therefore, under pure moment, the failure mode is tension yielding in the steel. Adding axial compression helps to alleviate some of the tension that is induced in the steel, under the influence of the moment.

To use the tables in Figures 5.47 and 5.48:

- Calculate the factored axial force P_u.
- Mark that value of P_u on the vertical axis of the appropriate chart (Figure 5.47 or 5.48).
- Draw a horizontal line through the mark.
- Calculate the applied magnified factored moment ϕM_u (where ϕ is the moment magnifier defined below).

CRITERIA

1. Concrete f'_c = 5,000 psi
2. Reinforcement f_y = 60,000 psi
3. Curves shown for full developement of reinforcement
4. Horizontal portion of curve is the maximum for tied columns = 0.80 ϕ P_c
5. Varies linearly from 0.9 for tension-controlled sections to 0.65 for compression-controlled sections in accordance with ACI 318-02 Section 9.3.2

USE OF CURVES

1. Enter at left with applied factored axial load, P_u.
2. Enter at bottom with applied magnified factored moment, δ M_u.
3. Intersection point must be to the left of curve indicating required reinforcement.

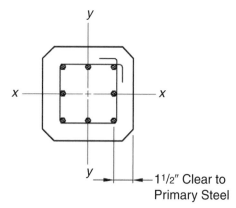

1¹/₂″ Clear to Primary Steel

NOTATION

ϕ P_n = design axial strength
ϕ M_n = design flexural strength
ϕ P_c = design axial strength at zero eccentricity
A_g = gross area of the column
δ = moment magnifier (Section 10.11–10.13 ACI 318-02)

The interaction curves have been smoothed for plotting purposes.
Exact calculated values may be slightly different.

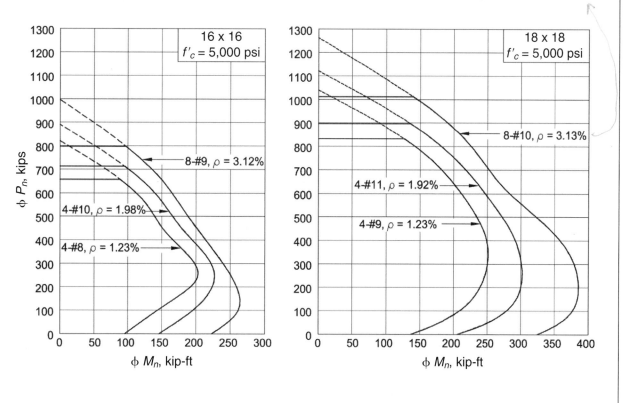

Figure 5.47 Design strength interaction curves for precast, reinforced concrete columns. (Reprinted from PCI Design Handbook, 6th edition. Copyright Precast/Prestressed Concrete Institute (PCI) and PCI Industry Handbook Committee, Leslie D. Martin, PE, editor. Reprinted with permission. All rights reserved.)

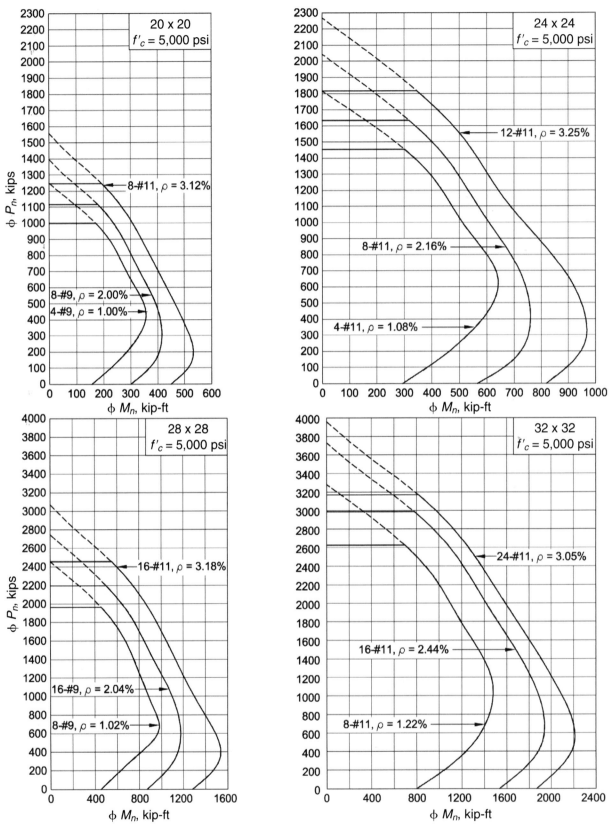

Figure 5.48 Design strength interaction curves for precast, reinforced concrete columns. (Reprinted from PCI Design Handbook, 6th edition. Copyright Precast/Prestressed Concrete Institute (PCI) and PCI Industry Handbook Committee, Leslie D. Martin, PE, editor. Reprinted with permission. All rights reserved.)

- Mark that value of ϕM_u on the horizontal axis.
- Draw a vertical line through the mark.

The intersection of the horizontal and vertical lines must be inside (to the left of) the curve.

Example Exercise for Sizing a Precast Column

Figure 5.49 shows a concrete column supporting an inverted-T concrete girder that supports double Ts. The image on the left shows the inverted double T. The image on the right shows the column with the force from the inverted T beam pressing down on the center of the haunch, P_2, and the axial force from the floors above, P_1.

The spacing of the girders is 30 ft. The length of the girders is 60 ft. Therefore, the girder supports an area of floor that is 30 ft (60 ft^2) = 900 ft^2. The dead load is 90 lb/ft^2, and the live load is 80 lb/ft^2.

Factored axial load from the girder is:

$$\text{Factored } P_2 = 1.2\left(90\frac{\#}{\text{ft}^2}\right)\left(900 \text{ ft}^2\right)$$
$$+1.6\left(80\frac{\#}{\text{ft}^2}\right)\left(900 \text{ ft}^2\right) \qquad \textbf{[5.8]}$$
$$= 212,400\# = 212 \text{ K}$$

There are two identical floors above the one shown here, so $P_1 = 2P_2 = 414$ K. The code allows an influence area reduction, based on the recognition that, statistically, it is extremely unlikely that the full floor load will be everywhere at the same time. Columns supporting very large floor areas benefit from this reduction more than most parts of the structure. Students interested in this load-reduction factor can consult the International Building Code. For the purposes of this illustrative example, the full load on the entire floor area is assumed.

The critical part of the column being sized is the part subject to the combined effect of P_1 and P_2, that is, the portion of the column below the bottom haunch. Therefore, the factored axial force is $P_1 + P_2 = 616$ K.

The moment induced by the force on the haunch is:

$$M = P_2\left(\frac{d}{2}+4 \text{ in.}\right) = 212 \text{ K}\left(\frac{d}{2}+4 \text{ in.}\right) \qquad \textbf{[5.9]}$$

This moment is absorbed partly by the part of the column above the haunch and partly by the part of the column below the haunch. To carefully size this column, a detailed analysis should be performed to determine the distribution of moment in the column. For the purposes of this exercise, assume that the portion of the column above the haunch provides half of the required moment and that the portion of the column below the haunch provides the other half of the required moment. In other words, the maximum moment induced in the column is about half of the moment shown in the preceding equation.

$$M = \frac{P_2\left(d_2+4 \text{ in.}\right)}{2} = 106 \text{ K}\left(\frac{d}{2}+4 \text{ in.}\right) \qquad \textbf{[5.10]}$$

This equation presents the classic chicken-and-egg dilemma so often encountered in design. The goal is to size the column, that is, decide what d should be. However, to calculate M in the equation, an assumption must be made about what d might be.

Assume that $d = 20$ in.

$$M = \frac{P_2\left(\dfrac{d}{2}+4 \text{ in.}\right)}{2} = 106 \text{ K}(14 \text{ in.})\left[\frac{\text{ft}}{12 \text{ in.}}\right] \qquad \textbf{[5.11]}$$
$$= 124 \text{ Kft}$$

Checking the interaction curves for 20 in. × 20 in. columns suggests that this is oversized.

Assume that $d = 16$ in.

$$M = \frac{P_2\left(\dfrac{d}{2}+4 \text{ in.}\right)}{2}$$
$$\qquad \textbf{[5.12]}$$
$$= 106 \text{ K}(12 \text{ in.})\left[\frac{\text{ft}}{12 \text{ in.}}\right] = 106 \text{ Kft}$$

Checking the interaction curves for 16 in. × 16 in. columns suggests that this is almost precisely the correct size. However, it is very close. To be conservative, you might want to choose an 18 in. × 18 in. column.

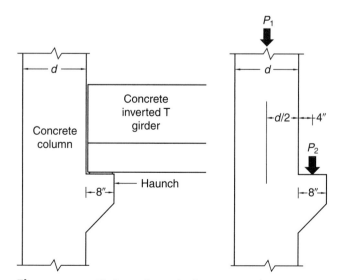

Figure 5.49 Girder on haunch of concrete column.

Assignment 5.3.4

Assuming the same concrete structural system as in the example above and the following conditions, size the column:

- Eight floors.
- Span of the girder is 50 ft.
- Spacing between girders is 60 ft.

Assignment 5.3.5

Assuming the same concrete structural system as in the example above and the following conditions, size the column:

- Three floors.
- Span of the girder is 60 ft.
- Spacing between girders is 40 ft.

CHAPTER

6

Beams

6.1 Generic Beam Issues

6.1.1 SHEAR, MOMENT, AND DEFLECTION

It is possible to determine internal forces, moments, and stresses by creating a freebody of a part of a beam. In that manner, forces and moments internal to the entire beam become external to the new freebody. Then the principles of equilibrium and action–reaction pairs can be applied to the new freebody to determine the forces and moments on the cut face of the new freebody.

Example 1: Simple-Span Beam with Uniform Load

Consider a simple-span beam with uniform load w over the entire length of the beam; see Figure 6.1.

The shear force V and the moment M shown on the freebody are the action of the part of the beam that has been removed from the diagram on the part of the beam remaining in the diagram.

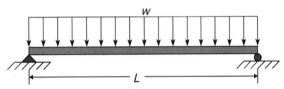

Replace the support structure with its equivalent actions:

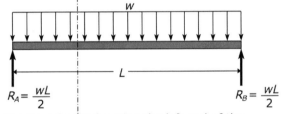

Create a freebody using the left end of the beam:

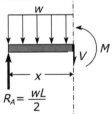

Replace the distributed force w with an equivalent point force:

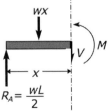

Figure 6.1 Creating a freebody to explore what is happening internal to the beam.

Summing the vertical forces yields:

$$\sum P_y = 0 \uparrow +$$

$$0 = \frac{wL}{2} - wx - V$$

$$V = \frac{wL}{2} - wx = \frac{w(L - 2x)}{2} \qquad \textbf{[6.1]}$$

Taking moments about the cut face eliminates V from the moment equation, yielding:

$$\sum M_F = 0$$

$$0 = \frac{wL}{2}x - wx\left(\frac{x}{2}\right) - M$$

$$M = \frac{wx(L - x)}{2} \qquad \textbf{[6.2]}$$

Plotting the shear and moment along the length of the beam yields Figure 6.2.

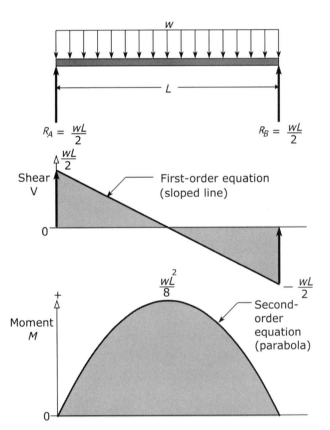

Figure 6.2 Shear and moment diagrams for the simple-span beam under uniform load.

Example 2: Simple Cantilever Beam under Uniform Load

See Figure 6.3. Summing the vertical forces produces:

$$\sum F_y = 0$$

$$0 = -wx - V$$

$$V = -wx \qquad \textbf{[6.3]}$$

See Figure 6.3. Summing the moments about the cut face F:

$$\sum M_F = 0$$

$$0 = -wx\left(\frac{x}{2}\right) - M$$

$$M = -\frac{wx^2}{2} \qquad \textbf{[6.4]}$$

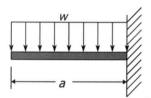

Replace the support structure with its equivalent actions:

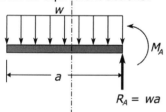

Create a freebody using the left end of the beam:

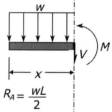

Replace the distributed force w with an equivalent point force:

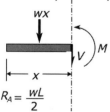

Figure 6.3 Freebodies for simple cantilever beam.

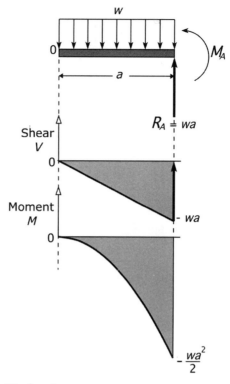

Figure 6.4 Shear and moment diagrams for simple cantilever under uniform load.

See Figure 6.5. Comparing a simple-span beam of length L to a cantilever of length a:

If $a = \dfrac{L}{2}$, the maximum moment in the cantilevered beam = maximum moment in the simple-span beam.

If $a > \dfrac{L}{2}$, then the maximum moment in the cantilevered beam is greater than the maximum moment in the simple span.

If $a < \dfrac{L}{2}$, then the maximum moment in the cantilevered beam is less than the maximum moment in the simple-span beam.

Some patterns are emerging from the examples of the simple-span beam and the simple cantilevered beam:

- Everywhere a point force occurs, there is an abrupt discontinuity in the shear diagram.
- Everywhere a point force occurs, there is an abrupt discontinuity in the slope of the moment diagram; that is, there is a cusp in the moment diagram.
- Everywhere the continuous load w occurs, the shear diagram is a straight line with slope equal to $-w$. (The negative sign means it is sloping down and to the right.)

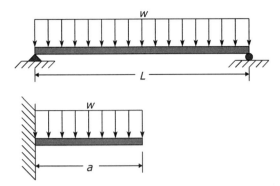

Figure 6.5 Comparing a simple-span beam of length L to a cantilever of length a.

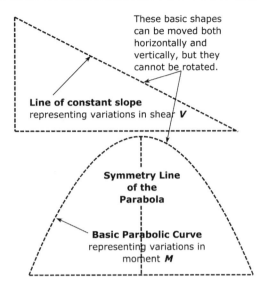

Figure 6.6 Triangular and parabolic templates for V and M, respectively.

- Everywhere the continuous load occurs, the moment diagram is a second-order equation:

$$M = -\frac{w}{2}(x-c)^2 + d$$

where c and d are constants. That is, the moment curve is a parabola, with a constant multiplier of $-\frac{w}{2}$. The negative sign means that the parabola has its maximum at the center and falls off to each side.
- The shear is zero at the end of a cantilevered beam.
- The moment is zero at the end of a cantilevered beam.
- The parabola representing the moment in a cantilevered beam peaks at the end of the cantilevered beam; that is, the centerline of the parabola occurs at the end of the parabola.

There is substantial discipline to be gained from creating templates for the shear and moments curves. These templates guide us and reduce the probability that we will draw the associated curves incorrectly. If the designer is drawing the diagrams by hand, these templates will be physical elements that can be moved around to construct various parts of the curves. If the designer is drawing the diagrams in a computer program, the curves can be constructed in the program and then replicated and moved around. Figure 6.6 shows what they might look like in the computer.

Figure 6.7 shows these templates being maneuvered to assist in the drawing of the shear and moment diagrams for a simple-span beam.

In using this construction technique:

- The left edge of the triangular template must always be kept vertical.
- The symmetry line of the parabolic template must also be kept vertical.
- The shear must be zero at the center of the beam, according to the symmetry of the forces on the beam, so the sloped edge of the triangle must intersect the zero-shear line at the center of the beam.

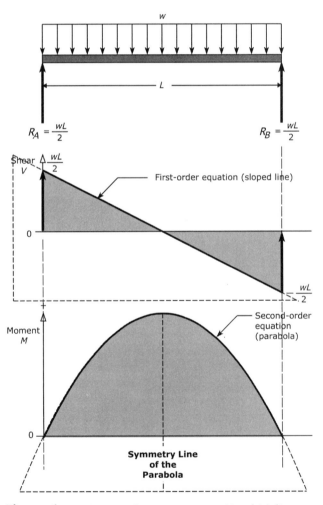

Figure 6.7 Using templates to construct V and M diagrams for a simple-span beam.

- The large discontinuity that takes the shear from zero shear just to the left of the left support (where there is no beam in which to have shear), to high positive shear just to the right of the left support, is caused by the point force of the support reaction. Similarly, at the right end of the beam, the sudden change from high negative shear just to the left of the right support, to zero shear just to the right of the right support, is caused by the support reaction at the right end of the beam.

- The parabola must be maneuvered so that it passes through the zero-moment line at both ends of the beam, because there is no agent at the end of the beam to cause any moment.

Figure 6.8 shows the triangular and parabolic templates being used to construct the shear and moment diagrams for a cantilevered beam that is cantilevering to the right. The following rules apply to this construction:

- The left edge of the triangular template must always be kept vertical.

- The symmetry line of the parabolic template must also be kept vertical.

- The shear must approach zero toward the right end of the beam, because there is no agent at the end of the beam to induce any shear there.

- The large discontinuity that takes the shear from zero shear just to the left of the left support (where there is no beam in which to have shear), to high positive shear just to the right of the left support, is caused by the point force of the support reaction.

- The parabola must be maneuvered so that it passes through the zero-moment line at both ends of the beam, because there is no agent at the end of the beam to cause any moment.

- The symmetry line of the parabola must pass through the end of the cantilevered beam; that is, the zenith of the parabola occurs at the end of the beam.

Figure 6.9 shows a beam with two supports and a cantilevered portion of the beam at each end. For the purposes of this problem, it is assumed that the lengths of the two cantilevers are the same.

Example 3: Beam with Equal-Length, Double Cantilevers under Uniform Load

For $0 < x < a$:

Summing the vertical forces produces:

$$\sum F_y = 0$$

$$0 = -wx - V$$

$$V = -wx \tag{6.5}$$

Summing the moments about the cut face F:

$$\sum M_F = 0$$

$$0 = -wx\left(\frac{x}{2}\right) - M$$

$$M = -\frac{wx^2}{2} \tag{6.6}$$

For $a < x < (a + b)$:

Summing the vertical forces produces:

$$\sum F_y = 0$$

$$0 = -wx + \frac{wL}{2} - V$$

$$V = w\left(\frac{L}{2} - x\right) \tag{6.7}$$

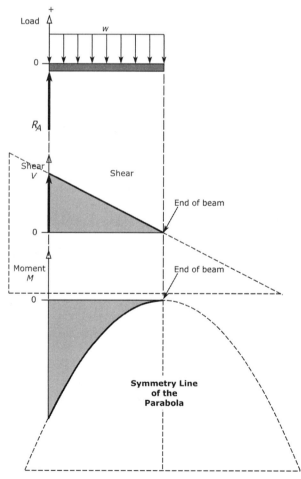

Figure 6.8 Using templates to construct V and M diagrams for a simple cantilever.

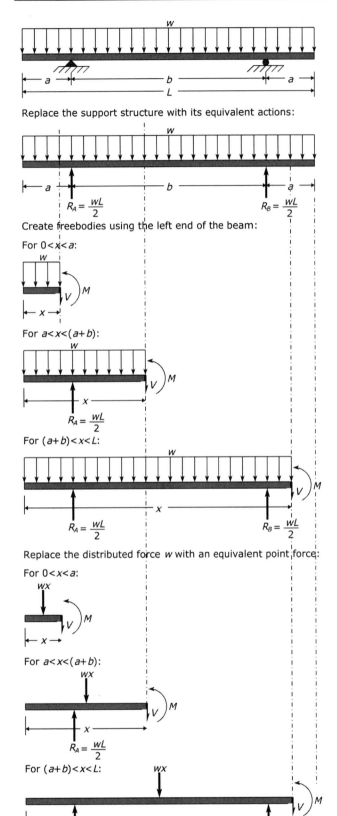

Figure 6.9 Freebodies for the various zones for a continuous beam with double cantilevers.

Replace the support structure with its equivalent actions:

Create freebodies using the left end of the beam:

For $0 < x < a$:

For $a < x < (a+b)$:

For $(a+b) < x < L$:

Replace the distributed force w with an equivalent point force:

For $0 < x < a$:

For $a < x < (a+b)$:

For $(a+b) < x < L$:

Summing the moments about the cut face F:

$$\sum M_F = 0$$

$$0 = -wx\left(\frac{x}{2}\right) + \frac{wL}{2}(x - a) - M$$

$$M = \frac{w}{2}(Lx - x^2 - La) \qquad \textbf{[6.8]}$$

To check the preceding expression, evaluate it at $x = a$:

$$M = \frac{w}{x}(La - a^2 - La) = -\frac{wa^2}{2} \qquad \textbf{[6.9]}$$

which matches the result derived from the expression for M on the interval $0 < x \leq a$, when it is evaluated at $x = a$. This is expected, because there is no agent at that point to cause a discontinuity in the moment.

As a further check of the equation for M, evaluate it at $x = a + b$:

$$M = \frac{w}{2}\left(L(a+b) - (a+b)^2 - La\right)$$

$$= -\frac{w}{2}\left(Lb - (a+b)^2\right) \qquad \textbf{[6.10]}$$

But $L = 2a + b$, so:

$$M = \frac{w}{2}\left((2a+b) \cdot b - (a+b)^2\right)$$

$$= \frac{w}{2}\left(2ab + b^2 - a^2 - 2ab - b^2\right) = -\frac{wa^2}{2} \qquad \textbf{[6.11]}$$

This is as expected, by the symmetry of the beam.

To help in visualizing the shear and moment distributions along the beam, the triangular and parabolic templates generated earlier can be used. In beginning this process, the following should be noted: A cantilever represents a load on whatever it is attached to. Whatever the cantilever is attached to is irrevocably changed by the action of the cantilever. In order to understand the nature of what the cantilever is attached to, one must first understand the cantilever. Fortunately, this does not complicate the process significantly, inasmuch as nothing loads the cantilever except for the applied load, which is always known at the start of the problem.

The fact that cantilevers are so straightforward and well understood makes them the logical place to begin drawing the shear and moment diagrams. The designer can then move on to other parts of the structure.

As shown in Figure 6.10:

• The left edge of any triangular template is always kept vertical.
• The symmetry line of any parabolic template is kept vertical.

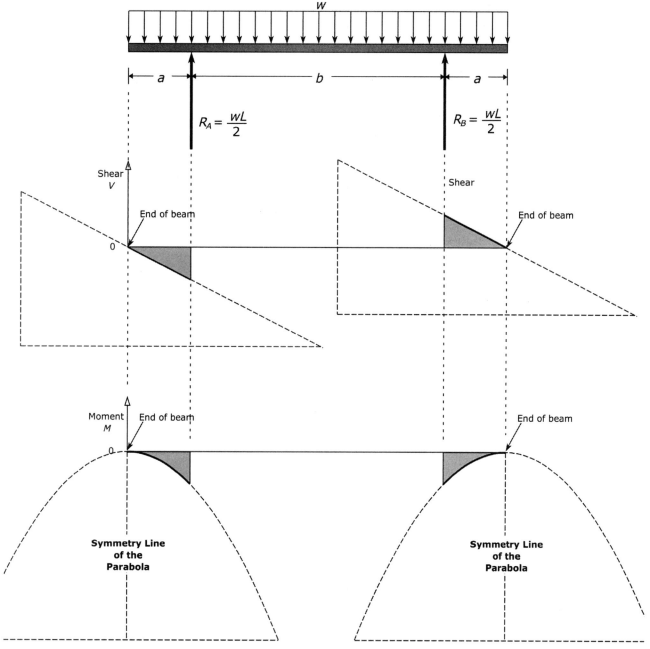

Figure 6.10 Using templates to construct V and M diagrams for the cantilevers.

- A triangular template is set so that the sloped edge passes through the $V = 0$ line at the left end of the left cantilever. A line is drawn along the sloped edge of the template, extending from the left end of the left cantilever to the dashed vertical line indicating the left support location.
- Another triangular template is set so that the sloped edge passes through the $V = 0$ line at the right end of the right cantilever. A line is drawn along the sloped edge of the template, extending from the right end of

the right cantilever to the dashed vertical line indicating the right support location.
- A parabola is maneuvered so that its zenith is aligned with the zero-moment line at the left end of the left cantilever. A curve is traced from the left end of the left cantilever to the dashed vertical line indicating the left support location.
- A parabola is maneuvered so that its zenith is aligned with the zero-moment line at the right end of the right cantilever. A curve is traced from the right end of the

right cantilever to the dashed vertical line indicating the right support location.

In Figure 6.11, the V and M curves are constructed between the two supports for the beam with two equal cantilevers. By the symmetry of the problem, the shear curve must go through zero at the center of the beam.

- A triangular template is set so that its sloped edge goes through the zero-shear line at the center of the beam. A line is drawn along the sloped edge from the vertical dashed line indicating the left support location, to the vertical line indicating the right support location.
- The discontinuities in the shear diagram at the support locations are the point forces exerted by the supports.

- A parabola is maneuvered so that it passes through the points of maximum negative moment at the bases of the cantilevers. Aligning the portions of the moment curve at the supports is crucial, because there is no agent to produce a discontinuity in the moment curve anywhere along the beam. (A local moment could be produced by a moment connection to the base support, but we started this problem by showing a pin joint and a roller joint for the supports.) The negative moment at the base of the cantilever represents the influence of the cantilever on the ends of the part of the beam between the supports. The fact that the location of the parabola representing the moment between the supports is shifted downward by the moments at the bases of the

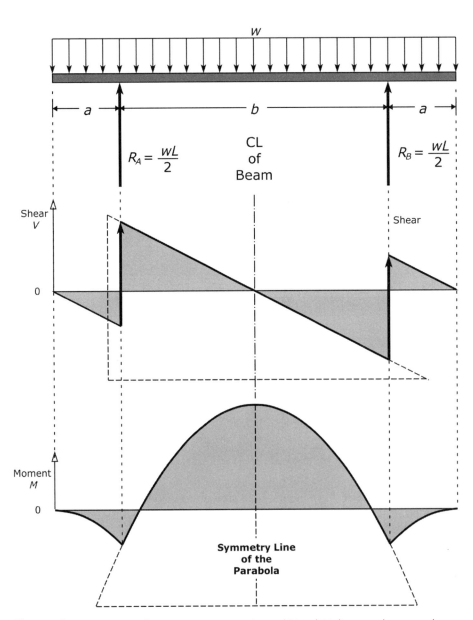

Figure 6.11 Using templates to construct portions of V and M diagrams between the supports.

cantilevers is the graphic indicator of the effect of the cantilevers on the part of the beam between the supports.

The maximum in the moment occurs at the center of the beam. To derive an expression for the moment at that point, substitute $x = \dfrac{L}{2}$ in the expression for M in the zone $a < x < (a + b)$:

$$M_+ = \frac{w}{2}\left(L \cdot \left(\frac{L}{2}\right) - \left(\frac{L}{2}\right)^2 - La\right) = \frac{wL}{2}\left(\frac{L}{4} - a\right) \qquad \textbf{[6.12]}$$

Does $M_+ = \dfrac{wL}{2}\left(\dfrac{L}{4} - a\right)$ make sense? To investigate the limits of this expression, slide the supports out to the ends, $a \rightarrow 0$, and:

$$M_+ = \frac{wL}{4}\left(\frac{L}{4} - 0\right) = \frac{wL^2}{8} \qquad \textbf{[6.13]}$$

This is as expected, for a simple span beam. Sliding the supports inward, that is, increasing a, $M_+ = \dfrac{wL}{2}\left(\dfrac{L}{4} - a\right)$ indicates that M_+ diminishes with increasing a, which is what would be expected for two reasons:

1. The span of the center section is diminishing, and the moment due to the load on that section is, therefore, diminishing.

$$M = \frac{w(\text{length})^2}{8} = \frac{w(L - 2a)^2}{8} \qquad \textbf{[6.14]}$$

2. The load on the cantilevers lifts the center section and relieves the positive moment. The longer the can-

tilevers, the greater the moments lifting up the portion of the beam between supports. When supports have been moved in to the quarter points, $a = \dfrac{L}{4}$ and $M = \dfrac{wL}{2}\left(\dfrac{L}{4} - \dfrac{L}{4}\right) = 0$.

This makes sense. The two halves of the beam tend to balance on their respective supports, and no moment is required at the center to stabilize the two parts, as illustrated in Figure 6-12.

Sliding the two supports together, so that $a = \dfrac{L}{2}$:

$$M_+ = \frac{wL}{2}\left(\frac{L}{4} - \frac{L}{2}\right) = \frac{wL}{2}\left(-\frac{L}{4}\right) = -\frac{wL^2}{8} \qquad \textbf{[6.15]}$$

or:

$$M_+ = -\frac{w}{2}\left(\frac{L}{2}\right)^2 = -\frac{w}{2} \cdot a^2 \qquad \textbf{[6.16]}$$

which is what can be expected for a cantilever of length $\dfrac{L}{2}$ (see Figure 6.13).

Because M tends to fail the beam, it would be helpful to minimize the magnitude of the worst moment. To do this with the cantilevered beam, move the supports in until the increasing negative moment just equals (in magnitude) the decreasing positive moment.

$$M_+ = |M_-|$$

$$\frac{wL}{2}\left(\frac{L}{4} - a\right) = \left|-\frac{wa^2}{2}\right| = \frac{wa^2}{2}$$

$$0 = a^2 + La - \frac{L^2}{4} \qquad \textbf{[6.17]}$$

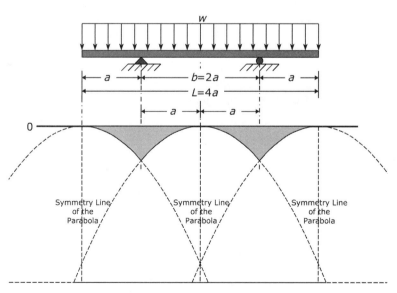

Figure 6.12 Making the cantilevers one-quarter of the length of the beam.

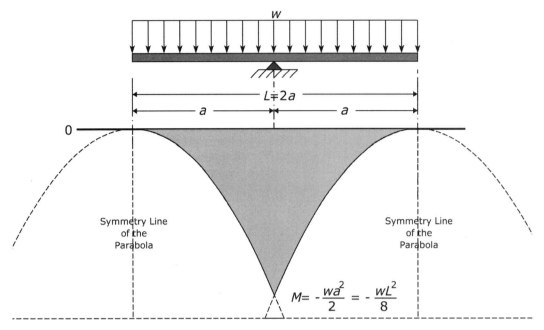

Figure 6.13 Making the cantilevers half the length of the beam.

The solution to an equation of the form $0 = ax^2 + bx + c$ is given by $x = \dfrac{-b \pm \sqrt{b^2 - 4ac}}{2a}$. Applying this solution form to equation [6.17] yields the following:

$$a = \frac{-L \pm \sqrt{L^2 - 4(1)\left(-\dfrac{L^2}{4}\right)}}{2(1)}$$

$$a = -\frac{L}{2} \pm \frac{L}{2}\sqrt{2} \qquad \qquad \textbf{[6.18]}$$

Only the positive term makes sense:

$$a = -\frac{L}{2} + \frac{L}{2}\sqrt{2} = \frac{L}{2}\left(-1 + \sqrt{2}\right) = L\left(\frac{-1 + 1.414}{2}\right) = 0.207L$$

$$a \approx 21\% L \qquad \qquad \textbf{[6.19]}$$

to minimize the worst moment.

Summary of results for the case of a continuous beam with two equal cantilevers:

$$M_+ = \frac{wL}{2}\left(\frac{L}{4} - a\right)$$

$$M_- = -\frac{wa^2}{2} \qquad \qquad \textbf{[6.20]}$$

If $a = 0.207L$, $M_+ = |M_-|$ and:

$$|M_{max}| = \frac{wa^2}{2} = \frac{w(0.207L)^2}{2} = 0.0214\, wL^2 \qquad \textbf{[6.21]}$$

Comparing the maximum moment (M_{max}) in the preceding beam with $a = 0.207L$ with the maximum moment in a simple-span beam (M_{ss}):

$$\frac{M_{max}}{M_{ss}} = \frac{0.0214\, wL^2}{\left(\dfrac{wL^2}{8}\right)} = 0.17 = 17\% \qquad \textbf{[6.22]}$$

By moving the supports in 20.7% from each end, M_{max} is reduced to 17% of what it would have been without moving the supports in from the ends.

Figure 6.14 shows families of shear and moment diagrams representing the effects of various lengths of cantilever beams. The heavy line outlines the moment curve corresponding to the minimal maximum magnitude for the moment along the length of the beam.

Example 4: Continuous Beam over a Support, with a Single Cantilever

Taking the entire beam as a freebody to find the reactions (see Figure 6.15):

$$\sum M_A = 0$$

$$0 = wL\left(\frac{L}{2}\right) - R_B(L - a)$$

$$R_B(L - a) = \frac{wL^2}{2}$$

$$R_B = \frac{wL^2}{2(L - a)} \qquad \qquad \textbf{[6.23]}$$

$$\sum M_B = 0$$

$$0 = R_A(L-a) - wL\left((L-a) - \frac{L}{2}\right)$$

$$R_A(L-a) = wL\left(\frac{L}{2} - a\right)$$

$$R_A = \frac{wL\left(\frac{L}{2}-a\right)}{L-a} = \frac{\frac{wL}{2}(L-2a)}{(L-a)} = \frac{wL(L-2a)}{2(L-a)} \quad [6.24]$$

Next, these reaction values are recorded on the beam diagram and freebodies are created for the two zones of the beam, as shown in Figure 6.16.

For $0 < x < (L-a)$:

$$\sum P_y = 0$$

$$0 = R_A - wx - V$$

$$V = R_A - wx = \frac{wL(L-2a)}{2(L-a)} - wx \quad [6.25]$$

$$\sum M_F = 0$$

$$0 = -M - wx\left(\frac{x}{2}\right) + R_A x$$

$$M = R_A x - \frac{wx^2}{2} = \frac{wL(L-2a)}{2(L-a)} \cdot x - \frac{wx^2}{2}$$

$$= \frac{wx}{2}\left(\frac{L(L-2a)}{(L-a)} - x\right) \quad [6.26]$$

This expression can be checked as follows:

At $x = 0$:

$M = 0$.

OK.

At $x = L - a$:

$$M = \frac{w(L-a)}{2}\left(\frac{L(L-2a)}{(L-a)} - (L-a)\right)$$

$$= \frac{w(L-a)}{2}\left(\frac{L(L-2a)}{(L-a)} - \frac{(L-a)(L-a)}{(L-a)}\right)$$

$$= \frac{w}{2}\left(L^2 - 2aL - (L^2 - 2aL + a^2)\right)$$

$$= \frac{w}{2}(L^2 - 2aL - L^2 + 2aL - a^2) = -\frac{wa^2}{2} \quad [6.27]$$

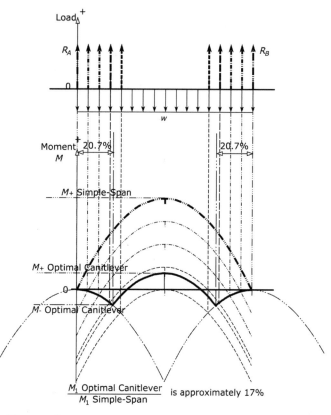

Figure 6.14 Shifting the support location to minimize the magnitude of the maximum moment.

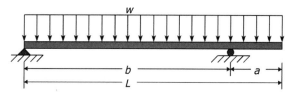

Replace the support structure with its equivalent actions:

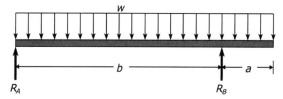

Figure 6.15 Beam continuous over a support with a single cantilever on one end.

which is what is expected at the base of the cantilever.

For $(L-a) \le x \le L$

$$\sum P_y = 0$$

$$0 = R_A - wx + R_B - V$$

$$V = R_A - wx + R_B = (R_A + R_B) - wx$$

$$R_A + R_B = wL \quad [6.28]$$

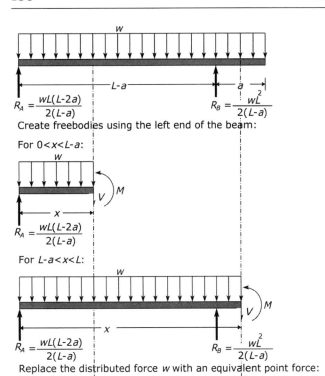

Create freebodies using the left end of the beam:

For $0 < x < L-a$:

For $L-a < x < L$:

Replace the distributed force w with an equivalent point force:

For $0 < x < L-a$:

For $L-a < x < L$:

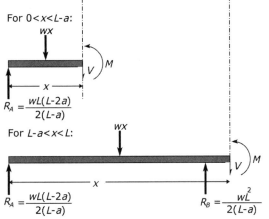

Figure 6.16 Freebodies for the various zones of the beam with one cantilever.

by equilibrium of entire beam, therefore:

$$V = wL - wx = w(L - x) \qquad [6.29]$$

Taking moments about the right end of the freebody:

$$0 = R_A(x) + R_B\left(x - (L-a)\right) - wx\left(\frac{x}{2}\right) - M$$

$$M = R_A(x) + R_B\left(x - (L-a)\right) - \frac{wx^2}{2}$$

$$= \frac{wL(L-2a)x}{2(L-a)} + \frac{wL^2(x-L+a)}{2(L-a)} - \frac{wx^2}{2}$$

$$= w\left(\frac{L(L-2a)x + L^2(x-L+a) - x^2(L-a)}{2(L-a)}\right)$$

$$= w\left(\frac{L^2x - 2Lax + L^2x - L^3 + L^2a - Lx^2 + ax^2}{2(L-a)}\right)$$

$$= w\left(\frac{2L^2x - 2Lax - L^3 + L^2a - x^2(L-a)}{2(L-a)}\right)$$

$$= w\left(\frac{2Lx(L-a) - L^2(L-a) - x^2(L-a)}{2(L-a)}\right)$$

$$= \frac{w}{2}(L^2 - 2Lx + x^2)$$

$$= -\frac{w}{2}(L-x)^2 \qquad [6.30]$$

Checks to be performed:

When $x = L$:

$M = 0$

OK.

When $x = L - a$:

$$M = -\frac{w}{2}(L - L - a)^2 = -\frac{wa^2}{2} \qquad [6.31]$$

which is the moment at the base of the cantilever.

One could have arrived at this answer almost by inspection and been spared most of the arithmetic by simply switching freebodies. To find the moment at the right end of the left freebody in Figure 6.17, the left end of the right freebody can be examined. The moments will be the same, according to the action–reaction pair principle.

Looking at the right freebody:

$$\sum M_F = 0$$

$$0 = M + w(L - x)\left(\frac{L - x}{2}\right)$$

$$M = -\frac{w}{2}(L - x)^2 \qquad [6.32]$$

In Figure 6.18, the shear and moment diagrams are constructed:

- A triangular template is set so that the sloped edge passes through the $V = 0$ line at the right end of the cantilever. A line is drawn along the sloped edge of the template, extending from the right end of the right cantilever to the dashed vertical line indicating the right support location.
- A parabola is maneuvered so that its zenith is aligned with the zero-moment line at the right end of the cantilever. A curve is traced from the right end of the right cantilever to the dashed vertical line indicating the right support location.

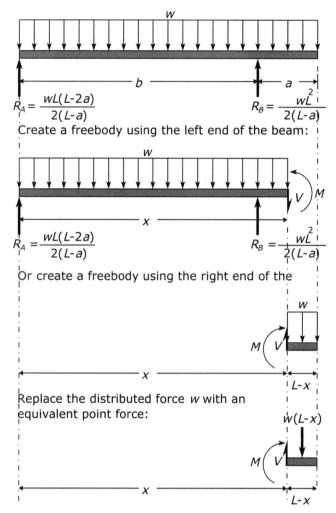

Figure 6.17 Freebody at right end of beam that is continuous over one support, with single cantilever.

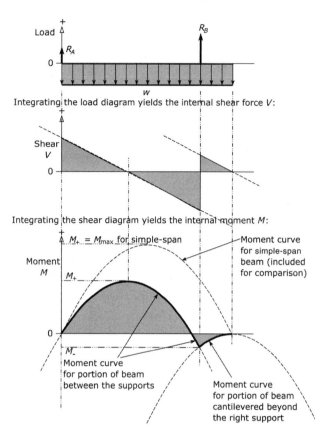

Figure 6.18 Shear and moment diagrams for continuous beam with one cantilever.

- The parabolic template is moved so that it passes through the zero-moment line at the left end of the beam and so that it intersects the moment curve for the cantilever at the right support of the beam. A curve is traced along the template from the left support to the right support.

- Before moving the parabolic template, extend the centerline of the template up to the zero-shear line in Figure 6.18. (The reason for doing this will become clear later. This is a quick and accurate way to establish the location of the rest of the shear curve.)

- Set a triangular template so that the sloped edge passes through the intersection of the zero-shear line and the parabola centerline drawn in the preceding step. Trace a sloped line from the left support to the right support.

The continuous beam with a single cantilever can be optimized in a manner similar to what was done with the beam with two equal cantilevers; that is, it is possible to find the cantilever that makes the positive moment be-

tween the supports equal to the magnitude of the negative moment over the support. To find an expression for the maximum positive moment, it is necessary to find the location of the maximum positive moment. Because the beam is not symmetric, this maximum moment does not occur at the center of the beam. As promised at the beginning of this text, the use of higher math, such as calculus, will be avoided as much as possible. However, there are some things that can be done only with calculus, and this is one of those things. The moment is a maximum where its derivative (slope) is zero. Between the supports:

$$M = \frac{wL}{2}\left(\frac{L-2a}{L-a}\right) \cdot x - \frac{wx^2}{2}$$

$$\frac{dM}{dx} = -\frac{wL}{2}\left(\frac{L-2a}{L-a}\right) - \frac{w(2x)}{2} = 0$$

$$0 = \frac{L}{2}\left(\frac{L-2a}{L-a}\right) - x$$

$$x = \frac{L(L-2a)}{2(L-a)} \tag{6.33}$$

Substituting the value of x back into the expression for M yields:

$$M_+ = \frac{wx}{2}\left(\frac{L(L-2a)}{L-a} - x\right)$$

$$= \frac{w}{2}\left(\frac{L(L-2a)}{2(L-a)}\right)\left(\frac{L(L-2a)}{L-a} - \left(\frac{L(L-2a)}{2(L-a)}\right)\right)$$

$$= \frac{w}{2}\left(\frac{L(L-2a)}{2(L-a)}\right)\left(\frac{2L(L-2a) - L - (L-2a)}{2(L-a)}\right)$$

$$= \frac{w}{2}\left(\frac{L(L-2a)}{2(L-a)}\right)\left(\frac{2L^2 - 4La - L^2 + 2La}{2(L-a)}\right)$$

$$= \frac{w}{2}\left(\frac{L(L-2a)}{2(L-a)}\right)\left(\frac{L^2 - 2La}{2(L-a)}\right)$$

$$= \frac{w}{2}\left(\frac{L(L-2a)}{2(L-a)}\right)\left(\frac{L(L-2a)}{2(L-a)}\right)$$

$$= \frac{w}{2}\left(\frac{L(L-2a)}{2(L-a)}\right)^2 \qquad \text{[6.34]}$$

Checks to be performed:

When $a = 0$:

$$M_+ = \frac{w}{2}\left(\frac{L(L-2\cdot 0)}{2(L-0)}\right)^2 = \frac{w}{2}\left(\frac{L}{2}\right)^2 = \frac{wL^2}{8} \qquad \text{[6.35]}$$

OK.

When $a = \dfrac{L}{2}$:

$$M_+ = \frac{w}{2}\left(\frac{L\left(L - 2\cdot\frac{L}{2}\right)}{2\left(L - \frac{L}{2}\right)}\right)^2 = 0 \qquad \text{[6.36]}$$

This is what would be expected. The positive moment goes to zero as a approaches $\dfrac{L}{2}$, and the moment diagram looks like Figure 6.13, with a single reaction force at the center and the reaction at the left end being zero.

Armed with the expression for M_+, we can minimize the maximum moment along the beam by setting:

$$M_+ = |M_-|$$

$$\frac{w}{2}\left(\frac{L(L-2a)^2}{2(L-a)}\right)^2 = \frac{wa^2}{2}$$

$$\frac{L(L-2a)}{2(L-a)} = a$$

$$L\left(\frac{L}{2} - a\right) = aL - a^2$$

$$0 = a^2 + (-2L)a + \left(\frac{L^2}{2}\right)$$

$$a = \frac{-(-2L) \pm \sqrt{(-2L)^2 - 4(1)\left(\frac{L^2}{2}\right)}}{2(1)}$$

$$= \frac{2L \pm L\sqrt{4-2}}{2}$$

$$= L \pm L\frac{\sqrt{2}}{2} = L(1 \pm 0.707)$$

$$= L\cdot 1.707 \text{ or } L\cdot 0.293 \qquad \text{[6.37]}$$

Only the answer $a = 0.293\ L$ makes sense. (The other answer is extraneous.) If the cantilever is 29% of the length, the maximum moment is a minimum with respect to position of the support.

Summary of the results for the case of a continuous beam with one cantilever:

$$M_+ = \frac{w}{2}\left(\frac{L(L-2a)}{2(L-a)}\right)^2 = \frac{wL^2}{8}\left(\frac{L-2a}{L-a}\right)^2$$

$$M_- = -\frac{wa^2}{2} \qquad \text{[6.38]}$$

If $a = 0.293\ L$, $M_+ = |M_-|$ and

$$|M_{max}| = -\frac{wa^2}{2} = \frac{w(0.293L)^2}{2} = 0.0429\ wL^2 \qquad \text{[6.39]}$$

Comparing with a simple span:

$$\frac{M_{max}}{M_{ss}} = \frac{0.0429\ wL^2}{\left(\frac{wL^2}{8}\right)} = 0.34 = 34\% \qquad \text{[6.40]}$$

If the support is moved in 29% from the end, M_{max} is reduced to 34% of M_{max} for the simple-span beam.

Figure 6.19 shows a family of shear and moment diagrams representing the effects of various cantilever lengths for the continuous beam with one cantilever. The bold line represents the optimal cantilever in terms of

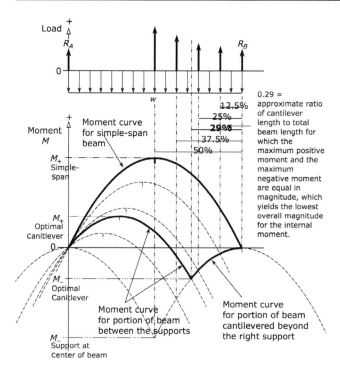

Figure 6.19 Shifting the support location to minimize the magnitude of the maximum moment.

minimizing the magnitude of the largest moment along the beam.

6.1.2 CROSS-SECTIONAL PROPERTIES OF BEAMS

Using the principles of equilibrium, beams have been torn apart and internal forces V and moments M have been examined. It has been learned that the internal shear force V and internal moment M can be determined from a knowledge of loads and supports. In a sense, the architectural context has indicated what V and M will be imposed on a beam. The function of the designer is to select a material and cross-sectional configuration that are adequate to resist these influences.

The behavior of materials has also, in a somewhat primitive way, been examined. The missing key to the puzzle is the effect of cross section. It is clear that cross section is important. But it is not yet clear how it affects the behavior of the beam. To begin exploring this issue, consider a foam rubber beam on which vertical sections are marked while the beam is unloaded, as shown in Figure 6.20.

When the beam is raised at each end, the self-weight of the beam provides a uniformly distributed load that induces substantial curvature and deflection. Under the load, the planar sections marked off in Figure 6.20 rotate so that they are no longer parallel. However, those sections remain *planar* after loading, as shown in Figure 6.21. This is an extremely important experimental fact that allows one to deduce a variety of things.

In Figure 6.22 are superimposed diagrams of the beam's central section, before and after loading.

Planar sections before loading remain planar after loading. The upper part of the beam is in compression, which squashes the material. The lower part of the beam is in tension, which stretches the material. At some point in between there is no stress and, therefore, no strain. The location on the cross section where the strain is zero is known as the neutral axis (N-A). For sections that are symmetric in both the vertical and horizontal directions, the N-A occurs halfway between the top and the bottom of the beam. For other shapes, such as a T-beam or a double-angle combination, the N-A occurs at the

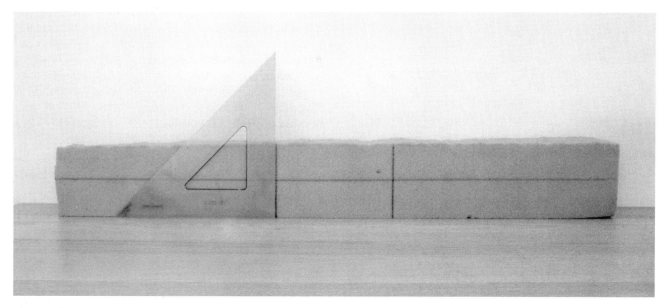

Figure 6.20 Foam rubber beam at rest on flat table top, being marked with vertical lines.

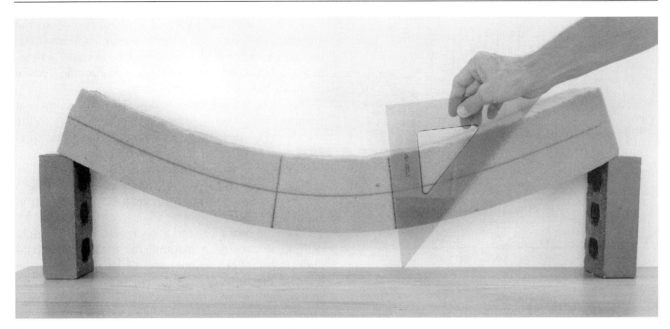

Figure 6.21 Foam rubber beam bending under its self-weight.

centroid, as defined in basic geometry. Finding centroids and other section properties for asymmetric shapes is beyond the scope of this book, but it is treated extensively in a variety of more specialized texts.

In Figure 6.22, a tiny horizontal slab of material has been shaded and its vertical position has been designated by y. This tiny slab of material has obviously been shortened by the compression stress. If you imagine dividing the entire central section into many similar thin, horizontal slabs, then it is apparent that the strain ε in any given slab is proportional to how far the slab is from the N-A. That is,

$$\varepsilon \propto y \qquad [6.41]$$

Over the working range of most common structural materials, the stress is proportional to the strain, with a constant of proportionality E. Therefore,

$$f = \varepsilon E$$
$$f \propto y \qquad [6.42]$$

Because stress is proportional to deformation and because deformation is proportional to the vertical distance from the neutral axis, it follows that the stress is directly proportional to the vertical distance from the neutral axis. For a rectangular cross section, the stress distribution would look like that shown in Figure 6.23, where f_b is the maximum bending stress, commonly referred to as the extreme fiber bending. This terminology is applied to all structural materials, including steel, concrete, and aluminum, even though none of these materials have fibers.

$$M = C \cdot \frac{2}{3}h \qquad [6.43]$$

But

$$C = f_{\text{average}} \cdot \frac{A}{2} = \frac{f_b}{2} \cdot \frac{bh}{2} \qquad [6.44]$$

Therefore,

$$M = \frac{f_b}{2} \cdot \frac{bh}{2} \cdot \frac{2}{3}h = f_b \cdot \frac{1}{6}bh^2 = f_b S \qquad [6.45]$$

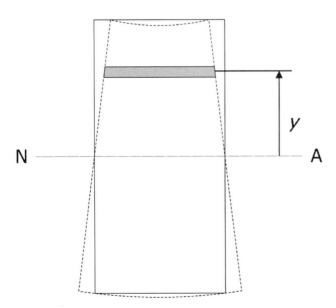

Figure 6.22 Deformed center section of the beam.

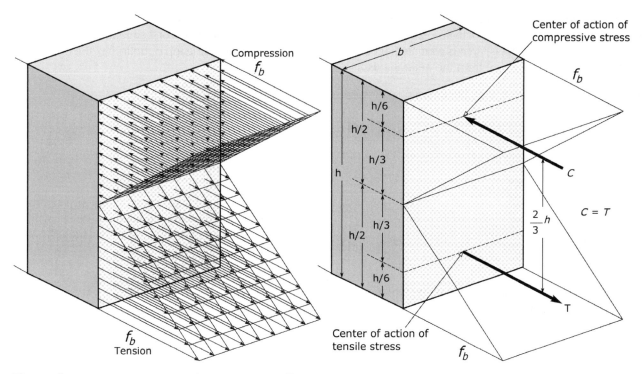

Figure 6.23 Moment stresses on the cross section of beam.

where:

$$S = \frac{1}{6}bh^2 \qquad \text{[6.46]}$$

S is the section modulus. This particular formula for S applies to a rectangular cross section of width b and depth h.

The best common-language descriptor of S is the strength of the cross section in generating internal resisting moment or the cross-sectional strength in resisting moment. Section moduli are tabulated for standard wood and steel sections, which greatly facilitates finding a beam that is both adequate and efficient in resisting the moments for which the beam is being designed.

As noted, the particular formula for S in Equation 6.46 is strictly for rectangular beams. It is useful to have a more generic definition and formula for S.

It is known that $f_b \propto y$, that is,

$$f_b = Ky \qquad \text{[6.47]}$$

where K is a constant. It may be expected that it will involve M and some cross-sectional properties. For example, one knows that the stresses will be greater if the moment inducing the stresses is higher. One also knows from experience that the stresses get higher when the cross section becomes shallower. Exploration of this issue can begin by calculating M in terms of f_b. In Figure 6.24, a generic cross section is depicted in an odd shape to emphasize that the mathematical formalism being de-

veloped is applicable to any doubly symmetric cross-sectional shape.

$$
\begin{aligned}
\Delta F_i &= \text{force on area } \Delta A_i \\
\Delta M_i &= \text{moment about N-A of } \Delta F_i \\
&= \Delta F_i \cdot y_i \\
M &= \text{total moment of stress on cross section} \\
&\cong \sum_{i=1}^{n} \Delta M_i = \sum_{i=1}^{n} \Delta F_i y_i \\
&\cong \sum_{i=1}^{n} f_b \Delta A_i y_i \cong \sum_{i=1}^{n} K y_i \Delta A_i y_i \\
&\cong K \sum_{i=1}^{n} y_i^2 \Delta A_i = K \lim_{n \to \infty} \sum_{i=1}^{n} y_i^2 \Delta A_i \\
&\equiv K \int y^2 dA \\
&\equiv KI \qquad \qquad \text{[6.48]}
\end{aligned}
$$

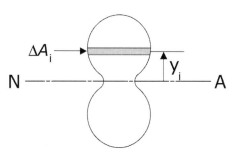

Figure 6.24 Cross section indicating area subdivisions.

where I is defined to be the integral of y^2 over the entire cross-sectional area. I is the area of the cross section with a weighting factor of y^2; that is, area is weighted according to the square of its distance from the neutral axis.

So $K = \dfrac{M}{I}$ and therefore $f_b = Ky$ becomes:

$$f_b = \frac{M}{I}y \qquad \qquad \textbf{[6.49]}$$

Consider I for a rectangle (see Figure 6.25):

$$I = \lim_{n \to \infty} \sum_{i=1}^{n} y_i^2 \Delta A_i = \lim_{n \to \infty} \sum_{i=1}^{n} y_i^2 b \Delta y_i$$

$$= \lim_{n \to \infty} b \sum_{i=1}^{n} y_i^2 \Delta y_i = 2b \lim_{\frac{n}{2} \to \infty} \sum_{i=1}^{\frac{n}{2}} y_i^2 \Delta y_i \qquad \textbf{[6.50]}$$

where the summation on the right side of the equation is over the upper half of the rectangle.

$$I = 2b \int_{0}^{\frac{h}{2}} y^2 dy = 2b \frac{y^3}{3} \Big|_{0}^{\frac{h}{2}}$$

$$= \frac{2b}{3} \left(\frac{h}{2}\right)^3 - 0 = \frac{1}{12} bh^3 \qquad \textbf{[6.51]}$$

$I = \dfrac{1}{12} bh^3$ for the rectangle. Note the dramatic effect of h. In the equation for S, the cubic power of h, as compared with the first power of b, explains why a 2×12 up on edge is much stronger and stiffer than when used as a beam lying flat. The beam will fail when the worst stress anywhere in the beam exceeds that allowed by the material. So the most important issue to designers is to keep the worst stress below a reasonable value.

Because $f_b = \dfrac{M}{I}y$,

$$\left(f_b\right)_{\max} = \frac{M_{\max}}{I} y_{\max} \qquad \qquad \textbf{[6.52]}$$

M varies along the length of the beam. Designers look for the worst moment to make sure that they have ac-

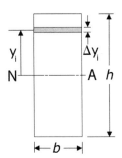

Figure 6.25 Rectangular cross section with representative sliver of area.

counted for the worst situation. Moreover, to ensure that they are dealing with the worst situation, they pick; the greatest y, which is at the top or bottom of the beam, that is, $y_{\max} = \dfrac{h}{2}$.

$$y_{\max} = \frac{h}{2}$$

$$\left(f_b\right)_{\max} = \frac{M_{\max}}{I} \left(\frac{h}{2}\right) \qquad \qquad \textbf{[6.53]}$$

Because h and I are both cross-sectional properties, they are combined into a single quantity, which will be designated with an S and which will be called the section modulus:

$$\left(f_b\right)_{\max} = \frac{\dfrac{M_{\max}}{I}}{\left(\dfrac{h}{2}\right)} \equiv \frac{M_{\max}}{S} \qquad \qquad \textbf{[6.54]}$$

$$S \equiv \frac{I}{\left(\dfrac{h}{2}\right)} \equiv \text{section modulus}$$

= indicator of cross-sectional strength of beam with respect to resisting moment

$(f_b)_{\max}$ = indicator of the strength of the material in the beam with respect to moment.

$S(f_b)_{\max}$ = best overall indicator of moment capacity of beam.

S and $(f_b)_{\max}$ always appear together.

I = an indicator of cross-sectional stiffness.

E = material stiffness.

EI = combined material and cross-sectional stiffness. E and I always appear together.

Δ = deflection of beam $\propto \dfrac{1}{EI}$ (Δ also depends on loads and support configuration).

Recall that for slender columns stiffness is the crucial issue. Lack of stiffness causes failure to be initiated by buckling (elastic instability). A suitable reformulation of Euler's buckling equation also indicates that the crucial combination is EI, as shown in the following equation:

$$P_{CR} = \frac{\pi^2 EI}{L^2}$$

The strength of the slender column is proportional to EI.

Miscellaneous Comments on Moments of Inertia

Consider the cross sections in Figure 6-26, all of which have the same area.

Because these beams all have the same amount of area, they have the same amount of material. They differ

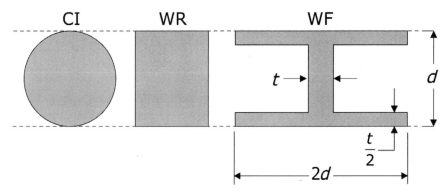

Figure 6.26 Three cross sections of equal area.

only in geometry—in the way in which the material is distributed.

Remember that $I \equiv \int y^2 dA$ ($\equiv$ means equals, by definition).

The moment of inertia is calculated by counting each little area increment dA, with a weighting factor y^2, which says that the area farthest from the N-A is most important. From this definition it is clear that those cross sections that have some of their area farther from the N-A will have the larger moments of inertia.

In Figure 6.27, the cross-hatched area is common to the circle and the rectangle. This area contributes equally to I_{CI} and I_{WR}. Therefore, the difference between I_{CI} and I_{WR} must be accounted for by the area that is not common to the two shapes. In Figure 6.28, the two shaded areas are equal. In rearranging the circle to get the rectangle, we have simply moved area away from the N-A. Therefore:

$$I_{WR} > I_{CI} \qquad\qquad \textbf{[6.55]}$$

The comparison of the WF to the WR is shown in Figures 6.29 and 6.30. Again the crosshatched area is common to the two shapes.

The noncommon areas make the difference in the two sections. The area indicated by shading on the rectangle in Figure 6.30 has moved upward as the rectangle evolves into the wide-flange section. Therefore:

$$I_{WF} > I_{WR} \qquad\qquad \textbf{[6.56]}$$

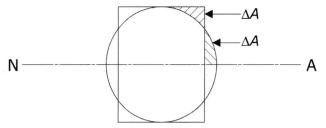

Figure 6.28 Showing the area of the circle that has been moved outward to form the rectangle.

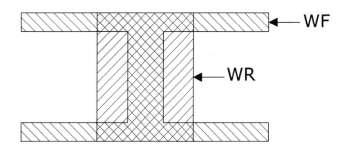

Figure 6.29 Comparing the wide rectangle WR to the wide flange WF.

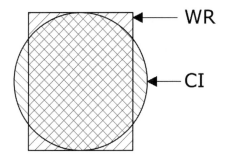

Figure 6.27 Comparing the circle CI to the wide rectangle WR.

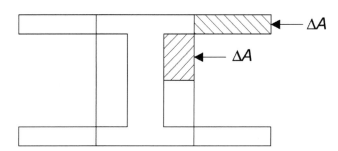

Figure 6.30 Showing the area of the WR that has been moved outward to create the WF.

Shear Stress (f_v)

Consider the beam in Figure 6.31. Starting at the top of the beam and moving downward, the horizontal shear stress starts off at zero, growing rapidly at first (where net f_b is large) and more slowly as the N-A approaches. The maximum shear occurs at the N-A. The variation in the shear stress is parabolic with the y position, as shown in Figure 6.32.

An important question is, What does $(f_v)_{horiz}$ have to do with the vertical shear stress $(f_v)_{vert}$, which is known to exist because of the shear force V? To answer the question, consider a very small cube extracted from the previous freebody, as shown in Figure 6.33. Select a cube so small that any stress will change a negligible amount from one side of the cube to the other. In that case, the bending stress f_b is essentially the same on both sides of the cube. Therefore, these two influences cancel each other out. Likewise, the two vertical shear effects balance each other out, and the two horizontal shear effects balance each other out. The only issue left is the two moments, one moment resulting from the two equal and opposite horizontal shear forces and the other moment resulting from the two equal and opposite vertical shear forces. These moments must be equal and opposite in order for the cube to be in rotational equilibrium. Because the lever arm for the vertical shear forces is equal to the lever arm for the two horizontal forces, the vertical forces must equal the horizontal forces. Because the areas over which the vertical and horizontal forces are distributed are equal, the vertical shear stress must equal the horizontal shear stress.

This leads to the following general conclusion: At any point in a solid, the shear stresses on any two perpendicular planes are equal. Therefore, consistent with the behavior of $(f_v)_{horiz}$, $(f_v)_{vert}$ varies parabolically with y, as shown in Figure 6.34.

From now on the symbol f_v will be used for $(f_v)_{horiz} = (f_v)_{vert}$. The average shear stress is given by the following expression:

$$(f_v)_{average} = \frac{V}{A}$$

Wood is very weak in shear parallel to the fibers. Aluminum and steel are so strong in shear that shear is rarely a design issue in aluminum or steel beams. This is fortunate, inasmuch as the formula for shear stress f_v in I-beams is quite complex. However, the maximum shear in rectangular beams is quite simple to calculate, as the following calculations indicate (see Figure 6.35).

For a parabola:

$$(f_v)_{max} = \frac{3}{2}(f_v)_{average} = \frac{3}{2} \cdot \frac{V}{A} \qquad \textbf{[6.57]}$$

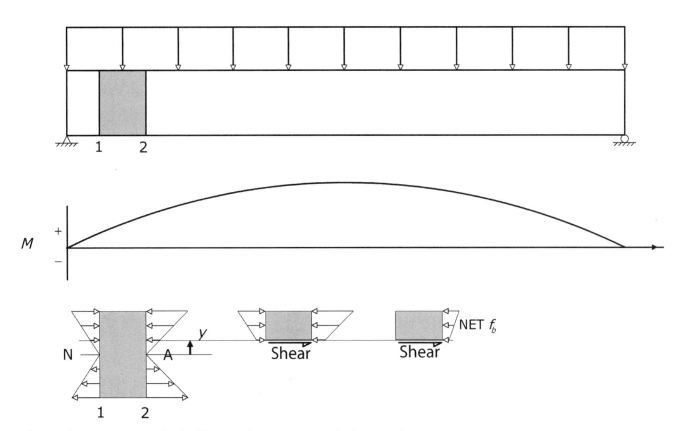

Figure 6.31 Selecting a chunk of beam with shear stress on the bottom edge.

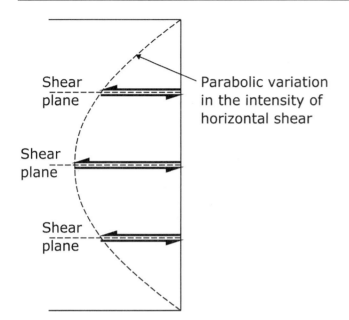

Figure 6.32 Parabolic variation in the horizontal shear stress $(f_v)_{horiz}$.

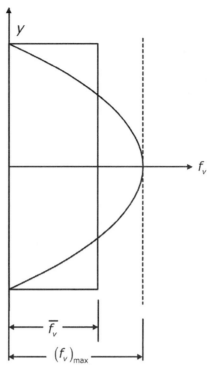

Figure 6.35 Comparison of average shear stress and parabolic variation in the shear stress.

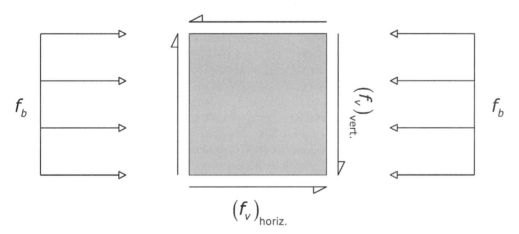

Figure 6.33 A very small cube showing shear and moment stresses.

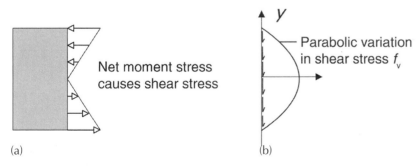

Figure 6.34 Effect of the net moment stress (a) in generating shear stress (b).

This is the maximum shear stress on the cross section of a rectangular beam of cross-sectional area A, subjected to total lateral shear force V. A is an indicator of the cross-sectional shear capacity of a rectangular beam. Doubling A doubles the total shear force capacity V. Note that A is also a measure of the amount of material in the beam. Shear sets a lower limit to the amount of material required. There is nothing one can do to re-arrange the cross section to get around this limit. The formula for the section modulus of a rectangular cross section can be rewritten in the following form:

$$S = \frac{1}{6}bh^2 = \frac{1}{6}Ah \qquad \textbf{[6.58]}$$

Similarly, the formula for the moment of inertia of a rectangular cross section can be rewritten in the following form:

$$I = \frac{1}{12}bh^3 = \frac{1}{12}Ah^2 \qquad \textbf{[6.59]}$$

Clearly, reducing b and increasing h, while keeping $A=bh$ constant, can take care of the cross-sectional strength in resisting moment, S, and cross-sectional stiffness I. In other words, moment and stiffness do not, per se, impose any theoretical lower limit on the amount of material required. So shear is a very significant design factor in wooden beams. (Lateral stability may limit depth.) The worst shear stresses occur at places exactly opposite from the worst moment stresses. The worst shear stress occurs at the ends of a simple span, at the N-A. The worst moment stresses occur near midspan at top and bottom of the beam (see Figure 6.36).

In an ordinary beam of rectangular cross section, the shear stresses are usually quite small as compared with the bending (moment) stresses. However, the design shear stress of wood is also small as compared with the design bending stress of wood. Therefore, for wood, a rectangular cross section is close to a balanced design for shear and moment. In comparison, for steel and aluminum, the design shear stress F_v is 0.6 of the design bending stress F_B. In other words, they are fairly comparable. Therefore, a 2×8 rectangular cross section would be drastically oversized for shear in either a steel or aluminum beam. This suggests that the designer should choose something other than a rectangular cross section for steel and aluminum. Because the shear stress is highest near the N-A, we expect that the material near the N-A provides the largest contribution to the shear force V. Because shear is apparently not a problem in a rectangular steel (or aluminum) beam, it can be expected that the proper approach to selecting a new cross section is to remove material near the N-A and add it near the top and bottom of the beam (see Figure 6.37).

This increases the section modulus S and hence increases the moment capacity.

$$M = F_bS \qquad \textbf{[6.60]}$$

This increased moment capacity implies increased load capacity. The increased load, coupled with a reduction in material near the N-A, causes the shear stress f_v to rise. Continued thinning of the web is ultimately limited by the rising shear stress. Usually, web buckling becomes a crucial issue long before the web stresses reach the design shear stress. Widening the flanges is desirable from the point of view of lateral stability of the beam, but is limited by flange buckling. A good cross section design balances all of these conflicting influences.

The following points are easily documented experimentally with models. Consider an I-section with a continuous web and discontinuous flange at the end of the beam, as shown in Figure 6.38. The web performs fine by itself in this situation, as indicated by the image on the right where the web is inserted in the slot of the support. It is common to cut back the flange near the end of a beam, to accommodate inserting the beam between flanges of a column. It is also customary to make the end connection only to the web of the beam, as that is the most effective part of the beam to transfer shear force.

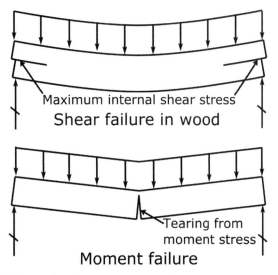

Figure 6.36 Modes of failure due to stress in a beam.

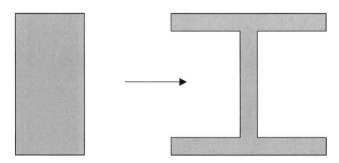

Figure 6.37 Reconfiguring the material in the cross section.

Figure 6.38 Effect of removing flanges at ends of beam where shear is high.

In contrast, the loss of the flanges at the center of the beam, where the moment is high, is disastrous, as shown in Figure 6.39. The beam is able to support only tiny weights before it begins to shift laterally.

Next, consider an I-section with continuous flanges and a discontinuous web at the end of the beam where the shear is high. The deformation in the flanges is extreme where the web has been removed (see Figure 6.40).

In contrast, the moment resistance of the beam is still quite good when part of the web is removed near the center of the beam, as shown in Figure 6.41.

These observations can be summarized in the following generalization: In an I-section, the bulk of the bending strength can be attributed to the flanges, and the bulk of the shear strength can be attributed to the web. Flange elements provide bending strength. Web elements provide shear strength.

Deflection in Beams

In addition to strength, deflection is an important issue in structures. Buildings with floors that move too much will be perceived as being unsafe or, at the very least, of poor quality. Roofs that are too flexible can fail owing to a process called ponding, wherein a heavy rain may induce a deflection, which creates a bowl shape that retains more water and causes more deflection. This process may not be self-limiting, in which case rain can

cause the roof to fail. Structures that are too flexible can move dangerously in the wind, such as was the case with the Tacoma Narrows Bridge. To address these issues, it is necessary to quantify how structures deflect under load. This is one of those topics that I do not know how to address without resorting to calculus. For those of you who do not have a working knowledge of calculus, it is worth noting that understanding this explanation in detail is not critical, and the only important thing is to understand the final equations and to be able to apply those equations to size beams.

A simple-span beam is used as an illustration. This makes things uncomplicated, and it also makes sense in that simple-span beams are the preponderance of the beams used in design practice.

In regard to simple tension or compression, the following equation is written:

$$\frac{\Delta L}{L} = \frac{P}{EA} \qquad [6.61]$$

In words, the fractional elongation (or shortening) of a member is proportional to the applied force and inversely proportional to the material stiffness E and the cross-sectional area of the member A.

Beams have a deformation equation of similar form, wherein the curvature at any point along the beam is proportional to the moment at that point along the beam

Figure 6.39 Poor moment performance when the flanges are removed.

Figure 6.40 Poor shear performance where the web is removed.

Figure 6.41 Moment performance is still good where the web has been removed.

and inversely proportional to the stiffness of the material and the stiffness of the cross section:

$$\text{Curvature} = \frac{M}{EI} \qquad \textbf{[6.62]}$$

This relationship between curvature and moment is immediately apparent in the deflected beam in Figure 6.21 in which the most severe curvature is occurring where the moment is most severe and the curvature approaches zero at the ends, where the moment is zero.

Both of the preceding equations express a deformation quantity (fractional elongation or curvature) in terms of the following:

1. An influence quantity (P or M), which depends on the magnitude and location of the loads
2. A quantity that expresses the stiffness of the material, E
3. A geometric quantity (A or I), which is a measure of stiffness due to geometric effects only

Because M can be found as a function of position x along the beam, the preceding equation allows one to find the curvature at any point along the beam. The equation is like a road map. As one proceeds along the beam, the map tells how much to curve (up or down). It, therefore, contains all the information necessary to describe the entire shape of the beam.

It would be helpful to be able to describe this shape in terms of a coordinate system (see Figure 6.42). In other words, the aim is to describe the curve assumed by the N-A of the beam, after loading, in terms of an equation of the form

$$y = f(x) \qquad \textbf{[6.63]}$$

which should be read, "y equals a function of x", which simply means that at any position x along the beam, the y coordinate of the N-A is determined by a clearly expressed relationship between y and x. The values of E (material stiffness) given in any of the design manuals are the best average values for the material in question. In other words, those values of E give the most accurate indication of actual deflection. Any margin of safety in the treatment of deflection is contained in the deflection condition itself.

By the definition of lateral shear force V, it is the force on the right cross section of the left freebody, which is necessary to equilibrate the loads on the freebody. In other words, V is equal in magnitude to the sum of all the loads on the left freebody. Therefore, the shear force V on any cross section of the beam is just the sum of all loads on the portion of the beam to the left of the cross section. In the language of calculus, the shear diagram is the integral of the load diagram. Furthermore, as will be demonstrated, the moment diagram is the integral of the shear diagram. To start the process of demonstrating that fact, a segment is sliced out of a simple-span beam (see Figure 6.43).

Taking the sum of the moments about the right end of the segment:

$$\sum M_F = 0$$

$$0 = M + V(\Delta x) - w\Delta x \left(\frac{\Delta x}{2} \right) - (M + \Delta M)$$

$$= V(\Delta x) - \frac{w(\Delta x)^2}{2} - \Delta M$$

$$\Delta M = V(\Delta x) - \frac{w(\Delta x)^2}{2}$$

$$\frac{\Delta M}{\Delta x} = \frac{V(\Delta x)}{\Delta x} - \frac{w(\Delta x)^2}{2\Delta x}$$

$$= V - \frac{w\Delta x}{2}$$

$$\lim_{\Delta x \to 0} \frac{\Delta M}{\Delta x} = \frac{dM}{dx} = V - 0 = V$$

$$\frac{dM}{dx} = \text{derivative of } M \text{ with respect to } x \qquad \textbf{[6.64]}$$

If V = derivative of M, then M is equal to the integral of V. Thus, the load diagram is integrated to get V, and V is integrated to get M. More specifically,

$$M_B = M_A + \int_A^B V dx$$

That is, M at point B is equal to M at A plus the integral (i.e., area) of the shear diagram between points A and B. Hence, if you know the shear diagram and M at any point, then you can find M at any other point.

The calculus metaphor can be used very effectively in the generation of curves describing the behavior of beams. For example, consider a simple-span beam with

Figure 6.42 Coordinates for describing shape of beam.

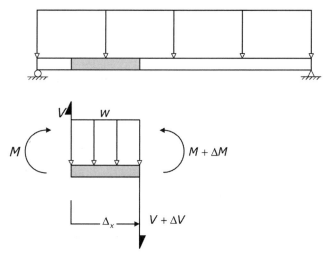

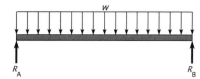

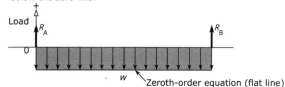

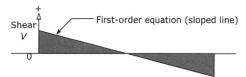

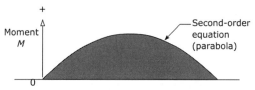

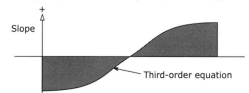

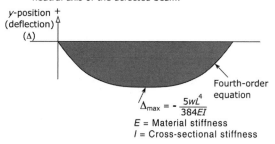

Figure 6.43 Shear forces and moments on a segment of the beam.

a uniform load over its entire length, as shown in the first diagram of Figure 6.44. The first diagram is drawn in the conventional sense, with the reactions pointing upward, but drawn below the beam, and the applied load pointing downward, but drawn above the beam. However, the forces on the beam can be *plotted* on a diagram, using the standard convention, in which upward forces are regarded as positive and are drawn above the zero line and downward forces are regarded as negative and are drawn below the zero line. This latter method of rendering the forces on the beam is shown in the second diagram in Figure 6.44. Drawing the forces as a plot in this format makes the process of integration to get the shear force *V* more easily comprehended in the classic calculus model.

The internal moment *M* involves compressive stress on one side of the beam, with an associated shortening of the material, and tension stress on the other side of the beam, with an associated lengthening of the material. These two deformations combine to produce a curvature; the greater the moment, the tighter the curvature; that is, the smaller the radius of curvature. In the terminology of calculus, curvature is the rate of change of slope. Because integration and differentiation are inverse operations, and differentiating the slope diagram yields the curvature, then integrating the curvature diagram will yield the slope diagram. Similarly, slope is the derivative of vertical position. Therefore, integrating the slope diagram will yield the vertical position diagram.

Over the range where the load is constant:

- The load is a zero-order polynomial.
- Integrating the uniform load yields a first-order polynomial (i.e., a sloped, straight-line function) for *V*.
- Integrating the sloped, straight-line function *V* yields a second-order polynomial (i.e., a parabolic curve) for *M*.

The forces on the beam can be plotted on a diagram, using the standard convention, in which upward forces are regarded as positive and are drawn above the zero line and downward forces are regarded as negative and are drawn below the zero line:

Integrating the force diagram yields the internal shear force *V*:

Integrating the shear diagram yields the internal moment *M*:

Integrating the moment diagram yields the slope of the beam:

Integrating the slope diagram yields the *y*-position of the neutral axis of the deflected beam:

$$\Delta_{max} = -\frac{5wL^4}{384EI}$$

E = Material stiffness
I = Cross-sectional stiffness

Figure 6.44 Generating shear, moment, and deflection diagrams.

- Integrating the parabolic function *M* yields a third-order curve for the slope of the beam.
- Integrating the third-order curve for the slope of the beam yields a fourth-order curve for the deflection of the beam.

For the simple-span beam of length *L* subjected to a uniform load *w*, this process of multiple integrations leads to the following fourth-order polynomial for the displacement of the beam:

$$y = \frac{w}{24EI}(-x^4 + 2Lx^3 - L^3x)$$

This equation yields $y = 0$ at both $x = 0$ and $x = L$, which is what would be expected. The maximum deflection occurs at the center of the beam, where $x = L/2$. Evaluating the preceding expression at $x = \frac{L}{2}$ produces the following expression:

$$y_{max} = -\frac{5\,wL^4}{384EI}$$

For simple-span beams, there are rules of thumb regarding deflections.

For most floors:

$$\frac{\Delta}{L} \le \frac{1}{360}$$

For flat roofs where ponding can occur (but with no plaster or other brittle material for the ceiling):

$$\frac{\Delta}{L} \le \frac{1}{240}$$

For least critical situations (sloped roofs with no plaster lining and walls under wind load):

$$\frac{\Delta}{L} \le \frac{1}{120}$$

This procedure of multiple integrations can be applied to any beam, under any support configuration and any load combination, to derive equations for shear V, moment M, and deflection y. For many common support and loading configurations, the equations for shear V, moment M, and deflection y can be gotten from tables such as those shown in the following pages of this chapter. These particular tables were reprinted courtesy of the American Institute of Steel Construction from the *Manual of Steel Construction*, which contains many more useful tables. In these particular tables, the nomenclature varies from that used in this book. In these tables, deflection at position x is given by Δ_x, which is expressed as positive downward, and the maximum deflection is given by Δ_{max}. In some references, if there are several maxima in the deflection curve, subscripts will be used to distinguish them. For example, for a beam that is continuous over a support to create a cantilever at one end, we are typically concerned about both the deflection between the supports and the deflection at the end of the cantilever (see Figures 6.45 and 6.46).

In summary, the following exact mathematical methods are available for dealing with shear, moment, and deflection in beams:

- Set up a freebody of length x; apply the principles of equilibrium to derive the equations for shear, moment, and deflection in terms of the variable x; and plot the curves from the equations.
- Look up the equations for shear, moment, and deflection in terms of the variable x in reference books, such as the *Manual of Steel Construction*, published by the American Institute of Steel Construction.
- Use a computerized structural analysis program to generate the curves and tabular data. For the purpose of this text, the discussion here tends to rely most often on computer analyses, which, in all cases, are based on the mathematical principles outlined in the preceding pages.

The following approximate graphic methods are available for dealing with shear, moment, and deflection:

- Make sketches by hand by creating physical templates of a triangle and a parabola, moving the templates around to the appropriate places, and tracing around the templates.
- Make sketches in a computer drawing program by setting up the shear and moment shapes described earlier and moving the shapes around to appropriate places along the beam.

6.2 Wood Beams

6.2.1 WOOD DECKING

Decking is a material used to span across beams or joists to create a floor or roof surface (see Figure 6.47).

The following are common examples of wood floor decking customarily used to span up to 16 in. between supporting joists:

- $\frac{3}{4}$ in.-thick tongue-in-groove plywood
- $\frac{5}{8}$ in.-thick particle board on top of $\frac{1}{2}$ in.-thick plywood
- Hardwood surfacing (such as $\frac{3}{4}$ in.-thick tongue-in-groove hardwood flooring) on top of $\frac{1}{2}$ in.-thick plywood

For roofs, $\frac{1}{2}$ in.-thick plywood is typically satisfactory up to spans of 24 in. between rafters or roof trusses. Typically, structural analysis of plywood decking is not performed, since it is dominated by extreme local loads that have the potential to produce punch-through. Selection of the appropriate material is also strongly influenced by perceptual issues regarding noise and movement. Over time, certain typical thicknesses and spans have been used, which are widely accepted and rarely questioned.

Laminated decking, for use in longer spans, usually consists of two, three, four, or five layers of $\frac{3}{4}$ in.-thick boards glued together in an offset manner. This creates a

Shears, Moments, and Deflections

1. SIMPLE BEAM—UNIFORMLY DISTRIBUTED LOAD

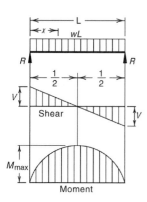

Total Equiv. Uniform Load .... $= wL$

$R = V$ .... $= \dfrac{wL}{2}$

V_x .... $= w\left(\dfrac{L}{2} - x\right)$

M_{max} (at center) .... $= \dfrac{wL^2}{8}$

M_x .... $= \dfrac{wx}{2}(L - x)$

Δ_{max} (at center) .... $= \dfrac{5\,wL^4}{384\,EI}$

Δ_x .... $= \dfrac{wx}{24\,EI}(L^2 - 2Lx^2 + x^3)$

2. SIMPLE BEAM—LOAD INCREASING UNIFORMLY TO ONE END

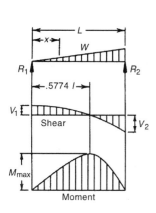

Total Equiv. Uniform Load .... $= \dfrac{16W}{9\sqrt{3}} = 1.03W$

$R_1 = V_1$ .... $= \dfrac{W}{3}$

$R_2 = V_2 = V_{max}$ .... $= \dfrac{2W}{3}$

V_x .... $= \dfrac{W}{3} - \dfrac{Wx^2}{L^2}$

M_{max} $\left(\text{at } x = \dfrac{L}{\sqrt{3}} = .577l\right)$ .... $= \dfrac{2WL}{9\sqrt{3}} = .128WL$

M_x .... $= \dfrac{Wx}{3L^2}(L^2 - x^2)$

Δ_{max} $\left(\text{at } x = L\sqrt{1 - \sqrt{\dfrac{8}{15}}} = .519l\right)$ .... $= 0.130 = \dfrac{WL^3}{EI}$

Δ_x .... $= \dfrac{Wx}{180EIL^2}(3x^4 - 10L^2x^2 + 7L^4)$

3. SIMPLE BEAM—LOAD INCREASING UNIFORMLY TO CENTER

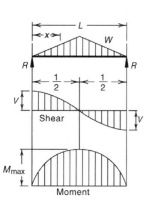

Total Equiv. Uniform Load .... $= \dfrac{4W}{3}$

$R = V$ .... $= \dfrac{W}{2}$ $\qquad L$

V_x (when $x < \dfrac{l}{2}$) .... $= \dfrac{W}{2L^2}(L^2 - 4x^2)$

M_{max} (at center) .... $= \dfrac{WL}{6}$

M_x (when $x < \dfrac{l}{2}$) .... $= Wx\left(\dfrac{1}{2} - \dfrac{2x^2}{3L^2}\right)$

Δ_{max} (at center) .... $= \dfrac{WL^3}{60EI}$

Δ_x (when $x < \dfrac{l}{2}$) .... $= \dfrac{Wx}{480EIL^2}(5L^2 - 4x^2)^2$

Figure 6.45 Shear, moment, and deflection for some simple-span beams. (Copyright American Institute of Steel Construction, Inc. Reprinted with permission. All rights reserved.)

Shears, Moments, and Deflections

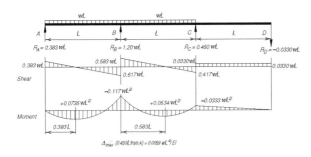

CONTINUOUS BEAM—THREE EQUAL SPANS—ONE END SPAN UNLOADED

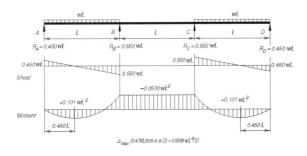

CONTINUOUS BEAM—THREE EQUAL SPANS—END SPANS LOADED

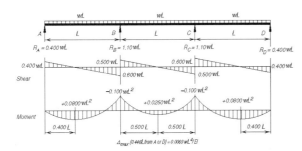

CONTINUOUS BEAM—THREE EQUAL SPANS—ALL SPANS LOADED

Figure 6.46 Shear, moment, and deflection for continuous three-span beams. (Copyright American Institute of Steel Construction, Inc. Reprinted with permission. All rights reserved.)

Figure 6.47 Plywood decking being nailed down to solid-sawn wood joists.

tongue-in-groove joint between adjacent decking boards. In situations where the decking is to be part of the finished ceiling surface, laminated decking works well. It is often used with glulam timbers (discussed later in this chapter) because their large size calls for wider spacing of the glulam elements, thereby requiring a decking material with substantial spanning capabilities. In addition, both materials are attractive as finished surfaces.

The following data relate to Potlatch Lock-Deck, a widely available decking product, but similar products are also available. (See Figure 6.48.)

Because decking is inherently wide, it gets much of its structural action from b (i.e., the width) in the formulas

$$S = \frac{bh^2}{6} \text{ and } I = \frac{bh^3}{12}$$

The great width b allows the depth h to be relatively small, resulting in a spanning member that is inherently shallow in its proportions. The sizing of members with very shallow proportions is governed by stiffness. Having continuity over supporting beams greatly increases the stiffness of the decking. Figure 6.49 shows a means of achieving continuity over multiple supports.

The pattern is called *random lengths continuous*. However, it is far from random in the mathematical sense of the word. There are several conditions to using the decking in this mode:

1. The decking must be continuous over three or more spans, with each piece of decking over at least one support.
2. The decking must be placed to disperse end joints as randomly as possible:
   a. The distance between end joints in adjacent rows of decking is at least 2 ft.
   b. The distance between end joints in rows of decking separated by only one row is at least 1 ft.
3. End spans must be carefully planned and placed. To ensure that end spans perform as indicated by the Span Tables, follow one of these practices:
   a. Eliminate end joints in the decking of the end bay or
   b. Provide a cantilever overhang, free of end joints, equal to 20% of the end span, or
   c. Shorten the end span by 10%.
4. Decking should be end matched and toe-nailed within 1 ft. of all ends.

Notice that the formulas for deflection and bending stress for using the decking in the continuous mode are modified, as compared with those for using the decking in simple-span mode, as depicted in Figure 6.50.

Figure 6.51 gives cross-sectional properties, which can be used in calculating structural performance

Nominal Sizes. 2 x 6, 2 x 8, 3 x 6, 3 x 8, 4 x 6, 4 x 8, 5 x 6, and 5 x 8. Following is the typical length assortment for 2", 3", 4" and 5" thicknesses.

2"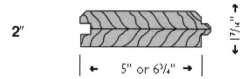

Minimum 15% combined 14' and/or 16', minimum 5% 16', maximum 85% 6' to 12', maximum 15% 6' to 9'.

3"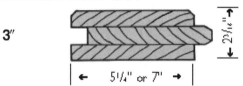

Minimum 20% combined 14' and/or 16', minimum 10% 16', maximum 80% 6' to 12', maximum 10% 6' to 9'.

4"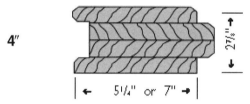

Minimum 35% combined 14' and/or 16', minimum 20% 16', maximum 65% 6' to 12', maximum 10% 6' to 9'.

5"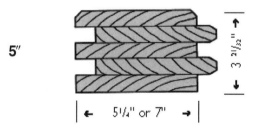

Minimum 45% combined 14' and/or 16', minimum 30% 16', maximum 55% 6' to 12', maximum 7% 6' to 9'.

Figure 6.48 Dimensions of laminated decking.

$$\blacktriangle = \frac{wL^4}{130\,EI} \qquad F_b = \frac{wL^2}{6.67\,s}$$

2' minimum
end joint spacing

Span

Figure 6.49 Decking pattern called *random lengths continuous*.

$$\blacktriangle = \frac{5}{384}\,\frac{wL^4}{EI} \qquad F_b = \frac{wL^2}{8\,s}$$

Span

Figure 6.50 Simple-span decking pattern.

Design Weights (lb/ft²)

Species	2" Nominal	3" Nominal	4" Nominal	5" Nominal	Shipping Wgts. lb/MBF
Western Red Cedar*	3	4	6	7	1,300
Cedar face with whitewood core	4	5	7	8	1,450
White Fir, Ponderosa Pine	4	5	7	9	1,550
Douglas Fir/Larch	4	6	8	11	1,750
Southern Pine	5	7	9	12	2,000

*Includes Inland Red Cedar.

Figure 6.51 Self-weights and shipping weights for laminated decking.

for situations to which the load tables in Figure 6.52 do not apply.

Figure 6.52 gives the allowable total unfactored uniform roof load, p_{total} (#/ft²), for horizontal, or nearly horizontal, roofs. Laminated decking is one of the materials for which loads are still expressed in terms of allowed unfactored loads.

Figure 6.53 permits the estimation of allowed total load for sloped roofs. It enables the generation of the allowed load p_{total} (#/ft²), where the square foot reference is

Lock-Deck	Span	Douglas Fir, Larch[4], Southern Pine E1.8 $F_b=2640^2$				Idaho White Pine[5], White Fir E1.5 $F_b=1850^2$				Ponderosa Pine, Western Red Cedar Face E1.3 $F_b=1590^2$				Western Red Cedar All Laminations E1.2 $F_b=1590^2$			
		Simple		Continuous[3]		Simple		Continuous[3]		Simple		Continuous[3]		Simple		Continuous[3]	
		L/180	L/240	L/180	L/240	L/180	L/240	L/180	L/240	L/180	L/240	L/180	L/240	L/180	L/240	L/180	L/240
2"	4'	245	183	368(f)	309(f)	206	155	247(f)	247(f)	176	132	252(f)	223	162	122	274(f)	206
	5'	125	93	212	158	106	79	158	134	90	68	152	114	83	63	180	105
	6'	72	54	123	92	61	46	103	78	52	39	88	66	48	36	81	61
	7'	46	34	77	58	38	29	65	49	33	25	56	42	30	23	52	39
	8'	31	23	52	39	26	19	44	33	22	16	37	28	20	15	34	26
	9'	21	16	36	27	18	14	31	23	15	12	26	20	14	11	24	18
3"	8'	107	80	181	136	89	67	151	113	77	58	127(f)	98	71	54	121	91
	9'	75	56	127	96	63	47	106	80	54	41	92	69	50	38	85	64
	10'	55	41	93	70	46	34	77	58	40	30	67	50	37	27	62	46
	11'	41	31	70	52	34	26	58	44	30	22	50	38	27	21	47	35
	12'	32	24	54	40	26	20	45	34	23	17	39	29	21	16	36	27
	13'	25	19	42	32	21	16	35	26	18	14	31	23	17	12	28	21
4"	10'	125	94	212	159	104	78	168(f)	132	90	68	144(f)	115	83	63	141	106
	11'	94	70	159	119	78	59	132(f)	99	68	51	115	86	63	47	106	79
	12'	72	54	122	92	60	45	102	77	52	39	88	66	48	36	82	61
	13'	57	43	96	72	47	36	80	60	41	31	70	52	38	28	64	48
	14'	46	34	77	58	38	28	64	48	33	25	56	42	30	23	51	39
	15'	37	28	63	47	31	23	52	39	27	20	45	34	25	19	42	31
	16'	31	23	52	39	25	19	43	32	22	17	37	28	20	15	34	26
5"	15'	72	54	121	91	63	47	107	80	55	41	93	70	51	38	86	64
	16'	60	44	100	75	52	39	88	66	45	34	76	57	42	31	71	53
	17'	49	37	83	62	43	33	74	55	38	28	64	48	35	26	59	44
	18'	42	31	70	53	37	27	62	46	32	24	54	40	29	22	50	37
	19'	35	26	59	44	31	23	53	40	27	20	46	34	25	19	42	32
	20'	30	23	51	39	27	20	45	34	23	17	39	29	21	16	36	27

Footnotes:
1. Values followed by (f) are governed by bending stress. Allowable loads for floors where governed by deflection are half of those listed in the I/180 column.
2. Bending stress relates to 2-month duration. It is not exceeded when the listed loads are applied based on recognized decking formulas.
3. Span/loads shown assume compliance to layup rules described elsewhere. Longer spans may require specific lengths differing from the standard shipment--consult your Disdero representative.
4. Nominal 5" Fir/Larch will have a MOE of 1.7 x 10⁶ psi unless special arrangements are made prior to manufacture.
5. Comparable values are obtained with Ponderosa Pine face and Douglas Fir/Larch centers and back.

Figure 6.52 Allowable total unfactored uniform roof load (lb/ft²) for horizontal, or nearly horizontal, laminated-deck roofs.

one square foot projected on the horizontal. This figure is used to determine a load adjustment factor (LAF), which is a function of the slope of the roof. That load adjustment factor is multiplied by the allowed total load p_{total} (#/ft²) for the corresponding situation in Figure 6.53 for horizontal roofs.

All the load adjustment factors are greater than 1, signifying that sloped decking will be stronger than horizontal decking in terms of its ability to support area-distributed load (as projected on the horizontal). The numbers listed in Figure 6.53 have been devised for making quick design decisions and tend to be conservative.

To achieve diaphragm action from this kind of decking, care must be taken in making the connection between elements forming the decking. Diaphragm action is achieved through the use of both nails and glue. Without the glue, there will not be a satisfactory diaphragm action. For the nominal 2 in.-thick decking, the action is achieved by nailing a layer of plywood on top of the decking. The plywood is easy to apply and resists shear better than thin laminated planks with the grain oriented in a single direction. For detailed specifications regarding diaphragm action in laminated decking, contact the manufacturer or consult an engineering expert in this area.

Sloped Roof Deck—Load Adjustment Factors*
To calculate the allowable load for a sloped roof deck, apply the coeffecent for the pitch to the load for a flat roof listed in the Allowable Load table in Figure 6.52.

Slope	Slope
4:12 – 1.05	9:12 – 1.25
4½:12 – 1.07	9½:12 – 1.28
5:12 – 1.08	10:12 – 1.30
5½:12 – 1.10	10½:12 – 1.33
6:12 – 1.12	11:12 – 1.36
6½:12 – 1.14	11½:12 – 1.39
7:12 – 1.16	12:12 – 1.41
7½:12 – 1.18	12½:12 – 1.44
8:12 – 1.20	14:12 – 1.54
8½:12 – 1.23	16:12 – 1.67

* Estimated

Figure 6.53 Load adjustment factors for sloped laminated-deck roofs.

Example Problem for Determining Span

Nominal 3 in.-thick southern pine laminated decking, configured in random lengths continuous, is to be used in a horizontal roofing application subject to the following design criteria:

Deflection limit is $\Delta = L/240$
Live load $= 20 \text{ lb/ft}^2$
Dead load $= 11 \text{ lb/ft}^2$
Total load $= 31 \text{ lb/ft}^2$

1. What is the maximum span of the decking between support joists, assuming simple-span decking between the support joists?

   See the table in Figure 6.52 on allowed uniform roof load on horizontal roofs. Look in the columns labeled "Douglas Fir, Larch, Southern Pine"; then look in the columns labeled "Simple," and in the column labeled "L/240." The units for the numbers in this column are lb/ft². Scan down to the rows that apply to 3 in. decking. According to the table, this decking can support 31 lb/ft² at a span of 11 ft. So the answer is 11 ft.

2. What is the maximum span of the decking between support joists, assuming continuous decking over the support joists?

   See the table in Figure 6.52. Look in the columns labeled "Douglas Fir, Larch, Southern Pine"; then look in the column labeled "Continuous," and then in the column labeled "L/240." Again, the units for the numbers in this column are lb/ft². Scan down to the rows that apply to 3 in. decking. According to the table, this decking can support 32 lb/ft² at a span of 13 ft. Because 32 > 31, the span limit has not quite been reached. The table could be extrapolated to determine what the span limit is for the load of 31 lb/ft². However, for the purposes of this solution, it is reasonable to indicate that the span limit is simply 13 ft.

3. What is the percent increase in span achieved via continuity over the joists?

   To answer this question with great precision, you would have to extrapolate beyond 13 ft to get the maximum allowed span for the continuous decking case. However, for the purposes of this solution, 13 ft is close enough to the correct value.

$$\text{Percent increase} = \frac{13 \text{ ft} - 11 \text{ ft}}{11 \text{ ft}} \cdot 100\% = 18.2\%$$

6.2.2 SOLID-SAWN WOOD BEAMS

The crucial data for sizing wooden beams are contained in Tables 4.4, 4.5, 4.6, and 4.7 in Chapter 4.

Example Sizing Solid-Sawn Wood Beams

Material: solid-sawn (S4S) #2 Hemlock-Fir
Span: simple-span, $L = 16$ ft.
Spacing of joists: 16 in. = 1.333 ft.

The dead load is estimated to be 10 lb/ft². This is a conservative number for this type of construction. For the purposes of this book, you can make this simplifying assumption:

$$P_{\text{dead}} = 10\frac{\#}{\text{ft}^2} \quad \text{and} \quad P_{\text{live}} = \frac{40\,\#}{\text{ft}^2}$$

$$w_{\text{factored}} = p_{\text{factored}} \cdot s = \left(\frac{1.2\,p_{\text{dead}} + 1.6\,p_{\text{live}}}{\lambda}\right) \cdot s$$

$$= \left(\frac{1.2\left(10\frac{\#}{\text{ft}^2}\right) + 1.6\left(40\frac{\#}{\text{ft}^2}\right)}{0.8}\right) \cdot 1.333 \text{ ft} = 126.7\frac{\#}{\text{ft}^2}$$

See Figure 6.54 and Table 6.1.

Options for dealing with moment strength:

1. Use 2 × 12 joists.
2. Change species.
3. Space the joists closer together to make 2 × 10s work. Spacing the joists closer together reduces the load proportionally, which reduces the required S_r proportionally. According to the calculations, a #2 Hemlock-Fir joist supporting a 16 in.-wide strip of floor must have a section modulus of 27.1 in.³. In contrast, a 2 × 10 has a section modulus of only 21.391 in.³. Therefore, the width of floor strip that a #2 Hemlock-Fir 2 × 10 can support is proportioned to be

   16 in. (21.391/27.1) = 12.6 in.

   The modular subdivision of the plywood sheet that is both less than 12.6 in. and close to 12.6 in. would be 96 in./8 = 12.0 in. Therefore, 2 × 10s in Hemlock-Fir at 12 in. OC will provide adequate strength in resisting moment.

Options for dealing with deflection:

1. Use 2 × 12 joists.
2. Change species.
3. Space the joists closer together to make 2 × 10s work: 16 in. (98.932/127.6) = 12.4 in. apart. The modular subdivision of the plywood sheet that is both less than 12.4 in. and close to 12.4 in. would be 96 in./8 = 12.0 in. Therefore, you could use 2 × 10s in Hemlock-Fir at 12 in. OC and still satisfy the deflection requirement.

In platform construction, which is typical of a situation in which solid-sawn lumber would be used, the floor platform has a uniform thickness throughout the structure. This thickness will be determined by the longest span,

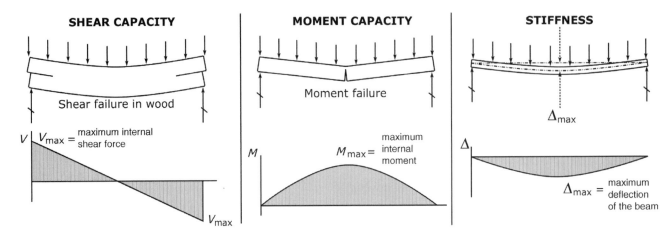

Figure 6.54 Modes of failure for wood beam.

with all of the shorter spans being deeper than necessary. Therefore, the greatest care is taken in selecting the depth of beam for the longest span, because that will determine the thickness of the entire floor. In most houses, a 16 ft span is the largest span that would occur. Therefore, in the preceding example, it would be most eco-nomical to use the 2 × 10s spaced 12 in. OC rather than the 2 × 12s spaced 16 in. OC. Moreover, 2 × 12s are harder to find and cost substantially more per board foot, so the floor with 2 × 12s at 16 in. OC might cost more than the floor with 2 × 10s at 12 in. OC, even without regard to the impact on the other spans in the building.

Table 6.1 Calculations for Shear, Moment, and Stiffness in a Solid-Sawn Wood Joist

$$V_{max} = \frac{w_{factored}L}{2} \qquad M_{max} = \frac{w_{factored}L^2}{8} \qquad \Delta_{max} = \frac{5(0.5w_{dead} + w_{live})L^4}{384\,EI}$$

$$E = \text{Material stiffness}$$
$$I = \text{Cross-sectional stiffness}$$

$$A_r = \frac{3V_{max}}{2F_v} \qquad S_r = \frac{M_{max}}{F_B} \qquad I_r = \frac{5(0.5w_{dead} + w_{live})L^4}{384E\Delta_{max}}$$

$$= \frac{\frac{3w_{factored}L}{2}}{2F_v} \qquad = \frac{\frac{w_{factored}L^2}{8}}{F_B} \qquad = \frac{5(0.5w_{dead} + w_{live})L^3}{384E} \cdot \frac{L}{\Delta_{max}}$$

$$= \frac{3w_{factored}L}{4F_v} \qquad = \frac{w_{factored}L^2}{8F_B} \qquad = \frac{5(0.5w_{dead} + w_{live})L^3(360}{384E}$$

$$= \frac{3 \cdot \left(126.7\frac{\#}{ft}\right) \cdot 16\,ft}{4F_v} \qquad = \frac{\frac{126.7\,\# \cdot (16\,ft^2)\left[\frac{12\,in.}{ft}\right]}{ft}}{8F_B} \qquad = \frac{5 \cdot 60\frac{\#}{ft} \cdot (16\,ft)^3 \cdot 360 \cdot \left[\frac{12\,in.}{ft}\right]\left[\frac{12\,in.}{ft}\right]}{384E}$$

$$= \frac{1{,}520\,\#}{F_v} \qquad = \frac{48{,}653\,\#\,in.}{F_B} \qquad = \frac{165{,}900{,}000\,\#\,in.^2}{E}$$

$$= \frac{1{,}520\,\#\left[\frac{in.^2}{in.^2}\right]}{243\frac{\#}{in.^2}} \qquad = \frac{48{,}653\,\#\,in.\left[\frac{in.^2}{in.^2}\right]}{1795\frac{\#}{in.^2}} \qquad = \frac{165{,}900{,}000\,\#\,in.^2\left[\frac{in.^2}{in.^2}\right]}{1{,}300{,}000\frac{\#}{in.^2}}$$

$$= 6.26\,in.^2 \qquad = 27.1\,in.^3 \qquad = 127.6\,in.^4$$

| For a 2 × 6: A = 8.250 in.²—Yes | For a 2 × 12: S = 31.641 in.³—Yes | For a 2 × 12: I = 177.98 in.⁴—Yes |
| For a 2 × 4: A = 5.250 in.²—No | For a 2 × 10: S = 21.391 in.³—No | For a 2 × 10: I = 98.932 in.⁴—No |

Allowed Span Tables for Solid-Sawn Wood Beams

Each of the following design equations can be re-arranged to solve for L, as limited by that particular structural issue. For example, L_{shear} is the maximum span, as limited by shear in the beam.

$$A_r = \frac{3w_{factored}L}{4F_v} \Rightarrow L_{shear} = \frac{4AF_v}{3w_{factored}}$$

$$S_r = \frac{w_{factored}L^2}{8F_B} \Rightarrow L_{moment} = \left(\frac{8SF_B}{w_{factored}}\right)^{0.5}$$

$$I_r = \frac{5(0.5w_{dead} + w_{live})L^3(360)}{384E} \Rightarrow L_{stiffness}$$

$$= \left(\frac{384IE}{5(360)(0.5w_{dead} + w_{live})}\right)^{0.33333}$$

Figure 6.55 shows a spreadsheet in which these computations have been carried out for a #2 grade in three different species of wood, for the following loads:

$$p_{dead} = 10\frac{\#}{ft^2} \quad \text{and} \quad p_{live} = 40\frac{\#}{ft^2}$$

These tables are popular, because they are very simple to use. They are generally limited to the most common loads encountered in wood construction, which include the following:

$$p_{dead} = 10\frac{\#}{ft^2} \quad \text{and} \quad p_{dead} = 20\frac{\#}{ft^2}$$

$$p_{live} = 30\frac{\#}{ft^2} \quad \text{and} \quad p_{live} = 40\frac{\#}{ft^2}$$

Span tables of this type are usually included in the International Residential Building Code.

For #2 Douglas Fir-Larch:

Cross Section	F_v (#/in.²) 292		F_b (#/in.²) 1,900		E (#/in.²) 1,600,000		Computed Span limit from All Factors for #2 Doug.Fir-Larch	Span limit from 2000 Residential Code for #2 Doug.Fir-Larch
	Area A (in.²)	$L_{shear}=$ Span limit set by Shear (ft)	Section Modulus S (in.³)	$L_{moment}=$ Span limit set by Moment (ft)	Moment of Inertia I (in.⁴)	$L_{stiffness}=$ Span limit set by Deflection (ft)	(ft)	(ft-in.)
2x6	8.250	25.35	7.563	8.70	20.797	9.37	8.70	9-9
2x8	10.875	33.42	13.141	11.46	47.635	12.35	11.46	12-7
2x10	13.875	42.64	21.391	14.62	98.932	15.75	14.62	15-5
2x12	16.875	51.85	31.641	17.79	177.979	19.16	17.79	17-10

For #2 Hemlock-Fir:

Cross Section	F_v (#/in.²) 243		F_b (#/in.²) 1,795		E (#/in.²) 1,300,000		Computed Span limit from All Factors for #2 Hemlock-Fir	Span limit from 2000 Residential Code for #2 Hemlock-Fir
	Area A (in.²)	$L_{shear}=$ Span limit set by Shear (ft)	Section Modulus S (in.³)	$L_{moment}=$ Span limit set by Moment (ft)	Moment of Inertia I (in.⁴)	$L_{stiffness}=$ Span limit set by Deflection (ft)	(ft)	(ft-in.)
2x6	8.250	21.10	7.563	8.45	20.797	8.74	8.45	9-1
2x8	10.875	27.81	13.141	11.14	47.635	11.52	11.14	12-0
2x10	13.875	35.48	21.391	14.21	98.932	14.70	14.21	15-2
2x12	16.875	43.15	31.641	17.29	177.979	17.88	17.29	17-7

For #2 Spruce-Pine-Fir:

Cross Section	F_v (#/in.²) 219		F_b (#/in.²) 1,636		E (#/in.²) 1,100,000		Computed Span limit from All Factors for #2 Spruce-Pine-Fir	Span limit from 2000 Residential Code for #2 Spruce-Pine-Fir
	Area A (in.²)	$L_{shear}=$ Span limit set by Shear (ft)	Section Modulus S (in.³)	$L_{moment}=$ Span limit set by Moment (ft)	Moment of Inertia I (in.⁴)	$L_{stiffness}=$ Span limit set by Deflection (ft)	(ft)	(ft-in.)
2x6	8.250	19.01	7.563	8.07	20.797	8.27	8.07	9-4
2x8	10.875	25.06	13.141	10.64	47.635	10.90	10.64	12-3
2x10	13.875	31.98	21.391	13.57	98.932	13.90	13.57	15-5
2x12	16.875	38.89	31.641	16.50	177.979	16.91	16.50	17-10

Figure 6.55 Allowed spans for #2-grade of various species, based on LRFD.

6.2.3 WOOD I-JOISTS AND LAMINATED VENEER LUMBER BEAMS

Figure 6.56 shows a wood structure with spanning members of various lengths subjected to a variety of loading intensities. The ridge beam is the longest and one of the most heavily loaded spanning members. It is a wide-flange steel I-beam, taking advantage of the exceptional stiffness and stress capacity of steel. The ends of the steel ridge beam are supported by tall, slender columns that are made of steel pipe, taking advantage of both the tubular shape and the stiffness of the steel to avoid buckling, while keeping the dimension of the column small enough to fit inside a stud-frame wall. The shortest members, such as the spanning members inside the dormers, the collar beams, and the wall studs, are solid-sawn lumber, inasmuch as the demands in terms of length of span and loading are both very small. Lightly loaded members that need to be longer, such as the rafters, are made from wood I-joists, which can be easily made long enough and deep enough to satisfy the spanning requirements. Longer members that are subjected to greater cumulative loads, such as the rafter beams supporting one side of the

dormers, are made of laminated veneer lumber (LVL) beams, which, like the wood I-beams, can be made both long and deep, but are able to handle much higher loads than the I-beams. LVL beams are also used for the wood headers carrying exceptionally high loads, such as the header spanning over the fireplace, where the load from the steel column must be transferred to the side so that the column does not come down in front of the fire. Headers carrying simple wall loads, or parts of minor floor loads, are made of solid-sawn lumber.

The tables and information given in Figures 6.57 through 6.65 are for Boise-Caskade engineered wood products. Similar products are sold by other manufacturers. These tables are presented as generally representative of what is available in the industry. Figure 6.57 shows the cross-sectional dimensions of the various BCI wood I-joists and LVLs, which Boise-Caskade calls VERSA-LAM. The LVLs come in thicknesses of $1\frac{1}{2}$ in., $1\frac{3}{4}$ in., $3\frac{1}{2}$ in., $5\frac{1}{4}$ in., and 7 in. Solid-sawn headers in 2 × 4 stud walls have to be made with two 2 x __ solid sawn boards plus a $\frac{1}{2}$ in. spacer block. The $1\frac{3}{4}$ in.-thick LVL can be doubled up to make a $3\frac{1}{2}$ in.-thick header without the trouble of having a space block. All these sec-

Figure 6.56 Wood framing involving members of various spans and loads.

tions are available in lengths up to 60 ft. It usually makes sense to order even the shallowest I-joists in the maximum length, as that reduces waste in the on-site cutting operations.

Figure 6.58 gives the allowed span for wood I-joists in flooring applications, assuming a dead load of 10 psf (unfactored) and a live load of 40 psf (unfactored). This table allows very rapid sizing of floor joists for this one particular loading condition, which happens to be the most widely applicable floor loading condition with which we deal. In setting up this table, three deflection conditions have been provided: L/360 (which is the common standard), L/480, and L/960. The I-joist manufacturers are able to provide very deep joists with very little additional cost. In promoting their products, they take advantage of that fact by emphasizing the higher floor stiffness that is easily and economically achieved using deep I-joists.

Example Wood I-Joist Floor Sizing Exercise 1

Joist spacing of 16 in., p_{dead} = 10 psf, p_{live} = 40 psf, deflection limit = L/480.

Find the shallowest joist that will span 16 ft.
Answer: A $9\frac{1}{2}$ in.-deep 5,000 s 1.8

Assignment:

For wood I-joists:

1. Joist spacing of 16 in., p_{dead} = 10 psf, p_{live} = 40 psf, deflection limit = L/360.
   Find the shallowest joist that will span 16 ft.
2. Joist spacing of 16 in., p_{dead} = 10 psf, p_{live} = 40 psf, deflection limit = L/480.
   Find the shallowest joist that will span 16 ft.
3. Joist spacing of 16 in., p_{dead} = 10 psf, p_{live} = 40 psf, deflection limit = L/960.
   Find the shallowest joist that will span 16 ft.
4. Joist spacing of 16 in., p_{dead} = 10 psf, p_{live} = 40 psf, deflection limit = L/360.
   Find the shallowest joist that will span 24 ft.
5. Joist spacing of 16 in., p_{dead} = 10 psf, p_{live} = 40 psf, deflection limit = L/480.
   Find the shallowest joist that will span 24 ft.
6. Joist spacing of 16 in., p_{dead} = 10 psf, p_{live} = 40 psf, deflection limit = L/960.
   Find the shallowest joist that will span 24 ft.

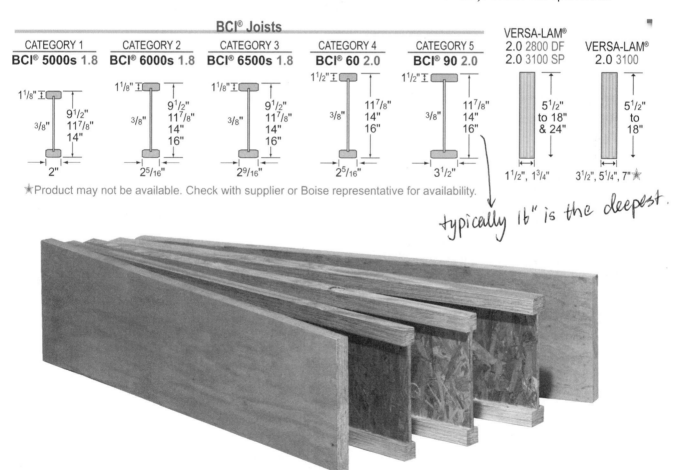

Figure 6.57 Wood I-joists and laminated veneer lumber (LVL).

Joist Depth	BCI® Joist Series	★ ★ ★ THREE STAR ★ ★ ★ Live Load deflection limited to L/480: The common industry and design community standard for residential floor joists, 33% stiffer than L/360 code minimum. However, floor performance may still be an issue in certain applications, especially with 9½" and 11⅞" deep joists without a direct-attached ceiling.					★ ★ ★ FOUR STAR ★ ★ ★ ★ Live Load deflection limited to L/960+: In addition to providing a floor that is 100% stiffer than the three star floor, field experience has been incorporated into the values to provide a floor with a premium performance level for the more discriminating homeowner.					CAUTION ★ MINIMUM STIFFNESS ALLOWED BY CODE ★ CAUTION Live Load deflection limited to L/360: Floors that meet the minimum building code L/360 criteria are structurally sound to carry the specified loads; however, there is a much higher risk of floor performance issues. This table should only be used for applications where floor performance is not a concern.				
		12" o.c.	16" o.c.	19.2" o.c.	24" o.c.	32" o.c.	12" o.c.	16" o.c.	19.2" o.c.	24" o.c.	32" o.c.	12" o.c.	16" o.c.	19.2" o.c.	24" o.c.	32" o.c.
9½"	5000s 1.8	17'-6"	16'-0"	15'-2"	14'-1"	12'-5"	11'-6"	11'-6"	10'-0"	10'-0"	9'-6"	19'-4"	17'-9"	16'-4"	14'-7"	12'-5"
	6000s 1.8	18'-2"	16'-8"	15'-8"	14'-8"	13'-4"	11'-6"	11'-6"	10'-0"	10'-0"	9'-10"	20'-2"	18'-5"	17'-5"	15'-9"	13'-8"
	6500s 1.8	18'-8"	17'-1"	16'-1"	15'-0"	13'-8"	11'-6"	11'-6"	10'-0"	10'-0"	10'-0"	20'-8"	18'-11"	17'-10"	16'-7"	14'-3"
11⅞"	5000s 1.8	20'-9"	19'-0"	17'-11"	16'-7"	13'-4"	15'-6"	14'-9"	13'-11"	12'-11"	11'-9"	23'-0"	20'-4"	18'-6"	16'-7"	13'-4"
	6000s 1.8	21'-7"	19'-8"	18'-7"	17'-4"	14'-10"	15'-6"	15'-4"	14'-5"	13'-5"	12'-1"	23'-10"	21'-10"	20'-0"	17'-11"	14'-10"
	6500s 1.8	22'-2"	20'-3"	19'-2"	17'-10"	14'-10"	16'-0"	15'-10"	14'-11"	13'-10"	12'-7"	24'-6"	22'-5"	21'-1"	18'-10"	14'-10"
	60 2.0	23'-3"	21'-3"	20'-1"	18'-8"	16'-4"	18'-0"	16'-7"	15'-7"	14'-6"	13'-2"	25'-9"	23'-6"	22'-3"	20'-9"	16'-4"
	90 2.0	26'-3"	23'-11"	22'-6"	20'-11"	19'-1"	19'-0"	18'-7"	17'-6"	16'-2"	14'-8"	29'-0"	26'-6"	25'-0"	23'-3"	19'-4"
14"	5000s 1.8	23'-7"	21'-7"	20'-2"	18'-0"	13'-11"	18'-6"	16'-10"	15'-11"	14'-9"	13'-5"	25'-7"	22'-1"	20'-2"	18'-0"	13'-11"
	6000s 1.8	24'-6"	22'-5"	21'-2"	19'-6"	15'-5"	19'-2"	17'-6"	16'-6"	15'-4"	13'-11"	27'-1"	23'-11"	21'-10"	19'-6"	15'-5"
	6500s 1.8	25'-2"	23'-0"	21'-8"	20'-2"	15'-5"	19'-8"	17'-11"	16'-11"	15'-8"	14'-3"	27'-9"	25'-2"	22'-11"	20'-6"	15'-5"
	60 2.0	26'-5"	24'-2"	22'-9"	21'-3"	16'-4"	20'-8"	18'-10"	17'-9"	16'-5"	14'-11"	29'-3"	26'-8"	25'-3"	21'-10"	16'-4"
	90 2.0	29'-9"	27'-1"	25'-6"	23'-8"	19'-6"	23'-3"	21'-1"	19'-9"	18'-4"	16'-7"	32'-10"	30'-0"	28'-3"	26'-0"	19'-6"
16"	6000s 1.8	27'-0"	24'-9"	23'-4"	20'-10"	15'-9"	21'-2"	19'-4"	18'-2"	16'-11"	15'-4"	29'-6"	25'-6"	23'-4"	20'-10"	15'-9"
	6500s 1.8	27'-9"	25'-4"	23'-11"	21'-1"	15'-9"	21'-9"	19'-9"	18'-8"	17'-4"	15'-8"	30'-8"	26'-11"	24'-6"	21'-1"	15'-9"
	60 2.0	29'-3"	26'-8"	25'-2"	21'-10"	16'-4"	22'-10"	20'-10"	19'-7"	18'-2"	16'-4"	32'-4"	29'-6"	27'-4"	21'-10"	16'-4"
	90 2.0	32'-11"	29'-11"	28'-2"	26'-2"	19'-7"	25'-8"	23'-4"	21'-11"	20'-3"	18'-4"	36'-4"	33'-2"	31'-3"	26'-2"	19'-7"

- Span table is based on a residential floor load of 40 psf live load and 10 psf dead load (12 psf dead load for 900 joists).
- Span values are a worst case of simple or multiple span applications. Joists spaced at 32" on-center require sheathing rated for such spacing (minimum ⅞" plywood/OSB).
- Spans are a clear distance between supports.
- Span table assumes that ²³/₃₂" min. rated sheathing is glued and nailed to joists.
- Repetitive loading increase has been included, where applicable.

(Shaded values do not satisfy the requirements of the North Carolina State Building Code. Refer to the THREE STAR table when spans exceed 20 feet.)

Figure 6.58 Allowed floor spans for I-joists under 10 psf dead load and 40 psf live load.

7. For $p_{dead} = 10$ psf, $p_{live} = 40$ psf, and a deflection limit of L/360, identify all the combinations of joist designation and joist spacing that will span 32 ft.

8. For $p_{dead} = 10$ psf, $p_{live} = 40$ psf, and a deflection limit of L/360, identify all the combinations of joist designation and joist spacing that will span 36 ft.

Figures 6.59 and 6.60 give the allowed uniform, unfactored load in pounds per linear foot (plf) for I-joists supporting floors. The 100% indicates that there is no adjustment allowed or required for duration of the load.

Example Floor Sizing Exercise 2

Joist spacing of 16 in., $p_{dead} = 10$ psf, $p_{live} = 80$ psf, deflection limit = L/480.

Find the shallowest joist that will span 16 ft.

The tables are set up for a deflection limit of L/480 under the live load, so the tables can be used directly. The live load along the beam will be

$$w_{live} = s \cdot p_{live} = 1.333 \text{ ft} \left(80\frac{\#}{\text{ft}^2}\right) = 106.7\frac{\#}{\text{ft}}$$

$$w_{total} = s \cdot p_{total} = 1.333 \text{ ft} \left(90\frac{\#}{\text{ft}^2}\right) = 120\frac{\#}{\text{ft}}$$

Answer: 14 in. is the shallowest I-joist that works. A 14 in.-deep 6,000 s 1.8 works, which is the lightest 14 in.-deep I-joist listed.

Example Floor Sizing Exercise 3

Joist spacing of 16 in., $p_{dead} = 10$ psf, $p_{live} = 80$ psf, deflection limit = L/960.

Find the shallowest joist that will span 16 ft.

The tables are set up for a deflection limit of L/480 under the live load. The live loads in the preceding tables have to be multiplied by 0.5 to determine the live-load limit set by the criterion that the deflection is limited to L/960. To make scanning the tables easier, you can multiply the live load by a factor of (1/0.5) = 2. So the live load that you need to seek in the tables is 2 (80 psf) = 160 psf.

The live load along the beam will be $w_{live} = s \cdot p_{live} = $ 1.333 ft (160 psf) = 212.8 plf.

Answer: Nothing works at 16 in. OC. We can try 12 in. OC, in which case, $w_{live} = s \cdot p_{live} = 1.00$ ft (160 psf) =

Allowable Uniform Floor Load
(in pounds per lineal foot [PLF])

	BCI® 5000s 1.8 Series 2" Flange Width						BCI® 6000s 1.8 Series 2⁵⁄₁₆" Flange Width							
	9½" BCI® 5000s 1.8		11⅞" BCI® 5000s 1.8		14" BCI® 5000s 1.8		9½" BCI® 6000s 1.8		11⅞" BCI® 6000s 1.8		14" BCI® 6000s 1.8		16" BCI® 6000s 1.8	
Span Length	Live Load	Total Load	Live Load	Total Load	Live Load	Total Load	Live Load	Total Load	Live Load	Total Load	Live Load	Total Load	Live Load	Total Load
6	-	280	-	300	-	313	-	320	-	333	-	346	-	353
7	-	240	-	257	-	268	-	274	-	285	-	297	-	302
8	-	210	-	225	-	235	-	240	-	250	-	260	-	265
9	-	186	-	200	-	208	-	213	-	222	-	231	-	235
10	163	168	-	180	-	188	183	192	-	200	-	208	-	212
11	126	152	-	163	-	170	141	174	-	181	-	189	-	192
12	99	140	-	150	-	156	112	160	-	166	-	173	-	176
13	79	128	129	138	-	144	89	147	144	153	-	160	-	163
14	64	111	105	128	-	134	73	129	117	142	-	148	-	151
15	53	96	86	120	-	125	60	112	97	133	-	138	-	141
16	44	85	72	108	104	117	50	98	81	125	117	130	-	132
17			61	96	88	110	42	84	68	112	99	122	-	124
18			51	86	75	101			58	100	84	115	112	117
19			44	77	64	91			50	89	72	106	96	111
20					55	82			43	81	62	96	83	106
21					48	74					54	87	72	99
22					42	68					47	79	63	90
23											42	72	56	83
24													49	76
25													44	70

- Total Load values are limited by shear, moment, or deflection equal to L/240.

- Live Load values are limited by deflection equal to L/480. For deflection limits of L/360 and L/960, multiply the Live Load values by 1.33 and 0.50 respectively.

- Both the Total Load and Live Load columns must be checked. Where a Live Load value is not shown, the Total Load value will control.

- Table values apply to either simple or multiple span joists. Span is measured center to center of the minimum required bearing length. Analyze multiple span joists with the BC CALC® software if the length of any span is less than half the length of an adjacent span.

- Table values assume that sheathing is nailed, but not glued, to the joists.

- Total Load values assume minimum bearing lengths without web stiffeners for joist depths of 16 inches and less.

Figure 6.59 Allowed total unfactored floor load on wood I-joists in pounds per linear foot (plf).

Allowable Uniform Floor Load
(in pounds per lineal foot [PLF])

	100%							
	BCI® 6500s 1.8 Series $2^9/_{16}$" Flange Width							
	$9^1/_2$" BCI® 6500s 1.8		$11^7/_8$" BCI® 6500s 1.8		14" BCI® 6500s 1.8		16" BCI® 6500s 1.8	
Span Length	Live Load	Total Load	Live Load	Total Load	Live Load	Total Load	Live Load	Total Load
6	-	320	-	333	-	346	-	353
7	-	274	-	285	-	297	-	302
8	-	240	-	250	-	260	-	265
9	-	213	-	222	-	231	-	235
10	-	192	-	200	-	208	-	212
11	153	174	-	181	-	189	-	192
12	121	160	-	166	-	173	-	176
13	97	147	-	153	-	160	-	163
14	79	137	129	142	-	148	-	151
15	65	124	106	133	-	138	-	141
16	54	109	89	125	127	130	-	132
17	46	92	75	117	107	122	-	124
18			64	110	91	115	-	117
19			54	99	78	109	104	111
20			47	89	68	104	90	106
21			41	81	59	96	78	100
22					51	88	69	96
23					45	80	60	92
24					40	74	53	84
25							47	77
26							42	72
27								
28								
29								
30								

Figure 6.60 Allowed total unfactored floor load on wood I-joists in pounds per linear foot (plf) (continued from Figure 6.59, with all the same conditions applying).

160 plf. Still nothing works. Finally, you can try 8 in. OC, in which case, $w_{live} = s \cdot p_{live} = 0.667$ ft (160 psf) = 106.7 plf.

Answer: 14 in. is the shallowest I-joist that works. A 14 in.-deep 6,000s 1.8 works, which is the lightest 14 in.-deep I-joist listed.

Figures 6.61, 6.62, and 6.63 give allowed spans for wood I-joists supporting roofs. Various unfactored dead and live loads are listed along with various slopes. The first column lists the spacing of the joists. The second column lists the allowed stress overloads associated with the fact that the loads are presumed to be of short duration, which are less deleterious for wood than loads of long duration. Values are labeled 115%, which repre-

sents the allowed stress overload for snow, and 125%, which represents the allowed stress overload for non-snow live load on the roof. The presumption is that snow will have a short duration and that non-snow live loads will have an even shorter duration. If the designer has any doubts regarding the duration of the loads, he or she should design for the 115% overload to be conservative. There is no snow live load of less than 25 lb/ft² in the 115% category, because such a small snow load is presumed to last for such a short time that it qualifies as a very short-term load; that is, it qualifies for a 125% stress overload.

Examples Using the Allowed Roof Span Tables

1. A flat roof is to span 32 ft, subject to a dead load of 10 lb/ft², a snow live load of 15 lb/ft², and a non-snow live load of 20 lb/ft². At a joist spacing of 16 in. OC, what is the shallowest I-joist that will work?

In Figures 6.61 through 6.63, scanning down to 16 in. spacing and jumping over to the third column of the figures, you can see that there is no snow load of 15 lb/ft². Therefore, you can focus on the non-snow load of 20 lb/ft², with the allowed stress overload of 125%. The shallowest I-joist that will work is a $11^7/_8$ in. BCI 90 2.0, which can span 34 ft-10 in. This would make an incredibly simple and inexpensive roof. It also allows a good depth of bat insulation between the I-joists. To provide proper insulation and some air space above the insulation, a designer would not want a shallower I-joist. There is little motive to provide an interior support wall to shorten the span, because the joists will have to be about $11^7/_8$ in. deep anyway.

2. A flat roof is to span 32 ft, subject to a dead load of 10 lb/ft², a snow live load of 15 lb/ft², and a non-snow live load of 40 lb/ft²; that is, the roof is being designed for human occupancy, rather than the occasional trip by a small number of people to inspect or repair the roof. Find a combination of I-joist and spacing that will work.

There is no non-snow load as great as 40 lb/ft². This is a limitation of the tables. The options are to use the portion of the table that allows the 115% overload, which will be on the conservative side, or to declare it a floor and use the allowed-load tables for floors. Starting with the former strategy, Figure 6.62 indicates that 16 in. BCI 6500s 1.8 spaced at 12 in. OC will span up to 31 ft.-5 in. The tables also indicate that 16 in. BCI 90 2.0 spaced at 16 in. OC can span up to 35 ft.-7 in. The tables in Figures 6.61 through 6.63 assume a deflection limit of L/240 under live load. Spanning this distance with I-joists will produce an occupiable roof with more than the normal amount of movement under live load. This could be perceived as a problem by the occupants. To get an occupiable roof with less deflection, you could use the data in Figures 6.59 and 6.60. Those tables indicate that no I-joist will span 32 ft. with acceptable stiffness.

Roof Span Tables

Maximum clear span in feet and inches, based on horizontal spans.

115% and 125%

				BCI® 5000s 1.8 Series 2" Flange Width									BCI® 6000s 1.8 Series $2^5/_{16}$" Flange Width											
				$9^1/_2$" BCI® 5000s 1.8			$11^7/_8$" BCI® 5000s 1.8			14" BCI® 5000s 1.8			$9^1/_2$" BCI® 6000s 1.8			$11^7/_8$" BCI® 6000s 1.8			14" BCI® 6000s 1.8			16" BCI® 6000s 1.8		
		Live Load [psf]	Dead Load [psf]	4/12 or Less	4/12 to 8/12	8/12 to 12/12	4/12 or Less	4/12 to 8/12	8/12 to 12/12	4/12 or Less	4/12 to 8/12	8/12 to 12/12	4/12 or Less	4/12 to 8/12	8/12 to 12/12	4/12 or Less	4/12 to 8/12	8/12 to 12/12	4/12 or Less	4/12 to 8/12	8/12 to 12/12	4/12 or Less	4/12 to 8/12	8/12 to 12/12
12" o.c.	Non-Snow 125%	20	10	24'-10"	23'-5"	21'-9"	29'-7"	27'-11"	25'-11"	33'-8"	31'-9"	29'-5"	26'-0"	24'-6"	22'-9"	30'-11"	29'-2"	27'-0"	35'-2"	33'-2"	30'-9"	38'-10"	36'-7"	34'-0"
		20	15	23'-6"	22'-1"	20'-5"	28'-0"	26'-4"	24'-4"	31'-10"	29'-11"	27'-7"	24'-7"	23'-1"	21'-4"	29'-3"	27'-6"	25'-4"	33'-3"	31'-3"	28'-10"	36'-9"	34'-6"	31'-10"
		20	20	22'-5"	21'-0"	19'-4"	26'-9"	25'-0"	23'-0"	30'-5"	28'-5"	26'-2"	23'-6"	22'-0"	20'-2"	27'-11"	26'-1"	24'-0"	31'-9"	29'-9"	27'-4"	35'-1"	32'-10"	30'-2"
	Snow 115%	25	10	23'-7"	22'-4"	20'-9"	28'-1"	26'-7"	24'-9"	31'-11"	30'-2"	28'-1"	24'-8"	23'-4"	21'-8"	29'-4"	27'-9"	25'-10"	33'-4"	31'-6"	29'-4"	36'-10"	34'-10"	32'-5"
		25	15	22'-6"	21'-2"	19'-7"	26'-10"	25'-3"	23'-4"	30'-3"	28'-8"	26'-7"	23'-6"	22'-2"	20'-6"	28'-0"	26'-4"	24'-5"	31'-10"	29'-11"	27'-9"	34'-11"	33'-1"	30'-8"
		30	10	22'-7"	21'-4"	19'-11"	26'-10"	25'-5"	23'-9"	30'-4"	28'-11"	27'-0"	23'-7"	22'-4"	20'-10"	28'-0"	26'-7"	24'-9"	31'-11"	30'-2"	28'-2"	35'-1"	33'-5"	31'-2"
		30	15	21'-7"	20'-5"	18'-11"	25'-9"	24'-4"	22'-7"	28'-6"	27'-8"	25'-8"	22'-7"	21'-4"	19'-9"	26'-11"	25'-4"	23'-6"	30'-7"	28'-10"	26'-9"	33'-0"	31'-11"	29'-7"
		40	10	20'-6"	19'-8"	18'-7"	24'-5"	23'-5"	22'-2"	27'-2"	26'-8"	25'-2"	21'-5"	20'-7"	19'-5"	25'-6"	24'-6"	23'-1"	29'-0"	27'-10"	26'-3"	31'-4"	30'-9"	29'-0"
		40	15	20'-2"	19'-1"	17'-10"	23'-8"	22'-9"	21'-3"	25'-10"	25'-4"	24'-1"	21'-1"	20'-0"	18'-7"	25'-1"	23'-9"	22'-2"	27'-11"	27'-1"	25'-2"	29'-10"	29'-3"	27'-10"
		50	10	19'-0"	18'-3"	17'-3"	22'-8"	21'-9"	20'-7"	24'-10"	24'-6"	23'-5"	19'-10"	19'-1"	18'-1"	23'-7"	22'-8"	21'-6"	26'-9"	25'-9"	24'-6"	28'-8"	28'-3"	27'-1"
		50	15	19'-0"	18'-1"	16'-11"	21'-10"	21'-5"	20'-2"	23'-9"	23'-4"	22'-10"	19'-10"	18'-11"	17'-8"	23'-7"	22'-6"	21'-0"	25'-8"	25'-3"	23'-11"	27'-5"	27'-0"	26'-5"
16" o.c.	Non-Snow 125%	20	10	22'-6"	21'-3"	19'-8"	26'-10"	25'-4"	23'-6"	30'-6"	28'-9"	26'-8"	23'-6"	22'-2"	20'-7"	28'-0"	26'-5"	24'-6"	31'-10"	30'-0"	27'-10"	35'-2"	33'-2"	30'-10"
		20	15	21'-4"	20'-0"	18'-6"	25'-5"	23'-10"	22'-0"	28'-11"	27'-1"	25'-0"	22'-3"	20'-11"	19'-4"	26'-6"	24'-11"	23'-0"	30'-2"	28'-4"	26'-2"	33'-4"	31'-4"	28'-11"
		20	20	20'-4"	19'-0"	17'-6"	24'-3"	22'-8"	20'-10"	27'-2"	25'-10"	23'-9"	21'-3"	19'-11"	18'-4"	25'-3"	23'-8"	21'-9"	28'-9"	26'-11"	24'-9"	31'-5"	29'-9"	27'-5"
	Snow 115%	25	10	21'-4"	20'-2"	18'-10"	25'-6"	24'-1"	22'-5"	28'-1"	27'-4"	25'-6"	22'-4"	21'-1"	19'-8"	26'-7"	25'-1"	23'-5"	30'-3"	28'-7"	26'-7"	32'-5"	31'-7"	29'-5"
		25	15	20'-5"	19'-2"	17'-9"	24'-0"	22'-10"	21'-2"	26'-2"	25'-6"	24'-1"	21'-4"	20'-1"	18'-7"	25'-4"	23'-10"	22'-1"	28'-3"	27'-2"	25'-2"	30'-3"	29'-5"	27'-9"
		30	10	20'-5"	19'-4"	18'-1"	24'-1"	23'-1"	21'-6"	26'-3"	25'-9"	24'-5"	21'-4"	20'-3"	18'-10"	25'-5"	24'-1"	22'-5"	28'-4"	27'-4"	25'-6"	30'-4"	29'-9"	28'-3"
		30	15	19'-7"	18'-6"	17'-2"	22'-8"	22'-0"	20'-5"	24'-8"	24'-1"	23'-3"	20'-6"	19'-4"	17'-11"	24'-4"	23'-0"	21'-4"	26'-8"	26'-0"	24'-3"	28'-6"	27'-10"	26'-10"
		40	10	18'-7"	17'-10"	16'-10"	21'-7"	21'-3"	20'-1"	23'-6"	23'-2"	22'-8"	19'-5"	18'-7"	17'-7"	23'-1"	22'-2"	20'-11"	25'-5"	25'-0"	23'-10"	27'-2"	26'-9"	26'-2"
		40	15	18'-1"	17'-4"	16'-1"	20'-6"	20'-1"	19'-3"	22'-4"	21'-11"	21'-4"	19'-1"	18'-1"	16'-10"	22'-2"	21'-6"	20'-1"	24'-2"	23'-8"	22'-10"	25'-10"	25'-4"	24'-8"
		50	10	17'-2"	16'-6"	15'-8"	19'-8"	19'-5"	18'-8"	21'-5"	21'-2"	20'-10"	18'-0"	17'-3"	16'-4"	21'-3"	20'-6"	19'-6"	23'-2"	22'-11"	22'-2"	24'-9"	24'-6"	24'-1"
		50	15	16'-8"	16'-4"	15'-4"	18'-10"	18'-6"	18'-1"	20'-7"	20'-2"	19'-9"	17'-11"	17'-1"	16'-0"	20'-4"	20'-0"	19'-0"	22'-2"	21'-10"	21'-4"	23'-9"	23'-4"	22'-10"
19.2" o.c.	Non-Snow 125%	20	10	21'-2"	19'-11"	18'-6"	25'-2"	23'-9"	22'-1"	28'-8"	27'-0"	25'-1"	22'-1"	20'-10"	19'-4"	26'-3"	24'-10"	23'-0"	29'-11"	28'-3"	26'-2"	33'-1"	31'-2"	28'-11"
		20	15	20'-0"	18'-10"	17'-4"	23'-10"	22'-5"	20'-8"	26'-7"	25'-6"	23'-6"	20'-11"	19'-8"	18'-2"	24'-11"	23'-5"	21'-7"	28'-4"	26'-7"	24'-7"	30'-8"	29'-5"	27'-2"
		20	20	19'-1"	17'-10"	16'-5"	22'-9"	21'-4"	19'-7"	24'-10"	23'-11"	22'-3"	19'-11"	18'-8"	17'-2"	23'-9"	22'-3"	20'-5"	26'-10"	25'-4"	23'-3"	28'-8"	27'-8"	25'-9"
	Snow 115%	25	10	20'-1"	19'-0"	17'-8"	23'-6"	22'-7"	21'-1"	25'-7"	25'-1"	23'-11"	21'-0"	19'-10"	18'-6"	24'-11"	23'-7"	22'-0"	27'-8"	26'-10"	25'-0"	29'-7"	28'-11"	27'-8"
		25	15	19'-2"	18'-0"	16'-8"	21'-11"	21'-4"	19'-11"	23'-10"	23'-3"	22'-5"	20'-0"	18'-10"	17'-5"	23'-8"	22'-5"	20'-9"	25'-9"	25'-1"	23'-7"	27'-7"	26'-10"	25'-11"
		30	10	19'-2"	18'-2"	16'-11"	22'-0"	21'-7"	20'-2"	23'-11"	23'-6"	22'-11"	20'-1"	19'-0"	17'-9"	23'-9"	22'-7"	21'-1"	25'-10"	25'-5"	24'-0"	27'-8"	27'-2"	26'-6"
		30	15	18'-3"	17'-4"	16'-1"	20'-8"	20'-2"	19'-2"	22'-6"	22'-0"	21'-3"	19'-3"	18'-2"	16'-10"	22'-4"	21'-7"	20'-0"	24'-4"	23'-9"	22'-10"	26'-0"	25'-5"	24'-7"
		40	10	17'-4"	16'-9"	15'-10"	19'-8"	19'-4"	18'-10"	21'-5"	21'-1"	20'-8"	18'-3"	17'-6"	16'-6"	21'-3"	20'-10"	19'-8"	23'-2"	22'-10"	22'-4"	24'-9"	24'-5"	23'-11"
		40	15	16'-6"	16'-2"	15'-2"	18'-8"	18'-4"	17'-10"	20'-4"	20'-0"	19'-5"	17'-10"	17'-0"	15'-10"	20'-2"	19'-10"	18'-10"	22'-0"	21'-7"	21'-0"	23'-6"	23'-1"	22'-6"
		50	10	15'-10"	15'-6"	14'-8"	17'-11"	17'-9"	17'-5"	19'-7"	19'-4"	19'-0"	16'-10"	16'-2"	15'-4"	19'-5"	19'-2"	18'-3"	21'-1"	20'-10"	20'-6"	22'-7"	22'-4"	21'-11"
		50	15	15'-2"	14'-11"	14'-4"	17'-2"	16'-11"	16'-6"	18'-9"	18'-5"	18'-0"	16'-4"	16'-1"	15'-0"	18'-7"	18'-3"	17'-10"	20'-3"	19'-11"	19'-5"	21'-8"	21'-3"	20'-10"
24" o.c.	Non-Snow 125%	20	10	19'-7"	18'-6"	17'-2"	23'-4"	22'-0"	20'-5"	25'-9"	25'-0"	23'-3"	20'-6"	19'-4"	17'-11"	24'-4"	23'-0"	21'-4"	27'-9"	26'-2"	24'-3"	29'-9"	28'-11"	26'-10"
		20	15	18'-6"	17'-5"	16'-1"	21'-10"	20'-9"	19'-2"	23'-9"	23'-1"	21'-9"	19'-4"	18'-2"	16'-10"	23'-0"	21'-8"	20'-0"	25'-8"	24'-8"	22'-9"	27'-5"	26'-7"	25'-2"
		20	20	17'-8"	16'-7"	15'-3"	20'-4"	19'-8"	18'-2"	22'-2"	21'-5"	20'-5"	18'-6"	17'-3"	15'-11"	22'-0"	20'-7"	18'-11"	23'-11"	23'-1"	21'-7"	25'-7"	24'-9"	23'-7"
	Snow 115%	25	10	18'-6"	17'-7"	16'-4"	21'-0"	20'-7"	19'-6"	22'-10"	22'-5"	21'-9"	19'-5"	18'-4"	17'-1"	22'-8"	21'-10"	20'-4"	24'-8"	24'-2"	23'-2"	26'-5"	25'-10"	25'-2"
		25	15	17'-3"	16'-8"	15'-5"	19'-7"	19'-1"	18'-4"	21'-4"	20'-9"	20'-0"	18'-6"	17'-5"	16'-2"	21'-2"	20'-7"	19'-3"	23'-0"	22'-5"	21'-8"	24'-8"	24'-0"	23'-2"
		30	10	17'-4"	16'-10"	15'-8"	19'-7"	19'-3"	18'-9"	21'-5"	21'-0"	20'-6"	18'-7"	17'-7"	16'-5"	21'-2"	20'-10"	19'-6"	23'-1"	22'-8"	22'-2"	24'-9"	24'-3"	23'-8"
		30	15	16'-3"	15'-11"	14'-11"	18'-5"	18'-0"	17'-5"	20'-1"	19'-8"	19'-0"	17'-7"	16'-9"	15'-7"	19'-11"	19'-6"	18'-7"	21'-9"	21'-3"	20'-6"	23'-3"	22'-8"	21'-11"
		40	10	15'-6"	15'-3"	14'-7"	17'-7"	17'-4"	16'-11"	19'-2"	18'-10"	18'-6"	16'-9"	16'-2"	15'-3"	19'-0"	18'-8"	18'-2"	20'-8"	20'-4"	20'-0"	22'-1"	21'-9"	21'-4"
		40	15	14'-9"	14'-5"	14'-0"	16'-8"	16'-4"	15'-11"	18'-2"	17'-10"	17'-4"	15'-11"	15'-7"	14'-8"	18'-0"	17'-8"	17'-2"	19'-8"	19'-3"	18'-9"	21'-0"	20'-7"	19'-8"
		50	10	14'-2"	13'-11"	13'-7"	16'-0"	15'-10"	15'-7"	17'-5"	17'-2"	16'-7"	15'-3"	14'-11"	14'-3"	17'-4"	17'-1"	16'-10"	18'-10"	18'-8"	18'-4"	19'-10"	19'-5"	18'-9"
		50	15	13'-6"	13'-4"	13'-0"	15'-4"	14'-11"	14'-3"	16'-2"	15'-8"	14'-11"	14'-7"	14'-4"	13'-11"	16'-7"	16'-4"	15'-11"	17'-11"	17'-4"	16'-6"	18'-3"	17'-8"	16'-10"

- Table values are limited by shear, moment, total load deflection equal to L/180 and live load deflection equal to L/240. Check the local building code for other deflection limits that may apply.
- Table values represent the most restrictive of simple or multiple span applications.
- Table values assume minimum bearing lengths without web stiffeners for joist depths of 16 inches and less.
- Slope roof joists at least ¼" over 12" to minimize ponding.
- Allowable spans and loads shall be adjusted and checked for wind load as required by local building code.

Figure 6.61 Allowed spans for wood I-joists supporting roofs.

Maximum clear span in feet and inches, based on horizontal spans.

115% and 125%

		Live Load [psf]	Dead Load [psf]	9½" BCI® 6500s 1.8			11⅞" BCI® 6500s 1.8			14" BCI® 6500s 1.8			16" BCI® 6500s 1.8		
				4/12 or Less	4/12 to 8/12	8/12 to 12/12	4/12 or Less	4/12 to 8/12	8/12 to 12/12	4/12 or Less	4/12 to 8/12	8/12 to 12/12	4/12 or Less	4/12 to 8/12	8/12 to 12/12
12" o.c.	Non-Snow 125%	20	10	26'-10"	25'-3"	23'-6"	31'-10"	30'-0"	27'-10"	36'-2"	34'-1"	31'-8"	40'-0"	37'-8"	35'-0"
		20	15	25'-5"	23'-10"	22'-0"	30'-2"	28'-4"	26'-1"	34'-3"	32'-2"	29'-8"	37'-10"	35'-7"	32'-10"
		20	20	24'-3"	22'-8"	20'-10"	28'-9"	26'-11"	24'-9"	32'-8"	30'-7"	28'-2"	36'-1"	33'-10"	31'-1"
	Snow 115%	25	10	25'-5"	24'-1"	22'-5"	30'-3"	28'-7"	26'-7"	34'-4"	32'-6"	30'-3"	37'-11"	35'-10"	33'-5"
		25	15	24'-3"	22'-10"	21'-2"	28'-10"	27'-2"	25'-1"	32'-9"	30'-10"	28'-7"	36'-2"	34'-1"	31'-7"
		30	10	24'-4"	23'-0"	21'-6"	28'-11"	27'-4"	25'-6"	32'-10"	31'-1"	29'-0"	36'-3"	34'-4"	32'-1"
		30	15	23'-4"	22'-0"	20'-5"	27'-8"	26'-2"	24'-3"	31'-6"	29'-9"	27'-7"	34'-8"	32'-10"	30'-6"
		40	10	22'-2"	21'-3"	20'-0"	26'-4"	25'-3"	23'-10"	29'-11"	28'-8"	27'-1"	33'-0"	31'-8"	29'-11"
		40	15	21'-9"	20'-7"	19'-3"	25'-11"	24'-6"	22'-10"	29'-5"	27'-10"	25'-11"	31'-5"	30'-9"	28'-8"
		50	10	20'-6"	19'-8"	18'-8"	24'-4"	23'-4"	22'-2"	27'-8"	26'-7"	25'-2"	30'-2"	29'-4"	27'-10"
		50	15	20'-6"	19'-6"	18'-3"	24'-4"	23'-2"	21'-8"	27'-0"	26'-4"	24'-8"	28'-11"	28'-5"	27'-3"
16" o.c.	Non-Snow 125%	20	10	24'-4"	22'-11"	21'-3"	28'-10"	27'-2"	25'-3"	32'-10"	30'-11"	28'-8"	36'-3"	34'-2"	31'-9"
		20	15	23'-0"	21'-7"	19'-11"	27'-4"	25'-8"	23'-8"	31'-1"	29'-2"	26'-11"	34'-4"	32'-3"	29'-9"
		20	20	21'-11"	20'-6"	18'-11"	26'-1"	24'-5"	22'-5"	29'-8"	27'-9"	25'-6"	32'-9"	30'-8"	28'-2"
	Snow 115%	25	10	23'-1"	21'-10"	20'-4"	27'-5"	25'-11"	24'-1"	31'-2"	29'-5"	27'-5"	34'-1"	32'-6"	30'-3"
		25	15	22'-0"	20'-8"	19'-2"	26'-1"	24'-7"	22'-9"	29'-8"	27'-11"	25'-11"	31'-10"	30'-11"	28'-7"
		30	10	22'-0"	20'-10"	19'-6"	26'-2"	24'-9"	23'-1"	29'-9"	28'-2"	26'-4"	31'-11"	31'-2"	29'-1"
		30	15	21'-1"	19'-11"	18'-6"	25'-1"	23'-8"	22'-0"	28'-1"	26'-11"	25'-0"	30'-0"	29'-4"	27'-7"
		40	10	20'-0"	19'-3"	18'-2"	23'-10"	22'-10"	21'-7"	26'-9"	26'-0"	24'-6"	28'-7"	28'-2"	27'-1"
		40	15	19'-9"	18'-8"	17'-5"	23'-4"	22'-2"	20'-8"	25'-5"	24'-11"	23'-6"	27'-2"	26'-8"	25'-11"
		50	10	18'-6"	17'-9"	16'-11"	22'-1"	21'-2"	20'-1"	24'-5"	24'-1"	22'-10"	26'-1"	25'-9"	25'-3"
		50	15	18'-6"	17'-8"	16'-6"	21'-5"	21'-0"	19'-8"	23'-5"	23'-0"	22'-4"	25'-0"	24'-7"	24'-0"
19.2" o.c.	Non-Snow 125%	20	10	22'-10"	21'-6"	20'-0"	27'-1"	25'-7"	23'-9"	30'-10"	29'-1"	27'-0"	34'-0"	32'-1"	29'-10"
		20	15	21'-7"	20'-3"	18'-9"	25'-8"	24'-1"	22'-3"	29'-2"	27'-5"	25'-4"	32'-3"	30'-3"	27'-11"
		20	20	20'-7"	19'-3"	17'-9"	24'-6"	22'-11"	21'-1"	27'-10"	26'-1"	24'-0"	30'-2"	28'-9"	26'-4"
	Snow 115%	25	10	21'-8"	20'-6"	19'-1"	25'-9"	24'-4"	22'-8"	29'-1"	27'-8"	25'-9"	31'-1"	30'-6"	28'-5"
		25	15	20'-8"	19'-5"	18'-0"	24'-6"	23'-1"	21'-5"	27'-2"	26'-3"	24'-4"	29'-0"	28'-3"	26'-11"
		30	10	20'-8"	19'-7"	18'-3"	24'-7"	23'-3"	21'-9"	27'-3"	26'-6"	24'-8"	29'-1"	28'-7"	27'-4"
		30	15	19'-10"	18'-9"	17'-5"	23'-6"	22'-3"	20'-8"	25'-7"	25'-0"	23'-6"	27'-5"	26'-9"	25'-11"
		40	10	18'-10"	18'-1"	17'-1"	22'-4"	21'-5"	20'-3"	24'-4"	24'-0"	23'-0"	26'-1"	25'-8"	25'-2"
		40	15	18'-6"	17'-6"	16'-4"	21'-3"	20'-10"	19'-5"	23'-2"	22'-9"	22'-1"	24'-9"	24'-4"	23'-8"
		50	10	17'-5"	16'-8"	15'-10"	20'-5"	19'-10"	18'-10"	22'-3"	22'-0"	21'-5"	23'-9"	23'-6"	23'-1"
		50	15	17'-3"	16'-7"	15'-6"	19'-7"	19'-3"	18'-5"	21'-4"	21'-0"	20'-6"	22'-10"	22'-2"	21'-2"
24" o.c.	Non-Snow 125%	20	10	21'-1"	19'-11"	18'-6"	25'-1"	23'-8"	22'-0"	28'-6"	26'-11"	25'-0"	31'-4"	29'-9"	27'-7"
		20	15	20'-0"	18'-9"	17'-4"	23'-9"	22'-4"	20'-7"	27'-0"	25'-5"	23'-5"	28'-11"	28'-0"	25'-11"
		20	20	19'-1"	17'-10"	16'-5"	22'-8"	21'-3"	19'-6"	25'-3"	24'-2"	22'-2"	26'-11"	26'-0"	24'-6"
	Snow 115%	25	10	20'-0"	18'-11"	17'-8"	23'-10"	22'-6"	21'-0"	26'-0"	25'-6"	23'-10"	27'-10"	27'-3"	26'-4"
		25	15	19'-1"	18'-0"	16'-8"	22'-3"	21'-5"	19'-10"	24'-3"	23'-7"	22'-6"	25'-11"	25'-3"	24'-4"
		30	10	19'-2"	18'-2"	16'-11"	22'-4"	21'-7"	20'-1"	24'-4"	23'-11"	22'-11"	26'-0"	25'-7"	24'-11"
		30	15	18'-4"	17'-4"	16'-1"	21'-0"	20'-6"	19'-1"	22'-10"	22'-4"	21'-7"	24'-5"	23'-11"	23'-1"
		40	10	17'-5"	16'-8"	15'-9"	20'-0"	19'-8"	18'-9"	21'-9"	21'-5"	21'-0"	23'-3"	22'-11"	22'-3"
		40	15	16'-9"	16'-2"	15'-1"	19'-0"	18'-7"	18'-0"	20'-8"	20'-4"	19'-3"	21'-7"	20'-9"	19'-8"
		50	10	16'-1"	15'-5"	14'-8"	18'-3"	18'-0"	17'-5"	19'-6"	19'-0"	18'-5"	19'-10"	19'-5"	18'-9"
		50	15	15'-5"	15'-2"	14'-4"	17'-3"	16'-8"	15'-11"	17'-11"	17'-4"	16'-6"	18'-3"	17'-8"	16'-10"

Figure 6.62 Allowed spans for wood I-joists supporting roofs.

Maximum clear span in feet and inches, based on horizontal spans.

		Live Load [psf]	Dead Load [psf]	11⅞" BCI® 90 2.0			14" BCI® 90 2.0			16" BCI® 90 2.0		
				4/12 or Less	4/12 to 8/12	8/12 to 12/12	4/12 or Less	4/12 to 8/12	8/12 to 12/12	4/12 or Less	4/12 to 8/12	8/12 to 12/12
12" o.c.	Non-Snow 125%	20	10	38'-5"	36'-3"	33'-8"	43'-7"	41'-2"	38'-2"	48'-4"	45'-7"	42'-3"
		20	15	36'-5"	34'-2"	31'-7"	41'-4"	38'-10"	35'-10"	45'-9"	43'-0"	39'-8"
		20	20	34'-9"	32'-6"	29'-11"	39'-5"	36'-11"	33'-11"	43'-8"	40'-10"	37'-7"
	Snow 115%	25	10	36'-6"	34'-6"	32'-1"	41'-5"	39'-2"	36'-5"	45'-10"	43'-4"	40'-4"
		25	15	34'-10"	32'-9"	30'-4"	39'-6"	37'-2"	34'-5"	43'-9"	41'-2"	38'-2"
		30	10	34'-11"	33'-1"	30'-10"	39'-7"	37'-6"	35'-0"	43'-10"	41'-6"	38'-9"
		30	15	33'-5"	31'-7"	29'-4"	38'-0"	35'-10"	33'-3"	42'-1"	39'-8"	36'-10"
		40	10	31'-9"	30'-5"	28'-9"	36'-0"	34'-7"	32'-8"	39'-11"	38'-3"	36'-2"
		40	15	31'-3"	29'-7"	27'-7"	35'-6"	33'-7"	31'-3"	39'-3"	37'-2"	34'-8"
		50	10	29'-5"	28'-2"	26'-9"	33'-4"	32'-0"	30'-5"	36'-11"	35'-5"	33'-8"
		50	15	29'-5"	28'-0"	26'-2"	33'-4"	31'-9"	29'-8"	36'-11"	35'-3"	32'-11"
16" o.c.	Non-Snow 125%	20	10	34'-10"	32'-10"	30'-6"	39'-6"	37'-4"	34'-7"	43'-9"	41'-4"	38'-4"
		20	15	33'-0"	31'-0"	28'-7"	37'-5"	35'-2"	32'-6"	41'-5"	38'-11"	36'-0"
		20	20	31'-6"	29'-6"	27'-1"	35'-8"	33'-5"	30'-9"	39'-7"	37'-0"	34'-1"
	Snow 115%	25	10	33'-1"	31'-3"	29'-1"	37'-6"	35'-6"	33'-1"	41'-7"	39'-4"	36'-7"
		25	15	31'-6"	29'-8"	27'-6"	35'-9"	33'-8"	31'-3"	39'-8"	37'-4"	34'-7"
		30	10	31'-7"	29'-11"	27'-11"	35'-10"	34'-0"	31'-9"	39'-9"	37'-8"	35'-2"
		30	15	30'-4"	28'-7"	26'-7"	34'-5"	32'-5"	30'-2"	38'-1"	35'-11"	33'-5"
		40	10	28'-9"	27'-7"	26'-1"	32'-7"	31'-4"	29'-7"	36'-2"	34'-8"	32'-9"
		40	15	28'-4"	26'-9"	25'-0"	32'-1"	30'-5"	28'-4"	35'-7"	33'-8"	31'-5"
		50	10	26'-7"	25'-6"	24'-3"	30'-2"	29'-0"	27'-6"	33'-5"	32'-1"	30'-6"
		50	15	26'-7"	25'-4"	23'-9"	30'-2"	28'-9"	26'-11"	33'-5"	31'-11"	29'-10"
19.2" o.c.	Non-Snow 125%	20	10	32'-9"	30'-11"	28'-8"	37'-2"	35'-0"	32'-6"	41'-2"	38'-10"	36'-0"
		20	15	31'-0"	29'-1"	26'-11"	35'-2"	33'-0"	30'-6"	38'-11"	36'-7"	33'-9"
		20	20	29'-6"	27'-8"	25'-5"	33'-6"	31'-5"	28'-11"	37'-2"	34'-9"	32'-0"
	Snow 115%	25	10	31'-1"	29'-5"	27'-4"	35'-3"	33'-4"	31'-1"	39'-0"	36'-11"	34'-5"
		25	15	29'-7"	27'-11"	25'-10"	33'-7"	31'-8"	29'-4"	37'-3"	35'-1"	32'-6"
		30	10	29'-8"	28'-1"	26'-3"	33'-8"	31'-11"	29'-10"	37'-4"	35'-4"	33'-0"
		30	15	28'-5"	26'-10"	24'-11"	32'-3"	30'-6"	28'-4"	35'-9"	33'-9"	31'-4"
		40	10	27'-0"	25'-11"	24'-6"	30'-7"	29'-5"	27'-9"	33'-11"	32'-7"	30'-9"
		40	15	26'-7"	25'-2"	23'-5"	30'-2"	28'-7"	26'-7"	33'-5"	31'-7"	29'-6"
		50	10	24'-11"	24'-0"	22'-9"	28'-4"	27'-2"	25'-10"	31'-5"	30'-2"	28'-8"
		50	15	24'-11"	23'-10"	22'-3"	28'-4"	27'-0"	25'-3"	29'-8"	28'-8"	27'-5"
24" o.c.	Non-Snow 125%	20	10	30'-4"	28'-7"	26'-7"	34'-5"	32'-5"	30'-2"	38'-1"	35'-11"	33'-5"
		20	15	28'-8"	26'-11"	24'-11"	32'-6"	30'-7"	28'-3"	36'-1"	33'-11"	31'-4"
		20	20	27'-4"	25'-7"	23'-7"	31'-0"	29'-1"	26'-9"	34'-4"	32'-2"	29'-8"
	Snow 115%	25	10	28'-9"	27'-2"	25'-4"	32'-7"	30'-10"	28'-9"	36'-2"	34'-2"	31'-10"
		25	15	27'-5"	25'-10"	23'-11"	31'-1"	29'-4"	27'-2"	34'-5"	32'-6"	30'-1"
		30	10	27'-6"	26'-0"	24'-4"	31'-2"	29'-7"	27'-7"	34'-6"	32'-9"	30'-7"
		30	15	26'-4"	24'-10"	23'-1"	29'-10"	28'-2"	26'-3"	33'-1"	31'-3"	29'-1"
		40	10	24'-11"	24'-0"	22'-8"	28'-4"	27'-2"	25'-9"	30'-11"	30'-0"	28'-6"
		40	15	24'-7"	23'-3"	21'-9"	27'-9"	26'-5"	24'-8"	28'-0"	26'-11"	25'-6"
		50	10	23'-1"	22'-2"	21'-1"	25'-7"	24'-11"	23'-11"	25'-9"	25'-2"	24'-4"
		50	15	23'-1"	22'-0"	20'-7"	23'-6"	22'-9"	21'-8"	23'-8"	22'-11"	21'-10"

Figure 6.63 Allowed spans for wood I-joists supporting roofs.

Assigment

A flat roof is to span 26 ft, subject to a dead load of 10 lb/ft², a snow live load of 15 lb/ft², and a non-snow live load of 40 lb/ft²; that is, the roof is being designed for human occupancy, rather than the occasional trip by a small number of people to inspect or repair the roof. Find a combination of I-joist and spacing that will work, using the allowed-load tables in Figures 6.59 and 6.60.

Figure 6.64 shows images of LVL. The data in Figure 6.65 are based on the allowed stress design. In other words, the allowable shear force (lb) and the allowable moment (ft-lb) are based on unfactored loads.

Example of Sizing LVL Beams

A plywood floor deck is to be supported by wood I-joists spanning L = 24 ft in simple-span mode. The loads are as follows:

$$p_{live} = 40 \text{ lb/ft}^2$$
$$p_{dead} = 20 \text{ lb/ft}^2$$

Single-loaded LVL girders spanning 24 ft supporting the ends of the I-joists that support the plywood deck. Assume the following uniformly distributed loads along the LVL:

$$w_{live} = p_{live} \cdot s = 40\frac{\#}{\text{ft}^2} \cdot 12 \text{ ft} = 480\frac{\#}{\text{ft}}$$

$$w_{dead} = p_{dead} \cdot s = 20\frac{\#}{\text{ft}^2} \cdot 12 \text{ ft} = 240\frac{\#}{\text{ft}}$$

$$w_{total} = 720\frac{\#}{\text{ft}}$$

In sizing for stiffness, assume that the deflection is $\Delta \le$ L/360 under the live load plus half the dead load. Table 6.2 presents the calculations for sizing the LVL beam.

6.2.4 GLUE-LAMINATED (GLULAM) WOOD BEAMS

Glulam members are very complex to design, as there are many options for width of member, depth of member, grades of wood in the core layers, grades of wood in the layers that are working substantially in compression, and grades of wood that are working substantially in tension. Furthermore, glulam members can be curved, which allows the fabrication of very elegant framed structures in which the effective bending depth of the glulam member varies in accordance with the intensity of the bending moment that must be resisted. Therefore, glulam members defy the reduction to simple load and span tables that is possible with solid-sawn lumber or wood I-joists. However, for simple-span beams, all the classic analytic methods of sizing for shear, moment, and deflection still apply to glulam beams. This section includes a few sizing exercises using simplified tables of properties.

In Table 6.3, the common-language names for the stress grades (lowest, moderate, good, best) were created for this particular text and do not represent titles of any official designating agency. However, for the purposes of this discussion, they will work well. The table gives material stiffness and design stresses (lb/in.²) for each grade. These design stresses are to be used with the load and resistance factor design (LRFD) method.

They are to be adjusted according the time effect factor, λ, as given in Table 6.4.

The data given represent a very simplified summary of the properties of glulam members, which can allow rapid and fairly accurate sizing of members used primarily in bending. The design and final sizing of glulam members is a very complex process, and the final sizing of all members should be done by an engineer with specialty training related to glulam timber design.

It is customary to use laminated decking in conjunction with glulam beams, since these materials are both structurally and visually appealing.

An Introduction to VERSA-LAM® Products

When you specify VERSA-LAM® laminated veneer headers/beams, you are building quality into your design. They are excellent as floor and roof framing supports or as headers for doors, windows, and garage doors and columns.

Figure 6.64 Laminated veneer lumber (LVL).

VERSA-LAM® Design Values

Grade	Width [in]	Depth [in]	Weight [lb/ft]	Allowable Shear [lb]	Allowable Moment [ft-lb]	Moment of Inertia [in⁴]
VERSA-LAM® 2.0 2800	1¾	3½	1.8	1164	956	6.3
		5½	2.8	1829	2245	24.3
		7¼	3.7	2411	3783	55.6
		9¼	4.7	3076	5994	115.4
		9½	4.8	3159	6304	125.0
		11¼	5.7	3741	8675	207.6
		11⅞	6.0	3948	9608	244.2
		14	7.1	4655	13112	400.2
		16	8.1	5320	16874	597.3
		18	9.1	5985	21079	850.5
		24	12.2	7980	36294	2016.0
VERSA-LAM® 2.0 3100	3½	5½	5.6	3658	4971	48.5
		7¼	7.4	4821	8377	111.1
		9¼	9.4	6151	13272	230.8
		9½	9.6	6318	13958	250.1
		11¼	11.4	7481	19210	415.3
		11⅞	12.1	7897	21275	488.4
		14	14.2	9310	29035	800.3
		16	16.2	10640	37364	1194.7
		18	18.3	11970	46674	1701.0
		20	20.3	13300	56952	2333.3
	5¼	5¼	8.0	5237	6830	63.3
		5½	8.4	5486	7457	72.8
		7¼	11.0	7232	12566	166.7
		9¼	14.1	9227	19908	346.3
		9½	14.5	9476	20937	375.1
		11¼	17.1	11222	28814	622.9
		11⅞	18.1	11845	31913	732.6
		14	21.3	13965	43552	1200.5
		16	24.4	15960	56046	1792.0
		18	27.4	17955	70011	2551.5
		20	30.4	19950	85428	3500.0
		24	36.5	23940	120549	6048.0

Grade	Width [in]	Depth [in]	Weight [lb/ft]	Allowable Shear [lb]	Allowable Moment [ft-lb]	Moment of Inertia [in⁴]
VERSA-LAM® 2.0 3100	7	9¼	16.6	12303	26544	461.7
		9½	17.1	12635	27916	500.1
		11¼	20.2	14963	38419	830.6
		11⅞	21.4	15794	42550	976.8
		14	25.2	18620	58069	1600.7
		16	28.8	21280	74728	2389.3
		18	32.4	23940	93348	3402.0
		20	36.0	26600	113904	4666.7
		24	43.2	31920	160732	8064.0

Design Property	VERSA-LAM® Beams		VERSA-LAM® Columns	VERSA-STUD® DF 1½"	VERSA-STUD® SP 1½"
	1¾"	1¾", 3½" & Wider			
Grade	2.0 2800	2.0 3100	1.7 2650	1.6 2250	2.0 3100 SP
Modulus of Elasticity $E(\times 10^6 \text{ psi})^{(1)}$	2.0	2.0	1.7	1.6	2.0
Bending F_b (psi)$^{(2)(3)}$	2800	3100	2650	2250	3100
Horizontal Shear F_v (psi)$^{(2)(4)}$	285	285	285	225	285
Tension Parallel to Grain F_t (psi)$^{(2)(5)}$	2150	2150	1650	1500	2150
Compression Parallel to Grain F_{cll} (psi)$^{(2)}$	3000	3000	3000	2500	3000
Compression Perpendicular to Grain F_{cll} (psi)$^{(1)(6)}$	750	750	750	525	750
Equivalent Specific Gravity for Fastener Design (SG)	0.5	0.5	0.5	0.42	0.5

1. This value cannot be adjusted for load duration.
2. This value is based upon a load duration of 100% and may be adjusted for other load durations.
3. Fiber stress bending value shall be multiplied by the depth factor, $(12/d)^{1/9}$ where d = member depth [in].
4. Stress applied perpendicular to the gluelines.
5. Tension value shall be multiplied by a length factor, $(4/L)^{1/8}$ where L = member length [ft]. Use L = 4 for members less than four feet long.
6. Stress applied parallel to the gluelines.

* Design properties are limited to dry conditions of use where the maximum moisture content of the material will not exceed 19%.

BUILDING CODE EVALUATION REPORT: ICC ESR 1040

Figure 6.65 Allowable shear force and moment in LVL.

Suppose nominal 3 in. laminated deck made of southern pine, constructed of continuous random lengths, is used in a flat roof to which we apply a deflection limit of L/240 to avoid ponding. Assume the LL/snow for the roof is 20 lb/ft² and that the dead weight of rigid insulation, recovery board, and waterproof membrane is 5 lb/ft².

The self-weight of the laminated decking is:

$$p_{deck} = \frac{D \cdot V}{A} = \frac{36\frac{\#}{ft^3}(ft^2)(2.25 \text{ in.})}{ft^2}\left[\frac{ft}{12 \text{ in.}}\right]$$

$$= \frac{6.75\,\#}{ft^2} \approx \frac{7\,\#}{ft^2}$$

The total unfactored load is $p_{total} = P_{deck} + P_{dead\ imposed} + p_{live} = (7 + 5 + 20)\text{lb/ft}^2 = 32$ lb/ft². As shown in Figure 6.52, giving spans for laminated decking, this roof deck system can span 13 ft from beam to beam. In this table, dead and live loads are both considered, even though the only governing issue is deflection. The reason that the dead load is included is that, for such a shallow spanning member, the phenomenon of creep can cause the deck to sag visibly under long-term loads. Thirteen feet is not a common beam spacing. Common modular spacings are 12 ft or 10 ft.

Suppose nominal 4 in. laminated deck made of southern pine, constructed of continuous random lengths, is used for a floor to which is applied a deflection limit

Table 6.2 Calculations for Sizing LVL Beams

Required Shear Force Capacity =	Required Moment Capacity =	Required X-sectional Stiffness
$V_r = \dfrac{w_{total}L}{2}$	$M_r = \dfrac{w_{total}L^2}{8}$	$I_r = \dfrac{(0.5w_{dead} + w_{live})L^3(360)}{384E}$
$= \dfrac{720\frac{\#}{ft}(24\,ft)}{2}$	$= 720\dfrac{\#}{ft}\dfrac{(24\,ft)(24\,ft)}{8}$	$= \dfrac{5(600)(24\,ft)(24\,ft)(24\,ft)(360)\frac{[12\text{ in.}]}{[ft]}\frac{[12\text{ in.}]}{[ft]}\frac{[\text{in.}^2]}{[\text{in.}^2]}}{384\left(2,000,000\frac{\#}{\text{in.}^2}\right)}$
$= 8,640\ \#$	$= 51,840\ \#\,ft$	$= 2,800\ \text{in.}^4$

Using the tables for $3\frac{1}{2}$ in.-wide Versa-Lam, what is the minimum cross-sectional depth required to safely resist the shear force?

Using the tables for $3\frac{1}{2}$ in.-wide Versa-Lam, what is the minimum cross-sectional depth required to the moment?

Using the tables for $5\frac{1}{4}$ in.-wide Versa-Lam, what is the minimum cross-sectional depth required to meet the stiffness criterion?

18 in.   20 in.   20 in.

Lightest section that works for all three issues: $5\frac{1}{4}$ in. $\times$ 20 in.

Table 6.3 Design Stress and Elastic Modulus for Glulam Beams, for Use with the LRFD Method

	Bending about the XX-Axis				Axial Loading		
Grade	F_B Bending Stress $\dfrac{\#}{\text{in.}^2}$	$F_{c\,perp}$ Compression Perpendicular to Grain $\dfrac{\#}{\text{in.}^2}$	F_v Shear Parallel to Grain $\dfrac{\#}{\text{in.}^2}$	E Material Stiffness $\dfrac{\#}{\text{in.}^2}$	F_t Tension Parallel to the Grain $\dfrac{\#}{\text{in.}^2}$	$F_{c\,parallel}$ Compression Parallel to the Grain $\dfrac{\#}{\text{in.}^2}$	E_c Material Stiffness $\dfrac{\#}{\text{in.}^2}$
Lowest	2,940	930	320	1,400,000	1,730	2,820	1,300,000
Moderate	3,670	930	320	1,500,000	1,730	2,920	1,400,000
Good	4,040	1,100	320	1,600,000	1,730	3,010	1,450,000
Best	4,400	1,100	320	1,700,000	1,900	3,110	1,500,000

Table 6.4 Time Effect Factor, λ, for Use with the LRFD Method with Glulam Beams

Load Combination	λ	
$1.2\,D + 1.6\,L + 1.6\,Lr$	0.7	when L is from storage
	0.8	when L is from occupancy
	1.25	when L is from impact
$1.2\,D + 1.6\,W +$		
$\quad 1.0\,L + 0.5\,Lr$	1.0	
$0.9\,D + 1.6\,W$	1.0	

Where:
$\quad D$ = dead load
$\quad L$ = live load
$\quad Lr$ = live/snow load on the roof
$\quad W$ = wind load

of L/360. Assume the live load for the floor is 100 lb/ft^2 and that the dead weight of ductwork and electric lighting is 2 lb/ft^2. According to the tables for sizing laminated decking, under a deflection limit of L/180, the decking can span 10 ft under a load of 212 lb/ft^2. Making the deflection limit L/360 cuts the deflection in half, which requires that the load be cut in half, to 106 lb/ft^2. This will not be quite enough to handle the combined effect of $p_{live} = 100$ lb/ft^2 and the self-weight of the deck, which is

$$p_{deck} = \frac{D \cdot V}{A} = \left(\frac{36\frac{\#}{ft^3}(ft^2)(3.0\text{ in.})}{ft^2}\right)\left[\frac{ft}{12\text{ in.}}\right]$$

$$= \frac{9\ \#}{ft^2}$$

However, with a slight relaxation of the deflection criterion, this deck will be sufficient to span 10 ft under the designated loads.

Example Sizing of Glulam Beams

Size glulam beams for the roof and floor of a two-story building.

- Column spacing is 30 ft in both directions.
- Roof joists are spaced 10 ft OC.
- Floor joists are spaced 10 ft OC.
- There are multiple bays, so that there are both perimeter and interior girders for both the roof and the floor.
- The best grade of glulam wood will be used, with the following design values: $F_v = 320$ lb/in.^{2}, $F_B = 4400$ lb/in.^{2}, $E = 1,700,000$ lb/in.^{2}.

For the roof, the loads will be:

$$p_{dead} = 12\frac{\#}{ft^2} \quad and \quad p_{live} = 20\frac{\#}{ft^2}$$

The roof joists will be subjected to the following factored applied loads:

$$w_{factored} = p_{factored} \cdot s = \left(\frac{1.2p_{dead} + 1.6p_{live}}{\lambda}\right) \cdot s$$

$$= \left(\frac{1.2\left(12\frac{\#}{ft^2}\right) + 1.6\left(20\frac{\#}{ft^2}\right)}{0.8}\right) \cdot 10ft = 580\frac{\#}{ft^2}$$

The roof joists will also have to safely support their own self-weight, with a load factor of 1.2.

In accounting for deflection in glulam beams, it is customary to use the live load plus half the dead load for dry wood and the total load for wood subjected to the weather. For the glulam roof beams:

$$0.5w_{dead} + w_{live} = \left(0.5p_{dead} + p_{live}\right) \cdot s$$

$$= \left(0.5\left(12\frac{\#}{ft^2}\right) + 1\left(20\frac{\#}{ft^2}\right)\right) \cdot 10ft = 260\frac{\#}{ft}$$

Half of the self-weight of the glulam roof joists will also have to be included with the applied load shown here.

For the floor, the loads will be as follows:

$$p_{dead} = 11\frac{\#}{ft^2} \quad and \quad p_{live} = 100\frac{\#}{ft^2}$$

The floor joists will be subjected to the following factored applied loads:

$$w_{factored} = p_{factored} \cdot s = \left(\frac{1.2p_{dead} + 1.6p_{live}}{\lambda}\right) \cdot s$$

$$= \left(\frac{1.2\left(11\frac{\#}{ft^2}\right) + 1.6\left(100\frac{\#}{ft^2}\right)}{0.8}\right) \cdot 10ft = 2,165\frac{\#}{ft^2}$$

The floor joists will also have to safely support their own self-weight, with a load factor of 1.2.

The following loads will be used to account for the deflection of the floor joists:

$$0.5w_{dead} + w_{live} = \left(0.5p_{dead} + p_{live}\right) \cdot s$$

$$= \left(0.5\left(12\frac{\#}{ft^2}\right) + 1\left(100\frac{\#}{ft^2}\right)\right) \cdot 10ft = 1060\frac{\#}{ft}$$

Half of the self-weight of the glulam roof joists will also have to be included with the applied load shown here.

The formulas for A_r, S_r, and I_r for a simple-span beam subjected to a uniform load are the same for glulam beams as for solid-sawn beams. In this book, the manner

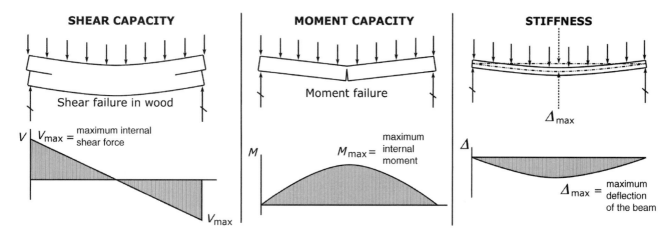

Figure 6.66 Modes of failure of glulam wood beams.

in which those computations are carried out will vary between the two materials in the following ways:

1. For solid-sawn beams, we will assume an approximate, but conservative value for the dead weight of the floor being supported by solid-sawn beams. A common value is $p_{dead} = 10$ lb/ft^2 for the total floor construction, including the beams. (There is the option to size the beams and then recalculate the total dead weight as a way of saving money by downsizing the beams. However, in practice this is almost never done.)

2. For glulam beams, the self-weight and the cost are often significant enough to justify performing the calculations in an iterative manner, to account more precisely for the self-weight of the glulam beams, thereby ensuring that the beams are not significantly oversized.

The modes of failure of a glulam beam are shown in Figure 6.66 and the equations governing the design are shown in Table 6.5.

To size the joists, perimeter girders, and interior girders, in both the roof and the floor of the structural grid, the equations in Table 6.5 have been incorporated into a spreadsheet calculation, the results of which are contained in Figure 6.67, 6.68, and 6.69. Students are encouraged to verify the computations in the spreadsheet. This spreadsheet file is included in the digital supplement and should be examined after a good-faith effort is made to work out the spreadsheet independently. In the

spreadsheet, more than one thickness of glulam member is considered. All of the dimensions in the spreadsheet are for Eastern Species glulams. The spreadsheet can be easily modified to accommodate Western Species dimensions. In the tables in Figures 6.67, 6.68, and 6.69, the self-weight of the beam is accounted for iteratively, with the self-weight in each calculation being based on the size of the beam that emerged in the previous calculation. The load $w_{factored}$ is the initial factored load from the live load and the decking plus the beam self-weight, based on the beam cross-sectional area calculated in the preceding step. For example, the roof joist, iteration-1, factored $w_{factored}$ is calculated in the following manner:

$$580\frac{\#}{ft} + \frac{1.2w_{beam}}{0.8} = 580\frac{\#}{ft} + \frac{1.2A_{beam} \cdot D_{beam}}{0.8}$$

$$= 580\frac{\#}{ft} + \left(\frac{1.2 \cdot 40.78 \text{ in.}^2}{0.8}\right)\left[\frac{ft}{12 \text{ in.}}\right]\left[\frac{ft}{12 \text{ in.}}\right]\left(35\frac{\#}{ft^3}\right)$$

$$= 594.9\frac{\#}{ft}$$

For each beam, three iterations are performed. In every case, the second and third iterations produce the same required cross-sectional area to three significant figures, indicating that the iterative calculation has converged. Once the spreadsheet is set up to perform iterative computations, they can be executed essentially at the push of a button. Furthermore, once the spreadsheet

---

Table 6.5 Computations for Sizing Glulam Beams

$$V_{max} = \frac{w_{factored}L}{2} \qquad M_{max} = \frac{w_{factored}L^2}{8} \qquad \Delta_{max} = \frac{5(0.5w_{dead} + w_{live})L^4}{384\,EI}$$

$$E = \text{material stiffness}$$
$$I = \text{cross-sectional stiffness}$$

For a beam of rectangular cross section:

$$A_r = \frac{3V_{max}}{2F_v} \qquad\qquad S_r = \frac{M_{max}}{F_B} \qquad\qquad I_r = \frac{5(0.5w_{dead} + w_{live})L^4}{384E\Delta_{max}}$$

$$= \frac{\frac{3w_{factored}L}{2}}{2F_v} \qquad\qquad = \frac{\frac{w_{factored}L^2}{8}}{F_B} \qquad\qquad = \frac{5(0.5w_{dead} + w_{live})L^3}{384E} \cdot \frac{L}{\Delta_{max}}$$

$$= \frac{3w_{factored}L}{4F_v} \qquad\qquad = \frac{w_{factored}L^2}{8F_B} \qquad\qquad = \frac{5(0.5w_{dead} + w_{live})L^3(360)}{384E}$$

Shear strength design

$$A = \frac{3w_T L}{4F_V}$$

	s	p_D	p_L	Factored w*	L	Design Shear Stress F_V	A	h for b=3.125"	h for b=5.125"	h for b=6.75"	h for b=8.75"	h for b=10.75"
	ft	#/ft²	#/ft²	#/ft	ft	#/in.²	in.²			h=A/b in.		
Roof Joists	10	12	20	580.0	30	320	40.78	13.05	7.96	6.04	4.66	3.79
Iteration 1				594.9			41.83	13.38	8.16	6.20	4.78	3.89
Iteration 2				595.2			41.85	13.39	8.17	6.20	4.78	3.89
Iteration 3				595.3			**41.85**	**13.39**	**8.17**	**6.20**	**4.78**	**3.89**
Roof Single Girder	15	12	20	892.9	30	320	62.78	20.09	12.25	9.30	7.18	5.84
Iteration 1				915.8			64.39	20.61	12.56	9.54	7.36	5.99
Iteration 2				916.4			64.43	20.62	12.57	9.55	7.36	5.99
Iteration 3				916.4			**64.43**	**20.62**	**12.57**	**9.55**	**7.36**	**5.99**
Roof Double Girder	30	12	20	1785.8	30	320	125.56	40.18	24.50	18.60	14.35	11.68
Iteration 1				1831.6			128.78	41.21	25.13	19.08	14.72	11.98
Iteration 2				1832.7			128.86	41.24	25.14	19.09	14.73	11.99
Iteration 3				1832.8			**128.87**	**41.24**	**25.14**	**19.09**	**14.73**	**11.99**
Floor Joists	10	11	100	2165.0	30	320	152.23	48.71	29.70	22.55	17.40	14.16
Iteration 1				2220.5			156.13	49.96	30.46	23.13	17.84	14.52
Iteration 2				2221.9			156.23	49.99	30.48	23.15	17.85	14.53
Iteration 3				2222.0			**156.23**	**49.99**	**30.48**	**23.15**	**17.86**	**14.53**
Floor Single Girder	15	11	100	3332.9	30	320	234.35	74.99	45.73	34.72	26.78	21.80
Iteration 1				3418.4			240.35	76.91	46.90	35.61	27.47	22.36
Iteration 2				3420.6			240.51	76.96	46.93	35.63	27.49	22.37
Iteration 3				3420.6			**240.51**	**76.96**	**46.93**	**35.63**	**27.49**	**22.37**
Floor Double Girder	30	11	100	6665.9	30	320	468.69	149.98	91.45	69.44	53.57	43.60
Iteration 1				6836.8			480.71	153.83	93.80	71.22	54.94	44.72
Iteration 2				6841.1			481.02	153.93	93.86	71.26	54.97	44.75
Iteration 3				6841.2			**481.03**	**153.93**	**93.86**	**71.26**	**54.97**	**44.75**

Figure 6.67 Sizing the glulam beams in the roof and floor to account for shear strength.

Moment strength design

$$S = \frac{w_T L^2}{8F_B} \frac{[12"]}{[ft]}$$

	s	p_D	p_L	Factored w_T	L	Design Moment Stress F_B	S	h for b=3.125"	h for b=5.125"	h for b=6.75"	h for b=8.75"	h for b=10.75"
	ft	#/ft²	#/ft²	#/ft	ft	#/in.²	in.³			$h=(6S/b)^{0.5}$ in.		
Roof Joists	10	12	20	580.0	30	4400	178.0	18.48	14.43	12.58	11.05	9.97
Iteration 1				619.1			189.9	19.10	14.91	12.99	11.41	10.30
Iteration 2				620.4			190.3	19.12	14.93	13.01	11.42	10.31
Iteration 3				**620.4**			**190.3**	**19.12**	**14.93**	**13.01**	**11.42**	**10.31**
Roof Single Girder	15	12	20	800.1	30	4400	245.5	21.71	16.95	14.77	12.97	11.71
Iteration 1				846.0			259.6	22.32	17.43	15.19	13.34	12.04
Iteration 2				847.3			260.0	22.34	17.45	15.20	13.35	12.05
Iteration 3				**847.3**			**260.0**	**22.34**	**17.45**	**15.20**	**13.35**	**12.05**
Roof Double Girder	30	12	20	1600.2	30	4400	491.0	30.70	23.97	20.89	18.35	16.55
Iteration 1				1665.1			510.9	31.32	24.46	21.31	18.72	16.89
Iteration 2				1666.4			511.3	31.33	24.47	21.32	18.72	16.89
Iteration 3				**1666.4**			**511.3**	**31.33**	**24.47**	**21.32**	**18.72**	**16.89**
Floor Joists	10	11	100	1732.0	30	4400	531.4	31.94	24.94	21.73	19.09	17.22
Iteration 1				1799.5			552.1	32.56	25.42	22.15	19.46	17.55
Iteration 2				1800.8			552.5	32.57	25.43	22.16	19.46	17.56
Iteration 3				**1800.8**			**552.5**	**32.57**	**25.43**	**22.16**	**19.46**	**17.56**
Floor Single Girder	15	11	100	2900.2	30	4400	889.8	41.33	32.28	28.12	24.70	22.29
Iteration 1				2987.5			916.6	41.95	32.76	28.54	25.07	22.62
Iteration 2				2988.8			917.0	41.96	32.77	28.55	25.08	22.62
Iteration 3				**2988.8**			**917.0**	**41.96**	**32.77**	**28.55**	**25.08**	**22.62**
Floor Double Girder	30	11	100	5800.3	30	4400	1779.6	58.45	45.65	39.77	34.93	31.52
Iteration 1				5923.8			1817.5	59.07	46.13	40.19	35.30	31.85
Iteration 2				5925.2			1817.9	59.08	46.13	40.20	35.31	31.85
Iteration 3				**5925.2**			**1817.9**	**59.08**	**46.13**	**40.20**	**35.31**	**31.85**

Figure 6.68 Sizing the glulam beams in the roof and floor to account for moment strength.

Deflection (stiffness design) $I = \dfrac{5(w_L+.5w_D)L^3(L/\Delta)\,[12"]\,[12"]}{384E\,[\text{ft}]\,[\text{ft}]}$								$h=(12I/b)^{0.3333}$ in.				
	s	p_D	p_L	w_L+ $0.5w_D$	L	L	E	I	h for	h for	h for	h for	h for
	ft	#/ft²	#/ft²	#/ft	ft	Δ	#/in.²	in.⁴	b=3.125"	b=5.125"	b=6.75"	b=8.75"	b=10.75"
Roof Joists	**10**	**12**	**20**	**260.0**	**30**	**240**	**1700000**	1858	19.25	16.32	14.89	13.66	12.75
Iteration 1				276.7				1977	19.65	16.66	15.20	13.94	13.02
Iteration 2				277.0				1980	19.66	16.67	15.21	13.95	13.02
Iteration 3				**277.0**				**1980**	**19.66**	**16.67**	**15.21**	**13.95**	**13.02**
Roof Single Girder	**15**	**12**	**20**	**415.5**	**30**	**240**	**1700000**	2970	22.50	19.08	17.41	15.97	14.91
Iteration 1				435.0				3109	22.85	19.37	17.68	16.21	15.14
Iteration 2				435.3				3111	22.85	19.38	17.68	16.21	15.14
Iteration 3				**435.3**				**3111**	**22.85**	**19.38**	**17.68**	**16.21**	**15.14**
Roof Double Girder	**30**	**12**	**20**	**831.0**	**30**	**240**	**1700000**	5939	28.35	24.04	21.93	20.11	18.78
Iteration 1				855.6				6115	28.63	24.27	22.15	20.31	18.96
Iteration 2				855.8				6117	28.63	24.28	22.15	20.31	18.97
Iteration 3				**855.8**				**6117**	**28.63**	**24.28**	**22.15**	**20.31**	**18.97**
Floor Joists	**10**	**11**	**100**	**1055.0**	**30**	**360**	**1700000**	11310	35.14	29.80	27.18	24.93	23.28
Iteration 1				1085.4				11636	35.47	30.08	27.44	25.17	23.50
Iteration 2				1085.7				11639	35.48	30.08	27.44	25.17	23.50
Iteration 3				**1085.7**				**11639**	**35.48**	**30.08**	**27.44**	**25.17**	**23.50**
Floor Single Girder	**15**	**11**	**100**	**1628.6**	**30**	**360**	**1700000**	17459	40.61	34.44	31.42	28.81	26.90
Iteration 1				1663.7				17836	40.90	34.68	31.64	29.02	27.09
Iteration 2				1664.0				17839	40.90	34.68	31.64	29.02	27.10
Iteration 3				**1664.0**				**17839**	**40.90**	**34.68**	**31.64**	**29.02**	**27.10**
Floor Double Girder	**30**	**11**	**100**	**3257.1**	**30**	**360**	**1700000**	34918	51.16	43.39	39.58	36.30	33.89
Iteration 1				3301.4				35393	51.39	43.58	39.76	36.46	34.05
Iteration 2				3301.6				35395	51.39	43.58	39.76	36.47	34.05
Iteration 3				**3301.6**				**35395**	**51.4**	**43.6**	**39.8**	**36.5**	**34.0**

Figure 6.69 Sizing the glulam beams in the roof and floor to account for stiffness.

has been created, it becomes a template that can be used repeatedly to perform sizing calculations.

The self-weight of the joists must be accounted for in the load on the girders. To do this, use the following factored formula:

$$\left(\frac{1.2}{0.8}\right)w_{\text{joists on girder}} = \left(\frac{1.2}{0.8}\right)s_{\text{girder}} \cdot p_{\text{joists}}$$

$$= \left(\frac{1.2}{0.8}\right)s_{\text{girder}} \cdot \frac{w_{\text{self-joists}}}{s_{\text{joists}}}$$

For the roof single girder, the factored load from decking and live load would be

$$w_{\text{factored}} = p_{\text{factored}} \cdot s = \left(\frac{1.2p_{\text{dead}}+1.6p_{\text{live}}}{\lambda}\right) \cdot s$$

$$= \left(\frac{1.2\left(12\frac{\#}{\text{ft}^2}\right)+1.6\left(20\frac{\#}{\text{ft}^2}\right)}{0.8}\right) \cdot 15\text{ft} = 870\frac{\#}{\text{ft}^2}$$

and the load from the joists would be

$$\left(\frac{1.2}{0.8}\right)w_{\text{joists on girder}} = \left(\frac{1.2}{0.8}\right)s_{\text{girder}} \cdot p_{\text{joists}}$$

$$= \left(\frac{1.2}{0.8}\right)s_{\text{girder}} \cdot \frac{w_{\text{self-joists}}}{s_{\text{joists}}} = \left(\frac{1.2}{0.8}\right) \cdot 15\text{ft} \cdot \frac{A_{\text{joist}} \cdot D_{\text{joist}}}{10\,\text{ft}}$$

$$= \left(\frac{1.2}{0.8}\right) \cdot 15\text{ft} \cdot \frac{41.85 \text{ in.}^2 \cdot \frac{35\ \#}{\text{ft}^3}\left[\frac{\text{ft}}{12\ \text{in.}}\right]\left[\frac{\text{ft}}{12\ \text{in.}}\right]}{10\,\text{ft}}$$

$$= 22.9\frac{\#}{\text{ft}}$$

The total starting factored load on the girder will be

$870\frac{\#}{\text{ft}} + 22.9\frac{\#}{\text{ft}} = 892.9\frac{\#}{\text{ft}}$, as shown in the spreadsheet.

In the tables in Figures 6.67, 6.68, and 6.69, the self-weight of the beam technically needs to be calculated for each beam base b and corresponding height h, because the cross-sectional area and weight will vary according to the width b. This is a result of the fact that narrow, deep beams are more efficient in generating resisting moment than are wide, shallow beams. However, to avoid making the spreadsheet unduly elaborate, it is

Final Solution for each beam:

Legend for this table:
Controlled by shear stress
Controlled by bending stress
Controlled by deflection

	h	h	h	h	h
Roof Joists	*19.66*	*16.67*	*15.21*	*13.95*	*13.02*
Roof Single Girder	*22.85*	*19.38*	*17.68*	*16.21*	*15.14*
Roof Double Girder	**41.24**	*25.14*	*22.15*	*20.31*	*18.97*
Floor Joists	**49.99**	*30.48*	*27.44*	*25.17*	*23.50*
Floor Single Girder	**76.96**	*46.93*	*35.63*	*29.02*	*27.10*
Floor Double Girder	**153.93**	*93.86*	**71.26**	**54.97**	*44.75*

Figure 6.70 Summary of sizing operations for the 30 ft-long glulam beams.

possible to account for the beam self-weight by using the heaviest beam to update the factored total load. The heaviest beam will always be the one for which $b = 10.75$ in. Using this approximation, the self-weight of the narrower beams will be slightly overestimated and those beams will be slightly oversized. The error made in this approximation is typically quite small. As an example computation, the roof-joist, iteration-1, factored w_{total} is calculated in the following manner:

$$580\frac{\#}{ft} + \frac{1.2 w_{beam}}{0.8} = 580\frac{\#}{ft} + \frac{1.2 A_{beam} \cdot D_{beam}}{0.8}$$

$$= 580\frac{\#}{ft} + \frac{1.2 \cdot 10.75 \text{ in.} \cdot h \cdot D_{beam}}{0.8}$$

$$= 580\frac{\#}{ft} + \left(\frac{1.2 \cdot 10.75 \text{ in.} \cdot 9.97 \text{ in.}^2}{0.8}\right)$$

$$\left[\frac{ft}{12 \text{ in.}}\right]\left[\frac{ft}{12 \text{ in.}}\right]\left(35\frac{\#}{ft^3}\right)$$

$$= 619.1\frac{\#}{ft}$$

Observations about the results of the sizing for glulam beams of the best grade, for which design bending stress $= F_B = 4400$ lb/in.^{2}, include the following:

- The material property that is most sensitive to the grade of material is F_B.
- For this high grade of material, bending stress does not control the sizing of any of the beams.
- For a lower grade of material, we would expect F_B to control in many more cases.
- The heavier the loads, the deeper the beams are.
- Deep beams are controlled by shear.
- Shallow beams are controlled by deflection.
- Bending stress has the greatest likelihood of controlling the size of the beams for beams of intermediate proportions, although, for this very high grade of wood, F_B does not control the sizing of any of the beam.
- For heavily loaded beams, the 3 in.-wide glulams are absurdly deep.
- For the most heavily loaded floor girders, even the 10.5 in.-wide glulams may be regarded as too deep.

- These beams need to be 44.75 in. deep, which is a depth $d = 0.144$ L = L/8.04.
- Typically, something closer to $d = 0.05$ L = L/20 is preferred.
- For these double-loaded girders, it may be desirable to double up two single-loaded 8.75 in. glulams.

Based on these results, what should the guidelines be for glulam beams in the spans and proportions guidelines in Chapter 1?

In every case, the governing depth would have to be rounded up to the nearest multiple of $1\frac{3}{8}$ in. to get the actual depth of the glulam beam in the Eastern Species system.

6.3 Steel Beams

6.3.1 CORRUGATED STEEL DECKING

6.3.1.1 Selecting Corrugated Steel Decking for the Roof

Assume that a roof is to be constructed of single-ply membrane on top of recovery board, on top of 4 in.-thick rigid Styrofoam insulation, on top of galvanized corrugated steel decking that is supported by steel truss joists. The spacing of the truss joists determines how far the decking must span. Typically, a designer wants the joists spaced far enough apart that the number and cost of the truss joists is not excessive, but close enough that the decking can span efficiently and so that the unbraced length of the chord members on the truss girders is not excessive. (The truss joists rest on panel points of the truss girders and that the length of the top chord of the truss girder must equal the spacing of the truss joists.) Five feet is generally a good spacing to choose, as it is a modular subdivision of common modular column grids, such as 30 ft, 40 ft, 50 ft, and 60 ft. However, the architect and engineer must work together to identify all the relevant architectural and structural factors that go into deciding on a joist spacing. For example, if at some point in the building there is a need for a 6 ft-wide stair to penetrate the floor, then it is not unreasonable to make all of the joist spacing consistent with the spacing required to accommodate the stair penetration (see Figure 6.71).

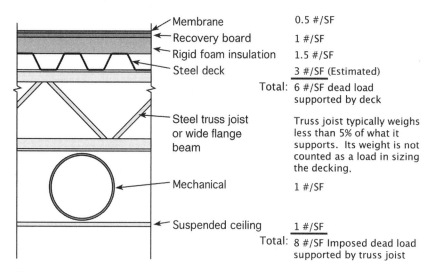

Membrane   0.5 #/SF

Recovery board   1 #/SF

Rigid foam insulation   1.5 #/SF

Steel deck   3 #/SF (Estimated)

Total: 6 #/SF dead load supported by deck

Steel truss joist or wide flange beam

Truss joist typically weighs less than 5% of what it supports. Its weight is not counted as a load in sizing the decking.

Mechanical   1 #/SF

Suspended ceiling   1 #/SF

Total: 8 #/SF Imposed dead load supported by truss joist

Figure 6.71 Typical roof decking construction in steel-frame buildings.

Figures 6.72 and 6.73 can be used to select corrugated steel roof decking. These tables give allowed total unfactored loads. The 1.5 in.-deep decking tends to be a little less expensive than 3.0 in.-deep decking, so unless there is some fairly compelling motive for using 3 in.-deep corrugations, we will stick to the shallower corrugations. The tables give construction limits, having to do with safety for the construction workers, and service load limits, having to do with how the building will perform after construction is complete. Construction safety issues often dictate the required strength of the decking.

The total load on the decking will be as follows:

$$\text{live/snow load} + \text{estimated dead load} = 20\frac{\#}{ft} + 6\frac{\#}{ft} = 26\frac{\#}{ft}$$

An examination of the tables for 1.5 in.-deep corrugations (both 1.5 B and 1.5 F) indicates that, in a three-span situation, all gauges of decking will safely support the 26 lb/ft² for a spacing between joists of 5 ft and that all gauges are serviceable under construction loads. The lightest decking is 24 gauge, weighing 1.46 lb/ft² in the galvanized version. To be conservative in calculating the loads on the roof trusses, the designer usually assumes that the total dead load of the membrane, recovery board, rigid insulation, steel decking, mechanical, and suspended ceiling is about 10 lb/ft². This slightly conservative number covers a multitude of possible misestimates in the elements listed. For construction done for many state governments, an additional 10 lb/ft² of dead load is added as a further measure of safety and to provide flexibility in future renovations.

Assignment

Under the 10 lb/ft² dead load and 20 lb/ft² live load, for both single-span and three-span decking, accounting for both construction load and service load:

- Find the longest span for 1.5 B decking. What is the depth–span ratio?
- Find the longest span for 1.5 F decking. What is the depth–span ratio?
- Find the longest span for 3.0 N decking. What is the depth–span ratio?
- How do these results compare with the spans and proportions for corrugated steel decking listed in Chapter 1?

6.3.2 SELECTING COMPOSITE CONCRETE/ CORRUGATED STEEL FLOOR DECKING

The superimposed live load for standard office spaces is prescribed to be 80 pounds per square foot of floor. However, for circulation areas, the live load is prescribed to be 100 pounds per square foot. In a speculative office building, where floor plans can be arranged in a variety of ways, it is not always clear what parts of this floor will be subjected to 100 pounds per square foot and which parts 80 pounds per square foot. A designer can be cautious by assuming 100 pounds per square foot everywhere. The cost penalty of doing this initially is small as compared with upgrading from 80 pounds per square foot to 100 pounds per square foot after the building is already constructed.

The tables in Figures 6.74, 6.75, 6.76, and 6.77 are for composite floor construction, consisting of concrete on top of corrugated steel decking. Figure 6.74 addresses 1.5 in.-deep corrugated decking with normal weight concrete. Figure 6.75 continues Figure 6.74, addressing 1.5 in.-deep corrugated decking in composite action with lightweight concrete. Figure 6.76 addresses 3 in.-deep corrugated decking in composite action with normal weight concrete. Figure 6.77 continues Figure 6.76,

ᐯULCRAFT

1.5 B, BI, BA, BIA

Maximum Sheet Length 42'-0
Extra Charge for Lengths Under 6'-0
Factory Mutual Approved (No. 0C847.AM, 0G1A4.AM, and 3Y1A6.AM) **
ICBO Approved (No.3415)

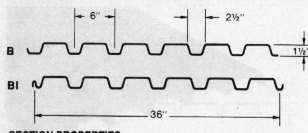

Type B (wide rib) deck provides excellent structural load carrying capacity per pound of steel utilized, and its nestable design eliminates the need for die-set ends.

1" or more rigid insulation is required for Type B deck.

Acoustical deck (Type BA, BIA) is particularly suitable in structures such as auditoriums, schools, and theatres where sound control is desirable. Acoustic perforations are located in the vertical webs where the load carrying properties are negligibly affected (less than 5%).

Inert, non-organic glass fiber sound absorbing batts are placed in the rib openings to absorb up to 65% of the sound striking the deck.

Batts are field installed and may require separation.

SECTION PROPERTIES

Deck Type	Design Thick.	Weight (PSF) Ptd.	Weight (PSF) Galv.	I in⁴/ft	Sp in³/ft	Sn in³/ft	Fy KSI
B24	0.0239	1.36	1.46	0.121	0.120	0.131	60
B22	0.0295	1.68	1.78	0.169	0.186	0.192	33
B21	0.0329	1.87	1.97	0.192	0.213	0.221	33
B20	0.0358	2.04	2.14	0.212	0.234	0.247	33
B19	0.0418	2.39	2.49	0.253	0.277	0.289	33
B18	0.0474	2.72	2.82	0.292	0.318	0.327	33
B16	0.0598	3.44	3.54	0.373	0.408	0.411	33

ACOUSTICAL INFORMATION

Deck Type	Absorption Coefficient 125	250	500	1000	2000	4000	Noise Reduction Coefficient*
1.5BA, 1.5BIA	.11	.20	.63	1.04	.66	.36	.65

* Source: Riverbank Acoustical Laboratories — RAL™ A94–185.
Test was conducted with 1.5 inches of 1.65 pcf fiberglass insulation on 3 inch EPS Plaza deck for the SDI.

[handwritten: steel decking institute.]

[handwritten: For roof: Dead is always 20#/ft². Live is always 20#/ft². So Dead + live = 40#/ft².]

VERTICAL LOADS FOR TYPE 1.5B

No. of Spans	Deck Type	Max. SDI Const. Span	Allowable Total (Dead + Live) Uniform Load (PSF) — Span (ft.-in.) C. to C. of Support 5'-0	5'-6	6'-0	6'-6	7'-0	7'-6	8'-0	8'-6	9'-0	9'-6	10'-0
1	B 24	4'-8	66	52	42	36	30	27	24	21	20		
	B 22	5'-7	91	71	57	47	40	34	30	27	24	22	20
	B 21	6'-0	104	81	64	53	44	38	33	29	26	24	22
	B 20	6'-5	115	89	71	58	48	41	36	31	28	25	23
	B 19	7'-1	139	107	85	69	57	48	41	36	32	29	26
	B 18	7'-8	162	124	98	79	65	55	47	41	36	32	29
	B 16	8'-8	206	157	123	99	81	68	58	50	44	39	34
2	B 24	5'-10	126	104	87	74	64	55	47	41	36	32	29
	B 22	6'-11	102	85	71	61	52	46	40	35	32	28	26
	B 21	7'-4	118	97	82	70	60	52	46	41	36	33	29
	B 20	7'-9	132	109	91	78	67	59	51	46	41	36	33
	B 19	8'-5	154	127	107	91	79	69	60	53	48	43	39
	B 18	9'-1	174	144	121	103	89	78	68	60	54	48	44
	B 16	10'-3	219	181	152	130	112	97	86	76	68	61	55
3	B 24	5'-10	130	100	79	65	54	45	39	34	31	27	25
	B 22	6'-11	128	106	89	76	65	57	50	44	39	34	31
	B 21	7'-4	147	122	102	87	75	65	56	49	42	38	34
	B 20	7'-9	165	136	114	97	84	72	61	53	46	41	36
	B 19	8'-5	193	159	134	114	98	84	71	61	53	47	41
	B 18	9'-1	218	180	151	129	111	96	81	69	60	52	46
	B 16	10'-3	274	226	190	162	140	119	100	85	73	64	56

Notes: 1. Load tables are calculated using sectional properties based on the steel design thickness shown in the Steel Deck Institute (SDI) Design Manual.
      2. Loads shown in the shaded areas are governed by the live load deflection not in excess of 1/240 of the span. A dead load of 10 PSF has been included.
      3. ** Acoustical Deck is not covered under Factory Mutual

Figure 6.72 Allowed loads on 1.5 in.-deep corrugated steel roof decking.

3 N, NI, NA, NIA

Maximum Sheet Length 42'-0
Extra Charge for Lengths Under 6'-0
ICBO Approved (No.3415)

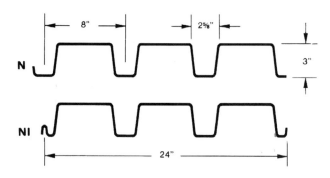

Acoustical deck (Type 3 NA, NIA) is particularly suitable in structures such as auditoriums, schools and theaters where sound control is desirable. Acoustic perforations are located in the vertical webs where the load carrying properties are negligibly affected (less than 5%).

Inert, non-organic glass fiber sound absorbing batts are placed in the rib openings to absorb up to 70% of the sound striking the deck.

Batts are field installed and may require separation.

SECTION PROPERTIES

Deck Type	Design Thick.	Weight (PSF) Ptd.	Weight (PSF) Galv.	I in⁴/ft	Sp in³/ft	Sn in³/ft	Fy KSI
N22	0.0295	2.16	2.26	0.772	0.382	0.433	33
N21	0.0329	2.40	2.50	0.876	0.445	0.497	33
N20	0.0358	2.61	2.71	0.964	0.501	0.552	33
N19	0.0418	3.05	3.15	1.153	0.597	0.659	33
N18	0.0474	3.46	3.56	1.334	0.688	0.749	33
N16	0.0598	4.36	4.46	1.745	0.893	0.944	33

ACOUSTICAL INFORMATION

Deck Type	Absorption Coefficient 125	250	500	1000	2000	4000	Noise Reduction Coefficient*
3NA, 3NIA	.14	.36	.89	.95	.53	.34	.70

* Source: Riverbank Acoustical Laboratories — RAL™ A95–21.
Test was conducted with 3 inches of 1.65 pcf fiberglass insulation on 3 inch EPS Plaza deck for the SDI.

VERTICAL LOADS FOR TYPE 3N

No. of Spans	Deck Type	Max. SDI Const. Span	Allowable Total (Dead + Live) Uniform Load (PSF) Span (ft.-in.) C. to C. of Support 10'-0	10'-6	11'-0	11'-6	12'-0	12'-6	13'-0	13'-6	14'-0	14'-6	15'-0
1	N22	11'-7	51	46	42	38	35	32	30	28	26	24	23
	N21	12'-5	59	53	47	43	39	36	33	30	28	26	25
	N20	13'-2	66	58	52	47	42	38	35	33	30	28	26
	N19	14'-7	79	69	61	55	50	45	41	38	35	32	30
	N18	15'-11	91	80	71	63	57	52	47	43	40	37	34
	N16	18'-6	119	105	93	83	74	66	60	55	50	46	43
2	N22	14'-9	58	52	48	44	40	37	34	32	29	27	26
	N21	15'-9	66	60	55	50	46	42	39	36	34	32	29
	N20	16'-6	74	67	61	56	51	47	44	40	38	35	33
	N19	18'-1	88	80	73	66	61	56	52	48	45	42	39
	N18	19'-5	100	91	83	76	69	64	59	55	51	47	44
	N16	22'-3	126	114	104	95	87	81	74	69	64	60	56
3	N22	14'-9	70	65	60	55	50	46	43	40	37		
	N21	15'-9	83	75	68	63	58	53	49	45	42		
	N20	16'-6	92	83	76	70	64	59	54	50	47		
	N19	18'-1	110	100	91	83	76	70	65	60	56		
	N18	19'-5	125	113	103	94	87	80	74	68	64		
	N16	22'-3	157	143	130	119	109	101	93	86	80		

Notes: 1. Load tables are calculated using sectional properties based on the steel design thickness shown in the Steel Deck Institute (SDI) Design Manual.
2. Loads shown in the shaded areas are governed by the live load deflection not in excess of 1/240 of the span. A dead load of 10 PSF has been included.
3. 3N, NI, NA, NIA are not covered under Factory Mutual.

Figure 6.73 Allowed loads on 3.0 in.-deep corrugated steel roof decking.

addressing 3 in.-deep corrugated decking in composite action with lightweight concrete. Conditions of support for decking are divided into three cases:

One span: The decking spans only from one supporting joist to the next supporting joist (i.e., simple span).

Two spans: The decking is supported by a joist at each end and is continuous across one interior joist.

Three or more spans: The decking is supported by a joist at each end and is continuous across at least two interior joists.

Continuity of the decking over interior support joists reduces deflection and increases the load-carrying capability of the corrugated deck while it is supporting the uncured concrete.

Thin corrugated steel decking is vulnerable to local buckling while it is supporting the uncured concrete. After the concrete has cured, the concrete braces the thin metal sheet, inhibiting buckling and allowing substantial additional load to be supported. The concrete also works in composite action with the steel decking, significantly increasing both the effective structural depth of the composite floor and the amount of material absorbing the stress. The composite of steel decking plus concrete is able to span much farther and support more weight than the steel decking by itself. The vulnerability of the thin steel sheet to buckling while the concrete is curing is a major limitation to the practical spans that can be achieved with the decking. This buckling problem can be addressed by putting in temporary supports (shoring) while the concrete is curing. However, the use of shoring adds substantially to the cost of construction, and normally it is avoided by either choosing a heavier gauge of corrugated steel or selecting a joist spacing that is small enough to allow the corrugated steel to safely support the concrete across that span. The decking comes in lengths up to 42 ft, which allows the possibility of continuous spanning across eight of the 5 ft spans between truss joists (40 ft total). In other words, the decking could span the entire width of a column bay. Scanning the tables in Figure 6.74 (for normal weight concrete) and Figure 6.75 (for lightweight concrete), we see that the lightest composite floor that will support this superimposed load is Lightweight Concrete (110PCF) on top of 1.5 in.-deep corrugated decking made from Type 22 (22-gauge, thickness = 0.0295 in.) sheet steel, with an overall slab depth of 3.5 in. ($t = 2$ in. = thickness of concrete above the top of the corrugations). This composite combination spanning 5 ft between truss joists will support a superimposed live load of 278 lb/ft^2. This is much more than the 100 lb/ft^2 for which we are designing. The tables clearly indicate that this decking will span much farther

than 5 ft for the office building application. However, the desire to avoid buckling of the unbraced chord members of the truss girders typically motivates us to not span the maximum distance that the deck could span. For reasons of fire rating and vibration suppression, substantially heavier deck is often chosen, such as 3 in.-deep corrugations with a 6 in. overall depth of lightweight concrete, which usually means that the decking will span much farther than the customary spacing between joists.

From Figure 6.75, in the left column the dead weight of the concrete in the 3.5 in.-thick, lightweight concrete composite slab is 26 lb/ft^2. From Figure 6.74, the weight of the steel is 1.78 lb/ft^2 for the 22-gauge decking with a galvanized finish. Therefore, the total dead weight of the floor decking is approximately 28 lb/ft^2. If we are designing the truss joists, then we need to add in 1 lb/ft^2 for the HVAC ducts and 1 lb/ft^2 for the hung ceiling, resulting in an overall total dead load of 30 lb/ft^2.

6.3.3 SIZING STEEL BEAMS FROM TABLES

For steel beams, shear is rarely a limiting factor under the load conditions typically encountered in building applications. The loads must be extremely high and the depth-to-span ratio for the beam must be extremely high before shear is the dominant issue. Common places in which shear might dominate are heavy rail bridges, where locomotives weighing several hundred tons produce shifting loads that can cause extremely high shear forces near the ends of the beams. For the purposes of this book, it can be assumed that shear is not an issue in sizing steel beams, although there may be situations in which the engineer on a project may need to check the shear capacity of a beam. This leaves three important issues:

1. Moment strength of the cross section
2. Stiffness
3. Buckling of parts of the cross section, such as the flanges or the webs

The second issue can be addressed in a manner similar to that used for sizing solid-sawn wood beams, wherein the required I_r is calculated and then a satisfactory beam is found in a tabulated list of sections sorted progressively by their I values. The only difference in the procedure is that the required cross-sectional stiffness of the steel beam is determined under the unfactored live load only, in contrast to the wood beam, for which the stiffness is determined under the unfactored live load plus half of the unfactored dead load. The difference is accounted for by the fact that the steel does not exhibit creep under long-term loads.

The first issue in the preceding list is handled in a manner somewhat similar to that used with solid-sawn

▼ULCRAFT

1.5 VL, VLI

Maximum Sheet Length 42'-0
Extra Charge for Lengths Under 6'-0
ICBO Approved (No. 3415)

STEEL SECTION PROPERTIES   Fy= 40 KSI

Deck Type	Design Thick.	Weight PSF	Ip in⁴/Ft	In in⁴/Ft	Sp in³/Ft	Sn in³/Ft
1.5VL22	0.0295	1.78	0.150	0.182	0.178	0.186
1.5VL21	0.0329	1.97	0.174	0.205	0.209	0.215
1.5VL20	0.0358	2.14	0.195	0.222	0.231	0.240
1.5VL19	0.0418	2.49	0.239	0.260	0.274	0.288
1.5VL18	0.0474	2.82	0.282	0.295	0.315	0.327
1.5VL17	0.0538	3.19	0.331	0.335	0.361	0.371
1.5VL16	0.0598	3.54	0.373	0.373	0.404	0.411

(N=9) NORMAL WEIGHT CONCRETE (145 PCF)

Total Slab Depth	Deck Type	SDI Max. Unshored Clear Span 1 Span	2 Span	3 Span	Superimposed Live Load, PSF — Clear Span (ft.-in.) 5'-0	5'-6	6'-0	6'-6	7'-0	7'-6	8'-0	8'-6	9'-0	9'-6	10'-0	10'-6	11'-0	11'-6	12'-0
3 1/2"	1.5VL22	5'-2	6'-11	7'-0	314	259	230	206	186	169	154	141	130	120	111	100	87	76	67
	1.5VL21	5'-9	7'-8	7'-9	331	294	243	218	197	179	163	150	138	127	118	104	91	80	70
(t=2")	1.5VL20	6'-2	8'-3	8'-4	345	306	275	228	206	187	171	157	144	133	124	108	94	82	73
	1.5VL19	6'-10	9'-2	9'-4	372	330	296	268	223	203	186	171	157	145	134	116	101	88	78
	1.5VL18	7'-6	9'-11	10'-2	395	351	315	285	260	238	199	182	168	156	142	123	107	94	82
33 PSF	1.5VL17	8'-2	10'-6	10'-10	397	353	316	286	261	239	221	183	169	157	145	131	114	99	87
	1.5VL16	8'-8	11'-0	11'-5	397	353	316	286	261	239	221	205	169	156	145	135	119	105	92
4"	1.5VL22	4'-11	6'-6	6'-7	342	301	267	240	216	196	179	164	151	139	129	119	111	103	96
	1.5VL21	5'-5	7'-3	7'-4	385	318	283	253	229	208	190	174	160	148	137	127	118	110	102
(t=2 1/2")	1.5VL20	5'-10	7'-9	7'-11	400	356	295	264	239	217	198	182	167	155	143	133	124	116	108
	1.5VL19	6'-6	8'-8	8'-10	400	383	344	311	259	235	215	197	182	168	156	145	135	126	115
	1.5VL18	7'-1	9'-5	9'-7	400	400	365	330	301	251	229	211	194	180	167	156	145	136	122
39 PSF	1.5VL17	7'-8	10'-0	10'-4	400	400	366	331	302	277	230	211	195	180	168	156	146	136	128
	1.5VL16	8'-2	10'-6	10'-10	400	400	365	330	301	276	255	211	194	180	167	155	145	136	127
4 1/2"	1.5VL22	4'-8	6'-3	6'-4	392	345	307	275	248	225	205	188	173	159	147	137	127	118	110
	1.5VL21	5'-2	6'-11	7'-0	400	364	324	290	262	238	217	199	183	169	157	145	135	126	117
(t=3")	1.5VL20	5'-6	7'-5	7'-6	400	400	338	303	274	249	227	208	192	177	164	152	142	132	123
	1.5VL19	6'-2	8'-3	8'-4	400	400	393	328	296	269	246	226	208	193	179	166	155	145	135
	1.5VL18	6'-8	8'-11	9'-2	400	400	400	378	315	287	262	241	222	206	191	178	166	155	145
45 PSF	1.5VL17	7'-3	9'-6	9'-10	400	400	400	378	345	287	263	241	223	206	191	178	166	155	146
	1.5VL16	7'-9	10'-0	10'-4	400	400	400	377	344	315	262	240	222	205	190	177	165	155	145
5"	1.5VL22	4'-6	6'-0	6'-1	400	391	347	311	280	254	232	213	195	180	167	155	143	133	124
	1.5VL21	4'-11	6'-8	6'-9	400	400	366	328	297	269	246	225	207	191	177	164	153	142	133
(t=3 1/2")	1.5VL20	5'-3	7'-1	7'-2	400	400	382	343	310	281	257	236	217	200	186	172	160	150	140
	1.5VL19	5'-10	7'-11	8'-0	400	400	400	370	335	304	278	255	235	218	202	188	175	163	153
	1.5VL18	6'-4	8'-7	8'-9	400	400	400	394	356	324	297	272	251	233	216	201	187	175	164
51 PSF	1.5VL17	6'-11	9'-1	9'-5	400	400	400	400	357	325	297	273	251	233	216	201	188	176	164
	1.5VL16	7'-4	9'-7	9'-10	400	400	400	400	388	323	295	271	250	232	215	200	187	175	164
5 1/2"	1.5VL22	4'-4	5'-9	5'-10	400	400	388	348	314	285	260	238	219	202	187	173	160	149	139
	1.5VL21	4'-9	6'-5	6'-6	400	400	400	367	332	301	275	252	232	214	198	184	171	159	148
(t=4")	1.5VL20	5'-1	6'-10	6'-11	400	400	400	383	346	315	287	263	243	224	208	193	179	167	156
	1.5VL19	5'-7	7'-7	7'-8	400	400	400	400	374	340	311	286	263	243	226	210	196	183	171
	1.5VL18	6'-1	8'-3	8'-4	400	400	400	400	399	363	332	305	281	260	241	225	210	196	183
57 PSF	1.5VL17	6'-7	8'-9	9'-0	400	400	400	400	399	363	332	305	281	260	242	225	210	196	184
	1.5VL16	7'-1	9'-2	9'-6	400	400	400	400	400	361	330	303	279	259	240	224	209	195	183
6"	1.5VL22	4'-2	5'-7	5'-8	400	400	400	385	347	315	288	263	242	223	207	191	178	165	154
	1.5VL21	4'-7	6'-2	6'-3	400	400	400	400	367	334	304	279	257	237	220	204	189	176	164
(t=4 1/2")	1.5VL20	4'-10	6'-7	6'-8	400	400	400	400	383	348	318	292	269	248	230	214	199	185	173
	1.5VL19	5'-5	7'-4	7'-5	400	400	400	400	400	377	344	316	291	270	250	233	217	202	189
	1.5VL18	5'-10	7'-11	8'-1	400	400	400	400	400	400	367	337	311	288	267	249	232	217	203
63 PSF	1.5VL17	6'-4	8'-5	8'-8	400	400	400	400	400	400	367	337	311	288	267	249	232	217	204
	1.5VL16	6'-9	8'-10	9'-2	400	400	400	400	400	399	365	335	309	286	266	248	231	216	202

Notes: 1. Minimum exterior bearing length required is 1.5 inches. Minimum interior bearing length required is 3.0 inches.
   If these minimum lengths are not provided, web crippling must be checked.
2. Always contact Vulcraft when using loads in excess of 200 psf. Such loads often result from concentrated, dynamic, or long term load cases
   for which reductions due to bond breakage, concrete creep, etc. should be evaluated.
3. All fire rated assemblies are subject to an upper live load limit of 250 psf.
4. Inquire about material availability of 17, 19 & 21 gage.

Figure 6.74 Weights and allowed loads on normal-weight concrete, composite decking with 1.5 in.-deep corrugations. (Reprinted courtesy of Vulcraft.)

SLAB INFORMATION

Total Slab Depth	Theo. Concrete Volume		Recommended Welded Wire Fabric
	Yds./ 100 Sq. Ft.	Cu. Ft./ Sq. Ft.	
3½"	0.78	0.210	6x6-W1.4xW1.4
4"	0.93	0.252	6x6-W1.4xW1.4
4½"	1.09	0.294	6x6-W1.4xW1.4
4¾"	1.16	0.314	6x6-W1.4xW1.4
5"	1.24	0.335	6x6-W2.1xW2.1
5½"	1.40	0.377	6x6-W2.1xW2.1
5¾"	1.47	0.398	6x6-W2.1xW2.1
6"	1.55	0.418	6x6-W2.1xW2.1

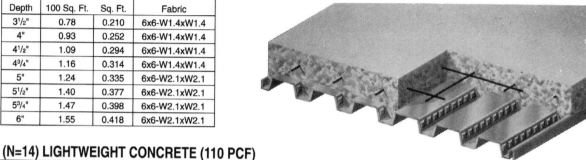

(N=14) LIGHTWEIGHT CONCRETE (110 PCF)

Total Slab Depth	Deck Type	SDI Max. Unshored Clear Span			Superimposed Live Load, PSF — Clear Span (ft.-in.)														
		1 Span	2 Span	3 Span	5'-0	5'-6	6'-0	6'-6	7'-0	7'-6	8'-0	8'-6	9'-0	9'-6	10'-0	10'-6	11'-0	11'-6	12'-0
3 1/2" (t=2") 26 PSF	1.5VL22	5'-7	7'-5	7'-6	278	247	206	185	167	152	139	124	105	89	76	66	57	50	44
	1.5VL21	6'-3	8'-3	8'-5	293	260	233	195	177	161	147	130	110	93	80	69	60	53	46
	1.5VL20	6'-8	8'-11	9'-0	305	271	243	220	185	168	154	135	114	97	83	72	62	54	48
	1.5VL19	7'-6	10'-0	10'-1	329	292	262	237	216	198	167	145	122	104	89	77	67	58	51
	1.5VL18	8'-2	10'-8	11'-0	350	311	279	252	230	211	184	153	129	110	94	81	71	62	54
	1.5VL17	8'-11	11'-4	11'-8	352	312	280	253	231	212	195	163	137	116	100	86	75	66	58
	1.5VL16	9'-6	11'-10	12'-3	352	312	280	253	231	212	195	171	144	122	105	91	79	69	61
4" (t=2 1/2") 30 PSF	1.5VL22	5'-4	7'-1	7'-2	324	269	239	215	194	177	161	148	136	126	113	98	85	75	66
	1.5VL21	5'-11	7'-11	8'-0	341	303	253	227	205	187	171	157	145	134	119	102	89	78	69
	1.5VL20	6'-4	8'-5	8'-7	355	315	283	237	214	195	178	164	151	140	123	106	92	81	71
	1.5VL19	7'-1	9'-6	9'-7	382	339	304	275	251	211	193	178	164	152	131	113	99	86	76
	1.5VL18	7'-9	10'-2	10'-6	400	360	323	292	266	244	206	189	175	162	139	120	104	91	80
	1.5VL17	8'-5	10'-10	11'-2	400	361	324	293	267	245	226	190	175	163	147	127	111	97	85
	1.5VL16	9'-0	11'-4	11'-9	400	360	323	292	266	244	225	209	195	162	151	134	116	102	90
4 1/2" (t=3") 35 PSF	1.5VL22	5'-1	6'-9	6'-10	372	309	275	246	223	202	185	170	156	145	134	125	116	106	93
	1.5VL21	5'-8	7'-7	7'-8	391	347	290	260	235	214	196	180	166	153	142	132	123	111	97
	1.5VL20	6'-0	8'-1	8'-2	400	361	324	272	246	223	204	188	173	160	149	139	129	114	101
	1.5VL19	6'-9	9'-0	9'-2	400	388	348	315	265	242	221	203	188	174	162	151	140	122	107
	1.5VL18	7'-4	9'-9	10'-0	400	400	369	334	305	257	236	217	200	186	173	161	147	129	114
	1.5VL17	8'-0	10'-4	10'-8	400	400	370	335	305	280	258	217	200	186	173	161	151	137	120
	1.5VL16	8'-6	10'-10	11'-3	400	400	369	334	304	279	257	239	199	185	172	160	150	140	126
4 3/4" (t=3 1/4") 37 PSF	1.5VL22	5'-0	6'-8	6'-9	396	329	293	263	237	216	197	181	167	154	143	133	124	116	108
	1.5VL21	5'-6	7'-5	7'-6	400	370	309	277	251	228	208	191	177	163	152	141	132	123	114
	1.5VL20	5'-11	7'-11	8'-0	400	385	322	289	262	238	218	200	185	171	159	148	138	129	118
	1.5VL19	6'-7	8'-11	8'-11	400	400	371	336	283	257	235	216	200	185	172	160	150	140	126
	1.5VL18	7'-2	9'-7	9'-9	400	400	393	356	324	274	251	231	213	198	184	171	160	150	133
	1.5VL17	7'-9	10'-2	10'-6	400	400	394	356	325	298	251	231	213	198	184	171	160	150	141
	1.5VL16	8'-4	10'-8	11'-0	400	400	392	355	324	297	274	230	212	197	183	171	159	149	140
5" (t=3 1/2") 39 PSF	1.5VL22	4'-11	6'-6	6'-7	397	350	311	279	252	229	209	192	177	164	152	141	131	123	115
	1.5VL21	5'-5	7'-3	7'-4	400	369	328	295	266	242	221	203	188	174	161	150	140	131	122
	1.5VL20	5'-9	7'-9	7'-10	400	400	342	307	278	253	231	212	196	181	168	157	146	137	128
	1.5VL19	6'-5	8'-8	8'-9	400	400	394	332	300	273	250	230	212	197	183	170	159	149	140
	1.5VL18	7'-0	9'-4	9'-7	400	400	400	378	344	291	266	245	226	210	195	182	170	159	150
	1.5VL17	7'-7	9'-11	10'-3	400	400	400	378	345	316	266	245	226	210	195	182	170	159	150
	1.5VL16	8'-2	10'-5	10'-9	400	400	400	377	343	315	291	244	225	209	194	181	169	159	149
5 3/4" (t=4 1/4") 46 PSF	1.5VL22	4'-7	6'-2	6'-3	400	400	367	329	297	270	247	227	209	193	179	166	155	145	135
	1.5VL21	5'-2	6'-11	7'-0	400	400	387	347	314	286	261	240	221	205	190	177	165	154	144
	1.5VL20	5'-6	7'-4	7'-5	400	400	400	362	327	298	272	250	231	214	199	185	172	161	151
	1.5VL19	6'-1	8'-2	8'-4	400	400	400	391	354	322	295	271	250	232	215	201	187	175	165
	1.5VL18	6'-7	8'-10	9'-1	400	400	400	400	376	343	314	289	267	247	230	214	200	188	176
	1.5VL17	7'-2	9'-5	9'-9	400	400	400	400	400	343	314	289	267	247	230	214	200	188	176
	1.5VL16	7'-8	9'-11	10'-3	400	400	400	400	400	371	312	287	265	246	229	213	199	187	175

Notes: 1. Minimum exterior bearing length required is 1.5 inches. Minimum interior bearing length required is 3.0 inches. If these minimum lengths are not provided, web crippling must be checked.
2. Always contact Vulcraft when using loads in excess of 200 psf. Such loads often result from concentrated, dynamic, or long term load cases for which reductions due to bond breakage, concrete creep, etc. should be evaluated.
3. All fire rated assemblies are subject to an upper live load limit of 250 psf.
4. Inquire about material availability of 17, 19 & 21 gage.

COMPOSITE

Figure 6.75 Weights and allowed loads on lightweight concrete, composite decking with 1.5 in.-deep corrugations. (Reprinted courtesy of Vulcraft.)

3 VLI

Maximum Sheet Length 42'-0
Extra Charge for Lengths Under 6'-0
ICBO Approved (No. 3415)

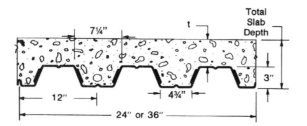

STEEL SECTION PROPERTIES — Fy= 40 KSI

Deck Type	Design Thick.	Weight PSF	Ip in⁴/Ft (in^4/Ft)	In in⁴/Ft (in^4/Ft)	Sp in³/Ft (in^3/Ft)	Sn in³/Ft (in^3/Ft)
3VLI22	0.0295	1.77	0.746	0.745	0.429	0.442
3VLI21	0.0329	1.97	0.850	0.848	0.495	0.511
3VLI20	0.0358	2.14	0.938	0.937	0.553	0.572
3VLI19	0.0418	2.50	1.105	1.103	0.677	0.700
3VLI18	0.0474	2.84	1.251	1.251	0.795	0.803
3VLI17	0.0538	3.22	1.421	1.421	0.913	0.913
3VLI16	0.0598	3.58	1.580	1.580	1.013	1.013

(N=9) NORMAL WEIGHT CONCRETE (145 PCF)

COMPOSITE

Total Slab Depth	Deck Type	SDI Max. Unshored Clear Span — 1 Span	2 Span	3 Span	Superimposed Live Load, PSF — Clear Span (ft.-in.) 7-0	7-6	8-0	8-6	9-0	9-6	10-0	10-6	11-0	11-6	12-0	12-6	13-0	13-6	14-0
5" (t=2") 44 PSF	3VLI22	7-8	9-7	9-7	216	195	149	133	120	109	99	90	83	76	70	64	59	54	50
	3VLI21	8-11	11-3	11-4	230	206	187	170	128	116	106	96	88	81	74	68	63	58	54
	3VLI20	9-6	11-11	12-4	241	216	196	178	163	150	111	101	93	85	78	72	66	61	57
	3VLI19	10-8	13-2	13-7	265	237	214	194	178	163	151	140	102	94	86	79	73	67	62
	3VLI18	11-8	14-1	14-6	289	261	238	218	201	186	173	161	151	142	106	98	92	86	80
	3VLI17	12-7	14-11	15-5	309	278	253	231	212	196	182	170	159	150	141	133	97	91	85
	3VLI16	13-4	15-8	15-11	327	294	267	243	223	206	191	178	167	156	147	139	132	96	89
5 1/2" (t=2 1/2") 50 PSF	3VLI22	7-0	8-9	8-9	247	190	170	152	137	124	113	103	94	87	80	73	67	62	57
	3VLI21	8-4	10-4	10-4	262	235	213	162	146	133	120	110	101	92	85	78	72	66	61
	3VLI20	9-0	11-5	11-9	275	247	223	203	186	140	127	116	106	97	89	82	76	70	65
	3VLI19	10-1	12-7	13-0	302	270	244	222	203	186	172	128	117	107	98	90	83	77	71
	3VLI18	11-1	13-5	13-11	330	298	271	248	229	212	197	184	173	130	121	112	105	98	92
	3VLI17	11-11	14-3	14-9	352	317	288	263	242	224	208	194	182	171	128	119	111	104	97
	3VLI16	12-8	15-0	15-5	373	335	304	277	255	235	218	203	190	178	168	159	117	109	102
6" (t=3") 57 PSF	3VLI22	6-5	8-1	8-1	242	214	191	171	154	140	127	116	106	97	89	82	76	70	65
	3VLI21	7-8	9-7	9-7	294	264	204	183	165	149	135	124	113	104	95	88	81	75	69
	3VLI20	8-7	10-11	10-11	309	277	250	228	173	157	143	130	119	109	100	92	85	79	73
	3VLI19	9-8	12-1	12-6	339	304	274	249	227	209	157	143	131	120	110	102	94	87	80
	3VLI18	10-7	12-11	13-4	370	334	304	279	257	238	221	207	158	146	136	126	118	110	103
	3VLI17	11-5	13-9	14-2	395	356	323	296	272	251	233	218	204	155	144	134	125	117	109
	3VLI16	12-0	14-5	14-11	400	376	341	311	286	264	245	228	213	200	189	141	132	123	115
6 1/2" (t=3 1/2") 63 PSF	3VLI22	6-0	7-5	7-5	268	237	212	190	171	155	141	129	118	108	99	91	84	78	72
	3VLI21	7-1	8-10	8-10	326	254	226	203	183	165	150	137	126	115	106	97	90	83	77
	3VLI20	8-1	10-1	10-1	343	307	278	214	192	174	158	144	132	121	111	103	95	87	81
	3VLI19	9-3	11-7	12-0	377	337	304	276	252	192	175	159	146	134	123	113	104	96	89
	3VLI18	10-1	12-5	12-10	400	371	338	309	285	264	246	189	175	162	151	140	131	122	115
	3VLI17	10-11	13-3	13-8	400	395	359	328	302	279	259	242	186	172	160	149	139	130	121
	3VLI16	11-6	13-11	14-4	400	400	378	345	317	293	272	253	237	222	169	157	146	136	128
7" (t=4") 69 PSF	3VLI22	5-7	6-11	6-11	295	261	233	209	188	171	155	142	130	119	109	101	93	86	79
	3VLI21	6-7	8-3	8-3	316	279	249	223	201	182	165	151	138	127	116	107	99	91	84
	3VLI20	7-6	9-5	9-5	377	338	262	235	212	192	174	159	145	133	122	113	104	96	89
	3VLI19	8-11	11-3	11-7	400	370	334	303	234	211	192	175	160	147	135	124	115	106	98
	3VLI18	9-9	12-0	12-5	400	400	371	340	313	290	226	208	192	178	166	154	144	135	126
	3VLI17	10-6	12-9	13-2	400	400	394	360	331	306	285	265	204	189	176	164	153	143	134
	3VLI16	11-1	13-5	13-10	400	400	400	379	348	322	298	278	260	200	185	172	161	150	140
7 1/2" (t=4 1/2") 75 PSF	3VLI22	5-2	6-6	6-6	321	285	254	228	205	186	169	154	141	130	119	110	101	93	86
	3VLI21	6-2	7-9	7-9	344	304	271	243	219	198	180	164	150	138	127	117	108	100	92
	3VLI20	7-1	8-10	8-10	400	321	286	256	231	209	190	173	158	145	134	123	114	105	97
	3VLI19	8-7	10-10	11-2	400	400	364	331	255	231	209	191	175	160	147	136	125	116	107
	3VLI18	9-4	11-7	12-0	400	400	400	370	341	316	269	246	210	195	181	168	157	147	138
	3VLI17	10-1	12-4	12-9	400	400	400	393	361	334	310	241	223	206	192	179	167	156	146
	3VLI16	10-8	13-0	13-5	400	400	400	400	380	351	325	303	235	218	202	188	175	164	153

NOTES:
1. Minimum exterior bearing length required is 2.5 inches. Minimum interior bearing length required is 5.0 inches. If these minimum lengths are not provided, web crippling must be checked.
2. Always contact Vulcraft when using loads in excess of 200 psf. Such loads often result from concentrated, dynamic, or long term load cases for which reductions due to bond breakage, concrete creep, etc. should be evaluated.
3. All fire rated assemblies are subject to an upper live load limit of 250 psf.
4. Inquire about material availability of 17, 19 & 21 gage.

Figure 6.76 Weights and allowed loads on normal-weight concrete, composite decking with 3.0 in.-deep corrugations. (Reprinted courtesy of Vulcraft.)

SLAB INFORMATION

Total Slab Depth	Theo. Concrete Volume Yds./100 Sq. Ft.	Cu. Ft./Sq. Ft.	Recommended Welded Wire Fabric
5"	1.08	0.292	6x6-W1.4xW1.4
5½"	1.23	0.333	6x6-W1.4xW1.4
6"	1.39	0.375	6x6-W1.4xW1.4
6¼"	1.47	0.396	6x6-W1.4xW1.4
6½"	1.54	0.417	6x6-W2.1xW2.1
7"	1.70	0.458	6x6-W2.1xW2.1
7¼"	1.77	0.479	6x6-W2.1xW2.1
7½"	1.85	0.500	6x6-W2.1xW2.1

(N=14) LIGHTWEIGHT CONCRETE (110 PCF)

Total Slab Depth	Deck Type	1 Span	2 Span	3 Span	8'-0	8'-6	9'-0	9'-6	10'-0	10'-6	11'-0	11'-6	12'-0	12'-6	13'-0	13'-6	14'-0	14'-6	15'-0
5" (t=2") 34 PSF	3VLI22	9'-1	11'-5	11'-5	141	127	115	83	75	67	60	54	49	45	40				
	3VLI21	9'-10	12'-4	12'-9	153	138	125	113	82	74	67	60	54	49	45	41			
	3VLI20	10'-6	13'-0	13'-5	163	147	133	121	110	102	72	65	59	54	49	44	40		
	3VLI19	11'-10	14'-4	14'-10	185	166	150	136	124	114	105	97	68	62	57	52	47	43	
	3VLI18	13'-0	15'-4	15'-10	244	222	204	188	174	162	151	142	133	126	119	90	85	79	75
	3VLI17	14'-0	16'-3	16'-6	262	238	218	201	185	172	161	150	141	133	126	119	113	85	80
	3VLI16	14'-5	16'-11	16'-11	277	254	234	217	202	189	177	166	157	149	141	134	127	99	94
5 1/2" (t=2 1/2") 39 PSF	3VLI22	8'-5	10'-6	10'-6	161	121	107	95	85	77	69	62	56	51	46	42			
	3VLI21	9'-5	11'-10	12'-2	175	157	142	105	94	84	76	69	62	56	51	47	42		
	3VLI20	10'-0	12'-6	12'-11	186	167	151	138	126	91	82	74	67	61	56	51	46	42	
	3VLI19	11'-3	13'-9	14'-3	211	189	171	155	142	130	120	86	78	71	65	59	54	49	45
	3VLI18	12'-4	14'-8	15'-2	278	253	232	214	198	184	172	161	152	118	110	103	97	91	85
	3VLI17	13'-4	15'-7	16'-0	299	272	248	229	211	196	183	171	161	152	143	110	103	97	91
	3VLI16	14'-0	16'-5	16'-5	316	289	267	247	230	215	202	190	179	170	161	153	146	114	107
6" (t=3") 43 PSF	3VLI22	7'-9	9'-9	9'-9	154	136	120	107	96	86	78	70	63	57	52	47	43		
	3VLI21	9'-0	11'-4	11'-6	196	176	160	118	106	95	86	77	70	64	58	52	48	43	
	3VLI20	9'-7	12'-0	12'-5	209	188	170	155	114	103	93	84	76	69	63	57	52	47	.43
	3VLI19	10'-9	13'-3	13'-8	237	212	192	174	159	146	107	97	88	80	73	67	61	56	51
	3VLI18	11'-9	14'-2	14'-8	312	284	261	240	223	207	193	181	142	133	124	116	109	102	96
	3VLI17	12'-9	15'-1	15'-7	335	305	279	257	237	221	206	192	181	170	132	124	116	109	102
	3VLI16	13'-5	15'-10	16'-0	354	325	299	277	258	241	226	213	201	190	181	143	135	128	121
6 1/4" (t=3 1/4") 46 PSF	3VLI22	7'-6	9'-5	9'-5	162	143	127	113	101	91	82	74	67	60	55	50	45	41	
	3VLI21	8'-10	11'-1	11'-1	207	186	140	125	112	100	90	82	74	67	61	55	50	46	42
	3VLI20	9'-5	11'-10	12'-2	221	198	179	134	120	108	98	88	80	73	66	60	55	50	46
	3VLI19	10'-6	13'-0	13'-6	250	224	202	184	168	154	113	102	93	84	77	70	64	59	54
	3VLI18	11'-6	14'-0	14'-5	329	300	275	253	235	218	204	191	150	140	131	122	115	108	101
	3VLI17	12'-5	14'-10	15'-3	354	322	294	271	250	233	217	203	191	150	140	131	122	115	108
	3VLI16	13'-2	15'-6	15'-10	374	343	316	293	272	254	239	225	212	201	190	151	143	135	128
6 1/2" (t=3 1/2") 48 PSF	3VLI22	7'-3	9'-1	9'-1	171	150	134	119	107	96	86	78	70	64	58	52	47	43	
	3VLI21	8'-7	10'-9	10'-9	218	196	147	131	117	106	95	86	78	71	64	58	53	48	44
	3VLI20	9'-2	11'-7	12'-0	232	209	189	141	127	114	103	93	84	77	70	63	58	53	48
	3VLI19	10'-4	12'-10	13'-3	263	236	213	193	176	131	119	108	98	89	81	74	68	62	57
	3VLI18	11'-4	13'-8	14'-2	346	316	289	267	247	230	215	170	158	147	138	129	121	113	107
	3VLI17	12'-2	14'-7	15'-0	372	338	310	285	263	245	228	214	201	158	147	138	129	121	114
	3VLI16	12'-11	15'-3	15'-7	393	360	332	308	286	268	251	236	223	211	169	159	150	142	134
7 1/4" (t=4 1/4") 55 PSF	3VLI22	6'-7	8'-3	8'-3	196	173	153	137	122	110	99	89	81	73	66	60	55	49	45
	3VLI21	7'-10	9'-9	9'-9	216	190	169	151	135	121	109	99	90	81	74	67	61	55	50
	3VLI20	8'-8	11'-1	11'-2	267	240	182	163	146	131	118	107	97	88	80	73	66	61	55
	3VLI19	9'-9	12'-2	12'-7	302	271	244	222	168	151	137	124	112	102	93	85	78	71	65
	3VLI18	10'-8	13'-0	13'-6	398	362	332	306	284	264	211	196	182	169	158	148	139	130	123
	3VLI17	11'-6	13'-10	14'-4	400	388	355	327	302	281	262	245	195	181	169	158	148	139	131
	3VLI16	12'-2	14'-7	15'-1	400	400	381	353	329	307	288	271	256	207	194	183	173	163	154

Header note for upper span columns: SDI Max. Unshored Clear Span (1 Span, 2 Span, 3 Span); Superimposed Live Load, PSF — Clear Span (ft.-in.)

COMPOSITE

NOTES:
1. Minimum exterior bearing length required is 2.5 inches. Minimum interior bearing length required is 5.0 inches. If these minimum lengths are not provided, web crippling must be checked.
2. Always contact Vulcraft when using loads in excess of 200 psf. Such loads often result from concentrated, dynamic, or long term load cases for which reductions due to bond breakage, concrete creep, etc. should be evaluated.
3. All fire rated assemblies are subject to an upper live load limit of 250 psf.
4. Inquire about material availability of 17, 19 & 21 gage.

Figure 6.77 Weights and allowed loads on lightweight concrete, composite decking with 3.0 in.-deep corrugations. (Reprinted courtesy of Vulcraft.)

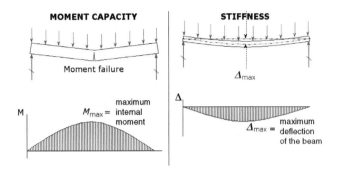

Figure 6.78 Primary modes of failure for steel beams.

wood, except that the steel beam will be chosen based on the plastic section modulus, Z, rather than the elastic section modulus, S. The plastic section modulus accounts for the fact that a steel beam has reserve capacity after it begins to yield. During the yielding process, the beam actually develops more resisting moment as more and more of the cross section reaches the yield stress. The plastic modulus is based on the ultimate moment capacity of the section, wherein all of the top part of the cross section is in one state of stress (e.g., compression) of a magnitude equal to the yield stress and all of the bottom part of the cross section is in the opposite state of stress (e.g., tension) of a magnitude equal to the yield stress. Typically, the plastic modulus Z for an I-beam is on the order of 13% to 15% higher than the elastic section modulus S. This means that using plastic design provides a moment capacity on the order of 1.13 times higher. For steel beams, however, a resistance factor of 0.9 is applied to provide a margin of safety. Multiplying the steel beam resistance factor by the ratio of the plastic section modulus to the elastic section modulus produces the following:

$$\phi \frac{Z}{S} = 0.9(1.13) \approx 1$$

In other words, the allowed moment in the beam will be approximately equal to the elastic section modulus times the yield stress. This is very convenient for facilitating the use of computerized structural analysis programs, which use the elastic section modulus S to calculate bending stresses. It means that in doing computerized structural analysis, one can target keeping the stress just below the yield stress.

The third issue in the preceding list is extremely difficult to address analytically and will be handled for standard steel sections by taking note of the following:

- All current wide-flange (W) sections, miscellaneous (M) I-sections, channel (C) sections, miscellaneous channel (MC) sections, and H-pile (HP) sections have compact webs at Fy ≤ 65 ksi.

- All current wide-flange (W) sections, miscellaneous (M) I-sections, channel (C) sections, and miscellaneous channel (MC) sections have compact flanges at Fy ≤ 50 ksi, except for the following: W 21 × 48, W 14 × 99, W 14 × 90, W 12 × 65, W 10 × 12, W 8 × 31, W 8 × 10, W 6 × 15, W 6 × 8.5, and M 4 × 6.

For the purposes of this text, steel beams in grades higher than 50 ksi will not be considered. Such high grades are rarely warranted, inasmuch as the beams will usually be limited by stiffness requirements. There are a huge number of steel shapes, and the small set of noncompact shapes listed here does not represent a significant part of the design repertoire. These sections are simply excluded from consideration in dealing with 50 ksi steel. For information about how to design for these sections, see "Load and Resistance Factor Design," *Manual of Steel Construction, Load and Resistance Factor Design*, Third Edition, from the American Institute of Steel Construction.

Figures 6.79 through 6.83 are reprinted from the *Manual of Steel Construction, Load and Resistance Factor Design*, Third Edition, published by the American Institute of Steel Construction. These figures list cross-sectional stiffness (moments of inertia I) and cross-sectional strength in resisting bending stresses (plastic section moduli Z) in descending order, for the most common steel beams, that is, for W-sections and M-sections. In each list, the section names are clustered into groups, with the section at the top of the group shown in bold type. In the cross-sectional stiffness list (I), these bold-type sections have the characteristic that no section occurring lower in the list has a higher I-value and no section occurring higher in the list weighs less. Similarly, in the cross-sectional strength list (Z), these bold-type sections have the characteristic that no section occurring lower in the list has a higher Z-value and no section occurring higher in the list weighs less. Therefore, to achieve maximum structurally efficiency, one need only look at the sections listed in bold type. If there are other goals than structural efficiency, such as the desire to keep the beam depths lower, then some of the non-bolded sections might be considered. The tables for plastic section modulus Z also list the design plastic resisting moment $\phi_B M_{px}$ for 50-ksi steel ($\phi_B M_{px} = 0.9\,F_y\,Z_x$). The tabulation of $\phi_B M_{px}$ simplifies the sizing calculations by eliminating the step to calculate the required Z.

For beams listed in the tables shown in Figures 6.79 through 6.83, the sizing procedure is to find the required resisting moment M_r and the required cross-sectional stiffness I_r. Then the tables are scanned to find the lightest section with a resisting moment $\phi_B M_{px}$ greater than or equal to the required moment M_r and the lightest section with a cross-sectional stiffness I_r greater than or equal to the required cross-sectional stiffness I_r. If the search

$$I_x$$

	$F_y = 50$ ksi
	$\phi_b = 0.90$
	$\phi_v = 0.90$

**W-Shapes
Selection by I_x**

Shape	I_x	Z_x	$\phi_b M_{px}$	Shape	I_x	Z_x	$\phi_b M_{px}$	Shape	I_x	Z_x	$\phi_b M_{px}$
	in.⁴	in.³	kip-ft		in.⁴	in.³	kip-ft		in.⁴	in.³	kip-ft
W36×798*	**62600**	**3580**	**13400**	**W40×215**	**16700**	**964.0**	**3620**	**W36×135**	**7800**	**509**	**1910**
				W27×368*	16200	1240	4650	W24×229	7650	675	2530
W40×593*	**50400**	**2760**	**10400**	W36×245	16100	1010	3790	W33×141	7450	514	1930
W36×650*	48900	2860	10700	W14×808*	16000	1830	6860	W14×455*	7190	936	3510
				W33×263	15900	1040	3900	W27×178	7020	570	2140
W40×503*	**41700**	**2320**	**8700**					W24×207	6820	606	2270
W36×527*	38300	2280	8550	**W40×211**	**15500**	**906**	**3400**				
				W36×230	15000	943	3540	**W33×130**	**6710**	**467**	**1750**
W40×431*	**34800**	**1960.0**	**7350**	W36×232	15000	936	3510	W30×148	6680	500	1880
								W14×426*	6600	869	3260
W40×397*	**32000**	**1800**	**6750**	**W40×199**	**14900**	**869**	**3260**	W27×161	6310	515	1930
				W30×292*	14900	1060	3980	W24×192	6260	559	2100
W44×335	**31100**	**1620**	**6080**	W27×336*	14600	1130	4240	W14×398*	6000	801	3000
W36×439*	31000	1870	7010	W14×730*	14300	1660	6230				
W40×392*	29900	1710	6410	W33×241	14200	940	3530	**W33×118**	**5900**	**415**	**1560**
W40×372*	29600	1680.0	6300	W24×370*	13400	1130	4240	W30×132	5770	437	1640
W40×362*	28900	1640	6150					W24×176	5680	511	1920
W36×393*	27500	1670	6260	**W40×183**	**13300**	**783**	**2940**	W27×146	5660	464	1740
				W36×210	13200	833	3120	W14×370*	5440	736	2760
W44×290	**27100**	**1420**	**5330**	W30×261	13100	943	3540	W30×124	5360	408	1530
W40×324	25600	1460	5480	W27×307*	13100	1030	3860	W21×201	5310	530	1990
W27×539*	25600	1890	7090	W33×221	12900	857	3210	W24×162	5170	468	1760
W36×359*	24800	1510	5660	W14×665*	12400	1480	5550				
W40×331	24700	1430	5360					**W30×116**	**4930**	**378**	**1420**
W40×327	24500	1410	5290	**W36×194**	**12100**	**767**	**2880**	W14×342*	4900	672	2520
W33×387*	24300	1560	5850	W27×281*	11900	936	3510	W27×129	4760	395	1480
				W24×335*	11900	1020	3830	W21×182	4740	477	1790
W44×262	**24200**	**1270**	**4760**	W30×235	11700	847	3180	W24×146	4580	418	1570
W40×297	23200	1330	4990								
W36×328*	22500	1380	5180	**W40×167**	**11600**	**693**	**2600**	**W30×108**	**4470**	**346**	**1300**
W33×354*	22000	1420	5330	W33×201	11600	773	2900	W14×311*	4330	603	2260
W40×277	21900	1250	4690	W36×182	11300	718	2690	W21×166	4280	432	1620
				W27×258	10800	852	3200	W27×114	4080	343	1290
W44×230	**20800**	**1100**	**4130**	W14×605*	10800	1320	4950	W12×336*	4060	603	2260
W30×391*	20700	1450	5440	W24×306*	10700	922	3460	W24×131	4020	370	1390
W40×278	20500	1190	4460	W36×170	10500	668	2510				
W36×300	20300	1260	4730	W30×211	10300	751	2820	**W30×99**	**3990**	**312**	**1170**
W40×249	19600	1120	4200					W14×283*	3840	542	2030
W33×318*	19500	1270	4760	**W40×149**	**9800**	**598**	**2240**	W21×147	3640	374	1400
W40×264	19400	1130	4240	W36×160	9760	624	2340	W27×102	3620	305	1140
W36×280	18900	1170	4390	W27×235	9700	772	2900				
W30×357*	18700	1320.0	4950	W24×279*	9600	835	3130				
W33×291	17700	1160	4350	W14×550*	9430	1180	4430				
W40×235	17400	1010	3790	W33×169	9290	629	2360				
W36×260	17300	1080	4050	W30×191	9200	675	2530				
W36×256	16800	1040	3900	W36×150	9040	581	2180				
W30×326*	16800	1190	4460	W27×217	8910	711	2670				
				W24×250*	8490	744	2790				
				W30×173	8230	607	2280				
				W14×500*	8210	1050	3940				
				W33×152	8160	559	2100				
				W27×194	7860	631	2370				

Figure 6.79 Moments of inertia for steel wide-flange sections. (Copyright American Institute of Steel Construction, Inc. Reprinted with permission. All rights reserved.)

[handwritten notes in right margin:] Only look at the bold numbers. ↓ most stiff + lightest in weight.

I_x	$F_y = 50$ ksi	W-Shapes
	$\phi_b = 0.90$	Selection by I_x
	$\phi_v = 0.90$	

Shape	I_x	Z_x	$\phi_b M_{px}$	Shape	I_x	Z_x	$\phi_b M_{px}$	Shape	I_x	Z_x	$\phi_b M_{px}$
	in.^{4}	in.^{3}	kip-ft		in.^{4}	in.^{3}	kip-ft		in.^{4}	in.^{3}	kip-ft
W30×90	**3610**	**283**	**1060**	**W24×55**	**1360**	**135**	**506**	**W18×35**	**510**	**66.5**	**249**
W12×305*	3550	537	2010	W21×62	1330	144	540	W14×48	485	78.4	294
W24×117	3540	327	1230	W18×76	1330	163	611	W12×58	475	86.4	324
W18×175	3450	398	1490	W16×89	1310	176	660	W10×77	455	97.6	366
W14×257*	3400	487	1830	W14×109	1240	192	720	W16×36	448	64.0	240
W27×94	3270	278	1040	W12×136	1240	214	803	W14×43	428	69.6	261
W21×132	3230	334	1250	W21×57	1170	129	484	W12×53	425	77.9	292
W12×279*	3110	481	1800	W18×71	1170	146	548	W10×68	394	85.3	320
W24×104	3100	289	1080					W12×50	391	71.9	270
W18×158	3060	356	1340	**W21×55**	**1140**	**126**	**473**	W14×38	383	61.1	229
W14×233*	3010	436	1640	W16×77	1120	151	566				
W24×103	3000	280	1050	W14×99††	1110	173	649	**W16×31**	**375**	**54.0**	**203**
W21×122	2970	308	1160	W18×65	1070	133	499	W12×45	348	64.2	241
				W12×120	1070	186	698	W10×60	341	74.6	280
W27×84	**2850**	**244**	**915**	W14×90††	999	157	589	W14×34	337	54.2	203
W18×143	2750	322	1210					W12×40	307	57.0	214
W12×252*	2720	428	1610	**W21×50**	**989**	**111**	**416**	W10×54	303	66.6	250
W24×94	2700	254	953	W18×60	984	123	461				
W21×111	2680	279	1050	W16×67	963	131	491	**W16×26**	**301**	**44.2**	**166**
W14×211	2660	390	1460					W14×30	288	46.9	176
W18×130	2460	290	1090	**W21×48††**	**959**	**107**	**401**	W12×35	285	51.2	192
W21×101	2430	253	949	W12×106	933	164	615	W10×49	272	60.4	227
W12×230*	2420	386	1450	W18×55	890	112	420	W10×45	248	54.9	206
W14×193	2400	355	1330	W14×82	882	139	521				
								W14×26	**243**	**39.9**	**150**
W24×84	**2370**	**224**	**840**	**W21×44**	**847**	**95.8**	**359**	W12×30	238	43.1	162
W18×119	2190	262	983	W12×96	833	147	551	W10×39	209	46.8	176
W14×176	2140	320	1200	W18×50	800	101	379				
W12×210*	2140	348	1310	W14×74	796	126	473	**W12×26**	**204**	**37.2**	**140**
				W16×57	758	105	394				
W24×76	**2100**	**200**	**750**	W12×87	740	132	495	**W14×22**	**197**	**32.8**	**123**
W21×93	2070	221	829	W14×68	722	115	431	W10×33	171	38.8	146
W18×106	1910	230	863	W10×112	716	147	551	W10×30	170	36.6	137
W14×159	1900	287	1080	W18×46	712	90.7	340				
W12×190	1890	311	1170	W12×79	662	119	446	**W12×22**	**156**	**29.3**	**110**
				W16×50	659	92.0	345	W10×26	144	31.3	117
W24×68	**1830**	**177**	**664**	W14×61	640	102	383				
W21×83	1830	196	735	W10×100	623	130	488	**W12×19**	**130**	**24.7**	**92.6**
W18×97	1750	211	791					W10×22	118	26.0	97.5
W14×145	1710	260	975	**W18×40**	**612**	**78.4**	**294**				
W12×170	1650	275	1030	W12×72	597	108	405	**W12×16**	**103**	**20.1**	**75.4**
W21×73	1600	172	645	W16×45	586	82.3	309	W10×19	96.2	21.6	81.0
				W14×53	541	87.1	327				
W24×62	**1560**	**154**	**578**	W10×88	534	113	424	**W12×14**	**88.5**	**17.4**	**65.2**
W18×86	1530	186	698	W12×65††	533	96.8	363	W10×17	81.9	18.7	70.1
W14×132	1530	234	878					W10×15	68.9	16.0	60.0
W16×100	1490	199	746	**W16×40**	**518**	**73.0**	**274**				
W21×68	1480	160	600					**W10×12††**	**53.8**	**12.6**	**47.3**
W12×152	1430	243	911								
W14×120	1380	212	795								

Figure 6.80 Moments of inertia for steel wide-flange sections (continued). (Copyright American Institute of Steel Construction, Inc. Reprinted with permission. All rights reserved.)

Z_x

	$F_y = 50$ ksi	
$\phi_b = 0.90$	**W-Shapes**
$\phi_v = 0.90$	**Selection by Z_x**

Shape	Z_x	I_x	$\phi_b M_{px}$	Shape	Z_x	I_x	$\phi_b M_{px}$	Shape	Z_x	I_x	$\phi_b M_{px}$
	in.³	in.⁴	kip-ft		in.³	in.⁴	kip-ft		in.³	in.⁴	kip-ft
W36×798*	3580	62600	13400	W44×262	1270	24200	4760	W40×183	783	13300	2940
				W33×318*	1270	19500	4760	W33×201	773	11600	2900
W36×650*	2860	48900	10700	W36×300	1260	20300	4730	W27×235	772	9700	2900
W40×593*	2760	50400	10400	W40×277	1250	21900	4690	W36×194	767	12100	2880
				W27×368*	1240	16200	4650	W30×211	751	10300	2820
W40×503*	2320	41700	8700	W40×278	1190	20500	4460	W24×250*	744	8490	2790
W36×527*	2280	38300	8550	W30×326*	1190	16800	4460	W14×370*	736	5440	2760
W40×431*	1960	34800	7350	W14×550*	1180	9430	4430				
W27×539*	1890	25600	7090	W36×280	1170	18900	4390	W36×182	718	11300	2690
W36×439*	1870	31000	7010	W33×291	1160	17700	4350	W27×217	711	8910	2670
W14×808*	1830	16000	6860	W40×264	1130	19400	4240	W40×167	693	11600	2600
W40×397*	1800	32000	6750	W27×336*	1130	14600	4240	W30×191	675	9200	2530
				W24×370*	1130	13400	4240	W24×229	675	7650	2530
W40×392*	1710	29900	6410	W40×249	1120	19600	4200	W14×342*	672	4900	2520
								W36×170	668	10500	2510
W40×372*	1680	29600	6300	W44×230	1100	20800	4130	W27×194	631	7860	2370
W36×393*	1670	27500	6260	W36×260	1080	17300	4050	W33×169	629	9290	2360
W14×730*	1660	14300	6230	W30×292*	1060	14900	3980				
				W14×500*	1050	8210	3940	W36×160	624	9760	2340
W40×362*	1640	28900	6150	W36×256	1040	16800	3900	W30×173	607	8230	2280
W44×335	1620	31100	6080	W33×263	1040	15900	3900	W24×207	606	6820	2270
W33×387*	1560	24300	5850	W27×307*	1030	13100	3860	W14×311*	603	4330	2260
W36×359*	1510	24800	5660	W24×335*	1020	11900	3830	W12×336*	603	4060	2260
W14×665*	1480	12400	5550	W40×235	1010	17400	3790				
				W36×245	1010	16100	3790	W40×149	598	9800	2240
W40×324	1460	25600	5480					W36×150	581	9040	2180
W30×391*	1450	20700	5440	W40×215	964	16700	3620	W27×178	570	7020	2140
W40×331	1430	24700	5360	W36×230	943	15000	3540	W33×152	559	8160	2100
				W30×261	943	13100	3540	W24×192	559	6260	2100
W44×290	1420	27100	5330	W33×241	940	14200	3530	W14×283*	542	3840	2030
W33×354*	1420	22000	5330	W36×232	936	15000	3510	W12×305*	537	3550	2010
W40×327	1410	24500	5290	W27×281*	936	11900	3510	W21×201	530	5310	1990
W36×328*	1380	22500	5180	W14×455*	936	7190	3510	W27×161	515	6310	1930
W40×297	1330	23200	4990	W24×306*	922	10700	3460				
W30×357*	1320	18700	4950					W33×141	514	7450	1930
W14×605*	1320	10800	4950	W40×211	906	15500	3400	W24×176	511	5680	1920
				W40×199	869	14900	3260	W36×135	509	7800	1910
				W14×426*	869	6600	3260	W30×148	500	6680	1880
				W33×221	857	12900	3210	W14×257*	487	3400	1830
				W27×258	852	10800	3200	W12×279*	481	3110	1800
				W30×235	847	11700	3180	W21×182	477	4740	1790
				W24×279*	835	9600	3130	W24×162	468	5170	1760
				W36×210	833	13200	3120				
				W14×398*	801	6000	3000				

Figure 6.81 Plastic modulus for steel wide-flange sections. (Copyright American Institute of Steel Construction, Inc. Reprinted with permission. All rights reserved.)

Z_x

$F_y = 50$ ksi
$\phi_b = 0.90$
$\phi_v = 0.90$

**W-Shapes
Selection by Z_x**

Shape	Z_x	I_x	$\phi_b M_{px}$	Shape	Z_x	I_x	$\phi_b M_{px}$	Shape	Z_x	I_x	$\phi_b M_{px}$
	in.³	in.⁴	kip-ft		in.³	in.⁴	kip-ft		in.³	in.⁴	kip-ft
W33×130	**467**	**6710**	**1750**	**W27×84**	**244**	**2850**	**915**	**W21×55**	**126**	**1140**	**473**
W27×146	464	5660	1740	W12×152	243	1430	911	W14×74	126	796	473
W30×132	437	5770	1640	W14×132	234	1530	878	W18×60	123	984	461
W14×233*	436	3010	1640	W18×106	230	1910	863	W12×79	119	662	446
W21×166	432	4280	1620					W14×68	115	722	431
W12×252*	428	2720	1610	**W24×84**	**224**	**2370**	**840**	W10×88	113	534	424
W24×146	418	4580	1570	W21×93	221	2070	829				
				W12×136	214	1240	803	**W18×55**	**112**	**890**	**420**
W33×118	**415**	**5900**	**1560**	W14×120	212	1380	795				
W30×124	408	5360	1530	W18×97	211	1750	791	**W21×50**	**111**	**989**	**416**
W18×175	398	3450	1490					W12×72	108	597	405
W27×129	395	4760	1480	**W24×76**	**200**	**2100**	**750**				
W14×211	390	2660	1460	W16×100	199	1490	746	**W21×48††**	**107**	**959**	**401**
W12×230*	386	2420	1450	W21×83	196	1830	735	W16×57	105	758	394
				W14×109	192	1240	720	W14×61	102	640	383
W30×116	**378**	**4930**	**1420**	W18×86	186	1530	698	W18×50	101	800	379
W21×147	374	3640	1400	W12×120	186	1070	698	W10×77	97.6	455	366
W24×131	370	4020	1390					W12×65††	96.8	533	363
W18×158	356	3060	1340	**W24×68**	**177**	**1830**	**664**				
W14×193	355	2400	1330	W16×89	176	1310	660	**W21×44**	**95.8**	**847**	**359**
W12×210*	348	2140	1310	W14×99††	173	1110	649	W16×50	92.0	659	345
				W21×73	172	1600	645	W18×46	90.7	712	340
W30×108	**346**	**4470**	**1300**	W12×106	164	933	615	W14×53	87.1	541	327
W27×114	343	4080	1290	W18×76	163	1330	611	W12×58	86.4	475	324
W21×132	334	3230	1250					W10×68	85.3	394	320
W24×117	327	3540	1230	**W21×68**	**160**	**1480**	**600**	W16×45	82.3	586	309
W18×143	322	2750	1210	W14×90††	157	999	589				
W14×176	320	2140	1200					**W18×40**	**78.4**	**612**	**294**
				W24×62	**154**	**1560**	**578**	W14×48	78.4	485	294
W30×99	**312**	**3990**	**1170**	W16×77	151	1120	566	W12×53	77.9	425	292
W12×190	311	1890	1170	W12×96	147	833	551	W10×60	74.6	341	280
W21×122	308	2970	1160	W10×112	147	716	551				
W27×102	305	3620	1140	W18×71	146	1170	548	**W16×40**	**73.0**	**518**	**274**
W18×130	290	2460	1090					W12×50	71.9	391	270
W24×104	289	3100	1080	**W21×62**	**144**	**1330**	**540**	W14×43	69.6	428	261
W14×159	287	1900	1080	W14×82	139	882	521	W10×54	66.6	303	250
W30×90	**283**	**3610**	**1060**	**W24×55**	**135**	**1360**	**506**	**W18×35**	**66.5**	**510**	**249**
W24×103	280	3000	1050	W18×65	133	1070	499	W12×45	64.2	348	241
W21×111	279	2680	1050	W12×87	132	740	495	W16×36	64.0	448	240
W27×94	278	3270	1040	W16×67	131	963	491	W14×38	61.1	383	229
W12×170	275	1650	1030	W10×100	130	623	488	W10×49	60.4	272	227
W18×119	262	2190	983	W21×57	129	1170	484	W12×40	57.0	307	214
W14×145	260	1710	975					W10×45	54.9	248	206
W24×94	254	2700	953								
W21×101	253	2430	949					**W14×34**	**54.2**	**337**	**203**

†† Indicates flange is non-compact.

Figure 6.82 Plastic modulus for steel wide-flange sections (continued). (Copyright American Institute of Steel Construction, Inc. Reprinted with permission. All rights reserved.)

Shape	Z_x	I_x	$\phi_b M_{px}$
	in.^{3}	in.^{4}	kip-ft
W16×31	**54.0**	**375**	**203**
W12×35	51.2	285	192
W14×30	**46.9**	**288**	**176**
W10×39	46.8	209	176
W16×26	**44.2**	**301**	**166**
W12×30	43.1	238	162
W14×26	**39.9**	**243**	**150**
W10×33	38.8	171	146
W12×26	**37.2**	**204**	**140**
W10×30	36.6	170	137
W14×22	**32.8**	**197**	**123**
W10×26	31.3	144	117
W12×22	**29.3**	**156**	**110**
W10×22	**26.0**	**118**	**97.5**
W12×19	**24.7**	**130**	**92.6**
W10×19	**21.6**	**96.2**	**81.0**
W12×16	**20.1**	**103**	**75.4**
W10×17	18.7	81.9	70.1
W12×14	**17.4**	**88.5**	**65.2**
W10×15	16.0	68.9	60.0
W10×12††	**12.6**	**53.8**	**47.3**

Z_x — $F_y = 50$ ksi
$\phi_b = 0.90$ **W-Shapes**
$\phi_v = 0.90$ **Selection by Z_x**

††Indicates flange is non-compact.

Figure 6.83 Plastic modulus for steel wide-flange sections (continued). (Copyright American Institute of Steel Construction, Inc. Reprinted with permission. All rights reserved.)

under these two criteria (moment strength and stiffness) yields two different cross sections, then the larger cross section must be checked to see if works for both criteria.

Example of Sizing Steel I-Beams

Selecting a steel W-section or M-section for a roof joist spanning 30 ft with a live load of $p_{live} = 20$ lb/ft^2, $p_{deck} = 10$ lb/ft^2, and a spacing of 5 ft.

$$w_{live} = 20\frac{\#}{ft^2} \cdot 5ft = 100\frac{\#}{ft}$$

Table 6.6 Computations for Sizing Steel Beams

$$M_r = \frac{w_{factored} \cdot L^2}{8} \qquad \Delta_{max} = \frac{5w_{live} \cdot L^4}{384EI}$$

E = material stiffness
I = cross-sectional stiffness

$$I_r = \frac{5w_{live}L^4}{384E\Delta_{max}}$$
$$= \frac{5w_{live}L^3}{384E} \cdot \frac{L}{\Delta_{max}}$$
$$= \frac{5w_{live}L^3(360)}{384E}$$

$$M_r = \frac{0.220\frac{K}{ft} \cdot (30\ ft)^2}{8} \qquad I_r = \frac{5\left(0.1\frac{K}{ft}\right)(30\ ft)^3(360)\left[\frac{12\ in.}{ft}\right]\left[\frac{12\ in.}{ft}\right]}{384\left(29{,}000\frac{K}{in.^2}\right)}$$

$$= 24.75\ K \cdot ft \qquad\qquad = 62.84\ K \cdot ft$$

$$w_{factored} = p_{factored} \cdot s = (1.2p_{dead} + 1.6p_{live}) \cdot s$$
$$= \left(1.2\left(10\frac{\#}{ft^2}\right) + 1.6\left(20\frac{\#}{ft^2}\right)\right) \cdot 5ft = 220\frac{\#}{ft}$$

For a W12 × 14 in. 50 ksi steel: $\phi_B M_{px} = 65.2$Kft and $I = 88.5$ in.^{4}, which works for both moment strength and stiffness. If the beam is close for moment capacity, it must be rechecked, accounting for the dead weight of the beam. That will not be necessary in this case, because the beam is substantially oversized for moment capacity. This beam is controlled by the deflection condition, which is the usual pattern for lightly loaded beams. It is also a very shallow beam, having a depth-to-length ratio of

$$\frac{14\ in.\left(\frac{ft}{12\ in.}\right)}{30\ ft} = 0.0389 = \frac{1}{25.7}$$

Assignment

A two-story steel-frame building has columns on a 30 ft × 30 ft grid, a flat roof with joists spaced at 5 ft OC, and a floor with joists spaced at 5 ft OC. Assuming 50 ksi steel W sections, size the roof joists, single-loaded roof girders, double-loaded roof girders, floor joists, single-loaded floor girders, and double-loaded floor girders. What do the beam sizes tell you about the guidelines for spans and proportions of wide-flange steel beams in Chapter 1?

6.4 Precast/Prestressed Concrete Beams

6.4.1 CONCRETE DOUBLE TS (DTS)

Concrete double Ts combine the joist and decking in an integrated, precast, prestressed spanning unit. High-strength steel cable is stretched to approximately 70% of its yield stress, and the concrete is cast around it. When the steel is released, it induces a camber in the double T. Adding load reduces the camber. The camber can be an aid in getting water off a roof. It can also be a problem in leveling a floor in a building. A concrete topping layer is an aid in the leveling process. Lightweight concrete double Ts tend to have more camber than normal-weight double Ts.

Concrete double Ts come in widths of 8 ft, 10 ft, 12 ft, and 15 ft. Because of space limits in this book, the design tables will be limited to double Ts of width 12 ft (see Figures 6.84 through 6.87). Additional design data and details are available from the PCI *Design Handbook*, Sixth Edition, of the Precast, Prestressed Concrete Institute. Overall depths for double Ts are 26 in., 30 in., and 34 in. So-called pretopped double Ts are the full depth, and the top surface of the pretopped double T is the working surface of the floor. Other double Ts are fabricated 2 in. shallower, to accommodate a 2 in.-deep concrete topping layer that is applied in the field. Pretopped members tend to be used in situations where they will be subject to weathering, and topped members tend to be used in most indoor installations.

Example of the use of precast double Ts and precast L-beams

- The footprint of a building is 60 ft in the north–south direction and 60 ft in the east–west direction, with a column on each of the corners of the building and a column at midspan of the east and west ends of the building.
- Precast L-beams (described in Figures 6.90 and 6.91) span 30 ft in the north–south direction (from column to column) along the east and west ends of the building.
- Precast double Ts (described in Figures 6.84 through 6.87) span 60 ft in the east–west direction between the L-girders at the east and west ends of the building.

Step 1: Size the double Ts, assuming a live load of 100 lb/ft². Assume that the double Ts are made of lightweight concrete. Choose the shallowest double Ts that will span the 60 ft while supporting the live load. If there is more than one double T that works, then pick the one with the least reinforcing. What is the strand pattern designation of the double T? What is the estimated camber at erection, in inches? What is the estimated long-time camber, in inches?

Step 2: Size the L-girders on the east and west ends of the building, accounting for the dead load of the double Ts and a live load of 100 lb/ft².

Solution to Step 1

Information about lightweight concrete double Ts is contained in the tables at the bottom of each of the Figures 6.84 through 6.91. From Figure 6.85, the shallowest lightweight double T that works under the live load is a 30-in. deep pretopped double T. The one with the least reinforcing has a strand pattern of 188-D1, which contains 18 strands of diameter $\frac{8}{16}$ in. $= \frac{1}{2}$ in. The D1 indicates that the strands are depressed at one point at the center of the span. In such situations, strands are held high near the ends of the beam and depressed at near mid-span to provide a favorable angle to resist the shear forces near the end of the double T. Where possible, the strands are only depressed at the center of the span (D1). For severe shear problems, the strands can be depressed twice (D2), producing a strand shape that more nearly follows the tension stress path in the beam. This double T supports a superimposed live load of 110 lb/ft² at a span of 60 ft, with an estimated camber at erection of 3.4 in. and an estimated long-time camber of 4.4 in.

Solution to Step 2

From the upper right-hand corner of Figure 6.85, the weight of the double T made from lightweight concrete is 62 lb/ft². At that weight, the load of the double Ts on the L-beam is:

$$w_{DoubleTsOnLbeam} = p_{DoubleTs} \cdot s = \frac{62\,\#}{ft^2} \cdot 30\,ft = 1860\frac{\#}{ft}$$

The live load on the L-beam is:

$$w_{LiveOnLbeam} = p_{Live} \cdot s = \frac{100\,\#}{ft^2} \cdot 30\,ft = 3000\frac{\#}{ft}$$

The total load on the L-beam is:

$$w_{TotalOnLbeam} = w_{DoubleTsOnLbeam} + w_{LiveOnLbeam}$$

$$= 1860\frac{\#}{ft} + 3000\frac{\#}{ft} = 4860\frac{\#}{ft}$$

An L beam with a designation of 20LB36 will span 30 ft under a safe superimposed service load of 5883 lb/ft (including dead and live), with an estimated erection camber of 0.6 in. and an estimated long-time camber of 0.2 in. The number 20 in the designation means that the width of the L-beam at the base is 20 in. The LB means L beam. The number 36 means the beam has a depth of 36 in. The strand pattern is 168-S, which means 16 strands of diameter $\frac{8}{16}$ in. $= \frac{1}{2}$ in., that are straight (S). The overall depth of the beam is 36 in., with a ledger that is 12 in.

Strand Pattern Designation

No. of strand (16)
S = straight D = depressed

16 8 - D 1 → *can have D1 or D2.*

No. of depression points
Diameter of strand in 16ths

Safe loads shown include dead load of 10 psf for untopped members and 15 psf for topped members. Remainder is live load. Long-time cambers include superimposed dead load but do not include live load.

Key
142 – Safe superimposed service load, psf
1.4 – Estimated camber at erection, in.
1.8 – Estimated long-time camber, in.

DOUBLE TEE
12'-0" x 28"

12'-0"
3'-0" 6'-0" 3'-0"
2" 7¾" 2"
28"
3" Chamfer
4¾"

$f'_c = 5{,}000$ psi
$f_{pu} = 270{,}000$ psi

Section Properties

	Untopped	Topped
A =	640 in.^{2}	–
I =	44,563 in.^{4}	61,410 in.^{4}
y_b =	20.21 in.	23.19 in.
y_t =	7.79 in.	6.81 in.
S_b =	2,227 in.^{3}	2,648 in.^{3}
S_t =	5,577 in.^{3}	9,018 in.^{3}
wt =	511 plf	822 plf
DL =	43 psf	68 psf
V/S =	1.62 in.	

12' width   depth inches + topping

Normal Weight Concrete | 12DT28 + 2 |

Double tee

Table of safe superimposed service load (psf) and cambers (in.)
2 in. Normal Weight Topping

Strand Pattern	y_s(end) in. / y_s(center) in.	40	42	44	46	48	50	52	54	56	58	60	62	64	66	68	70	72
108-S	6.00 / 6.00	127 0.8 0.8	110 0.9 0.8	95 0.9 0.8	82 0.9 0.8	70 0.9 0.7	60 0.9 0.6	51 0.9 0.5	42 0.8 0.3	35 0.8 0.1	29 0.7 -0.1							
128-S	7.00 / 7.00	154 1.0 1.0	134 1.0 1.0	117 1.1 1.0	102 1.1 1.0	88 1.1 1.0	77 1.1 0.9	66 1.1 0.8	57 1.1 0.7	49 1.1 0.5	41 1.0 0.3	32 0.9 0.0						
148-S	8.00 / 8.00	177 1.1 1.1	155 1.1 1.2	136 1.2 1.2	119 1.2 1.2	105 1.3 1.1	92 1.3 1.1	80 1.3 1.0	70 1.3 0.9	60 1.3 0.8	50 1.2 0.6	41 1.2 0.3	32 1.1 0.1					
168-S	9.00 / 9.00	197 1.1 1.2	173 1.2 1.3	152 1.3 1.3	134 1.3 1.3	118 1.4 1.3	104 1.4 1.2	90 1.4 1.2	78 1.4 1.1	66 1.4 0.9	56 1.4 0.8	47 1.3 0.5	39 1.3 0.3	31 1.2 0.0				
168-D1	13.00 / 3.75			199 1.5 1.7	177 1.6 1.7	157 1.7 1.7	140 1.8 1.8	125 1.9 1.7	111 1.9 1.7	97 2.0 1.6	84 2.0 1.5	72 2.0 1.3	62 2.0 1.1	52 1.9 0.8	43 1.8 0.5	36 1.8 0.2	30 1.6 -0.2	
188-D1	14.39 / 4.00							143 2.0 1.9	126 2.1 1.9	111 2.1 1.9	97 2.2 1.8	85 2.2 1.7	73 2.3 1.5	63 2.3 1.3	54 2.2 1.0	45 2.1 0.7	37 2.0 0.3	31 1.9 -0.2

straight

Lightweight Concrete | 12LDT28 + 2 |

Table of safe superimposed service load (psf) and cambers (in.)
2 in. Normal Weight Topping

Strand Pattern	y_s(end) in. / y_s(center) in.	40	42	44	46	48	50	52	54	56	58	60	62	64	66	68	70	72	74	76	78
108-S	6.00 / 6.00	137 1.4 1.4	120 1.5 1.4	104 1.6 1.4	91 1.6 1.4	80 1.7 1.3	69 1.7 1.2	60 1.8 1.1	52 1.8 0.9	45 1.8 0.7	38 1.8 0.5	32 1.8 0.2	27 1.7								
128-S	7.00 / 7.00	164 1.6 1.7	144 1.7 1.7	127 1.8 1.8	111 1.9 1.8	98 2.0 1.8	86 2.1 1.7	76 2.1 1.7	67 2.2 1.6	59 2.2 1.4	51 2.2 1.3	44 2.2 1.0	38 2.2 0.8	31 2.2 0.4	25 2.1 0.1						
148-S	8.00 / 8.00	187 1.8 1.9	165 1.9 2.0	146 2.0 2.0	129 2.1 2.1	114 2.2 2.1	101 2.3 2.1	90 2.4 2.0	80 2.5 1.9	70 2.5 1.8	61 2.6 1.7	52 2.6 1.5	45 2.6 1.2	38 2.6 0.9	31 2.5 0.6	25 2.4 0.1					
168-S	9.00 / 9.00		183 2.0 2.1	162 2.1 2.2	144 2.2 2.2	128 2.4 2.2	114 2.5 2.2	101 2.6 2.2	90 2.7 2.2	78 2.7 2.1	67 2.8 1.9	58 2.8 1.7	50 2.8 1.5	42 2.8 1.2	36 2.8 0.9	29 2.8 0.5					
168-D1	13.00 / 3.75							135 3.2 3.0	121 3.3 3.0	109 3.5 3.0	98 3.6 3.0	88 3.7 2.9	77 3.8 2.8	68 3.9 2.6	59 4.0 2.3	51 4.0 2.0	43 4.0 1.6	36 3.9 1.1	30 3.9 0.6		
188-D1	14.39 / 4.00												89 4.1 3.2	79 4.3 3.0	69 4.3 2.8	60 4.4 2.6	52 4.5 2.2	45 4.5 1.9	38 4.5 1.4	32 4.5 0.8	26 4.3 0.1

Shaded values require release strengths higher than 3500 psi.

1 point depression.

Figure 6.84 Allowed load on 12 ft-wide double T with topping layer and overall depth of 30 in. (Copyright Prestressed/Precast Concrete Institute (PCI). Reprinted with permission. All rights reserved.)

Strand Pattern Designation

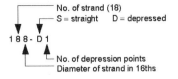

No. of strand (18)
S = straight   D = depressed

188-D1

No. of depression points
Diameter of strand in 16ths

Because these units are pretopped and are typically used in parking structures, safe loads shown do not include any superimposed dead loads. Loads shown are live load. Long-time cambers do not include live load.

Key
158 – Safe superimposed service load, psf
0.8 – Estimated camber at erection, in.
1.1 – Estimated long-time camber, in.

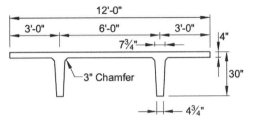

PRETOPPED DOUBLE TEE
12'-0" x 30"

12'-0"

3'-0" | 6'-0" | 3'-0"

7¾"

4"

3" Chamfer

30"

4¾"

$f'_c = 5,000$ psi

$f_{pu} = 270,000$ psi

Section Properties

	Normal Weight	Lightweight
A =	928 in.²	928 in.²
I =	59,997 in.⁴	59,997 in.⁴
y_b =	22.94 in.	22.94 in.
y_t =	7.06 in.	7.06 in.
S_b =	2,615 in.³	2,615 in.³
S_t =	8,498 in.³	8,498 in.³
wt =	967 plf	741 plf
DL =	81 psf	62 psf
V/S =	2.30 in.	2.30 in.

12DT30

Table of safe superimposed service load (psf) and cambers (in.)
Normal Weight — No Topping

Strand Pattern	y_s(end) in. y_s(center) in.	40	42	44	46	48	50	52	54	56	58	60	62	64	66	68	70	72	74	76	78	80	82
128-S	7.00 7.00	158 0.8 1.1	138 0.8 1.2	120 0.9 1.2	105 0.9 1.2	91 0.9 1.2	79 0.9 1.2	69 0.8 1.1	59 0.8 1.1	51 0.7 1.0	43 0.6 0.8	37 0.5 0.6	30 0.4 0.4										
148-S	8.00 8.00	182 0.9 1.3	160 1.0 1.3	140 1.0 1.4	123 1.0 1.4	108 1.1 1.4	95 1.1 1.5	83 1.0 1.4	73 1.0 1.4	63 1.0 1.3	55 0.9 1.2	47 0.8 1.0	41 0.7 0.9	34 0.5 0.6	29 0.3 0.4								
168-S	9.00 9.00		178 1.1 1.5	157 1.1 1.5	139 1.2 1.6	122 1.2 1.6	108 1.2 1.6	95 1.2 1.6	84 1.2 1.6	74 1.1 1.5	65 1.1 1.5	57 1.0 1.3	49 0.9 1.2	42 0.8 1.0	36 0.6 0.7	31 0.4 0.4							
188-S	10.00 10.00		194 1.1 1.6	171 1.2 1.6	152 1.2 1.7	134 1.3 1.7	119 1.3 1.8	106 1.3 1.8	93 1.3 1.8	83 1.3 1.7	73 1.2 1.7	64 1.1 1.6	56 1.0 1.4	49 0.9 1.2	43 0.8 1.0	36 0.6 0.7	29 0.4 0.4						
188-D1	14.39 4.00					184 1.6 2.2	165 1.7 2.3	148 1.7 2.4	132 1.8 2.4	119 1.8 2.4	107 1.8 2.4	96 1.8 2.3	86 1.7 2.2	77 1.7 2.1	68 1.6 2.0	61 1.4 1.9	54 1.3 1.7	48 1.1 1.4	42 0.9 1.1	35 0.6 0.7	29 0.3 0.2		
208-D1	15.50 4.25							166 1.9 2.6	149 2.0 2.7	135 2.0 2.7	121 2.0 2.7	109 2.1 2.7	97 2.1 2.7	86 2.0 2.6	76 1.9 2.4	68 1.8 2.3	61 1.7 2.1	54 1.5 1.9	48 1.3 1.7	43 1.1 1.4	37 0.8 1.0	31 0.5 0.5	26 0.1 -0.1

12LDT30

Table of safe superimposed service load (psf) and cambers (in.)
Lightweight — No Topping

Strand Pattern	y_s(end) in. y_s(center) in.	40	42	44	46	48	50	52	54	56	58	60	62	64	66	68	70	72	74	76	78	80	82	84	86	88	90
128-S	7.00 7.00	172 1.4 1.8	152 1.4 1.9	134 1.5 2.0	119 1.6 2.1	105 1.6 2.2	93 1.7 2.2	83 1.7 2.3	73 1.7 2.3	65 1.7 2.3	57 1.6 2.2	51 1.6 2.2	45 1.5 2.0	39 1.4 1.9	34 1.2 1.6	29 1.0 1.3											
148-S	8.00 8.00	196 1.5 2.1	174 1.6 2.2	154 1.7 2.3	137 1.8 2.4	122 1.9 2.5	109 1.9 2.6	97 2.0 2.6	87 2.0 2.7	77 2.0 2.7	69 2.0 2.7	61 2.0 2.7	55 1.9 2.6	48 1.8 2.5	43 1.7 2.3	38 1.6 2.1	33 1.4 1.8	29 1.1 1.4									
168-S	9.00 9.00		192 1.8 2.4	171 1.9 2.5	153 2.0 2.6	136 2.1 2.7	122 2.1 2.8	109 2.2 2.9	98 2.2 3.0	88 2.3 3.0	79 2.3 3.0	71 2.3 3.0	63 2.3 3.0	57 2.2 2.9	50 2.2 2.8	45 2.1 2.6	40 2.0 2.4	35 1.8 2.1	31 1.6 1.7	27 1.3 1.3							
188-S	10.00 10.00		185 2.0 2.6	166 2.1 2.8	148 2.2 2.9	133 2.3 3.0	120 2.3 3.1	108 2.4 3.2	97 2.5 3.3	87 2.5 3.3	78 2.5 3.3	70 2.5 3.3	63 2.4 3.2	57 2.3 3.1	51 2.2 3.0	45 2.1 2.8	40 1.9 2.5	36 1.7 2.2	31 1.4 1.8	27 1.1 1.3							
188-D1	14.39 4.00					179 2.8 3.8	162 2.9 4.0	147 3.1 4.1	133 3.2 4.3	121 3.3 4.4	110 3.4 4.4	100 3.4 4.5	90 3.5 4.5	81 3.5 4.5	73 3.4 4.4	65 3.2 4.2	58 3.1 4.0	52 2.9 3.7	46 2.7 3.4	42 2.4 3.2	38 2.1 2.8	35 1.8 2.5	31 1.4 2.0	28		1.5	
208-D1	15.50 4.25											123 3.7 4.9	111 3.8 5.0	101 3.8 5.1	91 3.9 5.1	82 3.9 5.1	74 3.9 5.0	67 3.9 4.9	60 3.8 4.7	53 3.6 4.4	48 3.4 4.0	42 3.1 3.6	38 2.9 3.3	35 2.6 2.8	31 2.2 2.4	28 1.8 1.9	26 1.3 1.3

Figure 6.85 Allowed load on pretopped, 12 ft-wide double T of depth of 30 in. (Copyright Prestressed/Precast Concrete Institute (PCI). Reprinted with permission. All rights reserved.)

Strand Pattern Designation

No. of strand (20)
S = straight   D = depressed

2 0 8 - D 1

No. of depression points
Diameter of strand in 16ths

Safe loads shown include dead load of 10 psf for untopped members and 15 psf for topped members. Remainder is live load. Long-time cambers include superimposed dead load but do not include live load.

Key
181 – Safe superimposed service load, psf
1.5 – Estimated camber at erection, in.
2.0 – Estimated long-time camber, in.

DOUBLE TEE
12'-0" x 32"

12'-0"
3'-0"   6'-0"   3'-0"
2"   7¾"   2"
3" Chamfer   32"
4¾"

$f'_c = 5{,}000$ psi
$f_{pu} = 270{,}000$ psi

Section Properties

	Untopped	Topped
A =	690 in.^{2}	–
I =	64,620 in.^{4}	88,305 in.^{4}
y_b =	22.75 in.	26.08 in.
y_t =	9.25 in.	7.92 in.
S_b =	2,840.4 in.^{3}	3,385.9 in.^{3}
S_t =	6,985.9 in.^{3}	11,149.6 in.^{3}
wt =	551 plf	851 plf
DL =	46 psf	71 psf
V/S =	1.70 in.	

Normal Weight Concrete   `12DT32 + 2`

Table of safe superimposed service load (psf) and cambers (in.)
2 in. Normal Weight Topping

Strand Pattern	y_s(end) in. / y_s(center) in.	40	42	44	46	48	50	52	54	56	58	60	62	64	66	68	70	72	74	76	78	80	82	84
128-S	7.00 / 7.00	190	167	146	128	113	99	87	76	66	57	49	42	36	30									
		0.8	0.9	0.9	1.0	1.0	1.0	1.1	1.1	1.1	1.0	1.0	1.0	0.9	0.8									
		0.9	1.0	1.0	1.0	1.0	1.0	0.9	0.9	0.8	0.7	0.5	0.3	0.1	-0.2									
148-S	8.00 / 8.00		194	171	151	133	118	104	92	81	71	62	54	47	40	32								
			1.0	1.1	1.1	1.2	1.2	1.2	1.3	1.3	1.3	1.3	1.2	1.2	1.1	1.0								
			1.1	1.1	1.2	1.2	1.2	1.1	1.1	1.0	0.9	0.8	0.7	0.5	0.2	-0.1								
168-S	9.00 / 9.00			192	170	151	135	120	106	94	84	74	65	56	48	39	32							
				1.2	1.2	1.3	1.3	1.4	1.4	1.4	1.4	1.4	1.4	1.4	1.3	1.3	1.2							
				1.3	1.3	1.3	1.3	1.3	1.3	1.2	1.1	1.0	0.9	0.7	0.5	0.3	0.0							
188-S	10.00 / 10.00				187	167	149	133	119	106	94	82	71	62	53	45	38	30						
					1.3	1.4	1.4	1.5	1.5	1.5	1.6	1.6	1.6	1.5	1.5	1.4	1.3	1.2						
					1.4	1.4	1.4	1.4	1.4	1.4	1.3	1.2	1.1	0.9	0.7	0.5	0.2	-0.1						
208-D1	15.50 / 4.25											132	118	105	93	82	72	63	54	46	39	32	27	
												2.3	2.4	2.4	2.5	2.5	2.5	2.5	2.4	2.3	2.2	2.1	1.9	
												2.2	2.1	2.0	1.9	1.8	1.6	1.4	1.1	0.7	0.3	-0.1	-0.6	
228-D1	16.41 / 4.50															93	83	73	64	55	48	41	34	28
																2.7	2.7	2.8	2.7	2.7	2.6	2.6	2.4	2.2
																2.1	2.0	1.8	1.5	1.2	0.9	0.5	0.0	-0.5

Lightweight Concrete   `12LDT32 + 2`

Table of safe superimposed service load (psf) and cambers (in.)
2 in. Normal Weight Topping

Strand Pattern	y_s(end) in. / y_s(center) in.	42	44	46	48	50	52	54	56	58	60	62	64	66	68	70	72	74	76	78	80	82	84	86	88	90
128-S	7.00 / 7.00	177	157	139	123	109	97	86	76	68	60	53	46	40	35	30	25									
		1.5	1.6	1.6	1.7	1.8	1.9	1.9	2.0	2.0	2.0	2.0	2.0	2.0	2.0	1.9	1.8									
		1.6	1.6	1.7	1.7	1.7	1.7	1.6	1.6	1.5	1.4	1.2	1.0	0.8	0.5	0.2	-0.2									
148-S	8.00 / 8.00		181	161	144	128	115	102	92	82	73	65	58	51	45	39	33	27								
			1.7	1.9	2.0	2.0	2.1	2.2	2.3	2.3	2.4	2.4	2.4	2.4	2.4	2.3	2.2								
			1.9	1.9	2.0	2.0	2.0	2.0	1.9	1.9	1.8	1.7	1.5	1.3	1.1	0.8	0.4	0.0								
168-S	9.00 / 9.00			181	162	145	130	117	105	94	84	76	67	59	51	44	38	32	27							
				2.0	2.1	2.2	2.3	2.4	2.5	2.6	2.7	2.7	2.7	2.7	2.7	2.7	2.7	2.6	2.5							
				2.1	2.2	2.2	2.3	2.3	2.2	2.2	2.1	2.0	1.9	1.7	1.5	1.2	0.9	0.5	0.1							
188-S	10.00 / 10.00			198	177	159	143	129	116	105	94	83	73	64	56	49	42	36	30	25						
				2.1	2.2	2.3	2.4	2.6	2.7	2.7	2.8	2.9	2.9	3.0	3.0	3.0	2.9	2.9	2.8	2.7						
				2.2	2.3	2.4	2.4	2.4	2.4	2.4	2.3	2.2	2.1	1.9	1.7	1.5	1.2	0.8	0.4	-0.1					
208-D1	15.50 / 4.25														98	88	78	69	61	54	47	41	35	29		
															4.4	4.5	4.6	4.7	4.7	4.8	4.8	4.8	4.7	4.5		
															3.6	3.5	3.3	3.1	2.8	2.5	2.1	1.6	1.1	0.4		
228-D1	16.41 / 4.50																	71	63	56	49	43	37	31	26
																		5.2	5.2	5.3	5.3	5.2	5.2	5.1	5.0
																		3.4	3.1	2.8	2.3	1.9	1.3	0.7	-0.1

Shaded values require release strengths higher than 3500 psi.

Figure 6.86 Allowed load on 12 ft-wide double T with topping layer and overall depth of 34 in. (Copyright Prestressed/Precast Concrete Institute (PCI). Reprinted with permission. All rights reserved.)

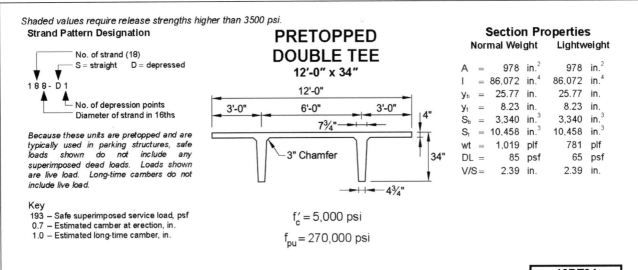

Shaded values require release strengths higher than 3500 psi.

Strand Pattern Designation

No. of strand (18)
S = straight   D = depressed

1 8 8 - D 1

No. of depression points
Diameter of strand in 16ths

Because these units are pretopped and are typically used in parking structures, safe loads shown do not include any superimposed dead loads. Loads shown are live load. Long-time cambers do not include live load.

Key
193 – Safe superimposed service load, psf
0.7 – Estimated camber at erection, in.
1.0 – Estimated long-time camber, in.

PRETOPPED DOUBLE TEE
12'-0" x 34"

12'-0"
3'-0"   6'-0"   3'-0"
7¾"
3" Chamfer
4"
34"
4¾"

$f'_c = 5{,}000$ psi

$f_{pu} = 270{,}000$ psi

Section Properties

	Normal Weight	Lightweight
A =	978 in.²	978 in.²
I =	86,072 in.⁴	86,072 in.⁴
y_b =	25.77 in.	25.77 in.
y_t =	8.23 in.	8.23 in.
S_b =	3,340 in.³	3,340 in.³
S_t =	10,458 in.³	10,458 in.³
wt =	1,019 plf	781 plf
DL =	85 psf	65 psf
V/S =	2.39 in.	2.39 in.

12DT34

Table of safe superimposed service load (psf) and cambers (in.)   Normal Weight — No Topping

Strand Pattern	y_s(end) in. y_s(center) in.	Span, ft																								
		40	42	44	46	48	50	52	54	56	58	60	62	64	66	68	70	72	74	76	78	80	82	84	86	88
128-S	7.00 7.00	193 0.7 1.0	169 0.7 1.0	149 0.8 1.1	131 0.8 1.1	115 0.8 1.1	101 0.8 1.1	88 0.8 1.1	77 0.8 1.1	67 0.7 1.0	59 0.7 09	51 0.6 0.8	43 0.5 0.7	37 0.4 0.5	31 0.3 0.4	25 0.2 0.1										
148-S	8.00 8.00		197 0.9 1.2	174 0.9 1.2	154 0.9 1.3	136 1.0 1.3	120 1.0 1.4	107 1.0 1.4	94 1.0 1.4	83 1.0 1.3	73 0.9 1.3	64 0.9 1.2	56 0.8 1.1	49 0.7 1.0	42 0.6 0.8	36 0.5 0.6	30 0.3 0.4	25 0.1 0.1								
168-S	9.00 9.00		197 1.0 1.4	174 1.0 1.4	155 1.1 1.5	138 1.1 1.5	123 1.1 1.6	109 1.1 1.6	97 1.1 1.6	86 1.1 1.5	76 1.1 1.5	67 1.0 1.4	59 1.0 1.3	52 0.9 1.1	45 0.7 1.0	39 0.6 0.8	34 0.4 0.5	28 0.2 0.2								
188-S	10.00 10.00			192 1.1 1.6	171 1.2 1.6	153 1.2 1.7	137 1.3 1.7	122 1.3 1.8	109 1.3 1.7	97 1.3 1.7	87 1.2 1.7	77 1.2 1.6	69 1.1 1.6	61 1.1 1.4	53 1.0 1.3	47 0.8 1.1	41 0.7 0.8	35 0.5 0.6	30 0.3 0.3							
188-D1	14.39 4.00							180 1.6 2.1	162 1.6 2.2	147 1.7 2.2	132 1.7 2.2	119 1.7 2.2	108 1.7 2.2	97 1.6 2.1	88 1.6 2.1	79 1.5 2.0	71 1.5 1.9	63 1.4 1.8	57 1.2 1.6	50 1.1 1.4	45 0.9 1.1	39 0.6 0.7	34 0.4 0.3	28 0.1 -0.1		
208-D1	15.50 4.25								183 1.8 2.4	166 1.8 2.5	150 1.9 2.6	136 1.9 2.6	123 2.0 2.6	112 2.0 2.6	101 1.9 2.5	92 1.9 2.4	82 1.8 2.3	74 1.7 2.2	67 1.6 2.1	61 1.5 1.9	55 1.3 1.7	49 1.1 1.4	43 0.9 1.1	37 0.6 0.7	31 0.3 0.2	26 -0.1 -0.3

12LDT34

Table of safe superimposed service load (psf) and cambers (in.)   Lightweight — No Topping

Strand Pattern	y_s(end) in. y_s(center) in.	Span, ft																											
		42	44	46	48	50	52	54	56	58	60	62	64	66	68	70	72	74	76	78	80	82	84	86	88	90	92	94	96
128-S	7.00 7.00	184 1.2 1.6	164 1.3 1.7	146 1.4 1.8	130 1.4 1.9	116 1.5 2.0	103 1.5 2.0	92 1.5 2.1	82 1.5 2.1	73 1.5 2.1	65 1.5 2.1	58 1.4 2.0	52 1.4 2.0	46 1.2 1.8	40 1.1 1.7	35 0.9 1.5	31 0.7 1.2	26 0.9											
148-S	8.00 8.00	189 1.5 2.0	169 1.6 2.1	151 1.6 2.2	135 1.7 2.3	121 1.8 2.4	109 1.8 2.4	98 1.9 2.5	88 1.9 2.5	79 1.9 2.5	71 1.9 2.5	64 1.8 2.4	57 1.8 2.3	51 1.7 2.2	45 1.6 2.0	40 1.5 1.7	35 1.3 1.4	31 1.1 1.1	27 0.9										
168-S	9.00 9.00	189 1.8 2.3	170 1.8 2.5	153 1.9 2.6	137 2.0 2.6	124 2.1 2.7	112 2.1 2.8	101 2.1 2.9	91 2.2 2.9	82 2.2 2.9	74 2.2 2.9	67 2.1 2.8	60 2.1 2.7	54 2.0 2.6	48 1.9 2.4	43 1.8 2.2	38 1.6 1.8	34 1.4 1.5	30 1.2 1.0	26									
188-S	10.00 10.00			186 2.0 2.7	168 2.1 2.8	152 2.2 2.9	137 2.2 3.0	124 2.3 3.1	112 2.4 3.1	102 2.4 3.2	92 2.4 3.2	83 2.4 3.2	76 2.4 3.2	68 2.3 3.1	62 2.3 3.0	56 2.1 2.9	50 2.0 2.7	45 1.8 2.4	40 1.6 2.1	36 1.3 1.7	32 1.0 1.2	28							
188-D1	14.39 4.00							195 2.6 3.5	177 2.7 3.7	161 2.8 3.8	147 3.0 3.9	134 3.1 4.1	123 3.2 4.2	112 3.2 4.2	103 3.2 4.2	94 3.2 4.2	86 3.3 4.1	78 3.3 4.0	71 3.1 3.9	64 3.0 3.7	57 2.9 3.5	53 2.7 3.3	48 2.6 3.1	44 2.4 2.9	40 2.1 2.6	36 1.8 2.2	33 1.5 1.8	29 1.1 1.2	25 0.6 0.5
208-D1	15.50 4.25							198 2.9 4.0	180 3.1 4.2	165 3.2 4.3	151 3.3 4.5	138 3.4 4.6	127 3.6 4.7	116 3.6 4.8	107 3.7 4.8	98 3.8 4.9	89 3.8 4.8	80 3.7 4.7	73 3.7 4.6	66 3.6 4.4	59 3.4 4.2	53 3.3 3.9	48 3.1 3.6	44 2.9 3.4	41 2.6 3.0	37 2.3 2.7	34 2.0 2.3	31 1.6 1.8	28 1.2 1.2

Figure 6.87 Allowed load on pretopped, 12 ft-wide double T of depth 34 in.

deep. So the stem of the L beam is 24 in. deep. The 24 in. stem of the L beam is less than the 30 in. depth of the double Ts, so the two beams are compatible, in the sense that the top of the L beam does not go above the top of the double Ts. If it is desired to get the top surface of the double Ts down even with the top of the surface of the L beam, the ribs of the double Ts can be notched upward by an amount of 6 in.

Assignment

Assuming a p_{live} = 100 lb/ft^2, what is the longest span and associated cambers, at erection and estimated long-time, for each of the double Ts in Figures 6.84 through 6.87?

6.4.2 CONCRETE HOLLOW-CORE PLANKS (HCPS)

Example of the use of precast hollow-core planks (HCPs)

- A building is supported on a grid of columns that is spaced at 30 ft OC in both the north–south and east–west directions. HCPs with a 2-in. topping span 30 ft in the east–west direction (see Figures 6.88 and 6.89 for span data on HCPs).
- Precast L beams span 30 ft in the north–south direction (from column to column) along the east and west ends of the building (see Figures 6.90 and 6.91 for span data on L beams).
- Precast inverted T beams span 30 ft in the north–south direction (from column to column) supporting the interior ends of the HCP. (Data is not provided in this textbook for inverted T beams.)

STEP 1: Size the HCPs, assuming a live load of 100 lb/ft^2. Choose the shallowest HCP that will span the 30 ft while supporting the live load. If there is more than one HCP of that depth that works, then pick the one with the least reinforcing. What is the strand pattern designation of the HCP? What is the estimated camber at erection, in inches? What is the estimated long-time camber, in inches?

STEP 2: Size the L girders on the east and west ends of the building, accounting for the dead load of the HCPs and a live load of 100 lb/ft^2.

Solution to Step 1:

From the bottom of Figure 6.88, the shallowest HCP that works under the live load is an 8 in. deep HCP. The HCP that works, with the least reinforcing, has a strand pattern of 68-S, which contains 6 strands of diameter $^8/_{16}$ in. = $^1/_2$ in. The S indicates that the strands are straight. The HCP supports a superimposed service load of 124 lb/ft^2 at a span of 30 ft. with an estimated camber at erection of 0.8 in. and an estimated long-time camber of 0.2 in.

Solution to Step 2:

From the upper right-hand corner of Figure 6.88, the weight of the HCP is 81 lb/ft^2. At that weight, the load of the HCPs on the L beam is

$$w_{HCPonLbeam} = p_{HCP} \cdot s = \frac{81\#}{ft^2} \cdot 15ft = 1215\frac{\#}{ft}$$

The live load on the L-beam is

$$w_{LiveonLbeam} = p_{Live} \cdot s = \frac{100\#}{ft^2} \cdot 15ft = 1500\frac{\#}{ft}$$

The total load on the L beam is

$$w_{TotalOnLbeam} = w_{HCPsonLbeam} + w_{LiveonLbeam}$$

$$= 1215\frac{\#}{ft} + 1500\frac{\#}{ft} = 2715\frac{\#}{ft}$$

An L beam with a designation of 20LB28 will span 30 ft under a safe superimposed service load of 3443 lb/ft (including dead and live), with an estimated camber at erection of 0.7 in. and an estimated long-time camber of 0.2 in. The number 20 in the designation means that the width of the L beam at the base is 20 in. The LB means L beam. The number 28 means a depth of 28 in. The strand pattern is 128-S, which means 12 strands of diameter $^8/_{16}$ in. = $^1/_2$ in. The S indicates that the strands are straight. The overall depth of the beam is 28 in., with a ledger that is 12 in. deep. So the stem of the L beam is 16 in. deep. The 16 in. stem of the L beam is more than the 10 in. overall depth of the HCP plus topping. This means that the top of the L beams is above the finished floor at the east and west ends of the building. To accommodate doorways at the east and west ends of the building, the top of the L beam must be flush with the top of the topping slab on the HCPs. To get the top surface of the L beam down, it is necessary to make the ledger 18 in. deep, so that the stem is only 10 in. deep. Making the ledger deeper will strengthen the L beam and may make it possible to go to an L beam that is only 24 in. deep. Further analysis or more extensive tables would be necessary to verify if that is possible.

Assignment 1 on HCP

With a normal-weight topping, what is the longest span possible with 8 in.-deep HCPs under a live load of 100 lb/ft^2?

Assignment 2 on HCP

With a normal-weight topping, what is the longest span possible with 12 in.-deep HCPs under a live load of 100 lb/ft^2?

6.4.3 CONCRETE L BEAMS

See Figures 6.90 and 6.91.

Strand Pattern Designation
76-S

- S = straight → no deflection.
- Diameter of strand in 16ths
- No. of Strand (7)

Safe loads shown include dead load of 10 psf for untopped members and 15 psf for topped members. Remainder is live load. Long-time cambers include superimposed dead load but do not include live load.

Capacity of sections of other configurations are similar. For precise values, see local hollow-core manufacturer.

Key
458 – Safe superimposed service load, psf
0.1 – Estimated camber at erection, in.
0.2 – Estimated long-time camber, in.

HOLLOW-CORE
4′-0″ x 8″
Normal Weight Concrete

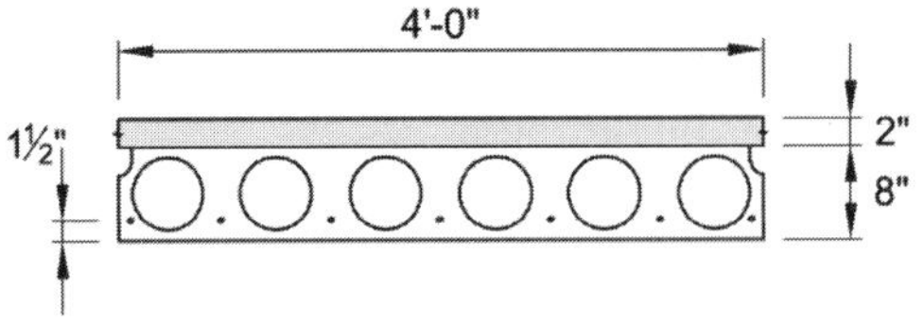

$f'_c = 5{,}000$ psi
$f_{pu} = 270{,}000$ psi

Section Properties

		Untopped		Topped	
A	=	215	in.^{2}	311	in.^{2}
I	=	1,666	in.^{4}	3,071	in.^{4}
y_b	=	4.00	in.	5.29	in.
y_t	=	4.00	in.	4.71	in.
S_b	=	417	in.^{3}	581	in.^{3}
S_t	=	417	in.^{3}	652	in.^{3}
wt	=	224	plf	324	plf
DL	=	56	psf	81	psf
V/S	=	1.92	in.		

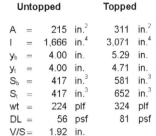

voids 4′ depth 8

Not load factored tables.

4HC8

Table of safe superimposed service load (psf) and cambers (in.) — **No Topping**

Strand Designation Code	11	12	13	14	15	16	17	18	19	20	21	22	23	24	25
66-S	458	415	378	346	311	269	234	204	179	158	140	124	110	98	87
	0.1	0.2	0.2	0.2	0.2	0.2	0.2	0.2	0.3	0.3	0.3	0.3	0.2	0.2	0.2
	0.2	0.2	0.2	0.3	0.3	0.3	0.3	0.3	0.3	0.3	0.3	0.3	0.2	0.2	0.1
76-S	470	424	387	355	326	303	276	242	213	188	167	149	133	119	106
	0.2	0.2	0.2	0.2	0.3	0.3	0.3	0.3	0.3	0.3	0.4	0.4	0.4	0.3	0.3
	0.2	0.2	0.3	0.3	0.3	0.4	0.4	0.4	0.4	0.4	0.4	0.4	0.4	0.3	0.3
58-S	464	421	384	352	323	300	280	260	244	229	211	194	177	160	144
	0.2	0.2	0.3	0.3	0.3	0.4	0.4	0.5	0.5	0.5	0.5	0.6	0.6	0.6	0.6
	0.3	0.3	0.4	0.4	0.5	0.5	0.6	0.6	0.6	0.7	0.7	0.7	0.7	0.7	0.7
68-S	476	430	393	361	332	309	286	269	253	235	223	209	200	180	165
	0.3	0.3	0.3	0.4	0.4	0.5	0.5	0.6	0.6	0.7	0.7	0.7	0.8	0.8	0.8
	0.3	0.4	0.5	0.5	0.6	0.6	0.7	0.7	0.8	0.8	0.9	0.9	1.0	1.0	1.0
78-S	488	442	402	370	341	318	295	275	259	241	229	215	203	195	180
	0.3	0.3	0.4	0.5	0.5	0.6	0.6	0.7	0.7	0.8	0.9	0.9	1.0	1.0	1.0
	0.4	0.5	0.5	0.6	0.7	0.8	0.8	0.9	1.0	1.0	1.1	1.2	1.2	1.2	1.3

Strand Designation Code	26	27	28	29	30	31	32	33	34	35	36	37	38	39	40
66-S	77	69	61	54	48	43	38	33	29						
	0.2	0.1	0.0	0.0	–0.1	–0.2	–0.3	–0.5	–0.6						
	0.0	–0.1	–0.2	–0.3	–0.5	–0.7	–0.9	–1.2	–1.4						
76-S	95	86	77	69	62	55	50	44	39	35	31	26			
	0.3	0.3	0.2	0.2	0.1	0.0	–0.1	–0.2	–0.4	–0.5	–0.7	–0.9			
	0.2	0.1	0.0	–0.1	–0.2	–0.4	–0.6	–0.8	–1.1	–1.4	–1.7	–2.0			
58-S	130	118	107	97	88	80	72	66	60	54	48	42	37	32	28
	0.6	0.6	0.5	0.5	0.5	0.4	0.3	0.2	0.1	0.0	–0.4	–0.3	–0.5	–0.7	–0.9
	0.6	0.6	0.5	0.4	0.3	0.2	0.0	–0.2	–0.4	–0.6	–0.9	–1.2	–1.6	–2.0	–2.4
68-S	153	142	132	121	110	101	92	84	77	70	63	56	51	45	40
	0.8	0.8	0.8	0.8	0.8	0.8	0.7	0.7	0.6	0.5	0.4	0.2	0.1	–0.1	–0.3
	1.0	0.9	0.9	0.9	0.8	0.7	0.6	0.4	0.2	0.0	–0.2	–0.5	–0.8	–1.1	–1.5
78-S	168	157	144	135	126	118	110	101	92	84	77	70	64	58	52
	1.1	1.1	1.1	1.1	1.1	1.1	1.1	1.1	1.0	0.9	0.8	0.7	0.6	0.5	0.3
	1.3	1.3	1.3	1.3	1.2	1.2	1.1	1.0	0.8	0.7	0.5	0.3	0.0	–0.3	–0.7

4HC8 + 2

Table of safe superimposed service load (psf) and cambers (in.) — **2 in. Normal Weight Topping**

Strand Designation Code	13	14	15	16	17	18	19	20	21	22	23	24	25	26
66-S	489	445	394	340	294	256	224	197	173	153	135	119	105	93
	0.2	0.2	0.2	0.2	0.2	0.2	0.3	0.3	0.3	0.3	0.2	0.2	0.2	0.2
	0.2	0.2	0.2	0.2	0.2	0.2	0.2	0.2	0.1	0.1	0.0	–0.1	–0.2	–0.3
76-S	498	457	420	387	347	304	267	235	208	184	164	146	130	116
	0.2	0.2	0.3	0.3	0.3	0.3	0.3	0.3	0.4	0.4	0.4	0.3	0.3	0.3
	0.2	0.2	0.3	0.3	0.3	0.3	0.3	0.3	0.2	0.2	0.2	0.1	0.0	–0.1
58-S	492	451	414	384	357	333	310	293	274	245	219	196	177	159
	0.3	0.3	0.3	0.4	0.4	0.5	0.5	0.5	0.5	0.6	0.6	0.6	0.6	0.6
	0.3	0.3	0.4	0.4	0.4	0.4	0.5	0.5	0.5	0.5	0.4	0.3	0.3	0.3
68-S		463	426	393	366	342	319	299	282	267	251	239	216	195
		0.4	0.4	0.5	0.5	0.6	0.6	0.7	0.7	0.7	0.8	0.8	0.8	0.8
		0.4	0.5	0.5	0.6	0.6	0.6	0.6	0.7	0.7	0.7	0.6	0.6	0.6
78-S		472	435	402	375	348	325	305	288	273	257	245	232	220
		0.5	0.5	0.6	0.6	0.7	0.7	0.8	0.9	0.9	1.0	1.0	1.0	1.1
		0.5	0.6	0.6	0.7	0.7	0.8	0.8	0.8	0.9	0.9	0.9	0.9	0.8

Strand Designation Code	27	28	29	30	31	32	33	34	35	36	37	38	39	40
66-S	82	68	56	45	36	26								
	0.1	0.0	–0.0	–0.1	–0.2	–0.3								
	–0.4	–0.6	–0.7	–0.9	–1.2	–1.4								
76-S	103	88	74	62	51	41	31							
	0.3	0.2	0.2	0.1	–0.0	–0.1	–0.2							
	–0.2	–0.4	–0.5	–0.7	–0.9	–1.2	–1.4							
58-S	143	126	110	95	82	70	59	49	40	32				
	0.6	0.5	0.5	0.5	0.1	0.3	0.2	0.1	0.0	–0.1				
	0.2	0.1	–0.1	–0.2	–0.4	–0.6	–0.9	–1.2	–1.5	–1.8				
68-S	177	158	140	124	110	97	84	73	62	53	44	36	28	
	0.8	0.8	0.8	0.8	0.8	0.7	0.7	0.6	0.5	0.4	0.2	0.1	–0.1	
	0.5	0.4	0.3	0.2	0.0	–0.2	–0.4	–0.6	–0.9	–1.2	–1.6	–2.0	–2.4	
78-S	207	186	167	149	133	119	106	94	83	73	64	55	46	38
	1.1	1.1	1.1	1.1	1.1	1.1	1.1	1.0	0.9	0.9	0.7	0.6	0.5	0.3
	0.8	0.7	0.7	0.6	0.4	0.3	0.1	–0.1	–0.3	–0.6	–0.9	–1.3	–1.7	–2.2

Figure 6.88 Allowed load on 4 ft-wide, 8 in.-deep hollow-core planks (HCPs). (Copyright Prestressed/Precast Concrete Institute (PCI). Reprinted with permission. All rights reserved.)

Strand Pattern Designation
76-S

S = straight
Diameter of strand in 16ths
No. of Strand (7)

Safe loads shown include dead load of 10 psf for untopped members and 15 psf for topped members. Remainder is live load. Long-time cambers include superimposed dead load but do not include live load.

Capacity of sections of other configurations are similar. For precise values, see local hollow-core manufacturer.

Key
258 – Safe superimposed service load, psf
0.3 – Estimated camber at erection, in.
0.4 – Estimated long-time camber, in.

HOLLOW-CORE
4'-0" x 12"
Normal Weight Concrete

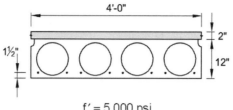

4'-0"
2"
12"
1½"

f'_c = 5,000 psi
f_{pu} = 270,000 psi

Section Properties

	Untopped	Topped
A =	262 in.²	358 in.²
I =	4,949 in.⁴	7,811 in.⁴
y_b =	6.00 in.	7.55 in.
y_t =	6.00 in.	6.45 in.
S_b =	825 in.³	1,035 in.³
S_t =	825 in.³	1,211 in.³
wt =	273 plf	373 plf
DL =	68 psf	93 psf
V/S =	2.18 in.	

4HC12

Table of safe superimposed service load (psf) and cambers (in.)   No Topping

Strand Designation Code	20	21	22	23	24	25	26	27	28	29	30	31	32	33	34	35	36	37	38	39	40	41	42	43	44	45	46
76-S	258	242	228	215	204	194	175	159	144	131	120	109	99	90	82	75	68	62	56	51	46	41	37	33	30	26	
	0.3	0.3	0.3	0.3	0.3	0.3	0.3	0.3	0.3	0.3	0.3	0.3	0.3	0.3	0.2	0.2	0.1	0.1	0.0	0.0	−0.1	−0.2	−0.3	−0.4	−0.5	−0.6	−0.8
	0.3	0.4	0.4	0.4	0.4	0.4	0.4	0.4	0.4	0.3	0.3	0.3	0.2	0.1	0.1	0.0	−0.1	−0.2	−0.3	−0.5	−0.6	−0.8	−1.0	−1.2	−1.5	−1.7	
58-S	258	242	228	215	204	194	182	174	167	157	151	143	138	128	118	108	100	92	84	78	71	66	60	55	51	46	42
	0.4	0.4	0.4	0.4	0.5	0.5	0.5	0.5	0.5	0.5	0.5	0.5	0.5	0.5	0.5	0.5	05	0.4	0.4	0.3	0.2	0.1	0.1	0.0	−0.1	−0.3	−0.4
	0.5	0.5	0.5	0.6	0.6	0.6	0.6	0.6	0.6	0.6	0.6	0.6	0.6	0.6	0.5	0.5	0.4	0.4	0.3	0.2	0.1	−0.1	−0.2	−0.4	−0.6	−0.8	−1.0
68-S	264	248	234	221	210	200	191	180	173	163	157	149	144	137	133	127	121	112	106	98	93	87	81	75	69	64	59
	0.4	0.5	0.5	0.5	0.6	0.6	0.6	0.7	0.7	0.7	0.7	0.7	0.7	0.7	0.8	0.8	0.7	0.7	0.7	0.7	0.6	0.6	0.5	0.5	0.4	0.3	0.2
	0.6	0.6	0.7	0.7	0.8	0.8	0.8	0.9	0.9	0.9	0.9	0.9	0.9	0.9	0.9	0.9	0.8	0.8	0.7	0.7	0.6	0.5	0.3	0.2	0.1	−0.1	−0.3	−0.5
78-S	273	257	243	230	216	206	197	186	179	169	163	155	150	143	136	133	127	121	115	110	105	98	93	86	82	78	72
	0.5	0.6	0.6	0.7	0.7	0.8	0.8	0.8	0.9	0.9	0.9	1.0	1.0	1.0	1.0	1.0	1.0	1.0	1.0	1.0	1.0	0.9	0.9	0.8	0.7	0.7	0.6
	0.7	0.8	0.8	0.9	0.9	1.0	1.0	1.1	1.1	1.1	1.2	1.2	1.2	1.2	1.2	1.2	1.2	1.1	1.1	1.0	1.0	0.9	0.8	0.7	0.5	0.3	0.2
88-S	282	266	252	236	225	212	203	192	185	175	169	161	153	149	142	136	130	127	121	116	114	107	102	95	91	84	81
	0.6	0.7	0.7	0.8	0.8	0.9	0.9	1.0	1.0	1.1	1.1	1.2	1.2	1.2	1.3	1.3	1.3	1.3	1.3	1.3	1.3	1.3	1.3	1.2	1.2	1.1	1.1
	0.8	0.9	1.0	1.0	1.1	1.2	1.2	1.3	1.3	1.4	1.4	1.5	1.5	1.5	1.5	1.6	1.6	1.5	1.5	1.5	1.4	1.4	1.3	1.2	1.1	1.0	0.8

4HC12 + 2

Table of safe superimposed service load (psf) and cambers (in.)   2 in. Normal Weight Topping

Strand Designation Code	20	21	22	23	24	25	26	27	28	29	30	31	32	33	34	35	36	37	38	39	40	41	42	43	44	45	46
76-S	295	276	258	246	232	217	196	177	160	144	131	118	107	96	87	78	71	63	56	50	43	35	28				
	0.3	0.3	0.3	0.3	0.3	0.3	0.3	0.3	0.3	0.3	0.3	0.3	0.3	0.2	0.2	0.1	0.1	0.0	0.0	−0.1	−0.2	−0.3	−0.4				
	0.3	0.3	0.3	0.3	0.3	0.3	0.2	0.2	0.2	0.1	0.1	0.0	−0.1	−0.2	−0.3	−0.4	−0.5	−0.7	−0.8	−1.0	−1.2	−1.4	−1.7				
58-S	292	273	258	243	229	216	205	195	186	175	167	160	151	139	127	116	106	97	89	81	72	63	55	47	39	32	26
	0.4	0.4	0.4	0.4	0.5	0.5	0.5	0.5	0.5	0.5	0.5	0.5	0.5	0.5	0.5	0.5	0.5	0.4	0.4	0.3	0.3	0.2	0.1	0.1	0.0	−0.1	−0.3	−0.4
	0.4	0.4	0.4	0.4	0.4	0.5	0.4	0.4	0.4	0.4	0.4	0.3	0.3	0.2	0.1	0.0	−0.1	−0.2	−0.3	−0.5	−0.7	−0.9	−1.1	−1.3	−1.6	−1.9	−2.2
68-S	301	282	264	249	235	222	211	201	192	181	173	166	157	152	144	139	132	127	117	107	98	88	78	69	61	53	46
	0.4	0.5	0.5	0.5	0.6	0.6	0.6	0.7	0.7	0.7	0.7	0.7	0.7	0.7	0.8	0.8	0.7	0.7	0.7	0.7	0.6	0.6	0.5	0.5	0.4	0.3	0.2	0.1
	0.5	0.5	0.6	0.6	0.6	0.6	0.6	0.6	0.6	0.6	0.6	0.5	0.5	0.4	0.3	0.2	0.1	−0.1	−0.2	−0.4	−0.6	−0.8	−1.0	−1.3	−1.6		
78-S	310	291	273	258	244	231	217	207	198	187	179	172	163	158	150	142	138	131	128	122	116	113	102	92	83	74	66
	0.5	0.6	0.6	0.7	0.7	0.8	0.8	0.8	0.9	0.9	0.9	1.0	1.0	1.0	1.0	1.0	1.0	1.0	1.0	1.0	1.0	0.9	0.9	0.8	0.7	0.7	0.6
	0.6	0.6	0.7	0.7	0.8	0.8	0.8	0.8	0.8	0.9	0.9	0.8	0.8	0.8	0.8	0.7	0.6	0.6	0.5	0.4	0.3	0.1	−0.1	−0.2	−0.5	−0.7	−0.9
88-S	319	300	282	267	250	237	226	213	204	193	185	175	169	161	156	148	141	137	131	125	122	117	111	106	103	94	86
	0.6	0.7	0.7	0.8	0.8	0.9	0.9	1.0	1.0	1.1	1.1	1.2	1.2	1.2	1.3	1.3	1.3	1.3	1.3	1.3	1.3	1.3	1.3	1.2	1.2	1.1	1.1
	0.7	0.8	0.8	0.9	0.9	1.0	1.0	1.0	1.1	1.1	1.1	1.1	1.1	1.1	1.1	1.0	1.0	0.9	0.9	0.8	0.7	0.6	0.4	0.3	0.1	−0.1	−0.3

Figure 6.89 Allowed load on 4 ft-wide, 12 in.-deep hollow-core planks (HCPs). (Copyright Prestressed/Precast Concrete Institute (PCI). Reprinted with permission. All rights reserved.)

L-BEAMS

Normal Weight Concrete

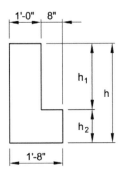

$f'_c = 5,000$ psi
$f_{pu} = 270,000$ psi
½ in. diameter
low-relaxation strand

Designation	h in.	h_1/h_2 in./in.	A in.²	I in.⁴	y_b in.	S_b in.³	S_t in.³	wt plf
20LB20	20	12/8	304	10,160	8.74	1,163	902	317
20LB24	24	12/12	384	17,568	10.50	1,673	1,301	400
20LB28	28	16/12	432	27,883	12.22	2,282	1,767	450
20LB32	32	20/12	480	41,600	14.00	2,971	2,311	500
20LB36	36	24/12	528	59,119	15.82	3,737	2,930	550
20LB40	40	24/16	608	81,282	17.47	4,653	3,608	633
20LB44	44	28/16	656	108,107	19.27	5,610	4,372	683
20LB48	48	32/16	704	140,133	21.09	6,645	5,208	733
20LB52	52	36/16	752	177,752	22.94	7,749	6,117	783
20LB56	56	40/16	800	221,355	24.80	8,926	7,095	833
20LB60	60	44/16	848	271,332	26.68	10,170	8,143	883

1. Check local area for availability of other sizes.
2. Safe loads shown include 50% superimposed dead load and 50% live load. 800 psi top tension has been allowed, therefore, additional top reinforcement is required.
3. Safe loads can be significantly increased by use of structural composite topping.

Key

6566 – Safe superimposed service load, plf.
0.3 – Estimated camber at erection, in.
0.1 – Estimated long-time camber, in.

Table of safe superimposed service load (plf) and cambers (in.)

Desig-nation	No. Strand	y_s(end) / y_s(center) in.	16	18	20	22	24	26	28	30	32	34	36	38	40	42	44	46	48	50
20LB20	98-S	2.44 / 2.44	6566	5131	4105	3345	2768	2318	1961	1674	1438	1243	1079							
			0.3	0.4	0.5	0.6	0.7	0.8	0.9	1.0	1.0	1.1	1.2							
			0.1	0.2	0.2	0.2	0.2	0.2	0.3	0.3	0.3	0.3	0.2							
20LB24	108-S	2.80 / 2.80	9577	7495	6006	4904	4066	3414	2896	2479	2137	1854	1617	1416	1244	1097	969			
			0.3	0.3	0.4	0.5	0.5	0.6	0.7	0.8	0.9	0.9	1.0	1.0	1.1	1.1	1.2			
			0.1	0.1	0.1	0.1	0.1	0.2	0.2	0.2	0.2	0.2	0.1	0.1	0.1	0.0	0.0			
20LB28	128-S	3.33 / 3.33			8228	6733	5596	4711	4009	3443	2979	2595	2273	2000	1768	1567	1394	1243	1110	992
					0.4	0.4	0.5	0.6	0.6	0.7	0.8	0.9	0.9	1.0	1.1	1.1	1.2	1.2	1.2	1.3
					0.1	0.1	0.2	0.2	0.2	0.2	0.2	0.2	0.2	0.2	0.2	0.1	0.1	0.0	0.0	
20LB32	148-S	3.71 / 3.71				8942	7446	6281	5356	4611	4001	3495	3071	2712	2406	2143	1914	1715	1540	1386
						0.4	0.5	0.5	0.6	0.7	0.7	0.8	0.9	1.0	1.0	1.1	1.2	1.2	1.3	1.3
						0.1	0.2	0.2	0.2	0.2	0.2	0.2	0.3	0.3	0.3	0.2	0.2	0.2	0.2	0.1
20LB36	168-S	4.25 / 4.25					9457	7988	6823	5883	5113	4476	3941	3489	3103	2771	2483	2231	2011	1816
							0.4	0.5	0.5	0.6	0.7	0.8	0.8	0.9	1.0	1.1	1.1	1.2	1.2	1.3
							0.2	0.2	0.2	0.2	0.3	0.3	0.3	0.3	0.3	0.3	0.3	0.3	0.3	0.2
20LB40	188-S	4.89 / 4.89						9812	8386	7235	6293	5513	4858	4305	3832	3425	3073	2765	2495	2257
								0.4	0.5	0.6	0.6	0.7	0.8	0.8	0.9	1.0	1.0	1.1	1.1	1.2
								0.2	0.2	0.2	0.2	0.2	0.2	0.3	0.3	0.3	0.3	0.3	0.3	0.3
20LB44	198-S	5.05 / 5.05								8959	7803	6845	6042	5363	4783	4284	3851	3474	3143	2850
										0.5	0.6	0.6	0.7	0.8	0.8	0.9	0.9	1.0	1.1	1.1
										0.2	0.2	0.2	0.2	0.2	0.2	0.2	0.2	0.2	0.2
20LB48	218-S	5.81 / 5.81									9226	8100	7158	6360	5678	5092	4584	4140	3751	3408
											0.5	0.6	0.6	0.7	0.8	0.8	0.9	0.9	1.0	1.1
											0.2	0.2	0.2	0.2	0.2	0.2	0.3	0.3	0.3	0.3
20LB52	238-S	6.17 / 6.17										9634	8521	7578	6774	6082	5482	4958	4499	4094
												0.6	0.6	0.7	0.7	0.8	0.9	0.9	1.0	1.0
												0.2	0.2	0.2	0.3	0.3	0.3	0.3	0.3	0.3
20LB56	258-S	6.64 / 6.64											9954	8860	7927	7124	6427	5820	5287	4816
													0.6	0.7	0.7	0.8	0.8	0.9	1.0	1.0
													0.2	0.2	0.3	0.3	0.3	0.3	0.3	0.3
20LB60	278-S	7.33 / 7.33													9089	8173	7380	6688	6080	5544
														0.7	0.7	0.8	0.9	0.9	1.0
														0.3	0.3	0.3	0.3	0.3	0.3

L-BEAMS

Normal Weight Concrete

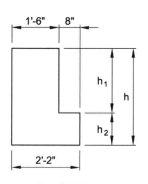

$f'_c = 5,000$ psi
$f_{pu} = 270,000$ psi
½ in. diameter
low-relaxation strand

Designation	h in.	h₁/h₂ in./in.	A in.²	I in.⁴	yb in.	Sb in.³	St in.³	wt plf
				Section Properties				
26LB20	20	12/8	424	14,298	9.09	1,573	1,311	442
26LB24	24	12/12	528	24,716	10.91	2,265	1,888	550
26LB28	28	16/12	600	39,241	12.72	3,085	2,568	625
26LB32	32	20/12	672	58,533	14.57	4,017	3,358	700
26LB36	36	24/12	744	83,176	16.45	5,056	4,255	775
26LB40	40	24/16	848	114,381	18.19	6,288	5,244	883
26LB44	44	28/16	920	152,104	20.05	7,586	6,351	958
26LB48	48	32/16	992	197,159	21.94	8,986	7,566	1,033
26LB52	52	36/16	1,064	250,126	23.83	10,496	8,879	1,108
26LB56	56	40/16	1,136	311,586	25.75	12,100	10,300	1,183
26LB60	60	44/16	1,208	382,118	27.67	13,810	11,819	1,258

1. Check local area for availability of other sizes.
2. Safe loads shown include 50% superimposed dead load and 50% live load. 800 psi top tension has been allowed, therefore, additional top reinforcement is required.
3. Safe loads can be significantly increased by use of structural composite topping.

Key

9672 – Safe superimposed service load, plf.
0.4 – Estimated camber at erection, in.
0.2 – Estimated long-time camber, in.

Table of safe superimposed service load (plf) and cambers (in.)

Designation	No. Strand	ys(end) in. / ys(center) in.	16	18	20	22	24	26	28	30	32	34	36	38	40	42	44	46	48	50
26LB20	158-S	2.67 / 2.67	9672	7563	6054	4938	4089	3428	2903	2480	2134	1847	1607	1403	1230	1080	950			
			0.4	0.5	0.6	0.7	0.8	1.0	1.1	1.2	1.4	1.5	1.6	1.7	1.8	1.9	1.9			
			0.2	0.3	0.3	0.4	0.4	0.5	0.5	0.6	0.6	0.7	0.7	0.7	0.7	0.7	0.6			
26LB24	158-S	2.67 / 2.67		9165	7493	6221	5231	4445	3811	3293	2863	2503	2198	1938	1714	1520	1350	1202	1070	
				0.5	0.5	0.6	0.7	0.8	0.9	1.0	1.1	1.2	1.3	1.3	1.4	1.5	1.5	1.5	1.5	
				0.2	0.2	0.2	0.2	0.3	0.3	0.3	0.3	0.3	0.3	0.3	0.2	0.2	0.1	0.1	0.0	
26LB28	188-S	3.33 / 3.33				8437	7170	6056	5207	4511	3935	3452	3043	2694	2394	2134	1907	1707	1532	
						0.6	0.6	0.7	0.8	0.9	1.0	1.1	1.2	1.3	1.3	1.4	1.5	1.5	1.6	
						0.2	0.2	0.3	0.3	0.3	0.3	0.3	0.3	0.3	0.3	0.3	0.2	0.2	0.2	
26LB32	218-S	4.00 / 4.00						9265	7906	6809	5912	5169	4545	4018	3568	3180	2844	2551	2294	2067
								0.6	0.7	0.7	0.8	0.9	1.0	1.1	1.2	1.2	1.3	1.4	1.5	1.5
								0.2	0.3	0.3	0.3	0.3	0.4	0.4	0.4	0.4	0.4	0.4	0.3	0.3
26LB36	248-S	4.50 / 4.50								8722	7585	6643	5854	5186	4615	4125	3699	3328	3002	2715
										0.7	0.8	0.9	0.9	1.0	1.1	1.2	1.3	1.3	1.4	1.5
										0.3	0.3	0.3	0.4	0.4	0.4	0.4	0.4	0.4	0.4	0.4
26LB40	278-S	5.11 / 5.11									9372	8216	7246	6426	5726	5123	4601	4145	3745	3392
											0.7	0.8	0.9	0.9	1.0	1.1	1.2	1.2	1.3	1.4
											0.3	0.3	0.4	0.4	0.4	0.4	0.4	0.4	0.4	0.4
26LB44	288-S	5.29 / 5.29											8992	7986	7127	6388	5748	5189	4698	4266
													0.8	0.8	0.9	1.0	1.0	1.1	1.2	1.2
													0.3	0.3	0.3	0.3	0.3	0.3	0.3	0.3
26LB48	328-S	5.75 / 5.75												9635	8609	7726	6961	6294	5708	5191
														0.8	0.9	1.0	1.0	1.1	1.2	1.3
														0.3	0.4	0.4	0.4	0.4	0.4	0.4
26LB52	358-S	6.29 / 6.29														9137	8241	7459	6773	6167
															0.9	1.0	1.1	1.1	1.2
															0.4	0.4	0.4	0.4	0.5
26LB56	378-S	7.00 / 7.00															9539	8641	7853	7158
																0.9	1.0	1.1	1.1
																0.4	0.4	0.4	0.4
26LB60	388-S	7.68 / 7.68																9904	9008	8217
																	0.9	0.9	1.0
																	0.3	0.3	0.3

Figure 6.91 Allowed load on 1.5 ft-thick L beams. (Copyright Prestressed/Precast Concrete Institute (PCI). Reprinted with permission. All rights reserved.)

6.5 Torsion

Beams can have torsional moments induced in them by loads. For example, a beam that is eccentrically loaded will tend to twist under such a load (see Figure 6.92).

Separating the system into freebodies produces the result shown in Figure 6.93.

The two forces on the girder are not along the same line, so they are a couple with a moment of magnitude $M = PL$. Moments that create a twisting along the long axis of the element are referred to as torsional moments. The deformational response is for the center parts of the beam to twist relative to the ends. The ends must be constrained if collapse is to be avoided (see Figure 6.94).

I-beams tend to be very poor in resisting torsional loading. To understand the torsional phenomenon, the stress patterns on the cross section of the member should be drawn and studied. The resistive torsional moment on the cross section depends on the intensity of the stress, the area over which the stress is applied, and the effective lever arm for the stresses. To understand the overall effect, it is useful to cluster the small incremental forces

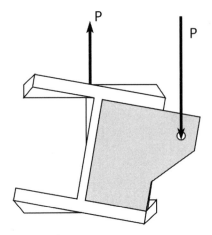

Figure 6.94 Torsional deformation.

on the cross section into couples, that is, two equal and opposite forces that together create a pure moment. The lever arms for these couples suggest a great deal about how intense the stresses must be to generate a given level of resistive torsional moment. If the lever arms for

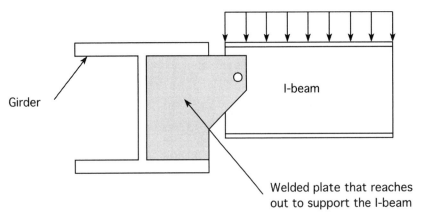

Figure 6.92 Plate connector creating eccentric loading on girder.

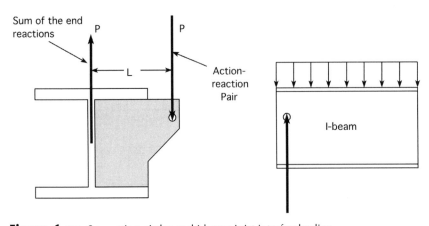

Figure 6.93 Separating girder and I-beam joist into freebodies.

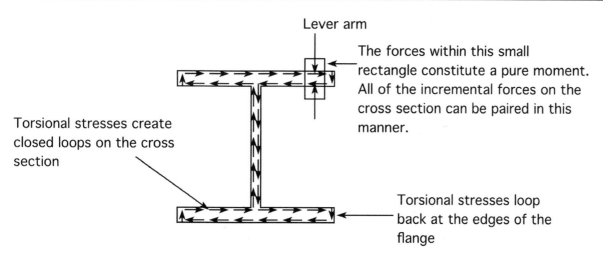

Figure 6.95 Stress path from torsional influence.

the small incremental force on the cross section tend to be small, then the stress level must be very high to achieve a given resistive torsional moment. For I-beams and wide-flange sections, the torsional stress pattern looks like that shown in Figure 6.95).

Torsional stresses create closed loops on the cross section. For a tubular cross section, they do not have to loop back the way they do for the I-section, but they simply keep going around the tube. A tube of circular cross section is ideal for resisting torsional moments (see Figure 6.96.)

Because I-sections are very poor at resisting torsional moments, it is highly desirable to avoid eccentric loading. In other words, connections to I-sections should be

made as near to the centerline of the members as possible. Clip-angle connections can be used to avoid eccentric loading (see Figure 6.97).

By making the connection directly to the web of the girder, the load is delivered right to the centerline of the girder. This avoids the eccentric loading that causes torsion in the girder. Furthermore, if the clip angles and the I-beam are rigidly connected together by a fillet weld or by widely spaced bolts, then the angles become an extension of the joists and they can help constrain the girder against any tendency to undergo a twisting rotation. The web is the logical place to make the connection at the end of the simple-span I-beam. Because shear forces are large near the ends of a simple-span beam, the connection

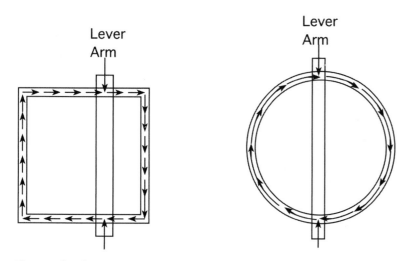

Figure 6.96 Stress path in a closed tube, showing larger lever arm for forces.

Top flange of I-beam is
notched to accommodate top
flange of the girder

Shop connection between clip
angles and I-beam can be by
welding or by bolts

Clip angle

*field bolting is done
by bolting clip angle to girder.*

I-beam

Girder

Field connection between clip
angles and girder is usually made
by bolting the clip angles to the
web of the girder

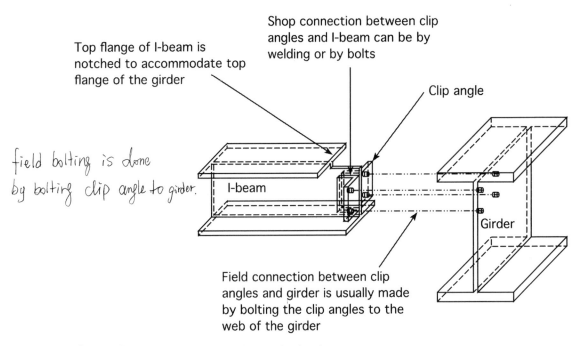

Figure 6.97 I-beam joist extends to web of girder.

should be made to the web, which is predominantly responsible for carrying shear forces. There is no need to involve the flanges in this connection, as the flanges are predominantly responsible for carrying bending moments and the moment is zero at the end of a simple-span beam.

Clip angles are even less effective than the I-beam itself in resisting torsional moments induced by eccentric loading, so eccentric loads on I-beams supported by clip-angle connections should be avoided.

7

Trusses

7.1 Flat-Top Trusses

7.1.1 JOINTS METHOD APPLIED TO SYSTEMS OF TWO-FORCE MEMBERS

Figure 7.1 shows an applied load w distributed along the top chord of a truss. Usually, decking, welded or nailed to the top chord of the truss, exerts this load, which includes the self-weight of the decking and dead, snow, or live loads on top of the decking. The estimated self-weight of the truss may also be included. The self-weights of individual members of the truss are small. A common accounting method for self-weight is to estimate the self-weight of the entire truss and add it to the applied load w distributed along the truss's top chord. In detailed computer analyses, the self-weight of each individual member is accounted for as part of the analysis of that member. However, to do longhand analysis, things are simplified by adding the truss self-weight to the other forces on the top of the truss.

The distributed load w is represented by many small arrows pointing down to indicate the direction of the force. The initial points of the arrows are connected together with a line, signifying that these arrows do not represent individual forces, but are part of a continuous load.

These arrows are tedious to draw, with the arrowheads often drawn at such a small scale in an attempt for clarity that they disappear altogether. Therefore, simple lines are often substituted for the arrows. The distributed-force direction is indicated by the side of the member on which the load is drawn. To make this convention work, it must be understood that the distributed force is always pushing on the member to which it is applied. For example, in Figure 7.2, the distributed force is pushing down on the top chord.

To express an upward force, such as wind suction on a roof, it would be represented as shown in Figure 7.3.

Point forces, such as reactions, are always represented by arrows, as shown in Figure 7.4.

For this truss, imagine pulling out one of the top chord members and representing it as a freebody (see Figure 7.5).

There can be a moment (M) at each end, a point force (P) at each end, and there will be bending induced by the applied lateral forces. If the joints in the truss are true pin joints, then the moments disappear.

Even if the joints are not pin joints, these moments are typically of minor significance, as will be shown in subsequent analyses. This leaves the force systems as shown in Figure 7.6.

There are forces on the ends of the members. It is the member's role to transmit these forces as part of the structural action of the truss. Refer to the diagram on the left in Figure 7.6. The directions of the arrows as depicted are arbitrary. The true directions will be deduced from the analysis. The diagram on the right represents local bending effects.

The analysis methods used for the axial and bending force systems are independent of each other, meaning that they can be analyzed separately and the results of the two analyses combined. The current focus will be on all the truss members' roles in the overall truss action, deferring discussion of local bending issues until later. To this end, it will be assumed that the top-chord members have the bending capacity to transfer the distributed loads to adjacent joints. Later, local bending will be accounted for to make sure that the top chord members can both withstand the forces of overall truss action and the bending moments induced by the locally applied lateral forces.

If the length of a top-chord member is s, then the force on that member is ws. This force is represented by the symbol P. To keep the member in equilibrium under this force, the joints at the end of the member must be exert-

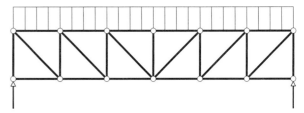

Figure 7.2 Truss subjected to uniform distributed load.

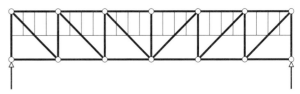

Figure 7.3 Truss subjected to uniform, upward distributed load.

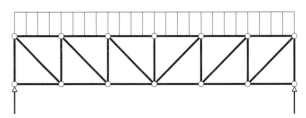

Figure 7.4 Truss subjected to uniform distributed load.

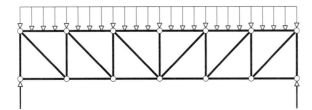

Figure 7.1 Truss subjected to uniform distributed load.

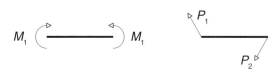

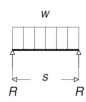

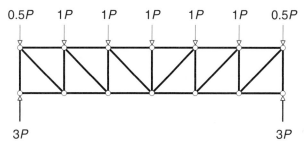

Figure 7.5 Actions on a top-chord member.

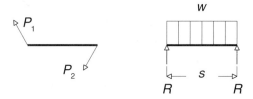

Figure 7.6 Actions on a top-chord member.

ing an upward force of $\frac{ws}{2}$, or $\frac{P}{2}$. According to the action–reaction pairs principle, the member must be pushing down on each of these joints with a force of equal magnitude (see Figure 7.7).

Each joint will receive a force of $\frac{ws}{2}$ from each of the members on each side of the joint. The joints at the end of the truss have a member on only one side, so they receive a force of $\frac{ws}{2}$, or simply $\frac{P}{2}$. Joints not at the end of the truss will have a member on each side, each contributing a force of $\frac{ws}{2}$, or $\frac{P}{2}$, for a total force on the joint of ws, or simply P. The conversion of the continuous distributed force on the top of the truss to these discrete forces on the joints is expressed in Figure 7.8

In Figure 7.8, the total downward force is 6 P aligned symmetrically about the truss center; therefore the reactions are $\frac{6P}{2} = 3\ P$. Once this transfer of forces from top-chord members to adjacent joints has occurred, the only remaining forces that need to be considered are those exerted by the joints at the ends of the members (see Figure 7.9).

In the context of this discussion, each member is referred to as a two-force member, since there are only two points at which any force is applied.

In order to satisfy the condition of equilibrium, these two forces must be equal in magnitude and opposite in direction, such as in Figure 7.10.

The condition of rotational equilibrium must also be satisfied, so these two forces must have zero lever arm. That is, they must lie along the same line, which means that they are either causing pure tension (see Figure 7.11) or pure compression (see Figure 7.12).

Figure 7.8 Equivalent point forces on joints of truss.

Figure 7.9 Forces on the ends of a top-chord member.

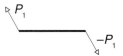

Figure 7.10 Equal and opposite forces.

Figure 7.11 Collinear forces.

Figure 7.12 Collinear forces.

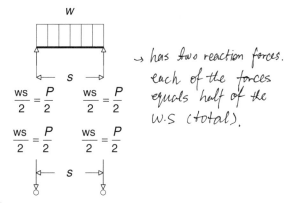

→ has two reaction forces.
each of the forces
equals half of the
w.s (total).

Figure 7.7 Actions on a top-chord member.

7.1.2 JOINTS METHOD APPLIED TO FOUR-BAY TRUSS USING EXPLODED DIAGRAM

A truss can be analyzed in detail by taking it one joint at a time, using an approach called the *joints method*. As will become apparent, it is called the joints method, rather than the members method, because the members are subjected to only two forces, which must be equal, opposite, and collinear. In contrast, the joints may be subjected to many forces. Resolving the forces at the joints is not only the challenge, but it is also the source of all useful information about force transmission through the system.

The discussion begins by considering an extremely simple truss, consisting of four square bays. To get at the force internal to the truss, an exploded diagram will be created, showing the joints and members as separate freebodies (see Figure 7.13).

In the exploded diagram in Figure 7.13, only three bays are shown. Because of the symmetry of the truss and the forces on the truss, the right-hand side of the truss solution will be symmetric with the left-hand side, so analysis of only two bays is required to get a complete picture of the internal forces in the truss. More than two bays have been included as a check on the solution, to verify that it is symmetric, as it must be.

The *P* forces are shown applied to the joints, consistent with the earlier discussion. The reaction force at joint B is also shown. It is crucial to get all the applied and reaction forces on the diagram before proceeding with the analysis. Otherwise, they are likely to be over-looked in the process of performing the analysis, negating the validity of the process. To simplify the image in Figure 7.13, we remove the dashed lines that indicate the relationship of points in the original diagram with points in the exploded diagram (see Figure 7.14).

To proceed with the solution, a choice must be made regarding at what joint to start the analysis. Logic suggests that we start at a joint with few unknowns, such as joint B, where only two members frame into the joint, one vertical, the other horizontal. In other words, there is one unknown vertical force on joint B, being exerted by the vertical member, and one unknown horizontal force on joint B, being exerted by the horizontal member.

Applying the equilibrium principle to the vertical forces on joint B:

The 2*P* upward reaction force on joint B must be equilibrated by a 2*P* downward force on joint B exerted by the vertical member between joint A and joint B. (Henceforth, this member will be referred to as member AB.) Vertical member AB is the only agent acting on joint B that is capable of exerting the required vertical force, since there is only one other member framing into joint B and that member, being horizontal, can exert only a horizontal force on the joint.

To illustrate this deduction in the following diagram, a downward force arrow 2 units long is drawn on joint B, indicating the 2 *P* downward force exerted by vertical member AB on joint B.

Applying the action–reaction pairs principle to the interaction between joint B and the vertical member AB:

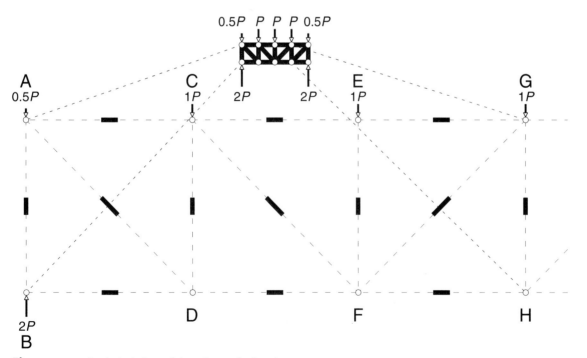

Figure 7.13 Exploded view of three bays of a four-bay truss.

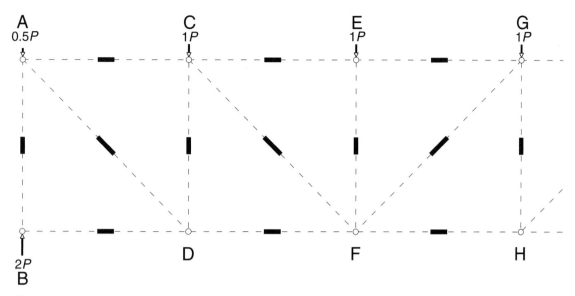

Figure 7.14 Exploded view of three bays of a four-bay truss.

Since the vertical member AB is pushing downward on joint B with a 2 *P* force, joint B must be pushing upward on vertical member AB with a 2 *P* force.

Draw an upward force arrow 2 units long on the bottom of vertical member AB, indicating the 2 *P* upward force exerted by joint B on the vertical member.

Applying the equilibrium principle to the vertical member AB:

The 2 *P* upward force on the bottom of vertical member AB, exerted by joint B, must be equilibrated by a 2 *P* downward force on the top of vertical member AB, exerted by joint A.

Draw a downward arrow 2 units long on the top of the vertical member AB, indicating the 2 *P* downward force exerted by joint A on the vertical member.

Applying the action–reaction pairs principle to the interaction between joint A and vertical member AB:

Since joint A is pushing down on vertical member AB with a 2 *P* force, vertical member AB must be pushing up on joint A with a 2 *P* force.

Draw an upward force arrow 2 units long on joint A, indicating the 2 *P* upward force exerted by vertical member AB on joint A. (See Figure 7.15.)

Applying the equilibrium principle to the horizontal forces on joint B:

Since there are no horizontal applied forces or horizontal reaction forces on joint B, the horizontal member BD is exerting no force on joint B. Any horizontal force from member BD would be unbalanced and would, therefore, upset the equilibrium of joint B.

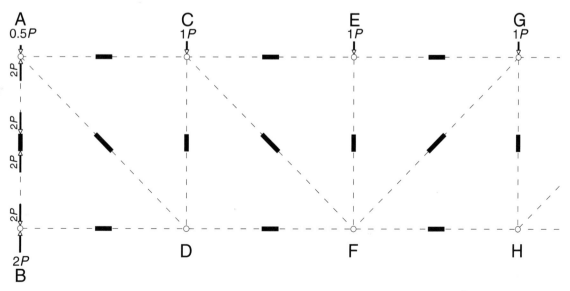

Figure 7.15 Resolving vertical forces on joint B, member AB, and joint A.

To illustrate this deduction in the following diagram, do not draw arrows on joint B, because there is no force exerted on the joint by the horizontal member BD.

Applying the action–reaction pairs principle to the interaction between joint B and horizontal member BD:

Since horizontal member BD is exerting no force on joint B, joint B must be exerting no force on member BD.

Do not draw arrows on horizontal member BD, because no force is exerted on it from joint B.

Applying the equilibrium principle to horizontal member BD:

Since joint B exerts no force on member BD, joint D must not exert any force on member BD either, because any force exerted by joint D on member BD would be unbalanced and would disturb the equilibrium of the member. Hence, horizontal member BD has no force in it.

Note: Whenever the analysis indicates a zero-force member, it is useful to imagine removing that member, to assess whether the structure looks stable without it. In this case, the structure remaining after removal of member BD would be balanced on top of the vertical member AB, indicating that no force would be required in member BD to keep the structure in equilibrium. The horizontal member BD only restrains the vertical member AB from toppling to the left or to the right. Member BD is a bracing member that is not directly engaged in transferring forces under the loads shown.

Do not draw arrows on horizontal member BD, because no force is exerted on it from joint D.

Applying the action–reaction pairs principle to the interaction between horizontal member BD and joint D:

Since joint D is exerting no force on horizontal member BD, member BD must be exerting no force on joint D.

Do not draw arrows on joint D, because there is no force exerted on the joint by the horizontal member BD.

Show the magnitude of the forces involved by writing 0 *P* along the line of action of horizontal member BD, indicating that no force is being transferred by this member and that the member has no axial force in it (see Figure 7.16).

Where to move next in the analysis? Joint D is not a good option, because there are two vertical forces, one from the vertical member CD and one from the vertical component of the diagonal member AD. There are also two horizontal forces, one from the horizontal member DF and one from the horizontal component of the diagonal member AD. There is only one vertical equilibrium equation and there are two vertical unknowns, so a direct solution to the vertical forces is not possible at joint D. Similarly, there is only one horizontal equilibrium equation and there are two horizontal unknowns, so a direct solution to the horizontal forces is not possible at joint D.

At joint A, there are two unknown horizontal forces, one from the horizontal member AC and one from the horizontal component of the diagonal member AD, which means that there is no direct solution to the horizontal forces. However, there is only one unknown vertical force, the vertical component of the diagonal member AD, meaning that the vertical equilibrium equation can be used to solve directly for the unknown vertical force.

Applying the equilibrium principle to the vertical forces on joint A:

The upward 2 *P* force of the vertical member AB on joint A combined with the downward 0.5 *P* applied force on joint A produces a net upward 1.5 *P* force that must

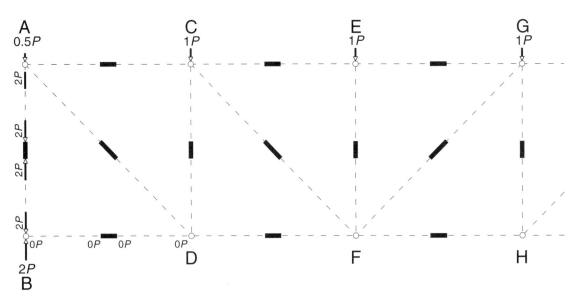

Figure 7.16 Resolving horizontal forces on joint B, member BD, and joint D.

be equilibrated by a 1.5 *P* downward force component exerted by the diagonal member AD on joint A.

These deductions are illustrated on Figure 7.17 by drawing a downward arrow 1.5 units long on joint A, indicating the downward force component of diagonal member AD on joint A.

This arrow is dashed, as a graphic indicator that it is a component of a diagonal force. Distinguishing the diagonal force components graphically from other forces makes the diagram easier to read and aids in tracking the solution. The use of a dashed arrow can be read as the arrow being incomplete without its corresponding orthogonal component. Throughout the rest of this analysis process, force components are drawn as dashed arrows. Furthermore, for the purposes of this particular analysis method, components are drawn rather than the net force along the diagonal. This makes the analysis easier to follow, since all forces in the diagram are either vertical or horizontal.

Applying the behavior principles of 2-force members to determine the horizontal force of the diagonal member AD on joint A:

Diagonal member AD must be pulling down and to the right on joint A with a net force along the centerline of member AD. Here, that centerline has a slope of 1-unit rise in 1-unit run. Therefore, any force along the diagonal member must have vertical and horizontal components that are equal in magnitude to each other. The downward vertical component must be 1.5 *P* (to keep joint A in equilibrium relative to upward vertical forces), so the rightward horizontal component must also be 1.5 *P*. In summary, diagonal member AD is exerting a downward force component of 1.5 *P* on joint A and a force component to the right of 1.5 *P* on joint A.

Draw a right-pointing dashed arrow 1.5 units long on joint A, indicating the horizontal force component of diagonal member AD on joint A.

Applying the action–reaction pairs principle to the interaction between joint A and diagonal member AD:

Since diagonal member AD is pulling down on joint A with a 1.5 *P* force component, joint A must be pulling up on member AD with a 1.5 *P* force component. Since member AD is pulling to the right on joint A with a 1.5 *P* force component, joint A must be pulling to the left on member AD with a 1.5 *P* force component.

Draw a dashed upward arrow 1.5 units long on the left end of diagonal member AD, indicating the vertical force component of joint A on member AD.

Draw a left-pointing dashed arrow 1.5 units long on the left end of the diagonal member AD, indicating the horizontal force component of joint A on the diagonal member AD.

Applying the equilibrium principle to diagonal member AD:

The 1.5 *P* upward force component exerted by joint A on the left end of diagonal member AD must be equilibrated by a 1.5 *P* downward force component exerted by joint D on the right end of member AD. The 1.5 *P* force component to the left exerted by joint A on the left end of member AD must be equilibrated by a 1.5 *P* force component to the right exerted by joint D on the right end of member AD.

Draw a dashed downward arrow 1.5 units long on the right end of the diagonal member AD, indicating the vertical force component of joint D on member AD.

Draw a right-pointing dashed arrow 1.5 units long on the right end of the diagonal member AD, indicating the horizontal force component of joint D on member AD.

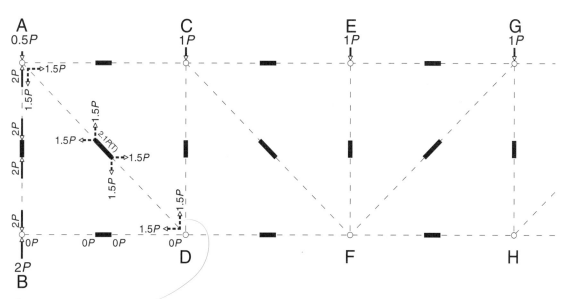

Figure 7.17 Resolving diagonal forces on joint A, member AD, and joint D.

Applying the action–reaction pairs principle to the interaction between diagonal member AD and joint D:

Since joint D is pulling down on diagonal member AD with a 1.5 P force component, member AD must be pulling up on joint D with a 1.5 P force component. Since joint D is pulling to the right on member AD with a 1.5 P force component, member AD must be pulling to the left on joint D with a 1.5 P force component.

Draw a dashed upward arrow 1.5 units long on joint D, indicating the vertical force component of the diagonal member AD on joint D.

Draw a left-pointing dashed arrow 1.5 units long on joint D, indicating the horizontal force component of the diagonal member AD on joint D.

For purposes of sizing the cross section of the diagonal member, it is crucial to calculate the total force in the diagonal member. Using geometry, it can be demonstrated that the sum of the two force components exerted by joints A and D on the ends of the diagonal member AD is a force of magnitude $\sqrt{(1.5\,P)^2 + (1.5\,P)^2} =$ 2.12 P pulling along the length of the member AD, since $\sqrt{(a)^2 + (b)^2} = c^2$. This pulling force implies that the member is in tension. The magnitude and nature of that force are indicated by writing 2.12 P(T), where T is tension, along the side of the diagonal member AD (see Figure 7.17).

Applying the equilibrium principle to the horizontal forces on joint A:

The 1.5 P force component to the right exerted by the diagonal member AD on joint A must be equilibrated by a 1.5 P force to the left exerted by the horizontal member AC on joint A.

Draw a left-pointing arrow 1.5 units long on joint A, indicating the force of horizontal member AC on joint A.

Applying the action–reaction pairs principle to the interaction between joint A and horizontal member AC:

Since horizontal member AC is pushing to the left with 1.5 P force on joint A, joint A must be pushing to the right with 1.5 P force on horizontal member AC.

Draw a right-pointing arrow 1.5 units long on the left end of member AC, indicating the force of joint A on horizontal member AC.

Applying the equilibrium principle to horizontal member AC:

The 1.5 P force to the right exerted by joint A on horizontal member AC must be equilibrated by a 1.5 P force to the left exerted by joint C on horizontal member AC.

Draw a left-pointing arrow 1.5 units long on the right end of member AC, indicating the force of joint C on horizontal member AC.

Applying the action–reaction pairs principle to the interaction between horizontal member AC and joint C:

Since joint C is pushing to the left with a 1.5 P force on horizontal member AC, member AC must be pushing to the right with a 1.5 P force on joint C.

Draw a right-pointing arrow 1.5 units long on joint C, indicating the force of horizontal member AC on joint C (see Figure 7.18).

Joint C is not a promising joint to address next, because there are two unknown vertical forces, neither of which can be determined directly with the single vertical equilibrium equation, and there are two unknown horizontal forces, neither of which can be determined directly with the single horizontal equilibrium equation.

However, joint D has only one unknown vertical force, from member CD, and one unknown horizontal force, from member DF.

Applying the equilibrium principle to the vertical forces on joint D:

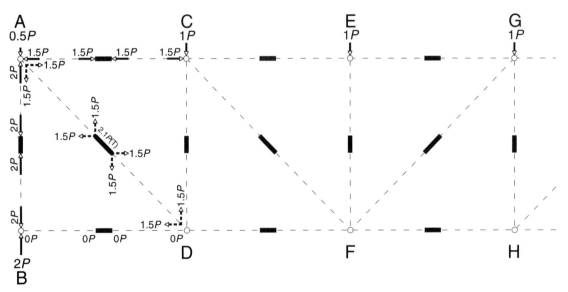

Figure 7.18 Resolving horizontal forces on joint A, member AC, and joint C.

The 1.5 *P* upward force component exerted by the diagonal member AD on joint D must be equilibrated by a 1.5 *P* downward force exerted by the vertical member CD on joint D.

Applying the action–reaction pairs principle to the interaction of joint D and the vertical member CD:

Since member CD is pushing down on joint D with a 1.5 *P* force, joint D must be pushing up on vertical member CD with a 1.5 *P* force.

Applying the equilibrium principle to the vertical forces on member CD:

The 1.5 *P* upward force exerted by joint D on vertical member CD must be equilibrated by a 1.5 *P* downward force exerted by joint C on vertical member CD.

Applying the action–reaction pairs principle to the interaction of joint C and the vertical member CD:

Since joint C is pushing down on vertical member CD with a 1.5 *P* force, vertical member CD must be pushing up on joint C with a 1.5 *P* force (see Figure 7.19).

Applying the equilibrium principle to the horizontal forces on joint D:

The 1.5 *P* force component to the left exerted by the diagonal member AD on joint D must be equilibrated by a 1.5 *P* force to the right exerted by the horizontal member DF on joint D.

Applying the action–reaction pairs principle to the interaction of joint D and horizontal member DF:

Since member DF is pulling to the right on joint D with a 1.5 *P* force, joint D must be pulling to the left on horizontal member DF with a 1.5 *P* force.

Applying the equilibrium principle to the horizontal forces on member DF:

The 1.5 *P* force to the left exerted by joint D on horizontal member DF must be equilibrated by a 1.5 *P* force to the right exerted by joint F on member DF.

Applying the action–reaction pairs principle to the interaction of joint F and horizontal member DF:

Since joint F is pulling to the right on horizontal member DF with a 1.5 *P* force, horizontal member DF must be pulling to the left on joint F with a 1.5 *P* force (see Figure 7.20).

Joint F is not a promising joint to address next, because there are three unknown vertical forces, none of which can be determined directly with the single vertical equilibrium equation, and there are three unknown horizontal forces, none of which can be determined directly with the single horizontal equilibrium equation.

At joint C, there are two unknown horizontal forces, one from the horizontal member CE and one from the horizontal component of the diagonal member CF, which means that there is no direct solution to the horizontal forces. However, there is only one unknown vertical force, the vertical component of the diagonal member CF, which means that the vertical equilibrium equation can be used to solve directly for that unknown force.

Applying the equilibrium principle to the vertical forces on joint C:

The upward 1.5 *P* force of the vertical member on joint CD combined with the downward 1 *P* applied force on joint C produces a net upward 0.5 *P* force. This must be equilibrated by a 0.5 *P* downward force component exerted by the diagonal member CF on joint C.

Draw a downward arrow 0.5 units long on joint C, indicating the downward force component of diagonal member CF on joint C.

Applying the behavior principle of 2-force members to determine the horizontal force of the diagonal member CF on joint C:

Diagonal member CF must be pulling down and to the right on joint C with a net force along the diagonal. The

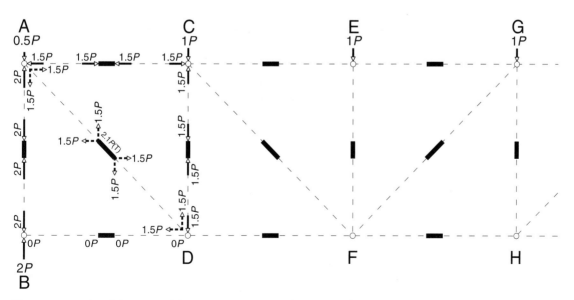

Figure 7.19 Resolving vertical forces on joint D, member CD, and joint C.

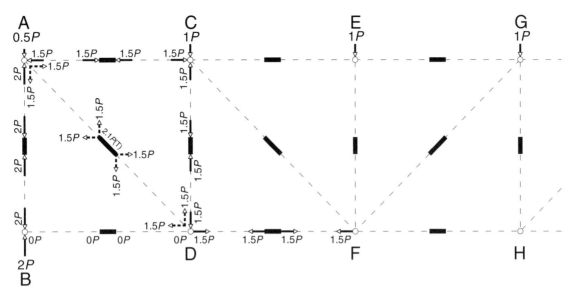

Figure 7.20 Resolving horizontal forces on joint D, member DF, and joint F.

vertical (downward) force component must be 0.5 *P* to equilibrate joint C, so the horizontal (right-pointing) force component must also be 0.5 *P*.

Draw a right-pointing arrow 0.5 units long on joint C, indicating the horizontal force component of diagonal member CF on joint C.

Applying the action–reaction pairs principle to the interaction between joint C and diagonal member CF:

Since diagonal member CF is pulling down on joint C with a 0.5 *P* force component, joint C must be pulling up on diagonal member CF with a 0.5 *P* force component. Since diagonal member CF is pulling to the right on joint C with a 0.5 *P* force component, joint C must be pulling to the left on diagonal member CF with a 0.5 *P* force component. The sum of the two force components exerted by joint C on the diagonal member is a force of magnitude $\sqrt{(0.5\,P)^2 + (0.5\,P)^2} = 0.707\,P$ pulling along the length of the member. This pulling force implies that the member is in tension, so the magnitude of that force is indicated by writing 0.717 *P*(*T*) along the side of the diagonal member.

Draw an upward arrow 0.5 units long on the left end of diagonal member CF, indicating the vertical force component of joint C on member CF.

Draw a left-pointing arrow 0.5 units long on the left end of diagonal member CF, indicating the horizontal force component of joint C on member CF.

Applying the equilibrium principle to diagonal member CF:

The 0.5 *P* upward force component exerted by joint C on the left end of diagonal member CF must be equilibrated by a 0.5 *P* downward force component exerted by joint F on the right end of member CF. The 0.5 *P* force component to the left exerted by joint C on the left

end of member CF must be equilibrated by a 0.5 *P* force component to the right exerted by joint F on the right end of member CF.

Draw a downward arrow 0.5 units long on the right end of diagonal member CF, indicating the downward force component of joint F on member CF.

Draw a right-pointing arrow 0.5 units long on the right end of diagonal member CF, indicating the horizontal force component of joint F on member CF.

Applying the action–reaction pairs principle to the interaction between diagonal member CF and joint F:

Since joint F is pulling down on diagonal member CF with a 0.5 *P* force component, diagonal member CF must be pulling up on joint F with a 0.5 *P* force component. Since joint F is pulling to the right on diagonal member CF with a 0.5 *P* force component, diagonal member CF must be pulling to the left on joint F with a 0.5 *P* force component.

Draw an upward arrow 0.5 units long on joint F, indicating the upward force component of the diagonal member CF on joint F.

Draw a left-pointing arrow 0.5 units long on joint F, indicating the horizontal force component of the diagonal member CF on joint F.

Write the magnitude of the net force (0.717 *P*) and state of stress (*T*) along the side of diagonal member CF (see Figure 7.21).

Applying the equilibrium principle to the horizontal forces on joint C:

Member AC pushes to the right with a 1.5 *P* force on joint C and diagonal member CF pulls to the right with a horizontal force component of 0.5 *P* on joint C, producing a combined force of 2 *P* to the right on joint C. This must be equilibrated by a 2 *P* force to the left exerted by horizontal member CE.

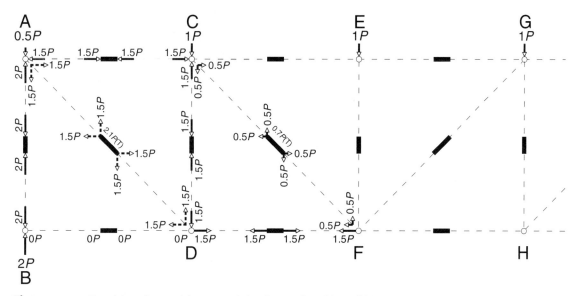

Figure 7.21 Resolving diagonal forces on joint C, member CF, and joint F.

Draw a left-pointing arrow 2 units long on joint C, indicating the force of horizontal member CE on joint C.

Applying the action–reaction pairs principle to the interaction between joint C and horizontal member CE:

Since horizontal member CE is pushing to the left with a 2 *P* force on joint C, joint C must be pushing to the right with a 2 *P* force on member CE.

Draw a right-pointing arrow 2 units long on the left end of horizontal member CE, indicating the force of joint C on member CE.

Applying the equilibrium principle to horizontal member CE:

The 2 *P* force to the right exerted by joint C on horizontal member CE must be equilibrated by a 2 *P* force to the left exerted by joint E on member CE.

Draw a left-pointing arrow 2 units long on the right end of horizontal member CE, indicating the force of joint E on member CE.

Applying the action–reaction pairs principle to the interaction between horizontal member CE and joint E:

Since joint E is pushing to the left with a 2 *P* force on horizontal member CE, member CE must be pushing to the right with a 2 *P* force on joint E.

Draw a right-pointing arrow 2 units long on joint E, indicating the force of horizontal member CE on joint E (see Figure 7.22).

Joint F is not a promising joint to address next, since there are three unknown vertical forces, none of which can be determined directly with the single vertical equilibrium equation. There are also three unknown

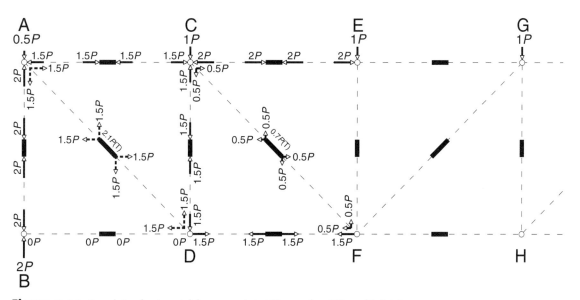

Figure 7.22 Resolving horizontal forces on joint C, member CE, and joint E.

horizontal forces, none of which can be determined directly with the single horizontal equilibrium equation.

At joint E, there is one unknown horizontal force being exerted by horizontal member EG, which means that the horizontal equilibrium equation can be used. Also at joint E, there is one unknown vertical force being exerted by vertical member EF, which means that the vertical equilibrium equation can be used.

Applying the equilibrium principle to the vertical forces on joint E:

The downward applied 1 *P* force must be equilibrated by an upward 1 *P* force exerted by vertical member EF on the joint E.

Applying the action–reaction pairs principle to the interaction between joint E and vertical member EF:

Since vertical member EF is pushing up on joint E with a 1 *P* force, joint E must be pushing down on member EF with a 1 *P* force.

Applying the equilibrium principle to vertical member EF:

The 1 *P* downward force exerted by joint E on the upper end of vertical member EF must be equilibrated by a 1 *P* upward force exerted by joint F on the lower end of member EF.

Applying the action–reaction pairs principle to the interaction between vertical member EF and joint F:

Since joint F is pushing up on vertical member EF with a 1 *P* force, member EF must be pushing down on joint F with a 1 *P* force (see Figure 7.23).

Applying the equilibrium principle to the horizontal forces on joint E:

The 2 *P* force to the right being exerted by horizontal member CE on joint E must be equilibrated by a 2 *P* force to the left being exerted by horizontal member EG on the joint E.

Applying the action–reaction pairs principle to the interaction between joint E and horizontal member EG:

Since horizontal member EG is pushing to the left with a 2 *P* force on joint E, joint E must be pushing to the right with a 2 *P* force on member EG.

Applying the equilibrium principle to horizontal member EG:

The 2 *P* force to the right exerted by joint E on horizontal member EG must be equilibrated by a 2 *P* force to the left exerted by joint G on member EG.

Applying the action–reaction pairs principle to the interaction between horizontal member EG and joint G:

Since joint G is pushing to the left on horizontal member EG with a 2 *P* force, member EG must be pushing to the right on joint G with a 2 *P* force (see Figure 7.24).

Now we can finally proceed to joint F, armed with sufficient information to resolve the forces at F.

Applying the equilibrium principle to the vertical forces on joint F:

The 1 *P* downward force of vertical member EF combined with the 0.5 *P* upward force component of diagonal member CF on joint F produces a net 0.5 *P* downward force. This must be equilibrated by a 0.5 *P* upward force component exerted by diagonal member FG on joint F.

Applying the behavior principle of 2-force members to determine the horizontal force of diagonal member FG on joint F:

Diagonal member FG must be pulling up and to the right on joint F with a net force along the diagonal. The vertical (upward) force component must be 0.5 *P* to equilibrate joint F, so the horizontal (right-pointing) force component must also be 0.5 *P*.

Applying the action–reaction pairs principle to the interaction between joint F and diagonal member FG:

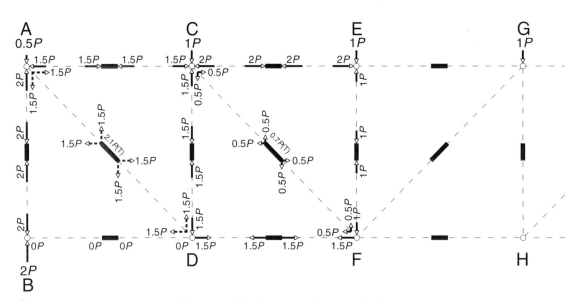

Figure 7.23 Resolving vertical forces on joint F, member EF, and joint E.

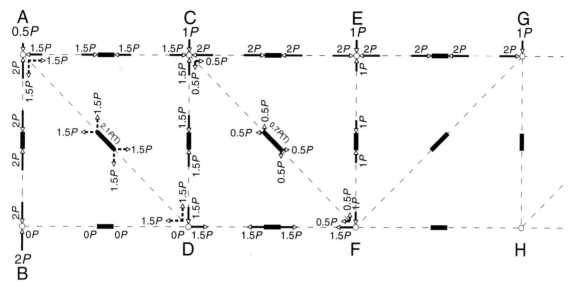

Figure 7.24 Resolving horizontal forces on joint E, member EG, and joint G.

Since diagonal member FG is pulling up on joint F with a 0.5 P force component, joint F must be pulling down on diagonal member FG with a 0.5 P force component. Since diagonal member FG is pulling to the right on joint F with a 0.5 P force component, joint F must be pulling to the left on diagonal member CF with a 0.5 P force component. The sum of the two force components exerted by joint F on diagonal member FG is a force of magnitude $\sqrt{(0.5\,P)^2 + (0.5\,P)^2} = 0.707\,P$ pulling along the length of the member. This pulling force is indicated by writing 0.717 $P(T)$ along the side of the diagonal member.

Applying the equilibrium principle to diagonal member FG:

The 0.5 P downward force component exerted by joint F on the left end of diagonal member FG must be

equilibrated by a 0.5 P upward force component exerted by joint G on the right end of member FG. The 0.5 P force component to the left exerted by joint F on the left end of member FG must be equilibrated by a 0.5 P force component to the right exerted by joint G on the right end of member FG.

Applying the action–reaction pairs principle to the interaction between diagonal member FG and joint G:

Since joint G is pulling up on diagonal member FG with a 0.5 P force component, member FG must be pulling down on joint G with a 0.5 P force component. Since joint G is pulling to the right on member FG with a 0.5 P force component, member FG must be pulling to the left on joint G with a 0.5 P force component (see Figure 7.25).

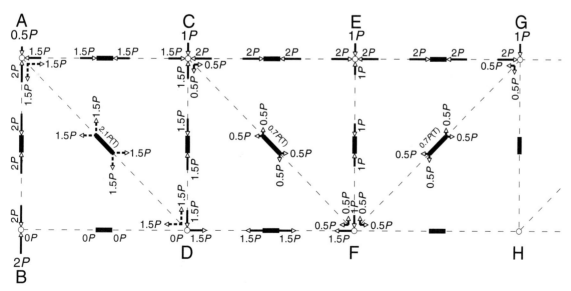

Figure 7.25 Resolving diagonal forces on joint F, member FG, and joint G.

Applying the equilibrium principle to the horizontal forces on joint F:

On joint F, there are three known forces:

Horizontal member DF pulls to the left with 1.5 P force.
Diagonal member CF pulls to the left with a horizontal force component of 0.5 P.
Diagonal member FG pulls to the right with a horizontal force component of 0.5 P.

These produce a combined force of 1.5 P to the left on joint F. This combined known force of 1.5 P to the left on joint F must be equilibrated by a 1.5 P force to the right exerted by the horizontal member FH pulling to the right on joint F.

Applying the action–reaction pairs principle to the interaction between joint F and horizontal member FH:

Since horizontal member FH is pulling to the right with a 1.5 P force on joint F, joint F must be pulling to the left with a 1.5 P force on member FH.

Applying the equilibrium principle to horizontal member FH:

The 1.5 P force to the left exerted by joint F on horizontal member FH must be equilibrated by a 1.5 P force to the right exerted by joint H on member FH.

Applying the action–reaction pairs principle to the interaction between horizontal member FH and joint H:

Since joint H is pulling to the right with a 1.5 P force on horizontal member FH, horizontal member FH must be pulling to the left with a 1.5 P force on joint H (see Figure 7.26).

Continuing on to joint G, the diagram shown in Figure 7.27 can be generated.

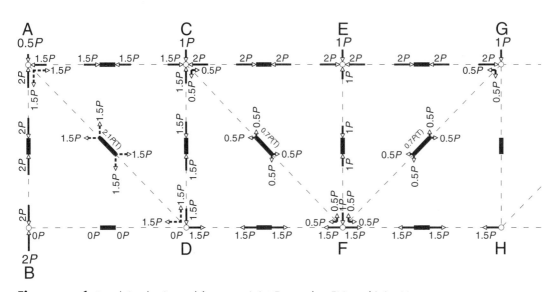

Figure 7.26 Resolving horizontal forces on joint F, member FH, and joint H.

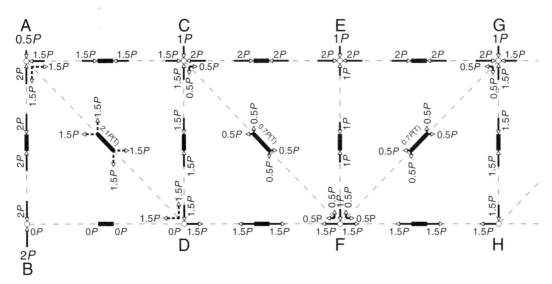

Figure 7.27 Resolving vertical forces on joint H, member GH, and joint G.

Continuing on to joint H, the diagram shown in Figure 7.28 can be generated.

Note the symmetry of forces about the center of the truss, which is consistent with our expectations, given the symmetry of both the truss geometry and the applied forces. Continuing this solution method throughout the rest of the truss would produce full force symmetry throughout the truss.

In the truss shown in Figure 7.28, diagonal members CF and FG form a sling, supplying equal support for the applied 1 *P* force transmitted down through member EF. Hence, each of these diagonals must supply a vertical force component of 0.5 *P*.

Diagonal members AD and HI (connected by DF and FH below) form a sling that must support the three applied *P* forces on joints C, E, and G. Each of these diagonal members must supply a vertical component that is one-half of this 3 *P* total force; that is, they each supply a vertical component of 1.5 *P*.

7.1.3 JOINTS METHOD APPLIED TO FIVE-BAY TRUSS USING EXPLODED DIAGRAM

Next we solve a truss consisting of five square bays, using the same solution method (see Figure 7.29).

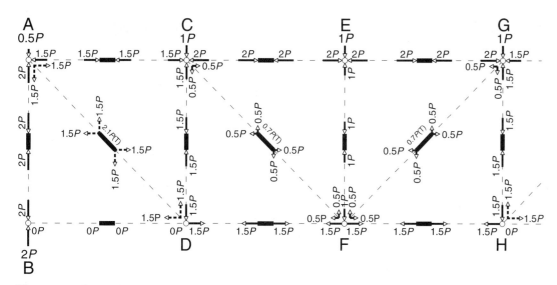

Figure 7.28 Resolving diagonal forces on joint H.

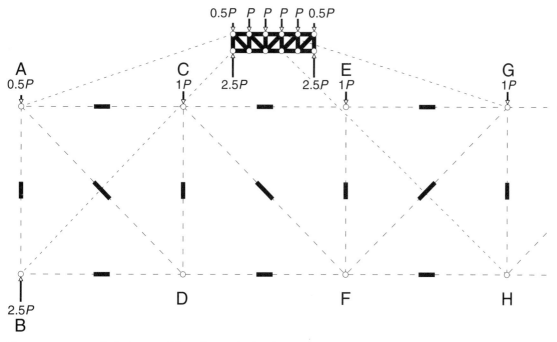

Figure 7.29 Exploded view of three bays of a five-bay truss.

Only three bays are shown in the diagram in Figure 7.29, as this is all that is required to find the truss's internal forces. Because the truss's symmetry and the forces on it, the right-hand side of the solution will be symmetric with the left-hand side.

The *P* forces are shown applied to the joints, consistent with the earlier discussion. The reaction force at joint B is also shown. It is crucial to get all the applied and reaction forces on the diagram before proceeding with the analysis. Otherwise, they are likely to be overlooked in the process of performing the analysis, negating the validity of the process. To simplify this image, remove the dashed lines that indicate the relationship of points in the original diagram with points in the exploded diagram (see Figure 7.30).

Applying the equilibrium principle to the vertical forces on joint B:

The 2.5 *P* upward reaction force on joint B must be equilibrated by a 2.5 *P* downward force on joint B exerted by the vertical member AB pushing down on joint B.

Applying the action–reaction pairs principle to the interaction between joint B and the vertical member AB:

Since the vertical member AB is pushing downward on joint B with a 2.5 *P* force, joint B must be pushing upward on member AB with a 2.5 *P* force.

Applying the equilibrium principle to the vertical member AB:

The 2.5 *P* upward force on the bottom of vertical member AB, exerted by joint B, must be equilibrated by a 2.5 *P* downward force on the top of member AB, exerted by joint A.

Applying the action–reaction pairs principle to the interaction between joint A and vertical member AB:

Since joint A is pushing down on vertical member AB with a 2.5 *P* force, member AB must be pushing up on joint A with a 2.5 *P* force (see Figure 7.31).

Applying the equilibrium principle to the horizontal forces on joint B:

Since there are no horizontal applied forces or horizontal reaction forces on joint B, the horizontal member BD is exerting no force on joint B. Any horizontal force from member BD would be unbalanced and would, therefore, upset the equilibrium of joint B.

Applying the action–reaction pairs principle to the interaction between joint B and horizontal member BD:

Since horizontal member BD is exerting no force on joint B, joint B must be exerting no force on horizontal member BD.

Applying the equilibrium principle to horizontal member BD:

Since joint B exerts no force on member BD, joint D must not exert any force on member BD either, as any force exerted by joint D on member BD would be unbalanced and would disturb the equilibrium of the member. Hence, horizontal member BD has no force in it.

Applying the action–reaction pairs principle to the interaction between horizontal member BD and joint D:

Since joint D is exerting no force on horizontal member BD, horizontal member BD must be exerting no force on joint D (see Figure 7.32).

Applying the equilibrium principle to the vertical forces on joint A:

The upward 2.5 *P* force of the vertical member AB on joint A combined with the downward 0.5 *P* applied force on joint A produces a net upward 2 *P* force that must be equilibrated by a 2 *P* downward force component exerted by the diagonal member AD on joint A.

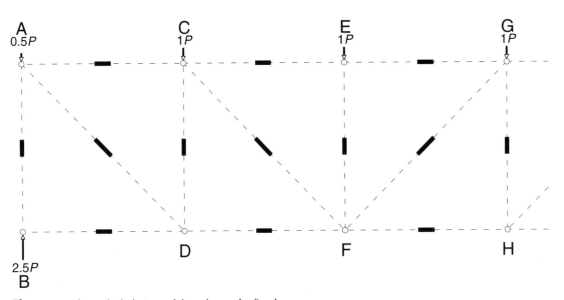

Figure 7.30 Exploded view of three bays of a five-bay truss.

Applying the behavior principle of 2-force members to determine the horizontal force of the diagonal member AB on joint A:

Diagonal member AD must be pulling down and to the right on joint A with a net force along the centerline of member AD. Here, that centerline has a slope of 1 unit rise in 1 unit run. Therefore, any force along the diagonal member must have vertical and horizontal components that are equal in magnitude to each other. The downward vertical component must be 2 P (to keep joint A in equilibrium relative to upward vertical forces), so the rightward horizontal component must be 2 P as well. In summary, diagonal member AD is exerting a downward force component of 2 P on joint A and a force component to the right of 2 P on joint A.

Applying the action–reaction pairs principle to the interaction between joint A and diagonal member AD:

Since diagonal member AD is pulling down on joint A with a 2 P force component, joint A must be pulling up on member AD with a 2 P force component. Since member AD is pulling to the right on joint A with a 2 P force component, joint A must be pulling to the left on member AD with a 2 P force component.

Applying the equilibrium principle to diagonal member AD:

The 2 P upward force component exerted by joint A on the left end of diagonal member AD must be equilibrated by a 2 P downward force component exerted by joint D on the right end of member AD. The 2 P force component to the left exerted by joint A on the left end

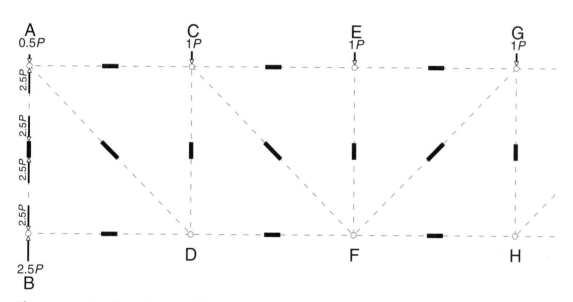

Figure 7.31 Resolving the vertical forces on joint B, member AB, and joint A.

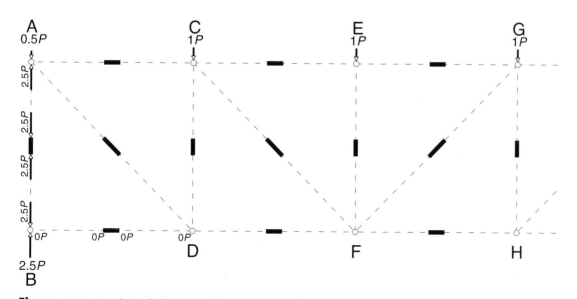

Figure 7.32 Resolving the horizontal forces on joint B, member BD, and joint D.

of member AD must be equilibrated by a 2 *P* force component to the right exerted by joint D on the right end of member AD.

Applying the action–reaction pairs principle to the interaction between diagonal member AD and joint D:

Since joint D is pulling down on diagonal member AD with a 2 *P* force component, member AD must be pulling up on joint D with a 2 *P* force component. Since joint D is pulling to the right on member AD with a 2 *P* force component, member AD must be pulling to the left on joint D with a 2 *P* force component (see Figure 7.33).

Applying the equilibrium principle to the horizontal forces on joint A:

The 2 *P* force component to the right exerted by diagonal member AD on joint A must be equilibrated by a 2 *P* force to the left exerted by horizontal member AC on joint A.

Applying the action–reaction pairs principle to the interaction between joint A and horizontal member AC:

Since horizontal member AC is pushing to the left with 2 *P* force on joint A, joint A must be pushing to the right with 2 *P* force on horizontal member AC.

Applying the equilibrium principle to horizontal member AC:

The 2 *P* force to the right exerted by joint A on horizontal member AC must be equilibrated by a 2 *P* force to the left exerted by joint C on horizontal member AC.

Applying the action–reaction pairs principle to the interaction between horizontal member AC and joint C:

Since joint C is pushing to the left with a 2 *P* force on horizontal member AC, member AC must be pushing to the right with a 2 *P* force on joint C (see Figure 7.34).

Examining the vertical equilibrium of joint D leads to the diagram in Figure 7.35.

Examining the horizontal equilibrium of joint D leads to the diagram in Figure 7.36.

Examining the diagonal equilibrium of joint C leads to the diagram in Figure 7.37.

Examining the horizontal equilibrium of joint C leads to the diagram in Figure 7.38.

Examining the vertical equilibrium of joint E leads to the diagram in Figure 7.39.

Examining the horizontal equilibrium of joint E leads to the diagram in Figure 7.40.

Applying the equilibrium principle to the vertical forces on joint F:

The 1 *P* downward force of the vertical member EF combined with the 1 *P* upward force component of diagonal member CF on joint F produces a net 0 P force. The only other vertical force that can be exerted on the joint would be from diagonal member FG. If diagonal member FG were to exert a force on joint F, it would not be balanced by any other force and, as such, it would upset the equilibrium of joint F. Therefore, diagonal member FG is not exerting vertical force on joint F.

Applying the behavior principle of 2-force members to determine the horizontal force of diagonal member FG on joint F:

If diagonal member FG is not exerting vertical force on joint F, then it must not be exerting horizontal force on joint F, since that horizontal force could not be along the centerline of diagonal member FG.

Applying the action–reaction pairs principle to the interaction between joint F and diagonal member FG:

Since diagonal member FG is not exerting force on joint F, joint F must not be exerting force on member FG.

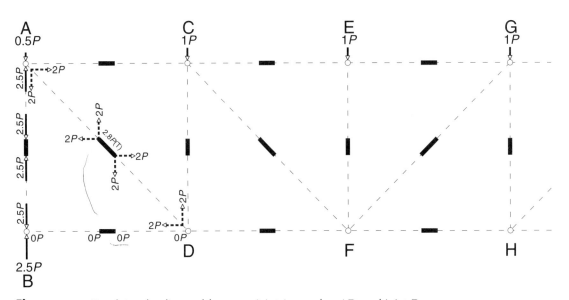

Figure 7.33 Resolving the diagonal forces on joint A, member AD, and joint D.

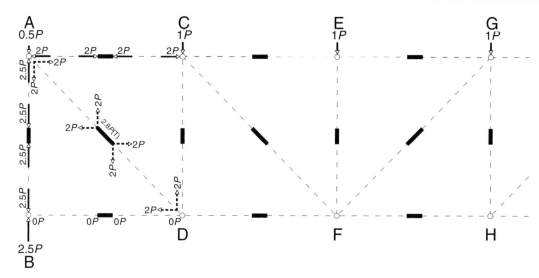

Figure 7.34 Resolving the horizontal forces on joint A, member AC, and joint C.

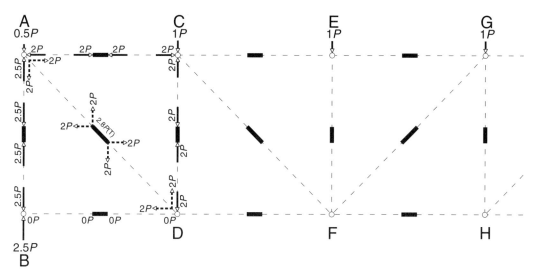

Figure 7.35 Resolving the vertical forces on joint D, member CD, and joint C.

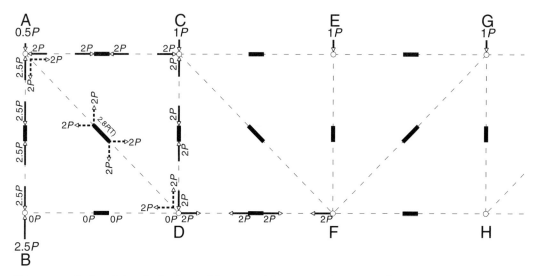

Figure 7.36 Resolving the horizontal forces on joint D, member DF, and joint F.

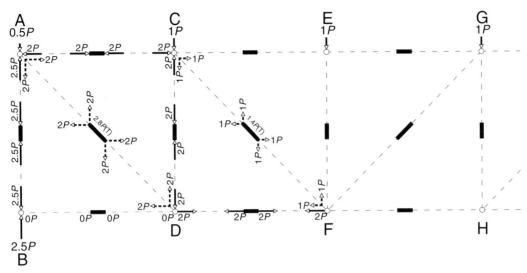

Figure 7.37 Resolving the diagonal forces on joint C, member CF, and joint F.

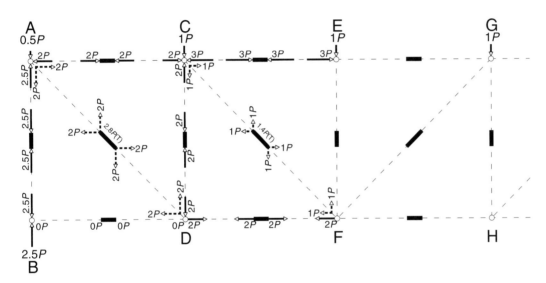

Figure 7.38 Resolving the horizontal forces on joint C, member CE, and joint E.

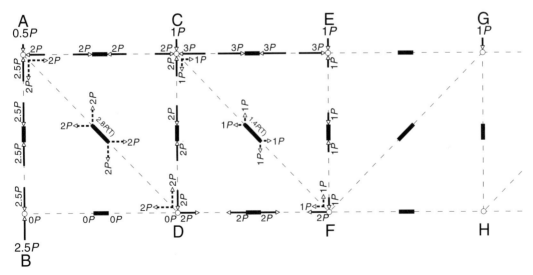

Figure 7.39 Resolving the vertical forces on joint F, member EF, and joint E.

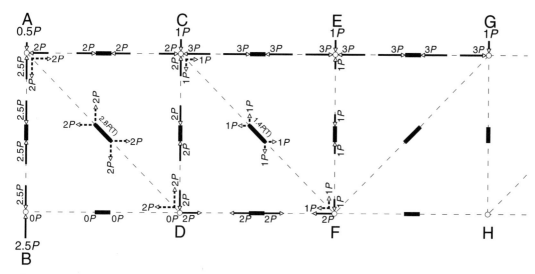

Figure 7.40 Resolving the horizontal forces on joint E, member EG, and joint G.

Applying the equilibrium principle to diagonal member FG:

Since joint F is not exerting force on diagonal member FG, equilibrium of member FG requires that joint G is also not exerting force on member FG.

Applying the action–reaction pairs principle to the interaction between diagonal member FG and joint G:

Since joint G is not exerting force on diagonal member FG, member FG is not exerting force on joint G.

Whenever the analysis indicates a zero-force member, it is useful to imagine removing that member, to assess whether the structure looks stable without it. In this case, the structure remaining after removal of member

BD would be balanced on top of vertical member AB, indicating that no force would be required in member BD to keep the structure in equilibrium. The horizontal member BD only restrains the vertical member AB from toppling to the left or to the right. Member BD is a bracing member that is not directly engaged in transferring forces under the loads shown. On a similar note, removing diagonal member FG under symmetric loads leaves a symmetric truss, a logical response to symmetric loads. Because the loads are symmetric about the center bay, vertical shear force is not expected in that bay. This means that neither truss half is expected to move up or down relative to the other truss half (see Figure 7.41).

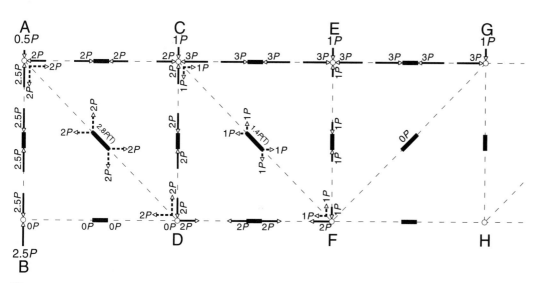

Figure 7.41 Resolving the diagonal forces on joint F, member FG, and joint G.

Applying the equilibrium principle to the horizontal forces on joint F:

On joint F, there are three known horizontal forces:

Horizontal member DF pulls to the left with a 2 *P* force.

Diagonal member CF pulls to the left with a horizontal force component of 1 *P*.

Diagonal member FG pulls to the right with a horizontal force component of 0 *P*.

These produce a combined force of 3 *P* to the left on joint F. This must be equilibrated by a 3 *P* force to the right exerted by horizontal member FH.

Applying the action–reaction pairs principle to the interaction between joint F and horizontal member FH:

Since horizontal member FH is pulling to the right with a 3 *P* force on joint F, joint F must be pulling to the left with a 3 *P* force on member FH.

Applying the equilibrium principle to horizontal member FH:

The 3 *P* force to the left exerted by joint F on horizontal member FH must be equilibrated by a 3 *P* force to the right exerted by joint H on member FH.

Applying the action–reaction pairs principle to the interaction between horizontal member FH and joint H:

Since joint H is pulling to the right with a 3 *P* force on horizontal member FH, member FH must be pulling to the left with a 3 *P* force on joint H (see Figure 7.42).

Continuing the analysis at joint G leads to the diagram in Figure 7.43.

Continuing the analysis at joint H leads to the diagram in Figure 7.44.

Parallel-Chord Trusses Assignment 1

Analyze a six-square-bay truss using an exploded diagram showing all joints and all members for at least half of the truss and showing all applied forces, reactions, and internal forces on all joints and all members drawn to scale; that is, the length of an arrow will be in proportion to the magnitude of the force, at a clearly identified scale.

Parallel-Chord Trusses Assignment 2

Analyze a seven-square-bay truss using an exploded diagram showing all joints and all members for at least half of the truss and showing all applied forces, reactions, and internal forces on all joints and all members drawn to scale; that is, the length of an arrow will be in proportion to the magnitude of the force, at a clearly identified scale.

7.1.4 SIMPLIFIED JOINTS METHOD APPLIED TO SYSTEMS OF TWO-FORCE MEMBERS

Using an exploded diagram with scaled forces to solve a truss, as illustrated in the previous sections, is effective in

Distilling "bite-sized" steps based on clear principles that are well illustrated in this solution method

Visualizing the magnitudes of forces both on, and internal to, the truss

However, using an exploded diagram with scaled forces to solve a truss takes a lot of paper and time. It also poses a dilemma: To choose the correct paper size and scale for the force arrows requires knowing the forces before solving the problem. This can lead to paralysis.

The simplified joints method abandons using scaled arrows, thus losing some visual information. However, this loss will be offset by greater simplicity and efficiency in the solution process.

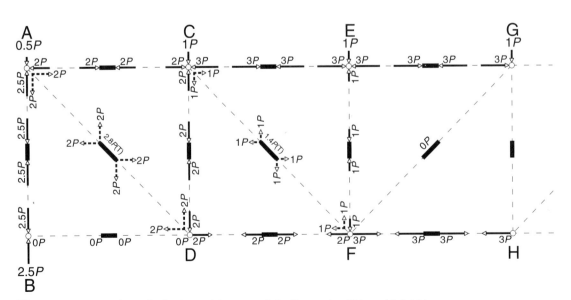

Figure 7.42 Resolving the horizontal forces on joint F, member FH, and joint H.

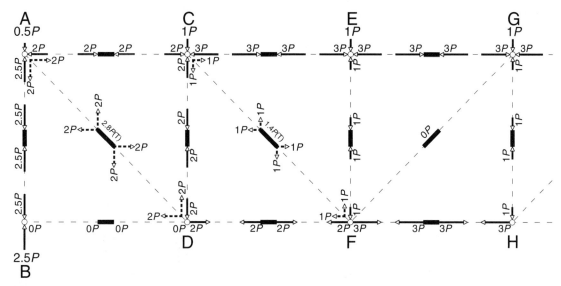

Figure 7.43 Resolving the vertical forces on joint H, member GH, and joint G.

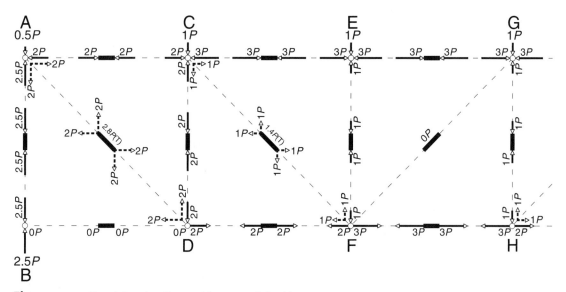

Figure 7.44 Resolving the diagonal forces on joint H.

In the simplified joints method, all the force arrows shown represent forces on the joints. Forces on the members have been omitted, since the members simply pass forces from one joint to the next. Including these forces would clutter the diagram and increase the work necessary to complete the solution, without substantially contributing to the diagram's useful information.

It was important to work the full problem in the early examples to become familiar with all the principles and steps in the process. Even in the simplified joints method, the members are active participants that must always satisfy the action–reaction pairs principle and the equilibrium principle. In the simplified method, verbalize the role of the forces on the members without recording the forces on the members on the solution diagram.

Finally, in the simplified method, draw diagonal force arrows rather than force component arrows. This further reduces the number of arrows that need to be shown on the diagram.

Example: Sixteen-Square-Bay, Simple-Span Truss Analysis Using the Simplified Joints Method

The diagram in Figure 7.45 shows the truss geometry with joints superimposed on it. It is useful to think of the members as removed from the diagram, since all the forces will be drawn on the joints. Only the left half of the truss has been depicted, to simplify the diagram and to show it large enough to get the required information on it. In accordance with truss symmetry, the forces in the right half will be the mirror image of the forces

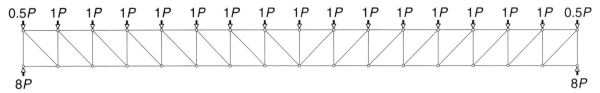

Figure 7.45 Sixteen-bay, square-bay truss.

calculated for the left half of the truss, so it is unnecessary to include both sides.

While tracing forces through the system, the same verbal arguments are made in the simplified method that were made for the exploded diagrams used earlier. The only difference in the two approaches is how the results of the deductive process are recorded (see Figure 7.46).

Applying the equilibrium principle to the vertical forces on joint B:

The 8 *P* upward reaction force on joint B must be equilibrated by an 8 *P* downward force on joint B exerted by the vertical member AB pushing down on joint B.

Draw a downward force arrow on joint B, indicating the downward force exerted by the vertical member on joint B. (Remember that only the forces on the joints are shown. The arrows showing the forces exerted on the members by the joints are omitted to avoid cluttering the diagram with too many arrows and numbers. However, knowing that there are forces on the members and understanding the role of those forces in this process is critical.)

Applying the action–reaction pairs principle to the interaction between joint B and the vertical member AB:

Since vertical member AB is pushing downward on joint B with an 8 *P* force, joint B must be pushing upward on member AB with an 8 *P* force.

Applying the equilibrium principle to the vertical member AB:

The 8 *P* upward force on the bottom of vertical member AB, exerted by joint B, must be equilibrated by an 8 *P* downward force on the top of member AB, exerted by joint A.

Applying the action–reaction pairs principle to the interaction between joint A and vertical member AB:

Since joint A is pushing down on vertical member AB with an 8 *P* force, member AB must be pushing up on joint A with an 8 *P* force.

Draw an upward force arrow on joint A, indicating the upward force exerted by the vertical member on joint A.

Show the magnitude of the forces involved by writing 8 *P* (C) along the side of the vertical member between joints A and B, indicating the compression force in the member. It is also the magnitude of the force that is being passed through the member from one joint to the next (see Figure 7.47).

Applying the equilibrium principle to the horizontal forces on joint B:

Since there are no horizontal applied forces or horizontal reaction forces on joint B, the horizontal member BD is not exerting force on joint B, since any horizontal force from member BD would be unbalanced and would, therefore, upset the equilibrium of joint B.

Applying the action–reaction pairs principle to the interaction between joint B and horizontal member BD:

Since horizontal member BD is not exerting force on joint B, joint B must not be exerting force on member BD.

Applying the equilibrium principle to horizontal member BD:

Since joint B exerts no force on horizontal member BD, joint D must not exert force on member BD either, as any force exerted by joint D on member BD would be unbalanced and would disturb the equilibrium of the member. Hence, member BD has no force in it. If this result is surprising, imagine removing the horizontal segment in question. When one examines the structure without that member, it becomes clear that the horizontal member's function is to balance the vertical member between A and B against toppling to the left or to the right. The horizontal member is a bracing member not directly engaged in transferring forces under the loads shown.

Applying the action–reaction pairs principle to the interaction between horizontal member BD and joint D:

Since joint D is not exerting force on horizontal member BD, member BD must not be exerting force on joint D.

Do not draw horizontal arrows on joint B or joint C, because no force is exerted on those joints by the horizontal member between them.

Show the magnitude of the forces involved by writing 0 *P* along the side of the horizontal member, indicating that no force is transferred through it and that the member has no axial force in it (see Figure 7.48).

Joint D has two unknown vertical forces and two unknown horizontal forces, making it unsuitable for the next step. There is only one equilibrium equation for vertical forces and one equilibrium equation for horizontal forces; therefore, there are not enough equilibrium equations to solve directly for forces on joint D.

Applying the equilibrium principle to the vertical forces on joint A:

The upward 8 *P* force of the vertical member AB on joint A combined with the downward 0.5 *P* applied force on joint A produces a net upward 7.5 *P* force that must be equilibrated by a 7.5 *P* downward force component exerted by diagonal member AD on joint A. (The diago-

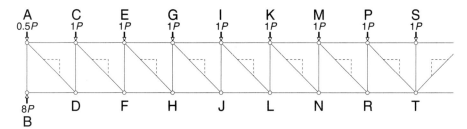

Figure 7.46 Closer view of half of the sixteen-bay truss.

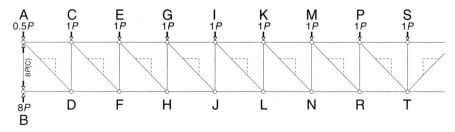

Figure 7.47 Resolved vertical forces on joint B.

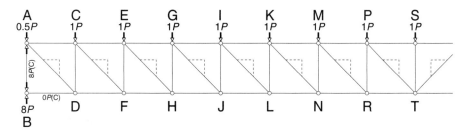

Figure 7.48 Resolved horizontal forces on joint B.

nal member is the only agent acting on joint A that is capable of exerting the required vertical force, since there is only one other member framing into joint A and that member, being horizontal, can exert only a horizontal force on the joint.) According to the previous argument regarding the behavior of 2-force members, this diagonal member between joints A and D must be pulling down on joint A with a force along the diagonal. For this particular problem, that diagonal has a slope of 1 unit rise in 1 unit run. Therefore, any force along that member must have equal vertical and horizontal components. The vertical component must be 7.5 P (to keep joint A in equilibrium relative to vertical forces), so the horizontal component must be 7.5 P as well. In summary, the diagonal is exerting a downward vertical force of 7.5 P on joint A and a horizontal force to the right of 7.5 P on joint A.

Applying the behavior principle of 2-force members to determine the horizontal force of diagonal member AD on joint A:

Diagonal member AD must be pulling down and to the right on joint A with a net force along the centerline of member AD. Here, that centerline has a slope of 1 unit rise in 1 unit run. Therefore, any force along the diago-

nal member must have vertical and horizontal components that are equal in magnitude to each other. The downward vertical component must be 7.5 P (to keep joint A in equilibrium relative to upward vertical forces), so the rightward horizontal component must be 7.5 P as well. In summary, diagonal member AD is exerting a downward force component of 7.5 P on joint A and a force component to the right of 7.5 P on joint A.

Applying the action–reaction pairs principle to the interaction between joint A and diagonal member AD:

Since diagonal member AD is pulling down on joint A with a 7.5 P force component, joint A must be pulling up on member AD with a 7.5 P force component. Since member AD is pulling to the right on joint A with a 7.5 P force component, joint A must be pulling to the left on member AD with a 7.5 P force component. The sum of the two force components exerted by joint on the diagonal member is a force of magnitude $\sqrt{(7.5\,P)^2 + (7.5\,P)^2} = 10.6\,P$ pulling along the member's length. This pulling force implies that the member is in tension, so the force magnitude is indicated by writing 10.6 P (T) along the side of the diagonal member. The

7.5 *P* force components of that 10.6 *P* force are indicated on the triangles along the side of the diagonal member.

Draw a downward force arrow on joint A along the diagonal member, indicating the force being exerted by the diagonal member pulling on joint A.

Applying the equilibrium principle to diagonal member AD:

The 7.5 *P* upward force component exerted by joint A on the left end of diagonal member AD must be equilibrated by a 7.5 *P* downward force component exerted by joint D on the right end of member AD. The 7.5 *P* force component to the left exerted by joint A on the left end of member AD must be equilibrated by a 7.5 *P* force component to the right exerted by joint D on the right end of member AD.

Applying the action–reaction pairs principle to the interaction between diagonal member AD and joint D:

Since joint D is pulling down on diagonal member AD with a 7.5 *P* force component, member AD must be pulling up on joint D with a 7.5 *P* force component. Since joint D is pulling to the right on member AD with a 7.5 *P* force component, member AD must be pulling to the left on joint D with a 7.5 *P* force component.

Draw an upward force arrow on joint D along the diagonal member, indicating the force being exerted by the diagonal member on joint D.

Show the magnitude of the forces involved by writing 10.6 *P* (T) along the side of the diagonal member, indicating the tension force in the member and that it is being passed through the member from one joint to the next.

Label the force components of the 10.6 *P* force (7.5 *P* for both vertical and horizontal components) on the triangle attached to the diagonal member (see Figure 7.49).

Applying the equilibrium principle to the horizontal forces on joint A:

The 7.5 *P* force component to the right, exerted by diagonal member AD on joint A, must be equilibrated by a 7.5 *P* force to the left, exerted by horizontal member AC on joint A.

Draw a left-pointing force arrow on joint A, indicating the force exerted by the horizontal member pushing on joint A.

Applying the action–reaction pairs principle to the interaction between joint A and horizontal member AC:

Since horizontal member AC is pushing to the left with a 7.5 *P* force on joint A, joint A must be pushing to the right with a 7.5 *P* force on member AC.

Applying the equilibrium principle to horizontal member AC:

The 7.5 *P* force to the right exerted by joint A on horizontal member AC must be equilibrated by a 7.5 *P* force to the left exerted by joint C on member AC.

Applying the action–reaction pairs principle to the interaction between horizontal member AC and joint C:

Since joint C is pushing to the left with a 7.5 *P* force on horizontal member AC, member AC must be pushing to the right with a 7.5 *P* force on joint C.

Draw a right-pointing force arrow on joint C, indicating the force exerted by the horizontal member on joint C.

Show the magnitude of the forces involved by writing 7.5 *P* (C) along the side of the horizontal member, indicating the compression force in the member and that it is being passed through the member from one joint to the next (see Figure 7.50).

Joint C has two unknown vertical and two unknown horizontal forces, making it an unsuitable next step.

Applying the equilibrium principle to the vertical forces on joint D:

The 7.5 *P* upward force component exerted by diagonal member AD on joint D must be equilibrated by a 7.5 *P* downward force exerted by vertical member CD on the joint D.

Applying the action–reaction pairs principle to the interaction of joint D and vertical member CD:

Since the vertical member CD is pushing down on joint D with a 7.5 *P* force, joint D must be pushing up on member CD with a 7.5 *P* force.

Draw a downward force arrow on joint D, indicating the downward force exerted by the vertical member on joint D.

Applying the equilibrium principle to the vertical forces on member CD:

The 7.5 *P* upward force exerted by joint D on vertical member CD must be equilibrated by a 7.5 *P* downward force exerted by joint C on member CD.

Applying the action–reaction pairs principle to the interaction of joint C and vertical member CD:

Since joint C is pushing down on vertical member CD with a 7.5 *P* force, member CD must be pushing up on joint C with a 7.5 *P* force.

Draw an upward force arrow on joint C, indicating the upward force exerted by the vertical member on joint C.

Show the magnitude of the forces involved by writing 7.5 *P* (C) along the side of the vertical member between joints C and D, indicating the compression force in the member and that it is being passed through the member from one joint to the next (see Figure 7.51).

Applying the equilibrium principle to the horizontal forces on joint D:

The 7.5 *P* force component to the left exerted by diagonal member AD on joint D must be equilibrated by a 7.5 *P* force to the right exerted by horizontal member DF on joint D.

Draw a right-pointing force arrow on joint D, indicating the force being exerted by the horizontal member between joints D and F pulling to the right on joint D.

Applying the action–reaction pairs principle to the interaction of joint D and horizontal member DF:

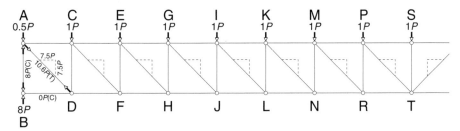

Figure 7.49 Resolved diagonal force on joint A.

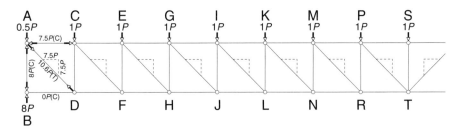

Figure 7.50 Resolved horizontal forces on joint A.

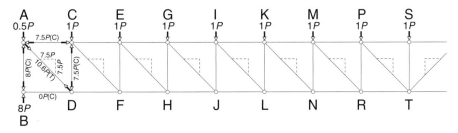

Figure 7.51 Resolved vertical forces on joint D.

Since horizontal member DF is pulling to the right on joint D with a 7.5 *P* force, joint D must be pulling to the left on member DF with a 7.5 *P* force.

Applying the equilibrium principle to the horizontal forces on member DF:

The 7.5 *P* force to the left exerted by joint D on horizontal member DF must be equilibrated by a 7.5 *P* force to the right exerted by joint F on member DF.

Applying the action–reaction pairs principle to the interaction of joint F and horizontal member DF:

Since joint F is pulling to the right on horizontal member DF with a 7.5 *P* force, member DF must be pulling to the left on joint F with a 7.5 *P* force.

Draw a left-pointing force arrow on joint F, indicating the force being exerted by the horizontal member between joints D and F pulling to the left on joint F.

Show the magnitude of the forces involved by writing 7.5 *P* (T) along the side of the horizontal member between D and F, indicating the tension force in the member and that it is being passed through the member from one joint to the next (see Figure 7.52).

Joint F has two unknown vertical and two unknown horizontal forces, making it unsuitable for the next step.

Applying the equilibrium principle to the vertical forces on joint C:

The upward 7.5 *P* force of the vertical member CD on joint C combined with the downward 1 *P* applied force on joint C produces a net upward 6.5 *P* force that must be equilibrated by a 6.5 *P* downward force component exerted by diagonal member CF on joint C.

Draw a downward force arrow on joint C along the diagonal member, indicating the force exerted by the diagonal member pulling on joint C.

Applying the behavior principle of 2-force members to determine the horizontal force of diagonal member CF on joint C:

Diagonal member CF must be pulling down and to the right on joint C with a net force along the diagonal. The vertical component must be 6.5 *P*, so the horizontal component must be 6.5 *P* as well.

Applying the action–reaction pairs principle to the interaction between joint C and diagonal member CF:

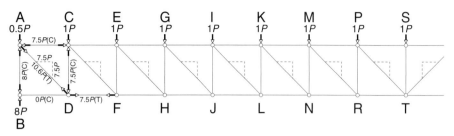

Figure 7.52 Resolved horizontal forces on joint D.

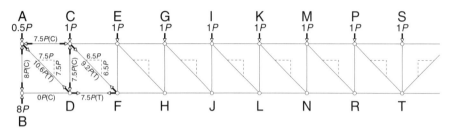

Figure 7.53 Resolved diagonal forces on joint C.

Since diagonal member CF is pulling down on joint C with a 6.5 *P* force component, joint C must be pulling up on member CF with a 6.5 *P* force component. Diagonal member CF is pulling to the right on joint C with a 6.5 *P* force component, so joint C must be pulling to the left on member CF with a 6.5 *P* force component. The sum of the two force components exerted by joint C on the diagonal member is a force of magnitude $\sqrt{(6.5\ P)^2 + (6.5\ P)^2} = 9.2\ P$ pulling along the length of the member.

Applying the equilibrium principle to diagonal member CD:

The 6.5 *P* upward force component exerted by joint C on the left end of diagonal member CF must be equilibrated by a 6.5 *P* downward force component exerted by joint F on the right end of member CF. The 6.5 *P* force component to the left exerted by joint C on the left end of member CF must be equilibrated by a 6.5 *P* force component to the right exerted by joint F on the right end of member CF.

Applying the action–reaction pairs principle to the interaction between diagonal member CF and joint F:

Since joint F is pulling down on diagonal member CF with a 6.5 *P* force component, member CF must be pulling up on joint F with a 6.5 *P* force component. Joint F is pulling to the right on member CF with a 6.5 *P* force component, so member CF must be pulling to the left on joint F with a 6.5 *P* force component.

Draw an upward force arrow on joint F along the diagonal member, indicating the force exerted by the diagonal member on joint F.

Show the magnitude of the forces involved by writing 9.2 *P* (T) along the side of the diagonal member, indicat-

ing the tension force in the member and that it is being passed through the member from one joint to the next.

Label the force components of the 9.2 *P* force (6.5 *P* for both vertical and horizontal components) on the triangle attached to the diagonal member between joints C and F (see Figure 7.53).

Applying the equilibrium principle to the horizontal forces on joint C:

Member AC pushes to the right with 7.5 *P* force on joint C and diagonal member CF pulls to the right with a horizontal force component of 6.5 *P* on joint C, producing a combined force of 14 *P* to the right on joint C. This combined force must be equilibrated by a 14 *P* force to the left exerted by horizontal member CE pushing to the left on joint C.

Draw a left-pointing force arrow on joint C, indicating the force exerted by the horizontal member between joints C and E pushing to the left on joint C.

Applying the action–reaction pairs principle to the interaction between joint C and horizontal member CE:

Since horizontal member CE is pushing to the left with a 14 *P* force on joint C, joint C must be pushing to the right with a 14 *P* force on member CE.

Applying the equilibrium principle to horizontal member AC:

The 14 *P* force to the right exerted by joint C on horizontal member CE must be equilibrated by a 14 *P* force to the left exerted by joint E on member CE.

Applying the action–reaction pairs principle to the interaction between horizontal member CE and joint E:

Since joint E is pushing to the left with a 14 *P* force on member CE, horizontal member CE must be pushing to the right with a 14 *P* force on joint E.

Draw a right-pointing force arrow on joint E, indicating the force exerted by the horizontal member between joints C and E pushing to the right on joint E.

Show the magnitude of the forces involved by writing 14 *P* (C) along the side of the horizontal member between joints C and E indicating the compression force in the member and that it is being passed through the member from one joint to the next (see Figure 7.54).

The next several steps are presented without explanation, other than the diagrams of resolved forces. The reader is encouraged to verbalize the application of the equilibrium principle and the action–reaction pair principle in resolving the forces in each of the steps shown in the diagrams in Figures 7.55 through 7.64.

Continuing this analytic process across the entire left half of the truss leads to the distribution of internal forces in the truss shown in Figure 7.65.

These results are summarized with the graphic technique shown in Figure 7.66, which uses flags beside the members, with the flag width proportional to the magnitude of the effect.

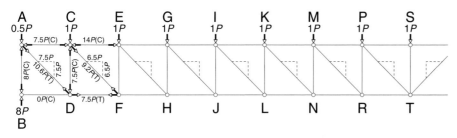

Figure 7.54 Resolved horizontal forces on joint C.

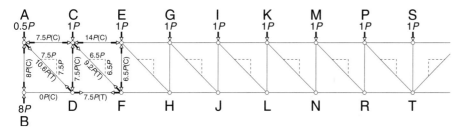

Figure 7.55 Resolved vertical forces on joint F.

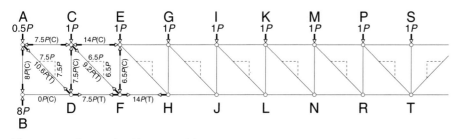

Figure 7.56 Resolved horizontal forces on joint F.

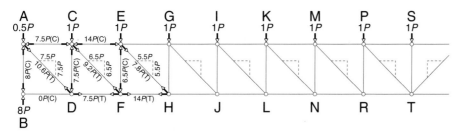

Figure 7.57 Resolved diagonal forces on joint E.

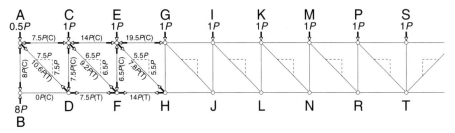

Figure 7.58 Resolved horizontal forces on joint E.

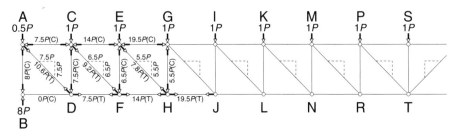

Figure 7.59 Resolved vertical and horizontal forces on joint H.

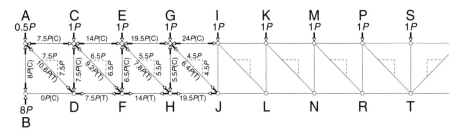

Figure 7.60 Resolved diagonal and horizontal forces on joint G.

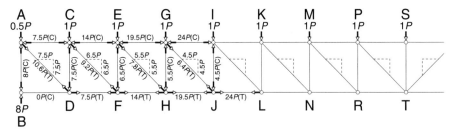

Figure 7.61 Resolved vertical and horizontal forces on joint J.

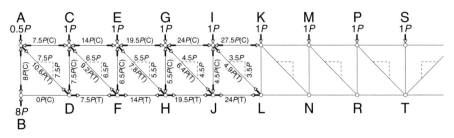

Figure 7.62 Resolved diagonal and horizontal forces on joint I.

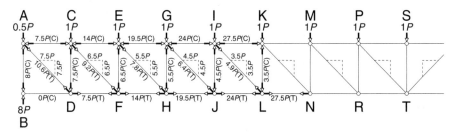

Figure 7.63 Resolved vertical and horizontal forces on joint L.

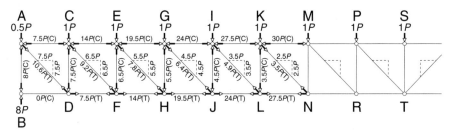

Figure 7.64 Resolved diagonal and horizontal forces on joint K.

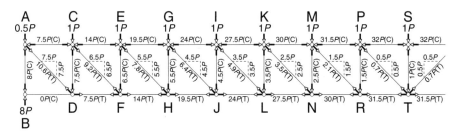

Figure 7.65 Complete analysis for left half of the sixteen-bay truss.

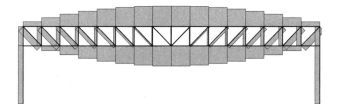

Figure 7.66 Graphic display of the member forces.

This graphic representation method is typical of most computer-based structural analysis programs: a flag is placed above the member to represent compression or below the member to represent tension. According to truss symmetry, it is expected that the forces in the members on the right half of the truss will mirror the forces in the corresponding members in the left half of the truss. The fact that the forces in the two diagonals at the center are equal in both magnitude and tension is the first check that the method has been correctly applied.

However, there is not a similarly simple check on the chord forces, because the way the chords meet at the center ensures symmetry, regardless of whether the calculations were done correctly. The importance of chord

forces requires an alternate computational method to verify the chord force results. This alternative method is called the sections method. The truss is sliced through the center with half of the truss used as a freebody. Chord forces can be determined by applying the equilibrium principle to the freebody.

Slicing the sixteen-square-bay truss through Bay 8 creates the freebody shown in Figure 7.67.

Taking moments about point P eliminates two unknowns (C and D) from the equation of equilibrium, leaving t as the single unknown.

$$\sum M_P = 0 \;\curvearrowright$$
$$0 = -7\,P(3\,s) + 8\,P(7\,s) - 0.5\,P(7\,s) - T(s)$$

Dividing both sides of the equation by s yields:

$$0 = -7\,P(3) + 8\,P(7) - 0.5\,P(7) - T$$

Collecting terms yields:

$$T = -21\,P + 56\,P - 3.5\,P$$
$$T = 31.5\,P$$

This result checks with the joints method.

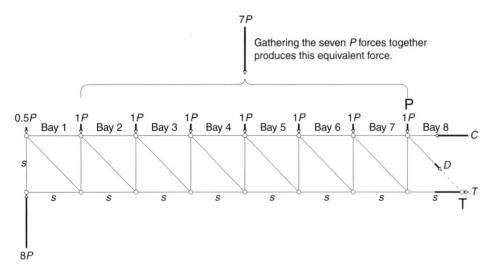

Figure 7.67 Applying sections method to freebody of half of the truss.

Taking moments about point T eliminates two unknowns (T and D) from the equation of equilibrium, leaving c as the single unknown.

$$\sum M_r = 0 \;\curvearrowright$$
$$0 = -7\,P(4\,s) + 8\,P(8\,s) - 0.5\,P(8\,s) - C(s)$$
$$C = -28\,P + 64\,P - 4\,P = 32\,P$$

This result checks with the joints method.

It may not be necessary to solve to the center of the truss using the joints method. For example, suppose that a single cross section is used for the top chord, a single cross section is used for the bottom chord, and a single cross section is used for all the web members. The sections method may be used to go straight to the bay with the largest chord forces, and the joints method may be used to find the worst web forces (at the supports). However, using both methods provides a check of the work, which is important.

7.1.5 FORCE PATTERNS IN SIMPLE-SPAN, PARALLEL-CHORD TRUSSES

Figure 7.68(a) shows the axial forces (P_x') in the members of three simple-span trusses of the same depth and subjected to the same distributed load w. Figure 7.68(b) shows the deformations of the same trusses.

For all simple-span trusses with the same depth and subjected to the same load per unit length of truss, the web forces for web members at the center are identical, regardless of span. (The center vertical web member is a column supporting the force on the joint above and supported at its base by the "sling" created by the two diagonal web members that meet at the bottom vertex. The vertical components in these two diagonal webs are both equal to 0.5 P, so they add up to the P force required to support the center vertical web. For trusses with an even number of bays, the force in the three most central web members is always the same: 1 P in compression in the

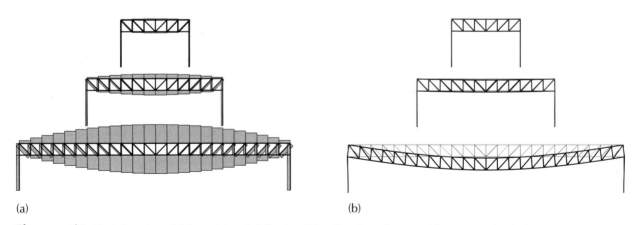

(a)   (b)

Figure 7.68 Variations in axial force (a) and deflection (b) as function of span, with constant depth.

vertical web member and 0.5 *P* vertical components in tension in the two diagonals' web members.)

For all simple-span trusses, the web forces are smallest at the center and increase in proportion to the distance from the truss's center.

These last two points imply that doubling the truss's span *L* doubles the most severe web force magnitudes. In the twenty-four–bay truss, the force in the last vertical web member is exactly twice the force in the last vertical web member of the twelve-bay truss. For the twenty-four–bay truss, the force in the last diagonal web member is close to twice the force in the last diagonal web member in the twelve-bay truss. It is not exactly twice, because these web members are not exactly at the end, but are about a half-bay in from the end. However, for all intents and purposes, doubling the length of span has also doubled the axial force in the most severely loaded diagonal web member.

The most severe top-chord force at the center of the twenty-four–bay truss is exactly four times the most severe top-chord force at the center of the twelve-bay truss. This is a manifestation of the fact that the internal resisting moment increases with the square of a spanning element's length (assuming that the load per unit length on the spanning member remains constant as the length is increased). For the truss, the compressive force in the top chord is one of two forces forming a couple that provides the internal resisting moment. The depth of the truss is the lever arm for the internal moment. Since the depth of the truss is not increased in moving from twelve bays to twenty four bays, the quadrupling of the internal resisting moment must be reconciled in a change in the force magnitude in the force couple providing the internal moment, that is, in the chord forces. By similar arguments, tripling the truss's length increases the maximum top-chord force by a factor of $3^2 = 9$. Quadrupling the span's length increases the maximum top-chord force by a factor of $4^2 = 16$.

The total floor area to be enclosed will be the same in each case. The difference is in deciding how many columns break up the space. Figure 7.69(a) shows axial force in the members and Figure 7.69(b) shows deflection of the trusses, using different spans and a constant truss depth.

The maximum chord force in the last case shown in Figure 7.69(a) will be sixteen times larger than the maximum chord force in the first case. Clearly, spanning longer distances will result in substantially more material expended in the spanning trusses. However, it has the advantages of simpler construction, fewer columns and footings, and fewer obstructions to space planning.

Of course, a shorter truss span means that the span depth can be less, which may save height on the building (see Figure 7.70).

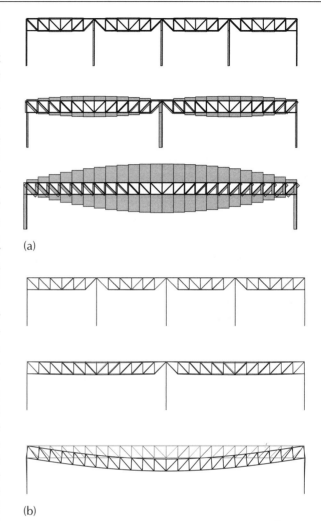

(a)

(b)

Figure 7.69 Variations in axial force (a) and deflection (b) as function of span, with constant depth.

Reducing the truss depth for the shorter span will increase the magnitude of the maximum chord force, somewhat offsetting the benefit of the shorter span.

Doubling the span increases the internal resisting moment by a factor of 4. However, doubling the depth increases the lever arm for the internal resisting moment by a factor of 2. Therefore, the net effect of doubling the span and doubling the depth of the truss is to increase the maximum chord force by a factor of $4 \cdot \frac{1}{2} = 2$. Doubling the depth of the truss does not significantly change the forces in the web members. However, longer web members are more vulnerable to buckling and they need to be larger in cross section to resist buckling. All of this suggests a general trend: For a fixed load per unit length of truss and for fixed truss proportions (i.e., constant depth-to-span ratio), the material in the truss increases approximately linearly with the span *L*.

Figure 7.71 shows the effect of truss depth on member forces (a) and deflection (b) for a fixed span and fixed load per unit length.

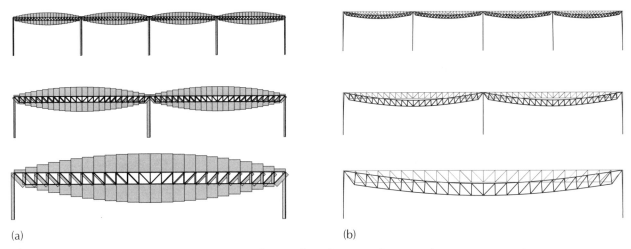

(a)   (b)

Figure 7.70 Variations in axial force (a) and deflection (b) as function of span, with constant proportions.

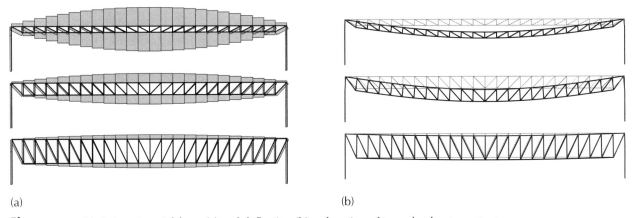

(a)   (b)

Figure 7.71 Variations in axial force (a) and deflection (b) as function of truss depth, at constant span.

Making the truss deeper reduces both the chord member forces and the truss deflection. However, there is a limit imposed on this process by the cost of longer web members. More vulnerable to buckling, longer web members need larger cross sections. Other economic factors also encourage shallow trusses, such as reducing the height of the building surface subjected to wind loading, reducing the building skin's first cost, and reducing the heat gains and losses through the building skin.

7.1.6 SIMPLIFIED JOINTS METHOD APPLIED TO A MODIFIED WARREN TRUSS

The truss configuration shown in Figure 7.72 is called a modified Warren truss.

Figures 7.73 and 7.74 show the solution to the modified Warren truss. This solution is presented without steps. Students should work out the truss, using the simplified joints method, as an exercise.

To check the solutions for the forces in the chord members, use the sections method (see Figure 7.75).

Using the sections method and taking moments about V (the intersection of the line of action of the C force and the line of action of the D force):

$$\sum M_v = 0 \ \curvearrowright$$
$$0 = +11.5 \, P(12 \, s) - 11 \, P(6 \, s) - T(s)$$
$$T = +13 \, P - 66 \, P = +72 \, P$$

This result checks with the bottom-chord force derived from the joints method.

It is desirable to have shallower slope on the end diagonal, to allow for a shallower end-bearing assembly. To achieve this effect, the repetitive pattern of diagonals is shifted over one bay and the shallow end diagonal is added, as shown in the geometry in Figure 7.76.

Figures 7.77 through 7.84 show steps in the solution to the modified Warren truss with shallow end diagonal, using the simplified joints method. These are presented without verbal explanation. Students should study these steps carefully and work out several additional steps.

Figures 7.85 and 7.86 show the complete solution, which had to be presented in two parts to fit on the page.

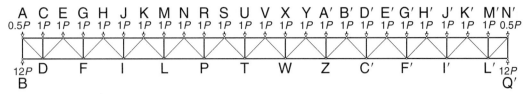

Figure 7.72 Geometry of modified Warren truss.

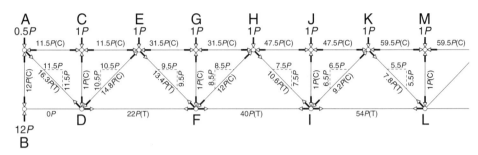

Figure 7.73 First part of the solution to the modified Warren truss.

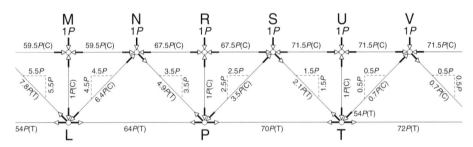

Figure 7.74 Second part of the solution to the modified Warren truss.

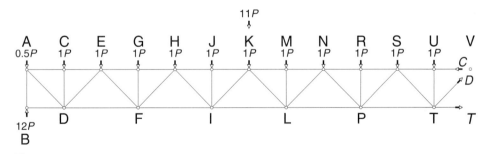

Figure 7.75 Sections method applied to modified Warren truss.

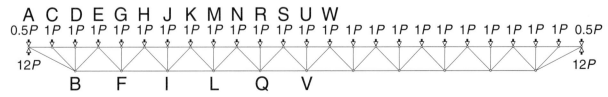

Figure 7.76 Geometry of modified Warren truss with shallow end diagonal.

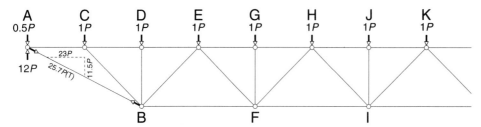

Figure 7.77 Resolved diagonal force on joint A.

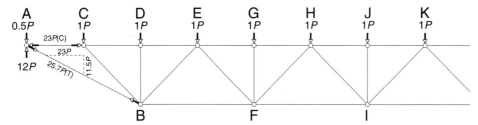

Figure 7.78 Resolved horizontal forces on joint A.

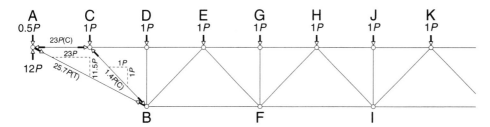

Figure 7.79 Resolved diagonal force on joint C.

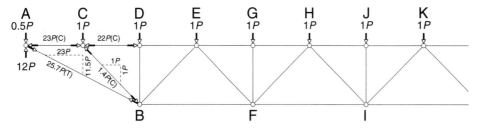

Figure 7.80 Resolved horizontal forces on joint C.

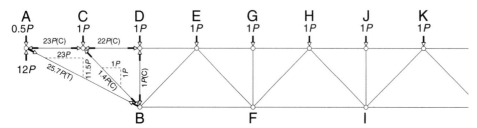

Figure 7.81 Resolved vertical forces on joint B.

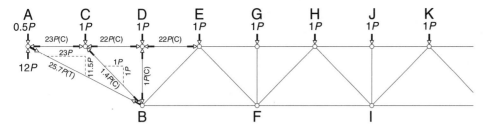

Figure 7.82 Resolved horizontal forces on joint D.

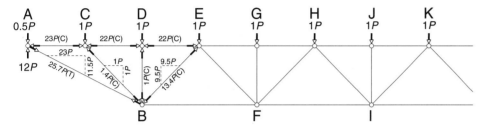

Figure 7.83 Resolved diagonal force on joint B.

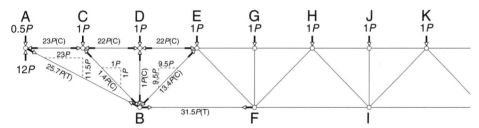

Figure 7.84 Resolved horizontal forces on joint B.

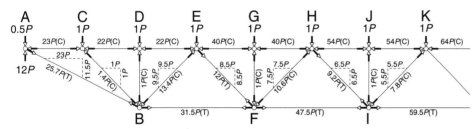

Figure 7.85 First part of solution to modified Warren truss with shallow end diagonal.

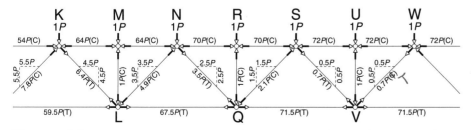

Figure 7.86 Second part of solution to modified Warren truss with shallow end diagonal.

To check the solutions for the forces in the chord members, use the sections method (see Figure 7.87).

Using the sections method and taking moments about R (the intersection of the line of action of the *C* force and the line of action of the *D* force):

$$\sum M_s \, \widehat{+} = 0$$

$$0 = +11.5\, P(11\,s) - 11\, P(5\,s) - T(s)$$

$$T = 71.5\, P$$

This result checks with the bottom chord force derived by the simplified joints method.

7.1.7 SIMPLIFIED JOINTS METHOD APPLIED TO RECTANGULAR BAY TRUSS

Many trusses have diagonals that are not sloped at 45°. For example, the truss in Figure 7.88 consists of eighteen bays that are 12 ft wide and 9 ft high. Using the simplified joints method, in Figure 7.89 a solution is generated for the left-hand side of the truss. A few representative

steps are presented in graphic form, without comment. Study them to make sure that you understand what is involved. (See Figures 7.90 through 7.93.)

To check the solutions for the forces in the chord members, use the sections method (see Figure 7.94).

Using the sections method and taking moments about R (the intersection of the line of action of the C force and the line of action of the D force):

$$\sum M_v \, \widehat{+} = 0$$

$$0 = +8.5\, P(10 \cdot 12 \text{ ft}) - 9\, P(5 \cdot 12 \text{ ft}) - T(9 \text{ ft})$$

$$\frac{0}{9 \text{ ft}} = \frac{+8.5\, P(120 \text{ ft}) - 9\, P(60 \text{ ft}) - T(9 \text{ ft})}{9 \text{ ft}}$$

$$= +8.5\, P(13.333) - 9\, P(6.667) - T$$

$$T = 113.331 \text{ ft} - 60.003 \text{ ft} = 53.33\, P$$

This result checks with the bottom-chord force derived from the simplified joints method.

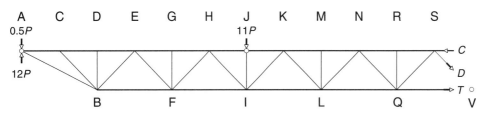

Figure 7.87 Sections method applied to the modified Warren truss with shallow end diagonal.

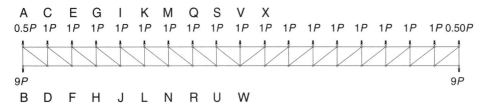

Figure 7.88 Eighteen-bay, rectangular-bay truss.

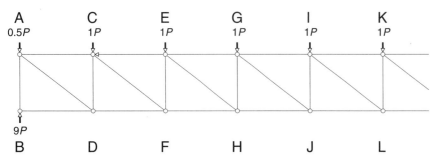

Figure 7.89 Drawing the left half of the truss as a freebody.

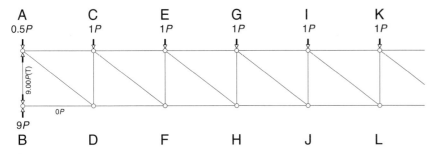

Figure 7.90 Resolved vertical and horizontal forces at joint B.

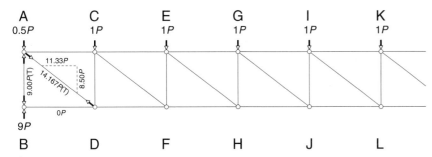

Figure 7.91 Resolved diagonal force at joint A.

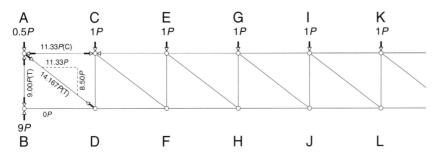

Figure 7.92 Resolved horizontal forces at joint A.

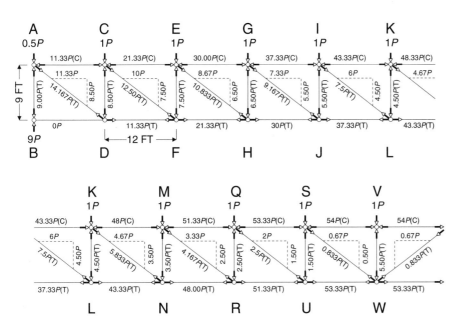

Figure 7.93 Solution to left half of eighteen-bay, rectangular-bay truss.

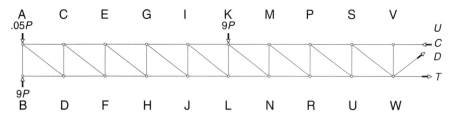

Figure 7.94 Sections method applied to eighteen-bay, rectangular-bay truss.

7.1.8 SIMPLIFIED JOINTS METHOD APPLIED TO TRUSSES WITH DOUBLE CANTILEVERS

Sometimes it is useful to move the supports in from the ends of the truss, producing column-free overhangs. This arrangement reduces the structural burden on the truss members and provides sheltering overhangs allowing unobstructed views and free access to the surrounding environment.

Figure 7.95 shows the configuration of a twenty-four–square-bay truss with five-bay cantilevers on both ends. Only the left half of the truss is depicted. By truss symmetry, the forces in the right half of the truss will be the mirror image of the forces calculated for the left half of the truss. Showing all twenty-four bays would be repetitious and make the type too small to read. By symmetry, each of the supports must be exerting an upward reaction of 12 P, to equilibrate the total downward force of 24 P on the top of the truss. Only half of the truss is needed to derive a complete solution.

To make the diagram easier to read, only seven bays at the left end of the truss are shown in Figure 7.96. After solving these seven bays in careful detail, the solution to the entire left-hand side of the truss will be shown.

Joint A is a good place to start, since there are only two members framing into that joint.

Applying the equilibrium principle to the vertical forces on joint A:

The applied downward 0.5 P force on joint A must be equilibrated by an upward 0.5 P force on joint A exerted by the vertical member connecting into joint A. (The vertical member is the only agent acting on joint A that is capable of exerting the required vertical force, since there is only one other member framing into joint A and that member, being horizontal, can exert only a horizontal force on the joint.)

Draw an upward force arrow on joint A, indicating the upward force exerted by the vertical member on joint A. (Remember that only the forces on the joints are shown. The arrows showing the forces exerted on the members

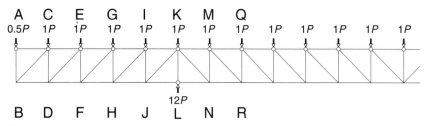

Figure 7.95 Twenty-four–bay, square-bay truss with five-bay cantilevers on both ends.

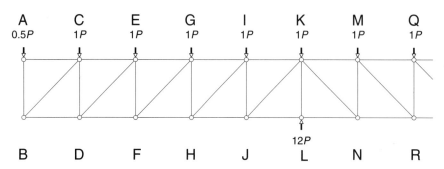

Figure 7.96 Close-up of twenty-four–bay, square-bay truss with five-bay cantilevers on both ends.

by the joints are omitted to avoid cluttering the diagram with too many arrows and numbers. However, knowing that there are forces on the members and understanding the role of those forces in this process is critical.)

Applying the action–reaction pairs principle to the interaction between joint A and the vertical member between joints A and B:

Since the vertical web member is pushing upward on joint A with a 0.5 P force, joint A must be pushing downward on the vertical member with a 0.5 P force.

Applying the equilibrium principle to the vertical member between joints A and B:

The 0.5 P downward force on the top of the vertical member, exerted by joint A, must be equilibrated by a 0.5 P upward force on the bottom of the vertical member, exerted by joint B.

Applying the action–reaction pairs principle to the interaction between joint B and the vertical member between joints A and B:

Since joint B is pushing upward on the vertical web member with a 0.5 P force, the vertical member must be pushing down on joint B with a 0.5 P force.

Draw a downward force arrow on joint B, indicating the downward force exerted by the vertical member on joint B.

Show the magnitude of the forces involved by writing 0.5 P (C) along the side of the vertical member between joints A and B, indicating the compression force in the member. It is also the magnitude of the force that is being passed through the member from one joint to the next (see Figure 7.97).

Applying the equilibrium principle to the horizontal forces on joint A:

The horizontal member is exerting no force on joint A, since there are no other horizontal forces present on the joint. Any force from the horizontal member would upset the joint's equilibrium.

Applying the action–reaction pairs principle to the interaction between joint A and the horizontal member between joints A and C:

Since the horizontal member between joints A and C is not exerting force on joint A, joint A must not be exerting force on that horizontal member.

Applying the equilibrium principle to the horizontal member between joints A and C:

Since joint A is not exerting force on the horizontal member, joint C must not exert force on that member either, because force exerted by joint C would disturb the horizontal member's equilibrium. Hence, the horizontal member between joints A and C has no force in it. If this result is surprising, imagine removing the horizontal segment in question. When one examines the structure without that member, it becomes clear that the horizontal member's function is to balance the vertical member between A and B against toppling to the left or to the right. The horizontal member is a bracing member not directly engaged in transferring forces under the loads shown.

Applying the action–reaction pairs principle to the interaction between joint C and the horizontal member between A and C:

Since the horizontal member between joints A and C is not exerting force on joint C, joint C must not be exerting force on the horizontal member.

Do not draw horizontal arrows on joint A or joint C, because no force is exerted on those joints by the horizontal member between them.

Show the magnitude of the forces involved by writing 0 P along the side of the horizontal member, indicating that no force is transferred through it and that the member has no axial force in it (see Figure 7.98).

Joint C has two unknown vertical and two unknown horizontal forces, making it unsuitable for the next step. There is only one equilibrium equation for vertical forces and one equilibrium equation for horizontal forces; therefore, there are not enough equilibrium equations to solve directly for forces on joint C.

Applying the equilibrium principle to the vertical forces on joint B:

The downward 0.5 P force on joint B, exerted by the vertical member between joints A and B, must be equilibrated by an upward 0.5 P force on joint B, exerted by the diagonal member connecting into joint B. (The diagonal member is the only agent acting on joint B that is capable of exerting the required vertical force, since there is only one other member framing into joint B and

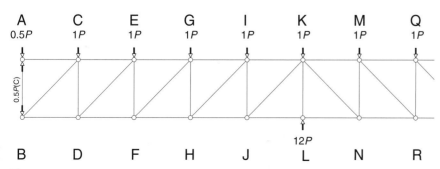

Figure 7.97 Resolved vertical forces at joint A.

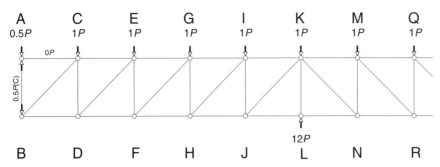

Figure 7.98 Resolved horizontal forces at joint A.

that member, being horizontal, can exert only a horizontal force on the joint.) Based on the previous argument regarding the behavior of 2-force members, this diagonal member between joints B and C must be pulling up on joint B with a force along the diagonal. For this particular problem, that diagonal has a slope of 1 unit rise in 1 unit run. Therefore, any force along that member must have equal vertical and horizontal components. The vertical component must be 0.5 P (to keep joint B in equilibrium relative to vertical forces), so the horizontal component must be 0.5 P as well. In summary, the diagonal is exerting an upward vertical force of 0.5 P on joint B and a horizontal force to the right of 0.5 P on joint B.

Applying the action–reaction pairs principle to the interaction between joint B and the diagonal member between joints B and C:

Since the diagonal member is pulling upward on joint B with a 0.5 P force, joint B must be pulling downward on the diagonal member with a 0.5 P force. Because the diagonal member is pulling to the right on joint B with a 0.5 P force, joint B must be pulling to the left on the diagonal member with a 0.5 P force. The sum of the two force components exerted by joint B on the diagonal member is a force of magnitude $\sqrt{(0.5\,P)^2 + (0.5\,P)^2} = 0.71\,P$ pulling along the member's length. This pulling force implies that the member is in tension, so the force is indicated by writing 0.71 P (T) along the side of the diagonal member. The 0.5 P force components of that 0.71 P force are indicated on the triangles along the side of the diagonal member.

Draw an upward force arrow on joint B along the diagonal member, indicating the force being exerted by the diagonal member pulling on joint B.

Applying the equilibrium principle to the diagonal member between joints B and C:

The 0.71 P force downward and to the left on the left end of the diagonal member, exerted by joint B, must be equilibrated by a 0.71 P force upward and to the right on the right end of the diagonal member, exerted by joint C.

Applying the action–reaction pairs principle to the interaction between joint C and the diagonal member between joints B and C:

Since joint C is pulling upward and to the right on the diagonal member with 0.71 P force, the member must be pulling down and to the left on joint C with 0.71 P force.

Draw a force arrow on joint C, downward and to the right along the diagonal member, indicating the force being exerted by the diagonal member on joint C.

Show the magnitude of the forces involved by writing 0.71 P (T) along the side of the diagonal member, indicating the tension force in the member and that it is being passed through the member from one joint to the next.

Label the force components of the 0.71 P force (0.5 P for both vertical and horizontal components) on the triangle attached to the diagonal member (see Figure 7.99).

Applying the equilibrium principle to the horizontal forces on joint B:

The horizontal member between B and D is exerting a 0.5 P force to the left on joint B, to equilibrate the 0.5 P force to the right exerted by the diagonal member between joints B and C.

Draw a left-pointing force arrow on joint B, indicating the force exerted by the horizontal member pushing on joint B.

Applying the action–reaction pairs principle to the interaction between joint B and the horizontal member between joints B and D:

Since the horizontal member between joints B and D is pushing to the left on joint B with a 0.5 P force, joint B must be pushing to the right with a 0.5 P force on that horizontal member.

Applying the equilibrium principle to the horizontal member between joints B and D:

Since joint B is pushing to the right on the horizontal member between joints B and D with a 0.5 P force, joint D must be pushing to the left on the horizontal member with a 0.5 P force.

Applying the action–reaction pairs principle to the interaction between joint D and the horizontal member between joints B and D:

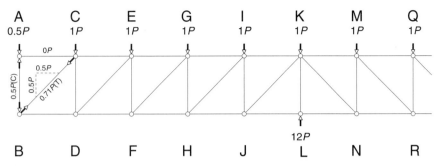

Figure 7.99 Resolved diagonal force at joint B.

Since joint D is pushing to the left on the horizontal member between joints B and D with a 0.5 *P* force, the horizontal member is pushing to the right on joint D with a 0.5 *P* force.

Draw a right-pointing force arrow on joint D, indicating the force exerted by the horizontal member on joint D.

Show the magnitude of the forces involved by writing 0.5 *P* (C) along the side of the horizontal member, indicating the compression force in the member and that it is being passed through the member from one joint to the next (see Figure 7.100)

Joint D has two unknown vertical and two unknown horizontal forces, making it unsuitable for the next step.

Applying the equilibrium principle to the vertical forces on joint C:

So far, there are two quantified vertical forces on joint C: a downward force of 1 *P*, which is part of the applied load, and a downward force of 0.5 *P* exerted by the diagonal member connecting to joint C. The sum of these forces is 1.5 *P* downward on joint C. This vertical force must be equilibrated by an upward force of 1.5 *P* exerted by the vertical member between joints C and D.

Draw an upward force arrow on joint C, indicating the upward force exerted by the vertical member on joint C.

Applying the action–reaction pairs principle to the interaction between joint C and the vertical member between joints C and D:

Since the vertical web member is pushing upward on joint C with a 1.5 *P* force, joint C must be pushing downward on the vertical member with a 1.5 *P* force.

Applying the equilibrium principle to the vertical member between joints C and D:

The 1.5 *P* downward force on the top of the vertical member, exerted by joint C, must be equilibrated by a 1.5 *P* upward force on the bottom of the vertical member, exerted by joint D.

Applying the action–reaction pairs principle to the interaction between joint D and the vertical member between joints C and D:

Since joint D is pushing upward on the vertical web member with a 1.5 *P* force, the member must be pushing down on joint D with a 1.5 *P* force.

Draw a downward force arrow on joint D, indicating the downward force exerted by the vertical member on joint D.

Show the magnitude of the forces involved by writing 1.5 *P* (C) along the side of the vertical member between joints C and D, indicating the compression force in the member and that it is being passed through the member from one joint to the next.

Applying the equilibrium principle to the horizontal forces on joint C:

There are two quantified horizontal forces on joint C: the 0 *P* force exerted by the horizontal between joints A and C and the 0.5 *P* pull to the left exerted by the diagonal between joints B and C. The sum of these forces is 0.5 *P* pulling to the left on joint C. This horizontal force must be equilibrated by a pull to the right of 0.5 *P* exerted by the horizontal member between joints C and E.

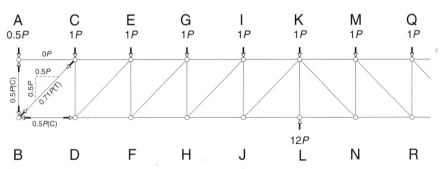

Figure 7.100 Resolved horizontal forces at joint B.

Draw a right-pointing force arrow on joint C, indicating the force being exerted by the horizontal member between joints C and E pulling to the right on joint C.

Applying the action–reaction pairs principle to the interaction between joint C and the horizontal member between C and E:

Since the horizontal member between joints C and E is pulling to the right with a 0.5 P force on joint C, joint C must be pulling to the left with a 0.5 P force on that horizontal member.

Applying the equilibrium principle to the horizontal member between joints A and C:

Since joint C is pulling to the left with a 0.5 P force on the horizontal member between joints C and E, joint E must be pulling to the right with a 0.5 P force on the horizontal member.

Applying the action–reaction pairs principle to the interaction between joint E and the horizontal member between C and E:

Since joint E is pulling to the right with a 0.5 P force on the horizontal member between joints C and E, the horizontal member is pulling to the left with a 0.5 P force on joint E.

Draw a left-pointing force arrow on joint E, indicating the force being exerted by the horizontal member between joints C and E pulling to the left on joint E.

Show the magnitude of the forces involved by writing 0.5 P (T) along the side of the horizontal member between C and E, indicating the tension force in the member and that it is being passed through the member from one joint to the next (see Figure 7.101).

Joint E has two unknown vertical and two unknown horizontal forces, making it unsuitable for the next step.

Applying the equilibrium principle to the vertical forces on joint D:

The downward 1.5 P force on joint D, exerted by the vertical member between joints C and D, must be equilibrated by an upward 1.5 P force on joint D, exerted by the diagonal member connecting into joint D. Based on previous arguments regarding the behavior of 2-force members, this diagonal member between joints D and E must be pulling up on joint D with a force along the di-

agonal. The vertical component must be 1.5 P (to keep the joint in equilibrium relative to vertical forces), so the horizontal component must be 1.5 P as well. In summary, the diagonal is exerting an upward vertical force of 1.5 P and a horizontal force to the right of 1.5 P on joint D.

Draw an upward force arrow on joint D along the diagonal member, indicating the force exerted by the diagonal member pulling on joint D.

Applying the action–reaction pairs principle to the interaction between joint D and the diagonal member between joints D and E:

Since the diagonal member is pulling upward on joint D with a 1.5 P force, joint D must be pulling downward on the diagonal member with a 1.5 P force. Since the diagonal member is pulling to the right on joint D with a 1.5 P force, joint D must be pulling to the left on the diagonal member with a 1.5 P force. The sum of the two force components exerted by joint D on the diagonal member is a force of magnitude $\sqrt{(1.5\,P)^2 + (1.5\,P)^2} = 2.12\,P$ pulling along the member's length. This pulling force implies that the member is in tension, so the magnitude of that force is indicated by writing 2.12 P (T) along the side of the diagonal member. The 1.5 P components of that 2.12 P force are indicated on the triangles along the side of the diagonal member.

Applying the equilibrium principle to the diagonal member between joints D and E:

The 2.12 P force downward and to the left on the left end of the diagonal member, exerted by joint D, must be equilibrated by a 2.12 P force upward and to the right on the right end of the diagonal member, exerted by joint E.

Applying the action–reaction pairs principle to the interaction between joint E and the diagonal member between joints D and E:

Since joint E is pulling upward and to the right on the diagonal member with a 2.12 P force, the member must be pulling down and to the left on joint E with a 2.12 P force.

Draw a force arrow on joint E, downward and to the right along the diagonal member, indicating the force exerted by the diagonal member on joint E.

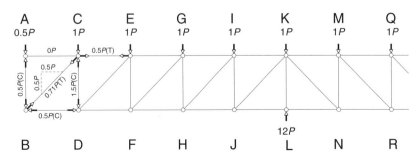

Figure 7.101 Resolved horizontal and vertical forces at joint C.

Show the magnitude of the forces involved by writing 2.12 *P* (T) along the side of the diagonal member, indicating the tension force in the member and that it is being passed through the member from one joint to the next.

Label the force components of the 2.12 *P* force (1.5 *P* for both vertical and horizontal components) on the triangle attached to the diagonal member between joints D and E (see Figure 7.102).

The next several steps of the solution are shown diagrammatically in Figures 7.103 through 7.111, without written explanation. Examine the steps to make sure that they make sense to you.

Resolving the forces at joint J leads to the diagram shown in Figure 7.112.

Joint K has two unknown vertical and two unknown horizontal forces, making it unsuitable for the next step. There is only one equilibrium equation for vertical forces

and one equilibrium equation for horizontal forces; therefore, there are not enough equilibrium equations to solve directly for forces on joint K.

Applying the equilibrium principle to the vertical forces on joint L:

The upward 12 *P* force on joint L, exerted by the support, must be equilibrated by an downward 12 *P* force on joint L, exerted by the vertical member between joints K and L.

Draw a downward force arrow on joint L, indicating the force exerted by the vertical member pushing down on joint L.

Applying the action–reaction pairs principle to the interaction between joint L and the vertical member between joints K and L:

Since the vertical member is pushing down on joint L with a 12 *P* force, joint L must be pushing up on the vertical member with a 12 *P* force.

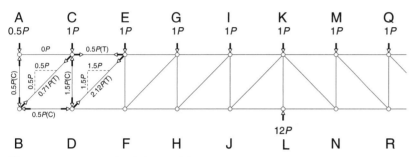

Figure 7.102 Resolved diagonal force at joint D.

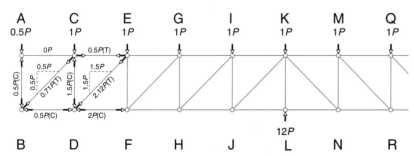

Figure 7.103 Resolved horizontal forces at joint D.

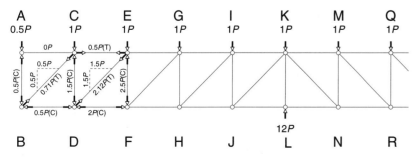

Figure 7.104 Resolved vertical forces at joint F.

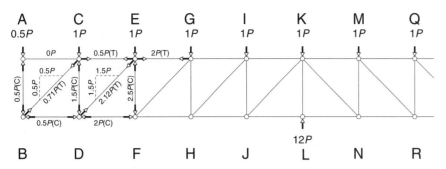

Figure 7.105 Resolved horizontal forces at joint E.

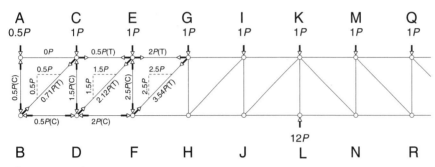

Figure 7.106 Resolved diagonal force at joint F.

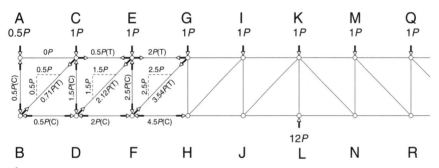

Figure 7.107 Resolved horizontal forces at joint F.

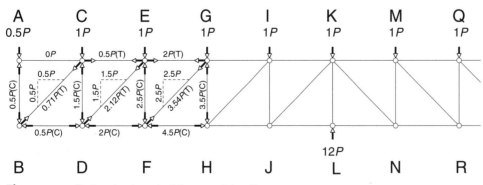

Figure 7.108 Resolved vertical forces at joint G.

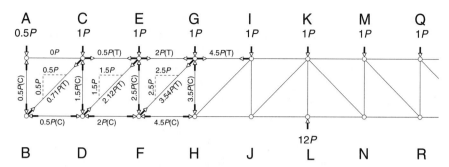

Figure 7.109 Resolved horizontal forces at joint G.

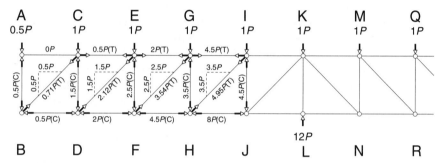

Figure 7.110 Resolved diagonal and horizontal forces at joint H.

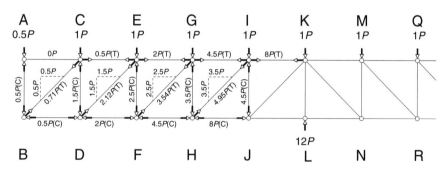

Figure 7.111 Resolved horizontal and vertical forces at joint I.

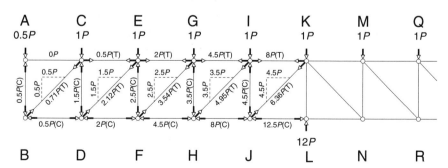

Figure 7.112 Resolved diagonal and horizontal forces at joint J.

Applying the equilibrium principle to the vertical member between joints K and L:

The 12 *P* upward force exerted by joint L on the bottom of the vertical member between joints K and L must be equilibrated by a 12 *P* downward force from joint K on the top of the vertical member between joints K and L.

Applying the action–reaction pairs principle to the interaction between joint K and the vertical member between joints K and L:

Since joint K is pushing downward on the vertical member with a 12 *P* force, the vertical member must be pushing up on joint K with a 12 *P* force.

Draw an upward force arrow on joint K, indicating the force exerted by the vertical member pushing up on joint K.

Show the magnitude of the forces involved by writing 12 *P* (C) along the side of the diagonal member, indicating the compression force in the member and that it is being passed through the member from one joint to the next (see Figure 7.113).

Applying the equilibrium principle to the horizontal forces on joint L:

There is only one quantified horizontal force on joint L: a pushing force of 12.5 *P* to the right exerted by the horizontal member between joints J and L. The horizontal member between L and N must equilibrate this force by pushing to the left with a 12.5 *P* force on joint L.

Draw a left-pointing force arrow on joint L, indicating the force exerted by the horizontal member between joints L and N pushing to the left on joint L.

Applying the action–reaction pairs principle to the interaction between joint L and the horizontal member between joints L and N:

Since the horizontal member between joints L and N is pushing to the left on joint L with a 12.5 *P* force, joint L must be pushing to the right with a 12.5 *P* force on the horizontal member.

Applying the equilibrium principle to the horizontal member between joints L and N:

Since joint L is pushing to the right with a 12.5 *P* force on the horizontal member between joints L and N, joint N must be pushing to the left with a 12.5 *P* force on the horizontal member between joints L and N, in order to keep the member in equilibrium.

Applying the action–reaction pairs principle to the interaction between joint N and the horizontal member between joints L and N:

Since joint N is pushing to the left with a 12.5 *P* force on the horizontal member between joints L and N, the horizontal member is pushing to the right with a 12.5 *P* force on joint N.

Draw a right-pointing force arrow on joint N, indicating the force exerted by the horizontal member between joints L and N pushing to the right on joint N.

Show the magnitude of the forces involved by writing 12.5 *P* (C) along the side of the horizontal member between joints L and N, indicating the compression force in the member and that it is being passed through the member from one joint to the next (see Figure 7.114).

Joint N has two unknown vertical and two unknown horizontal forces, making it unsuitable for the next step. There is only one equilibrium equation for vertical forces and one equilibrium equation for horizontal forces; therefore, there are not enough equilibrium equations to solve directly for forces on joint N.

Joint K represents a new condition, with two diagonals framing into the joint. In this case, there are two unknown horizontal forces and one unknown vertical force. Therefore, in attempting to resolve this joint, begin by resolving the vertical forces.

Applying the equilibrium principle to the vertical forces on joint K:

There are three quantified vertical forces on joint K: a downward force of 1 *P* applied load, a downward force of 4.5 *P* exerted by the diagonal member between joints J and K, and a vertical upward force of 12 *P* exerted by the vertical member between joints K and L. The sum of these forces is −4.5 *P* − 1 *P* + 12 *P* = +6.5 *P* upward on joint K. This vertical force must be equilibrated by a downward force of 6.5 *P* exerted by the diagonal member between joints K and N. Based on previous arguments regarding the behavior of 2-force members, this diagonal member between joints K and N must be pulling down and to the right on joint K with a net force along the diagonal. The vertical component must be 6.5 *P* (to keep joint K in equilibrium relative to vertical forces), so the horizontal force component of the diagonal on joint K must also be 6.5 *P*. The sum of the two force com-

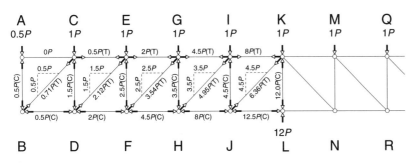

Figure 7.113 Resolved vertical forces at joint L.

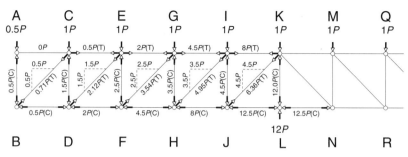

Figure 7.114 Resolved horizontal forces at joint L.

ponents exerted by the diagonal member on joint K is a force of magnitude $\sqrt{(6.5\,P)^2+(6.5\,P)^2}=9.19\,P$ pulling along the member's length.

Draw a force arrow on joint K, downward and to the right along the diagonal member, indicating the force exerted by the diagonal member pulling on joint K.

Applying the action–reaction pairs principle to the interaction between joint K and the diagonal member between joints K and N:

Since the diagonal member is pulling down and to the right on joint K with a 9.19 P force, joint K must be pulling up and to the left on the diagonal member with a 9.19 P force.

Applying the equilibrium principle to the diagonal member between joints K and N:

The force of 9.19 P pulling up and to left exerted by joint K on the left end of the diagonal member must be equilibrated by a force of 9.19 P pulling down and to the right, exerted by joint N on the right end of the diagonal member.

Applying the action–reaction pairs principle to the interaction between joint N and the diagonal member between joints K and N:

Since joint N is pulling down and to the right with a 9.19 P force on the diagonal member, the diagonal member is pulling up and to the left on joint N with a 9.19 P force.

Draw an upward force arrow on joint N along the diagonal member, indicating the force exerted by the diagonal member on joint N.

Show the magnitude of the forces involved by writing 9.19 P (T) along the side of the diagonal member, indi-

cating the tension force in the member and that it is being passed through the member from one joint to the next.

Label the force components of the 9.19 P force (6.5 P for both vertical and horizontal components) on the triangle attached to the diagonal member between joints K and N (see Figure 7.115).

Applying the equilibrium principle to the horizontal forces on the joint K:

There are three quantified horizontal forces on joint K: a pulling force of 8 P to the left exerted by the horizontal member between joints I and K, a pulling force component to the left of 4.5 P exerted by the diagonal member between joints J and K, and a pulling force component to the right of 6.5 P exerted by the diagonal member between joints K and N. The sum of these forces is $-8\,P-4.5\,P+6.5\,P=-6\,P$ to the left. The horizontal member between K and M must equilibrate this force by pulling to the right with a 6 P force on joint K.

Draw a right-pointing force arrow on joint K, indicating the force exerted by the horizontal member between joints K and M pulling to the right on joint K.

Applying the action–reaction pairs principle to the interaction between joint K and the horizontal member between joints K and M:

Since the horizontal member between joints K and M is pulling to the right on joint K with a 6 P force, joint K must be pulling to the left with a 6 P force on the horizontal member.

Applying the equilibrium principle to the horizontal member between joints K and M:

Since joint K is pulling to the left with a 6 P force on the horizontal member between joints K and M, joint M must be pulling to the right with a 6 P force on the

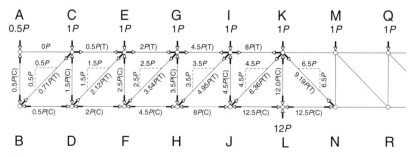

Figure 7.115 Resolved diagonal forces at joint K.

horizontal member, in order to keep the member in equilibrium.

Applying the action–reaction pairs principle to the interaction between joint M and the horizontal member between joints K and M:

Since joint M is pulling to the right with a 6 P force on the horizontal member between joints K and M, the horizontal member between joints K and M is pulling to the left with a 6 P force on joint M.

Draw a left-pointing force arrow on joint M, indicating the force exerted by the horizontal member between joints K and M pulling to the left on joint M.

Show the magnitude of the forces involved by writing 6 P (T) along the side of the horizontal member between

joints K and M, indicating the tension force in the member and that it is being passed through the member from one joint to the next (see Figure 7.116).

Continuing on in a similar manner to joints N, M, R, Q, T, S, and so forth, one arrives at a solution for the left side of the truss, shown in Figure 7.121.

The two diagonal web members at the center of the truss are both in tension and have the same vertical components and horizontal components. This is evidence that the web members are properly resolved, since symmetric results are expected by virtue of the structure's symmetry. There is not a similar check on the chord forces when arriving at the truss's center, because applying equilibrium principles at the center joints ensures

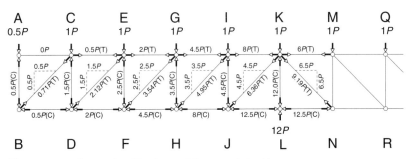

Figure 7.116 Resolved horizontal forces at joint K.

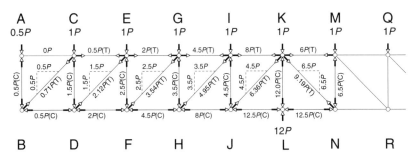

Figure 7.117 Resolved vertical forces at joint N.

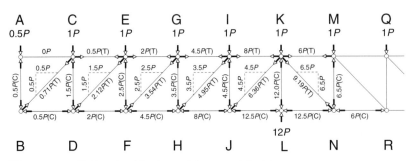

Figure 7.118 Resolved horizontal forces at joint N.

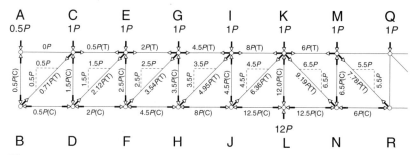

Figure 7.119 Resolved diagonal force at joint M.

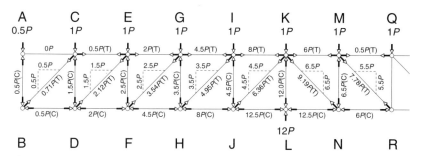

Figure 7.120 Resolved horizontal forces at joint M.

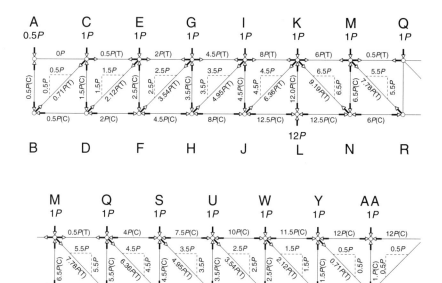

Figure 7.121 Axial forces for half of the twenty-four–bay, square-bay truss with two five-bay cantilevers.

symmetric chord forces, even if an error is committed in previous calculation stages. To check the chord forces, use the sections method. To do this, slice the truss through one of the two center bays and take the left part of the truss as a freebody (see Figure 7.122).

Then replace the eleven 1 P forces with a single 11 P force at the action center of the eleven 1 P forces (see Figure 7.123).

Taking moments about joint BB:

$$\sum M_{BB} \curvearrowright = 0$$

$$0 = -0.5\,P(12\,s) + 12\,P(7\,s) - 11\,P(6\,s) - C(s)$$

$$C = -6\,P + 84\,P - 66P = +12\,P$$

This result checks with the top-chord force derived from the simplified joints method.

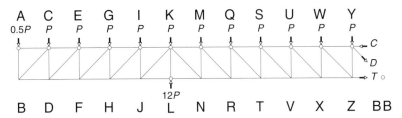

Figure 7.122 Applying the sections method to the twenty-four–bay, square-bay truss with two five-bay cantilevers.

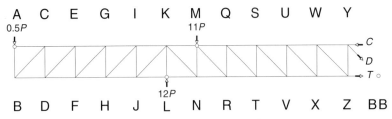

Figure 7.123 Clustering forces to simplify calculations.

Taking moments about joint Y:

$$\sum M_Y \curvearrowright = 0$$

$$0 = -0.5\,P(11\,s) + 12\,P(6\,s) - 11\,P(5\,s) - T(s)$$

$$T = -5.5\,P + 72\,P - 55\,P = +11.5\,P$$

This result checks with the bottom-chord force derived from the simplified joints method.

7.1.9 OPTIONAL DOUBLE CANTILEVERS IN CONTINUOUS PARALLEL-CHORD TRUSSES

The diagram in Figure 7.124 shows graphically the forces in twenty-four–bay trusses with various length double cantilevers. As before, the size of a flag is proportional to the force in the member. Light gray flags represent tension forces, and dark gray flags represent compression forces. For the simple-span structure on the top, the maximum compressive forces are on the top and the maximum tension forces on the bottom.

The shape of these diagrams is strongly suggestive of how the depth of the truss or the thickness of the members might be varied to respond to internal moment variations.

From an inspection of the diagram in Figure 7.124 for the twenty-four–bay trusses under uniform gravity load, the following inferences are clear:

1. The optimal cantilever to minimize the maximum web force is six bays, or ⁶/₂₄, or 25% of the overall truss length (tip-to-tip dimension) of the twenty-four–bay truss. Since the web forces are accounting for shear in the spanning member, it makes sense that the shearing force would be minimal when the material is balanced on each side of the supports. Shifting away from this balance increases the load on one side of the supports, thereby increasing the required shearing force.

Figure 7.124 Variations in axial forces as supports are pulled inward.

2. The optimal cantilever to minimize the maximum chord force is five bays, or $^5/_{24}$, or 20.8% of the overall truss length (tip-to-tip dimension) of the twenty-four–bay truss. Notice that the compression forces in the bottom chords at the supports are almost identical to the compression forces in the top-chord members at midspan between the supports. Shifting the supports in either direction would cause one or the other of these chord forces to increase, taking the chord forces higher.

3. The worst compression chord force for the twenty-four–bay simple-span truss occurs on the top of the truss, and the worst compression chord force in the twelve-bay cantilever truss is on the bottom of the truss. The maximum compressive chord force for the twenty-four–bay simple-span truss is equal to the maximum compressive chord force for the twelve-bay, cantilever truss. This leads to the following rules of thumb for trusses:

- A given truss cross section can span twice as far in simple-span mode as in cantilever mode.
- The depth-to-span ratio for a cantilever truss should be twice the depth-to-span ratio for a simple-span truss. For example, a typical simple-span truss depth might be $D = ^L/_{20}$ (depth = 0.05 · length), while a typical cantilever truss depth might be $D = ^L/_{10}$ (depth = 0.10 · length).

Items 2 and 3 are tempered by a number of caveats. These diagrams assume a uniformly distributed gravity load, such as snow on a roof. They do not represent shifting live loads on a floor or localized forces on a roof, such as a pallet of roofing material dropped from a crane by repairmen who lack understanding or respect for the roof's structural limits. Nor do they represent wind forces. Wind forces on overhangs can be the dominant load concern, particularly in environments with high winds, such as coastal areas. Overhangs can have an upward pressure on a cantilever's underside equal to the overpressure on a building's windward side ($C = +0.8$). There may also be a suction force on the cantilever's top surface equal to the maximum suction on a flat roof ($C = -0.7$). The overpressure and suction conspire to produce large forces on the overhang. The worst load case depends on the wind and snow zone in which the building is constructed. Given these facts, the optimizations under uniform load discussed earlier can be elegant and seductive, but they should not be taken as anything more than one of the many factors in the development of a rational design. For more on this issue, refer to the discussion on shifting live loads in Chapter 2.

Figure 7.125 shows the deflection of the trusses discussed above.

The optimal cantilever to minimize the deflection of the cantilever's end is five bays (20.8%), the same as the optimum for minimizing the maximum chord force.

Sometimes the span between columns cannot be changed, in which case shifting the columns inward

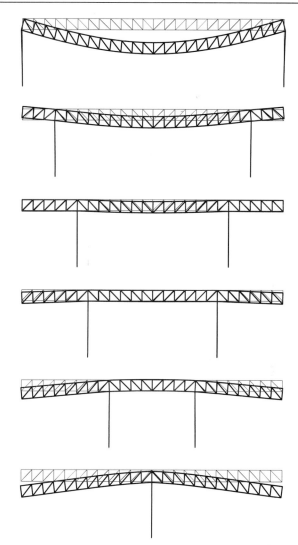

Figure 7.125 Variations in deflection as supports are moved inward.

from the truss ends is not an option. However, cantilevers may be added beyond the column supports to provide extra functional space, but the cost needs to be justified. One justification is the reduction in cost for the truss portions between the supports. The diagram in Figure 7.126 shows the progressive chord force changes for the truss portion between the supports, as longer and longer cantilevers are added beyond the columns.

For the last truss shown in Figure 7.126, the chord forces between the supports are reduced to 52 percent of what they are without cantilevers, suggesting that the material in the chords' cross sections between the supports can be reduced by a factor of 0.52. The additional chord material length included in the cantilevers is approximately 70% of the chord material length between the supports. Therefore, the overall truss length is increased by a factor of 1.7. Therefore, the total material in the chord members is changed by about $0.52 \cdot 1.7 = 0.884$. Adding cantilevers to the structure actually reduced the total required chord material. Furthermore,

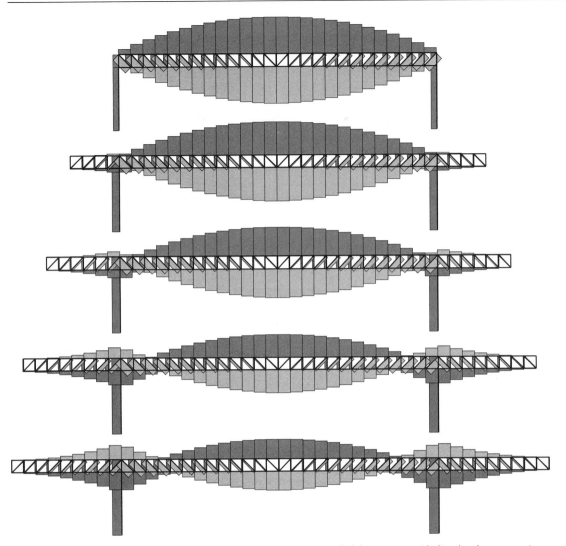

Figure 7.126 Variations in axial forces as cantilevers are extended from truss with fixed column spacing.

adding the cantilevers substantially reduced the deflec-tion between the supports, which reduced the roof's ponding failure threat, as illustrated in the diagram of deflections in Figure 7.127.

If the original truss design is governed by deflection, rather than stress, then adding the cantilevers may have an even more dramatic savings benefit in relation to the chord material. On the downside, adding the cantilevers is not beneficial for reducing web forces and it requires additional web members and roof decking. Moreover, wind uplift can become the governing issue. However, this illustration shows that adding cantilevers has struc-tural benefits, particularly under uniform gravity loads, and that adding the cantilevers may prove economically viable. However, in the final analysis, the major justifi-cation must be the gain of useful space under the over-hangs or getting solar protection from the overhangs.

7.1.10 SIMPLIFIED JOINTS METHOD APPLIED TO TRUSSES WITH SINGLE CANTILEVERS

Sometimes it is desirable to shift one support in from the end of the truss, but not shift the other support, resulting in a single cantilever on one end of the truss. The analy-sis of this truss is complicated by the lack of symmetry, meaning that the entire truss needs to be solved, rather than just half the truss. It is also complicated because the reactions are not typically round numbers. Non-round values, starting with the reactions, propagate throughout the structure, requiring that several significant figures be carried throughout the analysis to ensure accuracy.

Consider the seventeen-bay truss with a single five-bay cantilever in Figure 7.128.

The total load applied to the joints on the top of the truss is 17 *P*. Replacing all of those forces with a single

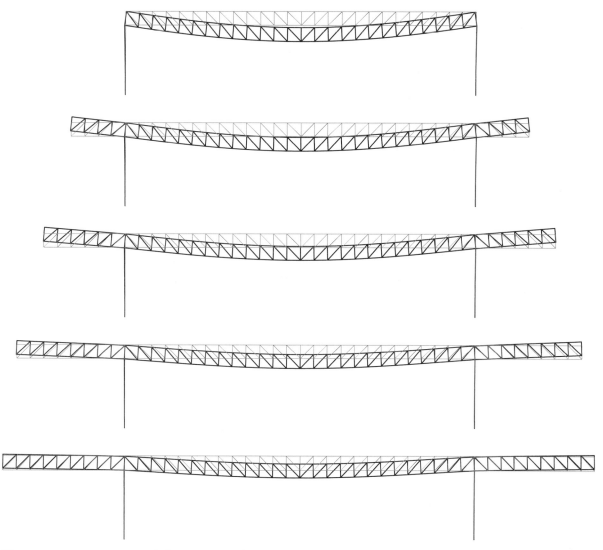

Figure 7.127 Variations in deflection as cantilevers are extended from truss with fixed column spacing.

17 P force at the truss's center yields the result shown in Figure 7.129.

Taking moments about point LL:

$$\sum M_{LL} \curvearrowright = 0$$

$$0 = \frac{+R_L(12\ s) - 17\ P(8.5\ s)}{12\ s} = R_L - 17\ P(0.70833)$$

$$R_L = 12.042\ P$$

Taking moments about point L:

$$\sum M_L \curvearrowright = 0$$

$$0 = +R_{LL}(12\ s) - 17\ P(3.5\ s) = \frac{R_{LL}(12\ s) - 17\ P(3.5\ s)}{12\ s}$$

$$= R_{LL} - 17\ P(0.29167)$$

$$R_{LL} = 4.958\ P$$

These reactions are not integers or half integers. They have an infinite number of digits after the decimal, which means that they must be rounded off. It is best to keep several digits to avoid accumulation of errors. However, writing out a lot of digits is time-consuming and inefficient. The number of digits in the preceding equations already exceeds the accuracy with which such things are known in real field conditions of construction. However, keeping all those digits is justified because, within the context of the idealized theory, they are accurate and known. Moreover, retaining extra digits can sometimes help in tracking errors in computations (see Figure 7.130).

The solution to the five-bay cantilever to the left is exactly the same as the solution to the five-bay cantilever on the double cantilever problem that previously worked (see Figure 7.131).

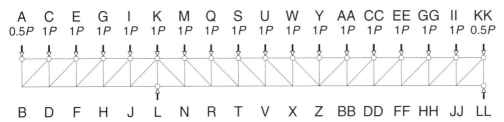

Figure 7.128 Seventeen-bay, square-bay truss with five-bay cantilever.

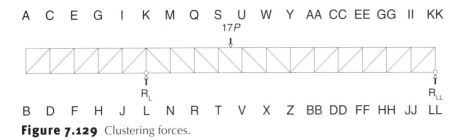

Figure 7.129 Clustering forces.

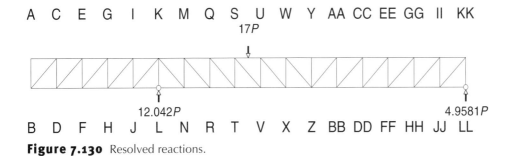

Figure 7.130 Resolved reactions.

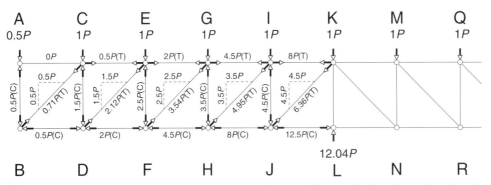

Figure 7.131 Writing out the solutions to the five-bay cantilever, which we have already solved.

Figures 7.132 through 7.137 resolve forces at the support and for joints to the right of the support.

Figure 7.138 shows the entire solution to the truss, in three parts, to make it fit on the page.

The diagonal between joints Z and AA is in compression. Up to this point, the web members in the trusses have been patterned so that the diagonals are all in tension. This has been done based on the logic that the diagonals, which are the longer members, are more vulnerable to buckling when put in compression. In laying out this asymmetric structure, the designer, lacking any knowledge to the contrary, made the transition from one diagonal slope to the alternative diagonal slope at midspan between the supports. Based on the evidence from the solution, this transition from one diagonal slope to the alternative diagonal slope would need to be one bay farther to the right to ensure that the diagonals are all working in tension. However, this may not be important, since the compression force in the diagonal in question is small and unlikely to cause serious

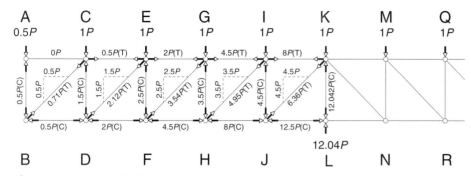

Figure 7.132 Resolved vertical forces at joint L.

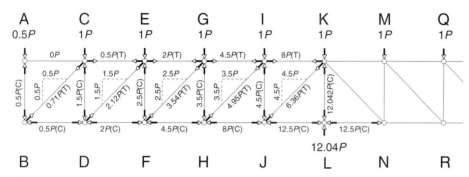

Figure 7.133 Resolved horizontal forces at joint L.

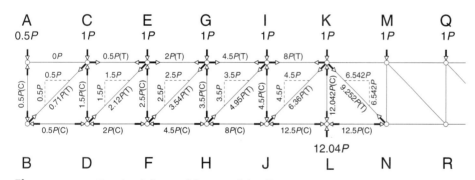

Figure 7.134 Resolved diagonal forces at joint K.

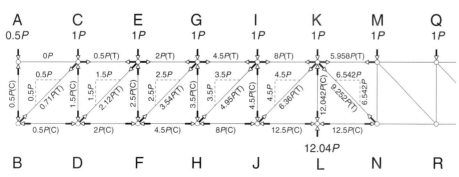

Figure 7.135 Resolved horizontal forces at joint K.

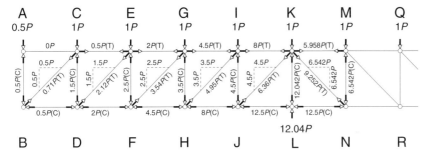

Figure 7.136 Resolved vertical forces at joint N.

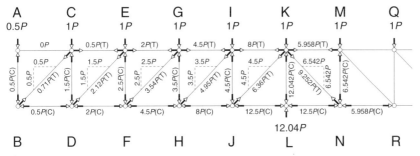

Figure 7.137 Resolved horizontal forces at joint N.

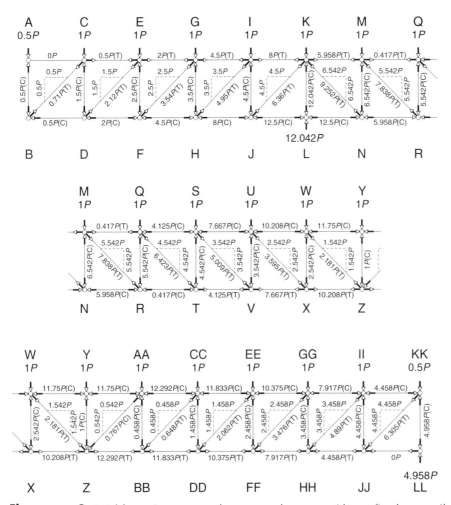

Figure 7.138 Axial forces in seventeen-bay, square-bay truss with one five-bay cantilever.

problems. Moreover, this analysis is for uniform gravity load; shifting loads could cause stress reversal in some of these diagonals regardless. Under all the possible load combinations, there will typically be some diagonals in compression, no matter how the truss is configured.

7.1.11 OPTIMAL SINGLE CANTILEVERS IN CONTINUOUS PARALLEL-CHORD TRUSSES

Figure 7.139 shows a progression of cantilevers caused by shifting one column varying distances in from the end of twenty-four–bay trusses. Figure 7.139(a) shows axial forces in the truss members, and Figure 7.139(b) shows deflections.

The deflections are greatly exaggerated to make them observable. The actual deflections would be much smaller and could be observed only by siting down the length of the truss. For the fourth truss down on the left, the greatest compression force in the top chord is about equal to the compression force in the bottom chord: seven bays/twenty-four bays = 0.2966, approximately 29%.

The optimum cantilever lengths to minimize the maximum internal moment are the following:

29% of the overall length for single cantilevers (ratio = 0.290).

20.8% of the overall length for double cantilevers (ratio = 0.208).

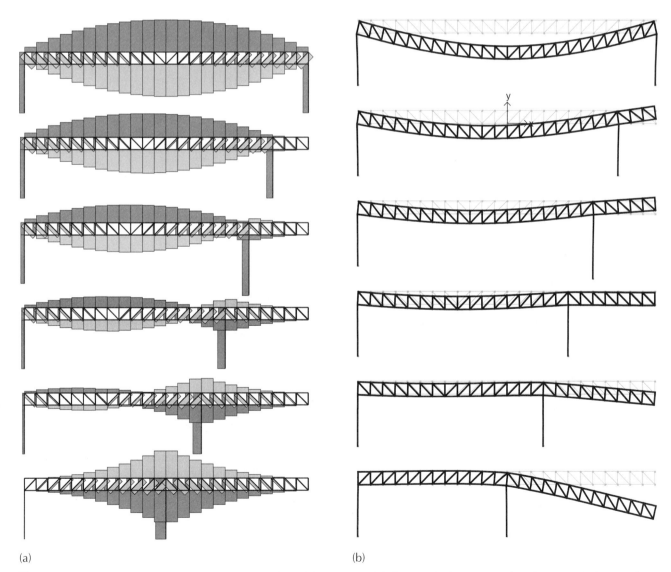

(a)   (b)

Figure 7.139 Effect of support location on internal axial forces (a) and deflection (b) for a twenty-four–bay truss with a cantilever at one end.

It is crucial that the supports occur under joints in a truss. Otherwise, severe bending is induced in chord members bearing on the supports. Therefore, finding the optimum cantilever solution is not a simple matter of multiplying the truss length by the ratios given here, because multiplying by those numbers may produce a cantilever that places the support at a chord member's midpoint. Table 7.1 calculates the optimum cantilevers for different numbers of bays and looks for numbers of bays that have a joint close to where the supports should land. Note that twenty-four–bay trusses and thirty-four–bay trusses represent good solutions for both double cantilevers and single cantilevers. The optimal cantilever based on multiplying by the ratios listed earlier is close to an integer number of bays for twenty-four–bay and thirty-four–bay trusses. The support can be placed under the nearest joint and come close to achieving the optimal cantilever.

The principle of judiciously adding a cantilever is well illustrated by the Virginia Beach Convention Center roof designed by the Skidmore, Owings & Merrill Chicago office (see Figure 7.140).

This is a long-span exhibit space that needs help to allow it to efficiently span the long distance. The loading dock also needs to be covered. By cantilevering the truss over the loading dock, some of the structural burden is removed from the truss portion over the main exhibit space, leaving the loading area free of columns so that truck traffic is uninhibited.

The cantilever is not precisely optimal in this case for minimizing moments. Furthermore, the shape of the truss was driven by aesthetics and the need to shed water off the roof as much as by structural optimization. However, the cantilever in this design is of a rational length and an elegant solution.

7.1.12 MODIFYING SIMPLE-SPAN TRUSSES BY MOMENT CONNECTING TO A STUFF COLUMN

Sometimes a column cannot be moved inward, because there is a functional requirement for a minimal spacing between columns. However, a cantilever may be added to a fixed-span system, thereby creating covering for additional space under the overhang and providing the beneficial, uplifting moment on the end of the truss portion between the supports (see Figure 7.141).

The cantilevers provide beneficial, uplifting moments on the ends of the truss portion between the supports. A similar benefit is achieved by connecting the ends of both the top and bottom chords of the truss to rigid columns. The net effect is that the columns exert a negative moment on the end of the truss, effectively lifting them up and reducing the axial forces on the top- and bottom-chord members at center span.

Table 7.1 Optimal Cantilevers and Possible Cantilevers for Trusses

N Total Number of Bays in Truss	.29N	Closest Integer Number of Bays to Optimal Single Cantilever	.207N	Closest Integer Number of Bays to Optimal Double Cantilever
10	2.90		**2.07**	2
11	3.19		2.28	
12	3.48		2.48	
13	3.77		2.69	
14	**4.06**	4	**2.90**	3
15	4.35		3.11	
16	4.64		3.31	
17	**4.93**	5	3.52	
18	5.22		3.73	
19	5.51		**3.93**	4
20	5.80		4.14	
21	**6.09**	6	4.35	
22	6.38		4.55	
23	6.67		4.76	
24	**6.96**	7	**4.97**	5
25	7.25		5.18	
26	7.54		5.38	
27	7.83		5.59	
28	8.12		5.80	
29	8.41		**6.00**	6
30	8.70		6.21	
31	**8.99**	9	6.42	
32	9.28		6.62	
33	9.57		6.83	
34	9.86		**7.04**	7
35	10.15		7.25	
36	10.44		7.45	
37	10.73		7.66	
38	**11.02**	11	7.87	
39	11.31		8.07	
40	11.6		8.28	
41	11.89		8.49	
42	12.18		8.69	
43	12.47		**8.90**	9
44	12.76		9.11	

This effect is illustrated in Figure 7.142(a), showing axial forces and deflection. At the top is the simple pinned connection of truss to the columns. Figure 7.142(b) shows the rigid connection to fairly slender, flexible columns. Figure 7.143 shows the effects of progressively stiffer columns, offering progressively greater resistance to truss rotation at the support locations. These analyses are computer generated and are beyond the scope of the hand analysis that is done in this book.

The trusses' rigid connection to the columns can provide a useful way to stabilize the building against wind and seismic forces. This topic is addressed in more detail in Chapter 10, "Lateral Bracing Systems."

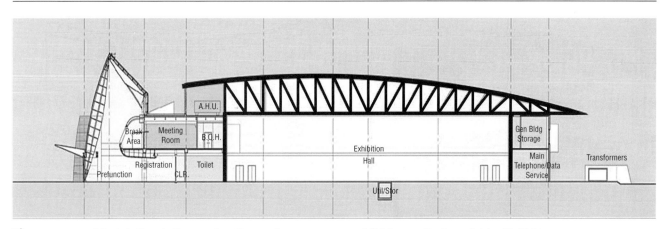

Figure 7.140 Virginia Beach Convention Center. (Image courtesy of Skidmore, Owings, & Merrill, LLP.)

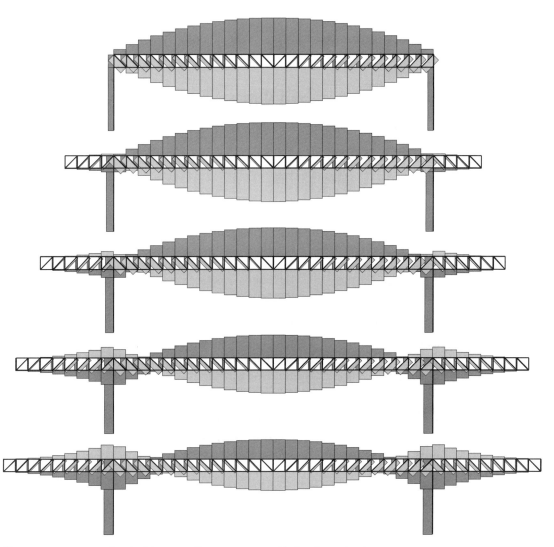

Figure 7.141 Benefit of adding cantilevers to truss with fixed spacing between supports.

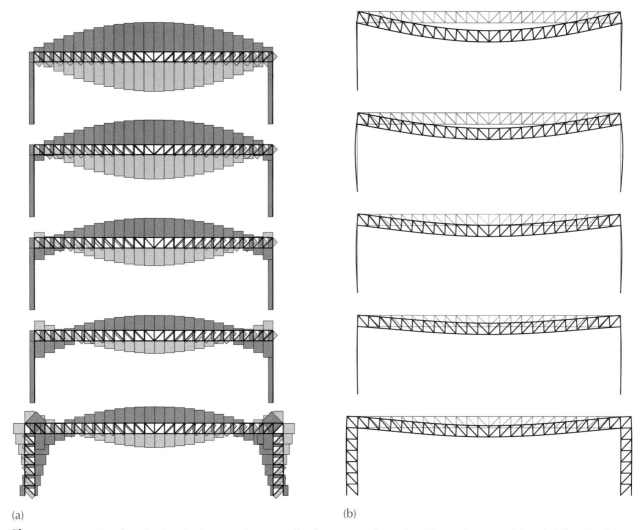

(a)

(b)

Figure 7.142 Benefits of using rigid connections to stiff columns to reduce chord forces in a truss (a) and deflection (b).

The structure in Figure 7.144 is a variation on the theme of using trussed elements at the ends of trusses to restrain the truss end's tendency to rotate. This truss is part of the Pompidou Museum in Paris (Architects: Richard Rogers and Lorenzo Piano; Engineers: Ove Arup and Partners and Peter Rice).

The bipod elements, at each end, connecting the top chord of a truss to the bottom chord of the truss above serve several important structural functions. As the lower truss begins to deflect, the bipods at the truss ends tend to rotate in such a manner that the two end bipods' top points start to move together. However, those points are connected to vertices on the truss above. The bottom chord of the truss above tends to compress as that truss below begins to deflect under load. The bottom chord of the truss above is pushing outward on the bipods' two top vertices, counteracting the tendency to move inward under the bottom chord's action.

The bipods' role at the centers of the trusses is to constrain all the trusses to deflect together. In this manner, if there is a large live load on one floor, it is shared among all the trusses in the truss network.

These bipod elements also serve to resist lateral forces, a topic that is covered in more detail in Chapter 10, "Lateral Bracing Systems."

7.1.13 CONCEPTS FOR TRUSSES WITH FLAT-TOP CHORDS

In Figures 7.145 and 7.146, flat-top trusses of various configurations are shown deforming under two load cases:

- A uniform load w across the full-truss span (symmetric, full load case)
- A uniform load w on the left half of the structure (asymmetric, partial load case)

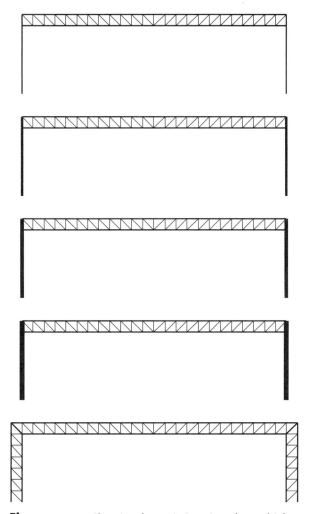

Figure 7.143 Showing the variations in column thickness for the simulations shown in Figure 7.142.

Figure 7.144 Trussed wall of the Pompidou Museum.

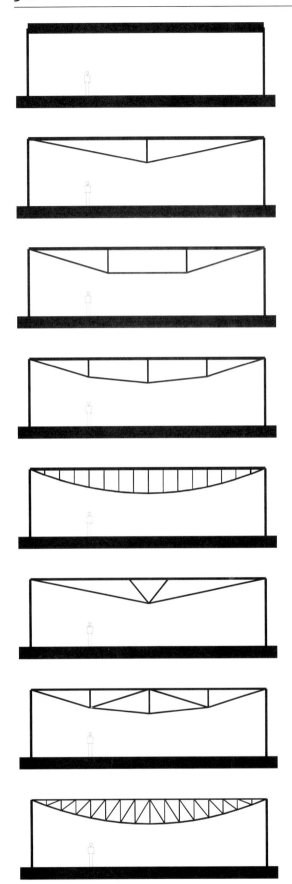

Figure 7.145 Configurations of sling trusses.

The asymmetric load has the same intensity as the symmetric load, but it is only on half of the truss, so the total downward force in the asymmetric, partial load is only half the total downward force of the symmetric, full load. All the deflections in the various diagrams are greatly exaggerated, as in all the previous deformation diagrams. However, they are all consistent in a relative sense.

The following observations can be made in regard to these two figures:

- The simple beam deforms more under symmetric, full load than under asymmetric, partial load.
- The king-post truss deflects about the same amount as the simple beam under full, symmetric load.
- The king-post truss exhibits much larger deflections under asymmetric, partial load than under symmetric, full load.
- A simple king-post supports only one point along the beam, and the angle for the sling elements is not favorable. To improve on both of these aspects, two posts are used to produce what is sometimes called a "queen-post" truss. The two points of support and a more favorable angle for the tension sling allow the queen-post truss to perform better than the king-post truss under symmetric full load. However, the extra post does nothing to help with the deformation under asymmetric, partial load.
- Adding a third post to the truss has a similar effect as adding the second post, in that it helps somewhat under symmetric, full load, but it does little to help with the deformation under asymmetric, partial load. The effect is the same for adding many more posts.
- Splitting the single king post into a bipod enhances resistance to deformation under symmetric, full load by reducing the span of the top beam between support points.
- The bipod is even more effective in resisting deformation under asymmetric, partial load, since the bipod resists tilting of the top beam over the center support.

The support posts allow the top beam to be made much shallower without the deformation becoming excessive under symmetric load. Making the top beam shallower makes it less effective in resisting the shear deformation that occurs under asymmetric load. Therefore, the simple posts are limited in terms of how much they allow the beam to be made shallower. Even under symmetric load, the benefit of the posts is not as good as the deformation diagrams would suggest, since the free vertical movement of the shallow beam makes it vulnerable to buckling under the compressive axial force. Therefore, simple posts are limited in their benefit. There are three typical ways to address this stiffness deficiency:

- Keep the beam deep.
- Use bipods.

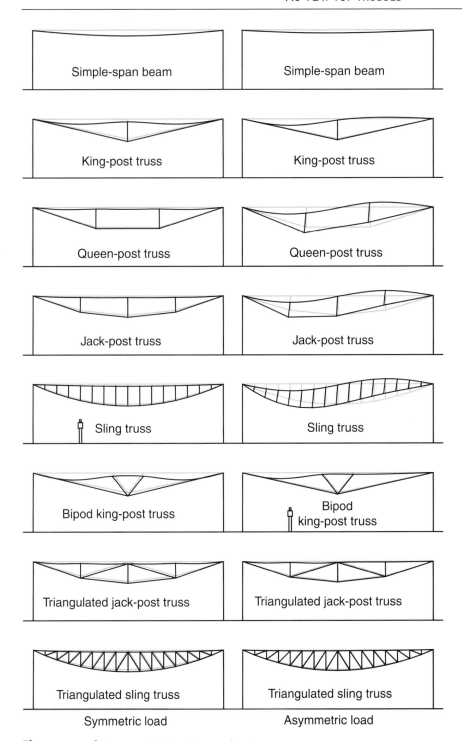

Figure 7.146 Asymmetric loading on sling trusses.

• Fully triangulate the truss (as shown in the two bottom diagrams in Figures 7.145 and 7.146). Clearly, the triangulation's stiffening effect has dramatically reduced the deformation under asymmetric load and the tendency to buckle under symmetric, full load. Note that the bottom-chord members are straight, rather than curved, since they are in pure tension and have no lateral forces to motivate the use of curved elements.

King-post trusses can be used as a simple, economical means to extend the range of certain spanning materials. For example, solid-sawn wood 2 × 10s can still be found in lengths up to 22 ft. By itself, a 2 × 10 is not suitable to span 22 ft. Adding a king post with steel rods for the sling elements turns the 2 × 10s into a very effective king-post truss that is suitable for spanning 22 ft. The kingpins also serve as sculptural elements, adding visual interest and elegance to a space. A single king post can also be used in a column grid, where one column needs to be removed to create a longer-span space. The column can be turned into a king post by cutting off its base and then supporting it with several slings from the tops of the adjacent columns that surround it.

The sling trusses shown at the bottom of Figures 7.145 and 7.146 are structurally very efficient, particularly under uniform load, for which the diagonal web members are zero-force members. However, they involve highly segmented bottom chords and webs of many different lengths, which tends to add to the fabrication costs. Therefore, a flat bottom chord is generally preferred for economy. The truss geometry at the bottom of Figures 7.145 and 7.146 can be morphed to create the parallel-chord geometry shown in Figure 7.148.

In the flat bottom-chord truss, the diagonal web members are major load-carrying members. Because of their orientation, the diagonal webs are in compression under a symmetric, uniform load on the truss. This role is expressed by fattening those members as compared to the vertical webs, which are shorter and predominantly acting in tension (they go into compression only under asymmetric loading or wind uplife). The truss geometry described here is not normally regarded as rational, since the long diagonal web members are in compression, which makes them vulnerable to buckling. However, this truss configuration makes sense when made of

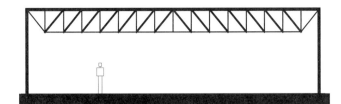

Figure 7.148 Parallel-chord truss with compression diagonals.

wood, since wood tolerates higher compression stresses than tension stresses. In addition, wood's low stress capacity means that wood members have cross sections large enough that they tend to be resistant to buckling.

This geometry does not make sense for steel, which has a high stress capacity, resulting in members that are intrinsically slender and, therefore, vulnerable to buckling. For steel, it is preferred to run the diagonal members inside the rectangle's opposite diagonal.

In the truss shown in Figure 7.149, the diagonals are in tension and the verticals are in compression under full symmetric loading. The vertical web members, being shorter than the diagonal web members, are less vulnerable to buckling. The truss in Figure 7.150 illustrates this point.

The diagonal web members are made of flat plates, which are thin and, therefore, suitable only for resisting tension forces. This truss design is not typical for roofing applications, where wind suction can lift a lightweight roof and cause stress reversal. That is, members such as these diagonals, which are in tension under uniform gravity load, go into compression under wind uplift. However, the roof depicted in Figure 7.150 is ballasted, with river rock holding down the roof membrane. River rock on the roof ensures that there is no net uplift under wind suction and that stress reversal does not occur in the diagonal web members. Hence, the trusses are designed to have the simple plate diagonals, taking advantage of the ballasting benefits by simplifying the truss design and detailing.

Sometimes, by the nature of the truss construction and the nature of the loads, the web members have fat

Figure 7.147 Fully triangulated, queen-post truss. Bridge in Exploris Museum, Raleigh, North Carolina (Architect: Clearscapes, Inc., Engineer: Lysaght and Associates).

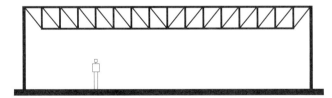

Figure 7.149 Parallel-chord truss with tension diagonals.

Figure 7.150 Parallel-chord truss with tension diagonals.

enough proportions that buckling is not a concern. In this case, square bays are not used, and a Warren truss is used instead (see Figure 7.151).

This is sometimes called a W-truss, which reflects the first initial of the inventor's name and the shape of the web members' pattern. The truss in Figure 7.152 is a classic example of this geometry. This truss is part of the Pompidou Museum in Paris (Architects: Richard Rogers and Lorenzo Piano; Engineers: Ove Arup and Partners and Peter Rice).

This truss is diagrammatically instructive. The compressive top chord is rendered with a much larger diameter than the tensile bottom chord, and the compressive web members are rendered larger in diameter than the tensile web members. Moreover, wherever a chord member passes through a joint that changes the chord member's force, the chord member's diameter changes from one side of the joint to the other, reflecting the changing magnitude of the force in the chord.

The truss in Figure 7.153 is a common example of the Warren truss geometry.

If there is a weak element in this truss, it is the long chord member, which is subjected to both axial compression and bending stress associated with vertical forces distributed along the chord member's top. Reducing the unbraced length of top chord is the best way to address these concerns.

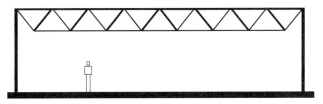

Figure 7.151 Warren truss, with both tension and compression diagonals.

Figure 7.152 Warren truss in the Pompidou Museum, Paris.

Figure 7.153 Warren truss with wood chords and steel-tube web members.

There are a number of methods to reduce the top chord's unbraced length. One way to achieve this in a Warren truss is to change the web members' angles, so that they are more closely spaced (see Figure 7.154).

Although this reduces the top chord's unbraced length, it does not help the long compression web members. The unbraced length of both the top chord and the compression web members can be reduced by superimposing the geometry of two Warren trusses that are offset by one half-bay (see Figure 7.155).

For the purposes of this text, this will be referred to as an interlaced Warren truss, with twice the normal Warren truss web frequency. In an interlaced Warren truss, the intersecting webs are braced at the midpoint against buckling. Of course, all these intersections create additional joints that can complicate both the design and fabrication, thereby increasing the cost of the truss.

The top chord is usually the primary concern, because it is subjected to both high compression and bending. A simple way to reduce the top chord's unbraced length is to use a modified Warren truss, which is shown in Figure 7.156.

As noted in the previous solution processes for trusses of this kind, the vertical webs all carry the same force. They are responsible for supporting the local loads delivered to the top chord's central part (and for bracing the top chord against buckling), but they do not play a role in the overall truss action. This truss is extremely common among standard manufactured trusses, such as those in the structure shown in Figure 7.157.

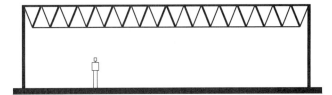

Figure 7.154 Warren truss with closely spaced panel points to produce short chord segments.

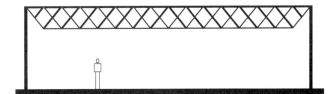

Figure 7.155 Interlaced Warren truss.

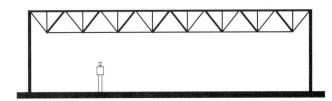

Figure 7.156 Geometry of modified Warren truss.

Figure 7.157 Modified Warren truss.

Figure 7.158 Truss with double angle.

The close-up in Figure 7.158 illustrates a common method used to make the connections in a truss of this geometry. The verticals serve as spacer elements connecting the two top-chord angles together and the two bottom-chord angles together. The diagonal webs, which are substantially more heavily loaded than are the vertical struts, are double angles welded to the outsides of the chord members.

The top-chord bracing method expressed in the geometry discussed here is carried further by splitting the verticals into multiple members that brace the top chord at multiple points (see Figure 7.159).

The truss shown in Figure 7.160 is an example of this general approach.

This limitation of this truss geometry is that the web members are long and unbraced. The modified Warren truss, with a Fink-sling substructure (shown in Figure 7.161), reduces the unbraced length of both the top chord and the web members.

In a similar vein, the parallel-chord, square-bay truss, shown in Figure 7.162 can be enhanced with a Fink-sling substructure to reduce the unbraced length of both the top chord and the web members, as shown in Figure 7.163.

The frequency of top-chord bracing for a square-bay truss can be increased by doubling the number of bays and making them rectangular, as shown in Figure 7.164.

Figure 7.160 Modified Warren truss with fanning webs, made by Vulcraft.

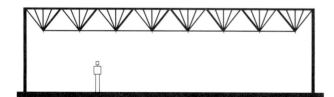

Figure 7.159 Modified Warren truss with fanning webs.

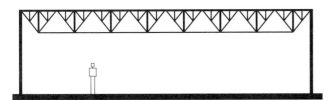

Figure 7.161 Parallel-chord truss enhanced with Fink-sling substructure.

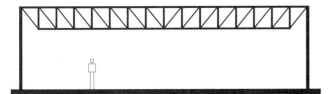

Figure 7.162 Square-bay truss.

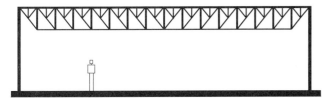

Figure 7.163 Square-bay truss with Fink-sling substructure.

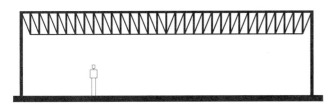

Figure 7.164 Rectangular-bay truss.

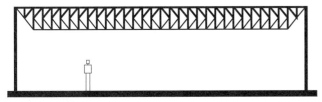

Figure 7.165 K-truss, with its short chord members and braced webs.

This still leaves the web members long and unbraced. A web pattern that provides more web member bracing is the K-truss, so named because the web pattern resembles the letter K repeated in a series. This is shown in Figure 7.165.

This pattern substantially inhibits web buckling within the truss plane. However, introducing the K-braces does not reduce the vertical web members' unbraced length with regard to buckling perpendicular to the truss plane. The effective length for vertical members buckling within the truss plane is half the effective length for buckling perpendicular to the truss plane. This suggests the use of unbalanced cross section web members, such as I-sections or rectangular tubing, with the web member cross section wide dimension set perpendicular to the truss plane. That is, make the cross section strong in the direction with less bracing. Examples of cross sections with greater moments of inertia about the y-y-axis than about the x-x-axis are shown in Figure 7.166.

Wide-flange sections lend themselves to being used with the section web perpendicular to the truss plane. For example, consider the structure in Figure 7.167, wherein the flat roof is supported at every other node on the top chord of the sloped truss.

The top chords are braced by the web members at every joint against buckling in the plane of the truss. The top chords are braced by the roof diaphragm at every other joint against buckling perpendicular to the plane of the truss. This is the classic situation that calls for a chord section that is stronger laterally than it is relative to movement within the plane of the truss. The design response was to make the top-chord member of a wide-flange section with the web perpendicular to the truss plane. For simplicity, all of the truss web members and the bottom-chord member are treated in the same manner, as shown in Figure 7.168.

The truss web members are miter cut, and the flanges of the truss web members are welded to the flanges of the truss chord members. No effort is made to ensure the continuity of the I-section web members into the center of the intersections. The I-section webs are not playing a role in the member connections. Not having part of the I-section participating in the connection process means that the connection has less cross-sectional area than the

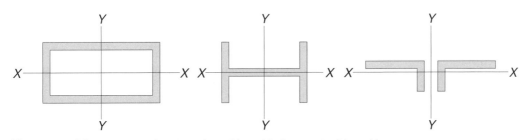

Figure 7.166 Sections with greater lateral breadth than vertical breadth.

Figure 7.167 Truss constructed of I-sections with their webs perpendicular to the plane of the truss.

members themselves. However, this does not mean that the joint is weaker than the members, since members in compression are limited by buckling to such a degree that they may not be as strong as the joint. This lack of I-section web connections is not typically a problem, since most of the I-section material is in the flanges, rather than the I-section web, so the joint cross section is more than sufficient to match the member's strength, after buckling is accounted for. Stopping the I-section web short of the intersection allows rainwater to drain down the trough created by the bottom-chord I-section. When a truss of this configuration is used internal to a building, this bottom-chord trough can be used to house fluorescent light fixtures or to carry power or signal wiring.

Another example of truss construction using I-sections with their webs perpendicular to the plane of the truss is the escalator support in CNN's lobby in Atlanta, Georgia (shown in Figure 7.169). Moment connections are used to create a rigid frame to stabilize the structure laterally.

Constructing a truss out of I-sections with their webs in the truss plane of the truss tends to produce a more complex connection, as shown in Figure 7.170.

The parabolic sling truss, shown in Figure 7.171, is the ideal geometry under uniform load.

However, for floors, the load can shift substantially, and one cannot assume that it is always uniformly distributed. Even on roofs, large localized forces associated with pallets of roofing materials may produce loads that deviate radically from uniformity. The ideal shape under

Figure 7.168 Truss constructed of I-sections with their webs perpendicular to the plane of the truss.

Figure 7.169 CNN headquarters, Atlanta, Georgia.

Figure 7.170 Joint in truss constructed with I-section webs in the plane of the truss.

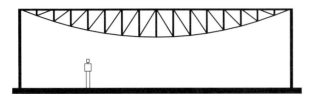

Figure 7.171 Parabolic sling truss.

a concentrated load near the left end is shown in Figure 7.172.

Figure 7.172 Shape response to point load.

The ideal shape under a concentrated load near the right end is shown in Figure 7.173.

Figure 7.173 Shape response to point load.

The truss in Figure 7.174 represents a reasonable compromise between the conflicting shape criteria outlined earlier.

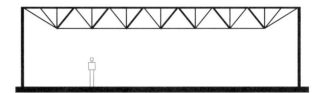

Figure 7.174 Compromise form.

This truss geometry is close to the ideal compromise for all the loads that may occur on a truss. It is also easier and more economical to produce than the parabolic truss shape. Notice that the truss in Figure 7.174 is terminated at a shallower angle than is the basic Warren truss, shown in Figure 7.175.

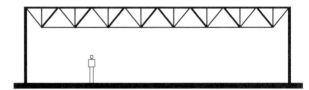

Figure 7.175 Modified Warren truss.

A shallower slope on the end web member allows for a shallower end-bearing assembly, which allows the end-bearing assembly to be less expensive and for the building to be shorter. Figures 7.176 and 7.177 show the end-bearing assemblies for roof joists resting on a

Figure 7.176 Method of supporting truss joists on truss girders, and truss girders on column tops.

Figure 7.177 Method of supporting truss joists on truss girders, and truss girders on column tops.

truss girder and for a truss girder resting on a plate on a column top.

The column top in Figure 7.176 is shown in the close-up photo in Figure 7.177.

For these manufactured trusses, the truss-joists' end-bearing assembly is 2.5 in. or 5 in. deep, and the girders' end-bearing assembly is 5.0 in., 7.5 in., or 10 in. More specifics are given regarding these trusses' characteristics in the Section 7.3, on selecting standard steel trusses.

7.1.14 TRUSS CONCEPTS FOR ADMITTING NATURAL LIGHT

Figure 7.178 shows a roof monitor with a combination of north- and south-facing glass. This roofing system is part of the Body Shop Corporate Headquarters in Wake Forest, North Carolina (Architect: Clearscapes, Inc.; Engineer: Lysaght & Associates; Daylighting Designer: Wayne Place).

Figure 7.179 is a photograph of the interior space.

The roof monitor in Figure 7.178 is retrofitted to an existing structure that encloses a space about 60 ft wide and about 300 ft long, with the long direction almost perfectly aligned to the east–west direction. This orientation facilitates long monitors with north and south exposures, which provides good daylighting without thermal overload. However, the situation is not optimal structurally or for drainage. The existing trusses slope toward the south, creating a challenge in handling the rainwater that flows toward the north side of the monitor. In the case of this building, the transfer of water past the monitor was accomplished with the use of leaders from the north–side to the south side of the monitor.

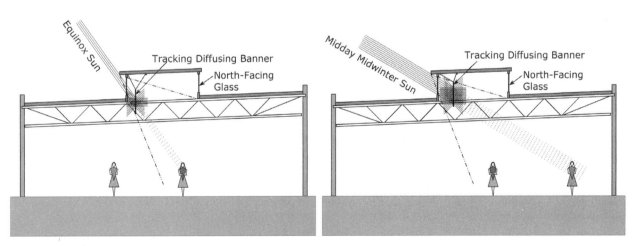

Figure 7.178 Roof monitor on the Body Shop Corporate Headquarters, Wake Forest, North Carolina.

Figure 7.179 Interior of Body Shop Corporate Headquarters in Wake Forest, North Carolina.

Incorporating the roof monitor involved removing the original roofing that was welded to the trusses' top chords. Additional bracing struts were required for the top chord members to replace the bracing function originally served by the roof deck diaphragm. These extra elements were required because the design was not originally conceived as a daylit building.

A structure designed from the beginning to have roof monitors may be framed in the manner shown in Figure 7.180. The rendering shows the structural frame partially covered with roof decking.

Both the top- and bottom-chord members are braced along their full length by decking. The web members interfere somewhat with the passage of the daylight through the aperture. However, with proper design, this effect is minimal, and the overall aesthetics can be pleasing. Care should be taken to minimize the cross section of the web members, and vertical webs should be located so that they are hidden behind glazing mullions.

7.2 Sizing Truss Members

The diagrams in Figures 7.181 and 7.182 represent a floor being supported by trusses spaced at 5 ft OC and spanning 60 ft. The first diagram is for 3 ft-deep trusses, which have a span-to-depth ratio of 20. The node-to-node spacing is assumed to be 3 ft, producing square bays. The second diagram is for 6 ft-deep trusses, which have a span-to-depth ratio of 10. The node-to-node spacing is assumed to be 6 ft, producing square bays.

For the 3 ft-deep truss, each node on the top chord supports a patch of floor stretching halfway to the node on each side (3 ft total) and halfway to the truss on each side (5 ft total); that is, the patch of floor is 3 ft by 5 ft, for a total area of 15 ft^2. Each node supports a force that is the distributed pressure on the floor times the area of the patch, which is 15 ft^2.

For the 6 ft-deep truss, each node on the top chord supports a patch of floor stretching halfway to the adjacent

Figure 7.180 Trussed roof admitting daylight through the trusses.

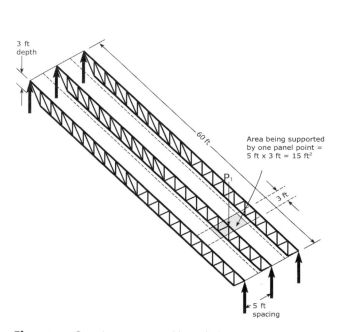

3 ft
depth

60 ft

Area being supported
by one panel point =
5 ft x 3 ft = 15 ft²

P₁

3 ft

5 ft
spacing

Figure 7.181 Floor supported by 3 ft-deep trusses.

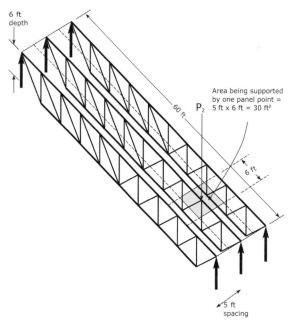

6 ft
depth

60 ft

Area being supported
by one panel point =
5 ft x 6 ft = 30 ft²

P₂

6 ft

5 ft
spacing

Figure 7.182 Floor supported by 6 ft-deep trusses.

Table 7.2 Computation of Truss Joint Loads

Truss	p_{dead} (#/ft²)	p_{dead} (K/ft²)	p_{live} (#/ft²)	p_{live} (K/ft²)	Node-to-Node Spacing (ft)	Truss-to-Truss Spacing (ft)	Floor Area per Node A (ft²)	P_{dead} $(= p_{dead} \cdot A)$ (K)	P_{live} $(= p_{liv} \cdot A)$ (K)	Factored Dead Load $1.2 \cdot P_{dead}$ (K)	Factored Live Load $1.6 \cdot P_{live}$ (K)	Factored Total Load $1.2 \cdot P_{dead} + 1.6 \cdot P_{live}$ (K)
3 ft deep	53	0.053	100	0.100	3	5	15	0.795	1.50	0.954	2.40	3.35
6 ft deep	53	0.053	100	0.100	6	5	30	1.59	3.00	1.908	4.80	6.71

node on each side (6 ft total) and halfway to the adjacent truss on each side (5 ft total); that is, the patch of floor is 6 ft by 5 ft, for a total area of 30 ft². Each node supports a force that is the distributed pressure on the floor times the area of the patch, which is 30 ft².

Table 7.2 summarizes the calculations to determine the factored total load on each node of the trusses shown in Figures 7.181 and 7.182.

In Figure 7.181, $P_1 = 3.35$ K.

In Figure 7.182, $P_2 = 6.71$ K.

Armed with the information given in Table 7.2, a designer can solve the trusses for the key internal forces. For a truss of this length, the chord members will be continuous members of constant cross section. The minimum cross section will be determined for the maximum force that occurs anywhere along the 60 ft of chord member. The webs will all be sized for the worst condition that can

exist at the location of the web in the truss. For the purposes of this example, the focus is on the web members with the highest forces, which will be those at the ends of the truss. A vertical web and a diagonal web near the end of the truss will be sized. Figure 7.183 shows the resolution of forces at the end of the 3 ft-deep truss.

The web forces shown in Figure 7.183 are expressed as multiples of P_1. Applying the multipliers to get the member forces will be done Table 7.3.

Figure 7.184 shows the resolved forces at the end of the 6 ft-deep truss. The resolution has expressed the web forces in terms of P_2, the node force for the truss. Applying the multipliers to get the member forces is done in Table 7.3.

The web forces shown in Figure 7.184 are expressed as multiples of P_2. Applying the multipliers to get the member forces is done in Table 7.3.

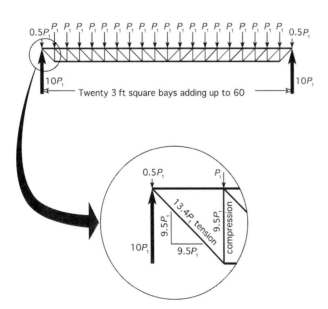

Figure 7.183 Resolved forces in webs at end of 3 ft-deep truss.

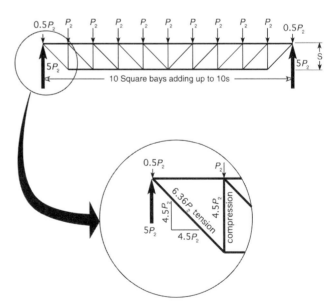

Figure 7.184 Resolved forces in webs at end of 6 ft-deep truss.

Figures 7.185, 7.186, and 7.187 show the sections method being applied to determine the chord forces at the center of the 3 ft-deep truss.

Divide the truss at the tenth bay to produce the following freebody (Figure 7.186).

Replace the nine P_1 forces with a single $9 P_1$ force acting at the center of action of the nine P_1 forces. At the left end of the freebody, group the upward $10 P_1$ force with the downward $0.5 P_1$ force to produce a net upward force of $9.5 P_1$ (Figure 7.187).

$$\sum M_Q = 0 \;\widehat{+}$$

$$0 = -T_1(3 \text{ ft}) - 9 P_1(4 \cdot 3 \text{ ft}) + 9.5(9 \cdot 3 \text{ ft})$$

$$T_1 = +49.5 P_1$$

$$\sum M_S = 0 \;\widehat{+}$$

$$0 = -C_1(3 \text{ ft}) - 9 P_1(5 \cdot 3 \text{ ft}) + 9.5(10 \cdot 3 \text{ ft})$$

$$C_1 = +50 P_1$$

The chord forces shown here are expressed as multiples of P_1. Applying the multipliers to get the member forces is done in Table 7.3.

Figure 7.188, 7.189, and 7.190 show the sections method being applied to determine the chord forces at the center of the 6 ft-deep truss.

Divide the truss at the fifth bay to produce the freebody shown in Figure 7.189.

Replace the four P_2 forces with a single $4 P_2$ force acting at the center of action of the four P_2 forces. At the left

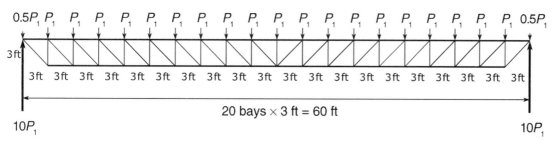

Figure 7.185 A 3 ft-deep, twenty-bay truss.

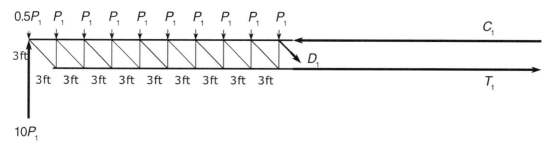

Figure 7.186 Creating a freebody of the left end of the 3 ft-deep, twenty-bay truss.

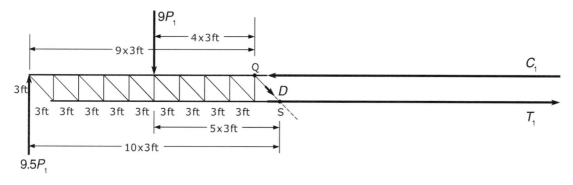

Figure 7.187 Clustering the forces.

Table 7.3 Computation of Web Forces

Factored Total Load $1.2 \cdot P_{dead} + 1.6 \cdot P_{live}$ (K)	Multiplier for Maximum Vertical Web Force	Maximum Vertical Web Force (K)	Multiplier for Maximum Diagonal Web Force	Maximum Diagonal Web Force (K)	Multiplier for Maximum Top-Chord Force	Maximum Top-Chord Force (K)	Multiplier for Maximum Bottom-Chord Force	Maximum Bottom-Chord Force (K)
$P_1 = 3.35$	9.5	**31.9**	13.4	**44.9**	50.0	**167.7**	49.5	**166.0**
$P_2 = 6.71$	4.5	**30.2**	6.36	**42.7**	12.5	**83.9**	12.0	**80.5**

end of the freebody, group the upward 5 P_2 force with the downward 0.5 P_1 force to produce a net upward force of 4.5 P_2 (Figure 7.190).

$$\sum M_Q = 0 \;\curvearrowright$$

$$0 = -T_2(6 \text{ ft}) - 4\,P_2(1.5 \cdot 6 \text{ ft}) + 4.5(4 \cdot 6 \text{ ft})$$

$$T_2 = +12\,P_2$$

$$\sum M_Q = 0 \;\curvearrowright$$

$$0 = -C_2(6 \text{ ft}) - 4\,P_2(2.5 \cdot 6 \text{ ft}) + 4.5(5 \cdot 6 \text{ ft})$$

$$C_2 = +12.5\,P_2$$

The chord forces shown here are expressed as multiples of P_2.

The force multipliers required to get member forces from P_1 and P_2 were derived in the preceding diagrams. They are applied in Table 7.3 to get the internal member forces.

The tables shown in Figures 7.191, 7.192, and 7.193 are excerpted from the *Manual of Steel Construction, Load and Resistance Factor Design (LRFD)*, Third Edition, a publication of the American Institute of Steel Construction. The tables chosen are for double angles assembled from angles with equal legs. Double angles can also be assembled from angles with longer legs

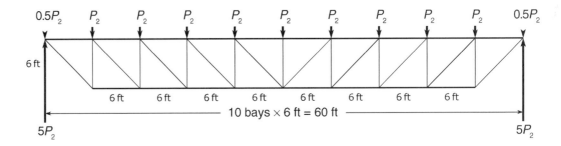

Figure 7.188
A 6 ft-deep truss.

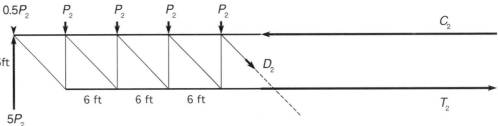

Figure 7.189
Creating a freebody from the left end of the 6 ft-deep truss.

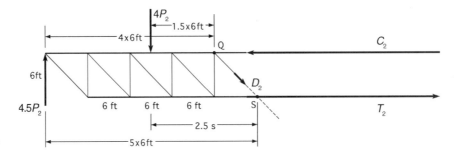

Figure 7.190
Clustering the forces.

$F_y = 36$ ksi
$\phi_c P_n = 0.85\, F_{cr}\, A_g$

Equal-Leg Double Angles
Design Strength in Axial
Compression, $\phi_c P_n$, kips

Shape	2L5×5×							No. of Connectors[a]	2L4×4×							No. of Connectors[a]
	7/8	3/4	5/8	1/2	7/16	3/8†	5/16†		3/4	5/8	1/2	7/16	3/8	5/16†	1/4†	
Wt/ft	54.6	47.5	40.1	32.6	28.7	24.8	20.9		37.0	31.3	25.5	22.5	19.4	16.3	13.2	
X-X Axis																
0	490	428	361	293	258	219	171		334	282	229	202	175	146	108	
2	483	423	356	289	255	217	169		326	276	224	198	171	144	106	
4	464	406	343	278	245	209	163		306	259	211	186	161	135	101	
6	433	379	321	261	230	196	154		274	233	190	168	146	123	92.0	
8	393	345	293	238	210	180	143		235	201	165	146	127	107	81.3	
10	348	306	260	212	188	161	129		194	166	137	122	106	89.6	69.3	
12	299	264	225	184	163	140	114	b	152	132	109	97.1	84.9	72.2	57.1	b
14	251	221	190	155	138	120	98.0		115	100	82.9	74.4	65.3	55.8	45.4	
16	204	181	156	128	114	99.2	82.6		87.8	76.8	63.5	56.9	50.0	42.7	35.0	
18	162	144	125	103	91.5	80.2	68.1		69.4	60.7	50.1	45.0	39.5	33.8	27.7	
20	132	117	101	83.1	74.1	65.0	55.3			49.1	40.6	36.4	32.0	27.3	22.4	
22	109	96.4	83.5	68.7	61.3	53.7	45.7									
24	91.4	81.0	70.1	57.7	51.5	45.1	38.4									
26							32.7									
Y-Y Axis																
0	490	428	361	293	258	219	171		334	282	229	202	175	146	108	
6	456	396	329	260	223	182	134		303	253	203	177	149	120	82.6	
9	426	369	307	243	208	171	127		273	228	183	159	135	109	76.4	
12	387	335	279	221	189	156	118		237	197	158	137	116	94.7	68.2	
15	343	296	246	195	166	139	106		197	163	130	113	96.2	78.7	58.3	
18	295	254	211	167	142	119	93.0		157	129	103	89.4	76.0	62.5	47.6	
22	231	198	165	130	110	92.8	74.5	2	109	89.5	71.3	61.6	52.5	43.3	34.0	
24	201	172	143	112	94.0	80.0	65.2		91.5	75.3	60.0	51.9	44.2	36.6	28.8	
26	172	147	122	96.2	80.5	68.6	56.3		78.0	64.2	51.2	44.3	37.8	31.3	24.7	
28	149	127	105	83.1	69.6	59.5	49.0		67.3	55.4	44.2	38.2	32.6	27.1	21.4	
30	130	111	91.9	72.6	60.8	52.0	42.9		58.7	48.3	38.5	33.3	28.5			3
32	114	97.4	80.9	63.9	53.6	45.9	37.9									
34	101	86.3	71.7	56.7	47.5	40.7	33.7									
36	90.1	77.0	64.0	50.6	42.5	36.4	30.2									
38	80.9							3								
40																

Effective length KL (ft) with respect to indicated axis

Properties of 2 angles - 3/8 in. back to back

	7/8	3/4	5/8	1/2	7/16	3/8	5/16		3/4	5/8	1/2	7/16	3/8	5/16	1/4	
A_g, in.^{2}	16.0	14.0	11.8	9.58	8.44	7.30	6.13		10.9	9.21	7.49	6.61	5.71	4.80	3.87	
r_x, in.	1.49	1.50	1.52	1.53	1.54	1.55	1.56		1.18	1.20	1.21	1.22	1.23	1.24	1.25	
r_y, in.	2.30	2.27	2.25	2.22	2.21	2.20	2.19		1.88	1.85	1.83	1.81	1.80	1.79	1.78	

Properties of single angle

	7/8	3/4	5/8	1/2	7/16	3/8	5/16		3/4	5/8	1/2	7/16	3/8	5/16	1/4	
r_z, in.	0.971	0.972	0.975	0.980	0.983	0.986	0.990		0.774	0.774	0.776	0.777	0.779	0.781	0.783	

[a] For Y-Y axis, welded or pretensioned bolted intermediate connectors must be used.
[b] For required number of intermediate connectors, see discussion of Table 4-9.
† Section is a slender-element cross-section.
Note: Heavy line indicates Kl/r equal to or greater than 200.

Figure 7.191 Design strength in axial compression for double angles, $\Phi_c P_n$, kips.

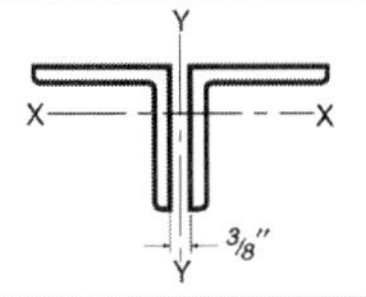

Equal-Leg Double Angles
Design Strength in Axial Compression, $\phi_c P_n$, kips

$F_y = 36$ ksi

$\phi_c P_n = 0.85\, F_{cr} A_g$

Shape		2L3½×3½×					No. of Connectors[a]	2L3×3×						No. of Connectors[a]
		1/2	7/16	3/8	5/16	1/4†		1/2	7/16	3/8	5/16	1/4	3/16†	
Wt/ft		22.2	19.6	17.0	14.3	11.6		18.7	16.6	14.3	12.1	9.77	7.41	
X-X Axis	0	200	177	153	129	101		168	149	129	109	87.8	60.8	
	1	198	175	152	128	100		167	147	128	108	87.0	60.3	
	2	194	172	149	126	98.2		162	143	124	105	84.8	58.9	
	3	188	166	144	122	95.3		155	137	119	100	81.1	56.6	
	4	179	158	138	116	91.2		145	128	112	94.1	76.2	53.5	
	5	168	149	130	110	86.3		133	118	103	86.8	70.4	49.8	
	6	156	138	121	102	80.7		120	106	92.9	78.6	63.9	45.7	
	7	143	127	111	93.7	74.5		106	94.3	82.5	69.9	56.9	41.2	
	8	129	115	100	85.0	67.9		91.8	82.0	71.9	61.1	49.9	36.6	
	9	114	102	89.5	76.1	61.2		78.2	70.0	61.5	52.4	42.9	32.0	
	10	100	89.9	78.9	67.3	54.4	b	65.3	58.7	51.7	44.2	36.3	27.5	b
	12	74.1	66.7	58.9	50.5	41.5		45.3	40.8	36.0	30.8	25.3	19.5	
	14	54.4	49.0	43.3	37.1	30.6		33.3	30.0	26.4	22.6	18.6	14.3	
	16	41.7	37.5	33.1	28.4	23.4								
	18				22.5	18.5								
	20													
Y-Y Axis	0	200	177	153	129	101		168	149	129	109	87.8	60.8	
	5	181	158	135	110	81.3		150	131	113	92.7	71.8	45.6	
	6	175	153	130	107	79.1		143	126	108	88.8	68.9	44.2	
	7	168	147	125	103	76.5		136	119	103	84.4	65.6	42.6	
	8	161	140	120	98.3	73.5		128	113	96.6	79.5	62.0	40.7	
	9	153	133	114	93.6	70.3		120	105	90.3	74.3	58.1	38.6	
	10	144	126	108	88.5	66.8		111	97.6	83.8	68.9	54.0	36.4	
	12	126	110	94.2	77.6	59.1		93.6	81.9	70.3	57.7	45.4	31.4	
	14	108	94.0	80.4	66.4	51.0		76.2	66.6	57.1	46.7	36.9	26.3	
	16	90.3	78.2	66.9	55.3	42.9		59.9	52.3	44.8	36.6	28.9	21.2	
	18	73.3	63.3	54.1	44.8	35.0	3	47.4	41.4	35.5	29.0	23.0	16.9	3
	20	59.5	51.4	44.0	36.5	28.6		38.4	33.6	28.8	23.6	18.7	13.9	
	22	49.2	42.6	36.4	30.3	23.8		31.8	27.8	23.8	19.5	15.5	11.5	
	24	41.4	35.8	30.7	25.5	20.1								
	26	35.3	30.5	26.2	21.8	17.1								
	28													

Effective length KL (ft) with respect to indicated axis

Properties of 2 angles - 3/8 in. back to back

	2L3½×3½×						2L3×3×					
A_g, in.²	6.53	5.77	5.00	4.21	3.41		5.50	4.86	4.22	3.55	2.87	2.18
r_x, in.	1.05	1.06	1.07	1.08	1.09		0.895	0.903	0.910	0.918	0.926	0.933
r_y, in.	1.63	1.61	1.60	1.59	1.57		1.43	1.42	1.41	1.39	1.38	1.37

Properties of single angle

r_z, in.	0.679	0.681	0.683	0.685	0.688		0.580	0.580	0.581	0.583	0.585	0.586

[a] For Y-Y axis, welded or pretensioned bolted intermediate connectors must be used.

[b] For required number of intermediate connectors, see discussion of Table 4-9.

† Section is a slender-element cross-section.

Note: Heavy line indicates Kl/r equal to or greater than 200.

Figure 7.192 Design strength in axial compression for double angles, $\Phi_c P_n$, kips.

$F_y = 36$ ksi

$\phi_c P_n = 0.85\, F_{cr}\, A_g$

Equal-Leg Double Angles
Design Strength in Axial
Compression, $\phi_c P_n$, kips

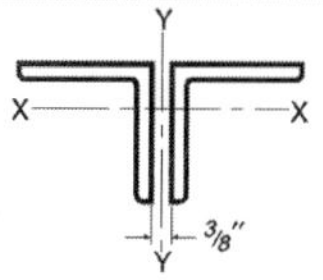

Shape		$2L2^{1}/_{2} \times 2^{1}/_{2} \times$					No. of Connectors[a]	$2L2 \times 2 \times$					No. of Connectors[a]
		$^{1}/_{2}$	$^{3}/_{8}$	$^{5}/_{16}$	$^{1}/_{4}$	$^{3}/_{16}$†		$^{3}/_{8}$	$^{5}/_{16}$	$^{1}/_{4}$	$^{3}/_{16}$	$^{1}/_{8}$†	
Wt/ft		15.3	11.8	9.96	8.07	6.13		9.30	7.89	6.43	4.91	3.34	
X-X Axis	0	138	106	89.7	72.5	54.1		83.5	71.0	57.8	44.1	27.4	
	1	136	105	88.5	71.6	53.4		81.7	69.5	56.6	43.2	26.9	
	2	130	101	85.0	68.9	51.4		76.6	65.2	53.2	40.6	25.5	
	3	121	94.0	79.6	64.5	48.3		68.7	58.7	48.0	36.7	23.3	
	4	110	85.5	72.5	58.9	44.3		59.0	50.6	41.5	31.9	20.5	
	5	97.0	75.7	64.4	52.4	39.5		48.6	41.8	34.5	26.6	17.5	
	6	83.1	65.3	55.6	45.4	34.5		38.2	33.1	27.4	21.3	14.3	
	7	69.2	54.8	46.8	38.4	29.3		28.8	25.1	20.9	16.3	11.4	
	8	56.1	44.7	38.4	31.6	24.3		22.1	19.2	16.0	12.5	8.74	
	9	44.5	35.6	30.6	25.3	19.6		17.4	15.2	12.7	9.87	6.90	
	10	36.0	28.8	24.8	20.5	15.9	b			10.3	7.99	5.59	b
	11	29.8	23.8	20.5	16.9	13.1							
	12	25.0	20.0	17.2	14.2	11.0							
	13												
Y-Y Axis	0	138	106	89.7	72.5	54.1		83.5	71.0	57.8	44.1	27.4	
	3	130	98.6	82.1	64.7	45.0		76.6	64.5	51.8	38.0	21.2	
	4	125	94.9	79.0	62.3	43.5		72.4	61.0	48.9	36.0	20.3	
	5	119	90.4	75.2	59.3	41.7		67.3	56.6	45.4	33.4	19.2	
	6	112	85.1	70.7	55.9	39.5		61.6	51.8	41.5	30.6	17.9	
	7	104	79.2	65.8	52.0	37.0		55.5	46.5	37.2	27.5	16.4	
	8	96.2	73.0	60.5	47.9	34.3		49.1	41.1	32.9	24.3	14.8	
	9	87.7	66.4	55.0	43.6	31.4		42.8	35.8	28.5	21.0	13.1	
	10	79.1	59.8	49.4	39.2	28.4		36.7	30.6	24.3	17.9	11.3	
	11	70.6	53.3	43.9	34.8	25.4		30.9	25.6	20.4	15.0	9.66	
	12	62.3	46.9	38.5	30.6	22.4		26.0	21.6	17.1	12.6	8.20	
	14	46.9	35.2	28.8	22.9	16.9	3	19.1	15.9	12.6	9.34	6.10	3
	16	36.0	27.0	22.1	17.6	13.1		14.6	12.2	9.68	7.17		
	18	28.4	21.4	17.5	13.9	10.4							
	20	23.0	17.3										
	22												

Effective length KL (ft) with respect to indicated axis

Properties of 2 angles - $^{3}/_{8}$ in. back to back											
A_g, in.^{2}	4.50	3.47	2.93	2.37	1.80		2.73	2.32	1.89	1.44	0.982
r_x, in.	0.735	0.749	0.756	0.764	0.771		0.591	0.598	0.605	0.612	0.620
r_y, in.	1.23	1.21	1.19	1.18	1.17		1.01	0.996	0.982	0.967	0.951

Properties of single angle											
r_z, in.	0.481	0.481	0.481	0.482	0.482		0.386	0.386	0.387	0.389	0.391

[a] For Y-Y axis, welded or pretensioned bolted intermediate connectors must be used.

[b] For required number of intermediate connectors, see discussion of Table 4-9.

† Section is a slender-element cross-section.

Note: Heavy line indicates Kl/r equal to or greater than 200.

Figure 7.193 Design strength in axial compression for double angles, $\Phi_c\, P_n$, kips.

back-to-back (LLBB) or shorter legs back-to-back (SLBB). Balanced design with regard to buckling about the two primary axes of the double-angle combination would favor LLBB. However, most manufacturers of trusses favor equal-leg angles, since the extra breadth of the chord members produces stiffer trusses that reduce the losses due to lateral buckling during handling. In the light of that preference, equal-leg angles are chosen for this design.

The tables from the *Manual of Steel Construction* list the member sizes across the top, the effective length for buckling down the left column, and the numbers in the table list the allowed axial force in the member, $\Phi_c P_u$, which is the resistance factor for the member times the ultimate load capacity of the member. The aim is to find values of $\Phi_c P_u$ in the vicinity of, but greater than, the member forces listed in Table 7.3. For the purposes of this exercise, the choice of double angle is made on the basis of the lightest member that satisfies the criterion that $\Phi_c P_u$ is greater than, or equal to, the design force in

Table 7.3. There are other factors to consider, such as length of weld required to make the connection at the joint and finding space to get all the required members to meet at a point, that is, at the node (see Figures 7.191, 7.192, and 7.193).

Table 7.4 and 7.5 summarize the choices for member cross sections, based on the criterion of choosing the lightest double-angle combination that will safely resist the loads.

Several trends in the numbers given in the preceding tables are worth noting:

- The web forces for the two trusses are very similar.
- The vertical web members in the deeper truss require a slightly heavier cross section than the vertical web members in the shallower truss, because the greater length of the vertical webs in the deeper truss makes them more vulnerable to buckling.
- The chord forces in the deeper truss are about half of the corresponding chord forces in the shallow truss.

Table 7.4 Summary of Information for the 3 ft-Deep Truss

	Vertical Web	Diagonal Web	Top Chord	Bottom Chord
Design force in member (K)	31.9	44.9	167.7	166.0
Effective length (ft)	3	0	3	0
Lightest member in table that works	2 L 2 × 2 × 3/16	2 L 2.5 × 2.5 × 3/16	2 L 4 × 4 × 7/16	2 L 3 × 3 × 1/2
Allowed axial force $\Phi_c P_n$ (from Table) (K)	36.7	54.1	192*	168
Weight of member (#/ft)	4.91	6.13	22.5	18.7
Number of members of this type	19	20	1	1
Linear feet per member (ft)	3	4.24	60	60
Total linear feet of member(s) (ft)	57	84.9	60.0	60.0
Total weight of this member type (#)	280	520	1,350	1,122
Total weight of all members in truss (#)	**3,272**			
Floor area supported by one truss (ft²)	300			
Weight of steel per sq ft of floor area (#/ft²)	**10.9**			
Weight of steel per lin ft of truss (#/ft)	**54.53**			

*interpolating between lengths of 2 ft and 4 ft

Table 7.5 Summary of Information for the 6 ft-Deep Truss

	Vertical Web	Diagonal Web	Top Chord	Bottom Chord
Design force in member (K)	30.2	42.7	83.9	80.5
Effective length (ft)	6	0	6	0
Lightest member in table that works	2 L 2.5 × 2.5 × 3/16	2 L 2 × 2 × 3/16	2 L 2 × 2 × 3/8	2 L 4 × 4 × 1/4
Allowed axial force $\Phi_c P_n$ (from Table)	34.5	44.1	92	83.5
Weight of member (#/ft)	6.13	4.91	13.2	9.3
Number of members of this type	9	10	1	1
Linear feet per member	6	8.485	60	60
Total linear feet of member(s)	54	84.85	60.00	60.00
Total weight of this member type (#)	331.0	416.6	792.0	558.0
Total weight of all members in truss (#)	**2,098**			
Floor area supported by one truss (ft²)	300			
Weight of steel per sq ft of floor area (#/ft²)	**7.0**			
Weight of steel per lin ft of truss (#/ft)	**34.96**			

- The bottom chord members in the deeper truss are about half of the weight of the bottom chord members in the shallower truss, since the bottom chord forces in the deep truss are about half of the bottom chord forces in the shallow truss and the bottom chord members are in tension, so there is no penalty for the greater length (the effective length for buckling is zero in both cases, since there is no possibility of buckling).
- The top chord members in the deep truss are lighter than the top chord members in the shallow truss, but not half the weight, since the reduced chord force is offset by a greater effective length, resulting in a greater potential for buckling.
- On net, the deep truss is substantially lighter and cheaper.

In light of this last point, why do the guidelines suggest trusses of much shallower proportions than the 60 ft-long, 6 ft-deep truss discussed here? The answer is that the guidelines are attempting to account, in an approximate way, for a variety of other economic factors, such as the cost of the building envelope, heat loss and gains through the building envelope, wind forces, foundation costs, and the like, which tend to favor keeping the depth of the trusses shallow. In some situations, other architectural factors motivate us to use deeper trusses. For example, in hospital design, essential interstitial spaces between floors often result in trusses deep enough to walk through. Staggered truss systems are designed with a similar concern. Restaurant spaces often benefit from high ceilings, which enhance the air circulation necessary to remove fumes and odors from a space. Such spaces tend to look better with deep trusses that add sculptural quality, rather than little, shallow trusses that hug the ceiling and produce the sense of a large, empty, minimal space. In these cases, architectural factors are acting with, rather than in opposition to, structural efficiency and economy.

7.3 Selecting Standard Steel Trusses

For most simple-span applications, it is not necessary to design all the truss members and connections. There are standard steel truss manufacturers who perform the analysis, choose the material grade, size the members, cut the members, lay out the truss, size the welds, do the welding, generate the details, provide specifications, and finish the final product—all guaranteed to meet the architectural and structural specifications. The quality and depth of service available for this structural type create a strong economic motivation for its use in many applications.

Typically, manufacturers do not stock trusses. Trusses are designed and fabricated to specifications upon receipt of an order. The architect and engineer of record provide the design specifications, including the span, overall geometry, and design loads.

To assist in preliminary design, the manufacturers provide a series of tables that allow quick and accurate truss sizing. Some of the tables in the following figures are reprinted from the *Catalog of Standard Specifications and Load Tables for Steel Joists and Joist Girders*, Forty-First Edition (August 2002), which is published by the Steel Joist Institute (SJI), the manufacturers association that sets the industry standard. These are copyrighted and are reprinted here with permission. All rights are reserved by SJI. Others of these tables are from Vulcraft Corporation.

The tables included in this book are for illustrative purposes only and are not complete. To obtain a copy of the catalog containing the complete set of tables and other valuable design information on detailing, bridging, camber, top-chord extensions, specifications, and code of standard practice, visit the website at http://www.steel joist.org/.

The tables include the following series of trusses:

Open-web steel joists, K-Series. These are lightweight trusses that are most suitable for roofing applications.

Long-span steel joists, LH-Series. These are medium-weight to heavyweight trusses suitable for floor applications.

Deep, long-span steel joists, DLH-Series. These are medium-weight to heavyweight long-span trusses.

Super-long-span steel joists, SLH-Series. These are medium-weight to heavyweight super-long-span trusses.

Joist girders. These are medium-weight to heavyweight trusses suitable for girders in floor and roof applications.

These trusses are commonly manufactured with double angles for the top and bottom chords. The web members may be:

Solid round bars welded between the double-angle chord members. These round bars are used for shallow trusses under light loads, for roofing applications.

Single angles welded between the double angles of the chord members.

Double angles welded to the outside vertical faces off the legs of the chord double angles.

Mixtures of single angles welded between the double angles of the chords and double angles welded to the outside vertical faces of the legs of the chord double angles.

Figure 7.194 illustrates most of these combinations.

Figure 7.194 Truss joists and truss girders.

The web members in the truss joists are solid, round bars. The vertical web members in the truss girder are single angles. These vertical angles have a light cross section, because they are lightly loaded. They are supporting a short top-chord segment against the gravity forces on the top chords, but they are not playing a role in the overall truss action. (See Section 7.1.6 for an example analysis of a modified Warren truss with this configuration.) The vertical, single-angle web members are mashed on the ends to give them a lateral 1 in. dimension. These web members serve as spacers and connectors for the double angles of the chord members. The truss girder web members that are more heavily loaded are double angles welded to the outside faces of the chord double

angles. The double-angle web members in compression are connected together with short angle lengths running laterally. These short angles make the web member's two angles work together to resist buckling.

The round-bar web members can be fabricated from a single bar bent in a zigzag pattern. However, a zigzag bar the length of a truss is flexible and unwieldy to handle. Therefore, the round-bar web members are usually fabricated as four web members forming a W-shape, as shown in Figure 7.195.

Figure 7.196 is a close-up of a truss with round-bar web members.

The mashed ends of the single-angle web members are shown in Figure 7.197.

Figure 7.195 Round bars bent into W-pattern for use as web members.

Figure 7.198 shows a truss made exclusively with single-angle web members, sandwiched between the double angles of the top and bottom chords.

Figure 7.199 is a close-up of a bottom chord with a vertical single angle sandwiched between the double angles of the chord. The double-angle web members are welded to the bottom chord's outside faces.

The trusses are carefully laid out on a welding table. Several welders work in a team, and each team member has a metal inert gas (MIG) welder with a huge spool of welding wire. The spool shown in Figure 7.200 is about 3 ft in diameter.

Welding wire is fed automatically through the welder. The welding team often lays out multiple trusses at once.

Figure 7.196 Close-up of solid-rod web members.

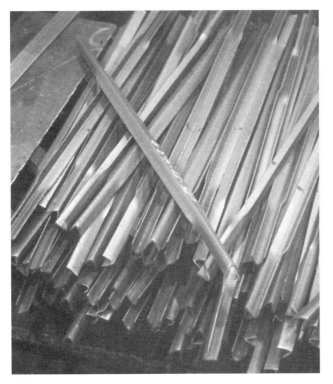

Figure 7.197 Single angles with mashed ends to provide 1 in. spacing between chord angles.

The team tack welds the web members to the chord members while the truss parts are lying horizontal on the table. Then they tilt the trusses to a vertical position to make it easier to get to the weld points. Figure 7.201 shows several trusses being finished in this vertical position.

The speed at which welds are executed and the weld penetration depths vary slightly among the team mem-

Figure 7.199 Joint at bottom chord of truss.

Figure 7.198 Truss with single-angle webs.

Figure 7.200 Spool of welding wire.

bers. The slight unevenness of the welds can cause lateral truss warping. If the difference is consistent from one side of the truss to the other, the warping may create a sweeping curve in the chords, as shown in Figure 7.202.

If the welding unevenness is not consistent along the truss length, then the warping may become a side-to-side wiggle of the chord members, as shown in Figure 7.203.

In previous chapters, it was shown that crooked compression members have drastic bending stresses induced by axial forces. However, the deformation in these chord members is not a structural concern, because the top chord is braced almost continuously by the decking diaphragm action and the bottom chord is not subjected to severe compression. The bracing standards for bottom chords, provided by the industry, account for the normal and expected deviations from straightness.

Although the side-to-side deformation induced by the residual welding stresses may be visually apparent, the deformation resulting from the welding in the truss's

Figure 7.202 Bottom chord warped into a sweeping curve.

Figure 7.201 Welding multiple trusses at one time.

Figure 7.203 Bottom chord warped into a wiggling curve.

Figure 7.204 Truss with built-in camber (in-plane curvature).

strong direction is not. However, many trusses are intended to have a camber, as shown in the truss in Figure 7.204.

This camber is designed to offset the deflection induced by a floor's dead load or to provide a positive slope for shedding rainwater off a roof.

This truss type is economical, having a high structural performance per dollar spent. The joints are more expedient than they are elegant, and the irregularities and weld spatter of these trusses make them suitable for hidden application behind finished surfaces. However, with proper painting and other visual distractions the trusses can be visually acceptable. For example, in the structure shown in Figure 7.205, the natural light produces such a wonderful glow that few people look critically at the steel structure's imperfections.

Figure 7.206 is a close-up of an end-bearing assembly created by butt-welding two short, inverted angles to the top chord's two angles.

End-bearing assemblies come in standard depths of 2.5 in., 5 in., 7.5 in., and 10 in. These depths correspond roughly to multiples of a brick course dimension, meaning that brick construction can be cleanly detailed around the wall pocket required by the end-bearing assembly. The 7.5 in. dimension is roughly equivalent to a course dimension for standard concrete masonry units. The butt-welded arrangement shown in Figure 7.206 is achieved by using 2.5 in. × 2.5 in. angles for both the chord members and the end-bearing assembly. The overall end-bearing assembly depth is 5 in. Using this butt-welded configuration requires that the lengths of the legs of the top-chord angle and the end-bearing angles add up to the required overall depth for the end-bearing assembly. When the right angle size is not available for the end-bearing angles, the end-bearing angles are lapped with the top-chord angles. Figure 7.207 shows the end-bearing angles lapped on the inside of the chord angles.

Figure 7.208 shows the end-bearing angles lapped on the outside of the chord angles.

This lapping system facilitates rotating the end-bearing angles so that they bear properly on a horizontal support while also accommodating sloped trusses that span from one elevation to another. Figure 7.209 shows such a truss, with the end-bearing angles at an angle relative to the top-chord members. (These trusses are being stored upside down.)

The delicate truss joists shown spanning from left to right in Figure 7.210 are powerful visual evidence of the minimal material requirements in such an efficient structural system.

Figure 7.211 shows the 2.5 in.-deep truss-joist end-bearing assemblies resting on the girders. The 5 in.-deep girder end-bearing assemblies sit on wide plates welded to the column tops.

Figure 7.205 Daylight passing through standard double-angle trusses.

Figure 7.206 Butt-welded end-bearing assembly.

Figure 7.207 End-bearing angles lapped inside the chord angles.

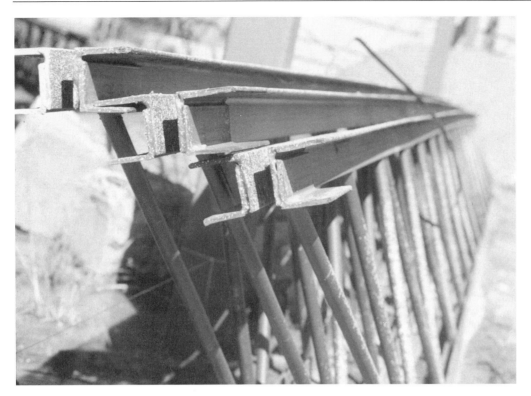

Figure 7.208 End-bearing angles lapped outside the chord angles.

Figure 7.209 Rotated end-bearing assemblies to accommodate sloping trusses.

Figure 7.210 Truss joists panning from left to right, resting on truss girder to the right.

Figure 7.211 Truss joists resting on truss girder.

Figure 7.212 Joist end-bearing assembly on girder end-bearing assembly on column top.

Figure 7.212 is a close-up view of the structure in Figure 7.211, showing the assembly of parts at the top of the column.

Figure 7.213 illustrates the complex interactions that occur when mixed systems need to bear on a column top. Truss-joist end-bearing assemblies rest on top of truss-girder end-bearing assemblies, which sit on top of a notched beam. The web of the beam is reinforced with stiffener plates to act as a short column perched on the real column top.

There are several ways to provide lateral stabilization for the truss joists:

- The bottom-chord ends can be stabilized by a plate welded to the column (as shown in Figure 7.213). The truss's chords straddle the plate, but are not otherwise connected to it. This slip joint inhibits lateral movement while preventing inadvertent compression in the truss's bottom chord.
- Linear bracing elements can be welded to the bottom chords of several trusses, as shown near the truss ends in Figure 7.214(a). Multiple linear braces are shown in the roof in Figure 7.214(b). These linear elements must

Figure 7.213 Beam notched to accommodate girder end-bearing assembly.

Figure 7.214 Linear bracing elements.

be attached to a rigid column, a sturdy wall, or a beam with a wide bottom flange at the end of the bracing run.

• Cross-bracing can be used to support adjacent trusses in a manner that reinforces both the top and bottom chords of the trusses as shown in Figure 7.215. This kind of bracing is crucial during construction, before the decking is in place, to stabilize the top chords of the trusses.

Struts can be connected to structural members running perpendicular to the braced truss. In Figure 7.216, struts connect the truss girder's bottom chord to the roof joists.

The analysis to determine the required type and frequency of bracing elements is complex. Extensive analyses and experiments have been performed to address the issue of lateral bracing. That knowledge has been distilled into guidelines for dealing with the issue. For more information on the lateral bracing requirements for standard manufactured trusses, see the publication *Steel Joists and Joist Girders* of the Steel Joist Institute.

Before using the tables for steel joists, presented later in this chapter, three numbers are required:

The live load per linear foot of truss w_{live}.
The total load (dead + live) per linear foot of truss (w_{total}).
The total load (dead + live) over the entire truss length (W_{total}).

All the loads used in these tables are unfactored loads. This method of accounting for loads is in contrast to load and resistance factor design (LRFD) method that is applied to most of the materials and structural elements addressed in this book. The truss design tables have already accounted for the uncertainty in predicting loads and in predicting the performance of this type of structural element. The loads in the tables are referred to as the safe, or allowed, loads.

The load tables list a series of joist designations. For example, on the first page of the K-Series table (Figure 7.220), the joist designations go from 8K1 to 16K9. The first number in the designation is the joist depth in inches. The letter indicates the series. The last number is an indication of the truss "sturdiness." For example, a 16K9 is heavier and stronger than a 16K4.

The second row of data listed is the joist depth in inches. This is redundant, given the significance of the first number in the joist designation.

The third row of data listed is the approximate weight per linear foot of joist.

The left-most column contains the span in feet. For example, the first page of the K-Series table addresses spans from 8 to 32 ft. This is clearly not the page to be on for this problem. However, it is worth noting a few things before leaving this page.

Figure 7.215 Methods of bracing the bottom of a truss joist.

Figure 7.216 Bracing a truss girder with struts connected to the truss joists.

For each combination of joist designation and span, there are two numbers listed. The top number represents the joist's *total* safe load-carrying capacity, given a uniform load, in pounds per linear foot of joist. The joist's self-weight must be deducted from this number to find the joist's total imposable, safe load-carrying capacity.

The second number represents the *live* load (in pounds per linear foot of joist), which produces a deflection of $\frac{L}{360}$ = 0.002778 L. Deflection is defined by the diagram in Figure 7.217.

$$\Delta = \frac{L}{360} = 0.00278\,L$$

For L = 30 ft:

$$\Delta = \frac{30\,\text{ft}}{360} \cdot \left[\frac{12\,\text{in.}}{\text{ft}}\right] = 1\,\text{in.}$$

For L = 40 ft:

$$\Delta = \frac{40\,\text{ft}}{360} \cdot \left[\frac{12\,\text{in.}}{\text{ft}}\right] = 1.33\,\text{in.}$$

For L = 60 ft:

$$\Delta = \frac{60\,\text{ft}}{360} \cdot \left[\frac{12\,\text{in.}}{\text{ft}}\right] = 2\,\text{in.}$$

This is a good deflection criterion to ensure that floor movement is not disturbing to the building occupants. Remember that live load is the critical issue, since the dead load deflection can be offset by cambering the member.

One may apply the less stringent deflection condition of less than or equal to $\frac{L}{240}$ of the span:

$$\Delta = \frac{L}{240} = 0.00417\,L$$

For L = 30 ft:

$$\Delta = \frac{30\,\text{ft}}{240} \cdot \frac{12\,\text{in.}}{\text{ft}} = 1.5\,\text{in.}$$

For the $\frac{L}{240}$ condition, the deflection is 1.5 times greater than the deflection for the $^L/_{360}$ condition.

Similarly for L = 40 ft:

$$\Delta = \frac{40\,\text{ft}}{240} \cdot \frac{12\,\text{in.}}{\text{ft}} = 2\,\text{in.}$$

This deflection condition makes the floor rigid enough that most people will not be nervous because of floor movement. It is also the condition applied to flat roofs to avoid ponding of water. For most applications, the more stringent requirement of $\Delta \le \frac{L}{360}$ is applied to floors to ensure a higher level of satisfaction in the building occupants. In addition, new vibration analyses may be applied, possibly leading to even more conservative truss designs.

For simple-span structures, the deflection induced by the live load w_{live} is given by the expression:

$$\Delta = \frac{5 \cdot w_{\text{live}} \cdot L^4}{384 \cdot E \cdot I} \quad \text{or} \quad \Delta = \frac{5 w_{\text{live}} L^4}{384\,E\,I}$$

Where:
  w_{live} is the live load per unit length on the spanning members.
  L is the spanning member's length.
  E is the material stiffness.
  I is the stiffness of the spanning member's cross section.

This expression indicates that the deflection is in direct proportion to the load w_{live}. Therefore, to generate twice the deflection, twice the load w_{live} needs to be applied. Or 1.5 times the deflection is generated by applying 1.5 times the live load w_{live}. It is apparent that relaxing the deflection condition from $\Delta_1 = \frac{L}{360} = 0.00278\,L$ to $\Delta_2 = \frac{L}{240} = 0.00417\,L$ allows the spanning member to carry 1.5 times the live load w_{live} without exceeding the deflection limit.

To find the acceptable live load w_{live} to keep the deflection at $\Delta = \frac{L}{240} = 0.004167\,L$, simply multiply the live load number from the allowable-loads tables by 1.5. The allowed load, as limited by deflection, may no

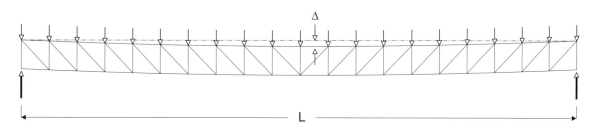

Figure 7.217 Truss deflection.

longer govern the design. Instead, strength may be the governing issue—but this is resolved by checking the first number in the allowable-loads tables.

After multiplying the loads, as limited by deflection, by 1.5 several times, it dawns on one that scanning the tables for an acceptable truss is simpler and more efficient if one multiplies the actual live load on the structure by $\frac{1}{1.5} = 0.6667 = \frac{2}{3}$. Use this number as the live load figure's upper limit in the allowable-loads tables. If the full load on the structure produces a deflection of $\Delta = \frac{L}{240}$, then $\frac{2}{3}$ of the load produces a deflection of $\Delta = \frac{L}{360}$.

The following trends are apparent in the safe load numbers:

- The deeper the joist, the longer the useful span.
- For a given joist, the longer the span, the lower the allowed load.

Load values are not listed for spans greater than 24 times the depth. Trusses of long, shallow proportions are not considered economical, and the deflection condition cannot be satisfied with spans greater than 24 times the depth.

The longer spans are limited by the second of the two numbers listed. (This is sometimes called the diving board effect: strong enough, but very flexible.)

Consider the case of a parallel-chord truss spanning 60 ft to support a floor.

The dead load on the top chord is

$$w_{dead} = \frac{50\ \#}{ft^2} \cdot 6\ ft = \frac{300\ \#}{ft}$$

The live load on the top chord is

$$w_{live} = \frac{80\ \#}{ft^2} \cdot 6\ ft = \frac{480\ \#}{ft}$$

The total imposed load (dead+live) on the top chord is

$$w_{total} = \frac{130\ \#}{ft^2} \cdot 6\ ft = \frac{780\ \#}{ft}$$

In the tables, the two numbers are stacked, with W_{total} on top and w_{live} below:

780
480

Before looking in the tables, write down the design loads in exactly this format. One calculates live load before calculating total load, but in the tables total load is listed first. Putting these two numbers in the order corresponding to that in the tables will reduce confusion and the number of mistakes in reading the tables.

For high-load situations, the truss failure may be in shear, making the web members or their welded con-

nections the limiting factor. Therefore, the shear force, $(w_{total}L)/2$, which is equal to $W_{total}/2$, must be addressed. The tables could have listed the allowed value of $W_{total}/2$. However, the designers of the tables chose to give the allowed value of W_{total} instead.

$$W_{total} = \frac{780\ \#}{ft^2} \cdot 60\ ft = 46{,}800\ \#$$

This must not exceed the number in any column labeled "SAFE LOAD in Lbs. Between."

Examining the tables reveals that K-Series trusses do not work for these high loads.

Looking at the LH-Series tables, one sees that the table format is altered. The joist designation is listed in the left-hand column, followed by the self-weight $\left(\frac{\#}{ft}\right)$ in column 2 and the truss depth (inches) in column 3.

Column 4 is titled "SAFE LOAD in Lbs. Between," under which are listed two span numbers (feet). For any span inclusive of or between those two span numbers, the allowed total load in pounds is listed in the column below. The SAFE LOAD in Lbs. Between applies to short spans where the web forces are large and web failure governs truss failure. Web forces depend on the total load on the truss W_{total} (or, more specifically $\frac{W_{total}}{2}$) and not on the truss length, which is why this column lists the total load in pounds and does not address different spans.

The remaining columns are labeled in 1 ft increments of clear span. For these spans, the governing issues is either of the following:

- The internal moment (the force in the chord members)
- Deflection

The allowed loads are listed in pounds per foot of joist.

A 36LH15, 36 in. deep and weighing $\frac{36\ \#}{ft}$, almost works for total load (769 < 780) and falls short for live load deflection (434 < 480).

A 40LH15, weighing $\frac{36\ \#}{ft}$ almost works for Safe Load in Lbs. Between (48,100), but when the truss's self-weight is accounted for, it fails by a slight amount. Therefore, the lightest section that works is a 40LH16, weighing 42 #/ft, which has a Safe Load in Lbs. Between of 53,000 #.

The tables do not list the precise truss weight, but the estimated truss weight. Uncertainty in the weight has to do with the fact that the manufacturer may substitute a slightly heavier member when the precise member size is not in stock.

One might think that oversizing the trusses could have serious consequences for the structure supporting the trusses, if these supporting elements are not designed for the additional load. However, a steel truss's self-weight is normally a small fraction of the total load on the truss. Therefore, slightly oversizing the truss will have a negligible effect on the structure below it.

Now take a detailed approach to sizing a 40 ft grid structure with floors and a flat roof (see Figure 7.218).

For roof-truss joists:

$$w_{dead} = \frac{\dfrac{10\ \#}{ft^2} \cdot 5ft \cdot 1ft}{ft} = \frac{50\ \#}{ft} = \frac{0.050\ K}{ft}$$

$$w_{live} = \frac{\dfrac{20\ \#}{ft^2} \cdot 5ft \cdot 1ft}{ft} = \frac{100\ \#}{ft} = \frac{0.100\ K}{ft}$$

$$w_{total} = w_{dead} + w_{live} = \frac{50\ \#}{ft} + \frac{100\ \#}{ft} = \frac{150\ \#}{ft} = \frac{0.150\ K}{ft}$$

$$W_{total} = w_{total} \cdot 40\ ft = \frac{150\ \#}{ft} = 6{,}000\ \#$$

For the floor system, assume the lightest composite of concrete and corrugated steel decking to meet the structural requirements. Remember that the desire for greater fire resistance and vibration suppression is motivation to use a thicker decking. For the floor:

$$w_{dead} = \frac{\dfrac{30\ \#}{ft^2} \cdot 5ft \cdot 1ft}{ft} = \frac{150\ \#}{ft} = \frac{0.150\ K}{ft}$$

$$w_{live} = \frac{\dfrac{100\ \#}{ft^2} \cdot 5ft \cdot 1ft}{ft} = \frac{500\ \#}{ft} = \frac{0.500\ K}{ft}$$

$$w_{total} = w_{dead} = w_{live} = \frac{150\ \#}{ft} + \frac{500\ \#}{ft} = \frac{650\ \#}{ft} = \frac{0.650\ K}{ft}$$

$$W_{total} = w_{total} \cdot 40\ ft = \frac{650\ \#}{ft} \cdot 40\ ft = 26{,}000\ \#$$

Consider the floor joist first:

To find a K-Series joist to span 40 ft, go to Figure 7.223. The deepest and heaviest joist listed is a 30K12, weighing $\dfrac{17.6\ \#}{ft}$. At a 40 ft span, it supports a total load

of 438 lb, below the $\dfrac{650\ \#}{ft}$ required capacity. The K-series joists are light and mainly suitable for lightweight roofing applications.

Moving on to the LH-Series trusses:

A 24LH10, which weighs $\dfrac{23\ \#}{ft}$, safely supports $\dfrac{702\ \#}{ft}$, including its self-weight, or $\dfrac{702\ \#}{ft} - \dfrac{23\ \#}{ft} = \dfrac{679\ \#}{ft}$ imposed load, which is greater than the $\dfrac{650\ \#}{ft}$ design load.

The live load that produces a deflection equal to $\dfrac{L}{360}$ is listed as $\dfrac{378\ \#}{ft}$. For this structure:

$$w_{live} = \frac{500\ \#}{ft}$$

So the 24LH10 joist does not satisfy the $\Delta \le \dfrac{L}{360}$ deflection condition. However, it may satisfy the less stringent $\Delta = \dfrac{L}{240}$ deflection condition. Adjusting the live load by $\frac{2}{3}$ leads to:

$$w_{live} = \frac{2}{3} \cdot \frac{500\ \#}{ft} = \frac{333\ \#}{ft}$$

This is less than $\dfrac{378\ \#}{ft}$, the load that produces the deflection $\Delta = \dfrac{L}{360}$ in the 24LH10.

The 24LH10 is 2 ft deep, exactly $d = \dfrac{L}{20}$, which is close to the midrange of proportions listed as parallel-chord truss guidelines.

To satisfy the more stringent deflection condition, use a deeper truss. The next deeper LH truss is 28 in. deep. The 40 ft span is not in a column's header by itself, but is part of the span range listed under "SAFE LOAD in Lbs. Between." To use this part of the table, reference the previously calculated value $W_{total} = 26{,}000\ \#$.

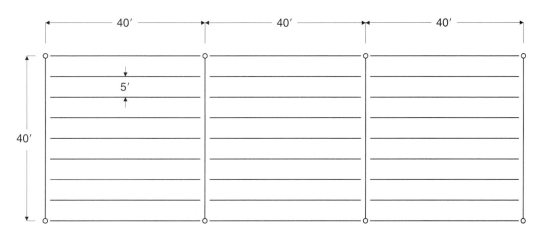

Figure 7.218 Framing plan for joists, girders, and columns on 40 ft × 40 ft grid.

A 28LH09, weighing $\frac{21\,\#}{ft}$, safely supports a total load of 27,700 lb between the supports. The total truss weight is $\frac{21\,\#}{ft} \cdot 40\,ft = 840\,\#$. Therefore, the total load, including the decking's imposed load and live load and the truss's self-weight, is 26,000 # + 840 # = 26,840 #, less than the 27,700 lb allowed. So this truss is strong enough.

Using the tables to search for deeper, more efficient trusses does not yield useful data. These tables are generated (and optimized) to cover the most common situations, where the truss depth is limited by several economic or architectural factors. These include the desire to limit the building's height and surface area (limiting the structural frame's cost, the building skin's cost, and energy costs of heat transmission through the building envelope). The tables do not cover other situations. If they did, there would be deeper, more efficient trusses shown. Deeper, more efficient structures can be designed by the architect or engineer, starting with basic principles of truss analysis and design, or they can be supplied by the truss manufacturer. The lack of such designs in these tables is an indication that they are not very common in practice. However, there are situations in which deeper trusses make both structural and architectural sense.

The 28LH09 truss safely supports a weight $\frac{27,700\,\#}{840\,\#}$ = 33 times its self-weight. The truss's self-weight is $\frac{840\,\#}{27,700\,\#} \cdot 100\% = 3.03\%$ of the weight that can be safely supported.

Deflection is not a serious concern for trusses listed in the column titled "SAFE LOAD in Lbs. Between," since those trusses have deep proportions. However, deflection must still be checked, particularly for those spanning members with lengths at the long end of the listed range, because those trusses have the shallowest proportions in that span range and are the most flexible.

For trusses listed in the column "SAFE LOAD in Lbs. Between," check the deflection starting with the data listed in the column to the right of that column. For the 28LH09, the column is headed 41 (feet) and the following two numbers are listed:

$$w_{total} = \frac{667\,\#}{ft}$$

$$w_{live} = \frac{428\,\#}{ft}$$

To check the 40 ft span's allowed live load, one needs a simple scaling method. Start with the deflection equation for a simple-span member:

$$\Delta = \frac{5\,w_{live}L^4}{384\,E\,I}$$

Dividing both sides of the equation by L reformulates the equation in terms of the ratio $\frac{deflection}{length}$:

$$\frac{\Delta}{L} = \frac{5\,w_{live}L^3}{384\,E\,I}$$

Solving for w_{live}:

$$w_{live} = \frac{384\,E\,I\frac{\Delta}{L}}{L^3}$$

Multiply both sides of the equation by L:

$$W_{live} = \frac{384\,E\,I\frac{\Delta}{L}}{5\,L^2}$$

In summary:

- The allowed distributed live load w_{live} varies *inversely* with the *cube* of the span L.
- The allowed live load force W_{live} varies *inversely* with the *square* of the span L.

The equation can be adjusted to account for end effects related to the end support's center of action. Both lengths used in the adjustment factor ratio are increased by 8 in. This rationale is illustrated in the diagram for an LH-Series truss, shown in Figure 7.219.

Clear span is the length listed in the tables. To find the effective structural span, one needs to add 4 in. on each end, for a total of 8 in., or 0.67 ft.

Method 1 for checking the truss for deflection under live load:

For the 28LH09, start with the live load on a reference length of 41 ft. The allowed live load for a length less than 41 ft is derived by multiplying the allowed live load W_{live} for the 41 ft truss by $\frac{(41+0.67)^2}{(L+0.67)^2}$. In this case, the span being checked is 40 ft, so the factor is $\frac{(41+0.67)^2}{(40+0.67)^2}$.

For comparison purposes, one needs to calculate W_{live} for the truss spanning 40 ft:

$$W_{live} = \frac{500\,\#}{ft} \cdot 40\,ft = 20,000\,\#$$

Next, calculate the allowed live load on the 28LH09 spanning 40 ft:

$$W_{live} = \frac{428\,\#}{ft} \cdot 41\,ft \cdot \frac{(41+0.67)^2}{(40+0.67)^2} = 18,425\,\#.$$

This does not work, because 20,000 > 18,425.

Check the allowed live load on the next larger truss, a 28LH10, spanning 40 ft:

$$W_{live} = \frac{466\,\#}{ft} \cdot 41\,ft \cdot \frac{(41+0.67)^2}{(40+0.67)^2} = 20,061\,\#$$

This works, because 20,000 < 20,061.

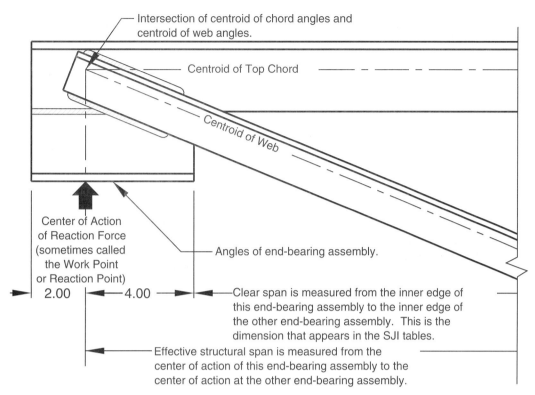

Intersection of centroid of chord angles and centroid of web angles.

Centroid of Top Chord

Centroid of Web

Center of Action of Reaction Force (sometimes called the Work Point or Reaction Point)

2.00   4.00

Angles of end-bearing assembly.

Clear span is measured from the inner edge of this end-bearing assembly to the inner edge of the other end-bearing assembly. This is the dimension that appears in the SJI tables.

Effective structural span is measured from the center of action of this end-bearing assembly to the center of action at the other end-bearing assembly.

Figure 7.219 Geometry of end-bearing assembly, showing intersections of centroid.

Method 2 for checking the truss for deflection under live load:

For the 28LH09, start with the distributed live load $w_{live} \left(\frac{\#}{ft} \right)$ on a reference length of 41 ft. The allowed distributed live load w_{live} for a length less than 41 ft is derived by multiplying the allowed distributed live load w_{live} for the 41 ft truss by $\frac{(41+0.67)^3}{(40+0.7)^3}$, since the allowed live load w_{live} varies inversely as the cube of the length L. The span being checked is 40 ft, so the factor is $\frac{(41+0.67)^3}{(40+0.67)^3}$.

For comparison purposes, remember that $w_{live} = \frac{500 \ \#}{ft}$ for the truss being designed.

$$w_{live} = \frac{428 \ \#}{ft} \cdot \frac{(41+0.67)^3}{(40+0.67)^3} = \frac{462 \ \#}{ft}$$

This is less than the $\frac{500 \ \#}{ft}$ live load.

Try a 28LH10:

$$w_{live} = \frac{466 \ \#}{ft} \cdot \frac{(41+0.67)^3}{(40+0.67)^3} = \frac{503 \ \#}{ft}$$

This works, because 500 < 503.

For the 28LH10:

$$W_{self} = w_{self} \cdot 40 \ ft = \frac{23 \ \#}{ft} \cdot 40 \ ft = 920 \ \#$$

The truss safely supports a weight $\frac{30,300 \ \#}{920 \ \#} = 32.9$ times its self-weight.

The truss's self-weight is $\frac{920 \ \#}{30,300 \ \#} \cdot 100\% = 3.04\%$ of the weight that it can safely support.

Selecting Steel Truss Girders from Standard Tables

Continuing with the 40 ft × 40 ft column grid example, assume the 28LH11 is used. With a self-weight of $\frac{25 \ \#}{ft}$, the support force under each truss joist end is

$$\text{(Design load + self-weight)} \cdot \frac{L}{2} = \left(\frac{650 \ \#}{ft} + \frac{25 \ \#}{ft} \right) \cdot \frac{40 \ ft}{2}$$

$$= \frac{27,700 \ \#}{2} = 13,500 \ \#$$

This force is provided by the truss girder. According to the action–reaction pairs principle, the downward force on the truss girder is equal and opposite to the truss girder's upward force on the truss joist. Each truss joist is exerting a localized downward force of 13,500 lb at the point at which it bears on the truss girder. To prevent excessive truss-girder top-chord bending, the 13,500 lb force must be delivered to a panel point—a joint into which supporting web members frame. Thus, the truss girder geometry is governed by the truss joist spacing, which is 5 ft on center.

The loading on a truss girder is twice as great when it is interior to a building, supporting truss joists on each side. The localized force becomes 27,000 lb on each truss-girder panel point.

Begin by designing a truss girder for the perimeter condition. In the tables for joist girders (Figures 7.230 through 7.234), the first column is "Girder Span" in feet. The second column is "Joist Spaces" in feet. The third column is "Girder Depth" in inches. The remaining columns fall under "Load on Each Panel Point," given in kips.

This case is a 40 ft span (column 1) with eight joists spaced 5 ft on center (column 2, row titled 8N @ 5.00). There is a load on each panel point of 13.5 K, rounded up to 14 K (column 14K):

The 32 in.-deep perimeter truss girder has a self-weight of $\frac{70\ \#}{\text{ft}}$.

The 36 in.-deep perimeter truss girder has a self-weight of $\frac{64\ \#}{\text{ft}}$.

The 40 in.-deep perimeter truss girder has a self-weight of $\frac{61\ \#}{\text{ft}}$.

For interior truss girders, the case is a 40 ft span with eight joists spaced 5 ft on center and a load on each panel point of 27 K. An examination of the tables shows that there is a column for a 25 K panel-point force and a column for a 30 K panel-point force. The difference is coarse. This jump is motivated by a desire to save paper when publishing the data. It has little to do with the truss's fabrication by the manufacturer, who takes the loads listed in the construction documents and designs an efficient truss to meet those requirements. In the meantime, one can get close to finding the truss's final self-weight by interpolating between the numbers in Table 7.6.

Hence, the 36 in.-deep interior truss girder has a self-weight of $\frac{124\ \#}{\text{ft}^2}$.

In the summary in Table 7.7, both the perimeter and interior truss girders are chosen to have a depth of 36 in. and the truss joists are 28LH11. This table summarizes the material expenditure for the floor trusses.

Selecting Roof Trusses

Assume that the roof joists support the loads shown in Table 7.8.

The load of $\frac{7.5\ \#}{\text{ft}^2}$ at the bottom of Table 7.8 is often

Table 7.6 Interpolating the Truss Girder Data in Figure 7.232

	Lower Weight/ Vertex (K)	Actual Weight/ Vertex (K)	Upper Weight/ Vertex (K)
	25	27	30
Girder Depth (in.)	Lower Self-Weight (#/ft)	Interpolated Self-Weight (#/ft)	Upper Self-Weight (#/ft)
32	121	133.4	152
36	111	124	144
40	105	111	119

Table 7.7 Summarizing the Floor Truss Self-Weights

	Trusses (No./bay)	Self-Weight per Foot (#/ft)	Length (ft)	Self-Weight (#/bay)	Self-Weight (#/ft²)
Truss joists	8	25	40	8,000	5.00
Perimeter girders	1	66	40	2,640	1.65
Interior girders	0.5	124	40	2,480	1.55
				Total:	8.20

Table 7.8 Roof Loads

Material	Estimated Weight (#/ft)
Single-ply membrane	0.5
Recovery board	1
4 in.-thick rigid Styrofoam insulation	1.5
Galvanized corrugated steel decking	2.5
Ducts	1
Hung ceiling and electrical lights	1
TOTAL	7.5

rounded up to $\frac{124}{\text{ft}^2}$, to be conservative. On many jobs, there is a requirement for another $\frac{10\ \#}{\text{ft}^2}$ for a total dead load of $\frac{20\ \#}{\text{ft}^2}$, to account for future loads that are yet to be identified. Among the possible catastrophic loads are large quantities of roofing materials deposited in a limited area on the roof, causing extreme local loading. Roofers are not structural engineers, and some give little thought to the effects of the loads they bring to the roof. The structural capacity cost of carrying the additional

$\dfrac{10\ \#}{\text{ft}^2}$ or $\dfrac{20\ \#}{\text{ft}^2}$ is small when it is part of the initial construction and high when it is a structural change implemented after construction is complete. For the moment, stick with the $\dfrac{10\ \#}{\text{ft}^2}$. However, in general, more conservative values are wise.

$$w_{\text{dead}} = \frac{10\ \#}{\text{ft}^2} \cdot 5\ \text{ft} = \frac{50\ \#}{\text{ft}}$$

$$w_{\text{live}} = \frac{20\ \#}{\text{ft}^2} \cdot 5\ \text{ft} = \frac{100\ \#}{\text{ft}}$$

$$w_{\text{total}} = w_{\text{dead}} + w_{\text{live}} = \frac{50\ \#}{\text{ft}} + \frac{100\ \#}{\text{ft}} = \frac{150\ \#}{\text{ft}^2}$$

$$w_{\text{total}} = w_{\text{total}} \cdot 40\ \text{ft} = \frac{150\ \#}{\text{ft}} \cdot 4\ \text{ft} = 6{,}000\ \#$$

Start in the tables of K-Series steel joists, since they are the best suited in lightweight roofing applications. For K-Series steel joists, there is never a column labeled "SAFE LOAD in Lbs. Between," because the loads are never high enough for shear failure to be the governing mode. The two numbers needed to look for in the tables are

150
100

A 24K4, with a self-weight of $\dfrac{8.4\ \#}{\text{ft}}$, has the following two numbers for a 40 ft span:

185
109

This is adequate for both moment strength (chord strength) and deflection. Note that it is most severely limited by deflection. If the deflection criterion is relaxed to $\dfrac{L}{240}$, then the adjusted live load for comparison with the tables would be $\dfrac{2}{3} \cdot \dfrac{100\ \#}{\text{ft}} = \dfrac{67\ \#}{\text{ft}}$, in which case a 20K4 with a self-weight of $\dfrac{7.6\ \#}{\text{ft}}$ works. Relaxing the deflection condition reduces the weight of steel required in the roof truss joists by $\dfrac{(8.4 - 7.6)}{8.4} \cdot 100\% = 9.5\%$.

To assess the truss's structural efficiency, the ratio of the total weight supported to the truss's self-weight is:

$$\frac{(\text{Weight imposed} + \text{self-weight})}{\text{Self-weight}} = \frac{158}{7.6} = 20.8$$

This means that the truss is supporting 20.8 times its weight. The truss's self-weight is $\dfrac{\text{Self-weight}}{(\text{Weight imposed} + \text{self-weight})} \cdot$ $100\% = \dfrac{7.6}{158} = \cdot 100\% = 4.8\%$ of the weight it supports.

This is not as efficient as the structure of floor trusses. The lower efficiency of the roof trusses is explained by the lower loads on the roof trusses than on the floor trusses:

- The roof truss members are more slender than the members in the floor trusses.
- The roof truss members are more vulnerable to buckling.
- The stress level in those members is limited by buckling, rather than by the material's crushing or tearing strength.
- The roof truss members are structurally less efficient than the floor truss members.

This argument runs parallel to the one regarding column efficiency for steel columns in Chapter 5.

Notice also that the roof trusses are limited by deflection. To make the web members less vulnerable to buckling, the roof trusses are made shallower. Shallower trusses are more flexible and exhibit greater deflection under load. The proportions of the roof trusses are: $\dfrac{L}{d} = \dfrac{40\ \text{ft}}{20\ \text{in.}} \cdot \left[\dfrac{12\ \text{in.}}{\text{ft}} \right] = 24.$

Selecting Steel Truss Girders for Roofs

Continuing with the 40 ft × 40 ft column grid example, assume the 24K4 is used. With a self-weight of $\dfrac{8.4\ \#}{\text{ft}}$, the support force under each truss joist end is (Design load + self-weight) $\cdot \dfrac{L}{2} = \left(\dfrac{150\ \#}{\text{ft}} + \dfrac{8.4\ \#}{\text{ft}} \right) \cdot \dfrac{40\ \text{ft}}{2} = \dfrac{6{,}336\ \#}{2}$ $= 3{,}168\ \#$. The girder is providing this support force. According to the action–reaction pairs principle, the force on the truss girder is equal and opposite to the truss-girder force on the truss joist. There is a localized downward force of 3,168 lb on the truss girder at the point where the truss-joist bears on it. To prevent excessive top-chord bending of the truss girder, the 3,168 lb force must be delivered to a panel point—a joint into which supporting web members frame. Thus, the truss-girder geometry is governed by the truss-joist spacing, which is 5 ft on center.

The loading on a truss girder is twice as great when it is interior to a building, supporting truss joists on each side. The localized force becomes 6,336 lb on each truss-girder panel point.

Begin by sizing a truss girder for the perimeter condition. Using the Joist Girder tables, this case is a 40 ft span with eight joist spaces of 5 ft. There is a load on each panel point of 3.17 K, which can be rounded up to 4 K to make using the tables easier. As indicated in the earlier discussion of floor girders, the tables' load differences are motivated by the desire to save paper in publishing. Interpolation is used in the tables to get a better estimate of the truss's manufactured weight. In this case, interpolation is not possible, because no column of data exists for loads lower than 4 K. One could interpolate, assuming that a zero load would produce a truss of zero self-weight (see Table 7.9).

However, these are incredibly light girders and the values can be taken from the column for a force/vertex of 4 K, without significantly overestimating the self-weights or the costs involved.

Since the weights involved are low, choose the shallowest truss.

The 32 in.-deep perimeter roof truss girder has a self-weight of $\frac{21\,\#}{\text{ft}}$.

For interior situations, the case is a 40 ft span with eight joist spaces of 5 ft and a load on each panel point of 6.336 K. Interpolation produces the results shown in Table 7.10.

Since the weights involved are low, choose the shallowest truss. The 32 in.-deep interior roof truss girder has a self-weight of $\frac{32.7\,\#}{\text{ft}}$.

Table 7.11 summarizes the material expenditure for the roof trusses.

The tables shown in Figures 7.220 through 7.234 are for simple-span, parallel-chord trusses. These represent a large fraction of the installations involving double-angle trusses. However, double-angle trusses are much more versatile and can be used for a wide range of applications and geometries. The photographs in Figures 7.235 and 7.236 give indications of what is possible. Figure 7.235 is a photo of Opryland (Trusses by Vulcraft). This structure has a shape that was motivated to a large degree by aesthetics, but it is also very rational structurally. The ends of the trusses are moment-connected to the support structure, producing a negative moment in the truss that makes it desirable to have some extra depth at the ends. There is a substantial positive moment at the center of the truss, which makes it desirable to have some extra depth there as well. This pattern of extra depth at the center and at the ends was discussed in Section 7.1, regarding the effect of moment connections to stiff columns, and it is discussed again in Chapter 10, "Lateral Bracing Systems."

Figure 7.236 shows the Brown and Root College workout center (Trusses by Vulcraft).

Table 7.9 Interpolating the Truss Girder Data in Figure 7.232 to Size the Interior Girder

	Lower Weight/ Vertex (K)	Actual Weight/ Vertex (K)	Upper Weight/ Vertex (K)
	0	3.168	4
Girder Depth (in.)	Lower Self-Weight (#/ft)	Interpolated Self-Weight (#/ft)	Upper Self-Weight (#/ft)
32	0	16.6	21
36	0	16.6	21
40	0	15.8	20

Table 7.10 Interpolating the Truss Girder Data in Figure 7.232

	Lower Weight/ Vertex (K)	Actual Weight/ Vertex (K)	Upper Weight/ Vertex (K)
	6	6.336	7
Girder Depth (in.)	Lower Self-Weight (#/ft)	Interpolated Self-Weight (#/ft)	Upper Self-Weight (#/ft)
32	31	32.7	36
36	29	30	32
40	27	28	30

Table 7.11 Summarizing the Roof Truss Self Weights

	Trusses (No./bay)	Self-Weight (#/ft)	Length (ft)	Self-Weight (#/bay)	Self-Weight (#/ft²)
Truss joists	8	8.4	40	2,688	1.68
Perimeter girders	1	21	40	840	0.53
Interior girders	0.5	32.7	40	654	0.41
				Total:	2.62

STANDARD LOAD TABLE/OPEN WEB STEEL JOISTS, K-SERIES
Based on a Maximum Allowable Tensile Stress of 30 ksi

Joist Designation	8K1	10K1	12K1	12K3	12K5	14K1	14K3	14K4	14K6	16K2	16K3	16K4	16K5	16K6	16K7	16K9
Depth (in.)	8	10	12	12	12	14	14	14	14	16	16	16	16	16	16	16
Approx. Wt (lbs./ft.)	5.1	5.0	5.0	5.7	7.1	5.2	6.0	6.7	7.7	5.5	6.3	7.0	7.5	8.1	8.6	10.0
Span (ft.)																
8	550/550															
9	550/550															
10	550/480	550/550														
11	532/377	550/542														
12	444/288	550/455	550/550	550/550	550/550											
13	377/225	479/363	550/510	550/510	550/510											
14	324/179	412/289	500/425	550/463	550/463	550/550	550/550	550/550	550/550							
15	281/145	358/234	434/344	543/428	550/434	511/475	550/507	550/507	550/507							
16	246/119	313/192	380/282	476/351	550/396	448/390	550/467	550/467	550/467	550/550	550/550	550/550	550/550	550/550	550/550	550/550
17		277/159	336/234	420/291	550/366	395/324	495/404	550/443	550/443	512/488	550/526	550/526	550/526	550/526	550/526	550/526
18		246/134	299/197	374/245	507/317	352/272	441/339	530/397	550/408	456/409	508/456	550/490	550/490	550/490	550/490	550/490
19		221/113	268/167	335/207	454/269	315/230	395/287	475/336	550/383	408/347	455/386	547/452	550/455	550/455	550/455	550/455
20		199/97	241/142	302/177	409/230	284/197	356/246	428/287	525/347	368/297	410/330	493/386	550/426	550/426	550/426	550/426
21			218/123	273/153	370/198	257/170	322/212	388/248	475/299	333/255	371/285	447/333	503/373	548/405	550/406	550/406
22			199/106	249/132	337/172	234/147	293/184	353/215	432/259	303/222	337/247	406/289	458/323	498/351	550/385	550/385
23			181/93	227/116	308/150	214/128	268/160	322/188	395/226	277/194	308/216	371/252	418/282	455/307	507/339	550/363
24			166/81	208/101	282/132	196/113	245/141	295/165	362/199	254/170	283/189	340/221	384/248	418/269	465/298	550/346
25						180/100	226/124	272/145	334/175	234/150	260/167	313/195	353/219	384/238	428/263	514/311
26						166/88	209/110	251/129	308/156	216/133	240/148	289/173	326/194	355/211	395/233	474/276
27						154/79	193/98	233/115	285/139	200/119	223/132	268/155	302/173	329/188	366/208	439/246
28						143/70	180/88	216/103	265/124	186/106	207/118	249/138	281/155	306/168	340/186	408/220
29										173/95	193/106	232/124	261/139	285/151	317/167	380/198
30										161/86	180/96	216/112	244/126	266/137	296/151	355/178
31										151/78	168/87	203/101	228/114	249/124	277/137	332/161
32										142/71	158/79	190/92	214/103	233/112	259/124	311/147

Figure 7.220 Standard load table for open web steel joists, K-Series. (Figures 7.220–7.228 copyright 2004 by Steel Joist Institute. Used with permission. All rights reserved.)

STANDARD LOAD TABLE/OPEN WEB STEEL JOISTS, K-SERIES
Based on a Maximum Allowable Tensile Stress of 30 ksi

Joist Designation	18K3	18K4	18K5	18K6	18K7	18K9	18K10	20K3	20K4	20K5	20K6	20K7	20K9	20K10	22K4	22K5	22K6	22K7	22K9	22K10	22K11
Depth (In.)	18	18	18	18	18	18	18	20	20	20	20	20	20	20	22	22	22	22	22	22	22
Approx. Wt. (lbs./ft.)	6.6	7.2	7.7	8.5	9	10.2	11.7	6.7	7.6	8.2	8.9	9.3	10.8	12.2	8	8.8	9.2	9.7	11.3	12.6	13.8
Span (ft.)																					
18	550	550	550	550	550	550	550														
	550	550	550	550	550	550	550														
19	514	550	550	550	550	550	550														
	494	523	523	523	523	523	523														
20	463	550	550	550	550	550	550	517	550	550	550	550	550	550							
	423	490	490	490	490	490	490	517	550	550	550	550	550	550							
21	420	506	550	550	550	550	550	468	550	550	550	550	550	550							
	364	426	460	460	460	460	460	453	520	520	520	520	520	520							
22	382	460	518	550	550	550	550	426	514	550	550	550	550	550	550	550	550	550	550	550	550
	316	370	414	438	438	438	438	393	461	490	490	490	490	490	548	548	548	548	548	548	548
23	349	420	473	516	550	550	550	389	469	529	550	550	550	550	518	550	550	550	550	550	550
	276	323	362	393	418	418	418	344	402	451	468	468	468	468	491	518	518	518	518	518	518
24	320	385	434	473	526	550	550	357	430	485	528	550	550	550	475	536	550	550	550	550	550
	242	284	318	345	382	396	396	302	353	396	430	448	448	448	431	483	495	495	495	495	495
25	294	355	400	435	485	550	550	329	396	446	486	541	550	550	438	493	537	550	550	550	550
	214	250	281	305	337	377	377	266	312	350	380	421	426	426	381	427	464	474	474	474	474
26	272	328	369	402	448	538	550	304	366	412	449	500	550	550	404	455	496	550	550	550	550
	190	222	249	271	299	354	361	236	277	310	337	373	405	405	338	379	411	454	454	454	454
27	252	303	342	372	415	498	550	281	339	382	416	463	550	550	374	422	459	512	550	550	550
	169	198	222	241	267	315	347	211	247	277	301	333	389	389	301	337	367	406	432	432	432
28	234	282	318	346	385	463	548	261	315	355	386	430	517	550	348	392	427	475	550	550	550
	151	177	199	216	239	282	331	189	221	248	269	298	353	375	270	302	328	364	413	413	413
29	218	263	296	322	359	431	511	243	293	330	360	401	482	550	324	365	398	443	532	550	550
	136	159	179	194	215	254	298	170	199	223	242	268	317	359	242	272	295	327	387	399	399
30	203	245	276	301	335	402	477	227	274	308	336	374	450	533	302	341	371	413	497	550	550
	123	144	161	175	194	229	269	153	179	201	218	242	286	336	219	245	266	295	349	385	385
31	190	229	258	281	313	376	446	212	256	289	314	350	421	499	283	319	347	387	465	550	550
	111	130	146	158	175	207	243	138	162	182	198	219	259	304	198	222	241	267	316	369	369
32	178	215	242	264	294	353	418	199	240	271	295	328	395	468	265	299	326	363	436	517	549
	101	118	132	144	159	188	221	126	147	165	179	199	235	276	180	201	219	242	287	337	355
33	168	202	228	248	276	332	393	187	226	254	277	309	371	440	249	281	306	341	410	486	532
	92	108	121	131	145	171	201	114	134	150	163	181	214	251	164	183	199	221	261	307	334
34	158	190	214	233	260	312	370	176	212	239	261	290	349	414	235	265	288	321	386	458	516
	84	98	110	120	132	156	184	105	122	137	149	165	195	229	149	167	182	202	239	280	314
35	149	179	202	220	245	294	349	166	200	226	246	274	329	390	221	249	272	303	364	432	494
	77	90	101	110	121	143	168	96	112	126	137	151	179	210	137	153	167	185	219	257	292
36	141	169	191	208	232	278	330	157	189	213	232	259	311	369	209	236	257	286	344	408	467
	70	82	92	101	111	132	154	88	103	115	125	139	164	193	126	141	153	169	201	236	269
37								148	179	202	220	245	294	349	198	223	243	271	325	386	442
								81	95	106	115	128	151	178	116	130	141	156	185	217	247
38								141	170	191	208	232	279	331	187	211	230	256	308	366	419
								74	87	98	106	118	139	164	107	119	130	144	170	200	228
39								133	161	181	198	220	265	314	178	200	218	243	292	347	397
								69	81	90	98	109	129	151	98	110	120	133	157	185	211
40								127	153	172	188	209	251	298	169	190	207	231	278	330	377
								64	75	84	91	101	119	140	91	102	111	123	146	171	195
41															161	181	197	220	264	314	359
															85	95	103	114	135	159	181
42															153	173	188	209	252	299	342
															79	88	96	106	126	148	168
43															146	165	179	200	240	285	326
															73	82	89	99	117	138	157
44															139	157	171	191	229	272	311
															68	76	83	92	109	128	146

Figure 7.221 Standard load table for open web steel joists, K-Series.

STANDARD LOAD TABLE/OPEN WEB STEEL JOISTS, K-SERIES
Based on a Maximum Allowable Tensile Stress of 30 ksi

Joist Designation	24K4	24K5	24K6	24K7	24K8	24K9	24K10	24K12	26K5	26K6	26K7	26K8	26K9	26K10	26K12
Depth (in.)	24	24	24	24	24	24	24	24	26	26	26	26	26	26	26
Approx. Wt. (lbs./ft.)	8.4	9.3	9.7	10.1	11.5	12.0	13.1	16.0	9.8	10.6	10.9	12.1	12.2	13.8	16.6
Span (ft.)															
24	520	550	550	550	550	550	550	550							
	516	544	544	544	544	544	544	544							
25	479	540	550	550	550	550	550	550							
	456	511	520	520	520	520	520	520							
26	442	499	543	550	550	550	550	550	542	550	550	550	550	550	550
	405	453	493	499	499	499	499	499	535	541	541	541	541	541	541
27	410	462	503	550	550	550	550	550	502	547	550	550	550	550	550
	361	404	439	479	479	479	479	479	477	519	522	522	522	522	522
28	381	429	467	521	550	550	550	550	466	508	550	550	550	550	550
	323	362	393	436	456	456	456	456	427	464	501	501	501	501	501
29	354	400	435	485	536	550	550	550	434	473	527	550	550	550	550
	290	325	354	392	429	436	436	436	384	417	463	479	479	479	479
30	331	373	406	453	500	544	550	550	405	441	492	544	550	550	550
	262	293	319	353	387	419	422	422	346	377	417	457	459	459	459
31	310	349	380	424	468	510	550	550	379	413	460	509	550	550	550
	237	266	289	320	350	379	410	410	314	341	378	413	444	444	444
32	290	327	357	397	439	478	549	549	356	387	432	477	519	549	549
	215	241	262	290	318	344	393	393	285	309	343	375	407	431	431
33	273	308	335	373	413	449	532	532	334	364	406	448	488	532	532
	196	220	239	265	289	313	368	368	259	282	312	342	370	404	404
34	257	290	315	351	388	423	502	516	315	343	382	422	459	516	516
	179	201	218	242	264	286	337	344	237	257	285	312	338	378	378
35	242	273	297	331	366	399	473	501	297	323	360	398	433	501	501
	164	184	200	221	242	262	308	324	217	236	261	286	310	356	356
36	229	258	281	313	346	377	447	487	280	305	340	376	409	486	487
	150	169	183	203	222	241	283	306	199	216	240	263	284	334	334
37	216	244	266	296	327	356	423	474	265	289	322	356	387	460	474
	138	155	169	187	205	222	260	290	183	199	221	242	262	308	315
38	205	231	252	281	310	338	401	461	251	274	305	337	367	436	461
	128	143	156	172	189	204	240	275	169	184	204	223	241	284	299
39	195	219	239	266	294	320	380	449	238	260	289	320	348	413	449
	118	132	144	159	174	189	222	261	156	170	188	206	223	262	283
40	185	208	227	253	280	304	361	438	227	247	275	304	331	393	438
	109	122	133	148	161	175	206	247	145	157	174	191	207	243	269
41	176	198	216	241	266	290	344	427	215	235	262	289	315	374	427
	101	114	124	137	150	162	191	235	134	146	162	177	192	225	256
42	168	189	206	229	253	276	327	417	205	224	249	275	300	356	417
	94	106	115	127	139	151	177	224	125	136	150	164	178	210	244
43	160	180	196	219	242	263	312	406	196	213	238	263	286	339	407
	88	98	107	118	130	140	165	213	116	126	140	153	166	195	232
44	153	172	187	209	231	251	298	387	187	204	227	251	273	324	398
	82	92	100	110	121	131	154	199	108	118	131	143	155	182	222
45	146	164	179	199	220	240	285	370	179	194	217	240	261	310	389
	76	86	93	103	113	122	144	185	101	110	122	133	145	170	212
46	139	157	171	191	211	230	272	354	171	186	207	229	250	296	380
	71	80	87	97	106	114	135	174	95	103	114	125	135	159	203
47	133	150	164	183	202	220	261	339	164	178	199	219	239	284	369
	67	75	82	90	99	107	126	163	89	96	107	117	127	149	192
48	128	144	157	175	194	211	250	325	157	171	190	210	229	272	353
	63	70	77	85	93	101	118	153	83	90	100	110	119	140	180
49									150	164	183	202	220	261	339
									78	85	94	103	112	131	169
50									144	157	175	194	211	250	325
									73	80	89	97	105	124	159
51									139	151	168	186	203	241	313
									69	75	83	91	99	116	150
52									133	145	162	179	195	231	301
									65	71	79	86	93	110	142

Figure 7.222 Standard load table for open web steel joists, K-Series.

STANDARD LOAD TABLE/OPEN WEB STEEL JOISTS, K-SERIES
Based on a Maximum Allowable Tensile Stress of 30 ksi

Joist Designation	28K6	28K7	28K8	28K9	28K10	28K12	30K7	30K8	30K9	30K10	30K11	30K12
Depth (In.)	28	28	28	28	28	28	30	30	30	30	30	30
Approx. Wt. (lbs./ft.)	11.4	11.8	12.7	13.0	14.3	17.1	12.3	13.2	13.4	15.0	16.4	17.6
Span (ft.)												
28	548	550	550	550	550	550						
	541	543	543	543	543	543						
29	511	550	550	550	550	550						
	486	522	522	522	522	522						
30	477	531	550	550	550	550	550	550	550	550	550	550
	439	486	500	500	500	500	543	543	543	543	543	543
31	446	497	550	550	550	550	534	550	550	550	550	550
	397	440	480	480	480	480	508	520	520	520	520	520
32	418	466	515	549	549	549	501	549	549	549	549	549
	361	400	438	463	463	463	461	500	500	500	500	500
33	393	438	484	527	532	532	471	520	532	532	532	532
	329	364	399	432	435	435	420	460	468	468	468	468
34	370	412	456	496	516	516	443	490	516	516	516	516
	300	333	364	395	410	410	384	420	441	441	441	441
35	349	389	430	468	501	501	418	462	501	501	501	501
	275	305	333	361	389	389	351	384	415	415	415	415
36	330	367	406	442	487	487	395	436	475	487	487	487
	252	280	306	332	366	366	323	353	383	392	392	392
37	312	348	384	418	474	474	373	413	449	474	474	474
	232	257	282	305	344	344	297	325	352	374	374	374
38	296	329	364	396	461	461	354	391	426	461	461	461
	214	237	260	282	325	325	274	300	325	353	353	353
39	280	313	346	376	447	449	336	371	404	449	449	449
	198	219	240	260	306	308	253	277	300	333	333	333
40	266	297	328	357	424	438	319	353	384	438	438	438
	183	203	222	241	284	291	234	256	278	315	315	315
41	253	283	312	340	404	427	303	335	365	427	427	427
	170	189	206	224	263	277	217	238	258	300	300	300
42	241	269	297	324	384	417	289	320	348	413	417	417
	158	175	192	208	245	264	202	221	240	282	284	284
43	230	257	284	309	367	407	276	305	332	394	407	407
	147	163	179	194	228	252	188	206	223	263	270	270
44	220	245	271	295	350	398	263	291	317	376	398	398
	137	152	167	181	212	240	176	192	208	245	258	258
45	210	234	259	282	334	389	251	278	303	359	389	389
	128	142	156	169	198	229	164	179	195	229	246	246
46	201	224	248	270	320	380	241	266	290	344	380	380
	120	133	146	158	186	219	153	168	182	214	236	236
47	192	214	237	258	306	372	230	255	277	329	372	372
	112	125	136	148	174	210	144	157	171	201	226	226
48	184	206	227	247	294	365	221	244	266	315	362	365
	105	117	128	139	163	201	135	148	160	188	215	216
49	177	197	218	237	282	357	212	234	255	303	347	357
	99	110	120	130	153	193	127	139	150	177	202	207
50	170	189	209	228	270	350	203	225	245	291	333	350
	93	103	113	123	144	185	119	130	141	166	190	199
51	163	182	201	219	260	338	195	216	235	279	320	343
	88	97	106	115	136	175	112	123	133	157	179	192
52	157	175	193	210	250	325	188	208	226	268	308	336
	83	92	100	109	128	165	106	116	126	148	169	184
53	151	168	186	203	240	313	181	200	218	258	296	330
	78	87	95	103	121	156	100	109	119	140	159	177
54	145	162	179	195	232	301	174	192	209	249	285	324
	74	82	89	97	114	147	94	103	112	132	150	170
55	140	156	173	188	223	290	168	185	202	240	275	312
	70	77	85	92	108	139	89	98	106	125	142	161
56	135	151	166	181	215	280	162	179	195	231	265	301
	66	73	80	87	102	132	84	92	100	118	135	153
57							156	173	188	223	256	290
							80	88	95	112	128	145
58							151	167	181	215	247	280
							76	83	90	106	121	137
59							146	161	175	208	239	271
							72	79	86	101	115	130
60							141	156	169	201	231	262
							69	75	81	96	109	124

Figure 7.223 Standard load table for open web steel joists, K-Series.

STANDARD LOAD TABLE
LONGSPAN STEEL JOISTS, LH-SERIES

Based on a Maximum Allowable Tensile Stress of 30 ksi
Adopted by the Steel Joist Institute May 25, 1983;
Revised to May 1, 2000 – Effective August 1, 2002

Joist Designation	Approx. Wt in Lbs. Per Linear Ft (Joists only)	Depth in inches	SAFE LOAD* in Lbs. Between	CLEAR SPAN IN FEET																
			21-24	25	26	27	28	29	30	31	32	33	34	35	36				
18LH02	10	18	12000	468	442	418	391	367	345	324	306	289	273	259	245				
				313	284	259	234	212	193	175	160	147	135	124	114				
18LH03	11	18	13300	521	493	467	438	409	382	359	337	317	299	283	267				
				348	317	289	262	236	213	194	177	161	148	136	124				
18LH04	12	18	15500	604	571	535	500	469	440	413	388	365	344	325	308				
				403	367	329	296	266	242	219	200	182	167	153	141				
18LH05	15	18	17500	684	648	614	581	543	508	476	448	421	397	375	355				
				454	414	378	345	311	282	256	233	212	195	179	164				
18LH06	15	18	20700	809	749	696	648	605	566	531	499	470	443	418	396				
				526	469	419	377	340	307	280	254	232	212	195	180				
18LH07	17	18	21500	840	809	780	726	678	635	595	559	526	496	469	444				
				553	513	476	428	386	349	317	288	264	241	222	204				
18LH08	19	18	22400	876	843	812	784	758	717	680	641	604	571	540	512				
				577	534	496	462	427	387	351	320	292	267	246	226				
18LH09	21	18	24000	936	901	868	838	810	783	759	713	671	633	598	566				
				616	571	527	491	458	418	380	346	316	289	266	245				
			22-24	25	26	27	28	29	30	31	32	33	34	35	36	37	38	39	40
20LH02	10	20	11300	442	437	431	410	388	365	344	325	307	291	275	262	249	237	225	215
				306	303	298	274	250	228	208	190	174	160	147	136	126	117	108	101
20LH03	11	20	12000	469	463	458	452	414	414	395	372	352	333	316	299	283	269	255	243
				337	333	317	302	280	258	238	218	200	184	169	156	143	133	123	114
20LH04	12	20	14700	574	566	558	528	496	467	440	416	393	372	353	335	318	303	289	275
				428	406	386	352	320	291	265	243	223	205	189	174	161	149	139	129
20LH05	14	20	15800	616	609	602	595	571	544	513	484	458	434	411	390	371	353	336	321
				459	437	416	395	366	337	308	281	258	238	219	202	187	173	161	150
20LH06	15	20	21100	822	791	763	723	679	635	596	560	527	497	469	444	421	399	379	361
				606	561	521	477	427	386	351	320	292	267	246	226	209	192	178	165
20LH07	17	20	22500	878	845	814	786	760	711	667	627	590	556	526	497	471	447	425	404
				647	599	556	518	484	438	398	362	331	303	278	256	236	218	202	187
20LH08	19	20	23200	908	873	842	813	785	760	722	687	654	621	588	558	530	503	479	457
				669	619	575	536	500	468	428	395	365	336	309	285	262	242	225	209
20LH09	21	20	25400	990	953	918	886	856	828	802	778	755	712	673	636	603	572	544	517
				729	675	626	581	542	507	475	437	399	366	336	309	285	264	244	227
20LH10	23	20	27400	1068	1028	991	956	924	894	865	839	814	791	748	707	670	636	604	575
				786	724	673	626	585	545	510	479	448	411	377	346	320	296	274	254

Figure 7.224 Standard load table for open web steel joists, LH-Series.

STANDARD LOAD TABLE/LONG SPAN STEEL JOISTS, LH-SERIES
Based on a Maximum Allowable Tensile Stress of 30 ksi

Each cell is given as **safe load (top) / load for L/360 deflection (bottom)** in lbs.

CLEAR SPAN IN FEET — 33 to 48

Joist Designation	Approx. Wt in Lbs. Per Linear Ft. (Joists only)	Depth in inches	SAFELOAD* in Lbs. Between 28-32	33	34	35	36	37	38	39	40	41	42	43	44	45	46	47	48
24LH03	11	24	11500	342/235	339/226	336/218	323/204	307/188	293/175	279/162	267/152	255/141	244/132	234/124	224/116	215/109	207/102	199/96	191/90
24LH04	12	24	14100	419/288	398/265	379/246	360/227	343/210	327/195	312/182	298/169	285/158	273/148	262/138	251/130	241/122	231/114	222/107	214/101
24LH05	13	24	15100	449/308	446/297	440/285	419/264	399/244	380/226	363/210	347/196	331/182	317/171	304/160	291/150	280/141	269/132	258/124	248/117
24LH06	16	24	20300	604/411	579/382	555/356	530/331	504/306	480/284	457/263	437/245	417/228	399/211	381/197	364/184	348/172	334/161	320/152	307/142
24LH07	17	24	22300	665/452	638/421	613/393	588/367	565/343	541/320	516/297	491/276	468/257	446/239	426/223	407/208	389/195	373/182	357/171	343/161
24LH08	18	24	23800	707/480	677/447	649/416	622/388	597/362	572/338	545/314	520/292	497/272	475/254	455/238	435/222	417/208	400/196	384/184	369/173
24LH09	21	24	28000	832/562	808/530	785/501	764/460	731/424	696/393	663/363	632/337	602/313	574/292	548/272	524/254	501/238	480/223	460/209	441/196
24LH10	23	24	29600	882/596	856/559	832/528	809/500	788/474	768/439	737/406	702/378	668/351	637/326	608/304	582/285	556/266	533/249	511/234	490/220
24LH11	25	24	31200	927/624	900/588	875/555	851/525	829/498	807/472	787/449	768/418	734/388	701/361	671/337	642/315	616/294	590/276	567/259	544/243

CLEAR SPAN IN FEET — 41 to 56

Joist Designation	Approx. Wt	Depth	SAFELOAD 33-39 / 40	41	42	43	44	45	46	47	48	49	50	51	52	53	54	55	56
28LH05	13	28	14000 / 14000	337/219	323/205	310/192	297/180	286/169	275/159	265/150	255/142	245/133	237/126	228/119	220/113	213/107	206/102	199/97	193/92
28LH06	16	28	18600 / 18600	448/289	429/270	412/253	395/238	379/223	364/209	350/197	337/186	324/175	313/166	301/156	291/148	281/140	271/133	262/126	253/120
28LH07	17	28	21000 / 21000	505/326	484/305	464/285	445/267	427/251	410/236	394/222	379/209	365/197	352/186	339/176	327/166	316/158	305/150	295/142	285/135
28LH08	18	28	22500 / 22500	540/348	517/325	496/305	475/285	456/268	438/252	420/236	403/222	387/209	371/196	357/185	344/175	331/165	319/156	308/148	297/140
28LH09	21	28	27700 / 27700	667/428	639/400	612/375	586/351	563/329	540/309	519/291	499/274	481/258	463/243	446/228	430/216	415/204	401/193	387/183	374/173
28LH10	23	28	30300 / 30300	729/466	704/439	679/414	651/388	625/364	600/342	576/322	554/303	533/285	513/269	495/255	477/241	460/228	444/215	429/204	415/193
28LH11	25	28	32500 / 32500	780/498	762/475	736/448	711/423	682/397	655/373	629/351	605/331	582/312	561/294	540/278	521/263	502/249	485/236	468/223	453/212
28LH12	27	28	35700 / 35700	857/545	837/520	818/496	800/476	782/454	766/435	709/408	682/383	656/361	632/340	609/321	587/303	566/285	546/270	527/256	/243
28LH13	30	28	37200 / 37200	895/569	874/543	854/518	835/495	816/472	799/452	782/433	766/415	751/396	722/373	694/352	668/332	643/314	620/297	598/281	577/266

CLEAR SPAN IN FEET — 49 to 64

Joist Designation	Approx. Wt	Depth	SAFELOAD 38-46 / 47-48	49	50	51	52	53	54	55	56	57	58	59	60	61	62	63	64
32LH06	14	32	16700 / 16700	338/211	326/199	315/189	304/179	294/169	284/161	275/153	266/145	257/138	249/131	242/125	234/119	227/114	220/108	214/104	208/99
32LH07	16	32	18800 / 18800	379/235	366/223	353/211	341/200	329/189	318/179	308/170	298/162	288/154	279/146	271/140	262/133	254/127	247/121	240/116	233/111
32LH08	17	32	20400 / 20400	411/255	397/242	383/229	369/216	357/205	345/194	333/184	322/175	312/167	302/159	293/151	284/144	275/137	267/131	259/125	252/120
32LH09	21	32	25600 / 25600	516/319	498/302	480/285	463/270	447/256	432/243	418/230	404/219	391/208	379/198	367/189	356/180	345/172	335/164	325/157	315/149
32LH10	21	32	28300 / 28300	571/352	550/332	531/315	512/297	495/282	478/267	462/254	445/240	430/228	416/217	402/206	389/196	376/186	364/178	353/169	342/162
32LH11	24	32	31000 / 31000	625/385	602/363	580/343	560/325	541/308	522/292	505/277	488/263	473/251	458/239	443/227	429/216	416/206	403/196	390/187	378/179
32LH12	27	32	36400 / 36400	734/450	712/428	688/406	664/384	641/364	619/345	598/327	578/311	559/295	541/281	524/267	508/255	492/243	477/232	463/221	449/211
32LH13	30	32	40600 / 40600	817/500	801/480	785/461	771/444	742/420	715/397	690/376	666/354	643/336	621/319	600/304	581/288	562/275	544/262	527/249	511/238
32LH14	33	32	41800 / 41800	843/515	826/495	810/476	795/458	780/440	766/417	738/395	713/374	688/355	665/337	643/321	622/304	602/290	583/276	564/264	547/251
32LH15	35	32	43200 / 43200	870/532	853/511	837/492	821/473	805/454	791/438	776/422	763/407	750/393	725/374	701/355	671/338	656/322	635/306	616/292	597/279

CLEAR SPAN IN FEET — 57 to 72

Joist Designation	Approx. Wt	Depth	SAFELOAD 42-46 / 47-56	57	58	59	60	61	62	63	64	65	66	67	68	69	70	71	72
36LH07	16	36	16800 / 16800	292/177	283/168	274/160	266/153	258/146	251/140	244/134	237/128	230/122	224/117	218/112	212/107	207/103	201/99	196/95	191/91
36LH08	18	36	18500 / 18500	321/194	311/185	302/176	293/168	284/160	276/153	268/146	260/140	253/134	246/128	239/123	233/118	227/113	221/109	215/104	209/100
36LH09	21	36	23700 / 23700	411/247	398/235	386/224	374/214	363/204	352/195	342/186	333/179	323/171	314/163	306/157	297/150	289/144	282/138	275/133	267/127
36LH10	21	36	26100 / 26100	454/273	440/260	426/248	413/236	401/225	389/215	378/206	367/197	357/188	347/180	338/173	328/165	320/159	311/152	303/146	295/140
36LH11	23	36	28500 / 28500	495/297	480/283	465/269	451/257	438/246	425/234	412/224	401/214	389/205	378/196	368/188	358/180	348/173	339/166	330/159	322/153
36LH12	25	36	34100 / 34100	593/354	575/338	557/322	540/307	523/292	508/279	493/267	478/255	464/243	450/232	437/222	424/213	412/204	400/195	389/187	378/179
36LH13	30	36	40100 / 40100	697/415	675/395	654/376	634/359	615/342	596/327	579/312	562/298	546/285	531/273	516/262	502/251	488/240	475/231	463/222	451/213
36LH14	36	36	44200 / 44200	768/456	755/434	729/412	706/392	683/373	661/356	641/339	621/323	602/309	584/295	567/283	551/270	535/259	520/247	505/237	492/228
36LH15	36	36	46600 / 46600	809/480	795/464	781/448	769/434	744/413	721/394	698/375	677/358	656/342	637/327	618/312	600/299	583/286	567/274	551/263	536/252

Figure 7.225 Standard load table for open web steel joists, LH-Series.

STANDARD LOAD TABLE/LONG SPAN STEEL JOISTS, LH-SERIES
Based on a Maximum Allowable Tensile Stress of 30 ksi

Joist Designation	Approx. Wt in Lbs. Per Linear Ft. (Joists Only)	Depth in inches	SAFELOAD* in Lbs. Between		CLEAR SPAN IN FEET															
			47-59	60-64	65	66	67	68	69	70	71	72	73	74	75	76	77	78	79	80
40LH08	16	40	16600	16600	254	247	241	234	228	222	217	211	206	201	196	192	187	183	178	174
					150	144	138	132	127	122	117	112	108	104	100	97	93	90	86	83
40LH09	21	40	21800	21800	332	323	315	306	298	291	283	276	269	263	256	250	244	239	233	228
					196	188	180	173	166	160	153	147	141	136	131	126	122	118	113	109
40LH10	21	40	24000	24000	367	357	347	338	329	321	313	305	297	290	283	276	269	262	255	249
					216	207	198	190	183	176	169	162	156	150	144	139	134	129	124	119
40LH11	22	40	26200	26200	399	388	378	368	358	349	340	332	323	315	308	300	293	286	279	273
					234	224	215	207	198	190	183	176	169	163	157	151	145	140	135	130
40LH12	25	40	31900	31900	486	472	459	447	435	424	413	402	392	382	373	364	355	346	338	330
					285	273	261	251	241	231	222	213	205	197	189	182	176	169	163	157
40LH13	30	40	37600	37600	573	557	542	528	514	500	487	475	463	451	440	429	419	409	399	390
					334	320	307	295	283	271	260	250	241	231	223	214	207	199	192	185
40LH14	35	40	43000	43000	656	638	620	603	587	571	556	542	528	515	502	490	478	466	455	444
					383	367	351	336	323	309	297	285	273	263	252	243	233	225	216	209
40LH15	36	40	48100	48100	734	712	691	671	652	633	616	599	583	567	552	538	524	511	498	486
					427	408	390	373	357	342	328	315	302	290	279	268	258	248	239	230
40LH16	42	40	53000	53000	808	796	784	772	761	751	730	710	691	673	655	638	622	606	591	576
					469	455	441	428	416	404	387	371	356	342	329	316	304	292	282	271

			52-59	60-72	73	74	75	76	77	78	79	80	81	82	83	84	85	86	87	88
44LH09	19	44	20000	20000	272	265	259	253	247	242	236	231	226	221	216	211	207	202	198	194
					158	152	146	141	136	131	127	122	118	114	110	106	103	99	96	93
44LH10	21	44	22100	22100	300	293	286	279	272	266	260	254	249	243	238	233	228	223	218	214
					174	168	162	155	150	144	139	134	130	125	121	117	113	110	106	103
44LH11	22	44	23900	23900	325	317	310	302	295	289	282	276	269	264	258	252	247	242	236	232
					188	181	175	168	162	157	151	146	140	136	131	127	123	119	115	111
44LH12	25	44	29600	29600	402	393	383	374	365	356	347	339	331	323	315	308	300	293	287	280
					232	224	215	207	200	192	185	179	172	166	160	155	149	144	139	134
44LH13	30	44	35100	35100	477	466	454	444	433	423	413	404	395	386	377	369	361	353	346	338
					275	265	254	246	236	228	220	212	205	198	191	185	179	173	167	161
44LH14	31	44	40400	40400	549	534	520	506	493	481	469	457	446	436	425	415	406	396	387	379
					315	302	291	279	268	259	249	240	231	223	215	207	200	193	187	181
44LH15	36	44	47000	47000	639	623	608	593	579	565	551	537	524	512	500	488	476	466	455	445
					366	352	339	326	314	303	292	281	271	261	252	243	234	227	219	211
44LH16	42	44	54200	54200	737	719	701	684	668	652	637	622	608	594	580	568	555	543	531	520
					421	405	390	375	362	348	336	324	313	302	291	282	272	263	255	246
44LH17	47	44	58200	58200	790	780	769	759	750	732	715	699	683	667	652	638	624	610	597	584
					450	438	426	415	405	390	376	363	351	338	327	316	305	295	285	276

			56-59	60-80	81	82	83	84	85	86	87	88	89	90	91	92	93	94	95	96
48LH10	21	48	20000	20000	246	241	236	231	226	221	217	212	208	204	200	196	192	188	185	181
					141	136	132	127	123	119	116	112	108	105	102	99	96	93	90	87
48LH11	22	48	21700	21700	266	260	255	249	244	239	234	229	225	220	216	212	208	204	200	196
					152	147	142	137	133	129	125	120	117	113	110	106	103	100	97	94
48LH12	25	48	27400	27400	336	329	322	315	308	301	295	289	283	277	272	266	261	256	251	246
					191	185	179	173	167	161	156	151	147	142	138	133	129	126	122	118
48LH13	29	48	32800	32800	402	393	384	376	368	360	353	345	338	332	325	318	312	306	300	294
					228	221	213	206	199	193	187	180	175	170	164	159	154	150	145	141
48LH14	32	48	38700	38700	475	464	454	444	434	425	416	407	399	390	383	375	367	360	353	346
					269	260	251	243	234	227	220	212	206	199	193	187	181	176	171	165
48LH15	36	48	44500	44500	545	533	521	510	499	488	478	468	458	448	439	430	422	413	405	397
					308	298	287	278	269	260	252	244	236	228	221	214	208	201	195	189
48LH16	42	48	51300	51300	629	615	601	588	576	563	551	540	528	518	507	497	487	477	468	459
					355	343	331	320	310	299	289	280	271	263	255	247	239	232	225	218
48LH17	47	48	57600	57600	706	690	675	660	646	632	619	606	593	581	569	558	547	536	525	515
					397	383	371	358	346	335	324	314	304	294	285	276	268	260	252	245

Figure 7.226 Standard load table for open web steel joists, LH-Series.

STANDARD LOAD TABLE
DEEP LONGSPAN STEEL JOISTS, DLH-SERIES

Based on a Maximum Allowable Tensile Stress of 30 ksi
Adopted by the Steel Joist Institute May 25, 1983;
Revised to May 1, 2000 – Effective August 1, 2002

Joist Designation	Approx. Wt in Lbs. Per Linear Ft (Joists only)	Depth in inches	SAFELOAD* in Lbs. Between	CLEAR SPAN IN FEET															
			61-88	89	90	91	92	93	94	95	96	97	98	99	100	101	102	103	104
52DLH10	25	52	26700	298	291	285	279	273	267	261	256	251	246	241	236	231	227	223	218
				171	165	159	154	150	145	140	136	132	128	124	120	116	114	110	107
52DLH11	26	52	29300	327	320	313	306	299	293	287	281	275	270	264	259	254	249	244	240
				187	181	174	169	164	158	153	149	144	140	135	132	128	124	120	117
52DLH12	29	52	32700	365	357	349	342	334	327	320	314	307	301	295	289	284	278	273	268
				204	197	191	185	179	173	168	163	158	153	149	144	140	135	132	128
52DLH13	34	52	39700	443	433	424	414	406	397	389	381	373	366	358	351	344	338	331	325
				247	239	231	224	216	209	203	197	191	185	180	174	170	164	159	155
52DLH14	39	52	45400	507	497	486	476	466	457	447	438	430	421	413	405	397	390	382	375
				276	266	258	249	242	234	227	220	213	207	201	194	189	184	178	173
52DLH15	42	52	51000	569	557	545	533	522	511	500	490	480	470	461	451	443	434	426	418
				311	301	291	282	272	264	256	247	240	233	226	219	213	207	201	195
52DLH16	45	52	55000	614	601	588	575	563	551	540	528	518	507	497	487	478	468	459	451
				346	335	324	314	304	294	285	276	267	260	252	245	237	230	224	217
52DLH17	52	52	63300	706	691	676	661	647	634	620	608	595	583	572	560	549	539	528	518
				395	381	369	357	346	335	324	315	304	296	286	279	270	263	255	247

Joist Designation	Approx. Wt in Lbs. Per Linear Ft (Joists only)	Depth in inches	SAFELOAD* in Lbs. Between	CLEAR SPAN IN FEET															
			66-96	97	98	99	100	101	102	103	104	105	106	107	108	109	110	111	112
56DLH11	26	56	28100	288	283	277	272	267	262	257	253	248	244	239	235	231	227	223	219
				169	163	158	153	149	145	140	136	133	129	125	122	118	115	113	110
56DLH12	30	56	32300	331	324	318	312	306	300	295	289	284	278	273	268	263	259	254	249
				184	178	173	168	163	158	153	150	145	141	137	133	130	126	123	119
56DLH13	34	56	39100	401	394	386	379	372	365	358	351	344	338	331	325	319	314	308	303
				223	216	209	204	197	191	186	181	175	171	166	161	157	152	149	145
56DLH14	39	56	44200	453	444	435	427	419	411	403	396	388	381	375	368	361	355	349	343
				249	242	234	228	221	214	209	202	196	190	186	181	175	171	167	162
56DLH15	42	56	50500	518	508	498	488	478	469	460	451	443	434	426	419	411	403	396	389
				281	272	264	256	248	242	234	228	221	215	209	204	198	192	186	182
56DLH16	46	56	54500	559	548	537	526	516	506	496	487	478	469	460	452	444	436	428	420
				313	304	294	285	277	269	262	254	247	240	233	227	221	214	209	204
56DLH17	51	56	62800	643	630	618	605	594	582	571	560	549	539	529	520	510	501	492	483
				356	345	335	325	316	306	298	289	281	273	266	258	251	245	238	231

Figure 7.227 Standard load table for open web steel joists, DLH-Series.

STANDARD LOAD TABLE/DEEP LONGSPAN STEEL JOISTS, DLH-SERIES
Based on a Maximum Allowable Tensile Stress of 30 ksi

Joist Designation	Approx. Wt in Lbs. Per Linear Ft (Joists only)	Depth in inches	SAFE LOAD* in Lbs. Between 70-99	100-104	105	106	107	108	109	110	111	112	113	114	115	116	117	118	119	120
60DLH12	29	60	31100	31100	295	289	284	279	274	270	265	261	256	252	248	244	240	236	232	228
					168	163	158	154	150	146	142	138	134	131	128	124	121	118	115	113
60DLH13	35	60	37800	37800	358	351	345	339	333	327	322	316	311	306	301	296	291	286	282	277
					203	197	191	187	181	176	171	167	163	158	154	151	147	143	139	135
60DLH14	40	60	42000	42000	398	391	383	376	370	363	356	350	344	338	332	327	321	316	310	305
					216	210	205	199	193	189	183	178	173	170	165	161	156	152	149	145
60DLH15	43	60	49300	49300	467	458	450	442	434	427	419	412	405	398	392	385	379	373	367	361
					255	248	242	235	228	223	216	210	205	200	194	190	185	180	175	171
60DLH16	46	60	54200	54200	513	504	494	485	476	468	460	451	444	436	428	421	414	407	400	393
					285	277	269	262	255	247	241	235	228	223	217	211	206	201	196	190
60DLH17	52	60	62300	62300	590	579	569	558	548	538	529	519	510	501	493	484	476	468	460	453
					324	315	306	298	290	283	275	267	261	254	247	241	235	228	223	217
60DLH18	59	60	71900	71900	681	668	656	644	632	621	610	599	589	578	568	559	549	540	531	522
					366	357	346	337	327	319	310	303	294	286	279	272	266	259	252	246

Joist Designation	Approx. Wt	Depth	75-99	100-112	113	114	115	116	117	118	119	120	121	122	123	124	125	126	127	128
64DLH12	31	64	30000	30000	264	259	255	251	247	243	239	235	231	228	224	221	218	214	211	208
					153	150	146	142	138	135	132	129	125	122	119	116	114	111	109	106
64DLH13	34	64	36400	36400	321	315	310	305	300	295	291	286	281	277	273	269	264	260	257	253
					186	181	176	171	168	163	159	155	152	148	144	141	137	134	131	128
64DLH14	40	64	41700	41700	367	360	354	349	343	337	332	326	321	316	311	306	301	296	292	287
					199	193	189	184	179	174	171	166	162	158	154	151	147	143	140	136
64DLH15	43	64	47800	47800	421	414	407	400	394	387	381	375	369	363	358	352	347	341	336	331
					234	228	223	217	211	206	201	196	191	187	182	177	173	170	165	161
64DLH16	46	64	53800	53800	474	466	458	450	443	435	428	421	414	407	401	394	388	382	376	370
					262	254	248	242	235	229	224	218	213	208	203	198	193	189	184	180
64DLH17	52	64	62000	62000	546	536	527	518	509	501	492	484	476	468	461	454	446	439	432	426
					298	290	283	275	268	262	255	248	243	237	231	226	220	215	210	205
64DLH18	59	64	71600	71600	630	619	608	598	587	578	568	559	549	540	532	523	515	507	499	491
					337	328	320	311	304	296	288	282	274	267	261	255	249	243	237	232

Joist Designation	Approx. Wt	Depth	80-99	100-120	121	122	123	124	125	126	127	128	129	130	131	132	133	134	135	136
68DLH13	37	68	35000	35000	288	284	279	275	271	267	263	259	255	252	248	244	241	237	234	231
					171	168	164	159	155	152	149	145	142	138	135	133	130	127	124	121
68DLH14	40	68	40300	40300	332	327	322	317	312	308	303	299	294	290	286	281	277	273	269	266
					184	179	175	171	167	163	159	155	152	148	145	141	138	135	133	130
68DLH15	44	68	45200	45200	372	365	360	354	348	343	337	332	327	322	317	312	308	303	299	294
					206	201	196	191	187	182	178	174	170	166	162	158	155	152	148	145
68DLH16	49	68	53600	53600	441	433	427	420	413	407	400	394	388	382	376	371	365	360	354	349
					242	236	230	225	219	214	209	204	199	195	190	186	182	178	174	171
68DLH17	55	68	60400	60400	497	489	481	474	467	460	453	446	439	433	427	420	414	408	403	397
					275	268	262	256	249	244	238	232	228	222	217	212	208	203	198	194
68DLH18	61	68	69900	69900	575	566	557	549	540	532	524	516	508	501	493	486	479	472	465	459
					311	304	297	289	283	276	269	263	257	251	246	240	234	230	225	219
68DLH19	67	68	80500	80500	662	651	641	631	621	611	601	592	583	574	565	557	548	540	532	525
					353	344	336	328	320	313	305	298	291	285	278	272	266	260	254	248

Joist Designation	Approx. Wt	Depth	84-99	100-128	129	130	131	132	133	134	135	136	137	138	139	140	141	142	143	144
72DLH14	41	72	39200	39200	303	298	294	290	285	281	277	274	270	266	262	259	255	252	248	245
					171	167	163	159	155	152	149	146	143	139	136	133	131	128	125	123
72DLH15	44	72	44900	44900	347	342	336	331	326	322	317	312	308	303	299	295	291	286	282	279
					191	187	183	178	174	171	167	163	160	156	152	150	147	143	140	137
72DLH16	50	72	51900	51900	401	395	390	384	378	373	368	363	358	353	348	343	338	334	329	325
					225	219	214	209	205	200	196	191	188	183	179	175	171	169	165	161
72DLH17	56	72	58400	58400	451	445	438	432	426	420	414	408	402	397	391	386	381	376	371	366
					256	250	245	239	233	228	224	218	213	209	205	200	196	191	188	184
72DLH18	59	72	68400	68400	528	520	512	505	497	490	483	479	470	463	457	450	444	438	432	426
					289	283	276	270	265	258	252	247	242	236	231	227	222	217	212	209
72DLH19	70	72	80200	80200	619	609	600	591	582	573	565	557	549	541	533	526	518	511	504	497
					328	321	313	306	300	293	286	280	274	268	263	257	251	247	241	236

Figure 7.228 Standard load table for open web steel joists, DLH-Series.

VULCRAFT SLH / GENERAL INFORMATION

VULCRAFT LOAD TABLE
SUPER LONGSPAN STEEL JOISTS, SLH-SERIES

JANUARY 1, 1991

Based on a Maximum Allowable Tensile Stress of 30,000 psi

Joist Designation	Approx. Wt. In Lbs. per Linear Ft. (Joists Only)	Depth In Inches	Safe Load In Lbs. Between 80-110	111	114	117	120	123	126	129	132	135	138	141	144	147	150	155	
80SLH15	40	80	52,000	466	442	421	401	383	366	350	335	321	307	295	283	272	261	244	228
				321	296	275	255	236	220	205	192	179	167	157	147	139	130	118	107
80SLH16	46	80	62,500	560	535	509	485	461	439	419	400	383	366	350	336	322	309	289	271
				375	347	321	297	276	257	240	224	209	196	184	172	162	162	138	126
80SLH17	53	80	72,200	647	617	587	559	533	510	487	466	446	427	410	393	378	363	340	319
				451	416	386	358	332	309	288	269	252	235	221	207	195	183	166	151
80SLH18	60	80	81,600	731	696	662	631	602	575	550	526	504	482	463	444	427	410	384	361
				516	477	441	409	380	354	330	308	288	270	253	237	223	210	190	173
80SLH19	67	80	95,200	853	812	773	736	701	670	640	612	585	560	537	516	495	476	445	418
				578	533	493	458	425	396	369	344	322	301	283	266	250	235	213	193
80SLH20	75	80	107,000	964	921	882	845	807	771	736	704	674	645	618	594	570	547	513	481
				646	596	552	512	475	443	412	385	360	337	316	297	279	263	238	216

Joist Designation	Approx. Wt. In Lbs. per Linear Ft. (Joists Only)	Depth In Inches	Safe Load In Lbs. Between 88-119	120	123	126	129	132	135	138	141	144	147	150	155	160	165	170	175
88SLH16	46	88	62,000	514	490	467	447	428	410	394	378	363	349	335	314	295	278	262	248
				361	336	313	291	272	254	238	223	210	197	186	168	153	140	127	117
88SLH17	51	88	70,100	581	553	526	502	479	458	439	420	403	386	371	347	326	306	288	271
				404	375	349	325	304	284	266	249	234	220	207	187	170	156	143	130
88SLH18	58	88	80,400	667	635	605	577	551	527	504	483	463	444	426	399	374	352	331	312
				460	427	397	370	346	323	303	284	267	250	236	214	195	177	162	149
88SLH19	65	88	93,000	771	734	699	666	636	608	582	557	534	513	492	461	432	406	382	360
				521	484	450	420	392	367	343	322	302	284	267	243	221	201	184	169
88SLH20	76	88	107,000	889	854	821	789	755	723	694	665	639	614	590	553	520	489	461	435
				623	579	539	502	469	438	410	385	361	340	320	290	264	241	220	202
88SLH21	89	88	132,000	1099	1045	996	950	907	867	829	794	762	731	702	657	616	579	544	513
				724	673	626	584	545	509	477	447	420	395	372	337	307	280	256	235

CLEAR SPAN IN FEET

NUCOR
VULCRAFT - GROUP

Figure 7.229 Standard load table for open web steel joists, SLH-Series. (Copyright 2004 by Steel Joist Institute and the Vulcraft Group of Nucor. Reprinted with permission. All rights reserved.)

VULCRAFT LOAD TABLE
SUPER LONGSPAN STEEL JOISTS, SLH-SERIES

Based on a Maximum Allowable Tensile Stress of 30,000 psi

Joist Designation	Approx. Wt. In Lbs. per Linear Ft. (Joists Only)	Depth In Inches	Safe Load In Lbs. Between	CLEAR SPAN IN FEET															
			96-128	129	132	135	138	141	144	147	150	155	160	165	170	175	180	185	190
96SLH17	52	96	70,000	540	517	496	474	456	438	421	405	380	357	335	316	298	281	266	252
				389	363	339	318	298	280	263	247	224	204	186	170	156	143	132	122
96SLH18	58	96	78,800	608	583	559	535	513	493	475	457	430	405	381	360	340	322	305	289
				443	413	386	362	340	319	300	282	256	232	212	194	178	163	150	139
96SLH19	66	96	94,200	727	697	667	638	611	585	561	539	505	474	445	419	396	373	353	334
				502	469	438	410	385	361	340	320	290	264	241	220	202	186	171	158
96SLH20	74	96	106,000	824	789	754	722	691	662	635	610	571	536	504	475	448	423	400	378
				569	531	496	465	436	409	385	362	329	299	272	249	229	210	193	178
96SLH21	90	96	133,000	1027	982	940	900	864	829	797	766	719	675	635	598	564	533	504	477
				698	652	610	571	535	503	473	445	404	367	335	306	281	258	238	220
96SLH22	102	96	149,000	1150	1108	1067	1028	991	957	921	886	832	782	736	694	656	620	587	556
				811	757	708	663	622	584	549	517	469	426	389	355	326	300	276	255

Joist Designation	Wt.	Depth	Safe Load **104-137**	138	141	144	147	150	155	160	165	170	175	180	185	190	195	200	205
104SLH18	59	104	76,800	554	532	512	489	172	444	418	396	374	354	335	318	302	287	273	260
				426	400	375	353	332	301	274	250	229	209	192	177	164	152	140	130
104SLH19	67	104	93,400	674	647	622	598	574	539	507	479	452	427	404	383	364	346	325	312
				484	453	426	401	377	342	311	284	260	238	218	201	186	172	160	148
104SLH20	75	104	105,000	764	738	714	688	661	621	583	548	516	487	460	435	413	391	371	353
				548	513	483	453	427	387	352	321	293	269	247	228	210	195	181	167
104SLH21	90	104	132,000	956	917	881	847	813	763	718	677	639	604	571	541	514	488	464	441
				673	632	593	558	525	476	433	395	361	331	301	280	259	240	222	206
104SLH22	104	104	148,000	1071	1034	999	966	934	883	830	783	738	698	660	626	594	564	536	511
				783	734	689	648	610	553	503	459	420	385	353	326	301	278	258	240
104SLH23	109	104	163,000	1181	1141	1096	1052	1009	945	887	834	785	741	700	662	628	595	565	537
				819	768	721	678	638	578	526	480	439	403	370	341	315	291	270	250

Joist Designation	Wt.	Depth	Safe Load **112-146**	147	150	155	160	165	170	175	180	185	190	195	200	205	210	215	220
112LSH19	67	112	91,900	623	600	564	530	500	472	446	424	402	382	362	345	329	314	300	286
				466	439	398	362	330	302	276	255	234	216	200	186	172	160	149	140
112SLH20	76	112	104,000	710	688	649	610	575	543	514	488	463	440	417	398	379	361	345	330
				528	497	450	410	374	342	313	288	266	245	227	210	195	181	169	158
112SLH21	91	112	131,000	891	858	805	757	713	673	637	603	572	543	516	491	468	446	426	407
				650	612	555	504	460	421	386	355	327	301	279	259	240	224	208	195
112SLH22	104	112	147,000	999	967	918	871	824	778	736	697	661	628	596	568	541	516	492	470
				755	711	644	586	535	489	449	412	380	350	324	301	279	260	242	226
112SLH23	110	112	162,000	1102	1067	1012	959	901	848	800	756	716	679	644	612	582	554	528	504
				790	744	674	613	560	512	469	431	397	367	340	315	292	272	253	236
112SLH24	131	112	192,000	1304	1263	1199	1139	1074	1014	959	909	862	819	778	741	706	673	642	613
				957	901	817	743	678	620	569	523	481	444	411	381	354	329	307	287

Joist Designation	Wt.	Depth	Safe Load **102-164**	165	170	175	180	185	190	195	200	205	210	215	220	230	235	240	
120SLH20	77	120	98,900	597	564	532	505	479	456	434	414	395	376	359	344	329	315	302	290
				430	393	361	332	306	282	261	242	225	209	195	182	170	159	149	140
120SLH21	92	120	123,000	748	706	667	632	599	570	542	516	492	469	448	428	410	392	376	360
				530	485	444	409	376	347	321	298	277	258	240	224	209	196	184	173
120SLH22	104	120	141,000	855	815	770	729	692	658	626	596	568	542	517	495	473	453	434	416
				616	564	516	475	438	404	374	347	322	300	279	261	244	228	214	201
120SLH23	111	120	156,000	943	898	848	804	763	725	690	657	626	596	569	543	519	496	475	455
				644	590	541	497	458	423	391	363	336	313	292	272	255	238	224	210
120SLH24	132	120	185,000	1117	1062	1003	950	902	858	816	777	741	706	675	645	617	591	566	543
				781	715	655	603	555	512	474	440	408	380	354	330	309	289	271	255
120SLH25	152	120	212,000	1284	1218	1152	1092	1036	984	936	891	850	811	775	741	709	678	650	623
				915	837	768	706	650	600	555	515	478	445	415	387	362	339	318	298

NUCOR
VULCRAFT - GROUP

Figure 7.230 Standard load table for open web steel joists, SLH-Series. (Copyright 2004 by Steel Joist Institute and the Vulcraft Group of Nucor. Reprinted with permission. All rights reserved.)

DESIGN GUIDE WEIGHT TABLE FOR JOIST GIRDERS
U. S. CUSTOMARY

Based on an allowable tensile stress of 30ksi

Girder Span (ft)	Joist Spaces (ft)	Girder Depth (in)	4K	5K	6K	7K	8K	9K	10K	11K	12K	14K	16K	18K	20K	25K	30K	35K	40K	50K	60K	70K	80K	100K
												Joist Girder Weight – Pounds Per Linear Foot — Load on Each Panel Point												
20	2N@10.00	16	16	16	16	16	16	16	16	17	18	21	23	26	30	35	41	47	54	69	83	100	108	140
		20	16	16	16	16	16	16	16	16	17	17	19	22	24	31	35	39	44	56	64	76	85	104
		24	16	16	16	16	16	16	17	17	17	17	17	19	20	26	29	34	37	48	57	66	73	88
	3N@6.67	16	16	16	16	16	16	18	20	22	24	27	31	35	38	48	54	69	79	101	114	141	152	187
		20	16	16	16	16	16	16	17	19	21	23	26	28	31	38	47	56	64	78	95	109	117	156
		24	16	16	17	17	17	17	17	18	19	23	25	26	31	34	38	45	51	67	80	97	109	122
	4N@5.00	16	16	16	18	20	22	26	28	29	32	38	42	50	54	66	83	100	108	140	162	188	209	314
		20	16	16	16	17	20	20	21	23	26	30	34	39	43	52	60	76	85	105	124	145	169	238
		24	16	16	16	16	17	19	20	21	22	25	28	32	38	44	54	61	75	89	107	126	149	189
	5N@4.00	16	16	18	19	24	26	29	33	37	39	47	54	59	66	83	101	113	140	172	212	247	296	
		20	16	16	17	19	21	26	28	29	32	37	41	49	53	65	80	95	104	134	167	198	221	296
		24	16	16	17	19	20	22	24	28	28	31	35	39	45	55	67	78	88	109	128	152	183	244
	10N@2.00	16	28	33	39	47	54	62	72	78	83	101	109	131	141	195	226	247	358					
		20	23	29	31	37	43	49	56	61	64	77	86	104	108	145	179	203	236	317				
		24	21	25	28	32	39	43	46	55	54	66	80	84	89	119	141	171		197	250	313		
30	2N@15.00	24	29	29	29	29	29	29	30	30	31	32	33	35	37	40	46	53	60	72	85	102	103	139
		28	29	29	29	29	29	30	30	30	30	32	32	34	36	38	41	44	49	65	74	86	92	115
		32	30	30	30	30	30	30	30	30	30	31	32	33	34	37	40	41	45	55	66	75	89	106
		36	30	30	30	30	30	30	30	30	30	31	32	32	33	36	38	41	42	51	60	68	76	95
	3N@10.00	24	15	16	16	16	18	19	22	24	25	29	31	34	38	48	57	65	74	91	109	130	151	176
		28	16	16	16	16	16	17	20	21	24	25	28	31	33	43	50	58	67	79	94	108	126	156
		32	16	16	16	16	16	17	18	19	21	25	26	29	30	38	45	51	60	69	89	96	110	136
		36	16	17	17	17	17	17	17	18	20	24	26	27	30	34	42	46	55	70	80	92	99	122
	4N@7.5	24	16	16	17	20	24	26	27	30	32	37	42	47	54	66	78	99	104	140	161	183	210	265
		28	16	16	17	18	21	23	25	27	28	33	37	42	46	56	71	79	93	110	143	156	179	223
		32	16	16	16	18	19	20	21	23	27	29	32	36	41	50	60	69	76	104	112	146	149	202
		36	16	16	17	17	18	19	21	22	24	27	30	35	38	45	54	62	71	87	106	115	147	184
	5N@6.00	24	16	17	20	23	26	29	32	34	38	45	53	58	62	78	100	108	131	162	193	231	262	
		28	16	16	19	21	24	27	28	31	34	38	46	49	56	71	79	102	107	143	166	195	224	285
		32	16	16	17	19	21	25	26	28	31	36	39	44	50	64	73	85	104	118	147	177	198	248
		36	16	17	17	19	21	22	25	27	29	31	38	40	44	58	66	76	88	108	127	151	179	220
	6N@5.00	24	17	19	24	28	31	34	39	42	47	54	62	69	78	100	109	140	161	190	237	288		
		28	16	19	20	26	28	31	34	37	40	46	52	60	67	84	102	111	143	167	195	222	289	
		32	16	17	20	22	26	28	31	32	35	41	47	53	60	74	87	106	113	148	175	200	237	304
		36	17	18	19	21	24	28	28	30	33	38	44	49	55	67	79	90	108	129	154	180	206	275
	8N@3.75	24	21	25	31	36	41	47	50	58	62	73	83	100	102	131	162	188	216	255				
		28	20	23	29	32	37	40	44	49	53	61	72	81	86	111	144	147	175	224	281			
		32	19	22	26	30	32	36	41	45	50	57	65	75	82	105	114	147	159	204	242	308	343	
		36	19	21	24	28	30	35	38	39	43	53	59	69	74	89	111	118	152	185	218	256	314	
	15N@2.00	24	40	50	58	66	78	92	101	106	115	142	165	181	196	257	326							
		28	34	41	52	60	68	76	85	103	105	113	137	152	176	216	265	329						
		32	30	39	47	54	62	73	77	83	91	111	117	133	159	195	242	275	325					
		36	29	35	42	49	56	66	72	79	82	103	117	127	142	183	222	260	290					

Bearing Depth	7 1/2 in.	10 in.

NUCOR
VULCRAFT - GROUP

Figure 7.231 Design guide weight table for joist girders. (Copyright by Steel Joist Institute and the Vulcraft Group of Nucor. Reprinted with permission. All rights reserved.)

DESIGN GUIDE WEIGHT TABLE FOR JOIST GIRDERS
U. S. CUSTOMARY

Based on an allowable tensile stress of 30ksi

Girder Span (ft)	Joist Spaces (ft)	Girder Depth (in)	Joist Girder Weight – Pounds Per Linear Foot — Load on Each Panel Point																				
			4K	5K	6K	7K	8K	9K	10K	11K	12K	14K	16K	18K	20K	25K	30K	35K	40K	50K	60K	70K	80K	100K
40	3N@ 13.33	32	22	23	23	23	24	24	25	26	27	30	34	38	40	51	60	69	81	94	108	124	150	185
		36	23	23	23	23	23	24	25	25	27	27	32	34	39	46	54	61	70	87	104	111	126	164
		40	23	23	23	23	23	23	24	25	27	27	28	32	35	43	49	55	62	84	93	107	125	156
		44	23	23	23	23	24	24	24	26	26	28	28	32	33	42	47	55	63	73	89	99	115	131
		48	23	24	24	24	24	24	24	26	26	29	29	29	32	38	44	51	57	70	80	92	102	131
	4N@ 10.00	32	16	16	19	22	25	26	28	30	33	39	45	50	53	68	77	90	104	129	152	173	202	252
		36	16	17	18	21	25	25	26	29	31	34	40	44	48	62	71	79	93	115	143	166	179	230
		40	17	17	17	19	23	25	26	27	29	32	38	41	46	56	68	77	93	109	119	150	172	212
		44	16	16	18	18	20	21	23	24	28	30	34	37	40	51	57	66	76	104	111	126	150	189
		48	17	17	18	18	19	20	23	25	26	28	32	34	37	49	58	66	74	87	108	116	139	178
	5N@ 8.00	32	16	18	22	25	28	31	34	37	40	46	54	58	65	78	100	106	130	157	188	227	255	
		36	16	17	20	23	25	27	31	34	35	41	46	54	59	71	91	102	107	143	167	196	230	298
		40	16	16	18	21	23	27	28	30	33	37	42	47	53	64	80	93	104	128	159	182	210	262
		44	17	17	17	20	23	24	28	29	31	35	39	46	49	60	73	81	96	116	138	161	186	245
		48	17	17	17	19	23	25	25	28	29	33	37	41	47	57	67	80	93	111	122	152	178	217
	6N@ 6.67	32	17	20	24	28	32	35	39	42	47	54	62	69	77	99	108	140	151	189	220	266		
		36	17	20	23	26	28	31	35	38	41	48	55	62	70	83	102	115	142	167	197	232	275	
		40	17	18	21	25	28	29	32	36	38	44	49	56	64	79	94	105	118	147	185	215	245	313
		44	17	18	21	22	27	29	30	33	36	42	49	53	58	74	86	105	111	148	177	199	227	294
		48	17	18	20	24	25	28	29	31	33	40	44	52	55	72	79	98	108	130	156	180	204	271
	7N@ 5.71	32	19	24	28	32	34	40	45	47	54	62	70	77	91	105	130	152	175	218	255			
		36	18	21	26	28	32	35	40	43	48	56	63	71	79	102	115	143	155	197	232	276		
		40	18	20	25	28	31	33	36	41	45	51	57	65	72	94	108	118	145	184	214	255	300	
		44	18	21	23	27	29	31	34	37	41	50	58	63	67	82	106	113	127	167	199	237	272	
		48	18	22	24	27	30	33	37	39	42	48	57	63	71	81	99	114	125	169	195	234	267	
	8N@ 5.00	32	21	27	31	36	39	47	50	58	62	70	83	100	101	121	152	175	197	241				
		36	21	25	29	32	37	40	48	51	56	64	72	84	93	111	144	156	182	222	277			
		40	20	23	27	30	35	38	41	46	51	61	69	76	86	105	119	148	171	203	257	294		
		44	20	24	29	30	34	38	41	45	50	58	66	75	78	98	113	129	153	193	240	278	320	
		48	19	24	26	29	32	35	40	43	46	55	60	72	76	90	111	118	144	183	218	261	295	
	10N@ 4.00	32	27	33	40	43	51	58	63	70	78	92	103	110	122	168	190	218	246					
		36	27	30	35	41	48	55	62	64	72	79	94	107	116	145	181	199	240	306				
		40	25	28	33	39	43	50	56	57	65	74	86	95	109	134	160	186	212	277				
		44	23	28	31	37	40	48	51	57	59	74	81	88	98	120	150	175	190	255	302			
		48	22	26	29	34	38	42	50	54	59	67	76	83	98	114	140	157	182	230	277	324		
50	4N@ 12.50	40	23	24	24	27	27	28	31	33	36	42	44	50	56	65	85	90	104	130	152	173	199	252
		44	23	24	24	26	28	28	29	31	34	38	43	49	51	66	74	87	104	115	153	174	180	230
		48	23	24	24	26	28	28	29	30	32	36	42	44	50	60	68	79	93	108	133	156	178	213
		54	27	27	27	28	28	28	28	30	31	33	38	42	45	55	62	73	82	106	112	137	159	197
		60	27	28	28	28	29	28	29	30	31	32	36	40	43	51	59	69	76	97	113	122	138	178
	5N@ 10.00	40	17	21	24	25	29	32	35	38	42	46	54	58	65	86	100	110	125	152	184	219	253	
		44	16	19	23	24	28	30	33	36	39	44	50	54	58	75	91	105	113	152	177	205	230	294
		48	17	19	22	25	25	29	31	33	36	40	46	53	59	68	88	94	107	134	159	183	209	269
		54	18	18	21	24	26	27	30	31	33	38	42	46	52	61	78	90	96	117	138	162	184	238
		60	18	20	20	22	25	27	28	31	31	35	41	46	48	62	70	79	93	112	133	163	166	217
	6N@ 8.33	40	18	22	26	29	32	36	41	46	47	54	62	70	78	100	109	131	151	188	226	260		
		44	17	22	24	27	30	34	37	40	46	49	55	63	71	92	106	116	142	168	205	246	281	
		48	17	22	23	26	28	32	35	38	39	47	56	63	65	80	103	109	123	159	191	222	258	
		54	18	20	23	25	29	29	32	35	37	43	49	57	58	73	87	105	112	148	174	197	226	293
		60	18	21	22	25	27	31	31	33	35	41	45	51	59	68	83	98	109	129	155	178	205	265
	8N@ 6.25	40	23	27	31	37	41	48	54	55	62	71	83	92	102	122	153	176	195	248				
		44	22	27	31	34	39	44	49	52	56	65	75	84	102	111	144	167	182	222	288			
		48	22	25	29	33	37	40	45	50	53	61	73	81	86	107	126	149	175	214	263	310		
		54	25	26	31	34	37	41	46	48	51	58	70	76	83	106	114	141	163	193	239	283	315	
		60	24	25	28	32	35	39	42	47	49	57	64	72	77	99	115	125	146	178	215	258	291	
	10N@ 5.00	40	28	33	41	46	55	62	66	74	78	92	105	115	131	156	193	229	267					
		44	27	32	37	44	49	56	63	67	72	88	102	107	116	155	180	208	239	302				
		48	27	32	35	41	48	54	57	64	68	80	94	103	109	135	160	186	214	274				
		54	26	29	33	40	43	50	55	58	62	74	82	96	106	121	152	173	188	251	306			
		60	25	28	32	38	41	45	51	54	58	68	77	84	98	114	142	167	180	225	275	317		

Bearing Depth	7 1/2 in.	10 in.

NUCOR
VULCRAFT - GROUP

Figure 7.232 Design guide weight table for joist girders. (Copyright by Steel Joist Institute and the Vulcraft Group of Nucor. Reprinted with permission. All rights reserved.)

DESIGN GUIDE WEIGHT TABLE FOR JOIST GIRDERS
U. S. CUSTOMARY

Based on an allowable tensile stress of 30ksi

Girder Span (ft)	Joist Spaces (ft)	Girder Depth (in)	Joist Girder Weight – Pounds Per Linear Foot																					
			\:Load on Each Panel Point																					
			4K	5K	6K	7K	8K	9K	10K	11K	12K	14K	16K	18K	20K	25K	30K	35K	40K	50K	60K	70K	80K	100K
60	5N@ 12.00	48	21	23	26	28	31	34	37	42	43	50	55	62	66	85	96	111	125	153	189	218	252	
		54	21	21	24	27	30	32	35	38	42	44	51	56	62	75	88	106	112	144	168	204	221	281
		60	21	22	23	26	28	30	33	35	38	44	46	51	57	68	86	95	108	128	158	182	208	256
		66	22	22	23	25	28	29	33	34	36	40	46	47	53	65	78	91	97	117	139	162	188	228
		72	22	23	23	24	27	29	31	34	35	38	44	47	52	62	72	81	93	113	135	164	177	217
	6N@ 10.00	48	21	23	26	31	34	38	40	46	47	58	66	70	77	100	114	131	152	188	227	262		
		54	19	23	25	29	32	35	38	41	45	53	59	67	71	92	106	117	119	169	204	229	269	
		60	19	22	26	28	31	34	36	39	42	48	55	61	68	81	95	110	134	160	181	209	242	
		66	20	22	25	27	30	32	34	67	41	47	50	58	62	77	96	106	112	140	175	198	216	278
		72	20	21	24	27	29	32	33	35	38	43	50	52	60	72	84	99	114	142	166	188	206	266
	8N@ 7.50	48	24	28	32	38	41	48	54	55	62	70	78	92	101	121	152	176	192	241				
		54	23	26	31	35	39	43	47	55	56	64	72	81	94	109	134	158	180	221	268			
		60	23	26	29	32	38	41	44	49	52	59	66	76	83	106	120	149	163	199	239	290		
		66	29	31	34	36	40	46	48	50	56	64	72	76	82	101	116	142	165	191	230	280	313	
		72	30	31	33	34	38	43	47	49	51	59	69	74	83	102	118	126	147	190	228	255	191	
	10N@ 6.00	48	30	36	43	50	58	65	66	75	78	92	106	116	132	157	193	229	265					
		54	29	34	40	46	51	59	60	68	76	88	95	107	144	147	180	205	232	296				
		60	27	33	38	41	47	53	61	61	70	79	90	97	110	136	162	183	210	272				
		66	27	32	36	40	46	49	55	62	64	75	81	97	99	120	143	165	190	254	296			
		72	27	32	35	39	43	48	53	58	61	73	77	86	100	116	137	169	191	225	283			
	12N@ 5.00	48	35	41	49	55	63	71	79	92	93	107	116	142	156	191	229	266						
		54	33	39	46	50	57	65	73	80	81	104	109	118	135	172	197	238	274					
		60	32	37	41	50	56	59	67	74	79	96	107	112	121	163	187	219	247	316				
		66	31	36	40	47	53	60	61	68	76	85	99	110	115	145	177	201	228	288				
		72	30	35	40	44	52	54	63	64	75	80	89	104	114	130	160	194	219	273	319			
	15N@ 4.00	48	39	49	62	70	78	92	101	106	110	132	155	167	189	228	289							
		54	37	47	56	64	73	81	94	95	105	118	135	158	171	208	254	298						
		60	35	42	51	59	68	76	83	88	98	112	122	141	164	197	229	276	307					
		66	36	44	54	57	65	73	80	88	94	113	118	130	158	193	221	261	294					
		72	36	43	49	57	67	75	77	84	91	107	121	126	143	178	219	240	283					
80	8N@ 10.00	60	29	32	38	43	47	52	58	65	66	78	91	100	105	131	153	189	205	253				
		66	29	32	36	40	46	48	53	59	63	71	79	93	105	126	154	177	192	233	284			
		72	30	32	34	38	43	47	79	54	61	69	78	89	95	115	136	159	182	260	258			
		84	30	32	34	38	43	47	48	54	61	69	78	89	95	115	134	157	179	217	264			
		96	30	32	34	38	43	47	49	54	61	69	78	89	95	115	126	141	163	199	225	272	301	
	10N@ 8.00	60	32	37	42	49	55	62	70	78	78	100	105	115	132	164	191	226	252					
		66	35	42	46	55	61	64	72	77	86	98	109	114	129	169	194	219	250					
		72	34	38	46	51	57	64	65	74	78	91	101	110	126	159	183	207	235					
		84	34	37	46	48	53	59	61	67	72	82	95	104	113	135	166	185	212	256				
		96	35	36	42	48	50	55	58	64	72	78	86	98	104	125	143	171	192	239	281			
	13N@ 6.15	60	40	47	59	66	71	78	92	101	106	116	143	155	175	206	252							
		66	38	47	54	60	68	77	80	94	103	109	134	145	157	195	231	261						
		72	37	44	50	59	67	71	79	83	96	111	120	137	152	186	213	253	298					
		84	36	43	50	54	59	67	75	79	84	101	112	119	128	170	193	229	255					
		96	37	42	47	53	57	66	72	81	79	94	109	118	124	155	177	201	235	294				
	16N@ 5.00	60	47	55	67	78	92	101	107	115	132	153	175	192	206	252								
		66	44	55	65	72	80	94	104	109	117	134	158	180	194	232	287							
		72	43	51	59	70	79	83	97	107	111	121	149	162	185	225	268							
		84	42	49	57	64	74	81	90	104	106	120	131	152	174	207	253	287						
		96	44	48	58	64	70	81	86	92	97	114	128	140	159	196	231	268	298					

Bearing Depth	7 1/2 in.	10 in.

NUCOR
VULCRAFT - GROUP

Figure 7.233 Design guide weight table for joist girders. (Copyright by Steel Joist Institute and the Vulcraft Group of Nucor. Reprinted with permission. All rights reserved.)

DESIGN GUIDE WEIGHT TABLE FOR JOIST GIRDERS
U. S. CUSTOMARY

Based on an allowable tensile stress of 30ksi

Girder Span (ft)	Joist Spaces (ft)	Girder Depth (in)	Joist Girder Weight — Pounds Per Linear Foot Load On Each Panel Point																					
			4K	5K	6K	7K	8K	9K	10K	11K	12K	14K	16K	18K	20K	25K	30K	35K	40K	50K	60K	70K	80K	100K
100	10N@ 10.00	84	56	57	58	62	64	72	76	88	90	103	118	129	142	172	200	225	257					
		96	58	58	59	61	64	67	70	78	88	94	106	120	131	152	180	204	228					
		108	58	60	60	61	63	68	70	73	77	93	96	111	111	139	170	188	209	258				
		120	60	60	62	64	66	67	68	71	74	85	99	108	113	139	157	188	201	242	289			
	12N@ 8.33	84	50	54	58	66	70	75	89	92	101	112	129	138	159	187	221	257						
		96	50	54	57	61	68	70	80	84	96	106	116	123	137	179	205	228	271					
		108	52	54	58	62	65	72	74	79	89	101	110	121	128	164	193	221	246	299				
		120	54	57	60	62	66	69	77	79	86	92	107	117	126	151	178	206	239	283				
	16N@ 6.25	84	55	60	71	76	83	96	110	112	119	139	161	184	199	235	288							
		96	56	60	67	75	79	88	102	105	119	128	145	168	191	218	265	301						
		108	58	63	67	72	81	87	93	106	111	125	136	157	180	204	251	292						
		120	60	65	68	74	79	90	93	98	110	117	134	147	166	208	248	275	304					
	17N@ 5.88	84	57	65	73	82	92	98	112	114	123	151	164	187	203	250								
		96	60	65	72	81	89	103	110	123	123	145	177	179	198	256	285							
		108	64	67	72	76	86	96	108	113	123	135	158	172	182	231	264	308						
		120	67	68	73	80	85	90	99	112	119	133	143	167	178	214	250	281	330					
	20N@ 5.00	84	67	77	87	105	115	122	132	148	159	193	208	226	246									
		96	67	73	82	95	111	120	120	135	152	177	199	211	227	279								
		108	66	72	79	91	101	116	125	130	131	162	184	197	207	267	316							
		120	71	75	82	88	96	106	120	123	136	149	170	193	205	246	289	332						
Bearing Depth			7 1/2 in													10 in.								

Joist Girder weights to the right of the heavy blue line have 10 inch bearing depths. Check with Vulcraft for material availability.

Figure 7.234 Design guide weight table for joist girders. (Copyright by Steel Joist Institute and the Vulcraft Group of Nucor. Reprinted with permission. All rights reserved.)

Figure 7.235 Curved bottom chords and sloped top chords. (Photograph courtesy of Vulcraft Corporation.)

Figure 7.236 Semicircular trusses. (Photograph courtesy of Vulcraft Corporation.)

7.4 Economic Implications of Truss Spans

Using the standard table for manufactured trusses, the effect of span on the depth, weight, and cost of standard steel truss construction can be explored.

The discussion begins with an examination of floors.

Assume a 5 ft joist-to-joist spacing, which is a common module that strikes an economical balance, accounting for typical modular layouts and an appropriate unbraced length for the top chords of the girder trusses.

Assume 2 in.-deep corrugated floor decking with composite construction, with an overall slab thickness of 6 in. using lightweight concrete. (For most applications, structural safety can be achieved with a much shallower slab. However, when vibration suppression and fire protection are accounted for, this 6 in.-thick slab becomes an attractive option.) See Figure 7.237.

Figures 7.238, 7.239, and 7.240 show the printouts from a spreadsheet that has been laid out for sizing both

Decking	Weight (#/ft²)
Concrete	49
Corrugated steel deck	1.62
Estimated HVAC	1
Estimated ceiling	1
TOTAL	52.62
Which can be rounded up to	**53**

For a 5 ft joist spacing:

$W_{dead} = 5\ ft*(53\#/ft^2)=$	265 #/ft
$W_{live} = 5\ ft*(100\#/ft^2)=$	500 #/ft
$W_{totalimposed}=$	765 #/ft

In the tables, the combination of numbers that we are seeking is:

765
500

Figure 7.237 Summary of dead weight in the floor assembly.

Joist L	Girder L
20	**20**
ft	ft

Design of joists:

Joist spacing: 5 ft

p_{dead} = 53 #/ft²

p_{live} = 100 #/ft²

w_{dead} = 265 #/ft

$w_{totalimposed}$ = 765 #/ft

w_{live} = 500 #/ft

$W_{totalimposed}$ = 15,300 #

From the *Steel Joist Institute* design tables for truss joists (Figures 7-220 through 7-230):

Joist Designation	Joist Depth d (in.)	Joist Proportions L/d	Joist w_{self} (#/ft)	Joist W_{self} (#)	Joist Self-Wt of Steel per ft² of floor (#/ft²)
18LH05	18	13.3	15	300	3.00

Adding in self-weight of the joist produces:

W_{total} = 15,600 #

Design of Girders:

Weight per vertex on Perimeter Girder:

7.8   *K*

Weight per vertex on Interior Girder:

15.6   *K*

Interpolating between values in the girder tables:		
	Perimeter Girder	
LowerWt/Vertex (*K*)	ActualForce (*K*)	UpperWt/Vertex (*K*)
7	7.8	8
LowerSelfWt/ft (#/ft)	InterpolatedSelfWt/ft (#/ft)	UpperSelfWt/ft (#/ft)
20	**21.6**	22
	Interior Girder	
LowerWt/Vertex (*K*)	ActualForce (*K*)	UpperWt/Vertex (*K*)
14	15.6	16
LowerSelfWt/ft (#/ft)	InterpolatedSelfWt/ft (#/ft)	UpperSelfWt/ft (#/ft)
38	**41.2**	42

From the *Vulcraft Corporation* design tables for truss girders, Figures 7-231 through 7-234:

	Girder Depth d (in.)	Girder Proportions L/d	Girder w_{self} (#/ft)	Girder W_{self} (#)	Girder Self-Wt of Steel per ft² of floor (#/ft²)
PerimeterGirder	**16**	**15.0**	21.60	432	2.16
InteriorGirder	**16**	**15.0**	41.20	824	2.06
			Overall weight of all trusses:		**7.22**

Overall depth of truss assembly: **21**

Overall depth = depth of girder + depth of end-bearing assembly of the joist (5 in.)

Figure 7.238 Design of floor framing for 20 ft × 20 ft grid.

Joist L	Girder L
40	**40**
ft	ft

Design of joists:

Joist spacing:	5	ft
p_{dead} =	53	#/ft²
p_{live} =	100	#/ft²
w_{dead} =	265	#/ft
$w_{totalimposed}$ =	**765**	#/ft
w_{live} =	**500**	#/ft
$W_{totalimposed}$ =	**30,600**	#

From the *Steel Joist Institute* design tables for truss joists (Figures 7-220 through 7-230):

Joist Designation	Joist Depth d (in.)	Joist Proportions L/d	Joist w_{self} (#/ft)	Joist W_{self} (#)	Joist Self-Wt of Steel per ft² of floor (#/ft²)
28LH11	28	17.1	25	1000	5.00

Adding in self-weight of the joist produces:

W_{total} =	31,600	#

Design of Girders:

Weight per vertex on Perimeter Girder:

15.8		*K*

Weight per vertex on Interior Girder:

31.6		*K*

Interpolating between values in the girder tables:		
Perimeter Girder		
LowerWt/Vertex (*K*)	ActualForce (*K*)	UpperWt/Vertex (*K*)
16	15.8	18
LowerSelfWt/ft (#/ft)	InterpolatedSelfWt/ft (#/ft)	UpperSelfWt/ft (#/ft)
83	**81.3**	100
Interior Girder		
LowerWt/Vertex (*K*)	ActualForce (*K*)	UpperWt/Vertex (*K*)
30	31.6	35
LowerSelfWt/ft (#/ft)	InterpolatedSelfWt/ft (#/ft)	UpperSelfWt/ft (#/ft)
150	**158**	175

From the *Vulcraft Corporation* design tables for truss girders, Figures 7-231 through 7-234:

	Girder Depth d (in.)	Girder Proportions L/d	Girder w_{self} (#/ft)	Girder W_{self} (#)	Girder Self-Wt of Steel per ft² of floor (#/ft²)
PerimeterGirder	**32**	**15.0**	81.30	3252	4.07
InteriorGirder	**32**	**15.0**	158.00	6320	3.95
			Overall weight of all trusses:		**13.02**

Overall depth of truss assembly:	37

Overall depth = depth of girder + depth of end-bearing assembly of the joist (5 in.)

Figure 7.239 Design of floor framing for 40 ft × 40 ft grid.

Joist L	Girder L
60	**60**
ft	ft

Design of joists:

Joist spacing:	5	ft
p_{dead} =	53	#/ft²
p_{live} =	100	#/ft²
w_{dead} =	265	#/ft
$w_{totalimposed}$ =	**765**	#/ft
w_{live} =	**500**	#/ft
$W_{totalimposed}$ =	**45,900**	#

From the *Steel Joist Institute* design tables for truss joists (Figures 7-220 through 7-230):

Joist Designation	Joist Depth d (in.)	Joist Proportions L/d	Joist w_{self} (#/ft)	Joist W_{self} (#)	Joist Self-Wt of Steel per ft² of floor (#/ft²)
40LH16	40	18.0	42	2520	8.40

Adding in self-weight of the joist produces:

W_{total} = 48,420 #

Design of Girders:

Weight per vertex on Perimeter Girder:
24.21   K

Weight per vertex on Interior Girder:
48.42   K

Interpolating between values in the girder tables:		
	Perimeter Girder	
LowerWt/Vertex (*K*)	ActualForce (*K*)	UpperWt/Vertex (*K*)
20	24.21	25
LowerSelfWt/ft (#/ft)	InterpolatedSelfWt/ft (#/ft)	UpperSelfWt/ft (#/ft)
121	**156.4**	163
	Interior Girder	
LowerWt/Vertex (*K*)	ActualForce (*K*)	UpperWt/Vertex (*K*)
40	48.42	50
LowerSelfWt/ft (#/ft)	InterpolatedSelfWt/ft (#/ft)	UpperSelfWt/ft (#/ft)
247	**305.1**	316

From the *Vulcraft Corporation* design tables for truss girders, Figures 7-231 through 7-234:

	Girder Depth d (in.)	Girder Proportions L/d	Girder w_{self} (#/ft)	Girder W_{self} (#)	Girder Self-Wt of Steel per ft² of floor (#/ft²)
PerimeterGirder	**60**	**12.0**	156.4	9382	5.21
InteriorGirder	**60**	**12.0**	305.1	18306	5.08
			Overall weight of all trusses:		**18.70**

Overall depth of truss assembly: **65**

Overall depth = depth of girder + depth of end-bearing assembly of the joist (5 in.)

Figure 7.240 Design of floor framing for 60 ft × 60 ft grid.

the truss joists and the truss girders. That same spreadsheet is applied three times on three consecutive pages to size the joists and girders for the following column grids:

20 ft × 20 ft
40 ft × 40 ft
60 ft × 60 ft

Since the cost of steel is sometimes volatile, cost data is not provided. Students can make economic assessments by finding current prices at the time of reading this book.

The three designs outlined here can be summarized in the graphs shown in Figure 7.241.

The trends noted in the preceding discussion are summarized here.

For modest spans, the self-weight of the spanning structure is very small as compared with the weights of the imposed loads. As long as the self-weight of the spanning structure is very small as compared with the imposed loads, the weight and depth of the structure increase in proportion to the span. However, when the span becomes very large, the self-weight of the spanning structure becomes more important and the weight and depth start to increase in a nonlinear manner. One way to think about it is that adding span increases the self-weight, which further increases the structural burden, which further increases the amount of material or depth of structure required to support the load. Figure 7.241 indicates that for spans up to 60 ft, both the cost of the spanning elements and the depth of the structure increase essentially linearly with the span, with a slight upturn in depth for a 60 ft span.

Exercises

Design the joists and girders for a trussed floor that is supported on a 30 ft × 30 ft column grid. Show how the depth and cost of the truss steel in your design fit on the graph in Figure 7.241.

Design the joists and girders for a trussed floor that is supported on a 50 ft × 50 ft column grid. Show how the depth and cost of the truss steel in your design fit on the graph in Figure 7.241.

Design the joists and girders for a trussed floor that is supported on a 100 ft × 100 ft column grid. Show how the depth and cost of the truss steel in your design fit on the graph in Figure 7.241.

Design roof joists to span 100 ft, assuming an imposed dead load of 10 lb/ft² and a live load of 20 lb/ft². Space the roof joists at 10 ft on center, and then redesign using the widest spacing (integer feet) that 3 in.-deep corrugated decking will allow used in 3-span mode.

What are the designations of the joists?
What is the depth of the joists?
How much material is required per square foot of roof?

Design roof joists to span 200 ft, assuming an imposed dead load of 10 lb/ft² and a live load of 20 lb/ft². Space the roof joists at 10 ft on center, and then redesign using the widest spacing (integer feet) that 3 in.-deep corrugated decking will allow.

What are the designations of the joists?
What is the depth of the joists?
How much material is required per square foot of roof?

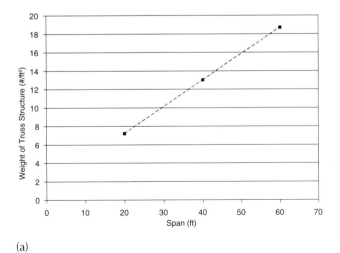

(a)

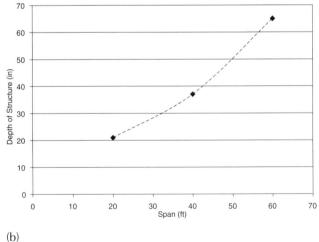

(b)

Figure 7.241 Cost (a) and depth (b) as a function of span.

7.5 Trusses Integrated with HVAC Systems

7.5.1 VARIATIONS OF THE COLUMN GRID

There can be significant advantages to column grids that are not square. For example, using a 60 ft span in one direction and a 30 ft span in the other direction still accommodates automotive parking at the lowest level of the building by keeping open the 60 ft aisles for double-loaded parking, while allowing for a more efficient span in the other direction. Since the goal is to keep the overall depth of the floor structure as shallow as possible, and since the depth of the girders tends to be greater than the depth of the joists, it is logical in this situation to span the short direction with the girders. (This is contrary to the usual choice when dealing with high-bay roofs in single-story applications, where the depth of the structure is usually not so critical and the goal is mainly structural efficiency. For roofs, the heavier loads on the girders makes the webs of the girders intrinsically larger, which means that the webs can be longer without having buckling problems. Longer webs make for a deeper truss, which can span more efficiently. Hence, in high-bay roofing systems, where the depth of the structure is not as critical as in a multistory application, the usual choice is to span the long direction with the girders.)

The trusses in the 30 ft × 60 ft column layout are sized in Figure 7.242.

The changes in truss weight and depth in going from the 60 ft × 60 ft column layout to the 30 ft × 60 ft column layout are summarized in Figure 7.243.

The 30 ft × 60 ft column layout still accommodates 60 ft freespan in one direction, but saves 24 in. in structural depth as compared to the 60 ft × 60 ft column layout. This is a height savings of three courses of concrete masonry units (CMUs).

7.5.2 INTEGRATING THE HVAC DUCTWORK INTO THE STRUCTURAL VOLUME

Also of extreme importance is the opportunity to integrate the HVAC ducts with the structural volume. As an example of this process, replace an interior girder with two side-by-side girders, each of half the weight of the original girder. (Remember that an interior girder weighs almost exactly twice as much as a perimeter girder, so there is no inefficiency in splitting the interior girder into two girders.) These girders (and the associated columns) can be moved apart by 8–10 ft to make a corridor. The decking can span across the corridor from girder to girder, leaving that volume completely free for a huge HVAC trunkline. Alternately, the corridor can be spanned by 5 in.-deep wide-flange steel beams (e.g., W 5 × 16) running in line with the joist end-bearing

assemblies. This facilitates running all the corrugated decking unbroken in the same direction, at the price of losing 5 vertical inches for the HVAC trunkline. The feeder ducts are run from the trunkline through the girders and out between the joists, as shown in the diagram in Figure 7.244. This requires a special pattern for the joist bracing, wherein bracing elements occur only in every other bay.

The Sears Tower is an excellent example of systems integration involving trusses. The Sears Tower consists of nine square structural tubes that are 75 ft × 75 ft in footprint, clustered together in a three-by-three array having an overall footprint that is 225 ft × 225 ft (see Figure 7.245).

There are no interior columns within the tubes, leaving an uninterrupted 75 ft × 75 ft of floor area to be configured in any manner appropriate to the occupants. Each square tube has four corner columns and four intermediate columns on each face. The column spacing is 15 ft on center. Horizontal I-beams at each floor are moment-connected to the columns to produce a rugged, stiff frame that forms the walls of the tube. The geometry of that rigid frame is most apparent in the lobby, which is more than a story high, revealing the pattern of the horizontal members unobstructed by floors (see Figure 7.246).

The role of these rigid-frame tubes in resisting lateral forces is discussed in more detail in Chapter 10, "Lateral Bracing Systems."

The floor decking is supported by the horizontal beams around the perimeter of the tube and by four 75 ft-long trusses spaced at 15 ft on center, spanning from the four columns on one face of the tube to the four columns on the opposite face of the tube. This produces a very simple flooring system, with large expanses of floor being supported by a very small number of trusses. The trusses were fitted with shear studs on the top to provide composite action with the concrete in the floor decking.

To distribute the gravity loads equally among the columns, the trusses run in one direction on half the floors and at 90° on the other half of the floors. This concept is illustrated in the floor framing plan shown in Figure 7.247. This layout of the trusses occurs for five floors before the direction of the trusses is switched.

Making the trusses 75 ft long created large expanses of unobstructed floor area. It also made the trusses deep enough that ductwork could be run through the trusses, rather than having to be placed below the trusses (see Figure 7.248).

Spacing the trusses so widely apart also made it easier to feed the ducts through the trusses, which was crucial to making the installation of the mechanical system cost-effective. To achieve this wide spacing of the trusses, the design team invented 3 in.-deep corrugated steel

Joist L	Girder L
60	**30**
ft	ft

Design of joists:

Joist spacing:	5	ft
p_{dead} =	53	#/ft²
p_{live} =	100	#/ft²
w_{dead} =	265	#/ft
$w_{totalimposed}$ =	**765**	#/ft
w_{live} =	**500**	#/ft
$W_{totalimposed}$ =	**45,900**	#

From the *Steel Joist Institute* design tables for truss joists (Figures 7-220 through 7-230):

Joist Designation	Joist Depth d (in.)	Joist Proportions L/d	Joist w_{self} (#/ft)	Joist W_{self} (#)	Joist Self-Wt of Steel per ft² of floor (#/ft²)
40LH16	40	18.0	42	2520	8.40

Adding in self-weight of the joist produces:

W_{total} =   48,420   #

Design of Girders:

Weight per vertex on Perimeter Girder:

24.21   *K*

Weight per vertex on Interior Girder:

48.42   *K*

Interpolating between values in the girder tables:		
	Perimeter Girder	
LowerWt/Vertex (*K*)	ActualForce (*K*)	UpperWt/Vertex (*K*)
20	24.21	25
LowerSelfWt/ft (#/ft)	InterpolatedSelfWt/ft (#/ft)	UpperSelfWt/ft (#/ft)
55	**65.1**	67
	Interior Girder	
LowerWt/Vertex (*K*)	ActualForce (*K*)	UpperWt/Vertex (*K*)
40	48.42	50
LowerSelfWt/ft (#/ft)	InterpolatedSelfWt/ft (#/ft)	UpperSelfWt/ft (#/ft)
108	**125.7**	129

From the *Vulcraft Corporation* design tables for truss girders, Figures 7-231 through 7-234:

	Girder Depth d (in.)	Girder Proportions L/d	Girder w_{self} (#/ft)	Girder W_{self} (#)	Girder Self-Wt of Steel per ft² of floor (#/ft²)
PerimeterGirder	**36**	**10.0**	65.1	1953	2.17
InteriorGirder	**36**	**10.0**	125.7	3770	2.09
			Overall weight of all trusses:		**12.66**

Overall depth of truss assembly: **41**

Overall depth = depth of girder + depth of end-bearing assembly of the joist (5 in.)

Figure 7.242 Design of floor framing for 30 ft × 60 ft grid.

Grid	Joist d (in.)	Girder d (in.)	Overall d (in.)	Weight of Steel (#/ft² of Floor)
60 x 60	40	60	65	18.70
30 x 60	40	36	41	12.66
		Reductions:	24	6.04

Figure 7.243 Comparison of 60 ft × 60 ft grid and 30 ft × 60 ft column grids.

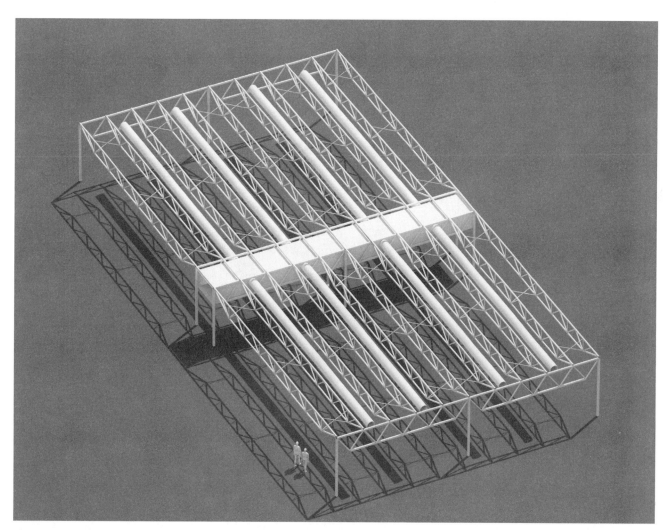

Figure 7.244 Integrating HVAC and structure in the 30 × 60 truss grid.

Figure 7.245 Sears Tower (Architects: Skidmore, Owings & Merrill; Engineers: Skidmore, Owings & Merrill).

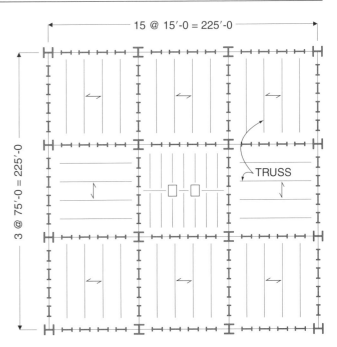

Figure 7.247 Framing plan of the Sears Tower.

Figure 7.246 Rigid frame as seen in the lobby of the Sears Tower.

LIGHTWEIGHT CONCRETE SLAB

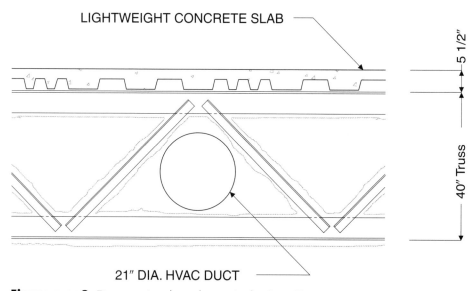

5 1/2"

40" Truss

21" DIA. HVAC DUCT

Figure 7.248 Duct running through truss in the Sears Tower.

decking. This was the first project on which 3 in.-deep corrugated decking was used.

The deep corrugations not only facilitated the support of the gravity loads over the 15 ft span from truss to truss, they also facilitated the integration of the electric power, telephone, and signal distribution systems, as shown in Figure 7.249.

Achieving the record height of the Sears Tower in an economical manner required that many floors be squeezed into the vertical dimension. Care was taken in the integration of the systems to keep the floor-to-floor

dimension as low as possible. Both the long span of the trusses and the long span of the decking opened opportunities for integrating elements that otherwise would not have fit within the depth of the structural elements.

Returning for a moment to the issue of the cost of spanning long distances: the designers of the Sears Tower did not consider the cost of spanning 75 ft exorbitant. In fact, they felt it was important to be competitive in a market where flexibility in space planning is crucial. For more information on the Sears Tower, see Chapter 2, "Loads," and Chapter 10, "Lateral Bracing Systems."

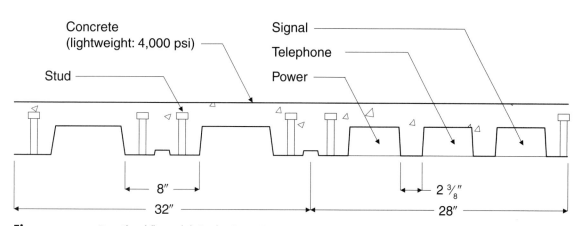

Concrete (lightweight: 4,000 psi)

Signal

Telephone

Stud

Power

8"

32"

2 3/8"

28"

Figure 7.249 Details of floor slab in the Sears Tower.

8

Compression
Structures

8.1 Arches and Bow Trusses

8.1.1 ACHIEVING TRUE ARCH ACTION

An arch must be buttressed by the earth or held together with a tie at the base if it is to exhibit true arch action and achieve good mechanical advantage. If it does not get good buttressing action, it will act like a beam and the effective depth of action will be drastically reduced.

If an arch is to exhibit true arch action, the stresses in the arch must be axial. Therefore, the force of the overall support reaction C must be tangent to the arch at the support point (see Figure 8.1). The tangential force at the support point can be broken down into horizontal and vertical components (see Figure 8.2).

One can cut through the arch and create a freebody that will help in understanding the internal forces (see Figure 8.3).

Because of the symmetry of the original structure and the loads on that structure, there can be no vertical internal force at the center of the arch where we sliced it to create the freebody. In other words, if we apply the laws of equilibrium to the vertical forces on the freebody, the vertical reaction V just equilibrates the downward force of the uniform load on the half of the arch that we are using as the freebody, and, therefore, the net vertical force on the surface where we sliced the freebody must be zero. Looked at another way, true arch action requires that the internal force be axial at all points; this implies that the internal force at the top of the arch must be horizontal, since the arch is horizontal at that point. Since there are only two horizontal forces, they must be equal in magnitude and opposite in direction. Therefore, they are both labeled with the same symbol, H, indicating that they have the same magnitude. The two H forces form a force couple that is the internal resisting moment of the spanning system. The lever arm for that force couple is shown in the diagram in Figure 8.3.

For the purposes of applying the laws of equilibrium to the new freebody, the uniform load can be replaced with an equivalent force at the center of the distribution (see Figure 8.4).

The vertical forces form a couple of strength VL_v tending to cause clockwise motion. The horizontal forces form a couple of strength HL_h tending to cause counterclockwise motion. Applying the moment equation about any point always produces the same equation:

$$0 = +VL_v - HL_h$$

This can be rewritten as

$$H = V\left(\frac{L_v}{L_h}\right) \tag{8.1}$$

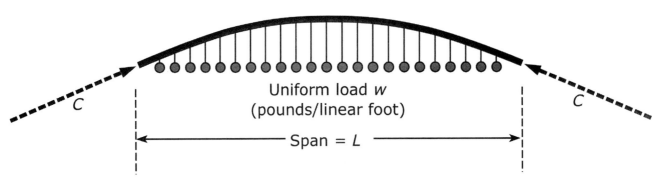

Figure 8.1 Tangential force at arch supports.

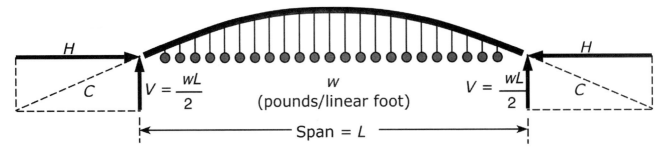

Figure 8.2 Resolving horizontal and vertical components.

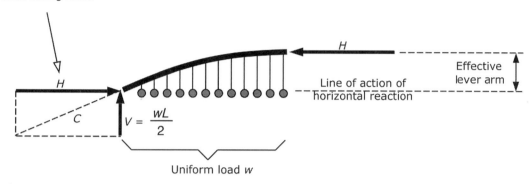

Figure 8.3 Creating a freebody.

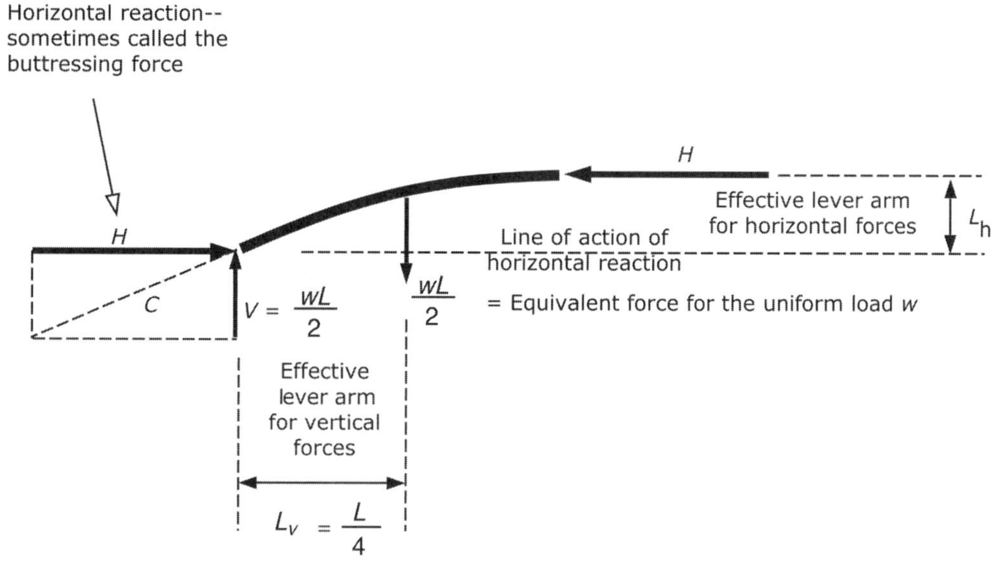

Figure 8.4 Simplifying the force system.

It is common to talk about the proportions of structural elements in terms of the span-to-depth ratio $\frac{L}{L_h}$, rather than the ratio of the lever arms $\frac{L_v}{L_h}$. Rearranging the preceding equation in terms of the span-to-depth ratio is straightforward, since $L_v = \frac{L}{4}$:

$$H = \left(\frac{L_v}{L_h}\right) = V\left(\frac{\frac{L}{4}}{L_h}\right) = V\left(\frac{L}{4 \cdot L_h}\right) = V\frac{\left(\frac{L}{L_h}\right)}{4} = V\frac{\left(\frac{L}{R}\right)}{4} \quad \textbf{[8.2]}$$

where R is the rise of the arch, which is the vertical distance from the horizontal line connecting the base points up to the centerline of the top of the arch. In other words,

H varies proportionally to the span-to-rise ratio for the arch. If the proportions of an arch are such that the span is four times the rise of the arch (i.e., the rise of the arch is one fourth of the span), the vertical reactions V are exactly equal to the horizontal force that exists everywhere in the arch.

As in the case of beams, arches can be analyzed by first calculating the moment generated by the vertical forces being supported in the process of spanning:

$$M_v = V \cdot L_v = V \cdot \frac{L}{4} = \frac{wL}{2} \cdot \frac{L}{4} = w\frac{L^2}{8} \quad \textbf{[8.3]}$$

The equation

$$M_v = w\frac{L^2}{8} \quad \textbf{[8.4]}$$

applies universally to any type of spanning element that is spanning a distance L under a uniform load w.

The moment from the horizontal forces is:

$$M_h = H \cdot L_h = H \cdot R \qquad \text{[8.5]}$$

$$M_h = H \cdot R \qquad \text{[8.6]}$$

The moment of the horizontal forces must equal the moment of the vertical forces, so:

$$M_h = M_v$$
$$H \cdot R = M_v$$
$$H = \frac{M_v}{R}$$
$$H = \frac{w\dfrac{L^2}{8}}{R} \qquad \text{[8.7]}$$

Suppose good arch action is not achieved. In other words, assume the structural element that one is calling an arch is not buttressed with a horizontal reaction at the base.

This situation could be achieved with a roller element at the support point (see Figure 8.5).

The equivalent of this situation can also occur by putting the curved structural element on top of support walls or columns that cannot provide significant resistance to horizontal thrust (see Figure 8.6).

These walls have a tremendous mechanical disadvantage in trying to resist the outward thrust of the curved element. The walls will deflect outward, allowing bending stresses to develop in the curved roof elements. These bending stresses will either support the roof or fail the curved structural element. The lack of a significant horizontal component at the support point means that no significant archlike action will be observed in the curved structural elements in the roof. Those elements are no longer arches; they are now curved beams.

Creating a freebody produces the diagram shown in Figure 8.7.

The question is, what is happening on the cut surface that was created when the freebody was sliced off from the original arch? Since all of the vertical forces on the freebody balance each other precisely, the vertical force on the cut surface must be zero. Moreover, there are no horizontal forces anywhere on the structure, so the net horizontal force on the cut surface must be zero. However, there must be a moment on the cut surface, since

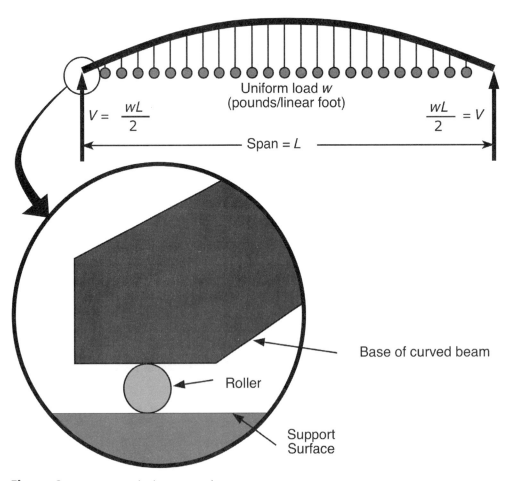

Figure 8.5 Removing the buttressing force.

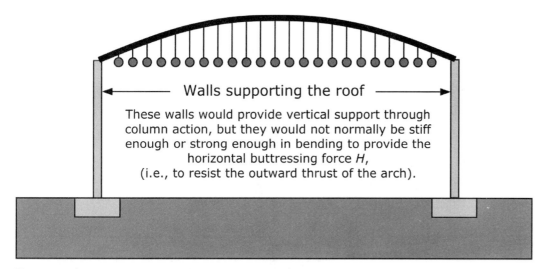

Figure 8.6 Situation of negligible buttressing force.

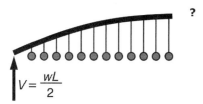

Figure 8.7 Freebody with no buttressing force.

the existing vertical forces do not lie along the same line. This can be visualized better by replacing the vertical distributed force with the equivalent force (see Figure 8.8).

The moment on the cut surface has been indicated with a curved arrow and the letter *M*. The details of the stress distribution that produces that moment *M* can be shown on a blowup drawing (see Figure 8.9).

By equilibrium, the two horizontal forces are equal to each other—that is, *C* = *T*—and, as in the case of the arch, we can designate this single horizontal force as H_b. In this

case, the subscript *b* has been added to the symbol *H* to indicate that we are dealing with the horizontal forces having to do with bending, which distinguishes H_b from the *H* symbol used in the case of the arch action described earlier. Applying the moment equation, produces the following equation:

$$0 = +VL_v - H_bL_h$$

This can be rewritten as

$$H_b = V\left(\frac{L_v}{L_h}\right)$$

[8.8]

The equation for the horizontal forces involved in beam action has exactly the same form as the equation for the horizontal forces involved in arch action, except that for beam action, L_h is very small (less than the depth of the cross section of the curved beam) as compared with L_h for arch action (equal to the rise of the arch). So the horizontal forces for the curved beam will be much larger than the horizontal forces for the arch.

Of course, these forces are not what will fail the beam. The maximum stress on the cross section will cause the failure of the beam. It would be a useful exercise to compare the maximum axial compressive stress for an arch to the maximum bending stresses that would occur when the buttressing action is removed from the arch. To do so, consider the following example. A curved glulam element spans 100 ft and rises 25 ft from its base to the centerline of the top. The element has a rectangular cross section that is uniform along its length, with a cross-sectional base *b* = 1 ft and a cross-sectional height *h* = 3 ft. The element is subject to a uniform distributed load $w = \dfrac{9,000 \; \#}{\text{ft}}$ including its own self-weight (see Figure 8.10).

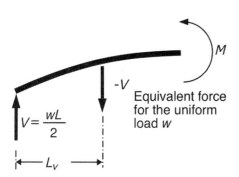

Figure 8.8 Simplifying the force system.

V = wL/2 (in figure)
-V (in figure)
Equivalent force for the uniform load *w*
M (in figure)
L_v (in figure)

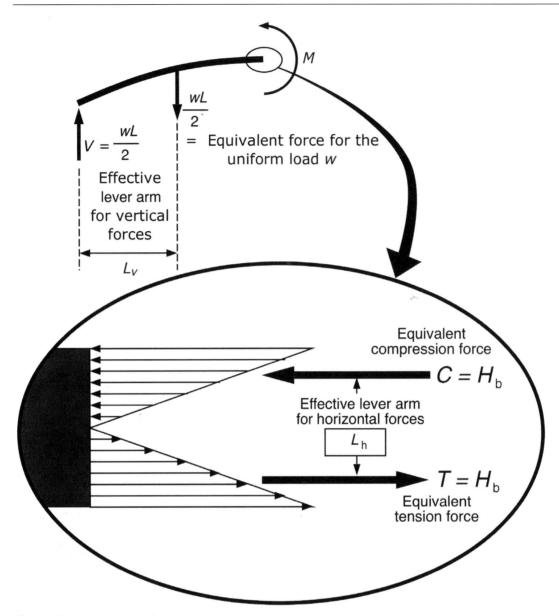

Figure 8.9 Showing the flexure stresses.

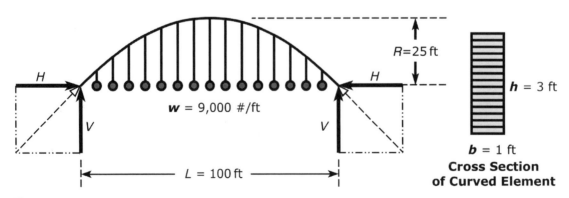

Figure 8.10 Example arch.

Whether the mode of structural action being addressed is arch action or bending action, the moment of the vertical forces is the same:

$$M_v = w \frac{L^2}{8} = \frac{9,000 \ \#}{ft} \cdot \frac{(100 \ ft)^2}{8} \cdot \left[\frac{12 \ in.}{ft} \right]$$
$$= 135,000,000 \ \# \cdot in. \qquad \textbf{[8.9]}$$

First, find the axial compressive stresses associated with arch action. From equation [8.7], the horizontal force associated with arch action is

$$H = \frac{M_v}{R} = \frac{135,000,000 \ \# \cdot in.}{25 \ ft \cdot \left[\dfrac{12 \ in.}{ft} \right]} = 450,000 \ \# \qquad \textbf{[8.10]}$$

The axial stress f_a at the top of the arch will be:

$$f_a = \frac{H}{A} = \frac{450,000 \ \#}{1 \ ft \cdot 3 \ ft \cdot \left[\dfrac{12 \ in.}{ft} \right] \cdot \left[\dfrac{12 \ in.}{ft} \right]} = \frac{1,042 \ \#}{in.^2} \qquad \textbf{[8.11]}$$

However, to find the most severe axial stress in the arch, the base must be considered, where there are both horizontal and vertical force components:

$$V = \frac{wL}{2} = \frac{\dfrac{9,000 \ \#}{ft} \cdot 100 \ ft}{2} = 450,000 \ \# \qquad \textbf{[8.12]}$$

The total force at the base is gotten from the Pythagorean theorem:

$$T = \sqrt{V^2 + H^2} = \sqrt{(450,000 \ \#)^2 + (450,000 \ \#)^2}$$
$$= 636,396 \ \# \qquad \textbf{[8.13]}$$

At the base of the arch, the axial stress due to arch action will be

$$f_a = \frac{T}{A} = \frac{636,396 \ \#}{1 \ ft \cdot 3 \ ft \cdot \left[\dfrac{12 \ in.}{ft} \right] \cdot \left[\dfrac{12 \ in.}{ft} \right]} = \frac{1,473 \ \#}{in.^2} \qquad \textbf{[8.14]}$$

Now, consider the bending stresses in the curved beam that result when the buttressing force is removed:

$$f_b = \frac{M_v}{S} = \frac{M_v}{\left(\dfrac{bh^2}{6} \right)} = \frac{135,000,000 \ \# \cdot in.}{\left(\dfrac{12 \ in. \cdot 36 \ in. \cdot 36 \ in.}{6} \right)}$$
$$= \frac{52,083 \ \#}{in.^2} \qquad \textbf{[8.15]}$$

For comparison purposes:

$$\frac{f_b}{f_a} = \frac{\dfrac{52,083 \ \#}{in.^2}}{\dfrac{1,473 \ \#}{in.^2}} = 35.4 \qquad \textbf{[8.16]}$$

In other words, the stress increases by a factor of 35.4 when the buttressing force is removed.

The diagram in Figure 8.11 provides a graphic comparison of the compressive stress at the base of a pure arch to the bending stress at the top when the buttressing action is removed.

Because of the far greater mechanical advantage of the true arch, as compared with the curved beam, the stresses are much lower on the cut surface of the true arch. In order to make the beam work efficiently, it must be made much deeper, so that its depth rivals the rise of the arch.

The arch can be thought of as part of a very deep "spanning system." The arch across the top of the spanning system carries the compression force, and a tie element joining the support points carries the tension force at the bottom of the spanning system. In a sense, the arch and tie member together are like a truss or a very deep beam from which much of the unnecessary material has been removed.

In addition to the leverage benefits associated with the great depth of the arch, as compared with the curved beam, the material in the arch is better utilized than the material in the beam, since all the material is fully stressed, as opposed to that in the beam, in which some of the material is highly stressed and some of the material has no stress.

However, getting true arch action requires a tie member or a very sturdy buttress, either of which will be called upon to supply a substantial horizontal force. As a general rule, soil is very poor in shear and, therefore, very poor in providing a horizontal force. Hence, using buttresses without a tie member is recommended only where the ground is very solid, preferably stone. The best place to use buttresses without tie members is in mountain gorges, such as with most of Maillart's bridges, where rocky mountains provide extremely stable and reliable buttressing action (see Figure 8.12). Otherwise, tie members are preferred.

Sometimes the forces on the arch and the tie member are huge, such as in the Broadgate Exchange House, designed by William Baker and Robert Sinn, of the Chicago office of Skidmore, Owings & Merrill, and H. Iyengar of Structural Design International. This structure spans 72 m (approximately 240 ft) and consists of ten stories of both dead and live load (see Figure 8.13).

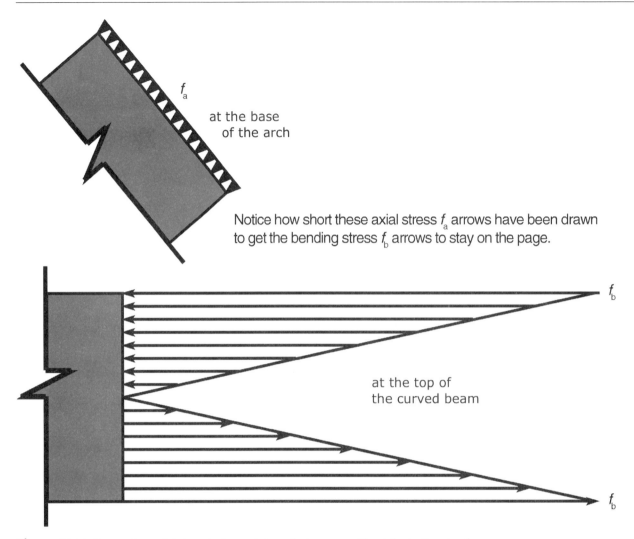

f_a

at the base
of the arch

Notice how short these axial stress f_a arrows have been drawn
to get the bending stress f_b arrows to stay on the page.

f_b

at the top of
the curved beam

f_b

Figure 8.11 Comparing axial stress to flexural stress that occurs without the buttressing force.

Figure 8.12 Maillart's Salginatobel bridge. (Image courtesy of Eugenio Pedrazzini.)

Figure 8.13 Broadgate Exchange House, London, England. (Architecture and Engineering by Skidmore, Owings & Merrill, LLP, Chicago office. Image courtesy of Hedrich Blessing.)

For such a long span and high load, the tie member has to be extremely strong and well connected (see Figure 8.14).

In Figure 8.15, the image on the left shows a series of tied arches supported at each end on a column. (These tied arches can be thought of as the simplest kind of bow truss, with no web members. If there are no web members, or very few web members, we typically use the term *tied arch*, rather than *bow truss*, but either term is appropriate.) The image on the right shows the deformation of the structure under snow and dead load on the arches and under self-weight of the structure. Note that the tie members exhibit far greater deflection than any other part of the structure. This is called deformation sag. The standard method of limiting sag is to use rods to suspend the tie member from the arch above. The deformation diagrams in Figure 8.15 give an indication of how effective the sag rods are.

Sag rods are extremely light and inexpensive. However, they do involve some material expenditure and

Figure 8.14 Broadgate Exchange House, London, England. (Architecture and Engineering by the Chicago office of Skidmore, Owings & Merrill, LLP. Photograph courtesy of SOM.)

fabrication costs. They begin to suggest the potential for adding a few more members and turning the arch into a full-fledged bow truss. The benefits of doing so are improved bracing of the curved compression members against roll-through buckling and improved resistance to asymmetric loading. These issues are discussed in more detail later in this chapter.

For the moment, attention is focused in the exact opposite direction, which is, how to free up the interior volume by getting rid of most of the tie members? Sometimes tie members may interfere with functions occurring in the high, open space under a structure. For example, pedestrian traffic, ship traffic, or basketball play may require maximum height under an arch, which precludes the use of a tie member. In such situations, the tie member can be eliminated by designing the spanning element as a curved beam or by providing buttressing through one means or another. One approach is to remove all the interior tie members and add horizontal trusses to provide the buttressing action (see Figures 8.16 through 8.19).

The horizontal trusses are being pushed outward by the thrusting action of the arches. The two tie members are providing the force reactions that allow the truss to span from one side of the building to the other and to resist the outward thrust of the arches. These tie members are carrying all of the collective force that was previously carried by nine tie members. As a consequence, the two tie

members have to be substantially larger than the nine tie members that they are replacing.

Continuing with the notion of freeing up space and making the interior more open and versatile, we can replace the interior columns with a truss suitable for providing the vertical component at the end of the arches (see Figures 8.20, 8.21, 8.22, and 8.23).

Figure 8.23 shows the vertical deformation associated with the vertical truss and the horizontal deformation associated with the horizontal trusses in the plane of the side roofs.

These horizontal buttressing trusses can be made curvilinear, as in Figures 8.24 through 8.27.

The addition to Union Station in Washington, D.C., designed by Benjamin Thompson and Associates, is an example of opening up the volume under the arches by removing most of the tie members (see Figure 8.28).

In designing a building like this, keep in mind that the roof diaphragm is very deep and, therefore, very stiff. Stiff elements tend to pick up a disproportionate share of the load. In other words, most of the load may go to the roof diaphragm, rather than to the horizontal truss that is part of the tubular truss. If the roof diaphragm is not designed to take the load, then it can fail, leaving the building without part of its envelope. If the roof diaphragm can take the load, then the diagonals on the top of the tubular truss can be omitted.

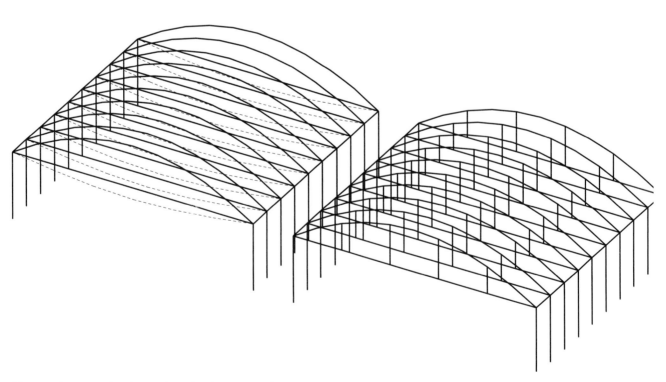

Figure 8.15 Tied arches with and without sag rods.

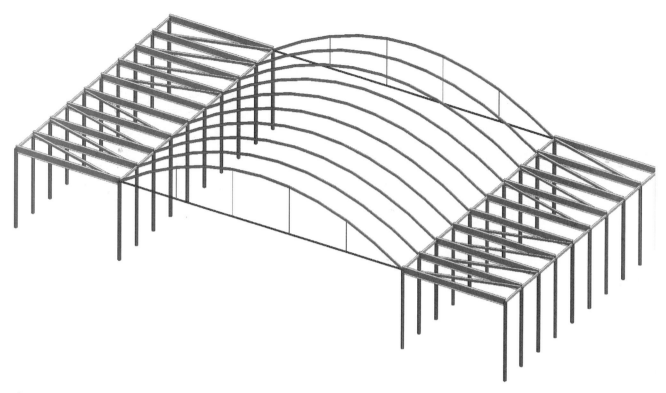

Figure 8.16 Arches buttressed with parallel-chord trusses.

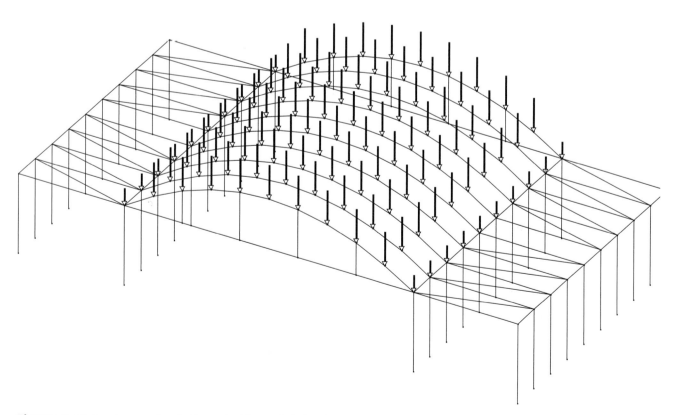

Figure 8.17 Loads on arches buttressed with parallel-chord trusses.

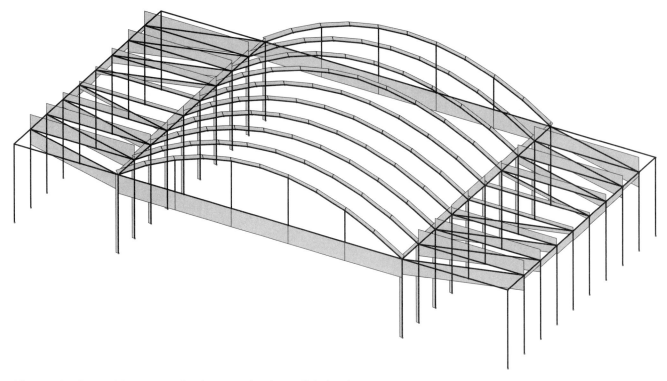

Figure 8.18 Axial forces in arches buttressed with parallel-chord trusses.

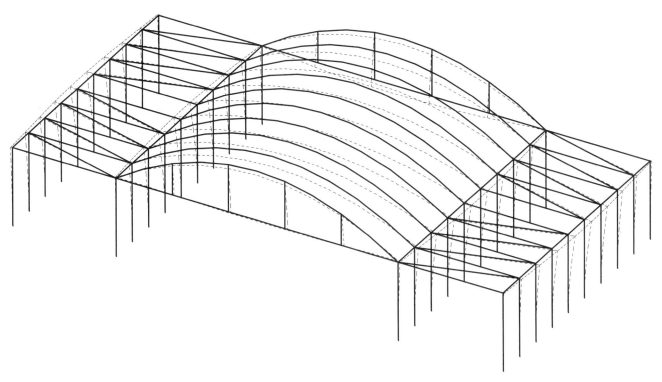

Figure 8.19 Deflection of arches buttressed with parallel-chord trusses.

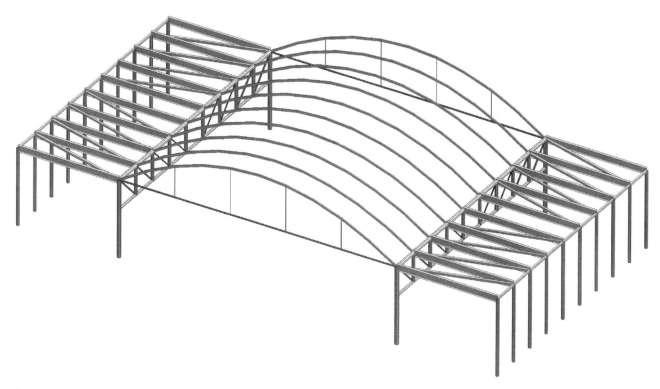

Figure 8.20 Arches buttressed and supported by parallel-chord trusses.

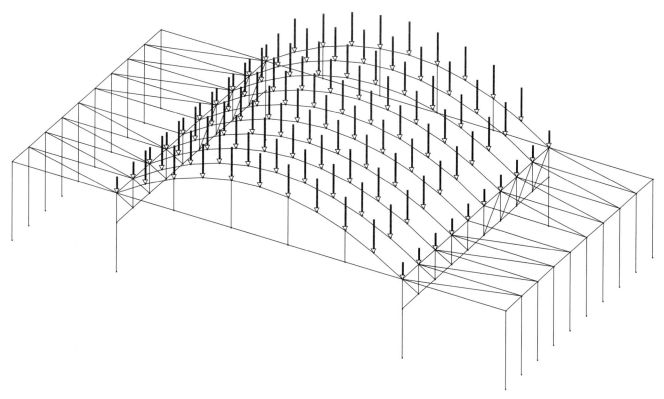

Figure 8.21 Loads on arches buttressed and supported by parallel-chord trusses.

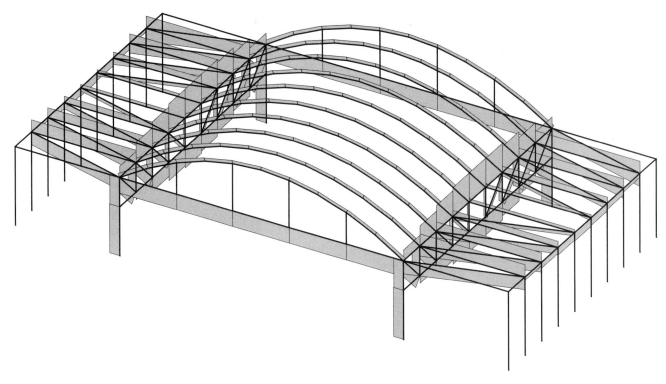

Figure 8.22 Axial forces in arches buttressed and supported by parallel-chord trusses.

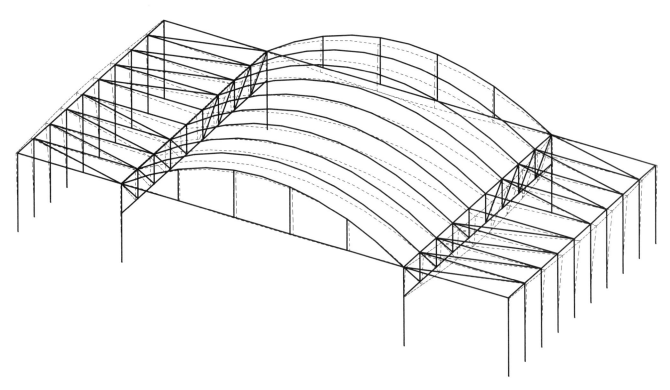

Figure 8.23 Deflection of arches buttressed and supported by parallel-chord trusses.

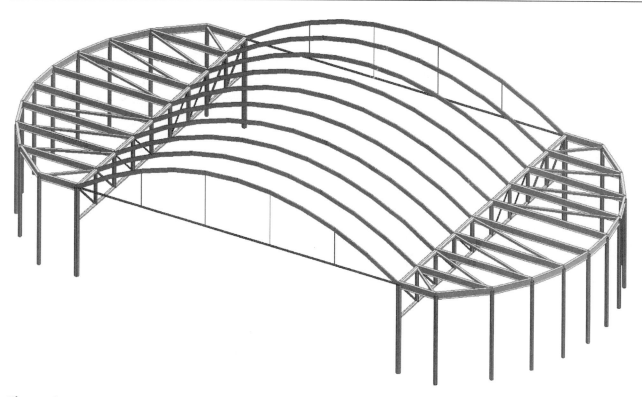

Figure 8.24 Arches buttressed by sling truss.

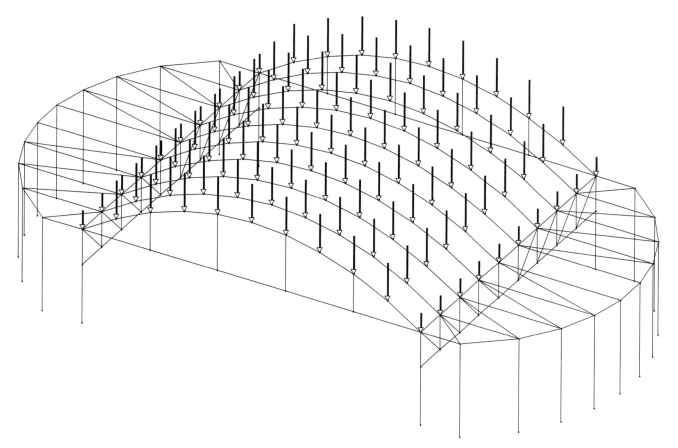

Figure 8.25 Loads on arches buttressed by sling truss.

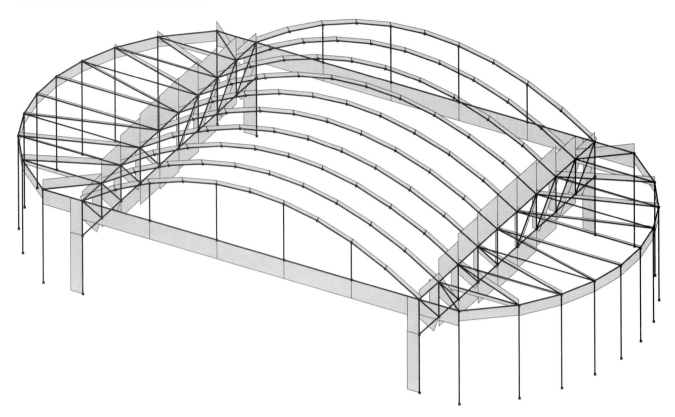

Figure 8.26 Axial force in arches buttressed by sling truss.

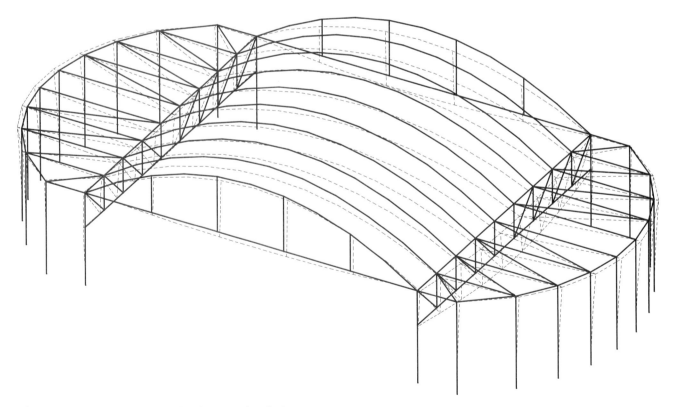

Figure 8.27 Deflection of arches buttressed with sling truss.

Figure 8.28 Union Station in Washington, D.C.

If you ever encounter something that looks like an arch, but has no tie member and no apparent buttressing action, then it is not an arch. Somewhere inside, there are other kinds of structural elements that make it work. For example, at the end bay of the structure in Figure 8.29, there is no buttressing element (a). The image in (b) shows that the actual structure is a series of 3 in.-diameter steel pipe columns supporting lightweight, wide-flange beams that span from column to column. The visual effect of the arch is achieved with the use of light framing covered with a thin skin. The appearance of fat columns is achieved with the use of lightweight prefab wraps.

8.1.2 REDUCING AXIAL FORCE BY INCREASING THE DEPTH-TO-SPAN RATIO FOR AN ARCH

The vertical loads, and, therefore, the vertical reactions, on an arch are "givens" of the design problem. If the arch is to exhibit true arch action, then the stresses in the arch must be axial. Therefore, the force of the overall support reaction C must be tangent to the arch at the support point. The lower the depth-to-span ratio, the lower the slope of the arch at the support point and the lower the slope of the reactive force C. Since the vertical reaction component V is fixed—that is, it is a "given" of the design problem—a shallow slope for C implies a large hor-

izontal component H and a large overall reaction force C. A high reaction force on the base of the arch implies high forces inside the arch. The first arch shown in Figure 8.30 has the lower depth-to-span ratio, which means that it has the higher forces in it. To resist this higher force, it must have more material in it.

The forces in the arch can also be compared by superimposing the images of several arches of differing rises, as shown in the diagram in Figure 8.31.

$$C_1 = \sqrt{(V)^2 + (0.5\ V)^2} = \sqrt{V^2 + 0.25\ V^2} = \sqrt{1.25\ V^2}$$
$$= V \cdot \sqrt{1.25} = 1.18\ V = 0.559\ W = 2.236\ H_1$$

$$C_2 = \sqrt{(V)^2 + (V)^2} = \sqrt{V^2} = V \cdot \sqrt{2} = 1.414\ V$$
$$= 0.707\ W = 1.414\ H_1$$

$$C_3 = \sqrt{(V)^2 + (2\ V)^2} = \sqrt{V^2 + 4\ V^2} = \sqrt{5\ V^2} = V \cdot \sqrt{5}$$
$$= V \cdot 2.236\ V = 1.118\ W = 1.118\ H_1$$

$$C_4 = \sqrt{(V)^2 + (4\ V)^2} = \sqrt{V^2 + 16\ V^2} = \sqrt{17\ V^2}$$
$$= V \cdot \sqrt{17} = 4.124\ V = 2.062\ W = 1.031\ H_1 \qquad \textbf{[8.17]}$$

There is an important related point involving bow trusses. A bow truss with an upwardly curved bottom chord does

(a)   (b)

Figure 8.29 Giving the appearance of being an arch (a) while concealing beam and columns (b).

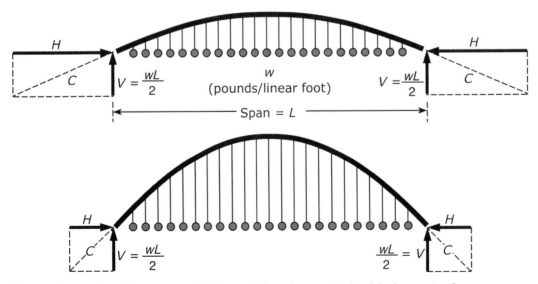

Figure 8.30 Effect of proportions (rise/span ratio) on the magnitude of the buttressing force.

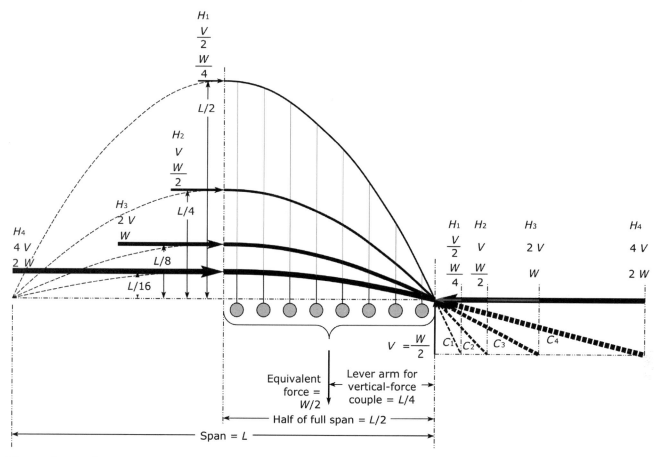

Figure 8.31 Effect of proportions (rise/span ratio) on the magnitude of the internal force.

not have a lever arm as large as one with a flat bottom chord. Therefore, the axial chord forces will be large in such a bow truss. This point is illustrated by the bow-truss configurations in Figures 8.32, 8.33, and 8.34. Figure 8.32 shows the shapes of the trusses and the applied forces on the trusses. Figure 8.33 shows the axial force in the members. The axial-chord forces for the truss on the bottom have doubled, as compared with the axial-chord force in the truss above, because the lever arm at the center of the bottom truss is half the lever arm for the truss above. There are also tensile web forces in the vertical webs of the bottom truss, since the tendency of the two curved chords is to pull apart. Figure 8.34 indicates that the deflection is much larger for the shallower truss.

8.1.3 VARIATIONS IN THE INTERNAL COMPRESSIVE FORCE IN AN ARCH

No matter where an arch is sliced to create a freebody, the horizontal component of the total force on the cut face must always equal the horizontal component of the reaction at the support. Hence, the horizontal component is constant throughout the arch. In order to keep the total

internal force tangent to the axial line of the arch, the vertical component must change along the arch. The maximum vertical force, and, therefore, the maximum total force, must occur where the slope of the arch is a maximum, that is, at the base of the arch.

At the top of the arch, the internal compressive force C is just equal to H. At the base of the arch, the internal compressive force is given by

$$C = \sqrt{H^2 + V^2}$$

where V is the vertical reaction at the base.

For arches with high proportions (i.e., the rise-to-span ratio is high), the lever arm for the H forces is very large relative to the lever arm for the vertical reaction V, so the H forces are small relative to the vertical reaction V. In such arches, V dominates the preceding expression given for C at the base of the arch, and the force C at the base is much larger than the force C at the top, which is only equal to H. In other words, in arches with high proportions, the variation in internal force along the arch is very significant. Hence, it becomes important in such structures to address this variation in force by varying the

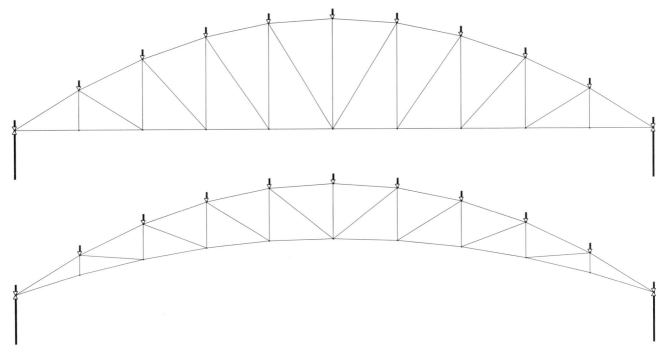

Figure 8.32 Standard bow truss and bow truss with curved bottom chord.

cross-sectional area of the arch, with the largest cross-sectional area occurring at the base of the arch. (Arches with very high proportions can be thought of as approaching freestanding columns, with the forces at the top being negligible and the forces at the bottom being quite significant.) An example of a structure with proportions of this kind is the Saint Louis Gateway Arch (Ar-

chitect: Eero Saarinen; Engineers: Severud and Associates). See Figure 8.35.

Of course, this is a complicated example that is not fully comprehended simply by consideration of the variations in the magnitude of *C*. For example, under wind loading, which is a significant issue in this structure, the "arch" is actually acting like a cantilever beam sticking

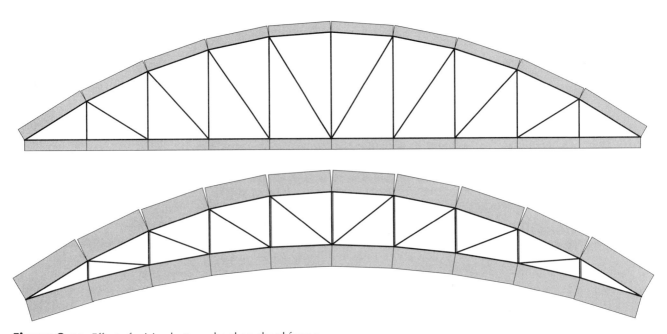

Figure 8.33 Effect of raising bottom chord on chord forces.

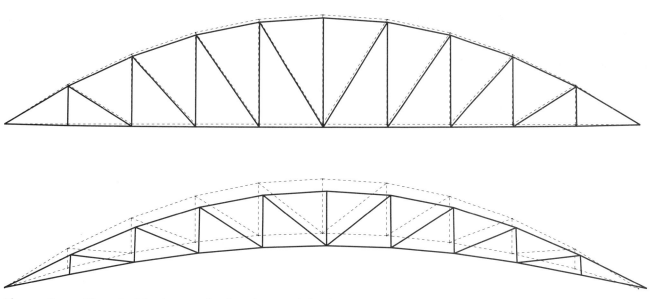

Figure 8.34 Effect of raising bottom chord on the truss deflection.

Figure 8.35 Gateway Arch. (Image courtesy of B. Mckinney.)

up out of the ground. For resisting wind loading, it is extremely important that we broaden the base of the structure, where the worst overturning moment is occurring. Putting most of the material at the base is also important simply from the point of view of lateral stability, since the arch is a compressive member that will fail by buckling if it is not stiff enough.

For arches with low proportions (i.e., the rise-to-span ratio is low), the lever arm for the H forces is very small relative to the lever arm for the vertical reaction V, so the H forces are large relative to the vertical reaction V. In such arches, H dominates the expression given earlier for C at the base of the arch, and the force C at the base is not much larger than H, which is the force C at the top. In other words, in arches with low proportions, the variation in internal force along the arch is modest. In such cases, adding thickness at the base may be more trouble than it is worth, and there may be other, more compelling motives for adding extra material elsewhere along the arch. This will become clear in upcoming discussions of buckling issues in regard to arches.

8.1.4 LATERAL STABILIZATION OF AN ARCH

Any arch is a compressive member, and like all other compressive members, it has a tendency to buckle. This buckling failure can involve either lateral or vertical movement.

If an arch has no other elements to help stabilize it against laterally buckling, lateral wind loads, and lateral loading from earthquakes, then its stability depends on its "lateral breadth," that is, on the lateral dimension of its cross section. Increasing the lateral dimension of an arch cross section will make the arch laterally more stable. This thickening can be made along the full extent of the arch, which may be the easiest thing to do for fabrication and construction (see Figure 8.36).

To achieve maximal design efficiency, however, it is desirable to preferentially increase the lateral dimension of the arch cross section at the base of the arch. Again, thinking of the arch as a freestanding column that is tending to collapse sideways, the logical response is to increase the dimension near the base (see Figure 8.37).

If the arch gets very high, it can be split at the base to give it an even wider stance (see Figure 8.38).

Stability against lateral buckling, lateral wind loads, and lateral loading from earthquakes can be achieved by other means than using a moment connection at the base of an arch. For example, multiple arches can be joined together using perpendicular bracing elements, with rigid joints where the perpendicular elements connect to the arches, thereby producing a curved Verendeel truss to resist lateral movement (see Figure 8.39).

If the Verendeel truss is not stiff enough against lateral movement, then the arches can be connected together with diagonal web members to produce a fully triangulated truss to resist lateral movement (see Figure 8.40).

Figure 8.36 Lateral stabilization through lateral breadth. (Image courtesy of Leonhardt, Andrä und Partner.)

Figure 8.37 Lateral stabilization through breadth at base. (Image courtesy of Leonhardt, Andrä und Partner.)

Figure 8.38 Lateral stabilization through breadth at base. (Image courtesy of Leonhardt, Andrä und Partner.)

Figure 8.39 Lateral stabilization through rigid-frame action. (Image courtesy of Leonhardt, Andrä und Partner.)

Figure 8.40 Lateral stabilization through trusswork. (Image courtesy of Leonhardt, Andrä und Partner.)

If there is a roof or working surface attached to the top of the arches, then this surface can be made into a diaphragm that stabilizes the arches against lateral movement. The diagram in Figure 8.41 is an example of such a roofing system.

8.1.5 VERTICAL STABILIZATION OF AN ARCH: RESISTING ROLL-THROUGH BUCKLING

Vertical buckling, sometimes called roll-through buckling, can occur in the manner depicted in Figure 8.42.

There are many methods of addressing this issue, the simplest of which is to thicken the arch in the vertical direction, such as shown in Figure 8.43.

This thickening can also be achieved with the use of a Verendeel-truss arch (see Figure 8.44).

It can also be achieved with the use of a fully triangulated trussed arch.

Roll-through buckling failure in arches is similar to lateral buckling in columns. Even in a perfectly straight column with a precisely axial force, lateral buckling can severely limit the stress that the column can endure. Similarly, even for an arch in which the internal force is exactly axial, roll-through buckling can occur. In the case of columns, the cross section was selectively increased near the center of the column in order to avoid buckling. If an analogy is sought between resisting buckling in columns and resisting buckling in arches, there may be a temptation to put most of the material at the center of the arch (see Figure 8.45).

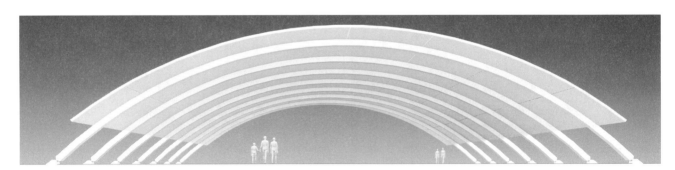

Figure 8.41 Lateral stabilization through diaphragm action. (Rendering by James Sweeney.)

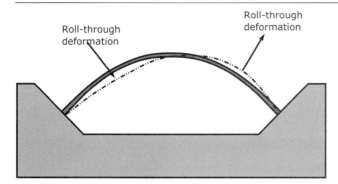

Figure 8.42 Roll-through buckling.

Figure 8.44 Using Verendeel trusses to resist roll-through buckling.

An arch, however, does not buckle in exactly the same manner as a column. As a column begins to buckle, the largest movements occur at the center. In the case of an arch, the largest movement does not occur at the center, but at the quarter points (see Figure 8.46).

In a sense, the top of an arch is constrained against vertical movement by the action of the other parts of the arch. Furthermore, the base points are also constrained against vertical movement. So the vertical movement occurs at the quarter points. Therefore, the proper column analogy is not a simple pinned-pinned column, such as

Figure 8.43 Resisting roll-through buckling by making the arch thicker. (Image courtesy of Leonhardt, Andrä und Partner.)

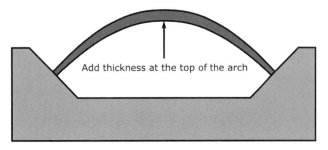

Figure 8.45 Adding thickness at the top of the arch.

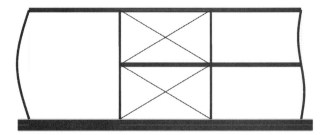

Figure 8.47 Column buckling shapes.

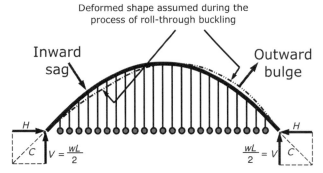

Figure 8.46 Movement at the quarter points.

Figure 8.48 Thickening the arch at the quarter points.

the one on the left in Figure 8.47, but rather a pinned-pinned column that is constrained at the center, such as the one on the right in Figure 8.47.

To address roll-through buckling, the aim is to add thickness away from the constrained parts, that is, near the quarter points (see Figure 8.48).

Maillart's bridges serve as an excellent example of this structural device (see Figure 8.49).

Roll-through buckling can also be resisted by bracing the arch at the quarter points using struts or tension members. This approach is beautifully illustrated by the example shown in Figure 8.50.

Figure 8.49 Bridge stabilized against roll-through by thickening at the quarter points. (Design by Robert Maillart; Image courtesy of Eugenio Pedrazzini.)

Figure 8.50 Broadgate Exchange House, London, England. (Image courtesy of Hedrich Blessing.)

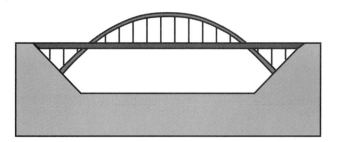

Figure 8.51 Bridge stabilized against roll-through by connection of road at the quarter points.

This particular structure is a crossover between a bowstring truss and a tied arch with bracing elements added to prevent roll-through buckling. This structure is discussed extensively later in this chapter. Roll-through buckling can also be resisted by a roadbed or roof that comes through the arch, and connects to the arch, at the quarter points. In the diagram in Figure 8.51, the roadbed (and associated beam structure) is stabilized by attachment to the land and, in turn, it connects to the quarter points of the arches to prevent roll-through of the arches.

Roll-through buckling can also be resisted by a thick, rigid roadbed or roof structure to which the arch is remotely connected (see Figure 8.52).

The diagram in Figure 8.53 demonstrates another variation on the theme of resisting roll-through buckling using a thick, rigid roadbed or roof structure to which the arch is remotely connected.

The working surface (be it roadbed, roof, or another surface) can be suspended from the arch with diagonal suspenders, as shown in Figure 8.54. Under uniform load, all of the suspenders have substantial tension because of the dead weight of the structure. Any roll-through deformation will cause some of the suspenders to slacken.

Figure 8.52 Arches stabilized against roll-through by connection to deep beam along roadway. (Image courtesy of Leonhardt, Andrä und Partner.)

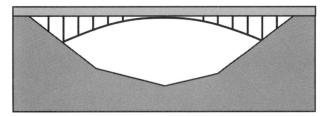

Figure 8.53 Bridge stabilized against roll-through by connection to thick beam along roadway.

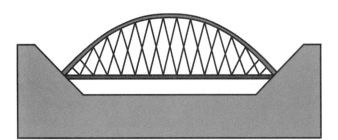

Figure 8.54 Bridge stabilized against roll-through using diagonal suspenders.

The suspenders that remain active in tension are at such an angle that they tend to restore the arch to its original shape, thereby inhibiting any tendency to roll-through.

One of the most effective ways to prevent roll-through buckling is to fully triangulate the arch to produce a classic bow truss, as shown in Figure 8.55. The behavior of bow trusses is discussed in depth later in this chapter.

Some arches are made thick at the base and thin near the top (see Figure 8.56).

Making the arch thick at the base has less to do with the function of the bridge in its service load than it does with simplifying construction, allowing the two ends of the bridge to cantilever under their self-weight during the construction process, thereby avoiding expensive centering to support the bridge during construction. Self-scaffolding structures tend to be much more efficient and economical to construct, even though the distribution of material may not be the most efficient for the final, in situ performance. This bridge and the Saint Louis Gateway Arch were both constructed in this manner. Figure 8.57

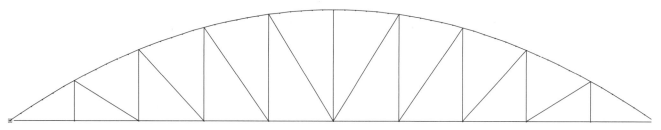

Figure 8.55 Web members of bow truss resist roll-through buckling.

Figure 8.56 Thickening the base of the arch. (Image courtesy of Leonhardt, Andrä und Partner.)

shows the Gateway Arch cantilevering out of the foundations during construction. The cantilevering action was adequate to support the two towering halves of the arch almost all the way to the top.

Figure 8.58 shows a trussed compression strut being used to push the two halves of the arch apart, to allow the final pieces to be installed. Figures 8.59 through 8.62 show other images of the construction of the St. Louis Arch.

Figure 8.57 Gateway Arch cantilevering out of foundations during construction. (Photograph courtesy of Jefferson National Parks Association.)

Figure 8.59 Gateway Arch. (Photograph courtesy of Jefferson National Parks Association.)

Figure 8.58 Two halves of the Gateway Arch being pushed apart by trussed compression strut. (Photograph courtesy of Jefferson National Parks Association.)

Figure 8.60 Inserting the final piece in the Gateway Arch. (Photograph courtesy of Jefferson National Parks Association.)

Figure 8.61 Crane on the Gateway Arch lifting another section into place. (Photograph courtesy of Jefferson National Parks Association.)

Figure 8.62 Installing the final segment in the Gateway Arch. (Photograph courtesy of Jefferson National Parks Association.)

8.1.6 FUNICULAR SHAPE UNDER THE PRIMARY LOAD

In compression structures, the funicular shape under a given load is the shape that allows the structure to work in pure axial compression, with no bending. Achieving the funicular shape under the primary load is important to achieving structural efficiency. It is particularly crucial in masonry construction where the material does not have tensile capacity. Gothic cathedrals are examples of masonry construction. Stacking the stones in exactly the right way was crucial to a building's standing up. The medieval builders used scale models to assess their designs. If the blocks fashioned for the model were not stable, then the real building surely would not stand. The designers also monitored their buildings during construction and made modifications as they seemed necessary. Many of the elements previously regarded as pure ornamentation are now known to have been motivated by structural concerns as well as aesthetic considerations. For example, in the Cathedral of Notre Dame in Paris, the weight of the spires perched on the flying buttresses is a part of the overall balance that keeps the structure stable (see Figure 8.63).

Spanish architect Antoni Gaudi generated very sophisticated designs for compression vaults by using tension models to establish the geometry of the structural form. He simply inverted the structural shapes assumed by complex assemblies of chains, loaded with weights distributed to simulate the loads on the intended structure.

Since Gaudi built with unreinforced masonry, it was critical that his structures have the right shape to ensure that no tensile stresses would occur. Using the chains, which cannot generate any bending resistance, he was able to ascertain the ideal shape for ensuring pure axial stress.

This text does not address in any detail structures of such complexity as Gothic cathedrals or Gaudi's vaults. The following discussion is devoted to understanding what the funicular shape would be for spanning elements subjected to various common loading conditions.

It is important to understand that the funicular shape is particular to the loading condition for which it is generated. Changing the load changes the funicular shape, just as the shape of a suspension bridge in a children's playground changes shape in response to the movement of a person walking across it. The funicular shape is typically derived for a dominant load condition. For example, Gothic cathedrals are large structures made out of stone, which is a very heavy material that induces high compressive stresses under self-weight. Gothic cathedrals are shaped to produce pure compression under self-weight. Under wind load, the stress patterns are completely different, producing significant bending stress. The bending stress induced by wind has associated with it a tensile

Figure 8.63 Notre Dame Cathedral.

component. If the building is designed properly, the tensile stress associated with wind-induced bending stress will never exceed the axial compressive stress induced by the self-weight of the structure. In other words, the dominant load is the self-weight, rather than the wind. The high self-weight of Gothic cathedrals has allowed them to remain stable under wind forces over the centuries.

An arch of uniform cross section under its own self-weight has a load that is uniform along its length. To achieve pure axial stress under its own self-weight, such an arch should be formed in the shape of a catenary. A rope or chain, suspended under its own self-weight, takes

on the shape of a catenary curve. A catenary curve is easy to generate experimentally by simply draping a rope. It is much more complicated to generate mathematically, as shown later in this section. The funicular shape for the structure shown in Figure 8.64, under its own self-weight, would be a catenary. If the arches and roof diaphragm are made out of concrete and the structure is in a location where the snow load is low, then the self-weight will be the dominant load and the appropriate shape would be a catenary. Snow is a load that is uniform on the horizontal. The appropriate shape for an arch subjected to a load that is uniform along the horizontal is a parabola. If

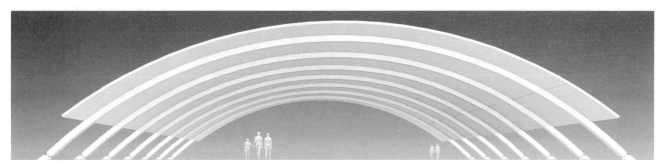

Figure 8.64 Arches and roof diaphragm of uniform cross section. (Rendering by James Sweeney.)

the arch shown in Figure 8.64 was built of a very light, efficient material and was located where the snow loads are high, then the snow load would be the dominant load and the parabola would be an appropriate shape for the arch.

In the building shown in Figure 8.65, the overwhelming load is the weight of the floors, which is uniformly distributed along the horizontal. For this building, the arch should definitely be a parabola.

Actually, the load on the arch in Figure 8.65 is not uniform in the sense of being continuous. Rather, the load consists of very large discrete forces spaced equally along the horizontal. The resulting arch is segmented, with cusps occurring at the points where the vertical elements

Figure 8.65 Parabolic arch of the Broadgate Exchange House, London, England. (Architecture and Engineering by the Chicago office of Skidmore, Owings & Merrill, LLP. Image from Hedrich Blessing.)

deliver the load to the arches and straight segments in between. The vertices where the cusps occur lie on a parabola (see Figure 8.66).

Figure 8.67 shows possible shapes for high arches.

Figure 8.68 shows possible shapes for low arches.

The obvious question is, How significant is the difference between these shapes? The answers are as follows:

- Using a parabola where a catenary is the funicular shape will produce significant bending stresses, often substantially in excess of the axial stresses.
- Using a catenary where a parabola is the funicular shape will also produce significant bending stresses, often substantially in excess of the axial stresses.
- The semicircle and ellipse deviate drastically from the funicular shape for most loading conditions, and using a semicircular or an elliptical element without bracing it to make it hold its shape will normally result in severe bending stresses that drastically exceed the axial stresses.

It is interesting that for many centuries, the semicircle was the dominant arch form. It survived because the infill material between the arches helped brace the arch against its tendency to bulge upward and outward at the quarter points, as shown in the structure in Figure 8.69.

Under movement induced by earthquake disturbances, the "arch" in Figure 8.69 has begun to give indications of its actual structural behavior: tensile cracks are occurring on the bottom side of the curve at the zenith and on the top side of the curve at the quarter points. No compressive stress can be transmitted across a crack. The actual stress path occurs where the stones are still pressing together. The actual stress path through the material is closer in shape to a catenary or a parabola than a semicircle. When structures like this are sufficiently disturbed, it is common for them to be shored up with interior walls to avoid total collapse.

In unreinforced masonry, the distinctions between these shapes can be a life-and-death matter. With most highly efficient modern materials that have both compressive and tensile capabilities (such as steel, wood, and reinforced concrete), the issue is not such an extreme concern. For structures made of these materials, the bending capacity of the material will compensate for minor errors associated with not getting the precise funicular shape. The efficiency of such a material also means that the self-weight associated with the material is small as compared with other loads on the structure, in which case the bending stress associated with these other forces will normally significantly exceed the axial stress associated with the compressive action under self-weight. By the time the structure has been given enough bending capacity to deal with these other forces, getting the precise funicular shape under self-weight is usually not particularly critical to the structural efficiency of the system.

Figure 8.66 Cusps in the arch of the Broadgate Exchange House, London, England. (Architecture and Engineering by the Chicago office of Skidmore, Owings & Merrill, LLP. Image from Hedrich Blessing.)

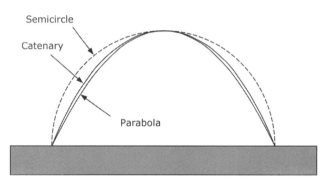

Figure 8.67 Common shapes for curved elements.

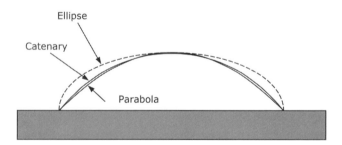

Figure 8.68 Shapes for low arches.

Again, it must be noted that the funicular shape applies to a specific, fixed-load distribution. The response to variable loads, such as wind load, road traffic, live loads, and drifting (nonuniform) snow load, has to be some kind of beam action; that is, the structure has to be thickened at strategic points to address the bending stresses induced by the variable loads.

Figure 8.69 Semicircular arch sagging at the center and bulging upward and outward at the quarter points. (Image courtesy of Rowland J. Mainstone from *Developments in Structural Form* [Architectural Press, 2001].)

Even the weakest of modern structural materials, such as concrete, are so inherently efficient that they allow designers to choose forms that deviate significantly from the ideal, because they simply want an expressive form. For example, the bridge shown in Figure 8.70 has two huge forces that, if properly accounted for in the shape, would produce pronounced cusp points where those forces are delivered. However, the designer has chosen a smooth, curved element for visual reasons. In the end, the dominant issue in the sizing of this curved structural element is the bending stress induced by the two large forces being delivered through the pillars resting on the curved element.

Figure 8.70 Curved element subjected to large localized forces. (Image courtesy of Leonhardt, Andrä und Partner.)

In the structure in Figure 8.71, the curved elements are loaded only by a localized force at the top of the curved element. The curved elements are not the funicular shape for addressing a concentrated force at the top. The strength of the steel elements allows them to work in bending to carry the load.

In the structure shown in Figure 8.72, the curved elements are semicircular in shape. Under snow load or the load of the roof decking, the bending stresses drastically exceed the axial stresses in semicircular elements. In this case, the desire for the optimum structural form under gravity loads was overridden by at least two other important factors: simplicity and economy of manufacture favored semicircular over catenary or parabolic curved elements.

Wind forces are comparable to gravity loads in such a lightweight structure, which means that serious bending stresses will occur under wind loads. Therefore, going to great lengths to choose the optimal shape under gravity loads is pointless, since the curved structural element must have substantial bending capacity anyway, to resist the effects of wind (see Figure 8.72).

The derivation of these funicular shapes is given in the following discussion. Also presented are analyses that help to clarify the design issues.

In the process of searching for the ideal structural shape, it is useful to look back at the results of previous studies to gain context and perspective. Chapter 7 addresses flat-top trusses. Parallel-chord trusses, such as that shown in Figure 8.73, are the most common form of flat-top trusses.

The main reason for this form is its simple fabrication from continuous, flat members used for the top and bottom chords. This avoids the need to shape the chords or to connect chord-member segments to each other. Supporting floors, which are flat, is a good use for flat-top trusses. However, parallel-chord trusses are so economical to produce that these trusses are used extensively in roofs despite their flatness, which is not ideal for shedding rain and snow (see Figure 8.74).

Parallel-chord truss chord forces are extremely variable (see Figure 8.75).

If the chord is made of a continuous member of uniform cross section, the maximum chord force along the truss length dictates the required cross-sectional area. Chord segments with less force have a larger cross-sectional area than the force in them requires. This means that more material is used than the structure requires.

Material is used more efficiently when each chord segment's cross-sectional area is adjusted to satisfy the segment's force requirements. This complicates the truss fabrication drastically, except when the truss length is such that handling it requires separate pieces for each truss segment. In almost all modest-span parallel-chord trusses (less than 60 ft), the simplicity of continuous-

Figure 8.71 Curved elements being loaded by a localized force at the top.

Figure 8.72 Semicircular, trussed arches at the Brown and Root Employee Center, Houston, Texas.

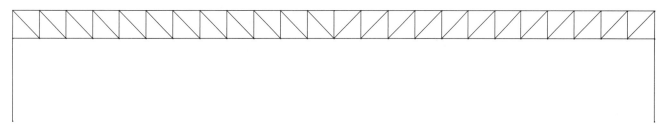

Figure 8.73 Twenty-four-bay, square-bay, parallel-chord truss.

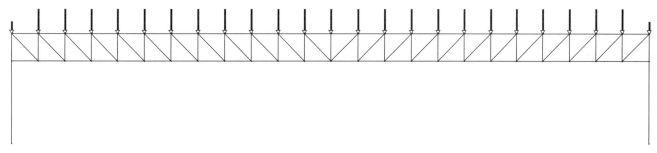

Figure 8.74 Loads on joints of the truss.

chord construction outweighs any material inefficiency resulting from oversizing some chord segments.

Despite structural deficiencies, the parallel-chord truss is so efficient and economical that it is a dominant form in American building construction. There is still a search for a more efficient form, particularly in areas where the parallel-chord truss needs improvement, such as in shedding rain.

In designing roofs, rather than floors, the top chord can be shaped to improve structural efficiency. There are at least two good ways to progress from the force diagram in Figure 8.75 to a more efficient structural form:

1. The internal moment in a simple-span truss varies parabolically along the spanning member's length. The maximum moment occurs at center span, and the zero moment occurs at each end. In the parallel-chord truss, the lever arm for the two chord members is a constant along the truss length. This lever arm can be made to fol-low a parabolic shape along the span, with a zero lever arm at the end supports and the maximum lever arm at center span.

2. The web forces increase toward the truss ends; the chord forces diminish. The top chord can be shaped to gather the web members' shear-resistance burden near the truss ends. The material in the chord segments is then engaged more, and the cross sections and the web members' connections are reduced in size.

Both of these arguments lead to the same new form—a bowstring truss (see Figure 8.76).

According to the reasoning outlined here, this truss has uniformly stressed chords, minimal web forces, and only two joints that transfer large forces, located where the two chords intersect at the ends. The top chord must be shaped to gain this structural efficiency and connection simplicity. Ways to shape the chord are discussed later in this chapter. The broad-brushstroke argument

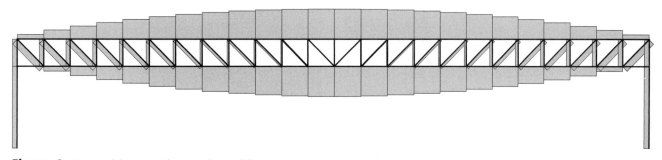

Figure 8.75 Axial forces in the members of the truss.

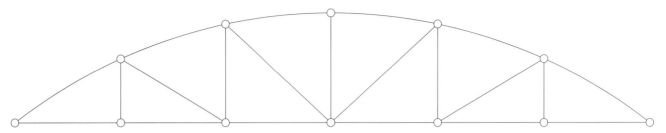

Figure 8.76 Bowstring truss, or bow truss.

outlined earlier shows the general idea behind the bow-string geometry. Structural analysis allows one to explore the various effects of load on form.

Equilibrium principles and action–reaction pairs are used to analyze and size members in a structure. The shape of that structure is chosen on the basis of factors other than the equilibrium principles and action–reaction pairs, such as the designer's intuitive sense of structures or aesthetics. It is also possible to use the equilibrium principles and action–reaction pairs as design tools, to help establish a rational basis for form.

To illustrate this idea, find the shape of a six-bay bow-string truss in which the web forces are zero under a uniform load of 1 P on each truss-top vertex. Under the uniform load, the web members are bracing members only; that is, they do not carry force. This top-chord shape is called the funicular shape under the prescribed load. The top chord works in pure compression, under this load, without bending, regardless of whether the web members are there or not.

Assume that the truss has six 20 ft-wide bays (for a 120 ft total span) and an overall 20 ft depth. This provides a span-to-depth ratio of 6, which is in the range of proportions listed for steel-bow trusses found in Chapter 1, in the guidelines for spans and proportions of common spanning members and systems. The diagram in Figure 8.77

shows the locations of the top-center joint D and the bottom-chord joints in proper proportion to each other. The top-chord joints B, C, E, and F are roughly drawn, as their locations are not known exactly until after the problem is solved.

To emphasize the point that the web members are zero-force members in this load condition, draw them as lightly dashed lines (see Figure 8.78).

In the drawing, there is an x–y coordinate system at the top of the truss's center. Write the coordinate of each top-chord vertex relative to this system. This system is chosen to simplify finding the current problem's solution: the y-axis is placed on the structure's symmetry line; the x-axis is located to avoid the requirement for an offset constant in the subsequent equation to describe the final truss geometry. When the problem is expanded or is altered, shift to another coordinate system that is more appropriate to the new problem. Because joint D has the coordinates $(x, y) = (0, 0)$ and because y is positive in an upward direction, the truss joints' coordinates have negative y values. Dealing with negative coordinates is a minor inconvenience for the sake of maintaining the long-standing mathematical convention of choosing up as the positive y direction.

The top-chord members' slopes are not known, nor are the forces in the top-chord members. Therefore, the joints

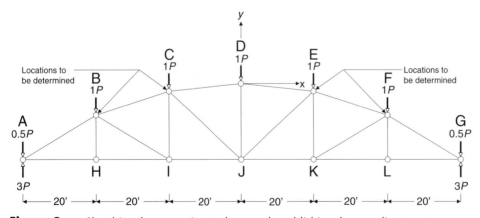

Figure 8.77 Sketching the approximate shape and establishing the coordinate system.

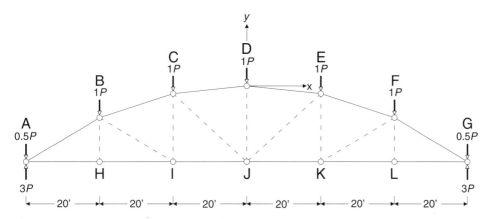

Figure 8.78 Dashing the webs to emphasize their role as zero-force, bracing members.

method cannot be directly applied at any location in the truss. The sections method can be applied to determine the force in the bottom chord at joint J and in the top chord at joint D. To do this, remove the truss's left side and draw the truss's right side with forces from the left side applied to the right side (see Figure 8.79).

In the diagram in Figure 8.79, directions are assumed for the forces the truss's left-hand side exerts on the truss's right-hand side. One is free to assume the force directions as long as an arrow representing each force is recorded so that one knows to account for it in the mathematics. Directions are assumed for the forces to be consistent with the anticipated outcome. It is expected that the correctness of each of those choices will be confirmed by a positive value for the force, as the result of the application of the equilibrium principle. The horizontal top-

chord force is labeled C (for compression), and the horizontal bottom-chord force T (for tension).

Take moments about joint D:

$$\sum M_D = 0 \,\widehat{+}$$
$$0 = P\,(20\text{ ft}) + P\,(40\text{ ft}) + 0.5\,P\,(60\text{ ft}) - 3\,P\,(60\text{ ft})$$
$$+ T(20\text{ ft})$$

Divide both sides of the equation by 20 ft:

$$0 = P\,(1) + P\,(2) + 0.5\,P\,(3) - 3\,P\,(3) + T\,(1)$$

Collect terms:

$$0 = -4.5\,P + 1\,T$$
$$T = +4.5\,P$$

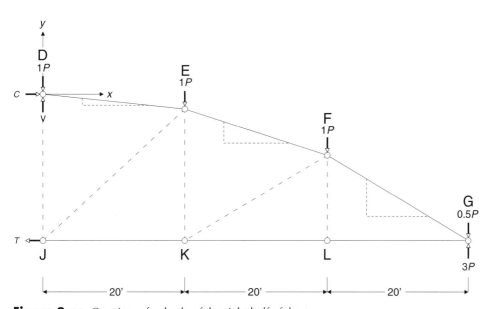

Figure 8.79 Creating a freebody of the right half of the truss.

As expected, the positive sign confirms the correctness of the *T* force's assumed direction. Summing the horizontal forces indicates that *C = T* = +4.5 *P* (see Figure 8.80).

Summing the vertical forces indicates that *V* = +0.5 *P*. The positive value confirms the correctness of *V*'s assumed direction (see Figure 8.81).

Now work through the truss, applying equilibrium principles at each joint to find the vertical and horizontal force components exerted by the chord segments that frame into those joints.

Applying the equilibrium principle to the horizontal forces on joint J:

The 4.5 *P* force to the left, exerted by the chord member IJ on joint J, must be equilibrated by a 4.5 *P* force to the right, exerted by the chord member JK on joint J.

Applying the action–reaction pairs principle to the interaction between joint J and chord member JK:

Since chord member JK is pulling to the right with a 4.5 *P* force on joint J, joint J must be pulling to the left with a 4.5 *P* force on chord member JK.

Applying the equilibrium principle to chord member JK:

The 4.5 *P* force to the left, exerted by joint J on chord member JK, must be equilibrated by a 4.5 *P* force to the right, exerted by joint K on member JK.

Applying the action–reaction pairs principle to the interaction between chord member JK and joint K:

Since joint K is pulling to the right with a 4.5 *P* force on chord member JK, member JK must be pulling to the left with a 4.5 *P* force on joint K (see Figure 8.82).

Similar deductive processes are applied at joints K and L, to arrive at the diagram shown in Figure 8.83.

Since the web members are not active, the only event at joints K and L is the chord force moving through the joints. From J to G is a continuous, uninterrupted chord member in which the force is a constant.

Applying the equilibrium principle to the horizontal forces on joint G:

The 4.5 *P* force to the left, exerted by the chord member LG on joint G, must be equilibrated by a horizontal 4.5 *P* force component to the right, exerted by the chord member FG on joint G.

Applying the action–reaction pairs principle to the interaction between joint G and chord member FG:

Since chord member FG is pushing to the right with a 4.5 *P* force component on joint G, joint G must be pushing to the left with a 4.5 *P* force component on member FG.

Applying the equilibrium principle to chord member FG:

The 4.5 *P* force component to the left, exerted by joint G on chord member FG, must be equilibrated by a 4.5 *P* force component to the right, exerted by joint F pushing on member FG.

Applying the action–reaction pairs principle to the interaction between chord member FG and joint F:

Since joint F is pushing to the right with a 4.5 *P* force component on chord member FG, member FG must be pushing to the left with a 4.5 *P* force component on joint F.

Applying the equilibrium principle to the vertical forces on joint G:

The 0.5 *P* applied force pushing down on joint G, combined with the 3 *P* reaction force pushing up on joint G, produce a net upward force of 2.5 *P*, which must be equilibrated by a downward 2.5 *P* force component, exerted by the chord member FG on joint G.

Applying the action–reaction pairs principle to the interaction between joint G and chord member FG:

Since chord member FG is pushing down with a 2.5 *P* force component on joint G, joint G must be pushing up with a 2.5 *P* force component on member FG.

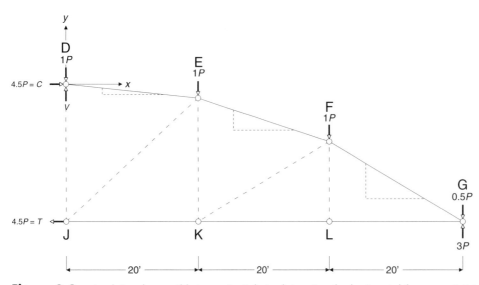

Figure 8.80 Applying the equilibrium principle to determine the horizontal forces on joints D and J.

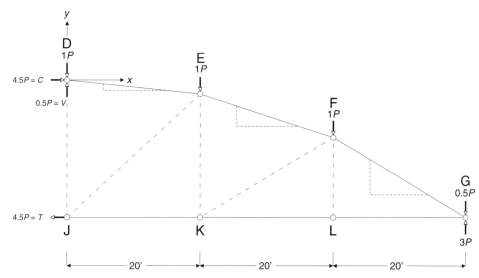

Figure 8.81 Applying the equilibrium principle to determine the vertical force on joint D.

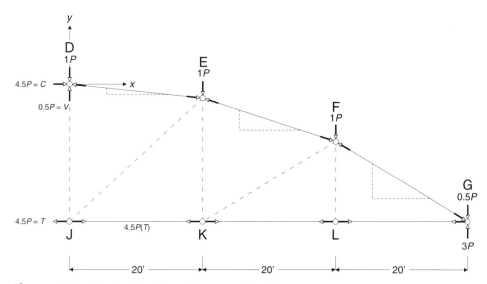

Figure 8.82 Resolved horizontal forces on joint J.

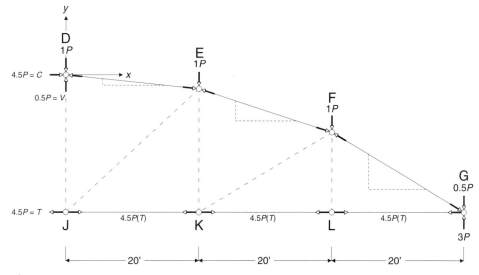

Figure 8.83 Resolved horizontal forces on joints K and L.

Applying the equilibrium principle to chord member FG:

The upward 2.5 *P* force exerted by joint G on chord member FG must be equilibrated by a downward 2.5 *P* force exerted by joint F on member FG.

Applying the action–reaction pairs principle to the interaction between chord member FG and joint F:

Since joint F is pushing downward with a 2.5 *P* force component on chord member FG, member FG must be pushing upward with a 2.5 *P* force on joint F (see Figure 8.84).

Applying the equilibrium principle to the horizontal forces on joint F:

The 4.5 *P* force to the left, exerted by chord member FG pushing on joint F, must be equilibrated by a horizontal 4.5 *P* force component to the right, exerted by chord member EF on joint F.

Applying the action–reaction pairs principle to the interaction between joint F and chord member EF:

Since chord member EF is pushing to the right with a 4.5 *P* force component on joint F, joint F must be pushing to the left with a 4.5 *P* force component on member EF.

Applying the equilibrium principle to chord member EF:

The 4.5 *P* force component to the left, exerted by joint F on chord member EF, must be equilibrated by a 4.5 *P* force component to the right, exerted by joint E on member EF.

Applying the action–reaction pairs principle to the interaction between chord member EF and joint E:

Since joint E is pushing to the right with a 4.5 *P* force component on chord member EF, member EF must be pushing to the left with a 4.5 *P* force component on joint E.

Applying the equilibrium principle to the vertical forces on joint F:

The 1 *P* applied force pushing down on joint F, combined with the upward 2.5 *P* force component exerted by chord member FG on joint F, produce a net upward 1.5 *P* force on joint F. This must be equilibrated by a downward 1.5 *P* force component exerted by chord member EF on joint F.

Applying the action–reaction pairs principle to the interaction between joint F and chord member EF:

Since chord member EF is pushing down with a 1.5 *P* force component on joint F, joint F must be pushing up with a 1.5 *P* force component on member EF.

Applying the equilibrium principle to chord member EF:

The upward 1.5 *P* force exerted by joint F on chord member EF must be equilibrated by a downward 1.5 *P* force exerted by joint E on member EF.

Applying the action–reaction pairs principle to the interaction between chord member EF and joint E:

Since joint E is pushing down with a 1.5 *P* force component on chord member EF, member EF must be pushing up with a 1.5 *P* force on joint E (see Figure 8.85).

Applying the equilibrium principle to the horizontal forces on joint E:

The 4.5 *P* force to the left exerted by the chord member EF pushing on joint E must be equilibrated by a horizontal 4.5 *P* force component to the right exerted by chord member DE on joint E.

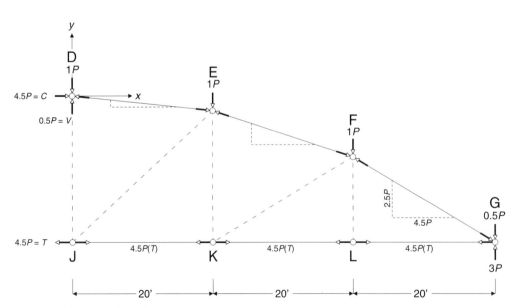

Figure 8.84 Resolved forces on joint G.

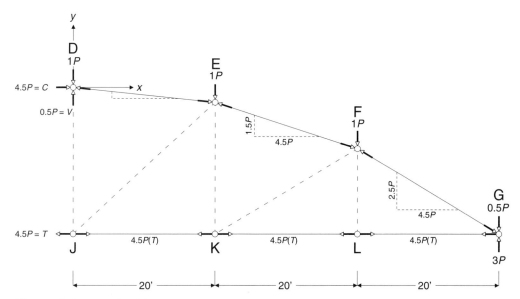

Figure 8.85 Resolved forces on joint F.

Applying the action–reaction pairs principle to the interaction between joint E and chord member DE:

Since chord member DE is pushing to the right with a 4.5 *P* force component on joint E, joint E must be pushing to the left with a 4.5 *P* force component on member DE.

Applying the equilibrium principle to chord member DE:

The 4.5 *P* force component to the left exerted by joint E on chord member DE must be equilibrated by a 4.5 *P* force component to the right exerted by joint D pushing on member DE.

Applying the action–reaction pairs principle to the interaction between chord member DE and joint D:

Since joint D is pushing to the right with a 4.5 *P* force component on chord member DE, member DE must be pushing to the left with a 4.5 *P* force component on joint D.

Applying the equilibrium principle to the vertical forces on joint E:

The 1 *P* applied force pushing down on joint E, combined with the upward 1.5 *P* force component exerted by chord member EF on joint E, produce a net upward force of 0.5 *P* on joint E. This must be equilibrated by a downward 0.5 *P* force component exerted by chord member DE on joint E.

Applying the action–reaction pairs principle to the interaction between joint E and chord member DE:

Since chord member DE is pushing down with a 0.5 *P* force component on joint E, joint E must be pushing up with a 0.5 *P* force component on member DE.

Applying the equilibrium principle to chord member DE:

The upward 0.5 *P* force, exerted by joint E on chord member DE, must be equilibrated by a downward 0.5 *P* force, exerted by joint D on member DE.

Applying the action–reaction pairs principle to the interaction between chord member DE and joint D:

Since joint D is pushing down with a 0.5 *P* force component on chord member DE, member DE must be pushing up with a 0.5 *P* force on joint D (see Figure 8.86).

The vertical and horizontal forces in the top-chord member of a bay determine that chord member's required slope in that bay. Because they are 2-force members, the forces must lie along the members. Therefore, the triangles representing the member's vertical and horizontal dimensions must be similar to the triangles for the vertical and horizontal force components (see Figure 8.87).

Using the proportions of similar triangles allows one to find the chord segment's vertical rise in the bay. Express the similarity of the two triangles for chord member DE:

$$\frac{\Delta y_1}{20 \text{ ft}} = \frac{0.5\,P}{4.5\,P}$$

Solve for Δy_1:

$$\Delta y_1 = \frac{0.5}{4.5} \cdot 20 \text{ ft} = 2.222 \text{ ft}$$

Express the similarity of the two triangles for chord member EF:

$$\frac{\Delta y_2}{20 \text{ ft}} = \frac{1.5\,P}{4.5\,P}$$

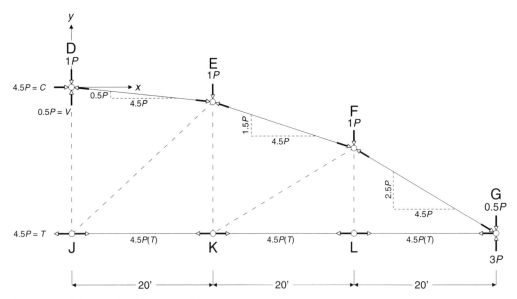

Figure 8.86 Resolved forces on joint E.

Solve for Δy_2:

$$\Delta y_2 = \frac{1.5}{4.5} \cdot 20 \text{ ft} = 6.667 \text{ ft}$$

Express the similarity of the two triangles for chord member FG:

$$\frac{\Delta y_3}{20 \text{ ft}} = \frac{2.5\, P}{4.5\, P}$$

Solve for Δy_3:

$$\Delta y^3 = \frac{2.5}{4.5} \cdot 20 \text{ ft} = 11.111 \text{ ft}$$

These results are summarized in Figure 8.88. The force arrows, web members, and bottom-chord members are removed for clarity.

The following generalized statement is made for bay n (where bays are counted moving away from the truss's center). V is vertical force and H is horizontal force:

$$\frac{\Delta y_n}{20 \text{ ft}} = \frac{V_n}{H}$$

Solve for Δy_n:

$$\Delta y_n = \frac{V_n}{H} \cdot 20 \text{ ft}$$

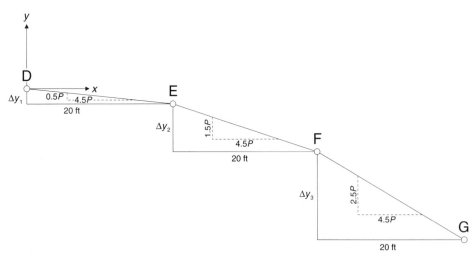

Figure 8.87 Similarity of slope triangles and force triangles.

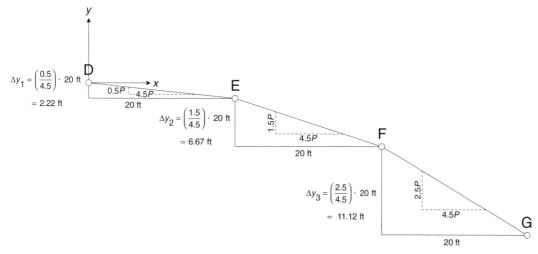

Figure 8.88 Resolved vertical dimensions.

The vertical shear force V_n increases by 1 P for each bay away from the truss's center:

$$V_{n+1} = V_n + P$$

In terms of P:

$$P = V_{n+1} - V_n$$

This 1 P force results in an increase in the chord member's vertical dimension, which is determined in the following manner:

$$\Delta\Delta y = \Delta y_{n+1} - \Delta y_n = \left(\frac{V_{n+1}}{H} \cdot 20\,\text{ft}\right) - \left(\frac{V_n}{H} \cdot 20\,\text{ft}\right)$$

$$= \frac{20\,\text{ft}}{H} \cdot (V_{n+1} - V_n) = \frac{20\,\text{ft}}{H} \cdot P = \frac{20\,\text{ft}}{4.5\,P} \cdot P = 4.44\,\text{ft}$$

The dimension $\Delta\Delta y$ is sometimes called the vertical difference from bay to bay:

$$\Delta y_n = \Delta y_{n+1} + \Delta\Delta y$$

These results are summarized in Table 8.1.

Table 8.1 Generation of Coordinates for Bow-Truss Vertices

Bay n	Δy_n (ft)	$\Delta\Delta y$ (ft)	Joint	x (ft)	y (ft)
			D	0	0.000
1	−2.222				
		−4.444	E	20	−2.222
2	−6.667				
		−4.444	F	40	−8.889
3	−11.111				
			G	60	−20.00

The shape output from the preceding analysis is shown in Figure 8.89.

This discussion of trusses began with curved-top chords, by noting the following:

• For a simple-span member under a uniform load, the internal moment varies parabolically along the member's length.

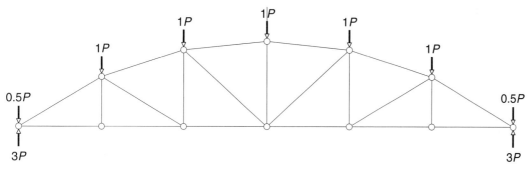

Figure 8.89 Correctly proportioned truss.

- In a truss, the top- and bottom-chord members provide the horizontal forces that constitute the force couple that is the internal-resisting moment.
- In a parallel-chord truss, the spacing of the top and bottom chords is a constant, meaning that the force couple's lever arm is a constant along the truss's length.
- The internal-resisting moment results from the magnitude of the horizontal force (in the force couple) times the lever arm. The internal-resisting moment's lever arm is a constant in a parallel-chord truss. The internal-resisting moment's parabolic variation in a parallel-chord truss must be accounted for by a parabolic variation in the chord members' horizontal forces. (This is apparent in the force diagram in Figure 8.75.)
- This variation in the chords' horizontal forces leads to the inefficient use of chord material.
- The chord members' horizontal forces can be made constant along the truss's length by changing the truss geometry so that the chord members' lever arm varies parabolically from zero at the ends to a maximum in the middle.

In the example worked out in Table 8.1, the horizontal forces are a constant. The question is, do the points that define the top chord's geometry actually lie on a parabola? This is checked by finding a parabola with a subset of nodes lying on it and testing to determine if the remaining top-chord vertices also lie along that parabola. Since the coordinate system is located so that the y-axis is the parabola's symmetry axis and so that $(x, y) = (0, 0)$ lies on the parabola, the appropriate parabolic function is:

$$y = kx^2$$

To determine the constant k, pick any point that represents a truss top-chord joint. For example, choose the first point, $(x, y) = (20 \text{ ft}, -2.222 \text{ ft})$:

$$-2.222 \text{ ft} = k\,(20 \text{ ft})^2$$

Solve for k:

$$k = \frac{-2.222 \text{ ft}}{(20 \text{ ft})^2} = \frac{-0.0056}{\text{ft}}$$

The parabola is given by the equation:

$$y = \left(\frac{-0.0056}{\text{ft}}\right)x^2$$

Test this parabola for the next top-chord vertex, for which $(x, y) = (40 \text{ ft}, -8.889 \text{ ft})$:

$$y = \frac{-0.0056}{\text{ft}}x^2 = \frac{-0.0056}{\text{ft}}(40 \text{ ft})^2 = -8.889 \text{ ft}$$

This checks with the vertex's y-coordinate.

Test this parabola for the next top-chord vertex, for $(x, y) = (60 \text{ ft}, -20 \text{ ft})$:

$$y = \frac{-0.0056}{\text{ft}}x^2 = \frac{-0.0056}{\text{ft}}(60 \text{ ft})^2 = -20 \text{ ft}$$

This checks for the vertex's y-coordinate.

There are two ways to extend this truss one more bay in each direction without altering the existing members' geometry or the forces in those members:

Method 1.   Use the parabola equation to find y for $x = 80$ ft:

$$y = \frac{-0.0056}{\text{ft}}x^2 = \frac{-0.0056}{\text{ft}}(80 \text{ ft})^2 = -35.556 \text{ ft}$$

Method 2.   Find Δy_4:

$$\Delta y_4 = \Delta y_3 + \Delta\Delta y = -11.111 \text{ ft} + -4.444 \text{ ft} = -15.556 \text{ ft}$$

Now add Δy_1 through Δy_4:

$$y = \Delta y_1 + \Delta y_2 + \Delta y_3 + \Delta y_4 = -2.222 \text{ ft} + -6.667 \text{ ft} + -11.111 \text{ ft} + -15.556 \text{ ft} = -35.556 \text{ ft}$$

The first method is faster. For certain design situations, however, the second method is often instructive.

Figures 8.90 and 8.91 show, respectively, the loads on and axial forces in, three arches that are all based on the same parabola, but differ in the number of segments and in length. In other words, for each arch, the generative geometry is the same, but some arches extend farther than others. If we number the segments of each arch, starting with the number one on the two center segments and counting progressively outward, then the corresponding segments on the three arches will all have the same slope, length, and axial force.

This notion of extending a spanning element's range without changing the spanning element's "core" or center design is useful in several design situations, including cross vaults, which are addressed in detail in Section 8.2.5, "Cross Vaults." In the cross vault shown in Figure 8.92, the minor arches (those parallel to the structure's boundary) deliver their loads to the major arches (those crossing diagonally from one corner of the structure to the other), which then transfer the loads to the foundations. The minor arches are truncated at various points as they engage the major arches:

The compressive forces in the center elements of the minor arches are identical (see Figure 8.93).

The minor-arch elements are all based on the same parabola and their geometry differs only in where they are terminated when they encounter the major arches. The corresponding segments of the minor arches all have the same axial force in them. The major arches are based on a single parabola, which is different from the parabola of the minor arches. The axial forces are the same in the

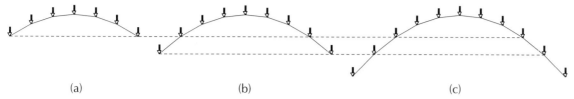

Figure 8.90 Extending arch outward and downward while maintaining same parabola.

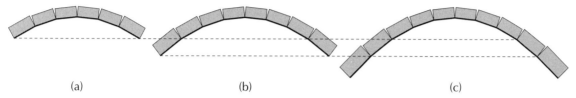

Figure 8.91 Invariant axial forces for center sections when extending arch outward and downward.

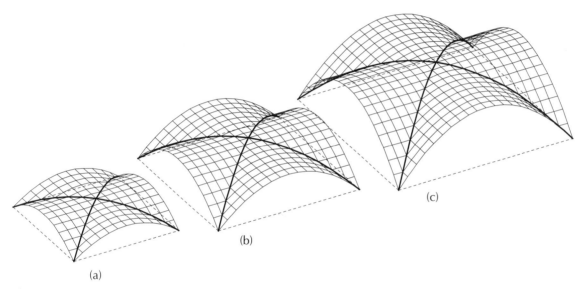

Figure 8.92 Extending cross vaults outward and downward while maintaining same parabola.

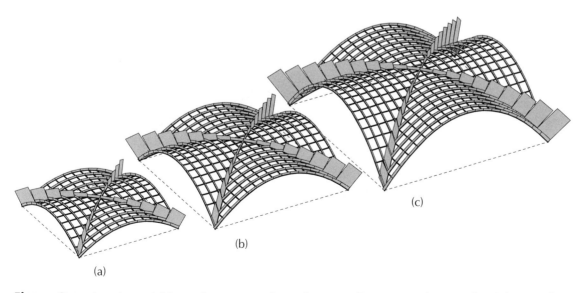

Figure 8.93 Invariant axial forces for center sections when extending cross vault outward and downward.

corresponding segments of the major arches in each of the three vaults.

Another variation on this theme relates to small-circle network domes, such as the Charter Spheres invented by T. C. Howard of Synergetics. This modular system is shown in Figures 8.94 and 8.95. Each dome is based on the same spherical geometry. The differences between the domes have to do with how far the geometry gets extended outward and downward.

The axial forces in corresponding members in the three domes will all be the same. In other words, dome (a) will serve as the center of dome (b), which will serve as the center of dome (c). This allows several dome diameters to be constructed from a single kit of parts.

Think of these trusses, vaults, or domes as multistory structures, not as spanning systems. In multistory build-

ings, the structural members are sized from the top down, so that each story's structural elements are sized to handle the weight of all the structural elements above.

Suppose there is a client who has commissioned the design of a 50-story office building. If the client suddenly changes his mind and wants a 70-story office building instead, there is no structural requirement to redesign the 50 stories that are already designed. Simply imagine elevating those 50 stories above 20 newly designed stories. Lifting a 50-story building is no small feat, but as the building is not built yet, this is easy to do. (Of course, the floors have to be renumbered. This may not be a small matter, since all of the original working drawings are labeled with the original floor numbers.)

If the fundamental control geometry of the arch, vault, or dome, is not changed, then the already designed part

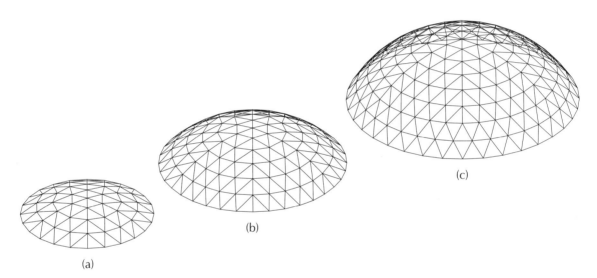

(a)

(b)

(c)

Figure 8.94 Extending domes outward and downward while maintaining same radius of curvature.

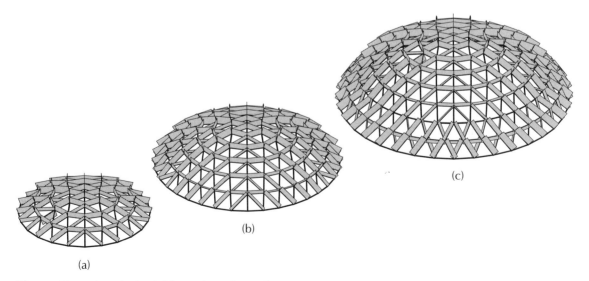

(a)

(b)

(c)

Figure 8.95 Invariant axial forces in center sections.

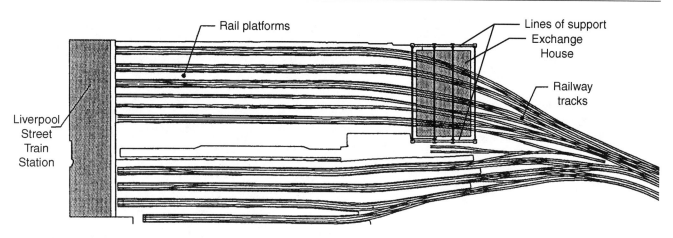

Figure 8.96 Rails on the site of the Broadgate Exchange House.

of the structure is raised and more structure underneath it is designed in a manner calculated not to alter the forces in the already designed part of the structure.

If the constant in the parabola equation governing the shape of the truss top chord or the vault is changed, then all of the forces in the member system will change and the system will need to be reanalyzed. Similarly, if the sphere radius controlling the dome geometry is changed, then all of the forces in the member system will change and the system will need to be reanalyzed.

8.1.7 BROADGATE EXCHANGE HOUSE (SOM)

This discussion of structural arcs began with trusses with curved top chords in roofing applications, but this structural form is not limited to roofs. An elegant design exploring this structural geometry is the Broadgate Exchange House, designed by William Baker and Robert Sinn, of the Chicago office of Skidmore, Owings & Merrill, LLP, and H. Iyengar of Structural Design International. The Exchange House is a multistory office development built in the railroad air rights located over the Liverpool Street Train Station in London, England. The railroad tracks covered most of the site and had to be kept intact and usable during and after construction. The Exchange House building site was located where the tracks begin to converge, which precluded column placement on an orderly grid, except for two lines spaced 78 m apart (see Figure 8.96).

Thus, the challenge was to produce an office tower that spanned 78 m. This represented an extreme structural challenge, since the loads were high and the span long. Among the spanning systems explored were a ten-story-deep truss, a ten-story-deep parabolic suspension system, and a parabolic arch system.[1] Both the truss and the

suspension structure involved longer load paths than the arch. Longer load paths require more linear feet of structural members, and the members' cross sections need to be larger to limit deflection related to material stretching along the load path. Therefore, the arch, with the minimal load path, is the most efficient spanning system. Figure 8.97 shows the building's final design.

This is a dramatic and powerful architectural image. It is also a rational structural concept. Figure 8.98 shows what the building looks like diagrammatically.

The plaza construction covers the railroad tracks, using story-deep trusses to span the somewhat randomly spaced columns threaded between the tracks. The plaza level creates a working platform for the main structure's construction above and protects the rail service below from the construction activities. Floor framing at the bottom chord of the story-deep truss supports parking.

In the literature on this structure, the primary spanning elements are called tied arches. They can also be called bow trusses, since a tied arch is the simplest bow truss and, in the case of the Exchange House, there are web members that brace the curved compression member under uniform load. These two web members become active load-carrying elements under asymmetric gravity loads and under lateral loads parallel to the arch plane. The Exchange House is cited earlier in this chapter and in Chapter 10, "Lateral-Bracing Systems."

The Exchange House has ten office levels, 78 m × 52 m in plan, supported on four segmental-tied arches spanning

[1]For an example of a ten-story parabolic suspension system, see the discussion of the Federal Reserve Bank Building in Chapter 9, Section 9.1, "Suspension Structures."

Figure 8.97 Broadgate Exchange House, London, England. (Architecture and Engineering by the Chicago office of Skidmore, Owings & Merrill, LLP. Image courtesy of Hedrich Blessing.)

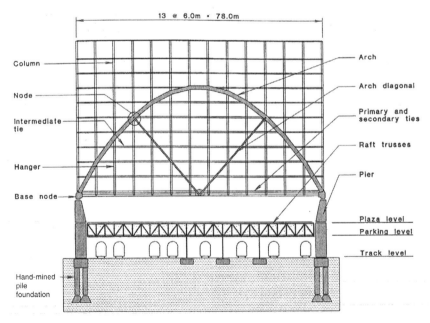

Figure 8.98 Broadgate Exchange House, London, England. (Architecture and Engineering by the Chicago office of Skidmore, Owings & Merrill, LLP. Drawing courtesy of Skidmore, Owings & Merrill, LLP.)

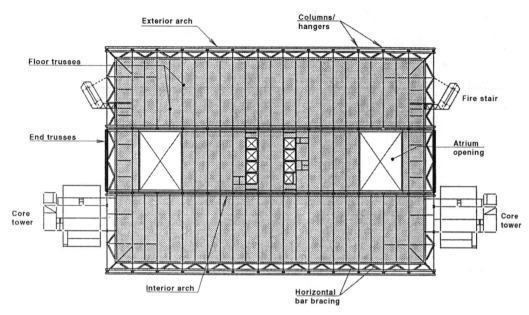

Figure 8.99 Broadgate Exchange House, London, England. (Architecture and Engineering by the Chicago office of Skidmore, Owings & Merrill, LLP. Drawing courtesy of Skidmore, Owings & Merrill, LLP.)

72 m and spaced 18.5 m, 15 m, and 18.5 m apart (see Figure 8.99).

The floor-to-floor spacing is 4.5 m. There are thirteen bays, or fourteen vertical elements, spaced 6 m apart. Diagrammatically, the tied arch and the vertical members look like the illustration in Figure 8.100.

The parts of the vertical members above the arch are in compression, carrying loads down to the arch. The parts of the vertical members below the arch are in tension, suspending loads off the arch. The elements in compression are susceptible to buckling and need bracing, whereas the vertical members below the arch do not. To help brace the compression verticals, horizontal elements are added (see Figure 8.101).

As shown in Figure 8.102, the structural frame is duplicated 18.5 m away from the first structural frame and some floor elements are added.

In the actual building, the floor elements spanning the 18.5 m from the plane of one arch to the plane of the other are trusses working in composite action with the floor slabs. For clarity, the trusses are rendered as solid-web beams. Moreover, to prevent visual clutter, only two of the four arches are shown and only two vertical planes of spanning members are shown. Each vertical member supports ten floor trusses and one roof truss. The load each element delivers to the vertical member corresponds to an influence area $6\ m \cdot \dfrac{18.5\ m}{2} = 55.5\ m^2 = 597$ ft. Such loads are huge as compared with the tied arch self-weight. When finding the right shape for the tied arch, focus on the floor structure's load, rather than the arch's self-weight. For a load distributed uniformly on the floors

and the roof, the forces delivered to the vertical members are the same for all verticals. Each vertical member transfers this force to the node intersecting the arch. In the case of such loads, the arch is subjected to point forces spaced every 6 m along the horizontal. As demonstrated earlier, the logical truss shape in response to this force system is a parabola.

To understand the tied-arch geometry, it is useful to use the mathematics developed earlier. Begin by using a formula based on fitting a parabola to the known building dimensions. Specifically, the tied-arch top nodes align with the seventh floor, which is $7 \cdot 4.5\ m = 31.5\ m$ above

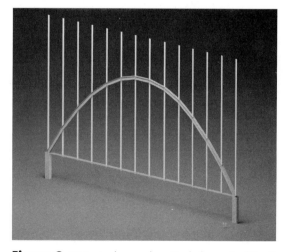

Figure 8.100 Arches and vertical element of the Broadgate Exchange House.

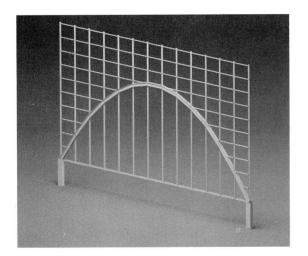

Figure 8.101 Horizontal braces.

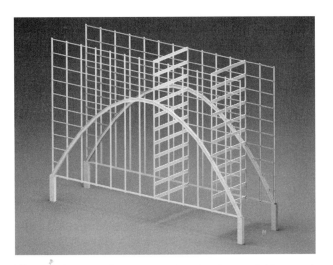

Figure 8.102 Floor trusses (rendered as solid beams for simplicity).

the bottom of the tied arch; the bottom nodes are at $x = 39$ m and $x = -39$ m.

In the earlier discussion, the xy-coordinate-system origin was located at the parabola's top. That location was chosen to ease the presentation of extending the parabola downward and outward to achieve greater spans, without altering the parts of the top chord already designed. The coordinate system's origin is typically located at the structure's base, the tied-arch spring line. Use the generalized-parabola equation:

$$y = c + kx^2 \qquad \text{[8.18]}$$

If the parabola depth is d and the span is L, then one parabola point is $(x, y) = (0, d)$. Substitute this point in equation [8.18]:

$$d = c + k(0)^2 \qquad \text{[8.19]}$$

This reduces to $c = d$. Therefore:

$$y = d + kx^2 \qquad \text{[8.20]}$$

Another parabola point is $(x, y) = \left(\dfrac{L}{2}, 0\right)$. Substitute this point in equation [8.20]:

$$0 = d + k\left(\frac{L}{2}\right)^2 \qquad \text{[8.21]}$$

Solve for k:

$$k = \frac{-d}{\left(\dfrac{L}{2}\right)^2} \qquad \text{[8.22]}$$

The complete equation is

$$y = d - \frac{dx^2}{\left(\dfrac{L}{2}\right)^2} \qquad \text{[8.23]}$$

Table 8.2 shows the depth $d = 31.5$ m, span $L = 78$ m, the x-values (in meters) corresponding to the horizontal positions of the nodes on the arch, and the node's y-values based on formula [8.23].

The nodes at $x = 3$ m and $x = -3$ m are not at $y = -31.5$ m, as expected. This is because the parabola was assumed to have an overall height of 31.5 m, as if the parabola's top point were located precisely at the seventh floor. In the Exchange House, there are an odd number of bays. Instead of a node at the center of the arch's parabolic shape, there are two nodes located symmetrically 3 m to each side of the centerline. The zenith of the Exchange House parabola extends slightly above the seventh floor, to allow the two nodes to align with the floor's base. The preceding mathematics are altered easily by adjusting slightly the constant that is multiplied times x^2. A scaling factor is used to boost 31.314 m up to 31.5 m (see Table 8.3).

Choosing an odd number of bays ensures that there is a center bay—a bay occurring at the building's centerline. This is an element in classical architecture: a building's opening is located at the building's centerline. In a repetitive-bay situation, such as a Greek temple, there is a bay at the center of the façade for entry. The Exchange House bays are elevated above the ground plane; entry is not through the center bay but through a separate structure at the ground level. An odd number of bays is visually appealing, which is undoubtedly why Mies van der Rohe arranged the façade patterns on all his buildings this way, even in places where the façades' vertical elements do not reach the ground plane.

Table 8.2 Computing y-Values Based on Formula [8.23]

d	L	x	For a parabola 31.5 m deep $y = d - \dfrac{d}{\left(\dfrac{L}{2}\right)^2} \cdot x^2$
(m)	(m)	(m)	(m)
31.5	78	−39	0
		−33	8.946746
		−27	16.402367
		−21	22.366864
		−15	26.840237
		−9	29.822485
		−3	31.313609
		3	31.313609
		9	29.822485
		15	26.840237
		21	22.366864
		27	16.402367
		33	8.946746
		39	0

Purists uncomfortable with using an adjustment factor to scale the parabola may fit the parabola to two data points for accuracy. To do so, begin again with the generalized-parabola equation. Use the two points $(x, y) = (39\ m, 0)$ at the base and $(x, y) = (3\ m, 31.5\ m)$ as a top vertex. The first equation:

$$y_1 = c + k(x_1)^2$$
$$0 = c + k(39\ m)^2 \qquad\qquad \textbf{[8.24]}$$

The second equation:

$$y_2 = c + k(x_2)^2$$
$$31.5\ m = c + k(3\ m)^2 \qquad\qquad \textbf{[8.25]}$$

The difference between equations [8.24] and [8.25]:

$$y_1 - y_2 = (c + k(x_1)^2) - (c - k(x_2)^2)$$
$$0 - 31.5\ m = (c + k(39\ m)^2) - (c - k(3\ m)^2)$$
$$-31.5\ m = k((39\ m)^2 - (3\ m)^2)$$
$$= km^2(39^2 - 3^2) = 1{,}512\ km^2 \qquad \textbf{[8.26]}$$

Solve for k:

$$-31.5\ m = 1{,}512\ km^2$$

$$k = \frac{-31.5\ m}{1{,}512\ m^2} = \frac{-0.020833}{m} \qquad\qquad \textbf{[8.27]}$$

Insert this value in Equation [8.24]:

$$0 = c + \left(\frac{-0.020833}{m}(39\ m)^2\right) \qquad \textbf{[8.28]}$$

Solve for c:

$$c = 31.69\ m \qquad\qquad \textbf{[8.29]}$$

The parabola's zenith overlaps slightly the 31.5 m height of the seventh floor, as expected. To compare this result with the generalized-parabola equation [8.18] solved earlier, apply the adjustment factor from Table 8.3 to the

Table 8.3 Adjusted y-Values That Allow Two Intersections at the Seventh Floor

d	L	x	For a Parabola 31.5 m deep $y = d - \dfrac{d}{\left(\dfrac{L}{2}\right)^2} \cdot x^2$	Adjustment Factor = $\dfrac{31.5}{31.313609} =$	$y_2 = y_1 \cdot$ Adjustment Factor
(m)	(m)	(m)	(m)		(m)
31.5	78	−39	0	1.00595238	0
		−33	8.946746		9
		−27	16.402367		16.5
		−21	22.366864		22.5
		−15	26.840237		27
		−9	29.822485		30
		−3	31.313609		31.5
		3	31.313609		31.5
		9	29.822485		30
		15	26.840237		27
		21	22.366864		22.5
		27	16.402367		16.5
		33	8.946746		9
		39	0		0

parabola with the zenith just touching the seventh floor (Table 8.2). The parabola's adjusted height is

$$c = \text{(adjustment factor)} \cdot 31.5 \text{ m}$$
$$= 1.006 \cdot 31.5 \text{ m} = 31.69 \text{ m} \qquad \textbf{[8.30]}$$

This checks with the result found in fitting the original parabola to the two known points $(x, y) = (39 \text{ m}, 0)$ [8.24] and $(x, y) = (3 \text{ m}, 31.5 \text{ m})$ [8.25].

Fitting the parabola to two known points is a complicated method, but a more satisfying one for mathematical purists.

The Exchange House is easier to analyze using the differences method, explained earlier in this chapter, than it is through fitting parabolas. Consider the freebody diagram for this structure shown in Figure 8.103.

Collecting the six 1 P forces together into a 6 P force, with a center of action 3.5 bays in from the end support, leads to the diagram shown in Figure 8.104.

Take moments about that support point:

$$\sum M_A = 0 \; \curvearrowright$$
$$0 = 6\,P(3.5 \cdot 6 \text{ m}) - H(31.5 \text{ m}) \qquad \textbf{[8.31]}$$

Solve for H:

$$H = \frac{126\,P \text{ m}}{31.5\,m} = 4\,P \qquad \textbf{[8.32]}$$

Applying the principle of equilibrium to all the joints along the bottom chord, it can be established that the force is a constant 4 P along the bottom-chord segments. Applying the principle of equilibrium at joint A and then to each subsequent joint along the top chord, the distribution of force components is derived, as shown in Figure 8.105.

Using the similarity of the force triangles and the dimension triangles, vertical dimensions are derived for each of the top-chord segments, as shown in Figure 8.106.

Once the basic process is understood diagrammatically, as shown in Figure 8.106, this problem can be set up in a spreadsheet such as that shown in Table 8.4. To get the fraction of the total rise that occurs within a single bay, take the ratio of the vertical force in that bay to the sum of all the vertical forces in all of the bays. Once the spreadsheet is set up, any of the input variables (such as total rise of the spanning element, the forces on the vertices, etc.) can be changed, the spreadsheet will automatically update the calculations to give the new rise in each bay.

Drawing the arch to proper scale results in the diagram in Figure 8.107.

A characteristic of the tied arch having an odd number of bays is that its zenith is a horizontal member carrying zero vertical shear force. The two bays on either side of

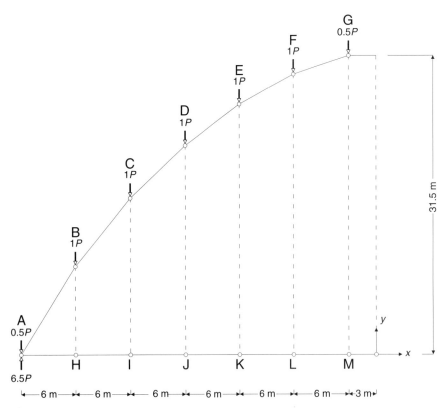

Figure 8.103 Force diagram for the Broadgate Exchange House.

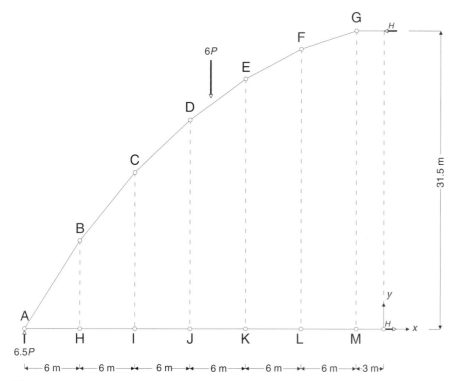

Figure 8.104 Clustering the forces to simplify the diagram.

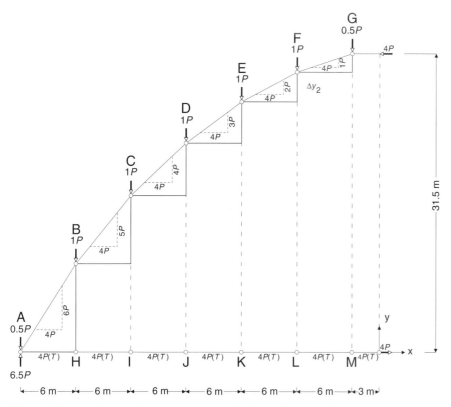

Figure 8.105 Resolved force components in the arch segments.

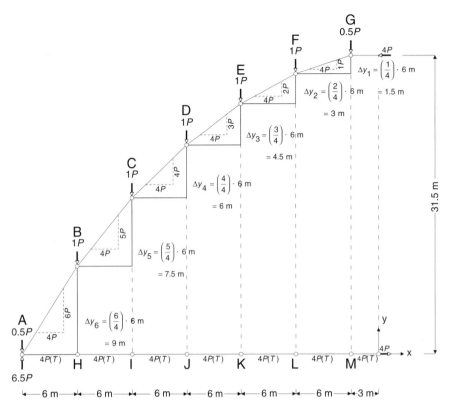

Figure 8.106 Resolved vertical dimensions of the arch segments.

Table 8.4 Computing Vertex Coordinates Based on Method of Differences

Consider a thirteen-bay truss where the center joints are labeled 1 and the numbering of joints and bays is done outward from the center:

Rise	31.5 m	
Span	78 m	
# of bays	13 bays	
Width of a bay	6 m	

Node #	Force on Node P	Bay	Shear Force in Bay P	Fraction of Total Rise Allocated to Bay	Δy in Bay ft	y Coordinate of Node ft	x Coordinate of Node ft	y Coordinate of Node ft
		Middle	0		0			
1	1	1	1	0.0476	1.500	0.000	3	0.000
2	1	2	2	0.0952	3.000	−1.500	9	−1.500
3	1	3	3	0.1429	4.500	−4.500	15	−4.500
4	1	4	4	0.1905	6.000	−9.000	21	−9.000
5	1	5	5	0.2381	7.500	−15.000	27	−15.000
6	1	6	6	0.2857	9.000	−22.500	33	−22.500
7	0.5					−31.500	39	−31.500
				Sum = 1.0000	Sum = 31.500			

Total of all components in all bays = 21

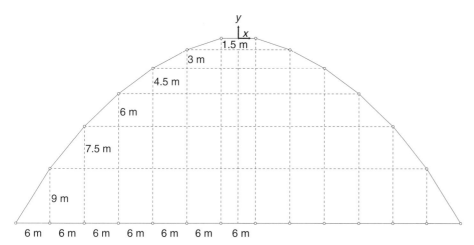

Figure 8.107 Drawn to appropriate shape.

the center bay each have a top-chord member carrying exactly 1 P vertical shear force. This is in contrast to the bow truss example that starts this chapter, which has a top chord with an even number of members. In that structure, the center two top-chord members each have a 0.5 P vertical shear force. This is similar to the parallel-chord truss examples, in which trusses with an odd number of bays have zero shear at the center bay; the bays to either side of the center bay each have a 1 P shear force. Trusses with an even number of bays have a 0.5 P vertical shear force in each of the two bays flanking the truss's center point. Parallel-chord trusses with an odd number of bays have vertical shears that are an integer multiple of P in every bay. Trusses with an even number of bays have vertical shears that are a half-integer multiple of P in every bay. The same is true for bow trusses and tied arches. Because the Exchange House has an odd number of bays, the vertical shear in each top-chord member is P times the bay number, counting away from the bow truss's center bay. This is summarized in the diagram in Figure 8.106, where the force triangles have 4 P on the base edge and 1, 2, 3, 4, 5, or 6 P on the vertical edge, depending on how many bays they are away from the center.

For an odd number of bays, it is more elegant and efficient to find the geometry using this differences method than trying to fit a parabola, the zenith of which does not have a straightforward relationship to the building's physical elements. The Exchange House's control geometry is not the parabola, but the intersections of the floors and the vertical support elements marking the boundaries between bays. Using the differences method describes the math without determining the parabola equation or the parabola's zenith location.

The geometry of the Broadgate Exchange House is simple and elegant. The final design's simplicity belies the complicated analysis involved in arriving at this geome-

try. At the start of the problem, the 78 m span was not precisely established. There was a wide range of possibilities for the number of bays, and the number and height of stories in the rise of the arch were not set. It was desired to have the arch joints coincide with the vertical members and to have the joints located at floor levels. An examination of the diagram in Figure 8.97 indicates that the only joints that do not align precisely with floors are the second joints from the top and the third joints from the bottom. Aligning the nodes with the floors is very helpful with regard to restraining the arch against buckling, minimizing deformation induced by nonuniform gravity loads, and providing lateral bracing for the building.[2] The design intention for the Exchange House was clarity and expressiveness in response to the uniform gravity loads. In response to nonuniform gravity loads and lateral loads, the building is more subtle and complicated. For the building's image to be as clear as possible, that is, to keep the arch the dominant visual element, design attention was devoted to keeping secondary elements to a minimum. These few structural elements serve many structural purposes, and the structural action of the system (under all loads other than uniform gravity load) is complex and highly redundant.

[2]For a more detailed discussion of the design and analysis of the Broadgate Exchange House, see H. Iyengar, W. F. Baker, and R. C. Sinn, "Broadgate Exchange House: Structural Systems," *Structural Engineer*, 71, no. 9 (1993).

For a series of superb pictures documenting the construction of the Broadgate Exchange House, see John Davies, *Phase 11*, published by Davenport Associates Ltd., 9 Sebastian Street, London EC1V 0HE, and The Photographers Gallery, 5 Great Newport Street, London WC2H 7HY.

8.1.8 PARABOLAS, CATENARIES, AND ARCS OF CIRCLES

8.1.8.1 Parabolas

Consider a 10 ft-deep bow truss spanning 60 ft that has a parabolic top chord. The solution methods developed earlier in this chapter can be used to generate the parabola that is the truss's control geometry. A spreadsheet can be used to do the arithmetic and to provide an orderly table of results (see Table 8.5).

The contents of the x and y columns can be copied from the spreadsheet and pasted into a structural analysis program to produce the segmental bow truss shown in Figure 8.108—a truss with a top chord consisting of straight segments between joints.

In this truss, the top and bottom chords are HSS $3 \times 3 \times \frac{3}{16}$ in. square tubes and the web members are HSS $2 \times 2 \times \frac{3}{16}$ in. square tubes. Structural sections need to be assigned to these members to facilitate the computer analysis. First consider the truss behavior under point loads on the joints shown in Figures 8.109 and 8.110.

The change from plotting axial force to plotting axial stress is to facilitate making comparisons in the following discussions. When calculating trusses by hand, one normally begins by calculating the axial force in each of the members. Each member's axial stress is found by dividing the axial force in the member by the member's cross-sectional area. Using the computer allows the luxury of bypassing axial force and starting with axial stress.

In the diagram in Figure 8.110, there is:

- Constant stress in the bottom chord.
- A slight variation in the stress in the top chord, representing the variation in the vertical shear force.
- No axial stress in the web members, which is expected, since, under this load, the top chord is shaped to handle the shear forces, leaving the web members with the sole purpose of bracing the top chord against roll-through buckling.

The minor variations in the top-chord stress are further reduced by curving both the top and the bottom chord as shown in Figures 8.111 and 8.112. This form is called a lenticular truss. Both chords have slope near the truss end and, therefore, share the shear force at the truss end.

Looking at the bow truss at the top versus the lenticular truss below it:

- The maximum axial stress along the top chord is reduced from 25.98 Ksi to 23.26 Ksi, meaning that it is changed by a factor of $\frac{23.26}{25.98} = 0.895$, a reduction of 10.5%.
- The maximum axial stress along the bottom chord has been increased from 22.28 Ksi to 23.26 Ksi, meaning that it is changed by a factor of $\frac{23.25}{22.28} = 1.044$, an increase of 4.4%.
- There is a slight net savings in material in the chord members.
- The vertical web members have acquired a significant structural role under this load condition; they transfer half of the load on the truss top joints to the bottom chord, which then provides half of the resistance to shear forces in the truss.

Lenticular truss fabrication can sometimes be simpler than the fabrication of the normal bow truss geometry, because the members do not curve as much. This is particularly beneficial in bow trusses made with bent wood chord members, where the wood's lack of flexibility means that to assume the curved shape, there are substantial bending stresses in the wood.

Using the lenticular truss shape has few structural or practical advantages over a normal bowstring truss shape. Many people think the lenticular shape attractive, and that is justification enough (see Figure 8.113).

The intention of bow trusses is to span, using members that work in pure tension and pure compression, rather than bending. Sometimes bending stresses occur inadvertently, in spite of our best intentions of avoiding them. It is useful to assess whether bending stresses are eliminated in the example of the parabolic bow truss that is subjected to uniform point loads on the joints. To determine whether a structure is acting primarily in axial action or bending action, similar quantities are needed.

Table 8.5 Generating the Vertex Coordinates From the Parabola

$$y = d - \frac{d}{\left(\frac{L}{2}\right)^2} \cdot x^2$$

d (ft)	L (ft)	x (ft)	(ft)
10	60	−30	0
		−24	3.6
		−18	6.4
		−12	8.4
		−6	9.6
		0	10
		6	9.6
		12	8.4
		18	6.4
		24	3.6
		30	0

Axial force Px′ and bending moment M are different types of quantities, like apples and oranges. Axial stress Sx′ and bending stress Sbz′ are similar quantities. Therefore, the relative levels of axial stress Sx′ and bending stress Sbz′ provide an indicator of whether the member is acting primarily in one mode or the other. Consider the loading conditions depicted in the diagram in Figure 8.114.

Continuous loading of the top chord occurs where corrugated decking rests directly on the truss's top chord, as shown in Figure 8.115.

The axial stresses for the two load cases are essentially the same. There are some differences, but they are difficult to detect with the eye (see Figure 8.116).

Figure 8.117 indicates that, for the load case with point forces on the joints, there is zero bending stress in the top chord segments. This is the intended outcome of the bow truss design: that all members work in pure compression or pure tension, and that bending is not a factor. For the uniformly distributed load on the top-chord members, bending stresses are occurring. In fact, the bending stresses in the top-chord members are greater than the axial stresses in the top-chord members. This is disturbing, because the intent of the bow truss design is that the members work in compression or in tension, and that bending not be a significant factor. The deformation causing this bending stress is seen in the deflection diagram

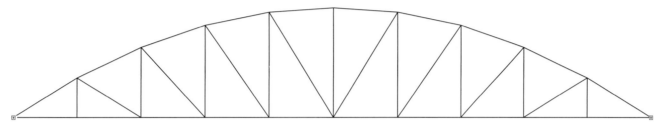

Figure 8.108 Segmented, parabolic bow truss.

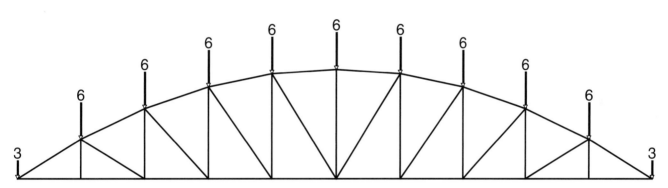

Figure 8.109 Joint forces.

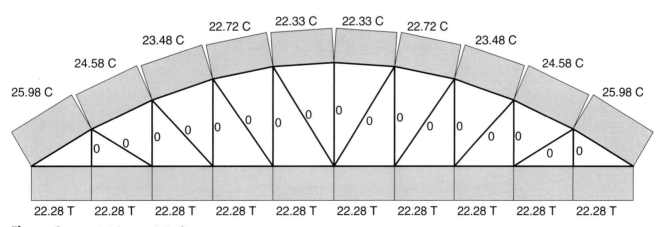

Figure 8.110 Axial stress (K/in.²).

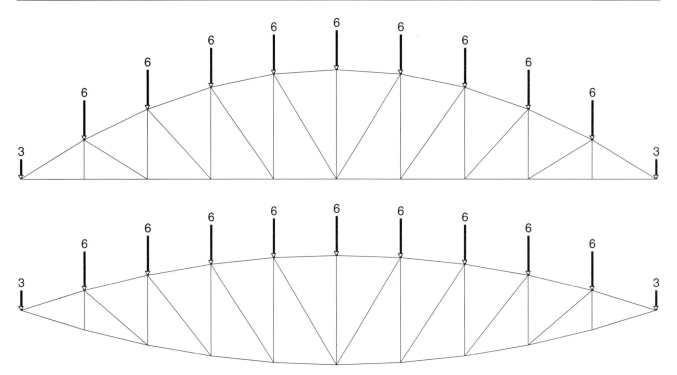

Figure 8.111 Parabolic bow truss and parabolic lenticular truss.

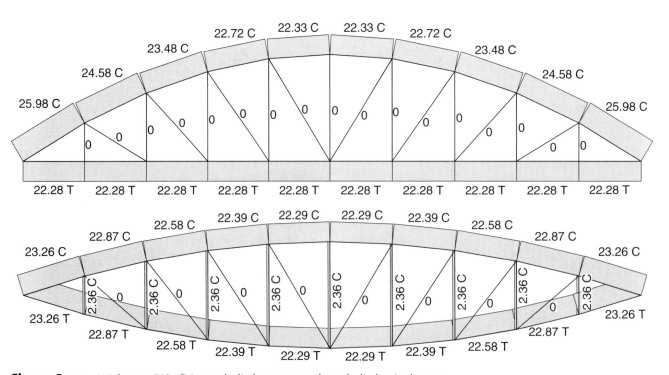

Figure 8.112 Axial stress (K/in.²) in parabolic bow truss and parabolic lenticular truss.

Figure 8.113 Royal Albert Bridge, Saltash, England, showing lenticular shape. (Image courtesy of Owen Dunn.)

Figure 8.115 Continuous, distributed force on the top-chord members of a bow truss.

in Figure 8.118. As usual, the deflections are exaggerated for illustration.

Clearly, the design concept needs to be altered to address the bending stress induced by the continuously distributed load. Shaping the top chord into a continuous, smooth curvature allows the entire top chord to act in compression. Most structural analysis programs do not simulate continuous curvature. Increasing the number of segments in the top chord approaches continuous-curvature behavior, as indicated in Figure 8.119 where there are six segments between the node points. Figure 8.120 shows the two load cases on the truss, and Figure 8.121 shows the axial stresses Sx'.

The axial stress diagram for this truss is very similar to the axial stress diagram for the segmented top chord (compare Figure 8.121 to Figure 8.116). Figure 8.122 shows the bending for the two load cases.

For point forces on the joints, the bending stresses in the top chord are larger than the axial stresses in the top chord. Continuous curvature of the top chord is clearly not the appropriate shape response to point forces on the nodes of the truss. For continuous loading of the top chord, the bending stress flags are very small. The fact that any bending stress occurs at all is a result of the simulation technique: the top chord is segmental, instead of being continuously curved. Increasing the number of

segments to more closely simulate continuous curvature will further decrease the bending stress.

The bending stress for the truss with the curved top chord subjected to point forces is severe and comparable to the bending stress observed for the segmental-top chord subjected to a continuous uniform load. When comparing the bending stress plots between the curved-top chord that has point forces at the nodes, with the segmental-top chord subjected to uniform load, the bending stresses are reversed. For the segmental-top chord subjected to a uniform load, the members are deflecting downward between the nodes, producing compression in the top of the chord members (see Figure 8.118(b)). For the curved top chord that has point forces applied to the nodes, the top chord's curved portions that are between node points bulge upward under the compression induced by the truss's action under the point load as shown in Figure 8.123(a). The resultant bending induces compression on the chord members' bottom sides. The forces are concentrated at the joints, and there is no force to hold down the curved segments that are between the joints to counteract bulging upward. Because the curved segments between the joints are in compression, they curve even more, with only the bending resistance within the segment counteracting the action.

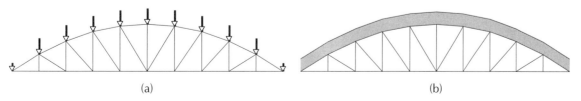

(a)   (b)

Figure 8.114 Two loading conditions: point forces on the joints (a) and uniform distributed load on the chord members (b).

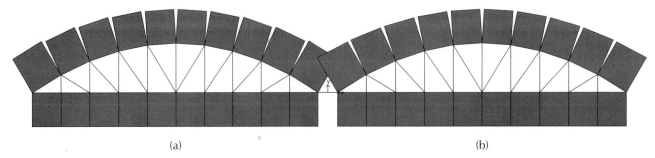

Figure 8.116 Comparison of axial stress (K/in.²) in the members, for the two load conditions.

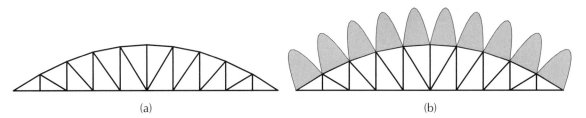

Figure 8.117 Comparison of bending stress (K/in.²) in the members, for the two load conditions.

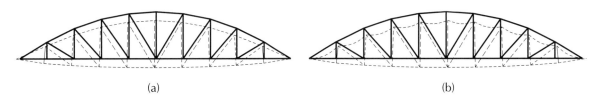

Figure 8.118 Comparing the truss deformation under the two load conditions.

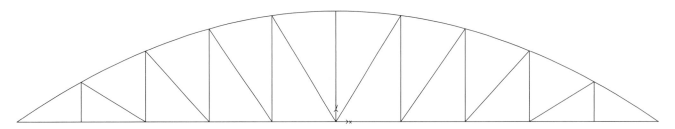

Figure 8.119 Top chord with many short segments approximating continuous curvature.

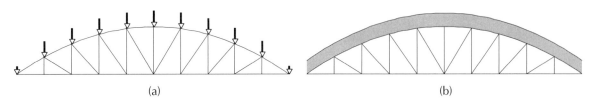

Figure 8.120 Two loading conditions: point forces on the joints (a) and uniform distributed load on the chord members (b).

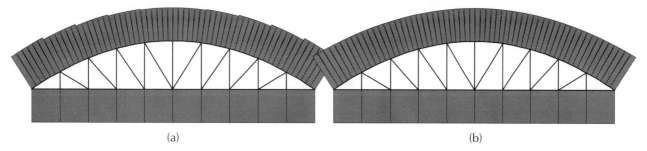

Figure 8.121 Comparison of axial stress (K/in.²) in the members, for the two load conditions.

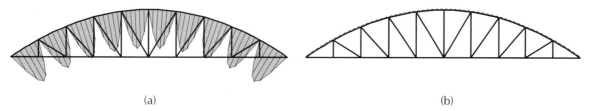

(a)   (b)

Figure 8.122 Comparison of bending stress (K/in.²) in the members, for the two load conditions.

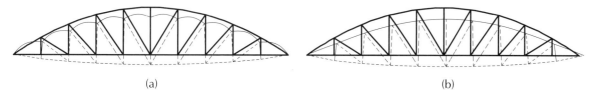

(a)   (b)

Figure 8.123 Comparing the truss deformation under the two load conditions.

In summary, segmental top chords are the ideal shape for point loading truss nodes. Curved-top chords are the ideal shape for continuous loading of the top chord. For the Broadgate Exchange House, the arches are loaded only at the joints and the segments between the joints are straight.

8.1.8.2 Catenaries

As mentioned earlier in this section, an arch of uniform cross section under its own self-weight has a load that is uniform along its length. To achieve pure axial stress under its own self-weight, such an arch should be formed in the shape of a catenary. A catenary curve can be generated experimentally by simply draping a rope. For many analytic purposes, draping a rope to get the catenary curve is not accurate enough. Therefore, it is useful to have an analytic method of generating the curve. The following mathematics is fairly complicated for the typical reader, and you may want to skip this discussion. It is included for completeness, for those advanced users who might have a need for it.

The equation for a catenary curve is the following:

$$y = a \cdot \cosh\left(\frac{x}{a}\right) + C = a\left(\frac{e^{\frac{x}{a}} + e^{\frac{-x}{a}}}{2}\right) + C \qquad \textbf{[8.33]}$$

where x and y are the standard spatial variables, a and C are arbitrary constants, and e is the natural log base. This equation is fairly easy to code up into a spreadsheet, and y can be calculated once a and C are specified. What makes the process slightly complicated is that a and C determine the overall shape of the catenary. The overall shape is typically not arbitrary and has been determined as the end product of a design process that has determined the span and the rise of the arch. Once those proportions have been established, the (x, y) coordinates at the center and ends of the arch have been established. Then one has to turn the process around and use the preceding equation to solve for a and C. Actually, C is fairly easy to deduce, if the center of the arch is to be at coordinate point $(0, 0)$. Thus,

$$0 = a\left(\frac{e^{\frac{0}{a}} + e^{\frac{-0}{a}}}{2}\right) + C = a\left(\frac{1+1}{2}\right) + C = a + C$$

$$C = -a \qquad \textbf{[8.34]}$$

Then equation [8.33] becomes

$$y = a\left(\frac{e^{\frac{x}{a}} + e^{\frac{-x}{a}}}{2}\right) - a \qquad \textbf{[8.35]}$$

If one wants a catenary that goes through (1, 1), then equation [8.35] becomes

$$1 = a\left(\frac{e^{\frac{1}{a}} + e^{\frac{-1}{a}}}{2}\right) - a \qquad [8.36]$$

There is no known algebraic way to solve this equation for a. However, it can be solved numerically by trial and error. A simple way to do this is to code up the expression on the right side of the preceding equation in a spreadsheet and keep adjusting the value of a until the right side of the equation comes extremely close to 1, as illustrated in the simple spreadsheet in Table 8.6.

To make the expression on the right side of the preceding equation very nearly equal to 1, make $a = 0.618759228$. When this value of a is substituted back into the original equation, it produces:

$$y = 0.618759228y\left(\frac{e^{\frac{x}{0.618759228}} + e^{\frac{-x}{0.618759228}}}{2}\right) - 0.618759228 \qquad [8.37]$$

This is the equation for a catenary curve that goes through (0, 0) and (1, 1). Once the x and y coordinates of the catenary curve have been generated using this equation, those coordinates can be scaled to get any catenary having the same proportions. Both coordinates have to be scaled equally in order for the scaled curve to be a catenary. In this sense, the catenary is like an arc of a circle, in that it cannot be scaled in just one coordinate. A semicircle, when scaled, produces half of an ellipse. This is in contrast to a parabola, which can be scaled differently on the two coordinates and the resulting shape is still a parabola. This allows you to mock up a parabola only once in a 3D computer-analysis program and then use that parabola as the starting point for any design process involving parabolas. Mathematically, parabolas are much easier to deal with than either circles or catenaries.

Points for the preceding catenary can be generated by substituting values of x and determining y. It will look like a suspension structure rather than an arch. To make it look like an arch, solve for y using formula 8.38 (below).

This can be calculated easily in a spreadsheet program. In Table 8.7, the coordinates for a parabola and a circle have been included along with the catenary.

Table 8.6 Using Spreadsheet Computation to Solve Numerically for a

a	e	$a\left(\frac{e^{\frac{1}{a}} + e^{\frac{-1}{a}}}{2}\right) - a$
1	2.718281828	0.543080635
0.7		0.844334722
0.618759228		0.999999999
0.6		1.045009696

When these are plotted, they look like the curves shown in Figure 8.124, with the catenary being between the parabola and the semicircle. The semicircle is almost vertical at the ends and needs more points near the ends to generate an approximation to a smooth curve.

8.1.9 METHODS OF FABRICATING BOW TRUSSES

Curved structural shapes are produced by passing them between rollers that are rotating. Placing the rollers closer together produces a tighter curvature—a smaller curvature radius. Pulling the rollers apart produces a gentler curvature—a larger curvature radius. When the rollers are placed at exactly the right distance apart, the member is rolled into the desired curvature radius (see Figure 8.125).

The diagram in Figure 8.126 shows the basic concept.

The following figures show some shapes that are rolled in this manner. Wide-flange sections and channels are easily rolled in the weak direction, as depicted in Figure 8.127. The end of the beam is not curved, because the rollers require a certain length of member to take effect.

Round pipe and tubing are also easily rolled, using concave rollers that cradle the pipe to prevent wall deformation; see Figure 8.128.

Curving wide-flange sections the strong way is much more challenging, because the pressure of the rollers tends to buckle the web of a wide-flange section. To avoid web buckling, additional rollers are provided to hook under the flange. These rollers try to counteract the compression in the web by pulling on the flanges in such a manner as to stretch the web. This system sometimes produces serious deformations of the flange and web during the rolling process. Rolling beams with thick webs produces smoother results than rolling beams with thinner webs.

Angles are rolled with the use of slotted rollers into which one angle leg is inserted. This stabilizes the angle and prevents it from twisting as it is rolled. Figure 8.129

$$y = 1 - \left(0.618759228\left(\frac{e^{\frac{x}{0.618759228}} + e^{\frac{-x}{0.618759228}}}{2}\right) - 0.618759228\right) \qquad [8.38]$$

Table 8.7 Coordinates of Catenary, Parabola, and Arc of a Circle

x	Catenary y	Parabola y	Arc of Circle y
	$y = 1 - \left(0.618759228 \left(\dfrac{e^{\frac{x}{0.618759228}} + e^{\frac{-x}{0.618759228}}}{2} \right) - 0.618759228 \right)$	$y = 1 - x^2$	$y = 1 - \sqrt{1^2 - x^2}$
0	1.0000000	1	1.000000
0.1	0.9919017	0.99	0.994987
0.2	0.9673949	0.96	0.979796
0.3	0.9258380	0.91	0.953939
0.4	0.8661432	0.84	0.916515
0.5	0.7867481	0.75	0.866025
0.6	0.6855743	0.64	0.800000
0.7	0.5599735	0.51	0.714143
0.8	0.4066581	0.36	0.600000
0.9	0.2216148	0.19	0.435890
1	0.0000000	0	0.000000

shows several angles that are rolled into rings and bolted together for easier transport.

These angles are rolled to a tight curvature. Angles can be rolled to even tighter curves than those shown here, but most bow trusses involve gentle curvature. Some bow trusses are fabricated with the use of angles that are bowed to the correct shape on the welding table. Members that are rolled into a curved shape have significant residual stresses; some of a member's material has not yielded and tries to return to its original shape, whereas other parts of the member have yielded and resist going back to the original shape. The yielded material holds the member to its new curved shape against the unyielded material's resistance.

The battle between the unyielded parts and the yielded parts causes significant residual stresses, reducing the member's capacity. Accounting for these residual stresses is beyond the scope of this book. It is often wise, however, to have specialized fabricators design spanning systems incorporating members that are rolled into curved shapes.

This rolling system produces an arc of a circle. There is no common system for producing continuously curved parabolic top chords. This would be a much more complicated shaping process. An important question is, how important is it to have the top chord in the shape of a parabola instead of in the shape of an arc of a circle? The next section of this chapter answers that question.

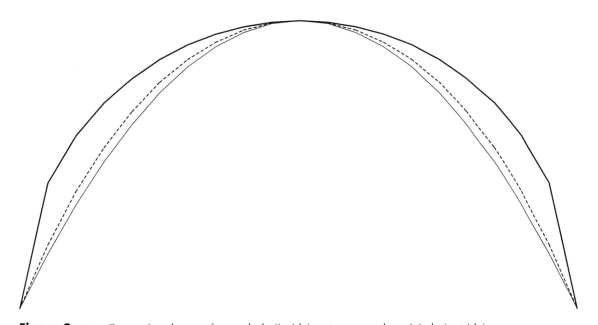

Figure 8.124 Comparing shapes of a parabola (inside), catenary, and semicircle (outside).

Figure 8.125 Chicago Metals roller system. Materials rest on a flat floor and are fed into the rotating rollers on vertical axles. The bearings and roller mounts are set down in a well, below the working surface.

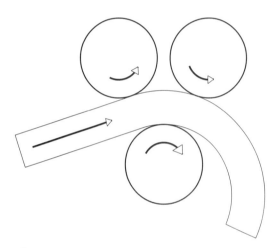

Figure 8.126 Rolling a straight member to a continuous curvature.

Figure 8.127 I-section curved in the weak direction.

(a)

(b)

Figure 8.128 Steel pipe (a) curved with the use of rollers like those shown in (b).

8.1.10 ANALYSIS OF BOW TRUSSES AND ARCHES IN THE FORM OF AN ARC OF A CIRCLE

To understand the difference in structural behavior between parabolas and arcs of circles, one must first develop a mathematical description of the circle's arc, similar to the mathematics developed for the parabola. In designing a bow truss, one typically sketches the shape to establish the desired proportions, or selects a depth-to-span ratio in the range set forth in the guidelines (see Chapter 1, Section 1.7, on rules of thumb and design guidelines for spans and proportions of common spanning members and systems). A depth of $\frac{L}{6}$ is within the recommended range for bow trusses and looks like that in Figure 8.130.

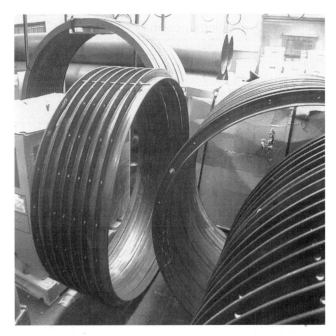

Figure 8.129 Angles curved by rolling.

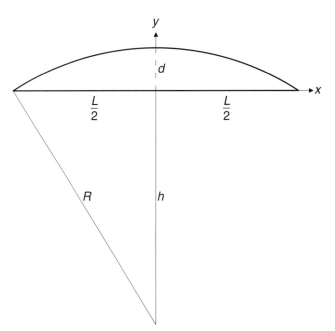

Figure 8.131 Identifying key geometric factors.

The coordinate axes are shown in the common location, with the x-axis along the bottom chord's centerline and the y-axis at the truss's symmetry line. These are the commonly chosen axes for working within a building's geometry, but it is not the ideal coordinate system for writing the circle equation. One needs to find its radius (R); see Figure 8.131:

In the triangle on the left in the diagram in Figure 8.131:

$$R^2 = \left(\frac{L_2}{2}\right)^2 + h^2 \qquad \textbf{[8.39]}$$

As a designer, one thinks that the important quantities are L and d. Mathematically, the important quantity is R. One wants to express R in terms of L and d. In the preceding equation, h is an extraneous quantity to be eliminated; one wants to express it in terms of other quantities of interest. Express h in terms of R and d:

$$h = R - d \qquad \textbf{[8.40]}$$

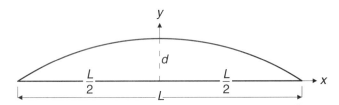

Figure 8.130 A top chord in the shape of an arc of a circle.

Substitute this expression in equation [8.39]:

$$R^2 = \left(\frac{L}{2}\right)^2 + (R-d)^2 = \left(\frac{L}{2}\right)^2 + (R^2 - 2Rd + d^2) \qquad \textbf{[8.41]}$$

Eliminate R^2 from both sides of the equation:

$$0 = \left(\frac{L}{2}\right)^2 - 2Rd + d^2 \qquad \textbf{[8.42]}$$

Solve for R:

$$2Rd = \left(\frac{L}{2}\right)^2 + d^2$$

$$R = \frac{\left(\frac{L}{2}\right)^2 + d^2}{2d} \qquad \textbf{[8.43]}$$

Now write the circle equation [8.39] using a new coordinate system (x', y') the origin of which is located at the circle's center (see Figure 8.132).

The circle equation is:

$$R^2 = (x')^2 + (y')^2 \qquad \textbf{[8.44]}$$

Solve for y':

$$y' = \sqrt{R^2 - (x')^2} \qquad \textbf{[8.45]}$$

Substitute x' = x:

$$y' = \sqrt{R^2 - x^2} \qquad \textbf{[8.46]}$$

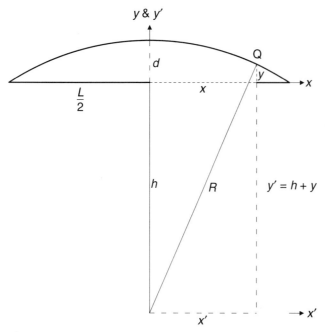

Figure 8.132 Establishing geometric relationships.

Substitute values:

$$y' = h + y = (R - d) + y \quad \text{[8.47]}$$

To find:

$$(R - d + y) = \sqrt{R^2 - x^2} \quad \text{[8.48]}$$

Solve for y:

$$y = \sqrt{R^2 - x^2} - R + d \quad \text{[8.49]}$$

Table 8.8 Generating Coordinates for Parabolas

			$y = d - \dfrac{d}{\left(\dfrac{L}{2}\right)^2} \cdot x^2$
d (ft)	L (ft)	x (ft)	(ft)
10	60	−30	0
		−24	3.6
		−18	6.4
		−12	8.4
		−6	9.6
		0	10
		6	9.6
		12	8.4
		18	6.4
		24	3.6
		30	0

Table 8.9 Coordinates for an Arc of a Circle

				For an arc 10 ft deep
				$y = \sqrt{R^2 - x^2} - R + d$
d (ft)	L (ft)	R (ft)	x (ft)	(ft)
10	60	50	−30	0.000
			−24	3.863
			−18	6.648
			−12	8.539
			−6	9.639
			0	10.000
			6	9.639
			12	8.539
			18	6.648
			24	3.863
			30	0.000

One can use this formula [8.49] in a spreadsheet to find the top-chord node coordinates for a bow truss that has a top chord in the shape of an arc of a circle. For comparison, it is instructive to find these nodes for the same span and depth used for the parabola in the previous illustration (see Tables 8.8 and 8.9).

A quick examination indicates that the two curves coincide at the end points and the zenith points, but that the other nodes of the arc of the circle are slightly higher than the corresponding parabola nodes. One can say that the arc of the circle is slightly fuller near the quarter points or that the parabola is slightly flatter near the quarter points. Figure 8.133 displays the relative shapes of the parabola and the arc of the circle by using the plot function in the spreadsheet program.

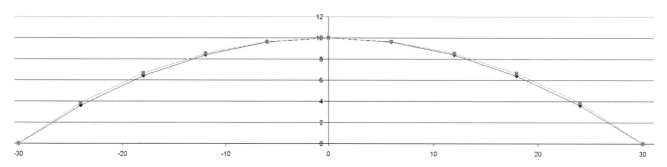

Figure 8.133 Displaying the parabola and the arc of a circle using the charting function of the spreadsheet program.

This charting function does not automatically plot the vertical and horizontal axes to the same scale, producing a sense of disproportion. The tabular data from the spreadsheet can be transported to an analysis program, where the two shapes are compared at the proper scale. Figure 8.134 shows the two shapes superimposed, as depicted by the analysis program.

As is known from the tabular data, the arc of the circle is slightly higher near the quarter points. These two shapes are so similar that the human eye has difficulty distinguishing between them when they are drawn accurately and superimposed on top of each other. However, under certain circumstances, they have substantially different structural behaviors.

Before performing the computer analysis, it is instructive to solve for the structure's internal forces using basic analysis principles. The forces on the system are shown in Figure 8.135.

For clarity, label the nodes and assign directions to the forces on the nodes. It is known that the top chords are in compression and the bottom-chord segments are in tension. So, put the force arrows from those members on the diagram (see Figure 8.136).

Web forces are less certain. Make a guess regarding the force directions in the web members. Then look at the results of the mathematics to see whether the right guess was made. Fortunately, one can always rely on the mathematics to lead to the right answer, regardless of the assumption made about the force arrow direction.

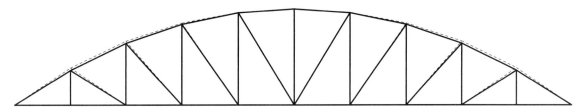

Figure 8.134 Displaying the parabola (solid line) and the arc of a circle (dashed line) using the structural analysis program.

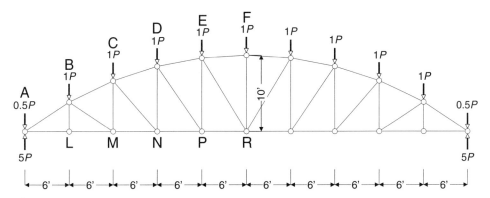

Figure 8.135 Point forces on the nodes of a bow truss in the shape of an arc of a circle.

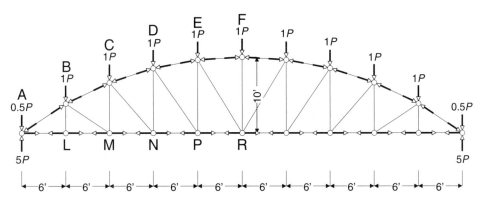

Figure 8.136 Putting the chord forces on the diagram.

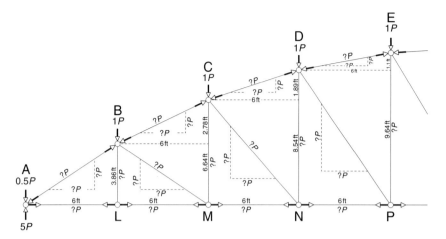

Figure 8.137 Recording the dimensions and providing places to record the forces.

On the truss diagram, provide:

Dimensions for the horizontal and vertical extent of each member
Places to record the force components' magnitudes

Focus on the truss's left four bays, as shown in Figure 8.137.

The dimensions in the diagram are obtained from the spreadsheet calculation shown in Table 8.10.

Start with joint A:

The 0.5 P applied force pushing down on joint A, combined with the 5 P reaction force pushing up on joint A, produce a net upward force of 4.5 P. This must be equilibrated by a downward 4.5 P force component exerted by the chord member AB on joint A.

Since chord member AB is pushing down with a 4.5 P force component on joint A, joint A reacts by pushing up with a 4.5 P force component on member AB.

The upward 4.5 P force exerted by joint A on chord member AB must be equilibrated by a downward 4.5 P force exerted by joint B on member AB.

Since joint B is pushing down with a 4.5 P force component on chord member AB, member AB reacts by pushing up with a 4.5 P force on joint B.

Table 8.10 Coordinates for an Arc of a Circle

				For an arc 10 ft deep	
d	L	R	x	$y = \sqrt{R^2 - x2} - R + d$	Δy
(ft)	(ft)	(ft)	(ft)	(ft)	(ft)
10	60	50	−30	0.000	
			−24	3.863	3.863
			−18	6.648	2.784
			−12	8.539	1.891
			−6	9.639	1.100
			0	10.000	0.361

Using similar triangles, the horizontal-force component in chord member AB must be

$$AB_x = \frac{6}{3.863} \cdot AB_y = \frac{6}{3.863} \cdot 4.5\,P = 6.989\,P$$

Using the Pythagorean theorem:

$$AB = \sqrt{(AB_x)^2 + (AB_y)^2} = \sqrt{(6.989\,P)^2 + (4.5\,P)^2}$$
$$= 8.312\,P$$

The 6.989 P force component to the left, exerted by chord member AB on joint A, must be equilibrated by a horizontal 6.989 P force to the right, exerted by chord member AL on joint A.

Since chord member AL is pulling to the right with a 6.989 P force on joint A, joint A reacts by pulling to the left with a 6.989 P force on member AL.

The 6.989 P force to the left, exerted by joint A on chord member AL, must be equilibrated by a 6.989 P force to the right, exerted by joint L on member AL.

Since joint L is pulling to the right with a 6.989 P force on chord member AL, member AL reacts by pulling to the left with a 6.989 P force on joint L (see Figure 8.138).

Move to joint L:

Since vertical member BL is the only member capable of exerting a vertical force on joint L, and since there are no applied forces on joint L, equilibrium of joint L requires that member BL does not exert force on joint L. Hence, member BL is a zero-force member.

The 6.989 P force to the left, exerted by chord member AL on joint L, must be equilibrated by a horizontal 6.989 P force to the right, exerted by chord member LM on joint L.

Since chord member LM is pulling to the right with a 6.989 P force on joint L, joint L reacts by pulling to the left with a 6.989 P force on member LM.

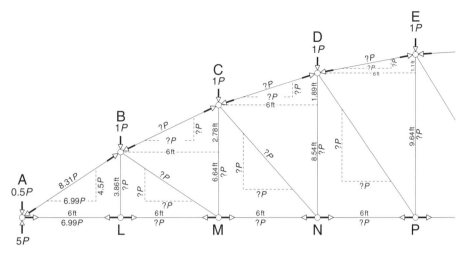

Figure 8.138 Resolved forces at joint A.

The 6.989 P force to the left, exerted by joint L on chord member LM, must be equilibrated by a 6.989 P force to the right, exerted by joint M on member LM.

Since joint M is pulling to the right with a 6.989 P force on chord member LM, member LM reacts by pulling to the left with a 6.989 P force component on joint M (see Figure 8.139).

Move to joint B:

To resolve joint B, assume a direction for diagonal member BM's force on joint B. This assumed direction is arbitrary. Assume that it is down and to the right, meaning that member BM is in tension. This single arrow is shown in the diagram in Figure 8.140.

This is where the problem becomes more challenging than in previous examples. Before, one could always move to a joint with sufficient information to resolve the forces at the joint without solving simultaneous equations. Here, there are two unknown vertical forces and

two unknown horizontal forces at joint B. Therefore, an orderly system has to be created to write the equations and solve them. In writing the equilibrium equations for joint B, the following nomenclature is used:

BC_x is the designation for chord member BC's horizontal force component on joint B.

BC_y is the designation for chord member BC's vertical force component on joint B.

BM_x is the designation for diagonal member BM's horizontal force component on joint B.

BM_y is the designation for diagonal member BM's vertical force component on joint B.

Force to the left is negative. Force to the right is positive. Apply the equilibrium equation to the horizontal forces on joint B:

$$0 = -BC_x + BM_x + 6.989\ P \qquad\qquad [8.50]$$

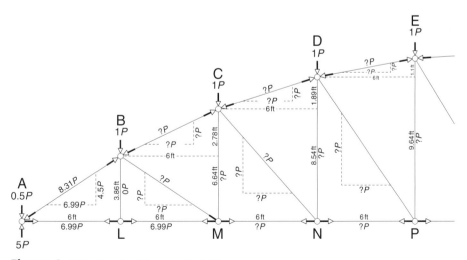

Figure 8.139 Resolved forces at joint L.

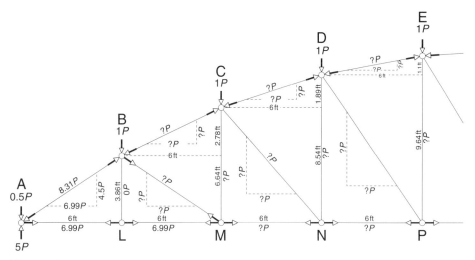

Figure 8.140 Assumed direction for the web force on joint B.

Apply the equilibrium equation to the vertical forces on joint B:

$$0 = -BC_y - BM_y + 4.5\,P - 1\,P \qquad \textbf{[8.51]}$$

There are two equations with four unknowns. The members' slopes are known, and, therefore, slopes of the forces produced by those members are known as well. Armed with this geometric information, rewrite equation [8.51], expressing the y-components in terms of the x-components of the forces. Based on member slopes:

$$BC_y = \frac{2.784}{6} \cdot BC_x = 0.464\,BC_x$$

$$BM = \frac{3.863}{6} \cdot BM_x = 0.644\,BM_x \qquad \textbf{[8.52]}$$

Substitute these relationships into the vertical forces' equilibrium equation [8.51]:

$$0 = -0.464\,BC_x - 0.644\,BM_x + 3.5\,P \qquad \textbf{[8.53]}$$

Multiply equation [8.53] by $-\dfrac{1}{0.464}$:

$$0 = +1\,BC_x + 1.388\,BM_x - 7.543\,P \qquad \textbf{[8.54]}$$

Add equation [8.54] to the horizontal forces' equilibrium equation [8.50]:

$$0 = -1\,BC_x + 1\,BC_x + 1\,BM_x + 1.388\,BM_x$$
$$\qquad + 6.989\,P - 7.543\,P$$

$$0 = +2.388\,BM_x - 0.554\,P \qquad \textbf{[8.55]}$$

Divide by 2.388:

$$0 = BM_x - 0.232\,P$$
$$BM_x = 0.232\,P \qquad \textbf{[8.56]}$$

The positive value indicates that the original direction choice for the force exerted by diagonal member BM on joint B was correct: member BM is in tension and is pulling on joint B. Using similar triangles:

$$BM_y = \frac{3.863}{6} \cdot BM_x = \frac{3.863}{6} \cdot 0.232\,P = 0.149\,P$$

$$BM = \sqrt{(BM_x)^2 + (BM_y)^2} = 0.276\,P \qquad \textbf{[8.57]}$$

This non-zero force proves that changing the top chord's shape from a parabola to an arc of a circle has altered the balance of forces in the system and introduced forces in the web members where previously none existed (see Figure 8.141).

Continue with the resolution of forces on joint B:

Apply the equilibrium equation to the horizontal forces on joint B:

$$0 = -BC_x + 0.232\,P + 6.989\,P \qquad \textbf{[8.58]}$$

Solve for BC_x:

$$BC_x = 7.221\,P \qquad \textbf{[8.59]}$$

Apply the equilibrium equation to the vertical forces on joint B:

$$0 = -BC_y - 0.149\,P + 4.5\,P - 1\,P \qquad \textbf{[8.60]}$$

Solve for:

$$BC_y = 3.351\,P$$

$$BC = \sqrt{(BC_x)^2 + (BC_y)^2} = \sqrt{(7.221\,P)^2 + (3.351\,P)^2}$$
$$= 7.960\,P \qquad \textbf{[8.61]}$$

See Figure 8.142.

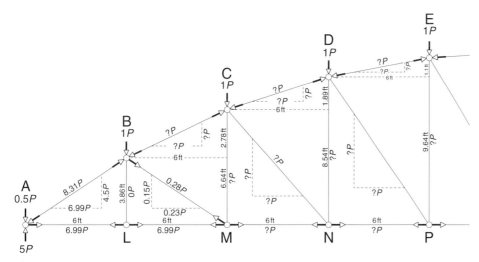

Figure 8.141 Resolved web force on joint B.

Resolve the forces to joint M:

The upward 0.149 *P* force component, exerted by diagonal member BM on joint M, must be equilibrated by a downward 0.149 *P* force, exerted by vertical member CM on joint M.

Since vertical member CM is pushing down with a 0.149 *P* force on joint M, joint M reacts by pushing up on member CM with a 0.149 *P* force.

The upward 0.149 *P* force, exerted by joint M on vertical member CM, must be equilibrated by a downward 0.149 *P* force, exerted by joint C on member CM.

Since joint C is pushing down with a 0.149 *P* force on vertical member CM, member CM reacts by pushing up with a 0.149 *P* force on joint C.

The 6.989 *P* force to the left exerted by chord member LM on joint M, combined with the 0.232 *P* horizontal force component to the left exerted by diagonal member BM on joint M, produce a net force to the left of 7.221 *P*

on joint M. This must be equilibrated by a horizontal 7.221 *P* force to the right, exerted by chord member MN on joint M.

Since chord member MN is pulling to the right with a 7.221 *P* force on joint M, joint M reacts by pulling to the left with a 7.221 *P* force on chord member MN.

The 7.221 *P* force to the left, exerted by joint M on chord member MN, must be equilibrated by a 7.221 *P* force to the right, exerted by joint N on chord member MN.

Since joint N is pulling to the right with a 7.221 *P* force on chord member MN, member MN reacts by pulling to the left with a 7.221 *P* force component on joint N (see Figure 8.143).

To resolve the forces on joint C, make an assumption about the force direction exerted by diagonal member CN on joint C. To ease this process, assume that CN is in tension; that it is pulling down and to the right on joint C, as shown in the diagram in Figure 8.144.

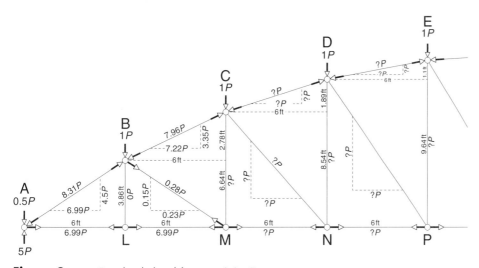

Figure 8.142 Resolved chord force on joint B.

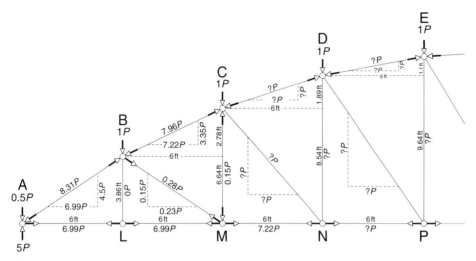

Figure 8.143 Resolved forces on joint M.

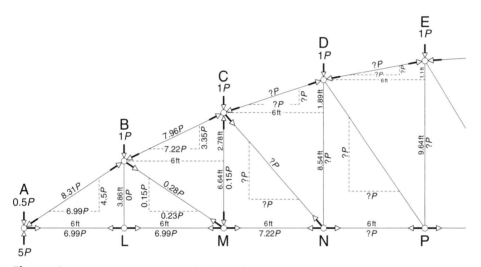

Figure 8.144 Assumed direction for the web force on joint C.

Apply the equilibrium equation to the horizontal forces on joint C:

$$0 = -CD_x + CN_x + 7.221 \, P \qquad \textbf{[8.62]}$$

Apply the equilibrium equation to the vertical forces on joint C:

$$0 = -CD_y - CN_y + 3.351 \, P - 1 \, P + 0.149 \, P \qquad \textbf{[8.63]}$$

There are two equations with four unknowns. The members' slopes are known, and, therefore, slopes of the forces produced by those members are known as well. Armed with this geometric information, rewrite equation [8.63], expressing the y-components in terms of the x-components. Based on member slopes:

$$CD_y = \frac{1.891}{6} \cdot CD_x = 0.315 \, CD_x$$

$$CN_y = \frac{6.648}{6} \cdot CN_x = 1.108 \, CN_x \qquad \textbf{[8.64]}$$

Substitute these relationships in the vertical forces' equilibrium equation [8.63] on joint C:

$$0 = -0.315 \, CD_x - 1.108 \, CN_x + 2.5 \, P \qquad \textbf{[8.65]}$$

Multiply equation [8.65] by $-\dfrac{1}{0.315}$:

$$0 = +1 \, CD_x + 3.515 \, CN_x - 7.932 \, P \qquad \textbf{[8.66]}$$

Add equation [8.66] to the horizontal forces' equilibrium equation [8.62] on joint C:

$$0 = -1 \, CD_x + 1 \, CD_x + 1 \, CN_x + 3.535 \, CN_x + 7.221 \, P - 7.932 \, P$$

$$0 = +4.515 \, CN_x - 0.712 \, P \qquad \textbf{[8.67]}$$

Divide by 4.515:

$$0 = CN_x - 0.158 \, P$$

$$CN_x = 0.158 \, P \qquad \textbf{[8.68]}$$

The positive value indicates that the original direction choice for the force exerted by the diagonal member CN on joint C was correct: member CN is in tension and is pulling on joint C.

$$CN_y = \frac{6.648}{6} \cdot CN_x = \frac{6.648}{6} \cdot 0.158\,P = 0.175\,P$$

$$CN = \sqrt{(CN_x)^2 + (CN_y)^2} = \sqrt{(0.158\,P)^2 + (0.175\,P)^2}$$

$$= 0.235\,P \qquad\qquad \textbf{[8.69]}$$

This non-zero force proves that changing the top chord's shape from a parabola to an arc of a circle altered the balance of forces in the system and introduced forces in the web members where previously none existed (see Figure 8.145).

Continue with the resolution of forces on joint C:

Apply the equilibrium equation to the horizontal forces on joint C:

$$0 = -CD_x + 0.158\,P + 7.221\,P \qquad\qquad \textbf{[8.70]}$$

Solve for CD_x:

$$CD_x = 7.378\,P \qquad\qquad \textbf{[8.71]}$$

Apply the equilibrium equation to the vertical forces on joint C:

$$0 = -CD_y - 0.175\,P + 3.351\,P - 1\,P + 0.149 \qquad \textbf{[8.72]}$$

Solve for CD_y:

$$CD_y = 2.325\,P$$

$$CD = \sqrt{(CD_x)^2 + (CD_y)^2} = \sqrt{(7.378\,P)^2 + (2.232\,P)^2}$$

$$= 7.736\,P \qquad\qquad \textbf{[8.73]}$$

See Figure 8.146.

Students are encouraged to resolve the forces on joints N, D, Q, and E to find the force components in the members DE, DQ, EF, and ER. The net forces in these members are provided in the diagram in Figure 8.147, along with the forces in all vertical and horizontal members, to provide checks for students' solutions. When working these equations, keep in mind that there are only two simultaneous equations per joint and each joint can be resolved before continuing to the next joint. Many structures in this book and in design practice involve solving hundreds, or even thousands, of simultaneous equations in complex arrays where individual joints cannot be resolved sequentially, as in the simple structure shown here. This example is given primarily to illustrate the mathematical and structural concepts, but it also begins to hint at the computation power provided by standard 3D analysis programs, which can solve such a problem almost in the time it takes to press the mouse button.

It will be instructive to use computer-based structural analysis to solve both the bow truss made from a parabola and the bow truss made from an arc of a circle. Figure 8.148 shows the loads on a truss in the shape of a parabola (top) and on a truss in the shape of an arc of a circle (bottom).

For the preceding trusses, the simulation is performed with a 1 K force on each of the interior top-chord nodes and a 0.5 K force on each of the end nodes. The units in the diagram in Figure 8.149 are in kips, and the C or T after the number indicates whether the member is in compression or in tension. Figure 8.149 gives the axial forces in the members of the two trusses calculated in the computer simulation.

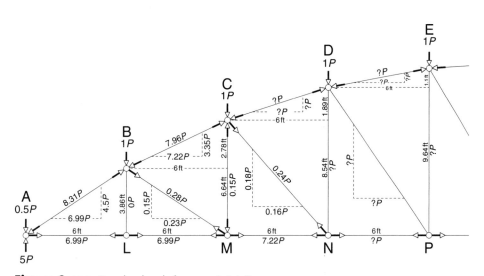

Figure 8.145 Resolved web force on joint C.

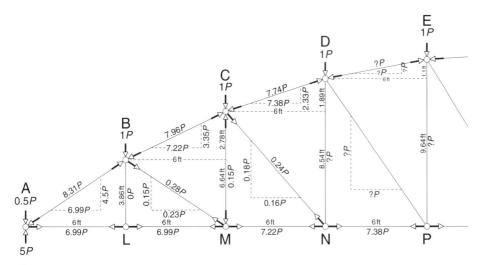

Figure 8.146 Resolved chord force on joint C.

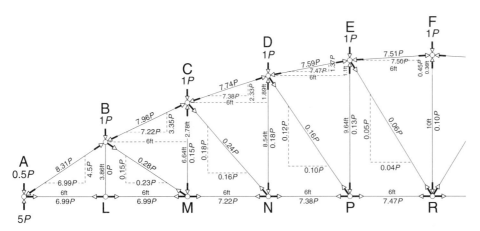

Figure 8.147 Complete solution to the truss with a chord in the shape of an arc of a circle.

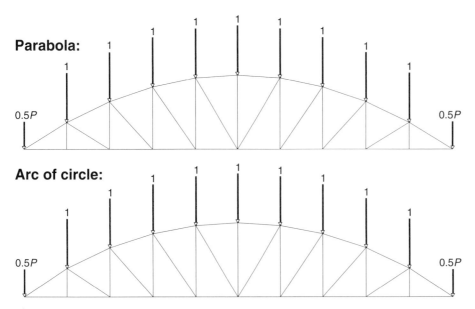

Figure 8.148 Load diagram from computer simulations for a top chord in the shape of a parabola (top) and an arc of a circle (bottom).

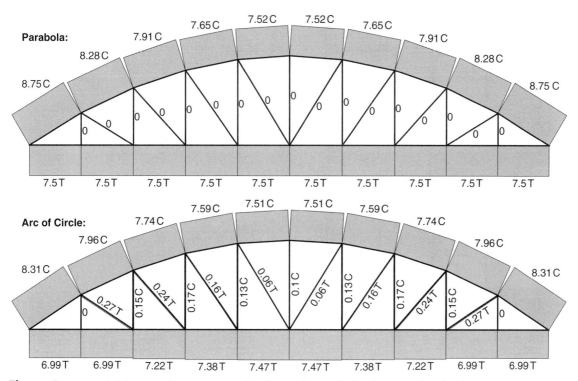

Figure 8.149 Axial forces in bow trusses in the shape of a parabola (above) and in the shape of an arc of a circle (below).

The chord forces for the two configurations are very similar. The most obvious difference between the two configurations is in the web forces. The web forces for the parabolic shape are zero, and the web forces are non-zero for the truss in the shape of an arc of a circle. The arc of a circle is not the correct shape to work in pure compression without help to hold it in shape. The web members are active to keep the compression chord that is in the shape of an arc of a circle from deforming under the load. The importance of the web members' bracing action can be assessed by simulating the truss with and without the web members. To do this, return to the previous example in which $P = 6$ K, the chord members are HSS $3 \times 3 \times \dfrac{3}{16}$ in., and the web members are HSS $2 \times 2 \times \dfrac{3}{16}$ in. See Figures 8.150 and 8.151.

The axial stresses are very similar for the two shapes, as shown in Figure 8.151. The major difference in the structural action of the two configurations is revealed by the bending stresses, shown in Figure 8.152.

As expected, the bending stresses in the arch in the shape of a parabola are zero. In comparison, the bending stresses in the arch in the shape of an arc of a circle are severe. The most severe bending stresses are more than twice the axial stresses. This is far from the intended ideal of pure axial action. The web members' action in bracing the chord member in the shape of an arc of a circle is crucial to the chord member's performance. The previous analyses demonstrate that a top chord in the

shape of an arc of a circle works well for bow trusses with frequent web members bracing the top chord. The web members are positioned favorably to hold the chord member's shape with modest stresses in the web members. In contrast, severe bending stresses occur in the chord member that has the shape of an arc of a circle if the chord member must use its bending strength to hold its shape when handling the compressive force. The arc of the circle works well for bow trusses but is not the preferred shape for unbraced arches.

Figure 8.153 shows the deformed shape of two arches in the shapes of a parabola and an arc of a circle. Notice the tendency of the center of the arc of the circle to sag downward and the tendency of the quarter points to bulge upward.

That tendency to sag can be inhibited by putting a post under the center of the arch. In order for that post to have the desired effect of lifting up on the arch, it must, in turn, be pushed up by the tie member. In order for the tie member to function to support the post, it must have some drape and a cusp under the center post, as in the structure designed by DeStefano + Partners shown in Figure 8.154.

The distinction between a parabola and an arc of a circle is crucial in a building like the Broadgate Exchange House, where the arches' depth would produce a radically different structural behavior in an arc of a circle as compared with a parabola. Figures 8.155, 8.156, and 8.157 explore more shapes for arches.

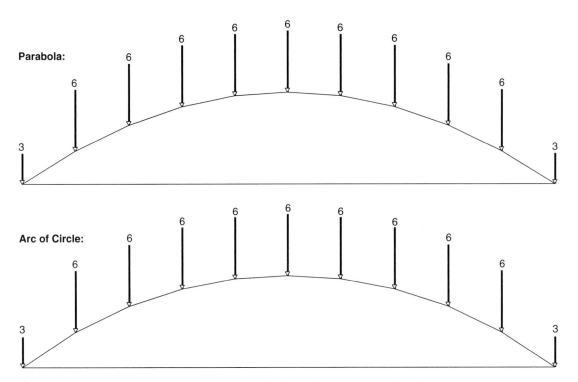

Figure 8.150 Tied arches in the shape of a parabola (top) and an arc of circle (bottom).

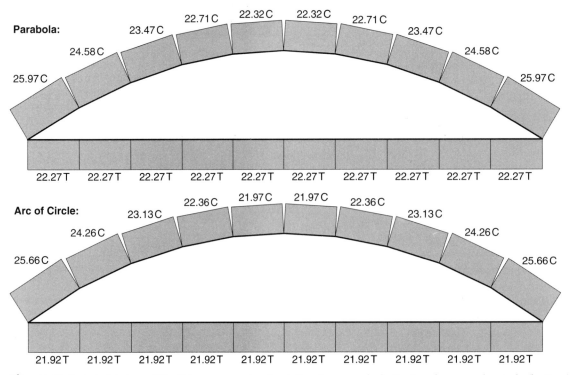

Figure 8.151 Axial stress (K/in.²) from computer simulation for a parabola (top) and an arc of a circle (bottom).

Parabola:

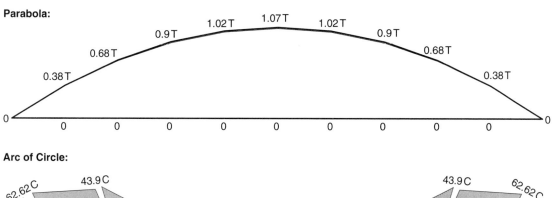

Arc of Circle:

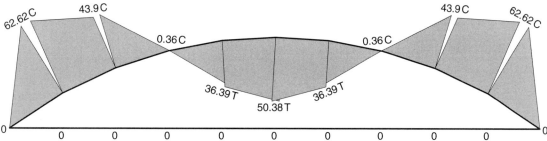

Figure 8.152 Bending stress (K/in.²) from computer simulation for a parabola (top) and an arc of a circle (bottom).

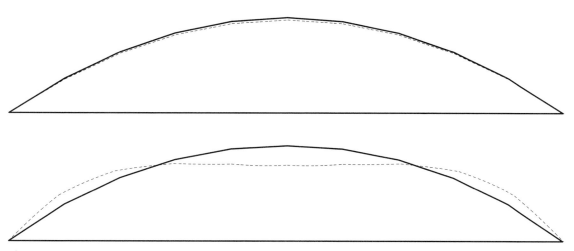

Figure 8.153 Deformation for an arch in the shape of a parabola (top) and an arc of a circle (bottom).

The flags in Figure 8.156 indicate the intensity of the bending stress on the same five spanning members. The parabolic spanning elements have no bending stress. The shallow arc of a circle has significant bending stress owing to the fact that it is not the ideal shape. The bending stresses in both the semicircle and the ellipse are extreme. Figure 8.157 indicates that the variation in deformation as a function of structural configuration follows a pattern similar to the variation in bending stress.

In addition to achieving structural efficiency, the Broadgate Exchange House designers desired to use the minimal number of web members to keep the structure as simple and visually clean as possible. The results of the simulation in Figures 8.156 and 8.157 make it clear that

more and heavier web members would have been required to make an arc of a circle or an ellipse work on that building.

The models in Figure 8.158 illustrate the difference in behavior between parabolas and semicircles. The model in (a) is a parabola, which remains stable when the centering supporting it is lowered away. Its stability is such that it can be nudged and deformed and it returns to its original shape, as shown in (b). The model in (c) is a semicircle supported by the centering. As soon as the centering is lowered away, as shown in (d), the semicircular arch begins to deform and collapse. Cracks are emerging on the outside of the arch at the quarter points and on the inside near the top center of the arch.

Figure 8.154 Arches with center post supported by tie member working as a sling.

Figure 8.155 Parabolic arches (left), arch in the shape of an arc of a circle (center), semicircular and elliptical arches (right), under uniform load.

The only way that a semicircular arch can be made functional structurally is for it to be very thick (so that the compressive stress path is comfortably contained within its dimensions) or to have material wedged around it (so that it cannot deform out of its original shape). The masonry wall in Figure 8.159 is based on that principle. When such a wall is seismically disturbed, it begins to

come apart quickly because of the uncomfortable balance that holds the semicircle in its shape.

Figure 8.160 illustrates how the arch in Figure 8.159 is able to work structurally. The arch benefits because there is more load over the parts of the arch that are tending to bulge upward and outward. It also benefits from the material wedged between it and the next arch. This ma-

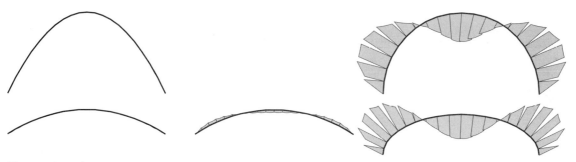

Figure 8.156 Bending stresses in parabolic arches (left), arch in the shape of an arc of a circle (center), semicircular and elliptical arches (right).

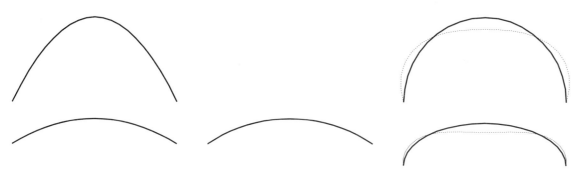

Figure 8.157 Deformation of parabolic arches (left), arch in the shape of an arc of a circle (center), semicircular and elliptical arches (right).

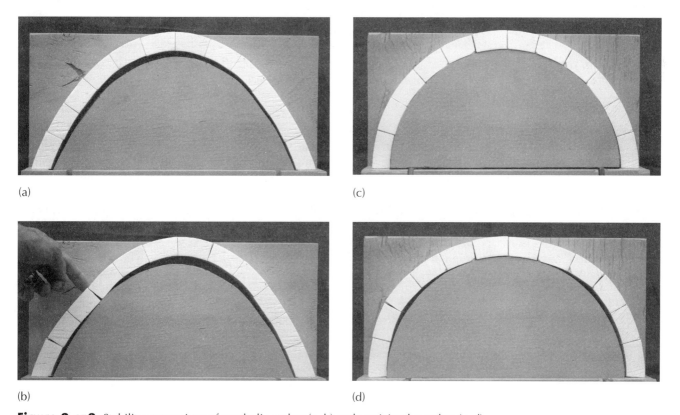

(a)

(c)

(b)

(d)

Figure 8.158 Stability comparison of parabolic arches (a, b) and semicircular arches (c, d).

Figure 8.159 Semicircular arch bulging upward and outward at the quarter-points and sagging inward at the top. (Photograph courtesy of Rowland J. Mainstone from *Developments in Structural Form* [Architectural Press, 2001].)

terial works in compression to keep the semicircle from bulging laterally. In Figure 8.159, the structure has moved over time, because of seismic disturbance, foundation settlement, or both. As the structural material has re-arranged itself, the stress path is now more apparent, being at the top of the arch at the center and on the inside of the arch at the quarter-points. Tracing the stress path would produce a shape more similar to a parabola or a catenary than to a semicircle.

8.1.11 SHAPE RESPONSES TO NONUNIFORM LOADS

Bow trusses are the ideal shape under a uniform load. In many instances, trusses are subjected to intense, local-ized, moving loads. To explore how a bow truss's design might change in response to concentrated loads, one needs to develop an analysis technique to find the ideal

shape for a truss subjected to a combination of a uni-formly distributed load and intense localized forces. Since one may want to look at many different load cases, it is nice to "program" the mathematics in a spreadsheet so that by changing one or two numbers, one can quickly find the new coordinates. To ease this process, revisit the differences method, discussed earlier in the context of the Broadgate Exchange House, now to be applied to the ten-bay bow truss example. Focus on symmetric loads—any concentrated force on the truss's left side has an equal concentrated force at the symmetric location on the truss's right side. Assume that the joints are labeled from the center outward, with the center top joint called Joint 1. The bays to each side of Joint 1 are called Bay 1, and subsequent bays are numbered with increasing numbers moving away from the center (see Figure 8.161).

According to truss symmetry, the 1 *P* force at the truss's center induces a 0.5 *P* shear force in each of the bays on

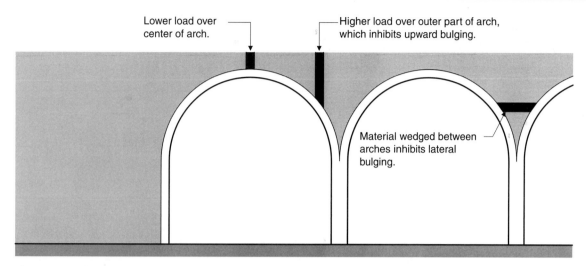

Figure 8.160 Influences that help semicircular arches hold their shape.

either side of the center point—in Bay 1 on each side. Moving out from the center, each time a joint is crossed, the shear force increases by the force's magnitude on the joint being crossed: A 5 P force on Joint 2 means that the shear force in Bay 2 is 5 P greater than the shear force in Bay 1. Since the shear force in Bay 1 is 0.5 P, the shear force in Bay 2 must be 0.5 P + 5 P = 5.5 P. A 1 P force on Joint 3 means that the shear force in Bay 3 must be 1 P greater than the shear force in Bay 2; the shear force in Bay 3 must be 6.5 P. These results are summarized in Table 8.11.

In the previous discussions, it was deduced that to maintain a chord's shape where the chord provides moment and shear capacity, each top chord segment must have a rise (Δy) that is in proportion to the shear force that it is resisting. Since one wants to set a limit on the truss height, the collective chord-segment rises cannot exceed the intended overall top-chord rise. Each chord segment

is allocated a fraction of the overall rise. This is equal to the shear force in that bay divided by the sum of all the shear forces in all the bays on one side of the truss:

$$\frac{\text{shear force in the bay}}{\Sigma \text{ of all shear force in all bays of that truss half}}$$

For Bay 4 in Figure 8.161:

$$= \frac{\text{shear force in bay 4}}{\substack{\text{shear force in} \\ (\text{Bay 1} + \text{Bay 2} + \text{Bay 3} + \text{Bay 4} + \text{Bay 5})}}$$

$$= \frac{7.5\,P}{0.5\,P + 5.5\,P + 6.5\,P + 7.5\,P + 8.5\,P}$$

$$= \frac{7.5\,P}{28.5\,P} = 0.263$$

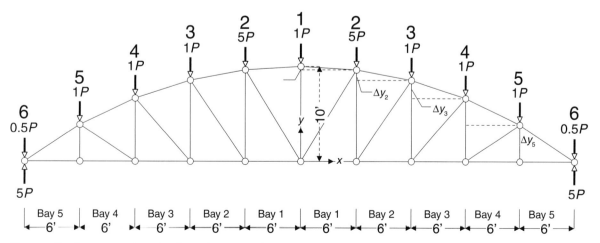

Figure 8.161 Nonuniform loads on the joints of a truss.

Table 8.11 Adjusting Truss Shape in Response to Large Force on Joint 2

Node #	Bay #	Force on Node (P)	Shear Force in Bay (P)	Fraction of Total Rise Allocated to Bay	Total Rise (R) (ft)	Δy in Bay (ft)	y coordinate of Node (ft)
1		**1**					10.000
	1		0.5	0.018	**10**	0.175	
2		**5**					9.825
	2		5.5	0.193		1.930	
3		**1**					7.895
	3		6.5	0.228		2.281	
4		**1**					5.614
	4		7.5	0.263		2.632	
5		**1**					2.982
	5		8.5	0.298		2.982	
6		**0.5**					0.000
			Total of all shear forces in all all bays = 28.5				

The chord-segment rise (Δy) in a bay is determined by multiplying that fraction by the overall top-chord rise (R):

$$\Delta y = R \cdot \text{chord-segment rise fraction}$$

For Bay 4 in Figure 8.161:

$$\Delta y = 10 \text{ ft} \cdot 0.263 = 2.63 \text{ ft}$$

A joint's vertical coordinate (y) is found by starting with the overall top-chord rise (R) and subtracting the sum of all the Δy's for the bays interior to the joint:

$$y = R - \sum \text{ of all interior bays' } \Delta y\text{'s}$$

For Joint 5 in Figure 8.161:

$$y = 10 \text{ ft} - (\Delta y_{Bay1} + \Delta y_{Bay2} + \Delta y_{Bay3} + \Delta y_{Bay4})$$
$$= 10 \text{ ft} = (0.175 \text{ ft} + 1.930 \text{ ft} + 2.281 \text{ ft} + 2.632 \text{ ft})$$
$$-7.018 \text{ ft} = 2.982 \text{ ft}$$

Using a spreadsheet saves one from performing hand calculations (see Table 8.11).

In this spreadsheet, bold numbers represent inputs to the spreadsheet. The forces are adjusted by changing the numbers. For example, shifting the 5 P forces outward to both Joints 5 produces the output shown in Table 8.12.

The coordinates change noticeably in response to shifting those forces. The spreadsheet is organized so that any symmetrical set of forces produces the correct coordinate output; the computations are not limited to 1 P and 5 P forces. Other changes are possible in the spreadsheet, as well. For example, by changing the shear force in both Bays 1 from 0.5 P to 1 P, the spreadsheet calculates the correct coordinates for an eleven-bay truss, in which the center bay is labeled Bay 0 and both Bays 1 are the first bays with non-zero shear. Similarly, additional joints and bays can be added to the spreadsheet,

Table 8.12 Adjusting Truss Shape in Response to Large Force on Joint 5

Node #	Bay #	Force on Node (P)	Shear Force in Bay (P)	Fraction of Total Rise Allocated to Bay	Total Rise (R) (ft)	Δy in Bay (ft)	y coordinate of Node (ft)
1		**1**					10.000
	1		0.5	0.030	**10**	0.303	
2		**1**					9.697
	2		1.5	0.091		0.909	
3		**1**					8.788
	3		2.5	0.152		1.515	
4		**1**					7.273
	4		3.5	0.212		2.121	
5		**5**					5.152
	5		8.5	0.515		5.152	
6		**0.5**					0.000
			Total of all shear forces in all bays = 16.5				

and it can be extended downward by copying the formulas. Moving the 5 *P* forces to each symmetric set of joints produces the shapes shown in Figures 8.162 and 8.163.

Performing an analysis of these shapes demonstrates that the web forces are zero, indicating that these are the desired shapes under the given loads, as shown in Figure 8.163.

In accounting for shifting loads, the most obvious change in shape occurs near the truss ends, where the smooth curve has a hump in response to the concentrated load. This truss shape is not uncommon on the sides of roadways (see Figure 8.164).

The added depth and the strange crook in the top chord is a response to the shifting loads created by vehicular traffic. The orientation of the wide flanges, in the truss shown in Figure 8.164, makes it easy to weld connections. Moreover, the truss's top chord is stabilized against lateral buckling by the vertical web members' moment connections to the horizontal beams supporting the roadbed. Orienting the vertical web members' cross sections in this way increases the lateral buckling resistance.

When trusses are deep, it is often desirable to provide lateral bracing elements at the truss top; this creates a need for the truss to be even deeper, particularly at the ends, to allow free movement of traffic onto and off the

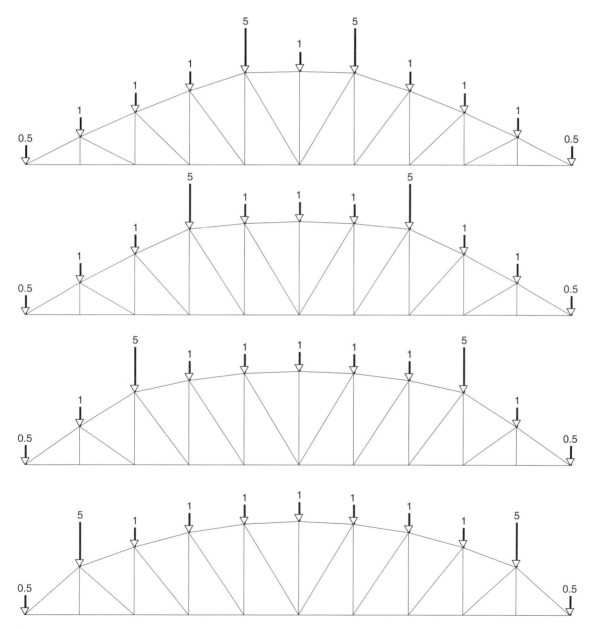

Figure 8.162 Derived shape responses to nonuniform loads.

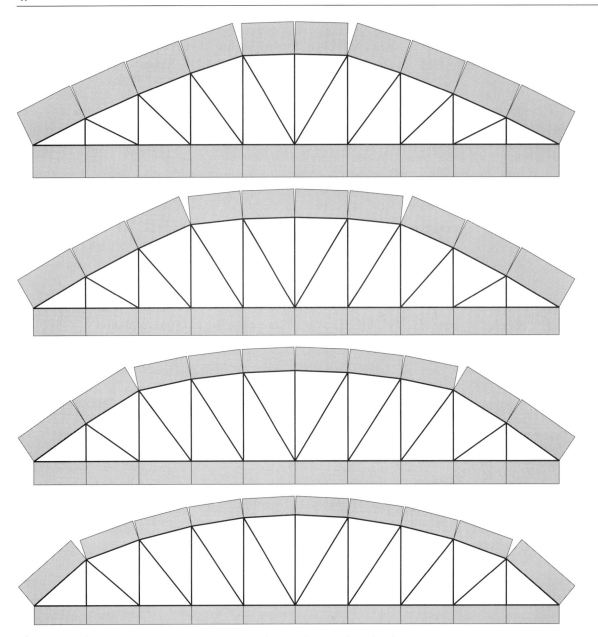

Figure 8.163 Axial forces from computer simulation of nonuniform loads.

bridge. Deepening the bridge ends works well for trains, inasmuch as a locomotive may weight 500 tons and create an intense and localized shifting load (see Figure 8.165).

This form has some curvature to express its response to the distributed load, and it is deep near the end to respond to shifting concentrated forces. The conceptual clarity and the elegance of the original bow truss—with two simple chords doing most of the work, zero-force web members, and only two highly stressed joints—is lost. The variety of load cases ensures that the web members are subjected to axial forces, and, to respond accordingly, the web members are thicker, losing their

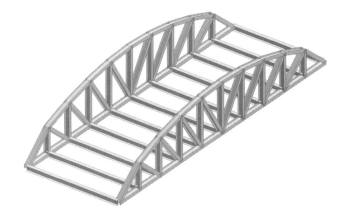

Figure 8.164 Bow truss with deep ends.

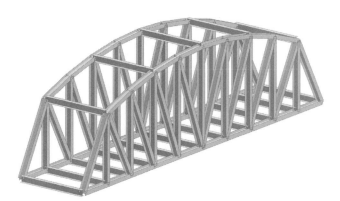

Figure 8.165 Bow truss with deeper ends to admit traffic through overhead bracing.

original slenderness and grace. The truss has not lost its beauty or functionality, however; people like the curved shape and, for overall balance, it is a functional form.

Even for roofing applications, where the loads are more uniform, there can be occasional concentrated loads, such as when a pallet of roofing materials is deposited on a roof. Consequently, many roof bow trusses are deep at the ends, similar to the shape shown in Figure 8.166.

When a truss has this modified shape, the web members are more active, even under uniform loads. An analysis of a truss under the load shown in Figure 8.167 produces the axial force diagram shown in Figure 8.168.

Since the top and bottom chords no longer meet, the sloped web members assume responsibility for transferring the large horizontal forces between the chord members. The lion's share of that burden falls on the last sloped web member. Vertical web members must be active to maintain the truss's shape. The bottom chord's last bay is a zero-force member. This bottom-chord segment is bypassed by the stress path. Now the bow truss has four major joints, and the importance of the other joints is increased by transferring major forces through the web members instead of connecting the two chords directly together. The force distribution in this truss is beginning to resemble the force distribution in a parallel-chord truss. The substantial forces in the web members are unavoidable if there are going to be concentrated shifting loads on the truss.

Web members are also active if the supports do not occur at the intersection of the chord members. In the uniform-load case shown in Figure 8.169, the supports are moved in one bay from the ends.

This produces the axial force diagram shown in Figure 8.170.

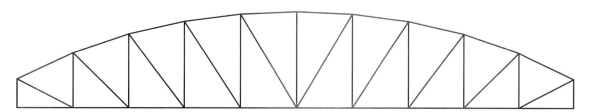

Figure 8.166 Bow truss with deep ends.

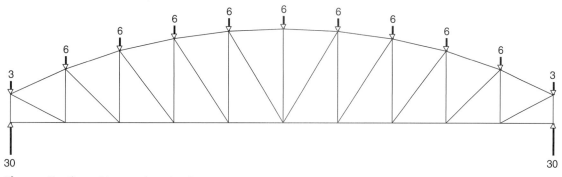

Figure 8.167 Adding uniform loads.

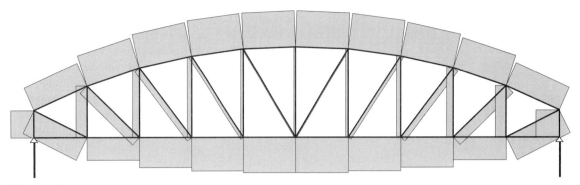

Figure 8.168 Axial forces generated by computer simulation.

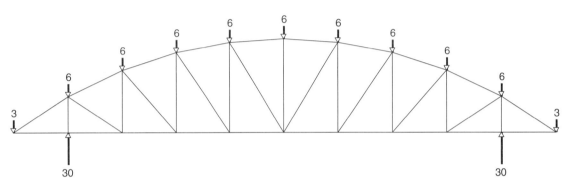

Figure 8.169 Moving the supports in by one bay to provide an overhand.

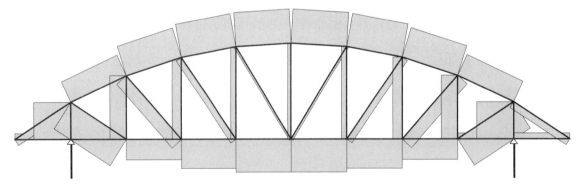

Figure 8.170 Axial forces generated by computer simulation.

8.1.12 BRACING RESPONSES TO NONUNIFORM FORCES ON ARCHES AND BOW TRUSSES

In the Broadgate Exchange House, symmetric, nonuniform loads were partially addressed by the connections of the arches to the floor diaphragms, which provided horizontal tie members at each floor level. In Figures 8.171, 8.172, and 8.173 are six versions of the Broadgate Exchange House. The three versions at the top of each figure have the floor ties present, and the three below lack floor ties. For the two versions on the left, the gravity loads on all the vertices are equal. For the two versions in the middle, the gravity loads on the outer vertices are greater than the loads on the inner vertices. For the two versions on the right, the gravity loads on the inner vertices are greater than the loads on the outer vertices. These variations in gravity force would be caused by shifting live loads.

Notice the following points:

• The deflection diagrams on the left in Figure 8.173 indicate no benefits from the floor ties, when the loads delivered to the arches are uniform as projected on the horizontal.

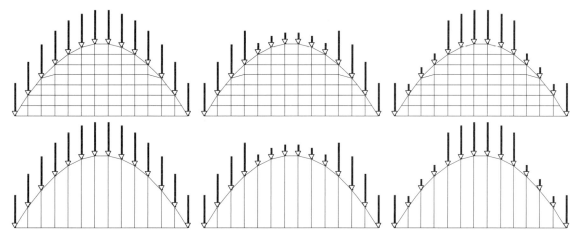

Figure 8.171 Nonuniform, symmetric loads on Broadgate Exchange House arch.

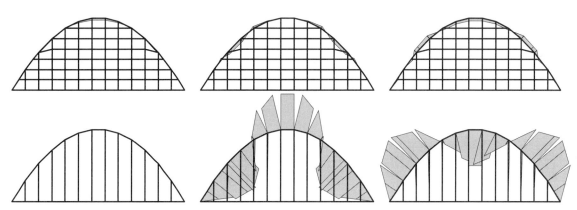

Figure 8.172 Bending stresses in the arch under nonuniform, symmetric loads.

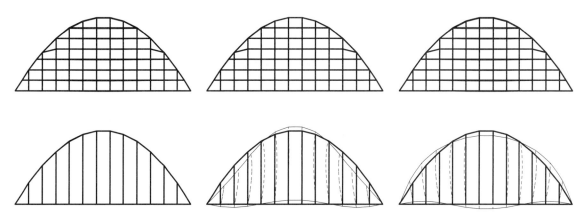

Figure 8.173 Deformation in the arch under nonuniform, symmetric loads.

- The bottom, middle deflection diagram in Figure 8.173 indicates that there is substantial inward sag of the arches where the forces are large in the outer bays, and an upward bulging of the arches where the forces are small in the center bays. The top, middle deflection diagram indicates that the floor ties essentially eliminate the deformation in the arches.

- The bottom, right deflection diagram in Figure 8.173 indicates that there is substantial inward sag of the arches where the forces are large in the inner bays, and an upward, outward bulging of the arches where the forces are small in the outer bays. The top, right deflection diagram indicates that the floor ties essentially eliminate the deformation in the arches.

- Figure 8.172 indicates that the floor ties dramatically reduce the bending stresses induced in the arches by the nonuniform, symmetric loads.

- Hiding the secondary tie members in the floor helps to keep an uncluttered appearance by avoiding visible web members.

8.1.13 RESPONSES TO SHIFTING LIVE LOADS, WIND LOADS, TEMPERATURE CHANGES, AND FOUNDATION SETTLEMENT IN ARCHES

The optimal shape to resist roll-through buckling under uniform load is also the optimal shape to resist shifting live loads, wind loads, thermal stress, and foundation settlement. Wind load, asymmetric snow load, and asymmetric live load all tend to produce bending stresses at the quarter points. Making the arch thick at the quarter points is an appropriate beamlike response to these stresses. Foundation settlement and thermal stresses both tend to produce bending stresses at the top of the arch. These stresses are not an essential part of the functioning of the spanning element, and the ideal response is to avoid these stresses. One method of avoiding such stresses is to provide hinges at the top of the arch and at the base points, producing what is called a three-hinged arch, as shown in Figure 8.174.

Maillart's bridges are exquisite examples of this structural type (see Figure 8.175).

Sometimes the three "hinge points" are true hinges with pins. In the case of the bridge in Figure 8.175, the three points have been made relatively very flexible by crossing the longitudinal rebar at those points. This ensures that there is essentially no bending resistance at these points and that any slight movement that occurs in the bridge cannot build up large bending stresses at these points.

Under some circumstances, arches that are not designed as three-hinged arches can develop substantial bending stress, even under uniform load. As load is added, the tie member stretches, causing the arch to splay apart and begin to act like a beam. This is particularly a problem on concrete arches with high-strength cable serving as the tie, where the self-weight of the concrete is high and the elongation of the cable is great. The sagging will induce bending stresses at the top of the arch, if the top of the arch is not designed as a hinge joint. One way of offsetting this effect is by posttensioning the tie member. This brings the arch back up to its appropriate form, so that the bending stresses are eliminated and a state of pure axial stress is restored in the compression material at the center of the arch. This posttensioning also facilitates the removal of the formwork under the arch, since posttensioning can raise the arch until it just lifts off the formwork. This technique was used in the Moscone Center in San Francisco, where long concrete arches span essentially the length of a city block to create an underground convention center beneath a large plaza area.

Diagonal braces stabilizing the quarter points of an arch can also be very effective in resisting asymmetric live load. Figure 8.176 is a computer simulation of the deformations in the Broadgate Exchange House, with and without the diagonal braces restraining the arch at the quarter points.

Fully triangulating the arch to produce a bow truss is also an excellent technique for resisting asymmetric

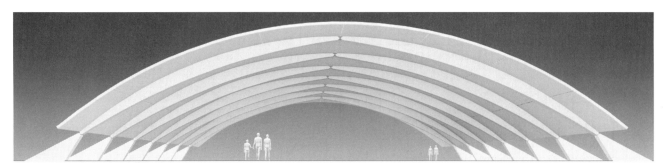

Figure 8.174 Three-hinged arch thickened at the quarter-points. (Rendering by James Sweeney.)

Figure 8.175 Salginatobel bridge, Schiers, Switzerland, designed by Robert Maillart. (Image courtesy of Eugenio Pedrazzini.)

loads. Figure 8.177 shows three bow trusses based on an arc of a circle. Two of these are simple tied arches, and one is fully triangulated. Figure 8.178 shows the loads applied to the three trusses. The top truss has a uniform load. The other two trusses have an asymmetric load, such as a drifting snow load.

For the load conditions, Figure 8.179 shows the deflections on the left and the bending stresses on the right. The deformation and bending stress for the asymmetric load case with no web members exceeds substantially the deformation and bending stress, respectively, for the symmetric load case with no web members. In other words,

asymmetric loading is an even more severe issue than the fact that the arch is not precisely the funicular shape under the uniform applied load. Note that the web members essentially eliminate all of the deflection and all of the bending stress induced by both the asymmetric and the symmetric loading condition.

Figure 8.180 shows two bow trusses in the shape of an arc of a circle, the one on top with an asymmetric load, such as a drifting snow load, and the one below with a uniform load. The diagrams on the left show the load distribution, and the diagrams on the right show the variations for the axial force. In both cases, the axial forces in

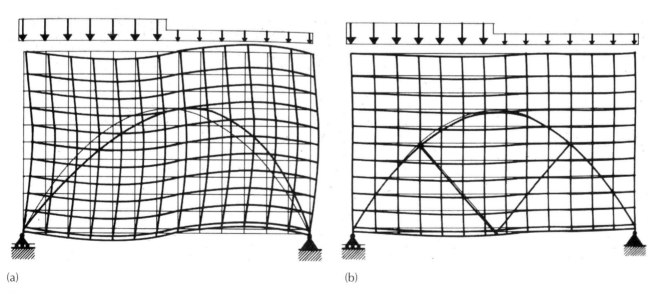

(a)   (b)

Figure 8.176 Deformation under asymmetric load without diagonals (a) and with diagonals (b). (Image courtesy of the Chicago office of Skidmore, Owings & Merrill, LLP.)

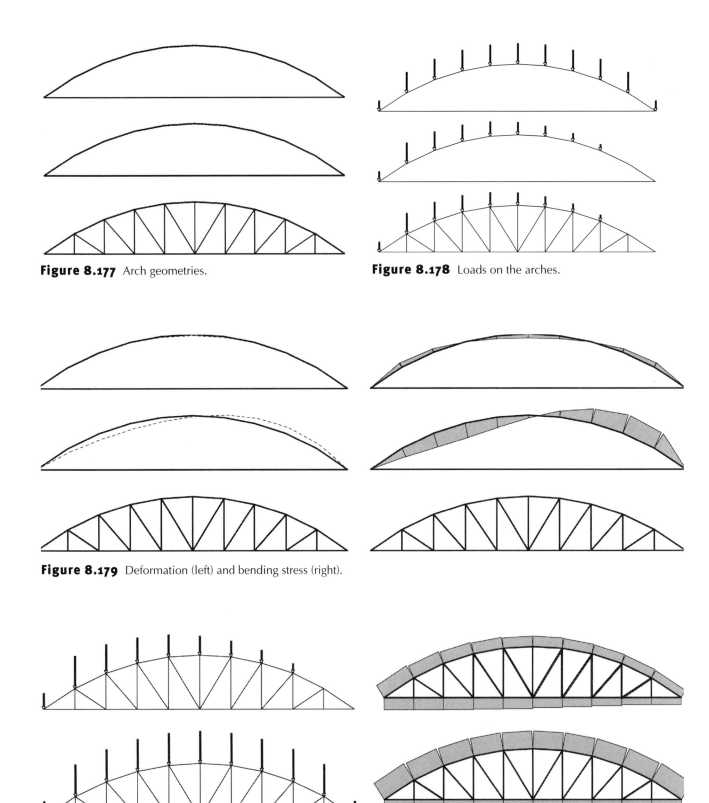

Figure 8.177 Arch geometries.

Figure 8.178 Loads on the arches.

Figure 8.179 Deformation (left) and bending stress (right).

Figure 8.180 Asymmetric and symmetric loads (left) and axial forces (right).

the web members are very small as compared with the axial forces in the chord members, which indicates that the web members are a very efficient means of holding the chord members in the proper shape under the primary (uniform) load and for any assistance in resisting secondary (nonuniform) load. This is also further illustration that choosing a top chord in the shape of an arc of a circle, rather than in the shape of a parabola, is not a significant structural issue for shallow bow trusses with frequent bracing by web members.

8.1.14 CANTILEVERED TRUSSES WITH CURVED TOP CHORDS

For a simple-span structure subjected to a continuous uniform load, the internal moment varies parabolically along the length of the spanning member, with zero moment at the supports and the maximum moment occurring at the center of the spanning member (see Figure 8.181).

For a cantilever subjected to a continuous uniform load, the internal moment varies parabolically along the length of the spanning member, with zero moment at the end of the cantilever and the maximum negative moment at the base of the cantilever (see Figure 8.182).

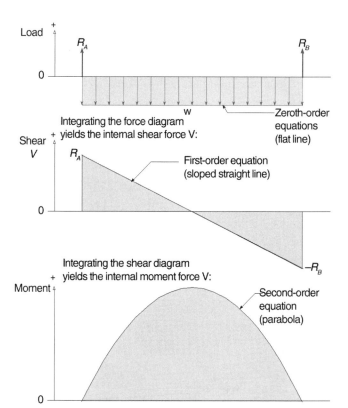

Figure 8.181 Shear and moment diagrams for a simple-span spanning element.

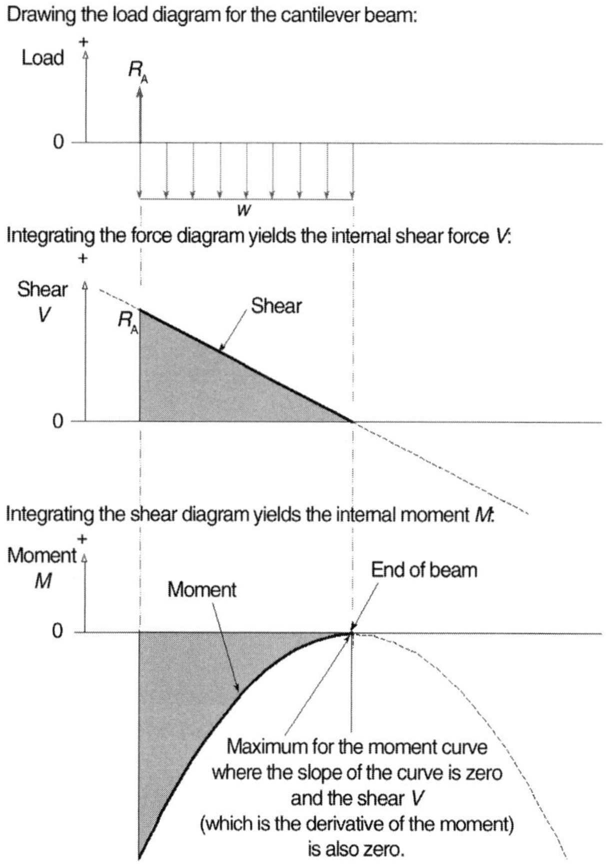

Drawing the load diagram for the cantilever beam:

Integrating the force diagram yields the internal shear force V:

Integrating the shear diagram yields the internal moment M:

Maximum for the moment curve where the slope of the curve is zero and the shear V (which is the derivative of the moment) is also zero.

Figure 8.182 Shear and moment diagrams for a cantilevered spanning element.

In the case of a simple-span truss, the optimal response was a parabolic chord shape. As will be demonstrated in the following discussion, the parabola is also the ideal shape for addressing moment in a cantilevered truss. Figure 8.183 shows the shape of the truss and the loads.

This shape produces the desired effect of zero web forces, as shown in the simulation of member axial force in Figure 8.184.

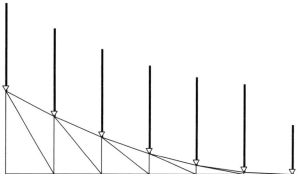

Figure 8.183 Parabolic, cantilevered truss under uniform loading of the joints.

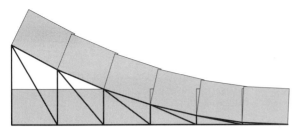

Figure 8.184 Axial forces in a parabolic, cantilevered truss.

Unfortunately, it has a very large deflection in the last bay, due to the shallowness of that portion of the cantilever (see Figure 8.185).

This bay-specific deformation is referred to as shear deformation. To reduce the amount of shear deformation, we customarily reduce the amount of "drape" in the top chord, so that the bays near the end of the cantilever are not so shallow. In making this change in geometry, the depth of the truss at the base of the cantilever is kept constant (see Figure 8.186).

In this new geometry, the web members become more active, and the forces in the chord members become more variable, as shown in the simulation of member axial force in Figure 8.187.

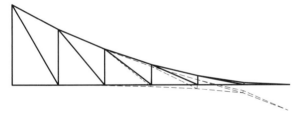

Figure 8.185 Deformation in a parabolic, cantilevered truss.

On the positive side, this change in shape drastically reduces the deflection problem in the end bay (see Figure 8.188).

This truss geometry has been used by Skidmore, Owings & Merrill in the design of the Korean Airlines hangar in Seoul. In that building, the extra depth of the cantilevered trusses accommodated the severe shifting loads associated with cranes attached to the roof structure. The depth of the end of the cantilevered trusses also accommodated large openings for venting smoke.

In Figure 8.189, the basic plan shows a hangar-door opening extending the full width of the hangar, with no columns interfering with the opening. Rather than cantilever out to this opening or use a deep, simple-span truss to support the roof over the opening, the decision was made to run two double-arch trusses from a column at the back center of the hangar diagonally out to two columns flanking the opening, as shown in the simplified framing plan (see Figure 8.189). Running the double-arch trusses on the diagonals reduced the longest span by a factor of 0.707.

Double arches were used to reduce the size of the tubes that were used and to provide lateral and torsional stiffness (see Figure 8.190).

The roof structure was assembled near the ground and elevated into place using a sliding mechanism to lift the roof up the supporting columns. Figure 8.191 shows the process of raising the roof. The tower along the centerline in front is strictly to assist in raising the roof and was removed once the erection was complete. Figure 8.192 shows the interior of the hangar after the roof was raised.

Apertures for admitting natural light are placed between the chord members in the double-arch trusses and

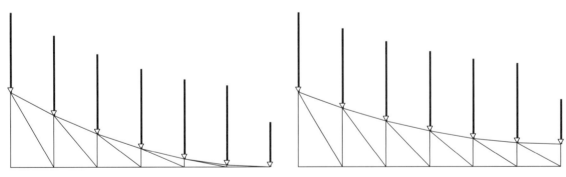

Figure 8.186 Making the end of the cantilevered truss deeper (right).

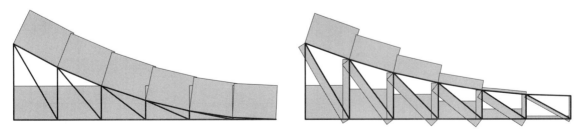

Figure 8.187 Axial forces in parabolic, cantilevered trusses.

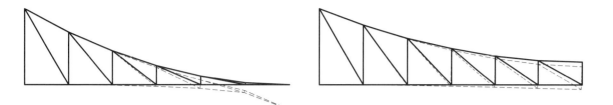

Figure 8.188 Deformation in parabolic, cantilevered trusses.

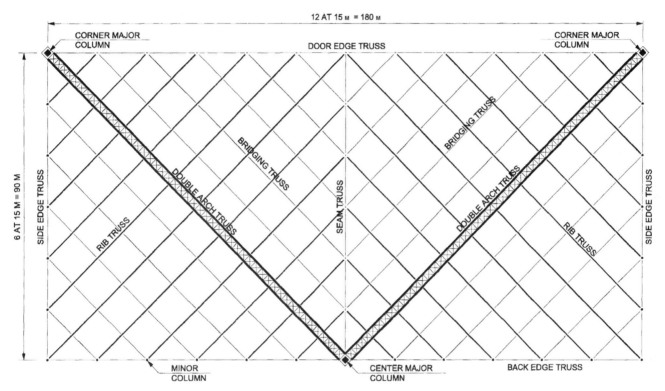

Figure 8.189 Korean Airlines headquarters and main hangar, Seoul, South Korea. (Architecture and engineering by the Chicago office of Skidmore, Owings & Merrill, LLP.)

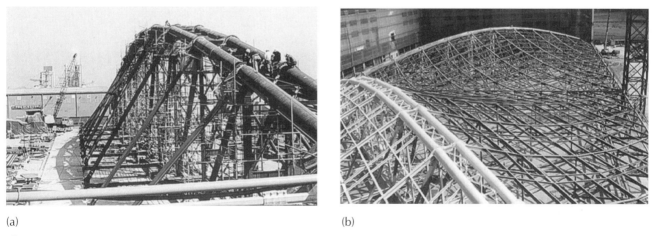

(a)   (b)

Figure 8.190 (a) Double-arch trusses and (b) completed roof framing assembled on the ground. (Architecture and engineering by the Chicago office of Skidmore, Owings & Merrill, LLP. Image courtesy of SOM.)

(a)

(b)

Figure 8.191 (a) Roof being raised and (b) roof in final position. (Architecture and engineering by the Chicago office of Skidmore, Owings & Merrill, LLP. Image courtesy of SOM.)

Figure 8.192 Korean Airlines headquarters and main hangar, Seoul, South Korea. (Architecture and engineering by the Chicago office of Skidmore, Owings & Merrill, LLP. Image courtesy of SOM.)

running parallel to the rib trusses. Having the daylight come through the double-arched trusses is a dramatic way of highlighting the structure. Having the bottom chords all running on the diagonal helps achieve a very high level of diaphragm action from the roof. The crane rails at 45° to the bottom chords help to further triangulate that plane (see Figure 8.192). Figure 8.193 shows an exterior view of the finished building.

Figure 8.193 Korean Airlines headquarters and main hangar, Seoul, South Korea. (Architecture and engineering by the Chicago office of Skidmore, Owings & Merrill, LLP. Image courtesy of SOM.)

8.2 Vaults

8.2.1 BARREL VAULTS

Arch structures can be made wide to serve both as structure and as enclosure, in which case they are referred to as barrel vaults. Thin-shell barrel vaults are strong and stiff in resisting forces on the edge of the vault parallel to the surface of the shell and parallel to the axis of the vault, as shown in Figure 8.194.

Thin-shell barrel vaults are weak and too flexible under forces against the surface of the shell, suggesting vulnerability to roll-through buckling under uniform loads and a severe vulnerability to roll-through deformation under asymmetric snow loading and wind loads against the shell. Figure 8.195 shows (a) an unloaded barrel vault and (b) a laterally loaded barrel vault.

In the ancient barrel vault structures of northern Europe, the stone vaults are extremely thick in order to compensate for the inherent weakness relative to roll-through deformation. They were also of very modest span, typically only a few feet.

In modern structures, this effective thickness can be achieved more efficiently by articulating the structure with ribs or other enhancements. For example, the structure shown in Figure 8.196 has ribs to stiffen it against roll-through buckling.

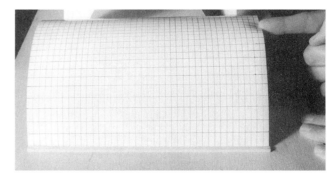

Figure 8.194 Force on a barrel vault parallel to the vault shell.

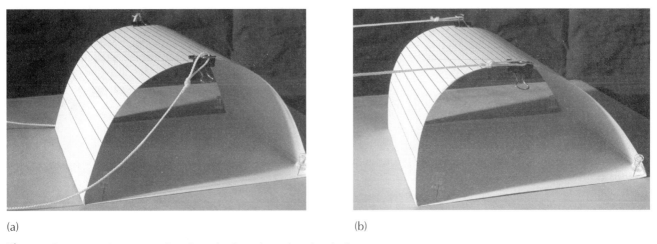

(a)   (b)

Figure 8.195 Deformation of vault under force lateral to the shell.

Figure 8.196 Interior ribs of the Leverone Field House, designed by Pierre Luigi Nervi. (Reprinted courtesy of the Rauner Special Collections of Dartmouth College Library.)

Barrel vaults have the architectural disadvantage that the openings for light naturally occur at the ends. For long vaults, this can produce an oppressive, tunnel-like space, with small openings at the ends. Barrel vaults tend to meet the foundations in a manner that creates dark, uninviting spaces at the bases of the vault. Additional openings can be created where the vault meets the foundation. In order to do that, the compressive forces carried by the ribs of the vault must be gathered together and delivered to discrete buttressing elements. A simple, but effective, way to do this is to use a deep, massive beam to span from buttress to buttress, as shown in Figure 8.197.

A more elegant way of gathering the forces is to start taking them out of the vault earlier via fan-shaped ribs converging on the buttresses, as shown in Figure 8.198.

In the Dartmouth Field House, the ribs are located inside the shell and the composite action of the ribs with the concrete shell is similar to that of a T-beam, in which the rib is the stem of the T-beam and the curved shell is the flange of the T-beam. T-beams are not as efficient as I-beams, which have material distributed away from the neutral axis on both sides of the neutral axis. By splitting the shell of the vault it is possible to achieve structural strength and stiffness more akin to that of an I-beam than that of a T-beam. The upper and lower portions of the roof shell are the flanges of the I-beam, and the rib between

Figure 8.198 The Salone Agnelli, designed by Pierre Luigi Nervi.

Figure 8.197 Forces of a vault being transferred by a deep, thick beam. (Reprinted courtesy of the Rauner Special Collections of Dartmouth College Library.)

Figure 8.199 Alternating high and low parts of the shell knit together with Verendeel truss ribs.

Figure 8.200 Pierre Luigi Nervi's Salone Agnelli, with Verendeel ribs to resist roll-through buckling and admit daylight. Image used with permission from the Visual Resources Center, Architecture Library, Ball State University.

the upper and lower portions of the shell is the web of the I-beam. In the case of the structure in Figure 8.199, the flanges are knit together by the Verendeel truss ribs, which produces a very strong structure and also facilitates admitting natural light for interior illumination. Using alternately high and low vault segments allows the shell material to resist roll-through deformation, either from roll-through buckling under uniform loading or deformation induced by bending associated with asymmetric loading.

A variation on the concept of high and low shells knit together by Verendeel elements is the structure in Figure 8.200.

The space between the alternating high and low vault segments can be uniform, as shown in the structure in Figure 8.200, or of variable depth, as shown in the structure in Figure 8.201.

Figure 8.201(a) shows the severe deformation associated with a lateral force on the top thin-shell arch.

Figure 8.201(b) shows the stiffening effect of adding trusswork between the upper and lower thin-shell arches.

Figure 8.201(c) shows the significant deformation associated with a lateral force on the outer part of the lower thin-shell arch.

Figure 8.201(d) shows the stiffening effect of adding vertical mullions anchored to a sturdy grade beam. Ideally, this lower opening would be fully trussed like the upper opening. However, the truss in the upper opening has already achieved most of the intended stabilization of the lower arched shell. Not fully trussing the lower opening means that the downward movement of some mullions and the upward movement of other mullions must be resisted by the beam action of the foundation. Usually, adding some thickness to the grade beam footing is more economical and architecturally less objectionable to fully triangulating the lower opening.

For shells with good diaphragm action, it is often possible to use widely spaced ribs to stabilize them. Adding an arched rib reinforcing the edges of a thin-shell barrel vault drastically increases the resistance of the structure to forces against the surface of the shell near the location of the rib, as demonstrated in Figure 8.202(a). The structural benefit of this rib diminishes for forces on the shell spatially removed from the rib, as indicated in Figure 8.202(b). However, the ribs at each end of the shell have substantially improved the structural performance everywhere along the shell surface. Highly distributed forces, such as wind, can often be effectively resisted, using ribs only at the ends of the vault.

Figure 8.203 shows horizontal wind forces on (a) a simple parabolic barrel vault and (b) a braced parabolic barrel vault. Figure 8.204 shows the deflection of the barrel vaults under the horizontal wind force, and Figure 8.205 shows the bending stresses.

Figures 8.204 and 8.205 clearly indicate that the stiffening elements at the ends of the vault have substantially reduced both the deflection and the bending stresses in the shell. However, an examination of both deflection and bending stresses in the shell indicate that they are still excessive, even with the stiffeners at the ends of the vault. The problem lies in the fact that the rigid frame constructed of slender elements does not achieve an adequate approximation in stiffness and strength to the

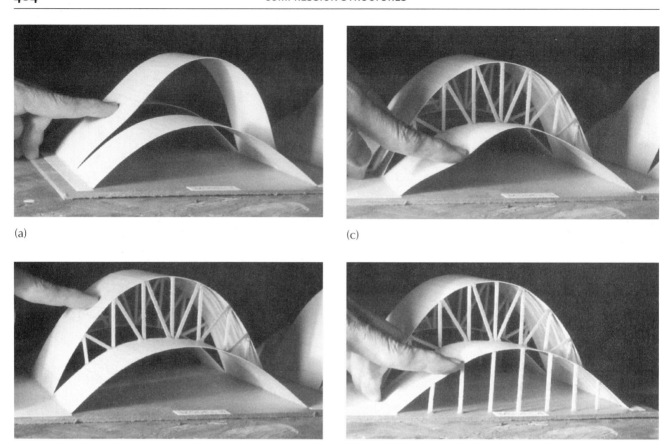

(a)

(c)

(b)

(d)

Figure 8.201 Stabilizing the edges of high and low thin-shell vaults.

diaphragm action of a continuous shell. To more closely approximate a continuous shell diaphragm, we must perform the simulation again with a fully triangulated frame. In Figures 8.206(a) and 8.207(a), the vault is the same un-triangulated vault that is shown in Figures 8.204(b) and 8.205(b), and the vault in Figures 8.206(b) and 8.207(b) is fully triangulated to effectively simulate a continuous diaphragm shell. The wind load has not been changed, but the diagrams of deflection and bending stress in Figures 8.206 and 8.207 are plotted at a more exaggerated scale, to allow a closer comparison with the triangulated shell, which is much stiffer and stronger.

The triangulated shell shown in Figures 8.206(b) and 8.207(b) is now strong enough and stiff enough for resisting wind load, even though it has stiffeners only at the ends of the shell.

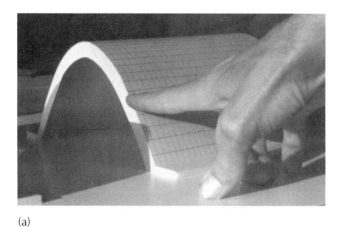

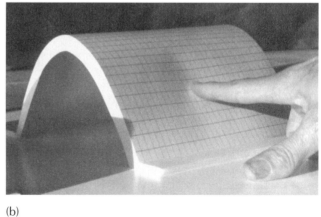

(a)

(b)

Figure 8.202 Adding perimeter arched ribs to resist roll-through buckling.

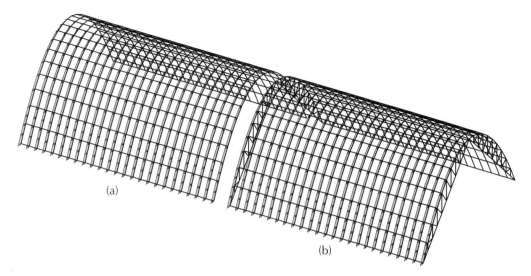

Figure 8.203 Wind loads on the vaults.

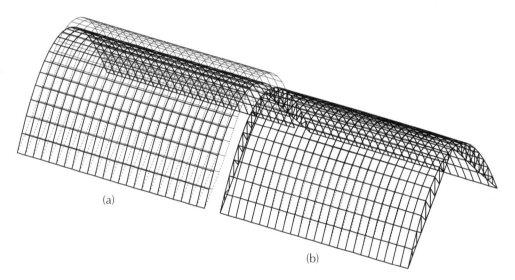

Figure 8.204 Deformations in the vaults under wind loads.

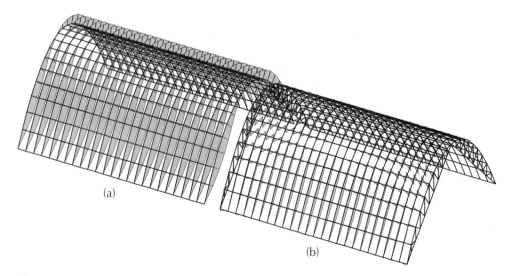

Figure 8.205 Bending stresses in the vaults.

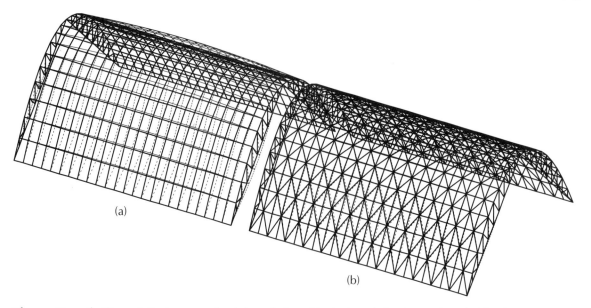

Figure 8.206 Effect of diaphragm action (triangulation of lattice) on deflection under wind load.

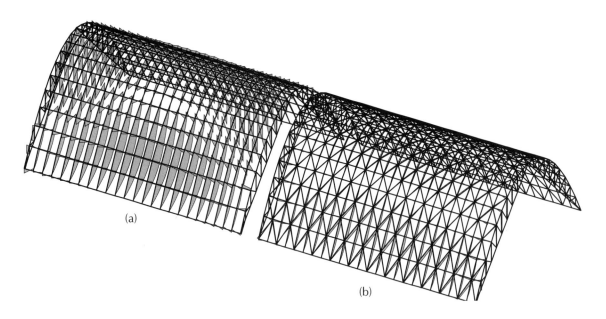

Figure 8.207 Effect of diaphragm action (triangulation of lattice) on bending stress under wind load.

8.2.2 HYPERBOLIC PARABOLOIDS (HYPARS)

Sometimes deep ribs near the boundary of a shell create shadows on the interior surface of the shell that make it seem dark and gloomy. The ribs can be located external to the shell to solve that problem. This is, however, a visually unappealing way of solving the problem. Curving the shell is a method of giving it effective depth against roll-through, while avoiding introducing ribs. The double curvature of the interior surface of the vault shell can provide a pleasing play of light. One way to introduce curvature is to create a shell in the form of a hyperbolic paraboloid. Rather than give a lengthy definition of a hyperbolic paraboloid, the discussion introduces this shape in a series of steps that will clarify the nature of the geometry. First, a parabola is constructed that spans the desired distance and has the desired proportions. For example, the parabola shown in Figure 8.208 spans 64 ft and has a rise of 16 ft.

Viewing the arch in 3D, it looks like the illustration in Figure 8.209.

Duplicate the parabola and rotate the duplicate by 90° to produce the image shown in Figure 8.210.

Mirror the second parabola about the y-coordinates to make it open upward rather than downward (see Figure 8.211).

Replicate the upper parabola in the positive x-direction by integer multiples of 4 ft and in the negative y-direction by an appropriate amount to attach to the vertices on the lower parabola. If the zenith of the lower parabola is set at the origin of the coordinate system, as is the case in Figure 8.211, the y-displacement and x-displacement in the

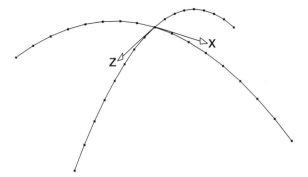

Figure 8.210 Two parabolas in vertical planes at 90° to each other.

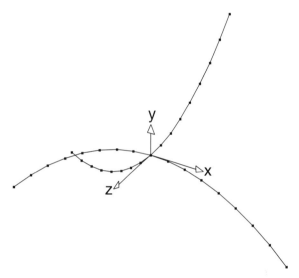

Figure 8.211 Two parabolas.

duplication process will just be equal to the y-coordinate and x-coordinate of the target vertex on the lower parabola (see Figure 8.212).

Mirror these new parabolas in the negative x direction (see Figure 8.213).

Replicate the lower parabola in the positive x-direction by integer multiples of 4 ft and in the positive y-direction by an appropriate amount to attach to the vertices on the upper parabola. If the zenith of the lower parabola is set at the origin of the coordinate system, as is the case in Figure 8.213, the y-displacement and x-displacement in the duplication process will just be equal to the y-coordinate and x-coordinate of the target vertex on the upper parabola (see Figure 8.214).

Mirror the new parabolas in the negative x-direction (see Figures 8.215, 8.216, and 8.217).

In Figure 8.217, all the curved elements appear as straight lines, indicating that each curve is in its own vertical plane, which we already know from the original

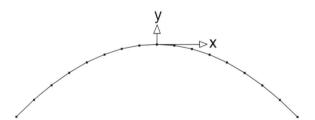

Figure 8.208 Frontal view of the parabola.

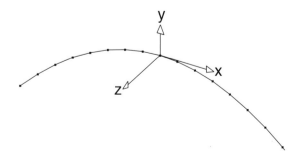

Figure 8.209 A 3D view of the parabola.

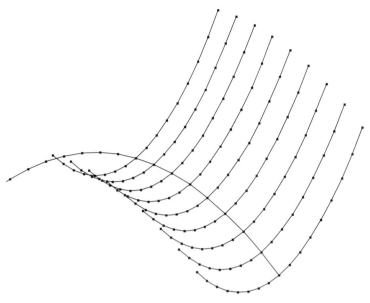

Figure 8.212 Family of upward-opening parabolas.

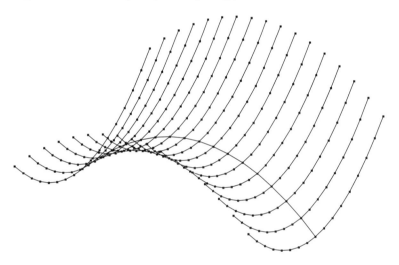

Figure 8.213 Complete family of upward-opening parabolas.

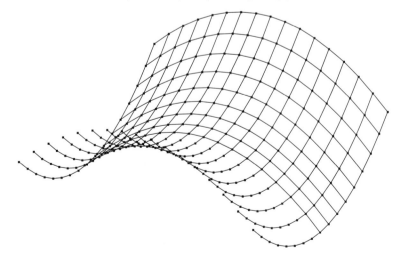

Figure 8.214 Family of downward-opening parabolas.

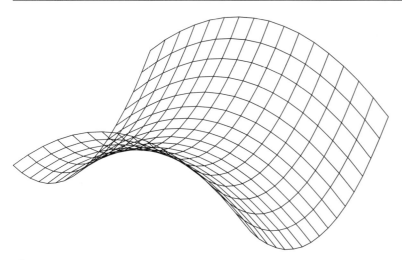

Figure 8.215 Complete family of downward-opening parabolas.

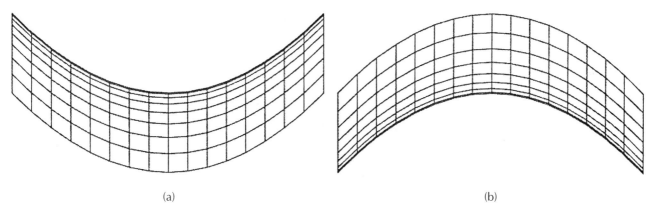

(a)

(b)

Figure 8.216 Looking along the *z*-axis (a) and along the *x*-axis (b).

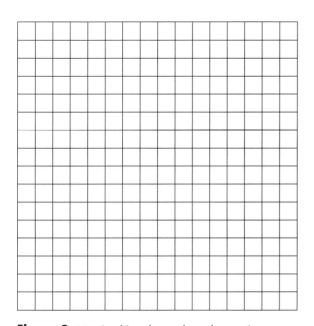

Figure 8.217 Looking down along the *y*-axis.

construction. The plan view is a grid of perfect squares, so snapping diagonal segments to the nodes produces straight lines at 45° to the original curves, as shown in Figure 8.218.

Shifting the view to 3D produces the image in Figure 8.219.

The image in Figure 8.219 can be rotated about the *y*-axis to view along the vertical plan that is at 45° relative to both the *x* = 0 plane and the *z* = 0 plane. In that view, the diagonal segments are all lined up in a vertical plane perpendicular to the picture plane (see Figure 8.220).

The image in Figure 8.220 can be rotated about the horizontal axis in the picture plane to produce the image in Figure 8.221. In the view in Figure 8.221, one set of diagonal segments has been reduced to a point, demonstrating that all those segments lie along a single line.

Continuing to rotate in the same direction reveals that there is always a view along the surface that reduces to a single point, indicating that there exists an infinite

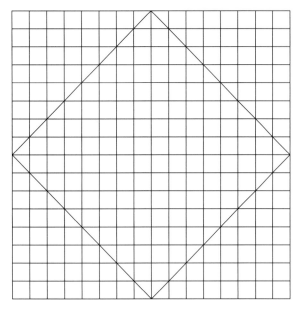

Figure 8.218 Plan view showing grid with diagonal lines.

number of straight lines that can be fitted to those portions of the surface (see Figure 8.222).

In Figure 8.223, a grid of diagonals has been added to the surface. These diagonals are all in vertical planes, and the vertical planes are all in a grid of parallel and perpendicular planes. However, the straight lines on the surface are not parallel to each other. They are skewed, consistent with being on a warped surface. These straight lines are referred to as the geometric directrices of the hyperbolic paraboloid.

The geometric directrices are generally not the useful lines for structure, but they can be very useful in setting accurate formwork for the support of the saddle surface during construction. They can also be useful for various kinds of geometric constructs or mathematical explorations. This issue is discussed again later in this chapter and in Chapter 9, "Tensile Spanning Structures."

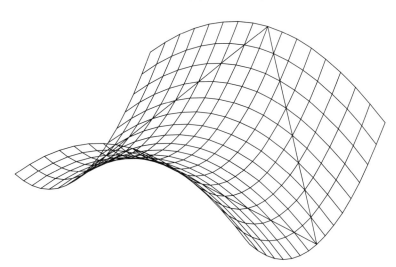

Figure 8.219 Hyperbolic paraboloid surface with diagonal segments in 3D view.

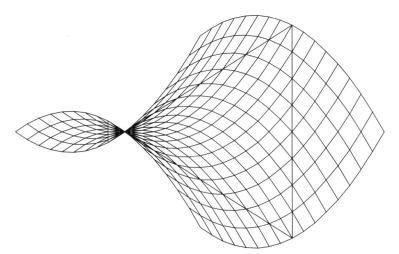

Figure 8.220 The 3D image rotated about the vertical axis.

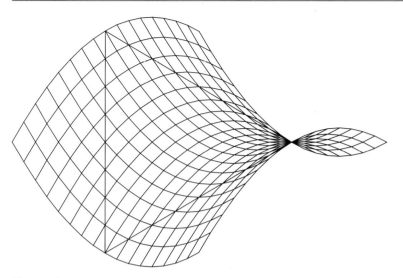

Figure 8.221 Viewing along a series of diagonal segments.

Figure 8.222 Viewing along one of the infinite number of straight lines in the surface.

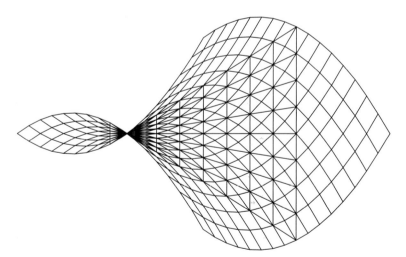

Figure 8.223 Geometric directrices of the hyperbolic paraboloid.

As demonstrated previously, a parabola can be scaled in either the horizontal or vertical direction and it will still be a parabola. This makes parabolas particularly easy to deal with mathematically, since once a parabola has been created, it can be used for any desired rise or span by simply applying proper horizontal and vertical scaling factors. Because a hyperbolic paraboloid surface has been generated from parabolic curves, it can also be scaled and will still be a hyperbolic paraboloid. Applying a vertical scaling factor of 0.5 to the hyperbolic paraboloid used in the previous images produces the shallower hyperbolic paraboloid shown in Figure 8.224.

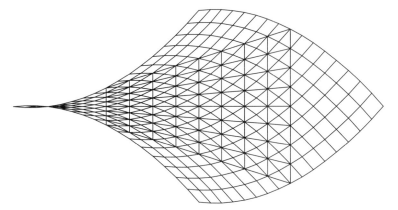

Figure 8.224 Shallower hyperbolic paraboloid.

Notice that the scaling factor has flattened the structure in both views along the horizontal axes, as shown in Figure 8.225.

In some instances, one may want to flatten the parabolas in one direction and make the parabolas deeper in the orthogonal direction. In that case, the construction of the hyperbolic paraboloid has to be started from the beginning, using different parabolas in the two directions.

In Figure 8.226, the image on the left is the same one used in the previous example, with both the downward-opening parabola and the upward-opening parabola having the same overall depth of 16 ft. In the image on the right, the downward-opening parabola remains unchanged, but the upward-opening parabola has been scaled by a factor of 0.5, which gives it an overall vertical dimension of 8 ft.

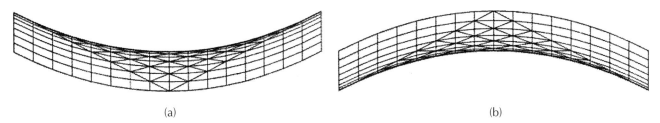

(a)   (b)

Figure 8.225 Looking along the x-axis (a) and along the z-axis (b).

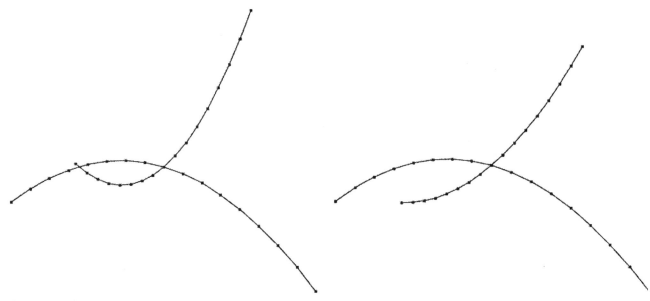

Figure 8.226 Rescaling the vertical dimension of the upward-opening parabola.

Constructing the hyperbolic paraboloid using the procedure outlined earlier leads to the geometry shown in Figure 8.227.

Now, in comparing views along the horizontal different curvatures can be seen, as shown in Figure 8.228.

This shape, with the deep arch and shallow drape, is more consistent with the structural design goals, since a deep arch is crucial to the primary structural function, which is to carry the gravity loads, as well as to the architectural function of providing an accommodating space beneath the arch. The curvature in the other direction is somewhat secondary, being there to help prevent roll-through buckling and to resist asymmetric loads.

To make this form serve as an arch, there must be buttressing elements that mediate between the geometry of the hyperbolic paraboloid and the ground plane, where tie elements can be located. These buttressing elements need to be tangential to the shell surface where they meet (see Figures 8.229 and 8.230).

Triangulating the surface of the shell gives it better diaphragm action and takes better structural advantage of the double curvature (see Figure 8.231).

For the surface in Figure 8.231, the diagonals do not line up along a straight line, because the upward-opening parabola and the downward-opening parabola used to generate the surface do not have the same depth. A slight curvature of the sequence of diagonal segments is apparent. There are straight lines, that is, geometric directrices, contained within the surface, but they are not at 45° in plan and they do not correspond to any sequence of vertices on the parabolas. Giving the upward parabolas a different curvature from the downward parabolas has shifted the direction of the straight lines away from 45° in the plan view.

The double-curved vault can be compared with a simple barrel vault to determine how useful the double curvature is in resisting asymmetric loads, such as drifting snow load or wind load (see Figures 8.232, 8.233, and 8.234).

Curving the vault has created a U-shaped cross section with an effective depth equal to the deviation of the curved surface from flatness, as shown in Figure 8.235.

The simulation results shown here, for both deflection and bending stress, clearly demonstrate the effectiveness of the U-shaped cross section in resisting roll-through deformation.

A hyperbolic paraboloid, such as the one in Figure 8.231, has the disadvantage that there are many distinct, oddly shaped panels that make up the surface. In fact, within a given quadrant of the surface, all of the panels

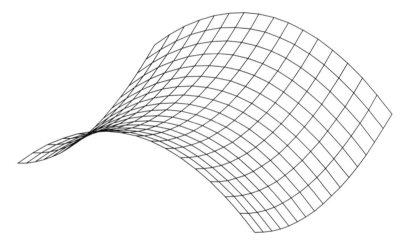

Figure 8.227 Hyperbolic paraboloid with the upward-opening parabolas half as deep as the downward-opening parabolas.

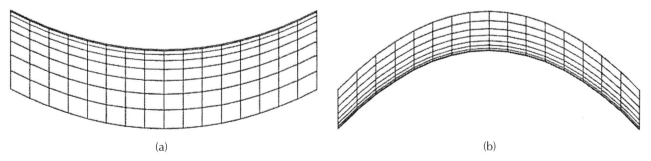

(a)   (b)

Figure 8.228 Looking along the x-axis (a) and along the z-axis (b).

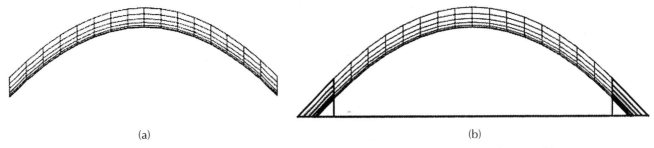

Figure 8.229 The basic geometry of the hyperbolic paraboloid (a) enhanced with buttressing elements (b).

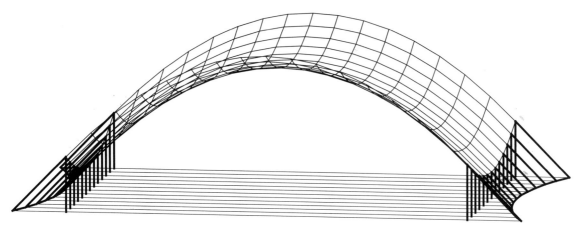

Figure 8.230 A 3D view of the basic arch and the buttressing elements.

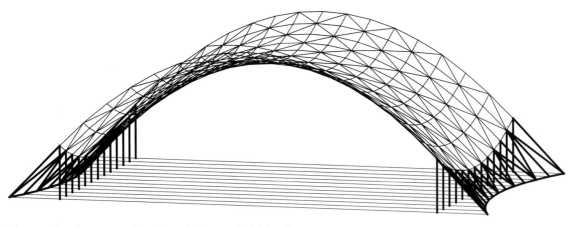

Figure 8.231 Triangulated hyperbolic paraboloid surface.

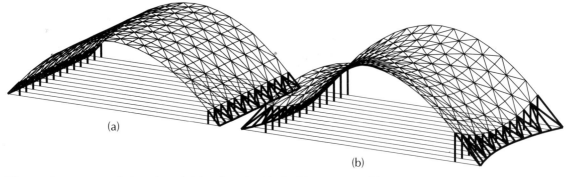

Figure 8.232 Simple barrel vault (a) and vault with double curvature (b).

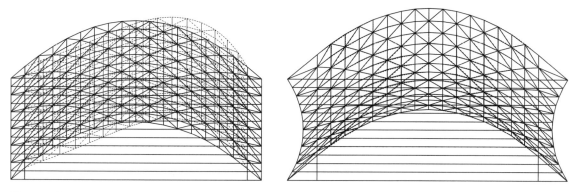

Figure 8.233 Deformation under asymmetric snow load.

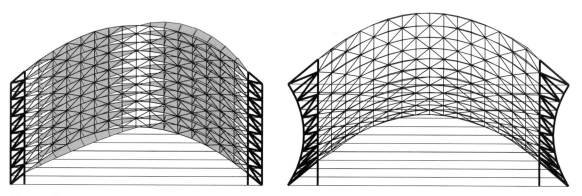

Figure 8.234 Bending stress under asymmetric snow load.

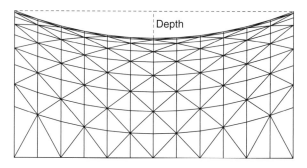

Figure 8.235 Deviation from flatness in the curved vault.

8.2.3 TOROIDAL VAULTS

In Section 8.1, in the case of bow trusses, it was deduced that a parabolic shape could be replaced with an arc of a circle with negligible consequences, assuming that the webs were sufficient in number to prevent roll-through buckling and resist asymmetric loads. The same principle applies to vaults that are provided with effective thickness to resist roll-through buckling and asymmetric loads. In the case of the vault, a circle can be chosen as the basis of the curvature in both directions. The shape can be generated by starting with the circle and rotating it through space with its center moving along a second circle, with the plane of the first circle always perpendicular to the tangent to the second circle. This produces a toroid, which is commonly referred to as a doughnut shape (see Figure 8.236).

A vault can be constructed using the outer portion of the toroidal surface (see Figure 8.237), which would be the choice for achieving a sense of shelter and protection from the elements, or it can be constructed using the inner portion of the toroidal surface (see Figure 8.238), which would be the choice for letting breezes blow through, maximizing the penetration of natural light, and projecting sound outward.

are unique in shape. These shapes can be mirrored about the two horizontal coordinates to fill out the rest of the surface. Assuming that the panels are flat and can be flipped over, each panel can be replicated exactly four times for use on the vault. If the panels have handedness (e.g., they have turned-down edges), there needs to be a left-handed and right-handed version of each shape and each panel can be replicated only twice for use in the vault. Simplifying the fabrication and construction of the vault would clearly be desirable.

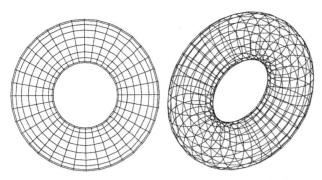

Figure 8.236 Toroid, generated by rotating a circle along a circular path.

In both Figure 8.237 and Figure 8.238, the three quadrilaterals that are marked with cross-bracing in the image on the right are all the facet shapes necessary to generate the entire 48 quadrilaterals that are highlighted in the image. Returning to the geometry of the hyperbolic paraboloid examined earlier, Figure 8.239 compares (a) the hyperbolic paraboloid with 192 facets to (b) a toroidal surface with 192 facets. To generate the hyperbolic paraboloid, there are a minimum of 48 unique facets. To generate the toroidal surface, there are a minimum of 6 unique facets. If the panels associated with each facet involve handedness, then the minimum number of panels required to cover the vault is double the number of unique facets.

An example of a structure using the inner portion of the toroidal surface is the Schubert Club Band Shell on Raspberry Island in Saint Paul, Minnesota (see Figures 8.240 through 8.243). This is a toroidal geometry that deviates only slightly from the shape in Figure 8.238 in that the outer band has been tapered in width on each side of the vault to give slightly more prominence to the center of the vault (see Figures 8.240 and 8.241).

The shape of the band shell projects sound in two directions. This shape lends itself acoustically to the option of providing seating on both sides of the shell, allowing the audience to sit closer to the stage.

Figure 8.242 shows a photograph of the primary connection and an exploded drawing of that connection.

The concrete buttresses of the Schubert Club Band Shell were precast and shipped to the site where they were bolted to the footings. The buttresses were set in a manner similar to that used in setting columns, using very thick leveling plates on the bottom, as shown in Figure 8.243.

The arch elements in the Schubert Club Band Shell are all buttressed by these two large pieces of concrete. Under uniform load, these arch elements are all about equally active in resisting the load; that is, they are about equally stressed. Some toroidal structures have buttressing only at the corners. Under those circumstances, the structural action of the network is radically altered.

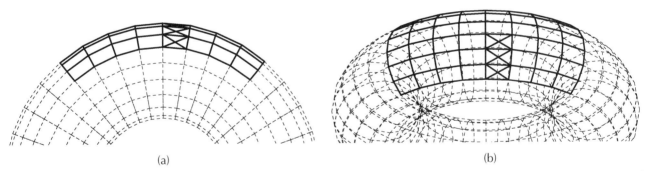

(a)   (b)

Figure 8.237 Generating vault geometry using a outer portion of the toroidal surface, viewed from the side (a) and at an angle from above (b).

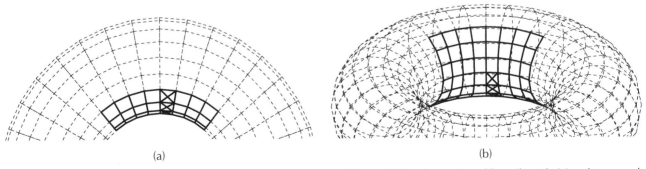

(a)   (b)

Figure 8.238 Generating vault geometry using the inner portion of the toroidal surface, viewed from the side (a) and at an angle from above (b).

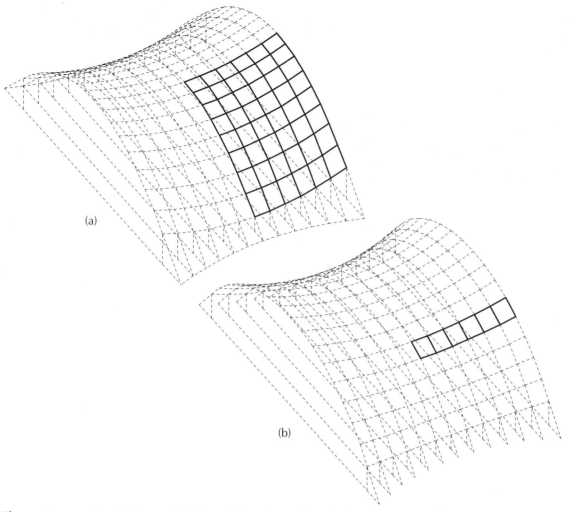

(a)

(b)

Figure 8.239 Hyperbolic paraboloid vault (a) and toroidal vault (b), each with 192 facets.

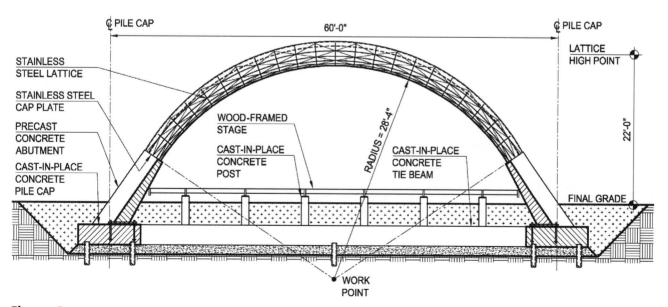

Figure 8.240 Schubert Club Band Shell on Raspberry Island. (Designer: James Carpenter; Structural Engineer: Shane Mc-Cormick of Skidmore, Owings & Merrill, LLP, Chicago; Component Specialists: TriPyramid Structures.)

Figure 8.241 Schubert Club Band Shell on Raspberry Island. (Designer: James Carpenter; Structural Engineer: Shane McCormick of Skidmore, Owings & Merrill, LLP, Chicago; Component Specialists: TriPyramid Structures.)

Figure 8.242 Details of Schubert Club Band Shell on Raspberry Island. (Designer: James Carpenter; Structural Engineer: Shane McCormick of Skidmore, Owings & Merrill, LLP, Chicago; Component Specialists: TriPyramid Structures.)

Figure 8.243 Concrete buttresses for the Schubert Club Band Shell. (Designer: James Carpenter; Structural Engineer: Shane McCormick of Skidmore, Owings & Merrill, LLP, Chicago; Component Specialists: TriPyramid Structures.)

Toroidal Vaults with Buttressing on the Corners

Figures 8.244, 8.245, and 8.246 each show the same two toroids. In those figures, the toroid labelled (a) is fully buttressed along two opposing edges and the toroid labelled (b) is buttressed on the four corners.

In the fully buttressed toroidal vault (a), the primary arches are running from left to right. These arches are sharing the load in a fairly uniform manner, as manifest by the consistent axial stress shown in Figure 8.246(a). The arches running perpendicular to the primary arches are secondary members, having minimal axial force, but serving a bracing function and possibly serving to resist bending induced by the panels covering the facets. The toroidal vault buttressed only at the corners is deforming much more than the fully buttressed vault (see Figure 8.245) and has concentrated axial forces in the members near the corners where the large reaction forces are introduced into the lattice (see Figure 8.246(b)). For the vault buttressed only at the corners, the buttressing forces are directed generally along the diagonal. Those forces are inducing severe bending stresses in the members near the corner, since there are no members on the diagonal to absorb the buttressing forces axially. (The bending stress diagram is not shown, because the bending stresses are far beyond the range of the axial forces and because the bending stress diagram is so jumbled.) To address the diagonal forces, we can add diagonal members, as shown in Figures 8.247, 8.248, 8.249, and 8.250.

The bending stresses in the triangulated shell (Figure 8.250(b)) are still very high owing to warpage of the lattice along the edges and near the supports. These bending stresses are a result of the fact that the lattice is not the funicular shape for the loads. This situation can be remedied by adding stiffening elements, such as trusses,

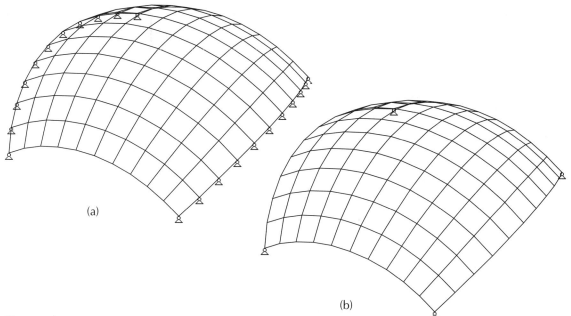

(a)

(b)

Figure 8.244 Fully buttressed toroidal vault (a) and a toroidal vault buttressed only on the corners (b).

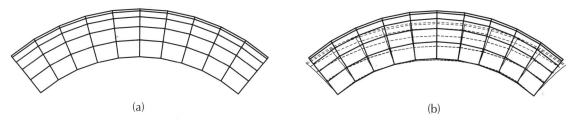

(a)

(b)

Figure 8.245 Deflection of fully buttressed toroidal vault (a) and a toroid vault buttressed only on the corners (b).

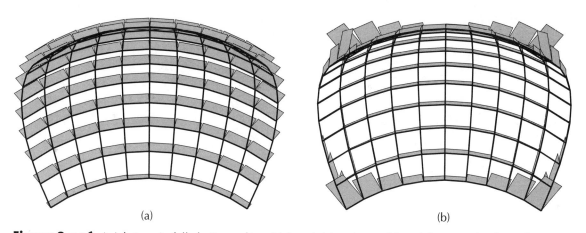

(a)

(b)

Figure 8.246 Axial stress in fully buttressed toroidal vault (a) and a toroid vault buttressed only on the corners (b).

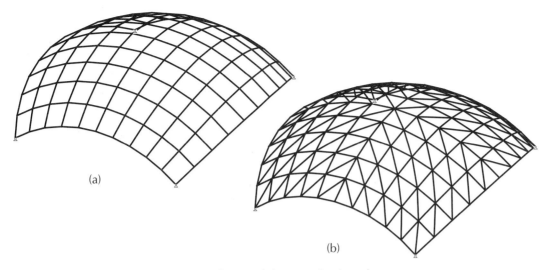

Figure 8.247 Triangulating the lattice for toroids buttressed only at the corners.

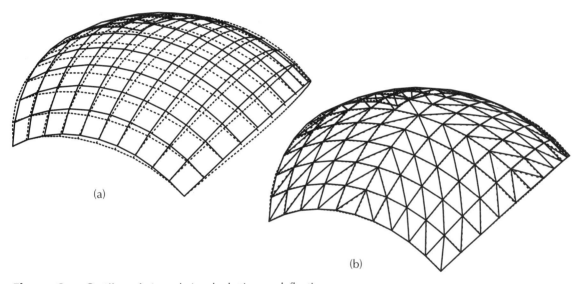

Figure 8.248 Effect of triangulating the lattice on deflection.

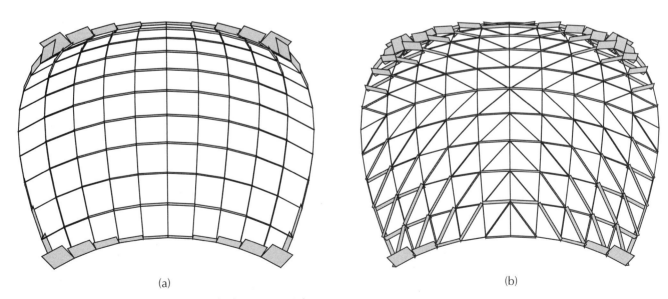

Figure 8.249 Effect of triangulating the lattice on axial stress.

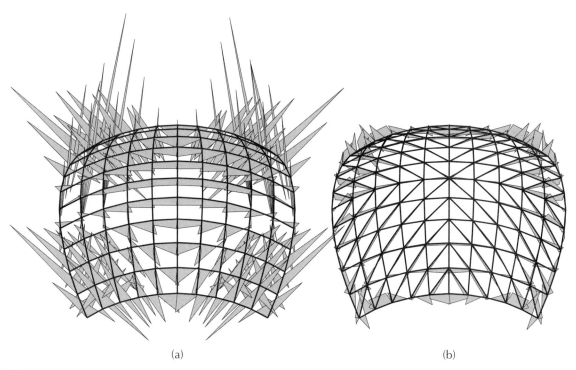

(a)   (b)

Figure 8.250 Effect of triangulating the lattice on bending stress.

to the boundary of the lattice, as shown in the (b) images in Figures 8.251, 8.252, 8.253, and 8.254.

The enhancements of adding diagonal members in the latticed surface and adding the stiffening trusses at the boundary have reduced the bending stresses (Figure 8.254(b)) to less than the axial stresses (Figure 8.253(b)). This seems like a reasonable goal to set, since the idea of a lattice structure of this sort is that the members act primarily in tension and compression, rather than in bending. Of course, there are no rigid rules in design and it is possible to build structures of this sort that rely on moment joints rather than triangulation. However, visual lightness and material economy will be improved by the structural enhancements outlined here.

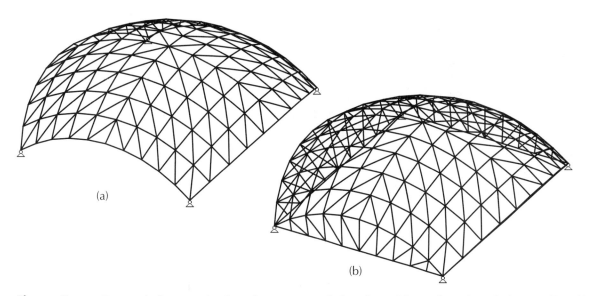

(a)

(b)

Figure 8.251 Two vaults buttressed only at the corners, with the edges of the vault on the right being stiffened by trusses.

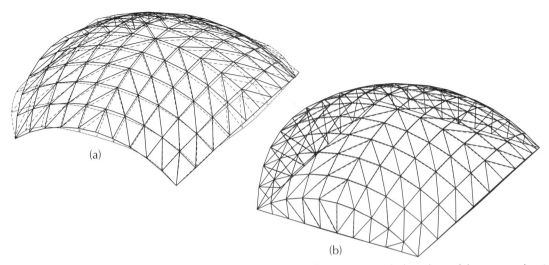

Figure 8.252 Deflection for two vaults buttressed only at the corners, with the edges of the one on the right being stiffened by trusses.

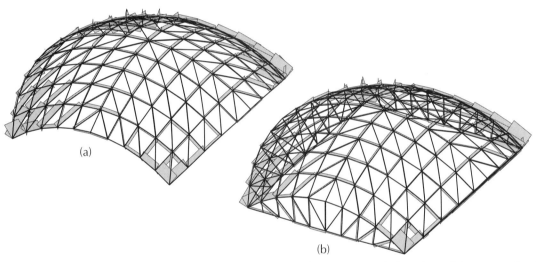

Figure 8.253 Axial stress for two vaults buttressed only at the corners, with the edges of the one on the right being stiffened by trusses.

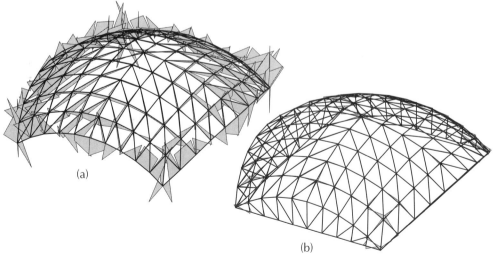

Figure 8.254 Bending stress for two vaults buttressed only at the corners, with the edges of the vault on the right being stiffened by trusses.

8.2.4 HYPERBOLIC PARABOLOIDS WITH BOUNDARY ELEMENTS ON THE GEOMETRIC DIRECTRICES

If the goal is to provide openings all around the structure, it is worthwhile revisiting the hyperbolic paraboloid form (see Figure 8.255).

All the lattice elements external to the directrices can be removed to produce the structural form shown in Figure 8.256.

As noted earlier, this structure is scalable, which means that it can be given any sized footprint by scaling the horizontal dimension, and any height by scaling the vertical dimension. Figure 8.257 is generated by scaling the y-dimension in Figure 8.256 by 0.5.

This structural form responds to uniform loads with greater structural clarity than does the toroid supported at the four corners, as indicated in the simulations in Figure 8.258.

The elements following the upward-opening (draped) parabolas are all in tension of fairly uniform magnitude. The elements following the downward-opening (arched) parabolas are all in compression of fairly uniform magnitude, with the exception that the arch running from foundation point to foundation point is carrying slightly more force than any of the other arches. This higher force is attributable to the fact that this arch is attached to the

rigid footings, which do not allow any movement. This makes this arch the slightly stiffer stress path, causing slightly more force in this arch. The bending stresses are generally negligible. The highest bending stresses are occurring in the draped members where they cross over the center arch. This is a further reflection of the fact that the center arch is moving slightly less than the others, by virtue of the fact that the ends are rigidly restrained. The bending stresses are very small as compared with the axial forces, so the shell structure is behaving as intended; that is, the elements are acting primarily in tension and compression, rather than bending. The consistent magnitude of forces in the lattice elements means that the same member cross section can be used everywhere in the lattice. Being able to use the same member cross section everywhere in the lattice means that the design and fabrication of the lattice can be very simple.

At every point that the lattice touches a boundary element, there are two lattice elements connecting to the boundary element, one lattice element at about 45° to the boundary element and one lattice element at about 135° to the boundary element. One of these lattice elements is in tension and the other is in compression, the tension force being about equal in magnitude to the compression force. When these two forces are resolved, the components perpendicular to the boundary essentially cancel each other and the components parallel to

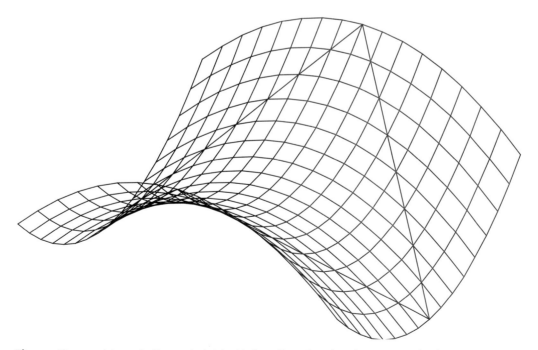

Figure 8.255 A hyperbolic paraboloid with four directrices forming a square in plan.

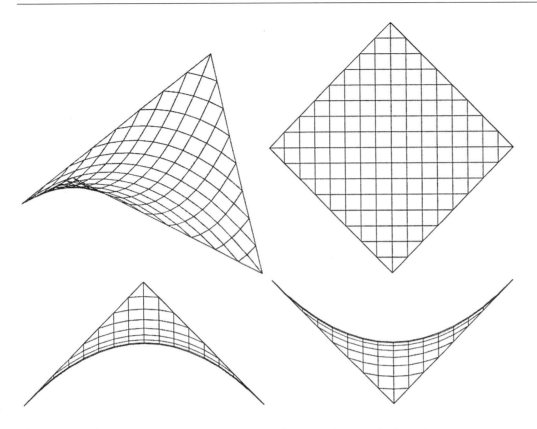

Figure 8.256 A hyperbolic paraboloid with four directrices forming the boundary.

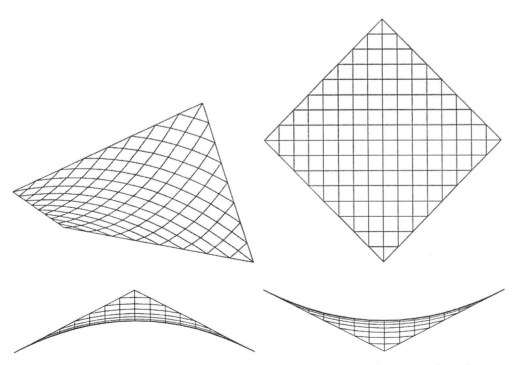

Figure 8.257 A shallower hyperbolic paraboloid with four directrices forming the boundary.

the boundary reinforce each other, producing a net force that is axial to the boundary element. This is a profoundly important point. It means that the boundary is not in bending and can be a fairly slender compression element. At each connection point on the boundary, the force in the boundary element is increased. The extremely variable axial force in the boundary elements is in direct contrast to the fairly uniform axial forces in the lattice. The logical response to this highly variable force in the boundary elements is a highly variable cross section. This is what one might expect from such a structure, which is a vault with a very wide cross section at the zenith and a very narrow cross section near the supports. The axial force that is being carried by many members near the zenith of the vault has to be carried by only

three members at the base of the arch. The cross section of the boundary elements has to increase near the base points to accommodate the loss of arch material near the base of the vault.

As the rendering in Figure 8.258(a) indicates, this is a remarkably delicate structure to be supporting its self-weight plus a $\frac{20\ \#}{\text{ft}^2}$ snow load. This is consistent with the original design goal to create a delicate, efficient structure that sits lightly on the ground. However, the effort may have succeeded too well with this goal, since this structural form is inherently unstable, tending to flop to one side or the other about the line connecting the two support points. This tendency is particularly pronounced under any kind of load that is asymmetric about the line

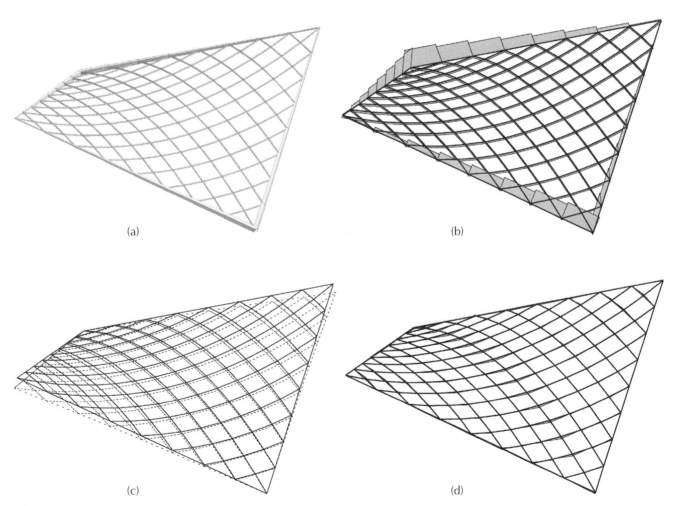

(a)

(b)

(c)

(d)

Figure 8.258 Hyperbolic paraboloid subjected to uniform load, showing boundary elements with variable cross sections (a), axial forces (b), deflection (c), and bending stress (d).

connecting the two support points. This structural form can be stabilized in a variety of ways, which are presented in the following discussion. The concrete structural model in Figure 8.259 was generated by students of Zubi Zubinzeretta, while he was teaching at the College of Design at North Carolina State University. Tipping the model from side to side is an irresistible response on the part of many observers, which is the kind of response that Zubi relished, since he was a great believer in active learning. This structure is a hyperbolic paraboloid made of reinforced concrete, with a steel tie member connecting the base points.

The structure represented in Figures 8.260, 8.261, 8.262, and 8.263 is a thin-shell hyperbolic paraboloid residence designed by Eduardo Catalano.

The large concrete element at the base point in the foreground of Figure 8.260 is one of the two buttresses providing the reactions that allow the arch action of the vault to occur. The structural shell consisted of three layers of $\frac{3}{4}$ in.-thick tongue-and-groove wood, with the bottom layer arching in the direction of the line connecting the base points, the middle layer draping in the direction of the line from high point to high point, and the top layer arching parallel to the bottom layer. This produced a wooden shell with an overall thickness of $2\frac{1}{4}$ in., with the upper and lower layers working in compression and the inner layer working in tension. The layers of wood were nailed together in the manner customary when putting down tongue-and-groove flooring. No glue was used in assembling the wooden shell. Steel compression elements were bolted along the edges of the shell, running

from the high tips down to the buttresses (see Figure 8.261). The shell was constructed on a formwork of straight timbers following the geometric directrices of the hyperbolic paraboloid. (Figures 8.223 and 8.224 show geometric directrices.)

The graceful sweep of the wood ceiling and glass walls on four sides combined to produce an extraordinary spatial experience. The wraparound glass walls created a wonderfully open feeling, and the sweeping wood canopy provided a sense of shelter. The building was particularly well suited to its site, which was buried in the woods, providing views in every direction (see Figure 8.261). It was strongly praised even by Frank Lloyd Wright, who rarely praised works other than his own.

The structural intention of the design was that the thin shell would span from base point to base point to resist gravity forces and that the mullions of the glass walls would stabilize the saddle shape against tipping from side to side. In other words, the mullions were envisioned as secondary structural elements to shore up the vault in the direction in which it was weak, that is, relative to lateral toppling. However, structures of this sort are complex and care has to be exercised in assessing the stiffness of various stress paths, so that the true structural burden on various elements can be properly assessed. The vertical wall mullions in the structure shown in Figure 8.261 are far stiffer in regard to gravity loads centered over the mullions than is the shell, which must carry the loads back to the footings that, in most instances, are displaced laterally quite some distance from the load. The point is amply demonstrated in the computer simulations of

Figure 8.259 Concrete hyperbolic paraboloid.

Figure 8.260 Residence with hyperbolic paraboloid roof, designed by architect Eduardo Catalano, in Raleigh, North Carolina.

Figure 8.261 Residence with hyperbolic paraboloid roof, showing the ample overhang of the roof, the boundary members, and the mullions in the glass walls.

Figure 8.262 to the computer simulations of Figure 8.258. Those two structures are the same except that columns have been added under the lattice for the structure in Figure 8.262.

The stiff columns are resisting the movement of the shell at the column tops, which is inducing bending in the lattice. The bending stresses in the lattice now exceed the axial stresses in the lattice, and the lattice is curving over the column tops. This phenomenon was in evidence in the Catalano residence. To ameliorate some of this problem, the boundary members were given substantial depth, so that they could act in bending in addition to resisting axial force, and a cable was strung between the upper tips of the vault. This cable was posttensioned to lift up on the boundary members. In this manner, the boundary elements began to take on a significant bending function in supporting the edge of the shell. Some of the deformation shown in computer simulation in Figure 8.262(c) is apparent in the photograph of the Catalano house shown in Figure 8.260, where the roof is "draping" over the corner mullions. The photograph in Figure 8.260 was taken after the building had been allowed to fall into disrepair. The wood roof had begun to decay after years

of exposure to moisture. As the decay progressed, the roof began to settle in a fairly pronounced way and the columns began to punch through the roof (Figure 8.263). The original shape of the building was more pleasing and more closely resembled the intended smooth shape of the hyperbolic paraboloid. However, even at the time of initial construction of the roof, the support role of the mullions and the edge beam was apparent in the slightly distorted shape of the thin shell roof.

There are other ways to stabilize a hyperbolic paraboloid that can be less problematic than the one used in this residence. For example, several hyperbolic paraboloids can be assembled to produce a larger structure within which the hyperbolic paraboloids are mutually stabilizing. In the structure in Figure 8.264, four hyperbolic paraboloids are assembled. Four of the boundary elements are now forming a pyramid with its peak at the center of the structure. This pyramid provides a very stable core for the structure.

The structure in Figure 8.265 is similar to the structure in Figure 8.264, except that Figure 8.265 shows distinct modules laced together at the boundaries. Figure 8.266 is similar to Figure 8.265, except that the modules have

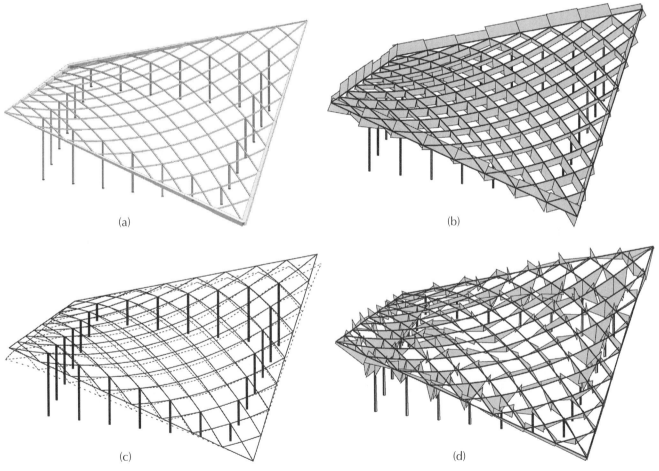

(a)   (b)

(c)   (d)

Figure 8.262 Hyperbolic paraboloid under uniform load, showing stabilizing columns (a), axial forces (b), deflection (c), and bending stress (d).

Figure 8.263 Mullion in glass wall punching through the deteriorating wooden shell.

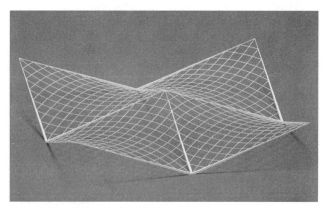

Figure 8.264 Four hyperbolic paraboloid shells bracing each other. Digital model by author; rendering by James Sweeney.

been tilted outward to increase the height of the central volume and lower the outer boundaries.

The structure in the photo in Figure 8.267, designed by Felix Candela, is based on the transformation concept illustrated in Figure 8.266.

The concrete shell in Figure 8.267 demonstrates some of the geometric variations achievable, starting with the basic saddle shape. A good way to describe the action of this structure is that it is like three saddle-shaped arches spanning from one support to the adjacent support. The saddle-shaped arches are leaning outward somewhat and would fall away from the center of the structure if they were not connected to each other. The tensional nature of the connection between the saddles has been expressed by splitting the saddles apart and then holding them in place with a steel trusswork that provides the tension function under gravity forces and the shear function under lateral forces. The aperture created by splitting the structure admits natural light in a manner that alleviates the darkness in the upper recesses and also allows the light to play off the curved shell, illuminating the form.

A structure of this form can be built without formwork by starting with a few bending members around the boundary, a cable network forming the surface geometry, and some tension cables holding down the tips of the bending members. The structure can be covered with several layers of fine steel mesh and then plastered with concrete that can be troweled or sprayed on. After the concrete cures, the shell works in compression to keep the cantilevered portions of the structure from yanking back under the influence of the tension cables in the cable network. Then the tension cables holding down the corners can be removed. This approach will become clearer in Chapter 9, which addresses cable networks.

The saddle-shaped arches can be used in a variety of arrangements, as long as there is some mechanism to keep them from rotating on the supports. In the arrangement shown in Figure 8.268, the high tips of two adja-

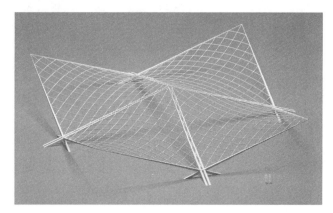

Figure 8.265 The hyperbolic paraboloid shells can be connected as a series of modular elements. Digital model by author; rendering by James Sweeney.

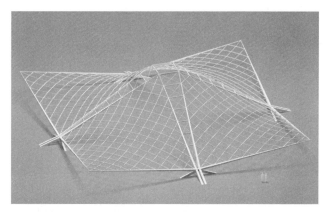

Figure 8.266 The hyperbolic paraboloid shells can be tilted or warped to produce a variety of spatial effects. Digital model by author; rendering by James Sweeney.

cent saddle arches are connected together so that the edges of the saddles form a four-sided pyramid that is open on two faces.

Figure 8.267 Concrete shell structure designed by Felix Candela. (Photo courtesy of Dorothy Candela.)

Figure 8.268 Mutually braced hyperbolic paraboloids designed by Felix Candela. (Photo courtesy of Dorothy Candela.)

8.2.5 CROSS VAULTS

Thin-shell barrel vaults pose a dilemma, in that they are strong in one direction and weak in another. Since a thin-shell barrel vault will always fail in the weak direction, the strength in the other direction is wasted. An effective way to deal with such a structure is to pair it with another element that is strong in the direction in which the first structure is weak. For example, two barrel vaults can be intersected so that they brace each other, similarly to how two plates are intersected to produce an angle or three plates to produce an I-section.

There are many classical examples of this technique, including Romanesque and Gothic cathedrals. A more modern example is the Bacardi Rum Factory designed by Felix Candela (see Figure 8.269).

A cross vault can be constructed on a computer using the procedure outlined in the diagrams in Figure 8.270.

When we simulate such a vault under uniform gravity loads, the forces in the minor arches of the cross vault are consistent with the forces that are in the arches of the barrel vault. What is dramatically different about the cross vault is the extreme concentration of force in the major arches crossing from support to support through the center of the vault (see Figure 8.271). This is not surprising, since the forces from the minor arches have to go somewhere, and the only stress path available is down the material at the intersection of the two thin sheets of material. This stress concentration is expressed in the vaults of Gothic cathedrals by having an extra thickness of stone forming a kind of rib down the intersection of the two stone vaults. It is expressed in the rendering in Figure 8.272 by having major arch elements that are larger than the minor arches and that are tapered, being relatively thin at the top and heavy at the bottom.

The intersecting arch vaults deliver their loads to the primary arches that cross from corner to corner. These

Figure 8.269 Parabolic cross vaults of the Bacardi Rum Factory, designed by Felix Candela. (Image courtesy of Dorothy Candela.)

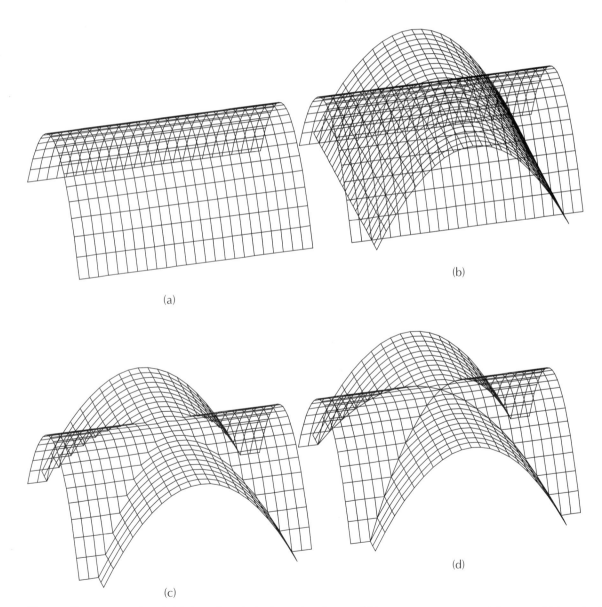

(a)

(b)

(c)

(d)

Figure 8.270 Barrel vault (a), barrel vault duplicated and rotated (b), excess interior material removed (c), and adding diagonal arches (d).

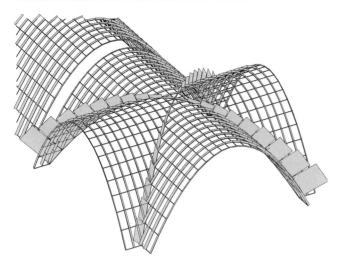

Figure 8.271 Axial forces in the barrel vault and cross vault under uniform snow load.

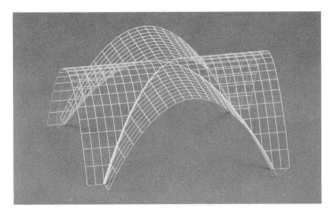

Figure 8.272 Form response to variations in forces along the primary arches. Digital model by author; rendering by James Sweeney.

primary arches are effectively braced by the intersection of the vault surfaces that create a local V-shape that is particularly pronounced at the quarter points. These "perpendicular" surfaces are mutually bracing, producing a very high resistance to roll-through at the quarter points of the primary arches.

The dilemma with this structure is that the surface area of the shell diminishes where the axial forces increase; that is, in the part of the shell approaching the support points. This increase in force must be accounted for by increasing the thickness of the shell; that is, by increasing the cross-sectional area of the material that constitutes the primary arches crossing from support to support through the center of the structure. In the case of a reinforced concrete shell, the problem can also be addressed by increasing the density of steel near the base of the shell. In the case of Candela's concrete shells, he increased both the thickness of the shell and the density of steel near the base of the shell (see Figure 8.273).

Although the shell seems to be coming to a point, Candela has used a visual trick to make it appear so, while actually dramatically thickening the shell and increasing the density of steel in the concrete. Over most of this structure, the shell is on the order of an inch thick, except close to the base where it gets much thicker.

To get better solar shading, these vaults can be cantilevered out over the glass enclosure walls. This produces a wonderful feeling of shelter. The overhangs are structurally very efficient, because they are effectively very deep beams. The overhangs cause a major redistribution in the stress pattern in the rest of the vault. The overhangs pull outward and upward on the parts of the vault interior to the supports, taking some of the stress off the "primary" arches and shifting that stress to the arch material spanning from one support point to the adjacent support point. This process of cantilevering can be carried to the point that there is no stress to speak of on the primary arches that cross through the center of the structure (see Figure 8.274).

Cross Vault Lateral Resistance

Cross vaults are much stiffer and stronger than barrel vaults in resisting lateral forces, as the diagrams in Figure 8.275 indicate.

Most of the bending stresses in the cross vault in (b) are due to the rigid frame action implicit in this particular lattice geometry. Those bending stresses would not exist if the cross vault was made of continuous thin-shell material, such as reinforced concrete or steel decking. Triangulating the lattice more closely simulates a continuous thin shell, as shown in Figure 8.276. The graphing scale for these figures is exaggerated, as compared with that in the previous diagrams, to make the deflections and bending stresses apparent.

Physical models can also be excellent indicators of the structural behavior of cross vaults (see Figure 8.277).

Cross vaults are substantially stronger and stiffer in resisting forces against the shell than are barrel vaults, particularly for forces against the part of the cross-vault shell surface near the groove where the two barrel shapes intersect. The resistance of cross vaults to lateral forces can be understood in terms of an analogy to something we discovered in dealing with arches. The observation was made that thickening the arch at the quarter points can dramatically improve resistance to roll-through buckling under uniform gravity load, and to roll-through deformation under asymmetric gravity loads and wind loads, as in the bridge shown in Figure 8.278(a). When viewed from the side (b), the thickest part of the cross vault is also near the quarter point.

The rugged behavior of cross vaults can also be understood in terms of the intersection of planes of material. The two sheets of material highlighted in Figure 8.279 are intersecting each other at angles that are suitable for

(a)

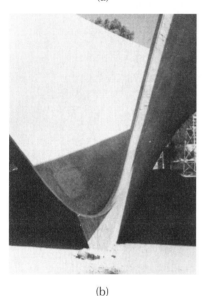

(b)

Figure 8.273 Xochilmico Restaurant, designed by Felix Candela. (Photo courtesy of Dorothy Candela.)

Figure 8.274 Extended shell creates overhang for solar shading in the Xochilmico Restaurant, designed by Felix Candela. (Photo courtesy of Dorothy Candela.)

mutual reinforcement of the sheets. Ideally, the angle of intersection would be 90°, but other angles can work well also.

One way of thinking about these structures is that the intersecting sheets of material stabilize each other near the intersection of the sheets, but, far from the intersection, the thin sheets need additional stiffening elements. The extremely thin shell is vulnerable to roll-through deformation out near the outer edges of the vault (see Figure 8.280).

The behavior is analogous to the plastic angle columns, which were very resistive to buckling near the intersection of the two sheets of material forming the angle, but vulnerable to buckling out near the ends of the thin legs of the angle. Vertical arched ribs can be very effective in stiffening the perimeter edge of the thin shell, either on the inside, as shown in Figure 8.281(a), or on the outside, as shown in Figure 8.281(b).

The configuration with the ribs on the outside allows for a smooth transition of the interior surface as the eye moves from the inside surface to the outside view, and it also allows the entire interior surface to be illuminated in a pleasing manner, without gloomy shadows cast on the ceiling by the arched ribs. The outer edges of the vault can be braced in a variety of ways, but whatever technique is used, it is generally aesthetically desirable to avoid making the thin shell appear very thick at the edges. The visual effect of thin edges can be achieved by using a light, highly transparent truss or by curving the shell, giving it the effect of a U-shaped beam to resist roll-through deformation. Both these techniques are illustrated in Figure 8.282, showing (a) the Church of San Antonio de las Huertas, in Caldaza, Mexico, and (b) the Exchange Hall, in Uruguay, both designed by Felix Candela. Note the high density of steel in the groove of the primary arches in Figure 8.282(b), reflecting the higher forces along those stress paths.

Where the vault surfaces intersect each other at a severe angle, which would describe the situation for the lower two-thirds of the vault, they strongly reinforce each other. Near the top of the structure, however, the vault surfaces intersect at a shallow angle and, at the very top (the zenith), they are "co-planar" to each other. At the zenith of the structure, the mutual benefit of thin sheets of material bracing each other disappears, producing a local weakness in the structure at the zenith. This weakness is manifest as a "shear deformation" (warping) of the locally flat part of the thin-shell cross vault at the center of the structure (see Figure 8.283).

Vertical arched ribs running across the center of the cross vault are extremely effective in reinforcing the locally flat part of the structure at the center and reducing the shear deformation associated with lateral forces (see Figure 8.284). In Figure 8.284, cords are used to exert lateral forces on the structure. The structure reinforced with

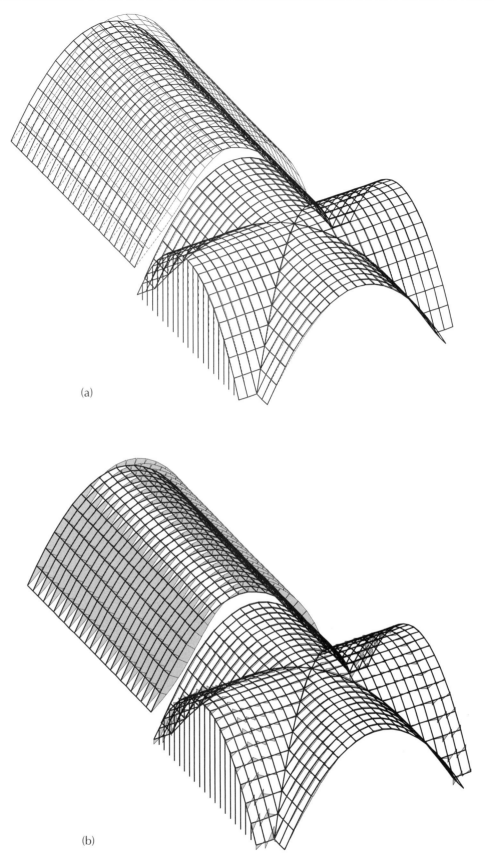

(a)

(b)

Figure 8.275 Comparison of barrel and cross vault under lateral forces, showing deflections (a) and bending stresses (b).

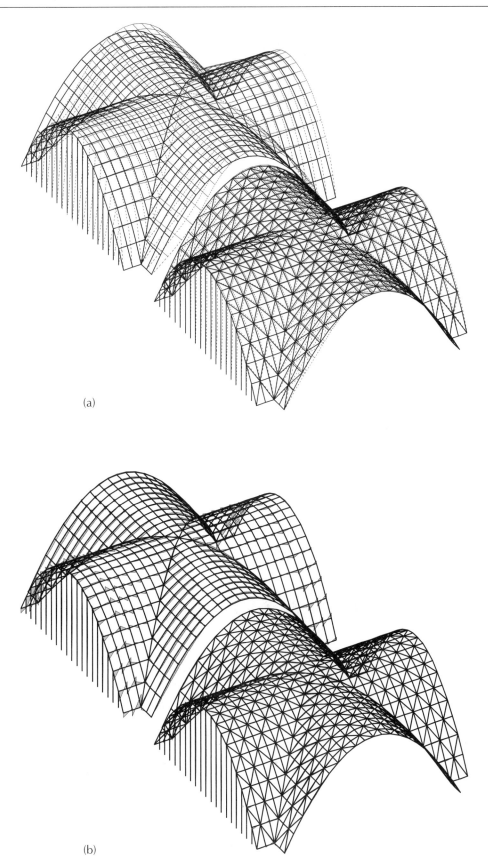

(a)

(b)

Figure 8.276 Effect of triangulating the lattice on deflection (a) and bending stress (b).

Figure 8.277 Lateral forces on the shell close to the intersection with adjoining shell.

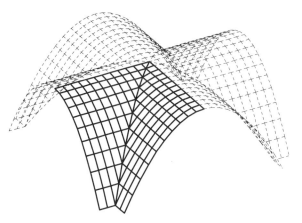

Figure 8.279 Highlighted curved sheets of intersecting materials form a V-shaped cross section.

(a)

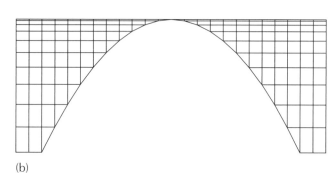

Figure 8.278 The Salginatobel bridge, designed by Malliart (a) and orthographic view of cross vault (b). (Photo courtesy of Eugenio Pedrazzini.)

(b)

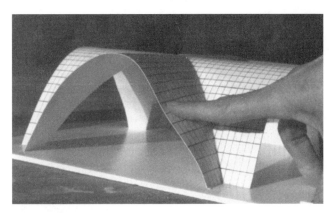

Figure 8.280 The thin-shell cross vault is vulnerable to forces against the shell near the perimeter.

the vertical ribs exhibits very little of the shear deformation apparent in the previous vault, which was not reinforced with ribs.

The vertical ribs shown in Figure 8.284 did little to help resist forces against the thin shell near the perimeter edge of the vault. Local forces produced severe warpage (Figure 8.285(a)) and pinwheel forces induced large pinwheel, roll-through deformation at the boundary of all the arches (Figure 8.285(b).

Ribs of triangular cross section in the grooves where the two shells intersect significantly stiffen the structure against pinwheel deformation. The torsional stiffness of the tubular ribs tends to inhibit pinwheel deformation, as shown in Figure 8.286(a). This enhancement is not quite

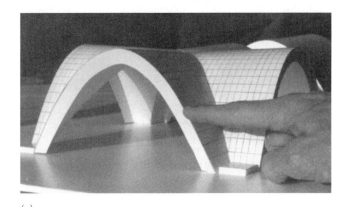

(a)

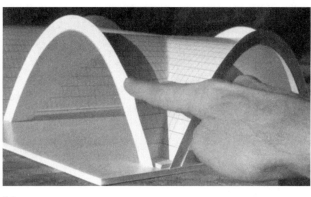

(b)

Figure 8.281 Vertical arched ribs stiffening the perimeter edges of the shell.

(a)

(b)

Figure 8.282 Designs by Felix Candela for inhibiting roll-through of the outer edge of the cross vault shell for the Church of San Antonio de las Huertas in Caldaza, Mexico. (Photos courtesy of Dorothy Candela.)

Figure 8.283 Shear deformation under edge force parallel to the shell.

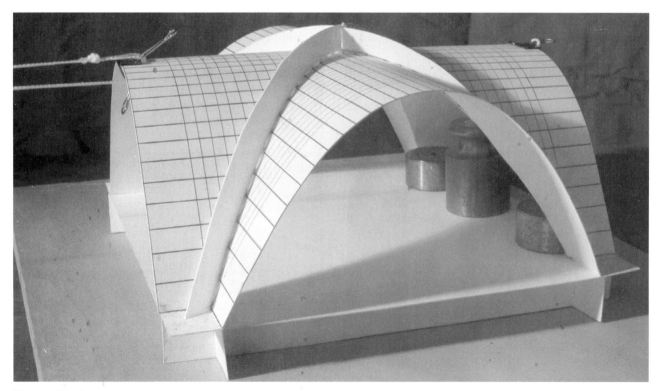

Figure 8.284 Using vertical ribs to stiffen the center of the vault.

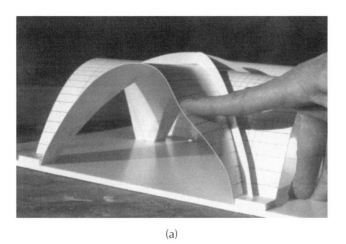 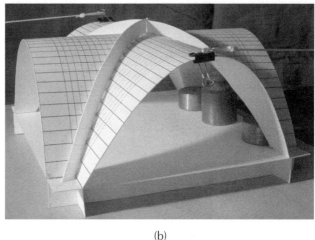

(a)   (b)

Figure 8.285 Models showing behavior of shell edges.

as effective in resisting this deformation as adding vertical arched ribs at the perimeter of the shell, but it may be regarded as aesthetically preferable by many people. The bands that form the tubular ribs also help somewhat with resisting shear deformation at the center of the vault under edge forces parallel to the vault, as shown in Figure 8.286(b), and also with resisting localized vertical forces at the center of the vault, but vertical ribs criss-crossing through the center of the vault are more effective in dealing with these issues. The bands creating the triangular cross sections in the grooves seem to strike a good balance of solving a lot of structural problems adequately, while being visually unobtrusive.

Semicircular and elliptical vaults tend to be flatter on the top and to bulge out more at the quarter points than is the case for the parabolic vaults (see Figure 8.287). This shape makes the semicircular vault and elliptical vault more vulnerable than the parabolic vault to vertical forces, either near the perimeter arches or near the center (see Figures 8.288(a) and 8.288(b)). This shape also makes the semicircular vault more vulnerable than the parabolic vault to edge forces parallel to the shell (see Figures 8.289(a)) and to pinwheel forces (Figure 8.289(b)).

The inherent deficiencies of the semicircular and elliptical vaults make enhancements, such as perimeter ribs, even more critical for semicircular and elliptical vaults than for parabolic vaults (see Figures 8.290(a) and 8.290(b)).

To produce the most open structure possible, the base points can be made very narrow. Making the base of the vault narrower makes the structure drastically less stiff against almost all forces, as the structure exhibits "skinny legged syndrome." This behavior is particularly acute in semicircular vaults, where the "leg" material is cut away higher up than is the case for the parabolic vaults (see Figure 8.291(a)). Because of their shape, parabolic vaults are

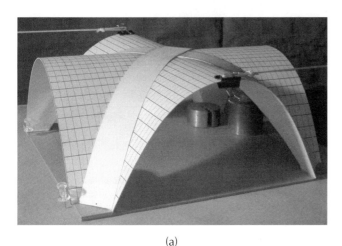 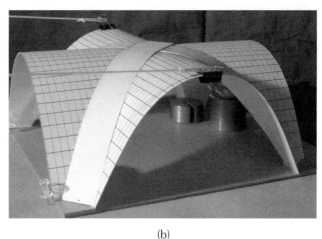

(a)   (b)

Figure 8.286 Model enhanced with bands that create triangular tubes in the grooves.

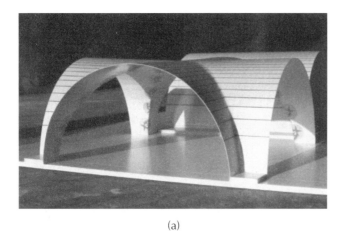

(a)

(b)

Figure 8.287 Semicircular (a) and elliptical vaults (b).

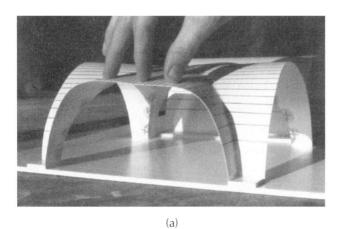
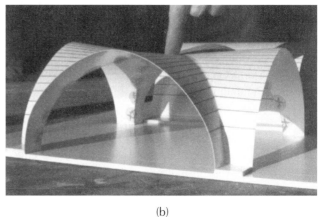

(a)

(b)

Figure 8.288 Deformation of semicircular vault under vertical forces at edge (a) and center (b).

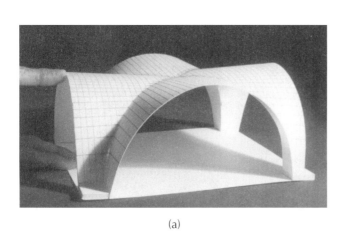
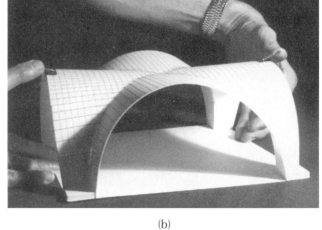

(a)

(b)

Figure 8.289 Deformation of semicircular vault under edge force parallel to shell (a) and pinwheel forces (b).

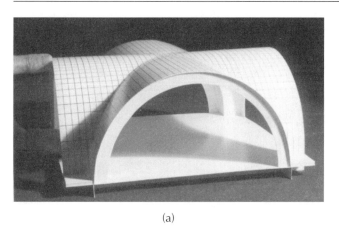

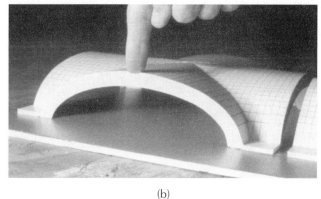

(a)   (b)

Figure 8.290 Semicircular (a) and elliptical (b) cross vaults with stiffening ribs at the perimeter of the shell.

less vulnerable to skinny legged syndrome (see Figure 8.291(b)).

For all the vaults shown previously, the tie member was buried in the base of the structure. When the vault is elevated on support columns, it is important to account for the buttressing force required for true arch action. Using a tie member to accomplish this function allows even fairly shallow vaults to work satisfactorily under vertical forces. Cutting the tie member completely destroys the effectiveness of the vault in resisting vertical forces, as shown in Figure 8.292.

Although the tie members help with gravity forces, they do nothing to help with lateral forces (see Figure 8.293(a)). For lateral stabilization, the openings between the columns can be cross braced or the columns can be thickened at the base and moment connected to deep grade beams, as shown in Figure 8.293(b).

Vaults with a fairly high rise, so that the outward thrust is not too great, and short columns radically thickened at the base and rigidly connected to a deep grade beam, can be designed to work without the tie member. The "C-clamp" structure created by the columns and grade beam working together can provide the necessary buttressing force for the vault action. The structure shown in Figure 8.294 worked reasonably well even after the tie members were cut.

Cross vaults can be produced in a variety of geometries other than quadripartite, some of which are shown in Figure 8.295.

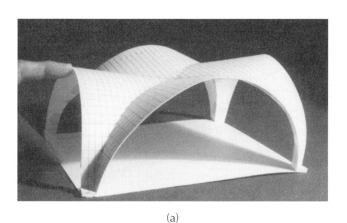

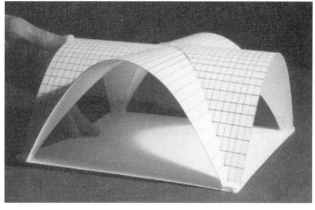

(a)   (b)

Figure 8.291 Narrow-based vaults under edge force parallel to the shell.

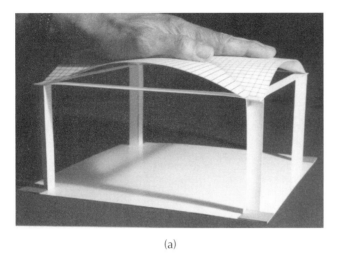

(a)

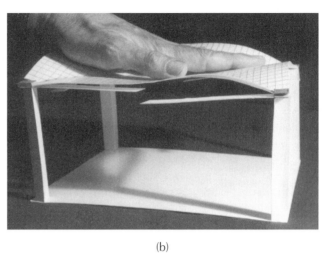

(b)

Figure 8.292 Elevated vault with elevated tie members.

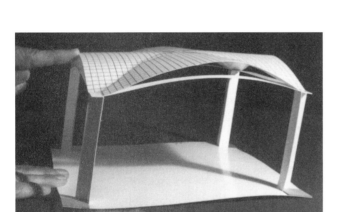

(a)

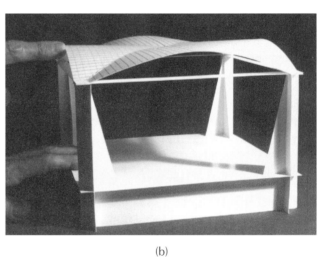

(b)

Figure 8.293 Response of elevated vault to lateral forces.

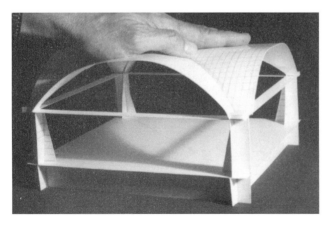

Figure 8.294 Short, thick columns and deep grade beams.

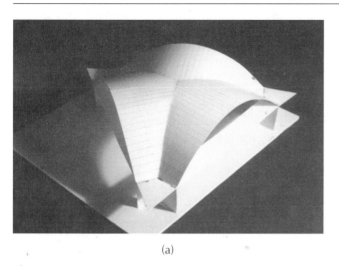 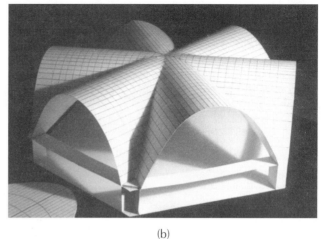

(a)   (b)

Figure 8.295 Tripartite and sexpartite cross vaults.

Assignment

Construct a cross vault using poster board, similar to the models in the preceding figures. Detailed instructions for this assignment are contained in the digital supplement, including digital files that can be plotted for making templates (see Figure 8.296).

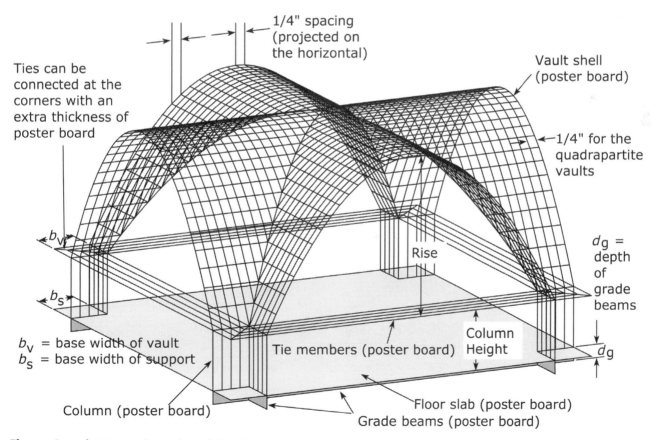

Figure 8.296 Diagram for vault model project.

9

Tensile Spanning Structures

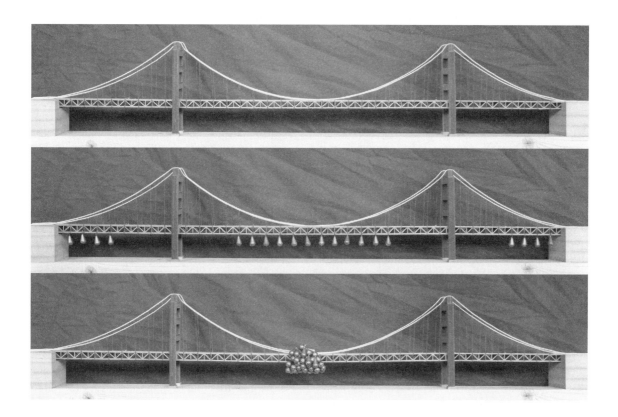

The primary stress in a tensile element is tension stress tangent to the long axis of the element. In addition to the primary stress, there may be some internal stress resulting from the pressure of a load distributed over the outside surface of the element. If the structural system is properly designed, this pressure from applied loads or reactions will be small as compared with the primary axial tension stress. However, there is some need to be concerned about this issue, since highly localized loads will produce high stresses that have a tendency to cut through the element.

Most elements that approximate a state of pure tension are so constructed that tension is the only state of stress that can be supported. For example, a thin wire or piece of string will support very large loads along the length of the element. In contrast, the wire or string will support essentially no load as a bending member spanning between two supports. Attempting to apply any significant force perpendicular to such an element will simply result in that element changing its shape until it either sheds the load or absorbs it in the form of a tension stress. In other words, the element assumes the shape that will result in a pure state of tension. The exact nature of that shape depends on the location and direction of applied forces and on the configuration of the supports.

A tension structure is one in which emphasis is placed on carrying as much of the applied load as possible through tension elements that are set at such an angle that those tension elements have a significant mechanical advantage in carrying the load. The term *tension structure* describes a state of mind or a design attitude more than a precisely definable structural system, since there is no such thing as a pure tension structure. All elements in tension achieve that state, because somewhere else in the structural system there is material in compression that is acting in such a way as to produce the state of tension in the tension element. Moreover, the concept of a "mechanical advantage" can be stretched to cover a variety of situations, ranging from very good mechanical advantage to borderline poor mechanical advantage. Hence, one is simply talking about a matter of degree when calling something a tension structure.

Tension structures tend to make highly efficient use of materials, for the following reasons:

1. Materials with the greatest stress capacity, such as drawn wire, glass fibers, and graphite fibers, are available only in a form suitable for tensile applications (i.e., they are very thin, which means that they tend to buckle under compression and they bend easily under lateral forces).
2. Tensile elements tend to be more efficient than compression elements, in which the stress level can be severely limited by buckling.

3. The stress in tensile elements can be uniform, which allows all of the material to be utilized at full stress, as compared with bending elements, in which much of the material is not fully stressed and, therefore, not fully utilized.

Tension structures are particularly appropriate for long-span applications.

9.1 Suspension Structures

If a tensile element is suspended between two supports, it will hang in a smooth curve called a *catenary*. When a localized force is applied at the center of the element, it changes shape until it is straight everywhere except at the point of the applied load, at which point the element changes abruptly from one direction to another. The point where the curve of the suspension element changes direction is called a *cusp*. This change is, in fact, not abrupt and does not occur at a single point. The highly localized load is not a point force, but is distributed in some way over some length of the tension member, and the tension member changes shape gradually over the region where the load is distributed. In Figure 9.1, the gradual change is shown for a forged suspender element.

However, in diagrams showing the "larger view" of the structure, the force is approximated as a point force and one speaks of a cusp in the tension element. This kind of "cusp" occurs at every localized force. It has been drawn in Figure 9.1 as occurring at a point where a major element is supported, but it also occurs at points where the suspension element itself is supported. For example, it can occur at the top of a bridge tower, such as shown in Figure 9.2.

The main suspension cable appears to have a cusp at the top of the tower. Closer examination reveals that a nicely rounded saddle surface has been provided to cradle the cable, making the change of direction less stressful for the cable and for the support structure.

For very strong tension elements subjected to very high point loads, the tension element will appear to be straight between the localized forces. However, there is always some curvature induced by the self-weight of the tension element. The images in Figure 9.3 show the effect of progressively increasing the magnitude of point forces. Figure 9.3(a) is the chain hanging in the shape of catenary. Below that, the images in (b) and (c) are for relatively light loads, which still leave a substantial curvature in the chain. The images in (d) and (e) involve heavier weights, which bring the chain closer to being straight. Increasing the point forces increases the tension in the chain, which tends to straighten out the portions of the chain between the point forces. However, no matter how much tension

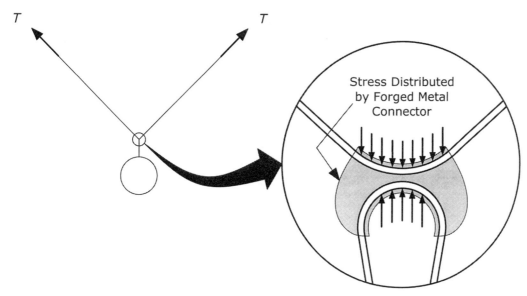

Figure 9.1 Suspender element.

is put into the chain, there will always be some curvature induced by the self-weight of the chain.

Along a similar line of reasoning, it is not possible to create a functional (i.e., load-carrying) suspension element with no drape or sag. Figure 9.4 shows a weight being supported on a suspension element. This weight can be thought of as the functional load. A vertical support force must be generated by the suspension element. The ends of the suspension element are looped over pulleys, and the tension required to keep the load from falling through is maintained by weights at the ends of the suspension element. The system finds it own equilibrium by virtue of the rotation of the pulleys. The tension in the suspension element is equal to the weight of one of the weights at the end of the suspension element. Figure 9.4(a) shows moderate weights at the end of the suspension element. Figure 9.4(b) has much larger weights.

Putting extremely large weights on the end of the chord would bring the chord close to straight. However, for reasons about to be demonstrated, there is no finite tension in the chord that could make it perfectly straight.

Figure 9.5 depicts the structural action of the tensile element with a single localized force applied to it.

The exploded diagram in Figure 9.6 shows three free-bodies:

1. A straight segment representing the left side of the suspension element
2. The weight that is responsible for the load
3. A straight segment representing the right side of the suspension element

(a)

(b)

Figure 9.2 Interface between cable and tower in Golden Gate Bridge. (Image in (b) courtesy of Rowland J. Mainstone from *Development in Structural Forms* [Architectural Press, 2001].)

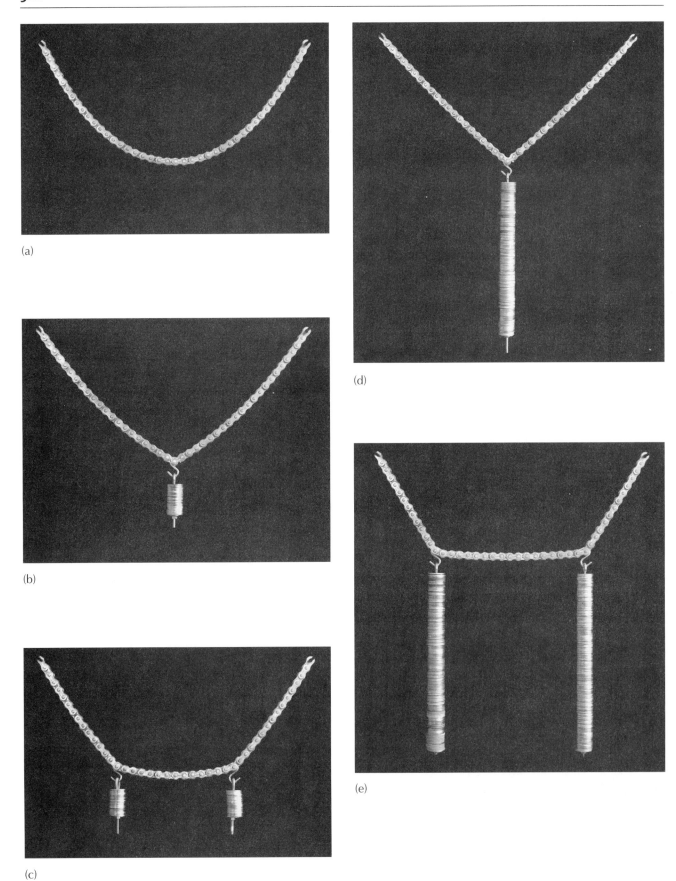

(a)

(b)

(c)

(d)

(e)

Figure 9.3 Effect of adding progressively heavier localized weights.

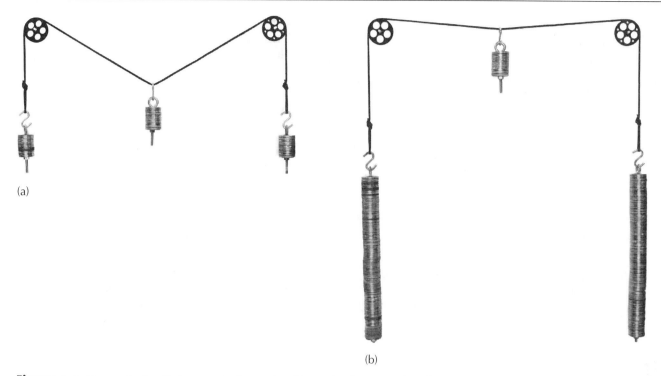

(a)

(b)

Figure 9.4 Demonstrating that sag varies inversely with tension in suspension element.

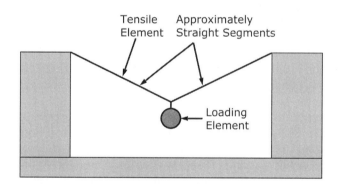

Figure 9.5 A single localized load.

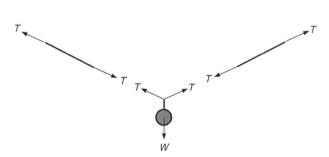

Figure 9.6 Creating freebodies of the diagram in Figure 9.5.

The assumption has been made that the applied load is much larger than the self-weight of the suspension element, so the two tensile segments are rendered as straight and they have forces only at the ends. Since there are only two forces on each tension segment, these forces must be equal and opposite, by the laws of equilibrium. Moreover, these two forces must be along the same line, since otherwise they would be a couple and would cause the segment to rotate. By simple geometry, the only line that the two forces can be along is the line passing through the end points of the segment. In other words, the two forces are along the segment, and they are equal and opposite. (Of course, one also knew that these forces had to be along the segment, by the nature of the flexible tensile element that would not sustain any load with a component perpendicular to the element.) Each of these forces has been labeled *T*. Each of these forces can be broken down into components in the horizontal and vertical directions, as shown in Figure 9.7.

The horizontal components on the bottoms of the two segments represent the action of the two segments on each other. The vertical components on the bottoms of the two segments represent the action of the loading element on the two segments. The sum of these two vertical components is the action of the loading element on the complete tensile element. The sum of these two vertical components at the bottoms of the tensile elements is, by Newton's second law, equal and opposite to the upward force on the loading element. By the laws of

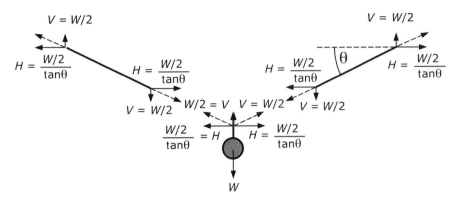

Figure 9.7 Drawing the components for forces in Figure 9.6.

equilibrium applied to the loading element, the upward force on the loading element due to the action of the tensile segments must be equal and opposite to the weight of the loading element. Hence, the vertical components at the bottoms of the segments are both equal to half the weight of the loading element.

The vertical components are determined by the weight of the loading element. The horizontal components on the tensile segments are then dependent on the vertical components and the slope of the tensile segments, as shown in Figure 9.8. As the slope approaches horizontal, that is, as Θ approaches zero, tanΘ approaches zero, H approaches ∞, and T approaches ∞.

Figure 9.9 shows the change in shape of the suspension element as more and more localized forces are added, until the forces are so close together that the situation approximates a uniform, distributed load. Each lateral force on the tension element changes the shape of the element, introducing a cusp in the tension element at the point of application of the force. If enough lateral forces are applied, the tension element will appear to be smoothly and continuously changing its direction, although close examination will reveal the straight segments between cusp points. In the diagram in Figure 9.9, the forces are all vertical and they are uniformly distributed along the horizontal, yielding a tension member shape with cusp points lying on a parabola.

The shape assumed by the suspending element under this load is a parabola, which is governed by the formula: $y = kx^2$, where k is a constant that correlates with the amount of sag. If k is small, then there is little sag.

The angle of the element at the support point indicates the direction of the reactive force T from the supports. If the reaction of the supports on the cable was in any other direction than along the length of the cable, then the cable would change its shape rather than resist the lateral component of the load. The force T can be resolved into its vertical and horizontal components, V and H (see Figure 9.10). By the laws of equilibrium, the vertical support components are each equal to half the total weight W of the balls suspended from the cable. (There is an assumption that the dead weight of the cable is negligible.) The magnitude of the horizontal components H depends on V and the angle of the force T. The less sag allowed in the suspension element, the greater will be the stress in the suspension element. As the sag in the suspension element approaches zero, the slope approaches horizontal, Θ approaches zero, tanΘ approaches zero, H approaches ∞, and T approaches ∞. Throughout this process, the vertical components of the reactions remain constant, being equal to half the total weight of the loading elements.

The increase in force H as the suspension element becomes shallower can be understood in terms of the tri-

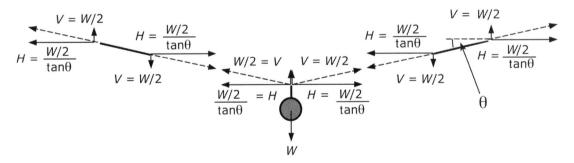

Figure 9.8 Larger horizontal component for shallower sag.

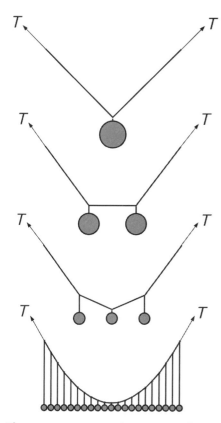

Figure 9.9 Approaching a smooth parabolic shape as the number of forces increases.

reinforces the fact that the vertical component is the same in each case ($V = W/2$). Only the horizontal component changes as the member becomes shallower. Note that even though we used freebodies and moment diagrams to arrive at the horizontal forces and subsequently to arrive at the overall tension forces, the tension forces at the end are in each case tangent to the suspension element at the point of support. In other words, T can be derived from the freebody argument or by constructing the tangent line to the suspension element and projecting that line until it rises an amount V; that is, until it is large enough to generate a vertical component of magnitude V.

$$T_1 = \sqrt{V^2 + (0.5\,V)^2} = \sqrt{V^2 + 0.25\,V^2} = \sqrt{1.25\,V^2}$$
$$= V \cdot \sqrt{1.25} = 1.18\,V = 0.599\,W = 2.236\,H_1$$

$$T_2 = \sqrt{V^2 + V^2} = \sqrt{2\,V^2} = V\sqrt{2} = 1.414\,V = 0.707\,W$$
$$= 1.414\,H_1$$

$$T_3 = \sqrt{V^2 + (2\,V)^2} = \sqrt{V^2 + 4\,V^2} = \sqrt{5\,V^2} = V \cdot \sqrt{5}$$
$$= V \cdot 2.236\,V = 1.118\,W = 1.118\,H_1$$

$$T_4 = \sqrt{V^2 + (4\,V)^2} = \sqrt{V^2 + 16\,V^2} = \sqrt{17\,V^2} = \sqrt{17}$$
$$= 4.12\,V = 2.062\,W = 1.031\,H_1$$

Notice that H is approaching T as the sag approaches zero, reflecting the fact that the vertical force becomes comparatively negligible as the horizontal force becomes very large. These relationships can also be established experimentally. Figure 9.13 shows such an experiment for a deep parabola and for a shallow parabola.

These images show that the weights used to tension the cable (so that it will hold its shape) are much larger for the shallow sag than for the deep sag, and that the weights tensioning the two ends of the cable are almost equal for the shallow sag and are quite different for the deep sag.

The condition of uniform loading along the horizontal is not the same as uniform loading along the length of the

angulation argument outlined earlier. It can also be understood in terms of leverage and equilibrium arguments, as outlined in Figures 9.11 and 9.12.

The couple of the horizontal forces = the couple of the vertical forces:

$$H_1 \cdot \frac{L}{2} = V \cdot \frac{L}{4}$$

The lever arm for horizontal-force couple = Sag.

Figure 9.12 shows the four diagrams in Figure 9.11 superimposed on each other. Using this graphic technique

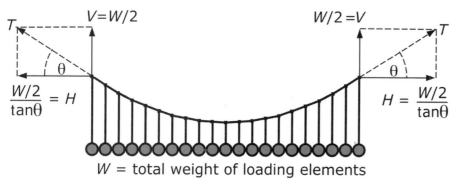

$V=W/2$ $W/2 =V$

$\dfrac{W/2}{\tan\theta} = H$ $H = \dfrac{W/2}{\tan\theta}$

W = total weight of loading elements

Figure 9.10 Geometry of support forces.

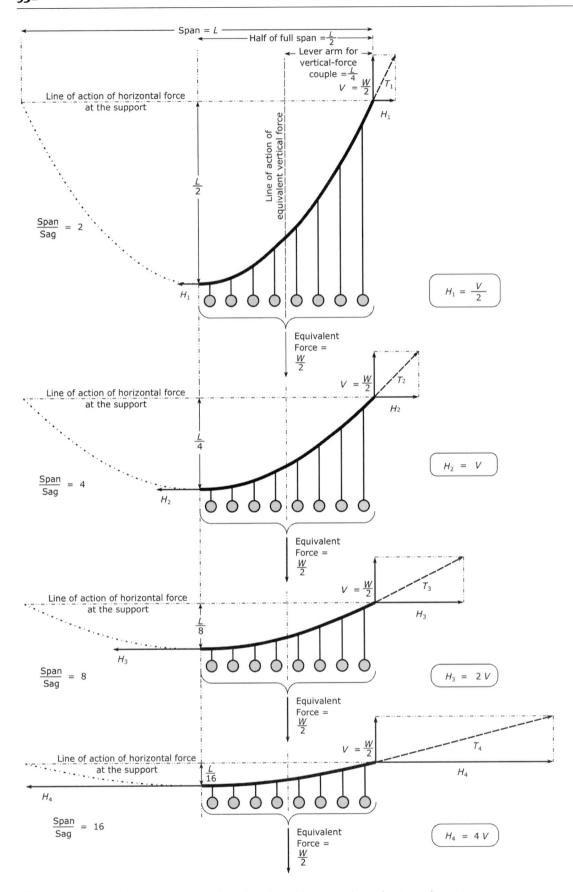

Figure 9.11 Applying the principle of rotational equilibrium to derive horizontal reactions.

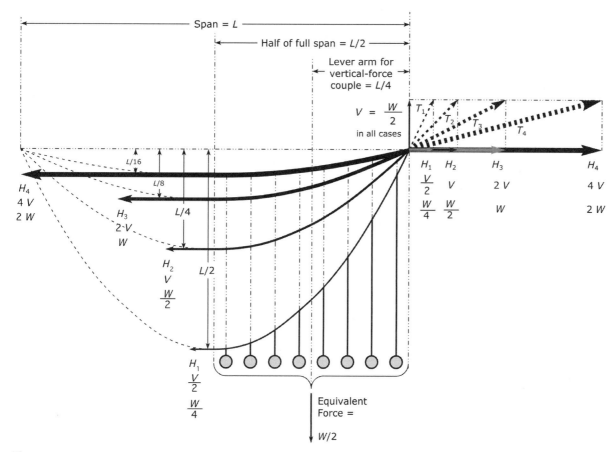

Figure 9.12 Suspension leverage: superimposing images of various sags on a single diagram.

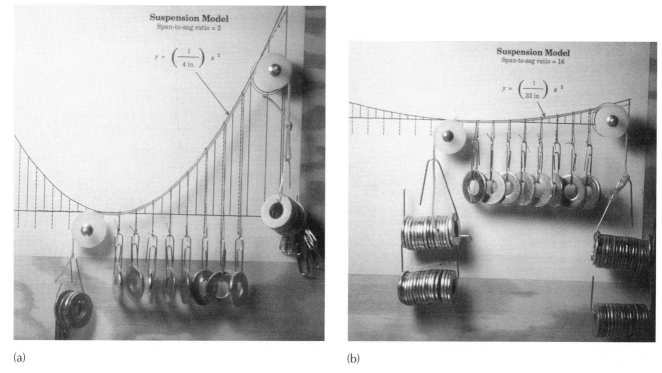

Figure 9.13 Variation in horizontal force with sag for deep sag (a) and shallow sag (b).

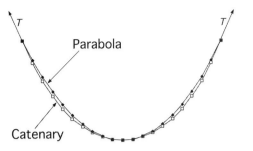

Figure 9.14 Comparing a catenary and a parabola.

suspension element, such as occurs for a cable or chain of uniform cross section hanging under its own dead weight. The suspension element has a short segment between the vertical suspender near the center part of the suspension element, but has longer segments between the vertical suspenders near the support points. In other words, the load due to the dead weight of the primary suspension element (as projected on the horizontal) is larger near the suspension points than it is near the center of the structure. This causes a suspension element to assume a shape under its own dead weight that bulges more at the sides than the parabola does. Under its own weight, the suspension element takes on the shape of a catenary (see Figure 9.14).

In tensile structures this difference is of little consequence, especially since the suspension element will automatically adjust itself to assume the "appropriate" shape. In arches, however, the difference between a parabola and a catenary can be quite significant. (For a

discussion of the mathematics of a catenary, see section 8.1.8.2 Catenaries.)

9.1.1 SUPPORTING THE SUSPENSION ELEMENT

Any suspension element subjected to gravity loads must be supported at the ends by vertical components that equilibrate the downward gravity loads. These vertical support forces must be provided by compression elements of some kind. (There is an ancient axiom that says, "What comes down must have gone up." Alternately, it can be said, "Even though there may be pure tension elements, there are no pure tensile systems.") Normally, a suspension structure is chosen because open space below is desired. This desire for space includes some minimum vertical clearance that is dictated by the functional requirements of the structure, whether it is to allow for the hurling of a football or the passage of a ship (see Figure 9.15).

The height of the lowest part of the suspension element is fixed by functional requirements. The higher the support points, the longer must be the compression elements providing the support. The longer a compression element is, the more it will cost. This is the classic design tradeoff:

- Increase the amount of sag, in order to reduce the tension force in the suspension element.
- Keep the sag small, in order to minimize the cost of the compression element.

In addition to the vertical components supporting the suspension element, there must be horizontal components as well. This follows from the fundamental axiom

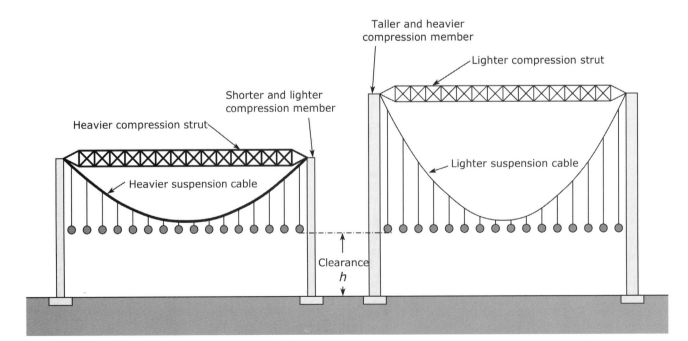

Figure 9.15 Design tradeoffs: heavier cable versus taller towers.

that the overall force must be tangent to the axis of the suspension element. For a suspension element with little sag, these horizontal components will be much larger than the vertical components. In a sense, this has created a monster. The designer of such a structure started off with a set of vertical loads, and in the process has put the structure at a mechanical disadvantage by shaping the structure, so that the overall tension force in the suspension element is much larger than the original load. Fortunately, there are tensile materials available that are extremely strong and structurally efficient, in the sense that they can support very large forces very efficiently.

The diagrams in Figure 9.16 depict several common methods of generating the horizontal force required at the support points of a suspension element.

When concrete-foundation anchorages are used to resist the pull of the tension elements, the force of the cables must be distributed throughout the mass of the concrete. Typically, the high-strength steel cable is not embedded directly in the anchor for two reasons:

1. The steel will elongate much more than the concrete can tolerate, creating severe stress concentrations where the steel exits the concrete mass. This stress concentration will break the bond of the concrete to the steel. Stress concentration will propagate this bond-breaking process along the cable until the cable pulls free from the concrete. This failure process is similar to the propagation of cracks in glass, which, once started, proceed with diminished resistance.

2. Massive, low-grade steel anchors embedded in the concrete and protruding from the concrete allow continuous strands of high-strength steel to be looped around the protruding ends of the low-grade steel anchors. In this manner of construction, a single strand of wire many miles long can be continuously looped back and forth across the expanse of the bridge, with no joints in the strand. Since joints in high-strength steel wire are hard to achieve, minimizing the joints is desirable.

The force transfer can be thought of as similar to the example of a high-strength steel column resting on a steel plate that distributes the force over the surface of a concrete pad, which, in turn, distributes the force over the soil on which it rests.

For suspension systems in which the suspension elements are attached to anchorages, the structural system is completed by the earth, which serves as the compression element that holds the anchorages apart. Figure 9.17 shows suspension elements with ends restrained against horizontal movement by stays running to anchorages in the earth. Figure 9.18 shows the system torn apart into its constituent freebodies.

The concrete anchorages must be large enough to distribute the horizontal forces over a sufficient area of soil that the stresses in the soil are not excessive. If the soil is of poor quality, using a suspension structure with the tension elements anchored in the ground is not a practical option. The structure in Figure 9.19 is an example of the structure in the two preceding figures.

In Figure 9.20, clamps are used to prevent the vertical suspenders from sliding down the sloped portion of the suspension element. The tangential forces along the suspension cable are generated by friction. The high-strength cable is too hard to drill and will detemper, if welded, so surface connections, such as by friction or gluing, are the only means to generate the tangential force. This friction connection is the same method used on very large suspension structures.

In the preceding structures, the walking surface between the towers and the anchorages is supported by the ground, rather than by the tension element. In that zone, there is no load on the tension element except for the self-weight of the element. The curvature in that zone is minimal. The situation here is in contrast to that shown in Figure 9.21, in which the portion of the working surface between the tower and the anchorage is supported by the suspension element. In this image, the towers are located at the quarter points of the suspension element and the cables between the towers, and the anchorages serve the dual function of supporting the roadbed (so they are curved) and anchoring the suspension system to the ground.

Figure 9.22 shows the preceding system broken into its constituent freebodies. In this diagram, the towers are at the quarter points of the suspension system, which is the customary geometric form. In some sense, each tower is supporting half the bridge at the center point of that half of the bridge. This produces cable shapes that are symmetric about the centerline of the tower (see Figure 9.23).

The symmetric shape shown in Figure 9.23 is normally preferred in suspension structures. However, sometimes the landform prompts placement of the towers in a slightly different location. In the case of the Golden Gate Bridge, the rocky support surface available below the water line falls off rapidly. Moving the towers all the way to the quarter points would have required constructing extremely tall towers and working in deep water. As a design compromise, the towers were located slightly away from the quarter points toward the anchorages, as shown in Figure 9.24. Note the different shape for the cables between the towers, as compared with the portions of the cable between the towers and the anchorages. This geometry is a little more complicated to design, and it results in a somewhat higher force in the cable. The force in the cable is dictated by the length of the span between the towers. If the towers could have been moved farther out, the force in the cable would have been somewhat

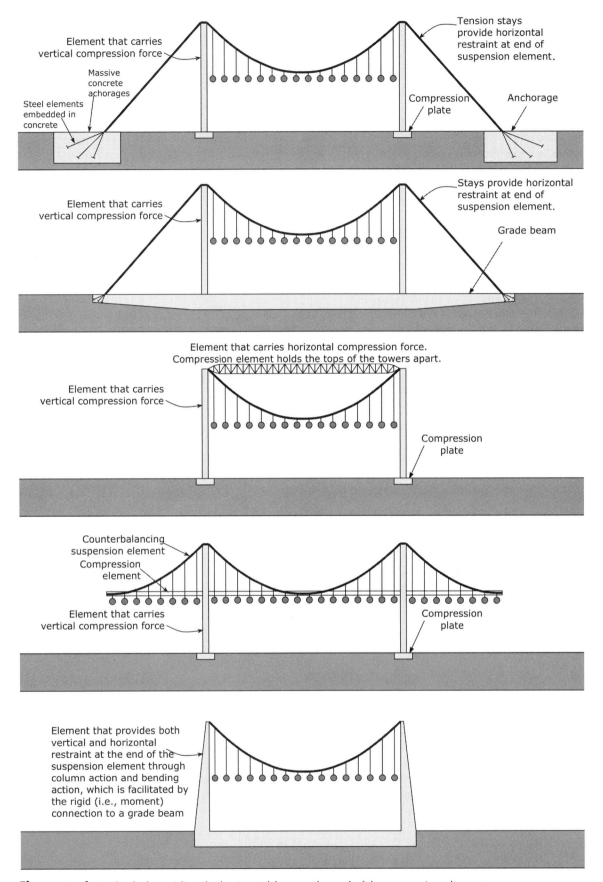

Figure 9.16 Method of providing the horizontal force at the end of the suspension element.

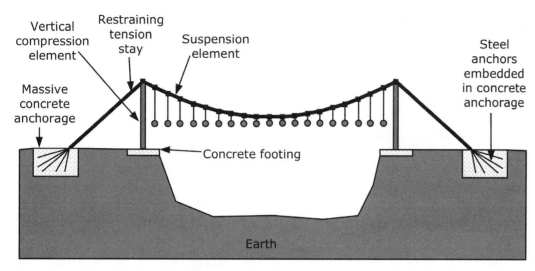

Figure 9.17 Ends of suspension element restrained against horizontal movement by stays running to anchorages in the earth.

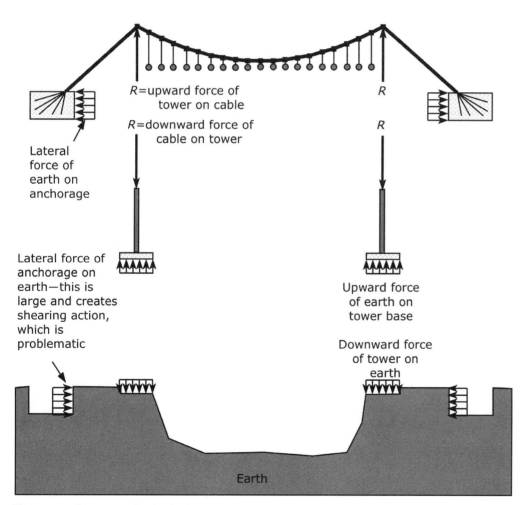

Figure 9.18 Creating freebody diagrams.

Figure 9.19 Ends of suspension element restrained against horizontal movement by stays running to anchorages in the earth.

Figure 9.20 Clamps hold suspenders against sliding down the suspension element.

smaller. However, in this situation, the cost savings in reduced cable force would not have paid for the added cost of the towers.

As discussed previously, the concrete anchorages must be large enough to distribute the horizontal forces over a sufficient area of soil, so that the stresses in the soil are not excessive. If the soil is of poor quality, using a suspension structure with the tension elements anchored in the ground is not a practical option. In the case of the Golden Gate Bridge, there was actually a rock mountain available to which the cables could be secured. Figure 9.25 shows the strategic location of the tower at the edge of the water and the anchorage on the other side of the rock mass. Pulling the anchorage loose would require ripping the mountain away. The efficiency and elegance of the high-strength steel spanning system is deceptive, since there are potentially huge costs associated with the hidden anchorages. If there is not an exceptionally solid landform to which the anchorages can be attached, the cost of the anchorages is usually prohibitive.

9.1.2 ADDRESSING SHIFTING LOADS

The primary function of a suspension element is to support gravity loads that are uniformly distributed along the horizontal. Suspension structures supporting live loads or moving vehicular loads are subjected to shifting forces that are not uniformly distributed along the horizontal. These loads cause the suspension element to radically change shape. This change in shape is acceptable in a bridge on a children's playground, where the excitement of the changing shape is stimulating to the curious minds of children playing on the structure, but not acceptable in a bridge handling high-speed vehicular traffic or in a building with glazing in the walls. To deal with shifting loads, some other structural element needs to be included. On the classic suspension bridges, this element

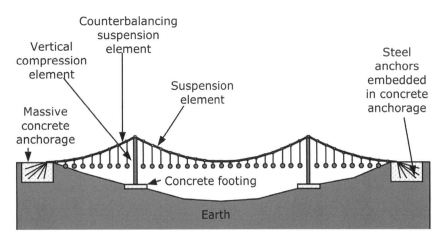

Figure 9.21 Suspension action on both sides of each tower.

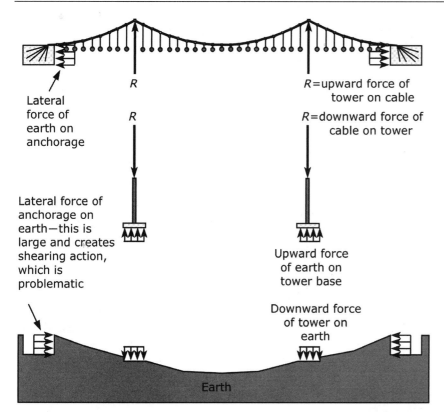

Figure 9.22 Freebody diagrams for the elements in the system shown in Figure 9.21.

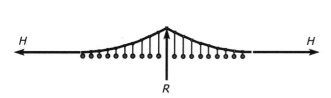

Figure 9.23 Symmetric, draped suspension elements.

Figure 9.25 Anchorage of the Golden Gate Bridge buried in a rock mountain.

Figure 9.24 Asymmetric cables of the Golden Gate Bridge.

is a truss along the side of the bridge roadbed. As compared with that of the suspension element, the effective structural depth of this truss is very small, as indicated in the preceding photographs of the Golden Gate Bridge. The suspension element is the primary load-carrying element, and the truss is there to "smooth out" the nonuniform load. This deep truss also helps inhibit wind-induced oscillations such as occurred in the failed Tacoma Narrows Bridge. In some cases, the depth of these trusses becomes so great that a second roadbed can be placed at the lower chords of the trusses, such as is the case for the Oakland-San Francisco Bay Bridge shown in Figure 9.26. This structure begins to suggest architectural possibilities, some of which are discussed later in this chapter.

The stiffening effect of the side trusses presents an interesting challenge during construction. As parts of the trusses are added, the shape of the suspension element changes in response to the added forces. To avoid pulling the towers to the side in a way that would severely stress the tower base, the trusses must be added in symmetric increments. In the case of the Bay Bridge, they were added starting at the middle of the spans and growing symmetrically toward each tower. In the case of the Golden Gate Bridge, the truss increments were added starting at the towers and moving symmetrically out from the towers. During construction, adding increments of the trusses causes significant deformations in the shape of the suspension element, which achieves the correct shape only after all the truss elements have been added, as demonstrated in Figure 9.27. In the first image, the suspension element is shown with minimal load. The second image demonstrates the response of the suspension element to a localized, asymmetric force, with the associated disturbing deformation. The remaining images show the progressive effects of adding weights symmetrically, starting at the center of the suspension span. This would be the mode of adding weight in the construction of the Oakland-San Francisco Bay Bridge.

To avoid inducing excessive stresses in the trusses while the suspension elements have the "wrong" shape, the bottom chords of the trusses can be left unbolted. Adding the last element of the trusses brings the suspension elements into the perfect shape, so that the bolt holes in the truss bottom chords line up, thereby allowing the bolts to be inserted. This tendency of suspension elements to change shape can be a serious concern during

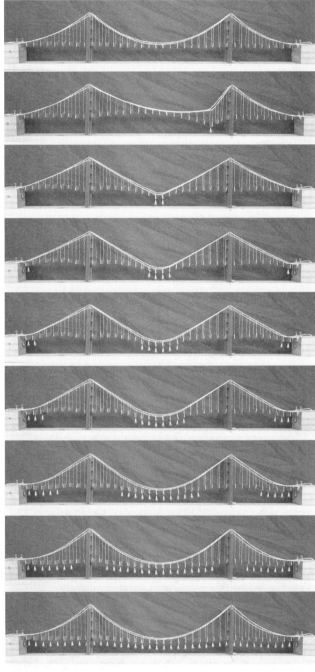

Figure 9.26 Deep trusses accommodating a second level at bottom chords of trusses.

Figure 9.27 Effect of local loads on the shape of the suspension element.

construction. Often, special measures, such as temporary scaffolding or adding false weights, are required during construction to compensate for the variability of the tension member geometry. These issues are discussed later in this chapter in regard to Dulles Airport and the Federal Reserve Bank.

Figure 9.28 shows a bridge with the stiffening effect of the side trusses. The first image is the unloaded bridge. The second image shows the deformation under a symmetric, non-uniform load. As compared with the sequence of images in Figure 9.27, it is apparent that the side trusses in Figure 9.28 are making a major contribution in distributing the localized load over the suspension cable, so that the suspension cable does not radically change shape. The third image shows the effect of adding all the weights to one side of the bridge. In this bridge, the side trusses and roadbeds on top and bottom are creating a tubular structure that is very effective in resisting the torsional deformation that would normally be induced by the load concentrated on one side of the roadway.

If the local soil is poor, or if there are reasons that it is not possible to get the tension elements down to the earth, one may choose to introduce a compression element that absorbs the inward thrust of the suspension elements. For example, on the classic suspension bridge, the roadbed structure can be made suitable for resisting compression and the cables can be connected to the end of that structure, as shown in Figure 9.29.

Figure 9.30 shows the constituent freebodies of the system in Figure 9.29. In Figure 9.30, anchorages have been provided to address two requirements:

1. Keep both towers from toppling over, either to the left or to the right.
2. Prevent vertical movement of the bridge roadbed at the end of the bridge, where substantial movement could result from the shifting load of the traffic on the bridge. (Having a 3 ft step suddenly occur at the end of the bridge would be very hard on automotive traffic attempting to drive onto the bridge at high speed.)

A structure can also be elevated, where anchorages are simply not available. Pierre Luigi Nervi's Burgo Paper Mill (Mantua, Italy), as seen in Figure 9.31, is an example of this kind of structure. The horizontal force on the end of the suspension elements is provided by the compression elements in the roof. The longitudinal lateral

Figure 9.28 Benefit of side trusses and tubular structure in resisting deformation under nonuniform and asymmetric loads.

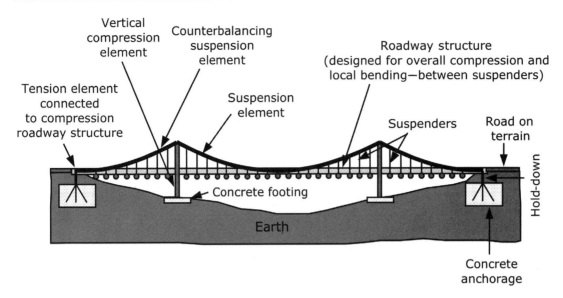

Figure 9.29 Suspension element with ends restrained against horizontal movement by connection to a compression element in the road structure.

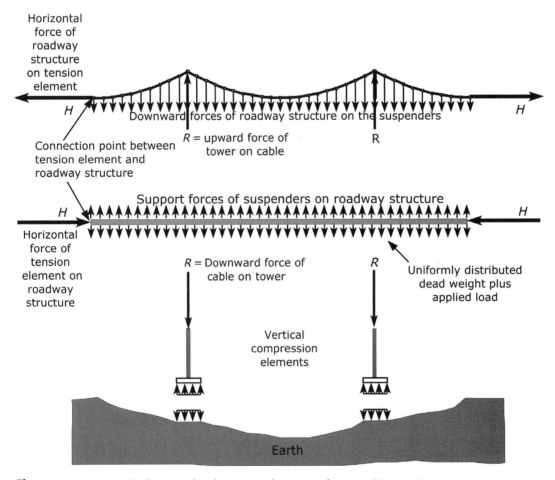

Figure 9.30 Freebody diagrams for elements in the system shown in Figure 9.29.

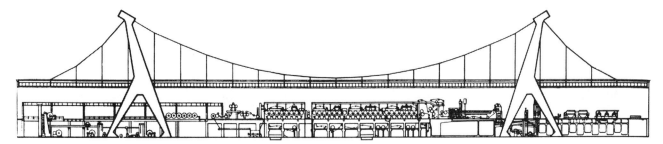

Figure 9.31 Burgo Paper Mill, designed by Pierre Luigi Nervi.

stabilization function has been taken over by the bipod bases of the towers. The transverse lateral stabilization is provided by the rigid-frame action of the vertical supports, which are moment-connected to the horizontal beam at the top and another horizontal beam just above the roof level. The roof is held down by the vertical mullions forming the walls around the building. Some of these mullions can be removed to allow for changing out of equipment. However, as few as possible should be removed, and only when wind loads will be low. Having a large opening in the wall aggravates the wind uplift on the roof, producing a wind overpressure inside the building that adds to the suction on the top of the building.

Figure 9.32 shows the horizontal and vertical elements forming the rigid frames that resist the transverse lateral forces. It also shows how the weight of the trusswork has been increased along the lines where connections are made to the suspension elements. This increased material allows that portion of the trusswork to serve its compressive function, as counterpoint to the tension in the suspension elements.

Thus far, the discussion has included using heavy anchorages and using horizontal compression members as

ways of providing the horizontal outward force required to allow the tensile element to function as a spanning element. There is also the brute force method of making the vertical support elements so that their bending capacity will resist the inward pull of the suspension element. In other words, the designer is asking these vertical support elements to resist the inward pull as beams cantilevering out of the ground. There is a price to be paid for this approach, since bending is generally less efficient than simple compression or tension. These vertical cantilevered beams must either be buried in huge foundations or have a grade beam stabilizing them.

Figure 9.33 illustrates some of the issues associated with this approach to supporting the suspension elements. The diagram in (a) shows an arrangement where the beam-columns simply continue down into the earth. This is something like what Frank Lloyd Wright referred to as the "tap root" footing. As the suspension element pulls inward on the tops of the vertical beam-columns, compression develops in the soil in such a way as to resist this moment. However, soils are a poor structural material. At the interface between the soil and the column, the soil is the weak element and controls the required geometry of the structure at that point. In order to transfer sufficient force between the soil and the vertical beam-column (at the lower stress capacity of the soil), the faces of the beam-columns must be broadened at that interface. Some of the inefficiencies of the soil can be alleviated by using a floor structure between the beam-columns to absorb the inward force of the beam-columns as shown in Figure 9.33(b). Then the floor structure acts as a horizontal column under the influence of the vertical beam-columns as they tilt inward.

Figure 9.34(a) shows a grade beam taking on all of the functions of stabilizing the vertical beam-columns. The approach of using cantilevered vertical beam-columns, emerging out of a deep grade beam, is more efficient than trying to use the compression in the soil to develop the structural capacity of the system. However, it is still inefficient as compared with what we typically expect with a predominantly tensile structure. The structural efficiency can be improved if a lower floor can be added, as shown in Figure 9.34. The top floor plate can then be

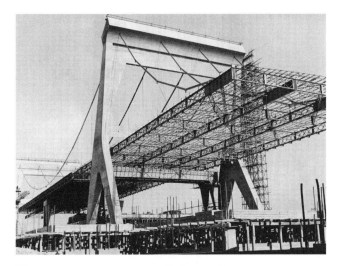

Figure 9.32 Burgo Paper Mill, designed by Pierre Luigi Nervi.

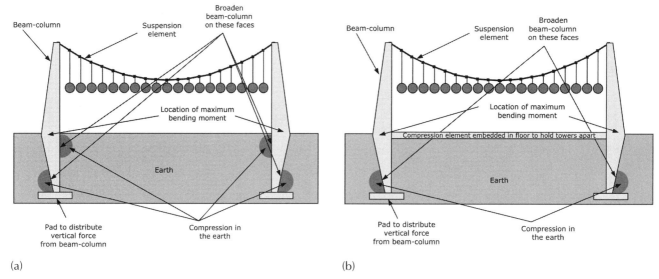

Figure 9.33 "Taproot" model of stability.

utilized as a compression element and the bottom floor as a tension element. In this manner, the lever arm for the floor elements acting on the vertical beam-columns is greater than the lever arm for the grade beam.

The Dulles Airport uses beam-columns to support its suspension roof (see Figure 9.35). The Dulles Airport design accomplishes the several things:

- The outward slope of the beam-columns locates the mass of the beam-columns where it can help resist the inward pull of the cables in the roof.
- The outward-sloping walls and the ample overhangs provide panoramic views while blocking most of the glare and excess solar gains through the glazed envelope.

- The outward slope of the beam-columns and the accentuated taper of the beam-columns are structurally very expressive and elegant.
- The design avoids compression struts across the roof, which would diminish the elegance of the form.
- The design avoids tension elements and anchorages that would interfere with movement around the exterior of the building.

To address some of the structural problem posed by the inward pull of the suspension cables, the massive beam-columns were tilted outward so that the dead weight of the beam-columns would partially offset the inward pull of the suspension elements and so that the forces delivered to the beam-columns would be more nearly axial. Some

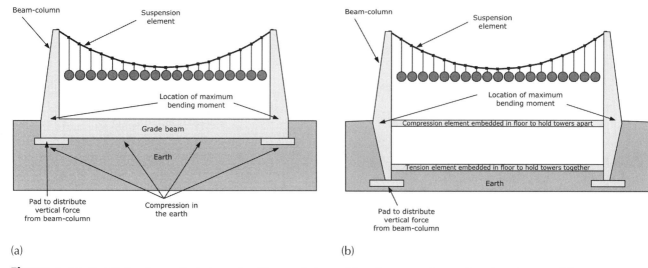

Figure 9.34 Stabilizing the vertical elements with a grade beam (a) and compression and tension elements (b).

Figure 9.35 Dulles Airport (Architect: Eero Saarinen; engineering: Severud and Associates.)

Figure 9.36 Steel rebar in supports of Dulles Airport. (Image courtesy of Erik V. Mehlman, AIA.)

people are under the impression that the weight of these outward-leaning beam-columns is adequate to offset the full inward pull of the roof cables. A detailed analysis will demonstrate that this is not the case. The tilting of the beam-columns is offsetting only a portion of the inward pull of the roof cables. This point is powerfully demonstrated by the construction photographs in Figures 9.36 and 9.37, showing the reinforcing steel in the beam-columns.

At the base of each beam-column, there is an extreme concentration of tension steel on the outside of the beam-column, suggesting that the beam action of the element is to resist a net inward pull. The beam-columns are sculpted to be thickest at the level of the top floor, where the moment in the beam-columns is highest.

9.1.3 WIND LOADING ON SUSPENSION STRUCTURES

An extremely lightweight roofing structure can be made using high-strength steel suspension elements covered with lightweight corrugated metal decking. Wind suction can cause wild oscillations and eventually fail such an unrestrained structure, as suggested in Figure 9.38.

Dead weight can be added to hold a suspension structure down against the upward suction of the wind. For example, in the Dulles Airport roof, concrete planks were laid across the steel suspension elements (see Figure 9.39).

If the dead weight added exceeds the wind suction, the structure will be held down against the upward suction of the wind. However, if the structure is still very flexible, the wind can cause a mode of oscillation in which the mass "sloshes" back and forth, as shown in the two diagrams in Figure 9.40.

To eliminate the sloshing action, either (1) energy-absorbing materials must be added, or (2) the roof structure must be stiffened. Designers of the Dulles Airport did both, using a layer of concrete on top of the prefabricated concrete planks, which helped to dampen motion, and then adding an integrated beam by allowing the monolithic concrete pour to go down between the planks, creating a concrete T-beam that stiffened the structure.

Figure 9.37 Steel rebar in supports of Dulles Airport. (Image courtesy of Erik V. Mehlman, AIA.)

If there is adequate dead weight or if there are appropriate tie-downs in the other parts of the structure, it may not be necessary to add dead weight to the suspension roof, since stiffening the roof is all that is necessary to stabilize it against wind loading. The roof can be stiffened in a number of ways, such as by filling the space between

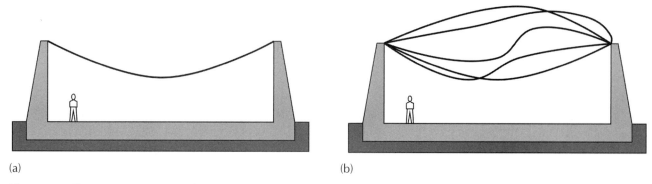

(a)   (b)

Figure 9.38 Gravity structure (a) does not necessarily resist wind well (b).

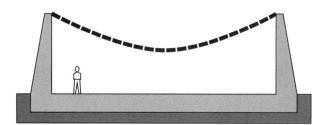

Figure 9.39 Using dead weight to keep the tensile roof from kiting.

top and bottom skins with material that connects the two skins together to create a stressed-skin roof. Examples of this technique include:

- Using structural plastic foam in the core.
- Providing shear diaphragms between top and bottom skins. Then the roof behaves like an I-beam with multiple webs and very wide flanges (the skins on the top and bottom of the sandwich panel being the flanges).
- Using truss webbing between top and bottom skins.

See Figure 9.41.

This deformation involving a shifting from one side to the other (sloshing) does not occur only with wind. It can also occur under shifting live loads, such as construction loads. This posed an interesting challenge in construction of the Dulles Airport, where concrete was being poured on a roof supported by thin cables that would exhibit sub-stantial deformation in response to nonuniform loads. The concrete could not be put on rapidly enough to ensure that the entire uniform roof load would be in place before any curing of the concrete occurred. There was a substantial risk of damage to the partially cured concrete as the shape of the roof changed under the influence of each new load of concrete deposited on the roof. To avoid this problem, the entire roof of the building was loaded with sandbags before the concrete pouring began. As concrete was added, sandbags were removed in a coordinated manner to keep the load uniform and avoid deformation. It was also important to pour the concrete on a day when wind would not induce a sloshing motion, which could also damage the partially cured concrete.

The building in Figure 9.42 uses curved I-sections as suspension elements under gravity loads. The stiffness of the I-sections serves to resist the bending associated with the wind-induced sloshing deformation discussed earlier. This stiffness also allows the roof to work as an arch in compression, under wind suction. This is a lightweight roof that would kite without that compressive action.

The sloshing movement in suspension elements can sometimes manifest itself in ways that mask the underlying causes, as shown in Figure 9.43. These oscillations were induced by a steady wind of 40 mph that was sustained long enough for the oscillations to build to this extraordinary amplitude. This bridge was so flexible that it was a natural oscillator in the presence of a steady wind,

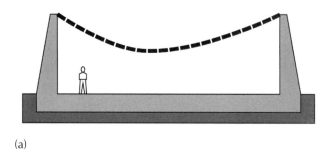 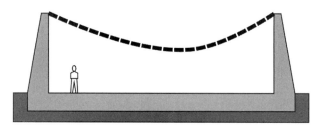

(a)   (b)

Figure 9.40 Moving to the left (a) and then to the right (b).

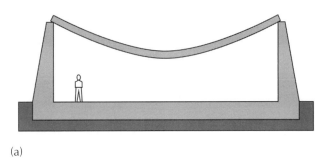

(a)

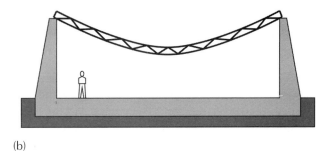

(b)

Figure 9.41 Sandwich-panel (a) and trussed roof (b).

similar to the reed of a reed instrument that vibrates under the influence of breath blowing over it at a steady rate. When the bridge was viewed along the length, the overwhelming visual impression was of an extreme torsional oscillation of the roadbed, twisting clockwise near one quarter point of the main span and counterclockwise near the other quarter point of the main span. When viewed from the side, as in the photograph in Figure 9.43, it is clear that the cable on the near side is sloshing down and to the right at the quarter point near the right end of the main span and the cable on the far side is sloshing down and to the left at the quarter point near the left end of the main span. These deformations are producing a clockwise twist at the far quarter point and a counterclockwise twist at the near quarter point. It is in the nature of the suspension elements to allow these movements to occur freely, without offering any resistance. Since the suspension elements cannot resist these movements, some other elements must provide the resistance. Typically, this is one of the roles of the trusses or beams along the side of the roadbed. Those trusses or beams are provided primarily for resisting shifting live loads. However, the cable shape changes associated with shifting live loads are similar to the shape changes apparent in Figure 9.43 (except that in the case of shifting live loads, the cables are typically sloshing in the same

direction). Therefore, the trusses or beams along the side of the roadbed are very appropriate for resisting these wind-induced oscillations. Unfortunately, in the case of the Tacoma Narrows Bridge, the beams along the side were not deep enough to serve this role. The span between towers was approximately 2,400 ft, and the depth of the side beams was about 8 ft. This is a span/depth ratio of 300, which is absurdly low. The extreme flexibility of the structure left it vulnerable to wind-induced oscillations. Using deep trusses in place of the side girders would also have improved the Tacoma Narrows Bridge, since such trusses tend to shed wind load better. Finally, adding horizontal trusses, top and bottom, further stiffens the bridge by creating a trussed tube, such as the one shown in Figure 9.48(a). These trussed tubes are extremely resistant to torsional deformations, such as those exhibited in the failure of the Tacoma Narrows Bridge.

In addition to deep side trusses and tubular trusses, inverted suspension cables or straight stays could have been used to help stabilize the Tacoma Narrows Bridge. This measure could have been implemented as a quick fix when the first serious oscillations were observed. However, the designer argued that what was happening

Figure 9.42 Lowara Offices, Vicenza, Italy. (Architect: Renzo Piano. Photograph by Gianni Berengo Gardin.)

Figure 9.43 Tacoma Narrows Bridge. (Image courtesy of University of Washington Libraries, Special Collections.)

should not be happening because it was contrary to the theory that he used in the design of the bridge. While he was defending his theory, disaster struck. This bridge provided many important lessons, one of which is: When something is clearly going wrong, fix it by any means possible as fast as possible, and debate the merits of the theory after things have been shored up enough to be safe.

Countertensioned cables offer an interesting method of resisting wind load. The structure shown in Figure 9.44 is an example of that approach.

In this structure, the set of cables with the normal drape is there to resist gravity loads, such as the roof decking or snow. Another set of cables is inverted and is there to resist wind suction upward. These two sets of cables are held together by vertical ties. The system should be countertensioned to the point that wind will not induce flutter in the roof. From a structural logic point of view, this structure is more satisfying than the Dulles Airport, because:

- The structure takes better advantage of the efficiency of tensile elements, using them to resist both gravity and wind forces.
- The inward pull of the cables is resisted by compression rings, thereby avoiding the inefficiencies of the extreme bending moments that had to be addressed in the Dulles Airport.

However, the Dulles Airport is a grand space and an incredibly beautiful structure that is significant for more than just structural efficiency. The structure shown in Figure 9.44 also relates to Section 9.2, "Cable and Fabric Structures," wherein countertensioned tension elements are explored as a theme.

An interesting variation of the structure shown in Figure 9.44 is to use the gravity cables as part of the reinforcement for a thin-shell concrete roof. That concrete forms the structural roof surface and also serves as an inverted dome to resist wind suction. In other words, the roof skin, acting in compression, allows the elimination

Figure 9.44 Countertensioning cables that are mutually stabilizing. (Digital model by author; rendering by James Sweeney.)

Figure 9.45 Oakland Alameda County Athletic Coliseum.

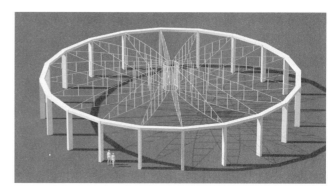

Figure 9.46 Cable truss roof. (Digital model by author; rendering by James Sweeney.)

of the wind-resisting cables. An example of this approach is the Oakland Alameda County Athletic Coliseum, in Oakland, California, designed by Skidmore, Owings & Merrill, LLP, shown in Figure 9.45. This structure is also distinguished in its approach to lateral stabilization, wherein every gravity-resisting element supporting the roof is also active in resisting lateral loads.

A bowl-shaped roof structure presents some difficulties in regard to getting water off the roof. An alternative to this structure is to put the inverted wind cables above and the draped gravity cables below, held apart by struts, as shown in Figure 9.46.

This is slightly less efficient in that the ties have been replaced with compression struts. However, it is more efficient in that there is only one compression ring and it now sheds water, assuming that the water-shedding roof surface is attached at the level of the wind cables on top. This kind of roof can also be used as a linear system. For example, the roof of the Dulles Airport could have been made using inverted wind cables above and draped gravity cables below. However, in linear form it would be less efficient, since the compression ring would be replaced by the rigid bending elements. An important question is, would it still have the artistry of the Dulles Airport?

Bowl-shaped roofs are not the only ones that pose challenges in getting water off their surfaces. In a deluge of rain, any very large roof area that is not favorably sloped can require special measures to remove water. For example, in the Dulles Airport the aerodynamic-looking element coming down from the center of the roof is a rain leader, taking water from the roof (see Figure 9.47).

Figure 9.47 Leader at center of the Dulles Airport roof.

(a)

(b)

Figure 9.48 Horizontal trusses in the Golden Gate Bridge (a) and the Oakland-San Francisco Bay Bridge (b). (Image of Golden Gate Bridge courtesy of Roy Abernathy.)

Lateral Wind Forces on a Suspension Structure

Suspension cables and suspenders draped in vertical planes are useless in resisting lateral forces of wind. The slightest breeze can cause substantial lateral movement. Lateral wind forces on a bridge roadway are resisted by two elements:

- Horizontal trusses at the tops and bottoms of the side trusses
- A concrete roadbed heavily reinforced with steel, which acts as a horizontal beam

The horizontal trusses absorb wind load during construction, and the roadbed beam assists after the concrete has had time to cure properly.

The photograph in Figure 9.48(a) is an upward view of the completed Golden Gate Bridge, showing the crossing web members in the horizontal truss at the level of the bottom chords of the side trusses. Although they are more difficult to see, there are also crossing web members just below the roadbed, at the top chords of the side trusses. These web members forming the horizontal trusses were installed during the erection of the steelwork, before the concrete roadbed was poured. Without these horizontal trusses, the slightest wind would have produced sufficient lateral movement to upset the curing process for the concrete in the roadbed. These horizontal trusses in conjunction with the vertical trusses on the side of the bridge form a trussed tube with a depth of roughly 30 ft and a width of roughly 70 ft. The Oakland-San Francisco Bay Bridge shown in Figure 9.48(b) uses a K-truss pattern for the horizontal truss resisting lateral forces.

The roles of all of the horizontal elements are crucial, which is apparent in a photograph of the underside of the Golden Gate Bridge shown in Figure 9.49.

Notice how narrow and long the horizontal trusses are. The span between towers for the bridge is 4,200 ft. Relative to horizontal forces, the span/depth ratio for these trusses is roughly (4,200 ft/70 ft) = 60, which means a very shallow structure. What makes this extreme ratio acceptable is that the horizontal structure is continuous past the towers, where the lateral constraints occur,

which stiffens the spanning system. Another factor is that an open bridge can tolerate greater lateral deflections than would be tolerated in a building enclosed in a brittle material such as glass. However, in spite of these factors, this bridge has been designed to the limits of acceptable tolerances. The problem of lateral forces under wind loading concerned one of the chief engineers for the Golden Gate Bridge sufficiently that he had the original steel railing on the bridge replaced with a sparser railing that presented a smaller effective cross section to wind forces.

Lateral forces on the roadway are carried to the towers, which subsequently carry those forces to the foundations of the towers. Figure 9.50 shows the towers of the Golden Gate Bridge. Above the roadbed, the forces on a tower are the wind on the tower itself and the force of the wind on the cables. These forces are resisted, in the case of this bridge, by the rigid-frame structure between the roadbed and the top of the tower. The lateral forces on the tower increase substantially in the portion of the tower below the roadbed, where the forces on the top section of the tower are supplemented by the extreme lateral forces delivered by the roadbed. The larger forces

Figure 9.49 Horizontal spanning trusses spanning from tower to tower in the Golden Gate Bridge. (Image courtesy of Roy Abernathy.)

Figure 9.50 Full triangulation of the tower below the roadway. (Image courtesy of Roy Abernathy.)

below the roadbed are resisted by fully triangulated bracing in the tower. The use of the rigid-frame bracing above the roadbed and fully triangulated bracing below the roadbed is one of the particularly expressive aspects of the Golden Gate Bridge towers.

In the case of the Dulles Airport, the beamlike elements cantilevering out of the footing resist both the inward pull of the cables and the lateral forces of the wind. A particularly appealing feature of the Dulles Airport is the way that it addresses the curtain walls. On the two long faces, the horizontal mullions are curved, allowing them to work in tension to resist wind against the glass. These tension mullions can be visually very light, and they are harmonious in form with the draped roof. The end walls are flat and are backed up with light, airy, cleanly detailed, and elegant trusses (see Figure 9.51).

9.1.4 FEDERAL RESERVE BANK BUILDING

The Federal Reserve Bank (FRB) in Minneapolis, Minnesota, was designed by Gunnar Birkerts and Associates, with engineering by Leslie Robertson and Associates. The structural concept for this building was based strongly on engineering precedents set in construction of the great ve-

hicular bridgs such as the Golden Gate Bridge. There are two distinct volumes of the building separated by a large open plaza. The lower volume has a variety of long-span, high-bay spaces that do not provide good opportunities to establish a regular array of columns. The decision was made to support the upper volume with a long-span structure, thereby stepping over the complex array of spaces in the lower volume. The resultant design problem was to support ten floors spanning approximately 300 ft between two vertical support structures (see Figure 9.52).

Spanning 300 ft with a commercially loaded floor is a fairly serious structural challenge. Roughly the same challenge was met by Skidmore, Owings & Merrill (SOM) in the Broadgate Exchange House discussed in Chapter 8. In that case, SOM used seven-story-high parabolic arches to span the width of a city block. The Broadgate Exchange House was designed and built after the Federal Reserve Bank (FRB) and may have benefited from the experience gained on the FRB.

If an attempt was made to span the full 300 ft with plate girders, they would have a depth of approximately $L/20$ = 300 ft/20 = 15 ft, which would consume the entire height of each floor in solid web beam—making the façade a solid mass with no windows. Parallel-chord

Figure 9.51 Glass curtain wall of Dulles Airport.

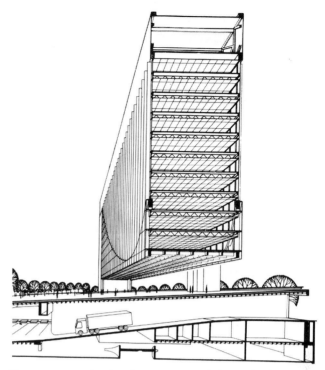

Figure 9.52 Sectional perspective of the Federal Reserve Bank. (Image courtesy of Gunnar Birkerts and Associates.)

trusses could provide light and some views, although every opening would be interrupted by truss webs (see Figure 9.53(a)). The system of trusses has some interesting structural issues. In the construction, the bottom chord of one floor would be connected with the top chord of the floor below. In that case, the tension in the bottom chord of the truss above would tend to counteract the compression in the top chord of the truss below. This "lost stress" is a manifestation of the fact that joining two trusses together creates a new truss that is twice as deep as the old truss. The deeper truss is more structurally efficient than the old one, and the forces in the truss chords are lower than they were before the two trusses were joined together. If all of the trusses are joined along their common chords, it creates a "truss network" with a depth of ten stories (approximately 140 ft) that spans approximately 300 ft between the two support structures (see Figure 9.53(b)). This new spanning system has excellent proportions, with a span-to-depth ratio of about 2 rather than about 20, which it would be for one truss alone. An unsatisfying aspect of this design is that the intermediate chord members are not very active. The network is acting more like a beam than a truss, in the sense that the stresses are not uniform over the cross section. The system has many parts to manufacture and assemble, and it would tend to be visually very noisy.

It would be desirable to generate a spanning system that is drastically simpler. There should be fewer members and, particularly, there should be fewer types of members. One approach to making the system struc-

turally more efficient, as well as simpler, is to eliminate the chord members at the intermediate floors and concentrate the "spanning material" at the extreme top and extreme bottom of the "spanning façade." Then the entire horizontal "chord material" is concentrated where it has the best lever arm. The diagram in Figure 9.54 shows the new configuration, with massive chord members at the top of the tenth floor and the bottom of the first floor and continuous web members running the full ten stories from the top chord to the bottom chord. The number of chord members has been reduced from eleven to two, and the number of web members has been reduced to one-tenth as many.

There is still a problem with the diagonals obstructing the view. It would be preferable to find a single structural element that would serve the structural function of the diagonal web members. Then the number of elements serving that structural function could be reduced again by a significant factor. The structural function of all of the diagonals and the bottom chord can be performed with a single suspension element (see Figures 9.55 and 9.56).

The diagram in Figure 9.57 is an axonometric detail of a section of the wall, showing the following:

- Steel cable suspension elements
- I-section suspension element
- Vertical 8 in. I-sections (columns) above the suspension element

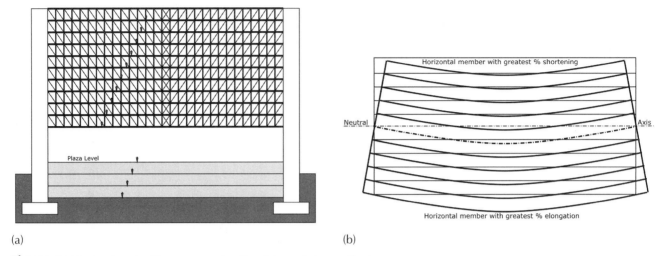

(a)   (b)

Figure 9.53 A network of trusses spanning the distance between the towers.

- Vertical 1 in. × 8 in. steel plates (hangers) below the suspension element
- Floor trusses attaching to those vertical elements
- Concrete slab floor diaphragms
- Deep mullions to add drama to the 8 in. I-section columns
- Recessed glazing above the I-section suspension element
- Front-mounted glazing below the I-section suspension element

In the Federal Reserve Bank Building:

1. The suspension element is parabolic.
2. The suspension element is the primary load-bearing element in supporting the uniform loads of the floors.
3. Each suspension element consists of two parts: high-strength steel cables and a 36 in.-deep I-section.

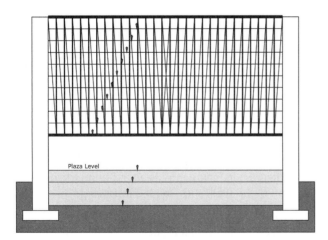

Figure 9.54 Using a truss of depth equal to the building height.

4. The steel cables are the primary support for the dead load of the structure. During construction, the cables were periodically posttensioned to counteract the deflection that occurred with the casting of the concrete in each floor deck. Once the final posttensioning was performed, the dead load was taken care of for the life of the building.
5. The 36 in.-deep I-section is the primary support for live load. Live load varies over time, causing movement that could potentially damage the glazing and/or be disturbing to the building occupants. Since deflection is a primary design criterion for the live load, using more steel is crucial. The steel in an I-section is slightly stiffer and much cheaper than steel cable. Therefore, the economical way to achieve greater stiffness is with an I-section, rather than with steel cables. This I-section is primarily serving a tension function and should not be thought of as an I-beam, since it is not a major bending element in the system.
6. The sag of the suspension element is ten floors, which is approximately half of the span.
7. The depth of the truss across the top of the building is about two floors, which is about one-tenth of the span of the structure and about one-fifth of the sag of the suspension element.
8. The depth of the cross section of the I-section in the suspension element is 36 in., which is about one-tenth of the depth of the truss across the top. This reconfirms the point made earlier, that in the context of this building, the I-section is not a major bending element.
9. The deep truss at the top works in compression to resist the inward pull of the suspension elements on the tops of the support towers.
10. The truss is the primary spanning element in resisting shifting live loads. This truss is the analog of the

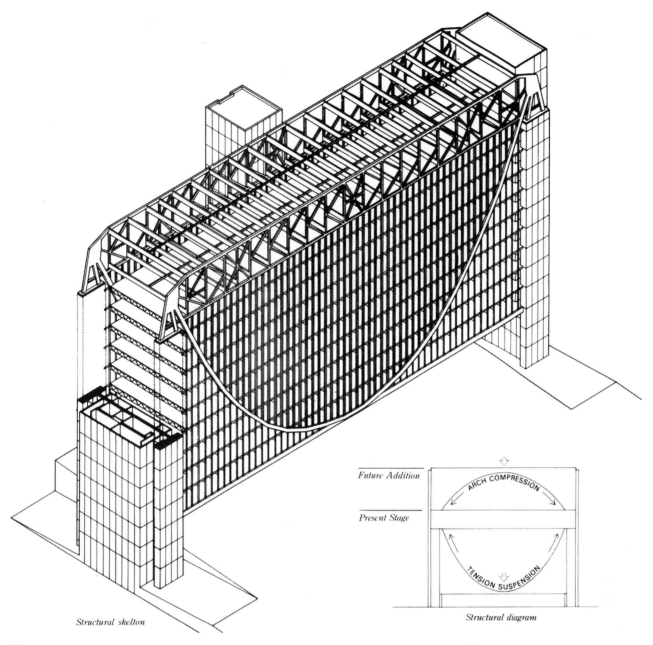

Structural skelton

Future Addition

Present Stage

ARCH COMPRESSION

TENSION SUSPENSION

Structural diagram

Figure 9.55 Isometric of the initial construction of the Federal Reserve Bank. (Image courtesy of Gunnar Birkerts and Associates.)

trusses along the side of the roads on the great vehicular suspension bridges, such as the Golden Gate Bridge and the Oakland-San Francisco Bay Bridge. In the Federal Reserve Bank, the truss is given a more exaggerated depth/length ratio as compared with the vehicular bridges, since the presence of large live loads and brittle glass in the curtain wall make racking of the structure under asymmetric loading an extremely critical concern.

11. The truss increases the robustness of the structure, redistributing loads in the event of failure at the base of one of the columns.

12. Under gravity loads, the floors are supported by trusses spanning from one broad face of the building to the other.

13. The ends of the trusses are supported by vertical members in the broad faces of the towers.

14. The vertical members above the suspension elements are in compression and have a wide-flange cross section.

15. These vertical compression elements can be as slender as they are because they are braced at every floor by the floor diaphragm, which is attached back to the rigid towers. The effective length for buckling of these

columns is the floor-to-floor dimension, rather than the full length of the vertical compression element.

16. The verticals below the suspension elements are in tension and have a cross section that is a 1 in. × 8 in. steel flat bar.

17. The use of the different cross sections of the verticals above and below the suspension element was partly motivated by structural logic and partly chosen as a means to an expressive end.

18. To further express the different nature and function of the vertical elements above and below the suspension element, the glazing above the suspension element is set back and the verticals have a thick, dark cladding that accentuates the visual size of the element. In comparison, the glazing below the suspension element is set flush with the outer face of the flat-bar suspender, thereby minimizing the visual size of the suspenders.

19. The verticals transfer gravity loads to the suspension element, either by pressing down from above or by hanging off the bottom of the suspension element.

20. Every attachment point on the suspension element is carrying the same number of floors and, therefore, has the same amount of load as any other point on the suspension element.

21. The suspension element carries the load to the tops of the towers, which subsequently carry the loads to the foundations.

22. The centerlines of the horizontal truss and the suspension element intersect at a point on the centerline of the tower. In this manner, gravity loads are delivered to the center of the tower, rather than creating an eccentric load that will induce unwanted moment in the tower.

23. Thick, vertical concrete elements have been centered under the intersection of the suspension element and the compression element.

24. These vertical concrete slab columns are knit together with a perpendicular plane of concrete that provides lateral stabilization for the columns under gravity forces.

25. The vertical compression slabs and perpendicular slab together create a huge I-section that is perfectly oriented to resist the horizontal wind force on the large faces of the building.

26. In addition to these huge vertical, concrete I-sections, the towers contain tubular sections that are useful in resisting torsion and lateral forces parallel to the long dimension of the building, which might result from wind on the narrow faces of the building or from seismic inertial forces. The tubular sections are not as deep as the I-sections, reflecting the lesser forces that the tubular sections must resist.

27. The towers are cantilevered beams embedded in the base of the building, where heavy footings and surrounding shear walls encase and stabilize the towers.

28. Under wind pressure on the broad faces of the building, pressure on the glass is transferred to the vertical elements, which transfer the loads to the floor diaphragms, which transfer the loads to the towers, which transfer the loads to the ground.

29. The suspension element in this building is quite a bit heavier than it would be in a suspension bridge of similar span. This should not be very surprising, since, in the building, the suspension element is effectively supporting eleven bridges (ten floors plus the roof), rather than one. Moreover, the loads on one floor of this building are generally greater than we would expect on a bridge supporting vehicular traffic. In a commercial building, we would design for a distributed live load of at least $\frac{80 \#}{ft}$, and in corridors we would have to design for $\frac{100 \#}{ft}$. On average, that would mean about $\frac{90 \#}{ft}$. For ten floors, the load that eventually contributes to the load on the suspension system would have to be ten times as great, or $\frac{900 \#}{ft}$. This load should be compared with a 4,000 lb automobile that, in bumper-to-bumper traffic, takes up an area of about 10 ft × 20 ft, producing a distributed load of $P = \frac{4,000 \#}{10\,ft \cdot 20\,ft} = \frac{20 \#}{ft}$. This is a very light load. In fact, the most intense load to which the Golden Gate Bridge has been exposed was not a rush-hour convoy of trucks, but rather the weight of pedestrians that piled onto the bridge to celebrate the fiftieth anniversary of the bridge. Comparing the typical service loads, the structural burden in the Federal Reserve Bank is on the order of 900/20 = 45 times as great as on a bridge. Even if we take the load of pedestrians on the Golden Gate Bridge as $\frac{100 \#}{ft}$, which is probably close to the load on the day of the fiftieth anniversary, the collective load on all the floors of the Federal Reserve Bank is still about nine times greater than the load on the Golden Gate Bridge.

30. The deflection criteria for the building also affect the size of the suspension element. Glass in the walls makes the building intolerant of deflections induced by changing live loads. Comparatively speaking, the bridge can deflect substantially more than the building without creating functional problems. This explains the presence of the thick I-section in the suspension element in the FRB, which is not present in any standard suspension bridge.

31. The arch of the addition, shown in Figure 9.56, generates an outward horizontal force equal to the inward horizontal pull of the suspension element in the original construction. This would be the case, regardless of the number of floors in the addition, assuming that the rise of the arch is always equal to the full height of the addition (see Figures 9.58 and 9.59).

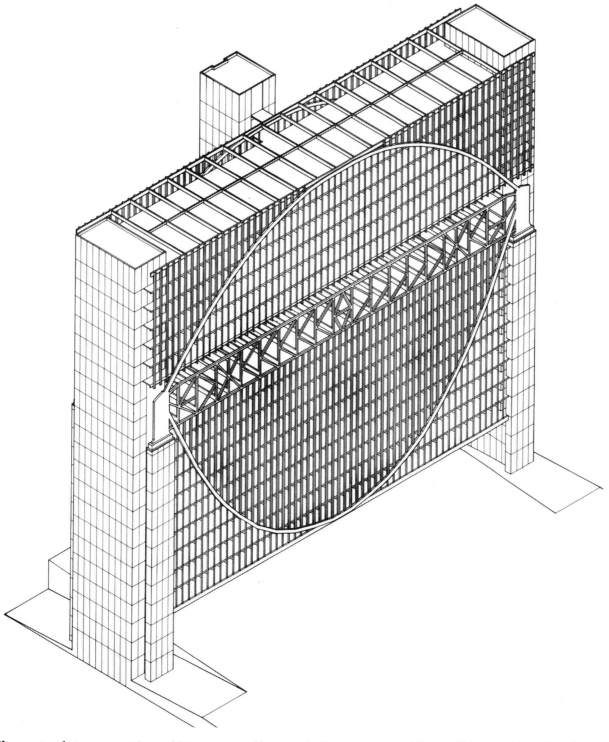

Figure 9.56 Structure with an addition supported by an arch. (Image courtesy of Gunnar Birkerts and Associates.)

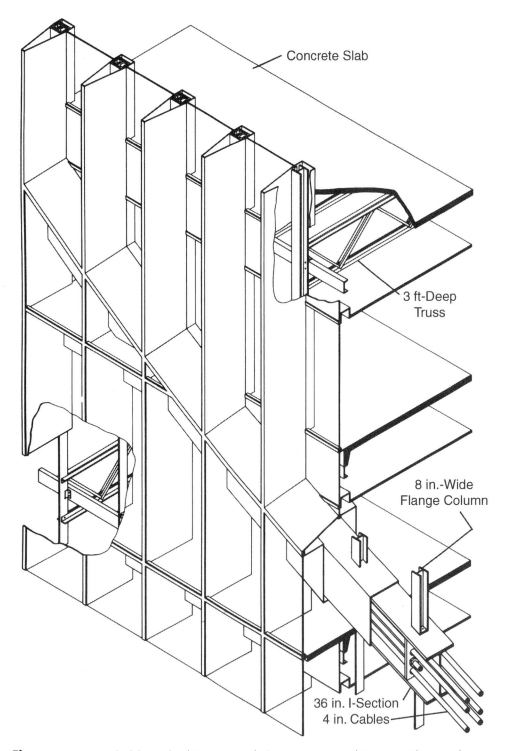

Concrete Slab

3 ft-Deep
Truss

8 in.-Wide
Flange Column

36 in. I-Section
4 in. Cables

Figure 9.57 Detail of the Federal Reserve Bank. (Image courtesy of Gunnar Birkerts and Associates.)

Figure 9.58 Federal Reserve Bank under construction. (Image courtesy of Minnesota Historical Society.)

Figure 9.59 Federal Reserve Bank Building. (Image courtesy of Minnesota Historical Society.)

9.2 Cable and Fabric Structures

9.2.1 CABLE TRUSSES OF THE VIRGINIA BEACH CONVENTION CENTER

For most of the suspension structures described in the previous section, tensile elements were used to support gravity loads, and the forces of wind suction were resisted by adding enough mass to the structure that the wind could not overcome the gravity forces. This approach of stabilizing super-lightweight tension elements using massive amounts of dead weight is oddly contradictory in terms

of design intent. This section addresses a more philosophically consistent design approach, involving the use of two different cable systems to account for forces in two different directions.

The suspension structure shown in Figure 9.60 involves a horizontal strut and a tensile sling for resisting gravity forces.

Under gravity loads, the effective structural depth of the spanning system is the vertical distance between the centroid of the horizontal strut and the centroid of the bottom tension member. Under wind suction, the bottom member would immediately buckle and the structural action would be reduced to the bending resistance of the horizontal strut. Under those circumstances, the effective structural depth of the spanning system would be contained within the vertical dimension of the cross section of the horizontal strut, as that member shifts from being in compression to being in bending. If that member is deep enough, acting as a member in bending, to resist the wind suction, then the roof will be fine. Such a system may be chosen in situations where the gravity forces are substantially larger than the wind forces, so that the deep spanning system is required for the gravity forces but not required for the wind suction forces. For lightweight roofing applications in many locations, the wind forces are comparable in magnitude, or even greater than, the gravity forces. For such situations, it is desirable to have a structural depth for resisting wind forces that is comparable to the structural depth for resisting gravity forces. One way to achieve this effect is to add wind cables (see Figure 9.61).

For the structure shown in Figure 9.61, under gravity forces, the active members are the horizontal compression strut and the lower sling cable (see Figure 9.62).

For the same structure under wind suction, the active members are the horizontal compression strut and the upper sling cable (see Figure 9.63).

There are two tensile systems, one set of tension members for resisting gravity forces and one set for resisting wind suction. For the purposes of this discussion, the terminology is simplified by referring to them as the gravity cables and the wind cables. Figure 9.64 is a classic example of this spanning concept. In thinking about these structures, keep in mind that the lever arm for the structure is always half of the breadth. In other words, the structure looks deeper than it actually is structurally.

For wall systems, wind forces can go in either direction and two sets of wind cables are also required. In this case, they are referred to as the left wind cables and the right wind cables (see Figure 9.64).

For the structure shown in Figure 9.64, under wind forces to the left, the active members are the vertical

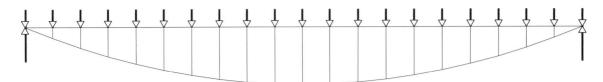

Figure 9.60 Cable for bottom chord and compression strut for top chord.

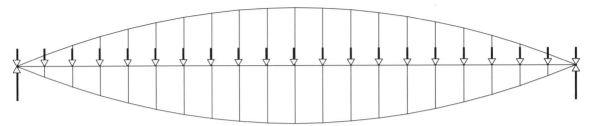

Figure 9.61 Cable truss with cables on top and bottom, with compression strut in the middle.

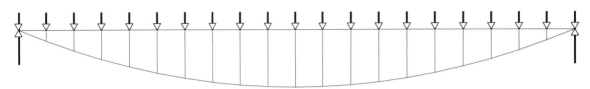

Figure 9.62 Active elements in resisting gravity.

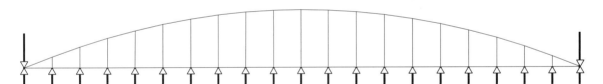

Figure 9.63 Active elements in resisting wind suction.

compression strut, the horizontal struts on the left, and the cable on the left. Under forces to the left, the structural depth is the horizontal distance from the centroid of the vertical compression strut to the centroid of the left cable. Under wind forces to the right, the active members are the vertical compression strut, the horizontal struts on the right, and the cable on the right. Under forces to the right, the structural depth is the horizontal distance from the centroid of the vertical compression strut to the centroid of the right cable. In essence, there are always two sets of tension elements that must be paid for, one of which is not active under any given loading condition. The need to pay for two sets of tension elements tends to offset some of the economic benefits derived from the structural efficiency of super-lightweight tension elements. However, sometimes structural elegance and the

lacy, diaphanous appearance of the structure is a greater motivation than minimizing first-cost of the building. Figure 9.65 shows a beautiful example of such a cable truss system. It is part of the glass curtain wall for the Virginia Beach Convention Center (Architects and Engineers: Skidmore, Owings & Merrill, Chicago).

The cable elements are countertensioned, so that neither cable goes slack under wind overpressure or wind suction. The horizontal struts are in compression and have a tendency to buckle to the side. To prevent this from happening, these struts are made thicker at the base where they are moment-connected to the vertical pipe strut. The vertical pipe strut has substantial torsional capacity that helps stabilize the horizontal struts against lateral movement. In this particular building, the horizontal mullions in the glazing system are also moment-

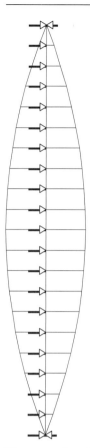

Figure 9.64 Cable truss designed to resist wind pushing left or right.

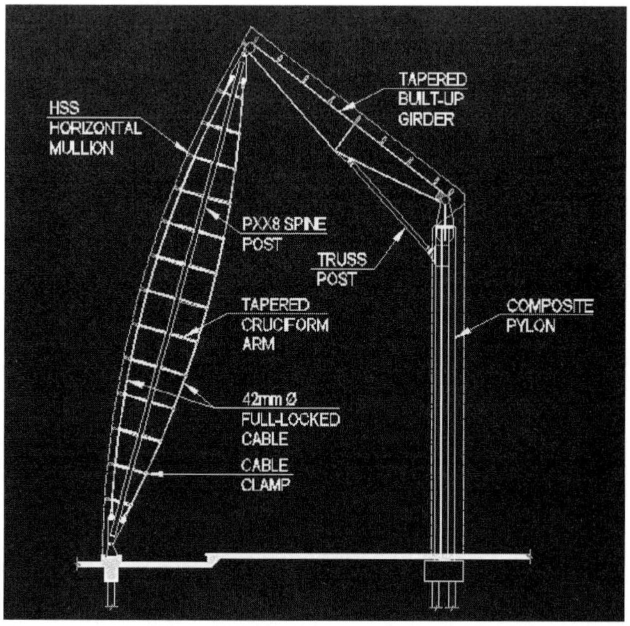

connected to the ends of the horizontal struts, providing substantial resistance to lateral movement of the horizontal struts. Figures 9.66 and 9.67 show the cable trusses at the manufacturing facility while they were waiting to be shipped to Virginia. Figure 9.68 shows the cable trusses installed. The moment connection of the horizontal struts to horizontal mullions provides lateral stabilization for the cable trusses, thereby avoiding the visual clutter associated with cross bracing.

Comparing these cable trusses to standard lenticular trusses:

- Cable trusses are similar in shape to lenticular trusses in that they are planar and have curved elements on each side.

Figure 9.66 Cable trusses for Virginia Beach Convention Center, ready for shipment. (Image courtesy of Skidmore, Owings & Merrill LLP, Chicago office.)

Figure 9.65 Cable truss for curtain wall of the Virginia Beach Convention Center. (Image courtesy of Skidmore, Owings & Merrill LLP, Chicago office.)

HSS HORIZONTAL MULLION
TAPERED BUILT-UP GIRDER
PXX8 SPINE POST
TRUSS POST
TAPERED CRUCIFORM ARM
COMPOSITE PYLON
42mm Ø FULL-LOCKED CABLE
CABLE CLAMP

Figure 9.67 Screw mechanism for adjusting tension in the cables. (Image courtesy of Skidmore, Owings & Merrill LLP, Chicago office.)

Figure 9.68 Cable truss in the curtain wall of the Virginia Beach Convention Center. (Image courtesy of Skidmore, Owings & Merrill LLP, Chicago office.)

- A cable truss has visually minimal tension elements at the boundary, concentrating the "visual bulk" into a single compression strut at the centerline of the structure, in contrast to the standard lenticular truss with no center strut and all the chord material is concentrated in the boundary.
- Only half of the cables in a cable truss are active under any given loading, whereas both the chords of a standard lenticular truss are active under any given loading.
- The effective structural depth of a cable truss is only half its overall depth, whereas the effective structural depth of a lenticular truss is equal to its overall depth, which means that the overall dimension of the cable truss has to be twice the overall dimension of the standard lenticular truss in order to get the same structural lever arm.

9.2.2 CABLE TRUSSES OF THE GENERAL MOTORS INTERNATIONAL HEADQUARTERS

Figure 9.69 shows cable trusses arrayed in a curved wall. For each cable truss, the two countertensioning cables are in the same plane.

As the next step in departure from a conventional truss, the countertensioning cables can run perpendicular to each other, as shown in Figure 6.70. The curvature of the wall makes it possible to sling horizontal cables over the cable trusses. The new horizontal cables can resist outward wind suction on the glazed wall and can countertension the inner cables of the cable trusses. As such, the new cables have replaced the structural function of the outer cables and outer struts of the cable trusses in Figure 9.69. In Figure 9.70, the cable trusses have been reduced to simple sling trusses; that is, half of the hori-

zontal struts and half of the cables have been eliminated from the original cable trusses.

For this system to work structurally, there must be reaction forces restraining the ends of the sling trusses and reaction forces on the ends of the horizontal cables to tension those cables. One way to achieve these reactive forces is to add a horizontal bow truss at the top of the wall and sling trusses at the ends, as shown in Figure 9.71.

The bow truss at the top has been chosen to be fully triangulated because the original shape of the wall in plan view was made an arc of a circle. This shape was chosen to simplify the layout and to make it easy to subdivide the wall into glazing panels of equal width. The shape of the top compression member along an arc of a circle makes triangulating crucial to avoid bending stresses in the curved member. The extreme variety of wind directions also makes it crucial that the top be triangulated to hold the shape of the wall. The horizontal cables in the walls stop at the sling cable of the end trusses, since that is where the force is introduced into the

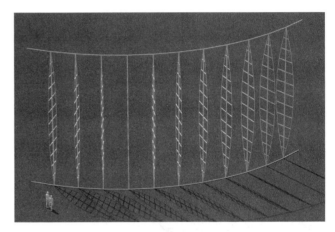

Figure 9.69 Cable trusses arrayed along a curved wall. (Digital model by author; rendering by James Sweeney.)

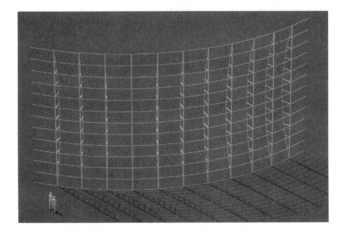

Figure 9.70 Inner cables in vertical planes and outer cables in horizontal planes. (Digital model by author; rendering by James Sweeney.)

horizontal cables. If the horizontal cables ran all the way to the vertical end struts, then they would be introducing bending stresses in the vertical end struts, and, thus, this is not an efficient or logical approach. The end slings were introduced specifically to provide the horizontal forces to tension the horizontal cables. Bypassing those cables and going straight to the end posts would defeat the intent of the end slings. It is desired to glaze the entire wall, including the parabolic opening between the vertical end strut and the end sling. This requires "infill" members that will be in bending under wind forces. To deal with the bending stresses, the elements filling that void will have to be thicker and sturdier than cables, as shown in Figure 9.72. There is a certain irony in the fact that these infill elements are heavier than the rest of the horizontal elements because they are *not* in tension. These horizontal struts help to stabilize the vertical compression members at the ends of the structure against lateral buckling. There is also a need for support for the roof, which can be provided by another sling truss supporting

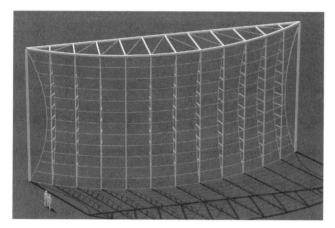

Figure 9.71 Adding bow truss on the top and cable-loaded, sling trusses at the ends. (Digital model by author; rendering by James Sweeney.)

the straight strut in the roof as shown in Figure 9.72. The structural elements in Figure 9.72 can be mirrored to produce the structure, as shown in Figure 9.73. The bottom chord of the central sling truss can be stabilized by inserting compression struts running from the bottom chord verices on the central sling truss up to the tops of the sling trusses in the walls, as shown in Figure 9.74. Figure 9.74 is the geometry of the entry to the General Motors International Headquarters (Architects and Engineers: Skidmore, Owings & Merrill, LLP, Chicago).

If the roof structure is made strong enough, it is possible to replace all the vertical compression struts in the walls.

The new, diagonal compression struts in the roof can provide the vertical forces at the upper ends of the sling trusses in the walls, eliminating the need for the compression struts in the sling trusses in the walls. In the design in Figure 9.73, large compressive forces are being carried by the verticals in the wall. When these verticals disappear, all of those forces will be transferred to the struts and the sling truss in the roof. This roof structure has to be very strong to handle gravity loads plus all the tension in the cables in the walls.

It is also possible to eliminate all the horizontal struts that were part of the original cable trusses. This may be accomplished by simply intersecting the vertical cables with the horizontal cables, as shown in Figure 9.75.

In the entry to the General Motors International Headquarters (shown in Figure 9.74), all of the glazing panels in the walls are identical. In the structure in Figure 9.75, with its toroidal-shaped wall surfaces, there are six trapezoidal shapes to make the bulk of the surface, plus six more special shapes at the ends. All the mullion fittings would be made substantially more complicated with this change in design. This structure is also problematic in that wind overpressure on one wall and wind suction on the other wall would tend to make the roof structure tilt to the side. There may have to be some straight members from

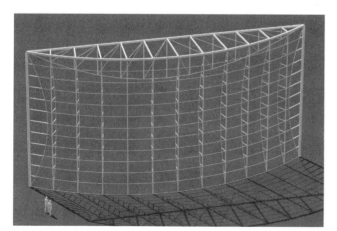

Figure 9.72 Adding infill members at ends and vertical sling truss under back edge of the roof. (Digital model by author; rendering by James Sweeney.)

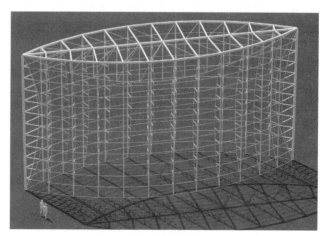

Figure 9.73 Replicating a mirror image of the structure completes an enclosed space. (Digital model by author; rendering by James Sweeney.)

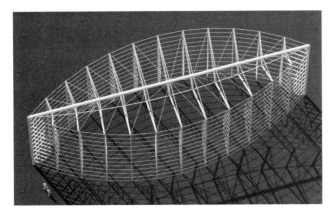

Figure 9.74 Entry to the General Motors International Headquarters. (Architects: Skidmore, Owings & Merrill LLP, Chicago office.) (Digital model by author; rendering by James Sweeney.)

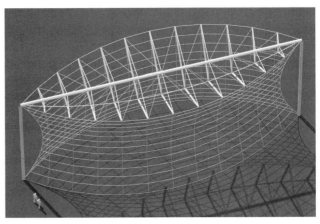

Figure 9.75 Modified structure without pure cable network in the walls. (Digital model by author; rendering by James Sweeney.)

the foundations up to the roof boundary to keep that tilting of the roof from occurring. This scheme, with the toroidal cable network, has simplified the structure by eliminating many members, but that simplification has been accomplished at the added complexity of the glazing system.

9.2.3 CABLE NETWORK OF THE SEATTLE-TACOMA INTERNATIONAL AIRPORT

A beautiful example of a toroidal cable-network glazing system is the Seattle-Tacoma International Airport Terminal, designed by Fentress Bradburn Architects, Ltd., Denver, Colorado (see Figure 9.76).

In the structure shown in Figure 9.76, the middle horizontal cable is neutral in that it has no tendency to slide up or down relative to the vertical cables. All of the horizontal cables in the lower half of the structure have a tendency to slide upward, and all of the horizontal cables in the upper half of the structure have a tendency to slide downward. To prevent the cables from sliding past each other in this manner, they must be clamped together. Figure 9.77 shows the two conditions where cables intersect. The most common is a simple crossing. The less common and more complicated intersection occurs at the columns, where the horizontal cable is discontinuous. The two ends of the horizontal cables meeting at that location are fitted with screw adjustments for fine-tuning the tension in the cables. Outriggers from the columns are provided to stabilize the cable network against lateral movement that would cause the glazing to rack. Figure 9.78 shows a closeup of the cable connection at the column.

The connection of the cable network to the column helps reduce movement of the glazing system under asymmetric wind loading. For uniform wind loading, the connection of the cable network to the columns is not necessary. The connections at the column provide screw adjustment for the horizontal cables, which stop and then start again at the connector. The lateral struts from the column to the connector are also provided with screw adjustments.

As in the case of the General Motors International Headquarters, the structure surrounding the cable network in the Seattle-Tacoma Airport must be extremely strong to resist the pull of all the cables in the cable network. If the structure is not extremely strong, then it will be destroyed as the cables are tensioned. In a sense, the incredibly minimal, transparent quality of the glazing system of the Seattle-Tacoma Airport has been achieved by moving most of the structural material normally seen in a glazing system somewhere else, where it does not encroach on the view. In the case of the Seattle-Tacoma Airport, this material has been so artfully hidden that only a person with a penchant for questioning how structures work wonders where the material has been put.

9.2.4 CABLE NETWORKS

In order for two sets of cables to stabilize each other, they must form a saddle surface, with one set of cables curved in one direction and the other set of cables curved in the other direction. There are many forms that a saddle surface can take, such as portions of a toroid, a hyperbolic paraboloid (hypar), or other surfaces that have not even been named. One of the challenges of designing such structures is to achieve an artful crafting of the space while keeping a simple, structurally efficient geometry for the cable network and for the elements stabilizing the boundary of the cable network. The following discussion explores some of the options.

Figure 9.76 Glazed wall of the Seattle-Tacoma International Airport Central Terminal. (Architects: Fentress Bradburn Architects, Ltd., Denver, Colorado; Design Engineers: Los Angeles Office of ATI; Fabricators: Mero; Photograph by James P. Scholz.)

Toroidal surfaces lend themselves well to wall glazing systems, such as the one in Figure 9.79.

In this system, the beams across the roof must cantilever and support the huge forces of tension in the cable network. The rim beam around the roof is curved and is subjected to substantial torsion under the forces from the cable network. These roof beams all have to be very strong to provide the boundary forces necessary to keep the cable network properly tensioned. As configured here, the footings have to be massive to resist the upward pull of the cables. Sometimes this upward pull is resisted by pilings penetrating deep into the earth. Such pilings

Figure 9.77 Spiders supporting the corners of the glazing panels. (Photograph by James P. Scholz.)

Figure 9.78 Cable-to-cable connector at the column. (Photograph by James P. Scholz.)

can take advantage of surface friction between the pilings and the surrounding soil, so that a substantial mass of the soil contributes to holding the footings down. Ground augers can also be used. A ground auger is basically a split plate welded to the end of a rod (see Figure 9.84). When the ground auger is rotated, this split plate augers itself into the ground. The plate then engages substantial amounts of soil in the form of an inverted cone. Ground augers can be extremely economical, since all of the mass holding the building down is the free mass of the local soil. Ground augers are problematic, however, in that they will be stopped when they encounter even fairly small rocks.

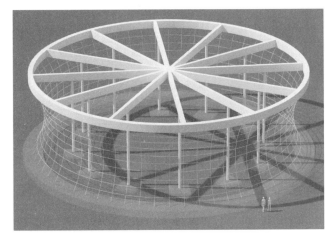

Figure 9.79 Toroidal glazed wall with a massive circular footing to hold down cable network. (Digital model by author; rendering by James Sweeney.)

Sometimes it is more economical to incorporate ground beams into the footings, rather than rely on massive amounts of dead weight in the concrete footings. For example, the structure shown in Figure 9.79 could be modified in the manner shown in Figure 9.80.

This cable network is particularly efficient, because the horizontal cables close on themselves and are, therefore, self-buttressing. Architecturally, this complete cable network is problematic because it does not provide an entry. Interrupting the horizontal cables to create an opening requires beams or trusses with substantial torsional capacity, such as those shown in Figure 9.81.

For roofing applications, both the toroid and the hyperbolic paraboloid are promising options (see Figure 9.82). Both of these shapes are discussed extensively in Chapter 8.

Figure 9.80 Toroidal glazed wall with grade beams to hold down cable network. (Digital model by author; rendering by James Sweeney.)

Figure 9.81 Entry openings flanked by tubular trusses to maintain tension in horizontal cables. (Digital model by author; rendering by James Sweeney.)

The following discussion and images focus on the hyperbolic paraboloid network, but most of the issues addressed apply equally well to the toroid network. Exceptions are noted as appropriate.

The vertical force component required at the ends of the gravity cables can be provided by columns, which are, in turn, supported on either individual spread footings or a long strip footing (as shown in Figure 9.83). The horizontal force component required at the ends of the gravity cables can be provided by stays, which are, in turn, restrained by anchorages in the ground. The stays require both vertical and horizontal components at the point of connection to the anchorages. The vertical restraint can be provided by piles, and the horizontal restraint by a wide, deep footing that provides enough area on the vertical face to avoid plowing through the soil.

For some applications, ground augers are an economical alternative to piles. Ground augers tend to be applied in temporary installations, such as for rides at state fairs, and in semipermanent installations, such as for stabilizing telephone poles and holding down mobile homes. Large ground augers commonly used in the power industry can generate up to 50,000 lb of anchoring force. They tend to be problematic in that even small rocks can stop their penetration and they may be subject to corrosion that will make their lifetime less than that of a concrete pile. However, they can be very economical and effective when properly applied (see Figure 9.84).

Wind cables can be extended to the ground and constrained in a similar manner, using a combination of piles (or augers) to prevent uplift and a deep vertical footing face to prevent lateral movement (see Figure 9.85).

The anchorages represent a smaller fraction of the cost of the structure when there are multiple cable networks that countertension each other, which then requires having anchorages only at the ends (see Figure 9.86).

The columns along the centerline become problematic if the entire volume needs to be connected internally. In that case, the columns can be replaced with an arch (see Figure 9.87).

The use of an arch has benefits beyond opening up the interior space. The arch is thrusting outward against the footing anchoring the wind cables, offsetting much of the inward pull of the wind cables. Of course, the outward force of the arch is not concentric with the force of the cables, so the cables and arch are acting in a manner to induce major moments in the wind cable footings. However, the net effect of the arch in this regard is beneficial. Figure 9.88 shows all of the interior columns replaced with arches.

It is possible to substantially reduce the footings associated with wind cables by introducing trusswork that follows the boundary of the cable network. This trusswork mediates the interaction of the arches pushing downward and outward and the wind cables pulling upward and inward (see Figure 9.89).

The stays and heavy anchorages can be replaced by compression struts, to provide the horizontal force for the

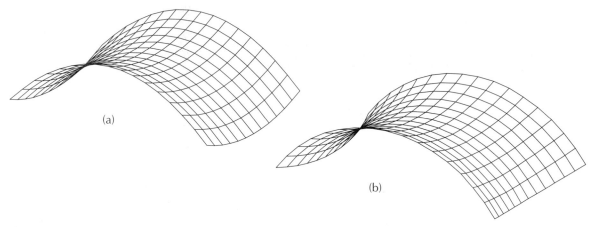

Figure 9.82 Hyperbolic paraboloid cable network (a) and toroid cable network (b).

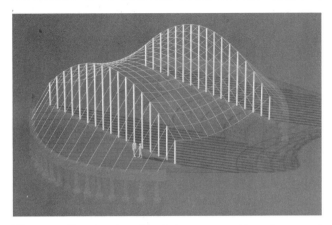

Figure 9.83 Gravity cables being supported by columns and stays. (Digital model by author; rendering by James Sweeney.)

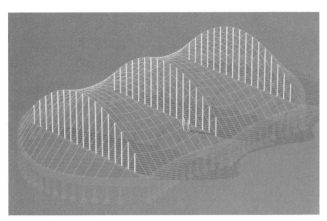

Figure 9.86 Multiple cable networks with anchorages at the ends. (Digital model by author; rendering by James Sweeney.)

Figure 9.84 A ground auger.

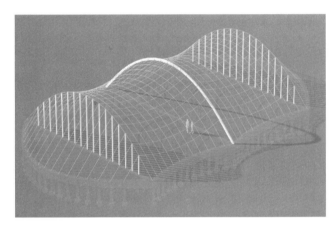

Figure 9.87 Replacing the interior columns with an arch. (Digital model by author; rendering by James Sweeney.)

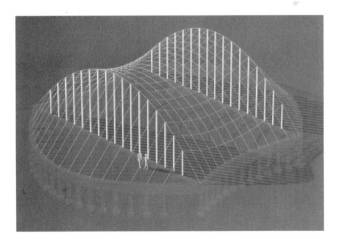

Figure 9.85 Anchoring both the stays and the wind cables to foundations. (Digital model by author; rendering by James Sweeney.)

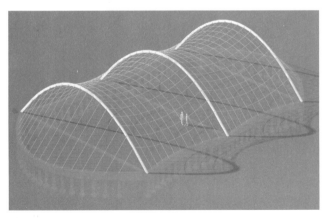

Figure 9.88 Replacing all of the interior columns with arches. (Digital model by author; rendering by James Sweeney.)

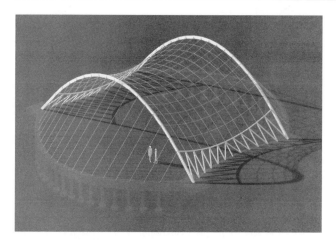

Figure 9.89 Boundary trusses helping to hold the wind cables. (Digital model by author; rendering by James Sweeney.)

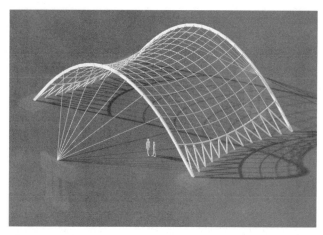

Figure 9.91 Pulling the stays to a common foundation point. (Digital model by author; rendering by James Sweeney.)

gravity cables, as shown in Figure 9.90. These struts have to be large in diameter to resist buckling under the compression forces induced by the gravity cables and to avoid excessive bending stress and deflection under their own self-weight. They tend to interfere visually with the curve of the cable network, which diminishes the aesthetics of the structure. To keep the arches from being stressed under lateral wind forces, some diagonal cables have been added to the cable network in Figure 9.90.

It is possible to open up the ends of the structure by pulling the stays to a more central location, as shown in Figure 9.91. This introduces some bending stresses into the arch and also challenges the localized footing to distribute the force into the soil. However, it provides a much-needed access to the interior.

The idea of using compression struts to hold the arches from collapsing inward under the force of the gravity cables can be carried a step further by consolidating all of

the compression struts into a single strut that extends beyond the planes of the arches and that is centered among all the points on the arch that need constraining, as shown in Figure 9.92. Then stays can connect from the ends of the compression strut to the points to be restrained on the arch.

As in the case of vaults, the hyperbolic paraboloid trimmed to the directrices can also be used for cable networks, as shown in Figure 9.93.

In the case of the vault, the parabolas opening downward were working in compression the and the parabolas opening upward were working in tension. Where those elements met at the boundary (at the directrices), their components lateral to the boundary elements offset each other and their components along the directrices reinforced each other, which put the boundary element in compression. When all the curved elements are cables, each of which is pretensioned, those elements are all

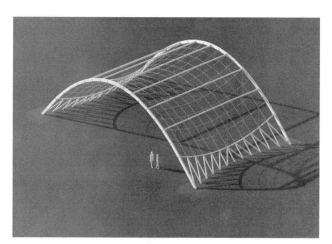

Figure 9.90 Compression struts providing horizontal forces for gravity cables. (Digital model by author; rendering by James Sweeney.)

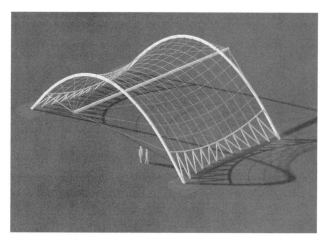

Figure 9.92 A single compression strut restraining the arches against collapsing inward. (Digital model by author; rendering by James Sweeney.)

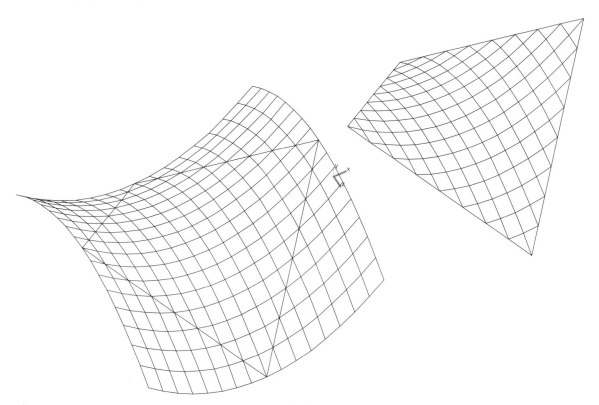

Figure 9.93 Hyperbolic paraboloid trimmed along the directrices.

pulling inward on the boundary elements. Therefore, the boundary elements are put in severe bending, even without snow or wind load on the roof. The bending induced by the cables can be addressed by making the boundary beams wide in the direction tangent to the surface, as shown in Figure 9.94. This necessitates having a twist in the boundary beams, or the beams need to be fairly thick in both their dimensions. For example, a rectangular tube with a sufficient dimension on both directions could work adequately to resist all the force components of the ca-

bles pulling on it. Having a twist in the boundary beams is more expressive of the geometry and the manner in which the beams and the cable network are interacting.

Using beams is an inefficient way to stabilize the cable network boundary. Using boundary trusses seems philosophically more consistent as a means to stabilize a lightweight structure like a cable network. For example, "parallel"-chord trusses can be used to stabilize the boundary, as shown in Figure 9.95. In that structure, the trusses have been given a twist, so the chords are

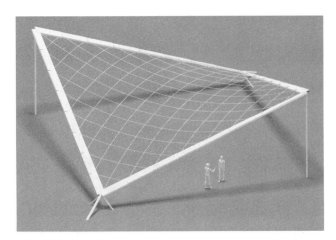

Figure 9.94 Cable network with boundary stabilized by beams. (Digital model by author; rendering by James Sweeney.)

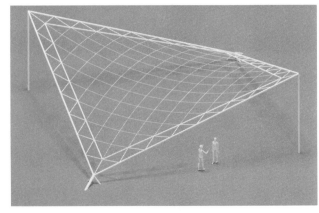

Figure 9.95 Cable network with boundary stabilized by "parallel"-chord trusses. (Digital model by author; rendering by James Sweeney.)

technically skewed, rather than parallel. The parallel-chord truss is geometrically well suited to the nature of this boundary problem in that the cables intersect cleanly with the vertices of the boundary trusses.

Bow trusses also work very well with the cable network, as shown in Figure 9.96.

As in the case of vaults, these modular units can be clustered together to form larger units, such as those shown in Figure 9.97.

Since these modules are square in plan, it is possible to cluster them together to cover larger squares, which allows for simple floor planning under a roof with a visual subtlety and richness that belies the simplicity of the plan beneath (see Figure 9.98).

The boundary can also be stabilized by sling trusses, as shown in Figure 9.99. These do not work as well with the geometry of the network, since the sling cable at the boundary intersects the cables of the network at odd points. However, this geometry does work well with fab-ric, which is a continuous medium, with which the discrete nature of the network cables is no longer an issue.

The compression members around the boundary can be removed, leaving a single cable along each edge of the cable network, as shown in Figure 9.100. To maintain tension in the boundary cables, stays have to be added to the high points to provide the horizontal force component.

Since parabolas can be scaled along either the vertical or horizontal axis, hyperbolic paraboloids can be also. With the use of a scaling factor, it is possible to squeeze the hypar down along one diagonal to produce a parallelogram in plan. If the proper scaling factor is applied, the angles of the parallelogram in plan can be made 60° and 120°. In that case, the modular units can be clustered

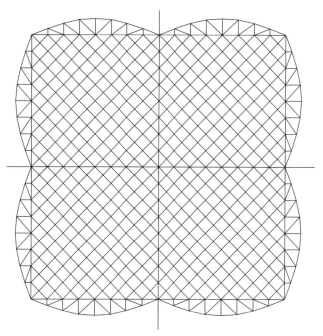

Figure 9.98 Plan view of modular cable networks assembled together into a large, square plan.

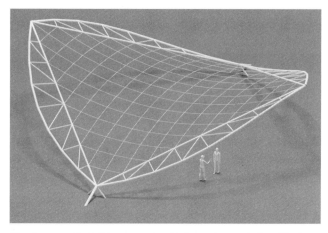

Figure 9.96 Cable network with boundary stabilized by bow trusses. (Digital model by author; rendering by James Sweeney.)

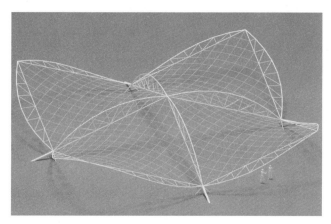

Figure 9.97 Modular cable networks assembled together. (Digital model by author; rendering by James Sweeney.)

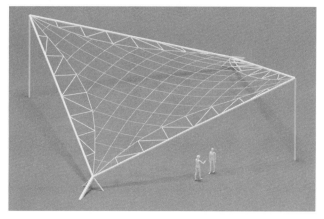

Figure 9.99 Sling trusses stabilizing the boundary of the cable network. (Digital model by author; rendering by James Sweeney.)

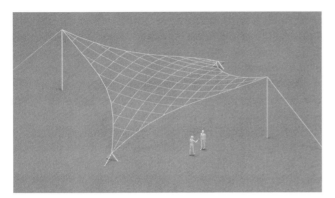

Figure 9.100 Cable stabilizing the boundary of the cable network. (Digital model by author; rendering by James Sweeney.)

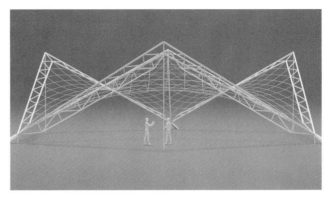

Figure 9.102 Three hypar modules connected around a center point (entry view). (Digital model by author; rendering by James Sweeney.)

together to produce hexagonal clusters, as in Figures 9.101, 9.102, and 9.103.

This structure could be used as formwork on which a dense mat of metal fabric or chicken wire could be stretched. That mesh could be hand-plastered with concrete or shot with concrete to produce a thin shell, similar to the designs by Felix Candela shown in Chapter 8. When the concrete hardens, the tendency of the cables to pull the points upward will be offset by the concrete acting in compression. Then the tie-down cables can be removed from the three high points, leaving unobstructed entry to the structure.

9.2.5 DORTON ARENA

All of the preceding examples of cable networks started with a particular shape of saddle surface, such as a toroid or a hyperbolic paraboloid, and the boundary support was configured to engage the chosen saddle surface. It is possible to generate a saddle surface by beginning with a boundary shape that was selected based on factors other than coordinating with a toroid or hyperbolic paraboloid geometry for the cable network. For example,

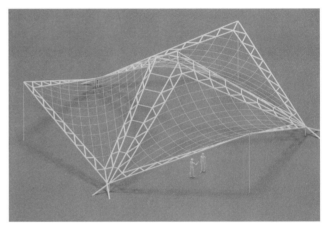

Figure 9.103 Three hypar modules tilted, with opening slots between them. (Digital model by author; rendering by James Sweeney.)

one could start with two sloped arches that are themselves in the shape of parabolas, such as those shown in Figure 9.104. The footings are also parabolic in plan (see also Figure 9.105).

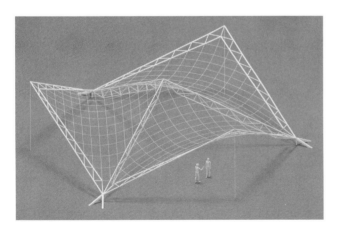

Figure 9.101 Three hypar modules connected around a center point. (Digital model by author; rendering by James Sweeney.)

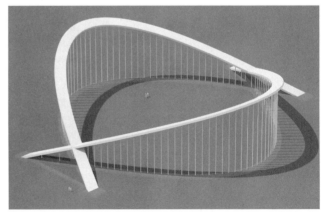

Figure 9.104 Sloped arches mutually buttressing. (Digital model by author; rendering by James Sweeney.)

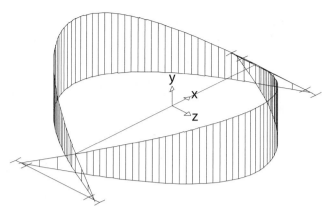

Figure 9.105 Identifying the coordinates and showing the centerlines of the members.

In constructing the model shown in Figures 9.104 and 9.105:

- The origin of the coordinate system is set vertically at the level of the intersections of the two arches.
- The distance from one intersection of the centerline of one parabolic footing with the centerline of the other

parabolic footing, to the corresponding intersection of the footings on the other side of the structure is 300 ft; that is, the intersections of the footing centerlines are at $(x, z) = (150, 0)$ and $(x, z) = (-150, 0)$.

- The distance from the zenith of the centerline of one parabolic footing to the zenith of the centerline of the other parabolic footing is 300 ft; that is, the centerline zeniths of the two parabolic footings are at $(x, z) = (0, 150)$ and $(x, z) = (0, -150)$.
- The spacing of the columns is 8 ft on center along the parabolic footing.
- The maximum vertical rise of the centerlines of the arches is 60 ft above the intersection of the centerlines of the two arches.
- The centerlines of the two footings is 24.5 ft below the intersection of the centerlines of the two arches.

The geometry of these arches can be generated by laying out the x- and z-coordinates of the foundations and then calculating the y-coordinates by multiplying the z-coordinates by $(60 \text{ ft}/150 \text{ ft}) = 0.4$, as outlined in the spreadsheet in Table 9.1. The spreadsheet shows the coordinates on the arch of the points of attachment for the gravity cables, for the spacing of 6 ft OC for the gravity cables.

Table 9.1 Coordinates on Arches for Attachment of the Gravity Cables

Node	d (ft)	L (ft)	x (ft)	$y = \left(\dfrac{60}{130}\right)z$	$z = d - \left(\dfrac{d}{\left(\dfrac{L}{2}\right)^2}\right)x^2$
1	150	300	−150	0.00	0.00
2			−144	4.70	11.76
3			−138	9.22	23.04
4			−132	13.54	33.84
5			−126	17.66	44.16
6			−120	21.60	54.00
7			−114	25.34	63.36
8			−108	28.90	72.24
9			−102	32.26	80.64
10			−96	35.42	88.56
11			−90	38.40	96.00
12			−84	41.18	102.96
13			−78	43.78	109.44
14			−72	46.18	115.44
15			−66	48.38	120.96
16			−60	50.40	126.00
17			−54	52.22	130.56
18			−48	53.86	134.64
19			−42	55.30	138.24
20			−36	56.54	141.36
21			−30	57.60	144.00
22			−24	58.46	146.16
23			−18	59.14	147.84
24			−12	59.62	149.04
25			−6	59.90	149.76
26			0	60.00	150.00

The arches are set at an angle of repose that will allow most of the gravity cables to be almost exactly tangent to the plane of the arch at the point of attachment to the arch. In this manner, the cables deliver most of their force to the arches in the plane of the arches, with minimal forces perpendicular to the plane of the arches. More specifically, the gravity cable that attaches to the zenith points of the two arches can be shaped as a parabola that is precisely tangent to the planes of the arches, at the points of attachment to the arches. This same parabola can be used as the basis of form for all the other gravity cables. In other words, the same parabola can be duplicated and moved so that it passes through the next point of attachment to the arch, and then the excess length is trimmed off. Assuming that the wind cables will also be spaced at 6 ft OC, the coordinates of the points along the gravity cable are calculated in the spreadsheet in Table 9.2.

Figure 9.106 shows the gravity cables attached to the arches.

There is no mathematical processing required for the wind cables. The shape of the wind cables is based on the attachment points on the gravity cables. Both gravity and wind cables are shown in Figure 9.107. Although the gravity cables are true parabolas, the wind cables are clearly not parabolic. The wind cables at the center of the

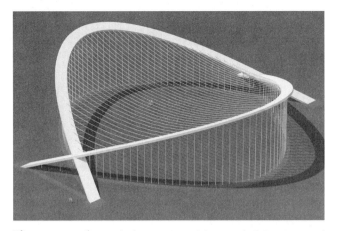

Figure 9.106 Parabolic gravity cables at 6 ft OC, supported by the arches. (Digital model by author; rendering by James Sweeney.)

structure actually have a slight dish, of about half an inch, which causes ponding if not corrected with tapered insulation. There are other ways that the surface could be configured. For example, the gravity cables could be made in progressively different parabolas, with the cable connecting the two zenith points on the arches being hung in a more shallow parabola (i.e., lower k in the for-

Table 9.2 Coordinates on Gravity Cables for Attachment of the Wind Cables

Node	d (ft)	L (ft)	x (ft)	$y = 60 - (d/([L/2] \cdot [L/2])) \cdot x \cdot x$ (ft)	z (ft)
1	31.3	300	0	60.000	−150
2			0	57.546	−144
3			0	55.192	−138
4			0	52.938	−132
5			0	50.785	−126
6			0	48.731	−120
7			0	46.778	−114
8			0	44.925	−108
9			0	43.172	−102
10			0	41.519	−96
11			0	39.967	−90
12			0	38.514	−84
13			0	37.162	−78
14			0	35.910	−72
15			0	34.758	−66
16			0	33.706	−60
17			0	32.755	−54
18			0	31.903	−48
19			0	31.152	−42
20			0	30.501	−36
21			0	29.950	−30
22			0	29.499	−24
23			0	29.149	−18
24			0	28.898	−12
25			0	28.748	−6
26			0	28.698	0

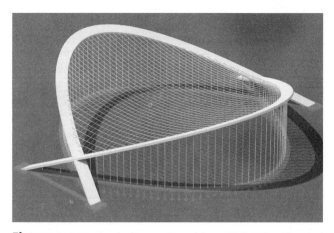

Figure 9.107 Parabolic gravity cables at 6 ft OC with wind cables crossing at 6 ft OC. Pilings holding footings down against uplift of the cables. (Digital model by author; rendering by James Sweeney.)

mula $y = kx^2$) and the gravity cables near the intersections of the arches being hung in a deeper parabola (i.e., higher k in the formula $y = kx^2$). If these parabolas are chosen correctly, the wind cable down the centerline of the structure can also be in the form of a parabola. Following this latter option, only the wind cable down the middle would be precisely a parabola, with the shape of all the other wind cables being dictated by the coordinates along the gravity cables where attachment occurred. This latter configuration would eliminate the dish at the center, leaving positive water runoff for all parts of the roof.

In the structure shown in Figure 9.107, the cable network is nearly tangent to the plane of the arches in the vicinity of the zeniths of the arches, but is tending substantially to pull the arches out of plane near the intersections of the planes. The out-of-plane forces are transmitted down the columns to the footings. To counteract this uplifting force, pilings of greater length can be placed near the portions of the footings where the greatest uplift forces are occurring, as shown in Figure 9.107.

This geometry is exactly what was built in the Dorton Arena in Raleigh, North Carolina, except that in the model of the structure shown in Figure 9.107, the cables are connected to the centerline of the arches, and in the Dorton Arena the cables are attached to the interior edges of the aches. Attaching the cables to the edges of the arches induces some torsion in the arches and some bending in the tops of the columns. Otherwise, the differences between the geometry shown in Figure 9.107 and the final geometry of the Dorton Arena are negligible. The dish, of about $\frac{1}{2}$ in. at the center of the geometry described earlier, is consistent with the ponding observed on the Dorton roof by William McClure, the engineer in charge of maintenance of the arena. This ponding was eliminated by installing tapered insulation, as shown in Figure 9.112.

This local depression in the cable network makes the network susceptible to wind uplift. To counteract this effect, cables were run from the center of the cable network down through the space, where they connected to the columns through dampers. Images of this damping system are presented in Figures 2.53 and 2.54 in the section on wind loads in Chapter 2. Figures 9.108, 9.109, and 9.110 show an aerial view, a ground-level view, and an interior view, respectively.

Figure 9.111 is a view of the adjustment mechanisms for the gravity and wind cables, where they attach to the inner rib of the hollow arch.

9.2.6 FABRIC STRUCTURES

Up to this point, the focus has been on networks of countertensioning cables. In many situations, fabric can be used as a satisfactory substitute for the cable network.

Figure 9.108 Aerial view courtesy of the North Carolina State Fairgrounds and the North Carolina Department of Motor Vehicles.

Figure 9.109 Exterior ground-level view showing the crossover of the arches.

Figure 9.110 The stands and the roof of the Dorton Arena, showing hanging acoustic tiles.

Figure 9.111 Adjustments on two of the gravity cables and turnbuckle on one wind cable.

Most structural fabric consists of fibers woven over and under each other in a mesh in which the fibers are at 90° to each other.

Most modern fabrics for architectural applications are coated with an agent that provides waterproofing. A very durable and strong choice is Teflon-coated fiberglass. Fiberglass is extremely light and strong. The Teflon coating provides a water barrier, bonds the fibers together, protects the fibers from abrasion, and generally makes it difficult for dirt to stick to the surface of the fabric. Teflon-coated fiberglass typically comes with a 20-year warranty and is very fire-resistant, so it is rated as a permanent building material. It is difficult to connect at the seams, and if it is creased, the strength is severely undermined. Therefore, care in handling is of extreme concern. The most common alternatives to Teflon-coated fiberglass are vinyl-coated nylon and vinyl-coated polyester. These materials are typically warranted for about half the life of Teflon-coated fiberglass and they burn in a flame. As compared with Teflon-coated fiberglass, they are much less expensive, are easier to connect at the seams, and can be handled much more roughly during transport and erection. Such alternatives, therefore, tend to be the materials of choice for transportable structures.

Fabrics can work well as a substitute for the cable network in the kinds of structural geometries that have been described so far in this chapter; that is, anywhere there is continuous support of the fabric along the boundary. The key is that the fabric has to be patterned so that the fibers are running in the same direction in which the cables would have been running. Just as in the case of cables, the fibers must have good curvature, and they cannot be running along the directrices of the hyperbolic paraboloid.

In addition to the methods of support outlined previously, it is possible to support a tent using a straight strut or column, as shown in Figure 9.113.

The tapered triangles in the tent shown here are called gores. They are joined at the seams by sewing, welding, or gluing. In Figure 9.113, the lines running along the gores from the boundary ring to the top of the support strut are the set of fibers running along the length of the fabric, called the warp. The perpendicular set of fibers, called the weft, run circumferentially around the tent. There are no fibers running along the seams. Seams are generally the weakest part of a fabric, but these seams are usually created by lapping and bonding the fabric from each of the two gores being joined. Therefore, even though there are no fibers running precisely along the seams, there is an extra thickness and density of the fibers. Whether those fibers are useful structurally depends on the nature of the tent fabric or, more specifically, the nature of the coating material. Fabric tends to be very strong and stiff when tensioned parallel to either the warp or the weft. However, it tends to stretch easily along the bias.

The lines on the tent surface in Figure 9.113 represent fabric fibers running in the gores. By simple observation, it is clear that the number of active fibers available for structural action is diminishing as the fabric approaches the point of support. At the point of support, the stress in the fabric approaches infinity. This method of support is clearly a design contradiction. Designers in this case want to safely support the fabric, without damaging it, but are choosing to support it by poking at it with a sharp stick.

To keep the stress in the fabric at the top within reasonable bounds, either the fabric would have to become progressively thicker or some other structural element would have to come down to engage the fabric along a line of sufficient length to transfer the support force. It is common to introduce a ring that terminates and clamps the fabric a substantial distance below the top of the strut (see Figure 9.114). This ring is usually supported by three heavy-duty tension rods with length adjustments, such as turnbuckles. Using three adjustable rods allows easy tensioning of the system. Using only three support points

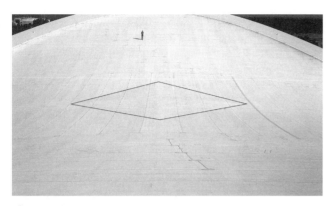

Figure 9.112 Diamond-shaped pyramid of tapered insulation to avoid ponding in the center.

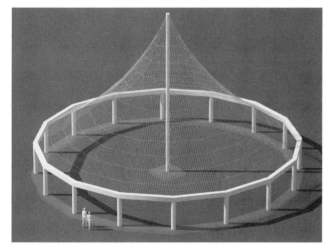

Figure 9.113 Fabric surface supported at a point by a strut. (Digital model by author; rendering by James Sweeney.)

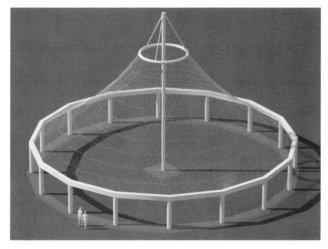

Figure 9.114 Ring supporting the upper edge of the fabric. (Digital model by author; rendering by James Sweeney.)

puts a fair amount of torsion in the ring, which must be designed accordingly. However, using three adjustable rods tends to be better than using four, since it is difficult to get four rods precisely tensioned. Only one tensioning rod has to be the wrong length in order to ensure that the rod on the opposite side will not be active either. In that case, there are only two active rods, which is worse than three. An analogy is a three-legged table, which is preferred to a four-legged table that is wobbling on only two legs.

The solution shown in Figure 9.114 is still less than ideal from the point of view of distributing the force on the fabric. The force on the fabric at the top will be greater than the force around the lower boundary and, furthermore, the length of the connection to the top ring is less than the length of connection at the lower boundary. Therefore, the stress in the fabric will be much greater near the top.

Cables pose the opposite problem to that posed by fabric, as indicated in the cable network shown in Figure 9.115. The density of cables increases drastically near the top of the support strut.

The cable network has excess structural capacity at the top, and the fabric has excess structural capacity near the lower boundary. A blending of cables and fabric has the potential to produce a balanced and economical solution, as shown in Figure 9.116.

The combination of cables and fabric is almost always the solution in systems using point supports. The cables can go all the way to the top of the support strut, or they can be terminated at the support ring. In either case, the cables are provided with individual adjustments to allow the fine-tuning of the system. The ring pulls up to provide longitudinal tensioning of the fabric. Adjusting the length of the cables causes them to straighten out, producing hoop tension in the fabric. When finally adjusted, a tent structure sounds a little like a drum when it is thumped. Fine-tuning a tent is an art that requires skill and a keen technical understanding of the nature of the material.

There can be more than one point of support for a tent. For example, two of the structures shown earlier can be merged and the material overlapping in the middle removed, similarly to conceptualizing a cross vault, as described in Chapter 8 (see Figure 9.117).

In the case of the cross vault, the stress that would have been carried in the material that was removed had to be transferred to other elements, specifically the major arches crossing through the center of the structure. The situation is similar in the case of these tents. The forces that would have been carried in the fabric and cables that have been removed at the intersection of the two tents have to be transferred to other elements, in this case, a very heavy cable running in the valley along the intersection of the two structures. This cable is pulling with an extreme concentrated force on the boundary element. The original boundary elements were complete rings,

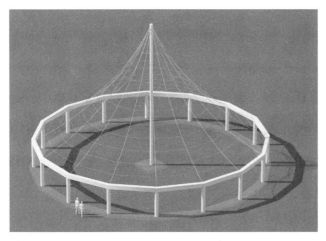

Figure 9.115 Cables concentrating together near the top of the compression strut. (Digital model by author; rendering by James Sweeney.)

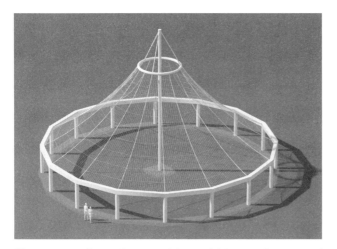

Figure 9.116 Combining cables and fabric to their mutual benefit. (Digital model by author; rendering by James Sweeney.)

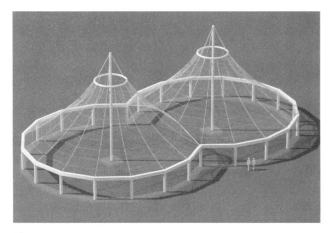

Figure 9.117 Combining two tent modules into a larger structure. (Digital model by author; rendering by James Sweeney.)

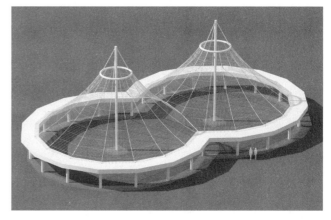

Figure 9.118 Boundary beam for resisting inward pull of cables. (Digital model by author; rendering by James Sweeney.)

being pulled inward with many distributed forces around the rings. In other words, they were acting as compression rings and have been rendered in a manner consistent with that role. In the structure shown in Figure 9.117, parts of the boundary rings have been removed, eliminating any possibility of their acting as compression rings. That fact, combined with the concentrated force from the valley cable, has turned the original boundary elements from compression rings to a combined element subject to major bending moments. To respond to that situation, the boundary has to be rendered as a seriously thick beam (see Figure 9.118) or a compression member has to be run horizontally from one end of the valley cable to the other. The compression member would be by far the more efficient structural solution, but it would tend to divide the space visually and psychologically.

9.2.7 DENVER INTERNATIONAL AIRPORT

One of the most dramatic examples of fabric architecture is the Denver International Airport (Architects: Fentress Bradburn Architects, Ltd.; Engineers: Severud Associates). It is designed to mimic the contours of the Rocky Mountains looming majestically in the background. Denver's location, at the point at which the high mountains rise out of a seemingly limitless plane, is one of the most visually dramatic sites in the world. The Denver Airport has accomplished the feat of introducing human habitation in a manner that is respectful to the spirit of such an extraordinary place (see Figures 9.119 and 9.120).

During the day, interior illumination is provided by the natural light admitted through the fabric roof. The transmission is on the order of 10%, which stops most of the heat of the sun but still produces a very bright space during most daylight hours. The lighting in such a space tends to be very mellow and diffuse. A space totally enclosed with diffusing fabric can make a sunny day seem like an overcast day. To avoid that feeling, the architects

Figure 9.119 View of Denver Airport against the Rocky Mountains. (Fentress Bradburn Architects, Ltd. Photograph by Timothy Hursley.)

provided windows around the perimeter of the space and glazing at the tops of some of the columns. These elements admit some beam sunlight to enliven the space (see Figure 9.121).

During the night, the artificial lighting for the interior is provided by fixtures mounted in sconces on the columns. Light is projected up on the white fabric roof, which serves as the source of indirect light for the space. Carefully hiding the electric lighting and the HVAC system has kept the interior space uncluttered and allows the eye to follow, and appreciate, the graceful curves of the fabric. Some of the electric lighting passes through the fabric, causing the structure to glow at night (see Figure 9.122).

Figure 9.123 is an early drawing of one of the column-top assemblies, showing the adjustable rods supporting the ring. The ring is shown as thin pipes connected together with perpendicular plates. The final version of the ring is fully triangulated.

Figure 9.124 is a photograph of one of the column-top assemblies. The ring alluded to in the previous paragraph has been constructed as a tubular truss. This provides bending and torsional capacity while keeping the structure light and transparent. In this figure, also note the cusps occurring at the valley points where the concentrated line-distributed force of the heavy cables is strongly influencing the local shape of the fabric.

This kind of fabric is very heavy as compared with what we commonly think of in clothing or small tarps, like those we might use in camping. Large expanses of the

Figure 9.120 Interior view of the Great Hall of the Denver Airport. (Fentress Bradburn Architects, Ltd. Photograph by Hedrich Blessing.)

Figure 9.121 Glazing at the tops of the columns. (Fentress Bradburn Architects, Ltd. Photograph by Ron Johnson.)

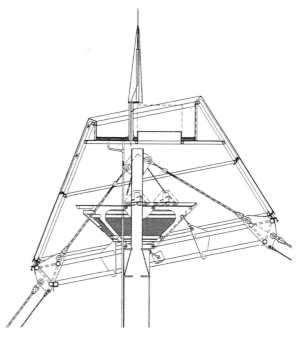

Figure 9.123 Drawing of column-top assembly of the Denver Airport.

fabric are heavy enough that they have to be handled with mechanical equipment, such as cranes. A huge roof like the Denver Airport's is assembled from many individual pieces of fabric, each of a size and weight suitable for manageable handling.

Figure 9.125 shows a detail of how the fabric is connected to a cable. The edge of the fabric is clamped between stiff plates, then glued and riveted, so that no stress concentration is introduced into the fabric. The same detail is used all around the boundary of a piece of fabric, including places where pieces of fabric meet in the val-

leys. The cables in the valleys bring the two pieces of fabric to a cusp, where they meet in the valley. Making the structure watertight in the valleys requires gluing, or welding, a strip of sealant fabric over the cable and associated connections.

The roof of the Denver Airport has two layers of fabric, which improves the thermal resistance, as compared

Figure 9.122 Denver Airport glowing at night. (Fentress Bradburn Architects, Ltd. Photograph by Timothy Hursley.)

very visible on the exterior of the building. For tents with a single layer of fabric, however, patches can be very visible inside, since the part of the fabric that is covered with the patch has a much lower light transmission than the rest of the structure. In other words, the patch is apparent as a dark patch in the roof. Adding the inner layer of fabric visually obscures the patch, making it much less apparent.

The fabric in a large roof like that of the Denver Airport moves a substantial amount under wind and snow load. The designers of the airport, however, did not want its glass walls to move. To solve the problem, the walls were cantilevered out of the floor structure. In other words, the walls are structurally independent of the roof. To allow the roof to move without disturbing the walls, a large inflated tube seals the space between the roof and the top of the walls, as shown in Figure 9.126.

The walls are restrained by a network of cables, as shown in Figure 9.127. Straight stays on each side of the vertical mullions restrain a point about two-thirds of the way up the mullions. At that stable point, struts project horizontally outward from the mullions. Cables from the tips of those horizontal struts to the top of the mullions create the cantilever that projects the remaining one-third of the way to the top of the wall.

Figure 9.124 Column-top assembly showing the tubular truss ring supporting the fabric and cables. (Fentress Bradburn Architects, Ltd. Photograph by Timothy Hursley.)

with a single layer. Adding the second layer of fabric prevents condensate from falling on the space below and provides a safety backup for the primary layer of fabric. The roof can be patched when it becomes punctured. The patches match the color of the fabric and are not

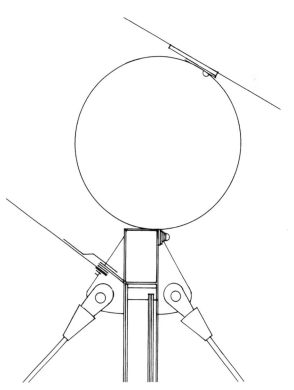

Figure 9.125 Edge detail of the Denver Airport fabric roof. (Fentress Bradburn Architects, Ltd. Photograph by Ron Johnson.)

Figure 9.126 Inflated tube between the outer layer of fabric and the top of the wall.

Figure 9.127 Cable restraints for cantilevered walls. (Fentress Bradburn Architects, Ltd. Photograph by Timothy Hursley.)

Figure 9.129 Canopy at Munich Olympic Stadium, by Frei Otto. (Image courtesy of TC Howard of Synergetics, Inc.)

9.2.8 MUNICH OLYMPIC VENUES

Another wonderful example of a countertensioned cable structure are the Munich Olympic Venues, designed by Frei Otto (see Figures 9.128 through 9.132).

9.2.9 FUNNEL CANOPY

The funnel shape associated with point supports can be inverted, as shown in Figure 9.133. In this configuration, wind passing over and under the canopy has a net tendency to suck the canopy downward. Since both wind and snow tend to pull the fabric downward, the force on the connection of the bottom of the fabric to the top of the column is not severe, and steel cables are not required for local reinforcement at that connection.

The canopy was to sit on an uneven plaza without any foundations being dug. It was conceived as a three-legged table stabilized by steel pipe legs moment-connected to cross trusses, as shown in Figure 9.134. A variety of cov-

Figure 9.128 Canopy at Munich Olympic Stadium, by Frei Otto. (Image courtesy of TC Howard of Synergetics, Inc.)

Figure 9.130 Canopy at Munich Olympic Stadium, by Frei Otto. (Image courtesy of TC Howard of Synergetics, Inc.)

Figure 9.131 Canopy over stadium, by Frei Otto. (Image courtesy of TC Howard of Synergetics, Inc.)

Figure 9.132 Canopy over entry bridge, by Frei Otto. (Image courtesy of TC Howard of Synergetics, Inc.)

Figure 9.133 Fabric canopy funneling water into columns that serve as leaders. (Designed and built by NLSU architecture students Nate James, Allen Owing, and Jean Donovan, under the supervision of Professor Place.)

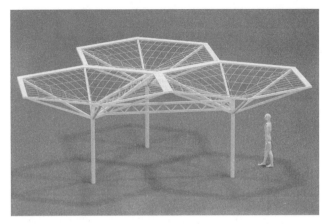

Figure 9.134 Trusses and columns moment-connected to make a three-legged table. (Digital model by author; rendering by James Sweeney.)

erings could be put on top of the columns of the three-legged table. In this case, a single hexagonal funnel "blossoms" from the top of each column. The frames of these hexagons are connected together to keep them from toppling from the column tops.

The final array consisted of three of these three-legged modules. The center module was higher than the other two, allowing more light in and giving the impression of plants growing to differing heights (see Figures 9.135 and 9.136).

9.2.10 TENSILE MODELS

The creation of models is a very useful way to explore tensile structures. Drawings can be made to do anything and look any way, but models are much more indicative of physical really. Every part of a tensile surface must be in double curvature. This is a serious design constraint. Tents communicate a lot about how they want to be shaped, and the tent designer had better listen. Otherwise, the fabric will tear apart and blow away. It is not possible to make cable or fabric surfaces take a shape that does not come naturally without using compression or bending elements to force the surface to take an alternative shape. This is a subject area in which the construction of physical models is an extremely important tool of exploration. Making a working model is the primary test of whether an idea is structurally rational. A working model must incorporate accurate materials and connections to properly simulate the behavior of the intended structure. Examples of such accuracy including the following:

- Elements that are intended to be tensile in the final structure cannot have bending resistance in the model.
- Elements that are intended to resist forces in tension cannot be simulated in the model with stretchy materials (such as knit fabric, which stretches excessively under minor forces).

Figure 9.135 Final design of canopy, consisting of three 3-legged tables. (Digital model by author; rendering by James Sweeney.)

Figure 9.136 Final construction, consisting of nine hexagonal funnels.

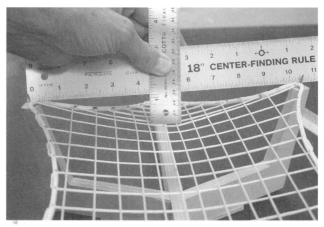

Figure 9.137 Model illustrating sag in cable network.

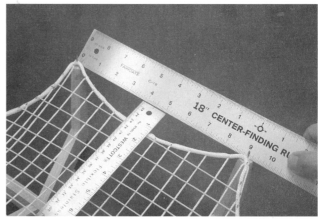

Figure 9.138 Model illustrating sag in boundary.

One seeks to achieve the same kind of mechanical advantage for a cable or fabric surface as for other structures: the greater the "sag," the more efficiently the cables will perform the structural functions of resisting wind or gravity loads. As a rough rule, the sag of any cable in the network should be at least one-tenth the span of the cable. More sag produces greater structural efficiency. Less sag produces larger forces in the cable and in the elements that restrain the ends of the cables. In Figure 9.137, the sag is 1.1 in. and the span is about 10.3 in. L/s = 10.3/1.1 = 9.36, or, put another way, $s = L/9.36$, which is deeper than the guideline of $L/10$.

The sag of cables around the boundary of the network should normally be even greater. An analogy is girder beams and joist beams, in which the more highly loaded member typically has deeper proportions. In Figure 9.138, the sag of the boundary cable is 1.3 in. and the span is 9.0 in., so the ratio of L/s = 9.0/1.3 = 6.92, so $s = L/6.92$ for the boundary cable.

More sag in the boundary cables means greater structural efficiency. More sag also means either that there is less coverage of space below the fabric surface or that the

structure has to extend farther into the landscape, consuming more terrain.

The appropriate shape for the network surface can be explored by two methods:

1. Stretch knit fabric over various support elements as a means to explore shape. Knit fabric is nonstructural in that it will dramatically change shape in response to the application of minor forces. However, this property of knit fabric makes it extremely well suited for geometric exploration, since the shape it assumes under loading is the appropriate shape for the actual structure to have in order to resist the applied forces. One way of thinking about it is that the very weak knit fabric reacts to the force distribution by taking on the best possible shape. If that shape works for the knit fabric, which is very weak and elastic, then it will work to resist much larger forces if a genuinely structural fabric is tailored to have the same shape. Another way of thinking about it is that the knit fabric is an amplifier that shows exaggerated deformation under loading.

2. Explore shape using geometric directrices, which are also not structural, but can be used to visualize and define the shape of the surface on which the structural members should be situated.

For the purposes of this text, the discussion focuses on using stretched fabric, which is the more versatile of the two methods. The following series of figures shows the sequence of construction of a tensile model. The first step is to lay out a plan for the structure, as shown in Figure 9.139, and design and build a support frame, as shown in Figure 9.140.

The frame shown in Figure 9.140 has sharp nails sticking out of the columns and eyelets for connecting to the low points of the support structure. In Figure 9.141, the knit fabric is stretched over these connection points. It is important to play with this fabric until it gives good curvature in both directions.

The boundary cable must be made of braided cord. Twisted cord will come unraveled when the connecting cords of the network pull along the length of the boundary chord. In Figure 9.142, the boundary cable has been attached with enough slack to give curvature around the boundary. In this case, very heavy cord is used everywhere in the model to make sure that it photographs clearly.

Using a template prepared for the purpose, check to make sure that the side boundary cables have the right amount of sag and mark the points for attachment of the gravity cables to the side boundary cable, as shown in Figure 9.143.

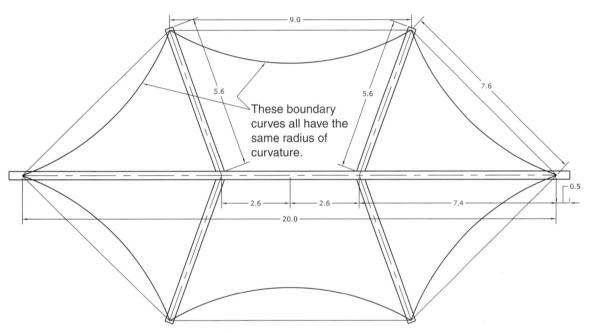

Figure 9.139 Plan diagram of the structural frame on which cable model is to be built.

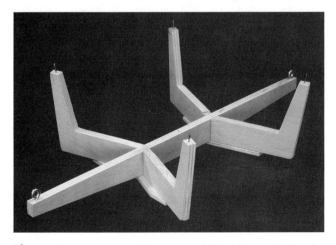

Figure 9.140 Structural frame on which cable model is to be built.

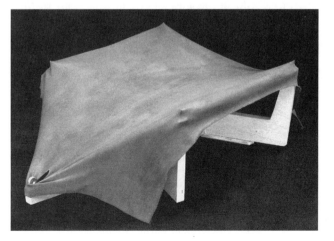

Figure 9.141 Stretching knit fabric over the frame.

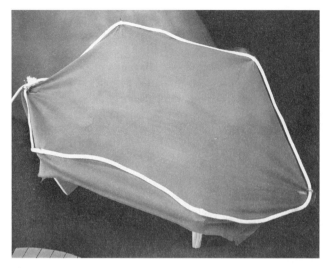

Figure 9.142 Securing the boundary cable to connection points.

Using another template prepared for the purpose, check to make sure that the other cables have the right amount of sag and mark the points for attachment of the wind cables to the boundary cable, as shown in Figure 9.144. In all cases, the lines dividing the template into equal spaces must be drawn in the same direction as one of the sets of cables to be attached to the boundary cable.

Using a template that is the mirror image of the last template, mark the points for the wind cable connections on the boundary cables on the other side of the model, as shown in Figure 9.145.

Sew the gravity cables through the boundary, as shown in Figure 9.146.

Sew the wind cables through the boundary cable, with the wind cables passing over the top of the gravity cables. Adjust the wind and gravity cables so that each type of cable has good sag and so that they countertension each

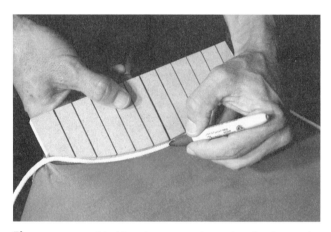

Figure 9.143 Marking the connection points for the gravity cables.

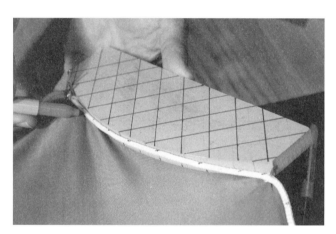

Figure 9.145 Using a mirror-image template to continue marking points.

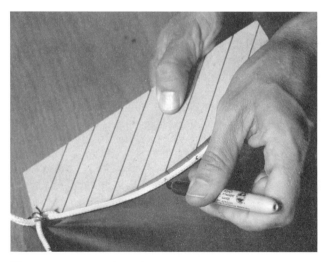

Figure 9.144 Marking the connection points for the gravity cables.

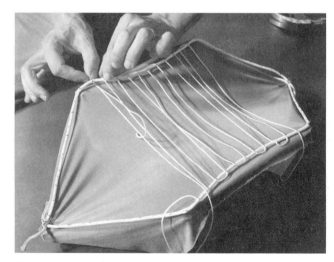

Figure 9.146 Sewing gravity cables through the boundary cable.

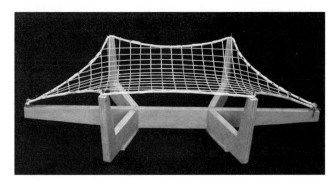

Figure 9.147 The finished model,

other to produce a good taut network. This is a little like adjusting your shoelaces. With a little practice, it will work out well, if the original markings on the boundary cable were properly located (see Figure 9.147).

Exercise: Cable Model Project

Design a canopy structure using counterstressing cables, with one set of cables predominantly resisting gravity loads and one set predominantly resisting the uplift force of wind suction. Sets of these cables would be pulled taut over each other, so that each cable is counterstressed by several other cables, producing the appearance of continually changing direction (i.e., smooth curvature). The countertensioning sets of cables then take on the appearance of a curvilinear surface of double curvature—more specifically, a saddle-type surface.

You may support the cables using:

1. Straight compression struts
2. Curvilinear compression elements, such as arches or bow trusses
3. Beams

The use of beams is generally discouraged, because they are relatively inefficient structurally and therefore philosophically inconsistent with the notion of a superlightweight cable network. However, they may be used, and if they are used, they should be of a shape that is structurally expressive and of a size appropriate to their role within the structure.

Design a structure and build a model that effectively simulates its structural behavior. In doing so, you may want to consider the following issues:

1. What is the intended function of the structure?
2. Where do people get in and out of it?
3. How does water run off it? (Water should not pool anywhere or fall over the accesses to the structure.)

4. How would the structure be constructed? Would it be easy to erect?
5. What is it that you think is elegant about the structure?

Remember that having the model effectively simulate structural behavior is much more important than having the model be pretty. In other words, making the joints strong is more important than making the joints look clean and neat. However, this should not be construed as meaning that the design should not be elegant or beautiful. The design should be something that pleases you and of which you will be proud. However, building a model with elegant joints is sometimes difficult. In fact, it is often more difficult to devise effective and elegant joints for the model than to do so in the actual structure.

Materials for the Cable Model Project

1. Heavy-duty thread for the cable network.
2. Woven chord for the perimeter of the model. Some students may not need this if the boundary of the cable network is not to be supported by cables.
3. 1 needle, for sewing the thread (through holes in the perimeter structure or the perimeter chord).
4. 1 piece of stretch fabric for simulating the shape of the cable-network surface. Large pantyhose are recommended, but other very stretchy knit fabrics can also work well. For some designs, the initial shape can be determined by the geometric directrices, in which case the stretch fabric is not required. If geometric directrices are used, it would be good to make them of a different color and a lighter-weight thread than the final, structural threads.
5. Other optional materials for supporting parts of the structure above the base: $\frac{1}{8}$ in.-diameter or $\frac{3}{16}$ in.-diameter PVC rods, wood dowel rods, drinking straws, or small-diameter tubing from a hobby shop. These can be made into spars, arches, or trusses. Wood or mat board can be fashioned into arches and grade beams that are part of the foundation.

The model should accurately express where material would be most structurally effective in the foundation, on which the stability of the cable network ultimately depends. Do *not* make a base out of a thick piece of plywood or fiberboard that would effectively represent a 10 ft-thick concrete pad the size of a football field. To do justice to the idea of a lightweight, super-efficient cable network structure, the structure should have an efficient and rational foundation. Foundations are the place that the beams (in the form of grade beams) become particularly attractive. Trenching provides very economical formwork for casting concrete grade beams and the depth of the trenches can be very easily varied to tailor the depth of the grade beams to the variation in moment induced by the various forces.

10

Lateral Bracing Systems

10.1 Basic Bracing Systems

Buildings require lateral bracing to remain stable, even under gravity loads. Most buildings are designed to be balanced in a state of equilibrium under pure gravity loads. Therefore, under pure gravity loads, the bracing members are zero-force members. Under lateral forces, such as wind and ground movement in an earthquake, the bracing members become active in resisting the forces. Under lateral forces, buildings are essentially cantilevers projecting out of their foundations. All the basic principles of horizontal cantilevers supporting gravity loads can be applied directly to vertical cantilevers resisting horizontal forces of the wind or an earthquake. The only difference is that, under horizontal forces, the cantilever is projecting out of the ground, where the materials are the weakest. Therefore, the guidelines for spans and proportions for vertical cantilevers should be modified in the direction of greater structural depth at the root of the cantilever. In other words, a wider base on the building is more crucial than a deeper root on a cantilever resisting gravity forces, simply because of the problematic nature of the material to which the base of the building is connecting. Ideally, the combination of building weight and breadth at the base should prevent any tendency for a building to lift up off the ground. If there is a tendency for a building to overturn, the dead weight of the footings has to be increased or advantage must be taken of the dead weight of the local soil by using ground anchors or piles projecting down into the ground. Figure 10.1 shows (a) a narrow building with a tendency to overturn and (b) a wider building with a tendency to skid sideways. If the footings are too shallow and the building is too light, skidding will occur. The footings need to

be made sufficiently deep that they engage enough soil mass to prevent skidding.

There are three common means to prevent a building from racking:

- Shear walls
- Triangulation
- Rigid-frame action

Figure 10.2 shows a building with no appreciable resistance being racked by a lateral force (a). That structure can be stabilized by shear walls (b). These shear walls are the structural analog of the solid-web beam in gravity systems. In solid-web beams, modest openings can be made in the web without undermining its structural function. Similarly, small openings can be made in a shear wall without significantly diminishing the role of that shear wall in resisting lateral forces.

The same structure can also be stabilized by triangulation, such as by cross bracing, as shown in Figure 10.3(a). Lateral bracing using triangulation is the analog of a truss being used to span against the forces of gravity. This structure can also be braced using beamlike elements forming a rigid frame, as shown in Figure 10.3(b).

Shear walls are stiff and strong. They tend to be very economical, since the enclosure material can often provide the shear resistance at no additional cost. Architecturally, they are the least flexible, offering the least opportunity for light, view, and movement through such walls. However, for low-rise construction, they can have fairly large openings that make them satisfactory for most applications. Common examples of shear walls are concrete bearing walls, concrete masonry walls, and wood stud walls with oriented strand board (OSB) or plywood sheathing. With regard to the latter, see the discussion and figures in Chap-

(a)

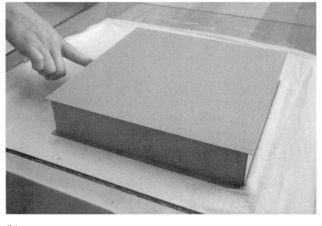

(b)

Figure 10.1 Benefit of a broad base in avoiding overturning of the building.

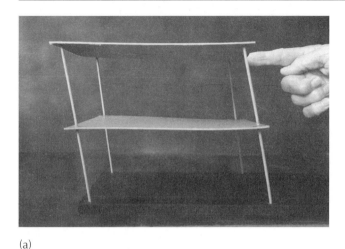

(a)

(b)

Figure 10.2 Structural frame stabilized by adding shear panels.

ter 1. Triangulation also produces a very stiff and strong bracing. Triangulation tends to limit movement through the walls, but can provide ample amounts of light and fairly good views, although, for some applications, the bracing elements are considered visually distracting. Rigid frames are architecturally the most flexible and accommodating of the three bracing systems, since they provide the kind of openings that allow human traffic to easily pass through at a variety of locations. They can also work very well for admitting natural light and providing views, as shown later in this chapter. Rigid frames tend to be structurally the least efficient system. However, for some very tall buildings, the inherently large dimensions of the columns make rigid-frame action very effective and practical. Moreover, the deep members required by rigid-frame action can often be located where they do not adversely affect the functions of admitting light or providing views.

It is extremely important that lateral bracing elements be located so that they can resist lateral forces in a balanced way. For example, it is not satisfactory to have only one bracing frame that is on only one side of the building, since a bracing frame in that location cannot create a force on the centerline of the lateral load. This point is illustrated in Figure 10.4, where one braced wall is provided parallel to the applied force. When the applied force is in the plane of the bracing, as shown in (a), the bracing is very effective in resisting the load. However, a wind force or seismic force will tend to be centered at the centerline of the building, as shown in (b), where the applied load and the resisting force are conspiring to cause a radical twist in the building structure.

To address this issue, the bracing must be on both sides of the building or along the centerline of the building.

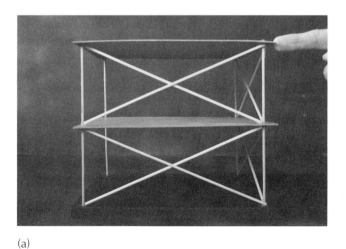

(a)

(b)

Figure 10.3 Bracing with triangulation (a) and rigid frame (b).

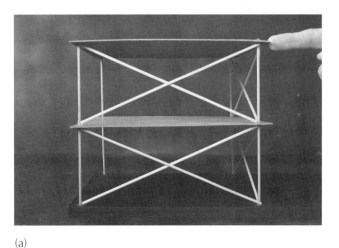

(a)

(b)

Figure 10.4 Effect of asymmetric resistance to lateral force.

10.2 Triangulated Lateral Bracing

For low-rise buildings, sufficient lateral bracing can be achieved by triangulating a single vertical bay, which we can call the braced frame (see Figure 10.5). In this situation, lateral forces on the building produce upward forces on the windward column in the braced frame and downward forces in the leeward column in the braced frame. These vertical forces in the columns induced by the lateral forces on the building are added on top of whatever gravity forces exist in the columns. In determining the potential upward forces on a footing under one of the columns, the upward vertical forces induced by the lateral forces on the building must be considered in conjunction with the least possible gravity load; that is, without any live load on the structure. For that load combination, there must be no net upward force after the weight of the footing has been accounted for. In fact, there must be a net compressive force on the bottom of the footing to provide for an adequate factor of safety against overturning. The downward vertical force in the columns in the braced frame must be considered in conjunction with the maximum gravity load, to ensure that the footing area is sized to account for the maximum possible downward force on the soil. Depending on the width of the braced frame and the relative magnitudes of the wind and gravity forces, the design of the area and weight of the spread footing under the columns in the braced frame may be governed by uplift or by downward force. The spread footings under the columns in the brace frame will always be larger in area and weight than the footings under the columns that support only gravity forces. The braced frame can be thought of as a kind of lever that is trying to lever up the footings to which it is attached. These footings have a special burden in resisting this lever effect. If the governing issue in the design

of these footings is downward force, the spread footing can be augmented with piles. If the governing issue in the design of these footings is uplift, the spread footings can be augmented with piles or ground augers (see Figure 10.5).

As the building gets taller, the lever effect increases and the spread footings under the braced frame will increase in size until they merge into one large footing (see Figure 10.6).

As the building gets even taller, the lever effect increases and the spread footings under the braced frame will have to be extended outward to become a grade beam. The longer the grade beam, the greater the lever arm for the action of the grade beam in stabilizing the base of the building. The longer the grade beam, the more effective the weight of the grade beam will be in keeping the building from toppling and the lower will be the stress on the soil associated with the overturning moment (see Figure 10.7).

The Wildlife Conservation Commission Headquarters Building on Centennial Campus in Raleigh, North Carolina, is an example of such a bracing system. Figure 10.8(a) shows most of the framing members in this structure, but has been simplified substantially. Figure 10.8(b)

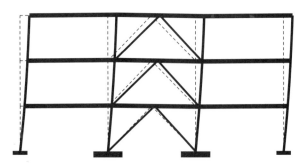

Figure 10.5 Three-story braced frame.

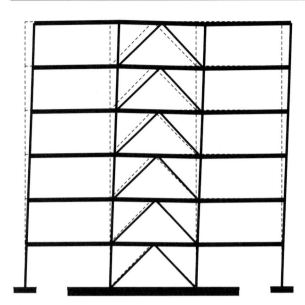

Figure 10.6 Six-story braced frame.

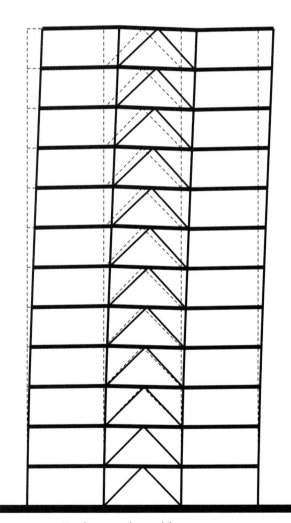

Figure 10.7 Twelve-story braced frame.

shows only the braced frames and the associated grade beams; in this image, the frame on the left is in the east wall. All the other braced frames are clustered together in the core of the building.

There are two braced frames for resisting forces in the east and west directions. These two frames are located symmetrically about the building centerline running in the east-west direction, which means that they share equally in the burden of resisting east-west forces. Doors were required in the center of the frame, which accounts for the use of chevron braces, which peak at the center of the frame. The relatively small east and west façades mean that the wind forces in the east and west directions are fairly modest. For this particular building, the governing issue for the east-west bracing elements was seismic force, rather than wind.

There are two braced frames for resisting forces in the north and south directions. The north-south frame at the east end of the building was placed where it would be obscured by the fire stairs. For fire stairs, the door openings have to be at one end of the stair. Diagonal braces that peak over the doors provided clearance for the doors while allowing completion of the triangulation in the frame. These are long diagonal members that have to be made fairly large in cross section to avoid buckling. This braced frame is at the extreme end of the building, which means that it is taking a smaller part of the north-south forces. The most severely loaded frame is the north-south frame set two bays in from the west end of the building. Because it is closer to the centerline of the building than the frame on the east end of the building, and because of the large wind forces on the large north and south façades, this frame is the most heavily loaded in the building. A chevron bracing pattern was chosen to keep the lengths of the bracing members short.

Figure 10.8 shows long grade beams under each of the braced frames. The largest grade beam is under the north-south braced frame located two bays in from the west end. This grade beam provides substantial hold-down force for the windward column in the braced frame and support for extremely high downward forces from the leeward column in the braced frame. The length of the grade beam was dictated by the need to distribute force over the soil, which was of relatively poor quality. Figure 10.9 shows the rebar in place for the grade beams on the lower level (which excludes the grade beam at the east wall, which is on a higher level off the left, well out of the field of view of the camera). The columns that form the three braced frames at the core of the building are marked by the plywood squares supporting the anchor bolts. The grade beams have steel both top and bottom, since there are both positive and negative moments in the grade beams and those moments reverse when the direction of the lateral force on the building reverses. Off to the right in Figure 10.9 are a few scattered spread footings that

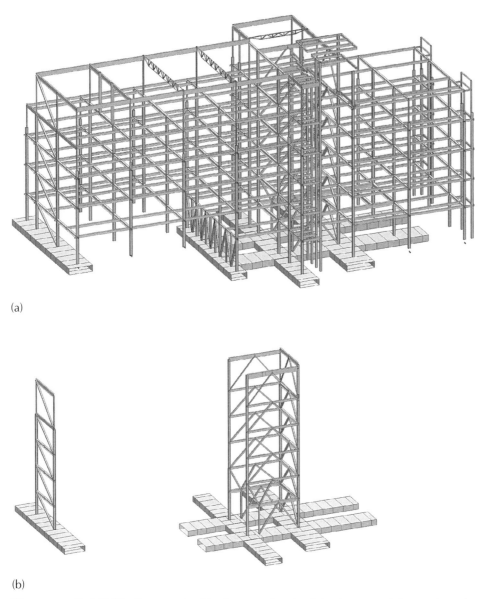

(a)

(b)

Figure 10.8 Wildlife Conservation Headquarters framing (viewing toward the southwest).

support columns that carry only gravity forces. To the left in this image are the vertical rebars of retaining walls that cantilever up out of wide footings. The retaining wall footings and the grade beams are so wide that they merge with each other to produce a continuous mat.

Figure 10.10 is a closer view of the intersection of two of the main grade beams, showing continuous steel running in both directions at both top and bottom of the grade beams.

Figure 10.11 is a closeup view of the anchor bolts for one of the columns at a intersection of two braced frames. These are held in proper alignment with a plywood template (a). This system requires some play in the holes in the column bases (b), so that the column bases can be lowered down over the bolts. Because of the play, the anchor bolts do not provide very good shear transfer. Transfer of the high shear forces is provided by the shear lugs that are welded to the bottom of the baseplates with full-penetration welds. The baseplates are 4 in. thick and the shear lugs are $2\frac{1}{4}$ in. thick. These shear lugs have to be solid-grouted into the concrete footings. This operation must be carefully performed, since any voids will undermine the force transfer.

In addition to the grade beams under the braced frames, this building utilizes spread footings under the stair towers and under the columns that resist only gravity force. Figure 10.12 shows anchor bolts supported by wood 2 × 4s spanning over a spread footing. A typical

Figure 10.9 Reinforcing for grade beams, retaining walls, and spread footings.

spread footing with no uplift force has rebar only in the bottom, since there is never any tension in the top of this kind of footing.

Zooming in closer on the image in Figure 10.12, Figure 10.13(a) shows a form of rebar called a form-saver. It screws to the inner surface of the formwork. The connection at the end of the form-saver has female threads. When the formwork is removed, threaded rebar can be screwed into the female connection. This provides for

Figure 10.10 Steel rebar at intersection of two grade beams.

continuous reinforcement from the spread footing into the wall footing (b). These images are presented as a sidelight, since they are not part of the subject of lateral bracing. However, they are pertinent in that they illuminate the differences between footings that address only gravity forces and footings that have to account for uplift.

Figure 10.14 shows steel reinforcing for a cantilevered retaining wall. Heavy dowels emerge vertically out of the wide footing, which contains steel both top and bottom. The heaviest steel in the footing is running perpendicular to the wall. The heaviest steel in the wall is the vertical rebar on the side where the soil is pressing against the wall. The footing has to be very wide so that the weight of the soil being retained can help in stabilizing the wall. The action of this wall is similar to that of a sheet metal bookend, in which the weight of the books helps to keep the bookends from toppling over. The cantilevered wall picks up the lateral load of the soil at the point of retention and keeps those forces from being transmitted into the rest of the building structure. Shear forces at the base of the wall are absorbed by the diagonal rebar that is embedded deep in the footing and in the wall.

Figure 10.15 is a closer view of the steel reinforcing for the cantilevered retaining wall.

Figure 10.16 shows a partially completed cantilevered retaining wall. Vertical rebar on the tension side of the wall has been overlapped by forty-eight bar diameters

(a)

(b)

Figure 10.11 Anchor bolts (a) and column baseplates with shear lugs (b).

Figure 10.12 Rebar at the bottom of a spread footing.

with the dowels that were cast as part of the original foundation pour. This overlap ensures that the binding action of the concrete will make the steel rebar act as if it were continuous. In some sense, the overlapping steel is wasted. A carefully executed weld could connect the new steel to the end of the dowels without this waste. However, the cost of that welding operation would exceed the cost of the steel that is lost because of the overlap.

Figure 10.17 shows the steel framing emerging out of the footings. This view is toward the southwest, which is the same general direction in which the framing diagrams were depicted earlier. At the left in this image is the east wall, with its braced frame. At the core of the building is a cluster of three braced frames. The frames in the core are all basically chevron braces, except for a slight vari-

(a)

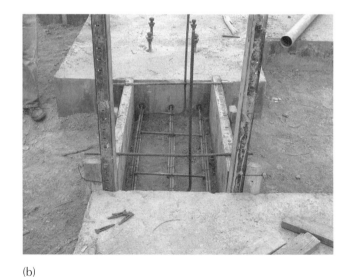

(b)

Figure 10.13 Form-savers (a) to be connected to rebar in bottom of wall footing (b).

Figure 10.14 Rebar for cantilevered retaining wall.

Figure 10.15 Closeup of rebar for cantilevered retaining wall.

Figure 10.16 Partially completed cantilevered retaining wall.

Figure 10.17 Steel frame, viewing toward the southwest.

ation in that geometry to accommodate door openings on the main floor.

Figure 10.18 is the view toward the west on the main floor at the cluster of braced frames. The chevron bracing straight ahead is typical of the construction of these frames. The bracing on the two side frames is unique to this story of the building.

Figure 10.19 shows the connection at the apex of the chevron bracing. The large gusset plate is welded to the beam in the fabrication shop. The diagonals are also cut to length, slotted, and drilled in the fabrication shop. Precisely located bolt holes serve to align the frame while the diagonals are field-welded to the gusset plate. In Figure 10.19(a), the diagonals have been bolted in place, but they have not yet been field-welded to the gusset plate. Figure 10.19(b) shows the top of one of the beams in the line of the bracing. Numerous large shear studs have been

Figure 10.18 View toward the west of three braced frames at core of building.

(a)   (b)

Figure 10.19 Top of chevron braces (a) and shear studs on beams connecting to braced frame (b).

welded to the top of the beam to ensure the transfer of forces between the braced frame and the floor diaphragm.

Figure 10.20 shows a typical connection at the bottom of the diagonals. The image in (a) shows the connection viewed from below, before the floor decking has been fully installed. The image in (b) shows the connection viewed from above, after the floor decking has been installed. The gusset plates have been welded to the tops of the beams in the shop. Angles have been welded to both the beam web and the gusset plate in the shop. The angles are bolted to the columns in the field. Again, precisely drilled holes hold the diagonal in place while it is

field-welded. This connection system illustrates important principles about steel construction: (1) try to do as much of the welding and precision work as possible in the fabrication shop, and (2) make the kit of parts sent to the field self-aligning so that the minimal amount of precision work and thinking needs to be done in the field. Field-work is complicated enough, and it is hard to think about or execute a quality weld with a freezing-cold wind howling by.

Figure 10.21 shows the connection for the steep diagonal in the special case on the first floor. For a steep diagonal, the connection is stretched out in the vertical

(a)   (b)

Figure 10.20 View of beam and associated gusset plate from below (a) and above (b).

Figure 10.21 View of beam and associated gusset plates for high-angle brace.

direction. In this case, gusset plates have been welded to both the top and the bottom of the beam.

These kinds of connections are described in detail in the *Manual of Steel Construction*, Vol. 2 (Connections ASD, Ninth Edition/LRFD, First Edition), from the American Institute of Steel Construction.

When the building becomes very tall, the forces in the columns of the braced frame and the moment in the grade beam become excessive and additional measures need to be taken to reduce these forces. In addition to providing more strength, measures must be taken to reduce lateral deflection in the building. For braced frames in buildings of only a few stories, the major source of lateral movement is shear deformation associated with the change in length of the diagonal members in the braced frame. This shear deformation is almost never severe enough to be a source of concern. When the braced frame becomes very tall, it begins to exhibit substantial moment deformation, associated with the change in length of the columns of the braced frame. When moment deformation becomes dominant, deflection can be very large and it is necessary to find ways to make the bracing system deeper. To do this, more bays can be braced, as shown in Figure 10.22. The left image shows the deflected frame with a single bay of bracing. The right image shows the deflected frame with all the bays braced, which effectively makes the braced frame the

entire depth of the building. In that case, instead of having a grade beam taking all the brunt of serving as an outrigger, a truss of depth equal to the height of the building is doing the work. This makes for a much more efficient structure. Sometimes bracing all the bays is more than is required. Moreover, architectural flexibility will incline us toward keeping as many of the bays open as possible. The middle image shows the effect of bracing some of the bays. Clearly, most of the reduction in deflection has been achieved with only a fraction of the expenditure in materials.

For very tall buildings, structural efficiency and economy motivate designers to take full advantage of the width of the building by making the depth of the bracing system equal to the width of the building. This gives birth to the concept of a stressed tube structure, which is designed to make all material on all the faces of a building active in resisting lateral forces. An excellent example of a trussed tube building is the John Hancock Building in Chicago, shown in Figure 10.23 (Architects: Skidmore, Owings & Merrill; Engineers: Skidmore, Owings & Merrill). The dramatic trussed tube on the perimeter of the building ensures that, regardless of the direction in which the wind is blowing, there will be truss webs to transfer shear forces from one side of the building to the other. Utilizing all the material at the perimeter of the building ensures maximum strength and stiffness and a very efficient structure.

The building tapers from base dimensions of 160 ft × 260 ft to top floor dimensions of 100 ft × 160 ft. The taper accomplishes several things, which include reducing the surface for wind exposure at the top; reducing the coherence of wind vortexes; providing a wider, more stable base; and getting more light down to the street. This taper is a subtle, but beautiful, gesture that has made the building one of the most revered skyscraper designs in the world. There are significant complications arising from the taper, including the fact that all the floor dimensions are different and the truss diagonals have many different lengths.

An even more severe complication of the taper arises from the following structural issue: when the trusses become active under lateral load, the diagonals can introduce force into the columns only at the intersection of two diagonals; that is, either at the corners of the building or at a column at the center of the face of the building. Columns intersecting a single diagonal simply bend that diagonal, without taking advantage of the axial strength of the diagonal. This is an example of a particular kind of shear lag across the face of the building. Allowing some of the columns to not participate in the process of resisting lateral forces goes against the design philosophy underlying the tubular truss, which has as its goal to take maximum structural advantage of all the material on the faces of a building.

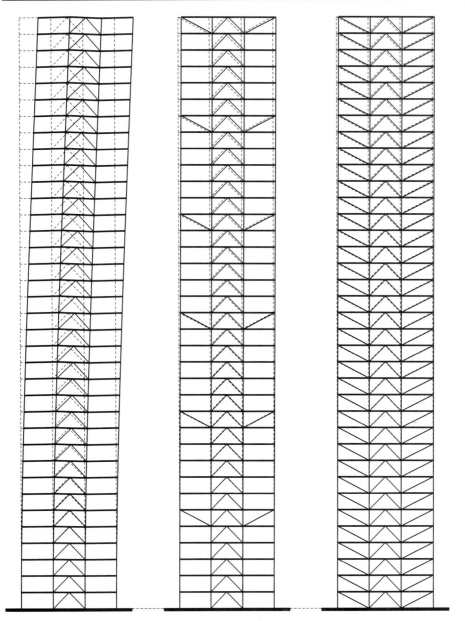

Figure 10.22 Computer simulations of different bracing patterns in a tall building.

All of the exterior columns could be made to participate in providing lateral resistance by judiciously adding more diagonals. This idea was discarded because it was thought that more diagonals would block too many windows and would make the building visually cluttered, detracting from the bold, dramatic quality of the façade. The solution turned out to be the addition of horizontal ties between the columns/diagonal intersections that were symmetric on each side of the building. These horizontal ties provide the additional force component to allow the diagonals to transfer force into the columns at those intersections. The structural analog can be gotten by taking the tension structure in Figure 10.24(a) and turning it upside down (b). Parts of the diagonals work with the horizontal to produce forces on the column where the diagonal and horizontal intersect.

To keep these horizontal elements from obscuring windows and becoming visually prominent, it was necessary to make a floor occur at each level where such an intersection occurs. Since the building is tapered, the vertical spacing between intersections of the columns and the diagonals is not uniform. In other words, the floor-to-floor spacing is governed in a complex way by the location of the intersections of columns and diagonals. In the end, this very complex patterning and analysis process was successfully completed, and the building stands as a beautiful testament to the effort involved. Few people viewing the building would ever imagine how such a

(a) (b)

Figure 10.23 Trussed tube of the John Hancock Building in Chicago.

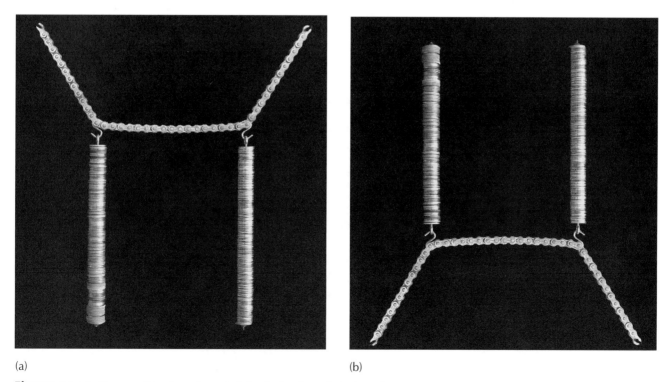

(a) (b)

Figure 10.24 Shapes of tension elements introducing force into the columns.

simple and elegant façade could have such an underlying complexity. The action of these horizontals also increases the robustness of the building, since any concentrated force is distributed quickly through the steel network in the façade.

10.3 Rigid-Frame Lateral Bracing

Figure 10.25 shows a simple building frame under the influence of wind force (a) and dead and snow load (b).

For the particular proportions of height to width in this frame, wind is producing greater deflection and greater internal moment than are the gravity loads. Furthermore, the most severe moment is occurring at the intersections of the vertical and horizontal elements. Creating that joint becomes a major focus and cost of this kind of frame. The diagrams suggest that perhaps material should be shifted from the center of the horizontal span and put at the joint. That approach can be tested analytically by simulating the same frame after introducing a pin joint at the center of the horizontal. This would be the extreme case of moving all the material away from the center toward the joints. Figure 10.26 shows the results of making that change. As in Figure 10.25, the wind-loaded frame is shown in (a) and the gravity-loaded frame is shown in (b).

Adding the pin joint at the center of the horizontal span had almost no effect on the moments under wind load. This is expected, since the moment under wind load was essentially zero at the center of the horizontal span before the pin joint was introduced. Under gravity loads, adding the pin joint has reduced the moment at center span to zero and has increased the moment at the intersections of the horizontal and vertical elements. After adding the pin joint, the most severe moment under gravity loading is similar in magnitude to the most severe moment under wind loading. This would suggest that once wind has been designed for, the gravity problem has taken care of itself. Continuing this thread of design thinking, if there must be a sturdy vertical for resisting wind-induced moments, perhaps that vertical can be used to support horizontal cantilevers spanning from each vertical to the center of the structure. This resonates well with something already discovered earlier in this book, which is that the moment in a simple-span beam is exactly equal to the moment in a cantilever of a length equal to half that of the simple-span beam. Figure 10.27 illustrates this point. On the left (a) is a simple-span beam and on the right (b) are two cantilevers connected at their tips by a pin joint. Both structures are subjected to gravity load. The most severe moment for the simple-span beam, which is a positive moment occurring at the center of the beam, is equal in magnitude to the most severe moment

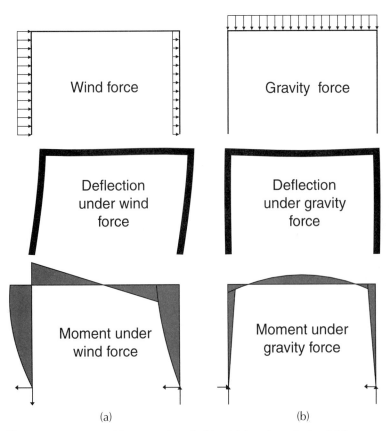

Figure 10.25 Rigid frame under wind load (a) and gravity load (b).

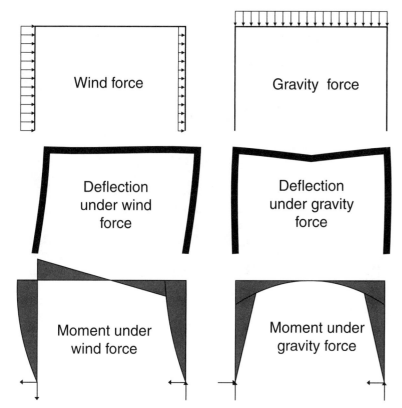

Figure 10.26 Rigid frame with pin joint at center of the horizontal span.

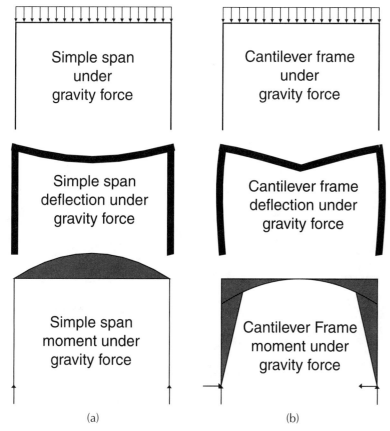

(a)   (b)

Figure 10.27 Simple-span beam (a) versus two cantilevers (b) of half the span each.

in one of the cantilevers, which is a negative moment occurring at the connection of the cantilever to the vertical. From the point of view of the gravity burden, one has made no sacrifice in going from the simple-span beam to the cantilevers. Complexity has been added by the requirement of fabricating a very sturdy joint at the top of each vertical. However, this had to be done for the wind load anyway. So, the wind load problem has led to a new paradigm that is quite different from that which a designer tends to arrive at in starting by thinking about gravity loads. However, the final resolution works very well for gravity as well as wind. A major advantage to using cantilevers, rather than a simple-span element that is twice as long, is simplified transport.

Figure 10.28(a) shows a structure based on the preceding design idea. Figure 10.28(b) shows the bracing of the bottom edge of the rigid frame being provided by the struts connecting back up to the purlins. This is the classic symbiotic relationship in which the rigid frame supports the purlins, which, in turn, brace the rigid frame. For this kind of frame, the bottom edge of the frame requires frequent bracing, particularly near the joint, because the negative moment is putting the bottom flange of the frame into severe compression. This additional bracing is a cost burden that this kind of framing incurs. In that sense, it is unlike the more common simple-span beams, in which the top flange is in compression and the top flange is stabilized by decking, which was put there for another purpose; that is, to complete the enclosure.

These rigid frames are welded up from plates. The triangular web plates are sometimes cut on a very large shear, but they can also be cut with a torch, laser, or water cutter.

When the moment at the joint gets very large, there is a strong tendency for the web plate to buckle. To address

Figure 10.29 Details of joint connection in a rigid frame.

this issue, a stiffener plate is often welded to the web along the centerline of the joint, as shown in Figure 10.29. This stiffener plate is very thin. It is representative of the thickness of the web plate. These frames are extremely lightweight and structurally efficient construction. The thickest plates in the frame are those used to make the bolted connection at the joint. The tension force in the outer flanges is transferred to the connecting plates through two paths: (1) directly from the flange plate to the connection plate where they are welded together, and (2) through the web. The connection plate is put in bending while transferring force from the flange plate and the web plate to the bolts. This bending influence accounts for the relatively large thickness required in the connection plates. To keep the bending from becoming too severe, every attempt is made to keep the bolts close

(a)

(b)

Figure 10.28 Rigid frame tapering to minimum at center of span.

in to the flange and the web plates. To keep the forces in the flanges and the connection bolts within reasonable bounds, the depth of the members at the joint is exaggerated. This is easy to do, once the commitment has been made to using tapered web plates.

Frames like this are planar elements. They are very strong in resisting forces in the plane of the frame and very weak in resisting forces perpendicular to the frame. To keep these frames upright, they are usually braced with X-bracing, as shown in Figure 10.30(a). This bracing can be removed after construction if the walls that are added provide adequate shear strength to keep the building up. The image in (b) shows the detail of how an X-bracing rod connects to the base of the frame. If an opening is needed through the side walls, it is usually possible to X-brace only one bay along each side wall. If even more opening is desired, rigid frames can be placed along the side walls to allow every bay to be open.

To keep the bases of the frame from kicking outward under gravity loads, a tie is provided at the base. Typically, there will be a concrete slab floor with substantial amounts of steel for preventing shrinkage cracks. This steel can be utilized as part of the tie from base point to base point. A piece of rebar with a 90° bend in the middle is wrapped around the column base, so that the two legs of the rebar extend out at 45° on each side of the frame. Extending the

rebar in this manner provides the force component in the desired direction and allows the rebar to reach laterally to engage many strands of wire mesh.

Figure 10.31 shows a frame with longer, shallower proportions under the same loads as the structure previously analyzed.

The new proportions cause a shift in the balance, with the moments induced by gravity forces becoming substantially larger than the moments induced by wind force. Under gravity loads, the moment in the horizontal portion of the frame is zero about 20% of the way in from the ends. At that same point, the wind moments are fairly small. The most severe gravity moments occur at the ends and at the center of the horizontal. The magnitude of the positive moment at the center is comparable to the magnitude of the negative moment at the supports. This moment pattern suggests using cantilevers at the ends, extending out to the point where the moment is zero, and a simple-span beam spanning across the gap between the ends of the cantilevers. The connection between the ends of the cantilevers and the simple-span beam cannot be a perfect pin joint, since there is still some moment at that location because of the influence of the wind loads. However, the gravity moments give the primary indicators of the desired shape, which is something like the structure shown in Figure 10.32. The frame is deepest at the center

(a)

(b)

Figure 10.30 X-bracing perpendicular to the frames.

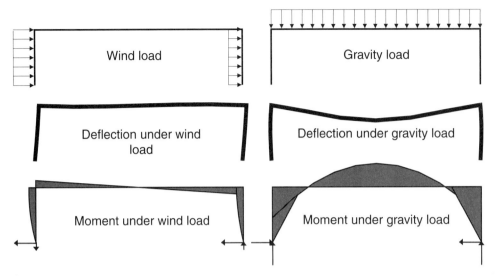

Figure 10.31 Loads, deformation, and moment for a long, shallow frame.

and at the joints. It is shallowest about 20% of the way in from the ends, where it is only thick enough handle the wind-induced moments. Some thickness would be required at those locations even if there was no wind force, inasmuch as putting pin joints there and at the bases of the verticals would create a four-hinged arch, which is inherently unstable.

Rigid-frame structures of the type described here are often lumped under the heading "prefabricated metal buildings." They are extremely efficient structurally and

very economical to build, requiring an absolute minimum of site work to prepare for the erection of the building. Because of their inherent simplicity and economy, they have tended to be used in low-end applications, such as warehouses and automobile repair shops. This "typecasting" is unfortunate, since this structural system has an inherent logic and beauty that, properly cultivated, can produce wonderful design results. The structure shown in Figure 10.33 is an example of what is possible with a good design eye.

Figure 10.32 Rigid frame with long, shallow proportions.

Sometimes a rigid frame is made to look like something else. For example, most people would look at the structure shown in Figure 10.34 and think of it as an arch, because of its shape. However, there is no buttressing action at the bottom of the curved element. The curved element participates in rigid-frame action with the verticals that support it.

Introducing a grade beam allows a moment connection at the base of each vertical, in addition to the moment connection already established at the top of the vertical. Figure 10.35 shows the deformation and moment pattern for three bays of this kind of rigid frame under the lateral force of wind.

The minimum moment occurs somewhere between halfway and one-third of the way up from the base, depending on which vertical we look at. The structure in Figure 10.36 is an example of such a configuration.

Frames can be stacked on top of each other to produce a multistory structure. In stacking frames, the opportunity arises to make a moment connection at the bottom of each vertical, similar to the moment connection being made at the top of each vertical. Figure 10.37 shows the deformation and moment distributions under lateral wind load.

This moment distribution is consistent with previous results, suggesting the structural logic of continuing the pattern of tapering the members to make the frame thicker at the joints and thinner at the midpoints between joints. Sometimes other practical factors motivate us to use simple, straight members. To begin with, there is a fabrication cost associated with tapering the members. Second, in a multistory structure there is often the requirement of having glass in the openings. Tapering the members requires that the window framing and glass be fabricated to special shapes as well. In most cases where there are windows in the openings in the frame, it is most practical to use straight members. A careful consideration of the preceding moment pattern can still yield an advantage. For example, it suggests that the joints must be very strong and should be shop-welded under controlled conditions that will ensure accurate, strong welds. It also suggests that the best place to make field connections is at midspan between joints. Using that technique, the members may not be tapered, but the joints are responsive to the dictates of the moment pattern shown in Figure 10.37.

Earlier in this chapter, it was noted that in very tall structures it is important to take maximum advantage of

(a)

(b)

Figure 10.33 An elegant rigid frame.

Figure 10.34 Curvilinear rigid frame.

the structural depth of the building by utilizing the concept of a structural tube. For a very tall building braced by triangulation, the example cited was the John Hancock Building in Chicago. For very tall buildings braced by rigid frames, two of the best examples are the World Trade Center (Architects: Yamasaki and Associates; engineers: Les Robertson Associates) and the Sears Tower in Chicago (Architects: Skidmore, Owings & Merrill, LLP, in Chicago; Engineers: Skidmore, Owings & Merrill, LLP, in Chicago). The World Trade Center was the supreme example of using a dense, rigid-frame tube. The horizontal elements were deep, and the vertical elements were both deep and closely spaced. The effectiveness of the rigid frame was apparent by the way the towers stood even after very large holes were blown out of the sides of both tubes. All of those rigid joints made the structure very ro-

bust and provided effective spanning action across large openings. The interior columns of the World Trade Center resisted only gravity, and all lateral loads were handled by the external tube. This produced an extremely open interior plan, with moderate size windows in the perimeter tube.

The Sears Tower has larger windows than the World Trade Center, which admit more light and provide larger views. The less dense exterior tube of the Sears Tower had the potential to cause greater shear lag across the windward and leeward faces of the building, owing to flexing of the members in the rigid frame. To reduce the amount of shear lag across these faces, four additional rigid frames were used in the interior of the building. These four rigid frames divided the plan of the building into 3 × 3 squares. These interior frames transmitted shear through the cen-

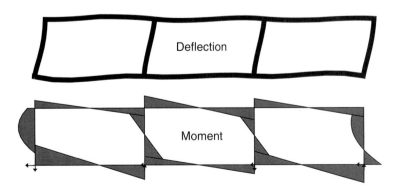

Figure 10.35 Deflection and moment for multibay frame under wind load.

Figure 10.36 Rigid frame with grade beam.

ter of the building and connected the windward and leeward walls at the one-third points. This shortened the windward and leeward walls to one-third of the span, in terms of shear lag. These interior frames cause more columns to interfere with interior space planning than was the case in the World Trade Center. In comparing the two structures, it is clear that the Sears Tower benefited by more light and larger viewing windows, whereas the World Trade Center had freer space planning.

The Sears Tower gave rise to the concept of bundled tubes. Instead of being one large tube, it became a bundle of nine tubes. These tubes were terminated at a variety of heights, which had the practical advantages of disrupting patterns in vortex shedding, reducing wind load at the top of the structure, suppressing wind oscillations by detuning the fundamental modes of oscillation of the various parts of the structure, providing a variety of floor sizes to fit a variety of clients, and allowing more light down to the street. On a personal note, the Sears Tower is one of the most elegant designs I have ever observed. There is a powerful and clear organizing principle. The huge windows up in the sky express a kind of openness and optimism that is contagious. Finally, there is the manner in which the tubes were terminated. There is a kind of randomness to them that suggests that the building is still a work in progress. I feel that one day the workers are going to show up and continue building even higher into the sky. This complexity created by the manner in which the tubes were terminated is the perfect counterpoint to the underlying clarity of everything else in the structure. I feel that I understand the essence of it, but that I will never fully figure it out (see Figure 10.38).

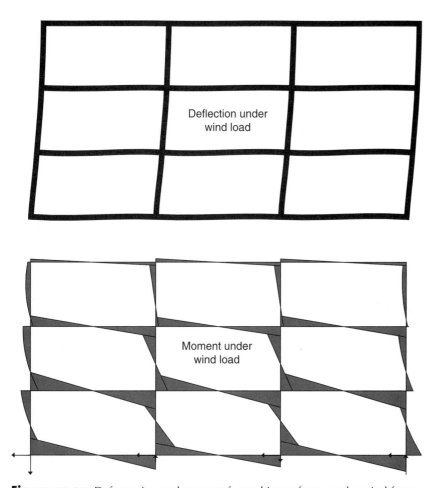

Figure 10.37 Deformation and moment for multistory frame under wind force.

Figure 10.38 Truncated tubes of the Sears Tower.

The Sears Tower is an example of designing the joints to fit the moment distribution. All of the joints were fabricated in a shop using a process called slurry welding, which fused the parts together as if they had been formed that way originally. The basic building elements were rigid frames consisting of one vertical and two horizontals. In this basic building element, the vertical member extends halfway from the top joint of the rigid frame to the bottom joint in the next rigid frame above, or halfway down from the bottom joint of the rigid frame to the top joint in the next rigid frame below. Similarly, horizontal elements in the frame extend halfway from their joints to the joints in the adjacent frame. Field connections were made by bolting plates to the webs of the verticals or horizontals being connected. These bolted joints were far from developing the full strength of the members connecting together. However, the joints were more than adequate to the task, since the frame has negligible moment at the locations of those joints (see Figure 10.39).

Figures 10.40 and 10.41 show parts of the rigid frame as they are experienced by visitors passing from the exterior lobby to an interior lobby of the Sears Tower.

A slightly different approach to rigid-frame construction was taken in One Liberty Plaza in New York City, shown in Figure 10.42(a) (Architects: Skidmore, Owings & Merrill, LLP; engineers: Skidmore, Owings & Merrill, LLP). In One Liberty Plaza, the horizontals were made very deep. This reduces the effective length of the verti-

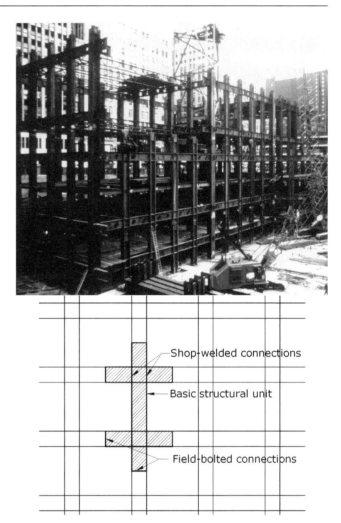

Figure 10.39 Prefabricated rigid-frame element being lifted into place.

cal elements' relative bending moment induced by lateral forces. The combination of reduced moment in the verticals and very deep beams allows the verticals to be spaced much farther apart, providing expansive panoramic views. As compared with the Sears Tower, the windows in One Liberty Plaza are not as high and do not admit as much natural light for interior illumination. On the positive side, the very thick spandrel beams in One Liberty Plaza provide substantial overhangs that limit unwanted solar gains through the windows (Figure 10.42(b)).

The Sears Tower and the John Hancock Building are both examples of tapering a building to provide a broad base for stability and a smaller top to reduce the wind force tending to turn the building over. There are other notable examples of this technique, the most extreme of which is probably the Transamerica Pyramid in San Francisco Architect: William L. Pereira Associates; engineers: Chin & Hensolt. This building tapers to a point at the top, which makes the design of occupiable space at the top of the structure somewhat problematic. The elements

Figure 10.40 Sears Tower rigid frame, clad in stainless steel.

Figure 10.41 One of the two interior lobbies of the Sears Tower.

(a)

(b)

Figure 10.42 Panoramic windows of One Liberty Plaza.

penetrating out of the pyramid at the top have to do with the elevator system. This building has succeeded in making itself the symbol of recognition for the San Francisco skyline, which is remarkable in a city with so many landmark structures. As a former resident of Berkeley, with a great fondness for the Bay Area, I always find that first glimpse of the Transamerica Pyramid very reassuring (see Figure 10.43).

At the base of the Transamerica Pyramid, lateral forces are absorbed by huge trusses. This is a very rational structural response at this level, where the shear forces associated with wind and earthquakes are at maximum. Unfortunately, it is difficult to enter a building through a maze of trusswork. Therefore, at the very lowest level, the building reverts to rigid frame. The columns are short and stubby and connected to a huge grade beam underground. Even though it is not triangulated, the entry portion of this structure is very rugged (see Figure 10.44).

Figure 10.43 San Francisco skyline from the University of California at Berkeley.

(a)

(b)

Figure 10.44 Two views of Transamerica Pyramid.

It is possible to taper a building in a curvilinear form reflecting the internal moment induced by lateral forces. This is similar to the cantilevered, draped trusses discussed in Chapter 7, except that now the structure is cantilevering out of the ground and the forces are horizontal rather than vertical. An example of this structural form is the Bank-One Plaza in Chicago (Architects: C.F. Murphy Associates; engineers: C.F. Murphy Associates), shown in Figure 10.45.

The Burg Dubai, designed by Skidmore, Owings & Merrill in Chicago, is under construction at the time of this writing. It has at its core a similar-shaped structure. To accommodate an orderly arrangement of floors, it does not follow a precisely smooth curve, but follows the curve in a series of steps. This building is remarkable in that it is a residential structure that will reach an unprecedented height. In plan, the building has three major fin walls that provide lateral stability. These interior walls are not considered disruptive to space planning, since they provide a kind of privacy and compartmentalization for the residential units. The three structural fin walls are stabilized against torsional deformation by a tubular wall surrounding the circulation core (see Figure 10.46).

High-rise buildings represent an odd and intensely contradictory set of design goals. Large footprints with a high density of structural elements are the logical structural response to high gravity loads and large overturning mo-

Figure 10.45 Bank-One Plaza in Chicago.

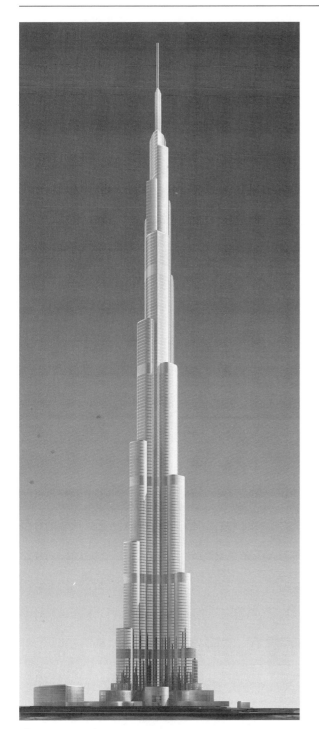

Figure 10.46 Burg Dubai, in Dubai, United Arab Emirates.

(a)

(b)

Figure 10.47 Citicorp Center in New York City.

ments. Yet the very high circulation rates, and the general urban density, at the bottom story of a building argue for spaciousness and openness.

Two designs that have pointed strongly in the direction of freeing up the ground plane are the Broadgate Exchange House, described in detail in Chapter 8 (Architects: Skidmore, Owings & Merrill, LLP; engineers: Skidmore, Owings & Merrill, LLP), and the Federal Reserve Bank Building (Architects: Gunnar Birkerts Associates; engineers: Leslie Robertson Associates), described in detail in Chapter 9. Both of those buildings were designed for circumstances that compelled long freespan responses. In other words, freeing up the urban ground plane was not the primary motivator, but it is a potential outcome of such designs. Another building that is particularly compelling in this regard is the Citicorp Center in New York City (Architects: Hugh Stubbins; engineers: LeMessurier Associates). Figure 10.47(a) shows the many floors of the building, which come to bear on four outrigger columns and a shear core (b).

The elevated, high-rise structure accommodates a church (in the left corner in Figure 10.47(a)), an outdoor plaza (Figure 10.48(a), and a large eating and shopping atrium (Figure 10.48(b)). These elements enhance the quality of urban life at the ground level.

Figure 10.49 shows sketches of the structural concept, generated by the structural engineer, William LeMessurier, during a design brainstorming session.

(a)

(b)

Figure 10.48 Open plaza (a) and atrium space (b) tucked underneath.

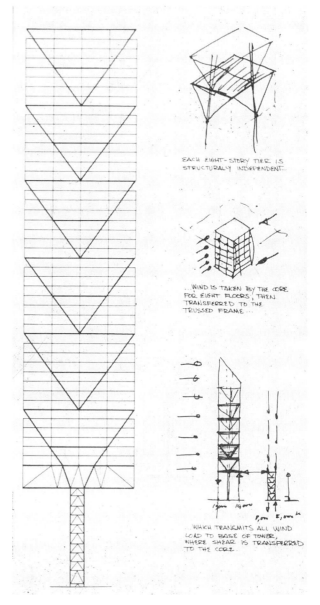

Figure 10.49 Design sketches of the structural design concept (by William LeMessurier).

10.4 Strategies for Admitting Natural Light to Multistory Buildings

In planning for daylighting, two of the keys are:

Locate the daylight glazing as high as possible in the wall.

Locate the ceiling as high as possible.

These objectives of locating the glazing and the ceiling as high as possible can be achieved by raising the overall height of the building. However, this is rarely an economically acceptable approach. Achieving an economical solution requires care in integrating the systems so that they require the minimal volume, thereby leaving the maximum volume for transport of natural light into the building. The most common approach to systems integration is not very aggressive in terms of achieving the goals outlined here. It consists of allocating discrete, layered volumes for structure, HVAC, and electric lighting and finished ceiling. This approach is expressed graphically in Figure 10.50.

In this process, vast amounts of hidden building volume are filled only with air, at the sacrifice of the human amenity of light, airy spaces with a wonderful sense of connection to the outside world. The design process has become more like volume allocation, rather than coordination or integration.

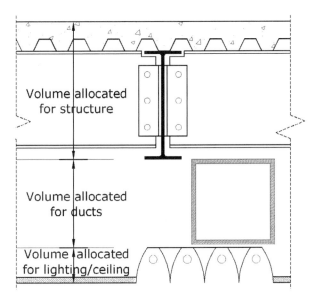

Figure 10.50 Layering of the systems.

Doing true systems integration has the virtues of:

Providing better architectural spaces for human occupation

Reducing lighting electricity consumption

To achieve these goals, it is necessary to focus design effort and research on ways of getting the subsystems to share volumes, to get the ceilings back up so that light can penetrate into the building.

An effective approach to systems integration is outlined in the following points:

- Beams running parallel to the daylight aperture wall have a greater obstructive influence in blocking light entering through the wall than do beams running perpendicular to the daylight aperture wall. Therefore, it is particularly compelling that the beams running parallel to the daylight aperture wall should be kept shallow.
- The more heavily loaded a beam is, the deeper the beam needs to be. Joists carry a lower load per unit length than do girders. Therefore, for a given span, joists are typically shallower than girders. This suggests that, for daylighting purposes, the joists should run parallel to the daylight aperture wall, and the girders should run perpendicular to the daylight aperture wall.
- To make the joists even shallower, it is desirable to use them in composite action with the floor slab. In a steel building, this is accomplished by using shear studs welded to the top of the beam. In concrete, this arrangement is naturally achieved by using double Ts where the decking and the ribs are integrally cast.
- To take advantage of the shallowness of the joist, it is important that the ceiling be set as close to the bottom of the joist as possible. Since the girders will be deeper than the joist, this implies that the ceiling must be placed between the girders, rather than below them. In other words, the girders will be visible, projecting downward through the ceiling surface.
- The longer the span of a beam, the deeper the beam needs to be. Therefore, it is important to keep the spans of the joists reasonably short so that their depth can be shallow, thereby allowing the ceiling to be kept high.

There is a limit to the process in the last bulleted item: a short span for the joists implies a close spacing of the supporting girders. Even though the girders run generally parallel to the direction of the daylight movement, much of the daylight is not moving directly perpendicular to the aperture wall, but rather is moving into the space at an angle. Much of this angled light will encounter the deep girders, which can absorb the light or scatter the light in an undesired direction (such as back out through the window or back into perimeter spaces that are already overlit). The closer the spacing of the girders, the more frequently these encounters will occur and the greater the interference to the light penetrating into the space.

Spacing the girders closer together also means there will be more columns to interfere with light entering through the daylight wall. This suggests that widely spaced girders trap less light and are better for light distribution than closely spaced girders.

For the purposes of the illustrations that follow, the spacing of the girders has been chosen to be 30 ft. The floor deck is lightweight concrete in composite action with 2 in.-deep corrugated steel decking, with an overall slab thickness of 6 in. (This depth was chosen to limit vibrations and for fire-rating purposes.) At a 30 ft span, the floor joists have been chosen to be 12 in.-deep wide-flange beams used in composite construction with the concrete deck, using $^3/_4$ in.-thick by 4 in.-long shear studs.

Figure 10.51 shows a building that is 60 ft deep from daylighting wall to daylighting wall. The floor joists are parallel to the daylighting wall, and the girders are perpendicular to the daylighting wall. The joists span 30 ft, and the girders span 30 ft. Lateral bracing is in a chevron pattern. Floor diaphragms absorb the wind forces on the daylighting wall and transfer the lateral force to the braces in the end walls. (From a daylighting point of view, the ideal situation would be with the daylighting walls facing north and south, and the end walls with the chevron braces facing east and west.)

The lateral braces on the building interior, which are resisting forces parallel to the daylighting walls, can be replaced by rigid frames in the daylighting walls. This may seem counterintuitive, since rigid frames tend to be heavier and to block more light and one would normally

not think of placing them in the daylighting wall, which is the wall through which any admitted light is desired. However, there are significant parts of the daylighting wall through which light would not be particularly useful anyway, so the structure can be put in those locations. Figure 10.52 shows a section through the daylighting wall.

Adding these deep spandrel beams to the rendering of the frame produces Figure 10.53.

The frame would continue up additional floors, but to avoid visual clutter and confusion, the framing has been omitted for all floors above the third floor and the columns have been truncated at the point of intersection with the spandrel beam for the third floor. The interior columns can be removed by making the girders deeper, as shown in Figure 10.54.

These deep girders interfere with the transport of thermally conditioned air along the length of the building (i.e., parallel to the daylight glazing). To solve this problem, the girders can be dropped down to pass underneath the joists. Return air can then be transported in the voids between the steel joists and over the girders. This framing arrangement is shown in Figure 10.55, which also shows:

- A cutaway view of the concrete floor deck on top of the joists
- A cutaway view of the ceiling just below the joists
- The steel joists extending beyond the end girder
- A horizontal manifold duct that gathers up the return air at the end of the building and delivers it to a vertical duct, which transports it back to the air-handling unit.

Figure 10.56 shows the same image as in Figure 10.55, with the addition of a cutaway view of an access floor and supply air ducts feeding air into the access-floor plenum.

Figure 10.57 is a cutaway view at the corner of the building, showing:

- The overhangs protecting the view glazing from excess solar gains
- The light shelves inside the glazing at the same level as the overhangs
- The return-air manifolds
- Small panoramic-view glazing on the end wall

In this version, the bottom of the spandrel beam has been moved up another foot and the extra glazing is accommodated with a section of sloped ceiling.

Figure 10.58 shows a section through the east wall, looking north. The glazing is for view only, so the height is limited and a substantial overhang is provided.

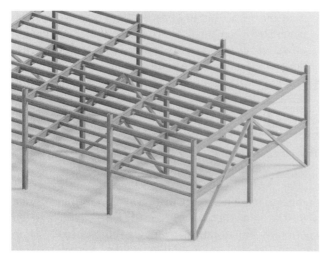

Figure 10.51 Steel framing with joist parallel to the daylighting wall. (Rendering by James Sweeney.)

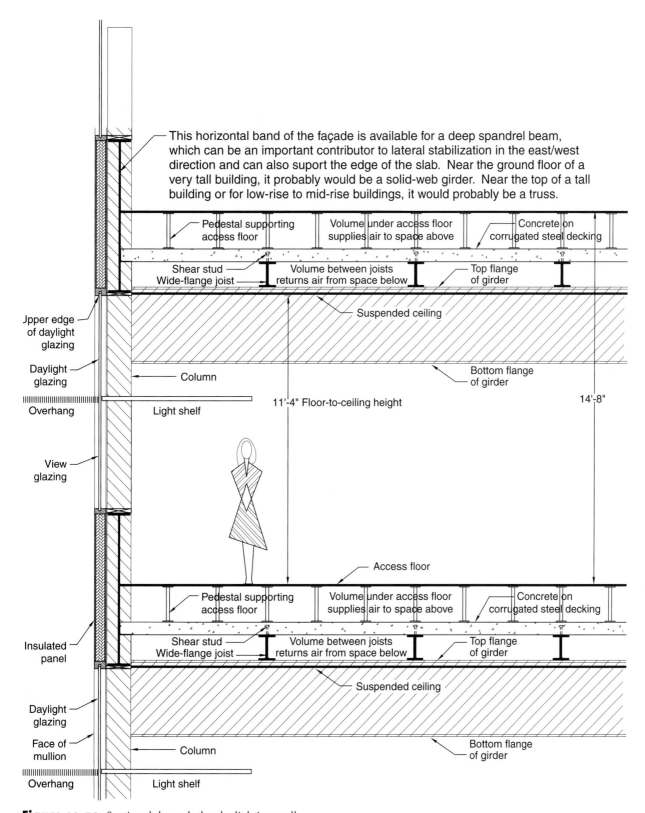

This horizontal band of the façade is available for a deep spandrel beam, which can be an important contributor to lateral stabilization in the east/west direction and can also suport the edge of the slab. Near the ground floor of a very tall building, it probably would be a solid-web girder. Near the top of a tall building or for low-rise to mid-rise buildings, it would probably be a truss.

Pedestal supporting access floor

Volume under access floor supplies air to space above

Concrete on corrugated steel decking

Shear stud
Wide-flange joist

Volume between joists returns air from space below

Top flange of girder

Suspended ceiling

Upper edge of daylight glazing

Daylight glazing

Column

Bottom flange of girder

Overhang

Light shelf

11'-4" Floor-to-ceiling height

14'-8"

View glazing

Access floor

Insulated panel

Pedestal supporting access floor

Volume under access floor supplies air to space above

Concrete on corrugated steel decking

Shear stud
Wide-flange joist

Volume between joists returns air from space below

Top flange of girder

Suspended ceiling

Daylight glazing

Face of mullion

Column

Bottom flange of girder

Overhang

Light shelf

Figure 10.52 Sectional through the daylighting wall.

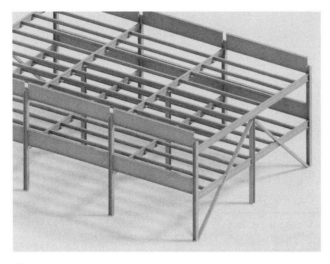

Figure 10.53 Deep spandrel beams as part of moment frame in daylighting wall. (Rendering by James Sweeney.)

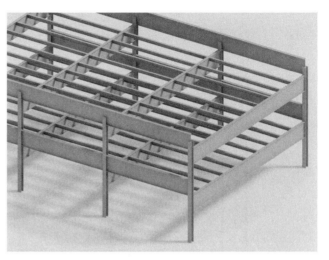

Figure 10.54 Rigid frames providing lateral stabilization in both directions. (Rendering by James Sweeney.)

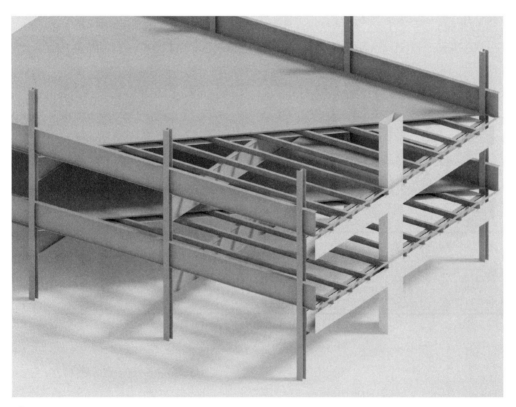

Figure 10.55 Return air volume between hung ceiling and the floor deck. (Rendering by James Sweeney.)

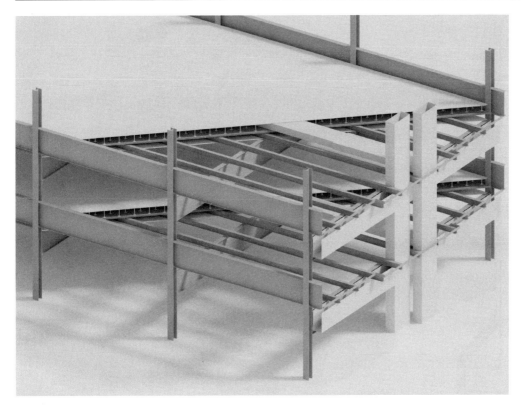

Figure 10.56 Ducts supplying the plenum under the access floor. (Rendering by James Sweeney.)

Figure 10.57 Cutaway view of corner of the building. (Rendering by James Sweeney.)

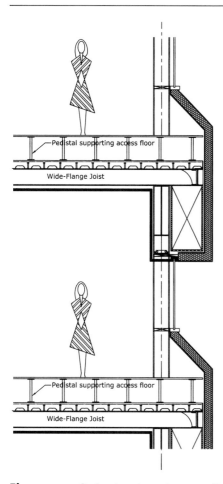

Figure 10.58 Section through east wall, looking north.

The same system can be constructed in precast con-crete, but there are some important differences in how it is framed. Figures 10.59 through 10.61 show a way that this can be done. The girder frames are moment-connected to the grade beam. The first spandrel beams are installed on two column ends of the girder frames, with one end of the spandrel beam cantilevering beyond the girder frame. This can be done in a way that minimizes the tendency of the spandrel beam to tilt where it rests on the girder frame. The spandrel beam is made hollow everywhere except where it rests on the girder frame. The solid part of the spandrel beam serves as a continuation of the col-umn portion of the girder frame. All of these connections are moment connections.

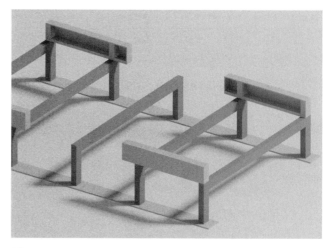

Figure 10.59 Girder frames and cantilevering spandrel beams. (Rendering by James Sweeney.)

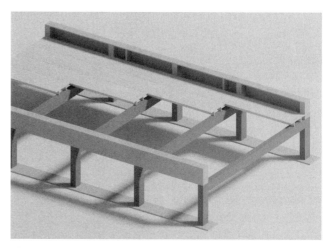

Figure 10.60 Adding the remaining spandrel beams and starting the double T decking. Return air goes between ribs of double Ts. (Rendering by James Sweeney.)

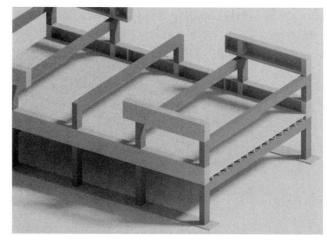

Figure 10.61 Adding more girder frames and cantilevering spandrel beams. (Rendering by James Sweeney.)

Index

INTRODUCTION

This appendix provides you with information on the contents of the CD that accompanies this book. For the latest and greatest information, please refer to the ReadMe file located at the root of the CD.

SYSTEM REQUIREMENTS

- A computer with a processor running at 120 Mhz or faster
- At least 32 MB of total RAM installed on your computer; for best performance, we recommend at least 64 MB
- A CD-ROM drive

NOTE: Many popular word processing programs are capable of reading Microsoft Word files. However, users should be aware that a slight amount of formatting might be lost when using a program other than Microsoft Word. The same is true for Microsoft Excel: Some popular spreadsheet programs are capable of reading these files, but users should be aware that a slight amount of formatting might be lost when using a program other than Microsoft Excel.

USING THE CD WITH WINDOWS

To install the items from the CD to your hard drive, follow these steps:

1. Insert the CD into your computer's CD-ROM drive.
2. The CD-ROM interface will appear. The interface provides a simple point-and-click way to explore the contents of the CD.

If the opening screen of the CD-ROM does not appear automatically, follow these steps to access the CD:

1. Click the Start button on the left end of the taskbar and then choose Run from the menu that pops up.
2. In the dialog box that appears, type **d:\start.exe**. (If your CD-ROM drive is not drive d, fill in the appropriate letter in place of *d*.) This brings up the CD Interface described in the preceding set of steps.

WHAT'S ON THE CD

The following sections provide a summary of the software and other materials you'll find on the CD.

Content

Any material from the book, including forms, slides, and lesson plans if available, are in the folder named "Content".

This Companion CD-ROM contains:

1. The Academic Version of the *Multiframe* structural analysis software developed, copyrighted, and provided by Formation Design Systems in Australia (http://www.formsys.com/). Analysis using the academic version of this software is limited to structures with 100 members or less. The academic version is also limited to five load cases. Files with more than 100 members and more than five load cases can be set up in the academic version of the software, but they require the full version of the software to perform the analysis. Students may exercise the option to construct such complex structures in the academic version of Multiframe and then perform the analysis on a copy of the full version of Multiframe. Full versions of the software may be available on your University computing system or a student version of the full-function software can be purchased from Daystar Software (http://www.daystarsoftware.com/academic/).
2. Exercises using Multiframe to do structural analyses.
3. Exercises using Microsoft Excel as a preprocessor for data to be input to Multiframe.
4. Exercises using Microsoft Excel in some stand-alone computations in which the full power of Multiframe in not needed.
5. Supplemental assignments not included in the hardcopy of the text.

For a typical Multiframe computer exercise, the reader will be provided with:

- A PDF file containing the instructions for the exercise. This document contains:
  - Images and text.
  - Instructions, which are preceded by a square bullet □.
  - Questions, which are preceded by bold numbers in the format: **1)**, **2)**, etc.
- A Microsoft Word worksheet document, which repeats the questions and provides a place for answering questions and for pasting images copied from Multiframe.
- In a few cases, special, preformatted starting files for Excel and Multiframe may also be provided.

The exercises are divided into parts, called sessions. One session corresponds approximately to one laboratory length session in an architectural structures course. A session might take anywhere from one to three hours, depending on the aptitude of the student (the laboratory session should be approached with the attitude that the student is going to work at it until it is done properly and not be preoccupied gauging themselves against other people who are finishing early).

These exercises can be completed in any sequence. However, early exercises devote more attention to helping learn to navigate through the programs. Therefore, the learning process will tend to be smoother when the exercises are done in proper order.

The exercises correspond to those in the book identified by the same numbers.

Applications

The following applications are on the CD:

Adobe Reader   Adobe Reader is a freeware application for viewing files in the Adobe Portable Document format.

Word Viewer   Microsoft Word Viewer is a freeware viewer that allows you to view, but not edit, most Microsoft Word files. Certain features of Microsoft Word documents may not display as expected from within Word Viewer.

Excel Viewer   Excel Viewer is a freeware viewer that allows you to view, but not edit, most Microsoft Excel spreadsheets. Certain features of Microsoft Excel documents may not work as expected from within Excel Viewer.

PowerPoint Viewer   Microsoft PowerPoint Viewer is a freeware viewer that allows you to view, but not edit, Microsoft PowerPoint files. Certain features of Microsoft PowerPoint presentations may not work as expected from within PowerPoint Viewer.

OpenOffice.org   OpenOffice.org is a free multi-platform office productivity suite. It is similar to Microsoft Office or Lotus SmartSuite, but OpenOffice.org is absolutely free. It includes word processing, spreadsheet, presentation, and drawing applications that enable you to create professional documents, newsletters, reports, and presentations. It supports most file formats of other office software. You should be able to edit and view any files created with other office solutions.

Shareware programs are fully functional, trial versions of copyrighted programs. If you like particular programs, register with their authors for a nominal fee and receive licenses, enhanced versions, and technical support.

Freeware programs are copyrighted games, applications, and utilities that are free for personal use. Unlike shareware, these programs do not require a fee or provide technical support.

GNU software is governed by its own license, which is included inside the folder of the GNU product. See the GNU license for more details.

Trial, demo, or evaluation versions are usually limited either by time or functionality (such as being unable to save projects). Some trial versions are very sensitive to system date changes. If you alter your computer's date, the programs will "time out" and no longer be functional.

CUSTOMER CARE

If you have trouble with the CD-ROM, please call the Wiley Product Technical Support phone number at (800) 762-2974. Outside the United States, call 1(317) 572-3994. You can also contact Wiley Product Technical Support at **http://support.wiley.com**. John Wiley & Sons will provide technical support only for installation and other general quality control items. For technical support on the applications themselves, consult the program's vendor or author.

To place additional orders or to request information about other Wiley products, please call (877) 762-2974.

CUSTOMER NOTE: IF THIS BOOK IS ACCOMPANIED BY SOFTWARE, PLEASE READ THE FOLLOWING BEFORE OPENING THE PACKAGE.